PETERSON'S®

ACT® PREP GUIDE:
THE ULTIMATE GUIDE TO MASTERING THE ACT

About Peterson's®

Peterson's is everywhere that education happens. For over five decades, Peterson's has provided products and services that keep students and their families engaged throughout the pre-college, college, and post-college experience. From the first day of kindergarten through high school graduation and beyond, Peterson's is a single source of educational content to help families maximize their student's learning and opportunities for success. Whether a fifth-grader needs help with geometry or a high school junior could benefit from essay-writing tips, Peterson's is the ultimate source for the highest quality educational resources.

Since 2005, Peterson's has been the leading publisher of prep guides for the ACT. Over the past ten years, more than one million students across 60 countries have prepared for the ACT with Peterson's titles.

For additional information about Peterson's range of educational products, please visit http://www.petersons.com.

ACT® is a registered trademark of ACT, Inc., which did not collaborate in the development of, and does not endorse, this product.

ACT® is a registered trademark of ACT, Inc., in the U.S.A. and other countries.

For more information, contact Peterson's, 3 Columbia Circle, Suite 205, Albany, NY 12203, 800-338-3282 Ext. 54229; or find us online at www.petersons.com.

Peterson's ACT® Prep Guide
ISBN 978-0-7689-4078-7

Peterson's ACT® Prep Guide PLUS
ISBN 978-0-7689-4091-6

Printed in the United States of America

10 9 8 7 6 5 4 3 2 1   18 17 16

First Edition

TABLE OF CONTENTS

INTRODUCTION TO *PETERSON'S ACT® PREP GUIDE*

Congratulations! If you're considering taking the ACT—and if you're reading this book, we'll assume you are—that means you probably intend to go to college. That's great news! You're preparing to transition into a really exciting (and maybe a *little* intimidating) period of your life. Taking the ACT will be one of the first steps of that transition, and *Peterson's ACT® Prep Guide: The Ultimate Guide to Mastering the ACT* will make that step a little easier for you.

Why This Is Your Best Choice for ACT Preparation

We won't lie to you: taking tests, especially important tests that can impact your future, can feel stressful and overwhelming. However, being well prepared will make the experience less stressful and overwhelming. That's where this book comes in. *Peterson's ACT® Prep Guide* will tell you everything you need to know to be prepared on test day. Seriously. We're not just talking about preparing you for the kinds of questions you are going to have to answer. We're talking about everything: how many questions are on the test, how to register for it, how to study for it, what to do and bring on test day, how the test is scored, and how those scores are reported. Think of it as your one-stop resource for all things ACT.

Peterson's ACT® Prep Guide is designed to help you excel on test day. There is a lot of information in this book, but you can rest assured that it is all relevant to the ACT, which is a pretty big test. The great thing about *Peterson's ACT® Prep Guide* is how faithfully it mirrors the ACT content. Every aspect of the ACT's content is addressed, and each skill is explained in detail and illustrated with test-like examples, so you don't have to fear any unpleasant surprises when you sit down to take the actual ACT. We understand; you have a lot of information to absorb while preparing for the ACT, and you have no time to waste on irrelevant information and filler. You need to know the ins and outs of the ACT, as accurately and thoroughly as possible, period. That is exactly what you will find in *Peterson's ACT® Prep Guide*.

How This Book Is Organized

Peterson's ACT® Prep Guide is organized to give you a clear and thorough understanding of the ACT and the skills tested on each of the ACT's five tests.

- **Chapters 1 and 2** tell you everything you need to know about the ACT and how to prepare for it: what it includes, how to register for the test, how to decide where and when to take it, how it is scored, and how those scores are reported to the colleges of your choice. Chapter 2 includes study tips that will come in handy as you prepare for the ACT.

- **Chapter 3** introduces you to your first full-length ACT practice exam—**the diagnostic test**. This section shows you how to approach this important test, which will help you identify your strengths and weaknesses in all the subjects covered on the ACT. You will then take the diagnostic test and complete a self-assessment to help you plan your study path.

- **Chapters 4–14** comprise the review chapters—the meat of the book. These chapters explain every skill you'll need to sharpen to master the ACT's English, Mathematics, Reading, Science, and Writing tests.

- **Chapters 15** gives you more opportunities to prepare with **four full-length practice tests**. Each test features detailed explanations for each question, designed to help you understand *why* an answer choice is correct or incorrect.

- **Chapter 16** shows you how to score your tests. Here you will find answer keys to each test broken down into subject areas and subscores. Included also are conversion charts to help you approximate what your scale scores would be, based on the number of questions you answer correctly on the test. This information is vital to helping you work toward reaching your goal score.

Special Study Features

You will find four kinds of special study features scattered throughout the book. Each study feature highlights specific types of information:

 Tips point out valuable information you need to know when taking the ACT. Tips provide quick and simple hints for selecting the correct answers for the most common ACT question types.

 Alerts identify potential pitfalls in the testing format or question types that can cause common mistakes in selecting answers.

NOTES: **Notes** address information about the test structure itself.

 Cautions provide warnings about possible errors in computation or formulas that can result in choosing incorrect answers on the math test.

How to Use This Book

It's understandable that all of the information you'll be reading about the ACT might seem a little overwhelming. But even if you are feeling confused by everything the ACT requires, take some comfort in the knowledge that you are holding the best resource guide to help you do well on the test. This book's job is not to make you a genius; its job is to make sure you are prepared to take the ACT. If you become a genius in the process, consider that a bonus.

Following the four steps listed below will help you get the most out of using this guide.

Step 1: First Things First—Get to Know the Exam

You will get the most out of *Peterson's ACT® Prep Guide* by using this book as it is organized. You may feel compelled to skip Chapter 1 because you're anxious to get right to the lessons, since that's where the real preparation begins. However, Chapter 1 is very useful for giving you a picture of the exam's content as a whole. There is also important information in it about what you need to do to qualify to take the exam.

 ALERT: If you skip Chapter 1, you may not realize that you neglected some important steps in registration or forgot to pay a particular testing fee. Chapter 1 will not prepare you to answer science or math questions, but it is as important as any other chapter in this book.

Step 2: The Diagnostic Test Is Your Friend—Don't Skip It!

Once you've learned all the essential information about the ACT in general, you will need to take the first step toward getting your scores where you want them to be by taking the diagnostic test. The diagnostic test is a full-length practice test that you should take before you start studying or reviewing any subject material.

Understandably, taking a long diagnostic test may not be your ideal way of getting started on your test preparation path. However, the point of a diagnostic test is to give you an idea of what your strengths and weaknesses are before you dive in to your ACT preparation. By taking the diagnostic test and analyzing your answers, you may discover that you retained more information from your English classes than you realized. You might also learn that you aren't quite the science expert you thought you were. Or maybe you'll find that most of your math skills are really strong, but you need some help when it comes to quadratic equations. Getting a clear idea of your strengths and weaknesses will help you to know which chapters of this book really demand your focus. The diagnostic test will help you get that clear idea.

Step 3: Build Your Skills—Practice, Practice, Practice!

After evaluating your diagnostic test results, you should know the skills on which you need to focus. By diligently studying the information presented, you will become familiar with not only the question types that will appear on the ACT, but also the language of the exam to help you be prepared for how the test will be worded.

 Familiarizing yourself with the way particular questions are worded on the ACT may help you figure out the kind of question you are answering, which may help you select the best answer.

Practice With the Most Test-like Questions Available

Sprinkled throughout each review chapter are practice questions related to the ACT-specific skill they assess—these questions will familiarize you with the language and presentation of the ACT.

Chapters 4–13 each end with a 20-question, multiple-choice quiz that tests your understanding of each skill assessed on the English, Mathematics, Science, and Reading portions of the ACT. Thorough explanations of why the given answer choices are correct and incorrect follow. **Don't skip over these explanations; understanding why an answer is right or wrong can stop you from repeating the same mistakes.** These explanations also function as mini-refresher courses, as they often repeat information you learned in the lessons that precede the practice tests.

Chapter 14, "Mastering the ACT® Writing Test," concludes with a practice essay prompt, followed by examples of both a poor and an excellent essay response.

Be sure to answer the questions scattered throughout the book as they appear. These questions test your understanding of the skills you just learned, and answering those questions reinforces concepts while the skills are still fresh in your mind. Similarly, taking the short quizzes at the end of each chapter will make the most of all the knowledge you gained while reading those chapters.

Step 4: See What You Have Learned—Test Yourself Again

At the end of the book, you will have the opportunity to take four complete ACT practice tests. With each practice test, you should see an improvement in your score since taking the diagnostic test. After all, you've now read all of the lessons and answered all the questions scattered throughout the book. However, you may still feel you can make improvements. So before taking the final full-length test, you might want to dive back into the book to review and study the skills you need to improve.

You should take these tests under the same circumstances you will encounter on test day. That means completing the English test in 45 minutes, the Math in 60 minutes, and so on. Official test times will be listed on the first page of every practice test. It also means using a calculator on the Math test if you so choose, but not using it on the Science test, which does not allow calculators. We'll talk more about test day rules in Chapter 1.

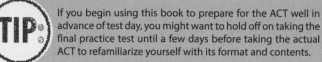 **TIP** If you begin using this book to prepare for the ACT well in advance of test day, you might want to hold off on taking the final practice test until a few days before taking the actual ACT to refamiliarize yourself with its format and contents.

THE PETERSON'S SUITE OF ACT® PRODUCTS

In addition to *Peterson's ACT® Prep Guide*, Peterson's has an array of cutting-edge ACT preparation resources designed to give you the best test preparation possible. Our online course, interactive practice tests, engaging mobile app, and DVD can be used alone or combined with other Peterson's ACT-focused products to help you succeed and get the high test scores you want. Take a few minutes to discover what's available in Peterson's suite of ACT products or visit our website at ***www.petersons.com/act***.

Peterson's ACT® Prep Guide

Peterson's ACT® Prep Guide features content and strategies that will help you master the newly revised ACT. It contains a full-length diagnostic test and access to six full-length practice tests (four within the book and two accessible online). *Peterson's ACT® Prep Guide's* skill-specific drills and practice quizzes help familiarize you with the ACT's unique content, structure, and format. Test-taking tips and advice guide you smoothly from registration to test day.

Peterson's ACT® Prep Guide PLUS—DVD

Peterson's ACT® Prep Guide PLUS offers bonus content that can enhance your test preparation experience. Bonus content includes videos to help you focus on your problem areas, useful articles to help you navigate the ACT process, and direct access to college and scholarship search. After reading *Peterson's ACT® Prep Guide PLUS* and taking the practice tests, you'll understand the areas where you need more work, so you can choose from videos that offer step-by-step instruction. These professional videos help you learn the material and master the strategies to increase your ACT scores. Use your Peterson's code at ***www.petersons.com/act*** to access all your bonus material, including everything on this DVD: 73834750-ACT.

Peterson's ACT® Online Practice Tests

Taking online practice tests is ideal because you get immediate feedback and automated scoring. *Peterson's ACT® Prep Guide* gives you access to two full-length online ACT practice tests with detailed feedback to help you understand the concepts presented.

If you find you enjoy the online test-taking experience, you can extend your preparation sessions with *Peterson's ACT® Online Practice Tests for the ACT*. This set of three full-length practice tests allows you to first diagnose your readiness for the exam and focus your studies on areas in which you need to improve your score. After studying, you can take the second practice test to measure how much you have improved. If further study is needed, a third practice test is provided to gauge your final readiness prior to taking the actual ACT test.

Peterson's ACT® Online Course

Peterson's ACT® Online Course is a comprehensive test prep course that is customized for you. In addition to practice tests, the online course allows access to supplemental content, including additional subject-specific strategies and lessons, tips and college search options tailored to your projected test scores and interests.

Here's how the course works:

1) An initial diagnostic pretest determines your strengths and weaknesses.

2) Based on your diagnostic test results, interactive lessons teach you the subject areas you need to learn.

3) Quizzes after each lesson gauge how well you have learned the materials just taught.

4) Full-length practice tests allow you to apply all the skills you've learned and monitor your progress.

Peterson's ACT® Online Course provides short, medium, and full-length options to enable you to get the most out of the course—no matter how close it is to test day!

Interested in going the extra mile and using the supplemental practice tests or the online course? Take advantage of customer-friendly discounts available only to customers who purchase *Peterson's ACT® Prep Guide*. For more information, go to **www.petersons.com/act**.

Peterson's ACT® Prep Guide Mobile App

Test prep doesn't have to be boring—and you don't have to be tied to your desk at home, either. Now you can purchase *Peterson's ACT® Prep Guide* mobile app for your Apple device. The mobile app features 10 interactive skill-building exercises. Simple and fun to use, these games will sharpen your thinking and standardized test-taking skills that are essential to mastering the ACT. The app also includes keywords and advice on how to convert the skills you learn into points on the ACT. To purchase the mobile app, search *Peterson's ACT* in the iOS store.

Now that you know why *Peterson's ACT® Prep Guide* is an essential resource to prepare you to take a very important test, it's time to make the most of this powerful preparation tool. Turn the page and find out everything you need to know about the ACT!

PART I: BASIC FACTS ABOUT THE ACT®

Chapter 1: All About the ACT®

Chapter 2: Test-Taking Strategies for the ACT®

CHAPTER 1:
ALL ABOUT THE ACT®

OVERVIEW

- Who Takes the ACT and Why?
- What's on the ACT?
- Registering for the ACT
- Registration Fees
- When and How Often to Take the ACT
- Choosing Your Test Day and Location
- Test Day: What to Expect, What to Bring, and What to Leave Home
- Scoring
- A Quick Word Before Moving On …
- Summing It Up

So what exactly is the ACT, and how is it used? ACT stands for American College Testing, and ACT, Inc., is the organization that produces the standardized test, the ACT college readiness assessment, or the ACT. The ACT measures how well you have learned critical thinking skills and the information taught in your classes in high school. Admission boards use ACT scores as one predictor of academic success when considering your application to their college or university. Don't let that alarm you. There are a lot of other factors that will affect an admission board's decision, including grades, an admissions essay, interviews, letters of recommendation, and other achievements, but the ACT is an important one. It tests your proficiency in some of the most essential subjects you've studied throughout your high school career: English, mathematics, reading, and science. Most of the questions are multiple choice, which require you to select the best of several possible answer choices. If you choose to take the ACT with the optional Writing test, you will be required to write an essay. We'll talk more about that option later on in this chapter.

WHO TAKES THE ACT AND WHY?

Who takes the ACT? In general, students from grades 6 through 8 who are invited to participate in an academic talent search program, or students in grades 11 and 12 who are planning to apply to college take the ACT (all four-year colleges and universities in the United States accept ACT results). But chances are if you're reading this book, there's only one answer to that question that matters to you: "I'm taking the ACT!"

Why take the ACT? Colleges examine your ACT scores to determine how you might measure up to other applicants. Naturally, a good score will give you the edge. Your grade point average (GPA) will be a major factor in admissions too, but your GPA does not provide as clear a portrait of what you know as your ACT score will. There are too many factors that affect your GPA, and those factors can vary from school to school. For example, some teachers are easier graders than others. Different schools may also use different scoring systems. However, your score on the ACT will be more objective, giving colleges a better idea of how strong your particular skills are. This will also help your college advisor place you in the courses that best suit your strengths and weaknesses. If your Mathematics test score is amazing, it will let your advisor know that you probably belong in advanced math classes. If you don't perform as well on the Science test, then maybe your science classes should be less advanced.

NOTE: Some states now use the ACT to assess school performance and require all high school students to take the ACT, whether or not they plan to attend college. If you live in one of these states, consider yourself lucky—you will be registered automatically and can take the test free of charge. And if you happen to hit the scores out of the ballpark, you can submit them to prospective colleges when the time comes. Who knows? Maybe seeing how well you've done will give you the confidence to pursue the college of your dreams, or, if you thought college wasn't an option, the opportunity to rethink your future plans. Check with your high school to see if your state requires you to take the ACT. To find out more about state-administered ACT testing, go to www.petersons.com/act.

WHAT'S ON THE ACT?

The ACT consists of four different tests: **English**, **Mathematics**, **Reading**, and **Science**. These tests are multiple choice. The optional Writing test asks you to write a timed essay. We'll explore these sections in detail as we cover them in the book, but let's look at a basic overview of each.

THE ENGLISH TEST

The English test is a 45-minute assessment consisting of 75 questions. It tests your skills in usage and mechanics, as well as rhetoric:

1) **Usage and mechanics** involve punctuation, grammar, and sentence structure.

2) **Rhetoric** is more about the writer's thought process—the strategy, organization, and style of a passage.

There are five passages, or essays, presented on the English test. They contain underlined portions that *may* contain errors in usage and mechanics. If there is an error or errors, you will select the best correction offered from four answer choices. If there aren't any errors, you will select the choice that reads NO CHANGE.

Rhetoric questions generally will ask you a specific question about the best way to rethink, reorganize, or restyle part of the passage. The relevant portions in the passages will always be numbered, and those numbers will refer to the number of the particular question that relates to those portions.

THE MATHEMATICS TEST

The Mathematics test is a 60-minute assessment consisting of 60 questions. There are six different content areas grouped into three subscore categories on the Math test—all designed to evaluate skills the ACT assumes most high school students have learned by their senior year:

1) **Pre-Algebra/Elementary Algebra**

    - Pre-Algebra questions include basic operations using whole numbers, decimals, fractions, and integers; square roots; exponents; scientific notation; factors; ratio, proportion, and percent; linear equations in one variable; absolute value; simple probability; and understanding simple descriptive statistics.

    - Elementary Algebra questions focus on properties of exponents and square roots, using variables to express functional relationships, understanding algebraic operations, evaluation of algebraic expressions through substitution, and the solution of quadratic equations by factoring.

2) **Intermediate Algebra/Coordinate Geometry**

    - Intermediate Algebra questions assess understanding of the quadratic formula, rational and radical expressions, absolute value equations and inequalities, sequences and patterns, systems of equations, quadratic inequalities, functions, modeling, matrices, roots of polynomials, and complex numbers.

    - Coordinate Geometry questions focus on graphing and the relations between equations and graphs, including points, lines, polynomials, circles, and other curves; graphing inequalities; slope; parallel and perpendicular lines; distance; midpoints; and conics.

3) **Plane Geometry/Trigonometry**

    - Plane Geometry questions are based on the relationships and properties of plane figures; the concept of proof and proof techniques; volume; and applications of geometry to three dimensions.

    - Trigonometry questions focus on understanding trigonometric relations in right triangles; values and properties of trigonometric functions; graphing trigonometric functions; modeling using trigonometric functions; use of trigonometric identities; and solving trigonometric equations.

Each question is multiple choice, although, unlike the English test, there are five possible choices for each question. While you will have to know basic formulas and computations for the Math test, you will not be expected to remember more complex ones—they will be provided for you along with the question. You are permitted to use a calculator on the Math test, though a calculator is not required. You will learn about what kinds of calculators are permitted on the ACT toward the end of this chapter.

THE READING TEST

The Reading test is a 35-minute assessment consisting of 40 questions. The ACT will present you with four different kinds of passages on the Reading test:

1) **Literary Narrative** passages are from short stories, novels, memoirs, or personal essays.
2) **Social Studies** passages discuss anthropology, archaeology, biography, business, economics, education, geography, history, political science, psychology, and sociology.
3) **Natural Science** passages discuss anatomy, astronomy, biology, botany, chemistry, ecology, geology, medicine, meteorology, microbiology, natural history, physiology, physics, technology, and zoology.
4) **Humanities** passages discuss architecture, art, dance, ethics, film, language, literary criticism, music, philosophy, radio, television, and theater.

The questions are multiple choice, each with four possible answers. Reading test questions require you to determine meanings stated explicitly and implicitly, main ideas, and the meanings of words as they are used in the context of the passage. You will also have to locate and interpret significant details, understand the sequence of events, comprehend cause-effect relationships, analyze the tone, and draw generalizations.

Some passages will consist of a pair of shorter passages, and some of the accompanying questions will test your ability to think of how those two passages relate to each other—mostly how they are different or similar.

THE SCIENCE TEST

The Science test is a 35-minute assessment consisting of 40 questions. The test includes various passages and pieces of scientific information, each followed by multiple-choice questions with four possible answers. The information presented is taken from the following natural science topics: biology, chemistry, physics, Earth science, and astronomy.

The Science test questions are presented in one of three different formats:

1) **Data representation** questions require you to read and interpret information on graphs, scatterplots, and tables.

2) **Research summary** questions require you to read about experiments and draw conclusions about their designs and results.

3) **Conflicting viewpoints** questions feature pairs of contrasting hypotheses about data or premises and require you to understand, analyze, compare, and contrast those viewpoints.

 ALERT: Calculators are not allowed on the Science test because it does not require you to make any calculations.

THE WRITING TEST

The optional Writing test is a 40-minute assessment consisting of a single essay question. You will receive three different perspectives on a particular issue. After reading each perspective carefully, you will compose an essay that evaluates the perspectives, while also creating your own perspective. Finally, you will explain how your perspective relates to the ones with which you were provided. Don't try to get into the mind of an essay grader. The quality of your ideas and writing—*not* your opinions—will affect your score. There are no multiple-choice questions on the Writing test.

The Writing test is optional because not every college requires you to take it. You can find the Writing test requirements of the college of your choice on the official ACT website at ***www.act.org.***

 ACT Timing: In total, the ACT is a 3-hour and 30-minute test consisting of 215 multiple-choice questions. Add in an extra 40 minutes if you're taking the Writing test. That's a long time, but it also includes a 30-minute break so you can refresh yourself a bit.

REGISTERING FOR THE ACT

Once you've decided to take the ACT, one of the first things you'll need to do is register, which you can do online at *www.actstudent.org/regist/*. Be prepared to create an account on the ACT website if you register online. You may also use the official ACT website to request extended time to take the test if you have a disability or request a standby online test if you missed the late registration deadline. You may also request an online test if you are homebound or confined or you are not within 75 miles of a testing center. All of these arrangements can be made by visiting *www.actstudent.org/regist*.

Registering online is the quickest method, but if you are under age 13 or you cannot pay with a credit card, you may order a Register-By-Mail packet by filling out a form online at *www.actstudent.org/forms/stud_req/*.

> **NOTE:** Please go to *www.petersons.com/act* for up-to-date fee information.

When you register for the ACT, you will receive a registration ticket with your photo. *You MUST bring this ticket with you on test day.*

Photo ID

All students must provide a photo ID to register for the ACT for test security purposes. Basically, they don't want you sending some test-taking wizard to the test center to take the ACT for you. A photo ID lets the test administrators know that you are you. You can find out how to upload a photo of yourself to the official ACT website using a computer or mobile device by visiting *www.actstudent.org/regist/add-photo.html*.

You will have to present your photo ID on test day, as well as your ACT admission ticket, which includes your photo. Your photo ID must be current, valid, and legal. Your ID must be hard plastic, such as a student ID or driver's license. If you do not have an acceptable photo ID, you must obtain an ACT Student Identification Letter with Photo from the ACT website at *www.act.org/aap/pdf/Identification-Letter-Form.pdf*.

Students taking the test on standby—those who missed the late registration date or requested a test date or test center change—must also bring a standby ticket with a photo of themselves on test day. Find out more about obtaining that ticket on the ACT site at *www.actstudent.org/regist/standbytest.html*.

 ALERT: Paper and electronic photo IDs are not permissible.

REGISTRATION FEES*

The fee for taking the ACT is $39.50. For that fee, you, your high school, and as many as four college choices will receive your score reports. If you are taking the ACT with the optional Writing test, the total fee is $56.50. That extra $17 fee is refundable in the event you either cannot attend test day or you decide to take the ACT without the Writing test.

There is a $12 fee for each additional college you want to receive your scores beyond the initial four you choose.

Other fees include:

- Standby testing: $49

- International testing outside the U.S. and Canada: $40

- Changing the date of your test: $23

- Changing the location of your test: $24

- Requesting a copy of your test and answers (Test Information Release or TIR): $20 (not every test center offers this service)

---

* Registration fees at the time of publication. Go to *www.petersons.com/act* for up-to-date information.

WHEN AND HOW OFTEN TO TAKE THE ACT

In the U.S. territories and Canada, the ACT is given six times a year—in September, October, December, February (except in New York), April, and June. Internationally, the ACT is given in September, October, December, April, and June. The best time to take the ACT is February or April of your junior year. By that time you will have learned most of the skills tested on the ACT, and there will be plenty of time for your college choices to receive your score.

It is also wise not to drag your feet too much in case you want to take the ACT more than once. That may sound a bit crazy—why would anyone want to take the same test more than once? Well, crazy at it may seem, there are several good reasons why students choose to retake the test—they are called *scores*. You want your scores to be the best they can be, right? Well perhaps, in spite of your best efforts on test day, you don't do as well as you hoped. Maybe your scores are perfectly acceptable—for *most* colleges, but not the college you *really* want to attend. If either of these situations applies to you—good news! Research has shown that your score is likely to improve if you take the ACT a second time. Taking the ACT is one of those situations in which life gives you a chance at a do-over, if you don't procrastinate.

> **NOTE:** There is no administration of the ACT in February internationally or in New York, U.S.A, so plan accordingly.

If you are preparing to take the ACT for the first time, try setting a score goal for yourself after reading through this book and making your way through the practice quizzes and practice tests, which should give you an idea of how well you will do on the actual test. If you reach that goal the first time you take the ACT, you may not want to take it again. But it's good to have the option of a do-over if you need it. You probably shouldn't take the test more than four times, though. After the fourth time, it is more likely that your score will go down rather than up. Nevertheless, taking the test multiple times is also a good idea if your college (or colleges) of choice practices superscoring. More on that later…

CHOOSING YOUR TEST DAY AND LOCATION

Even if reading this book makes you an expert ACT test taker with sky-high confidence, you should still be prepared for your test day to be a big deal. Try not to take the ACT test on a day when your schedule is crammed with other tasks. Also be mindful of how far away your test center is. Having to travel a long distance on test day is hardly ideal either.

You can make your most informed decision about when and where to take your test by visiting *www.petersons.com/act*. There are numerous centers that administer the ACT in the U.S., Canada, and other countries. Find the most convenient one for you in the U.S. or Canada by visiting *www.petersons.com/act*.

Just be aware that the longer you wait to register for the ACT, the more likely it is that your preferred test location will fill to capacity. So do your best to register early so you won't have to travel too far to take your test.

TEST DAY: WHAT TO EXPECT, WHAT TO BRING, AND WHAT TO LEAVE HOME

Okay, so it's the big day, the day for which you have been preparing. Just imagine how you'd feel if you did all that hard work studying, reading, and taking practice tests and you weren't allowed in the testing center on test day. That could happen if you show up late! So it's probably smart to plan to arrive a little early. You may want to leave yourself as much as an extra 30 minutes if you are driving to a testing center you have never visited. You don't want to get turned away at the testing center because you or the person driving you got a little lost on the way there.

Be sure to take all possible factors into account to ensure you don't arrive late to the test center: traffic, adverse weather conditions, a detour to the gas station, etc. You might even want to consider taking a dry-run drive to the test center just to get the very best idea of how long the trip takes and to make sure you don't get lost on test day.

Testing always begins at 8:00 a.m., by which time the test takers should all be present and in their seats. Read that again—not running in the front door, not pulling into the parking lot, but *in your seat*, ready to go! The tests are administered in the following order: English, Mathematics, Reading, Science, and finally, if you've chosen to take it, Writing. Your 30-minute break occurs after the Mathematics test. There is also an extra 10-minute break before the Writing test if you're taking it.

Test Day Checklist

All students must provide a photo ID to register for the ACT for test security. Before going to take the ACT, you may want to use the following checklist to make sure you have everything you need:

 TEST TICKET

 ACCEPTABLE PHOTO ID

 SHARP PENCILS WITH ERASERS

 PERMISSIBLE CALCULATOR

SNACK AND BOTTLE OF WATER

A SWEATER OR SWEATSHIRT IN CASE OF COOLER TEST CENTER CONDITIONS (OPTIONAL)

> **NOTE:** ACT testing begins at 8 a.m. Plan to arrive at the test site 15 to 30 minutes early to make sure you are seated, settled, and ready to begin. The ACT is generally dismissed at 12:15 p.m. The ACT with Writing concludes at 1:15 p.m.

CALCULATOR INFO

Although calculators are allowed for the Mathematics test, the following calculators are prohibited according to the official ACT website:

- Texas Instruments calculators with model numbers beginning with TI-89 or TI-92, as well as the TI-Nspire CAS

- Hewlett-Packard models HP Prime and HP 48GII and all models with model numbers beginning with HP 40G, HP 49G, or HP 50G

- Casio models fx-CP400 (ClassPad 400), ClassPad 300, ClassPad 330, and Algebra fx 2.0, as well as all models with model numbers that begin with CFX-9970G

Other prohibited devices include tablets, laptop computers, electronic writing pads (with the exception of the Sharp EL 9600), cell phone calculators, calculators with typewriter keypads, and calculators that make noise or require power cords. Furthermore, test takers are not permitted to share calculators.

You may bring your cell phone to use during the 30-minute break, but it must be turned off or set on silent while taking the test. You might also want to bring a little snack or a bottle of water to have during the break. It could give you just the right amount of energy to get you through the rest of the test.

SCORING

The ACT is a multiple-choice test that does not penalize you for selecting a wrong answer. However, a blank answer will be marked as incorrect. Therefore, it is important to **answer every question on the test,** even if you only guess. **Never** leave a question blank.

 ALERT: It's worth repeating. Your score will NOT be marked down for a wrong answer—only correct answers count toward your score. That means any answer, even a guess, is better than none!

Each of the four multiple-choice tests—English, Mathematics, Reading, and Science—is worth 36 points. Your total score, which the ACT calls your **composite score**, is the average score of those tests. That means the highest score you can get on the ACT is 36. Clearly, that's a great score—a perfect score. Scoring higher than 30 is great too. Whether or not a score below 30 is considered a "great" score will largely depend on the college to which you are applying. Some schools may consider 25 to be a truly exceptional score. Most ACT test takers tend to get a score of 21. So, if you score above that, you've beaten the national average.

The Writing test essay is scored a bit differently. Two scorers individually read your essay and assign subscores on a scale from 1–6 in each of four writing domains. The subscores from each domain are combined to create four final domain scores (each ranging from 2–12), and your writing score is calculated from the four final domain scores and reported on a scale of 1–36. That number is distinct from the score you receive for the multiple-choice tests. If you take the Writing test, you will also receive an English Language Arts (ELA) score, which is an average of the English, Reading, and Writing tests.

Superscoring

If you take the ACT multiple times, some colleges will **superscore** your test results. A superscore is obtained when a college chooses to recognize your *best* scores on each of the multiple-choice tests from a combined pool of all the times you take the ACT. That means if you had a terrible day in math one test day, studied up, and took the ACT again to raise your score by a lot, your superscore would reflect only the good math score and ignore the lower one.

The number of colleges that superscore ACT results is growing. To find out if the college you are interested in attending offers super-scoring, visit its website or contact the admissions office.

In addition, more than 500 colleges use the Common Application, an application that can be submitted to multiple schools, which gives you the option of entering your *highest* scores for the English, Mathematics, Reading, and Science tests on the ACT, as well as your highest composite score. It does not matter if you earned each of those scores on different dates. This application feature gives you the best ACT score you can receive. Superscoring is definitely another convincing reason to take the ACT more than once.

Viewing Scores

Student score reports are generally posted for viewing within two weeks after test day. You will be able to see your ACT scores by accessing your ACT Web account on the official ACT website. You can find the earliest date your score might be posted by visiting *http://www.actstudent.org/scores/viewing-scores.html.*

Try not to get too frustrated if your scores are not posted on that earliest date. Just keep checking back in once a week, since all scores are posted on a weekly basis. Eventually, you'll be able to view your score. The score for your Writing test will be posted about two weeks after your scores for the multiple choice tests. Official score reports are released and mailed to you within 3 to 8 weeks.

Reporting Scores to Your High School and Selected Colleges

ACT prepares three reports for you after you've taken the ACT: the Student Report (explained above, which is viewable online and mailed to you); the High School Report, which is sent to your school; and the College Report, which is sent to the colleges or agencies you listed upon registering to take the ACT. Keep in mind that ACT sends these scores out automatically, which is why you should take care when deciding which colleges to list.

If you're pleased with your scores and would like to send them to more colleges after receiving your results—congrats, that's great! You must go to *www.actstudent.org* and fill out a form to send the score of your choice to the extra college or colleges of your choice. You can also complete the form by phone or mail. There is a $12 fee for each additional college you want to receive your score per each test date you are reporting.

CANCELING SCORES

Sometimes, in spite of their best intentions and effort, students do not do well on a test. It happens. If you think you may have gotten a low score on the ACT, you can choose to cancel it. The catch: You will have to go with your gut since you *cannot* see your score before you cancel it. In fact, you have to make the decision to cancel by 12 p.m. (CT) the Thursday immediately after your Saturday test date.

If, after you have taken the test, you see your scores and are unhappy with them, you can request to delete a test date record. If you do decide to go this route, you will have to submit a letter to:

> ACT Institutional Services
> P.O. Box 168
> Iowa City, IA 52243-0168
> USA

Be sure to include your name and address on your letter specifying that you want to have your score for a particular test date deleted. After ACT receives your cancellation request, it will send you another form that you will have to fill out and return. Keep in mind that all the scores for that test date will be removed, including those for the tests on which you may have scored well.

A QUICK WORD BEFORE MOVING ON...

Well, that was a lot of information, wasn't it? Reading this chapter must have been like that first day of class when you find out everything you are expected to do and learn all year long. Those classes are always a bit intense. But then what happens? You get used to your workload and figure out the best way to manage your time. You can do it. We believe in you.

Don't feel obligated to memorize every useful piece of information in this chapter. In fact, you may want to give it a quick review the night before test day just to make sure you are completely prepared.

So take a deep breath. It's time to turn the page and start the next chapter, which will tell you everything you need to know about the best way to study for the ACT and provide some indispensable tips for taking the actual test. Remember that the second day of class is almost always less stressful than the first!

11

SUMMING IT UP

- **The ACT college readiness assessment** is a component used to help colleges and universities decide whether or not they want to accept applicants.

- **The ACT consists of four multiple-choice tests on English, Mathematics, Reading, and Science** with a total of 215 questions. You will have 3 hours and 30 minutes to complete the tests. There is also an optional Writing test that takes an additional 40 minutes to complete. Some colleges do not require the Writing test.

- **The English test consists of 75 questions** that test your grammar and usage and rhetorical skills. You will read passages that may contain errors and choose the answers that best correct those errors. You will also be asked to improve certain portions of a passage by means of reorganization, clarification, or addition or deletion of sentences.

- **The Mathematics test consists of 60 questions** that test your knowledge of pre-algebra, elementary algebra, intermediate algebra, coordinate geometry, plane geometry, and trigonometry.

- **The Reading test consists of four passages (literary narrative, social studies, science, and humanities)** and 60 questions that test your ability to comprehend what you have read.

- **The Science test consists of 40 questions** assessing your reasoning and problem-solving skills and your ability to interpret, analyze, and evaluate data representation, research summaries, and conflicting viewpoints. These questions are derived from information taught in the natural sciences course of study: biology, chemistry, physics, Earth science, and astronomy.

- **The Writing test consists of an essay** that requires you to evaluate three perspectives on an issue, create your own perspective on that issue, and explain how your perspective relates to the ones provided. There are no multiple-choice questions on the optional Writing test.

- **Register for the test online at *www.actstudent.org/regist/*.** During registration, you will choose where and when you will take the test. You will also receive a registration ticket that you MUST bring with you on test day. Registration fees apply.

- **Arrive at the test center on test day well before test time (8:00 a.m.)** with everything you will need to be admitted into the test center and everything you need to take the ACT.

- **There is no penalty for choosing an incorrect answer on the ACT,** so you should answer every question. Unanswered questions are considered to be wrong answers.

- **The maximum score you can get on the ACT is 36,** and that score is determined by averaging your score on each of its four multiple-choice tests.

- **The maximum score you can get on the Writing test is 36,** and that score is distinct from the one you receive for the multiple-choice tests.

- **Scores are posted online for you to view about two weeks after the test date.** Writing test scores are usually posted two weeks after multiple-choice scores are posted. Score reports are released and mailed within three to eight weeks after the test dates. If you take the Writing test, your score reports will be released only after the Writing scores are available, within five to eight weeks after the test date.

- **Scores will automatically be submitted to the colleges you listed when applying for the ACT.** You also have the option of canceling your score if you think you might not have performed well on the ACT, but only before you have seen your scores—by the Thursday after your Saturday test date.

CHAPTER 2:
TEST-TAKING STRATEGIES FOR THE ACT®

OVERVIEW

- General Study Strategies
- Sample Study Plans
- The Night Before Test Day
- Summing It Up

Studying is a personal matter, and everyone has his or her own way of working. Some students find that studying for a short period every day is the best way to comprehend and retain information. Others insist that waiting until the night before the test day and cramming for seven hours is the only thing that works.

If the procrastination method works best for you, maybe you're reading this book the night before the test. In that case, you certainly have a long night ahead of you—best of luck! But if you have several weeks to go and need a way to focus your studying, read on for some tips on how to get started with a plan that will yield winning results.

Remember that the ACT is not like most of the tests you have taken. It is long, requires knowledge of several subjects and dozens of skills, and takes hours to complete. Really, there is no way to fully cram for a comprehensive test like the ACT. However, there are some general tips you may find useful when studying for the exam.

GENERAL STUDY STRATEGIES

SPREAD OUT YOUR STUDYING

Some students try to devote only one or two days a week to ACT prep, but no matter how well intentioned, this method often fails. They get bored or burnt out, spend days "off," and then lose all momentum they might have gained.

Instead of spending an entire day studying so you have maximum free time for the next three days, try spreading out that one long session into four short ones. Think **two hours a night** for **four days a week**. Two hours is not that big of a chunk of your night. Set aside two hours, four nights a week for some quality, well-paced studying instead of hours of crazed—and likely ineffective—cramming. Pick a quiet spot in which to do your reading and practice, set a timer, and do your best to avoid any distraction—think of ACT prep as a nonnegotiable part of your week. And, most important, try not to let more than two days go by without a study session.

A few words about your study time and taking the practice tests: For your ACT preparation to be the most effective, you should try your best to simulate the test-taking experience. That means setting aside enough time to take the entire test. The ACT session lasts either 175 minutes (without Writing) or 215 minutes (with Writing). You *can* break up the test sections to fit into your standard two-hour study timeframe, but to simulate the actual ACT experience (including breaks between tests), you will need to set aside *at least* four hours. You will want to consider this time commitment as you include your study plan in your regularly scheduled life. You might have to pass on a trip to the mall or a movie date, but it's worth the sacrifice.

WRITE IT DOWN

Writing helps you to remember and comprehend. If there is a particularly tough concept you're having trouble mastering, try writing it down. It may sound too simple to be effective, but it often works. If there is a grammar or math rule you simply keep forgetting, write it down on an index card and carry it with you. Tackle each troublesome concept one at a time, focusing on it consistently for a few days until you have it memorized. You could carry your index card with you for quick review throughout the day, or you might want to tape your index card or a sheet of paper with the information written on it in a place you will see it every day—your bathroom mirror, the refrigerator, or on a wall in your designated study area. Eventually, it will become a deposit in your memory bank. Once you have the information memorized, move on to the next concept or formula. Simple as it sounds, it really does work!

Something to keep in mind before you start writing: Research has shown that memory is affected by color, and that the colors red and orange in particular stimulate the brain. So when you write down information you want to remember, *use color*. Get a couple of markers if you're going to use index cards, or take advantage of the font colors available on your computer or mobile device.

> **TIP**
>
> If you're more the technology type, use a "sticky notes" app or a list tool on your mobile device to keep track of each concept. You could also create a master list of the concepts in a text document on your computer titled something like "Tricky ACT Concepts." Just be sure to focus on one concept at a time.

PRACTICE, PRACTICE, PRACTICE

In order to be confident on test day, it's important to get used to the layout and format of the ACT exam. You will also be your most prepared if you're familiar with the language of the test and the way questions are asked. Think of all the time you will save on test day if you already know the directions, the test breakdown, and all the question types when you open up your test booklet.

The good news is that this book comes equipped with hundreds of practice questions, a full-length diagnostic test, and six full-length practice tests—four in the book and two online—that mirror the actual ACT you will see on test day, so you should be quite familiar with the ACT after using this guide. Just follow these steps to success:

1) First, before you begin reviewing all the concepts tested on the ACT, take the diagnostic test in Chapter 3 to get a sense of your strengths and weaknesses.

2) Next, make your way through the review sections and answer the 20-question practice sets at the end of each chapter.

3) Finally, throughout your preparation, continue to take practice tests (in Chapter 15) to see the results of what you've learned and to determine where you need to focus for even more review.

DON'T SKIP THE ESSAYS!

When taking practice tests, you may be tempted to skip over the actual "writing" part of the ACT Writing test. One major bit of advice: unless you are absolutely sure you will not be taking the ACT with Writing, don't skip the writing.

You will never get used to the process of reading an essay prompt, perspectives, and task…then taking a stance on the issue to plan out an essay…then writing the essay in its entirety…then editing it…unless you practice the process several times before test day. And remember, you have to do all four of the steps in 40 minutes! Writing isn't even the most difficult part of the process—you need to think on your feet and feel comfortable forming a solid opinion.

There are two full-length practice essays in Chapter 14, and one in each of the four practice tests at the end of this guide. There is also one practice essay in each of the two online practice tests. That's eight opportunities to sharpen your essay writing skills. We recommend that you practice writing at least one ACT essay per week, so if you're following the one- or two-month plan, you're in great shape. But if you've given yourself more time to prepare, where will you find the source of your prompts outside of this book?

We've got you covered.

When you're ready to practice writing essays based on prompts and perspectives like those you will see on the ACT Writing test, go to **www.petersons.com/act**. There you can access and choose from a collection of essay topics. Pick a topic, grab some paper, a few pencils, and a timer, and get ready to write!

You will find instructions much like those on the ACT Writing test for you to follow. Be sure to read them carefully so that you can be sure to craft your essay properly. This isn't the classic five-paragraph persuasive essay you're used to writing--you're going be evaluating, analyzing, and comparing different points of view and relating them to your own.

"But," you may ask, "what if I don't have a point of view?" Look to the world around you.

Make a habit of reading the newspaper (online or print) and looking at news and opinion articles about controversial topics. Choose articles that cover the topics thoroughly, and try to think in terms of multiple perspectives and how you may or may not agree with them. Forming opinions about different topics pulled from actual events will improve your ACT score in a few ways. First, you will greatly expand your vocabulary and comprehension skills if you read well-written journalism. Second, you will practice the skill of forming a solid opinion—a big part of your success on the test. Finally, reading about the world around you will keep you informed about everything from politics to science to pop culture—you'll begin to widen your knowledge base, which will lead to you having more things to say.

Developing the skills of forming opinions and using that skill to express yourself with the prompts we've provided is an unbeatable combination that will lead you to ACT Writing test success.

15

Chapter 2

Test-taking Strategies for the ACT®

KEEP TRACK OF WHAT WORKS—AND WHAT DOESN'T

While taking as many practice tests as you can is always a good thing, it's definitely not an effective exercise unless you use what you've learned from the tests to help you pinpoint the concepts you need to work on and sharpen your skills. Using index cards is a great way to help you remember formulas and general concepts, but you might need more detailed information to help you learn to reason and recognize how to approach and solve specific problem types.

Putting it in writing is still the best way to keep a record of what you need to work on. It doesn't matter how you "write" it—jot it down in a notebook, create a document on your computer or mobile device, or use some of the blank pages at the end of this guide. What should you write down? Anything that will help. Keep track of the items you didn't answer correctly when taking the practice tests, and use the explanations as your tutor. You will find the best way to solve a specific problem type in the explanation given for each question. Record that information so you will be able to solve similar questions in future practice tests and when you encounter them on the ACT. You might also want to list some of the tips you come across in this guide to explain the *why*s and *how*s of the problems giving you trouble.

Take a look at an example of a note that will help a student deal with a probability question. Notice that he included not only the way to solve any problem of this type, but also personal reminders.

Location:	Practice Test 1, Math Test, Question 8
Page:	123
Problem:	Probability—If John can guess a person's age correctly 4/5 of the time, if he guesses four people's ages in a row, what is the probability that he will guess all four ages correctly?
How to Solve:	<u>To calculate the probability of consecutive events occurring, find the product of their individual probabilities.</u> I should have multiplied 80% (the equivalent of 4/5) by itself four times to get the solution, then simplified. Better be careful with exponents—USE CALCULATOR for percentage problems!

You can customize your notes so that they are the most helpful to you; just be sure to include enough information to be useful, but not so much it becomes overwhelming. The goal is to get the trouble spots identified and written down, along with how to solve them so you can focus on mastering the concepts.

TIP Always review your notes and index cards before you take a practice test to be sure that you have all the concepts, tips, and hints you've gathered well in mind.

SAMPLE STUDY PLANS

Now that you've learned some tried-and-true study skills and strategies, you're going to want to make a study plan to tackle all of this material. On the next few pages, you will find some sample study plans based on how much time you have before your test date. But before you get started, here are few tips to help make your study sessions the best they can be.

Study Plan Tips

- **Choose and stick to a study plan.** Set a realistic plan based on your schedule, but keep in mind that the more you put into your test preparation, the better chance you'll have to get the ACT scores you want.

- **Attempt to write one essay a week.** At the very least, look at one essay topic a week and give yourself 3-5 minutes to decide how you would relate your opinion about the topic to the three perspectives provided.

- **Write it down.** Keep a record of the questions and explanations you answer incorrectly on the practice tests and the associated rules, techniques, and formulas. Be specific so your notes will be informative and useful. Make flashcards when necessary. Use a bright-colored marker on the flashcards for an extra memory boost.

- **Pace yourself.** The best test-taking strategy is to answer the easy questions first on your practice tests and skip the questions you have trouble with. If you have time after answering the easy questions, return to the more difficult questions and answer them.

- **Never leave a question blank.** When taking your practice tests, do your best to answer all of the questions in the allotted time, even if you have to guess to complete a section—the ACT does *not* penalize you for a wrong answer!

- **Turn off your cell phone during prep time.** You won't be allowed to have your phone during the test, so now is a good time to learn to live phone-free for a few hours!

- **Get to know your calculator before test day.** Make sure it's an approved calculator and try to figure out which question types are best solved using a calculator and which you should solve without it.

- **Simulate the actual test-taking experience as closely as possible.** Always time yourself during practice tests, and whenever possible, take the whole test at once.

The chapters we suggest you read through every week are just that—suggestions. If you find you have already mastered the math on the ACT, feel free to review just the math practice questions instead of making your way through the entire chapters. Instead, spend your time on English, reading, science, and writing. We created the following plans with the student who needs to tackle all the test sections in mind.

Six-Month Plan

Month 1	
Week 1	• Read Introduction. • Read Chapter 1. • Read Chapter 2.
Week 2	• **Take the Diagnostic Test and review your results.**
Week 3	• Read Chapter 4, "Usage/Mechanics"; answer all practice questions. • Read Chapter 9, "Social Studies and Natural Sciences Passages"; answer all practice questions.
Week 4	• Read Chapter 6, "Pre-Algebra and Elementary Algebra"; answer all practice questions.

Month 2	
Week 5	• Read Chapter 11, "Data Representation"; answer all practice questions.
Week 6	• **Take and review Practice Test 1.**
Week 7	• Read Chapter 14, "Mastering the ACT® Writing Test"; write practice essays.
Week 8	• Read Chapter 5, "Rhetorical Skills"; answer all practice questions. • Read Chapter 10, "Literary Narrative/Prose Fiction and Humanities Passages"; answer all practice questions.

Month 3	
Week 9	• Review notes from previous chapters and tests.
Week 10	• Review Chapter 7, "Intermediate Algebra and Coordinate Geometry"; answer all practice questions.
Week 11	• **Take and review Practice Test 2.**
Week 12	• Read Chapter 12, "Research Summaries"; answer all practice questions.

Month 4	
Week 13	• Read Chapter 8, "Plane Geometry and Trigonometry"; answer all practice questions.
Week 14	• Read Chapter 13, "Conflicting Viewpoints"; answer all practice questions.
Week 15	• **Take and review Practice Test 3.**
Week 16	• Review notes from previous chapters and tests.

Month 5	
Week 17	• Review notes from previous chapters and tests.
Week 18	• **Take and review Practice Test 4.**
Week 19	• Review notes from previous chapters and tests.
Week 20	• Review notes from previous chapters and tests.

Month 6	
Week 21	• **Take and review Practice Test 5.**
Week 22	• Review notes from previous chapters and tests.
Week 23	• **Take and review Practice Test 6.**
Week 24	• Complete final review of trouble spots. • Relax, get sleep, eat well, and mentally prepare for your exam.

THREE-MONTH PLAN

Month 1	
Week 1	• Read Introduction. • Read Chapter 1. • Read Chapter 2. • **Take the Diagnostic Test and review your results.**
Week 2	• Read Chapter 4, "Usage/Mechanics"; answer all practice questions. • Read Chapter 9, "Social Studies and Natural Sciences Passages"; answer all practice questions.
Week 3	• Read Chapter 6, "Pre-Algebra and Elementary Algebra"; answer all practice questions. • Read Chapter 11, "Data Representation"; answer all practice questions.
Week 4	• **Take and review Practice Test 1.** • Read notes from previous chapters and tests.

Month 2	
Week 5	• Read Chapter 14, "Mastering the ACT® Writing Test"; write practice essays. • Read Chapter 5, "Rhetorical Skills"; answer all practice questions.
Week 6	• Read Chapter 10, "Literary Narrative/Prose Fiction and Humanities Passages"; answer all practice questions. • **Take and review Practice Test 2.**
Week 7	• Read Chapter 7, "Intermediate Algebra and Coordinate Geometry"; answer all practice questions. • Read Chapter 12, "Research Summaries"; answer all practice questions.
Week 8	• **Take and review Practice Test 3.** • Review notes from previous chapters and tests. • Read Chapter 13, "Conflicting Viewpoints"; answer all practice questions.

Month 3	
Week 9	• Read Chapter 8, "Plane Geometry and Trigonometry"; answer all practice questions. • **Take and review Practice Test 4.** • Review notes from previous chapters and tests.
Week 10	• Review notes from previous chapters and tests. • **Take and review Practice Test 5.**
Week 11	• Review notes from previous chapters and tests. • **Take and review Practice Test 6.**
Week 12	• Complete final review of trouble spots. • Relax, get sleep, eat well, and mentally prepare for your exam.

Month 1	
Week 1	<ul><li>Read Introduction.</li><li>Read Chapter 1.</li><li>Read Chapter 2.</li><li>**Take the Diagnostic Test and review your results.**</li><li>Read Chapter 4, "Usage/Mechanics"; answer all practice questions.</li></ul>
Week 2	<ul><li>Read Chapter 9, "Social Studies and Natural Sciences Passages"; answer all practice questions.</li><li>Read Chapter 6, "Pre-Algebra and Elementary Algebra"; answer all practice questions.</li><li>Read Chapter 11, "Data Representation"; answer all practice questions.</li><li>**Take and review Practice Test 1.**</li></ul>
Week 3	<ul><li>Review notes from previous chapters and tests.</li><li>Read Chapter 14, "Mastering the ACT® Writing Test"; write practice essays.</li><li>Read Chapter 5, "Rhetorical Skills"; answer all practice questions.</li></ul>
Week 4	<ul><li>Read Chapter 10, "Literary Narrative/Prose Fiction and Humanities Passages"; answer all practice questions.</li><li>Read Chapter 12, "Research Summaries"; answer all practice questions.</li><li>**Take and review Practice Test 2.**</li></ul>
Month 2	
Week 5	<ul><li>Read Chapter 7, "Intermediate Algebra and Coordinate Geometry"; answer all practice questions.</li><li>**Take and review Practice Test 3.**</li></ul>
Week 6	<ul><li>Read Chapter 13, "Conflicting Viewpoints"; answer all practice questions.</li><li>Read Chapter 8, "Plane Geometry and Trigonometry"; answer all practice questions.</li><li>**Take and review Practice Test 4.**</li></ul>
Week 7	<ul><li>Review notes from previous chapters and tests.</li><li>**Take and review Practice Test 5.**</li></ul>
Week 8	<ul><li>**Take and review Practice Test 6.**</li><li>Complete final review of trouble spots.</li><li>Relax, get sleep, eat well, and mentally prepare for your exam.</li></ul>

20

Chapter 2

Test-taking Strategies for the ACT®

Month 1	
Week 1	• Read Introduction. • Read Chapter 1. • Read Chapter 2. • **Take the Diagnostic Test and review your results.** • Review one English, mathematics, reading, and science chapter.
Week 2	• **Take and review Practice Tests 1 and 2.** • Review one additional English, mathematics, reading, and science chapter. • Review writing chapter; write practice essays. • Review notes from previous chapters and tests.
Week 3	• **Take and review Practice Tests 3 and 4.** • Review remaining mathematics and science chapters. • Review notes from previous chapters and tests.
Week 4	• **Take and review Practice Tests 5 and 6.** • Complete final review of trouble spots. • Relax, get sleep, eat well, and mentally prepare for your exam.

As you can see, the less time you have, the more work you have to do in order to prepare for the test. There is a lot of information to learn and retain in order to do well on the test—waiting to prepare makes this a huge challenge. Remember, the ACT is not a test with minimal content you can cram into your brain in a few days—it's comprehensive and complex. You really need to give yourself time to absorb the techniques and practice using them on tests.

THE NIGHT BEFORE TEST DAY

There are some simple things you can do to ensure test day goes as smoothly as possible. It's probably not very helpful to tell you "Relax! Don't let the test stress you out!" Look, taking tests is stressful, and it's natural to feel very anxious about test day. However, there are measures you can take to make it a little less nerve-wracking while you're in the moment.

Our first helpful hint may actually be the exact thing you want to hear: don't study. Well, at least you shouldn't study too much. If you need to cram all night before the test, you probably haven't prepared well enough to give your best effort anyway. So give yourself the night before test day off. Do something fun and relaxing. Spend time with a friend. Watch a movie. Read a book. If you must study, just don't overdo it. You certainly do not want to spend all night studying.

Instead of cramming, you may want to spend the night before test day organizing your supplies. You'll need at least two sharpened No. 2 pencils with fresh erasers (pens and mechanical pencils are not allowed). Pack your calculator, and triple check to make sure it fits the ACT requirements (turn back to page 9 of Chapter 1 for a reminder on calculator rules). Review your route to the testing site one last time to make sure you're not frazzled in the morning. Make sure you have your admission ticket and photo ID. If you think you will need a snack during your 30-minute break, pack it now. If you think you might need a light jacket or sweatshirt in case the testing site is cool, set it aside now.

Getting a good night's sleep before test day is important. Minimize distractions if you can, turn out the lights early, and set an alarm (or two, if you need them!). Rest assured that you are prepped and ready for the ACT. After making your way through this book, you will know the exam inside and out—from the simplest questions to the hardest—and exactly how to answer all of them. Don't forget to take a deep breath and approach every question as if you know the answer. Confidence is key!

SUMMING IT UP

- **Spread out your study time.** Studying a few hours multiple times a week is preferable to studying many hours one or two nights a week.

- **Write down concepts that give you the most trouble.** Doing so is a great way to sear them into your brain. Using color (for example, a red or orange marker) can help you retain the concepts you write down.

- **Keep track of what works—and what doesn't.** Keep a detailed record of the questions you answer incorrectly on the practice tests and their explanations, and the associated rules, techniques, and formulas. This collection of information will give you a one-stop resource of "trouble spots" to review again and again until you master them.

- **Create a study plan and stick with it.** Take full advantage of the practice quizzes provided in each chapter, and treat your practice tests like the real ACT: turn off your phone, find a quiet space with no interruptions, and time yourself while you take the entire test as you would on test day.

- **Relax.** The night before test day should be spent relaxing and organizing any supplies you will need for the test, including your admission ticket and photo ID, No. 2 pencils with erasers, a calculator that meets ACT requirements, and a snack or drink if you think you'll need some refreshment during the 30-minute break.

PART II: THE DIAGNOSTIC TEST

Chapter 3: The Diagnostic Test

DIAGNOSTIC TEST INTRODUCTION

Now that you are familiar with the format of the ACT and how to approach your study plan, it's time to assess your skills in all test areas using the diagnostic test. This test mirrors the ACT you will see on test day—it has the exact number of questions as the ACT, and the questions presented reflect the subject matter you will see on the actual ACT. Use your diagnostic test results to determine the subject areas giving you the most trouble—then focus your most intensive studying there first.

We suggest that you take this exam under conditions that mimic the test as closely as possible. Find a quiet spot where you will have limited or, ideally, no interruptions. As hard as it may be, silence your phone and put it in another room so you're not tempted to look at it. It should go without saying, but turn off the television and don't listen to any music. Treat this like you would an actual exam.

Each subject test will note a time limit at its start. Set a timer and try to answer all of the section's questions in the allotted time. If you find you can't, make a note—time management is an issue you will have to practice before test day. See? That's what this diagnostic test is for—to see where your strengths and weaknesses lie so you can work on them.

Here are a few more suggestions before you start.

- **Get your answer sheets ready.** The answer grid sheets and the pages on which you can plan and write your essay are provided on the next several pages. Cut them out (or if you prefer, photocopy them) and get them organized before you begin your test session.

- **Include breaks in your test session.** Be sure to include a 30-minute break after you take the math test. If you plan on taking the writing test, take a 10-minute break after completing the science test before you begin. That way, you will give yourself the same mental breaks you will get on test day.

- **Use the calculator you will take with you to the ACT.** Be sure that the calculator you intend to use on test day is allowed (see the list of prohibited calculators in Chapter 1, page 9).

- **Don't look for answer choice patterns.** There is no correct answer letter quota on the ACT. Do not feel you have to select a particular answer choice letter (A, B, C, D, etc.) just because you have not selected it in a while.

After the exam you will find full answers and explanations for each test question, sample essays at different levels, and a chart that explains where you can find preparation to help you learn the info in every single test question.

CHAPTER 3:
THE DIAGNOSTIC TEST

OVERVIEW

- Answer Sheets
- English Test
- Mathematics Test
- Reading Test
- Science Test
- Writing Test
- Answer Keys and Explanations
- Diagnostic Test Assessment Grid
- Diagnostic Test Conclusion

English Test

1. Ⓐ Ⓑ Ⓒ Ⓓ   16. Ⓕ Ⓖ Ⓗ Ⓙ   31. Ⓐ Ⓑ Ⓒ Ⓓ   46. Ⓕ Ⓖ Ⓗ Ⓙ   61. Ⓐ Ⓑ Ⓒ Ⓓ
2. Ⓕ Ⓖ Ⓗ Ⓙ   17. Ⓐ Ⓑ Ⓒ Ⓓ   32. Ⓕ Ⓖ Ⓗ Ⓙ   47. Ⓐ Ⓑ Ⓒ Ⓓ   62. Ⓕ Ⓖ Ⓗ Ⓙ
3. Ⓐ Ⓑ Ⓒ Ⓓ   18. Ⓕ Ⓖ Ⓗ Ⓙ   33. Ⓐ Ⓑ Ⓒ Ⓓ   48. Ⓕ Ⓖ Ⓗ Ⓙ   63. Ⓐ Ⓑ Ⓒ Ⓓ
4. Ⓕ Ⓖ Ⓗ Ⓙ   19. Ⓐ Ⓑ Ⓒ Ⓓ   34. Ⓕ Ⓖ Ⓗ Ⓙ   49. Ⓐ Ⓑ Ⓒ Ⓓ   64. Ⓕ Ⓖ Ⓗ Ⓙ
5. Ⓐ Ⓑ Ⓒ Ⓓ   20. Ⓕ Ⓖ Ⓗ Ⓙ   35. Ⓐ Ⓑ Ⓒ Ⓓ   50. Ⓕ Ⓖ Ⓗ Ⓙ   65. Ⓐ Ⓑ Ⓒ Ⓓ
6. Ⓕ Ⓖ Ⓗ Ⓙ   21. Ⓐ Ⓑ Ⓒ Ⓓ   36. Ⓕ Ⓖ Ⓗ Ⓙ   51. Ⓐ Ⓑ Ⓒ Ⓓ   66. Ⓕ Ⓖ Ⓗ Ⓙ
7. Ⓐ Ⓑ Ⓒ Ⓓ   22. Ⓕ Ⓖ Ⓗ Ⓙ   37. Ⓐ Ⓑ Ⓒ Ⓓ   52. Ⓕ Ⓖ Ⓗ Ⓙ   67. Ⓐ Ⓑ Ⓒ Ⓓ
8. Ⓕ Ⓖ Ⓗ Ⓙ   23. Ⓐ Ⓑ Ⓒ Ⓓ   38. Ⓕ Ⓖ Ⓗ Ⓙ   53. Ⓐ Ⓑ Ⓒ Ⓓ   68. Ⓕ Ⓖ Ⓗ Ⓙ
9. Ⓐ Ⓑ Ⓒ Ⓓ   24. Ⓕ Ⓖ Ⓗ Ⓙ   39. Ⓐ Ⓑ Ⓒ Ⓓ   54. Ⓕ Ⓖ Ⓗ Ⓙ   69. Ⓐ Ⓑ Ⓒ Ⓓ
10. Ⓕ Ⓖ Ⓗ Ⓙ   25. Ⓐ Ⓑ Ⓒ Ⓓ   40. Ⓕ Ⓖ Ⓗ Ⓙ   55. Ⓐ Ⓑ Ⓒ Ⓓ   70. Ⓕ Ⓖ Ⓗ Ⓙ
11. Ⓐ Ⓑ Ⓒ Ⓓ   26. Ⓕ Ⓖ Ⓗ Ⓙ   41. Ⓐ Ⓑ Ⓒ Ⓓ   56. Ⓕ Ⓖ Ⓗ Ⓙ   71. Ⓐ Ⓑ Ⓒ Ⓓ
12. Ⓕ Ⓖ Ⓗ Ⓙ   27. Ⓐ Ⓑ Ⓒ Ⓓ   42. Ⓕ Ⓖ Ⓗ Ⓙ   57. Ⓐ Ⓑ Ⓒ Ⓓ   72. Ⓕ Ⓖ Ⓗ Ⓙ
13. Ⓐ Ⓑ Ⓒ Ⓓ   28. Ⓕ Ⓖ Ⓗ Ⓙ   43. Ⓐ Ⓑ Ⓒ Ⓓ   58. Ⓕ Ⓖ Ⓗ Ⓙ   73. Ⓐ Ⓑ Ⓒ Ⓓ
14. Ⓕ Ⓖ Ⓗ Ⓙ   29. Ⓐ Ⓑ Ⓒ Ⓓ   44. Ⓕ Ⓖ Ⓗ Ⓙ   59. Ⓐ Ⓑ Ⓒ Ⓓ   74. Ⓕ Ⓖ Ⓗ Ⓙ
15. Ⓐ Ⓑ Ⓒ Ⓓ   30. Ⓕ Ⓖ Ⓗ Ⓙ   45. Ⓐ Ⓑ Ⓒ Ⓓ   60. Ⓕ Ⓖ Ⓗ Ⓙ   75. Ⓐ Ⓑ Ⓒ Ⓓ

Math Test

1. Ⓐ Ⓑ Ⓒ Ⓓ Ⓔ   16. Ⓕ Ⓖ Ⓗ Ⓙ Ⓚ   31. Ⓐ Ⓑ Ⓒ Ⓓ Ⓔ   46. Ⓕ Ⓖ Ⓗ Ⓙ Ⓚ
2. Ⓕ Ⓖ Ⓗ Ⓙ Ⓚ   17. Ⓐ Ⓑ Ⓒ Ⓓ Ⓔ   32. Ⓕ Ⓖ Ⓗ Ⓙ Ⓚ   47. Ⓐ Ⓑ Ⓒ Ⓓ Ⓔ
3. Ⓐ Ⓑ Ⓒ Ⓓ Ⓔ   18. Ⓕ Ⓖ Ⓗ Ⓙ Ⓚ   33. Ⓐ Ⓑ Ⓒ Ⓓ Ⓔ   48. Ⓕ Ⓖ Ⓗ Ⓙ Ⓚ
4. Ⓕ Ⓖ Ⓗ Ⓙ Ⓚ   19. Ⓐ Ⓑ Ⓒ Ⓓ Ⓔ   34. Ⓕ Ⓖ Ⓗ Ⓙ Ⓚ   49. Ⓐ Ⓑ Ⓒ Ⓓ Ⓔ
5. Ⓐ Ⓑ Ⓒ Ⓓ Ⓔ   20. Ⓕ Ⓖ Ⓗ Ⓙ Ⓚ   35. Ⓐ Ⓑ Ⓒ Ⓓ Ⓔ   50. Ⓕ Ⓖ Ⓗ Ⓙ Ⓚ
6. Ⓕ Ⓖ Ⓗ Ⓙ Ⓚ   21. Ⓐ Ⓑ Ⓒ Ⓓ Ⓔ   36. Ⓕ Ⓖ Ⓗ Ⓙ Ⓚ   51. Ⓐ Ⓑ Ⓒ Ⓓ Ⓔ
7. Ⓐ Ⓑ Ⓒ Ⓓ Ⓔ   22. Ⓕ Ⓖ Ⓗ Ⓙ Ⓚ   37. Ⓐ Ⓑ Ⓒ Ⓓ Ⓔ   52. Ⓕ Ⓖ Ⓗ Ⓙ Ⓚ
8. Ⓕ Ⓖ Ⓗ Ⓙ Ⓚ   23. Ⓐ Ⓑ Ⓒ Ⓓ Ⓔ   38. Ⓕ Ⓖ Ⓗ Ⓙ Ⓚ   53. Ⓐ Ⓑ Ⓒ Ⓓ Ⓔ
9. Ⓐ Ⓑ Ⓒ Ⓓ Ⓔ   24. Ⓕ Ⓖ Ⓗ Ⓙ Ⓚ   39. Ⓐ Ⓑ Ⓒ Ⓓ Ⓔ   54. Ⓕ Ⓖ Ⓗ Ⓙ Ⓚ
10. Ⓕ Ⓖ Ⓗ Ⓙ Ⓚ   25. Ⓐ Ⓑ Ⓒ Ⓓ Ⓔ   40. Ⓕ Ⓖ Ⓗ Ⓙ Ⓚ   55. Ⓐ Ⓑ Ⓒ Ⓓ Ⓔ
11. Ⓐ Ⓑ Ⓒ Ⓓ Ⓔ   26. Ⓕ Ⓖ Ⓗ Ⓙ Ⓚ   41. Ⓐ Ⓑ Ⓒ Ⓓ Ⓔ   56. Ⓕ Ⓖ Ⓗ Ⓙ Ⓚ
12. Ⓕ Ⓖ Ⓗ Ⓙ Ⓚ   27. Ⓐ Ⓑ Ⓒ Ⓓ Ⓔ   42. Ⓕ Ⓖ Ⓗ Ⓙ Ⓚ   57. Ⓐ Ⓑ Ⓒ Ⓓ Ⓔ
13. Ⓐ Ⓑ Ⓒ Ⓓ Ⓔ   28. Ⓕ Ⓖ Ⓗ Ⓙ Ⓚ   43. Ⓐ Ⓑ Ⓒ Ⓓ Ⓔ   58. Ⓕ Ⓖ Ⓗ Ⓙ Ⓚ
14. Ⓕ Ⓖ Ⓗ Ⓙ Ⓚ   29. Ⓐ Ⓑ Ⓒ Ⓓ Ⓔ   44. Ⓕ Ⓖ Ⓗ Ⓙ Ⓚ   59. Ⓐ Ⓑ Ⓒ Ⓓ Ⓔ
15. Ⓐ Ⓑ Ⓒ Ⓓ Ⓔ   30. Ⓕ Ⓖ Ⓗ Ⓙ Ⓚ   45. Ⓐ Ⓑ Ⓒ Ⓓ Ⓔ   60. Ⓕ Ⓖ Ⓗ Ⓙ Ⓚ

Diagnostic Test—Answer Sheet

Reading Test

1. Ⓐ Ⓑ Ⓒ Ⓓ   11. Ⓐ Ⓑ Ⓒ Ⓓ   21. Ⓐ Ⓑ Ⓒ Ⓓ   31. Ⓐ Ⓑ Ⓒ Ⓓ
2. Ⓕ Ⓖ Ⓗ Ⓙ   12. Ⓕ Ⓖ Ⓗ Ⓙ   22. Ⓕ Ⓖ Ⓗ Ⓙ   32. Ⓕ Ⓖ Ⓗ Ⓙ
3. Ⓐ Ⓑ Ⓒ Ⓓ   13. Ⓐ Ⓑ Ⓒ Ⓓ   23. Ⓐ Ⓑ Ⓒ Ⓓ   33. Ⓐ Ⓑ Ⓒ Ⓓ
4. Ⓕ Ⓖ Ⓗ Ⓙ   14. Ⓕ Ⓖ Ⓗ Ⓙ   24. Ⓕ Ⓖ Ⓗ Ⓙ   34. Ⓕ Ⓖ Ⓗ Ⓙ
5. Ⓐ Ⓑ Ⓒ Ⓓ   15. Ⓐ Ⓑ Ⓒ Ⓓ   25. Ⓐ Ⓑ Ⓒ Ⓓ   35. Ⓐ Ⓑ Ⓒ Ⓓ
6. Ⓕ Ⓖ Ⓗ Ⓙ   16. Ⓕ Ⓖ Ⓗ Ⓙ   26. Ⓕ Ⓖ Ⓗ Ⓙ   36. Ⓕ Ⓖ Ⓗ Ⓙ
7. Ⓐ Ⓑ Ⓒ Ⓓ   17. Ⓐ Ⓑ Ⓒ Ⓓ   27. Ⓐ Ⓑ Ⓒ Ⓓ   37. Ⓐ Ⓑ Ⓒ Ⓓ
8. Ⓕ Ⓖ Ⓗ Ⓙ   18. Ⓕ Ⓖ Ⓗ Ⓙ   28. Ⓕ Ⓖ Ⓗ Ⓙ   38. Ⓕ Ⓖ Ⓗ Ⓙ
9. Ⓐ Ⓑ Ⓒ Ⓓ   19. Ⓐ Ⓑ Ⓒ Ⓓ   29. Ⓐ Ⓑ Ⓒ Ⓓ   39. Ⓐ Ⓑ Ⓒ Ⓓ
10. Ⓕ Ⓖ Ⓗ Ⓙ   20. Ⓕ Ⓖ Ⓗ Ⓙ   30. Ⓕ Ⓖ Ⓗ Ⓙ   40. Ⓕ Ⓖ Ⓗ Ⓙ

Science Test

1. Ⓐ Ⓑ Ⓒ Ⓓ   11. Ⓐ Ⓑ Ⓒ Ⓓ   21. Ⓐ Ⓑ Ⓒ Ⓓ   31. Ⓐ Ⓑ Ⓒ Ⓓ
2. Ⓕ Ⓖ Ⓗ Ⓙ   12. Ⓕ Ⓖ Ⓗ Ⓙ   22. Ⓕ Ⓖ Ⓗ Ⓙ   32. Ⓕ Ⓖ Ⓗ Ⓙ
3. Ⓐ Ⓑ Ⓒ Ⓓ   13. Ⓐ Ⓑ Ⓒ Ⓓ   23. Ⓐ Ⓑ Ⓒ Ⓓ   33. Ⓐ Ⓑ Ⓒ Ⓓ
4. Ⓕ Ⓖ Ⓗ Ⓙ   14. Ⓕ Ⓖ Ⓗ Ⓙ   24. Ⓕ Ⓖ Ⓗ Ⓙ   34. Ⓕ Ⓖ Ⓗ Ⓙ
5. Ⓐ Ⓑ Ⓒ Ⓓ   15. Ⓐ Ⓑ Ⓒ Ⓓ   25. Ⓐ Ⓑ Ⓒ Ⓓ   35. Ⓐ Ⓑ Ⓒ Ⓓ
6. Ⓕ Ⓖ Ⓗ Ⓙ   16. Ⓕ Ⓖ Ⓗ Ⓙ   26. Ⓕ Ⓖ Ⓗ Ⓙ   36. Ⓕ Ⓖ Ⓗ Ⓙ
7. Ⓐ Ⓑ Ⓒ Ⓓ   17. Ⓐ Ⓑ Ⓒ Ⓓ   27. Ⓐ Ⓑ Ⓒ Ⓓ   37. Ⓐ Ⓑ Ⓒ Ⓓ
8. Ⓕ Ⓖ Ⓗ Ⓙ   18. Ⓕ Ⓖ Ⓗ Ⓙ   28. Ⓕ Ⓖ Ⓗ Ⓙ   38. Ⓕ Ⓖ Ⓗ Ⓙ
9. Ⓐ Ⓑ Ⓒ Ⓓ   19. Ⓐ Ⓑ Ⓒ Ⓓ   29. Ⓐ Ⓑ Ⓒ Ⓓ   39. Ⓐ Ⓑ Ⓒ Ⓓ
10. Ⓕ Ⓖ Ⓗ Ⓙ   20. Ⓕ Ⓖ Ⓗ Ⓙ   30. Ⓕ Ⓖ Ⓗ Ⓙ   40. Ⓕ Ⓖ Ⓗ Ⓙ

WRITING TEST

PLAN YOUR ESSAY

_____
_____
_____
_____
_____
_____
_____
_____
_____
_____
_____
_____
_____
_____
_____
_____
_____
_____
_____
_____
_____
_____
_____
_____
_____
_____
_____
_____
_____
_____
_____
_____
_____

WRITE YOUR ESSAY

_____

_____

_____

_____

_____

_____

_____

_____

_____

_____

_____

_____

_____

_____

_____

_____

_____

_____

_____

_____

_____

_____

_____

_____

_____

_____

_____

_____

_____

_____

_____

_____

_____

ENGLISH TEST

45 MINUTES—75 QUESTIONS

DIRECTIONS: In this section, you will see passages with words and phrases that are underlined and numbered. In the right-hand column you will see a question corresponding to each number which provides alternatives to the underlined part. In most of the items, you are to choose the best alternative. If no change is needed, choose NO CHANGE.

In other items, there will be either a question about an underlined portion of the passage or a question about a section of the passage, or about the passage as a whole. This question type will correspond to a number or numbers in a box.

For each question, choose the best alternative or answer and fill in the corresponding circle on the answer sheet.

PASSAGE I

Code Talking

[1]

In September of 1992, a group of American heroes who had gone unrecognized for many years was honored by the United States Pentagon. <u>Consisted of</u> thirty-five Navajo code talkers.
₁

[2]

During World War II, the United States Marines needed to develop a <u>code, for communicating</u> top-secret information.
₂

<u>It being the case that they would then have access to information</u>
₃
<u>about United States Marines tactics and troop movements, it</u>
₃
<u>was crucial that enemy forces not be able to decipher the code.</u>
₃

[3]

The military recruited a small group of Navajos to create a code based on their language. The Navajo language made an excellent code for several essential reasons. First, it was extremely difficult to learn and virtually unknown outside the Navajo community in the American Southwest. <u>However,</u> the Navajo language
₄
does not have a written form; it uses no alphabet. Its complexity and obscurity made it the perfect basis for a code.

1. **A.** NO CHANGE
    B. Having consisted of
    C. A group which were made of
    D. It consisted of

2. **F.** NO CHANGE
    G. code for communicating
    H. code, for communicating,
    J. code for communicating,

3. **A.** NO CHANGE
    B. It was crucial to the United States, that enemy forces not be able to decipher the code, having access to information about Marines tactics and troop movements.
    C. It was crucial that enemy forces not be able to decipher the code, because if they did they would have access to information about the Marines' tactics and troop movements.
    D. Crucially, the enemy forces were not able to decipher the code, which would have access to the Marines' tactics and troop movements.

4. **F.** NO CHANGE
    G. Furthermore
    H. Likewise
    J. As a result

CONTINUE

[4]

The first group of Navajo recruits attended boot camp in
1942. <u>Afterward</u>, they set to work developing a vast dictionary
　　　　5
of code words for military terms, based on the Navajo language.
Each code talker had to memorize the dictionary before being
sent to a Marine unit. <u>Using telephones and radios to transmit</u>
　　　　　　　　　　　　　　　　　6
<u>encoded orders and information, once the code talkers were</u>
　　　　　　　　　　　　　　　　6
<u>stationed with a unit.</u>
　　　　6

[5]

While the Navajo language was complicated, the code was even
more complex. A code talker receiving a message heard a stream
of Navajo words. The receiver had to translate the words into

<u>English, and</u> then use the first letter of each English equivalent
　　　7

to spell out a word. <u>Adding to the difficulty,</u> of breaking the code
　　　　　　　　　　　　　　　8
was the fact that most letters could be indicated by the code
talkers with more than one Navajo word. Also, there were certain
military terms that were not spelled out letter by letter, so
although the military terms did not translate to words, the creators
of the code matched Navajo words to them. 9

5.　A.　NO CHANGE
　　B.　As a result
　　C.　However
　　D.　OMIT the underlined portion.

6.　F.　NO CHANGE
　　G.　Once, the code talkers used telephones and
　　　　radios to transmit encoded orders and infor-
　　　　mation, when they were stationed with a unit.
　　H.　Once stationed with a unit, using telephones and
　　　　radios to transmit encoded orders and
　　　　information.
　　J.　Once they were stationed with a unit, the code
　　　　talkers used telephones and radios to transmit
　　　　encoded orders and information.

7.　A.　NO CHANGE
　　B.　English and
　　C.　English and,
　　D.　English, so to

8.　F.　NO CHANGE
　　G.　(Begin new paragraph) Adding to the difficulty
　　H.　(Do NOT begin new paragraph) More difficulty,
　　J.　(Do NOT begin new paragraph) Adding to the
　　　　difficulty

9.　At this point, the writer would like to help readers
　　understand how the code worked. Which of the
　　following sentences, if added here, would most
　　effectively accomplish this?

　　A.　The code was not like Morse code, which used a
　　　　system of dots and dashes to signify letters of the
　　　　alphabet.
　　B.　For example, *besh-lo*, Navajo for "iron fish," was
　　　　the code word for submarine.
　　C.　Prior to this, other Native American languages
　　　　had been used in military codes.
　　D.　The code, which was so difficult, should have
　　　　been acknowledged earlier by the Pentagon.

[6]

Though able to crack the codes of other military branches, enemy forces never managed to decipher what the Marines' Navajo code talkers said. The code talkers were renowned for the speed,
10
and accuracy, with which they worked,
10

and also they were credited by officers for the U.S. Marines' success
11
in World War II.

[7]

The code talkers were acknowledged until quite recently because
12
the Navajo language remained part of a security classified code. At last, though, half a century later, thirty-five former code talkers and their families attended the dedication of the Navajo code talker exhibit at the United States Pentagon, officially taking their place in military history. 13

10. **F.** NO CHANGE
    G. speed, and accuracy
    H. speed and accuracy
    J. speed and accuracy,

11. **A.** NO CHANGE
    B. and officers credited them
    C. they were credited by officers
    D. OMIT the underlined portion.

12. **F.** NO CHANGE
    G. had been unknown
    H. remained unacknowledged
    J. did not get known

13. The writer would like to add an introductory sentence to Paragraph 7 that emphasizes the secrecy surrounding the role of the Navajo code talkers. Which of the choices does that best?

    A. Despite its important role, the work of the Navajo code talkers was virtually unknown outside the military.
    B. The work of the Navajo code talkers was one part of a complex military system.
    C. Many people joined the military looking for glory.
    D. Although code talkers were also involved in the First World War, they did not use the Navajo language.

Questions 14 and 15 ask about the essay as a whole.

14. The writer is planning to add the following sentence to the essay:

So complicated was the code that even a Navajo soldier who had been taken prisoner by the enemy was unable to understand it.

This sentence would best be placed after the last sentence in Paragraph:

    F. 4.
    G. 5.
    H. 6.
    J. 7.

CONTINUE

15. Suppose the writer had been assigned to write an essay describing the contributions of minority soldiers in World War II. Would this essay successfully fulfill the assignment?

   A. Yes, because it describes the contributions of Navajo soldiers.
   B. Yes, because it describes a military maneuver that was crucial to the success of the war.
   C. No, because it discusses the contributions of only one minority group of soldiers.
   D. No, because the essay does not focus on the positive effects of the Navajo soldiers' work.

PASSAGE II

The Real World

[1]

Our college employment counseling center recommended that students have mock interviews before setting out into the world for the real thing. For some reason, I believed that this applied to other people but not to I. Midway through my senior
                                16
year of college, I sent out resumes to several law firms in the area.

16. F. NO CHANGE
    G. to me
    H. for I
    J. applying to me

Nobody was consulted about how to begin seeking a job. My
          17
plan was to work at a law firm for a couple of years before attending law school. I received a couple of responses and was thrilled to set up my first interview, at a prestigious law firm that had offices all over the world. It was exactly the type of environment in which
                            18
I envisioned myself.

17. A. NO CHANGE
    B. With nobody I consulted
    C. Nobody consulted me
    D. I didn't consult with anybody

18. F. NO CHANGE
    G. There was
    H. Here is
    J. And so it was

[2]

The position for which I was interviewing was a clerical job that, the interviewer made clear from the outset, would require long hours, late nights; and a great deal of filing and photo-
                        19
copying. I confidently announced to the interviewer that I didn't mind long hours and thankless assignments. After all, I happily informed him my aim was to work my way up and someday be
        20

19. A. NO CHANGE
    B. nights: and
    C. nights and
    D. nights, and

20. F. NO CHANGE
    G. informed him, my aim
    H. informed, him my aim
    J. informed him my aim,

his boss. I figured the surprised look on his face was because he wasn't used to seeing young men as ambitious and articulate as I was. 21

21. The writer considered deleting the previous sentence and instead writing, "I can't believe I made such a foolish mistake." If the writer had done this, it would have diminished the reader's understanding of:

    I. the narrator's point of view at the time of the interview.

    II. what type of job the narrator wished to obtain.

    III. the interviewer's opinion of the narrator.

  A. I only

  B. II only

  C. I and III only

  D. I, II, and III

I <u>would of</u> kept going, had he not suggested moving on to
22
another topic.

[3]

    In the next phase of the interview, I was asked to list my strengths and weaknesses. I'm sorry to say that here I left nothing to the imagination. I believed that my interviewer would value my stark honesty when I told him that <u>our greatest</u> weaknesses
23
included not getting along with other people very well and a tendency to make more enemies than friends. The interviewer <u>raises</u> his eyebrows but said nothing, and I was certain that he
24

knew he'd found his candidate. After <u>all, I figured,</u> I wouldn't need
25
to get along with people to photocopy and file, so I'd hit upon the perfect answer to a tricky question.

22. **F.** NO CHANGE

     G. could of

     H. would have

     J. would to have

23. **A.** NO CHANGE

     B. my greatest

     C. his great

     D. it was not that my greatest

24. **F.** NO CHANGE

     G. was raising

     H. had raised

     J. raised

25. **A.** NO CHANGE

     B. all I figured,

     C. all I, figured

     D. all I figured

CONTINUE

[4]

(1) I did not get offered that job, nor <u>the next several firms</u>
<u>at which I interviewed for one</u>.
26

26. **F.** NO CHANGE
G. ones for interviewing from the next several firms
H. the next several for which I interviewed at other firms
J. any interviews from the next several jobs at firms

27 (2) Eventually I paid a long-overdue trip to the college job counseling office and got a few pointers on my technique. (3) I am happy to say that while I never did end up going to law

school, I have become a high school guidance counselor who specializes in helping students find internships in community businesses. 28

27. Which of the following sentences, if added here, would most effectively signal the shift in focus that occurs at this point in the essay?

A. I felt very angry at the firms that rejected me as a job candidate.
B. Time and time again, I tried and failed to get a job.
C. Every interview I gave ended much like the first one had: with no promise of a job.
D. After a few months, I finally had to admit that the problem might be with my approach.

28. The writer wants to add a sentence here that would give the essay a sense of completion by tying the ending back to the beginning. Which choice would best accomplish this?

F. Not all of my students are interested in an internship, but I encourage them to give it a try.
G. I conduct practice interviews with every student because, as I tell them, it's a lot harder to give a good interview than one might think!
H. I can't believe that so many of my students have never interviewed for a job before!
J. I can only hope that one of my students will accomplish my early dreams of becoming a lawyer.

29. The writer is considering adding the following sentence to Paragraph 4:

I began to think that perhaps my extra-candid approach was doing me more harm than good, after all.

The most logical and effective place for this sentence would be:

A. before Sentence 1.
B. before Sentence 2.
C. before Sentence 3.
D. after Sentence 3.

PASSAGE III

Tamarin Families

[1]

Deep in the rainforests of Brazil, tiny creatures known as "kings of the jungle" inhabit the trees. These creatures, similar in size to squirrels, have bright, reddish-orange coats and hairless faces; the fur <u>obscuring</u> their faces resembles the mane of a lion.
30
Accordingly, these highly endangered monkeys are called golden lion tamarins.

30. Which choice gives the most appropriate image?

   F. NO CHANGE

   G. encircling

   H. covering

   J. marking

[2]

Tamarins live in small family units of up to nine individuals. Offspring are generally born in <u>pairs, and</u> all members of the
31

31. **A.** NO CHANGE

   B. pairs, which

   C. pairs so

   D. pairs then

<u>group will</u> pitch in to help care for them. Younger tamarins who
32

32. **F.** NO CHANGE

   G. group do

   H. group can

   J. group

participate in caring for <u>it's</u> newborn siblings tend to become
33
better parents themselves.

33. **A.** NO CHANGE

   B. their

   C. its

   D. they

[3]

Tamarins are diurnal, meaning they are active <u>among</u> the
34
daytime. However, they dislike direct sunlight, and so are well-suited to the dense foliage of the forest. At night, they seek shelter in tree hollows. They are omnivorous, eating fruits, insects, and occasionally small lizards and <u>snakes and they</u> spend their time
35

34. **F.** NO CHANGE

   G. amidst

   H. during

   J. withstanding

35. **A.** NO CHANGE

   B. snakes; and they

   C. snakes: they

   D. snakes. They

in <u>trees, using</u> their fingers to grip the branches.
36

36. **F.** NO CHANGE

   G. trees they use

   H. trees to use

   J. trees, use

CONTINUE

[4]

Golden lion tamarins inhabit a distinct ecological <u>niche,</u>
37

37. **A.** NO CHANGE
    B. niche they,
    C. niche they
    D. niche; they

<u>they</u> are found only <u>toward</u> the eastern rainforests of Brazil. As
37   38
farmers clear the rainforest to grow cash crops, the habitat of

38. **F.** NO CHANGE
    G. within
    H. between
    J. below

the tamarins has decreased drastically, <u>but</u> the survival of the
39
species is in extreme danger. Ecologists estimate that there are

only one thousand tamarins remaining in the wild.

39. **A.** NO CHANGE
    B. however
    C. so
    D. nonetheless

[5]

(1) A conservation campaign was initiated in the 1970s to
save the tamarins. (2) The movement began as a collaboration
among the National Zoological Park in <u>Washington, where an</u>
40
<u>Asian elephant was recently born,</u> the Smithsonian Institute,
40
and the Rio de Janeiro Primate Center. (3) Research and education

40. **F.** NO CHANGE
    G. Washington; where an Asian elephant was recently born,
    H. Washington where an Asian elephant was recently born,
    J. Washington,

are also important components of the movement. [41] (4) The
program has grown to address the problem from several angles,

41. For the sake of logic and coherence, Sentence 3 in this paragraph should be placed:

    A. where it is now.
    B. immediately before Sentence 1.
    C. immediately before Sentence 2.
    D. immediately after Sentence 4.

including <u>managing, and restoring</u> the disappearing habitat of
42
the tamarins, breeding tamarins in captivity and in the wild, and
reintroducing tamarins into their natural environment.

42. **F.** NO CHANGE
    G. managing and restoring
    H. managing, and restoring,
    J. managing and restoring,

[6]

So far, efforts to relocate these animals from captivity back into rainforests have been fruitful, making golden lion tamarins one of very few species to be successfully reintroduced into the wild. 43

43. The writer wishes to end on a cautionary note, reminding the reader that the problem of tamarins' endangerment has not yet been solved. Which choice would best accomplish this?

A. Luckily, there are many dedicated professionals who continue to work for the benefit of the tamarin.

B. However, it is only with an unwavering dedication to restoring and preserving their natural habitat that we can expect tamarins to survive.

C. It seems as though the future is bright for the tamarin.

D. Unfortunately, many other species have not been as lucky as the tamarins.

Questions 44 and 45 ask about the essay as a whole.

44. The writer is considering adding the following sentence to the essay:

I, myself, have witnessed the tiny and majestic sight of the golden lion tamarin, and I personally urge that every effort be made to restore this species to health.

Given that this statement is true, should it be added to the essay, and, if so, where?

F. Yes, at the beginning of the first paragraph, to introduce the idea that the tamarin is in danger.

G. Yes, at the end of the last paragraph, to emphasize in the conclusion that the tamarin is worth saving.

H. No, because the passage is not about the need to try to preserve the tamarin.

J. No, because such a personal statement does not fit in with the narrative style of the rest of the essay.

CONTINUE

45. Suppose the editor of a magazine had assigned the author to write an essay describing dangers to the rainforests of Brazil. Does the essay successfully fulfill the assignment?

A. Yes, because the essay mentions that the rainforest is being cleared to make way for cash crops.

B. Yes, because the essay discusses an endangered species in the rainforest.

C. No, because the essay focuses on one endangered species rather than on the rainforest itself.

D. No, because the essay does not mention that the rainforest is in any kind of danger.

PASSAGE IV

Defied Expectations

[1]

On January 23, 1849, in the town of Geneva, New York, Elizabeth Blackwell stepped onto the altar, of the Presbyterian church. And received her Doctor of Medicine degree from the
₄₆

46. **F.** NO CHANGE
G. altar of the Presbyterian church and
H. altar of the Presbyterian church; and
J. altar of the Presbyterian church, and

president of Geneva Medical College. The effect was, she took
₄₇
her place in history. Blackwell had defied the expectations of

47. **A.** NO CHANGE
B. Therefore
C. In doing so
D. Even so

most of her teachers and classmates to become the countries
₄₈
first female doctor.
₄₈

48. **F.** NO CHANGE
G. countries' first female
H. first female country's
J. country's first female

[2]

As a young woman, Blackwell had worked as a teacher, but she found herself unsatisfied. Once she realized that her dream was to be a doctor, she faced tremendous obstacles. There had never before been a female physician in America; girls often
₄₉
didn't even receive the same basic education that boys did. Blackwell's education did not prepare her for the challenges of

49. **A.** NO CHANGE
B. America; as a result, girls
C. America and therefore girls
D. America, but girls

medical school, and <u>to catch up she had to do much</u>. To make
50
up for the gaps in her education, she arranged to live in the

household of a physician, where <u>having access</u> to educational
51
resources and received some medical training.

[3]

As she prepared to apply to medical school, Blackwell sought

advice from physicians in New York and Philadelphia. She found

that they <u>doubted</u> she would be admitted to medical school; at
52
least one advisor went so far as to suggest that she might disguise

herself as a man in order to gain admittance. Her advisors were

not far from wrong in their prediction. Blackwell <u>applies</u> to well
53
over a dozen medical <u>colleges; and received admission to only</u>
54
<u>one. Geneva Medical College.</u>
54

[4]

Gaining admission to the college <u>became</u> the first in a long
55
line of obstacles. Blackwell discovered that her fellow <u>students</u>
56
<u>who were all men and had</u> elected as a joke to admit her, and
56
were <u>astonishing</u> and bewildered when she actually showed up.
57
The students were embarrassed by her presence in lectures on

topics—such as human anatomy—that they considered

unsuitable for mixed company.

50. **F.** NO CHANGE
    G. to catch up she would have
    H. there was for her to do much catching up
    J. she had to catch up

51. **A.** NO CHANGE
    B. she had access
    C. she has access
    D. she did have access

52. **F.** NO CHANGE
    G. debated
    H. insisted
    J. supposed

53. **A.** NO CHANGE
    B. applied
    C. has applied
    D. applying

54. **F.** NO CHANGE
    G. colleges, and received admission to only one,
    Geneva Medical College.
    H. colleges but received admission to only one:
    Geneva Medical College.
    J. colleges. But received admission to only one:
    Geneva Medical College.

55. **A.** NO CHANGE
    B. was not
    C. becomes
    D. were

56. **F.** NO CHANGE
    G. students were all men and they
    H. men students had
    J. students, all of whom were men, had

57. **A.** NO CHANGE
    B. astonished
    C. astonishment
    D. having astonishment

CONTINUE

[5]

Steadily, and with perseverance, Blackwell gained acceptance

among the students and faculty. <u>After,</u> she completed her degree,
58

she continued to <u>face prejudice and outright barriers to her career.</u>
59
She was unable to establish the private practice she had

hoped for, <u>but she had the chance to do other things instead.</u>
60

58. **F.** NO CHANGE
    G. Afterward,
    H. After
    J. After to

59. **A.** NO CHANGE
    B. face outright barriers to her career, that was prejudice
    C. face outright prejudice that was a barrier to her career
    D. face barriers that were outright prejudice to her career

60. Which of these choices, assuming they are all accurate, should the writer use here to show that Elizabeth Blackwell found success as a doctor?

    F. NO CHANGE
    G. and she is remembered for having been the first woman in America to receive a medical degree
    H. but she had a distinguished career as a promoter of preventative medicine and as a champion of medical opportunities for women
    J. and when she went to study at a hospital in Paris, she was assigned the same duties as young girls with no education at all

PASSAGE V

Form and Function in the Roman Aqueducts

[1]

The use of a system of pipes to carry water from its source

to the place where it is needed is an <u>imperious</u> idea, one that
61

can be traced back to several ancient <u>civilizations including,</u>
62
<u>Persia, India, and Egypt.</u> The Roman Empire is generally considered
62

61. **A.** NO CHANGE
    B. unsettling
    C. inimitable
    D. ingenious

62. **F.** NO CHANGE
    G. civilizations, including Persia, India, and Egypt
    H. civilizations including Persia, India and Egypt
    J. civilizations, including: Persia and India and Egypt

to have <u>created the most advancing system</u> of water transport
63
in the ancient world, roughly two thousand years ago.

[?]

The Roman Empire's water transport—or aqueduct—system

was a feat of engineering <u>it combined</u> form and function. The
64
aqueducts were built in Italy, Greece, Spain, France, and other

regions that were within the vast reach of the Roman Empire.

The original Roman aqueducts were quite <u>truly</u> tunnels that ran
65
down hillsides to transport water used to irrigate the plains.

Later, the structures became more <u>elaborate, they</u> were able to
66

conduct water over distances in excess of fifty miles. [67]

[3]

The most famous Roman aqueducts are those that consisted

of tiers of granite arches reaching across valleys. The Romans

used a trial-and-error <u>system; some</u> of their aqueducts
68

<u>failed, for</u> those that succeeded were used as models for subse-
69
quent ones. The principles of engineering that held up the

---

63. **A.** NO CHANGE
   B. created the most advanced system
   C. created in advance of the system
   D. created a system of the most superlative advancement

64. **F.** NO CHANGE
   G. which had been combining
   H. that made a combination of
   J. that combined

65. **A.** NO CHANGE
   B. simply
   C. actually
   D. quickly

66. **F.** NO CHANGE
   G. elaborate but they
   H. elaborate; they
   J. elaborate! So they

67. Which of the following sentences, if inserted here, would best support the writer's point that the aqueducts were an impressive accomplishment?

   A. Today's water transport systems, of course, are far more effective.
   B. The Roman Empire's accomplishments also included finely engineered roads, bridges, and buildings.
   C. Several modern European countries still contain evidence of the aqueducts.
   D. Amazingly, some of these aqueducts are still in use.

68. **F.** NO CHANGE
   G. system, some
   H. system: some
   J. system! Some

69. **A.** NO CHANGE
   B. failed, but
   C. failed, so
   D. fail, but

CONTINUE

successful arches are the same ones that <u>will be applied</u> in modern

70

architecture <u>(for example on many impressive American</u>

71
<u>landmarks).</u>

71

[4]

The stone <u>arches':</u> while well-known, actually consisted of

72
a relatively small portion of the aqueduct system.

<u>The rest of the aqueducts were different</u>. The system took

73
advantage of the force of gravity, which caused the water to flow

from the source to the city, passing through a series of distribution

tanks along the way, providing water to the people of the cities

and to the famous majestic fountains of the Roman Empire.

[5]

Water conduit systems have, of course, undergone hundreds

of decades' worth of modernization. While modern-day aqueduct

systems <u>would</u> transport far more water over far greater distances,

74

they lack the grandeur of the arched Roman aqueducts. 75

---

70. F. NO CHANGE
G. are applied
H. had been applied
J. were applying

71. A. NO CHANGE
B. architecture, for example, on many impressive American landmarks
C. architecture
D. architecture—for example—on many, impressive American landmarks

72. F. NO CHANGE
G. arches
H. arches;
J. arches,

73. Which choice best supports the paragraph by giving the most specific details?

A. NO CHANGE
B. The rest of the aqueduct consisted of a series of underground pipes that were made mostly of stone and terra cotta.
C. The graceful curves of the stone arches are, of course, much more interesting than the rest of the aqueducts.
D. The rest of the system was different, made of several kinds of materials.

74. F. NO CHANGE
G. should
H. will
J. OMIT the underlined portion.

75. The writer wants the final sentence of the last paragraph to reflect the main idea of the whole essay. Which of the following sentences would best accomplish this?

A. NO CHANGE
B. It's too bad that modern technology is not as aesthetically pleasing as it was during the days of the Roman Empire.
C. The Roman Empire will long be remembered for its aqueducts, as well as for its advanced system of political governance.
D. As far as modern technology advances, it will always be indebted to the aesthetic and mechanical achievements of the Roman Empire.

STOP

MATHEMATICS TEST

60 Minutes—60 Questions

DIRECTIONS: For each of the following items, solve each problem, choose the correct answer, and then fill in the corresponding circle on the answer sheet.

If you encounter problems that take too much time to solve, move on. Solve as many problems as you can; then return to the others in the time remaining for the test.

You may use a calculator on this test for any problems you choose, but some of the problems may best be solved without the use of a calculator.

SHOW YOUR WORK HERE

Note: Unless otherwise stated, assume the following:

1. Illustrative figures are NOT necessarily drawn to scale.
2. Geometric figures lie in a plane.
3. The word *line* indicates a straight line.
4. The word *average* indicates arithmetic mean.

---

1. If $a + 2b = a + 18$, then $b =$

   A. 6
   B. 9
   C. 16
   D. 18
   E. 36

2. Barbie answered 2 of the 20 questions on her math test incorrectly. What percent of the questions did Barbie answer correctly?

   F. $\dfrac{2}{20} \times 100\%$

   G. $\dfrac{2}{20 \times 100}\%$

   H. $\dfrac{18}{20} \times 100\%$

   J. $\dfrac{18}{20 \times 100}\%$

   K. $\dfrac{18}{100\%} \times 20$

CONTINUE

3. A delicatessen offers a lunch special composed of a sandwich, a beverage, and a snack. The deli offers 5 kinds of sandwiches, 4 kinds of beverages, and 6 kinds of snacks. How many different lunch special combinations are possible?

A. 20

B. 24

C. 30

D. 60

E. 120

SHOW YOUR WORK HERE

4. If the measure of $\angle A$ is 53°, then the measure of $\angle B$ is 127°.
The measure of $\angle B$ is NOT 127°.

If these statements are both true, then it follows that the measure of:

F. $\angle A$ is NOT 53°.

G. $\angle A$ is 53°.

H. $\angle A$ is 127°.

J. $\angle B$ is 53°.

K. $\angle B$ is NOT 53°.

5. If $0.65 < x < 85\%$, which of the following could be x?

A. $\dfrac{2}{5}$

B. $\dfrac{5}{12}$

C. $\dfrac{5}{8}$

D. $\dfrac{2}{3}$

E. $\dfrac{7}{8}$

6. Set $S = \{0, x + 2, x + 4, x + 6\}$. What is the average of Set S?

F. $\dfrac{3}{4}x + 3$

G. $x + 6$

H. $x + 3$

J. $x + 4$

K. $3x + 12$

7. What is the measure of angle *ABC* in the figure below?

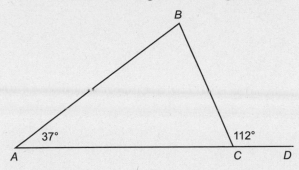

   A. 53°
   B. 68°
   C. 75°
   D. 105°
   E. 143°

8. Which of the following expressions is equal to $15a + 6b$?

   F. $90ab$
   G. $21(a + b)$
   H. $3(5a + 2b)$
   J. $6(5a + b)$
   K. $5(3a + b)$

9. Jamie went out to dinner and paid a total of $42, which included the amount due plus a $7 tip. What percent of the amount due does this tip represent?

   A. 7%
   B. $16\dfrac{2}{3}$%
   C. 20%
   D. 25%
   E. 35%

10. If $\dfrac{n}{6}$ and $\dfrac{n}{8}$ are both integers, all of the following could be *n* EXCEPT:

   F. 192
   G. 96
   H. 48
   J. 24
   K. 12

11. If $a = 6$, then $2a(a - 2)^2 + a \div 3 =$

   A. 32.67
   B. 96
   C. 98
   D. 194
   E. 384

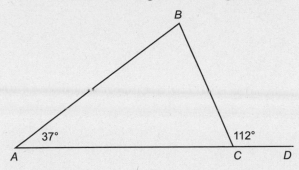
CONTINUE

12. When 64 is divided by x, the quotient is a negative integer. Which of the following could be x?

    F. 16

    G. 6

    H. 1

    J. −8

    K. −12

SHOW YOUR WORK HERE

13. If $17 + x = -23$, then $x =$

    A. −40

    B. −16

    C. −6

    D. 6

    E. 40

14. A group of students fills an entire row in the school auditorium. Counting from the left, Matt is seated in the fourth chair in the row; counting from the right, he is seated in the fifteenth chair in the row. What is the total number of chairs in this row?

    F. 11

    G. 12

    H. 18

    J. 19

    K. 20

15. The area of a rectangle is $x^2 + 4x - 12$ square units. If its length is $x + 6$ units, what is its width, in units?

    A. $\dfrac{x^2 + 3x}{2}$

    B. $(x + 2)$

    C. $(x + 3)$

    D. $(x - 2)$

    E. $(x - 3)$

16. The clock below shows a time of 3:05. What time will the clock show when the minute hand has moved 60° clockwise?

    F. 3:00

    G. 3:15

    H. 3:45

    J. 4:05

    K. 5:05

17. If $a = (x + 1)$ and $b = (x - 1)$, then what is the value of $2ab$?

A. $2x + 2$

B. $2x^2$

C. $x^2 - 1$

D. $2x^2 - 1$

E. $2x^2 - 2$

18. If, in the figure below, point A is the vertex of a square with area 9, which of the following could be another vertex of this square?

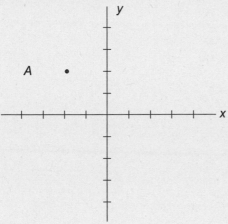

F. $(-9, 2)$

G. $(-5, 5)$

H. $(-2, -7)$

J. $(3, 2)$

K. $(7, 2)$

19. The dimensions in inches of two rectangular solids are given below. If they have equal volumes, what is the value of h in inches?

Box 1: $20 \times 8 \times 12$

Box 2: $4 \times 10 \times h$

A. 6

B. 12

C. 24

D. 48

E. 80

CONTINUE

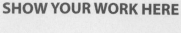

20. How many sections on the spinner below should be colored red in order to make the probability of the arrow NOT landing on red 0.375 in a single spin?

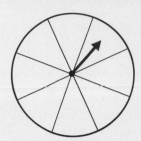

   F.   1
   G. 3
   H. 5
   J.   7
   K. 8

21. Of the triangles with the side lengths given below, which is a right triangle?

   A.   6, 13, 14
   B.   8, 10, 12
   C.   12, 16, 18
   D.   15, 22, 23
   E.   20, 21, 29

22. A corner market sells individual cans of soda for $1.25 each. A superstore sells cases of 24 cans of this soda for $19.20. How much more would it cost to buy 24 individual cans at the market instead of a case from the superstore?

   F. $0.45
   G. $4.80
   H. $4.20
   J. $10.80
   K. $30

23. Martha is wrapping a gift. She wants to put a ribbon around the box and then attach a bow onto the ribbon as shown in the illustration. The ribbon must go completely around the box, and the bow itself will take 25 inches of ribbon. What is the minimum length of ribbon Martha will need, in inches?

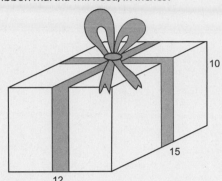

    A. 62
    B. 79
    C. 94
    D. 95
    E. 119

24. $x^5 (x^3)^2 =$
    F. x^{10}
    G. x^{11}
    H. x^{14}
    J. x^{16}
    K. x^{30}

25. The ratio of sugar to flour in a recipe is 2:5. If $1\frac{1}{2}$ cups of sugar are used, how many cups of flour are used?

    A. $\dfrac{3}{5}$

    B. $2\dfrac{1}{4}$

    C. $3\dfrac{3}{4}$

    D. 4

    E. $10\dfrac{1}{2}$

26. What are the roots of the equation $x^2 - 12 = -4x$?

    F. −2 and 6
    G. 2 and −6
    H. −3 and 4
    J. 3 and −4
    K. 1 and −12

CONTINUE

27. Joanie's scores for 3 tests are 100, *x*, and 80. If the median of her scores is higher than the mean of her scores, then which of the following numbers could be *x*?

   A. 60
   B. 70
   C. 80
   D. 90
   E. 100

SHOW YOUR WORK HERE

28. For the complex number *i* such that $i = \sqrt{-1}$, what is the value of $(i^2 - 5)^2$?

   F. −36
   G. −16
   H. −6
   J. 16
   K. 36

29. What is the smallest positive value (in radians) of *x* for which $\cos 3x = 0$?

   A. 0
   B. $\dfrac{\pi}{6}$
   C. $\dfrac{\pi}{3}$
   D. $\dfrac{\pi}{2}$
   E. $\dfrac{2\pi}{3}$

30. Jamal needs to drive 220 miles to City *X* and plans to drive at 55 miles per hour. If he needs to arrive at 3:00 p.m., what is the latest time he can leave?

   F. 9:30 a.m.
   G. 10:30 a.m.
   H. 11:00 a.m.
   J. 11:30 p.m.
   K. 12:00 p.m.

31. Which of the following represents the solution set to the inequality $-5 - 2x < -1$?

   A. ←⊕————————— x
         −4

   B. ——⊕————————→ x
         −4

   C. ——⊕——⊕————— x
        −4 −2

   D. ←————⊕————— x
            −2

   E. ——————⊕————→ x
            −2

32. A fish tank has a length of 24 inches, a width of 8 inches, and a height of 10 inches. If the tank contains 1,728 cubic inches of water, what is the depth, in inches, of water in the tank?

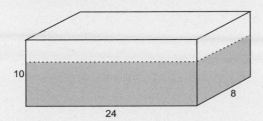

   F.   6
   G.   7
   H.   8
   J.   9
   K.   10

33. A car rental company charges $20 per day for a rental car, plus $0.50 for each mile driven. If Kecia kept a car for 3 days and was charged $156, how many miles did she drive?

   A.   432
   B.   312
   C.   192
   D.   156
   E.   96

34. What is the area, in square feet, of a triangle with sides of length 12 feet, 16 feet, and 20 feet?

   F.   192
   G.   160
   H.   120
   J.   96
   K.   Cannot be determined from the given information

35. If the equation of a line is given as $y = mx + b$, $m =$

   A. $y - b$

   B. $\dfrac{y - b}{x}$

   C. $x(y - b)$

   D. $\dfrac{y + b}{x}$

   E. $\dfrac{x}{y - b}$

CONTINUE

36. The point with coordinates (2, 1) lies on the circumference of a circle with center (2, –3). What is the equation of this circle?

SHOW YOUR WORK HERE

- **F.** $(x - 2)^2 + (y + 3)^2 = 16$
- **G.** $(x + 2)^2 + (y - 3)^2 = 16$
- **H.** $(x - 2)^2 + (y + 3)^2 = 4$
- **J.** $(x + 2)^2 + (y - 3)^2 = 4$
- **K.** $(x - 2)^2 + (y - 1)^2 = 9$

37. $\dfrac{x^2 - y^2}{3x - 3y} =$

- **A.** $\dfrac{3}{x + y}$
- **B.** $\dfrac{x - y}{3}$
- **C.** $\dfrac{x + y}{3}$
- **D.** $\dfrac{x^2 - 3x}{y^2 - 3y}$
- **E.** $\dfrac{1}{3}$

38. In right triangle *ABC* below, $\cos A = \dfrac{1}{2}$. What is the value of $\cos B$?

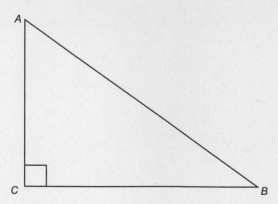

- **F.**   2
- **G.** $\sqrt{3}$
- **H.** $\dfrac{\sqrt{3}}{2}$
- **J.** $\dfrac{\sqrt{3}}{3}$
- **K.** $\dfrac{1}{2}$

39. In △RST, if RS = RT, then which of the following statements about angles S and T MUST be true?

    A. They are acute angles.
    B. They are obtuse angles.
    C. They are right angles.
    D. They are complementary angles.
    E. They are supplementary angles.

40. A packing company is looking to reduce costs by changing the size of its boxes. It wants to create a new box that has the same volume as its current box, but a smaller surface area. The current box is shown below. What are the dimensions, in feet, of the box with the same volume and the smallest surface area?

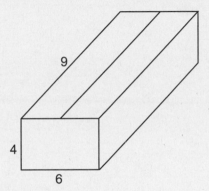

    F. 2 × 3 × 36
    G. 2 × 4 × 27
    H. 3 × 6 × 12
    J. 3 × 8 × 9
    K. 6 × 6 × 6

41. If line *l* is defined by the equation 2y − x = 5, which of the following equations could define a line that is perpendicular to line *l* ?

    A. $y = -\dfrac{1}{2}x + 3$

    B. $y = \dfrac{1}{2}x + \dfrac{5}{2}$

    C. $y = -x - 5$
    D. $y = x + 2$
    E. $y = -2x + 2$

42. Rain is falling at a rate of 0.25 cm each hour. At this rate, how many hours would it take for *c* centimeters of rain to fall?

    F. $\dfrac{c}{0.25}$

    G. $\dfrac{0.25}{c}$

    H. 0.25c
    J. c + 0.25
    K. c − 0.25

CONTINUE

43. The table shows how the variable y depends on various values of x. Which equation best represents this relationship?

x	−2	0	2	4
y	−3	−2	−1	0

A. $y = x - 1$

B. $y = 2x + 1$

C. $y = -2x - 2$

D. $y = \dfrac{1}{2}x - 2$

E. $y = -\dfrac{1}{2}x - 2$

44. If $x > y$ and $z > y$, which of the following MUST be true?

F. $x > z$

G. $z > x$

H. $x^2 > y^2$

J. $z^2 > y^2$

K. $x + z > 2y$

45. If $y + 2x = 5$ and $3y + 2x = 9$, what is the value of $y + x$?

A. $1\dfrac{1}{2}$

B. 2

C. $3\dfrac{1}{2}$

D. 10

E. 14

46. In the figure below, a circle is inscribed within a square. If the perimeter of the square is 36 feet, what is the area of the shaded region, in square feet?

F. $9 - 4.5\pi$

G. $36 - 9\pi$

H. $36 + 9\pi$

J. $81 - 20.25\pi$

K. $81 - 36\pi$

47. A carnival game involves a spinner with congruent sections numbered 1 through 50. On a given spin, the spinner has an equal chance of landing on any number. If Greg bets on numbers 32 through 46, what is the probability that the spinner will land on one of Greg's numbers?

A. $\dfrac{1}{50}$

B. $\dfrac{7}{25}$

C. $\dfrac{3}{10}$

D. $\dfrac{7}{10}$

E. $\dfrac{23}{25}$

48. In the rectangular box shown below, what is the sine of angle *QSR*?

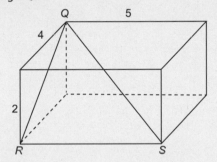

F. $\dfrac{3}{2}$

G. $\dfrac{2}{3}$

H. $\dfrac{\sqrt{5}}{3}$

J. $\dfrac{2\sqrt{5}}{5}$

K. $\dfrac{3\sqrt{5}}{5}$

CONTINUE

49. If the graph of the equation $y = 2x^2 - 4x + c$ never intersects the *x*-axis, which of the following could be the value of *c*?

A. −1

B. 0

C. 1

D. 2

E. 3

SHOW YOUR WORK HERE

50. The length of the radius of circle *A* is 3 times as long as the radius of circle *B*. If the area of circle *A* is *x*, what is the area of circle *B*?

F. $\dfrac{x}{9}$

G. $\dfrac{x}{6}$

H. $\dfrac{x}{3}$

J. $3x$

K. $9x$

51. Which of the following lines is parallel to the line graphed below?

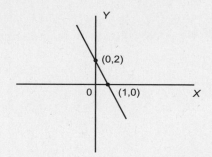

A. $y = x + 2$

B. $y = 2x - 3$

C. $y = -2x + 2$

D. $y = \dfrac{1}{2}x - 5$

E. $y = -\dfrac{1}{2}x + 2$

52. If the area of △ABC is 24 square feet, what is the perimeter of parallelogram *BCED*, in feet?

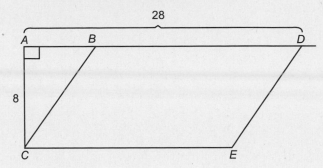

F. 76 feet

G. 72 feet

H. 68 feet

J. 64 feet

K. $44 + 2\sqrt{73}$ feet

53. A ball thrown upward from ground level is *s* feet high after *t* seconds, where $s = 80t - 16t^2$. At which of the following times will the ball be 96 feet above the ground?

A. $\frac{1}{4}$ second

B. 1 second

C. 2 seconds

D. $2\frac{1}{2}$ seconds

E. 4 seconds

54. Working together, a standard printer and a high-speed printer can complete a certain print job in $3\frac{1}{3}$ hours. If it takes the high-speed printer 5 hours to do the job alone, how many hours would it take the standard printer to do the job alone?

F. $1\frac{2}{3}$

G. $4\frac{1}{6}$

H. $6\frac{2}{3}$

J. $8\frac{1}{3}$

K. 10

CONTINUE

55. Increasing a number by 30% and then decreasing the result by 50% is the same as decreasing the number by:

  A. 10%

  B. 15%

  C. 20%

  D. 35%

  E. 65%

SHOW YOUR WORK HERE

56. In the figure below, if Line 1 is parallel to Line 2, all of the following are true EXCEPT:

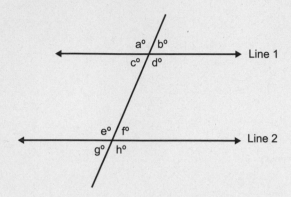

  F. $a + b = g + h$

  G. $f - h = c - d$

  H. $a + h = g + c$

  J. $d + b - f = e + c - g$

  K. $h - c = d - f$

57. In the figure below, what is the value of n?

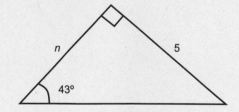

  A. $\dfrac{5}{\sin 43°}$

  B. $\dfrac{5}{\cos 47°}$

  C. $\dfrac{5}{\tan 43°}$

  D. $5 \sin 47°$

  E. $5 \tan 43°$

58. The average of a set of 6 integers is 22. When one of these numbers is removed, the average of the set increases to 25. What is this number?

    F. 3

    G. 7

    H. 15

    J. 16

    K. 18

59. What is the equation of the parabola graphed below?

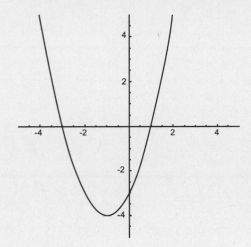

    A. $y = x^2 - 2x - 3$

    B. $y = x^2 - 2x + 3$

    C. $y = x^2 + 2x - 3$

    D. $y = x^2 + 2x + 3$

    E. $y = -x^2 - 2x - 3$

60. If a fair coin is tossed four times, what is the probability of NOT obtaining exactly three heads?

    F. $\dfrac{1}{4}$

    G. $\dfrac{5}{16}$

    H. $\dfrac{5}{8}$

    J. $\dfrac{3}{4}$

    K. $\dfrac{15}{16}$

SHOW YOUR WORK HERE

Ⓧ
STOP

READING TEST

35 Minutes—40 Questions

> **DIRECTIONS:** There are four passages in this test. Each passage is followed by several questions. Read each passage, select the best answer to each related question, and fill in the corresponding circle on the answer sheet. You may look back at the passages as often as you need.

PASSAGE I

PROSE FICTION: Passage A is an excerpt from *The Strange Case of Dr. Jekyll and Mr. Hyde* by Robert Louis Stevenson. Passage B is an excerpt from *The Invisible Man* by H.G. Wells.

Passage A
by Robert Louis Stevenson

Six o'clock struck on the bells of the church that was so conveniently near to Mr. Utterson's dwelling, and still he was digging at the problem. Hitherto it had touched him on the intellectual side alone; but now his imagination also was engaged, or rather
5   enslaved; and as he lay and tossed in the gross darkness of the night and the curtained room, Mr. Enfield's tale went by before his mind in a scroll of lighted pictures. He would be aware of the great field of lamps of a nocturnal city; then of the figure of a man walking swiftly; then of a child running from the doctor's;
10 and then these met, and that human Juggernaut trod the child down and passed on regardless of her screams. Or else he would see a room in a rich house, where his friend lay asleep, dreaming and smiling at his dreams; and then the door of that room would be opened, the curtains of the bed plucked apart, the sleeper
15 recalled, and lo! there would stand by his side a figure to whom power was given, and even at that dead hour, he must rise and do its bidding. The figure in these two phases haunted the lawyer all night; and if at any time he dozed over, it was but to see it glide more stealthily through sleeping houses, or move the more
20 swiftly and still the more swiftly, even to dizziness, through wider labyrinths of lamplighted city, and at every street corner crush a child and leave her screaming. And still the figure had no face by which he might know it; even in his dreams, it had no face, or one that baffled him and melted before his eyes; and thus it
25 was that there sprang up and grew apace in the lawyer's mind a singularly strong, almost an inordinate, curiosity to behold the features of the real Mr. Hyde. If he could but once set eyes on him, he thought the mystery would lighten and perhaps roll altogether away, as was the habit of mysterious things when
30 well examined. He might see a reason for his friend's strange preference or bondage (call it which you please) and even for the startling clause of the will. At least it would be a face worth seeing: the face of a man who was without bowels of mercy: a face which had but to show itself to raise up, in the mind of the
35 unimpressionable Enfield, a spirit of enduring hatred.

From that time forward, Mr. Utterson began to haunt the door in the by-street of shops. In the morning before office hours, at noon when business was plenty, and time scarce, at night under the face of the fogged city moon, by all lights and
40 at all hours of solitude or concourse, the lawyer was to be found on his chosen post.

"If he be Mr. Hyde," he had thought, "I shall be Mr. Seek."

Questions 1–3 ask about Passage A.

1. As it is used in line 12, the word *rich* most nearly means:
    - A. wealthy.
    - B. affluent.
    - C. abundant.
    - D. plush.

2. Mr. Utterson starts spending time by the door in the by-street of shops:
    - F. while having a nightmare about Mr. Enfield.
    - G. after deciding he needs to see Mr. Hyde.
    - H. before talking to his friend about Mr. Hyde.
    - J. on his way to his place of work.

3. It can be inferred from the passage that the relationship between Mr. Utterson and Mr. Hyde is most similar to that between:
    - A. two brothers.
    - B. a police officer and a criminal.
    - C. an employee and a boss.
    - D. former co-workers.

Passage B
by H.G. Wells

The stranger came early in February one wintry day, through a biting wind and a driving snow, the last snowfall of the year, over the down, walking as it seemed from Bramblehurst railway station and carrying a little black portmanteau in his thickly
5   gloved hand. He was wrapped up from head to foot, and the

CONTINUE

brim of his soft felt hat hid every inch of his face but the shiny tip of his nose; the snow had piled itself against his shoulders and chest, and added a white crest to the burden he carried. He
10 staggered into the Coach and Horses, more dead than alive as it seemed, and flung his portmanteau down. "A fire," he cried, "in the name of human charity! A room and a fire!" He stamped and shook the snow from off himself in the bar, and followed Mrs. Hall into her guest parlour to strike his bargain. And with that much introduction, that and a ready acquiescence to terms
15 and a couple of sovereigns flung upon the table, he took up his quarters in the inn.

Mrs. Hall lit the fire and left him there while she went to prepare him a meal with her own hands. A guest to stop at Iping in the winter-time was an unheard-of piece of luck, let alone a guest
20 who was no "haggler," and she was resolved to show herself worthy of her good fortune. As soon as the bacon was well under way, and Millie, her lymphatic aid, had been brisked up a bit by a few deftly chosen expressions of contempt, she carried the cloth, plates, and glasses into the parlour and began to lay them
25 with the utmost clat. Although the fire was burning up briskly, she was surprised to see that her visitor still wore his hat and coat, standing with his back to her and staring out of the window at the falling snow in the yard. His gloved hands were clasped behind him, and he seemed to be lost in thought. She noticed
30 that the melted snow that still sprinkled his shoulders dripped upon her carpet. "Can I take your hat and coat, sir," she said, "and give them a good dry in the kitchen?"

"No," he said without turning.

She was not sure she had heard him, and was about to repeat
35 her question.

He turned his head and looked at her over his shoulder. "I prefer to keep them on," he said with emphasis, and she noticed that he wore big blue spectacles with side-lights and had a bushy side-whisker over his coat-collar that completely hid his
40 face.

"Very well, sir," she said. "As you like. In a bit the room will be warmer."

He made no answer and had turned his face away from her again; and Mrs. Hall, feeling that her conversational advances
45 were ill-timed, laid the rest of the table things in a quick staccato and whisked out of the room.

Questions 4–6 ask about Passage B.

4. What does the first paragraph (lines 1–16) suggest about the stranger?

- F. He has something to hide.
- G. He is a wanted criminal.
- H. He is the strangest man Mrs. Hall has ever met.
- J. He is about to die.

5. As it is used in line 2, the word *biting* most likely means:

- A. snapping.
- B. freezing.
- C. abrasive.
- D. hateful.

6. Which of the following statements does NOT describe Mrs. Hall's attitude toward the stranger?

- F. She cares about his well-being.
- G. She is uneasy in his presence.
- H. She is amused by his odd behavior.
- J. She feels she is professionally obligated to him.

Questions 7–10 ask about both passages.

7. Both passages are mainly about:

- A. people who are enslaved by a mysterious stranger.
- B. people with friends who are in trouble.
- C. people who must deal with a mysterious person.
- D. people who must perform tasks they feel uncomfortable doing.

8. It can be reasonably inferred that one way Mr. Utterson in Passage A is DIFFERENT from Mrs. Hall in Passage B is:

- F. he is intrigued by a mysterious person.
- G. he finds someone's behavior baffling.
- H. he feels concern for other people.
- J. he likes to solve mysteries.

9. It can be reasonably inferred that these two passages:

- A. occur on the final pages of the novels from which they were excerpted.
- B. are the most important incidents in the novels from which they were excerpted.
- C. were intended to be humorous tangents in the novels from which they were excerpted.
- D. occur early in the novels from which they were excerpted.

10. Paragraph 1 of Passage A and Paragraph 2 of Passage B are both mainly about:

- F. the arrivals of mysterious people.
- G. the effects mysterious people have on others.
- H. the evil deeds mysterious people do.
- J. the demanding nature of mysterious people.

PASSAGE II

SOCIAL SCIENCE: This passage is adapted from an article in a popular economics magazine.

For more than two centuries, the bull and the bear have symbolized two opposing forces in stock exchanges. A bull represents a market that is rising, strong, and profiting. A bear

represents a market that is falling, weak, and losing. These terms
5 are also used for the people whose attitudes are fundamentally
supportive of one force over the other. A bullish stockbroker is
positive and confident, believing that stock prices will rise,
whereas a bearish investor is negative and cautious, believing
that stock prices will fall.

10 Why was this particular pair of animals chosen? In the seventeenth and eighteenth centuries, bull-baiting and bear-baiting
were cruel yet popular sports. The prevalence of such heartless
games caused bulls and bears to be commonly associated as
opposites. In terms of their roles in nature, however, they don't
15 seem to be particularly disparate in build or character, as, for
instance, a lion and a sheep might be. Bulls and bears are both
large, powerful, aggressive creatures. Perhaps a bull is considered
to be more powerful and aggressive than the average bear, but
even smaller breeds of bears can become quite mean when
20 provoked. Surely there must be a better animal than the bear
to represent falling share prices. How about the chicken?
Remember Chicken Little, the comical coward who, when a leaf
landed on his tail, believed that the entire sky was falling? And
although the bull seems to make a perfectly fine symbol for
25 strong market activity, there are plenty of other candidates for
the role. How about the little piggy who went to market? Certainly
as years pass and economies grow, more people have become
piggish about stocks.

Consider also that life does not always progress in a linear
30 fashion but moves in cycles, like the seasons: growing, maturing,
harvesting, and regenerating. In light of this viewpoint, the bear
and the bull might not be the best representatives of stock
market swings. Should the various moods and supporters of the
markets be reduced to mere ups and downs? What about markets
35 that are indecisive, always bobbing up and down like rabbits or
frogs? Perhaps these are more appropriate symbols to reflect
the fickle tendencies of markets.

Despite these alternative options, history has chosen the bull
and the bear—and a powerful image, once ordained, usually
40 sticks. There are a few theories, some stronger than others, as
to why the bull and the bear reign as the market's mascots. One
such theory suggests that the two directions any market can
take are symbolized by the way each of these creatures attacks:
the bear slashes with his claws in a downward motion, while the
45 bull charges and gores upward with his horns.

A more probable theory involves fur traders on the early
American frontier. Some bear hunters were called "bearskin
jobbers" because they sold bearskins before they actually caught
the bears. Likewise, in the stock market, some speculators had
50 a strategy of selling shares "short," meaning that they sold shares
of stock they did not yet actually own. They made these advance
sales hoping that the share price would go down before they

were actually due to pay for them. If the price did fall as anticipated, the speculator made a profit on the difference between
55 the high selling price and the lower buying price. So this similar
attitude of "sell now, catch later" was applied to the speculators,
and they were nicknamed bears.

In 1785, an Englishman named Thomas Mortimer wrote one
of the earliest known references to the two types of market
60 players as being bulls and bears. Perhaps he was already familiar
with the American bearskin jobber slang, but he took the metaphor a step further. Remember that the bears employed the
strategy of selling shares short, hoping the price would fall once
payment was due. Mortimer claimed that this type of trader
65 went to the exchange hungrily seeking "whose property he can
devour," eager to hear of "any misfortune that may bring about
the wished-for change of falling stocks." The bulls employed a
strategy nearly opposite that of the bears. They optimistically
bought stocks on margin—a method similar to the bearish
70 strategy of selling shares short. The main difference, however,
was that a bull bought stocks at a lower price—with little or no
money—then hoped that the prices would rise by the time
payment was due. If the price went up between the time of
purchase and the time of payment, then the bull sold the shares
75 and kept the difference as profit. According to Mortimer, this
kind of trader tended to act like a bull, hoping to unload "his
heavy burden by selling it to another person."

Perhaps more retrospective consideration has been given to
the notion of the bull and bear as stock market symbols than
80 was ever given to the choice when it was initially made. In our
efforts to make sense of the symbols, we may inadvertently have
ascribed more significance to them than they were ever intended
to have. Whatever their origin, and however meaningful their
earliest designation as stock market symbols, the bear and the
85 bull are destined to be permanently pitted against one another
in the arena of the trading room floor.

11. According to the passage, bearskin jobbers were:

   A. hunters who cheated their customers out of
      money.
   B. hunters who sold bearskins before they caught
      them.
   C. speculators who short-sold shares of stock.
   D. speculators who bought shares of stock on margin.

CONTINUE

12. The author suggests that bulls and bears "don't seem to be particularly disparate in build or character" (line 15) because:

    F. stock markets can be difficult to predict.
    G. lions and sheep are a better combination.
    H. most breeds of bears are bigger than bulls.
    J. both animals are big, strong, and fierce.

13. In the fifth paragraph (lines 46–57), the main point is that the expression of a speculator being a bear:

    A. originally represented how the short-seller acted.
    B. has been the subject of a few theories about its origin.
    C. came from the early American fur trade.
    D. came from the way a bear attacks with its claws.

14. The passage states that when buying stocks on margin, speculators hope that:

    F. the price will fall before the shares are bought.
    G. the price will rise before the payment is due.
    H. they can borrow money to buy the stocks.
    J. a bull will optimistically buy shares from them.

15. As it is used in line 28, the word *piggish* most likely means:

    A. optimistic.
    B. greedy.
    C. immoral.
    D. unpredictable.

16. Which of these statements is supported by the third paragraph (lines 29–37)?

    F. Bulls and bears might not be the best animals to represent complex stock market forces.
    G. There are many theories about how bulls and bears came to be symbols of the stock market.
    H. Ups and downs are the only two forces that control the stock market.
    J. The strategy of bearish speculators is riskier, but the rewards can be greater too.

17. Bearish speculators, in contrast to bullish ones, are described as:

    A. having a more scientific approach to investing.
    B. buying shares with little or no money.
    C. losing money when share prices drop.
    D. hoping to profit from falling share prices.

18. The author's attitude toward bull-baiting and bear-baiting is one of:

    F. curiosity.
    G. disapproval.
    H. admiration.
    J. wrath.

19. Together with other information in the passage, Mortimer's writings suggest that:

    A. there are many theories about bulls and bears.
    B. speculators even acted like bulls and bears.
    C. the market tends to favor bulls over bears.
    D. bulls and bears are recent symbols of the market.

20. Based on the last paragraph (lines 78–86), the author believes that:

    F. symbols should not become more important than the facts they represent.
    G. the bull and bear are misleading symbols that have negatively affected the market.
    H. people might be attributing too much meaning to the bull and bear symbols.
    J. without symbols, it is difficult to understand the complexities of the market.

PASSAGE III

HUMANITIES: This passage is adapted from an essay about Javanese performance art.

In a public square on the Indonesian island of Java, dusk falls. Families gather; it is a festival day, and the air hums with excitement. Children dart around while, on the edges of the square, vendors hawk snacks and toys. A large screen, lit from
5 behind, stands prominently in the square. A twenty-piece percussion orchestra, or *gamelan*, prepares to play. Soon, a performance will begin that will last all night long.

The scene is modern-day Java, or perhaps Java hundreds of years ago. The performance is *wayang kulit*, or shadow puppetry,
10 one of the world's oldest storytelling traditions. The origins of *wayang kulit* stretch back to the ancient spiritual practices of Indonesia's original inhabitants, who believed that the spirits of the ancestors governed the living world. Ceremonial puppet plays addressed the spirits, asking them to help the living.

15 Over two thousand years ago, islands such as Java, Bali, and Sumatra saw their first migrants from India, a nation to which Indonesia was linked through trade relations. In the centuries that followed, Indian culture influenced not only Indonesia's language, religion, and arts, but virtually every aspect of
20 Indonesian life. Indonesian government imitated the monarchal system of India, Indonesian laborers were categorized by class,

or caste, and the Indian religion of Hinduism took root on the islands.

The traditional puppet plays reflected these cultural changes.
25 They began to depict narratives from Hindu religious texts, including the *Mahabharata*, the *Ramayana*, and the *Serat Menak*. Traditional Indonesian stories were either blended into Hindu epics or lost altogether. Later, when Islam began to spread throughout Indonesia, puppet plays again transformed. The
30 Islamic religion prohibited the display of gods in human form, so Indonesians adapted their art by making flat, leather puppets that cast shadows on a screen. The puppets themselves remained unseen during the performance; only their shadows were visible. *Wayang kulit* was born.

35 Java is particularly well known for its continuation of the shadow puppet tradition. Performances are truly epic events, lasting from sunset to sunrise with no break. They take place in public spaces, generally temple yards or village squares, and are performed on holidays and festival days and at family celebrations.
40 At the center of the performance is a large screen, backlit by a gas or electrical light. Behind this screen sits the *dalang*, or shadow master, who is traditionally a man. The *dalang* is the driving force behind the show. He manipulates the puppets—sometimes more than a hundred of them in a single show—with rods, voicing
45 and singing all of the roles. Simultaneously, he directs the *gamelan*, the large percussive orchestra that accompanies the play. While sticking primarily to the traditional narrative, he occasionally improvises to add humor and topical references.

The artistry of *wayang kulit* is apparent in even the smallest
50 details of the performance. Each puppet is carefully crafted, a flat figure that is intricately perforated to project a highly detailed shadow. Artists begin creating a puppet by tracing the outline of a paper model on leather, marking where holes will be cut. The leather figure is painstakingly smoothed and treated before
55 being passed onto another craftsperson, who paints it. Then, the puppet's moving parts—the arms and hands—are added, along with the sticks used to manipulate its parts. These puppets follow an established set of conventions: evil characters have grotesque, exaggerated faces, while noble ones have more refined features.
60 They are highly stylized caricatures, rather than realistic figures.

Javanese audiences traditionally split in half at *wayang kulit* performances, with women on one side of the screen watching the shadows, and men on the other viewing the actual puppets. Viewers who see the puppets gain an additional level of infor-
65 mation during the performance, because the puppets' colors are significant. In the course of a play, characters often appear in different colors to indicate changes in their emotions or circum- stances. A red character, for instance, has a hot temper; a white

character is youthful and innocent. Certain characters are always
70 painted the same color. For example, the face of the Hindu god Vishnu is always painted black, while the god Shiva's face is always painted gold.

As it endures, shadow puppetry continues to evolve. Female *dalangs*, though still uncommon, are no longer unheard of. In
75 addition to filling public spaces, productions are broadcast reg- ularly on Indonesian television. Javanese artists perform around the world, often incorporating the art, music, and dance of other cultures. The centuries-old art form flourishes, bridging Indonesia's rich past with its future.

21. Which of the following is NOT characteristic of shadow puppets?

    A. They are made of leather.

    B. They are painted different colors.

    C. They have moveable parts.

    D. They have natural-looking faces.

22. One can reasonably infer that at traditional *wayang kulit* performances:

    F. the *dalang* encourages the audience to participate.

    G. children are not welcome.

    H. there are several puppeteers working at one time.

    J. women do not see the colors of the puppets.

23. The creation of *wayang kulit* was influenced by:

    I.   the traditional ceremonies of ancient Indonesians.

    II. the spread of Islam in Indonesia.

    III. early Christian texts.

    A. I and II only

    B. I and III only

    C. II and III only

    D. I, II, and III

24. As it is used in line 73, the word *endures* most nearly means:

    F. suffers.

    G. tolerates.

    H. manages.

    J. lasts.

CONTINUE

25. The main point of the third paragraph (lines 15–23) is that:

   A. Indonesia lost its identity once migrants from India arrived.
   B. Indian culture greatly influenced Indonesian culture.
   C. Indonesians lacked religious beliefs before the spread of Hinduism.
   D. the traditional arts of Indonesia shaped much of Indian culture.

26. The passage implies that:

   F. modern-day *wayang kulit* performances differ drastically from traditional ones.
   G. Hindu gods are regular characters in *wayang kulit* performances.
   H. shadow puppetry is equally popular throughout all of Indonesia.
   J. *dalangs* must be talented craftspeople in addition to storytellers.

27. According to the sixth paragraph (lines 49–60), the rods used to move the puppets' arms are added:

   A. immediately after the leather outline of the puppet is cut.
   B. after the puppets are painted.
   C. before the leather is treated.
   D. before the arms and hands are added.

28. All of the following are said to have been influenced by Indian migrants EXCEPT:

   F. architecture.
   G. government.
   H. language.
   J. religion.

29. Based on the passage, one way that *wayang kulit* has changed is that:

   A. a large proportion of *dalangs* are now female.
   B. fewer of the performances are based on traditional texts.
   C. people don't have to be in public spaces to view performances.
   D. performances have become similar to the plays and movies of Western culture.

30. The sentence "The scene is modern-day Java, or perhaps Java hundreds of years ago" (lines 8–9) suggests that:

   F. the island of Java has resisted modernization.
   G. the people of Java dress as they did in ancient times.
   H. shadow puppet performances have changed little over the centuries.
   J. Java does not welcome visitors from other countries.

PASSAGE IV

NATURAL SCIENCE: This passage is adapted from a scientific website.

Smell is considered to be the most delicate of our five senses. It has many practical functions—allowing us, for example, to determine whether food has gone bad or to detect smoke when something is burning. Our noses are powerful tools for recog-
5 nizing familiar people and places or recalling old memories: we can smell things that remind us of our aunt's cooking or our second grade classroom, just as an infant can identify the individual scents of its mother and father. Smell also factors into romance, which is why the perfume industry labors to extract
10 and mix pleasure-provoking aromas. The nose even plays a complementary role in tasting: if you plug your nose while eating, you will find that your food seems to lose some of its taste. It is certainly true that we can perceive much more subtle olfactory variations than visual or auditory ones.

15 Despite all of these known applications, our knowledge of just *how* the nose knows is less than that of how our other senses operate. First of all, it's often difficult to describe how something smells. It's relatively easy to identify a D major chord or paint a verbal picture of something that is silvery-blue, but the fragrance
20 of a rose is more elusive. The scent of one rose might be "flowery and sweet, with a touch of citrus," while that of another might be more "like honey and freshly-cut grass." Even those employed in the perfume and food industries often have trouble agreeing on how to describe and categorize particular scents.

25 Sights and sounds are measured in terms of their wavelengths, which can be assessed with scientific instruments. Scent molecules are not as easy to quantify. We know that molecules up to a certain mass have scents, but there are conflicting theories as to what determines their smell and how the nose records and
30 transmits this information to the brain. Until recently, most experts believed us able to recognize a certain smell based on a molecule's shape. Such a theory asserts that when a scent molecule of a certain shape enters the nose and touches a receptor, like a key, it unlocks and triggers a particular smell, which is then sent to
35 the brain. Likewise, a variety of different scent molecules can open a combination of locks, sending a mixture of scent signals

to the brain ("smells like this spaghetti sauce has basil and garlic in it"). This "lock-and-key" theory does hold true for the shape and smell of many molecules. For instance, most molecules that
40 contain an amine group will have a fishy smell. There are, however, many instances of similarly shaped molecules with different smells, and vice versa. For example, two differently shaped compounds will still smell like rotten eggs if they both contain sulfur.

Luca Turin, a biophysicist and perfume enthusiast, questioned
45 these discrepancies and resolved to form a new theory of his own. Turin has performed many experiments that refute the lock-and-key theory. He believes that out of literally millions of different smells, there are too many cases in which the shape does *not* determine the smell. He once demonstrated this
50 assertion by comparing a hydrocarbon called camphane (the main component of camphor, sometimes used in cold medicines) with decaborane. Decaborane resembles camphane structurally, except that it has boron atoms where camphane has carbon atoms. According to the lock-and-key theory, both compounds
55 should smell like camphor. However, the decaborane instead smells like rotten eggs (which is surprising, as it contains no sulfur). This example proves that molecular shape is not always the determining factor of smell.

Then what exactly *is* the determining factor? Turin theorizes
60 that it's the *vibration* of a molecule's atoms that provides its signature smell. The number of atoms and electrons connected within a molecule determines that molecule's particular vibration. The result of these minute shakes and quivers can be recorded as a particular frequency. The receptors in the nose, therefore,
65 actually record the vibration of the molecules and transmit that information to the brain as a scent. This theory puts smell in the same category as sight and sound. Colors can be measured along a spectrum of light according to their wavelengths; tones can be measured along a spectrum of octaves according to their
70 wavelengths. Turin claims that the same types of measurements can be taken with smells.

Although the frequencies of scents are much more complicated to measure, measuring them is exactly what Turin has set out to do.

Because many scientists (not to mention perfume executives)
75 disagree with him, Turin has struggled to gain recognition for his theory. However, a rare condition known as synaesthesia, which is characterized by a scrambling of the senses, seems to offer support. People with synaesthesia claim that they have heard colors, smelled sounds, or seen odors. For instance, a
80 musician may be immersed in playing a song and interpret everything he perceives as being sounds—not only the music, but sights and smells as well. Doctors believe that some babies are unable to distinguish among sight, smell, and sound until their brains develop the ability to process each sense
85 separately.

If Turin's theory turns out to be true, then it may be possible to design specific scents by creating molecules of particular frequencies. The perfume industry has traditionally created scents by mixing varieties of essential oils and other aromatic ingredients.
90 However, it may become possible to re-create synthetic odor molecules that have floral, citrine, or musky scents. A computerized molecular modeling program, if perfected, could create such synthetic molecules; it would display and define a spectrum of smell vibrations, and then predict where along the spectrum
95 any particular scent molecule's vibration would place it. To this end, an important goal should be to create perfumes that are biodegradable and less expensive, yet still appealing to the nose.

31. What is the main idea of the first paragraph (lines 1–14)?

    A. Our sense of smell has many practical and pleasurable functions.

    B. Our sense of smell is not as well understood as our senses of sight and sound.

    C. People can recognize very subtle smells, such as that of their home or of their parents.

    D. It is more difficult to describe how something smells than how it looks.

32. Luca Turin compared camphane with decaborane to prove that:

    F. they have similar smells but different shapes.

    G. they have similar shapes but different smells.

    H. one has a fishy smell and the other has a sulfur smell.

    J. they both smell like the same kind of cold medicine.

33. The passage mentions that Luca Turin is a:

    A. perfume executive.

    B. biophysicist.

    C. computer programmer.

    D. medical doctor.

34. It can be inferred from the third paragraph (lines 25–43) that molecules above a certain mass:

    F. do not have a scent.

    G. smell like rotten eggs.

    H. have a stronger scent.

    J. can be tasted in food.

CONTINUE

35. According to the author, babies:

    I. depend mainly on their sense of smell right after birth.

    II. are usually able to recognize their parents by their scents.

    III. sometimes confuse their senses of smelling, seeing, and hearing.

    A. II only

    B. I and II only

    C. II and III only

    D. I, II, and III

36. The author claims that Turin's theory "puts smell in the same category as sight and sound" (lines 66–67) because:

    F. they are all interpreted in terms of their particular vibrations.

    G. people sometimes confuse sights, sounds, and smells.

    H. they are all easy to measure and define.

    J. the sense of taste is enhanced by these other three senses.

37. The passage states that the "lock-and-key" theory of smell:

    A. was developed by Luca Turin.

    B. was challenged by Luca Turin.

    C. measures the vibration of a scent molecule.

    D. measures the strength of a particular smell.

38. Luca Turin's theory of smell asserts that:

    I. differently shaped molecules may have the same smell.

    II. the size of the molecule determines the smell.

    III. the vibrations of atoms determine the smell.

    F. I only

    G. II only

    H. II and III only

    J. I and III only

39. As it is used in line 45, the word *discrepancies* most nearly means:

    A. inconsistencies.

    B. disagreements.

    C. similarities.

    D. definitions.

40. The author concludes that artificially creating perfume scents:

    F. has helped to prove Turin's theory of scent frequencies.

    G. would be too complicated to ever achieve.

    H. will never be as good as using natural ingredients.

    J. may make them cheaper and more environmentally friendly.

STOP

SCIENCE TEST

35 MINUTES—40 QUESTIONS

DIRECTIONS: There are seven passages in this test. Each passage is followed by several questions. Read each passage, select the best answer to each related question, and fill in the corresponding circle on the answer sheet. You may look back at the passages as often as you need.

You are NOT allowed to use a calculator on this test.

PASSAGE I

Transpiration is the process by which land plants lose water through evaporation from tiny pores on the underside of leaves called *stomata*. Some plants close their stomata at certain points to stop additional water loss and prevent wilting. Some plants cease transpiring when the humidity level in the surrounding air reaches a point of saturation at which it can bear no more moisture. Students carried out experiments to explore how the rate of transpiration is influenced by environmental conditions as well as the surface area of plant leaves.

Experiment 1

Students studied the effects of temperature on the transpiration rates of plants A, B, and C. They used a *potometer* (a device that allows one to calculate the amount of moisture lost by a plant over time) to measure the amount of water lost in milliliters (mL) from the plants at five 10-minute intervals at each of three temperature settings: room temperature, in a refrigerator, and under a heat lamp.

All factors other than temperature were kept constant. The results are recorded in Table 1.

Table 1															
Temperature and Time Variables		**Room Temperature**					**Refrigerator**					**Heat Lamp**				
		Intervals (min.)					**Intervals (min.)**					**Intervals (min.)**				
		10	20	30	40	50	10	20	30	40	50	10	20	30	40	50
Water Loss (mL)	Plant A	.5	.45	.45	.6	.55	.02	.03	.01	.03	.01	1.0	.9	1.2	1.1	1.0
	Plant B	2.1	1.9	1.8	2.0	1.9	1.1	1.3	.9	1.2	1.3	2.8	2.5	.7	0	0
	Plant C	.35	.4	.25	.3	.3	0	0	0	0	0	.7	.7	.6	.75	.8

Diagnostic Test — SCIENCE

CONTINUE

Experiment 2

The students tested the effects of humidity levels on the same plants and at the same intervals as Experiment 1. All factors other than humidity were kept constant. The results are shown in Table 2.

Humidity and Time Variables		No Humidity Intervals (min.)					Medium Humidity Intervals (min.)					High Humidity Intervals (min.)				
Table 2																
		10	20	30	40	50	10	20	30	40	50	10	20	30	40	50
Water Loss (mL)	Plant A	0.7	0.75	0.6	0.6	0.65	0.2	0.15	0.15	0.2	0.25	0.05	0.1	0.1	0.05	0.05
	Plant B	0.45	0.4	0.5	0.4	0.45	0.03	0.04	0.04	0.04	0.02	0	0	0	0	0
	Plant C	2.9	2.9	3.1	2.8	2.8	2.2	2.3	2.2	2.1	2.2	1.6	1.4	0	0	0

Experiment 3

The students repeated the heat lamp experiment on three different specimens of Plant A: one with 10 leaves, one with 50 leaves, and one with 100 leaves. Water loss figures were recorded over five 10-minute intervals, and the mean water losses per 10-minute interval were calculated. Each specimen was observed under the same environmental conditions. The results are indicated in Table 3.

Table 3		
Plant A Specimen	Number of Leaves	Mean Water Loss Under Heat Lamp per 10-minute Intervals (mL)
1	10	0.3
2	50	1.8
3	100	3.4

1. The information in the passage suggests that humidity and temperature:

    A. are the only factors determining plant transpiration rates.
    B. have the same effect on plant transpiration rates.
    C. have opposite effects on plant transpiration rates.
    D. have no effect on plant transpiration rates.

2. The students used different specimens of the same plant in Experiment 3 most probably because:

    F. they wished to isolate a single factor for observation.
    G. they wished to compare the effects of the two factors studied in Experiments 1 and 2.
    H. only Plant A can be examined under a heat lamp.
    J. transpiration is more likely to occur in plant A than in any other plant.

3. One can deduce from the results that the Plant A specimen used in Experiment 1 had:

    A. fewer than 10 leaves.
    B. 10 leaves.
    C. between 10 and 50 leaves.
    D. more than 50 leaves.

4. Which of the following explanations best accounts for the results of Experiment 3?

    F. Plants with more leaves close their stomata more often.
    G. Plants with more leaves contain more stomata.
    H. Plants with fewer leaves are more vulnerable to heat.
    J. Plants with fewer leaves live in more humid environments.

5. Assume that the students varied the leaf number in Experiment 3 in order to determine how increases in a plant's leaf surface area influence the plant's rate of transpiration. Which of the following, if true, would invalidate the experiment?

A. The leaves on all three specimens of Plant A are roughly the same size.

B. The leaves on all three specimens of Plant A are on average larger than the leaves on specimens of Plant C.

C. The leaves on all three specimens of Plant A are of a different shape than the leaves on specimens of Plant B.

D. The leaves on the specimen of Plant A with 10 leaves are on average 10 times the size of the leaves on the specimen of plant A with 50 leaves.

6. At what point is it most likely that plant stomata closed to prevent wilting?

F. In Plant A in the refrigerator at the 20-minute mark

G. In Plant B under the heat lamp at the 40-minute mark

H. In Plant B at high humidity at the 10-minute mark

J. In Plant C at medium humidity at the 30-minute mark

PASSAGE II

Waves are believed to be caused by the transference of energy from wind to a body of water as the wind pushes the water ahead of it. Based on this theory, wave height should be proportional to the speed of the wind that generates the wave. Scientists exploring this hypothesis performed the following experiments.

Experiment 1

A recording station was constructed to measure wind speeds and wave heights at an ocean location. For each wave detected, the height of the wave as it passed the station was recorded, as was the wind speed at the station at the precise moment of crossing. The information recorded by the station's sensors is presented in Figure 1.

FIGURE 1

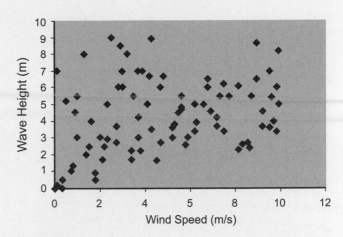

Experiment 2

Swell waves are waves that originate in storm centers. When a swell wave moves faster than the storm that produced it, it often maintains its height and spreads to further regions beyond the storm. Over the course of a week, scientists observed the percentage of waves crossing the recording station used in Experiment 1 that did not originate in the station's vicinity. The results are depicted in Table 1.

Table 1	
Day	**Percentage of Swell Waves**
Monday	13
Tuesday	37
Wednesday	7
Thursday	21
Friday	6
Saturday	3
Sunday	28

CONTINUE

Experiment 3

A recording station was constructed to measure the wind speeds and wave heights in a small lake with minimal access to larger water bodies. Wind speed and wave height measurements, collected in the same manner as described in Experiment 1, are represented in Figure 2.

FIGURE 2

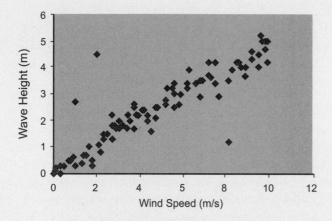

7. The significance of Experiment 2 is that it:

   A. demonstrates that swell waves are just as likely to appear in ocean areas as in lake areas.
   B. raises the possibility that the wind speeds observed by the recording station were skewed by the effects of storms taking place in regions beyond the testing site.
   C. reveals that the recording station used in Experiment 1 primarily detected waves created by distant storms.
   D. establishes the likelihood that some waves measured in Experiment 1 were not created by the winds present at the recording station.

8. One is most likely to accurately predict the approximate height of a wave when the wind is blowing 12 m/s at:

   F. neither the ocean station nor the lake station.
   G. both the ocean station and the lake station.
   H. the ocean station but not the lake station.
   J. the lake station but not the ocean station.

9. The results of Experiments 2 and 3:

   A. disprove the hypothesis stated in the passage's introduction.
   B. help to explain the shape of the data depicted in Figure 1.
   C. demonstrate that the measurements taken in Experiment 1 were improperly interpreted.
   D. call into question the ability of recording stations to accurately measure wind and wave properties.

10. The data in the passage lend most support to which of the following statements?

   F. Wave height is influenced by wind speed in lakes but not in oceans.
   G. The ocean area observed in Experiment 1 contained more swell waves than the lake area observed in Experiment 3.
   H. Swell waves are invariably larger than wind waves.
   J. It is impossible to use wind speed to predict wave height.

11. Figure 2 suggests that swell waves of which of the following heights crossed the recording station used in Experiment 3?

   A. 1.2 m and 2.7 m
   B. 0.5 m and 2.0 m
   C. 2.7 m and 5.0 m
   D. 1.2 m and 6.0 m

12. In order to lend further support to the hypothesis stated in the passage's introduction, scientists could:

   F. repeat the lake experiment on a day with severe thunderstorms.
   G. repeat the ocean experiment on a perfectly wind-free day.
   H. collect data on wave height and wind speed from an indoor pool exposed to a powerful electronic blower.
   J. collect data on wave height and wind speed from a body of water not as open as an ocean but not as enclosed as a lake.

PASSAGE III

A *projectile* is defined as an object upon which the only force is gravity. In order to observe the parameters of a projectile, a student hit a tennis ball with a racquet and filmed the ball's trajectory. She then viewed the film and used equations to simulate the ball's trajectory in terms of its horizontal distance from the point of impact and its corresponding vertical height above the ground. Various readings, presented in chronological order from the beginning of the ball's movement until the end, are recorded in Table 1.

Table 1			
Horizontal Distance (m)	Vertical Height (m)	Horizontal Distance (m)	Vertical Height (m)
0	1	15	0.9
1.5	2.3	16.5	1.2
3.0	3.3	18	0
4.5	4.0	19.5	0.5
6.0	4.5	21	0
7.5	4.7	22.5	0
9.0	4.1	24.0	0
10.5	3.2	22.0	0
12.0	2.1	20.0	0
13.5	0	18.0	0

Figure 1 indicates the ball's horizontal distance from the point of impact as plotted against time.

FIGURE 1

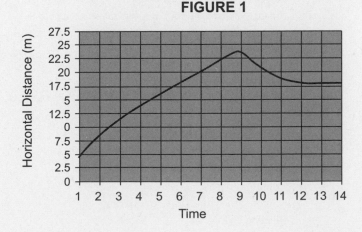

13. The data indicates that the ball bounced approximately:
   A. 3 seconds after impact.
   B. 6 seconds after impact.
   C. 9 seconds after impact.
   D. 13 seconds after impact.

14. The data indicates that exactly 8 seconds after impact, the ball was:
   F. flying in the air away from the point of impact.
   G. flying in the air toward the point of impact.
   H. rolling on the ground away from the point of impact.
   J. rolling on the ground toward the point of impact.

15. The information in the passage suggests that the ball:
   A. continued moving for 14 seconds.
   B. encountered an obstacle toward the end of its movement.
   C. maintained a single direction during the course of its movement.
   D. increased steadily in height for 9 seconds following impact and then decreased gradually in height after that.

16. If the vertical height of the ball is plotted against time, how would the general shape of the resulting graph compare to the shape of the graph in Figure 1?
   F. It would be the same, because the vertical and horizontal parameters of the ball's trajectory are nearly identical.
   G. It would be different, because the horizontal parameter of the ball's trajectory varies with time while the vertical parameter of the ball's trajectory does not.
   H. It would be the same, because both the horizontal distance from the point of impact and the vertical height of the ball first increase and then decrease with time.
   J. It would be different, because the vertical height of the ball follows a repeating pattern of increases and decreases over time.

CONTINUE

17. Which of the following can be inferred from the data in the passage?

- **A.** The ball rolled on the ground from 8 seconds after the student hit it to 12 seconds after the student hit it.
- **B.** The ball traveled away from the point of impact from 7 seconds after the student hit it to 12 seconds after the student hit it.
- **C.** The ball rolled on the ground from 12 seconds after the student hit it to 14 seconds after the student hit it.
- **D.** The ball flew in the air from 7 seconds after the student hit it to 10 seconds after the student hit it.

PASSAGE IV

The number of cases of childhood asthma has risen dramatically in the past few decades. The following hypotheses attempt to account for the increasing incidence of this disease among children.

Contaminants Hypothesis

The dramatic increase in childhood asthma in recent decades can be explained by the fact that children today are more exposed to environmental contaminants, including dust, pollen, molds, pesticides, air pollution, second-hand cigarette smoke, and food additives. Taken together, these chemicals form a "toxic soup" that envelops children, either attacking their lungs directly, triggering the wheezing and shortness of breath characteristic of asthma, or compromising their immune systems, making them more susceptible to a wide range of diseases. Moreover, because they spend a greater amount of time indoors watching television, playing video games, or using computers, children today have greater exposure to indoor allergens than in the past.

Hygienic Hypothesis

The dramatic increase in childhood asthma in recent decades can be attributed to the over-obsession with health and clean-liness that has pervaded our culture. We increasingly sanitize our homes with disinfectants, immunize our children to ward off even minor, non-life-threatening diseases, and shield children from "unclean" animals and other children with the slightest sign of a cold. However, the human body evolved over millions of years in close proximity to its natural surroundings, including dirt, germs, and all kinds of noxious elements; the human immune system evolved specifically to recognize and fight such elements. If children have not been sufficiently exposed to germs and impurities at an early age, their underused immune systems become hypersensitized when they do eventually encounter these elements. Such immune system deficiencies predispose children to asthma and other similar diseases.

18. Adherents to the two hypotheses would disagree most strongly on the issue of whether:

- **F.** increased television viewing correlates with increased exposure to allergens.
- **G.** there has been a significant recent increase in the incidence of childhood asthma.
- **H.** exposure to environmental impurities is conducive to a child's health.
- **J.** children today are less exposed to germs than children were in the past.

19. If a child who moves from a rural countryside to a congested metropolitan area develops asthma for the first time, this could support:

- **A.** the Contaminants Hypothesis but not the Hygienic Hypothesis.
- **B.** the Hygienic Hypothesis but not the Contaminants Hypothesis.
- **C.** both the Contaminants Hypothesis and the Hygienic Hypothesis.
- **D.** neither the Contaminants Hypothesis nor the Hygienic Hypothesis.

20. Proponents of the Contaminants Hypothesis could use which piece of evidence from the Hygienic Hypothesis to support their own theory?

- **F.** The increase in childhood immunizations, if it could be shown that sometimes these immunizations cause severe side effects
- **G.** The decrease in children's exposure to animals, if it could be shown that this negatively affects the development of such children's immune systems
- **H.** The increased use of household sanitizers, if it could be shown that such products contain chemicals that can trigger asthma attacks
- **J.** The increase in childhood immunizations, if it could be shown that such immunizations are extremely successful in warding off major human diseases, such as polio

21. Proponents of the two theories agree on which of the following propositions?

- **A.** Environmental factors can affect a child's immune system.
- **B.** Today's children have hypersensitive immune systems.
- **C.** Asthma is the worst disease currently afflicting children.
- **D.** Childhood asthma will be cured if steps are taken to clean up the environment.

22. Believers in the Hygienic Hypothesis would be likely to characterize the effect of what they describe as our society's preoccupation with health as:

    F. detrimental because it causes us to disregard the effects of the noxious elements of our environment.

    G. beneficial because it leads people to immunize their children against a multitude of diseases.

    H. unquantifiable because the effects of our society's obsession with health and cleanliness cannot be precisely determined.

    J. ironic because current actions intended to promote health actually diminish it.

23. A parent is considering applying a synthetic mosquito repellent to his six-month-old child. Which of the following reactions would be most expected based on the information in the passage?

    A. Supporters of the Hygienic Hypothesis would encourage the use of the repellent.

    B. Supporters of the Hygienic Hypothesis would discourage the use of the repellent.

    C. Supporters of the Hygienic Hypothesis would not have an opinion on the use of the repellent.

    D. Supporters of the Contaminants Hypothesis would encourage the use of the repellent.

24. Some scientists believe that an increase in the survival rate of low-birth-weight babies has greatly increased the number of children susceptible to asthma. How does this theory relate to the two theories presented in the passage?

    F. It supports the Contaminants Hypothesis but not the Hygienic Hypothesis.

    G. It supports the Hygienic Hypothesis but not the Contaminants Hypothesis.

    H. It supports both the Contaminants Hypothesis and the Hygienic Hypothesis.

    J. It supports neither the Contaminants Hypothesis nor the Hygienic Hypothesis.

PASSAGE V

It has long been hypothesized that the average adult needs 7 to 8 hours of sleep daily to ensure optimal functioning of mind and body, and that sleep deprivation causes not only physical impairments but mental abnormalities as well. Researchers conducted studies to explore the ways in which sleep deprivation affects the performance of mental tasks and the physiological activities of the brain.

Study 1

Ten healthy adults volunteered to remain awake for an entire night and participate in cognitive tests over the course of a 30-hour sleepless period. Each subject was awoken at 7:00 a.m. on Day 1 of the study for the first set of tests and, subsequently, was tested every 3 hours until 1:00 p.m. on Day 2. Each testing trial consisted of verbal, math, and short-term memory tasks, rated at the same difficulty level from trial to trial. The researchers measured both the speed and the accuracy of responses to test items, combining these scores into a mean Proficiency Quotient on a scale from 1 to 10. Results are depicted in Figure 1.

FIGURE 1

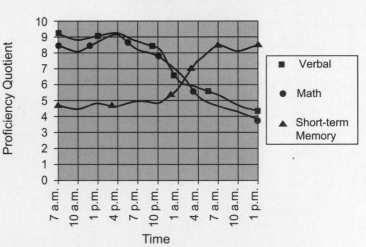

Study 2

A sleep-deprived volunteer, awake for 25 straight hours, and a fully rested volunteer, observed 1 hour after waking from a restful 8-hour sleep, were monitored while responding to the questions and tasks listed in Table 1. Functional magnetic resonance imaging (MRI) scans were used to indicate brain activity while the subjects responded. The *temporal lobe* and the *parietal lobe* are two regions of the cerebral cortex. The activity status of these regions during the responses to the specific questions and tasks are indicated in Table 1, with a checkmark signifying activity in that lobe and an "X" signifying lack of activity.

Table 1				
Question / Task	Sleep-Deprived Subject		Rested Subject	
	Temporal Lobe	Parietal Lobe	Temporal Lobe	Parietal Lobe
What is 642 divided by 27?	X	X	X	✓
Read the following text from Lincoln's Gettysburg Address [text provided].	X	✓	✓	X
Define "loyalty."	X	✓	✓	X
Fill in the blank in the following sequence: 3, 7, 15, 31, ___, 127	X	X	X	✓
Describe a memorable dream you had during childhood.	X	✓	✓	X
Calculate: (232 + 464 − 117) × 6	X	X	X	✓

25. It is reasonable to conclude that the researchers selected the specific questions and tasks used in Study 2 with the intention of:

　A. supplementing some of the findings of Study 1.
　B. refuting the findings of Study 1.
　C. defending the method employed in Study 1.
　D. invalidating the method employed in Study 1.

26. The study results indicate that definite but substandard math capability is most probably exhibited by:

　F. both the temporal and parietal lobes of sleep-deprived people.
　G. some lobe other than the temporal and parietal lobes of sleep-deprived people.
　H. the temporal lobe of rested people.
　J. the parietal lobe of rested people.

27. The results of Study 2 best support which of the following hypotheses?

　A. The temporal lobe may, in some instances, compensate for inactivity of the parietal lobe in the brains of sleep-deprived people.
　B. The parietal lobe may, in some instances, compensate for inactivity of the temporal lobe in the brains of sleep-deprived people.
　C. The temporal lobe may, in some cases, supersede the parietal lobe in the processing of short-term memory tasks.
　D. Math tasks are primarily processed in brain regions outside of the cerebral cortex.

28. A weakness of Study 1 is that its results do not allow one to differentiate between:

　F. the general impact of sleep deprivation on memory and verbal proficiency.
　G. the respective functions of the temporal and parietal lobes.
　H. the speed of responses and the accuracy of responses.
　J. the subject areas addressed in the study.

29. Insomnia is an inability to sleep. The methodology of Study 1 would be most flawed if it were found that:

　A. all ten participants reported experiencing episodes of insomnia at some points in their lives.
　B. five of the participants reported changes in their sleep patterns during the week following the study.
　C. four of the ten participants suffered from severe insomnia during the middle of the night prior to Day 1 of the study.
　D. all ten participants experienced insomnia during the entire 30-hour study.

30. The short-term memory performance indicated in Study 1 would be more understandable if it were found that short-term memory tasks are processed primarily by:

　F. the entire cerebral cortex.
　G. lobes exterior to the cerebral cortex.
　H. the temporal lobe.
　J. the parietal lobe.

PASSAGE VI

Coagulation of the blood—commonly called *clotting*—is the process by which blood solidifies to stop the flow of bleeding. Clotting requires numerous proteins called *clotting factors*, which generally circulate in the bloodstream in an inactive state. These factors are activated in a series of steps when clotting is required.

The clotting process begins with the appearance of Tissue Factor emitted by damaged cells. Tissue Factor binds to activated Factor 7 and forms an enzyme called TF-7, which activates Factor 10; Factor 10, in turn, binds to and activates Factor 5. This creates an enzyme called *prothrombinase*, which converts *prothrombin* to *thrombin*. Thrombin helps to form soluble molecules of fibrin and also activates Factor 13, which converts the soluble fibrin molecules into an insoluble meshwork forming the clot. This process is summarized in Figure 1.

FIGURE 1

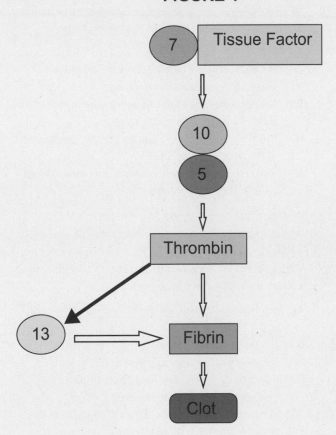

This initial clotting process is *amplified* by the further activation of these and other factors which are inserted back into the clotting process to enhance its effect. Table 1 lists four proteins that play a role in this amplification process.

Table 1	
Protein	**Activates Factor:**
TF-7	9
Thrombin	5, 8, 11
Complex Formed from Factors 8 and 9	10
Factor 11	9

Calcium ions are also required for clotting to take place.

31. The clotting mechanism resulting from the combination of processes depicted in Figure 1 and Table 1 can best be characterized as a/an:

    A. efficient cycle of positive reinforcement.
    B. negative feedback loop.
    C. random interaction.
    D. inherently flawed design.

32. Certain blood diseases are caused by malfunctions in the amplification stage of the clotting process. Based on the information in the passage, which of the following would be least likely to be implicated in the onset of such diseases?

    F. A deficiency in the activation of Factor 9
    G. A deficiency in the activation of Factor 11
    H. A deficiency in the binding of Factor 8 and Factor 9
    J. A deficiency in the activation of Factor 13

33. A chelating agent is used to bind calcium ions, rendering them ineffective. Which of the following people would be most likely to benefit from this agent?

    A. A doctor treating a bleeding accident victim
    B. A technician in a blood donation facility
    C. A geneticist researching the molecular makeup of blood
    D. A hemophiliac suffering from an inability to form blood clots

CONTINUE

34. Factor 8 circulates naturally in the blood and is stabilized by a protein called von Willebrand Factor. A deficiency of or mutation in von Willebrand Factor causes it to lose its protective impact on Factor 8, resulting in von Willebrand disease, a clotting disorder that mimics hemophilia. This condition is most likely to lead to a deficiency in:

F. Factor 7.
G. TF-7.
H. prothrombinase.
J. prothrombin.

35. Some scientists theorize that treatable human bleeding disorders are caused by abnormalities in the amplification process and are characterized by a Factor 9 deficiency. This hypothesis would be most strengthened if it were true that:

A. human bleeding disorders occasionally result in death when not treated in time.
B. Factor 11 deficiencies are fatal to humans.
C. clotting could not occur without the further activation of factors during the amplification stage.
D. Factors 8 and 11 are activated by thrombin, while Factor 9 is activated by TF-7.

PASSAGE VII

The study of *psychoacoustic effects* explores how sounds are perceived under various circumstances. Researchers discovered that a sustained sound steadily increased in intensity (volume) will seem to a listener to change in pitch. This was dubbed "Stevens's Rule" after the scientist who explored and documented this phenomenon. Sounds with frequencies below 2,000 hertz (Hz) are considered low-frequency sounds, and sounds with frequencies above 2,000 Hz are considered high-frequency sounds. A *pure tone* is a single frequency tone consisting of a fundamental harmonic with no harmonic overtones.

Table 1 indicates the effect that an increase in intensity from 60 to 90 decibels (dB) has on the perceived pitch of pure tones at various frequencies. The perceived change in pitch is measured in *cents*, a unit of pitch based upon the equal-tempered octave. A *semitone* (the difference between a C and a C sharp on a piano, for example) is equal to 100 cents.

Table 1	
Effect on pitch of intensity increase from 60 to 90 dB	
Frequency of Pure Tone (Hz)	Perceived Change in Pitch (Cents)
6,000	30
4,000	20
2,000	0
1,000	0
200	−20
50	−30

Because the pitch of such complex sounds as speech and music is perceived by listeners as an amalgamation of several harmonics, such sounds are impacted by Stevens's Rule to a lesser extent than are pure tones.

36. Which of the following generalizations about psychoacoustic effects is supported by the information in Table 1?

F. The pitch of some high-frequency pure tones seems higher at lower intensities.
G. The pitch of some high-frequency pure tones seems lower at higher intensities.
H. The pitch of some low-frequency pure tones seems higher at lower intensities.
J. The pitch of some low-frequency pure tones seems lower at higher intensities.

37. Assume that a singer sings into a microphone that is amplified by a public address system. If the singer holds a note at a frequency of 200 Hz for 10 seconds while the volume of the PA is increased from 60 to 90 decibels, the audience would most likely perceive:

A. no change in pitch from the beginning of the note to the end.
B. a decrease in pitch of less than 20 cents from the beginning of the note to the end.
C. a decrease in pitch of exactly 20 cents from the beginning of the note to the end.
D. a decrease in pitch of more than 30 cents from the beginning of the note to the end.

38. Which of the following inferences regarding Stevens's Rule is best supported by the data presented in Table 1?

F. It is not operative for pure tones in certain frequency ranges.

G. It applies uniformly to sounds across all frequency ranges.

H. It is most observable for pure tones above 90 dB.

J. It is least observable for pure tones below 50 Hz.

39. A pure tone at a frequency of 5,000 Hz is played for 10 seconds while the intensity is raised from 60 to 90 decibels. Based on the information in Table 1, one would expect the perceived difference in pitch from the beginning to the end of the tone to be:

A. greater than 1 semitone.

B. equal to 1 semitone.

C. between 0.5 and 1 semitone.

D. between 0 and 0.5 semitone.

40. A pure tone at a frequency of 6,000 Hz is amplified through a public address system and played at an intensity of 100 dB. At the end of 10 seconds, a listener is expected to perceive:

F. an increase in the tone's pitch.

G. a decrease in the tone's intensity.

H. no change in the tone's pitch.

J. an increase in the tone's intensity.

Ⓧ
STOP

WRITING TEST

40 MINUTES

> **DIRECTIONS:** This is a test of your writing skills. You have forty (40) minutes to write an essay in English. Be sure to carefully read the issue and three perspectives presented before planning and writing your essay so you understand clearly the task you are being asked to do. Your essay will be graded on the evidence it provides of your ability to analyze the issue; evaluate and analyze the perspectives; state and develop a personal perspective; and describe the relationship between the given perspectives and your own, while effectively using organization, logic, and language according to the conventions of standard written English.

THE CLASSROOM OF THE FUTURE

Most of us are accustomed to learning in traditional classrooms—with walls, windows, teachers, and fellow classmates all together in rooms, in pursuit of common educational goals. But advances in technology and online learning may change the shape of the future classroom. We conduct a wide array of important daily tasks online: paying bills, making purchases, maintaining relationships with friends and family, and conducting important research. Online learning opportunities are available for students from the primary through postgraduate level, and they continue to expand. Weighing the potential advantages and disadvantages of a learning environment that makes complete use of modern technology and the Internet's capabilities, we must look at the possibility of the physical classroom of the past being replaced by the virtual classroom of the future.

Read and carefully consider these perspectives. Each suggests a particular way of thinking about how the classroom of the future should work.

PERSPECTIVE ONE

Physical classrooms will and should always exist. The Internet and modern technology clearly provide life-changing and time-saving benefits, but also include too many distractions. Effective, focused learning can only occur in a traditional classroom alongside other students, under the direct guidance of a teacher keeping everyone on task.

PERSPECTIVE TWO

Physical classrooms will and should eventually be replaced by online classrooms. Technological advances have made traditional classrooms unnecessary and have revealed their limitations. In the future, the modern, virtual classroom will be free of the constraints and limitations that inhibit learning and impede the achievement of each student's educational goals.

PERSPECTIVE THREE

The classroom of the future will continue to integrate the best of both worlds—the traditional and the virtual—for a blended, effective learning experience. Students will benefit from guided classroom learning that also takes advantage of technology for additional opportunities to achieve educational goals.

ESSAY TASK

Write a cohesive, logical essay in which you consider multiple perspectives on the classroom of the future. In your essay, be sure to:

- examine and assess the perspectives given
- declare and explain your own perspective on the issue
- discuss the relationship between your perspective and those given

Your perspective may be in full or partial agreement, or in total disagreement, with any of the others. Whatever the case, support your ideas with logical reasoning and detailed, persuasive examples.

PLAN AND WRITE YOUR ESSAY

Use the first two pages of the Writing test answer sheet (found at the beginning of the test) to generate ideas and plan your essay. Then use the following four pages to write your essay. Consider the following as you compose your essay:

What are the strengths and weaknesses of the three perspectives provided?

- Identify the insights they present and what they fail to consider.
- Ascertain why a given perspective might persuade or fail to persuade.

How can you apply your own experience, knowledge, and values?

- Express your perspective on the issue, identifying the perspective's strengths and weaknesses.
- Formulate a plan to support your perspective in your essay.

ENGLISH

1.	D	20.	G	39.	C	58.	H
2.	G	21.	C	40.	J	59.	A
3.	C	22.	H	41.	D	60.	H
4.	G	23.	B	42.	G	61.	D
5.	A	24.	J	43.	B	62.	G
6.	J	25.	A	44.	J	63.	B
7.	A	26.	H	45.	C	64.	J
8.	J	27.	D	46.	G	65.	B
9.	B	28.	G	47.	C	66.	H
10.	H	29.	B	48.	J	67.	D
11.	B	30.	G	49.	A	68.	F
12.	H	31.	A	50.	J	69.	B
13.	A	32.	J	51.	B	70.	G
14.	G	33.	B	52.	F	71.	C
15.	C	34.	H	53.	B	72.	J
16.	G	35.	D	54.	H	73.	B
17.	D	36.	F	55.	A	74.	J
18.	F	37.	D	56.	J	75.	D
19.	D	38.	G	57.	B		

1. **The correct answer is D.** As written, this sentence is a fragment requiring a subject, such as "the group." The pronoun *it* in choice D makes this antecedent clear. Choices B and C do not work because the specific subject doesn't have a verb—*having* and *were* are part of the descriptive phrase, not the direct action of the subject.

2. **The correct answer is G.** The phrase "for communicating" is set off by a comma in the passage, but because the description "for communicating" modifies *code* (defining the purpose of that code), "for communicating" is what is called a restrictive phrase. It should not be separated from the word or phrase it modifies. The same is true for "top secret," which eliminates choices H and J.

3. **The correct answer is C.** Avoid such wordy constructions as "it being the case that they would," especially when good alternatives are available. "It was crucial that enemy forces not be able to decipher the code" puts "enemy forces" (the subject) at the front of the sentence. Choice D also places "enemy forces" near the beginning of the sentence, but the second clause is constructed in such a way as to imply that the *code*, not the enemy forces, would have access to the tactics and troop movements. Choice B's "having access" is ambiguous

about who would have that access. Only choice C makes clear who has the access.

4. **The correct answer is G.** The essay cites the fact that the Navajo language has no written form as an additional reason why it made an excellent code. In choice F, *However* indicates a contrast to the previous sentence, which is about what an excellent code the Navajo language made. The correct answer should instead mean something like "in addition." The best answer is choice G, *Furthermore*. Choice H would make sense only if the sentence were making a comparison, such as between Navajo and another language. Choice J would only make sense if the sentence was completing a cause and effect relationship.

5. **The correct answer is A.** This sentence shows a simple progression from one event to the next, so choice A, *Afterward*, is the best choice. Choice B is a transitional phrase that indicates the completion of a cause and effect relationship, and there is no such relationship in this sentence. Choice C, *However*, indicates a contradiction. Omitting *Afterward* would not alter the sentence's meaning dramatically; however it would not improve the sentence either, so D is not the best choice.

6. **The correct answer is J.** Choices F and H can be eliminated because neither sentence has a subject ("the code talkers"). In choice G, the comma after *Once* indicates that the action happened only one time; the sentence implies that the actions of the code talkers were ongoing, so *once* does not make sense in the context. Only choice J is a complete sentence that does not alter the original sentence's meaning incorrectly.

7. **The correct answer is A.** A comma is used here to separate a long sentence into two logical clauses. Choice B is a possible alternative, but reading the sentence aloud makes it clear that a pause between *English* and *and* is necessary. Choice C is incorrect because in a compound sentence like this, the comma is placed before the conjunction. The phrase "so to" indicates a cause and effect relationship, and there is no such relationship in this sentence; therefore, choice D is incorrect.

8. **The correct answer is J.** This phrase should not begin a new paragraph, because it does not introduce a new idea, so choice G is incorrect. It lists another supporting detail to the main idea of the paragraph (which is that the code was complicated). No comma is needed because the underlined words do not serve as an introductory phrase. They are part of the larger phrase, "adding to the difficulty of breaking the code," which is the actual full introductory phrase. Choice H is incorrect because "More difficulty" is not a complete transitional phrase and is a grammatically incorrect way to begin a sentence.

9. **The correct answer is B.** The best way to help the reader understand how the code worked would be with a specific example of the code, rather than with general facts about other languages, codes, etc. Only choice B addresses details about the code. Choice A goes off on an unnecessary tangent about Morse code. Choice C confuses the flow by backtracking to discuss military codes used in the past. Choice D contributes to the author's larger argument, but the difficulty of the code is not a detail that will help a reader better understand the specifics of the code itself.

10. **The correct answer is H.** The commas in the original sentence are not needed to separate "speed and accuracy" from the rest of the sentence, as the adverbial phrase does not need to be set off from the verb (the work of the code talkers). Choices G and J fail to delete all of the unnecessary commas.

11. **The correct answer is B.** The current sentence uses both the passive voice and an awkward construction. Choice B corrects the error with a clear, active phrase. Choice C loses the conjunction *and* to create a comma splice, and choice D, omitting the underlined portion entirely, makes no sense.

12. **The correct answer is H.** This question asks you to resolve a logical contradiction in the original sentence. Earlier in the passage, the author explained that the military only recently acknowledged the efforts of the Navajo code talkers. The phrase "remained unacknowledged" best describes this theme. Choice G, "had been unknown," incorrectly uses the past perfect tense, and choice J, "did not get known," has the right meaning but uses awkward language.

13. **The correct answer is A.** Only choice A conveys the idea of secrecy, using the words "virtually unknown outside the military" to describe the work of the code talkers. "Complex military system" in choice B might imply secrecy, but it does not clearly state that the Navajo code talkers' work was unknown outside the military. Choices C and D are unrelated to the topic.

14. **The correct answer is G.** The sentence belongs in the paragraph that is about the complexity of the Navajo code, Paragraph 5, in which the author states, "While the Navajo language was complicated, the code was even more complex." Paragraph 4 is about the development and memorization of the code, so choice F is incorrect. Paragraph 6 is about the effectiveness of the code, so choice H is incorrect. Choice J is incorrect because Paragraph 7 is about the code talkers' legacy.

15. **The correct answer is C.** This essay is focused on the specific contributions of one minority group: the Navajos. An essay describing the contributions of minority soldiers would have to be more inclusive by talking about the involvement of various minority groups in the war effort, so choices A and B are incorrect. Choice D is incorrect because the essay does focus on the positive effects of the Navajo soldiers' work. Only choice C explains why this essay does not describe the contributions of various groups of minority soldiers in World War II.

16. **The correct answer is G.** When you are trying to determine the correct form of the first person pronoun (*me* or *I*), you need to first determine whether the pronoun is an object (it receives the action of the sentence) or a subject (it performs the action of the sentence). In this case, at the end of the sentence, the author is the person to whom he believes the rule does not apply; *me* is the appropriate object here, so choice G is correct, and the original sentence is incorrect. Choice H uses both the wrong pronoun (*I*) and the wrong preposition (*for*), and choice J violates the parallelism by adding the word *applying*.

17. **The correct answer is D.** "Nobody was consulted me" (choice C) is an example of passive voice—giving the action to the object of the sentence, not the author—and it makes the existing sentence very unclear. Only choice D, "I didn't consult with anybody," corrects the problem. The reversal of word order in choice B, "With nobody I consulted," makes the sentence awkward. "Nobody consulted me" (choice C) changes the meaning of the sentence, implying that the author should have been consulted about his interviewing.

18. **The correct answer is F.** The current sentence correctly uses the pronoun *it* to refer to the environment of the law firm, and remains in the past tense like the rest of the paragraph. "There was" (choice G) replaces the pronoun with a vague descriptive that doesn't make sense in context. "Here is" (choice H) incorrectly uses the present tense. "And so it was" (choice J) begins the sentence with an inappropriate transition.

19. **The correct answer is D.** The underlined portion belongs to a list, so all of the items in the list should be separated by commas. As it is written, the sentence incorrectly uses a semicolon as if to begin a new sentence. Choice B incorrectly adds a colon as if to signal a new list. Choice C removes the punctuation, causing the last two items to run together ambiguously. Only choice D gets it right.

20. **The correct answer is G.** The narrative phrase, "I happily informed him" should be set off by commas, because it describes the manner in which the speaker described his aim to the interviewer. Only choice G accomplishes this. Choice F is incorrect because the original sentence lacks the necessary comma after *him*. Choices H and J misplace the comma.

21. **The correct answer is C.** Deleting the previous sentence would eliminate the writer's description of what he believed at the time of the interview (Statement I)—that his interviewer was impressed with how ambitious and articulate he was. It would also take away the reference to "the surprised look" on the interviewer's face, which tells the reader something about the interviewer's opinion of the narrator (Statement III). The idea that the author is trying to communicate here is the distance between his feelings

about himself and the interviewer's feelings about him; Statements I and III describe exactly that. Choice A does not encompass everything the reader would not know if the writer had replaced the sentence. Statement II is not relevant to the sentence, so choices B and D can be eliminated.

22. **The correct answer is H.** The correct phrase is "would have." "would of" (choice F) and "could of" (choice G) are never correct, although they are common mistakes due to pronunciation. Choice J is grammatically incorrect in any context.

23. **The correct answer is B.** The underlined phrase refers to the narrator only, so it should contain the pronoun *my*. Choices A and C use the wrong pronoun, and choice D changes the meaning of the sentence by adding an extra negative.

24. **The correct answer is J.** The underlined verb should be in the simple past tense, in keeping with the rest of the sentence. Choice F should be used in the present tense. Choice G should only be used if the sentence is in the past continuous tense. Choice H is incorrect since the sentence does not require the simple past perfect tense.

25. **The correct answer is A.** Try reading the sentence without "I figured"; it makes sense, which means "I figured" is an extra informational phrase that needs to be set off by commas. The phrase is correct as written. Choices B and C each eliminate a necessary comma. Choice D eliminates both necessary commas.

26. **The correct answer is H.** This question requires you to figure out the clearest wording to explain that the writer did not get the next several jobs for which he interviewed. The first part of the sentence talks about not being offered "that job," so the *nor* implies that *several* should refer to jobs, not firms, which is the mistake the original sentence makes. Choice H makes this distinction clear. Choice G retains the error, and choice J changes the meaning by suggesting that the author was offered no more interviews.

27. **The correct answer is D.** The shift in focus that the question mentions is the narrator's understanding that his failure to get a job might be his own fault. The best clue to this is the next sentence, in which the author calls his visit to the job counseling office "long overdue." Only choice D shows the narrator realizing that his approach might be to blame. Choices A, B, and C merely recycle information that the author has presented in the first part of the paragraph: that he has failed to get any of the jobs for which he applied.

Answer Keys and Explanations

28. The correct answer is G. The essay begins with the narrator saying that his college employment office recommended mock interviews for students about to begin a job search. Choice G ties the ending to the beginning by mentioning the practice interview and implying that the writer is helping his students to learn from his mistakes. Choices F and J are not necessarily off topic, but they do not tie the end of the essay back to its beginning. Choice H does not tie back to the beginning and it makes a jarring shift to a less formal tone than the rest of the passage.

29. The correct answer is B. This sentence describes the narrator's realization that he is doing something wrong. It logically should go right before the sentence in which he decides to seek help to correct his mistakes. Placing it before Sentence 1 (choice A) or before or after Sentence 3 (choices C and D) would jumble the paragraph's flow of ideas.

30. The correct answer is G. The first part of the sentence describes their "hairless faces," so the notion of fur *obscuring* (choice F) or *covering* (choice H) the face is inappropriate. Similarly, the mane of a lion does not *mark* (choice J) a lion's face: it encircles it. The best choice to complete the author's metaphor is choice G.

31. The correct answer is A. The best word is *and*, because it connects the two ideas and includes the comma that belongs before the conjunction. Choices B and C suggest a cause and effect relationship that is not present in the sentence. Choice D makes the mistake of indicating a sequential relationship.

32. The correct answer is J. The future "will pitch" does not fit the overall present tense of the sentence. Choice G not only is redundant but also suggests that a previous sentence might have challenged the helpfulness of the group. Choice H is inappropriate, because *can* addresses their ability to pitch in (not the fact that they actually do) and might even reduce the task to an optional luxury. Choice J most simply and clearly expresses the author's meaning.

33. The correct answer is B. The sentence requires a plural possessive pronoun. Choice A, *it's*, is a contraction meaning "it is," so eliminate it. Choice C, *its*, is possessive but not plural, and choice D, *they*, is plural but not possessive. *Their* matches both the plural subject ("younger tamarins") and the possessive requirement ("newborn siblings").

34. The correct answer is H. This question requires you to find the appropriate preposition to complete the

sentence. *Among* (choice F) means part of a group, so it does not make sense with *daytime*. *Amidst* (choice G) means "within," which is wrong as well. Choice J, *withstanding*, means "resisting," which does not make sense in this context. The only choice that fits is choice H, *during*.

35. The correct answer is D. The *and* in the middle of the current sentence separates two different ideas and forms a run-on sentence. It is best rewritten as two separate sentences, as in choice D. The semicolon in choice B might serve the same purpose, but the *and* following the semicolon makes the sentence incorrect. The colon in choice C does not belong, because the second part is neither a list nor a clarifying example of the first part.

36. The correct answer is F. The sentence correctly uses a comma to separate the modifying phrase at the end of it. Choices G and H create run-on sentences, while choice J creates a fragment.

37. The correct answer is D. The underlined phrase contains a comma splice. Choices B and C do nothing to fix the problem. Because the phrase on each side of it can stand on its own as a sentence, the correct punctuation is a semicolon rather than a comma.

38. The correct answer is G. The sentence describes where tamarins live, citing eastern Brazilian rainforests as their habitat. Choice F, *toward*, implies that they are moving closer to the forests from somewhere else. Choice H, *between*, suggests that there are only two forests. Choice J, *below*, places the tamarins underground. The correct preposition is *within* (choice G) because it accurately explains that they live among the rainforests themselves.

39. The correct answer is C. The underlined word should indicate cause and effect, since the endangerment of the tamarins is a direct result of their decreasing habitat. Choice A, *but*, choice B, *however*, and choice D, *nonetheless*, all indicate contrast. The best choice is *so*, which communicates that because of their decreasing habitat, the tamarins are in greater danger.

40. The correct answer is J. The information that an elephant was just born, while loosely related to animals, is unrelated to the subject of the passage (tamarins) and breaks the flow of the sentence. It should be eliminated entirely. Choices G and H fail to eliminate the unnecessary phrase and introduce punctuation errors.

41. The correct answer is D. The sentence lists additional components of the movement to save the tamarins, so it should logically go after the sentence that lists several components of the movement, sentence 4. Leaving the sentence where it is now (choice A) or placing it before sentences 1 (choice B) or 2 (choice C) would disrupt the paragraph's logical flow of ideas.

42. **The correct answer is G.** "Managing and restoring" do not need to be set off by commas or separated from each other, because they are neither part of an informational phrase nor part of a list of more than two parts. Therefore, choices F, H, and J are incorrect. If a third item were added (e.g., "managing, restoring, and preserving"), commas between the elements would be justified, but the conjunction *and* works just fine here.

43. **The correct answer is B.** The word *however* signals a contrast to the previous sentence about the success of the tamarin program. The phrase "it is only with unwavering dedication" warns the reader that much hard work must still be done to preserve the tamarin. Choices A and C do not include the cautionary note that the author intends; choice D is cautionary but doesn't talk about tamarins.

44. **The correct answer is J.** The added sentence would completely contradict the narrative style of the essay, which is entirely in the third person and refrains from involving the narrator, so choices F and G are incorrect. The essay is about the need to preserve the tamarin, so choice H is incorrect.

45. **The correct answer is C.** While the essay does mention the danger to the rainforest, it focuses on the resultant danger to the tamarin, not on the rainforest in general, so choices A and B are incorrect, and choice C is correct. Choice D misidentifies why the essay does not fulfill the assignment because the essay does mention that the rainforest is in danger.

46. **The correct answer is G.** The words "altar of the Presbyterian church" form one descriptive phrase, so no commas are needed in it—choice F can be eliminated. No comma (choice J) or semicolon (choice H) is needed before the conjunction *and* in this sentence, because receiving her degree is the second of two actions carried out by the same subject (Elizabeth Blackwell).

47. **The correct answer is C.** You can tell by context that the underlined phrase should mean something like "By receiving her degree," but the original sentence is awkward and contains an unnecessary comma. Choice C best accomplishes this. *Therefore* does imply a cause and effect (choice B), but "in doing so" communicates that her action had significance. *Even so* (choice D)

means "in spite of," which does not make sense in this context.

48. **The correct answer is J.** The right choice must use the singular possessive form of *country*. Choice F is neither singular nor possessive, choice G is possessive but plural, and choice H scrambles the word order and distorts the meaning. Only choice J does the job.

49. **The correct answer is A.** Each of the two halves of the sentence can stand on its own, so the semicolon is correct. The other choices provide the wrong links between the two ideas, falsely indicating cause and effect, as in choices B and C, or contrast, as in choice D.

50. **The correct answer is J.** As it is written, the phrase is confusing, placing the verb awkwardly before the subject. Choices G and H are even more confusingly phrased. The simplest and clearest wording is choice J.

51. **The correct answer is B.** The sentence only makes sense if the underlined section contains a subject and a verb. "Having access" (choice A) lacks a subject. Choice B includes the subject and employs the correct tense. Choice C has a subject but is the present tense, and choice D is awkward and redundant.

52. **The correct answer is F.** You can tell from context that the underlined word should be something that means "didn't believe," so choice F, *doubted*, is the best choice. The doctors Blackwell consulted didn't think she would be admitted to medical school because no women had ever been admitted to medical school. Choices G, H, and J do not make any sense in this context.

53. **The correct answer is B.** This sentence takes place in the past tense, so the correct choice is B, *applied*. "Has applied" would imply that her applications were pending, but all of the events of this passage are described in the past tense because Elizabeth Blackwell lived in the nineteenth century. Choices A and D would only be used if the sentence took place in the present tense. Choice C uses the simple past perfect tense incorrectly.

54. **The correct answer is H.** Both the semicolon and the period in the underlined portion create new standalone sentences, but neither punctuation mark is followed by something that can stand on its own, so choice F is incorrect. While choice G comes close to fixing the problem, the comma after *colleges* is misplaced, and the comma before *Geneva* is not as strong as a colon would be. Choice H works best—the first punctuation mark is gone, *and* is replaced by the more effective *but*, and the

colon appropriately denotes the final clarifying example. Choice J creates a fragment.

55. **The correct answer is A.** The phrase is correctly written in the past tense: *became* implies that her admission to medical school was at the head of a long line of obstacles. Choices C and D are grammatically incorrect, while choice B changes the sentence's meaning.

56. **The correct answer is J.** The current sentence lacks an action verb; choice J corrects this problem and appropriately sets off the modifying phrase with commas. Choice G changes both the meaning and the tense. Choice H is awkward because the phrase "men students" does not make sense.

57. **The correct answer is B.** The underlined word must be a past-tense verb. Choice A, *astonishing*, is an adjective; choice C, *astonishment*, is a noun, and choice D, "having astonishment," is a descriptive phrase.

58. **The correct answer is H.** "After she completed her degree" is the correct introductory phrase, because it establishes the time sequence involved (Blackwell faced prejudice after she completed her degree). There is no need to separate the word *after* from the rest of the phrase, so the comma is inappropriate (choice F). Choice G is not the correct introductory word and reintroduces the unnecessary comma. "After to" is not a proper introductory phrase, so choice J is wrong.

59. **The correct answer is A.** In this sentence, *prejudice* and "outright barriers to her career" are two distinct items: *prejudice* describes feelings directed against her, and *outright barriers* are actions possibly taken by those who felt that prejudice. Therefore, the sentence should include both items separately to preserve the author's meaning. Choice C makes the mistake of combining these items. Choices B and D do not make grammatical sense.

60. **The correct answer is H.** As it is written, the sentence does not explain what "other things" Blackwell did, and does not tell the reader whether or not she had any success as a doctor, both of which would successfully complete the passage. Choice G also does not describe anything that Blackwell went on to do after she got her degree, and choice J describes an occurrence that could not be construed as success. Only choice H describes the successes that Blackwell had after becoming a doctor, despite the obstacles she faced.

61. **The correct answer is D.** *Ingenious* means "clever and inventive," making it the best choice to describe a *brilliant* idea. Choice A, *imperious*, means "arrogant";

choice B, *unsettling*, means "disturbing"; choice C, *inimitable*, means "unable to be imitated."

62. **The correct answer is G.** The comma in this sentence belongs in the place where it will distinguish the start of the list from the rest of the sentence. Putting the comma after "ancient civilizations" and before *including* indicates that Persia, India, and Egypt are items included on the list of ancient civilizations. The original sentence (choice F) and choice H are missing the comma after *civilizations*. Choice J uses a semicolon, which is not needed before a list when *including* is used. It also should link the first two items in the list with a comma and not the conjunction *and*.

63. **The correct answer is B.** The sentence as written contains the incorrect form of the adverb *advance*. To describe something technologically complex, you would say that it is *advanced*, not *advancing*. Choice C implies that something was created in advance of, or before, the system, but since the system itself is what you are trying to describe, this choice doesn't make sense in the context. "Superlative advancement" is, in fact, superlative: it doesn't provide additional understanding of the high level of technology used by the Romans to create the aqueducts, so choice D is wrong. On the ACT, always err on the side of the least complex construction with the fewest words.

64. **The correct answer is J.** As it is written, this is a run-on sentence. Using *that* instead of *it* (choice F) makes it clear that you are describing what the aqueduct system combined (form and function) and not adding a separate thought that describes the aqueduct system in this manner. Choices G and H are awkward and wordy.

65. **The correct answer is B.** *Simply* is the idiom that works with *quite*. It also manages to convey the author's meaning: that the first aqueducts were not complicated. Choices A and C are awkward in this context, and choice D does not make sense.

66. **The correct answer is H.** A semicolon, not a comma, should separate two stand-alone phrases. The fact that the structures were elaborate is related to the fact that they could conduct water over large distances, but each thought can stand alone. The conjunctions *but* and *so* in choices G and J are inappropriate, because the relationship between the two parts of the sentence is not one of contrast or of cause and effect.

67. **The correct answer is D.** Choice A makes the aqueducts seem less impressive by highlighting the superiority of today's systems. Choice B might indicate

that the Roman Empire was impressive, but it doesn't say anything about aqueducts. Choice C indicates that the aqueducts might still stand, which is impressive enough, but choice D adds the fact that the aqueducts are still in use, which is even more impressive.

68. **The correct answer is F.** The existing sentence correctly uses a semicolon to separate two phrases that each form a complete sentence. A comma (choice G) or colon (choice H) do not perform this function. The first phrase is not an exclamation, so choice J does not make sense.

69. **The correct answer is B.** *Failed* is the correct verb form (it corresponds with the use of the past tense in the rest of the passage), which allows you to eliminate choice D. Choices A and C imply cause and effect, which isn't the most suitable relationship. The better choice offers a contrast: some aqueducts failed, but those that didn't were used as models. This implies a difference between the failing models and the successful models, and the Romans' different response to each situation.

70. **The correct answer is G.** This sentence compares the past to the present. The application of principles in modern architecture takes place in the present, so it should be written as are applied (choice G). The original phrase indicates an action that will happen in the future. Choices H and J indicate actions that happened in the past.

71. **The correct answer is C.** In the original sentence, the information in the parentheses does not add to our understanding of the Roman aqueducts, so it should be eliminated entirely (choice C). Choices B and D fail to eliminate that information entirely.

72. **The correct answer is J.** *Arches* is plural. Because it is not a possessive, it does not need an apostrophe (choice F). It should be followed by a comma to set off the informational phrase ("while well-known"), and not a semicolon (choice H), which separates two complete clauses. Choice G fails to follow it with any punctuation at all.

73. **The correct answer is B.** Choice B provides specific information about the aqueducts that didn't fall into the category of the famous stone arch aqueducts. Choice C discusses one feature of the stone arches but adds nothing about their role in the greater system. Choice D explains that the other aqueducts were made of different materials but doesn't specify what these materials were, making it a less desirable possibility than choice B.

74. **The correct answer is J.** The best way to maintain the proper tense and appropriately contrast the technologies of past and present is to omit the underlined word altogether, as choice J suggests. Leaving it as is (choice F) or changing it to another word (choices G and H) do not correct the error.

75. **The correct answer is D.** A main theme of the essay is the legacy of ancient Roman aqueducts in modern architecture. Choice C is close, but it mentions the Romans' advanced system of government, which is an idea not mentioned in the essay. Choices A and B do not reflect the main idea.

MATHEMATICS

1.	B	16.	G	31.	E	46.	J
2.	H	17.	E	32.	J	47.	C
3.	E	18.	G	33.	C	48.	G
4.	F	19.	D	34.	J	49.	E
5.	D	20.	H	35.	B	50.	F
6.	F	21.	E	36.	F	51.	C
7.	C	22.	J	37.	C	52.	J
8.	H	23.	E	38.	H	53.	C
9.	C	24.	G	39.	A	54.	K
10.	K	25.	C	40.	K	55.	D
11.	D	26.	G	41.	E	56.	H
12.	J	27.	E	42.	F	57.	C
13.	A	28.	K	43.	D	58.	G
14.	H	29.	B	44.	K	59.	C
15.	D	30.	H	45.	C	60.	J

1. **The correct answer is B.** Since a appears on both sides of the equation, eliminate a and solve for b:

$$a + 2b = a + 18$$
$$2b = 18$$
$$b = 9$$

Choice A is incorrect because it needs $3b$, not $2b$, on the left side of the equation. Choice C subtracts 2 from both sides of the equation instead of dividing. Choice D represents $2b$, not b. For choice E, you multiplied both sides of the equation by 2 when you should have instead divided by 2.

2. **The correct answer is H.** If Barbie answered 2 of the 20 questions incorrectly, then she answered $20 - 2 = 18$ correctly. Percent is equal to $\frac{\text{part}}{\text{whole}} \times 100$, so Barbie answered $\frac{18}{20} \times 100\%$ of the questions correctly, choice H. Choice F represents the percentage of questions answered *incorrectly*. For choice G, the 100 should be in the numerator so that you are taking a proportion of 100%, and even then, the result would be the percentage of questions answered *incorrectly*. For choice J, the 100 should be in the numerator so that you are taking a proportion of 100%. For choice K, you need to interchange the 20 and 100 in this expression.

3. **The correct answer is E.** There are 5 choices for the sandwich, 4 for the beverage, and 6 for the snack, so there are a total of $5 \times 4 \times 6 = 120$ possible lunch combinations.

For choice A, you likely ignored "6 kinds of snacks" when forming the combinations, and for choice B, you likely ignored "5 kinds of sandwiches." For choice C, you likely ignored "4 kinds of beverages" when forming the combinations. Choice D is one-half of the correct answer.

4. **The correct answer is F.** If the measure of $\angle A$ is 53°, then the measure of $\angle B$ is 127°. The contrapositive of this says that if the measure of $\angle B$ is NOT 127°, then the measure of $\angle A$ cannot be 53°. Therefore, choice F is correct. For choice G, think about how the contrapositive of "if p then q" is "if not q, then not p." This shows choice F to be true, so choice G cannot be true. For choices H, J, and K, in each case, you have the wrong measures associated with angles A and B.

5. **The correct answer is D.** To compare fractions, decimals, and percentages, convert them all to the same form. Since $85\% = 0.85$, $0.65 < x < 0.85$. Choices A and B are both less than $\frac{1}{2}$, or 0.5, so they can be eliminated. As a decimal, $\frac{5}{8} = 0.625$, so choice C can

also be eliminated as too small. As a decimal, $\frac{2}{3} = 0.\overline{66}$. This does fall between 0.65 and 0.85, so choice D is correct. For the record, $\frac{7}{8} = 0.875$, so it is too big.

6. **The correct answer is F.** The average is equal to the sum of the terms divided by the number of terms:

$$\text{Average} = \frac{0 + (x+2) + (x+4) + (x+6)}{4}$$

$$= \frac{3x+12}{4}$$

$$= \frac{3x}{4} + \frac{12}{4}$$

$$= \frac{3}{4}x + 3$$

Choice G is the maximum, not the average. Choice H is the median, not the mean. For choice J, you divided the sum by 3, not 4; remember, you must include "0" data points in the size of the data set. Choice K is incorrect because you must divide it by 4 to be correct.

7. **The correct answer is C.** Angle BCD is supplementary to angle BCA, so $\angle BCA = 180° - 112° = 68°$. The interior angles of a triangle sum to 180°, so $\angle ABC = 180° - 68° - 37° = 75°$, choice C.

Choice A is the complement of angle BAC, but it does not account for the fact that angle BCA is 68 degrees. Choice B is the measure of angle BCA. Choice D is the supplement of the correct angle measure. Choice E cannot be the case because the sum of all three angles in a triangle must be 180 degrees.

8. **The correct answer is H.** Factoring a 3 out of $15a + 6b$ gives you $3(5a + 2b)$, which matches choice H. Choice F is the product, not the sum. Choice G is incorrect because you cannot add the coefficients of unlike terms and then factor in this manner. For choice J, note that $6(5a)$ does not equal $15a$. Choice K is incorrect because after distributing the 5, you would get $5b$, not $5a$.

9. **The correct answer is C.** If $42 included the amount due plus a $7 tip, the amount due must have been $42 – $7 = $35. As a percent of the amount due, $7 represents $\frac{\$7.00}{\$35.00} \times 100\% = \frac{1}{5} \times 100\% = 20\%$ choice C. For choice A, note that 7 does not equal 7%. For choice B, you likely divided 7 by 42, but should have divided by 35. Choice D would require the original bill

to be $28, not $35. For choice E, $35 is the amount of the bill before tip, which is not equal to 35%.

10. **The correct answer is K.** If $\frac{n}{6}$ and $\frac{n}{8}$ are both integers, then n must be divisible by both 6 and 8. The question asks for the one value that does NOT satisfy this condition, so you're looking for the one choice that is not divisible by both 6 and 8.

Choice F: (192)

$192 \div 6 = 32$; $192 \div 8 = 24$; eliminate

Choice G: (96)

$96 \div 6 = 16$; $96 \div 8 = 12$; eliminate

Choice H: (48)

$48 \div 6 = 8$; $46 \div 8 = 6$; eliminate

Choice J: (24)

$24 \div 6 = 4$; $24 \div 8 = 3$; eliminate

Choice K: (12)

$12 \div 6 = 2$; $12 \div 8 = 1$ with a remainder of 4; CORRECT

11. **The correct answer is D.** Plug $a = 6$ into the expression and follow PEMDAS to solve:

$$2a(a-2)^2 + a \div 3 = 2(6)[6-2]^2 + 6 \div 3$$

$$= 12[4]^2 + 2$$

$$= 12[16] + 2$$

$$= 192 + 2$$

$$= 194$$

For choice A, you did not properly use the order of operations; $6 \div 3$ should be computed first. For choice B, in the last line of the simplification, you divided instead of adding. For choice C, $4^2 = 16$, not 8. For choice E, in the final step, you used multiplication instead of addition.

12. **The correct answer is J.** A negative times a negative is positive, so a positive divided by a negative is negative. Therefore, x must be negative, and you can eliminate choices F, G, and H. In order for the quotient to be an integer, 64 must be divisible by x; only –8 divides evenly into 64, so choice J is correct. Choice K is not possible because 64 is not divisible by –12.

13. **The correct answer is A.** Solve the equation algebraically:

$$17 + x = -23$$
$$x = -23 - 17$$
$$= -40$$

Choices B, C, D, and E can be ruled out by plugging in their values for x and seeing that you do not get a true statement.

14. **The correct answer is H.** Counting from the right side, Matt is in the fifteenth chair, so you know that there are at least 15 seats; eliminate choices F and G. Counting from the left side, he's in the fourth chair, so there must be three seats to the left of him. That means that there are a total of $15 + 3 = 18$ seats (choice H). Therefore, choices J and K are too large.

15. **The correct answer is D.** The area of a rectangle is equal to lw, where l and w are its length and width respectively. You're given that the area of the rectangle is $x^2 + 4x - 12$, and that its width is $x + 6$. You need to find the other factor that, when multiplied by $(x + 6)$, produces $x^2 + 4x - 12$. To produce x^2 you need a first term of x, so eliminate choice A. You need a second term that, when multiplied by 6, produces -12; since $6(-2) = -12$, choice D, $(x - 2)$, is correct. Choice A cannot be correct because of the square term—single dimensions can only be linear. For choices B, C, and E, you incorrectly factored the expression for the area.

16. **The correct answer is G.** There are 12 numbers on the clock. A circle contains 360°, so the distance between each pair of consecutive numbers is $360° \div 12 = 30°$. If the minute hand moves 60°, it will move from 1 to 2 to 3. That means that both the hour hand and minute hand will be on 3, which represents a time of 3:15, choice G. Choice F represents a move 30° counter-clockwise, and choice H is 240° clockwise. Choice J is 360° clockwise, and choice K is 720° clockwise.

17. **The correct answer is E.** Plug in the given values, and then solve using FOIL:

$$2ab = 2(x + 1)(-1)$$
$$= 2(x^2 - 1)$$
$$= 2x^2 - 2$$

Choice A leaves out the $(x - 1)$ term. In choice B, the constant term is wrong; when you multiply a and b, you should get $x^2 - 1$, which you then multiply by 2. For choice C, you dropped the 2 in $2ab$. For choice D, you forgot to distribute the 2 through $2(x^2 - 1)$.

18. **The correct answer is G.** The area of a square is equal to s^2, where s is a side of the square. Since the area of this square is 9, s must be 3. Point A has coordinates $(-2, 2)$, so any other vertex of the same square must have an x-coordinate that is either equal to or 3 units away from -2.

This means that the x-coordinate can be $-5, -2,$ or 1; eliminate choices F, J, and K. The vertex must also have a y-coordinate that is either equal to or 3 units away from 2. This means that the y-coordinate can be $-1, 2,$ or 5; eliminate choice H. Only choice G, $(-5, 5)$, meets both conditions.

19. **The correct answer is D.** The volume of a rectangular solid is lwh, where l is the length, w the width, and h the height. That means that the volume of box 1 is $(20)(8)(12) = 1,920$ cubic inches. Box 2 must also have a volume of 1,920 cubic inches, so use this volume to solve for h:

$$(4)(10)(h) = 1,920$$
$$40h = 1,920$$
$$h = \frac{1,920}{40}$$
$$= 48$$

In choice A, you likely left out the 8 when calculating the volume of the first solid. In choice B, you likely added an extra 4 when calculating the volume of the second solid. Choice C is incorrect because you might have switched the 4 from the second solid with the 8 from the first solid when calculating the volume of the second solid. Choice E is incorrect because you would need to divide by 24 to get an answer of 80, and you can see that 4×10 already exceeds this factor.

20. **The correct answer is H.** The spinner is divided into 8 equal sections. As a fraction, $0.375 = \frac{3}{8}$. For the probability of NOT landing on red on a single spin to be $\frac{3}{8}$, then 3 of the sections must NOT be red. That means that the remaining $8 - 3 = 5$ sections must be red. Choice F is incorrect because there are 8 congruent wedges, so this would imply that the probability of not landing on red is 0.875. Choice J would make the probability of not landing on red 0.125. Choice K would make the probability of not landing on red 0.

21. **The correct answer is E.** The sides of any right triangle are related by the Pythagorean theorem, which states that the sum of the squares of the legs is equal to the square of the hypotenuse. This is often written as $a^2 + b^2 = c^2$, where a and b are the legs, and c is the hypotenuse. Test each set of sides to see which satisfies the Pythagorean theorem and is therefore a right triangle:

    Choice A: (6, 13, 14)

    $$6^2 + 13^2 = 14^2$$
    $$36 + 169 = 196$$
    $$205 \neq 196; \text{ eliminate}$$

    Choice B: (8, 10, 12)

    $$8^2 + 10^2 = 12^2$$
    $$64 + 100 = 144$$
    $$164 \neq 144; \text{ eliminate}$$

    Choice C: (12, 16, 18)

    $$12^2 + 16^2 = 18^2$$
    $$144 + 256 = 324$$
    $$400 \neq 324; \text{ eliminate}$$

    Choice D: (15, 22, 23)

    $$15^2 + 22^2 = 23^2$$
    $$225 + 484 = 529$$
    $$709 \neq 529; \text{ eliminate}$$

    Choice E: (20, 21, 29)

    $$20^2 + 21^2 = 29^2$$
    $$400 + 441 = 841$$
    $$841 = 841 \; \therefore \; \text{right triangle}$$

22. **The correct answer is J.** 24 cans at $1.25 each would cost a total of $30. The superstore sells a case of 24 cans for $19.20, which is a savings of $30 − $19.20 = $10.80, choice J. Choice F is the savings per can, not per case. For choice G, you have incorrectly multiplied 12 times $1.25 to get the cost of a case from the corner store. For choice H, you used $1 per can instead of $1.25 per can at the corner store. Choice K is the cost of 24 cans.

23. **The correct answer is E.** The ribbon must go all the way around the box as shown in the figure. This will require sections of ribbon along the length of the top and bottom of the package, for a total of 2(12) = 24 inches. It

will require sections of ribbon along the width of the top and bottom of the package, for a total of 2(15) = 30 inches. This will also require sections of ribbon along the height of each of the four sides of the package, for a total of 4(10) = 40 inches. Adding this to the length needed for the bow itself, 25 inches, will require a total of 24 + 30 + 40 + 25 = 119 inches of ribbon. Choice A is incorrect because you did not account for the fact that there are multiple sides with the above dimensions along which the ribbon must be laid. For choice B, you forgot to include the length of the four sides (4 × 10). For choice C, you forgot to include the length of the bow (25). For choice D, you forgot to include the section of the ribbon along the length of the top and the bottom of the package (2 × 12).

24. **The correct answer is G.** According to PEMDAS, you must perform exponential operations before multiplication. This means that you need to evaluate $(x^3)^2$ before multiplying this expression by x^5. To raise a power to a power, multiply the exponents: $(x^3)^2 = x^{3 \times 2} = x^6$. To multiply two powers with the same base, add the exponents: $x^5(x^6) = x^{5+6} = x^{11}$. Choice F is incorrect because you added all the exponents—for $(x^3)^2$, you should have multiplied them. Choice H is incorrect because $(x^3)^2$ does not equal x^9; you should multiply 3 times 2, not raise 3 to the second power. For choice J, you applied the exponent rules in the wrong order; this is equal to $(x^5 \times x^3)^2$. For choice K, you multiplied all the exponents.

25. **The correct answer is C.** Set up a proportion to determine the number of cups of flour needed for the recipe, setting this unknown equal to x. Cross-multiply to solve for x:

    $$\frac{2}{5} = \frac{1\frac{1}{2} \; (\text{cups of sugar})}{x \; (\text{cups of flour})}$$

    $$2x = 5 \times \frac{3}{2}$$

    $$2x = \frac{15}{2}$$

    $$x = \frac{15}{4} = 3\frac{3}{4}$$

    For choice A, you inverted half of the proportion before solving for x. For choice B, you likely treated the mixed number incorrectly; you cannot multiply the whole and fractional parts. Choice D rounds up instead of giving the exact answer. Choice E is incorrect because the ratio 2:5 is not equivalent to the ratio 1:7.

26. **The correct answer is G.** Put the equation into standard quadratic form $ax^2 + bx + c = 0$, and then solve by factoring:

$$x^2 - 12 = -4x$$
$$x^2 + 4x - 12 = 0$$
$$(x + 6)(x - 2) = 0$$

$$x + 6 = 0 \quad x - 2 = 0$$
$$x = -6 \quad\quad x = 2$$

The two roots are –6 and 2, choice G. Choice F is incorrect because the signs of the two roots should be changed. For choices H, J, and K, you factored incorrectly. Once you bring all terms to the left side, the correct factored form is $(x + 6)(x - 2)$.

27. **The correct answer is E.** Find the median and mean for each choice; the correct choice will produce a median greater than its mean.

Choice A: $(x = 60)$

60, 80, 100 — median = 80;

$$\text{mean} = \frac{60 + 80 + 100}{3} = \frac{240}{3} = 80$$

The median is equal to the mean, so eliminate.

Choice B: $(x = 70)$

70, 80, 100, — median = 80;

$$\text{mean} = \frac{70 + 80 + 100}{3} = \frac{250}{3} = 83.3$$

The median is less than the mean, so eliminate.

Choice C: $(x = 80)$

80, 80, 100 — median = 80;

$$\text{mean} = \frac{80 + 80 + 100}{3} = \frac{260}{3} = 86.6$$

The median is less than the mean, so eliminate.

Choice D: $(x = 90)$

80, 90, 100 — median = 90;

$$\text{mean} = \frac{80 + 90 + 100}{3} = \frac{270}{3} = 90$$

The median is equal to the mean, so eliminate.

Choice E: $(x = 100)$

80, 100, 100 — median = 100;

$$\text{mean} = \frac{80 + 100 + 100}{3} = \frac{280}{3} = 93.3$$

The median is greater than the mean, so this is the correct answer.

28. **The correct answer is K.** If $i = \sqrt{-1}$, then $i^2 = -1$.

Plug this into $(i^2 - 5)^2$ and evaluate: $\left(i^2 - 5\right)^2 = (-1 - 5)^2$
$$= (-6)^2$$
$$= 36$$

Choice F is incorrect because $(-6)^2 = 36$, not –36. For choice G, you seem to have used $i^2 = 1$, not –1 and calculated $(-4)^2 = -16$, which is also incorrect. In choice H, you forgot to square –6. For choice J, remember that $i^2 = -1$, not 1.

29. **The correct answer is B.** First, find the angle with a cosine of 0. Using the cos–1 or Arccos function on your calculator will yield 90°, which is equal to $\left(\dfrac{\pi}{2}\right) = 0$ radians. This means that $3x = \dfrac{\pi}{2}$, and $x = \dfrac{\pi}{6}$.

Choice A is incorrect because cos(0) = 1, so this is not a solution. In choice C, cos(π) = –1, not 0, so this is not a solution. For choice D, while $\cos\left(\dfrac{\pi}{2}\right) = 0$, this is not the smallest value of x that makes the equation true. For choice E, cos(2π) = 1, so this is not a solution.

30. **The correct answer is H.** Use the formula $D = RT$, where R = rate, T = time, and D = distance:

$$55T = 220$$
$$T = \frac{220}{55}$$
$$= 4$$

This means that it will take Jamal 4 hours to drive to City X. If he needs to be at City X at 3:00 p.m., then he needs to leave 4 hours earlier, at 11:00 a.m. Choices F and G are incorrect, because he will arrive early. For choice J and K, he will arrive late.

31. **The correct answer is E.** Isolate x on one side of the inequality, remembering to flip the direction of the inequality sign when you multiply or divide by a negative:

$$-5 - 2 < -1$$
$$-2x < -1 + 5$$
$$-2x < 4$$
$$x > -2$$

Answer Keys and Explanations

Only choice E properly represents the inequality $x > -2$ on a number line. For choice A, you likely forgot to divide by –2 and switch the sign. For choice B, you likely forgot to divide by –2. Choice C has 2 restrictions on x instead of 1. For choice D, you forgot to switch the sign when dividing by a negative number.

32. **The correct answer is J.** The length and width of the water are the same as those of the tank. Therefore, the water's volume is equal to the area of the tank's base (length × width) times the water's depth. Since you are given the water's volume and the length and width of the tank's base, you can solve for the water depth d:

$$1,728 = (4)(8)(d)$$
$$1,728 = 192d$$
$$\frac{1,728}{192} = d$$
$$d = 9$$

The dimensions for depth in choices F, G, and H result in a volume less than 1,728 cubic inches, since the 8 and 24 are fixed. For choice K, this would mean the tank was full, which would result in a volume of 1,920 cubic inches.

33. **The correct answer is C.** Kecia had the car for 3 days, so 3($20) = $60 of the charges were due to the daily fee. That means that the remaining $156 – $60 = $96 were mileage charges. Each mile is charged at $0.50, so Kecia must have driven $96 ÷ $0.50 = 192 miles. For choice A, you have incorrectly added $156 and $60 (charge for a 3-day rental) instead of subtracting $60 from $156. For choice B, you did not subtract $60 from $156. Choice D, 156, is a dollar amount and not the mileage driven. For choice E, you forgot to divide by $0.50.

34. **The correct answer is J.** This is a multiple of a 3-4-5 right triangle: 3(4) = 12, 4(4) = 16, 5(4) = 20. Since it is a right triangle, its area is half the product of its legs: $\frac{12 \times 16}{2} = 96$ square feet . For choice F, you forgot to divide by 2; remember the area for a triangle is $\frac{1}{2} \times$ base $\times$ height . For choices G and H, you used the hypotenuse in place of the base or height in the area formula. Choice K is incorrect because you are given a right triangle, so you can easily identify the base and height.

35. **The correct answer is B.** Isolate m on one side of the equation:

$$y = mx + b$$
$$y - b = mx$$
$$\frac{y - b}{x} = m$$

Choice A has not been divided by x. Choice C results from multiplying by x instead of dividing. Choice D results from adding b instead of subtracting it. Choice E is the reciprocal of the correct expression.

36. **The correct answer is F.** A circle is defined by the equation $(x - h)^2 + (y - k)^2 = r^2$, where (h, k) is the center of the circle and r is its radius. Point (2, –3) is given as the center of the circle, so plug it in for (h, k): $(x - 2)^2 + (y + 3)^2 = r^2$. This eliminates choices G, J, and K, which don't have center (2, –3). To find the radius, use the two points given. If (2, –3) is the center of the circle and (2, 1) lies on the circumference, then the radius must connect these two points. This makes the radius equal to 1 – (–3) = 4. Plug in $r = 4$ to complete the equation:

$$(x - 2)^2 (y + 3)^2 = (4)^2$$
$$(x - 2)^2 + (y + 3)^2 = 16$$

37. **The correct answer is C.** Factor both the numerator and denominator of the fraction, then cancel any common factors:

$$\frac{x^2 - y^2}{3x - 3y} = \frac{(x + y)(x - y)}{3(x - y)}$$
$$= \frac{x + y}{3}$$

Choice A is the reciprocal of the correct answer. For choice B, you likely canceled the wrong factor in the numerator and denominator. Choice D is incorrect because you cannot group terms across the numerator and denominator in this manner. For choice E, you likely canceled $(x - y)$ with $(x^2 - y^2)$ as though they were equal, but there is a remainder when doing so.

38. The correct answer is H. Cosine is equal to $\dfrac{\text{adjacent side}}{\text{hypotenuse}}$, so $\dfrac{AC}{AB} = \dfrac{1}{2}$ as shown in the figure below.

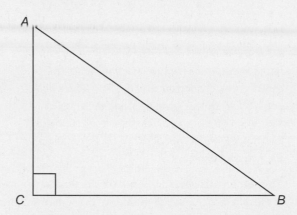

To find the cosine of angle B, you need to know the length of the side adjacent to it, segment BC. Since the length of a leg of this triangle is related to the length of its hypotenuse in the ratio of 1:2, this is a 30-60-90 right triangle, whose three sides are related in the ratio of $1 : \sqrt{3} : 2$. This means that $BC = \sqrt{3}$ and $\cos B = \dfrac{\sqrt{3}}{2}$, choice H. Choice F is $\csc B$. Choice G is $\cot B$. Choice J is $\tan B$. Choice K is $\sin B$.

39. The correct answer is A. In any triangle, the angles opposite equal sides are equal to each other. Since $RS = RT$, $\angle S = \angle T$, and since the three angles of a triangle must total 180°, $\angle R + \angle S + \angle T = 180°$. Choice B cannot be correct, because if the two angles were obtuse, their sum would be greater than 180°, which would be larger than the triangle itself. Choice C also cannot be correct, because if each angle measured 90°, the two right angles would total 180° and leave no room for a third angle; this same reasoning makes choice E incorrect. It follows that if they can't both be obtuse angles and they can't both be right angles, then they must both be acute angles, choice A. Choice D might have been tempting because it *could* be true, but remember that the question asks which statement MUST be true. If the angles were complementary—that is, if their sum were 90°—then $\angle S = \angle T = 45°$. This would make $\angle R = 90°$, which is fine. However, it is just as possible that $\angle S = \angle T = 60°$, making $\angle R = 60°$. This still satisfies the conditions of the question, but does not make angles T and S complementary.

40. The correct answer is K. Start by finding the volume and surface area of the current box:

$$V = lwh$$
$$= 6 \times 9 \times 4$$
$$= 216$$

$$SA = 2lw + 2lh$$
$$= 2(6)(9)(4) + (6)(4)$$
$$= 108 + 72 + 48$$
$$= 228$$

Now find the answer choice with a volume of 216 and a surface area less than 228.

Choice F:

$$V = 2 \times 3 \times 36 = 216$$

$$SA = 2(6) + 2(108) + 2(72) = 372; \text{ eliminate}$$

Choice G:

$$V = 2 \times 4 \times 27 = 216$$

$$SA = 2(8) + 2(108) + 2(54) = 340; \text{ eliminate}$$

Choice H:

$$V = 3 \times 6 \times 12 = 216$$

$$SA = 2(18) + 2(72) + 2(36) = 252; \text{ eliminate}$$

Choice J:

$$V = 3 \times 8 \times 9 = 216$$

$$SA = 2(24) + 2(72) + 2(27) = 246; \text{ eliminate}$$

Choice K:

$$V = 6 \times 6 \times 6 = 216$$

$$SA = 2(36) + 2(36) + 2(36) = 216$$

This is the only surface area smaller than 228, so it is correct.

41. The correct answer is E. Put the equation for line *l* in slope-intercept form:

$$2y - x = 5$$
$$2y = x + 5$$
$$y = \frac{1}{2}x\frac{5}{2}$$

This shows that line *l* has a slope of $\dfrac{1}{2}$. The slopes of perpendicular lines are negative reciprocals, so the slope of a line perpendicular to line *l* is $-\dfrac{1}{\left(\dfrac{1}{2}\right)} = -2$.

Only choice E, $y = -2x + 2$, has the correct slope of –2. The slope is incorrect in choices A, C, and D; the product of the slopes must be –1 if the two lines are perpendicular. Choice B is equivalent to the given line and so cannot be perpendicular to it.

Answer Keys and Explanations

42. The correct answer is F. Set up a proportion equating the ratio of rainfall per hour to the ratio of rainfall per x hours, and cross multiply to solve for x:

$$\frac{0.25}{1} = \frac{c}{x}$$
$$0.25x = c$$
$$x = \frac{c}{0.25}$$

Choice G is the reciprocal of the correct expression. For choice H, you have multiplied by 0.25 instead of dividing by it; you likely inverted half of the proportion to get this answer. For choice J, when solving the equation $0.25x = c$, divide by 0.25, don't add it to both sides. For choice K, when solving the equation $0.25x = c$, divide by 0.25, don't subtract it from both sides.

43. The correct answer is D. The table lists coordinates of points on the line. All of the answer choices are in slope-intercept form, $y = mx + b$, where m is the slope and b is the y-intercept. The second pair of coordinates listed in the table is $(0, -2)$, giving the y-intercept of the line as -2. Choices A and B can be eliminated, since neither equation has a y-intercept of -2. The slope of a line is equal to the change in its y-coordinates divided by the change in its x-coordinates. Looking at the row of x-coordinates, you can see that they change in increments of 2; the y-coordinates change in increments of 1. This means that the slope of the line is $\frac{1}{2}$, so choice D,

$y = \frac{1}{2}x - 2$, correctly represents the relationship in the

table. In choice A, the point $(-2, -3)$ does not satisfy this equation. In choice B, $(0, -2)$ does not satisfy this equation. In choice C, $(-2, -3)$ does not satisfy this equation. In choice E, $(2, -1)$ does not satisfy this equation.

44. The correct answer is K. You know that both x and z are greater than y, but you aren't given any information about how they relate to one another. This means that you cannot tell which, if either of them, is greater than the other, so choices F and G can be eliminated. You might assume that since $x > y$, $x^2 > y^2$, but this is not necessarily true. If $x = 2$ and $y = -3$, for example, then $2^2 < (-3)^2$, making $x^2 < y^2$. This allows you to eliminate choices H and J, leaving choice K as correct. It must be true that $x + z > 2y$; since both x and z are greater than y, their sum must be greater than $2y$.

45. The correct answer is C. Stack the two equations and add them:

$$
\begin{array}{r}
y + 2x = 5 \\
3y + 2x = 9 \\
\hline
4y + 4x = 14
\end{array}
$$

Factoring out a 4 yields $y + x = 3\frac{1}{2}$. For choice A, you did not treat mixed numbers correctly—you cannot multiply the whole part and fractional part. For choice B, you divided incorrectly; $14 \div 4$ does not equal 2. For choice D, when solving the equation $4(x + y) = 14$ for $(x + y)$, divide by 4, don't subtract it. For choice E, you forgot to divide by 4 after adding the two equations.

46. The correct answer is J. The area of the shaded region is the difference between the area of the square and the area of the circle. The perimeter of the square is 36 square feet, so each of its sides is $36 \div 4 = 9$ feet. If you draw a diameter through the center of the circle, you will see that it is equal to a side of the square, so the diameter of the circle is also 9 feet, as shown in the figure.

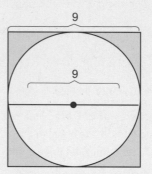

Now find the areas of both known regions. Area of a square is equal to s^2, so the area of this square is $9^2 = 81$ square feet. Area of a circle is equal to πr^2. Since the diameter of the circle is 9, its radius is 4.5, making its area $\pi(4.5)^2 = 20.25\pi$ square feet. Therefore, the area of the shaded region is $81 - 20.25\pi$ square feet. For choice F, you have forgotten to square the side and the radius when finding the area of the square and circle, respectively. Choice G is incorrect because the area of the square is 81 square feet, not 36 square feet, and the radius of the circle is 4.5 feet, not 3 feet. Choice H is the perimeter of the shaded region, not its area. Choice K is incorrect because the radius of the circle is 4.5 feet, not 6 feet.

47. The correct answer is C. There are a total of 50 numbers on the wheel, so figure out how many of these 50 will make Greg win. Greg bets on numbers 32 through 46. Be careful not to settle for 46 – 32, because this difference does not include both 32 and 46 as possibilities. To include both endpoints, add one to the difference between them; that means there are 46 – 32 + 1 = 15 winning numbers. Therefore, the probability that the spinner will land on one of Greg's numbers is $\frac{15}{50} = \frac{3}{10}$. Choice A is the probability of landing on any given number, but Greg placed his bet on 15 of the 50 numbers. Choice B is incorrect because there are 15 numbers on which Greg placed his bet, not 14. Choice D is the probability that the spinner does not land on one of Greg's numbers. Choice E is incorrect because Greg did not bet on 46 numbers; he only bet on 15 of them.

48. **The correct answer is G.** In any right triangle, $\text{sine} = \dfrac{\text{opposite}}{\text{hypotenuse}}$, so $\sin\angle QSR = \dfrac{QR}{QS}$. This means that you'll need to determine the lengths of segments QR and QS.

$\overline{QR}$ is the hypotenuse of a right triangle with legs 2 and 4, so use the Pythagorean theorem to find its length:

$$QR = \sqrt{2^2 + 4^2}$$
$$= \sqrt{4 + 16}$$
$$= \sqrt{20}$$
$$= 2\sqrt{5}$$

$\overline{QS}$ is the hypotenuse of ΔQRS, which has legs $\overline{QR}$ and $\overline{RS}$. You just found that $QR = 2\sqrt{5}$, and it's given that $RS = 5$. Therefore:
$$QS = \sqrt{(QR)^2 + (RS)^2}$$
$$= \sqrt{(2\sqrt{5})^2 + 5^2}$$
$$= \sqrt{20 + 25}$$
$$= \sqrt{45}$$
$$= 3\sqrt{5}$$

Now use these two values to calculate the sine of the angle:
$$\sin\angle QSR = \frac{QR}{QS}$$
$$= \frac{2\sqrt{5}}{3\sqrt{5}}$$
$$= \frac{2}{3}$$

Choice F is csc(QSR). Choice H is cos(QSR). Choice J is tan(QSR). Choice K is sec(QSR).

49. **The correct answer is E.** The number of x-intercepts that a parabola has is the same as the number of real roots it has. The given parabola never intersects the x-axis, so it must have no real roots. The discriminant, $b^2 - 4ac$, of a quadratic equation reveals whether a parabola will have 0, 1, or 2 real roots. When the discriminant is positive, the equation has two real roots and intersects the x-axis at two points; when it is zero, the equation has one real root and intersects the x-axis at exactly one point; when it is negative, the equation has no real roots and does not intersect the x-axis. Find the discriminant of the given quadratic equation, $y = 2x^2 - 4x + c$.

$$b^2 - 4ac = (-4)^2 - 4(2)(c)$$
$$= 16 - 8c$$

Since the parabola has no real roots, the value of this discriminant must be negative. Try the answer choices to see which one will make $16 - 8c$ negative:

Choice A: 16 – 8(–1) = 16 + 8 = 24; eliminate

Choice B: 16 – 8(0) = 16 – 0 = 16; eliminate

Choice C: 16 – 8(1) = 16 – 8 = 8; eliminate

Choice D: 16 – 8(2) = 16 – 16 = 0; eliminate

Choice E: 16 – 8(3) = 16 – 24 = –8; CORRECT

50. **The correct answer is F.** The ratio of the areas of two figures is equal to the *square* of the ratios of their corresponding linear measurements. Since the ratio of the radius of circle A to the radius of circle B is 3:1, the ratio of their areas must be $3^2:1^2 = 9:1$. That means that the area of circle B is $\dfrac{1}{9}$ the area of circle A, or $\dfrac{x}{9}$.

Choice G is incorrect because $3^2 = 9$, not 6. Choice H is incorrect because you must square the 3 for the denominator. Choices J and K are incorrect because circle A is larger than circle B, so its area must be larger.

51. **The correct answer is C.** Parallel lines have equal slopes. Plugging into the slope formula, you'll find that the slope of the line shown is $\dfrac{2-0}{0-1} = \dfrac{2}{-1} = -2$. Since all of the answer choices are already in slope-intercept form $y = mx + b$, where m is the slope, a quick scan reveals that the only line with a slope of –2 is $y = -2x + 2$, choice C. Choices A, B, and D are incorrect because the graphed line falls from left to right, so it must have a negative slope—each of these lines has a positive slope. In choice E, the slope is wrong; remember that the slope of a line is the change in y divided by the change in x.

52. **The correct answer is J.** The area of a triangle is equal to $\frac{1}{2}bh$. The area of $\triangle ABC$ is 24 and its height, segment AC, has a length of 8, so its base, segment AB, must have a length of 6. Given that $AD = 28$, it follows that $BD = 28 - 6 = 22$. Now that you have the length of a pair of sides of the parallelogram, you just need the length of the other pair of sides to solve. Since segment BC happens to be the hypotenuse of a right triangle with legs of 6 and 8, its length must be 10. That makes the perimeter of parallelogram $BCED$ equal to $2(22 + 10) = 2(32) = 64$ feet. For choice F, you likely used AD in place of BD when computing the perimeter. For choice G, you likely used the length of AC instead of the length of BC, and AD instead of BD, when computing the perimeter. For choice H, you likely used AD in place of BD and AB instead of BC when computing the perimeter. For choice K, you miscomputed the length of BC.

53. **The correct answer is C.** You want to know the value of t when $s = 96$. Plugging in $s = 96$ gives you $96 = 80t - 16t^2$. Put this equation into standard quadratic form and solve:

$$96 = 80t - 16t^2$$
$$16t^2 - 80t + 96 = 0$$
$$16\left(t^2 - 5t + 6\right) = 0$$
$$16(t - 3)(t - 2) = 0$$
$$t = 3 \text{ or } t = 2$$

Only 2 is a choice, so choice C is correct. All other choices listed for t do not yield 96 when substituted into the expression.

54. **The correct answer is K.** Let x equal the number of hours it takes the standard printer to do the job alone. That means that every hour it does $\frac{1}{x}$ of the job. The high-speed printer can complete the job alone in 5 hours, so every hour it does $\frac{1}{5}$ of the job. Working together, the two printers complete the job in $3\frac{1}{3} = \frac{10}{3}$ hours, so each hour they do $\frac{1}{\left(\frac{10}{3}\right)} = \frac{3}{10}$ of the job. The sum of the individual rates is equal to the rate working

together, so you can write the following equation and solve for x:

$$\frac{1}{x} + \frac{1}{5} = \frac{3}{10}$$
$$\frac{1}{x} = \frac{3}{10} - \frac{1}{5}$$
$$\frac{1}{x} = \frac{1}{10}$$
$$x = 10$$

Choices F and G cannot be correct because the standard printer would take longer than the high-speed printer to do the job alone. If you selected choice H, you likely made an arithmetic error. Choice J is the result of adding the rates, which is incorrect—these two printers are going to work *together*, which does not accurately portray the comparison of job completion rates of the two printers.

55. **The correct answer is D.** Pick a number, then apply the percent changes to it and see what happens. Use 100, since it's the easiest number for which to find percentages. 30% of 100 is 30, so increasing 100 by 30% results in $100 + 30 = 130$. 50% of 130 is 65, so decreasing 130 by 50% results in $130 - 65 = 65$. Since you started with 100, this is a net decrease of $100 - 65 = 35$. As a percent of 100, 35 represents 35%, so choice D is correct. Choice A is too low and likely the result of an arithmetic error. Choice B is the result of multiplying 0.30 times 0.50, but this implies that the percentages both serve to increase a quantity or decrease a quantity to which they are being applied; here, one percentage is an increase and the other is a decrease. Choice C is incorrect because you cannot simply add or subtract percentages unless they are being applied to the same amount; in this case, the percentages are being applied in succession and hence, to different amounts. You must subtract choice E from 100% to get the correct percentage.

56. **The correct answer is H.** When parallel lines are crossed by a transversal, 8 angles are formed. Unless the transversal is perpendicular to the pair of parallel lines (and it isn't in this case), 4 of the angles are acute and 4 of the angles are obtuse. All of the acute angles are equal to each other, all of the obtuse angles are equal to each other, and each acute angle is supplementary to each obtuse angle. Evaluate the expression in each choice to see which is NOT true:

Choice F: $(a + b = g + h)$:

obtuse + acute = acute + obtuse

True; eliminate

Choice G: $(f - h = c - d)$:

acute – obtuse = acute – obtuse

True; eliminate

Choice H: ($a + h = g + c$):

obtuse + obtuse = acute + acute

NOT true; CORRECT

Choice J: ($d + b - f = e + c - g$):

obtuse + acute – acute = obtuse + acute – acute

True; eliminate

Choice K: ($h - c = d - f$):

obtuse – acute = obtuse – acute

True; eliminate

57. **The correct answer is C.** You're given the side opposite the 43° angle, as well as the side adjacent to it. Choose the trig function that uses both the opposite and adjacent sides to an angle in a right triangle. Since

$$tangent = \frac{opposite\ side}{adjacent\ side},\ tan43° = \frac{5}{n}.$$ To solve for n,

isolate it on one side of the equation:

$$tan43° = \frac{5}{n}$$
$$n(tan43°) = 5$$
$$n = \frac{5}{tan43°}$$

Choices A and B are the hypotenuse, not n. In choice D, you are not using the correct definition of sine of an angle. For choice E, you should divide by tan 43°, not multiply by it.

58. **The correct answer is G.** Since

$$average = \frac{sum}{number\ of\ terms},\ sum = average \times number$$

of terms. The sum of the set of 6 integers, therefore, is $22 \times 6 = 132$. When one of the 6 numbers is removed, the average of the remaining 5 integers is 25, so their sum is $25 \times 5 = 125$. The number that was removed must be $132 - 125 = 7$. Choice F is too small; the resulting set would need to have a larger average. Choices H and J are too large; the resulting set would need to have a smaller average. In choice K, you multiplied 25 by 6, but you should have multiplied it by 5 because the new set contains 5 numbers.

59. **The correct answer is C.** The graph opens upward, which means that the coefficient of x^2 must be positive,

so you can eliminate choice E immediately. The graph also indicates a y-intercept of –3, which means that $y = -3$ when $x = 0$, so you can eliminate choices B and D as well. Now pick a specific point from the graph and plug its coordinates into the remaining answer choices. Since the x-intercept (1, 0) is easily identifiable and makes the arithmetic simplest, let $x = 1$ and $y = 0$ to see which equation works:

Choice A: $y = x^2 - 2^x - 3$ for (0):

$$0 = 1^2 - 2(1) - 3$$
$$0 = 1 - 2 - 3$$
$$0 \neq -4$$

Eliminate choice A.

Choice C: $y = x^2 + 2^x - 3$ for (0):

$$0 = 1^2 + 2(1) - 3$$
$$0 = 1 + 2 - 3$$
$$0 = 0$$

This is the correct answer.

60. **The correct answer is J.** Start by determining the total number of possible outcomes. Each coin toss has two possibilities (either heads or tails), so for all four coin tosses there are $2 \times 2 \times 2 \times 2 = 16$ possibilities. The question asks how many of these 16 outcomes will NOT contain exactly three heads. It is probably easiest to look for outcomes that *do* contain exactly three heads, which are as follows:

H H H T

H H T H

H T H H

T H H H

If, as shown above, 4 out of 16 possibilities contain exactly three heads, then 12 out of 16 will NOT contain exactly three heads. This is a probability of $\frac{12}{16} = \frac{3}{4}$. Choice F is the probability of getting exactly three heads. Choice G is the probability of getting at least three heads. For choice H, you seem to have disregarded some of the ways of not getting three heads. Choice K is the probability of not getting exactly four heads.

READING

1.	D	11.	B	21.	D	31.	A
2.	G	12.	J	22.	J	32.	G
3.	B	13.	A	23.	A	33.	B
4.	F	14.	G	24.	J	34.	F
5.	B	15.	A	25.	B	35.	C
6.	H	16.	F	26.	G	36.	F
7.	C	17.	D	27.	B	37.	B
8.	J	18.	G	28.	F	38.	J
9.	D	19.	B	29.	C	39.	A
10.	G	20.	H	30.	H	40.	J

1. **The correct answer is D.** This is a vocabulary-in-context question about the word *rich*, which appears in the fourth sentence of the first paragraph. While choices A, B, and C are all definitions of the word, only choice D makes sense in this context. The synonyms *wealthy* (choice A) and *affluent* (choice B) can only describe people, not houses. Choice C, *abundant*, cannot describe a house on its own; what is the house abundant in? Choice D, *plush*, however, can describe a house, so it best captures the meaning of *rich* as it is used in the context of Paragraph 1.

2. **The correct answer is G.** This is a detail question that requires a close reading of the first paragraph in which Mr. Utterson decides that the only way to understand why his friend feels compelled to do the bidding of Mr. Hyde is to see Mr. Hyde for himself. The first sentence of the second paragraph says, "From that time forward, Mr. Utterson began to haunt the door in the by-street of shops." Although Mr. Utterson has a dream about Mr. Hyde in the story, he does not have a nightmare about Mr. Enfield, so choice F is not correct. You can eliminate choice H since there is no mention of who, exactly, is Mr. Utterson's friend who feels compelled to do the bidding of Mr. Hyde, and there is no mention of whether or not Mr. Utterson ever discussed Mr. Hyde with that friend. The reader only knows that he discussed Mr. Hyde with someone named Mr. Enfield. There is also no indication that the door in the by-street of shops is on the way to Mr. Utterson's place of work, so choice J is incorrect.

3. **The correct answer is B.** This is an inference question about Mr. Utterson and Mr. Hyde. Based on information in this passage, the reader can conclude that Mr. Hyde is evil, and at the end of the passage, Mr. Utterson decides to pursue him. Choice B is correct because this relationship is most similar to that of a police officer pursuing a criminal. Some brothers and former

co-workers do not get along, but that is not enough to conclude that choice A or choice D is correct. Although there is a sense that Mr. Hyde has a certain amount of power over Mr. Utterson's thoughts, the relationship is not like that of an employee and a boss, so choice C does not make sense.

4. **The correct answer is F.** This is an inference question. The stranger who comes to the Coach and Horses seems to want to keep his face and body hidden in his outerwear, and is making a conscious effort to conceal his identity from Mrs. Hall. Clearly, he has something to hide, so choice F is the best answer. However, there is not enough information in this passage to conclude that he is a criminal (choice G), and there is not enough information about Mrs. Hall to conclude that the stranger is the strangest man she has ever met (choice H). Although the stranger seemed "more dead than alive," this is merely a colorful description of him and not a concrete indication that he was actually about to die, so choice J is not the best answer.

5. **The correct answer is B.** This is a vocabulary-in-context question for the word *biting*, which appears in the first sentence of the passage. In this sentence, *biting* describes the wind on a wintry day, so *freezing* is the best definition of the word in this particular context. Although the other answer choices are synonyms for *biting*, none of them describe how the word is used in this context. Wind cannot really be *snapping* (choice A) or *abrasive* (choice C). Wind cannot express emotions, so *hateful* (choice D) does not make sense in this context.

Answer Keys and Explanations

6. **The correct answer is H.** This is an except question, so eliminate choices that *are* supported by the passage. Mrs. Hall does her best to make the stranger comfortable, so she does seem to care about his well-being, which eliminates choice F. However, she also works at the Coach and Horses, so it is probably her job to care about his well-being. Therefore, you can conclude that she feels professionally obligated to see to his comfort (choice J). Based on the way she sets his table quickly before rushing out of the room, you can conclude that she feels uneasy in his presence, which eliminates choice G. However, as odd as the stranger is, his behavior never seems to amuse Mrs. Hall, so choice H is the best answer.

7. **The correct answer is C.** This is a main idea question about the two passages. The best answer is choice C since Mr. Utterson in Passage A must deal with the mysterious Mr. Hyde and Mrs. Hall in Passage B must deal with the mysterious stranger who comes to the Coach and Horses. Only Mr. Utterson's friend is enslaved by a mysterious stranger, so choices A and B describe ideas only in Passage A. Only Mrs. Hall seems uncomfortable performing tasks for a stranger, so choice D describes only Passage B.

8. **The correct answer is J.** This question is asking you to make an inference by contrasting two characters in similar situations. Since it is asking you to find a difference between those two people, you should try to eliminate all the answer choices that suggest ways they are similar. Mr. Utterson is intrigued by the mysterious Mr. Hyde and Mrs. Hall is intrigued by the mysterious stranger who comes to the Coach and Horses, so this is one way they are similar. Therefore, you can eliminate choice F. Both Mr. Utterson and Mrs. Hall find the behavior of those two mysterious people baffling, so choice G is wrong. Mr. Utterson seems to care about his friend who is obsessed with Mr. Hyde and Mrs. Hall cares about the troubled stranger who comes to the Coach and Horses, so choice H does not describe a way they are different. However, only Mr. Utterson wants to seek out a mysterious person to learn more about him, and Mr. Utterson's enthusiasm about it makes it seem as though he likes to solve mysteries. Even though the stranger who comes to the Coach and Horses intrigues Mrs. Hall, she wants to flee from him, not solve the mystery that apparently surrounds him. So choice J describes a difference between Mr. Utterson and Mrs. Hall.

9. **The correct answer is D.** This is an inference question about how these passages function in the novels from which they were excerpted. Since each passage seems to set up something—Passage A sets up Mr. Utterson's pursuit of Mr. Hyde, and Passage B sets up the arrival of a mysterious stranger at the Coach and Horses—it is unlikely they occur on the final pages of the novels from which they were excerpted (choice A). A passage that merely sets up a plot thread probably won't be the most important incident in a novel, no matter how important the plot thread that follows will be, so you can eliminate choice B. However, since both passages set up plot threads that will likely be important, it is more likely that they occur early in the novels from which they were excerpted, so choice D is the best answer. Neither passage is particularly humorous, so choice C does not make sense.

10. **The correct answer is G.** This is a main idea question about Paragraph 1 of Passage A and Paragraph 2 of Passage B. Choice F is incorrect because Mr. Hyde does not actually arrive anywhere in Passage 1. However, only he seems particularly evil, so choice H cannot apply to Passage 2. Mr. Hyde may demand things of Mr. Utterson's friend, and the stranger who comes to the Coach and Horses demands that Mrs. Hall light a fire and get him a room at the inn, but neither captures the main idea of the paragraphs in question. Therefore, choice J is not the best answer. The only choice that really captures the main ideas of the paragraphs is choice G, since Paragraph 1 of Passage A describes how Mr. Hyde is affecting Mr. Utterson's thoughts and dreams, and Paragraph 2 of Passage B describes how the stranger affects Mrs. Hall's behavior, since she is working to attend to the stranger's needs.

11. **The correct answer is B.** This is a detail question about bearskin jobbers, who appear in the fifth paragraph. The second sentence provides the correct answer (choice B). The passage doesn't mention anything about hunters cheating customers (choice A). Choice C relates to sentence three, which describes speculators, not bear jobbers. Choice D refers to bull speculators, as seen in the fifth sentence of the following paragraph.

12. **The correct answer is J.** This is a detail question. Locate the phrase, which appears in the fourth sentence of the second paragraph. Neither this phrase nor the paragraph as a whole has anything to do with predicting the stock market (choice F). Choice G may refer to the end of the selected phrase, but lions and sheep have

nothing to do with why bears and bulls don't seem opposite in build or character. Nothing in the passage supports choice H. The fifth sentence provides the desired detail, making choice J correct.

13. **The correct answer is A.** This is a main idea question related to the fifth paragraph. The majority of the paragraph describes how short-selling speculators acted, making choice A correct. Choice B appears in the second sentence of the fourth paragraph. The origin of the term in the American fur trade (choice C), is a detail mentioned only at the beginning of the fifth paragraph, setting up the more central discussion about the way certain speculators did business. Choice D appears in the last sentence of the fourth paragraph.

14. **The correct answer is G.** This is a detail question. Scan for the word *margin*, which first appears in the sixth sentence of the sixth paragraph. The next sentence provides the answer, "…then hoped that the prices would *rise* by the time payment was due," making choice G correct. Choice F refers to bear speculators, as discussed in the fifth paragraph. There is no evidence to support choice H. Someone who buys on margin is described as a bull, so choice J doesn't make sense.

15. **The correct answer is A.** This is a vocabulary-in-context question about the word *piggish*, which appears in the last sentence of the second paragraph. The sentence states that people become piggish about stocks as economies grow, which suggests optimism, choice A. Remember also that the pig is specifically introduced as a potential replacement for the bull. This further supports choice A, because the sixth paragraph describes bulls as *optimistically* buying stocks. Choice B, therefore, is contradictory because bears, not bulls, are said to "hungrily seek property to devour." There is no evidence to support choice C. Choice D does not fit the context; stocks may be unpredictable, but people would not feel unpredictable about them.

16. **The correct answer is F.** This is a detail question that also points to the main idea. Examine each choice as it relates to the third paragraph. The second sentence provides the correct answer, choice F. The number of theories is discussed in the fourth paragraph, so choice G is wrong. Up and down cycles (choice H) are what happen in the stock market, not the forces that control it. There is no support for choice J.

17. **The correct answer is D.** This is an inference question asking you to describe the attitude of bear speculators as compared with that of bull speculators. There is no support for choice A or choice B. Choice C is wrong because bears *make* money when stock prices go down. The author states this in the next-to-last sentence of the fifth paragraph, which also supports choice D.

18. **The correct answer is G.** This is an inference question referring to the beginning of the second paragraph. Curiosity (choice F), is felt only toward the choice of these two animals as economic symbols, not toward bull-baiting or bear-baiting. The author calls these sports "cruel" and "heartless," which indicates strong disapproval and makes choice G correct. Admiration (choice H), is the exact opposite of the answer. Choice J goes too far, as nothing suggests that the author disapproves so strongly as to become wrathful.

19. **The correct answer is B.** This is a detail question about Thomas Mortimer, who appears in the sixth paragraph. Mortimer did not discuss other theories but proposed a theory himself, so choice A is wrong. The fourth sentence begins a description of the animalistic behavior of speculators as noted by Mortimer, making choice B the right answer. There is no support for choice C. The fact that Mortimer wrote in 1785 makes choice D incorrect.

20. **The correct answer is H.** This is a main idea question. The first two sentences of the paragraph convey the narrator's idea that people might be attributing more to the symbols than they should be, choice H. There is no specific evidence to support choices F, G, or J.

21. **The correct answer is D.** This is an except question that requires you to scan the passage for details about shadow puppets. The sixth paragraph says that the puppets "are highly stylized caricatures, rather than realistic figures." This means that they do not look natural, so choice D is the correct answer, as it is the only choice *not* supported by the passage. Choices A, B, and C are characteristics described in the passage.

22. **The correct answer is J.** This is an inference question. The answer lies in the next-to-last paragraph, which tells us that traditionally, men sit on one side of the screen and watch the actual puppets, while women sit on the other and watch the shadows. The paragraph also explains that viewers who see the actual puppets (men) get to see the colors of the puppets. You can infer that women, who see only the shadows cast by the puppets, do not get to see how the puppets are painted. There is nothing to support choice F. The first paragraph specifically mentions children darting around at the performance, so you can eliminate choice G. The passage also explains that there is a single *dalang* working the puppets, so eliminate choice H.

23. **The correct answer is A.** This is a two-part detail question. The second paragraph says that the origins of *wayang kulit* stretch back to ancient Indonesian religious beliefs. This makes Statement I true, so eliminate choice C. The fourth paragraph explains that after the spread of Islam, which prohibited displaying gods in human form, Indonesians adapted by creating shadow puppets. This means that Statement II is also true, so eliminate choice B. There is no mention of early Christian texts—the stories of *wayang kulit* are based on Hindu texts. This makes Statement III false, so eliminate choice D. The correct answer is choice A.

24. **The correct answer is J.** The line says that as Javanese shadow puppetry *endures*, it continues to evolve, or change. One definition of *enduring* is lasting a long time, and that's the one that makes sense here. Choices F, G, and H do not work in this context, although each is a possible definition for *endures*.

25. **The correct answer is B.** The third paragraph describes all of the aspects of Indonesian life that were influenced by migrants from India. Choice A goes too far—the paragraph doesn't say that Indonesians lost their identity, just that their culture was heavily influenced. Choice C is unsupported, especially since we learn elsewhere in the passage that Indonesians already had a belief system in place before the arrival of Hinduism. Choice D contradicts the answer because the paragraph is about how India shaped Indonesian culture, not the other way around.

26. **The correct answer is G.** The fourth paragraph states that *walang kulit* is based on Hindu religious texts, and the next-to-last paragraph mentions the way puppets of the Hindu gods Vishnu and Shiva are painted. You can reasonably infer that Hindu gods are regular, recurring characters in the performances. Choice F is wrong because, while the last paragraph mentions certain changes to *walang kulit*, the passage makes it clear that a modern-day performance is extremely similar to performances of hundreds of years ago. Choice H is not supported by the passage, which says that shadow puppetry is particularly popular in Java, and choice J is wrong because the passage does not state or imply that *dalangs* make their own puppets.

27. **The correct answer is B.** This is a detail question that requires you to understand the order in which events occur. The third paragraph from the end explains the process of making shadow puppets. The fifth sentence describes when the rods that control the moving parts are added—it's after the puppet has been painted. The sentence makes it sound as though the rods and the moving parts are added at the same time, so eliminate choice D. The leather is treated early in the process, so eliminate choice C.

28. **The correct answer is F.** Refer to the third paragraph to solve this except question. It mentions government (choice G), language (choice H), and religion (choice J), but not architecture (choice F).

29. **The correct answer is C.** This is a detail question. The last paragraph describes the ways that *wayang kulit* has changed in modern times. One of those ways is that performances are now broadcast on television—in other words, people don't have to be in public spaces to view the performances. Choice A distorts the answer—female *dalangs* do exist but are said to be uncommon. Choice B is not supported. Choice D might have been tempting because the paragraph says that some performances have incorporated elements from other cultures, but there is no support for the idea that the performances resemble Western plays and movies.

30. **The correct answer is H.** The purpose of the line is to illustrate that a performance today would have basically the same elements as a performance hundreds of years ago: the same lit screen, the same kinds of puppets, the audience milling around a public square. Choice F is too broad—the sentence does not refer to all of Java, just the traditions of a particular art form. Choice G goes too far—the sentence is not intended to imply that the people of Java are completely unchanged, just that shadow puppetry has not changed very much. There is nothing to support choice J.

31. **The correct answer is A.** This is a main idea question about the first paragraph. The author mentions the function of smell for both pleasure (such as romance) and practicality (such as determining whether food has gone bad), so choice A is correct. Choice C is a detail, not a main point. Choices B and D are not discussed until the second paragraph.

32. **The correct answer is G.** This is a detail question about Turin's experiment with camphane and decaborane, discussed in the fourth paragraph. The opposite of choice F is true, making choice G the correct answer, supported by the third, fourth, and next-to-last sentences. Neither choice H nor choice J is what Turin set out to prove.

33. **The correct answer is B.** This is a detail question. Luca Turin is introduced in the first sentence of the fourth paragraph, which states that he is a biophysicist, choice B. Choice A is incorrect because a perfume enthusiast is not the same thing as a perfume executive. The final

paragraph of the passage mentions that Turin uses a computer, but it never suggests he is a computer programmer, so choice C is wrong. Biophysicists and medical doctors are both scientists, but they are not the same kind of scientist, so choice D is wrong.

34. **The correct answer is F.** This is an inference question about the third paragraph. The third sentence states that "molecules up to a certain mass have scents." Therefore, those over that mass would not have a smell, making choice F correct and disproving choice H. The last sentence of the paragraph mentions the rotten egg smell (choice G), but does not relate it to mass. Choice J is wrong because taste, which is mentioned only in the first paragraph, is never discussed in relation to mass.

35. **The correct answer is C.** This is a two-part detail question regarding babies. Scan the entire passage for any mention of infants and examine all of the numbered statements. The last sentence of the sixth paragraph both refutes Statement I and supports Statement III. Therefore, eliminate choices B and D for containing Statement I and choice A for *not* containing Statement III. This leaves choice C; Statement II is verified by the third sentence of the first paragraph.

36. **The correct answer is F.** This is an inference question. Begin by locating the phrase, which appears in the sixth sentence of the fifth paragraph. The author explains the phrase in the following sentences, drawing a parallel between measuring sight and sound as well as smell in terms of vibrations. This makes choice F correct. Choices G, H, and J do not make sense as applied to the quote.

37. **The correct answer is B.** This is a detail question about the "lock-and-key" theory, which first appears in the third paragraph. Luca Turin challenged this theory, as mentioned in the first and second sentences of the fourth paragraph, making choice B correct. Choice A says the opposite, so it's wrong. Choice C refers to Luca Turin's theory, not the "lock-and-key" theory. There is no support for choice D.

38. **The correct answer is J.** This is a two-part detail question about Luca Turin's theory. Examine each statement to see whether it applies. Statement I is supported by the final sentence of the fourth paragraph, so eliminate choices G and H for not containing Statement I. Because Statement III is supported by the fifth paragraph, the correct answer is choice J.

39. **The correct answer is A.** This is a vocabulary-in-context question about the word *discrepancies*, which appears in the first sentence of the fourth paragraph. This sentence refers back to the information at the end of the preceding paragraph. Choice A is correct as *discrepancies* means "differences." Choice B might be tempting, but it's not quite right in this context; chemical compounds cannot disagree. The opposite of choice C is true. Choice D does not make sense.

40. **The correct answer is J.** This is a detail question about the author's conclusion, located in the final sentence of the last paragraph. Choice J paraphrases this conclusion and is the correct answer. There is no evidence to support choices F, G, or H.

SCIENCE

1.	C	11.	A	21.	A	31.	A
2.	F	12.	H	22.	J	32.	J
3.	C	13.	B	23.	B	33.	B
4.	G	14.	H	24.	J	34.	H
5.	D	15.	B	25.	A	35.	B
6.	G	16.	J	26.	G	36.	J
7.	D	17.	A	27.	B	37.	B
8.	J	18.	H	28.	H	38.	F
9.	B	19.	C	29.	C	39.	D
10.	G	20.	H	30.	J	40.	H

1. **The correct answer is C.** A comparison of the figures in Tables 1 and 2 shows that transpiration rates increase as temperature increases from refrigerator levels to room temperature to heat lamp, while transpiration rates decrease as humidity levels go from no humidity to medium humidity to high humidity. Humidity and temperature thus have opposite effects on transpiration rates, not the same effect (choice B), or no effect at all (choice D). Choice A is incorrect, as nothing indicates that temperature and humidity are the only factors affecting transpiration rates. In fact, leaf surface area is another factor that is explored in this set of experiments, indicating that transpiration is indeed affected by other things besides temperature and humidity.

2. **The correct answer is F.** Experiment 3 is designed to shed light on the way in which leaf surface area affects transpiration rates. The students varied surface area by varying the number of leaves on each plant studied. As seen in Experiments 1 and 2, however, different plants have different transpiration rates, even though they all follow the same basic pattern. To avoid unnecessary variables introduced by differences among plant species, the students relied on one plant species in Experiment 3 so that the single issue of surface area's relationship to transpiration could be isolated and observed. Choice G is incorrect, as the factors in Experiments 1 and 2, temperature and humidity, were not compared in Experiment 3, which focused on leaf surface area while keeping other environmental conditions stable. Choice H directly contradicts Experiment 1, in which plants B and C were also observed under a heat lamp. Choice J directly contradicts Experiments 1 and 2, which show that plants B and C are just as likely as plant A to transpire, not to mention the thousands of other plant species about which we know nothing. As noted above, plant A was chosen

exclusively for Experiment 3—not presumably for any intrinsic quality of that particular plant species, but because it made sense to choose a single species and stick with it to eliminate unnecessary and confusing variables.

3. **The correct answer is C.** Glancing at the choices tells us that we need to determine the number of leaves in plant A of Experiment 1, so it's likely we'll need a clue from the experiment focusing specifically on leaf count, Experiment 3. There we see that the mean amount of water lost under the heat lamp every 10 minutes was .3 mL in a specimen of plant A with 10 leaves, 1.8 mL in a specimen with 50 leaves, and 3.4 mL in a specimen with 100 leaves. Our task is to determine how these numbers relate to plant A's heat lamp figures from Experiment 1. Eyeballing the relevant information in Table 1, we can estimate the mean water loss per 10-minute interval for plant A's heat lamp to be somewhere around 1.0 mL. That's more than the corresponding .3 figure observed in Experiment 3 for the specimen with 10 leaves, but less than the 1.8 figure yielded by the specimen with 50 leaves. We can deduce, therefore, that the number of leaves on the specimen of plant A used in Experiment 1 was somewhere between 10 and 50 (choice C). If the plant had fewer than 10 leaves (choice A), or exactly 10 leaves (choice B), the mean water loss would have been much less than displayed in Experiment 1's results. If the plant had more than 50 leaves, choice D, the mean water loss would have been greater than the results displayed.

4. **The correct answer is G.** Table 3 suggests that plants with more leaves lose more water than plants with fewer leaves. What can account for this? Considering that stomata are defined as the tiny pores on leaves through which water is lost, it's

reasonable to deduce that a greater number of leaves might contain a greater number of stomata, thus accounting for the extra water lost in plants with more leaves. Choice F tends to oppose the results of Experiment 3, as one would expect plants that close their stomata more often to lose less water than other plants. Yet in Experiment 3, plants with more leaves lost more water. Choice H is incorrect, as the experiment results suggest that the heat has a greater effect on plants with more leaves, which lose more water. Choice H does nothing to explain why transpiration rate increases with the addition of leaves. Choice J is incorrect. The plants in Experiment 3 are tested under a heat lamp, and other factors, such as humidity, are kept constant. So a correlation between leaf number and humidity doesn't help to explain the experiment's results.

5. **The correct answer is D.** The question stem reinforces the reasonable deduction that the purpose of Experiment 3 was to see how transpiration varies with leaf surface area; after all, the passage introduction indicates that surface area is a subject of the experiments, and the first two experiments focused on temperature and humidity. So it's reasonable to assume what's stated in the question stem—that varying the number of leaves was the students' attempt to vary leaf surface area. However, this methodology is valid only if the leaves of each specimen are roughly the same size. If, for example, the leaves of the 10-leaf plant were so big compared to the leaves of the other specimens that the leaf surface area of the 10-leaf plant was actually the same as or greater than those of the 50-leaf and 100-leaf plants, then using leaf number to represent surface area would yield misleading results. Choice A is incorrect. As noted above, the scenario described in this choice is required for the validity of the experiment, because it ensures that increasing the number of leaves on plant specimens also increases their surface areas. Choices B and C are incorrect, as plants B and C are not part of Experiment 3 and thus have no bearing on the final experiment's methodology. While choice B at least hints at a reference to the right issue, leaf surface area, choice C, focusing on leaf *shape*, is even less relevant to Experiment 3.

6. **The correct answer is G.** The passage introduction indicates that some plants close their stomata at certain points to stop additional water loss and prevent wilting. So we need to find a point at which water loss was occurring but then stopped suddenly, presumably in response to the plant's own requirement to retain water. The cessation of transpiration must be marked by a zero

in the charts, which eliminates the points listed in choices F and J. Since transpiration continues to take place, we cannot conclude that stomata have closed at these points. The points indicated in choices G and H both indeed contain zeros, but with one important difference: plant B at high humidity does not transpire at all, suggesting that the surrounding atmosphere is too saturated to allow this plant to release water into the atmosphere. The lack of transpiration from this plant at this point, therefore, is probably not a matter of closing stomata. Choice G, however, is more promising. Transpiration rate dropped significantly for plant B under the heat lamp at the 30-minute mark, indicating the plant's sudden strong reaction to water loss while under the heat lamp. At the 40-minute mark, when transpiration has ceased entirely, an inferable reason is that stomata closed to prevent wilting.

7. **The correct answer is D.** Experiment 1 yields a somewhat unusual and unexpected result. While one can detect a general upward trend in some spots, there are too many outlying values that suggest a more random pattern than one would expect, given the hypothesis that wave height and wind speed are proportional. This leads logically to Experiment 2's focus on swell waves. The results of this experiment suggest that at least some of the waves measured in Experiment 1 were not created by local winds. This is important because it helps to make the unusual, wide-ranging results of Experiment 1 less mysterious. Choice A is incorrect, because the table in Experiment 2 does not include data on lake areas. It is not until Experiment 3 that a lake takes center stage. Choice B is incorrect. While the waves of distant storms might appear at the testing site, nothing indicates that the winds from such storms skewed the wind readings taken during Experiment 1. Wherever such winds might originate, they have a definite speed at the point of observation, and nothing suggests that these measurements were inaccurate. Choice C is factually inaccurate. The percentage of swell waves never exceeded 50%, which means that most of the waves detected were not created by distant storms.

8. **The correct answer is J.** This question requires you to notice the difference between the scatterplots in Figures 1 and 2. There is a far higher variability in wave heights associated with specific wind speeds in the ocean data than in the lake data. That is, the range of wave heights is much smaller for each wind speed recorded in the lake than in the ocean, which makes the lake a safer bet for predicting wave heights associated

with a 12 m/s wind. At wind speeds of 10 m/s in the lake, waves were roughly 4 to 5 meters high. At 12 m/s, we can expect a wave to be somewhere between 5 and 6 meters. By contrast, the ocean waves at a wind speed of 10 m/s ranged from around 3 to 8 meters in height, so it would be far more difficult to accurately predict what a 12 m/s wind would produce, making choice G incorrect. Choices F and H are incorrect because the lake station would provide an accurate prediction.

9. **The correct answer is B.** The randomness of the scatterplot shown in Figure 1 is surprising. Why, if wave height and wind speed are supposedly proportional, is there such a large range of wave heights at each wind speed indicated? Perhaps the hypothesis is incorrect, as choice A states? No—Experiments 2 and 3 provide a plausible reason: swell waves originating in distant storm centers were recorded and associated with local wind speeds measured at the ocean recording station. So while there is a general upward slope in Figure 1 indicated by numerous readings that would support the hypothesis, there are numerous outlying values (such as the 7-meter wave recorded when wind speed was nearly 0 m/s) that may be explained as swell waves. Experiment 3 further confirms this notion, exhibiting a pattern one might expect if wave height and wind speed are indeed proportional. An isolated lake is less likely to contain swell waves originating far away, so without significant interference from swell waves, the results accord better with the hypothesis. Choices C and D are incorrect, as nothing in Experiments 2 and 3 indicates a flaw in the analysis of or measurements taken in Experiment 1. Experiment 1 does not appear faulty, just surprising. As noted above, Experiments 2 and 3 help to explain why the results of Experiment 1 appear as they do.

10. **The correct answer is G.** It is reasonable to infer that the wide range of wave heights recorded in Experiment 1 is due to the existence of numerous swell waves at the ocean station, while the more compact upward sloping scatterplot of Experiment 3 results from the presence of far fewer swell waves in the relatively enclosed lake. Choice F is incorrect. The data suggest not that wind speed doesn't influence ocean wave height, but rather that the winds local to the ocean recording station may not be responsible for some of the waves observed at that station (namely, the swell waves that originated far away). Choice H is incorrect, as the passage does not supply enough information for a definitive comparison between the heights of swell waves created by storms and by normal wind waves. In fact, the idea in choice H

seems doubtful since there are outlying wave heights, presumably representing swell waves, on both sides of the normal range in each scatterplot. Choice J is contradicted by the relatively proportional graph in Figure 2. In the lake area observed, it would be quite possible to predict a wave height based on wind speed by observing the general trend of the graph.

11. **The correct answer is A.** Any of the waves indicated in the graph could, in theory, be a swell wave, but there's no way to tell which points on the general upward curve represent waves that originated elsewhere. However, the three very noticeable outlying points on the graph are most likely swell waves, since there's no other way to explain why their heights would be so different from the mass of other waves recorded at those same wind speeds. The first outlying point corresponds to a wave with a height of a little under 3 meters, while the third outlying point, on the right side of the graph corresponding to a wind speed of a little over 8 m/s, comes in at just over 1 meter. The waves that are 1.2 and 2.7 meters high are good approximations for these outlying points that are likely to represent swell waves. Choices B, C, and D do not represent outlying points.

12. **The correct answer is H.** Experiment 3 added validity to the original hypothesis by using a lake setting, which significantly reduced the number of swell waves that might obscure the relationship between wave height and wind speed. Still, in addition to outlying values, there was some variation even among the points composing the solidly upward trend. Observing the effect of a wind blower on an indoor pool would eliminate possible outside interference even more, thus providing an excellent opportunity to further support the original hypothesis. In the absence of any mitigating factors, one could determine whether the resulting graph is precisely linear as the theory would suggest. Choice F is incorrect, as thunderstorms would likely only complicate the data by introducing additional variables into the experiment. Choice G is incorrect, as the point of the experiments is to observe the effect of wind on wave height. Not much would be gained, therefore, by conducting trials during a wind-free period. Choice J leans in the opposite direction of correct choice H. Rather than reduce the chance of swell waves even further in order to observe the pure effect of wind on wave height, choice J proposes to observe a body of water likely to have even more swell waves than the lake. One would expect the results to be somewhat in between those recorded in the ocean and those

recorded at the lake, which is not likely to lend additional support to the hypothesis.

13. **The correct answer is B.** Figure 1 shows that 6 seconds after impact, the ball was roughly 18 meters horizontally from where the student hit it. Referencing this number in Table 1, we see that the first time the ball achieved a horizontal distance of 18 meters, its vertical height was 0, meaning that it was on the ground. Just before this, the ball was 1.2 meters above the ground, and just afterward, it was 0.5 meters above the ground. It's reasonable to infer, therefore, that the ball bounced roughly 6 seconds after being hit. Choice A is incorrect. Figure 1 shows that at the 3-second mark, the ball was roughly 11 meters from the point of impact. Referencing this number in Table 1 shows that the ball still had a positive vertical height at this point, which means it hadn't bounced yet. Choices C and D are incorrect. Figure 1 shows that at 9 seconds after impact, the ball was roughly 24 meters away, which corresponds in Table 1 to a point at which the ball was on the ground (vertical height of 0). Table 1 further indicates that the ball had been on the ground both before and after the 24-meter mark. This does not suggest a bounce at these points, as a bounce would be characterized by a vertical height of 0 followed by a positive vertical height, as in correct choice B.

14. **The correct answer is H.** According to Figure 1, 8 seconds after impact corresponds to a horizontal distance of roughly 22.5 meters from the point of impact. Table 1 indicates that at this distance, the vertical height of the ball is 0, which means it's on the ground. This makes choices F and G incorrect. The next reading shows the ball at 24 meters, further from the point of impact, yet the vertical height remains at 0. This indicates that at the 8-second mark the ball was rolling on the ground away from the point of impact, making choice H correct and choice J incorrect.

15. **The correct answer is B.** The shape of Figure 1 shows that the ball's horizontal distance from the point of impact increased steadily until 9 seconds after the student hit it, whereupon it decreased and then remained constant. The final three horizontal readings in Table 1 indicate the same change in direction, as the ball actually got closer to the point of impact. The only thing that can account for this reversal is contact with an obstacle toward the end of the ball's movement, around the 9-second mark. Choice A is incorrect, as Figure 1 indicates that the horizontal distance of the ball stopped decreasing and remained constant around the 12-second mark until the end. This means that the

ball stopped moving before 14 seconds had elapsed. Choice C is incorrect. As mentioned in the discussion of correct choice B, the data in both Table 1 and Figure 1 indicate that the ball must have reversed direction, because after reaching 24 horizontal meters from the point of impact, that number began to decrease. The ball, therefore, could not have traveled in a single direction. Choice D attempts to confuse you by presenting a close description of the shape of the graph in Figure 1. However, that graph depicts *horizontal* distance as plotted against time. Vertical height, which is what choice D refers to, did not vary in the same way. Table 1 shows that the ball increased to a maximum of 4.7 meters above the ground, then decreased until it hit the ground (vertical height 0), increased again, hit the ground, increased a lesser amount again, and then stayed on the ground the rest of the way—far different from the description given in choice D.

16. **The correct answer is J.** The height of the ball as plotted against time can be ascertained from the figures in Table 1, since we're told that these figures follow the chronology of the ball's flight. And we just discussed the ball's vertical pattern in our discussion of choice D of the previous question: Table 1 shows that the ball increased to a maximum of 4.7 meters above the ground, then decreased until it hit the ground (vertical height 0), increased again, hit the ground, increased a lesser amount again, and then stayed on the ground the rest of the way. This pattern of increases and decreases, corresponding to bounces, repeats numerous times. No such repeating pattern is exhibited by the shape of the graph in Figure 1. Choices F and H are incorrect, as we've seen how the shape of a graph plotting the ball's vertical height against time would differ greatly from the shape of the graph in Figure 1. Choice G is incorrect. While the shape of a graph plotting vertical height against time would indeed be different from the shape of the graph in Figure 1, it would not be different for the reason cited in this choice. Both the horizontal and vertical elements of the ball's trajectory vary with time; they just don't vary in the same way.

17. **The correct answer is A.** Figure 1 shows that at the 8-second mark, the ball was roughly 22.5 meters from the point of impact. Table 1 shows that at this horizontal distance, the vertical height of the ball was 0 and had been for a few meters. The height of the ball continues to be 0 for the rest of the way, meaning that it was on the ground at this point. The horizontal distance continues to increase to a maximum of 24 meters from the student, whereupon it decreases back to 18 meters away, which corresponds to the point at which the

distance curve flattens out on Figure 1 at the 12-second mark. So between 8 and 12 seconds, the ball was moving with a height of 0, meaning it was rolling on the ground. Choice B is incorrect, because Figure 1 indicates that from 9 to 12 seconds after impact, the ball's distance from the student decreased, meaning that it traveled back toward the point of impact for part of the time period mentioned in this choice. Choice C is incorrect, because Figure 1 indicates that after 12 seconds, the ball's horizontal distance remained unchanged, which means the ball stopped moving between 12 and 14 seconds after the point of impact. Choice D is incorrect, because at the 7-second mark, the ball was roughly 20 meters from the start point, and from there traversed the distances (listed at the end of Table 1) that correspond to vertical heights of 0. Figure 1 shows the ball moving back toward the point of impact at the 10-second mark. So between 7 and 10 seconds, the ball must have been rolling on the ground, not flying through the air.

18. **The correct answer is H.** Supporters of the Contaminants Hypothesis believe that increased exposure to environmental impurities has a detrimental effect on children's health, while supporters of the Hygienic Hypothesis think that exposure to environmental impurities is *necessary* for the proper development of the immune system and thus conducive to children's health. Choice F is incorrect, because the Hygienic Hypothesis doesn't touch on the relationship between TV and allergens. Choice G is incorrect, as supporters of both theories purport to explain what's causing the "dramatic increase" in childhood asthma. Choice J is incorrect, as only the Hygienic Hypothesis deals with exposure to germs.

19. **The correct answer is C.** Since environmental contaminants are more likely to be present in larger quantities in a congested metropolitan area than a rural countryside, it's possible that the child in question, upon moving, would be significantly exposed to them for the first time. The Contaminants Hypothesis is based on the assertion that environmental impurities (such as smoke and pollution) may be a contributing factor in the development of asthma, so the evidence presented in this case could support this theory. This means you can eliminate choice D. Yet it could also support the Hygienic Hypothesis, since it's possible that the child's immune system has been compromised by a lack of exposure to environmental contaminants, and the move to the congested city atmosphere has overwhelmed his underdeveloped immune system, making

him susceptible to the disease. Choice C is correct because both hypotheses could be supported, making choices A and B incorrect.

20. **The correct answer is H.** Supporters of the Hygienic Hypothesis argue that household sanitizers are bad because they eliminate the type of contaminants with which children's immune systems need to come in contact in order to develop. However, if these sanitizers themselves contain the kind of chemicals included in the "toxic soup" that supporters of the Contaminants Hypothesis cite, these supporters could claim that sanitizers contribute to asthma for the reason *they* state, not the reason put forth by supporters of the Hygienic Hypothesis. Choice F is incorrect, because potential side effects of immunizations are beyond the scope of both hypotheses. Nothing about side effects speaks to the main issue of rising asthma rates. Choice G is incorrect, because the result it states—the negative effect on the development of children's immune systems—is exactly what proponents of the Hygienic Hypothesis predict will happen when children are less exposed to animals and other natural environmental elements. Choice J is incorrect, as the Hygienic Hypothesis does not maintain that immunizations are entirely unnecessary or state that warding off major diseases is not beneficial to children. Proponents of the hypothesis take issue with the overuse of immunizations to ward off minor, non-fatal diseases. It is this overuse of immunizations that Hygienic theorists believe may prevent the kind of contact with germs necessary for the proper development of the immune system.

21. **The correct answer is A.** Both theories are based on the idea that environmental factors can affect the immune system, though in different ways. Believers in the Contaminants Hypothesis think that environmental contaminants, such as pollution and smoke, compromise children's immune systems, while proponents of the Hygienic Hypothesis think that exposure to noxious environmental elements aids in the proper development of children's immune systems. Choice B is incorrect. Supporters of the Hygienic Hypothesis believe that today's children have hypersensitive immune systems, but we have no reason to believe that supporters of the Contaminants Hypothesis believe this as well. They believe that the immune system of children may be compromised by chemicals in their environment; that's not the same as an endorsement of the hypersensitive argument of the Hygienic Hypothesis. Choice C is incorrect, for while both groups believe that asthma is on the rise, neither states an

opinion on the relative severity of asthma as compared with other childhood diseases. Choice D is incorrect. First, supporters of the Hygienic Hypothesis believe the opposite: that sanitizing the environment is causing *increases* in childhood diseases such as asthma. Secondly, the statement in choice D is too extreme even for supporters of the Contaminants theory; although they're likely to believe that cleaning up the environment will be a good step toward preventing asthma, we have no indication they would go so far as to say that it would constitute a total "cure."

22. **The correct answer is J.** Our obsession with health and cleanliness is clearly intended to make us healthier, but supporters of the Hygienic Hypothesis believe it can also have an opposite effect on children by stunting the development of their immune systems. It's reasonable to say that this qualifies as ironic (that is, peculiar or paradoxical). Choice F is incorrect, considering that our obsession with health and cleanliness has an effect contrary to the one stated in this choice. We don't disregard the noxious elements of our environment; we attempt to stamp them out, much to the consternation of the Hygienic Hypothesis supporters. Choice G is incorrect, because proponents of the Hygienic Hypothesis believe that excessive reliance on immunizations is detrimental, not beneficial. Choice H is incorrect, as the Hygienic Hypothesis does cite a specific effect of our obsession with health and cleanliness: it negatively impacts our immune systems by underexposing us to natural elements.

23. **The correct answer is B.** Supporters of the Hygienic Hypothesis believe that some steps we're taking to sanitize our lives are weakening children's immune systems. They feel that the overuse of immunizations and excessive sanitizing of our living spaces have a negative effect on health. They also consider natural elements of our environment, presumably even noxious ones like mosquitoes, to play a part in the proper development of our immune systems. Therefore, it is reasonable to infer that they would not be in favor of protecting a child from mosquitoes with a man-made repellent; this is, most likely, an example of the kind of thing they would believe to have negative consequences in the long run. This eliminates choices A and C in favor of choice B. Choice D is incorrect, because it would be reasonable to infer that bug spray is similar to pesticides and other chemicals contributing to the "toxic soup" the supporters of the Contaminants Hypothesis loathe; therefore, they would be more likely to oppose its use than to encourage it.

24. **The correct answer is J.** At the heart of both theories lies the idea that environmental factors are responsible for the dramatic increase in childhood asthma. The first theory states that the environment has become too dirty; the second argues that the environment has become too clean. Both, however, relate the rise in asthma directly to environmental changes. The theory presented in this question ignores environmental factors altogether, while citing a biological factor that may account for the increased susceptibility to asthma. It thus supports neither theory presented in the passage, making choices F, G, and H incorrect.

25. **The correct answer is A.** The questions and tasks fall into the general categories of math and verbal, two of the three subject areas tested in Study 1. It is reasonable to assume, then, that these specific questions and tasks were chosen in order to shed light on how lobe activity in the brain might relate to the sleep deprivation findings associated with the math and verbal drills from Study 1. Choice B is incorrect, because merely indicating which lobes of the brain are involved with tackling different tasks in people with different amounts of sleep can't, by itself, refute the results of Study 1. If this were the intention, a study would need to be set up that allows researchers to demonstrate performance levels other than those noted in Study 1, and Study 2 has no means of accomplishing this. Choices C and D are incorrect, as the questions and tasks presented in Study 2 offer no commentary, good or bad, on the method used in Study 1. They are employed simply to determine which areas of the brain are active in handling each type of task, something which may be of use in understanding what's happening in the brain as the patterns in Study 1 play out.

26. **The correct answer is G.** The table in Study 2 indicates that during the math-based questions, neither the temporal lobe nor the parietal lobe was active. However, Study 1 indicates that even after 30 hours of continuous wakefulness, the very sleep-deprived subjects exhibited some math proficiency; while the proficiency quotient certainly declined, it did not fall to 0. This suggests the likelihood that in sleep-deprived people, some math capability—albeit a diminished one—is exhibited by some area of the brain other than the temporal and parietal lobes. Choice F is incorrect, because Table 1 shows that both of these lobes are inactive in sleep-deprived people working out math problems. Choices H and J are incorrect. Table 1 shows that the temporal lobe of rested people is not active while working on math problems, and while the parietal lobe

is active in this situation, nothing indicates that the math capability of this lobe in these circumstances is substandard.

27. **The correct answer is B.** The temporal lobe, but not the parietal lobe, is active while the rested subject attempts the three verbal tasks presented in Table 1. In the sleep-deprived subject, the situation is reversed, suggesting that as one gets very tired, the temporal lobe shuts down while the parietal lobe springs to life in an attempt to compensate for the inactivity of the temporal lobe. Choice A is incorrect. The temporal lobe of the sleep-deprived subject is not active at all during Study 2, so we cannot say that this lobe is in any way compensating for the parietal lobe's inactivity. As noted in the discussion of correct choice B, it seems to be the other way around. Choice C is incorrect, as no short-term memory tasks are assigned in Study 2. The question regarding a childhood experience concerns the verbal articulation of a long-term memory. Choice D is incorrect. In the rested subject, the temporal lobe, noted as part of the cerebral cortex, is active during math questions. This suggests that it is just as plausible that math tasks are mostly processed within the cerebral cortex, as opposed to outside of it. While some other area might become active when sleep-deprived people attempt math problems, nothing suggests that math processing generally takes place outside the cerebral cortex.

28. **The correct answer is H.** The researchers were interested in both the speed and accuracy of responses to the tasks presented in the study, but by combining the performances in these areas into a single proficiency quotient, they lost the opportunity to convey how the subjects fared in each respect. Although we know, for example, that verbal performance declined with increasing sleep deprivation, we can't tell whether decreases in speed, accuracy, or some combination of both caused the decline. For all we know, the speed of responses may have dropped dramatically while subjects got roughly the same number of questions right—or vice versa. Having more detailed breakdowns, instead of a single speed/accuracy indicator for each subject area, would have revealed much more about the effects of sleep deprivation. Choice F is incorrect, as the study results make quite clear that in response to sleep deprivation, overall verbal performance worsened while memory performance improved. Thus the study does allow one to differentiate between these two effects. Choice G is incorrect, because brain physiology is the focus of Study 2 but is not addressed in Study 1.

So while it is true that Study 1 does not illustrate the difference suggested by this choice, this does not constitute a weakness of the study since its designers did not set out to do so. Choice J is incorrect, as the study's subject areas are precisely delineated. The participants are observed performing math, verbal, and memory tasks.

29. **The correct answer is C.** Note that Study 2 explicitly indicates that the rested volunteer received 8 hours of quality sleep, something never indicated in regard to Study 1's subjects, who were awakened for tests at 7 a.m. If nearly half of them slept terribly just prior to the study, then the study, which supposedly differentiates between performances while rested and performances while sleep-deprived, would already be questionable. If the designers of a sleep deprivation study wish to compare rested subjects with sleep-deprived ones, they must be sure that the rested subjects are truly rested. Choice A is incorrect. The study is designed to show how performance after rest might differ from performance while sleep-deprived. As long as the subjects tested didn't suffer major bouts of insomnia immediately preceding the study, it would make little difference whether they had experienced insomnia sometime in the past. Choice B is incorrect because results following the study are irrelevant to the methodology of the study itself. It would not be unusual for some subjects to experience changes in sleep patterns after participating in such a study, but that has no bearing on what the study set out to show and whether it was designed properly to show it. Choice D in no way invalidates the study's methodology, since the point all along was to keep participants awake for 30 straight hours. As the question defines insomnia as an inability to sleep, we would suspect that something was amiss only if the subjects *didn't* experience insomnia during the study.

30. **The correct answer is J.** Study 2 suggests that the parietal lobe, inactive during verbal tasks in the rested subject, seems to be active during verbal tasks in the sleep-deprived subject. If the parietal lobe is associated with short-term memory, it's a bit easier to understand why this capability may increase in sleep-deprived subjects, as indicated by the upward sloping line in Figure 1. Called into service to help the sleep-deprived subjects handle verbal tasks, the parietal lobe may be hyperactive in these people, accounting for the improved performance in memory tasks as the study progressed. As far as we know, the structures listed in the other choices do not possess this singular quality of

the parietal lobe—that is, the tendency to become more active in sleep-deprived people. Choices F and H are incorrect because, according to Table 1, the temporal lobe is more active in the rested subject, meaning it would not account for the strong short-term memory results in the sleep-deprived subject. Choice G is not discussed in the study.

31. **The correct answer is A.** The process depicted in Figure 1 initiates clotting; key elements in the process are Factors 5 and 10, which bind to form thrombin. But in the amplification stage, thrombin itself activates more Factor 5 and also activates Factors 8 and 11, which both play a role in activating more Factor 10. These newly activated proteins are filtered back into the process, presumably causing additional Factor 5 and 10 to bind to form more thrombin, and so it goes in a continual loop. This is best characterized as a cycle of positive reinforcement: a loop in which one substance (thrombin) helps to produce more of the very substances (Factors 5 and 10) from which it continues to be derived. This efficient design eliminates choices C and D, because the clotting process as described is neither random nor inherently flawed. Choice B is incorrect, as a negative feedback loop would cause a progressive lessening and eventual elimination of certain elements in the process. Here, the process instead builds on itself through the positive reinforcement of factors until a clot is formed.

32. **The correct answer is J.** Since these malfunctions are said to occur in the amplification stage, it makes sense to look for some step of the process that does not take place during this stage if we are to find a deficiency *not* likely to be implicated in the onset of the blood diseases in question. The factors listed in choices F, G, and H are all involved in the amplification stage, as indicated in Table 1. Factor 13, however, is created only by thrombin and is not directly involved in the amplification process. While it's possible that a Factor 13 malfunction occurs late in the process, Factors 8, 9, and 11 are more directly involved in the reinforcement process and are, therefore, more likely to be at fault if something in the amplification stage breaks down.

33. **The correct answer is B.** This is inferable if we closely follow the chain of cause and effect. The chelating agent interferes with the effectiveness of calcium ions. Since calcium ions are required for clotting, we can deduce that the chelating agent would prevent clotting. Of the people in the choices, only the technician in choice B would benefit from *preventing* clotting, since he or she would not want donated blood stored for later use to clot in the storage bags. In contrast, the doctor and the hemophiliac in choices A and D would presumably want to aid, not inhibit, clotting. It's also difficult to see any reason for the researcher in choice C to be interested in clotting in anything other than a theoretical sense, so without further information, we cannot presume that this person would have a use for the chelating agent.

34. **The correct answer is H.** As part of the amplification process, Factor 8 binds to Factor 9 to produce more Factor 10, which is reinserted back into the reactions summarized in Figure 1. If von Willebrand Factor is deficient or defective, Factor 8 will be deficient and will likely not bind properly with Factor 9 to activate the additional Factor 10 needed to spur the process forward. Since Factor 10 is needed to activate Factor 5 to form prothrombinase, we would expect a deficiency of prothrombinase under these circumstances. Choices F and G are incorrect, because the production of Tissue Factor and its binding with activated Factor 7 occur at a point in the initial clotting process before the influence of Factor 8 is felt. Choice J is incorrect, as prothrombin is a substance that's acted upon by prothrombinase. A lack of prothrombinase (which would likely occur in the absence of stabilized Factor 8) doesn't imply there will be a lack of prothrombin. If anything, there may even be an *excess* of prothrombin, since it wouldn't be converted to thrombin in the usual fashion when bleeding occurs.

35. **The correct answer is B.** The hypothesis concerns the point during the clotting process at which abnormalities arise, resulting in bleeding disorders. Scientists theorize that this happens during the amplification stage—that is, after the initial process has begun and when the process needs to be reinforced by the additional activation of factors listed in Table 1. Because Factor 11 is introduced only during amplification and plays no role in the initial process, choice B strengthens this hypothesis by making it less likely that these treatable abnormalities arise in the initial steps of clotting. Fatal deficiencies in Factor 11 (which directly activates Factor 9 during amplification) would make it plausible that the treatable abnormalities in question are related to amplification problems concerning Factor 9. Choice A is incorrect, because it deals with a possible result of bleeding disorders instead of supporting a hypothesis regarding their cause. Choice C is incorrect. It explains why the amplification stage is necessary for clotting, but not why bleeding disorders are caused by deficiencies in the amplification stage as opposed to earlier in the clotting process. Choice D is incorrect, as it

merely restates information already contained in Table 1.

36. **The correct answer is J.** At low frequencies such as 50 and 200 Hz, the perceived change in pitch has a negative value, indicating that these tones appear to drop in pitch as intensity is increased over time. The pitch of at least some low-frequency tones, therefore, seems to get lower as they get louder. Choices F and H are incorrect, as Stevens's Rule applies only to sounds that increase in intensity. There is no indication in the table that pitches are perceived to go up as volume goes down. Choice G states the opposite of the trend noted in Stevens's Rule. The table indicates that the pitch of some high-frequency pure tones seems to rise, not fall, as intensity increases.

37. **The correct answer is B.** The parameters in this question are nearly identical to the ones established in the passage introduction, so we would expect Stevens's Rule to apply, immediately making choice A incorrect. Table 1 indicates that a 200 Hz tone whose intensity increases from 60 to 90 dB would seem to drop in pitch by 20 cents. However, there is one difference: the tone in question is not a pure tone, but rather the human voice. We're told that speech and musical sounds are impacted by Stevens's Rule to a *lesser* extent than are pure tones, so while we'd expect the singer's note to appear to drop in pitch, we wouldn't expect it to drop as much as indicated in the table, making choices C and D incorrect. The pitch should decrease, but by less than 20 cents.

38. **The correct answer is F.** Considering that there is no perceived change in pitch for tones at 1,000 and 2,000 Hz, it is reasonable to infer that Stevens's Rule doesn't apply to pure tones in certain frequency ranges. Choice

G is incorrect; this is, in fact, the opposite of what's suggested by the data. As cited in correct choice F, there is no perceived change in pitch for tones at frequencies of 1,000 and 2,000 Hz, so there are some frequencies for which the effect doesn't apply at all. In addition, in high-frequency ranges (above 2,000 Hz), pitch seems to increase with increasing intensity, while at low frequencies (below 2,000 Hz), pitch seems to decrease with increasing intensity, further suggesting that the effect is not uniform at all. Choice H is incorrect, as we have no way of knowing at what intensity the phenomenon is most observable. Moreover, the issue is not what happens at any single volume, but what happens in the context of volume *increases*. Choice J is not inferable; in fact, the opposite of choice J seems evident, because the trend indicates that the effect becomes more pronounced as low tones get lower in frequency. Extrapolating from the trend, it's reasonable to believe that the perceived change will be even greater for tones below 50 Hz.

39. **The correct answer is D.** A frequency of 5,000 Hz falls right between 4,000 and 6,000 Hz, so we can extrapolate from the information in the table that a 5,000-Hz tone would seem to rise in pitch between 20 and 30 cents if its intensity increased from 60 to 90 dB in intensity. Since there are 100 cents in a semitone, that corresponds to an increase between 20% and 30% of a semitone—greater than 0, but less than half a semitone. Choices A, B, and C are too high.

40. **The correct answer is H.** There is no indication that the intensity of the note is varied, so choices G and J are incorrect. Moreover, without an increase in intensity, it is unlikely that Stevens's Rule would be in effect. The pitch of the tone should, therefore, remain constant.

SAMPLE ESSAY: SCORE 1

Ideas and Analysis:	Score = 1
Development and Support:	Score = 1
Organization:	Score = 1
Language Use and Conventions:	Score = 1

I already learn what I need to know online from the websites I go to, Facebook and Twitter and more they have everything that's going on. I can get everything from a book or teacher that I can get from them on my laptop or phone, so why bother going into school and wasting my time? I can even play games and listen to my music and show off all my photos to my friends and whoever so why cant I skip school and do what I need to do on my own schedule and finally live like adults? I get really bored in school anyway and so do my friends and we'd all be much rather spending our time doing almost anything else. My school's a waste of money too so they can stop paying the teachers and everyone there and maybe they can start paying the students for a change?

Scoring Explanation

Ideas and Analysis: Score = 1

This essay fails to establish a unifying thesis that addresses the given prompt. The writer provides some ideas regarding the value of traditional classrooms (a waste of time and money), but fails to utilize them in a cohesive or effective manner. There is little or no effort to create a piece of writing that responds to the specific essay task.

Development and Support: Score = 1

The writer of this piece does little to develop the few ideas provided into an effective argument that addresses the essay task. As a result, we do not get the writer's perspective on the future of the classroom, or the impact technology will have on it. Furthermore, the writer doesn't provide any additional external support for his or her ideas, and the resulting essay lacks depth, authority, or credence.

Organization: Score = 1

This essay response lacks a coherent, effective flow of ideas connected to an overarching theme. Instead, we are given a disjointed set of thoughts that are at best tangentially related to the writing task. The response indicates that the author believes traditional school is a waste of money and time, time that is better spent on a computer or phone, but it lacks an effective overall structure and doesn't progress toward a central idea regarding the future of the classroom.

Language Use and Conventions: Score = 1

The response demonstrates a significant skill deficit in the effective use of language mechanics and conventions. The essay contains several errors in grammar and usage, and uses a limited word choice range, which adversely impact a reader's ability to comprehend the author's intent.

Diagnostic Test— ANSWERS

SAMPLE ESSAY: SCORE 6

Ideas and Analysis:	Score = 6
Development and Support:	Score = 6
Organization:	Score = 6
Language Use and Conventions:	Score = 6

It can be argued that technological advances in recent decades have helped us learn as much about the classroom as we learn inside the classroom. Although it's certainly clear that the traditional classroom has equipped generations of students with the knowledge and skills required to lead America and other countries around the world into the modern technological era, with great change comes the responsibility to pause and reflect. What should happen now? We need to take a hard and thoughtful look at the current design of the average classroom, at both its strengths and its limitations, and design a new and unabashedly modern learning environment—one that takes full advantage of modern technological innovations while retaining the healthy structural roots that have allowed us to flourish thus far.

The traditional classroom does provide educational nourishment for fertile minds that are eager to learn. A skilled and motivated teacher, equipped with an effective lesson plan and learning goals, can make a real and measurable difference in the minds of students inside of these rooms. But the technological advances that have flooded into our everyday lives have changed the way we live, and in turn are changing how we think and learn. These are just a few examples: More of us now get our news from our phones instead of newspapers. Most of us stay in touch with the people in our lives through social media websites as much or more than in person. If we need to handle our daily responsibilities we go over to our computers as often as we roll up our sleeves and head out the front door. With so much of our lives unfolding online, why shouldn't the modern classroom follow suit?

As previously mentioned, the way we learn has already changed. We read on tablets and phones, consume information through websites, communicate online as much as in person—an effective learning environment (the word *classroom* even feels outdated) takes this into consideration and mirrors the society and culture in which it exists.

What should the classroom of the future look like? An effective modern classroom will integrate the best of both worlds. It will acknowledge that real learning objectives can be met when students gather together in rooms under the direct guidance of qualified, capable teachers. It will also acknowledge that technology has advanced to the level where each student can use modern tools to address his or her individual educational goals in a virtual learning environment, wherever they are. Envision less time spent in an actual classroom but just as much time spent learning, only in a more effective fashion that takes into consideration each student's individual skill set and goals. Modified classroom learning can be supplemented with time spent on a tablet, phone, or laptop, at home or anywhere else, in pursuit of customized academic objectives. Students can use emails, texts, chats, tweets, or Skype to contact trained educators for guidance and feedback. Students can collaborate using these tools as well. Assignments, research, and projects can use modern computer applications—the same tools used in a wide range of professions—further preparing students for life beyond the classroom. In schools across the country and around the world this has already happened, though in limited ways. We're squarely in the middle of an "educational evolution," and if logic and forward-thinking were allowed to lead the way, this evolution will continue to follow this path. It has or is occurring in nearly every facet of society, from medicine and banking, to shopping and entertainment—and far beyond—don't our classrooms deserve the same respect, resources, and consideration?

Scoring Explanation

Ideas and Analysis: Score = 6

The writer provides a nuanced, thoughtful argument regarding the future of the classroom. From its insightful and engaging opening to its provocative closing question, the essay presents a wealth of ideas on why the traditional classroom needs to "evolve," as well as ideas for how this can occur. It's clear that the writer of this piece has thoughtfully analyzed the issue and framed it within a larger societal context (learning environments should mirror societal modes of consuming information), lending credence to the balanced, carefully considered perspective provided.

Development and Support: Score = 6

The writer begins the argument with an insightful perspective on the value of technology in learning about effective classroom operation, and progresses with a well-reasoned development of ideas that support a clear perspective on the issue. The argument includes a historical perspective that supports the notion that traditional classrooms once had a clear purpose, and provides compelling details on how an evolving society needs an evolving learning environment for its fertile and hungry minds. An intriguing set of ideas on how this evolution might occur is provided as the argument moves forward, and culminates with an inspirational call to action.

Organization: Score = 6

The writer demonstrates a command of effective essay structure, organization, and flow. A clear perspective on what the classroom of the future should be like is provided, and an array of persuasive material is galvanized and carefully presented in support of this viewpoint. It progresses from a thought-provoking introduction to a well-reasoned argument in support of a blended (traditional and virtual) learning environment, and ends with an urgent—and moving—call for change.

Language Use and Conventions: Score = 6

The writer employs an impressive use of language and nuance in the development of a compelling essay. Strong and varied word choices and effective transitions are used throughout, alongside a wealth of emotion, to convince the reader that this perspective on the complex issue of the future of learning is a worthy one. The writer also displays an impressive command of grammar and syntax, lending authority to this argument.

DIAGNOSTIC TEST ASSESSMENT GRID

Now that you've completed the diagnostic test and read through the answer explanations, you can use your results to target your studying. The following tables show you exactly where you can find thorough coverage for every single subject area on the multiple-choice portion of the test. Find the question numbers from the diagnostic test that gave you trouble and highlight or circle them below. The chapters with the most markings are your ideal starting points on your preparation journey.

ENGLISH TEST

Usage/Mechanics (Chapter 4)	
Question Type	**Question Numbers**
Grammar and Usage	16, 22, 24, 33, 48, 53, 55, 57, 63, 70, 72, 74
Punctuation	2, 10, 19, 20, 25, 37, 42, 46, 62, 68
Sentence Structure	1, 6, 7, 11, 18, 26, 31, 32, 35, 36, 40, 49, 51, 54, 58, 64, 66, 69

Rhetorical Skills (Chapter 5)	
Question Type	**Question Numbers**
Organization	4, 5, 8, 14, 27, 29, 39, 41, 44, 47, 73
Style	3, 12, 17, 23, 34, 38, 50, 52, 56, 59, 65, 71
Strategy	9, 13, 15, 21, 28, 30, 43, 45, 60, 61, 67, 75

What English test question types gave you the most trouble?

Grammar and Usage ☐   **Organization** ☐

Punctuation ☐   **Style** ☐

Sentence Structure ☐   **Strategy** ☐

Chapters to focus on first: _____

Pre-Algebra and Elementary Algebra
(Chapter 6)

Question Type	Topic	Question Numbers
Pre-Algebra		
	Data Interpretation	27, 58, 60
	Elementary Counting Techniques and Simple Probability	3, 14, 20, 47
	Linear Equations in One Variable	3, 33
	Operations Using Decimals	22
	Operations Using Fractions	5, 9
	Operations Using Integers	12
	Percent	2, 55
	Proportion	25
Elementary Algebra		
	Evaluation of Algebraic Expressions Through Substitution	1
	Understanding Algebraic Operations	6, 8, 10, 30, 31, 42
	Using Variables to Express Functional Relationships	43

Intermediate Algebra and Coordinate Geometry
(Chapter 7)

Question Type	Topic	Question Numbers
Intermediate Algebra		
	Complex Numbers	28
	Functions	11, 53
	Inequalities	44
	Rational Expressions	17, 24, 37, 54
	Roots of Polynomials	26
	Systems of Equations	45
Coordinate Geometry		
	Graphing	18
	Relations Between Equations, Graphs, Including Circles	36

Plane Geometry and Trigonometry
(Chapter 8)

Question Type	Topic	Question Numbers
Plane Geometry	Application of geometry to three dimensions	23, 32, 40
	Concept of proof and proof techniques	4
	Properties and relations of plane figures, including angles	16, 39
	Properties and relations of plane figures, including circles	46, 50
	Properties and relations of plane figures, including parallelograms	52
	Properties and relations of plane figures, including rectangles	15
	Properties and relations of plane figures, including triangles	7, 21, 34
	Volume	19
Trigonometry		
	Values and properties of trigonometric functions	29, 38, 48, 57

Which Mathematics test question types gave you the most trouble?

Pre-Algebra ☐ _____
_____
_____
_____

Elementary Algebra ☐ _____
_____
_____
_____
_____

Intermediate Algebra ☐ _____
_____
_____
_____

Coordinate Geometry ☐ _____
_____
_____
_____

Plane Geometry ☐ _____
_____
_____
_____

Trigonometry ☐ _____
_____
_____
_____

Chapters to focus on first: _____

Reading Test

Social Studies/Natural Sciences Passages (Chapter 9)	
Question Type	Question Numbers
Detail	11, 12, 14, 16, 19, 32, 33, 35, 37, 38, 40
Inference	17, 18, 34, 36
Vocabulary	15, 39
Main Idea	13, 20, 31

Literary Narrative/Prose Fiction and Humanities Passages (Chapter 10)	
Question Type	Question Numbers
Detail	2, 6, 21, 23, 27, 28, 29
Inference	3, 4, 8, 9, 22, 26, 30
Vocabulary	1, 5, 24
Main Idea	7, 10, 25

Which Reading test question types gave you the most trouble?

Social Studies/Natural Sciences Passages		Literary Narrative/Prose Fiction and Humanities Passages	
Detail	☐	Detail	☐
Inference	☐	Inference	☐
Vocabulary	☐	Vocabulary	☐
Main Idea	☐	Main Idea	☐

Chapters to focus on first: _____

SCIENCE TEST

Data Representation (Chapter 11)

Question Type	Question Numbers
Inferences	15, 17, 32, 33, 34, 35, 38
Looking Up Answers	13, 14, 36, 37
Spotting Trends	16, 31, 39, 40

Research Summaries (Chapter 12)

Question Type	Question Numbers
Inferences	1, 3, 4, 7, 9, 10, 25, 26, 27, 30
Looking Up Answers	11
Scientific Method	2, 5, 8, 12, 28, 29
Spotting Trends	6

Conflicting Viewpoints (Chapter 13)

Question Type	Question Numbers
Inferences	22
Compare/Contrast	18, 19, 20, 21, 23, 24

What Science test question types gave you the most trouble?

Data Representation		Research Summaries		Conflicting Viewpoints	
Inferences	☐	**Inferences**	☐	**Inferences**	☐
Looking Up Answers	☐	**Looking Up Answers**	☐	**Compare/Contrast**	☐
Spotting Trends	☐	**Scientific Method**	☐		
		Spotting Trends	☐		

Chapters to focus on first: _____

A WORD ABOUT THE WRITING TEST

If you took the writing test and found that your essay did not compare well to the level 6 essay sample, don't worry. We're here to help you with that too. Chapter 14, "Mastering the ACT® Writing Test," has the information you need to strengthen your writing skills. It also includes a full essay grading rubric, which tells you what the graders are looking for in a high-quality essay. Use the rubric as you would use the grids to help you focus on the areas you need to work on.

DIAGNOSTIC TEST CONCLUSION

Taking the diagnostic test should have given you more insight into the ACT: what it feels like to take such a long test, how you perform on a timed exam, and where you now need to focus your energy in the days, weeks, and months leading up to your test day.

Here are some questions to keep in mind as you move on to the preparation part of your ACT study plan:

How did I do under timed conditions?

Did you find yourself rushing to answer the final questions in every test section? Did one particular section give you more problems than others? Take note of how timing affected you in this test, and see if you can make small changes to your test-taking approach. For example, maybe you spent too much time reading the passages in the Reading test and then didn't actually have time to answer all the questions. The good news? Every section in this book offers tips on how to efficiently and quickly answer ACT test questions. Study up, and when you take Practice Test 1 you can see if your method improves.

Did I just not know how to answer questions in a particular section?

Maybe you sailed through the Math test but could barely get through a Science test passage. Or maybe the Reading test was a breeze, but you couldn't for the life of you remember anything about trigonometry. Whatever your situation, this book has extensive preparation for it. Now that you have a better understanding of your strengths and weaknesses as they relate to the ACT, you can customize your study plan.

Did I make careless mistakes or second-guess myself?

Well, first of all, you're not alone. Testing is *hard*—you're under timed conditions and you want to do very well. The best part about taking on a plan of study with this book is that when you are done, you will be *prepared*. First, you will know the test inside and out. This is a very important bit of knowledge, as you won't even have to stop to read directions or familiarize yourself with the test come exam day—you will be ready to go! Second, you will have a deeper understanding not only of all the different topics tested on the ACT, but also how the exam presents them (the language it uses and how it asks questions). The key to excelling on the ACT is to speak the language of the test maker, and that's what we're here to help you do.

No matter what challenges you faced on the diagnostic test, there's a section in this book to help you overcome them. Stay focused, commit the time, and take your practice tests—if you do that, you are sure to get the score you want on the ACT.

PART III: ENGLISH STRATEGIES FOR THE ACT®

Chapter 4: Usage/Mechanics

Chapter 5: Rhetorical Skills

ENGLISH STRATEGIES FOR THE ACT®

Do you know what an editor does? After a writer finishes a book or article, that piece of writing goes to the editor, who checks it over for errors in usage and mechanics, as well as rhetoric. That's basically what you're going to do on the ACT English test. You'll play the role of editor by reading and editing brief passages that can be made better by correcting errors or deleting, adding, or moving details. Don't worry, though. Your job will be easier than the job of a professional editor since you'll have four possible corrections to choose from. The next two chapters will help you to select the best answer choices.

First of all, you need to become familiar with the style of the passages and questions on the ACT English test, since you may not have taken a test quite like this one before. Each passage is fairly short, about 350 to 450 words. Each paragraph in that passage is numbered, and each paragraph contains underlined phrases followed by numbers. Those numbers refer to a corresponding question.

Sometimes, several complete sentences in a paragraph will begin with a number in brackets. These numbers are used for identification when you have to decide the best way to reorganize sentences or choose which sentence needs to be deleted. The question that asks you to do this task will correspond to a number in a box. This number soup may sound a little confusing, but it will be less confusing when you see what an English passage on the ACT looks like. So let's look at one:

· ·

PASSAGE 1

Sample ACT English Passage

[1]

This is a sample of a passage in the English section of the ACT test. Isn't it fabulous? Watch out, though, because this passage contains some errors. Remember, <u>it's your job to find them errors</u> and figure out the best way to correct them.
10

10. **A.** NO CHANGE
    B. it's your job to find those errors
    C. it's your job to find this errors
    D. it's your job to find that errors

[2]

(1) This is the second paragraph of the sample passage. (2) You may notice that it's a bit different from the first paragraph. (3) However, <u>your job is still the same; you still have to</u> find the
11
errors and choose the answers that best correct them. (4) I like pancakes. (5) This is the final sentence in this sample passage—aren't you sorry it's finished? 12

11. **F.** NO CHANGE
    G. your job is still the same you still have to
    H. your job is still the same, you still have to
    J. your job is still the same) you still have to

12. For the sake of the unity and coherence of this paragraph, which sentence should be omitted?

    A. Sentence 1
    B. Sentence 2
    C. Sentence 3
    D. Sentence 4

· ·

As you probably noticed, this extra-short sample passage contains two underlined portions with a number beneath each of them. That means two multiple-choice questions will ask about it. However, unlike most multiple-choice questions you've probably answered throughout your school career, in Usage/Mechanics questions, the first answer choice is always the same: NO CHANGE. You see, the underlined words in an ACT English passage will not always contain errors, and if they don't, you should select NO CHANGE. Pretty tricky!

Still confused about what all the numbers mean? Let's take a closer look.

[2] ← Boldfaced numbers in brackets identify the paragraph order.

(1) This is the second paragraph of the sample passage. (2) You may notice that it's a bit different from the first paragraph. (3) However, <u>your job is still the same; you still have to find the</u> 11 errors and choose the answers that best correct them. (4) I like pancakes. (5) This is the final sentence in this sample passage— aren't you sorry it's finished? 12

Numbers that appear below the <u>underlined</u> portion of the passage correspond to specific usage questions.

Numbers in parentheses before each sentence within a paragraph identify sentence order.

Numbers that appear in a box correspond to questions that relate to a paragraph's strategy, organization, or style.

Now that you have the key to ACT English by the numbers, we can focus on the answers and explanations that go with the sample passage. Something to keep in mind--when you are answering questions on the ACT English test, be sure to read the entire sentences as they appear in the passage and not just the short portions in the answer choices. Seeing how the words in the answer choices work in the greater context of the passage may help you to answer the questions. Now--on to the explanations!

Did you see the error in question 10? There is a lack of agreement between the pronoun *them* and the noun *errors*. Try saying the sentence out loud. Doesn't it sound wrong to say "them errors"? It does, because it is grammatically incorrect. The sentence should read "it's your job to find *those* errors." Therefore, you can conclude that **choice B is the best answer** to question 10. Just remember that when you actually take the ACT, you should only think of how the sentence sounds and not actually say it out loud. A room full of babbling test-takers can be a little distracting.

NOTE: Most rhetorical skills questions will probably be a bit more familiar since they tend to contain an actual question and the first answer choice will not always be NO CHANGE.

Question 11 is a different story. This is one of those tricky questions about underlined words that don't actually contain any errors. Choices G, H, and J actually introduce new punctuation errors to a sentence that is already written correctly. Therefore, **the best answer choice is F:** NO CHANGE.

Question 12 is yet another story because, as you can see, it begins with a direct question and the first answer choice is not NO CHANGE. Those clues should help you conclude that question 12 is a rhetorical skills question. This particular question tests your ability to find the sentence that does not belong in the paragraph. This particular paragraph is about how ACT English passages look. It isn't about food. So what is a sentence about the author's preference for pancakes doing in it? The clever editor will select **answer choice D** to omit this irrelevant sentence about pancakes —even though pancakes are really tasty.

The next two chapters will get deeper into the kinds of errors you will find on the ACT English test. You will look out for mistakes in punctuation, grammar, sentence structure, strategy, organization, and style. Each of these errors falls into one of two categories: Usage/Mechanics and Rhetorical Skills. First up—Usage/Mechanics!

CHAPTER 4:
USAGE/MECHANICS

OVERVIEW

- Punctuation
- Grammar and Usage
- Sentence Structure
- Summing It Up
- Practice

On the ACT, Usage/Mechanics errors may really jump out at you. For example, a sentence that asks a question but ends in an exclamation point *(Is that your sock!)* just looks wrong. Of course, you'll need to know a little more than "find the sentences that look wrong" to answer Usage/Mechanics questions correctly. The good news is that you've probably learned most of the rules discussed in this chapter already.

But let's not get ahead of ourselves. First of all, we should probably define the terms *usage* and *mechanics*. **Usage** refers to the way words are used in a sentence. Obviously, you'll want to make sure they're used correctly to select the best answers on the ACT. **Mechanics** refers to the more technical components of sentences, such as punctuation, which will be the first topic in this chapter.

141

Chapter 4

**Usage/
Mechanics**

PUNCTUATION

Periods. Commas. Semicolons. Apostrophes. There are quite a few different kinds of punctuation, and each punctuation mark has its own purpose. On the ACT, 10 to 15 percent of the Usage/Mechanics questions will test your ability to recognize the correct way to use these little symbols.

END-OF-SENTENCE PUNCTUATION

Every sentence must come to an end. That means the one form of punctuation you will see in every complete sentence is end-of-sentence punctuation. These were probably the very first punctuation marks you learned about.

- **The period (.):** good for ending most sentences.

- **The exclamation point (!):** handy for ending exclamations, which indicate extreme excitement.

- **The question mark (?):** absolutely necessary for ending questions.

 A question can be asked excitedly, but it still needs to end with a question mark, not an exclamation point.

End-of-sentence marks are pretty straightforward. You probably already know that you shouldn't end a question with a period or an exclamation with a question mark. These marks become slightly tricky only when quotation marks are added to the punctuation mix.

For the most part, end-of-sentence punctuation belongs *within* the quotation marks. Like this:

Tessa asked, "Have you seen my superhero costume?"

The only exception occurs when the quotation marks indicate a title and placing end-of-sentence punctuation within the marks might give the false impression that the mark is part of the title:

Have you read Tessa's article, "I Am a Superhero"?

COMMAS

Let's continue with one of the most common forms of punctuation and one of the most misused: the **comma.** Some writers use commas like salt—they sprinkle them all over their sentences. And just as sprinkling around too much salt will make your food taste pretty bad, sprinkling around too many commas without rhyme or reason will make sentences pretty bad too. Here's an example of a sentence with way too many commas:

If there is one thing I love, it's fresh bread, straight from the oven, of Gomer's Bakery.

While there is the odd situation in which the use of a comma is up to the writer, there are almost always very definite rules for comma use.

Introductory or Transitional Words and Phrases

Commas should be used to offset introductory words or phrases from the words that follow. Here are some examples:

Suddenly, I realized I was locked out of the house.

At that moment, the entire room began to shake.

My alarm never went off. Therefore, I missed my job interview.

 Commas are not used to separate compound predicates, which explain more than one thing about the subject.

For example:

Adriana rides the bus, and reads a book. (Incorrect!)

Adriana rides the bus and reads a book. (Correct!)

Compound Sentences

Compound sentences consist of two independent clauses, which means both parts of the sentence would be complete sentences on their own. When independent clauses are joined by a conjunction to form a compound sentence, a comma is used before the conjunction to separate the clauses. For example:

Chandra is going to see that new movie at the theater, but Mason is going to watch it on demand.

Chandra is going to see that new movie at the theater is the first independent clause. *Mason is going to watch it on demand* is the second. The conjunction is *but,* and a comma is used to separate those clauses correctly.

Nonrestrictive Words, Phrases, and Clauses

A nonrestrictive word, phrase, or clause is not essential to the meaning of the sentence and should be separated with one comma if it comes at the beginning or end of the sentence and two commas if it is placed in the middle.

Nonrestrictive phrase at the beginning of the sentence: *The most delicious of all fruits, apples grow in orchards.*

Nonrestrictive phrase in the middle of the sentence: *Apples, the most delicious of all fruits, grow in orchards.*

Nonrestrictive phrase at the end of the sentence: *In the orchard I grew apples, the most delicious of all fruits.*

Read this sentence:

My pants, which I bought at the mall, are too tight.

This sentence would still make sense without the clause *which I bought at the mall*. It would read *My pants are too tight*, which is a perfectly fine sentence. That means the clause is nonrestrictive and should be enclosed in commas like it is in the sentence above. However, if that clause were *restrictive*—essential to the meaning of the sentence—no commas would be needed (Example: *The pants I bought at the mall are too tight*.).

Series

Each item in a series of three or more in a list should be separated with a comma. For example:

I keep my cell phone, e-reader, pens, and wallet in my desk drawer.

In this sentence a comma also precedes the conjunction *and*, although this is not a hard-and-fast rule. Some writers prefer not to use that extra comma. So the following sentence is also technically correct:

I keep my cell phone, e-reader, pens and wallet in my desk drawer.

The decision to place a comma before the conjunction in a series of items is up to the writer. Passages on the ACT use the comma before the conjunction, but you will not be expected to answer questions about such situations without concrete rules.

Appositives

An appositive is a noun, noun phrase, or noun clause that describes or renames a noun. An appositive contains a noun or pronoun and often one or more modifiers, and it appears directly before or after the noun it describes. Appositives need to be set off with commas.

For example:

My car, a real piece of garbage, keeps breaking down on the highway.

In this sentence, the appositive is *a real piece of garbage*, and commas are used to set it off correctly.

Quotations

When quoting a complete phrase someone said, one or more commas are needed to separate it from the rest of the sentence. See how the commas are used in these examples:

Buddy said, "That sandwich made me feel sick."

"That sandwich made me feel sick," Buddy said.

"That sandwich," Buddy began, "made me feel sick."

However, if that quotation includes end-of-sentence punctuation, a comma is not needed.

For example:

"That sandwich made me feel sick!," Buddy said. **(Wrong!)**

"That sandwich made me feel sick!" Buddy said. **(Right!)**

Now answer this quick exercise question. Keep in mind that all questions on the ACT will relate to a larger passage and not a stand-alone statement like this one. You will get the chance to answer questions that relate to passages at the end of each English chapter and in the practice tests.

. . . .

This story <u>a medieval thriller written by Shirley Jackson,</u> is
really scary.   1

1. **A.** NO CHANGE
    B. This story, a medieval thriller written by Shirley Jackson, is really scary.
    C. This story a medieval thriller written by Shirley Jackson is really scary.
    D. This story, a medieval thriller written by Shirley Jackson is really scary.

The correct answer is B. The appositive phrase *a medieval thriller by Shirley Jackson* must be set off from the rest of the sentence with commas.

. . . .

APOSTROPHES

Apostrophes look like commas that have floated up to the top of words, but they serve very different functions from commas. Apostrophes are most often used to indicate that a word is a contraction or to show possession.

Correct use of apostrophes in **contractions** mostly depends on placing the apostrophe in the right place (*Do'nt*—**incorrect!** *Don't*—**correct!**) and recognizing when a word that looks like a contraction is not a contraction (for example, *it's* is a contraction of *it is*; *its* is the possessive form of *it*).

Using apostrophes in possessive words is a little trickier. For the most part, the apostrophe will be placed before the letter *s*.

> *Madison's keys*
>
> *the dog's bone*
>
> *the car's headlights*
>
> *the sun's beams*

However, if the possessive word ends with an *s*, the apostrophe belongs after the *s*.

> *the glasses' lenses*
>
> *the two kittens' guardian*
>
> *the brass' gleam*
>
> *the bus' wheels*

This rule is different when a specifically named person is doing the possessing. For people whose names end in *s*, an apostrophe and an extra *s* is required.

> *Mavis's hair*
>
> *Augustus's shoes*
>
> *Venus's lunch*
>
> *Charles's smile*

When more than one noun is doing the possessing, only the last noun in the pair or list needs an apostrophe.

> *my father and mother's favorite restaurant*
>
> *the bedspread and the curtains' pattern*
>
> *Cherie and Gladys's address*
>
> *the bass and drums' sounds*

COLONS

Colons look like a stack of two periods, though they are always used within a sentence. Colons are usually used to introduce a list or series of examples:

> *My pack contains everything I need for school: books, pens, a calculator, and a lunch bag.*

Colons are also used to offset and emphasize an example:

> *That book taught me the most important lesson of all: true friendship never dies.*

Colons can also be placed after a salutation in a letter (*To whom it may concern:*) or used to separate a title from a subtitle (*Green Peas: The Movie*). However, colons should not be used to separate objects and verbs (**Incorrect:** *My opinion is: irrelevant*) or prepositions and objects (**Incorrect:** *Gluten is found in: bread, pasta, and many other basic foods.*).

SEMICOLONS

A semicolon looks like a period floating over a comma, and it should not be confused with a colon. Semicolons can be used in place of conjunctions in compound sentences, joining the independent clauses just as *and, or, but,* or *because* would:

> *I spent the day reorganizing my bedroom; it was a complete mess.*

Semicolons are also necessary in lists that contain items with commas. To keep all those commas from becoming confusing, semicolons separate each individual item.

> *This meal contains only the freshest ingredients: tomatoes and onions, which I bought at the farmer's market; basil, which I grew in a pot in the kitchen; and peppers, which I grew in the backyard garden.*

 ALERT: Colons and semicolons are not interchangeable. Each punctuation mark has its own function.

Now answer this quick exercise question.

- -

There are a variety of creatures other than fish in this book about

<u>sea animals: dolphins and whales, which are mammals; crabs</u>
2
<u>and lobsters, which are crustaceans; and octopi and squid, which</u>
2
<u>are mollusks.</u>
2

2. **F.** NO CHANGE
   G. sea animals; dolphins and whales, which are mammals; crabs and lobsters, which are crustaceans; and octopi and squid, which are mollusks.
   H. sea animals: dolphins and whales, which are mammals, crabs and lobsters, which are crustaceans, and octopi and squid, which are mollusks.
   J. sea animals: dolphins and whales; which are mammals; crabs and lobsters; which are crustaceans; and octopi and squid; which are mollusks.

The correct answer is F. The sentence is correct as is. The colon is used properly to signal a list of upcoming examples. Since the items listed contain commas, it is best to separate them using semicolons.

146

Chapter 4

Usage/ Mechanics

DASHES

Much like the comma, the dash tends to get overused and misused. A big problem with dashes is that they're almost never needed according to the rules of mechanics, so a lot of writers just aren't sure what to do with them. You're about to become one of the lucky few who do know when to use the pesky dash.

Like the colon, a dash can be used to offset and emphasize a single example:

> *In trying times, I knew I could always turn to the one individual who understood me—my dog, Blinky.*

A dash can also be used to separate an example or examples in the middle of a sentence:

> *Everything—boxes, hats, and games—came tumbling from the top shelf during the earthquake.*

Dashes are also useful for indicating a pause or interruption in dialogue:

> *Marcus asked, "Can I borrow your—"*

> *"Sure! Whatever! Take what you want!" Paulette enthused before Marcus could complete his question.*

PARENTHESES

Sometimes, a few extra details are needed to make a sentence as informative as it can be, but those details aren't always easy to cram into the natural flow of the sentence. In such cases, parentheses are in order. Like dashes, parentheses are used to enclose bonus examples, but the examples in parentheses tend to be a little less relevant to the sentence than the ones you'd place between dashes.

Watch out for sentences that overuse parentheses. They clutter sentences with too much nonessential information. You may be expected to delete unnecessary parenthetical information on the ACT.

Mrs. Gale (my brother's high school Earth Science teacher) is going to be teaching biology next quarter.

Now you will put everything you have learned about punctuation to the test by reading this sample passage and answering the questions that follow.

An avalanche occurs when a mass of <u>snow, rock, soil, or ice, breaks</u>
3
away from a mountainside and slides down the slope. Factors

such as seasonal thawing, wind, and vibrations can cause

avalanches. <u>Consequently, avalanches can make numerous</u>
4

recreations very <u>dangerous; skiing, mountain climbing, and</u>
5
<u>hiking.</u> However, there are methods for preventing major ava-
5
lanches before they happen. One such approach is accomplished

with <u>explosives (deployed from helicopters or shot from small</u>
6
<u>howitzers) that trigger</u> minor avalanches before major ones
6
can occur.

3. **A.** NO CHANGE
   B. snow rock, soil, or ice, breaks
   C. snow, rock, soil or ice, breaks
   D. snow, rock, soil, or ice breaks

The correct answer is D. There is no comma needed between *ice* and *breaks*.

4. **F.** NO CHANGE
   G. Consequently avalanches can make numerous
   H. Consequently— avalanches can make numerous
   J. Consequently; avalanches can make numerous

The correct answer is F. The sentence is correct as is. A comma is the correct punctuation here.

5. **A.** NO CHANGE
   B. dangerous skiing, mountain climbing, and hiking.
   C. dangerous: skiing, mountain climbing, and hiking.
   D. dangerous, skiing, mountain climbing, and hiking.

The correct answer is C. A colon is needed after *dangerous* because it introduces a list of examples.

6. **F.** NO CHANGE
   G. explosives, deployed from helicopters or shot from small howitzers, that trigger
   H. explosives deployed from helicopters or shot from small howitzers that trigger
   J. explosives' deployed from helicopters or shot from small howitzers that trigger

The correct answer is H. The fragment *deployed from helicopters or shot from small howitzers* is important to the sentence, so it should not be set off by parentheses or commas.

GRAMMAR AND USAGE

Grammar and usage questions appear with a bit more frequency on the ACT than punctuation questions do—15 to 20 percent of the test's questions require you to understand how words work with each other and in the context of the passage as a whole. Do subjects and verbs agree? How about pronouns and their antecedents or modifiers and the words they modify? Does the writer use idioms correctly?

Answering grammar and usage questions can be a bit more complicated than answering punctuation questions, but knowing the rules is still key. And while incorrect punctuation won't necessarily make a sentence sound wrong, poor grammar will. So thinking about how these sentences sound can help you select the best answers to grammar and usage questions.

NOUNS

If a sentence is like a galaxy, then the subject of that sentence is the sun around which all the other words revolve. The subject is always a **noun**: the person, place, or thing doing the action the sentence describes. A number of grammar and usage questions on the ACT will involve a sentence's subject, often in terms of how it agrees with verbs or pronouns. However, before we discuss how nouns interact with other words, let's look at some special forms of nouns.

Plural Nouns

The nice thing about nouns is that they really have only two essential forms: the singular and the plural. The **singular noun** form requires nothing fancy at all. *Cat, dog, otter, lampshade, avocado, eyebrow*—these are all nouns in their most basic singular form. Making nouns plural is often as simple as adding the letter *s* to the end. Stick an *s* to the end of *cat*; now you have many *cats*. Done.

Plural nouns get tricky only when they are irregular—hard-and-fast rules are often tough to apply to a language as complicated as English. Ideally, we could say that you're always safe adding *-es* to the end of all nouns that end in *o* to make them plural. Unfortunately, this is not always the case. For example, the plural of *avocado* is *avocados*.

148

Chapter 4

**Usage/
Mechanics**

While you cannot be expected to memorize every single irregular plural noun for the ACT, you can familiarize yourself with some of the most common. Take a look at this table:

Noun ends with-	Creating the plural form	Examples	
-f	change *f* to *v* and add *-es*	**singular:** calf	**plural:** calves
		singular: elf	**plural:** elves
		singular: half	**plural:** halves
		singular: leaf	**plural:** leaves
		singular: shelf	**plural:** shelves
		singular: thief	**plural:** thieves
		singular: wolf	**plural:** wolves
-fe	change *f* to *v* and add *-s*	**singular:** knife	**plural:** knives
		singular: wife	**plural:** wives
		singular: life	**plural:** lives
-is	change to *-es*	**singular:** axis	**plural:** axes
		singular: analysis	**plural:** analyses
		singular: parenthesis	**plural:** parentheses
-o	add *-es*	**singular:** echo	**plural:** echoes
		singular: hero	**plural:** heroes
		singular: potato	**plural:** potatoes
		singular: tomato	**plural:** tomatoes
-ouse	change to *-ice*	**singular:** louse	**plural:** lice
		singular: mouse	**plural:** mice
-s	add *-es*	**singular:** class	**plural:** classes
		singular: boss	**plural:** bosses
-us	*change to -i*	**singular:** alumnus	**plural:** alumni
		singular: fungus	**plural:** fungi

There are a few other variations of irregular plural nouns that do not involve changing the last letter or two of the singular form. Fortunately, most of these should be very familiar to you.

Nouns that require -oo- to be changed to -ee- for their plural form:

singular: foot	**plural:** feet
singular: goose	**plural:** geese
singular: tooth	**plural:** teeth

Nouns that require the addition or substitution of -en for their plural form:

singular: man	**plural:** men
singular: ox	**plural:** oxen
singular: woman	**plural:** women
singular: child	**plural:** children

Finally, there are the nouns that require no change whatsoever to become plural:

singular: deer	**plural:** deer
singular: fish	**plural:** fish
singular: offspring	**plural:** offspring
singular: series	**plural:** series
singular: sheep	**plural:** sheep
singular: species	**plural:** species

Now answer this quick exercise question.

There are <u>mouses</u> living under the foliage.

7

7. **A.** NO CHANGE
   B. mouse's
   C. mice
   D. mices

The correct answer is C. The plural of *mouse* is *mice*.

Collective Nouns

Collective nouns are interesting because they have some of the flavor of plural nouns since they seem to describe more than one thing: a bunch of students in a *class*, a group of sailors in a *navy*, several fish in a *school*, etc. However, while the individuals (*students, sailors, fish*) in these collections are plural, the collections themselves (*class, navy, school*) are singular. Recognizing when a collective noun is used as a singular or plural subject will be particularly important when we deal with subject-verb agreement and noun-pronoun agreement in the next section of this book.

First, you should familiarize yourself with some common collective nouns.

army	audience	band	board	class
committee	company	corporation	council	department
faculty	family	firm	flock	group
herd	jury	majority	navy	public
school	senate	society	team	unit

AGREEMENT

Words in a sentence are a little like people. When they agree, things go smoothly. When they don't, there might be trouble. You can ensure that the elements in sentences don't clash by recognizing when they aren't in agreement. Subjects and verbs need to be on the same page in terms of number. The same is true of pronouns and antecedents, which also need to agree in terms of gender.

Subject/Verb Agreement

Every complete sentence has a **subject** and a **verb.** The subject is the noun doing the action. The verb is the action the subject is doing. Simple, right? Actually, it is fairly simple, and a sentence with just a subject and a verb can be really simple.

> *The dog growls.*

That sentence only has three words, but it's still a complete sentence because it has a subject and a verb. Just as important, the subject and verb agree: the singular subject *dog* agrees with the singular verb *growls*. That's right: the verb is singular even though it ends with the letter *s*. Okay, maybe it's slightly complicated. Nevertheless, if you can remember that rule, you're on your way to identifying when subjects and verbs are in agreement. Furthermore, you can say the sentence out loud. Does *The dog growl* sound right to you?

Determining whether or not subjects and verbs are in agreement can get a little more complicated in sentences with compound subjects.

> *The dog and the bear growl.*

Neither *dog* nor *bear* ends with an *s*, so they may not look plural, but they work together as a compound subject when joined with a conjunction such as *and*. That means they require a plural verb, and as you may have guessed, a plural verb does not end in an extra *s*. The compound subject and verb are in agreement in the sentence above. However, if the conjunction were *or* or *nor*, a singular verb would be required.

> *Neither the dog nor the bear growls.*

Once again, the compound subject and verb are in agreement.

When dealing with collective nouns, the agreement rule depends on what the collective noun is doing. If every member of the collective noun is doing the exact same thing, it is operating as a single unit and the verb should be singular:

Subject-verb agreement can get confusing when there is a word or phrase between the subject and verb. Make sure you have identified the entire subject and verb correctly before figuring out whether or not they agree.

*The committee **agrees** that Wednesday is the best day to meet.*

However, if all the members of that collective noun are doing their own things, those members should be specified and a plural verb is required.

*The **committee** disagree on the best day to meet; they may never hold another meeting.*

Although the sentence above is grammatically correct, many writers will avoid the awkward construction of using a collective noun with a plural verb by adding the word members to the sentence:

*The **committee members** disagree on the best day to meet; they may never hold another meeting.*

Pronoun/Antecedent Agreement

Pronouns and **antecedents** also need to agree. A pronoun replaces a specific noun. Its antecedent is the noun the pronoun replaces. To illustrate, look at a simple example with the following sentences.

Luisa lives in the red house. She has lived there for nearly 20 years.

The subject of both sentences is *Luisa*. But rather than repeat Luisa's name, which might sound awkward, we can use a subject pronoun for the second reference. In the example, the antecedent to the pronoun *she* is *Luisa*. The noun and pronoun agree, both in number (*Luisa* is a singular subject; *she* is a singular pronoun) and gender (*Luisa* is a female; *she* is a female pronoun). Perfect!

Let's look at another example, but this time, we'll use a possessive pronoun instead of a personal pronoun. Since it would be redundant to say *Luisa drives Luisa's car*, most writers would replace the second *Luisa* with a possessive pronoun.

Luisa drives her car.

Much better, right? In this sentence, *Luisa* is the antecedent and the pronoun is *her*. Both are in agreement in this sentence if we understand that Luisa is female. *Her* is a female possessive pronoun. It is also singular, which is appropriate since Luisa is only one woman. Now, if the sentence read *Luisa drives his car*, it would lack pronoun-antecedent agreement in terms of gender (unless, of course, if Luisa was borrowing some guy's car). If it read *Luisa drives their car*, it would sound as if Luisa were driving a car owned by two or more people other than herself.

However, *their* would be necessary in a sentence with a **compound antecedent.** For example, maybe Luisa co-owns her car with a friend named Ginnie. Then the sentence should read, *Luisa and Ginnie drive their car on alternating days.* Compound antecedents are a bit more complicated when the conjunction is *or* or *nor* instead of *and*. In such cases, you will select your pronoun based on the antecedent to which it is nearest.

1) *Neither my wife nor my daughters brought **their** luggage out to the car.*

2) *Neither my daughters nor my wife brought **her** luggage out to the car.*

Both of these sentences are written correctly. Since the plural antecedent *daughters* is closer to the pronoun in sentence 1, the plural pronoun *their* is required. Since the singular antecedent *wife* is closer to the pronoun in sentence 2, the singular pronoun *her* is required.

Now, if your antecedent is a collective noun, selecting the right pronoun depends on what the collective noun is doing and how it is doing it. If every member of the collective noun is doing the exact same thing as a single unit, the singular pronoun is needed.

*The soccer team played **its** game magnificently.*

In this example, everyone on the team is playing the same game, and the singular pronoun *its* is used correctly. However, if all of the members of that collective noun are doing their own thing, a singular pronoun is in order.

*The soccer team played **their** individual positions magnificently.*

This example describes how the members of the team handled their individual positions (goalkeeper, defenders, midfielders, forwards), and it uses the plural pronoun *their* correctly.

Now answer this quick exercise question.

. . . .

Neither Henrietta nor Alexandra has <u>their</u> ticket to the show.
                                        8

8. **F.** NO CHANGE
       G. its
       H. she
       J. her

The correct answer is J. This is a compound antecedent using the word *nor*. The verb must agree with the subject closest to it.

. . . .

SELECTING PRONOUNS

Person will be another factor when figuring out the best way to use pronouns on the ACT. A first-person pronoun (*I*, *me*, *we*, *us*) is necessary when a writer is referring to herself.

A second-person pronoun (*you*) is needed when the writer is addressing the reader. When the pronoun refers to a third person who is neither writing nor reading the passage, a third-person pronoun (*she, he, her, him, they, them*) is needed.

Choosing the right pronoun can be tricky in sentences that pair them with nouns. Is *Ricky and I went to the game* or *Ricky and me went to the game* correct?

In such cases, try removing the noun and saying the sentence with just the pronoun (*I went to the game; me went to the game*). Chances are the wrong pronoun will now sound wrong.

Relative Pronouns

Relative clauses are like adjectives: they exist to describe. You can recognize a relative clause from the presence of a relative pronoun. The relative pronouns *who, whom, whose,* and *that* all refer to people; the relative pronouns *that* and *which* refer to things.

The relative clauses in the following sentences are underlined:

Mr. Marshall, <u>who used to live next door to me</u>, is the head manager at my new job.

The person <u>whom you are seeking</u> is not at home.

Florida, <u>which is where I went on vacation last year</u>, is located in the southern region of the United States.

The <u>truck that is parked across the street</u> belongs to Francois.

153

Chapter 4

Usage/
Mechanics

Reflexive Pronouns

When a subject needs a pronoun to refer to itself, a reflexive pronoun fits the bill. In fact, *itself* is a reflexive pronoun, as is any pronoun that ends with *-self* or *-selves*. There are five singular reflexive pronouns (*myself, yourself, himself, herself, itself*) and three plural reflexive pronouns (*ourselves, yourselves, themselves*).

Reflexive pronouns are often misused when included as part of a list of subjects. For example:

Feel free to contact Bob, Jerry, and **myself**.

Don't do it! The best way to tell if a reflexive pronoun is needed is to write or say the sentence as if you were the only subject:

Feel free to contact **me**.

A good rule of thumb is to use the reflexive pronoun when the subject and the object of the sentence are the same (*I* heard **myself**.), and the regular object pronoun when they are different (**You** heard **me**.).

Interrogative Pronouns

To interrogate is to question, and interrogative pronouns are used to ask questions. There are five main interrogative pronouns: *whose, who,* and *whom* refer to people exclusively; *what* refers to things exclusively; and *which* can refer to people or things.

The addition of the suffix *-ever* also creates five less common interrogative pronouns. These are w*hatever, whichever, whoever, whomever,* and *whosoever.*

Perhaps the most common confusion regarding interrogative pronouns is when to use *who* and when to use *whom*.

- *Who* is used as the subject of a question. (Example: *Who called at 3 a.m. this morning?*)
- *Whom* is used as the object of a question. (Example: *To whom am I speaking?*)

Possessive Pronouns

In an earlier section of this book, you learned a thing or two about apostrophes. As you may recall, they are important elements when indicating that a noun possesses something. More often than not, you can just pop an apostrophe and an *s* onto the end of a word to make it possessive.

That guitar is Jimi's.

There is a goldfish in Jess's bathtub.

You also learned that the extra s is not necessary with a possessive noun that already ends in s but is not someone's name.

The lions' cubs played in the grass.

Those books' covers are falling apart.

Pronouns, however, usually have their very own forms to show possession. Since pronouns such as *his, her, its, their, my, mine, yours, their,* and *theirs* already show possession, they don't need an apostrophe or an extra *s*.

The game is **mine.**

Their *friend is coming to the beach with us.*

Her *father is coaching the team.*

The cat licked **its** *paws.*

The only pronouns that do need that apostrophe and extra *s* are the indefinite pronouns an*ybody, anyone, everybody, everyone, no one*, and *nobody*.

> **Anybody's** *guess is as good as mine.*

> **Everybody's** *weekend will be spent studying.*

 ALERT: Remember that *it's* is not the possessive form of *it*; it is a contraction of *it is.*

VERB TENSE

Verbs are words that refer to actions, and their tense indicates when that action happened. Is the action happening now? The verb is in the present tense. Did the action already happen? Well, then the verb is in the past tense. Are you still waiting for it to happen? Then the verb is in the future tense.

Past, present, and future are the most basic points in time. However, there are quite a few more than three verb tenses.

- **Simple present tense** indicates an action happening now: *I am here*.
- **Present progressive tense** indicates an action happening now that will continue into the future: *I am walking*.
- **Present perfect progressive tense** indicates an unfinished action: *I have been studying* all day.
- **Present perfect simple tense** indicates an action that occurred in the past but continues to be relevant: *I have eaten artichokes*.
- **Past perfect simple tense** indicates an action that occurred in the past but is now complete: *When I woke up this morning, I realized that it had rained last night*.
- **Past simple tense** indicates an action that happened already: *I was asleep*.
- **Past progressive tense** pairs a past tense verb with a continuous verb ending in *-ing*: *I was dreaming*.
- **Past perfect progressive tense** reflects on an ongoing action from the past: *By the 1990s, hip-hop had been a popular form of music for several years*.
- **Future simple tense** indicates an action that will happen later: *I will be home by 5:00*.
- **Future progressive tense** indicates an action that will happen later and continue: *I will be working all day tomorrow*.
- **Future perfect simple tense** indicates the completion of an action that will happen later: *I will have finished cleaning the house by noon today*.
- **Future perfect progressive tense** indicates an incomplete action that will happen later: *I will have been cooking for three hours by the time my guests arrive*.

> **NOTE:** You will not be expected to identify the various verb tenses on the ACT, but familiarizing yourself with them will help you to spot errors and select the best answer choices.

ADJECTIVES AND ADVERBS

As we've already established, the only completely essential elements of a sentence are its subject and verb.

The dog barks.

Once again, that is a complete sentence. But is it a particularly interesting sentence? Writing a sentence with nothing but a subject and a verb is like making soup with nothing but water and tomatoes. Where are the other flavors? In a sentence, **adjectives** (words that describe nouns) and **adverbs** (words that describe verbs) add some extra flavor. Think of them as the spices of a sentence.

The furious dog barks uncontrollably.

Now there's a sentence that paints a picture! The adjective *furious* shows the dog is not barking playfully. The adverb *uncontrollably* shows that the dog is really worked up and probably won't calm down anytime soon. In this section, we will take a look at the different forms of adjectives and adverbs you have to know before taking the ACT.

Comparative and Superlative

Big! Bigger! Biggest! Adjectives and adverbs change form when they are used to make a comparison.

The **comparative** form is used when comparing two things.

Comparative adjectives:

> This street is <u>wider</u> than the last one.
>
> I feel <u>more limber than</u> I did before I stretched.

Comparative adverbs:

> This week seemed to go by <u>more quickly</u> than last week did.
>
> I am taking my studies <u>more seriously</u> than I ever have before.

The **superlative** form is used when comparing three or more things.

Superlative adjectives:

> This is the <u>longest</u> book I own.
>
> Alshad is the <u>politest</u> boy in my class.
>
> Craig is the <u>most ambitious</u> candidate.

Superlative adverbs:

> Out of everyone in the office, Peri works the <u>hardest</u>.
>
> This is the <u>quickest</u> I have ever run.

As you may have noticed, simply adding *-er* to the end of comparative and *-est* to the end of superlative adjectives is not always enough. Once again, there are a number of exceptions you need to understand to use comparative and superlative adjectives correctly.

Case	Adjective	Comparative	Superlative
One- and two-syllable adjectives ending in *-e* do not need an extra *-e*.	*close* *large* *simple*	*closer* *larger* *simpler*	*closest* *largest* *simplest*
One-syllable adjectives ending in a consonant need to have that consonant doubled.	*big* *sad* *thin*	*bigger* *sadder* *thinner*	*biggest* *saddest* *thinnest*
One- and two-syllable adjectives ending in *-y* change that *-y* to an *-i*.	*dry* *heavy* *tiny*	*drier* *heavier* *tinier*	*driest* *heaviest* *tiniest*
Certain adjectives with two or more syllables remain the same but need the addition of *more* for comparatives and *most* for superlatives.	*beautiful* *complete* *important*	*more beautiful* *more complete* *more important*	*most beautiful* *most complete* *most important*
Irregular adjectives require their own special alterations in the comparative and superlative forms.	*bad* *far* *good* *many*	*worse* *farther* *better* *more*	*worst* *farthest* *best* *most*

For comparative adverbs, adding *more* is usually enough, and superlative adverbs usually only need *most*.

> *I sang <u>more quietly</u> than Enid did.*

> *The car runs <u>most smoothly</u> on paved roads.*

As you may have guessed, there are exceptions to this rule, but don't worry because there aren't as many exceptions for adverbs as there are for adjectives. Basically, any adverb that does not end in *-ly* should be treated the same way you would treat it if it were being used to modify a noun instead of a verb.

Adverb	Comparative	Superlative
bad	worse	worst
far	farther	farthest
fast	faster	fastest
good	better	best
hard	harder	hardest
little	less	least
long	longer	longest
loud	louder	loudest
many	more	most
quick	quicker	quickest

157

Chapter 4

**Usage/
Mechanics**

Another thing you need to make sure of on the ACT is that comparatives and superlatives are actually being used to make a comparison. You may have seen an advertisement that boasts, "Our product is better!" You might ask, "Better than *what*?" Obviously, the implication is that the product is better than other similar products, but the comparison is not correct and complete if that information is not stated directly.

Our product is better than other similar products!

Maybe that isn't the catchiest slogan in the world, but it is a complete comparison. Remember that incomplete comparisons are incorrect when you're reading English passages on the ACT.

Incomplete comparisons involving superlatives may not sound as awkward as incomplete comparisons involving comparatives, but they are still grammatically incorrect. For example, it is grammatically incorrect to say *"You're the best."*

IDIOMS

A recurring theme in this book so far has been "the English language can be tricky." For nonnative English speakers, there are few things trickier than idioms. Idioms are so confusing because they use words to mean something other than their literal meanings. If you were to "pull the wool over someone's eyes," you probably would not literally grab a wool scarf and pull it over that person's eyes. However, you may deceive them, which is the idiomatic meaning of "pull the wool over someone's eyes." See what we mean? Idioms are tricky.

English is a rich language, and it is very, very rich with idioms. There is no way to address all of them in this book. Be prepared for the possibility that you may encounter completely unfamiliar idioms on the ACT. Even if you are not 100 percent familiar with the meaning of a particular idiom, you may still recognize it as an idiom if it sounds a bit familiar and does not make literal sense in the context of the passage. Idiom questions on the ACT often require you to identify mistakes in their wording. So even if you don't know what the idiom "bite off more than you can chew" means, you may still have heard it. Therefore, you should be able to recognize that "bite off more than you can see" is not a correctly composed idiom. You may also deduce that biting with your eyes, which you use for seeing, is both difficult and uncomfortable.

NOTE: A good way to become familiar with a wide variety of idioms is to read a lot. Writers love to use idioms!

Here are some other common idioms:

Idiom	Meaning
Actions speak louder than words.	What one does is more important than what one says.
Back to the drawing board!	Time to start all over again!
Barking up the wrong tree	Drawing the wrong conclusion
Beat around the bush	Avoid the topic
Bite off more than you can chew	To take on too large of a task
Costs an arm and a leg	Very expensive
Cry over spilt milk	Complain about something that cannot be changed
Feel under the weather	Feel ill
Is on the ball	Is very competent
Hit the sack	Go to bed
Kill two birds with one stone	Accomplish two tasks with a single action
Let sleeping dogs lie	Do not provoke a potentially unpleasant situation

Let the cat out of the bag	Reveal a secret
Piece of cake	Easy
Take with a grain of salt	Not to take something too seriously
The whole nine yards	Everything

PREPOSITIONAL PHRASES

As the old lesson goes, a preposition is anywhere a mouse can go: *over, under, sideways, down, in, out, at, from, above, to, inside, outside, before, after, forward, toward,* etc. **Prepositions** indicate time and direction, and—pun intended—are pretty straightforward. Prepositional phrases, however, are less straightforward. In fact, they're very similar to idioms in that they cannot be explained with simple rules. You just have to get familiar with them and decide what sounds the best.

A **prepositional phrase** combines a preposition with one or more words. For example, *at home* is a common prepositional phrase. You will need to be aware of the most commonly used prepositional phrases on the ACT. Here are a few common prepositions you should remember:

among friends	at school	in the family	in the yard
at home	at work	in the grass	in your mind
at the office	at the beach	in the room	on the lawn
at play	in my heart	in the tree	on the road
	in the doorway	in the window	on the roof

NOTE: Sometimes, you may have to read a sentence more than once to figure out whether or not it contains an error.

Now you will put everything you have learned about grammar and usage to the test by reading this sample passage and answering the questions that follow.

. . . .

By the time you attend college, you probably have a very clear idea of what your <u>interests, strengths, and weakness are</u>, which
₉
means you probably also have an idea of what your ideal major is. However, you may discover that idea can evolve once you actually start taking classes.

9. **A.** NO CHANGE
    B. interests, strengths, and weaknesss are
    C. interests, strengths, and weakness's are
    D. interests, strengths, and weaknesses are

The correct answer is D. The plural of *weakness* is *weaknesses*.

<u>When I began our undergraduate studies</u>, I was a journalism
₁₀
major. I loved writing, and journalism seemed like a practical writing career. However, after taking a couple of journalism classes, I realized that I simply did not have much aptitude for interviewing people and "rooting out the story." Since I was already part of the communications department as a journalism major, I decided to stay within that department but <u>attempt my</u>
₁₁
<u>hand at a totally different major.</u>
₁₁

10. **F.** NO CHANGE
     G. When I began my undergraduate studies
     H. When we began our undergraduate studies
     J. When you began our undergraduate studies

The correct answer is G. The passage takes on a first-person point of view, so all parts should be singular.

11. **A.** NO CHANGE
     B. try my hand at a totally different major
     C. try my mind at a totally different major
     D. attempt my hand in a totally different major

The correct answer is B. The correct idiom is *try my hand*.

Realizing I had <u>most interest in movies than journalism</u>,
₁₂
I decided to major in film studies. I'm happy to say that it was a perfect fit, and I ended up getting my bachelor's degree in film studies. When I started college, I never imagined I would get a degree in watching and writing about movies!

12. **F.** NO CHANGE
     G. the most interest in movies than journalism
     H. more interest in movies than journalism
     J. many interest in movies than journalism

The correct answer is H. When comparing two items, the correct word to use is *more*.

. . . .

SENTENCE STRUCTURE

We started this chapter with a close-up look at tiny punctuation marks. Then our scope widened a bit to examine how words relate to each other by studying grammar and usage. Now we're going to explore entire sentences. Are you ready to take a look at the big picture?

Sentence structure questions are the most common Usage/Mechanics questions on the ACT English test; 20 to 25 percent of those Usage/Mechanics questions will test your ability to understand the relationships between and among clauses, the placement of modifiers, and shifts in construction. You will have to spot little bits of sentences known as *fragments* and sentences that go on and on and on, known as *run-ons*.

CLAUSES

Just as you can't have a sentence without a subject and verb that express a complete thought, you can't have a sentence without clauses. We'll let you in on a little secret: a phrase that contains a subject and verb is a **clause.** If the clause expresses a complete thought, it's an **independent clause,** because it can stand on its own. A clause that has its own subject and verb but cannot stand on its own is a **dependent (or subordinate) clause.**

> **Independent clause:** *The rooster crows.*

> **Dependent clause:** *when the sun rises*

A dependent clause needs to be paired with an independent clause to be part of a complete sentence.

> *When the sun rises, the rooster crows.*

In English writing, there are four different sentence structures. Notice that each one always includes at least one independent clause.

A **simple sentence** has only one independent clause:

> *The dog barks.*

A **compound sentence** has two or more independent clauses joined with a conjunction or semicolon:

> *The dog barks, and the cat meows.*

> *The dog barks; the cat meows.*

A **complex sentence** has one independent clause and at least one subordinate clause:

> *When the mail carrier arrives, the dog barks.*

A **compound-complex sentence** has at least two independent clauses and at least one subordinate clause:

> *When the mail carrier arrives, the dog barks; the cat meows.*

 ALERT: A semicolon is the most used punctuation mark that can join independent clauses without a conjunction. Using only a comma to join independent clauses without a conjunction creates a **comma splice,** which is considered incorrect punctuation usage.

You may have noticed the important role conjunctions play in these various sentence structures. When a conjunction joins independent clauses of equal importance, it is known as a **coordinating conjunction.**

> *The movie was very good, but the book was terrible.*

In this compound sentence, *but* is the coordinating conjunction. If you divide the sentence before and after the coordinating conjunction, you will still have two independent clauses of equal importance:

The movie was very good.

The book was terrible.

However, if a conjunction joins a subordinate clause to an independent clause, it is known as a **subordinating conjunction.**

The movie that I didn't want to see was actually very good.

In this sentence, the subordinate clause is *that I didn't want to see*, which is not a complete sentence on its own. The subordinating conjunction is *that*. Here are some other coordinating and subordinating conjunctions:

Coordinating Conjunctions
and
but
for
nor
or
so
yet

Subordinating Conjunctions	
after	until
although	when
as	whenever
because	whereas
before	wherever
even though	whether
if	which
since	while
that	who
though	why
unless	

Now answer this quick exercise question.

. . . .

The <u>jacket, I bought this afternoon, fits</u> me perfectly.
13

13. **A.** NO CHANGE
    B. jacket those I bought this afternoon fits
    C. jacket I bought this afternoon, fits
    D. jacket that I bought this afternoon fits

The correct answer is D. The subordinate clause in this sentence is *that I bought this afternoon*.

. . . .

FRAGMENTS AND RUN-ONS

Two of the most common sentence structure errors are fragments and run-ons. The names of these writing errors say a lot about what they are. A fragment is a piece of a complete object. The same is true in English. A **fragment** is a piece of a sentence, but it is not a complete one.

> *Bouncing on the waves.*

What was bouncing on the waves? This phrase needs a subject. Otherwise, it's nothing more than a fragment.

> *The little boat is bouncing on the waves.*

Ah, that's more like it. The subject-verb pair *The little boat* and *is* rescued this sentence from the fragment heap.

Run-on sentences are the opposite of fragments, but they are just as incorrect. They combine two or more independent clauses without using a coordinating conjunction or proper punctuation. In effect, the sentences "run on" (and into each other) without stopping. Unlike a fragment, in which there is a shortage of words, run-on sentences have too many words improperly joined together.

NOTE: Sometimes, writers use fragments and run-on sentences on purpose to achieve a particular effect. However, as far as the ACT English test is concerned, fragments and run-on sentences are always wrong.

> *The sea is rough and stormy the little boat is bouncing on the waves.*

This run-on sentence needs the correct punctuation, but adding a comma is not quite enough:

> *The sea is rough and stormy, the little boat is bouncing on the waves.*

Now the sentence has graduated from a run-on sentence to a comma splice. It needs one more element to make it grammatically correct. However, that little boat need not fear. This comma splice can be repaired by adding a coordinating conjunction.

> *The sea is rough and stormy, and the little boat is bouncing on the waves.*

Run-on sentences can also be corrected without adding a conjunction by using the correct punctuation, such as a semicolon, a dash, or a period.

The ACT will never ask you to choose between stylistic differences such as the different ways to correct a run-on sentence. There will be only *one* correct answer.

> **Semicolon:** *The sea is rough and stormy; the little boat is bouncing on the waves.*

> **Dash:** *The sea is rough and stormy—the little boat is bouncing on the waves.*

> **Period:** *The sea is rough and stormy. The little boat is bouncing on the waves.*

You could also make one of the clauses dependent on the other by adding a subordinate conjunction.

> *Because the sea is rough and stormy, the little boat is bouncing on the waves.*

As you can see, there are several ways to express the thought clearly.

Now answer this quick exercise question.

. . . .

Irina <u>was surfing a jellyfish</u> stung her.
　　　　14

14. **F.** NO CHANGE
    G. was surfing, a jellyfish
    H. surfing when a jellyfish
    J. was surfing when a jellyfish

The correct answer is J. The original run-on sentence has been corrected by making the second clause (*a jellyfish stung her*) dependent on the first (*Irina was surfing*).

. . . .

MODIFIERS AND THEIR PROBLEMS

As we said while discussing adjectives and adverbs, descriptive parts of speech add spice to sentences. However, you cannot just sprinkle these particular spices anywhere. Modifiers such as adjectives, adverbs, and descriptive phrases and clauses need to be placed correctly in sentences. Otherwise, you can end up with a very bewildering brew.

The two most common modifier issues are misplaced modifiers and dangling modifiers. A **misplaced modifier** is not placed next to the word it is supposed to modify.

> *I tiptoed across the floor because I didn't want to wake the people sleeping in the room below mine carefully.*

In this sentence, the modifier *carefully* is a long way from home. In fact, its placement makes it seem as though the people were sleeping carefully. How do you sleep carefully? You have to be conscious to be careful. The adverb *carefully* would be put to better use modifying *tiptoed*. The best way is to pluck it from the end of the sentence and drop it immediately after *tiptoed*.

> *I tiptoed carefully across the floor because I didn't want to wake the people sleeping in the room below mine.*

Excellent! In this sentence, the modifier *carefully* is no longer misplaced.

Dangling modifiers are even more confusing than misplaced ones. They don't modify anything at all because there's nothing in the sentence for them to modify. Take a look at this sentence:

> *Worried about the time, breakfast was left on the table.*

The modifier in this sentence is *Worried about the time*. The problem is we don't know exactly who was worried about the time—it certainly can't be breakfast! This sentence leaves the modifier dangling without anything to modify. Someone needs to add a subject to give the modifier something to do. We'll handle this one.

> *Worried about the time, Greta left her breakfast on the table.*

The addition of the subject *Greta* gives the phrase *worried about the time* something to modify.

NOTE: On the ACT, make sure you choose the right noun to give the modifier something to modify. You will make the best selection by reading the passage very carefully.

Now answer this quick exercise question.

. . . .

The man <u>did not show up to work today who runs the store</u>.
15

15. **A.** NO CHANGE
    B. did not show up to work who runs the store today.
    C. did not show up who runs the store to work today.
    D. who runs the store did not show up to work today.

The correct answer is D. The modifier *who runs the store* should directly follow the word it describes: *man*.

. . . .

PARALLEL STRUCTURE

When two things are parallel, they are moving in the same direction. All parts of a group of words in a sentence need to move in the same direction too. You can't place a word or phrase that's going backward into the past alongside one that's moving into the future. In fact, you cannot combine different tenses into any single group. Parallel structure crumbles when groups of words combine different types of phrases, clauses, and parts of speech.

> *I start my day by brushing my teeth, eating breakfast, and then head to school.*

This sentence describes something that is happening in the present, and the writer uses the present continuous tense to indicate that she is brushing her teeth and eating breakfast. Everything is smooth until that final phrase: *then head to school*. It is written in the simple present tense, which violates the parallel structure of a sentence otherwise written in the present continuous tense.

> *I start my day by brushing my teeth, eating breakfast, and heading to school.*

This sentence corrects the parallel structure by putting that pesky final verb in its present continuous tense. Now all parts of the sentence are moving in the same direction.

You need to be aware of parallel structure when using other parts of speech in lists as well. To be grammatically correct, the words have to be the same part of speech and used correctly in the structure of the sentence.

TIP

A sentence does not need to be written entirely in the same tense to be correct. It just needs to be structured correctly. The sentence *I ate an apple yesterday, and I am going to eat an orange tonight* does not violate parallel structure.

Incorrect: *Sean was brave, courage, and kind.* (*Courage* is a noun; *brave* and *kind* are adjectives.)

Correct: *Sean was brave, courageous, and kind.*

Incorrect: *In the snow I drive carefully, defensively, and slow.* (*Slow* is an adjective; *carefully* and *defensively* are adverbs.)

Correct: *In the snow I drive carefully, defensively, and slowly.*

CORRELATIVE CONJUNCTIONS

You must also be mindful of parallel structure when dealing with correlative conjunctions. These are conjunctions that work in pairs: *either . . . or, neither . . . nor,* and *not only . . . but also.* Mixing your correlative conjunctions is another way to violate parallel structure.

> *Neither the pants or the shirt suit my taste in clothing.*

Oops! *Neither* indicates a negative, and *or* indicates a positive. So what does this sentence mean? Do the pants and shirt suit the writer's very particular tastes, or don't they? We will know only if the parallel structure is repaired.

> *Neither the pants nor the shirt suit my taste in clothing.*

Oh, the writer doesn't like either piece of clothing! Too bad!

 ALERT: To say something like *I am not only a son, but a brother* is incorrect because the *not only…but also* conjunction is missing the word *also* in this instance.

Now you will put everything you have learned about grammar and usage to the test by reading this sample passage and answering the questions that follow.

. . . .

Back in the 1970s, few members of the movie industry believed

in a strange, little, movie called *Star Wars* .
 ‾‾‾‾‾‾‾‾‾‾‾‾‾‾‾‾‾‾‾‾‾‾‾‾‾‾‾‾‾‾‾‾
        16

16. F.   NO CHANGE
     G.   in a strange little movie called *Star Wars*
     H.   in a movie strange, little movie called *Star Wars*
     J.   in a strange called *Star Wars*

The correct answer is G. No commas are needed to set off the adjectives modifying *movie.*

George Lucas's <u>outer space fantasy. It was full</u> of odd robots and
                                17
creatures very out of step with the vogue for gritty, realistic, and

rather pessimistic movies.

17. A.   NO CHANGE
     B.   outer space fantasy was full
     C.   outer space fantasy; it was full
     D.   outer space fantasy will be fulls

The correct answer is B. *George Lucas's outer space fantasy* is a fragment that cannot be a stand-alone sentence or set off by a semicolon.

However, <u>it has outlasted most of the movies of its day and</u>
                                18
<u>continuing</u> to delight audiences well into the twenty-first century.
   18
In fact, *Star Wars* seems more popular than ever lately, spawning

18. F.   NO CHANGE
     G.   it has outlasted most of the movies of its day; and continues
     H.   it has outlasted most of the movies of its day and continues
     J.   it has outlasted most of the movies of its day, continues

The correct answer is H. Since *has outlasted* and *continues* are the compound predicate to the subject pronoun *it,* no punctuation is needed before the coordinating conjunction *and.*

a recent stream of feature films and <u>television series, as well as</u>

<u>all of the merchandise</u> that has been an important part of this
19

pop-culture juggernaut since its inception some four decades

ago.

19. A. NO CHANGE

B. television series. As well as all of the merchandise

C. television series, all of the merchandise

D. television series all of the merchandise

The correct answer is A. The section is correct as is.

. . . .

SUMMING IT UP

- **End-of-sentence punctuation** includes the period, the exclamation mark, and the question mark. When a sentence ends with quotation marks used to indicate dialogue, the end-of-sentence punctuation is placed within the quotation marks. If the quotation marks indicate a title and placing end-of-sentence punctuation within the marks might give the false impression that the mark is part of the title, the end-of-sentence punctuation is placed outside of the closing quotation marks.

- **Commas** are used to separate introductory words, phrases, and clauses; clauses in compound sentences, nonrestrictive phrases, items in series, appositives, and quotations.

- **Apostrophes** are used to separate letters in contractions and indicate possession. When indicating possession, an apostrophe is usually followed by the letter *s*. However, no extra *s* is necessary if the possessing word ends in *s* and is not someone's name.

- **Colons** are used to introduce a list of items or offset an example.

- **Dashes** are used to offset examples and indicate a pause or interruption in dialogue.

- **Parentheses** enclose bonus information that cannot be fit into a sentence naturally.

- **Plural nouns** do not always end with *s*; there are several variations among plural nouns depending on the words' letters. **Collective nouns** are singular nouns in most cases; they act as plural nouns only when individual members are not acting in unison.

- **Subjects and verbs** are in agreement when they are in the same form. They both need to be either singular or plural.

- **Pronouns and antecedents** (the words for which the pronouns stand in) need to be in agreement. They need to agree in terms of number, gender, and person.

- **Relative pronouns** signal relative clauses, which are used to describe nouns; **reflexive pronouns** refer back to their subjects; **interrogative pronouns** are used when asking a question; **possessive pronouns** show ownership.

- **Verb tense** indicates when the action the verb describes takes place.

- **Comparative adjectives and adverbs** are used when comparing two things. They usually end in *-er*. **Superlative adjectives and adverbs** are used when comparing three or more things. They usually end in *-est*.

- **Idioms** use words to mean something other than their literal meanings.

- **Prepositional phrases** combine a preposition with other words to indicate direction and time.

- **Independent clauses** contain a subject and a verb and make sense on their own. **Subordinate clauses** contain a subject-verb pair but must be linked to an independent clause to be correct.

- **Fragments** are partial sentences that lack either a subject or a verb. They are grammatically incorrect.

- **Run-on sentences** are complete sentences that are connected without the necessary conjunction or punctuation.

- **Modifiers** are words and phrases that describe something. **Misplaced modifiers** are not placed next to the words they are supposed to modify. They are grammatically incorrect. **Dangling modifiers** fail to modify any word at all.

- **Parallel structure** occurs when all groups of words in a sentence are written in the same tense and form. When such words are not in the same tense or form, the sentence is grammatically incorrect. Failing to pair correlative conjunctions correctly also violates parallel structure.

167

Chapter 4

Usage/
Mechanics

Pump up your test prep power with *Peterson's ACT Online Course*. The course will give you access to customized lessons designed to strengthen your skills in the Grammar and Usage topics covered on the ACT English test:

- Pronouns, Nouns, and Verbs
- Adjectives and Adverbs
- Connection Words
- What Makes a Sentence?
- Using Modifiers
- Common Sentence Mistakes
- Sentence Enders
- Setting off Phrases
- Apostrophes
- Agreement
- Verb Tenses
- Shift in Person

To purchase and access the course, go to ***www.petersons.com/act***.

168

Chapter 4

**Usage/
Mechanics**

PRACTICE

Now it's time to take your first English practice quiz. The passages in this quiz are similar in length to those that will appear on the actual ACT. Read each one very carefully before answering the questions. When you've finished answering all 20 questions, check the answers and explanations that follow to figure out how well you did and why you may have selected some incorrect answer choices.

PASSAGE I

The Great Chicago Fire

[1]

On October 8, 1871, a fire ignited in Chicago, Illinois, and continued to engulf the city for the next two days. One of the most monumental disasters on U.S. soil, the Great Chicago Fire ultimately killed as many as 300 people left more than 100,000 [1] others without homes, and ravaged 3.3 square miles of land. This is a tragic story, yet not one without hope, as anyone which has [2] visited or lived in the city of Chicago can confirm today.

[2]

The most famous tale of the Great Chicago Fire's cause almost [3] seem like something out of a children's story: a cow owned by Patrick and Catherine O'Leary had kicked over a lantern in their barn. The lantern set fire to the barn, and then the fire [4] swept through the entire city. However, this story has no more validity than the average children's story.

1. **A.** NO CHANGE
   B. many as 300, people left more
   C. many as 300 people; left more
   D. many as 300 people, left more

2. **F.** NO CHANGE
   G. as anyone who has visited
   H. as anyone those has visited
   J. as anyone which have visited

3. **A.** NO CHANGE
   B. most famous tale of the Great Chicago Fire's cause almost seeming
   C. most famous tale of the Great Chicago Fire's cause almost seems
   D. most famous tale of the Great Chicago Fire's cause almost will seem

4. **F.** NO CHANGE
   G. fire to the barn, though then the fire swept
   H. fire to the barn, after then the fire swept
   J. fire to the barn, until then the fire swept

A dozen years after the fire, <u>Michael Ahern admitted he made</u>
                                                              5
<u>up the story, a reporter from the</u> *Chicago Republican*, because
         5
he thought people would find it interesting. The truth is that no
one knows exactly how the Great Chicago Fire started, though
it did indeed begin in the O'Leary's barn.

[3]

What is known is <u>how rapidly and ruthlessly the fire</u> spun out
                                                        6
of control. Since most of the buildings in Chicago were constructed of wood at the time, the fire had a lot of material to
consume. Even the sidewalks in Chicago were made of wood. As
the wind <u>lifted up burning debris and carried</u> it throughout the
                             7
city, new conflagrations broke out.

[4]

<u>Chicagos' mayor Roswell B. Mason</u> sent out a distress call to
                   8
get help from neighboring towns while his own fire department
continued to fight the flames. However, the end of the Great
Chicago Fire was mostly brought about naturally as it died down
on its own. The rainfall that began on October 9 helped drown
the already dying fire. It was out by the morning of October 10,
1871.

[5]

The Great Chicago <u>Fire was now over Chicago's troubles had</u>
                                                      9
<u>barely begun.</u> With many people dead and homeless, and many
      9

buildings <u>destroyed including the courthouse and waterworks</u>
                                    10
<u>a difficult period</u> of repairs lay ahead. Reconstruction began
         10
immediately, though another major fire in 1874 was a tremendous
setback. However, the use of terra cotta tiles in many newly
constructed buildings would make Chicago one of the most

5. A. NO CHANGE
    B. Michael Ahern, a reporter from the *Chicago Republican*, admitted he made up the story
    C. reporter Michael Ahern admitted he from the *Chicago Republican* made up the story
    D. Michael Ahern, a reporter from the *Chicago Republican*

6. F. NO CHANGE
    G. how much rapider and more ruthless the fire
    H. how rapider and ruthlesser the fire
    J. how rapid and ruthless the fire

7. A. NO CHANGE
    B. lifted up burning debris and carries
    C. lifted up burning debris and carrying
    D. Lifts up burning debris and carries

8. F. NO CHANGE
    G. Chicagos mayor Roswell B. Mason
    H. Chicago is mayor Roswell B. Mason
    J. Chicago's mayor Roswell B. Mason

9. A. NO CHANGE
    B. Fire was now over, Chicago's troubles had barely begun
    C. Fire was now over, but Chicago's troubles had barely begun
    D. Fire was now and Chicago's troubles had barely begun

10. F. NO CHANGE
    G. destroyed; including the courthouse and waterworks; a difficult period
    H. destroyed. Including the courthouse and waterworks. A difficult period
    J. destroyed—including the courthouse and waterworks—a difficult period

fireproof cities in the United States. By 1893, it was ready to host

a major international fair called the World's Columbian Exposition.

Today, Chicago is one of the most popular cities in the United

States. Its fire department training academy is now located on

the site where the O'Leary's barn once stood. It is a reminder of

how much Chicago has endured and how much it has overcome.

PASSAGE II

Rock Opera

[1]

Are there two kinds of music more different than <u>opera and</u>

<u>rock music. Opera is</u> an artful form of music sung by professionally
11

trained singers that conveys complex stories. Rock music is rough

and raw and is played on loud electric guitars by people who

often don't even know how to read music. <u>Opera is for serious</u>
12

<u>and cultured.</u> Rock music is for everyone, and the less serious
12

and <u>cultured they are, the better</u>.
13

[2]

Of course, these stereotypes were shattered in the 1960s when

several rock musicians schemed to unite that most serious of

music forms with the wildest pop music around. It all began with

a British <u>called The Who</u> and their manager Kit Lambert. Rock
14

bands of the time did not get any wilder than The Who. <u>The band</u>
15

<u>was known to smash his instruments</u> to pieces at the end of
15

concerts so loud they actually broke world records for volume.

Lambert was more of a serious music lover, and his father,

Constant Lambert, was the musical director of the Royal Ballet

at England's Covent Garden.

11. **A.** NO CHANGE
    B. opera and rock music: opera is
    C. opera and rock music? Opera is
    D. opera and rock music, opera is

12. **F.** NO CHANGE
    G. Opera is for serious and cultured people.
    H. Opera is for serious, cultured.
    J. Opera is for serious and culture.

13. **A.** NO CHANGE
    B. cultured they be, the better
    C. cultured they was, the better
    D. cultured they is, the better

14. **F.** NO CHANGE
    G. The Who
    H. popular called The Who
    J. rock band called The Who

15. **A.** NO CHANGE
    B. The band was known to smash their instruments
    C. The band was known to smash its instruments
    D. The band was known to smash our instruments

[3]

Feeling the band he managed needed a good <u>gimmick as if</u>
                                                           16
<u>smashing instruments was not a good enough gimmick on its</u>
                                                           16
<u>own,</u> Lambert encouraged The Who's main songwriter, Pete
   16
Townshend, to try putting more complex stories into his songs.

Realizing The Who's second album <u>was neither long enough or</u>
                                                        17
<u>progressive enough</u> to compete with what the most interesting
          17

other bands of the time were doing, Townshend strung together

six <u>unfinished songs, gave them a storyline, had his first</u>
                            18
"mini-opera."

[4]

<u>However it was The Who's full-length opera</u> that made them
                            19

international celebrities and <u>made "rock opera" a household</u>
                                              20
<u>word.</u> The opera was called *Tommy* and told the story of a boy
   20
with multiple disabilities who ends up becoming a pinball

champion and reluctant religious leader. As strange as the story

was, the public loved it. Artists such as Andrew Lloyd Webber,

Pink Floyd, Green Day, and The Decemberists would follow,

making their own successful unions of opera and rock and roll.

16. F. NO CHANGE
    G. gimmick. As if smashing instruments was not a good enough gimmick on its own.
    H. gimmick (as if smashing instruments was not a good enough gimmick on its own)
    J. gimmick (as if smashing instruments was not a good enough gimmick on its own

17. A. NO CHANGE
    B. was neither long enough and progressive enough
    C. was either long enough or progressive enough
    D. was neither long enough nor progressive enough

18. F. NO CHANGE
    G. unfinished songs, gave them a storyline, and had his first
    H. unfinished songs, had his first
    J. unfinished songs, gave them a storyline, as had his first

19. A. NO CHANGE
    B. However, it was The Who's full-length opera
    C. However: it was The Who's full-length opera
    D. It was The Who's full-length opera

20. F. NO CHANGE
    G. made "rock opera" a house word
    H. made "rock opera" a holding word
    J. made "rock opera" a household

ANSWERS AND EXPLANATIONS

Be sure to read each explanation thoroughly to help you understand why the incorrect answer choices are incorrect, why you may have selected them, and how to avoid making the same errors on the actual ACT.

1. **The correct answer is D.** Items in a series need to be separated with commas, even if those items consist of phrases. This particular series describes the various disastrous results of the Great Chicago Fire. As the sentence is originally written, the first two items in that list—the number of people who died in the fire, and the number of people who were left homeless—are not separated with any punctuation, so choice A is incorrect. Items in a list should be separated with semicolons only if those items already contain commas. Since this is not the case, choice C is incorrect. Choice B includes a comma, which is the correct punctuation for separating the items in this particular series, but it is misplaced in the middle of the first item, so choice B is wrong. Only choice D correctly places the comma after the first item (*killed as many as 300 people*), and it is therefore the correct answer choice.

2. **The correct answer is G.** As it is written, the sentence uses the wrong relative pronoun. The antecedent is the indefinite pronoun *anyone*, which indicates a person, yet the relative pronoun *which* should be used only to replace a thing. So you can eliminate choices F and J. Choice J makes the additional error of matching the plural verb *have* with the singular pronoun *anyone*. Choice H mistakenly uses the plural pronoun *those* to indicate the singular antecedent *anyone*. Only choice G offers the relative pronoun *who* and the correct agreement.

3. **The correct answer is C.** This is a somewhat tricky subject-verb agreement question because of all the words that appear between the subject *tale* and the verb *seem*. However, a careful reading of the sentence reveals that these words are, indeed, its subject and verb. It should also reveal that the singular noun *tale* needs a singular verb, and *seem* is a plural verb. Therefore, you can eliminate choice A. Rewriting the verb in the progressive tense (*seeming*) does not correct the error, so go ahead and eliminate choice B too. The same is true of rewriting it in the future tense (*will seem*), so choice D is incorrect too. That leaves choice C, which correctly rewrites the verb in the singular form (*seems*).

4. **The correct answer is F.** This sentence contains two ideas of equal importance: the lantern set fire to the barn, and then the fire swept through the entire city. That means it needs a coordinating conjunction to join those two ideas, and since *and* is a coordinating conjunction, the sentence is correct as it is written and choice F is the right answer. Choices G, H, and J all replace the correct coordinating conjunction with various incorrect subordinating conjunctions.

5. **The correct answer is B.** There is a misplaced modifier in this sentence as it is written. The modifier is *a reporter from the Chicago Republican*, and it needs to modify the subject *Michael Ahern*. However, the way it is placed in the original sentence makes it seem as though the story about the O'Leary's cow was a reporter from the *Chicago Republican*. That means choice A is incorrect. Only choice B moves the modifier so it follows the subject directly. Therefore, choice B is the best answer. Choice C is worded confusingly, and choice D deletes words, which would turn the sentence into a fragment, so these two answer choices are both incorrect.

6. **The correct answer is F.** In this sentence, the words *rapidly* and *ruthlessly* modify the verb *spun*. Since they are written in the adverb form, and adverbs modify verbs, the sentence is correct as written, and choice F is the best answer. Since nothing is being compared in this sentence, the comparative form is not required in this sentence, and choice G is incorrect. That answer choice makes the additional error of transforming the adverbs into adjectives. Choice H further misuses the comparative form with the word *ruthlesser*, which is not a real word. Choice J does not attempt to use the comparative form, but it is still wrong since *rapid* and *ruthless* are adjectives, not adverbs.

7. **The correct answer is A.** The underlined portion in this sentence uses parallel structure, and it is balanced since both *lifted* and *carried* are written in the past tense. Choice A is the right answer. Choices B and C violate that parallel structure by mixing the past and present tenses (choice B), and the past and progressive tenses (choice C). Choice D is parallel, but it rewrites the two verbs in the present tense, and this is incorrect since the sentence describes something that happened in the past.

8. **The correct answer is J.** This question tests your knowledge of how to use apostrophes to show possession. As the sentence is originally written, the apostrophe is used incorrectly. It makes it seem as though there is more than one Chicago, or that the name of the city ends with the letter *s*. Eliminate choice F. Choice G fails to use the apostrophe, and choice H deletes the apostrophe and the *s*. Both elements are needed when a singular word that does not end with *s* is in its possessive form. Only choice J uses both essential elements in their correct places.

9. **The correct answer is C.** This is a run-on sentence as written. The two clauses in this compound sentence—*The Great Chicago Fire was now over* and *Chicago's troubles had barely begun*—need to be joined with a coordinating conjunction. Eliminate choice A. Choice B uses a comma instead of a conjunction; that is known as a comma splice, and comma splices are always incorrect. Eliminate choice B. Choice D uses a coordinating conjunction, but it is not the right coordinating conjunction. The choice also randomly deletes the adjective *over*, and the comma before the conjunction is missing. Since the second clause is a counterpoint to the first, the coordinating conjunction *but* is in order, making choice C is the best answer.

10. **The correct answer is J.** In this sentence, *including the courthouse and waterworks* is an example, and it needs to be offset from the rest of the sentence. The best way to accomplish this is with dashes, so choice J is the best answer. As the sentence is originally written, there is no offsetting punctuation at all, so choice F is wrong. Choice G mistakenly uses semicolons instead of dashes. Choice H not only uses periods, which is the wrong punctuation to use to offset examples, but also turns the example into a fragment.

11. **The correct answer is C.** The first sentence of the passage asks a question, and, therefore, it should end with a question mark. As originally written, it ends with a period, which belongs at the end of a statement. Choice A is wrong. Choice B attempts to correct the problem by joining the first two sentences of the passage with a colon, yet the colon would be appropriate only if placed before both parts of the example. Since only the example relating to opera follows the first sentence (the example relating to rock music is in its own sentence that comes next), the colon is not the right punctuation for this particular circumstance, which makes choice B incorrect. Choice D creates a comma splice, which is never a correct solution. Choice

C offers the simplest solution to a fairly simple problem by replacing the period with a question mark.

12. **The correct answer is G.** Opera is for serious and cultured *what*? As this sentence is written, we simply do not know because it lacks an object for the preposition *for*. Therefore it is incomplete, and you can eliminate choice F. Choice H fails to correct the problem; it only replaces the coordinating conjunction with a comma. Choice J turns the adjective *cultured* into a noun, leaving the sentence nonsensical. To correct this sentence, you need to make an assumption about what or who is serious and cultured. *People* is a good guess that makes sense within the context of the passage, so choice G is the best answer.

13. **The correct answer is A.** This underlined portion contains a variation of the idiomatic expression *the less . . . the better*. The idiom is used correctly and everything is in agreement, so choice A is the best answer. Choices B, C, and D ruin a perfectly good sentence with various verbs that fail to agree with the subject pronoun *they*.

14. **The correct answer is J.** In this sentence, *called The Who* is a modifier; it explains what something is called. But what is that thing? We do not know because it is a dangling modifier, making choice F wrong. Introducing a subject for the modifier to modify will correct this sentence. Since this passage makes it clear that The Who is a rock band, introducing that information to the sentence will correct it. Choice J accomplishes this task well. Choice G makes it seem as though there are several *The Who*s, and it just so happens that the British one invented the rock opera. Eliminate choice G. *Popular* is an adjective, not a noun, and though The Who became popular, this adjective does not correct the dangling modifier problem, so choice H is incorrect.

15. **The correct answer is B.** This is a pronoun-antecedent question, and the sentence as written makes it seem as though The Who was one person. It was actually a band of four people, so choice A does not make sense. Since The Who is a band, it is a collective noun, so collective noun rules apply here. Think about what The Who are doing in this sentence: they are smashing their instruments. Chances are every member of the Who does not play the same instrument; otherwise the sentence might read something like *the band was known to smash its guitars*. Since most band members play different instruments, each member of The Who is doing something a little different, even though they are all smashing something. Therefore, the best way to write this sentence is as it is written in choice B, not choice C. Choice D makes it sound as if you, the reader,

and the writer of this passage owned instruments that The Who took away and smashed.

16. **The correct answer is H.** This sentence contains a little bonus information about how The Who already had a gimmick before inventing the rock opera. Bonus information should not be dropped in the middle of a sentence without any punctuation to separate it. This is how it appears in the sentence as originally written, so choice F is wrong. It belongs within a set of parentheses, as it appears in choice H. Choice J has the right idea but fails to close up the parentheses. Choice G creates a fragment by splitting off the subordinate clause before the bonus information with a period.

17. **The correct answer is D.** As it is written, this sentence mismatches the words in a correlative conjunction. The negative *neither* does not belong with the positive *or*, so choice A is wrong. Now, your job is to figure out if this sentence requires the *neither . . . nor* correlative conjunction or the *either . . . or* one. Since the sentence indicates that Pete Townshend made an effort to make The Who's second album something that it was not (long enough or progressive enough to compete with what the most interesting other bands of the time were doing), you can conclude that this sentence requires the *neither . . . nor* combination. That means you can eliminate choice C and select choice D as the best answer. There is no *neither . . . and* correlative conjunction, so you should have eliminated choice B.

18. **The correct answer is G.** The sentence as originally written is incorrect because it lacks a conjunction between the two final items in the series of things Pete Townshend did to make his first "mini-opera." Eliminate choice F. Since these items are of equal importance, a coordinating conjunction is needed, and choice G contains the best option. Choice H senselessly eliminates one of the important items in this series. Choice J uses a subordinating conjunction that makes no sense in this context.

19. **The correct answer is B.** *However* is a transitional word, and a transitional word needs to be offset with a comma. Since the sentence as written fails to do this, you can eliminate choice A. Since choice B does do this, you can select it as the best answer. Choice C uses the wrong punctuation. Choice D deletes the transitional word completely. While this is not grammatically incorrect, the transitional word improves the flow of ideas between the final two paragraphs, so choice D is not the very best option.

20. **The correct answer is F.** This question expects you to be familiar with the idiom "household word," which is a word or term so common that people seem to use it in every household. The sentence as originally written uses the idiom correctly, so choice F is correct. Choices G and J delete elements necessary to the idiom's common use. There is no such idiom as "a holding word," so choice H is incorrect.

175

Chapter 4

Usage/
Mechanics

CHAPTER 5: RHETORICAL SKILLS

OVERVIEW

- Strategy
- Organization
- Style
- Summing It Up
- Practice

Now that you know everything you need about the usage/mechanics questions on the ACT English test, it's time to get familiar with the test's other question type. Rhetorical skills questions are a bit trickier than usage/mechanics questions because the error may not be quite as obvious. These questions deal with subtler matters of strategy, organization, and style. They deal with making sure a piece of writing is as clear and convincing as it can be.

Take a look at this paragraph.

Have you ever heard the song of a prairie warbler? The bird makes a buzzing sound that rises and falls, changing pitch. Male cardinals appear to have red feathers because of the way the light catches them and not because the feathers contain red pigment. The prairie warbler's song is quite enchanting.

NOTE: Rhetorical skills questions may sometimes seem as though they have more than one correct answer. That will never be the case, so be sure to contrast those answers against each other to select the very best one.

Grammatically speaking, there's nothing wrong with this paragraph. The punctuation is in the right place. The sentences are well constructed. However, there is definitely something wrong with it. What's a sentence about cardinal feathers doing in a paragraph about a prairie warbler's song? Your guess is as good as ours, because the inclusion of that sentence about cardinals and their lovely feathers has nothing to do with the paragraph's topic. In fact, it is downright distracting—it weakens the author's attempt to convince you that the prairie warbler's song is unique and enchanting. This is the kind of subtle error you will have to recognize when answering rhetorical skills questions on the ACT.

Obviously, all rhetorical skills questions do not deal with off-topic details. They also involve making sure that the tone and mood of a piece of writing are consistent and appropriate, deleting redundant details, making sure the transitions between ideas are strong, avoiding wordiness, and so on. You basically learned how to fix the major errors in a piece of writing in the previous chapter. In this chapter you will learn how to make a piece of writing really worth reading, which is something that all the best editors do.

STRATEGY

Just as a well-prepared team studies the competing team's strategies to plot out its moves as effectively as possible, a strong writer plots out her or his ideas to reach an audience as effectively as possible. Writers choose the expressions that will best affect their particular readers. They delete, revise, and delete again the details most likely to fall flat with that audience. They choose only the most relevant and convincing details to support their writing. All of this is part of the writer's strategy, a concept covered on 15 to 20 percent of the rhetorical skills questions on the ACT English test.

SUPPORTING EXAMPLES AND EVIDENCE

A piece of writing has two main elements: 1) a topic; and 2) the examples and evidence that support that topic. You can't have one without the other. Simply stating a topic is neither very informative nor convincing.

> *Hawaii is the best place to take a vacation. That's it! I'm sure you'll start planning your vacation right now!*

We're sure Hawaii is a lovely state and a great place to vacation, but it's going to take a bit more convincing than that.

> *Hawaii is the best place to take a vacation. The weather is warm and sunny. The Pacific Ocean is clear, blue, and perfect for swimming or surfing. The local cuisine and music are unique and fabulous. Once you go to Hawaii, you may never want to go home again!*

We were right! Hawaii *is* a lovely state and a great place to vacation! All it took to convince us were a few relevant pieces of evidence to explain why Hawaii is so nice.

Not everything that is remotely related to a topic is actually relevant. Had the above paragraph boasted about how great the snowy Swiss Alps are for skiers, it would not belong in this paragraph just because it relates to the topic of a great vacation spot. The vacation spot in this paragraph is very specific, and all of the paragraph's details need to be relevant to that spot: Hawaii.

As another way to access your ability to recognize relevant details, supporting examples and evidence questions may ask you to identify what kind of information the passage would lose if a particular example or piece of evidence was deleted.

NOTE: Some questions may ask you to assess the author's use of particular strategies and details. For such questions, you should think about whether those elements improve or harm the passage, and why.

ACT English questions may ask you to select examples and evidence to support a piece of writing that needs to be more convincing. You can get a good idea of how those questions will look by trying the following exercise question. Start by reading the paragraph.

(1) There is an ongoing debate about the use of practical special effects versus computer-generated effects in movies. (2) Practical effects are physical props and models built by expert craftspeople. (3) Computer-generated effects are complex visuals made by digital animators. (4) Supporters of practical effects feel that they bring a sense of realism to a film. (5) Those who prefer computer-generated effects do so because such effects are on the cutting edge of technology, and therefore look more modern and realistic to their eyes. [1]

1. Which of the following sentences, when inserted after Sentence 4, would provide a concrete example of a statement made by the author?

   A. Practical effects might also include masks and costumes that might otherwise be created digitally by a computer effects department.

   B. Practical effects do not require actors and actresses to interact with animated characters and objects that are not really there.

   C. Before computer-generated effects came into use in the 1980s, almost all movie special effects were created by practical means.

   D. Even though most modern audiences seem to prefer computer-generated effects, some filmmakers continue to use practical ones.

The correct answer is B. The new sentence is to be inserted into the paragraph after a sentence about those who support practical special effects. Choice B provides evidence and explanation for this preceding sentence.

OFF-TOPIC AND REDUNDANT DETAILS

Building an argument is a bit like making a dish. If you were making a salad, you probably wouldn't toss chocolate chips into it just because chocolate chips are food and you happen to have a bag of them lying around. You would choose only the ingredients that belong in the particular salad you're making: some fresh lettuce, a few ripe tomatoes, maybe a nice sprinkling of dill, etc. You'd probably have a hard time convincing anyone to eat that salad if it were also full of chocolate chips.

Similarly, you would not just toss any old idea into a piece of writing simply because it happened to pop into your head. You would select only the ideas, details, and examples most relevant to your topic.

Remember that paragraph about what a wonderful vacation spot Hawaii is? Do you also remember how a sentence about how wonderful a vacation spot the Swiss Alps are would not belong in that paragraph? That's because details about the Swiss Alps are **off-topic** in a paragraph about Hawaii. If you see such an off-topic detail in a passage on the ACT test, you'll probably be expected to delete it.

> **TIP** Pay attention to the precise location of details you are going to add to a passage. Just because a detail might be relevant in the passage, it might not be relevant in the particular spot designated in the question.

You'll have to make a similar tough decision if you find **redundant** details. These are details that repeat information already stated in the passage. A writer does not need to keep saying the same thing over and over again. He or she does not need to include the same ideas over and over and…oops. Our apologies. The information in this paragraph is starting to get a bit redundant. Well, think of these redundant details as examples of the kinds you will have to delete on the ACT.

Take a look at the following example question to get familiar with ACT questions that require you to delete details.

(1) Thunderstorms, powerful winds, relentless rain, and dangerous ocean waves are all by-products of tropical cyclones. (2) The cyclones themselves are storm systems that rotate with great speed. (3) They spin in circular movements. (4) They usually form over warm bodies of water, and gain their power as surface water evaporates and builds saturated storm clouds. ☒

2. For the sake of unity and coherence, which of the following sentences does NOT belong in the paragraph?

   F. Sentence 1
   G. Sentence 2
   H. Sentence 3
   J. Sentence 4

The correct answer is H. Sentence 3 is redundant—the preceding sentence already says that storm systems *rotate with great speed*.

APPROPRIATE EXPRESSIONS

When a writer is plotting out a piece of writing, he or she has to think about who is going to be reading that piece of writing. If it is going to be an article in a science journal, it probably shouldn't contain expressions like "I was totally *crushing it* in the chemistry lab!" Such journals are aimed at professional people in a particular field who know all the technical jargon and expect the articles they read to be formal and written at an academic level. To those readers, informal language seems unprofessional and indicates that the writer probably isn't taking her or his work very seriously. However, using slang like *crushing it* might be completely appropriate to use in a blog post for a wide audience that doesn't have the patience to decode a lot of technical language.

ALERT: Not every kind of writing demands either formal or informal language. The most important factor is consistency. No matter what kind of writing it is, the entire piece should be written entirely either in formal or informal language and not a haphazard combination of both.

This strategy involves knowing exactly who your audience is and choosing the most appropriate language to reach them. Take a look at the following table to see examples of the kinds of writing in which it's usually appropriate to use informal expressions and the kinds that usually utilize formal expressions.

Formal	Informal
Academic journal	Blog post
Academic paper	Entertainment magazine article
Newspaper article	Fictional story
Scientific studies	Novel
Sociological studies	Personal essay
Textbook	Post on social media site

Passages on the ACT won't necessarily announce the kinds of writing they are, but you will be able to tell if they require formal or informal language based on how they are written, the topic being discussed, and the overall tone. Chances are if you're reading a formally written passage that suddenly includes a single slang expression, that slang expression does not belong, and there will be a question requiring you to delete it from the passage…kind of like this example question:

· ·

(1) Everybody these days seems obsessed with wasting every waking moment blathering away on social media sites. (2) These are computer-mediated tools for the creation and exchange of information. (3) People seem to think their every thought and item of personal business is so precious that it needs to be announced to the entire world. (4) Personally, I think that people need to consider their own privacy a little more. ③

3. For the sake of unity and coherence, which of the following sentences does NOT belong in the paragraph?

   A. Sentence 1
   B. Sentence 2
   C. Sentence 3
   D. Sentence 4

The correct answer is B. The tone of Sentence 2 is too formal for the rest of the paragraph, which seems like a personal essay or blog post on social media.

· ·

ORGANIZATION

Now that we've discussed the kinds of ideas that belong in a particular piece of writing, we're going to examine the best ways to put those ideas together. Nothing undermines a piece of writing like bad organization—no matter how solid its ideas may be. Imagine building a brick house by sticking those bricks together with chewing gum. Bricks are nice and sturdy, but that chewing gum isn't going to hold them together very well. Good organization is more like using good old cement to adhere those bricks together.

The organizational techniques that cement ideas in a piece of writing include choosing effective opening, transitional, and closing sentences. Just as you would not build a house with the smallest bricks on the bottom, writers also need to make sure their ideas are in the right order, and reorganizing for the sake of clarity and logic is another important organizational skill. On test day, 10 to 15 percent of the ACT English test questions will cover organization.

NOTE: Organization questions may ask you the best way to improve paragraphs by moving sentences to the spots where they are most logical.

STRONG OPENING SENTENCES

All journeys begin with a single step, and all pieces of writing begin with a single sentence. It's okay to stumble on the first step of that journey, but it is not okay to stumble when composing an opening sentence. The opening sentence sets the tone for all the other sentences that follow. It is also the sentence that most needs to hook the reader's interest. Imagine reading an article with a long, boring, meandering opening sentence. How much will you want to keep reading after that? However, an opening sentence that hooks your interest will make you want to keep reading.

TIP: A strong opening sentence does not just grab the reader's interest. It is also relevant to the topic of the passage as a whole and leads into the second sentence naturally.

Here are a few suggestions for making an opening sentence that really grabs the reader's attention.

- State the topic of the piece briefly and clearly. (Example: *Without question, Shakespeare was the finest playwright who ever lived.*)

- Use exciting words. (Example: *Although William Shakespeare wrote his plays four hundred years ago, they still have the* **power** *to* **thrill** *and* **dazzle** *audiences today.*)

- Ask a question. (Example: *Who is generally considered to be the finest playwright who ever lived?*)

- Use a point-counterpoint structure. (Example: *Most people think William Shakespeare is the finest playwright who ever lived. However…*)

- Use a surprising fact or theory. (Example: *William Shakespeare is generally regarded as the finest playwright who ever lived, but there is a pervasive theory that he didn't actually write some of his most well-known plays.*)

- If appropriate, try using a bit of humor. (Example: *If William Shakespeare is the great playwright everyone seems to think he is, why do I fall asleep every time I have to sit through one of his plays?*)

- Start with a quotation. (Example: *"The remarkable thing about Shakespeare is that he is really very good — in spite of all the people who say he is very good." –poet Robert Graves in "Sayings of the Week,"* The Observer, *1964*).

Now read this paragraph and answer the example question that follows.

The problem began when the state decided to use butterfly ballots. These are paper ballots that require voters to punch out perforated dots known as *chads*. However, a lot of voters had difficulty punching out these chads, leaving the dots hanging out of the ballots. Consequently, the press questioned whether or not Florida had tallied its votes correctly. This was an important issue, since Florida's votes were the deciding factor in who would be the next president of the United States. 4

4. The writer wishes to open the essay with a sentence that will set its theme and tone. Which of the following would most effectively accomplish this?

A. In 2000, United States voters had to decide who the next president would be, and their choice was either George W. Bush, a Republican, or Al Gore, a Democrat who'd been the Vice President of the United States for the past eight years.

B. Have you ever wondered how different states count the votes of their citizens in a presidential election?

C. The 2000 U.S. presidential election was thrown into turmoil when Florida decided to recount its votes.

D. Supporters of 2000 presidential candidate Al Gore were really hoping a recount in Florida would put him in the White House

The correct answer is C. It is the most ideal introduction and topic sentence for the sentences that follow.

ORGANIZING FOR CLARITY

Now you know what writers need to do to hook their readers, but no piece of writing can rest on its opening sentence alone. Every sentence and paragraph that follows needs to be strong too, and they also need to be well organized. Let's continue our comparison of a piece of writing to a brick house. Imagine you walked into the entry hallway and the first room you entered was…the attic? Doesn't the attic belong at the very *top* of the house? Yes, it does.

Every part of a piece of writing needs to be in a sensible place so that the piece is clear, logical, and completely readable. This is true of both sentences and paragraphs. Basically, the ideas in a piece of writing should not jump out of closets and yell "Surprise!" Writers need to lead up to their ideas with each one linking to the next in a sensible order. Take a look at the following sentences:

1) In the window was the cutest puppy I'd ever seen.

2) I decided she was the right puppy for me, and I've been happy ever since I brought her home.

3) When I woke up this morning, I thought to myself, "I wish I had a dog."

4) So after eating breakfast and getting dressed, I went to the pet shop.

Isn't that an adorable experience? Well, maybe it isn't that adorable in the order it is written. Take a second to see if you can put these sentences in their correct order.

Are you ready for the solution? These sentences belong in the following order: 3, 4, 1, 2. They simply do not make any sense in any other order.

Organization questions on the ACT may not be as clear-cut as this rather simplistic example. However, there will always be a *best* way to organize sentences in paragraphs. There will also be a *best* way to organize paragraphs, since some questions may require you to consider the organization of the passage as a whole. Just as the sentences in a paragraph need to be ordered clearly and logically, paragraphs need to follow each other in the same manner.

Keep an eye out for transitional words when answering organization questions. For example, a word like *however* should signify an idea contrary to the one before, or a word like *also* should signify an idea that builds on the one before it.

The most obvious paragraph organization errors occur when the opening and closing paragraphs are incorrectly placed. The reason this error is obvious is that there are very clear ways to identify these paragraphs: the opening paragraph will include its topic statement, and the closing paragraph will include the concluding statement. If the topic statement or concluding statement suddenly pops up in the middle of a passage and basically yells "Surprise!" you know those paragraphs are not in the correct order. However, when the body paragraphs—the ones in the middle—are out of order, it may be a little tougher to recognize the problem.

The key is to read the paragraphs carefully to make sure that there are no surprise details in them. Each detail needs to be introduced clearly. If the introduction of a detail in one paragraph follows a deeper explanation or description of that detail in a previous paragraph, then those body paragraphs are probably out of order. If you read carefully and yet continue to find a passage confusing, that might also be a clue that the paragraphs are not in the right order. Just as our little example about the adorable puppy had a very definite order, the sentences and paragraphs in a passage will always have a definite order too. They simply won't make sense if they aren't in that order.

See if you can select the best order for the following paragraph by answering this example question.

(1) Anoles all have slender bodies with long, thin tails. (2) There are 165 species of the small lizard known as the anole. (3) However, each species is so similar that scientists often have a tough time distinguishing them. (4) They also all have adhesive pads at the ends of their claws, which help them climb and stick to flat surfaces. [5]

5. Which of the following sentence sequences will make the paragraph most logical?

    F. NO CHANGE
    G. 3, 4, 2, 1
    H. 2, 3, 1, 4
    J. 2, 4, 1, 2

The correct answer is H. It is the only order that makes sense. Starting the paragraph introducing the topic, the anole, with information about the number of species, and then following with a sentence with contradictory information, and then adding details about the lizard's appearance with the third and fourth sentences presents the topic in a clear and logical order.

TRANSITIONAL WORDS AND PHRASES

As we've learned, an important factor in strong organization is how ideas connect to each other. Transitional words and phrases are the fasteners that link ideas. Without transitional words and phrases, you could end up with something like this:

> *I met Rahul in front of the movie theater. We were supposed to see* Avengers: Age of Ultron. *We decided to see* Ant-Man *instead. We made the right decision. It was great.*

Who went to see this movie, a robot? There has to be a less choppy way to express these thoughts. Adding a few transitional words and phrases should do the trick.

> *I met Rahul in front of the movie theater **since** we were supposed to see* Avengers: Age of Ultron. ***However**, we decided to see* Ant-Man *instead. **Ultimately**, we made the right decision **because** it was great.*

Different transitional words and phrases perform different functions. Take a look at the following table:

Function	Transitional Words and Phrases
introduction	to begin, first of all, to start with
an addition	additionally, also, furthermore, in addition, moreover, secondly
clarification	in other words, that is to say, to put it another way
the passage of time	afterwards, later, meanwhile, next, subsequently
examples	for example, for instance, to demonstrate, specifically, to illustrate
cause	because, since
effect	as a result, consequently, therefore
comparison	comparatively, in comparison, in similar fashion, likewise, similarly
contrast	at the same time, however, in contrast, nevertheless, notwithstanding, on the contrary, yet
conclusion	in conclusion, in short, to conclude, to sum up, to summarize, ultimately

Sometimes writers use entire sentences to transition between ideas. The transitional sentence in the following example is underlined.

> *People currently understand that the earth is spherical. <u>However, this was not always the case.</u> The common belief used to be that the world was flat.*

Although this sentence makes complete sense without the transitional sentence, that transitional sentence helps connect the contrasting ideas *(people now know the earth is spherical; people once thought the earth was flat)* in a way that holds the reader's interest.

. . . .

(1) There is an attitude in our culture that certain art forms qualify as "high art" and others qualify as "low art." (2) European films are often distinguished as "high art" for the most sophisticated and intellectual people, while comic books are "low art" aimed at children and people with average or below-average educations. (3) Many European films are as silly and insubstantial as the worst American movies, while there have been comic books with incredibly rich characterizations and plot developments. 6

6. Which of the following sentences, if inserted at this point, would provide the most effective transition between the second and third sentences of the paragraph?

A. Subsequently, there has been a great explosion in the number of comic books on the market.
B. In contrast, fine literature is considered to be a "high art" and is taught in classes around the world.
C. For example, people who did not attend a college might be thought of as uneducated.
D. However, a closer look at this stereotype reveals that it is both patronizing and untrue.

The correct answer is D. It transitions from one point of view (thoughts on how all European films are "high art" and comic books are "low art") to another (thoughts on how many European films are silly and many comic books are complex).

. . . .

STRONG ENDINGS

So we've covered the best ways to get a piece of writing started and moving through its details and ideas. All that's left is to wrap it up. That's where the closing sentence comes in. It's the cap on a piece of writing, and it should leave the reader feeling satisfied.

A closing sentence doesn't have to be too fancy. At this point, the writer has already introduced and discussed all necessary topics and supporting details. There shouldn't be anything new that requires further explanation in the closing sentence. Here are some different qualities of a strong closing sentence:

- It is short and clear.
- It repeats key words or phrases from the first paragraph to provide satisfying continuity.
- It uses compound structure for the sake of clarity and balance after what may have been acomplicated collection of details.
- It redefines an important idea or detail in the passage.
- It captures an accepted attitude regarding the topic.

TIP Beginning a concluding sentence with "In conclusion" is technically appropriate, but it is not a very interesting way to signal the conclusion of a piece of writing.

To close this section on organization questions, try another practice paragraph-question pair.

When construction of the Empire State Building concluded and Governor Al Smith declared it open on May 1, 1931, New York City had become the home to the tallest building in the world. In subsequent years, more than 20 taller buildings would be constructed across the globe, stripping the Empire State Building of its tallest building status. 7

7. The writer wishes to improve the conclusion of this paragraph. Which of the following would most effectively accomplish this if placed after the final sentence?

F. One such building is the Burj Khalifa in Dubai, which stands 2,717 feet tall.

G. The Empire State Building began construction on March 17, 1930, two months after the excavation crew broke the ground of its site.

H. The Empire State Building has been an iconic location in such films as *King Kong, An Affair to Remember,* and *Sleepless in Seattle.*

J. However, for the impact the building has made on our culture and its sheer iconic design, it will forever be one of the most recognizable and celebrated skyscrapers in the world.

The correct answer is J. It ties up all the information in the paragraph and leaves a lasting impression.

STYLE

Style: everyone wants to have some, and pieces of writing are no different. Style does not necessarily mean making everything tidy and neat or putting everything in its proper place. That is organization. Style means achieving something with a bit of flair; it means eliminating the elements that do not work and taking advantage of the ones that really add some interest…maybe even a little excitement. Style also requires knowing exactly who the audience is and the best way to reach that audience. Style involves tailoring the images, words, tone, and mood of a piece of writing to that audience's particular specifications.

Elements such as ambiguous pronoun references, wordiness, and redundancy are likely to distract any audience and need to be cleaned up or cut out. That's what you will have to do when answering style questions, which make up 15 to 20 percent of the questions on the ACT English test.

Tone and Mood

When you read a piece of writing, you should be able to tell what the writer feels about the topic. Does she or he seem against it or in favor of it? A good piece of writing should also make you feel something. Does it make you happy or sad, angry or soothed?

A piece of writing with style should be written with feeling *and* stir feelings. If it does, then the writer has mastered the tone and mood of the piece.

- **Tone** is the author's attitude toward the subject she or he is discussing.
- **Mood** is the author's way of making the reader feel certain emotions.

 TIP Contractions can help create an informal tone.

Sometimes it is very easy to recognize the tone of a piece. If a writer declares, "I think soft cheeses are disgusting!" it doesn't take a genius to figure out that he is not a fan of soft cheeses. A lot of writers opt for greater subtlety than this.

For some reason, many people have developed a taste for soft cheese.

This writer does not do anything as blunt as declaring soft cheeses "disgusting," but she still makes her opinion known by using the subtle phrase *For some reason*. This phrase indicates that she does not understand the reason many people have developed a taste for soft cheeses, which indicates that she is not one of those soft-cheese-loving people. With that phrase, she makes the tone of her argument clear.

NOTE: Rhetorical skills questions may ask you to identify the audience for a particular piece of writing. To answer such questions, you should think about its tone and mood.

Despite the writer's intentions, different people may react to a piece of writing differently. One person may find an article to be inspirational, while another might think it is utterly boring. Nevertheless, a writer will still put forth his or her best effort to make you feel a particular emotion by manipulating the mood of a piece. Carefully chosen words help establish a particular atmosphere. Let's think of something as mundane as a dog. What if a writer described that dog like this:

The mutt's mile-long tongue dripped drool puddles the size of the Atlantic Ocean.

Have you stopped rolling all over the floor in a fit of laughter yet? Okay, maybe it wasn't that funny, but you can probably tell that the writer was going for a humorous mood by focusing on a sillier aspect of the dog (its drooling) and using absurdly exaggerated descriptions (the dog's tongue was a mile long; the puddles of drool were the size of the Atlantic Ocean).

Another writer may see the same dog and decide to describe it like this:

The snarling mongrel dripped rank saliva from its powerful, snapping jaws.

Well, there's a dog we hope we never have to meet. Although the dog is basically doing the same thing it was in the previous example (drooling), the writer has completely altered the humorous mood by using unpleasant words like *snarling* and *rank* and focusing on the powerful snapping of the dog's *jaws*. Even the decision to refer to the dog as a *mongrel* instead of the somewhat more comical (and slightly affectionate) *mutt* contributes to the threatening mood of this second example.

Writers often signal the tone or mood of their work by using certain key words. The following table provides a small sampling of words they use to indicate negative and positive tones and moods.

Positive Words	Negative Words
adorable	abhorrent
celebratory	annoying
cheerful	angering
comforting	belligerent
comic	bitter
compassionate	boring
confident	cold
delightful	condescending
ebullient	contemptuous
fascinating	derogatory
friendly	despairing
funny	desperate
hilarious	disrespectful
hopeful	dull
joyful	embarrassing
laudatory	frustrating
lively	harsh
passionate	hopeless
playful	lethargic
respectful	melancholy
reverent	miserable
romantic	pathetic
sympathetic	pretentious
whimsical	solemn
	upsetting

One of your many jobs on the ACT English test is to ensure that the tone or mood of a passage is consistent. If a writer seems like he is in favor of a particular topic, and then suddenly seems to take a negative stance without rhyme or reason, this is an error in style and you have to correct it. If a writer seems to be establishing a jolly mood, then suddenly starts dropping in negative words—possibly because she doesn't really understand what they mean—you're going to have to correct that too. Get started by reading this example passage and deciding what to do with its underlined portion in the question that follows:

NOTE: While many types of rhetorical skills questions refer to entire sentences or paragraphs, some use the same underlined portion format of usage/mechanics questions.

When my mother told me she wanted to move in with my wife and me, I was knocked two ways from Sunday. You see: my wife and I had established a quiet little existence in our small suburban house. We were perfectly happy gardening, reading, and doing other activities that would probably bore most normal people to tears. The idea of my <u>tornado of a mom</u> living with us would
8
basically take that happy existence and stomp all over its head.

8. **A.** NO CHANGE
    B. dear mother
    C. maternal caregiver
    D. most beloved family member

The correct answer is A. The underlined portion is ideal as is. *Tornado of a mom* is an interesting and descriptive phrase that precisely describes the image and feel the author wants to convey.

PRECISE AND APPROPRIATE IMAGES AND WORDS

Gigi asked, "Steve, can you please put my stuff in the thing?"

Huh? What exactly is Gigi asking Steve to do? What stuff? What thing? Gigi needs to choose her words more precisely!

Gigi asked, "Steve, can you please put my luggage in the overhead compartment?"

Oh, they're on an airplane! See how much clearer an image we get when reading precise words?

Precise words and images make writing come alive. They help the reader to know exactly what is being discussed and give the reader a clear picture of how things look, sound, feel, and smell.

The moon came up.

So what? The moon comes up all the time. Why should we care that it came up again?

The full moon arose and emitted a glow that bathed the landscape in a soft, enchanting glow.

Wow! That is an image that would get us up off the sofa and go outside to see it for ourselves. So, do you see how precise images can make writing really sparkle?

On the ACT test, you will examine passages to determine whether more precise words and images will make them clearer and more stylish. If a writer lapses into describing specific items as *stuff* and *things*, it's your job as editor to clarify what that writer is trying to say. You will determine the most appropriate words and images by reading the passage carefully and completely.

You will also consider tone and mood when answering questions about precise and appropriate words and images, since the most appropriate ones should suit the overall mood and tone of the passage.

187

Chapter 5

Rhetorical Skills

Try this next example question:

No other artist did more to propel surrealism into the mainstream than Salvador Dali. Dali's bizarre images of melting clocks crawling with ants and elephants with legs as long and thin as stilts can be seen on wall posters, T-shirts, coffee mugs, and calendars throughout the world. Perhaps this is because people respond to the playfulness of his images or the way they resemble the odd dreams that <u>someone experiences</u> while sleeping.
9

9. **F.** NO CHANGE
   G. all the strangest people experience
   H. even the most straight-laced person experiences
   J. a few students experience

The correct answer is H. *Someone* is not a precise enough word. You'll want to look for the most specific and appropriate replacement for words that don't convey any information about a person or thing.

AMBIGUOUS PRONOUN REFERENCES

As we've just seen, using imprecise words and images can really confound readers. Another baffling mistake is the ambiguous pronoun reference.

> *I spent the morning searching for my keys and my wallet, but I found only it.*

Once again, we are going to need some clarification. Specifically, what is *it*? There are two possible antecedents in this sentence: *keys* and *wallet*. The pronoun *it* can refer to only one of them. As this sentence is written, the pronoun reference is ambiguous. The best way to clarify this ambiguity is to get rid of the pronoun completely:

> *I spent the morning searching for my keys, which I found, and my wallet, which I didn't.* (**Correct!**)

> *I spent the morning searching for my keys and my wallet, but I found only my wallet.* (**Also correct!**)

Multiple pronouns can make the ambiguous pronoun situation even more confusing:

> *Solveig and Jelynne were supposed to meet me at 3:00 p.m., but she was stuck in traffic, and she overslept.*

Who was stuck in traffic and who overslept? We can't tell from this sentence.

> *Solveig and Jelynne were supposed to meet me at 3:00 p.m., but Jelynne was stuck in traffic, and Solveig overslept.* (**Correct!**)

Now we know who might need a wake-up call next time.

> **ALERT:** Using the passive voice weakens style. Passive voice is when the action is being done by the subject (*The book was read by me.*) instead of having the subject do the action (*I read the book*).

Ambiguous pronoun references also occur when there is no antecedent at all.

> *I called her but she wasn't home.*

Called who? There are two pronouns in this sentence and no antecedent. We need a specific idea of who is being called for this sentence to be clear.

> *I called my sister but she wasn't home.* (**Correct!**)

So once again, precise words save the day. Now it's your chance to put on the superhero cape and tights and save the day by fixing an example that desperately needs your help:

. . . .

The plot of this novel is riveting, but <u>their</u> prose style was not very involving.
10

10. **A.** NO CHANGE
    B. the pages'
    C. the author's
    D. the plot's

The correct answer is C. The prose style of a novel belongs to its author.

. . . .

A WORD ON WORDINESS

This is the final lesson section of this rhetorical skills chapter of this book, which is a kind of publication, and it discusses an error called wordiness.

In case you didn't notice, the above sentence is an example of that error!

Wordiness occurs when writers get a little overenthusiastic about words. They use more words than necessary. Maybe that's a good strategy if you're a professional writer who gets paid by the word, but you probably won't get a lot of jobs if all your work suffers from wordiness. The simplest way is often the best way. So let's see what we can do to simplify that mess of a sentence that began this lesson. Unfortunately, that means we're going to have to read it again. Here it is:

> *This is the final lesson section of this rhetorical skills chapter of this book, which is a kind of publication, and it discusses an error called wordiness.*

Let's examine the various problems with the sentence.

- You could probably already tell that the lessons in this book are divided into sections. Eliminate the word *section*.

- The second instance of the pronoun *this* is unnecessary. It implies that there is more than one rhetorical skills chapter in this book. Don't worry, there is only one rhetorical skills chapter, and it's almost finished. Eliminate *this*.

- We trust that you already know what a book is. There is no reason to define it as *a kind of publication*.

- In fact, you already know the rhetorical skills chapter is in this particular book, so let's eliminate the mention of this *book* altogether. Eliminating that also eliminates the pronoun *it* that refers to the antecedent *book*.

- The words *lesson* and *rhetorical skills* can be consolidated. This is a rhetorical skills lesson, after all. That eliminates the need for *chapter*.

By making those eliminations, you can construct a clearer and more concise sentence like this:

> *This final rhetorical skills lesson discusses an error called wordiness.*

189

Chapter 5

Rhetorical
Skills

It's time to answer another example question.

There are 120 species of pine trees in the Northern Hemisphere,

<u>but only one species, the Sumatran pine, can</u> be found below
11
the equator.

11. **F.** NO CHANGE
   G. but only the Sumatran pine can
   H. but only one species, a species called the Sumatran pine, can
   J. but only one can

The correct answer is G. Deleting one species, which is not needed, is the most clear and concise way to revise the sentence.

> **ALERT:** Some incorrect answer choices in wordiness questions may delete necessary words as well as unnecessary ones. The correct answers will address the wordiness without depriving the original sentence of its details and meaning.

SUMMING IT UP

- **Supporting examples** and **evidence** support the topic of a passage, but **off-topic** and **redundant details** need to be deleted. Off-topic details are distracting because they introduce ideas that have little or nothing to do with the topic being discussed. Redundant details repeat information needlessly.

- **Appropriate expressions** suit the formal or informal style of a particular piece of writing. Expressions too informal for a formal piece of writing need to be revised. Expressions too formal for an informal piece of writing also need to be revised.

- **Strong opening sentences** hook the reader's interest and set the tone for the rest of the passage.

- **Organizing for clarity** involves placing sentences and paragraphs in the clearest and most logical order. Ideas should flow into each other naturally.

- **Transitional words and phrases** improve the connection of ideas between sentences and paragraphs.

- **Strong closing sentences** bring passages to satisfying conclusions with clarity, impact, and relevance to the overall passage.

- **Tone** is the author's attitude toward the subject she or he is discussing, which is apparent from the words the author chooses. Tone needs to be consistent throughout a piece of writing.

- **Mood** is the author's way of making the reader feel certain emotions, which the author achieves by the use of either positive or negative descriptive words. Mood needs to be consistent throughout a piece of writing.

- **Precise and appropriate images and words** need to be used in place of vague language. Vague language can render ideas and details unclear and uninteresting.

- **Ambiguous pronoun references** occur when a pronoun's antecedent is unclear or missing. A noun needs to be used in place of the ambiguous pronoun.

- **Wordiness** occurs when writers use more words than is necessary, and it renders writing cluttered and unclear. Correcting wordiness involves picking out all of the unnecessary words without deleting any essential details and reconstructing the sentence.

Want to Know More?

Access more practice questions, lessons, helpful hints, and strategies for the following Rhetorical Skills topics in *Peterson's ACT Online Course*.

- Strategy
- Style
- Organization
- Using Modifiers

To purchase and access the course, go to **www.petersons.com/act**.

191

Chapter 5

Rhetorical Skills

PRACTICE

Now it's time to take your second English practice quiz. Read each passage very carefully before answering each question. When you're finished answering all 20 questions, check the answers and explanations that follow to figure out how well you did and why you may have selected some incorrect answer choices.

Feathered Dinosaurs

[1]

⬚1 (1) The image of the dinosaur changed in 1995 when a surprising discovery was made in Liaoning, China. (2) Paleontologists found dinosaur fossils with well-preserved feathers. ⬚2 (3) The iconic lizard-like appearance of the dinosaur had morphed into a more bird-like creature. (4) Some of the common birds include sparrows, pigeons, and seagulls. ⬚3

1. The writer wishes to open Paragraph 1 with a sentence that will set the theme and tone of the passage. Which of the following would most effectively accomplish this?

   A. Most people think of dinosaurs as big scary monsters covered in scales a lot like the ones you can see on an alligator in your local zoo!

   B. For a century and half, the most common concept of the dinosaur was a giant creature with scales not unlike those of an alligator or iguana.

   C. The common image of dinosaurs as large beasts covered in scales was completely changed when scientists realized several dinosaurs actually have feathers.

   D. Dinosaurs in movies always seem to be covered in lizard-like scales, but you'll never see another dinosaur like that after the discovery scientists made in 1995.

2. The writer wishes to improve the transition between Sentences 2 and 3 in Paragraph 1. Which of the following would most effectively accomplish this if placed at the beginning of Sentence 3?

   F. Consequently,
   G. In conclusion,
   H. Suddenly,
   J. In similar fashion,

3. For the sake of unity and coherence, which of the following sentences does NOT belong in Paragraph 1?

   A. Sentence 1
   B. Sentence 2
   C. Sentence 3
   D. Sentence 4

[2]

(1) One dissimilarity Huxley noted was that the *Archaeopteryx* had feathers while the *Compsognathus* did not. (2) However, Huxley may have been wrong on that matter. (3) Actually, scientists had been drawing connections between birds and dinosaurs since the mid-nineteenth century when biologist Thomas Henry Huxley suggested that birds had evolved from dinosaurs. (4) <u>He based his thing</u> on the skeletal similarities between the
4

dinosaur *Campsognathus* and *Archaeopteryx*, the creature generally regarded as the first bird. 5

[3]

The Liaoning discovery of 1995 led to a deeper exploration of the possibility that several dinosaur species had feathers, and *Compsognathus* is believed to be one such dinosaur. Others include the more iconic *Velociraptor* and the mighty *Tyrannosaurus rex*. You heard me right: the *Velociraptor* and the *Tyrannosaurus* had feathers! 6 Considered two of the most threatening dinosaurs,

<u>these fearsome beasts took on a somewhat comic appearance</u>
7
<u>when artists began creating conceptual renderings of them with</u>
7
<u>the feathers scientists believe they sported.</u> However, feathered
7
dinosaurs still did not dominate pre-history. In fact, recent studies indicate that the original concept of the creatures was the most common: most dinosaurs were covered in scales, not feathers. The current theory is that feathers evolved throughout dinosaur history, and though there was the odd early dinosaur with

4.
F. NO CHANGE
G. He based his idea
H. He based his theory
J. He made his thing

5. Which of the following sentence sequences will make Paragraph 2 most logical?

A. NO CHANGE
B. 3, 4, 1, 2
C. 2, 1, 4, 3
D. 1, 2, 4, 3

6. For the sake of unity and coherence, what should the writer do with this sentence?

F. move it to the beginning of the paragraph
G. move it to the end of the paragraph
H. delete it entirely
J. divide it into two sentences at the colon

7.
A. NO CHANGE
B. these fearsome beasts took on a somewhat comic appearance when artists began creating conceptual renderings of them with all the feathers professional scientists believe they sported all over their bodies
C. these fearsome beasts took on a somewhat comic appearance when artists began creating conceptual renderings of them, which are drawings and other kinds of pictures that artists make, with the feathers scientists believe they sported
D. these beasts took on a somewhat comic appearance when artists began creating them with feathers

feathers, feathers did not become more common until closer to the end of the dinosaur age. ⑧

[4]

Still, there is much to learn about which dinosaurs were feathered and when feathers evolved to the point that they were most common. Scientists believe dinosaurs grew feathers because

they provided warmth and attracted mates. So feathers may also
9
have much to teach about basic dinosaur biology. Regardless of which dinosaurs had feathers, when those feathers evolved, and the functions those feathers performed, there is no question that feathered velociraptors and tyrannosauruses have transformed our concept of these fascinating, extinct creatures completely.

8. Which of the following parenthetical statements, when inserted in the preceding sentence, would provide a concrete example of a statement made by the author?

  F. (dinosaurs lived between 230 million years ago and 65 million years ago)

  G. (the Cretaceous period was the final one to see the existence of dinosaurs)

  H. (among the last dinosaurs to walk the earth were the iguanodon, the centrosaurus, the triceratops, and the troodon)

  J. (2014 saw the discovery of the feathered *Kulindadromeus*, a 150 million-year-old herbivore)

9. A. NO CHANGE

  B. that

  C. dinosaurs

  D. those feathers

Question 10 refers to the passage as a whole.

10. Is the writer's decision not to use contractions appropriate in the passage?

  F. No, because it makes the passage inaccessible to a general audience.

  G. No, because it creates an informal tone that is inappropriate for the subject.

  H. Yes, because it creates a formal tone that is appropriate for the nature of the subject.

  J. Yes, because it helps to focus the essay on the feathered dinosaurs.

Goodbye, Car!

[1]

(1)You do not realize how much of a car-culture exists in the suburbs until you move to an urban environment. (2) I lived in the suburbs of Long Island for most of my life. (3) I was born on this little island by Manhattan, and continued to live there when
11
I got my driver's license as a teenager. (4) Like many a suburban dweller, I was hooked on my car. (5) That changed drastically after I moved to the city. (6) That's when I went from being a suburban dweller to a city boy. ⑫

11. A. NO CHANGE

  B. a stone's throw from

  C. around

  D. somewhere near

12. For the sake of unity and coherence, which of the following sentences does NOT belong in the paragraph?

  F. Sentence 1

  G. Sentence 4

  H. Sentence 5

  J. Sentence 6

[2]

Long Island was not <u>without public transportation for getting around on</u>. It had buses and the famous Long Island railroad. However, without any subway system; plenty of garages, driveways, free parking lots, and street parking spots; and a gas station on every corner, Long Islanders were <u>much more likely to own and drive their own cars</u> than take advantage of the buses and trains. I was no different, and the way I used my car now makes me cringe. If I had to pop a letter in the mailbox a block away, I'd literally get into my car and drive <u>it.</u> It was as if I didn't have a pair of functioning legs!

[3]

(1) When I moved to New York City's borough of Brooklyn at the age of 25, I arrived in my car. (2) Yet I discovered a very different environment from that of Long Island. (3) Instead of bucolic streets lined with houses, there were bustling blocks of apartment buildings. ☐16 (4) Parking was hard to come by, and street-sweeping laws meant I had to find a new parking spot almost every day even if I'd found the perfect parking spot and didn't need to use my car again for a while. (5) Those laws meant I could get a parking ticket for leaving my car on the wrong side of the street, and I received my share of tickets during my first year in Brooklyn. ☐17 (6) Furthermore, the abundance of public transportation meant I usually didn't have to use my car anyway. (7) I took the subway to work in Manhattan, and the cost of subway fare was much less than the price of gas. (8) Plus, the less often I drove my car, the less often I needed to get it repaired at an expensive auto shop.

[4]

(1) Since then I have never considered getting another car. (2) Ultimately, I decided my car was more trouble than it was worth and gave it up completely. (3) Aside from the amount of

13. **A.** NO CHANGE
    B. without public transportation
    C. without public transportation for getting around Long Island
    D. without transportation

14. **F.** NO CHANGE
    G. much more likely to own their own cars
    H. much more likely to own cars
    J. much more likely to own and drive their cars

15. **A.** NO CHANGE
    B. that
    C. that one block
    D. my car

16. For the sake of unity and coherence, Sentence 3 in Paragraph 3 should be:
    F. where it is now.
    G. placed at the end of paragraph 3.
    H. placed at the beginning of paragraph 4.
    J. deleted altogether.

17. The writer is considering eliminating Sentence 5 in Paragraph 3. If the writer removed this sentence, the essay would primarily lose:
    A. an example of how laws are created to hurt people, not help them.
    B. the main point of the author's argument against car ownership.
    C. evidence to support the idea that street sweeping laws can cause problems for car owners.
    D. an explanation of what made him finally decide to give up his car and never get another one

money I save (let's not forget about the costs of car insurance or annual inspections, either!), there is also the safety and environmental benefits of using public transportation exclusively. (4) One is much less likely to get injured or worse in a bus or subway than a car. (5) Buses that carry many people cause less air pollution than all the private cars needed to transport those individuals would. 18 19

18. The writer wishes to improve the organization of Paragraph 4. Which of the following would most improve the paragraph?

   F. moving the second sentence to the end of the paragraph

   G. moving the second sentence in front of the first sentence

   H. introducing a new sentence about how cars are more dangerous than buses

   J. deleting the second sentence altogether

19. The writer wishes to improve the conclusion of this paragraph. Which of the following would most effectively accomplish this if placed after the final sentence?

   A. I am not trying to convince anyone else to travel the same route that I did, but I can attest that my life has improved in several ways since I decided to say "goodbye" to my car!

   B. As Booth Tarkington wrote in the novel *The Magnificent Ambersons*, "I'm not sure he's wrong about automobiles…With all their speed forward they may be a step backward in civilization – that is, in spiritual civilization."

   C. I have also begun taking taxicabs more often, though they can actually be very expensive if I'm going a long distance.

   D. But since buses do create some pollution, the very best to get around is to use your feet and walk everywhere.

Question 20 refers to the passage as a whole.

20. Which of the following assignments would this essay most clearly fulfill?

   F. Write a persuasive essay for a general audience about the pros and cons of car ownership.

   G. Write a persuasive essay for an audience of children about road safety.

   H. Write a persuasive essay for an audience of automotive manufacturers about the changing attitudes about car ownership.

   J. Write a persuasive essay for a general audience about something you decided to give up.

ANSWERS AND EXPLANATIONS

1. **The correct answer is B.** This question tests your ability to select the very best opening sentence for the passage. Since the mood of the passage is formal, and referring to dinosaurs as *big scary monsters* is pretty informal, choice A is not the best opening sentence and you can eliminate it. Choice C reveals too much since the paragraph builds to the discovery that some dinosaurs had feathers. Choice D is not the most relevant opening sentence since it dwells on the way dinosaurs look in movies, and this is not something the rest of the passage discusses. Only choice B is a completely relevant opening sentence that suits the tone of the rest of the passage.

2. **The correct answer is H.** This question expects you to choose the best transitional phrase or word. For such questions, it is important to think about what each sentence is doing. Sentence 2 describes a discovery. Sentence 3 describes how that discovery changed long-held perceptions. That change was pretty sudden, so *suddenly* is the best transitional word, and choice H is correct. Choice F would be correct only if there were a cause-and-effect relationship between the sentences. Choice G indicates the drawing of a conclusion when the passage has barely begun. Choice J indicates a comparison, and the author does not compare ideas between Sentences 2 and 3 in Paragraph 1.

3. **The correct answer is D.** This question asks you to eliminate an off-topic sentence from Paragraph 1, which is about how paleontologists discovered that some dinosaurs have feathers. Although birds are related to feathered dinosaurs, they are not the main topic of the paragraph, and a list of types of birds does not belong in it. That means choice D is the best answer. The sentences indicated in choices A, B, and C are all relevant to the topic of the discovery of feathered dinosaurs.

4. **The correct answer is H.** As written, the sentence lacks precise wording. The word *thing* is much too vague, which means choices F and J are incorrect. Choice G is more precise, but it is not the best choice since scientists do not devise scientific *ideas*; they devise scientific *theories*. Choice H is the most precise answer.

5. **The correct answer is B.** This question tests your ability to organize sentences in their most logical order. As Paragraph 2 is originally written, Thomas Henry Huxley's conclusions are discussed before he has been introduced. A good signal that the paragraph is disorganized is the fact that Huxley's full name does not appear until the third sentence. You can also conclude that the first two sentences of the paragraph belong after Sentence 4 since those first two sentences discuss the dinosaur *Compsognathus* and the bird *Archaeopteryx*, which are introduced in Sentence 4. Therefore, choice B describes the best sequence of sentences for the paragraph. Choices A, C, and D do not organize it effectively.

6. **The correct answer is H.** This question expects you to deal with an inappropriate expression. This is a formal scientific passage, and the expression *you heard me right* is very informal. It also shifts the third-person point of view of the overall passage to the second person. Deleting it altogether is the best approach, so choice H is correct. Neither moving the sentence (choices F and G) nor dividing it into two sentences (choice J) makes it any more appropriate.

7. **The correct answer is A.** This sentence is correct as written, so choice A is the best answer. Choices B and C take a perfectly fine sentence and make it wordy. Choice B wastes space by distinguishing that the scientists are *professional* and that the feathers were *all over the bodies of the dinosaurs*. The reader can probably assume that the scientists in question were professional and the feathers were on the dinosaurs' bodies. Choice C wastes space by overexplaining conceptual renderings when the reader can probably figure out what conceptual renderings are from the information in the sentence. Choice D makes the opposite error by deleting necessary details, making it seem as though feathered dinosaurs were fictional monsters created by artists.

8. **The correct answer is J.** The sentence in Paragraph 3 mentions that some early dinosaurs had feathers, and choice J provides an example of one such early, feathered dinosaur. Choice F goes off topic by explaining when dinosaurs lived. Choice G mentions the final dinosaur period, not an early one. Choice H lists an assortment of dinosaurs that lived at the end of the dinosaur era, and we do not even know whether or not they had feathers.

9. **The correct answer is D.** Choice A is incorrect because there is an ambiguous pronoun reference in the sentence as it is originally written. Does *they* refer to

197

feathers or *dinosaurs*? Since it does not make much sense that dinosaurs provided warmth to dinosaurs (were the dinosaurs snuggling with each other?), you can conclude that the best substitute for *they* is *those feathers* (choice D) and not *dinosaurs* (choice C). Choice B just substitutes one ambiguous pronoun for another, and it also introduces a pronoun-antecedent agreement error since *dinosaurs* and *feathers* are both plural, and *that* is a singular pronoun.

10. **The correct answer is H.** The tone of this passage is fairly formal, and since contractions contribute to an informal tone, choice H is the best answer, and choice G can be eliminated. Formal writing does not have to be inaccessible to a general audience, and a general audience will probably grasp this passage with or without contractions, so choice F is not the best answer. Contractions do not create focus, so choice J does not make sense.

11. **The correct answer is B.** As the sentence is originally written, it lacks precise wording. *By* is too vague a word to clearly indicate the relative positions of Manhattan and Long Island, so choice A is not the best answer. Choices C and D are equally vague and can be eliminated. Choice B uses a descriptive idiom to indicate that Long Island is very close to Manhattan. It is the best answer choice.

12. **The correct answer is J.** In Sentence 4, the author explains that he was once a suburban dweller. In Sentence 5, he explains that he moved to the city. He does not need to immediately repeat that information in Sentence 6. It is redundant, which means choice J is the best answer. Choices F, G, and H would all deprive the paragraph of essential details.

13. **The correct answer is B.** As originally written, the sentence is too wordy. The reader should already know the purpose of public transportation, so the additional phrase for *getting around on* is unnecessary and awkward. Therefore, choice A is incorrect. Choice C introduces redundant information to an already wordy sentence by mentioning Long Island a second time. Choice D removes an important detail. Without the word *public* we do not know if the writer is discussing public transportation like buses and trains, or private transportation like a car. Only choice B corrects the wordiness of the original sentence without deleting important information.

14. **The correct answer is H.** As it is originally written, the sentence contains redundant information, so choice F is not the correct answer. The ownership of cars is mentioned twice (Long Islanders were much more likely to *own* and drive their *own* cars). Also, the reader can assume that these car owners also drive their cars, so that detail can be deleted. Only choice H corrects this redundant and wordy sentence. Choice G fails to correct the redundancy. Choice J fails to correct the wordiness.

15. **The correct answer is C.** Choice A is incorrect because there is an ambiguous pronoun reference in the sentence as it is originally written. Is the writer driving the car or the block? We do not know, because he uses the ambiguous pronoun *it*. Choice B is just another ambiguous pronoun, so you can eliminate it. Replacing *it* with the best concrete noun clears up the ambiguity, so you have to decide if the writer intended the pronoun to refer to the car or the block. Try replacing *it* with choices C and D to get a better idea of the best answer. Choice D makes it unclear where or why the writer was driving his car. Choice C makes it clear that he was driving that one block to mail a letter. Choice C is the best answer choice.

16. **The correct answer is J.** Think about what the sentence contributes to the topic of owning a car in the city. Does it contribute anything by explaining how homes in the city were different from the ones in the suburbs? This passage is not about general differences between suburban and urban life; it is very specifically about owning a car in those environments. The sentence does not belong in this passage, and should be deleted as per the instructions in choice J. Leaving it where it is (choice F) or moving it elsewhere in the passage (choices G and H) does not make the sentence any less off topic.

17. **The correct answer is C.** This sentence describes how street sweeping laws often caused the writer to receive parking tickets. Therefore, choice C is the best answer. While the writer probably didn't enjoy getting those tickets, choice A is an extreme conclusion to draw. The sentence describes only one of many reasons the writer decided to give up his car; it is not significant enough to conclude that choices B or D are correct.

18. **The correct answer is G.** The second sentence of Paragraph 4 finds the writer deciding to give up his car once and for all. The rest of the paragraph deals with the consequences of that decision. Therefore, it belongs at the beginning of the paragraph (choice G). Moving the sentence even further from the beginning of the paragraph, as choice F suggests, would make the paragraph even less organized. Since the sentence can function as a strong introduction to the paragraph, deleting it (choice J) is not the best approach. Introducing an extra sentence describing information that already appears later in the passage does not make much sense either, so choice H is wrong.

19. **The correct answer is A.** This question asks you to choose the best closing sentence for a passage that lacks one. Choice A sums up the writer's attitude about car ownership while also tying in the title of the passage, so it is a very effective closing sentence. Good closing sentences often contain quotes, but the one in choice B doesn't suit this passage's friendly, informal tone, and its spiritual element has nothing to do with the rest of the passage. Choice C suddenly introduces a new detail about taxicabs, which is something not discussed elsewhere in the passage, so this answer choice fails to wrap up the discussion well. Choice D contradicts the writer's argument in favor of public transportation and would be a very odd way to close the passage.

20. **The correct answer is J.** Think about what the writer is explaining and the words he uses to explain that. Is this passage particularly technical? It isn't, so it is unlikely he wrote it for an audience of automotive manufacturers (choice H). However, the passage is not particularly simplistic. The complex sentence structure and relatively advanced vocabulary the writer uses suggests he did not write his essay for children. Furthermore, road safety is a very minor discussion point in this passage, so choice G is not the best answer. While the writer's approachable language indicates that he wrote his essay for a general adult audience, he does not describe the pros and cons of car ownership; he discusses only the cons. Therefore, choice F cannot be correct. That leaves choice J as the best answer.

PART IV: MATHEMATICS STRATEGIES FOR THE ACT®

Chapter 6: Pre-Algebra and Elementary Algebra

Chapter 7: Intermediate Algebra and Coordinate Geometry

Chapter 8: Plane Geometry and Trigonometry

MATHEMATICS STRATEGIES FOR THE ACT®

The ACT Mathematics test covers the main concepts from the high school mathematics curriculum, including pre-algebra, elementary algebra, intermediate algebra, coordinate geometry, basic plane geometry, and elementary trigonometry. On test day, you will have 60 minutes to answer 60 multiple-choice questions.

Think of math as a construction project you have to tackle, beam by beam, nail by nail. Your job is to get to the end result—but in order to do so, you need to have the proper tools and to know the most efficient way to use them. This section of Peterson's *ACT® Prep Guide* is your toolkit and your instruction manual. We'll walk you through the nitty-gritty of all the math you will encounter on the exam and show you the best method to find an answer, prove it is right, and move on to the next question.

The exam is very skills-oriented, so while there are indeed many concepts to review, the exam doesn't include tricky questions involving obscure facts or convoluted reasoning. You'll need to know your rules and how to apply them—and that's where this chapter will come in handy as you prepare for your exam.

The three chapters in this section will review the main concepts, formulas, and techniques you should be comfortable with before you take the ACT. In addition to the math review, we'll also give you lots of tips and problem-solving strategies that you can use to efficiently attack problems on this exam, as well as cautionary remarks highlighting potential pitfalls and the most common errors that students make. At the end of each chapter, you will find a 20-question practice exam reviewing the main concepts with test-like questions. Make sure to read through the explanations—each one not only explains why the correct answer is right, but also why you might have arrived at one of the incorrect choices.

Upon completing these three sections, you will be armed with the tools and strategies to be victorious on the ACT Mathematics test! So, without further delay, let's begin with a review of pre-algebra and elementary algebra.

203

Part IV:

Mathematics Strategies for the ACT®

CHAPTER 6:
PRE-ALGEBRA AND ELEMENTARY ALGEBRA

OVERVIEW

- Basic Arithmetic Operations
- Exponents, Radicals, and Approximation
- Basic Logarithms
- Ratios, Proportions, and Percentages
- Linear Equations in One Variable
- Absolute Value
- Algebraic Expressions
- Introduction to Quadratic Equations
- Counting Techniques
- Simple Probability
- Basic Statistics and Data Collection
- Summing It Up
- Practice

205

Chapter 6
Pre-Algebra
and
Elementary
Algebra

This chapter focuses on the main elements of pre-algebra and elementary algebra. It may have been a very long time since you actually considered some of these topics, and you are likely on autopilot when working with numbers and expressions. But there are many subtleties that you may have forgotten, and the majority of questions on the ACT Mathematics test will require you to call upon these concepts. So, even if this material *seems* easy and you feel the urge to skip it, we encourage you to reconsider! It will be worth your review even if just one single concept is made clearer as a result.

BASIC ARITHMETIC OPERATIONS

The study of mathematics begins with the set of **whole numbers**, namely 1, 2, 3, 4... The table below provides a quick way to determine if a number can divide evenly into another whole number—that is, no remainder is produced when dividing.

These are the most common divisibility rules:

Whole Number	A whole number n is divisible by the number in the left column if...
2	the number n ends in 0, 2, 4, 6, or 8.
3	the digit sum of n is divisible by 3.
4	the last two numbers of n, taken as a number in and of itself, is divisible by 4.
5	the number n ends in 0 or 5.
6	the number n is divisible by both 2 and 3.
9	the digit sum of n is divisible by 9.
10	the number n ends in 0.

These rules are useful when determining the factors of a whole number. A whole number n whose only factors are the numbers 1 and n is called **prime**; if it has other factors, it is called **composite**. Every composite number can be written as a product of prime numbers, which is called its **prime factorization**. For instance, $90 = 2 \times 3 \times 3 \times 5$.

> The **digit sum** is the sum of all digits in the numeral n. For example, the digit sum of 234 is $2 + 3 + 4 = 9$, which means it is divisible by both 3 and 9.

Two related concepts are the **greatest common factor (GCF)** and the **least common multiple (LCM)** of two or more whole numbers. The GCF of two whole numbers n and m is the largest whole number that **divides *into both* n and m evenly**. The LCM of two whole numbers n and m is the smallest whole number *into which* both n and m divide.

For instance, consider the whole numbers 8 and 28. Even though 2 is a common factor of both 8 and 28, it is not the *greatest* common factor. Rather, 4 is the GCF. Also, the smallest whole number into which both 8 and 28 divide is 56—this is their LCM. These definitions also apply to three or more whole numbers. See if you can identify the GCF and LCM in this sample question.

Which of the following sets contains two elements with a greatest common factor of 6 and a least common multiple of 72?

- **F.** {6, 30}
- **G.** {12, 18}
- **H.** {18, 24}
- **J.** {24, 72}
- **K.** {6, 144}

The correct answer is H. You should use the answer choices provided to you and test them all out to find the pair of numbers with a greatest common factor of 6 and a least common multiple of 72. If a choice does not meet one of the two conditions, stop and move on—do not bother testing for the other condition.

Choice F: {6, 30}
   GCF = 6; LCM = 30; eliminate
Choice G: {12, 18}
   GCF = 6; LCM = 36; eliminate
Choice H: {18, 24}
   GCF = 6; LCM = 72; DONE!

The set of **integers** is comprised of the whole numbers, their negatives, and 0. We write this as the set {... −4, −3, −2, −1, 0, 1, 2, 3, 4 ...}. Arithmetic involving integers is similar to the arithmetic involving whole numbers, but with the caveat that you must learn how to take negative signs into consideration.

The following rules and terminology are useful when working with integers:

1. $-(-a) = a$, for any integer a	**5.** Sums of positive integers are positive.
2. $a - (-b) = a + b$, for any integers a, b	**6.** Sums of negative integers are negative.
3. An integer is *even* if it is a multiple of 2.	**7.** A product of two negative integers is positive.
4. An integer is *odd* if it is not a multiple of 2.	**8.** A product of one positive and one negative integer is negative.

Here's a handy rule to keep in mind. If you have a product or quotient of more than two integers, count the number of negative signs to determine the sign of the product or quotient. If there is an even number of negative signs, the product or quotient is positive; if there is an odd number of negative signs, the product or quotient is negative.

FRACTIONS AND DECIMALS

A **fraction** is a quotient of two whole numbers, denoted by $\frac{a}{b}$, where $b \neq 0$. The top number is called the **numerator,** and the bottom number is the **denominator.** A fraction is *simplified* or *in reduced form* if the numerator and denominator do not share any common factors.

An important fact to remember through the ACT Mathematics test, which will likely come up in the form of an incorrect answer choice, is that you can never divide by 0! If an answer choice results in a denominator of 0, you know for sure it cannot be correct.

When performing arithmetic operations involving fractions, simplifying all fractions *first* will lead to smaller numbers that are easier to work with.

With that in mind, the **reciprocal** of $\frac{a}{b}$ can be computed by flipping the fraction over to get $\frac{b}{a}$, if, and only if, $a \neq 0$!

Here is a quick reference chart for you that shows how to handle arithmetic operations involving fractions. You can bookmark this page and come back to it if you get caught on a fraction problem and are unsure of the rules and how to apply them.

207

Chapter 6

Pre-Algebra
and
Elementary
Algebra

Arithmetic Operation	Rule (in Symbols)	Interpretation
Adding/Subtracting	$\dfrac{a}{b} \pm \dfrac{c}{d} = \dfrac{ad \pm cb}{bd}$	When fractions have different denominators, first find a common denominator. Apply it to the fractions and then add or subtract the numerators.
Simplifying/Reducing	$\dfrac{a \bullet c}{b \bullet c} = \dfrac{a}{b}$	You can cancel like factors in the numerator and denominator of a fraction to reduce it to lowest terms.
Multiplying by –1	$-\dfrac{a}{b} = \dfrac{-a}{b} = \dfrac{a}{-b}$	When multiplying a fraction by –1, you can multiply either the numerator or the denominator by –1, but NOT both.
Multiplying	$\dfrac{a}{b} \bullet \dfrac{c}{d} = \dfrac{ac}{bd}$	When multiplying two fractions, you can simply multiply their numerators and their denominators.
Dividing	$\dfrac{a}{b} \div \dfrac{c}{d} = \dfrac{a}{b} \bullet \dfrac{d}{c} = \dfrac{ad}{bc}$ $\dfrac{\frac{a}{b}}{\frac{c}{d}}$ means $\dfrac{a}{b} \div \dfrac{c}{d}$	When dividing two fractions, start by converting the quotient into a multiplication problem.

Error	Comment
$\dfrac{a}{b+c} \neq \dfrac{a}{b} + \dfrac{a}{c}$	You cannot pull a fraction apart as a sum of two fractions when the sum occurs in the denominator.
$\dfrac{a}{b} + \dfrac{c}{d} \neq \dfrac{a+c}{b+d}$	When adding fractions, do not simply add the numerators and denominators. First, get a common denominator.
$\dfrac{a}{a+b} \neq \dfrac{\cancel{a}}{\cancel{a}+b}$	You cannot cancel *terms* that are the same in the numerator and denominator. You can only cancel *factors* common to both.

CAUTION There are several errors test-takers often make when working with fractions. You can prevent yourself from choosing incorrect answers on the ACT by avoiding these inequality errors.

Sometimes, fractions will be written as **mixed numbers.** Often, it is easier to convert such a number to an **improper fraction,** or one whose numerator is larger than the denominator. For instance: $4\dfrac{2}{5} = \dfrac{4 \cdot 5 + 2}{5} = \dfrac{22}{5}$.

Don't lose all sense of your rules of arithmetic when a decimal point is introduced into the mix. Arithmetic involving decimal numbers is just like arithmetic involving integers, with the extra step of correctly positioning the decimal point. The same sign conventions for integers (your rules for positives and negatives from page 207) apply here.

The following are some rules of thumb to apply when working with decimal numbers:

- When *adding or subtracting decimal numbers*, line up the decimal points and add or subtract as you would whole numbers, simply keeping the decimal point in the same position.
- When *multiplying* decimal numbers, remove the decimal points and then multiply the numbers as you would whole numbers. Then, to determine the position of the decimal point, count the number of digits after the decimal point in all original numbers being multiplied. Move that number of steps left from the far right of the product, and place the decimal point there.

Any fraction can be converted into a decimal number by dividing the numerator by the denominator. All such decimal numbers will either terminate or repeat. Any decimal number that neither repeats nor terminates is called **irrational.** A **real number** is any number that is either rational or irrational.

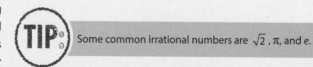
TIP: Some common irrational numbers are $\sqrt{2}$, π, and e.

When performing arithmetic operations on numbers expressed in different ways (e.g., fractions, mixed numbers, and decimal numbers), convert all numbers to the same format and then proceed as usual.

208

Chapter 6

Pre-Algebra
and
Elementary
Algebra

Let's look at some problems in action.

Examples:

Perform the following computations:

1. $3\dfrac{5}{8} \div \dfrac{3}{4} = \underline{\hspace{2cm}}$

2. $(0.02)(-1.4)(-0.3) = \underline{\hspace{2cm}}$

3. $\dfrac{3}{5} - 1.2 - 4\dfrac{1}{2} = \underline{\hspace{2cm}}$

Solutions:

1. $3\dfrac{5}{8} \div \dfrac{3}{4} = \dfrac{29}{8} \div \dfrac{3}{4} = \dfrac{29}{8} \cdot \dfrac{4}{3} = \dfrac{29}{\cancel{4} \cdot 2} \cdot \dfrac{\cancel{4}}{3} = \dfrac{29}{6}$

2. $(0.02)(-1.4)(-0.3) = 0.0084$

3. $\dfrac{3}{5} - 1.2 - 4\dfrac{1}{2} = 0.6 - 1.2 - 4.5 = -5.1$

Now let's look at a conversion question as it might appear on the ACT.

....

$\dfrac{0.0378}{0.21}$ is equal to how many thousandths?

A. 0.180
B. 1.8
C. 18
D. 180
E. 7,938

The correct answer is D. Convert the fraction: $\dfrac{0.0378}{0.21}$, or 180 thousandths. The problem asks how many thousandths, not simply the value of the decimal number to which the quotient is equal. Be careful to read *exactly* what the question is asking for; all of the natural wrong answers will be included among the choices!

209

Chapter 6

Pre-Algebra
and
Elementary
Algebra

....

Scientific Notation

Decimals with several digits before and/or after the decimal point are often expressed using **scientific notation**, a way of writing a complicated decimal as a product of a simpler decimal and a power of 10. For example:

$2{,}345 = 2.345 \times 10^3$ (digits before the decimal point) $0.00000342 = 3.42 \times 10^{-6}$ (digits before the decimal point)

The "simpler decimal" has only one place *before* the decimal point. The power of 10 then tells you how many places the decimal point must move in the simpler decimal to get the original one. For instance, in the first example above, we used the power 3 because the decimal point must move 3 places *to the right* to get from 2.345 back to the original number 2,345. Likewise, in the second example, we used the power −6 because the decimal point must move 6 places *to the left* to get from 3.42 back to the original number 0.00000342.

Now, try some on your own.

Examples:

Rewrite the following two numbers using scientific notation:

1. $0.06054 =$ _____

2. $231.2 =$ _____

Solutions:

1. 6.054×10^{-2}

2. 2.312×10^{2}

Some answers (possibly the correct answer!) on the ACT might be expressed in scientific notation in place of the decimal you originally calculate.

REAL NUMBER PROPERTIES

The following properties apply for *all* real numbers *a, b,* and *c*:

Property Name	Rule (in symbols)	Interpretation
Commutative	$a+b=b+a$ $a \bullet b = b \bullet a$	You can add or multiply real numbers in any order.
Associative	$(a+b)+c=a+(b+c)$ $(a \bullet b) \bullet c = a \bullet (b \bullet c)$	You can group the terms of a sum or a product of more than two terms in any manner you like.
Distributive	$a \bullet (b \pm c) = a \bullet b \pm a \bullet c$	To multiply a sum or difference by a real number, first multiply each term by the number and then add/subtract the results.
FOIL	$(a+b) \bullet (c+d) =$ $a \bullet c + a \bullet d + b \bullet c + b \bullet d$	The acronym FOIL means "First, Outer, Inner, Last" and represents all combinations of terms to be multiplied. FOILing means using the distributive property twice.
Zero Factor Property	If $a \cdot b = 0$, then either $a = 0$ or $b = 0$, or both.	If a product of real numbers is zero, then at least one of the factors must be zero.

The ACT will often ask you to simplify an arithmetic expression involving all types of numbers and operations. In order to do so correctly, you must use the following rules: the **order of operations.**

Step 1: Simplify all expressions contained within parentheses.

Step 2: Simplify all expressions involving exponents.

Step 3: Perform all multiplication and division as it arises from left to right.

Step 4: Perform all addition and subtraction as it arises from left to right.

If there are multiple groupings, apply the same steps *within* each grouping.

To help you remember the correct order of operations, try using the acronym PEMDAS: **P**arentheses, **E**xponents, **M**ultiplication and **D**ivision, **A**ddition, and **S**ubtraction.

Try your hand with these problems.

Examples:

Simplify the following arithmetic expressions using the order of operations.

1. $-2(3-1) + 4 \times 3 - 2 = $ _____

2. $-3[10 - (2+3) \times (1 - (-1))] = $ _____

Solutions:

1. $-2(3-1) + 4 \times 3 - 2 = -2(2) + 4 \times 3 - 2 = -4 + 12 - 2 = 8 - 2 = 6$

2. $-3[10 - (2+3) \times (1-(-1))] = -3(10 - 5 \times 2) = -3(0) = 0$

Don't rush when faced with what looks like basic arithmetic! Work slowly and methodically, and make sure you stick to the rules. Some of the answer choices provided on the ACT are sure to be incorrect solutions that would result if you perform operations in the wrong order.

Read word problems just as you would numerical expressions—carefully, making sure to interpret each sentence so you know what's being asked of you. There will be a question or two on the ACT that is a word problem whose solution requires only basic arithmetic. The trick is to carefully extract the given information and answer the question being asked.

See if you can figure out what's being asked in the word problem below.

• •

A car rental company charges $40 per day for a rental car, plus $0.25 for each mile driven. If Dan kept a car for 5 days and drove 248 miles, what was the cost of the rental?

    A. $445
    B. $262
    C. $200
    D. $150
    E. $62

The correct answer is B. Dan had the car for 5 days, so $5(\$40) = \$200$ for the daily fee. Since he drove 248 miles, the cost of the mileage is $248(\$0.25) = \$62$. So, the cost of the rental is $\$200 + \$62 = \$262$.

• •

EXPONENTS, RADICALS, AND APPROXIMATION

It is convenient to express a product involving multiple identical terms, such as $2 \times 3 \times 3 \times 3 \times 5$, in a more compact manner. This is where exponents come into play. If b and n are natural numbers, then $b^n = \underbrace{b \times \ldots \times b}_{n \text{ times}}$. Here, b is called the **base** and n is the **exponent.**

The table below outlines the properties of exponents that will be useful to know when solving various algebra problems. Again, this is a good table to bookmark and return to as you work to remember exponent rules.

For the following, assume that the bases a and b are greater than 1, and that the exponents n and m are real numbers.

Exponent Rule (in symbols)	Interpretation
$a^0 = 1$	The result of raising any nonzero real number to the zero power is 1.
$a^{-n} = \dfrac{1}{a^n}, \quad a^n = \dfrac{1}{a^{-n}}$	A term in the numerator that is raised to a negative exponent is equivalent to a term in the denominator with the same base, but positive exponent, and vice versa.
$a^n \bullet a^m = a^{n+m}$	When multiplying terms with the same base raised to powers, add the powers.
$\dfrac{a^n}{a^m} = a^{n-m}$	When dividing terms with the same base raised to powers, subtract the powers.
$\left(a^n\right)^m = a^{n \bullet m}$	When raising a term that is already raised to a power to another power, multiply the powers.
$(a \bullet b)^n = a^n \bullet b^n$	When raising a product to a power, apply the power to each term and multiply the results.
$\left(\dfrac{a}{b}\right)^n = \dfrac{a^n}{b^n}$	When raising a quotient to a power, apply the power to each term and divide the results.
If $a = b$, then $a^n = b^n$, for any exponent n.	If two real numbers are equal, then their powers are also equal.

212

Chapter 6

Pre-Algebra
and
Elementary
Algebra

 When you are rushing, it is very common to apply the exponent rules incorrectly and to even make up rules that do not exist! The following are some common misapplication of rules to avoid when working with exponents.

Error	Interpretation
$-a^2 \neq (-a)^2$	If the negative sign is *outside* the parentheses of a quantity being squared, then the square does not apply to it.
$(a+b)^n \neq a^n + b^n$	The power of a sum is not equal to the sum of the powers.
$\dfrac{a^n}{b^m} \neq \left(\dfrac{a}{b}\right)^{n-m}$	You cannot write the quotient of terms with different bases raised to different powers as a single quotient raised to a power.
$a^n \bullet b^m \neq (a \bullet b)^{n+m}$	You cannot write the product of terms with different bases raised to different powers as a single product raised to a power.

Let's do some practice with exponents.

Examples:

Simplify the following expressions using the appropriate exponent rule(s):

1. $(-2)^3 \times 3^{-2} = $ _____

2. $\left(\dfrac{2}{3}\right)^{-3} \bullet \left(2^{-1}\right)^{-2} = $ _____

Solutions:

1. $(-2)^3 \bullet 3^{-2} = \dfrac{(-1)^3 \bullet 2^3}{3^2} = \dfrac{-8}{9} = -\dfrac{8}{9}$

2. $\left(\dfrac{2}{3}\right)^{-3} \bullet \left(2^{-1}\right)^{-2} = \dfrac{2^{-3}}{3^{-3}} \bullet 2^{(-1)(-2)} = \dfrac{3^3}{2^3} \bullet 2^2 = \dfrac{27}{8} \bullet 4 = \dfrac{27}{2}$

The **square root** of a nonnegative real number a is another number b whose square is a—that is $b^2 = a$. In such case, we write $\sqrt{a} = b$.

For instance, $\sqrt{36} = 6$, and $\sqrt{121} = 11$. Note that $(-6)^2$ also equals 36, and $(-11)^2$ also equals 121; therefore -6 and -11 are also square roots of 36 and 121, respectively.

A **cube root** of a real number a is another number b whose cube is a—that is $b^3 = a$. In such case, we write $\sqrt[3]{a} = b$. For instance, $\sqrt[3]{27} = 3$ and $\sqrt[3]{-64} = -4$.

Square roots and cube roots are called **radicals.** In both cases, the a in $\sqrt{a}$ and in $\sqrt[3]{a}$ is called the **radicand**.

The following are useful properties of radicals to master before you take the ACT.

213

Chapter 6

Pre-Algebra
and
Elementary
Algebra

Radical Rule (in symbols)	Interpretation
$\left(\sqrt{a}\right)^2 = a, \ \left(\sqrt[3]{a}\right)^3 = a$	Raising an nth root to the nth power gives back the original radicand.
$\sqrt{a \bullet b} = \sqrt{a} \bullet \sqrt{b}$, when $a \geq 0$ and $b \geq 0$.	The square root of a product is the product of the square roots.
$\sqrt{\dfrac{a}{b}} = \dfrac{\sqrt{a}}{\sqrt{b}}$, when $a \geq 0$ and $b > 0$.	The square root of a quotient is the quotient of the square roots.
$\dfrac{1}{\sqrt{a}} = \dfrac{1}{\sqrt{a}} \bullet \dfrac{\sqrt{a}}{\sqrt{a}} = \dfrac{\sqrt{a}}{a}$, when $a > 0$.	You can clear a square root from the denominator of a fraction by multiplying the numerator and denominator of the fraction by the square root. (This is often called "multiplying by the *conjugate*" or "*rationalizing* the denominator.")
If $0 < a < b$, then $\sqrt{a} < \sqrt{b}$.	If a is less than b, then you can take the square root on both sides of the inequality without having to reverse the sign.

These properties can be used to simplify radicals. For instance:

$$\sqrt{72} = \sqrt{2 \bullet 4 \bullet 9} = \sqrt{2} \bullet \sqrt{4} \bullet \sqrt{9} = \sqrt{2} \bullet 2 \bullet 3 = 6\sqrt{2}$$

ADDING AND SUBTRACTING RADICAL EXPRESSIONS

If the terms you want to add have the *same* radical parts, just add or subtract the coefficients:

$$2\sqrt{5} - 6\sqrt{5} =$$
$$(2-6)\sqrt{5} = -4\sqrt{5}$$

However, terms that have *different* radical parts cannot be combined:

$$3\sqrt{5} + 4\sqrt{7} - 9\sqrt{5} =$$
$$(3-9)\sqrt{5} + 4\sqrt{7} = -6\sqrt{5} + 4\sqrt{7}$$

ALERT: A common error is to apply the radical to each individual term of a sum. Note that the square root of a sum is *not* the sum of the square roots. In this example, note that $-6\sqrt{5} + 4\sqrt{7} \neq (-6+4)\sqrt{5+7}$! The same goes for cube roots.

Let's work through a problem together.

Simplify $\dfrac{56\sqrt{7}}{28\sqrt{42}}$.

Let's use the properties of radicals and apply the rules of multiplying fractions to simplify this expression:

$$\frac{56\sqrt{7}}{28\sqrt{42}} = \frac{2 \bullet 28\sqrt{7}}{28\sqrt{7 \bullet 6}} = \frac{2\sqrt{7}}{\sqrt{7} \bullet \sqrt{6}} = \frac{2}{\sqrt{6}}$$

Finally, we rationalize the denominator (removing its root symbol) by multiplying the numerator and denominator by $\sqrt{6}$:

$$\underbrace{\frac{56\sqrt{7}}{28\sqrt{42}} = \frac{2}{\sqrt{6}}}_{\text{From above}} = \underbrace{\frac{2}{\sqrt{6}} \bullet \frac{\sqrt{6}}{\sqrt{6}}}_{\substack{\text{Rationalizing the} \\ \text{denominator}}} = \frac{2\sqrt{6}}{6} = \frac{\sqrt{6}}{3}$$

APPROXIMATION

Computations often arise in which either numbers are so large that working with them directly is difficult or expressions involve roots or irrational numbers that can make you stop in your tracks and not be able to proceed. In these cases, you should resort to approximation, where you round a number to one that is easier to manipulate. There are a couple of methods that can help you arrive at an answer more quickly when approximating or estimating real numbers.

A common technique is to round large numbers to the nearest thousand, ten thousand, etc. Suppose you want to round a whole number to the nearest thousand. Look at the digit to the immediate right, which in this case is the hundreds place. If that digit is 5 or greater, increase the digit in the thousands place by 1 and replace all digits to its right with zeros; if the digit is 4 or less, keep the thousands place as is and replace all digits to its right with zeros.

For example, 343,783 rounded to the nearest thousand is 344,000, while 214,332,499 rounded to the nearest thousand is 214,332,000. The same technique works when rounding any real number expressed as a decimal number to any place desired.

1,	0	0	0,	0	0	0	.	0	0	0	0
Millions	Hundred thousands	Ten thousands	Thousands	Hundreds	Tens	Ones		Tenths	Hundredths	Thousandths	Ten thousandths

Decimal number place values from millions to ten thousandths.

Estimating roots, such as $\sqrt{47}$ and $\sqrt[3]{11}$, can be tricky. Sometimes, though it's not easy to provide a single estimate, providing a range of values is easier. For instance, it's not easy to compute $\sqrt{47}$. In a case like this, you can determine numbers with more obvious square roots on either side of 47. You know

TIP Rounding the numbers involved in a problem can help you to eliminate some choices right off the bat!

$6^2 = 36$ and $7^2 = 49$ and that $36 < 47 < 49$. Therefore, you know $\underbrace{\sqrt{36}}_{=6} < \sqrt{47} < \underbrace{\sqrt{49}}_{=7}$, so that $6 < \sqrt{47} < 7$. The answer $\sqrt{47}$ must lie somewhere between 6 and 7.

The same trick works for estimating cube roots, except in that case you want to find two numbers for which the cube root, not square root, is easily computed.

Other irrational numbers, such as π and e, enter into computations. Common approximations for these are $\pi \approx 3.14$ and $e \approx 2.718$.

Try this question working with irrational numbers.

. . . .

What is the smallest positive integer value of x for which $x - \sqrt{7} > 7$ is true?

    F. 11
    G. 10
    H. 9
    J. 8
    K. 7

The correct answer is G. Rewrite the inequality to solve for the range of x:

$$x - \sqrt{7} > 7$$
$$x > 7 + \sqrt{7}$$

Since $\sqrt{7}$ is between 2 and 3, $7 + \sqrt{7}$ must be between 9 and 10.

Therefore, the smallest positive integer value of x is 10.

. . . .

ORDERING REAL NUMBERS BY VALUE

A real number p is *less than* another real number q, written $p < q$, if q lies further to the right along the real number line than p. We also say that q is *greater than p*. The same process can be used to compare whole numbers, decimals, and fractions—you can compare two fractions by first converting them to decimal numbers and using the same process.

For instance, $-2 < -\dfrac{7}{5}$, $3 \leq 4.102$, $\pi \geq 3.14$, and $0 > -0.001$.

The questions related to ordering on the ACT Mathematics test can be a bit tricky, primarily because they are often asked in a more abstract manner. That is, they usually involve variables rather than numbers.

TIP When dealing with problems involving variables and inequalities, it is always a good idea to plug in actual numbers to eliminate choices. Always try to find a way to make the problem less abstract!

The following important properties will be very helpful to know when handling these types of questions.

Rule	Explanation
If $0 < a < b$, then $a^n < b^n$, for any positive exponent n.	If a is less than b, then you can raise both sides of the inequality to a positive exponent without reversing the inequality sign. (NOTE: You reverse the inequality sign whenever you multiply or divide both sides by a negative number.)
If $0 < a < b$, then $-b < -a < 0$.	If a and b are both positive, and a is less than b, then the reverse inequality is true for the negatives of a and b.
If $a < b$ and $c < d$, then $a + c < b + d$.	You can add the left sides and right sides of inequalities that have the same signs; the resulting sums satisfy the same inequality.
If $0 < a < 1$, then $a^2 < a$.	Squaring a real number between 0 and 1 produces a smaller real number.
If $a > 1$, then $a^2 > a$.	Squaring a real number greater than 1 produces a larger real number.
If $0 < a < b$, then $\dfrac{1}{b} < \dfrac{1}{a}$.	If a and b are both positive, and a is less than b, then the reverse inequality is true for the reciprocals of a and b.

See if you can solve these ACT-style sample questions.

- -

If $x > y$ and $z > y$, which of the following MUST be true?

- **F.** $z^2 > y^2$
- **G.** $x^2 > y^2$
- **H.** $x > z$
- **J.** $x + z > 2y$
- **K.** $z > x$

The correct answer is J. You know that both x and z are greater than y, but you are not given any information about how they relate to one another. This means that you cannot tell which, if either of them, is greater than the other. So, you can eliminate choices H and K. You might assume that since $x > y$, $x^2 > y^2$, but this is not necessarily true. If $x = 2$ and $y = -3$, for example, then $2^2 < (-3)^2$, making $x^2 < y^2$. This allows you to eliminate choices F and G, leaving choice J as correct. It must be true that $x + z > 2y$ since both x and z are greater than y, their sum must be greater than $2y$.

If $65\% < x < 0.85$, which of the following could be x?

- **A.** $\dfrac{5}{12}$
- **B.** $\dfrac{5}{8}$
- **C.** $\dfrac{2}{5}$
- **D.** $\dfrac{2}{3}$
- **E.** $\dfrac{7}{8}$

The correct answer is D. To compare fractions, decimal numbers, and percentages, convert them all to the same form. Since $65\% = 0.65$, $0.65 < x < 0.85$. Choices A and C are both less than 0.5, so they can be eliminated. As a decimal number, choice B can also be eliminated as too small. As a decimal number, $\dfrac{2}{3} = 0.\overline{66}$. This number does fall between 0.65 and 0.85, so choice D is correct.

- -

BASIC LOGARITHMS

Logarithms are not tested heavily on the ACT Mathematics test, but they do arise occasionally, so it's best to be prepared. A logarithm is simply an exponent. The key formula to remember is $y = \log_a x$ means the same thing as $x = a^y$. So, for instance, $\log_4 64 = x$ can be written as $4^x = 64$, and the answer is, of course, $x = 3$. So, $\log_4 64 = 3$, meaning the quantity $\log_4 64$ is the exponent to which you raise 4 in order to get 64.

Try these logarithm problems on your own.

Examples:

Compute the following logarithms.

1. $\log_2 128 = $ _____

2. $\log_6 1 = $ _____

3. $\log_3 \sqrt{3} = $ _____

Solutions:

1. $\log_2 128 = 7$

2. $\log_6 1 = 0$

3. $\log_3 \sqrt{3} = \dfrac{1}{2}$

RATIOS, PROPORTIONS, AND PERCENTAGES

A **ratio** is a comparison of one quantity x to another quantity y, expressed as a fraction $\dfrac{x}{y}$, or sometimes using the notation $x{:}y$ (read "x to y"). In plain English, this is interpreted as, "For every x of one type, there are y of the second type."

For example, if there are 3 girls to every 1 boy in a class, we say that the ratio of girls to boys is 3:1, or 3 to 1, and write the fraction $\dfrac{3}{1}$. Similarly, if there are 5 dogs for every 2 cats in an animal shelter, we say that the ratio of dogs to cats is 5:2, or 5 to 2, and write the fraction $\dfrac{5}{2}$. We could have instead described the ratio as 2 cats for every 5 dogs, and say the ratio of cats to dogs is 2:5 and write the fraction $\dfrac{5}{2}$. This conveys the same information. However, since $\dfrac{2}{5} \neq \dfrac{5}{2}$, the two ratios are not equal. The order in which the quantities appear in a ratio is important because we represent the ratio as a fraction.

A **proportion** is an equation relating two ratios. In symbols, a proportion is expressed by setting two fractions equal to each other, say $\dfrac{a}{b} = \dfrac{c}{d}$. Proportions arise when solving many different types of problems—you'll use them in problems that ask you to change units of measure and find side lengths of similar triangles.

Proportions are often formulated when one ratio is known and one of the two quantities in an equivalent ratio is unknown. Here is an example of a simple scenario you might see on the ACT:

There are 3 binders for every 5 boxes of pens in a supply closet. If the last count was 80 boxes of pens, how many binders are in the supply closet?

217

Chapter 6

Pre-Algebra
and
Elementary
Algebra

To solve this problem, let b denote the number of binders in the supply closet. You can set up the proportion $\frac{3}{5} = \frac{b}{80}$. To solve for b, cross-multiply to get $3(80) = 5b$, or $240 = 5b$. Dividing both sides by 5 then yields $b = 48$. So, there are 48 binders in the supply closet.

Now, look at this sample question.

. . . .

A new unit of measure called the *wobble* is a unit of length equivalent to 8 inches. If the length of a giraffe's neck is 6 feet, what is the length of the giraffe's neck in wobbles?

    F.   0.11
    G.   7.5
    H.   8
    J.   9
    K.   64

The correct answer is J. First, you know that 1 foot = 12 inches, so 6 feet is equivalent to 6(12) = 72 inches. You are given that 1 wobble = 8 inches, and you want to determine how many wobbles are in 72 inches. Let x be the number of wobbles in 72 inches and set up a proportion:

$$\frac{1}{8} = \frac{x}{72}$$
$$8x = 72$$
$$x = \frac{72}{8}$$
$$x = 9$$

. . . .

 ALERT: The answer obtained by reversing the ratio is sure to be one of the wrong answer choices for ratio and proportion problems!

The word **percent** means "per hundred." A percentage is used to express the number of *parts* of a *whole*. For instance, 34 percent means "34 parts of 100," which can be expressed as the fraction $\frac{34}{100}$ and as the decimal 0.34. It is also denoted as 34%. These three representations are all equivalent.

218

Chapter 6

Pre-Algebra
and
Elementary
Algebra

 To convert from decimal form to percent form, you simply move the decimal point two units to the right and affix the % sign; to convert in the opposite manner, move the decimal point two units to the left, insert a decimal point, and drop the % sign.

Problems involving percentages on the ACT can be whittled down to three basic calculations:

Problem Type	Method Used to Solve the Problem	Example
Compute $x\%$ of y.	Convert $x\%$ to a decimal and multiply by y.	**Q:** Compute 54% of 8. **A:** 0.54(8) = 4.32
What percent of x is y?	Divide x by y.	**Q:** What percent of 150 is 45? **A:** $\frac{45}{150} = 0.30 = 30\%$
x is $y\%$ of what number z?	Convert $y\%$ to a decimal, multiply it by z, and set equal to x. Solve for z.	**Q:** 18 is 40% of what number z? **A:** Solve $0.40z = 18$ for z to get $z = 45$.

Sometimes, questions on the ACT will be as straightforward as one of the examples above. But more likely, you will be given a word problem involving percentages, and you will need to identify which of these scenarios applies. For instance, consider the following problem.

. . . .

Max went out to dinner and paid a total of $36, which included the amount due plus a $9 tip. What percentage of the amount due does this tip represent?

A. 9%

B. 20%

C. 25%

D. $33\frac{1}{3}$%

E. 40%

The correct answer is D. If $36 included the amount due plus a $9 tip, the amount due must have been $36 – $9 = $27. As a percentage of the amount due, $9 represents

$$\frac{\$9}{\$27} \times 100\% = 33\frac{1}{3}\% \cdot$$

Make certain to read the problem carefully! You are asked for the percent of the amount *due*, not the amount *paid*.

. . . .

LINEAR EQUATIONS IN ONE VARIABLE

Linear equations are equations in which the variable is raised to the first power, like $5x = 13$ and $4(y - 1) = 5$. The process of solving linear equations involves simplifying expressions by clearing fractions and using the order of operations and the distributive property of multiplication to get the variable on one side of the equation.

The basic rule to remember is *balance both sides of the equation*. If you add or subtract a number from one side, you MUST do so to the other; if you divide or multiply one side by a number, you MUST do it to the other.

Let's solve an example problem together.

Example: _____

If $3(1 - 2x) + 4(2x - 1) = -x$, what is the value of x^2 ? _____

Solution: _____

First, you must solve the given equation. The order of operations applies to solving linear equations—after all, the variable x represents a real number. Simplify the left side and then get the x-terms on the left side and constants on the right. Then combine like terms, and finally divide by the coefficient of x:

$$3(1 - 2x) + 4(2x - 1) = -x$$
$$3 - 6x + 8x - 4 = -x$$
$$2x - 1 = -x$$
$$2x + x = 1$$
$$3x = 1$$
$$x = \frac{1}{3}$$

219

Chapter 6

Pre-Algebra
and
Elementary
Algebra

Remember to read carefully! Note that you were not asked for the solution, but rather an expression involving it.

So, the final step here is to compute x^2, which is $\left(\dfrac{1}{3}\right)^2 = \dfrac{1}{9}$.

Sometimes, a linear equation can involve more than one variable, and you can be asked to solve for one of them in terms of the others. The same exact procedure applies! For instance, you can solve the equation $y - y_1 = m(x - x_1)$ for x_1 as follows:

TIP. If you are asked to solve a linear equation like this, a quick way to get the solution is to substitute the given choices for the variable. Whichever one results in a true statement, like $1 = 1$, is the solution.

$$y - y_1 = m(x - x_1)$$
$$y - y_1 = mx - mx_1$$
$$y - y_1 - mx = -mx_1$$
$$\dfrac{y - y_1 - mx}{-m} = x_1$$

The fraction on the left side can be expressed in various equivalent ways, and often the correct choice listed will not be the solution you come up with, but rather a variant of your solution. Using the properties of fractions, all of the following are equivalent to this fraction. All of these answers would be correct:

$$\dfrac{-y + y_1 + mx}{m}, \quad \dfrac{y_1 - y + mx}{m}, \quad \dfrac{y_1}{m} - \dfrac{y}{m} + x$$

220

TIP. If a linear equation involves fractions, first multiply both sides of the equation by the LCD of all fractions occurring in the equation. Then, you can just deal with arithmetic involving integers, which is quicker than working with fractions!

Chapter 6

Pre-Algebra and Elementary Algebra

See how this method is put into practice in the following problem.

If $\dfrac{1}{4}y - \dfrac{1}{12} = \dfrac{5}{8}y + \dfrac{3}{4}$, then what is the value of $\dfrac{1}{y}$?

- **A.** 20
- **B.** −11
- **C.** 11
- **D.** $-\dfrac{20}{9}$
- **E.** $-\dfrac{9}{20}$

The correct answer is E. Multiply both sides of the equation by the LCD, 24, to eliminate the fractions. Then solve the equation for y:

$$\frac{1}{4}y - \frac{1}{12} = \frac{5}{8}y + \frac{3}{4}$$
$$24 \bullet \left(\frac{1}{4}y - \frac{1}{12}\right) = 24 \bullet \left(\frac{5}{8}y + \frac{3}{4}\right)$$
$$6y - 2 = 15y + 18$$
$$-20 = 9y$$
$$-\frac{20}{9} = y$$

Therefore, $\dfrac{1}{y} = -\dfrac{9}{20}$

ABSOLUTE VALUE

A **number line** is a convenient way of illustrating the position of real numbers with respect to zero. The integers 7 and −7 are both 7 units away from 0, even though they exist on either side of 0. For any real number a, we use the **absolute value** of a, denoted $|a|$, to measure the distance between a and 0. Since distance is a nonnegative quantity, the definition has two parts:

$$|a| = \begin{cases} a, \text{ if } a \geq 0 \\ -a, \text{ if } a < 0 \end{cases}$$

For instance, $|8| = 8$ and $|-8| = -(-8) = 8$. This definition works for any type of real number: integers, fractions, decimal numbers, or irrational numbers.

The following are some useful properties of absolute value you should master before taking the ACT:

Property (in symbols)	Property (in words)
$|a| = b$ whenever $a = b$ or $a = -b$	The real numbers b and $-b$ are both $|b|$ units from the origin.
$|a \cdot b| = |a| \cdot |b|$	The absolute value of a product is the product of the absolute values.
$\left|\dfrac{a}{b}\right| = \dfrac{|a|}{|b|}$, whenever $b \neq 0$	The absolute value of a quotient is the quotient of the absolute values.

 Remember, when a and b have opposite signs, $|a+b| \neq |a|+|b|$.

For example, $|-5+4| \neq |-5|+|4|$.

The correct way of simplifying $|-5 + 4|$ is by first simplifying the whole expression inside the absolute value bars (much like parentheses). Then, when there is a single number enclosed by the absolute value bars, compute the absolute value.

So, $|-5 + 4| = |-1| = 1$. This is not equivalent to $|-5| + |4|$, which equals 9.

Let's try some practice problems.

Examples:

Simplify these expressions involving absolute value:

1. $-5 - |2 - 6| = \underline{\hspace{2cm}}$

2. $|-5|^{-1} - |-1|^3 = \underline{\hspace{2cm}}$

Solutions:

1. $-5 - |2 - 6| = -5 - |-4| = -5 - 4 = -9$

 When applying the order of operations, treat absolute values like parentheses. Remember PEMDAS: what's inside the parentheses (or in this case, absolute value bars) is always simplified first.

2. $|-5|^{-1} - |-1|^3 = (5)^{-1} - (1)^3 = \dfrac{1}{5} - (1)^3 = \dfrac{1}{5} - 1 = -\dfrac{4}{5}$

Question 2 may look a bit intimidating, but just remember—compute the absolute values first. Then, apply the order of operations as usual.

ALGEBRAIC EXPRESSIONS

A **variable** is an unknown quantity represented by a letter, like x, y, or z. A **constant** is a real number whose value does not change. A **term** is a variable or constant, or products of powers thereof, and an **algebraic expression** is an arithmetic combination of terms, like $5x - 3yz$ or $2xy^3 - 5xz + 3$.

If two terms have the same variables, they are called **like terms.** For instance, $21a^5$ and $-8a^5$ are like terms because they have the same variable: a^5. Likewise, if two terms have different variables—such as $10zy$ and $10xy$—then they are not like terms. Different powers of the same variable—such as $3m^3$ and $4m^6$—are also not like terms. The powers must also be the same.

When evaluating algebraic expressions for specific values of the variables, simply substitute the values in and simplify the arithmetic expression, as in the problem below.

· ·

If $a = 4$, then $3a(a - 1)^2 + a \div 2 = ?$

  A. 56
  B. 108
  C. 110
  D. 194
  E. 216

The correct answer is C. Plug $a = 4$ into the expression:

$$3a(a - 1)^2 + a \div 2 = 3(4)(4 - 1)^2 + 4 \div 2$$

Note that at this point, it is just an **arithmetic expression,** so you follow those rules (specifically the order of operations) to simplify it:

$$3(4)(4-1)^2 + 4 \div 2 = 3(4)(3)^2 + 4 \div 2$$
$$= 3(4)(9) + 4 \div 2$$
$$= 108 + 2$$
$$= 110$$

· ·

Since variables represent real numbers, all of the rules (exponent rules, order of operations, etc.) and properties of arithmetic (commutative property, associative property, etc.) must apply to algebraic expressions.

To add (or subtract) like terms, you add (or subtract) the coefficients of the terms and keep the variable parts the same. For instance: $5x^6 + 8x^6 = 13x^6$.

When multiplying or dividing terms, use the exponent rules just as when simplifying arithmetic expressions. Remember the FOIL method when multiplying two binomials? It is often used when multiplying algebraic expressions. For example:

$$(2x + 3y)(x - 5) = 2x(x) + 2x(-5) + 3y(x) + 3y(-5) = 2x^2 - 10x + 3xy - 15y$$

This same process works for multiplying trinomials and polynomials with even more terms.

>  When expanding the square of a binomial, like $(a + b)^2$, remember that this means $(a + b)(a + b)$, and you must apply the FOIL method. A common error is to distribute the exponent to get $a^2 + b^2$.
> This is incorrect! If you FOIL as in the above example,
> you get $a^2 + \boxed{2ab} + b^2$!

Observe this polynomial term.

. . . .

What is the sum of the polynomials $4ab^3 + 3a^2b^3$ and $-a^2b - 2a^2b^3$?

F. $4ab^3 - a^2b + 3a^2b^3$

G. $3ab^3 + a^2b^3$

H. $3ab^3 + 5a^2b^3$

J. $4ab^3 - a^2b + a^2b^3$

K. $4ab^3 + a^3b + 5a^3b^3$

The correct answer is J. Do not be thrown by the variables—simply combine like terms. In the expression $(4ab^3 + 3a^2b^3) + (-a^2b - 2a^2b^3)$, there are two multiples of a^2b^3. Since $3a^2b^3 + (-2a^2b^3) = a^2b3$, the entire expression simplifies to $4ab^3 - a^2b + a^2b^3$.

. . . .

SIMPLIFYING EXPRESSIONS

The basic rules of factoring are important to review, including factoring out a GCF and factoring differences of squares and basic trinomials. More sophisticated factoring techniques (like factoring differences/sums of cubes, factoring by regrouping, etc.) are not covered on the exam, so you do not need to sweat those! Try the following problems as a quick review of factoring.

Examples:

Factor the following expressions completely:

1. $12x^2y^3 - 4xy^2 + 16x^3y^3 = $ _____

2. $6x^2 + x - 2 = $ _____

3. $2x^2 - 8x - 10 = $ _____

4. $x^2 - 81 = $ _____

Solutions:

1. $12x^2y^3 - 4xy^2 + 16x^3y^3 = 4xy^2(3xy - 1 + 4x^2y)$

2. $6x^2 + x - 2 = (3x + 2)(2x - 1)$

3. $2x^2 - 8x - 10 = 2(x + 1)(x - 5)$

4. $x^2 - 81 = (x - 9)(x + 9)$

The exponent rules are also applicable when simplifying algebraic expressions. Try the following problems to practice manipulating exponents when working with variables instead of whole numbers.

Examples:

Simplify the following algebraic expressions:

1. $(3a^2b)^2 = $ _____

2. $\dfrac{v^{-3}\left(wx^2\right)^3}{w^2xv^2} = $ _____

223

Chapter 6

Pre-Algebra
and
Elementary
Algebra

Solutions:

1. $(3a^2b)^2 = 3^2a^4b^2 = 9a^4b^2$

2. $\dfrac{v^{-3}\left(wx^2\right)^3}{w^2xv^2} = \dfrac{v^{-3}w^3x^6}{w^2xv^2} = \dfrac{w^3x^6}{v^3w^2xv^2} = \dfrac{w^3x^6}{w^2xv^2} = \dfrac{1}{v^{-1}} \cdot \dfrac{w^3x^6}{w^2xv^2} \cdot \dfrac{wx^5}{v^5} = vwx^5$

EXPRESSIONS IN WORD PROBLEMS

One of the most challenging parts of algebra, and a major part of the ACT Mathematics test, is translating words describing a math scenario into symbols. Several word problems involving arithmetic, linear equations, systems of equations, basic geometry, and elementary triangle trigonometry are typically included on the ACT, so it is definitely in your best interest to practice solving them.

When creating an algebraic expression, equation, or inequality that describes a relationship between one or more quantities, you must first identify what the unknowns are and how many of them you have. Use a different letter for each unknown. Then, identify common words and phrases (like *is*, *of*, *less than*, *greater than*, etc.) and translate them, piece by piece, into algebraic expressions.

Let's try some practice problems.

Example:

Translate the following statements into algebraic expressions.

1. A number is three less than two times another number. _____

2. The square of the sum of two numbers is greater than 4. _____

3. The sum of two numbers is twice the product of two other numbers. _____

Solutions:

1. $x = 2y - 3$

2. $(x + y)^2 > 4$

3. $x + y = 2wz$

INTRODUCTION TO QUADRATIC EQUATIONS

Another common type of equation is a **quadratic equation,** which is an equation in the form $ax^2 + bx + c = 0$, where a, b, and c are real numbers and $a \neq 0$. There can be 0, 1, or 2 solutions to a quadratic equation. The methods you can use to solve these equations include factoring, the quadratic formula, and completing the square. We will give you an in-depth look at factoring in this section.

To master the process of solving a quadratic equation by factoring, it's important to follow these steps in order every time. First, put the equation into the standard form $ax^2 + bx + c = 0$. Take note! Do NOT factor until you put the equation in this form—zero MUST be on one side of the equation before you proceed.

224

Chapter 6

Pre-Algebra
and
Elementary
Algebra

Next, if possible, factor the quadratic expression into a product of two factors. Once factored, set each factor equal to zero and solve for x.

For example, let's look at $6x^2 + x = 2$.

First, rewrite the equation in the correct form: $6x^2 + x - 2 = 0$.

Next, factor the left side to get an equivalent equation that is the product of two factors: $(3x + 2)(2x - 1) = 0$.

Finally, set each factor equal to zero and solve for x:

$$3x + 2 = 0 \implies x = -\frac{2}{3}$$

$$2x - 1 = 0 \implies x = \frac{1}{2}$$

So the solutions of the equation are $-\frac{2}{3}$ and $\frac{1}{2}$.

 TIP When you are able to factor the expression into a product of two factors, it is possible that there is only one factor, but it will be squared.

Examples:

Determine the real solutions of the following quadratic equations.

1. $5x^2 + 35x = 0$ _____

2. $x^2 + 11x + 10 = 0$ _____

3. $9x^2 + 6x + 1 = 0$ _____

4. $x^2 - 144 = 0$ _____

5. $x^2 + 4 = 0$ _____

Solutions:

1. $5x^2 + 35x = 5x(x + 7) = 0$, so $x = 0, -7$

2. $x^2 + 11x + 10 = (x + 10)(x + 1) = 0$, so $x = -10, -1$

3. $9x^2 + 6x + 1 = (3x + 1)^2 = 0$, so $x = -\frac{1}{3}$ (NOTE! Only one solution!)

4. $x^2 - 144 = (x - 12)(x + 12) = 0$, so $x = -12, 12$

5. $x^2 + 4 = 0$ does not have real solutions.

 ALERT: The expression $a^2 + b^2$ does NOT factor!

225

Chapter 6

Pre-Algebra
and
Elementary
Algebra

COUNTING TECHNIQUES

There are two main types of counting problems that commonly occur on the ACT Mathematics test.

One type of problem will ask you to determine the number of combinations that can be formed from *a* of quantity 1, *b* of quantity 2, *c* of quantity 3, etc. Assuming that order is not important and that all of the quantities are different, you simply need to multiply *a*, *b*, *c*, together.

Example:

A deli offers a lunch special composed of a salad, a beverage, and a dessert. The deli serves 7 kinds of salads, 5 kinds of beverages, and 3 kinds of desserts. How many different lunch special combinations are possible?

Solution:

There are 7 kinds of salads, 5 kinds of beverages, and 3 kinds of desserts, so there are a total of $7 \times 5 \times 3 = 105$ possible lunch combinations.

In another type of counting problem, you will be asked to find the number of ordered arrangements of *n* objects.

Example:

At a track meet, five athletes are running a relay race, and the coach records the order in which they cross the finish line. In how many different orderings can these five athletes cross the finish line, assuming that ties are not allowed?

Solution:

To get started, note there are five possible people that could cross the finish line first. Now that one athlete is out of the running, how about the second place? Well, there are 4 remaining athletes, any of whom can come in second. So, at this point, there are 5×4 ways of getting the first- and second- place winners. We are not yet done! There are 3 remaining athletes, any of whom can come in third place. So, there are $5 \times 4 \times 3$ different ways of getting the first-, second-, and third-place winners. Continuing in a similar way, there are $5 \times 4 \times 3 \times 2$ different ways in which the first four athletes can cross the finish line, leaving the fifth athlete as the only one who can come in fifth place. So, all told, there are $5 \times 4 \times 3 \times 2 \times 1$ such orderings. We write this expression more compactly using **factorials;** that is, we write $5! = 5 \times 4 \times 3 \times 2 \times 1$.

Try a practice problem much like one you might see on the exam.

· ·

A group of four friends meets four days a week to study. For each meeting, a different friend is responsible for bringing snacks, and nobody is allowed to bring snacks on more than one day. In how many different ways can the friends be matched up with the day on which they are each responsible to bring the snacks?

    A. 10
    B. 12
    C. 24
    D. 64
    E. 120

The correct answer is C. Let us call the days A, B, C, and D. There are four different ways to assign the friend responsible for bringing snacks on day A. Once that is decided, that friend can no longer bring snacks on the remaining three days, leaving three choices for day B. Similarly, there are then two options for day C, and only one for day D. As such, just as in the example, we multiply $4 \times 3 \times 2 \times 1$ to get the total number of orderings. This product is 24.

· ·

SIMPLE PROBABILITY

All experiments that involve uncertainty or chance (e.g., predicting the stock market or weather, guessing the percentage of votes a candidate will receive, or simply flipping a coin) involve probability.

The result of a single trial of a probability experiment is called an **outcome.** The collection of all outcomes is the **sample space**, which is written as a set. For instance, if you roll a typical six-sided die and record the number of the face on which it comes to rest, the outcomes are the labels on the faces: $S = \{1, 2, 3, 4, 5, 6\}$. An **event** is a subset of the sample space and is usually described using one or more conditions. For instance, the event that "the die lands on an odd number" is the subset $E = \{1, 3, 5\}$.

Suppose E and F represent events of some probability experiment. Some common events formed using them are as follows:

Event	Description in words
E or F	All outcomes in E or in F or in both
E and F	All outcomes in common to E and F
Complement of E	All outcomes NOT in E

You are likely familiar with the notion of chance, such as the percent chance of snow today or the likelihood that a professional baseball player will hit a home run. The **probability** of an event A, denoted by $P(A)$, is a number between 0 and 1, inclusive, that describes the percent chance that event A has of occurring.

How do you determine the probability of an event? The answer can be rather complicated, but for most of the experiments you will encounter, each outcome in the sample space is *equally likely*. So, if the sample space contains N outcomes, then the probability of any *one* of them occurring is $\frac{1}{N}$.

This can be extended to events in the sense that if A contains k elements, then $P(A) = \dfrac{\text{Number of outcomes in } A}{\text{Number of possible outcomes}} = \dfrac{k}{N}$.

For the above dice experiment, since the event "the die lands on an odd number" is the subset $E = \{1, 3, 5\}$, and all outcomes are equally likely, $P(E) = \dfrac{3}{6} = \dfrac{1}{2}$. So, there's a 50% chance of the die landing on an odd number, which is intuitive!

Take a look at this probability question.

. . . .

A board game involves a spinner with congruent sections numbered 1 through 25. On a given spin, the spinner has an equal chance of landing on any number. What is the probability that the spinner will land on a number that is divisible by 3?

- **A.** $\dfrac{17}{25}$
- **B.** $\dfrac{14}{25}$
- **C.** $\dfrac{8}{25}$
- **D.** $\dfrac{7}{25}$
- **E.** $\dfrac{3}{25}$

The correct answer is C. There are a total of 25 numbers on the wheel, so we must determine how many of these 25 numbers are divisible by 3. Writing them down, we see that 3, 6, 9, 12, 15, 18, 21, and 24 are precisely the numbers from 1 to 25 that are divisible by 3. Since there are 8 of them and 25 numbers in all, the probability that the number on which the spinner lands is divisible by 3 is $\dfrac{8}{25}$.

. . . .

BASIC STATISTICS AND DATA COLLECTION

Statistics is a collection of procedures and principles used for gathering data and analyzing information that aids in making decisions and inferences when faced with uncertainty. Suppose you have certain data—such as the number of sit-ups you can do in 75 seconds, or the number of people who attend different yoga classes at a local studio. Each measurement in the data set originates from a distinct source called a **unit**. The complete collection of units about which information is sought is called the **population**. A **variable** is a characteristic of the population of units we are interested in, and the **data** are the observed values of a variable.

There are two main types of variables: qualitative and quantitative. A **qualitative** variable is one with values that are categories (e.g., gender, hair color, demographic information). There is not a unique numerical ordering of these outputs. A **quantitative** variable is one whose values are numerical quantities (e.g., height, temperature, number of heads obtained in three flips of acoin).

It is rarely possible to collect data for each and every unit in a population because resources are often limited. So, a representative subset of the population of units, called a **sample,** is chosen for which you will attempt to gather information for the variable of interest.

An ideal sample should be reasonably large. For instance, if the population of your study were the entire U.S. population, you would not want to choose your sample to consist of merely eight people from Connecticut. The sample should also be devoid of bias. A study is **biased** if it systematically favors certain outcomes. For instance, suppose you were investigating a question in which females would likely respond differently than males, and that your population was equally split between males and females. In such case, a sample consisting of 98 percent males could potentially yield biased results.

COMPUTING MEAN

Questions involving data and statistics on the ACT will sometimes require you to compute the average (or **mean**) of a list of numbers in some applied context. To compute the mean of a list of numbers, simply add the numbers and then divide by how many numbers you added:  $\text{mean} = \dfrac{\text{sum of values}}{\text{number of values}}$

228

Chapter 6

**Pre-Algebra
and
Elementary
Algebra**

> **CAUTION**
>
> You must include any zeros in the total count when computing a mean.
>
> For instance, the mean of the set {0, 2, 5, 6, 7}
>
> is $\dfrac{0+2+5+6+7}{5}=4$, not $\dfrac{0+2+5+6+7}{4}=5$.

SUMMING IT UP

- The **greatest common factor** (GCF) of two whole numbers n and m is the largest whole number that divides into both n and m evenly. The **least common multiple** (LCM) of two whole numbers n and m is the smallest whole number into which both n and m divide.

- The **order of operations** when simplifying an expression is first parentheses, then exponents, then multiplication and division from left to right, and finally addition and subtraction from left to right.

- If b and n are natural numbers, then $b^n = \underbrace{b \times \ldots \times b}_{n \text{ times}}$. Here, b is called the **base** and n is the **exponent.**

- **Scientific notation** is simply a way of expressing a number as a product of a decimal number between 1 and 10 and an appropriate power of 10.

- The **square root** of a nonnegative real number a is another number b whose square is a, that is $b^2 = a$. In such case, we write $\sqrt{a} = b$. A **cube root** of a real number a is another number b whose cube is a, that is $b^3 = a$. In such case, we write $\sqrt[3]{a} = b$.

- A **logarithm** is simply an exponent. When working with logarithms, remember that $y = \log_a x$ means the same thing as $x = a^y$.

- A **ratio** is a comparison of one quantity x to another quantity y, expressed as a fraction $\dfrac{x}{y}$, or sometimes using the notation $x{:}y$.

  In words, this is interpreted as, "for every x of one type, there are y of the second type." A **proportion** is an equation relating two ratios. In symbols, a proportion is expressed by setting two fractions equal to each other, say $\dfrac{a}{b} = \dfrac{c}{d}$.

- **The word *percent* means "per hundred."** A percentage is used to express the number of *parts* of a *whole*.

- **Linear equations** are equations in which the variable is raised to the first power. The process of solving linear equations involves simplifying various expressions by clearing fractions and using the order of operations and the distributive property of multiplication in order to get the variable on one side of the equation.

- The **absolute value** of a, denoted $|a|$, measures the distance between a and 0.

- A **variable** is an unknown quantity represented by a letter, like x, y, or z; a **constant** is a real number whose value does not change.

- An **algebraic expression** is an arithmetic combination of terms. All of the rules (exponent rules, order of operations, etc.) and properties of arithmetic (commutative property, associative property, etc.) must apply to algebraic expressions.

- **Like terms** are two or more terms that have the same variables.

- A **quadratic equation** is an equation of the form $ax^2 + bx + c = 0$, where a, b, and c are real numbers, and $a \neq 0$.

- **There are two main types of counting problems assessed on the ACT:**

  1. If you want to determine the number of combinations that can be formed from a of quantity 1, b of quantity 2, c of quantity 3, assuming that order is not important and that all of the quantities are different, you simply need to multiply a, b, c, together.

  2. The number of ordered arrangements of n objects is $n!$

- An **outcome** is the result of a single trial of a probability experiment. The collection of all outcomes is the **sample space**. An **event** is a subset of the sample space and is usually described using one or more conditions.

- The **probability** of an event A, denoted by $P(A)$, is a number between 0 and 1, inclusive, that describes the percent chance that event A has of occurring.

  - If each outcome in the sample space is *equally likely* and the sample space contains N outcomes, then the probability of any *one* of them occurring is $\dfrac{1}{N}$.

    This can be extended to events in the sense that if A contains k elements, then $P(A) = \dfrac{\text{Number of outcomes in } A}{\text{Number of possible outcomes}} = \dfrac{k}{N}$.

  - To compute the **mean** of a list of numbers, simply add the numbers and divide by how many numbers are added:

$$\text{mean} = \frac{\text{sum of values}}{\text{number of values}}.$$

229

Chapter 6

Pre-Algebra
and
Elementary
Algebra

Access more practice questions, lessons, helpful hints, and strategies for the following pre-algebra and elementary algebra topics in *Peterson's ACT Online Course*:

- Averages
- Converting Fractions
- Factoring
- Fractions and Decimals
- Inequalities
- Number Properties
- Operations with Fractions
- Percents
- Powers and Roots
- Probability
- Quadratics
- Ratios
- Solving Equations
- Word Problems

To purchase and access the course, go to ***www.petersons.com/act***.

230

Chapter 6

Pre-Algebra and Elementary Algebra

PRACTICE

Now it's time to take your first mathematics practice quiz. When you're finished answering all 20 questions, check the answers and explanations that follow to figure out how well you did and why you may have selected an incorrect answer choice.

1. If $\frac{n}{4}$ and $\frac{n}{14}$ are both integers, all of the following could

    be n EXCEPT:

    A. 56
    B. 70
    C. 112
    D. 168
    E. 224

2. If $\frac{x^3 y^2}{z}$ is negative, then which of the following could

    be true?

       I. x and z are both negative.
      II. x is negative and z is positive.
     III. x is zero.

    F. I only
    G. II only
    H. I and II
    J. II and III
    K. I, II, and III

3. In order to set up the Internet connection in a computer lab, the following amounts of cable are needed for each computer in the lab:

       2 cables, each measuring 3 feet
       3 cables, each measuring 9 inches
       1 wire, measuring 5 feet

    If the room requires 25 computers and cable costs $0.15 per inch, approximately how much will it cost to set up the computers for the lab?

    A. $23.85
    B. $72.00
    C. $159.00
    D. $596.25
    E. $3,975.00

4. $(0.01)^{-3} =$

    F. 10^{-6}
    G. 10^{-5}
    H. 10^{-3}
    J. 10^3
    K. 10^6

231

Chapter 6

Pre-Algebra
and
Elementary
Algebra

5. What is the largest possible value for the product xy if $x + y = 20$ and x and y are both prime numbers?

A. 19
B. 36
C. 51
D. 91
E. 96

6. Which of the following is the prime factorization of 3,780?

F. $2^2 \times 3^3 \times 35$
G. $2 \times 3 \times 5 \times 7$
H. $2^2 \times 3^3 \times 5 \times 7$
J. $2 \times 3^2 \times 5 \times 6 \times 7$
K. $2^2 \times 3^4 \times 5 \times 7$

7. If x is a real number such that $x^3 = 160$, between which two consecutive integers does x lie on the number line?

A. 2 and 3
B. 3 and 4
C. 4 and 5
D. 5 and 6
E. 6 and 7

8. If $\log_6 216 = x$, then $x =$

F. $\dfrac{\log 216}{6}$
G. $\sqrt[6]{216}$
H. 36
J. 3
K. 6^{216}

9. Phillip answered 4 of the 35 questions on his driving exam incorrectly. What percentage of the questions did Phillip answer correctly?

A. $\dfrac{4}{35} \times 100\%$

B. $\dfrac{31}{35} \times 100\%$

C. $\dfrac{4}{35 \times 100}\%$

D. $\dfrac{31}{35 \times 100}\%$

E. $\dfrac{31}{100\%} \times 35$

232

Chapter 6

Pre-Algebra
and
Elementary
Algebra

10. Increasing a positive number by 40% and then decreasing the result by 30% is the same as which of the following?

    F. Increasing the original number by 10%
    G. Increasing the original number by 12%
    H. Decreasing the original number by 12%
    J. Increasing the original number by 2%
    K. Decreasing the original number by 2%

11. The ratio of butter to chocolate chips in a cookie recipe is 2:3. If $2\frac{1}{4}$ cups of butter are used, how many cups of chocolate chips are used?

    A. $\frac{2}{3}$

    B. $1\frac{1}{2}$

    C. 3

    D. $3\frac{3}{8}$

    E. 5

12. If $3x + 2 = 9x + 14$, then $4x^3 =$

    F. -108
    G. -32
    H. -24
    J. -2
    K. 32

13. $-6 - |-6| =$

    A. -12
    B. -6
    C. 0
    D. 6
    E. 36

14. For real numbers a, b, and c, $a < b$ and $c < 0$. Which of the following inequalities must be true?

    F. $ab > 0$
    G. $ac < 0$
    H. $a + c < 0$
    J. $\dfrac{a}{c} > \dfrac{b}{c}$
    K. $\dfrac{a}{c} < \dfrac{b}{c}$

233

Chapter 6

Pre-Algebra and Elementary Algebra

15. What is the value of $m^2 - 6mn^3 + n$ when $m = -2$ and $n = -1$?

   A. -17
   B. -13
   C. -9
   D. 9
   E. 17

16. Which of the following is equivalent to $(-4x^3)^2$?

   F. $-4x^5$
   G. $-3x^6$
   H. $-16x^6$
   J. $8x^6$
   K. $16x^6$

17. Which of the following is the completely factored form of $6d^4e^2 - 18de^3$?

   A. $6(d^4e^2 - 18de^3)$
   B. $6de^2(d^3 - 3e)$
   C. $6(d^4e^2 - 18de^3)$
   D. $6d(d^3e^2 - 3e^3)$
   E. $-12d^3e^{-1}$

18. There is only one real solution for x for the equation $4x^2 + 12x = k$. Which of the following could be k?

   F. 0
   G. 4
   H. 9
   J. -9
   K. -18

19. A bag contains only white, yellow, and purple cubes. There are a total of 40 cubes in the bag, and the probability of NOT selecting a yellow cube is $\frac{3}{4}$. How many yellow cubes are in the bag?

   A. 4
   B. 5
   C. 8
   D. 10
   E. 30

234

Chapter 6

Pre-Algebra
and
Elementary
Algebra

20. A lab technician took a measurement of new rainfall once a day during a five-day work week. The table below indicates how many inches of new rainfall were recorded on each day.

Day	Inches of New Rainfall
Monday	1.0
Tuesday	1.5
Wednesday	0
Thursday	1.0
Friday	0.5

What is the average number of inches per day for this work week?

- **A.** 4
- **B.** 1
- **C.** 0.8
- **D.** 0.4
- **E.** 0

1. **The correct answer is B.** Since $\frac{n}{4}$ and $\frac{n}{14}$ are both integers, then n must be divisible by both 4 and 14. The question asks for the one value that does *not* satisfy this condition, so you are looking for the one choice that is not divisible by both 4 and 14. Since it is difficult to do this by inspection, start with the first one and move through the list until you find the correct number.

Choice A: 56

$56 \div 4 = 14$; $56 \div 14 = 4$; eliminate

Choice B: 70

$70 \div 4 = 17$ with remainder 2; $70 \div 14 = 5$; correct

Once you have determined that B is the correct choice, stop here!

Each of the remaining choices are numbers that are divisible by both 4 and 14.

2. **The correct answer is G.** In order for the expression to be negative, you must have an odd number of negative signs. Since y is squared, the term y^2 cannot be negative. However, both x^3 and z are negative whenever x and z are negative, respectively.

Statement I is false because if x and z are both negative, then x^3 and z are both negative, making the quotient positive. Statement II is true because if x is negative, then so is x^3. So, you have a quotient with one negative term all told; so, it must be negative. Statement III is false because if $x = 0$, the entire quotient is zero and thus not negative. Using this information, you can conclude that choice G is the correct answer and that all other choices are incorrect.

3. **The correct answer is D.** First, get the total inches for each type of cable. Two 3-foot cables are $2 \times 3 = 6$ feet, which converts to $6 \times 12 = 72$ inches. Three 9-inch cables are $3 \times 9 = 27$ inches. And the last cable is $5 \times 12 = 60$ inches. Adding together the inches for all cables gives $72 + 27 + 60 = 159$ inches of cable needed to connect *one* computer to the Internet. At a cost of $0.15 per inch, the cost of connecting one computer in the lab to the Internet is $159(\$0.15) = \$23.85$. Hence, the cost of connecting all 25 computers to the Internet is $25(\$23.85) = \$596.25$. So, choice D is correct.

Choice A is the cost of connecting one computer to the Internet, not 25 of them. Choice B is only the number of inches for two cables measuring 3 feet each. Choice C is incorrect because each computer requires 159 inches of cable for the Internet setup, but this is neither the cost of doing so for one computer nor the cost for doing so for all 25 computers in the lab. Choice E is the number of inches of cable needed to connect all 25 computers in the lab to the Internet.

4. **The correct answer is K.** The value in parentheses, 0.01, can be rewritten as 10^{-2}.
Therefore, $(0.01)^{-3} = (10^{-2})^{-3} = 10^{(-2)(-3)} = 10^6$.

Choice F is incorrect because 0.01 equals 10^{-2}, not 10^2. In choice G, you added the exponents, but should have multiplied them. Choice H is incorrect because the value in parentheses is 10^{-2}, not 10. Choice J is incorrect because the value in parentheses is 10^{-2}, not 10^{-1}.

5. **The correct answer is D.** Two pairs of prime numbers sum to 20: $3 + 17$ and $7 + 13$. The largest resulting product is $7 \times 13 = 91$, so 91 is the largest possible value of xy if x and y are both prime numbers for which $x + y = 20$. So, choice D is the correct answer.

Choice A represents a common math mistake—be careful, because the number 1 is not considered to be prime. Choice B is the result of using 2 and 18, but 18 is not prime. Choice C is the smaller of the two such products. Choice E is the result of using 8 and 12, neither of which is prime.

6. **The correct answer is H.** A prime factorization is the product of the powers of the prime factors of a whole number. The prime factorization of 3,780 is $2^2 \times 3^3 \times 5 \times 7$. The best way to get the prime factorization is by using the divisibility rules. In choice G, although 2, 3, 5, and 7 are the prime factors of 3,780, both 2 and 3 occur more than once in the correct factorization. Choices F and J involve non-prime numbers, and so can be eliminated immediately. Choice K contains one too many factors of 3.

Try to eliminate as many choices as possible first. Here, since choices F and J involve non-prime numbers and you are looking for the prime factorization, they can be eliminated immediately.

236

Chapter 6

Pre-Algebra
and
Elementary
Algebra

7. The correct answer is D. The problem is asking you to find two consecutive integers, the first of which has a cube less than 160, and the second of which has a cube greater than 160. Use the answer choices to help you. The cubes of 2, 3, 4, 5, and 6 are, respectively: 8, 27, 64, 125, and 216. Since 160 falls between 125 and 216, you know that x is between 5 and 6, and you do not need to go any further. As such, the other choices are not possible.

8. The correct answer is J. The equation $\log_6 216 = x$ is the same as saying $6^x = 216$. Note that $6^3 = 216$, so that the answer is 3, which is choice J.

Choice F is incorrect because the denominator should be $\log_6$, not just 6. Choice G is incorrect because $\log_6 216 = x$ is equivalent to $6^x = 216$, not $216^{\frac{1}{6}} = \sqrt[6]{216} = x$. For choice H, $6^2 = 36$, not 216.

Choice K is incorrect because $\log_6 216 = x$ is equivalent to $6^x = 216$, not $6^{216} = x$.

9. The correct answer is B. If Phillip answered 4 of the 35 questions incorrectly, then he answered $35 - 4 = 31$ correctly. By definition, the percentage is equal to $\dfrac{\text{part}}{\text{whole}} \times 100\%$. So, Phillip answered $\dfrac{31}{35} \times 100\%$ of the questions correctly, which is choice B.

Choice A is the percentage of questions he answered *incorrectly*. Choice C is incorrect because the 100 should be in the numerator so that you are taking a proportion of 100%; even then, the result would be the percentage he answered *incorrectly*. Choice D is incorrect because the 100 should be in the numerator so that you are taking a proportion of 100%. For choice E, you need to interchange the 35 and 100 in this expression.

10. The correct answer is K. Let x represent some number. Increasing the number by 40% produces the new number $(1 + 0.40)x = 1.40x$. Now, decreasing this result by 30% means to subtract 30% of $1.40x$ from $1.40x$: $(0.30)(1.40x) = 0.42x$, and subtracting this from $1.40x$ yields $0.98x$. So, comparing this to the original number x shows that the end result is $0.02x$ less than x. You could have decreased the number by 2% to arrive at the same result. Therefore, the answer is K.

TIP: If thinking with variables is problematic for you, you can follow the same process by using a specific number for x, for example, 100.

Choice F is incorrect because you cannot simply add or subtract percentages unless they are being applied to the same amount. In choices G and H, you multiplied 0.40 times 0.30, but this implies that the percentages both serve to increase a quantity or decrease a quantity to which they are being applied; here, one percentage is an increase and the other is a decrease. For choice J, your calculations are likely correct, but the end result is $0.98x$, which is smaller than x, not larger than it—the process described leads to a *decrease*, not an increase.

11. The correct answer is D. Set up a proportion to determine the number of cups of chocolate chips needed for the recipe, setting this unknown equal to x. Cross-multiply to solve for x:

$$\frac{2}{3} = \frac{2\frac{1}{4}}{x}$$

$$\frac{2}{3} = \frac{\frac{9}{4}}{x}$$

$$2x = 3\left(\frac{9}{4}\right)$$

$$2x = \frac{27}{4}$$

$$x = \frac{27}{8} = 3\frac{3}{8}$$

Choice A, the ratio itself, is not the number of cups of chocolate chips needed. You must set up a proportion to solve for this unknown. In choice B, you inverted half of the proportion before solving for x. Choice C is incorrect because you can't round down; you should give the exact answer. In choice E, you simply multiplied the two quantities in the ratio; you must set up a proportion to solve for this unknown.

12. The correct answer is G. First, solve the given equation for x:

$$3x + 2 = 9x + 14$$
$$2 = 6x + 14$$
$$-12 = 6x$$
$$-2 = x$$

Now, evaluate $4x^3$ at $x = -2$ to get $4(-2)^3 = 4(-8) = -32$. So choice G is the correct answer.

Choice F would imply $x = -3$, not -2. For choice H, when computing $(-2)^3$, you multiplied the base times the exponent, but this is not how you compute a power. For choice J, this is the value of x, not $4x^3$. For choice K, this should be negative, not positive.

13. **The correct answer is A.** First, note that $|-6| = 6$. So $-6 - |-6| = -6 - 6$. Now, just add these integers as usual to get -12. So, the correct answer is A.

   For choice B, you dropped one of the two terms from the expression. For choice C, $-|-6| = -6$, not 6. For choice D, since $-6 - |-6| = -6 - 6$ and you are

   adding two negative integers, the result cannot be positive. For choice E, you multiplied -6 and $-|-6|$ instead of adding them.

14. **The correct answer is J.** If you divide both sides of the inequality $a < b$ by c, since c is negative, you must reverse the inequality sign when doing so. This yields the inequality $\dfrac{a}{c} > \dfrac{b}{c}$. So choice J is the correct answer.

   For choice F, if $a = -3$ and $b = 2$, then $a < b$, but $ab < 0$, not > 0. For choice G, take $a = -5$, $b = -3$, and $c = -1$. Note that $ac > 0$. For choice H, take $a = 4$, $b = 5$, and $c = -1$. Note that $a + c = 3 > 0$. For choice K, you need to reverse the inequality sign.

15. **The correct answer is C.** Plug the given values of m and n into the expression and evaluate:

$$
\begin{aligned}
m^2 - 6mn^3 + n &= (-2)^2 - 6(-2)(-1)^3 + (-1) \\
&= 4 - 6(-2)(-1) - 1 \\
&= 4 - 12 - 1 \\
&= -8 - 1 \\
&= -9
\end{aligned}
$$

   In choice A, you said $m^2 = -4$ when it is actually 4. In choice B, you dropped m^2 from the expression. Choice D should be -9, not 9. In choice E, you disregarded all negative signs throughout the expression.

16. **The correct answer is K.** For this problem, it is important to remember the rules of exponents. When a product is raised to a power, each of the terms must be raised to that power. So $(-4x^3)^2$ is equal to $(-4)^2 \times (x^3)^2$. When a power is raised to another power, you multiply the exponents. So $(-4)^2 \times (x^3)^2$ is equal to $(-4)^2 \times (x^6)$. Now evaluate: $(-4)^2 \times (x^6) = 16 \times (x^6) = 16x^6$.

   In choice F, note that $\left(a^b\right)^c \neq a^{b+c}$; you must apply the exponent to the coefficient, -4, as well. Choice G is incorrect because you must apply the exponent to the coefficient, -4. In choice H, you forgot to square the -1. In choice J, $(-4)^2 = (-4)(-4)$, you do not multiply the base times the exponent.

17. **The correct answer is B.** To factor the expression, look for terms that are common to both quantities. For example, 6 can be divided out of both terms, as can d and e^2. Thus, you can factor out $6de^2$, leaving $(d^3 - 3e)$. So, the completely factored form is: $6de^2(d^3 - 3e)$.

   In choice A, you forgot to factor the 6 out of the second term, and the GCF actually consists of more than just 6; it also includes powers of d and e. Choice C is incorrect because the GCF actually consists of more than just 6; it also includes powers of d and e. In choice D, the expression is not *completely* factored; you can still factor out e^2. In choice E, you cannot subtract unlike terms by subtracting their coefficients and exponents in this manner.

18. **The correct answer is J.** If a quadratic equation of the form $ax^2 + bx + c = 0$ has only one solution, or root, it means that the expression on the left can be factored as a binomial squared, or $(Mx + N)^2$. First, put the given equation in standard form:

$$
4x^2 + 12x - k = 0
$$

   If you substitute $k = -9$, you get the expression $4x^2 + 12x + 9 = 0$ on the left side, which factors as $(2x + 3)^2$, which implies the equation has only one real solution: $-\dfrac{3}{2}$.

   All other choices of k lead to an expression that cannot be written in the form $(Mx + N)^2$. So, the equations corresponding to the other choices of k either have two real solutions or no real solutions.

19. **The correct answer is D.** If the probability of NOT selecting a yellow cube is $\dfrac{3}{4}$, then the probability of selecting a yellow cube is $1 - \dfrac{3}{4} = \dfrac{1}{4}$. Let x represent the number of yellow cubes in the bag. Set up the following proportion to solve for x:

$$
\frac{1}{4} = \frac{x}{40}
$$
$$
40 = 4x
$$
$$
10 = x
$$

   Therefore, there are 10 yellow cubes in the bag.

   Choice A is incorrect because it would mean that the probability of not selecting a yellow cube is $\dfrac{9}{10}$, not $\dfrac{3}{4}$. Choice B is incorrect because it would mean that the probability of not selecting a yellow cube is $\frac{7}{8}$,

not $\frac{3}{4}$. Choice C is incorrect because it would mean

that the probability of not selecting a yellow cube is

$\frac{4}{5}$, not $\frac{3}{4}$. Choice E is the number of cubes in the

bag that are NOT yellow.

20. **The correct answer is C.** Remember that

$$average = \frac{\text{sum of values}}{\text{number of values}}.$$ To find the average

number of inches of rainfall per day for this data, divide
the total number of inches of rainfall for the week by the
number of days, 5:

$$\frac{(1.0+1.5+0+1.0+0.5)}{5}=\frac{4.0}{5}=0.8$$

So, the mean daily rainfall is 0.8 inches.

Choice A is the total number of inches of rain
recorded for the entire week; you must divide this by
5 (the number of measurements) to get the mean. In
choice B, you divided the total number of inches by 4
instead of 5; remember, you must include "0" data
values among the number of measurements. In
choice D, you divided the total number of inches by
10, not 5. Choice E is incorrect because it would
imply that there was absolutely no rain during
this week.

239

Chapter 6

**Pre-Algebra
and
Elementary
Algebra**

CHAPTER 7: INTERMEDIATE ALGEBRA AND COORDINATE GEOMETRY

OVERVIEW

- Lines
- Rational Expressions
- Radical Expressions
- Complex Numbers
- Quadratic Equations and the Quadratic Formula
- Linear Inequalities
- Systems of Linear Equations

- Basic Coordinate Geometry
- Functions
- Modeling
- Sequences
- Matrices
- Summing It Up
- Practice

Now that you have brushed up on your pre- and elementary algebra skills in Chapter 6, we'll start building upon those foundations to tackle the next level of ACT Mathematics: intermediate algebra and coordinate geometry. Before you begin this chapter, you should feel confident about the math we presented in the last chapter—go ahead and give it another review if you still feel shaky on the concepts, because most of the information here will combine many of the rules and practices we covered before.

You'll notice that this chapter contains a lot of formulas that give you a direct path to finding correct answers. As we mentioned before, the ACT assumes you have knowledge of basic formulas (which include most of the ones we present in this chapter). Many times, there will be a way to figure out an answer without using a formula—but rest assured, if you study and master the tactics in this chapter, you will be armed with the fastest and most efficient way to answer questions on test day.

LINES

Knowing how to work with lines and linear equations in two variables is an important part of succeeding on the ACT Mathematics test. Let's review the basic features of lines and look at several common ACT problem types.

THE EQUATION OF A LINE

The two most common forms you will see for the equation of a line are **standard form** ($Ax + By = C$), and **slope-intercept form** ($y = mx + b$). In these, A, B, C, m, and b represent real numbers. The more useful of these is the slope-intercept form, since the two numbers m and b actually tell you something about the graph of the line. First, b is the line's **y-intercept,** meaning that the graph of the line crosses the y-axis at the point $(0, b)$. Next, m indicates the **slope** of the line, which measures steepness of the line, or the change in y-value per unit change in x-value.

If you have two points on the line, say (x_1, y_1) (x_2, y_2), the slope is the change in y over the change in x, which we calculate as shown here:

$$m = \frac{y_1 - y_2}{x_1 - x_2} = \frac{y_2 - y_1}{x_2 - x_1}$$

 ALERT: Make certain to always subtract the y-coordinates in the same order as the x-coordinates. Otherwise, you will get the negative of the correct slope.

- If m is positive, the graph of the line rises from left to right.
- If m is negative, it falls from left to right.
- If $m = 0$, then the equation becomes $y = b$ and the graph is a horizontal line—all points have a y-coordinate of b.

Likewise, the graph of the equation $x = a$ is a vertical line (where $y = 0$). All points in this line have an x-coordinate of a, and such a line is said to have an **undefined slope**.

If you are given a point (x_1, y_1) on a line and you know its slope m, then you can find the **point-slope** form for the equation using the formula $y - y_1 = m(x - x_1)$.

 TIP: There is no reason to first determine the y-intercept of the line if you have these two pieces of information. Note that if you solve this equation for y and simplify, you will get the following: $y = mx + \underbrace{(-mx_1 + y_1)}$
This is the y-intercept b

Here are some common ACT math problems that ask you to find the equation of a line, along with the best method of attack for each.

Problem Type	Method of Attack
1. Given a point and a slope (either written or by way of a graph), determine the equation of the line.	Use the point-slope formula immediately.
2. Given two points on a line (either written or by way of a graph), determine the slope or the equation of the line.	First, find the slope of the line. (If this is what the question asks for, you are done.) Use the point-slope formula to find its equation.
3. Given a table of points that describe a linear relationship between variables x and y, determine the equation of the line.	Use any two of the points to find the slope. Then, use any of the points from the table with the slope to find the equation of the line.
4. Given a scenario in which two quantities are related linearly, find the equation of the line, or determine the value of one of the variables given the value of the other.	Identify one quantity as the input (x) and the other as the output (y). Typically, the input variable x is the quantity you change; the output variable y is the quantity you observe. Extract information from the description—either two points or a point and slope. Proceed as above.

For all of the problem types listed in the table, depending on the way the choices are listed, you might then need to put the equation into slope-intercept form or standard form.

Consider the following sample question.

. . . .

Suppose that the points $(1, -5)$ and $(2, -1)$ lie on a line. Which of the following is the equation of this line?

A. $y = x - 8$

B. $y = 4x - 9$

C. $y = 4x + 9$

D. $y = x + 8$

E. $y = \dfrac{1}{4}x - 9$

The correct answer is B. First, determine the slope:

$$\text{slope} = m = \frac{-5 - (-1)}{1 - 2} = 4$$

Using the point $(2, -1)$ with the point-slope formula, the equation of the line passing through these two points is $y - (-1) = 4(x - 2)$. This is equivalent to $y = 4x - 9$.

. . . .

 ALERT: Be careful with the negative signs when using a point that has a negative coordinate, as in this case. The equation obtained by subtracting incorrectly will likely be among the choices.

Now, let's look at another question.

. . . .

What is the y-intercept of the line represented by the equation $8x + 4y = 20$?

F. $\dfrac{1}{2}$

G. 2

H. 4

J. 5

K. 8

The correct answer is J. Put the equation into slope-intercept form, $y = mx + b$, where b is the y-intercept:

$$8x + 4y = 20$$
$$4y = -8x + 20$$
$$y = -2x + 5$$

This shows that the y-intercept of the line is 5.

Your first step should always be to put the equation into slope-intercept form. A common mistake people often make is thinking the constant term 20 in the equation $8x + 4y = 20$ is the y-intercept, which is incorrect.

. . . .

PARALLEL AND PERPENDICULAR LINES

Consider two lines whose equations are $y = m_1x + b_1$ and $y = m_2x + b_2$. The lines are **parallel** if the slopes are the same (i.e., $m_1 = m_2$) and **perpendicular** if the product of the slopes is -1 (i.e., $m_1 \times m_2 = -1$).

By definition, lines are parallel if they lie on a plane, always the same distance apart, and never meet.

Perpendicular lines intersect each other on a plane at right (90-degree) angles.

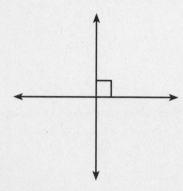

A common question on the ACT will ask you to compare two lines, or to use information about the relationship between two different lines to determine the equation of one of the lines.

For instance, consider the following problem:

Lines m and n are perpendicular in the standard (x, y) coordinate plane below. Which of the following is the equation for line m?

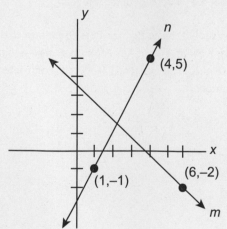

- **F.** $x - 2y = 2$
- **G.** $x + 2y = 1$
- **H.** $x + 2y = 2$
- **J.** $2x + y = -14$
- **K.** $2x - y = 14$

The correct answer is H. First, we need to determine the equation of line n. The slope of n is $\frac{5-(-1)}{4-1} = 2$. Using the point $(4, 5)$ and this slope with the point-slope formula, we see that the equation of n is $y - 5 = 2(x - 4)$, which simplifies to $y = 2x - 3$. Since this line is perpendicular to line m, the slope of m must be $-\frac{1}{2}$ (since the product of these slopes must be -1).

Using the point $(6, -2)$ on m with the point-slope formula yields the equation $y - (-2) = -\frac{1}{2}(x - 6)$, which simplifies to $y = -\frac{1}{2}x + 1$. Since the choices are given in standard form, we must go one step further to write this as $x + 2y = 2$.

RATIONAL EXPRESSIONS

Do you remember the arithmetic rules for fractions? If you need to brush up on the rules, do a quick review of Chapter 6, because we're going to take the math one step further now—working with fractions that have expressions in the numerator and denominator.

The math here is similar to what you have already seen—you simply add, subtract, multiply, and divide polynomials like you did before and cancel like factors in the top and bottom as you would when simplifying a fraction involving only numbers.

Let's look at a few examples in action and solve the following problems.

Examples:

1. Simplify: $\dfrac{8x^2+2x-3}{1-2x}$. _____

2. Add and simplify: $\dfrac{2x-4}{x^2-1}+\dfrac{3-x}{x^2-1}$. _____

3. Subtract and simplify: $\dfrac{x}{5-2x}-\dfrac{1}{2+x}$. _____

4. Multiply and simplify: $\dfrac{2x^2+2x}{x^2-4}\bullet\dfrac{x+2}{x^2-1}$. _____

Solutions:

1. First, factor the numerator and see if anything can be canceled in the top and bottom:

$$\frac{8x^2+2x-3}{1-2x}=\frac{(4x+3)(2x-1)}{-(2x-1)}\quad\text{Factor!}$$

$$=\frac{(4x+3)\cancel{(2x-1)}}{-\cancel{(2x-1)}}\quad\text{Cancel like factors in top and bottom}$$

$$=-(4x+3)$$

Note that we factored a –1 out of the denominator. Always be on the lookout for negatives when factoring—a common error (and likely one of the incorrect answer choices) is a final expression that drops the –1.

2. In this case, we can simply add the numerators while keeping the denominator the same because the two fractions already have the same denominator. Then, we simplify the result as much as possible:

$$\frac{2x-4}{x^2-1}+\frac{3-x}{x^2-1}=\frac{2x-4+3-x}{x^2-1}\quad\text{Combine the fractions.}$$

$$=\frac{x-1}{x^2-1}\quad\text{Simplify.}$$

$$=\frac{\cancel{x-1}}{\cancel{(x-1)}(x+1)}\quad\text{Factor and cancel like factors in top and bottom.}$$

$$=\frac{1}{x+1}$$

3. First, find a common denominator—remember, you can't add or subtract without one. You can simply multiply the denominators already present: $(5 - 2x)(2 + x)$. Express both fractions using this denominator, and then combine and simplify:

$$\frac{x}{5-2x} - \frac{1}{2+x} = \frac{x(2+x)}{(5-2x)(2+x)} - \frac{5-2x}{(5-2x)(2+x)}$$

$$= \frac{x^2+2x}{(5-2x)(2+x)} - \frac{5-2x}{(5-2x)(2+x)}$$

$$= \frac{x^2+2x-5+2x}{(5-2x)(2+x)}$$

$$= \frac{x^2+4x-5}{(5-2x)(2+x)}$$

$$= \frac{(x+5)(x-1)}{(5-2x)(2+x)}$$

Note that the final expression cannot be simplified further since there are no factors common to the top and the bottom.

4. Factor all expressions and then cancel those common to the top and bottom:

$$\frac{2x^2+2x}{x^2-4} \bullet \frac{x+2}{x^2-1} = \frac{2x\,(x+1)}{(x-2)\,(x+2)} \bullet \frac{x+2}{(x+1)\,(x-1)} = \frac{2x}{(x-2)(x-1)}$$

Beware—do not multiply the numerators and the denominators *before* factoring. Doing so will create a huge mess that is nearly impossible to simplify.

 TIP If you are asked to *divide* two rational expressions, the process is practically identical to multiplication, with the additional step of first rewriting the division problem as a multiplication problem, just as with division of numerical fractions.

Let's look at three more.

. . . .

Simplify the following rational expression: $\frac{x^2-y^2}{5x-5y}$.

A. $\frac{x-y}{5}$

B. $\frac{5}{x+y}$

C. $\frac{x+y}{5}$

D. $\frac{1}{5}$

E. $\frac{x^2-5x}{y^2-5y}$

The correct answer is C. First, factor both the numerator and denominator of the fraction, and then cancel any common factors:

$$\frac{x^2-y^2}{5x-5y} = \frac{(x-y)(x+y)}{5\,(x-y)} = \frac{x+y}{5}$$

. . . .

If x and y are positive numbers, $\dfrac{x}{5} - \dfrac{2}{y} =$

F. $\dfrac{xy-2}{5y}$

G. $\dfrac{xy-10}{5+y}$

H. $-\dfrac{2x}{5y}$

J. $\dfrac{xy-10}{5y}$

K. $\dfrac{x-2}{5-y}$

The correct answer is J. To solve, you need a common denominator. The common denominator is $5y$. Write the first fraction, $\dfrac{x}{5}$, as an equivalent one with a denominator of $5y$: $\dfrac{y}{y} \bullet \dfrac{x}{5} = \dfrac{xy}{5y}$.

Likewise, rewrite the fraction after the minus sign as one with a denominator of $5y$: $\dfrac{5}{5} \times \dfrac{2}{y} = \dfrac{10}{5y}$. Since the denominators are now the same, you can subtract: $\dfrac{xy}{5y} - \dfrac{10}{5y} = \dfrac{xy-10}{5y}$.

If $a = xy$ and $b = y^2z$, what is $\dfrac{b}{a}$ in terms of x, y, and z?

A. $\dfrac{yz}{x}$

B. $\dfrac{x}{z}$

C. $\dfrac{x}{yz}$

D. $\dfrac{xy}{z}$

E. xy^3z

The correct answer is A. You are given the values of a and b in terms of x, y, and z, so substitute these into the expression $\dfrac{b}{a}$.

Then you have $\dfrac{b}{a} = \dfrac{y^2z}{xy}$, which reduces to $\dfrac{yz}{x}$ using exponent rules.

 **CAUTION** Make certain you divide in the correct order. A common error is to compute the reciprocal, $\dfrac{a}{b}$.

RADICAL EXPRESSIONS

In the previous chapter, we covered the rules for simplifying radicals. As a quick review, try solving the following practice questions.

Examples:

 **TIP** The exponent rules you learned in Chapter 6 also apply to algebraic expressions!

Simplify the following arithmetic expressions involving radicals:

1. $\left(3\sqrt{5}\right)^2 = $ _____

2. $(4+\sqrt{3})(5-\sqrt{3}) = $ _____

Solutions:

1. $\left(3\sqrt{5}\right)^2 = 3^2 \bullet \left(\sqrt{5}\right)^2 = 9 \bullet 5 = 45$

2. $(4+\sqrt{3})(5-\sqrt{3}) = 4 \bullet 5 - 4 \bullet \sqrt{3} + 5 \bullet \sqrt{3} - \left(\sqrt{3}\right)\left(\sqrt{3}\right) = 20 + \sqrt{3} - 3 = 17 + \sqrt{3}$

The same rules used in the previous questions can also be used to simplify more complicated algebraic expressions involving radicals. Try your hand at the next three examples:

Examples:

1. Suppose that x, y, and z are positive real numbers. Simplify the following radical expression:

$\sqrt{8x^8y^2z^3} = $ _____

2. Suppose that x, y, and z are positive real numbers. Simplify the following radical expression:

$\dfrac{\sqrt{64x^3y^5}}{xy\sqrt{y}} = $ _____

3. Simplify the following algebraic expressions involving radicals:

   a) $\left(2-\sqrt{x}\right)\left(x+3\sqrt{x}\right) = $ _____

   b) $2\sqrt{a^5b^3c} \bullet \sqrt{abc^2} = $ _____

Solutions:

1. Two properties are at play here, namely $\sqrt{a \bullet b} = \sqrt{a} \bullet \sqrt{b}$ and $\sqrt{a^2} = a$ whenever $a > 0$.

   The idea is to express the radicand as a product of squared terms and everything that is left over.

   Employing that strategy, we see that:

   $$\sqrt{8x^8y^2z^3} = \sqrt{2} \bullet \sqrt{4} \bullet \sqrt{\left(x^4\right)^2} \bullet \sqrt{y^2} \bullet \sqrt{z^2} \bullet \sqrt{z}$$
   $$= \sqrt{2} \bullet 2 \bullet \left(x^4\right) \bullet y \bullet z \bullet \sqrt{z}$$
   $$= 2 \bullet x^4 \bullet y \bullet z \bullet \sqrt{2} \bullet \sqrt{z}$$
   $$= 2 \bullet x^4 \bullet y \bullet z \bullet \sqrt{2z}$$

2. This problem is similar to the previous example, but now we need to simplify a rational expression. Indeed, we have:

   $$\frac{\sqrt{64x^3y^5}}{xy\sqrt{y}} = \frac{\sqrt{8^2x^2 \bullet x \bullet y^4 \bullet y}}{xy\sqrt{y}}$$
   $$= \frac{8x \bullet y^2 \bullet \sqrt{xy}}{x \bullet y \bullet \sqrt{y}}$$
   $$= \frac{8\cancel{x} \bullet y\cancel{^2} \sqrt{x} \bullet \cancel{\sqrt{y}}}{\cancel{x} \bullet \cancel{y} \bullet \cancel{\sqrt{y}}}$$
   $$= 8y\sqrt{x}$$

3. **a)** $\left(2-\sqrt{x}\right)\left(x+3\sqrt{x}\right) = 2x+6\sqrt{x}-x\sqrt{x}-3\left(\sqrt{x}\right)^2 = 2x+6\sqrt{x}-x\sqrt{x}-3x = -x+6\sqrt{x}-x\sqrt{x}$

   b) $2\sqrt{a^5b^3c} \bullet \sqrt{abc^2} = 2\sqrt{\left(a^5b^3c\right) \bullet \left(abc^2\right)} = 2\sqrt{a^6b^4c^3} = 2a^3b^2c\sqrt{c}$

COMPLEX NUMBERS

Remember that the square root of a negative real number is *not* a real number. However, it is **imaginary**, meaning that it involves *i*, where $i^2 = -1$. We can use this to further simplify some radicals. For instance:

$$\sqrt{-36} = \sqrt{-1} \bullet \sqrt{36} = i \bullet 6 = 6i$$

$$\sqrt{81} - \sqrt{-125} = 9 - \sqrt{-1} \bullet \sqrt{125} = 9 - i \bullet 5\sqrt{5} = 9 - 5i\sqrt{5}$$

A **complex number** is a number of the form $a + bi$, where a and b are both real numbers. The number a is called the **real part** and the number b is called the **imaginary part.** The following are the basic rules of arithmetic and some important computations involving complex numbers:

Definition (in Symbols)	Definition (in Words)
Sum $(a + bi) + (c + di) = (a + c) + (b + d)i$	When adding complex numbers, add the real parts and the imaginary parts separately, and form the complex number using those sums.
Difference $(a + bi) + (c + di) = (a + c) + (b + d)i$	When subtracting complex numbers, subtract the real parts and the imaginary parts separately, and form the complex number using those differences.
Product $(a + bi) \bullet (c + di) = (ac + bd) + (bc + ad)i$	To multiply two complex numbers, apply the FOIL technique and use the fact that $i^2 = -1$.
Complex Conjugate The *complex conjugate* of $z = a + bi$ is $a - bi$.	To form the complex conjugate of a complex number, change the sign of the imaginary part, but leave the real part the same.
Quotient $\dfrac{a + bi}{c + di} = \dfrac{a + bi}{c + di} \bullet \dfrac{c - di}{c - di}$ $= \dfrac{(ac + bd) + (bc - ad)i}{c^2 + d^2}$	To divide two complex numbers, multiply top and bottom by the conjugate of the denominator and simplify.

See how these rules can be applied in the next problem.

. . . .

Which of the following is equivalent to $-\sqrt{-48} + 2\sqrt{27} - \sqrt{-75}$?

A. $9\sqrt{3} - 6i\sqrt{3}$

B. $6\sqrt{3} + 9i\sqrt{3}$

C. $6\sqrt{3} - 6i\sqrt{3}$

D. $6\sqrt{3} - 9i\sqrt{3}$

E. $9\sqrt{3} + 6i\sqrt{3}$

The correct answer is D. Simplify each radical term and then combine those with the same radical part:

$$\begin{aligned} -\sqrt{-48} + 2\sqrt{27} - \sqrt{-75} &= -\sqrt{-4^2 \bullet 3} + 2\sqrt{3^2 \bullet 3} - \sqrt{-5^2 \bullet 3} \\ &= -4i\sqrt{3} + 6\sqrt{3} - 5i\sqrt{3} \\ &= (-4 - 5)i\sqrt{3} + 6\sqrt{3} \\ &= 6\sqrt{3} - 9i\sqrt{3} \end{aligned}$$

. . . .

Examples:

Perform the indicated arithmetic operations and express the final answer in the form $a + bi$:

1. $(3 - 2i)(1 - 3i) =$ _____

2. $\dfrac{2}{4 - 3i} =$ _____

Solutions:

1. $(3 - 2i)(1 - 3i) = 3 - 2i - 9i + 6i^2 = 3 - 11i - 6 = -3 - 11i$

2. $\dfrac{2}{4 - 3i} \cdot \dfrac{4 + 3i}{4 + 3i} = \dfrac{2(4 + 3i)}{(4 - 3i)(4 + 3i)} = \dfrac{8 + 6i}{16 - 9i^2} = \dfrac{8 + 6i}{16 + 9} = \dfrac{8 + 6i}{25} = \dfrac{8}{25} + \dfrac{6}{25}i$

QUADRATIC EQUATIONS AND THE QUADRATIC FORMULA

In the last chapter, we looked at quadratic equations and learned to solve them when the quadratic expression is factorable. But, this is not always the case. When you cannot factor a quadratic expression, the **quadratic formula** comes to the rescue!

The solutions of the equation $ax^2 + bx + c = 0$ can be found by using the quadratic formula:

$$x = \frac{-b \pm \sqrt{b^2 - 4ac}}{2a}$$

 When using the quadratic formula, don't forget to divide *the entire numerator*, not just $-b$, by the denominator $2a$.

Just as when you applied factoring to solve a quadratic equation, you must get all terms to one side before identifying the coefficients a, b, and c in the quadratic formula.

The resulting solutions can be one of three types, depending on the sign of the radicand $b^2 - 4ac$, called the **discriminant**:

$b^2 - 4ac > 0$	Two distinct real solutions
$b^2 - 4ac = 0$	One repeated real solution
$b^2 - 4ac < 0$	Two complex conjugate solutions

Solve the following quadratic equations using the quadratic formula.

Examples:

1. $16x^2 + 9 = -24x$ _____

2. $2x^2 - 5x + 2 = 0$ _____

3. $3x^2 + x + 1 = 0$ _____

250

Chapter 7

Intermediate
Algebra and
Coordinate
Geometry

Solutions:

1. First, write the equation in standard form by bringing $-24x$ to the left: $16x^2 + 24x + 9 = 0$. Now, identify $a = 16$, $b = 24$, and $c = 9$ and apply the quadratic formula:

$$x = \frac{-24 \pm \sqrt{24^2 - 4(16)(9)}}{2(16)} = \frac{-24 \pm \sqrt{0}}{32} = -\frac{3}{4}$$

So this equation has only one real solution.

2. Identify $a = 2$, $b = -5$, and $c = 2$ and apply the quadratic formula:

$$x = \frac{-(-5) \pm \sqrt{(-5)^2 - 4(2)(2)}}{2(2)} = \frac{5 \pm \sqrt{25 - 16}}{4} = \frac{5 \pm \sqrt{9}}{4} = \frac{5 \pm 3}{4} = -\frac{1}{2}, 2$$

So this equation has two distinct real solutions.

3. Identify $a = 3$, $b = 1$, and $c = 1$ and apply the quadratic formula:

$$x = \frac{-(1) \pm \sqrt{(1)^2 - 4(3)(1)}}{2(3)} = \frac{-1 \pm \sqrt{-11}}{6} = \frac{-1 \pm i\sqrt{11}}{6}$$

So this equation has two complex conjugate solutions.

Let's take a look at the way this concept would be tested on the ACT.

If the graph of the equation $y = 2(x - 4)^2 + k$ never intersects the x-axis, which of the following could be the value of k?

A. -4
B. -2
C. -1
D. 0
E. 1

The correct answer is E. The number of x-intercepts a parabola has is the same as the number of real roots the corresponding quadratic equation has (found by setting it equal to 0). Since the given parabola never intersects the x-axis, this equation must have no real roots. This occurs when the discriminant, $b^2 - 4ac$, is negative.

To compute the discriminant in this situation, set up the quadratic equation in standard form:

$$2(x - 4)^2 + k = 0$$
$$2x^2 - 16x + (32 + k) = 0$$

So, the discriminant is
$b^2 - 4ac = (-16)^2 - 4(2)(32 + k) = 256 - 256 - 8k = -8k$.

The only values that make this discriminant negative are positive values of k. So the correct answer must be choice E.

 For exam questions that ask about the nature of solutions of a quadratic equation, the discriminant is often the most efficient tool to use!

LINEAR INEQUALITIES

The same basic strategy used to solve linear equations is also used to solve linear inequalities, with one additional step—the inequality sign must be switched whenever both sides of the inequality are multiplied by a negative real number. Another distinguishing factor of linear inequalities in contrast to linear equations is that the **solution set** of an inequality (that is, the set of real numbers that satisfies the inequality) contains infinitely many values. The solution set is often depicted on a number line, as follows:

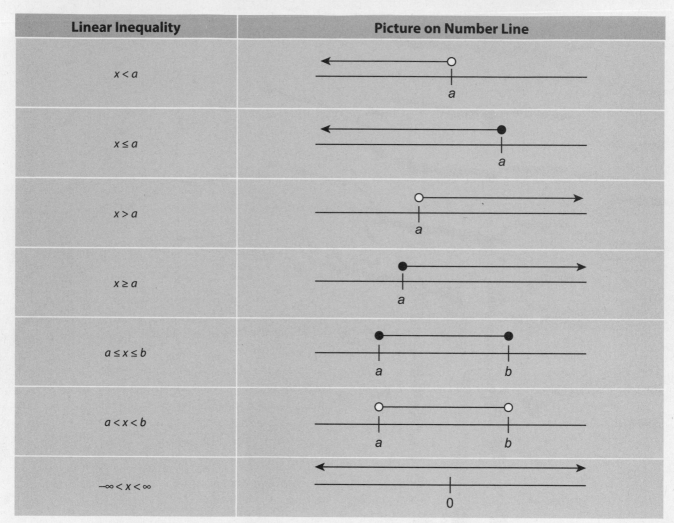

Linear Inequality	Picture on Number Line
$x < a$	
$x \le a$	
$x > a$	
$x \ge a$	
$a \le x \le b$	
$a < x < b$	
$-\infty < x < \infty$	

252

Chapter 7

Intermediate
Algebra and
Coordinate
Geometry

www.petersons.com

Problems involving inequalities come in different varieties on the ACT. The following table gives typical forms in which these questions are frequently asked, along with some suggestions about how to attack them:

Problem Type	Method of Attack
Solve a given inequality, where the answer choices are given symbolically (like the left-hand column of the previous table).	Solve the inequality as you would a linear equation, being careful with the inequality sign. The final step will have the variable on one side and a number on the other. This should be one of the choices.
Solve a given inequality, where the choices are given graphically on the number line (like the right-hand column of the previous table).	Solve the inequality as you would a linear equation, being careful with the inequality sign. Once you have the variable on one side and a number on the other, match that to the correct picture. Double-check whether each circle over its correct numerical value is open or closed.
You are given a ray on the number line and are asked to identify which of the inequalities listed is its solution set.	If the pictured ray has a closed circle at its endpoint, you can discard any of the choices involving a *strict* inequality (that is, one with < or >). Likewise, if there is an open circle on the endpoint of the ray, discard any of the choices involving a ≤ or ≥ sign. To distinguish among the remaining choices, choose an extreme x-value (very large or very small) that is in the graphed ray, plug it into the inequalities, and see the one it satisfies. That is the solution.
You are given a verbal description whose translation into symbols results in an inequality, and you are asked for the solution set.	Translate the verbal scenario into an inequality, and solve as above.

Consider the following ACT-like problem.

. . . .

When 2 times a number x is decreased by 8, the result is less than 20. Which of the following represents the solution set of this relationship?

- **F.** $x < 2$
- **G.** $x < 6$
- **H.** $x < 14$
- **J.** $x < 20$
- **K.** $x < 28$

The correct answer is H. First, translate the given information into an inequality: $2x - 8 < 20$. Now solve the inequality for x:

$$2x - 8 < 20$$
$$2x < 28$$
$$x < 14$$

. . . .

Sometimes, you will be asked to solve a double inequality, as in the following example. Give it a try.

Example:

Determine the solution set for the double inequality $-4 < 8 - 3x < 20$. _____

Solution:

The strategy behind solving such inequalities is to get the variable *in the middle* by itself. To do that here, simply subtract 8 from all parts of the inequality, and then divide all parts by –3. When you perform this division, make certain to switch *both* signs since you are working with a negative number:

$$-4 < 8 - 3x < 20$$
$$-12 < -3x < 12$$
$$4 > x > -4$$

The last line is the solution set and can be written equivalently as $-4 < x < 4$.

ABSOLUTE VALUE EQUATIONS AND INEQUALITIES

You should also be comfortable working with linear equations and inequalities involving absolute values. Solve these problems by writing them in equivalent forms involving plain old vanilla linear equations and inequalities *without* absolute values, as follows:

Absolute Value Equation/Inequality	Solution
$\lvert x \rvert = a$	$x = a$ or $x = -a$
$\lvert x \rvert \geq a$	$x \geq a$ or $x \leq -a$
$\lvert x \rvert > a$	$x > a$ or $x < -a$
$\lvert x \rvert \leq a$	$-a \leq x \leq a$
$\lvert x \rvert < a$	$-a < x < a$

Use these definitions when x is replaced by some linear expression in x, and then solve the resulting equation(s) or inequality in the same manner that you would solve other more standard linear equations and inequalities. Work through the following examples.

Examples:

1. Solve the equation $\lvert 4x - 1 \rvert = 3$. _____

2. Determine the solution set of the inequality $\lvert 2 - 3x \rvert < 7$. _____

Solutions:

1. We must adapt the fact that the solutions of $\lvert x \rvert = a$ are $x = a$ and $x = -a$ to this situation. To do so, we create two equations: $4x - 1 = 3$ and $4x - 1 = -3$. Then, solve each for x.

   For the first equation, $4x = 4$, so $x = 1$. For the second equation, $4x = -2$, so $x = -\frac{1}{2}$.

   Therefore, the solutions of the original equation are 1 and $-\frac{1}{2}$.

2. In this scenario, we must adapt the fact that the solution set of $\lvert x \rvert < a$ is $-a < x < a$. The absolute value inequality can be written equivalently as the double inequality $-7 < 2 - 3x < 7$.

   Solve this inequality by subtracting 2 from all parts to get $-9 < -3x < 5$, and then divide all parts by –3, remembering to reverse the signs.

   The final solution set is $3 > x > -\frac{5}{3}$. This can be rewritten as $-\frac{5}{3} < x < 3$.

Now see how a question of this type would appear on the ACT.

Which of the following inequalities gives the complete solution set for the inequality $|2x - 3| < 8$?

F. $x < -\dfrac{5}{2}$ or $x > \dfrac{11}{2}$

G. $x < \dfrac{11}{2}$

H. $x > -\dfrac{5}{2}$

J. $-5 < x < 11$

K. $-\dfrac{5}{2} < x < \dfrac{11}{2}$

The correct answer is K. Express the absolute value inequality as the equivalent double inequality $-8 < 2x - 3 < 8$. Then add 3 to all parts of the inequality to get $-5 < 2x < 11$. Finally, divide all parts by 2 to get the solution set $-\dfrac{5}{2} < x < \dfrac{11}{2}$.

 If you have to solve an absolute value inequality of the forms $|ax + b| < c$ or $|ax + b| \leq c$, the solution set cannot be a ray (like choices G and H in this problem)! You can discard those answer choices immediately.

Sometimes, absolute value problems sneak in subtly in the form of a word problem, as in this next sample question:

Zane earns an annual salary of Z dollars, and Wendi earns an annual salary of W dollars. If the difference between Zane's and Wendi's average monthly salaries is $450, which of the following represents the relationship between Z and W?

A. $|Z - W| = 5,400$

B. $\left|\dfrac{Z + W}{2}\right| = 5,400$

C. $|Z + W| = 5,400$

D. $|Z + W| = 450$

E. $|Z - W| = 450$

The correct answer is A. The difference between Zane's and Wendi's average monthly salaries is $450, so the difference between their annual salaries is $450 \times 12 = \$5,400$. We do not know who earns more, but the difference between their annual salaries is $|Z - W|$ dollars. Thus, $|Z - W| = 5,400$.

 ALERT: Read the problem carefully. Choice E, for instance, is the difference between *monthly* salaries, not *annual* salaries.

QUADRATIC INEQUALITIES

A quadratic inequality is an inequality involving a quadratic expression. Here are some examples:

$$x^2 + 6 < 5x, \quad 2x^2 \geq 1, \quad (3 - x)(4 + x) \leq 0$$

Solving these problems is a little tricky since, unlike linear inequalities, the goal is *not* to get x on one side by itself. Here are the steps used to solve quadratic inequalities:

1) Gather all terms on one side so that you get 0 on one side of the inequality.

2) Factor the resulting quadratic expression, if possible, to determine its roots (that is, where the expression *equals* zero). If you cannot factor it, use the quadratic formula to find the roots.

3) Draw a number line and label the roots. Choose any number in each interval of the number line before, between, or after the roots. Plug this number into the quadratic expression and note its sign.

4) The solution set is those intervals where the sign determined in step 3 satisfies the inequality. If the inequality is *strict* (that is, either < or >), then do NOT include the roots in the solution set; if the inequality includes equals (that is, either ≤ or ≥), DO include the roots in the solution set.

Let's walk through an example together.

Solve the quadratic inequality $x^2 + 6 < 5x$.

Step 1: Write the inequality as $x^2 - 5x + 6 < 0$. (Note: Put the terms in decreasing order according to the exponents on x; this will make it easier to factor.)

Step 2: Factor the left side as $(x - 3)(x - 2) < 0$. The roots of the left side are 2 and 3.

Step 3: Form the following number line:

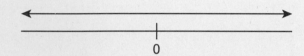

0

Choose the point 0 in the leftmost interval, 2.5 in the middle interval, and 5 in the rightmost interval, and plug them into the factored expression. The sign shown above each interval is the sign of the quadratic expression on the respective interval.

Step 4: The solution set is the open interval (2, 3).

Now try a couple on your own.

Examples:

Solve these quadratic inequalities.

1. $(3 - x)(x + 6) > 0 =$ _____

2. $2x^2 + x - 1 \geq 0$ _____

Solutions:

1. $(-6, 3)$

2. $\left(-\infty, -1\right] \cup \left[\dfrac{1}{2}, \infty\right)$

256

Chapter 7

Intermediate
Algebra and
Coordinate
Geometry

SYSTEMS OF LINEAR EQUATIONS

A **system of linear equations** is a pair of linear equations involving x and y that must be satisfied *at the same time*. To solve a system means to identify ordered pairs (x, y) that satisfy not just one, but *both* equations.

There are only three possibilities that can occur when trying to find the solution to a system:

Number of Solutions	Geometric Interpretation
0	The graphs of the lines in the system are *parallel*. Hence, there is no point that is on both lines simultaneously.
1	The graphs of the lines in the system intersect in a *single* point. The intersection point is the solution of the system.
Infinitely many	The graphs of the lines in the system are exactly the same. Every point on the line is a solution of the system.

There are two algebraic methods that you can use to solve a system: the **elimination method** and the **substitution method.** Let's look at how to use both methods to solve the same system.

ELIMINATION METHOD

First, we'll use the elimination method to solve a system.

$$\text{Solve the system: } \begin{cases} 2x + 3y = -1 \\ 3x + y = 2 \end{cases}$$

The strategy behind this method is to multiply both equations by a number or numbers so that when you add the left sides and the right sides, one of the variables drops out (or is eliminated). Then you solve for that remaining variable and plug the value you get back into either equation to find the value of the first variable. When that step is complete, you have your ordered pair.

For instance, suppose our goal was to eliminate the variable x. One way to do so is to multiply both sides of the first equation by 3 and both sides of the second equation by –2:

$$\begin{cases} 6x + 9y = -3 \\ -6x - 2y = -4 \end{cases}$$

Now add the left sides and right sides to get the equation $7y = -7$. (Note that the x has indeed been eliminated!) Solving this equation for y yields $y = -1$.

Finally, substitute this value back into either equation in the original system (it does not matter which one!) and solve for x. If we use the second equation, we get $3x + (-1) = 2$. Solving for x yields $3x = 3$, and so $x = 1$. Thus, the solution of the system is $(1, -1)$.

257

Chapter 7

Intermediate Algebra and Coordinate Geometry

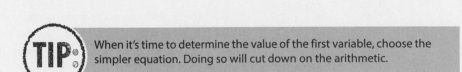

TIP: When it's time to determine the value of the first variable, choose the simpler equation. Doing so will cut down on the arithmetic.

SUBSTITUTION METHOD

Now we'll solve the same system again, but this time, let's use the substitution method.

$$\text{Solve the system: } \begin{cases} 2x + 3y = -1 \\ 3x + y = 2 \end{cases}$$

The strategy behind this method is to solve one of the equations for a variable (either x or y, whichever is slightly easier to isolate) and *substitute* that expression for the variable into the other equation (doing so results in an equation involving only one variable). Solve that equation and then plug the value you get back into either equation to find the value of the unknown variable. When that step is complete, you have your ordered pair.

Solve the second equation for y to get $y = 2 - 3x$. Substitute this expression for y in the first equation to obtain $2x + 3(2 - 3x) = -1$. This equation involves only x, so you can now solve for x, as follows:

TIP When applying the substitution method, choose the equation in which you can solve for one of the variables easily.

$$2x + 3(2 - 3x) = -1$$
$$2x + 6 - 9x = -1$$
$$-7x + 6 = -1$$
$$-7x = -7$$
$$x = 1$$

Finally, plug this value of x back into $y = 2 - 3x$ to get $y = 2 - 3(1) = -1$. Thus, the solution of the system is $(1, -1)$.

What kinds of problems involve solving such systems on the ACT Mathematics test? As usual, there is a variety. You could simply be given two equations and asked which one of the given choices is a solution to the system. In a case like this, it is more efficient to plug the given values into the system to determine which one satisfies both.

258

Chapter 7

Intermediate Algebra and Coordinate Geometry

ALERT: If you are given a system and asked which of a list of choices is a solution, remember that the ordered pair must satisfy BOTH equations, not just one of them. Among the choices will be points that satisfy one of the equations, but not the other!

It is more likely that the problem involving systems will have a little extra twist to it. For instance, you might be asked to evaluate an expression involving the x- and y-coordinates of the solution rather than simply identifying the solution itself, as in the following problem.

· ·

If $x - 4y = -2$ and $2x + y = 23$, what is the value of $5xy$?

    A. 10
    B. 13
    C. 30
    D. 50
    E. 150

The correct answer is E. The two methods are equally convenient to use, so let's apply the substitution method. Solve the first equation for x to get $x = 4y - 2$ and substitute this in for x in the second equation to get $2(4y - 2) + y = 23$. Solving for y yields $8y - 4 + y = 23$, which is equivalent to $9y = 27$, so $y = 3$. Plugging this value back into the substitution expression yields $x = 4(3) - 2 = 10$.

The final step here is to evaluate the expression $5xy$ using $x = 10$ and $y = 3$ (since these are the only values of x and y for which both equations hold simultaneously). Doing so yields $5(10)(3) = 150$.

· ·

Another type of problem will ask you to identify the value of a coefficient, such that the nature of the solutions of a given system satisfies some condition. For instance, consider the following problem.

Suppose the system $\begin{cases} x + ky + 1 = 4x \\ -3x = 5 - 2y \end{cases}$ has no solution.

What must be the value of k?

F. -2

G. 2

H. $\dfrac{1}{2}$

J. $-\dfrac{1}{2}$

K. 4

The correct answer is G. The only way a linear system can have *no solution* is for the two lines to be parallel, which means they have the same slope. So in order to determine the value of k, put each of the lines into slope-intercept form and equate the slopes:

$$x + ky + 1 = 4x \;\Rightarrow\; ky = 3x - 1 \;\Rightarrow\; y = \frac{3}{k}x - \frac{1}{k}$$

$$-3x = 5 - 2y \;\Rightarrow\; -5 - 3x = -2y \;\Rightarrow\; y = \frac{3}{2}k + \frac{5}{2}$$

In this form, the slopes of the lines are $\dfrac{3}{k}$ and $\dfrac{3}{2}$. Setting them equal and solving for k yields $k = 2$. This is the only value for which these two lines are parallel.

BASIC COORDINATE GEOMETRY

If you are on the road to taking the ACT, you are likely familiar with the (x, y)-coordinate plane and know how to plot points. But you may have forgotten some of the associated terminology and formulas that will probably come up on the exam, the numbering of quadrants, and the distance and midpoint formulas. We'll review the language and application of coordinate geometry concepts in this section.

The (x, y) coordinate plane is divided into four congruent **quadrants** numbered I, II, III, and IV counterclockwise as shown below. This image is also a good reference for the signs of coordinates that lie in each quadrant.

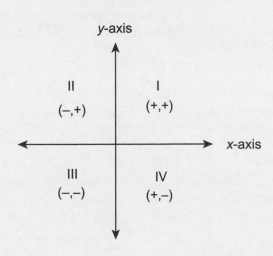

259

Chapter 7

Intermediate
Algebra and
Coordinate
Geometry

IMPORTANT COORDINATE GEOMETRY FORMULAS

You can quickly compute the length of any vertical or horizontal line segment by simply subtracting its y- or x-coordinates, respectively, and taking the absolute value of the result (since length cannot be negative). For diagonal segments, the **distance formula** comes in handy:

The distance between two points $P(x_1, y_1)$ and $Q(x_2, y_2)$ is $\sqrt{(x_2 - x_1)^2 + (y_2 - y_1)^2}$.

Likewise, the midpoint of the line segment with endpoints $P(x_1, y_1)$ and $Q(x_2, y_2)$ is the point with coordinates $\left(\dfrac{x_1 + x_2}{2}, \dfrac{y_1 + y_2}{2} \right)$.

Often, the problems on the ACT Mathematics test that involve the distance and midpoint formulas are word problems, such as the following question.

. . . .

A map is laid out in the standard (x, y) coordinate plane. How long in units is the path from City A located at (4, 11) to City B located at (8, 9), given that the path is a straight line between the cities?

   F. 2 units

   G. $\sqrt{6}$ units

   H. $2\sqrt{5}$ units

   J. 6 units

   K. 20 units

The correct answer is H. You can use the distance formula to find the straight-line distance between any two points in the (x, y) plane.

$$
\begin{aligned}
d &= \sqrt{(x_1 - x_2)^2 + (y_1 - y_2)^2} \\
&= \sqrt{(4 - 8)^2 + (11 - 9)^2} \\
&= \sqrt{-4^2 + 2^2} \\
&= \sqrt{16 + 4} \\
&= \sqrt{20} \\
&= 2\sqrt{5}
\end{aligned}
$$

260

Chapter 7

Intermediate
Algebra and
Coordinate
Geometry

. . . .

 ALERT: Be careful to avoid making these common errors when using the distance formula:

- Forgetting to square the differences inside the radical
- Subtracting the coordinates of a given point rather than subtracting the x-coordinates and y-coordinates of the two points
- Forgetting to take the square root

These errors are reflected in the distractor choices for these problems.

See how the midpoint formula might be used in an ACT question.

. . . .

Suppose that $P(-1, 6)$ is one of the endpoints of a line segment PQ and that its midpoint is $M(4, -5)$. What is point Q?

   A. $\left(\dfrac{3}{2}, \dfrac{1}{2} \right)$

   B. $(-5, 11)$

   C. $(5, -11)$

   D. $(9, -16)$

   E. $(-9, 16)$

The correct answer is D. Since we do not know the coordinates of Q, let's call that point (x, y); we must determine the values of both x and y. Using the midpoint formula, we can express the midpoint of PQ as $\left(\dfrac{-1 + x}{2}, \dfrac{6 + y}{2} \right)$. Since we are given that the midpoint is (4, -5), we know that $\dfrac{-1 + x}{2} = 4$ and $\dfrac{6 + y}{2} = -5$.

Solving each of these yields $x = 9$ and $y = -16$. Hence, the coordinates of Q are (9, -16).

. . . .

CIRCLES IN THE COORDINATE PLANE

Circles and their graphs appear on the ACT occasionally as well. The equation of a circle with center (h, k) and radius r, as pictured below, is $(x - h)^2 + (y - k)^2 = r^2$:

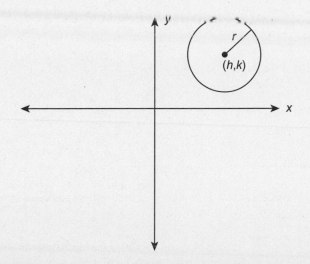

 Be careful when identifying the coordinates of the center. If the equation of the circle is $(x + 3)^2 + y^2 = 16$, then the center is $(-3, 0)$, not $(3, 0)$!

The following is a typical ACT mathematics question involving the equation of a circle.

The circle with equation $(x + 2)^2 + (y - 9)^2 = 25$ lies completely inside a square. What is the least possible length of one of the sides of the square?

- **F.** 4
- **G.** 8
- **H.** 10
- **J.** 14
- **K.** 16

The correct answer is H. In order for the circle to lie completely inside the square, the side length of the square must be at least as large as the diameter of the circle. The diameter of a circle is twice its radius. Here, the equation of the circle is in standard form; the right side is the square of the radius. So the radius is 5, which means the diameter is 10 units.

FUNCTIONS

A **function** is a rule that associates a corresponding y-value to each input x. Commonly, functions are described using algebraic expressions (which can then be illustrated by a graph). Functions are denoted using letters, like f or g. When we want to emphasize the input/output-defining relationship of a function, an expression in the form $y = f(x)$ (read "y equals f of x") is often used.

The **domain** of a function is the set of all values of x that can be substituted into the expression and yield a meaningful output. The **range** of a function is the set of all possible y-values attained at some member of the domain. Try working through these examples.

Examples:

What are the domains of the following functions?

1. $f(x) = 2 + \dfrac{3}{x+5}$ _____

2. $g(x) = \sqrt{4-x}$ _____

3. $h(x) = \dfrac{x+5}{\left(x^2+9\right)(x-4)}$ _____

4. $j(x) = x^3 + x^2 - 5x + 3$ _____

Solutions:

1. The domain is the set of all real numbers *except* –5, because we can substitute any value other than –5 for *x* and get a well-defined real number as an output.

2. The domain of the function $g(x) = \sqrt{4-x}$ consists of all real numbers *x* for which the radicand, 4 – *x*, is nonnegative—we want the output to be a real number, and we know that the square root of a negative number involves *i*. As such, we will allow any *x* that satisfies the inequality 4 – *x* ≥ 0, which is equivalent to 4 ≥ *x*, to be an input into the function. So the domain is all real numbers for which *x* ≤ 4.

3. All real numbers except 4.

4. All real numbers.

 For a rational function like *h(x)*, only the *x*-values that make the *denominator* equal to zero are excluded from the domain. You do NOT exclude values that make the *numerator* equal to zero.

When working with functions on the ACT test, you will likely be asked to compute the value *f(x)* (called the *functional value of x*) for various inputs. Get some practice with these computations by solving these examples.

Examples:

1. Consider the function $f(x) = 2x^2 - x + 1$. Compute *f*(3) and *f*(*a* + 2) _____

2. How do we compute *f*(*a* + 2)? _____

3. If $f(x) = -3x^2 + 1$, compute *f*(*x* + 2). _____

Solutions:

1. To compute $f(3)$, simply plug in 3 for x to obtain $f(3) = 2(3)^2 - 3 + 1 = 18 - 3 + 1 = 16$.

2. Here, the input happens to be an algebraic expression instead of a number. We must substitute the *entire* quantity within the parentheses for x everywhere it occurs in the formula:

$$f(a+2) = 2(a+2)^2 - (a+2) + 1$$
$$= 2(a^2 + 4a + 4) - (a+2) + 1$$
$$= 2a^2 + 8a + 8 - a - 2 + 1$$
$$= 2a^2 + 7a + 7$$

3. $f(x+2) = -3(x+2)^2 + 1$
$$= -3(x^2 + 4x + 4) + 1$$
$$= -3x^2 - 12x - 12 + 1$$
$$= -3x^2 - 12x - 11$$

 **CAUTION** A common error is to say $f(x + 2) = f(x) + f(2)$. This is wrong! You cannot distribute the function in this manner. You must compute as above.

FUNCTIONS AND ARITHMETIC

We can define arithmetic operations on functions in the same manner that we perform arithmetic on real numbers. Let f and g be functions. The sum $(f+g)(x)$ is defined to be $f(x) + g(x)$. Likewise, the difference function $(f-g)(x)$ is defined to be $f(x) - g(x)$; the product function $(f \bullet g)(x)$ is defined to be $f(x) \bullet g(x)$; and the quotient function $\left(\dfrac{f}{g}\right)(x)$ is defined to be $\dfrac{f(x)}{g(x)}$. Another function that is important is the **composition** of f and g, denoted by $(f \circ g)$. This value is defined by $(f \circ g)(x) = f(g(x))$, as in the example below.

263

Chapter 7

Intermediate
Algebra and
Coordinate
Geometry

Example:

Let $f(x) = 3x - 2$ and $g(x) = 4x^2 + 1$. Compute $(f \circ g)(x)$ and $(g \circ f)(x)$.

Solution:

$$(f \circ g)(x) = f(g(x)) = f(4x^2 + 1) = 3(4x^2 + 1) - 2 = 12x^2 + 1$$
$$(g \circ f)(x) = g(f(x)) = g(3x - 2) = 4(3x - 2)^2 + 1 = 4(9x^2 - 12x + 4) + 1 = 36x^2 - 48x + 17$$

 **CAUTION** Note that, in general, $(f \circ g) \neq (g \circ f)$. The order in which you compose functions matters!

GRAPHING FUNCTIONS

The following are the graphs of some of the most common functions you will encounter on the ACT.

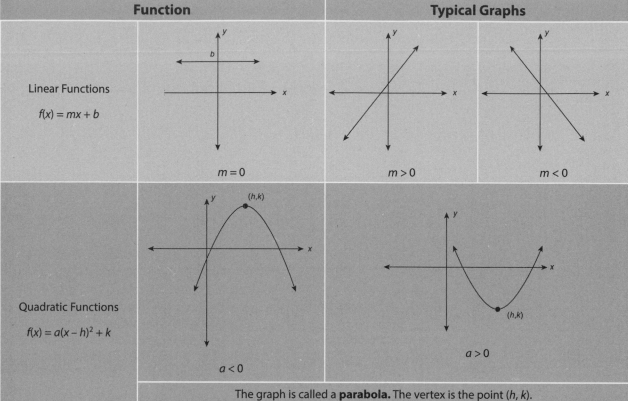

Function	Typical Graphs

Linear Functions
$f(x) = mx + b$

$m = 0$ $m > 0$ $m < 0$

Quadratic Functions
$f(x) = a(x - h)^2 + k$

$a < 0$ $a > 0$

The graph is called a **parabola.** The vertex is the point (h, k).

Note that the maximum or minimum value of a parabola occurs at the vertex.

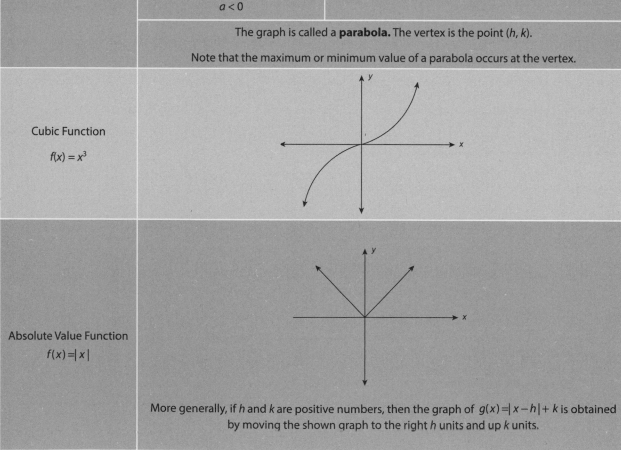

Cubic Function
$f(x) = x^3$

Absolute Value Function
$f(x) = |x|$

More generally, if h and k are positive numbers, then the graph of $g(x) = |x - h| + k$ is obtained by moving the shown graph to the right h units and up k units.

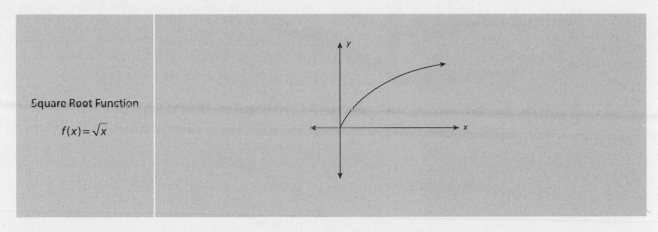

Square Root Function

$f(x) = \sqrt{x}$

Note that when you have a graph of a function, you can determine if an *x*-value belongs to the domain of *f* by simply determining if an ordered pair with that *x*-value belongs to the graph of *f*. You should be familiar with the following features of the graph of a function $y = f(x)$:

- The *minimum of f* is the smallest *y*-value in the range of *f*; it is the *y*-value of the lowest point on the graph of *f*.

- The *maximum of f* is the largest *y*-value in the range of *f*; it is the *y*-value of the highest point on the graph of *f*.

- *f* is *decreasing* if its graph falls from left to right as you progress through the interval from left to right.

- *f* is *increasing* on an interval if its graph rises from left to right as you progress through the interval from left to right.

- An *x-intercept of f* is a point of the form (*x*, 0). You determine the *x*-intercepts of a function by solving the equation $f(x) = 0$.

- A *y-intercept of f* is the point (0, *f*(0)).

Let's look at another sample question.

What is the equation of the parabola graphed below?

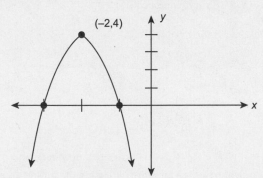

(−2,4)

A. $y = -4x^2 - 16x - 12$
B. $y = -x^2 - 2x + 3$
C. $y = -x^2 + 2x - 3$
D. $y = 4x^2 - 16x - 12$
E. $y = 4x^2 + 16x + 12$

The correct answer is A. Factor the expression to get $-4x^2 - 16x - 12 = -4(x^2 + 4x + 3) = -4(x + 3)(x + 1)$.

This equals zero at $x = -3$ and $x = -1$; as shown, the *y*-intercept is −12; the parabola opens downward because the coefficient of x^2 is negative. So this is the equation of the graph shown. The other choices can be discarded. The graph opens downward, which means that the coefficient of x^2 must be reactive, so you can eliminate choices D and E immediately. The graph also has *x*-intercepts at −3 and −1. If you factor the expression in choice B, you get $-(x + 3)(x - 1)$, which is zero at 1 and −3, not −1 and −3. So this can be discarded. For a similar reason, you can discard choice C.

Which of the following could be the equation for the graph below?

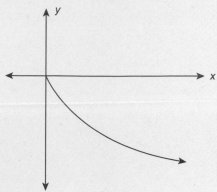

The correct answer is K. Even if you didn't immediately recognize that this graph of $y = \sqrt{x}$ reflected over the *x*-axis, you can still answer this question using the process of elimination. Choice F can be immediately eliminated because it is a linear equation, and its graph would therefore be a straight line. Choices G, H, and J can be eliminated because they are defined for *negative x*-values, but such values are not used to get the graph shown.

F. $y = Ax$

G. $y = Ax^2$

H. $y = Ax^3$

J. $y = Ax^4$

K. $y = A\sqrt{x}$

. . . .

All of these functions can be moved within the coordinate plane using horizontal and vertical **translations** and **reflections,** defined as follows. Here, let *h* and *k* stand for positive real numbers.

New Function	Verbal Description of How to Graph This Function By Translation or Reflecting the Graph of $y = f(x)$
$F(x) = f(x) + k$	Translate the graph of **$y = f(x)$** *k* units vertically upward.
$F(x) = f(x) - k$	Translate the graph of **$y = f(x)$** *k* units vertically downward.
$F(x) = f(x - h)$	Translate the graph of **$y = f(x)$** *h* units to the right.
$F(x) = f(x + h)$	Translate the graph of **$y = f(x)$** *h* units to the left.
$F(x) = -f(x)$	Reflect the graph of **$y = f(x)$** over the *x*-axis.

POLYNOMIALS

A polynomial is a function of the form $f(x) = a_n x^n + a_{n-1}x^{n-1} + \ldots + a_1 x + a_0$, where $a_0, a_1, \ldots, a_n$ are real numbers, and *n* is a nonnegative integer. We say the polynomial has **degree _n_.** The graphing of polynomials is a bit more difficult to grasp, and you will likely see a question or two about graphing polynomials on the ACT. Often, such questions focus on the terminology involved instead of some obscure property or trick. The three main concepts with which you should be familiar are *x-intercept*, **zero**, and **factor.**

Term	Definition
x-intercept	A point $(a, 0)$ on the graph of $y = p(x)$ (In such case, a is a solution of the equation $p(x) = 0$.)
zero (or root)	A real number a such that $p(a) = 0$
factor	An expression of the form $(x - a)$ in which a is a zero of $p(x)$

A high-powered theorem known as the **fundamental theorem of algebra** tells us that a polynomial with degree n has at most n x-intercepts, and these occur at the x-values that make each linear factor equal to zero. Consider the following problem.

In the standard (x, y) coordinate plane, how many roots does the graph of $y = 2(x - 3)(x + 5)(x + 7)$ have?

- **A.** 1
- **B.** 2
- **C.** 3
- **D.** 4
- **E.** 5

The correct answer is C. The graph will have a root at any x-value for which y equals zero, and this occurs when any of its factors equals zero. Set the expression equal to zero and solve for x:

$$0 = 2(x - 3)(x + 5)(x + 7)$$

The right side is zero when x is 3, –5, or –7. This means that the graph has 3 roots.

MODELING

You will encounter all kinds of word problems on the ACT Mathematics test. Some will involve simple arithmetic, while others will require you to set up equations, inequalities, or systems of equations, or to use a trigonometric relationship to identify the value of an unknown. The common link? Your goal is always to first identify the variable(s), and then interpret the information provided into a mathematical expression so that you can make use of all of the rules and methods discussed so far in this chapter.

At this point in our review, you have all of the pieces needed to solve the following word problems.

A ball thrown upward from ground level is s feet high after t seconds, where $s = 112t - 16t^2$. At which of the following times will the ball be 96 feet above the ground?

- **A.** 0.25 second
- **B.** 0.5 second
- **C.** 2 seconds
- **D.** 4 seconds
- **E.** 6 seconds

The correct answer is E. You want to know the value of t when $s = 96$. Plugging in $s = 96$ gives you $96 = 112t - 16t^2$. Put this equation into standard quadratic form and solve for t:

$$96 = 112t - 16t^2$$
$$16t^2 - 112t + 96 = 0$$
$$16(t^2 - 7t + 6) = 0$$
$$16(t - 6)(t - 1) = 0$$
$$t = 1, 6$$

So the ball is at this height at both 1 and 6 seconds. Since 6 seconds is the only one of the two answers that is listed, it must be the correct answer.

Working together, a standard desktop computer and a supercomputer can complete a data analysis job in 2.5 hours. If it takes the standard desktop computer 6 hours to do the job alone, how many hours would it take the supercomputer to complete the job alone?

F. $\dfrac{1}{6}$ hour

G. $\dfrac{2}{5}$ hour

H. 2 hours

J. $4\dfrac{2}{7}$ hours

K. 5 hours

The correct answer is J. Let x equal the number of hours it takes the supercomputer to complete the job alone. The standard desktop computer can complete the job alone in 6 hours, so every hour it does $\dfrac{1}{6}$ of the job. That means every hour, the supercomputer does $\dfrac{1}{x}$ of the job. Working together, the two printers complete the job in 2.5 hours, so each hour they do $\dfrac{1}{2.5} = \dfrac{1}{\frac{5}{2}} = \dfrac{2}{5}$ of the job. The sum of the individual rates equals the rate working together. As such, we have the following equation involving x: $\dfrac{1}{x} + \dfrac{1}{6} = \dfrac{2}{5}$.

Solving this equation yields:

$$\frac{1}{x} + \frac{1}{6} = \frac{2}{5}$$
$$30 + 5x = 12x$$
$$30 = 7x$$
$$x = \frac{30}{7} = 4\frac{2}{7}$$

In which of the following equations is p inversely proportional to the square root of q and directly proportional to the cube of r?

A. $\dfrac{r^3}{\sqrt{q}} = p$

B. $\dfrac{\sqrt{p}}{r^3} = q$

C. $\dfrac{\sqrt{r}}{q^3} = p$

D. $\dfrac{\sqrt{q}}{p^3} = r$

E. $\dfrac{\sqrt{q}}{r^3} = p$

The correct answer is A. The equation must contain p, $\sqrt{q}$, and r^3. The only two answer choices that have these are A and E, so immediately eliminate choices B, C, and D. Then, you must remember what both *directly* proportional and *inversely* proportional mean. If a and b are *directly* proportional, there must be a constant k such that $a = kb$, and if they are *inversely* proportional, there must be a constant k such that $a = k \cdot \dfrac{1}{b}$. Of the two choices, A is the correct one, while E is the two relationships reversed.

While shopping, Dennis finds that one pair of jeans and three T-shirts cost $140, while two pairs of jeans and one T-shirt cost $120. If the store charges the same price for all of its T-shirts and the same price for all of its jeans, what is Dennis's cost if he decides to simply buy one pair of jeans and one T-shirt?

F. $32
G. $44
H. $50
J. $64
K. $76

The correct answer is K. Let j be the cost of one pair of jeans and t the cost of one T-shirt. The condition, "one pair of jeans and three T-shirts cost $140" translates to $j + 3t = 140$, and the condition, "two pairs of jeans and one T-shirt cost $120" translates to $2j + t = 120$. These two equations must be satisfied *simultaneously*, so we must solve a system to determine the cost of one pair of jeans and one T-shirt.

Let's use the elimination method. Multiply both sides of the first equation by -2: $-2j - 6t = -280$. Then add this to the second equation to obtain $-5t = -160$, so that $t = 32$. So we know the price of one T-shirt is $32.

Now, plug this into the second equation for t and solve for j: $2j + 32 = 120$, so that $2j = 88$ and $j = 44$. So one pair of jeans costs $44. Finally, to answer the question posed, one pair of jeans and one T-shirt cost $32 + $44 = $76.

Marlene needs an average of 74% on five quizzes in order to get her desired grade in biology. Her first four quiz scores are 64%, 80%, 70%, and 78%. What does she need to score on her fifth quiz to attain her desired average?

F. 74
G. 78
H. 82
J. 86
K. 90

The correct answer is G. Let x represent the fifth quiz score. To compute the average of five numbers, sum them and divide by five. Since we are given percentages for all the scores, as well as the desired average, you can drop the percent sign momentarily and affix it to the final value of x:

$$\frac{64+80+70+78+x}{5}=74$$

$$\frac{292+x}{5}=74$$

$$292+x=370$$

$$x=78$$

So she needs 78% on the fifth quiz to attain the desired average.

SEQUENCES

Some ACT questions will ask you to find the value of an unknown term if given a sequence of terms. There are two special types of sequences for which we can find explicit formulas for the nth term rather easily.

An **arithmetic sequence** is a sequence with terms obtained by adding a fixed constant to the previous term. For instance, the sequence 8, 12, 16, 20, 24, …is an arithmetic sequence because the constant 4 is added to one term to get the next term. Likewise, the sequence 5, 1, –3, –7, –11, …is an arithmetic sequence because the constant –4 is added to one term to get the next term. However, the sequence 3, 6, 10, 15, 21, …is *not* an arithmetic sequence because the *same* constant is not added to each term to get the next. To get the second term, you add 3 to the first one; but, to get the third term, you must add 4 to the second term, and to get the fourth term, you must add 5 to the third one, and so on.

In general, if a sequence is arithmetic (and you add d to a term to get the next term), then the formula for its nth term is given by $a_n =$ (first term) $+ (n - 1)d$.

A **geometric sequence** is a sequence with terms obtained by multiplying the previous term by a fixed constant r. For instance, the sequence $\frac{1}{3}$, $\frac{1}{9}$, $\frac{1}{27}$, $\frac{1}{81}$, …is a geometric sequence because each term is multiplied by $\frac{1}{3}$ to get the next term. However, the sequence 8, 4, 0, –4, –8, … is *not* geometric because there is no single number by which you can multiply each term to get the next term.

In general, if a sequence is geometric (and you multiply a term by r to get the next term), then the formula for the nth term a_n is given by $a_n = r^{n-1} \times a_1$.

Here's a sequence question problem like you might encounter on the ACT.

What is the seventh term of the sequence 6, 12, 18, …?

F. 24
G. 30
H. 36
J. 42
K. 108

The correct answer is J. To answer this question, we must determine a pattern that the numbers of the sequence follow. Here the pattern is to add 6 to the previous term to get the next one. So the next term in the sequence is 24. But that's not the answer, as that is only the fourth term. We need the seventh term. So we continue to expand, getting 30, 36, and 42. So the seventh term is 42.

MATRICES

A **matrix** is an array of real numbers. If a matrix **A** has r rows and c columns, we say **A** is an $r \times c$ (read "r by c") matrix. A matrix is written by listing all of its entries in an array, enclosed by brackets. Here are some examples:

$$\underbrace{\begin{bmatrix} a & b \\ c & d \end{bmatrix}}_{2\times2 \text{ matrix}} \qquad \underbrace{\begin{bmatrix} 1 & -2 & 3 \\ 1 & 0 & 2 \\ 5 & 2 & 1 \end{bmatrix}}_{3\times3 \text{ matrix}} \qquad \underbrace{\begin{bmatrix} 1 \\ 3 \\ 2 \\ 1 \end{bmatrix}}_{4\times1 \text{ matrix}}$$

The basic arithmetic operations involving matrices are performed "component-wise," which means you need to pay attention to each entry's position in a matrix. The following is a list of the basic operations on 2×2 matrices that may occur on the ACT Mathematics test, though such questions occur infrequently. (All letters stand for real numbers.)

Term/Operation	Definition
Equality: $\begin{bmatrix} a & b \\ c & d \end{bmatrix} = \begin{bmatrix} e & f \\ g & h \end{bmatrix}$	$\begin{bmatrix} a & b \\ c & d \end{bmatrix} = \begin{bmatrix} e & f \\ g & h \end{bmatrix}$ whenever $\underbrace{a=e,\ b=f,\ c=g,\ d=h}_{\text{corresponding entries are equal}}$
Sum: $\begin{bmatrix} a & b \\ c & d \end{bmatrix} + \begin{bmatrix} e & f \\ g & h \end{bmatrix}$	$\begin{bmatrix} a & b \\ c & d \end{bmatrix} + \begin{bmatrix} e & f \\ g & h \end{bmatrix} = \begin{bmatrix} a+e & b+f \\ c+g & d+h \end{bmatrix}$ In words, add corresponding entries to get the sum.
Difference: $\begin{bmatrix} a & b \\ c & d \end{bmatrix} - \begin{bmatrix} e & f \\ g & h \end{bmatrix}$	$\begin{bmatrix} a & b \\ c & d \end{bmatrix} - \begin{bmatrix} e & f \\ g & h \end{bmatrix} = \begin{bmatrix} a-e & b-f \\ c-g & d-h \end{bmatrix}$ In words, subtract corresponding entries to get the difference.
Scalar Multiplication: $k\begin{bmatrix} a & b \\ c & d \end{bmatrix}$	$k\begin{bmatrix} a & b \\ c & d \end{bmatrix} = \begin{bmatrix} ka & kb \\ kc & kd \end{bmatrix}$ In words, multiply all entries by the constant k.

The following is a typical mathematics question on the ACT test involving matrices.

. . . .

Determine the value of x that makes the following equation true:

$$3\begin{bmatrix} x & -1 \\ 1 & 1 \end{bmatrix} - \begin{bmatrix} 3 & 1 \\ 0 & -1 \end{bmatrix} = \begin{bmatrix} 9 & -4 \\ 3 & 4 \end{bmatrix}$$

A. -6

B. 3

C. 1

D. 12

E. 4

The correct answer is E. First, simplify the left side of the equation using the rules for multiplying a matrix by a scalar and subtracting matrices. Then, equate corresponding entries to get an equation to solve for x:

$$3\begin{bmatrix} x & -1 \\ 1 & 1 \end{bmatrix} - \begin{bmatrix} 3 & 1 \\ 0 & -1 \end{bmatrix} = \begin{bmatrix} 9 & -4 \\ 3 & 4 \end{bmatrix}$$

$$\begin{bmatrix} 3x & -3 \\ 3 & 3 \end{bmatrix} - \begin{bmatrix} 3 & 1 \\ 0 & -1 \end{bmatrix} = \begin{bmatrix} 9 & -4 \\ 3 & 4 \end{bmatrix}$$

$$\begin{bmatrix} 3x-3 & -4 \\ 3 & 4 \end{bmatrix} = \begin{bmatrix} 9 & -4 \\ 3 & 4 \end{bmatrix}$$

Since two matrices are equal only when their corresponding entries are the same, then $3x - 3$ must equal 9. Solving this equation yields $x = 4$. So choice E is the correct answer.

. . . .

Chapter 7

Intermediate Algebra and Coordinate Geometry

SUMMING IT UP

- The **equation of a line** can come in different forms; the two most common are **standard form**, ($Ax + By = C$), and **slope-intercept form,** ($y = mx + b$).

- **The slope of a line** measures steepness of the line, or the change in y-value per unit change in x-value. If you have two points on a line, say (x_1, y_1) and (x_2, y_2), the slope is the "change in y over the change in x," written as $m = \dfrac{y_1 - y_2}{x_1 - x_2} = \dfrac{y_2 - y_1}{x_2 - x_1}$. The **point-slope form** for the equation of a line is $y - y_1 = m(x - x_1)$.

- Two lines $y = m_1x + b_1$ and $y = m_2x + b_2$ are **parallel** if the slopes are the same, that is $m_1 = m_2$. They are **perpendicular** if $m_1 \times m_2 = -1$.

- **A rational expression is a quotient of polynomials.** You can add, subtract, multiply, and divide rational expressions in the same manner as fractions—you're now just combining algebraic expressions.

- The **imaginary number** i satisfies $i^2 = -1$.

- A **complex number** is a number of the form $a + bi$, where a and b are both real numbers. The number a is called the **real part** and the number b is called the **imaginary part.** There are several rules that dictate the arithmetic of complex numbers, and they are very similar to how you perform arithmetic on binomials.

- The **solutions of $ax^2 + bx + c = 0$** are given by the **quadratic formula:** $x = \dfrac{-b \pm \sqrt{b^2 - 4ac}}{2a}$.

- The **discriminant** of $ax^2 + bx + c = 0$ is $b^2 - 4ac$. The sign of the discriminant determines the number and nature of the quadratic equation's solutions.

- **Linear inequalities** can be solved by using the same basic strategy used to solve linear equations, with the additional step of switching the inequality sign whenever both sides of the inequality are multiplied by a negative real number.

- A **system of linear equations** is a pair of linear equations involving x and y that must be satisfied *at the same time*. To solve a system means to identify ordered pairs (x, y) that satisfy *both* equations—not just one, but both! A linear system can have 0, 1, or infinitely many solutions, which can be determined using the **elimination method** or **substitution method.**

- The **distance between two points** $P(x_1, y_1)$ and $Q(x_2, y_2)$ is $\sqrt{(x_2 - x_1)^2 + (y_2 - y_1)^2}$.

- The **midpoint of the line segment** with endpoints $P(x_1, y_1)$ and $Q(x_2, y_2)$ is the point with coordinates $\left(\dfrac{x_1 + x_2}{2}, \dfrac{y_1 + y_2}{2} \right)$.

- The **equation of a circle** with center (h, k) and radius r is $(x - h)^2 + (y - k)^2 = r^2$.

- A **function** is a rule that associates to each input x a corresponding y-value. They are typically named using letters, like f or g. The notation $f(x)$ represents the functional value at x.

- The **domain** of a function is the set of all values of x that can be substituted into the expression and yield a meaningful output. The **range** of a function is the set of all possible y-values attained at some member of the domain.

- **The sum $(f + g)(x)$ is defined as $f(x) + g(x)$.** Likewise, the difference function $(f - g)(x)$ is defined as $f(x) - g(x)$, the product function $(f \cdot g)(x)$ is defined as $f(x) \cdot g(x)$, and the quotient function $\left(\dfrac{f}{g} \right)(x)$ is defined as $\dfrac{f(x)}{g(x)}$.

- The **composition of f and g**, denoted by ($f \circ g$), is defined by $(f \circ g)(x) = f(g(x))$. Generally, $(f \circ g) \neq (g \circ f)$.

- The **minimum** of f is the smallest y-value in the range of f; it is the y-value of the lowest point on the graph of f. Likewise, **maximum** of f is the largest y-value in the range of f; it is the y-value of the highest point on the graph of f.

- f is **decreasing** on an interval if its graph falls from left to right as you progress through the interval from left to right; f is **increasing** on an interval if its graph rises from left to right as you progress through the interval from left to right.

272

Chapter 7

Intermediate
Algebra and
Coordinate
Geometry

- An **x-intercept of f is a point of the form (x, 0).** You determine the x-intercepts of a function by solving the equation $f(x) = 0$.

- A **y-intercept of f is the point (0, $f(0)$).**

- A **polynomial** is a function of the form $f(x) = a_n x^n + a_{n-1} x^{n-1} + \ldots + a_1 x + a_0$, where $a_0, a_1, \ldots, a_n$ are real numbers and n is a nonnegative integer. We say the polynomial has *degree n*. Its graph has at most n x-intercepts.

- An **arithmetic sequence** is a sequence whose terms are obtained by adding a fixed constant to the previous term. A formula for its nth term is $a_n = (\text{first term}) + (n-1)d$.

- A **geometric sequence** is a sequence whose terms are obtained by multiplying the previous term by a fixed constant r. A formula for the nth term a_n is $a_n = r^{n-1} \times a_1$.

- A **matrix** is an array of real numbers. If a matrix **A** has r rows and c columns, we say **A** is an $r \times c$ matrix. The basic arithmetic operations involving matrices are performed "component-wise."

ONLINE
PREP

WANT TO KNOW MORE?

Access more practice questions, lessons, helpful hints, and strategies for the following math topics in *Peterson's ACT Online Course:*

- Rational and Radical Expressions

- 2 Equations, 2 Unknowns

- Inequalities

- Quadratic Formula

- Functions

- Coordinate Geometry

To purchase and access the course, go to ***www.petersons.com/act***.

273

Chapter 7

Intermediate
Algebra and
Coordinate
Geometry

PRACTICE

It's time once again to assess what you have learned with another mathematics practice quiz. When you're finished answering all 20 questions, check the answers and explanations that follow to figure out how well you did and why you may have selected some incorrect answer choices.

1. If line l is defined by the equation $2y - x = 8$, which of the following equations could define a line that is parallel to line l?

   A. $y = -\dfrac{1}{2}x + 4$

   B. $y = \dfrac{1}{2}x + 5$

   C. $y = -x - 8$
   D. $y = x + 6$
   E. $y = -2x + 1$

2. Which of the following lines is perpendicular to the line graphed below?

   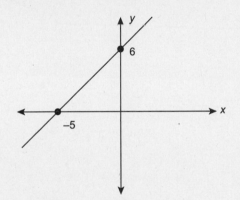

   F. $5y = 6x + 2$
   G. $5y = -6x + 8$
   H. $y = -x + 6$
   J. $6y + 5x = -1$
   K. $6y - 5x = 0$

3. Which of the following is equal to $\dfrac{3i}{2i - 1}$?

   A. $1 - \dfrac{3}{5}i$

   B. 3

   C. $-\dfrac{3}{5}i$

   D. $-\dfrac{3}{5} + \dfrac{6}{5}i$

   E. $\dfrac{6}{5} - \dfrac{3}{5}i$

4. If $x^2 - 10x + 4 = 0$, what are the possible values of x?

   F. $5 \pm \sqrt{21}$

   G. $5 \pm 2\sqrt{21}$

   H. $-5 \pm \sqrt{21}$

   J. $10 \pm 2\sqrt{21}$

   K. $5 \pm i\sqrt{21}$

5. Which of the following represents the solution set to the inequality $-7 - 3x > 2$?

   A.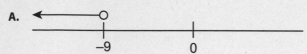

   B.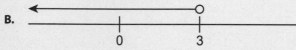

   C.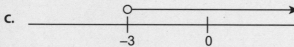

   D.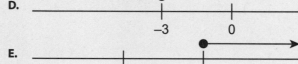

   E.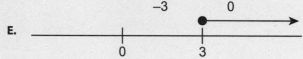

6. What is the solution set for the inequality $|4x + 1| < 5$?

   F. $x < 1$

   G. $-\dfrac{3}{2} < x < 1$

   H. $-1 < x < \dfrac{3}{2}$

   J. $-\dfrac{3}{2} < x$

   K. $-\dfrac{5}{4} < x < \dfrac{5}{4}$

276

Chapter 7

Intermediate Algebra and Coordinate Geometry

7. If $z - w = \dfrac{1}{4}$ and $w + z = 1$, then what is the value

of $\dfrac{z}{w - z}$?

A. $-\dfrac{5}{32}$

B. $\dfrac{5}{8}$

C. $-\dfrac{2}{5}$

D. $\dfrac{5}{2}$

E. $-\dfrac{5}{2}$

8. Which of the following is equivalent to $\dfrac{24 + 6x}{42x}$?

F. $\dfrac{6x + 4}{7x}$

G. $\dfrac{5}{7}$

H. $24\dfrac{1}{7}$

J. $\dfrac{x + 4}{7x}$

K. $\dfrac{24 + 6x}{7x}$

9. If x is a positive real number, which of the following is equal to $\dfrac{x^2 + x}{2x + 4} \div \dfrac{3x}{x + 2}$ in simplified form?

A. $\dfrac{x + 1}{6}$

B. $\dfrac{3x^3 + 3x}{2x^2 + 8x + 8}$

C. $\dfrac{6}{x + 1}$

D. $x + \dfrac{1}{6}$

E. $\dfrac{2x^2 + 8x + 8}{3x^3 + 3x}$

277

Chapter 7

Intermediate Algebra and Coordinate Geometry

10. For all nonnegative values of a and b, $\sqrt{5^4y^3z^6} =$

    F. $5^8y^6z^{12}$

    G. $25y^{\frac{2}{3}}z^{\frac{1}{3}}$

    H. $25y^{\frac{3}{2}}z^3$

    J. $25y^{-\frac{3}{2}}z^{-3}$

    K. $5^4y^3z^6$

11. What is the length of a line segment with endpoints $(-3, 2)$ and $(5, -1)$?

    A. $\sqrt{11}$

    B. $\sqrt{61}$

    C. 11

    D. $\sqrt{73}$

    E. 73

12. What is the minimum value of the expression $|x+6|-1$?

    F. -6
    G. -1
    H. 0
    J. 1
    K. 6

13. The equation of a polynomial is given by $y = 8(2x + 3)$ $(x + 5)(3x - 1)(x - 2)(x + 6)$. How many times does its graph cross the x-axis?

    A. 6
    B. 5
    C. 3
    D. 2
    E. 0

14. Which of the following equations defines a circle in the (x, y) coordinate plane with a center at $C(-3, 2)$ that passes through $P(5, -4)$?

    F. $(x - 3)^2 + (y - 2)^2 = 100$
    G. $(x + 3)^2 + (y + 2)^2 = 100$
    H. $(x + 3)^2 + (y - 2)^2 = 10$
    J. $(x + 3)^2 + (y - 2)^2 = 100$
    K. $(x + 3)^2 + (y - 2)^2 = 106$

15. For which real values of x is $\dfrac{5^x(x+2)}{(x-6)^3}$ defined?

    A. All real numbers
    B. All except $x = 6$
    C. All except $x = 6$ and $x = -2$
    D. All except $x = -6$
    E. All except $x = -6$ and $x = -2$

16. If $f(x) = -3x^2 + 4x - 2$, what is the value of $f(-2)$?

    F. -22
    G. -20
    H. -6
    J. 18
    K. 22

17. If $f(x) = 1 - 2x$ and $g(x) = 3x^2 - x$, what is the value of $f(g(x))$?

    A. $1 - 6x^2 - x$
    B. $-(6x^2 - 2x - 1)$
    C. $12x^2 - 10x + 2$
    D. $-(6x^2 + 2x + 1)$
    E. $-6x^3 + 5x^2 - x$

18. Snow is falling at a rate of 0.50 inch per hour. At this rate, how many hours would it take for S inches of snow to fall?

    F. $\dfrac{S}{2}$
    G. $\dfrac{1}{2S}$
    H. $2S$
    J. $S + \dfrac{1}{2}$
    K. $S - \dfrac{1}{2}$

19. A general contractor calculates that it costs him m dollars per hour in materials costs and l dollars per hour in labor costs to complete a job. Which of the following expressions would provide him with the total cost of a job requiring h hours to complete?

    A. ml
    B. mlh
    C. $m + l$
    D. $h(m + l)$
    E. $(mh)(lh)$

20. If $M = \begin{bmatrix} 0 & 2 \\ -1 & 3 \end{bmatrix}$ and $N = \begin{bmatrix} -5 & 2 \\ 0 & 1 \end{bmatrix}$ then

$3M - N =$

SHOW YOUR WORK HERE

F. $\begin{bmatrix} 5 & 0 \\ -1 & 2 \end{bmatrix}$

G. $\begin{bmatrix} 15 & 0 \\ -3 & 6 \end{bmatrix}$

H. $\begin{bmatrix} 0 & 6 \\ -3 & 9 \end{bmatrix}$

J. $\begin{bmatrix} -5 & 8 \\ -3 & 10 \end{bmatrix}$

K. $\begin{bmatrix} 5 & 4 \\ -3 & 8 \end{bmatrix}$

Answers and Explanations

1. **The correct answer is B.** First, rewrite the equation for line *l* in slope-intercept form:

$$2y - x = 8$$
$$2y = x + 8$$
$$y = \frac{1}{2}x + 4$$

Now you can see that the line *l* has a slope of $\frac{1}{2}$. The slopes of parallel lines are equal, so the slope of a line parallel to line *l* is also $\frac{1}{2}$. Only choice B satisfies this condition. Choices A, C, D, and E all have different slopes. It is worth noting that the line in choice E is actually perpendicular to *l*: $\frac{1}{2} \times -2 = -1$.

2. **The correct answer is J.** The product of the slopes of perpendicular lines is −1. So first determine the slope of the graphed line and then determine which line listed among the choices has a slope that is its negative reciprocal. Using the slope formula with the points (−5, 0) and (0, 6), we see that the slope of the graphed line is $\frac{6-0}{0-(-5)} = \frac{6}{5}$. So the correct answer will be the line with a slope of $-\frac{5}{6}$. Rewriting the equation in choice J in slope-intercept form yields $y = -\frac{5}{6}x - \frac{1}{6}$.

The line in choice F is parallel to the graphed line since it has the same slope. In choice G, the slope is $-\frac{6}{5}$, not $-\frac{5}{6}$. In choice H, while the lines have the same *y*-intercept, the product of their slopes is not −1, so they cannot be perpendicular. In choice K, the slope is $\frac{5}{6}$, not $-\frac{5}{6}$.

3. **The correct answer is E.** In order to compute this quotient, multiply the numerator and the denominator by the conjugate of the denominator, $2i + 1$. Then, simplify:

$$\frac{3i}{2i-1} = \frac{3i}{2i-1} \bullet \frac{2i+1}{2i+1} = \frac{3i(2i) + 3i(1)}{(2i)^2 - 1^2} = \frac{-6+3i}{-5} = \frac{6}{5} - \frac{3}{5}i$$

Therefore, choice E is the correct answer.

In choice A, the real part is wrong. In choice B, you mistakenly canceled out the *i*'s from the numerator and denominator. In choice C, you forgot to include the real part, which is $\frac{6}{5}$. In choice D, you interchanged the real and imaginary parts.

4. **The correct answer is F.** Use the quadratic formula to complete this problem. Since $x^2 - 10x + 4 = 0$ is in the form $ax^2 + bx + c = 0$, you know that $a = 1$, $b = -10$, and $c = 4$.

$$x = \frac{-b \pm \sqrt{b^2 - 4ac}}{2a}$$
$$= \frac{-(-10) \pm \sqrt{(-10)^2 - 4(1)(4)}}{2(1)}$$
$$= \frac{10 \pm \sqrt{100 - 16}}{2}$$
$$= \frac{10 \pm \sqrt{84}}{2}$$
$$= \frac{10 \pm 2\sqrt{21}}{2}$$
$$= 5 \pm \sqrt{21}$$

In choice G, you only divided the number before the "$\pm$" sign by the denominator, but should have also divided the term after the "$\pm$" sign by the denominator. For choice H, −5 should be 5 because in the quadratic formula the first term in the numerator is −*b*, not *b*. In choice J, you forgot the denominator; in the quadratic formula, you are supposed to divide by 2*b*. In choice K, the *i* should not be part of the solution because the radicand was positive, not negative.

5. **The correct answer is D.** Isolate *x* on one side of the inequality, remembering to flip the direction of the inequality sign when you multiply or divide by a negative number:

$$-7 - 3x > 2$$
$$-3x > 9$$
$$x < -3$$

Only choice D properly represents the inequality $x < -3$ on a number line.

In choice A, you forgot to divide both sides by 3. In choice B, the sign of the endpoint of the ray is wrong—it should be −3, not 3. In choice C, you forgot to reverse the inequality sign when dividing both sides by a negative number. In choice E, the endpoint of the ray should be −3, not 3, and it should have an open circle on it instead of a filled circle.

6. **The correct answer is G.** First, rewrite the absolute value inequality as the double inequality $-5 < 4x + 1 < 5$. To solve this inequality, subtract 1 from all parts to get $-6 < 4x < 4$ and then divide all parts by 4 to get $-\frac{3}{2} < x < 1$. This is the solution set.

In choice F, you forgot the left part when converting the absolute value inequality to a double inequality. In choice H, the endpoints of the interval should be reversed and have opposite signs. In choice J, you forgot the right part when converting the absolute value inequality to a double inequality. In choice K, you forgot to subtract 1 from all parts of the double inequality before dividing by 4.

7. **The correct answer is E.** You already have the value for the denominator of the fraction from the first equation (just multiply both sides by -1 to get $w - z = -\frac{1}{4}$). But, we still need to find the value of z. To do so, add the two given equations to get $2z = \frac{5}{4}$, so that $z = \frac{5}{8}$.

Now substitute the values for z and $w - z$ into the expression:

$$\frac{z}{w-z} = \frac{\frac{5}{8}}{-\frac{1}{4}} = \frac{5}{8} \div \left(-\frac{1}{4}\right) = \frac{5}{8} \times (-4) = -\frac{5}{2}$$

You do not need to solve the system to find *both z* and *w* here, since you already know the value of half of the expression from one the equations. This will save you a little time.

In choice A, you multiplied instead of dividing when computing the value of the given expression. Remember, $\frac{a}{b} \div \frac{c}{d} = \frac{a}{b} \bullet \frac{d}{c}$. Choice B is just the value of z; you did not account for the denominator. Choice C is the reciprocal of the correct answer. Choice D has the opposite sign of the correct answer.

8. **The correct answer is J.** Begin by factoring out the greatest common factor, which is 6, in the numerator. This yields $\frac{24+6x}{42x} = \frac{6(4+x)}{42x}$.

Then cancel the common factor 6 from the numerator and denominator:

$$\frac{24+6x}{42x} = \frac{6(4+x)}{42x} = \frac{4+x}{7x}$$

This is equivalent to $\frac{x+4}{7x}$. The correct answer is J.

In choice F, you should have canceled the 6 in the $6x$ as well. In choice G, $24 + 6x$ does not equal $(24 + 6)x$; you cannot add coefficients of like terms. In choice H, while you can split up the fractions into a sum of two, the same denominator must be applied to both: $\frac{(24+6x)}{42x} \ne 24 + \frac{6x}{42x}$. In choice K, you should have canceled a 6 in the numerator as well.

9. **The correct answer is A.** Dividing rational expressions is similar to multiplying them, with the exception that the first step is to transform the division problem into a multiplication problem by multiplying the first fraction by the reciprocal of the second fraction. Then, factor whatever you can and cancel common factors in the top and bottom:

$$\frac{x^2+1}{2x+4} \div \frac{3x}{x+2} = \frac{x^2+1}{2x+4} \bullet \frac{x+2}{3x}$$
$$= \frac{\cancel{x}(x+1)}{2\cancel{(x+2)}} \bullet \frac{\cancel{x+2}}{3\cancel{x}}$$
$$= \frac{x+1}{6}$$

In choice B, you multiplied instead of divided. In choice C, you flipped the wrong fraction. When converting a quotient of fractions to a product, you take the reciprocal of the fraction *after* the division sign. In choice D, you likely had the correct answer, but then simplified incorrectly. You should have applied the denominator to the x-term as well. In choice E, you multiplied the fractions and *then* took the reciprocal. You should have rewritten the division problem as a multiplication problem by taking the reciprocal of the fraction following the division sign, and *then* multiplied those fractions.

10. **The correct answer is H.** Simplify the expression by taking the square root of each factor separately, as follows:

$$\sqrt{5^4 y^3 z^6} = \sqrt{5^4} \times \sqrt{y^3} \times \sqrt{z^6}$$
$$= 5^2 \times y^{\frac{3}{2}} \times z^3 = 25 y^{\frac{3}{2}} z^3$$

In choice F, you squared the expression instead of taking its square root. Choice G is incorrect because $\sqrt{y^3} = y^{\frac{3}{2}}$, not $y^{\frac{2}{3}}$. In choice J, the exponents of y

and z should not be negative. In choice K, you completely ignored the radical sign.

11. **The correct answer is D.** Use the distance formula to find the length:

$$\sqrt{(-3-5)^2+(2-(-1))^2}=\sqrt{(-8)^2+(3)^2}$$
$$=\sqrt{64+9}$$
$$=\sqrt{73}\text{ units}$$

In choice A, you computed the differences of the coordinates of single points rather than the x-coordinates of both points and the y-coordinates of both points, and you forgot to square these differences. In choice B, you computed the differences of the coordinates of single points rather than the x-coordinates of both points and the y-coordinates of both points. In choice C, you mistakenly computed $\sqrt{a^2+b^2}=a+b$; remember, you cannot distribute the square root across a sum. In choice E, you forgot to take the square root.

12. **The correct answer is G.** The smallest absolute value of any expression is 0. The absolute value of $x+6$ equals 0 only when x is -6. For this value of x, the value of the expression is -1. Choice F is the x-value at which the minimum occurs. Choice H is the minimum value of just the absolute value expression—you still need to subtract 1 from it. Choices J and K are incorrect because there are smaller possible values produced by this expression, so they cannot be the minimum value of the expression.

13. **The correct answer is B.** A graph intersects the x-axis every time $y=0$, which occurs whenever one of the factors of the polynomial is equal to 0. Each of the terms inside the parentheses is distinct, so there will be five different values of x for which $y=0$: $-\dfrac{3}{2}, -5, \dfrac{1}{3}, 2$, and -6. Thus the graph crosses the x-axis 5 times.

Choice A is incorrect because while the constant 8 is a factor, it cannot be zero. Choices C and D are incorrect because you must set all factors equal to zero, not just those with a "+" (as in choice C) or those with a "−" (as in choice D). Choice E is way off since each of the five factors equals zero at a different x-value, and these are the values at which the graph crosses the x-axis.

14. **The correct answer is J.** The general formula for a circle is $(x-h)^2+(y-k)^2=r^2$, where (h, k) is the center of the circle and r is the radius. Of the equations given, only $(x+3)^2+(y-2)^2=100$ has a center at $(-3, 2)$ and a radius equal to the distance between C and P, which is

$$\sqrt{(-3-5)^2+(2-(-4))^2}=10.$$

In choices F and G, the radius is correct, but the center is $(-3, 2)$, not $(3, 2)$ or $(-3, -2)$. In choice H, the right side should be squared. In choice K, the radius is incorrect; you should use the distance formula to compute the distance between C and P.

15. **The correct answer is B.** A fraction is not defined whenever the denominator equals 0. Set the denominator equal to 0, and note that $(x-6)^3$ will equal 0 only when $x=6$. Therefore, the fraction is undefined when $x=6$.

Choice A is incorrect because if $x=6$, the denominator would equal 0. Choices C and E are incorrect because -2 makes the numerator of the fraction equal to zero, which is permissible—this simply means the fraction itself is equal to zero. For choices D and E, the denominator equals 0 when $x=6$, not -6.

16. **The correct answer is F.** To find $f(-2)$, plug in -2 for every instance of x in the function, and remember to use the order of operations:

$$f(-2)=-3(-2)^2+4(-2)-2$$
$$=-3(4)-8-2$$
$$=-12-8-2$$
$$=-22$$

In choice G, you forgot to include the constant term in the calculation. In choice H, you computed $4(-2)$ as 8 instead of -8. In choice J, you did not apply the order of operations correctly: the -3 only applies to x^2, not the entire rest of the polynomial. In choice K, you dropped the negative sign off the answer.

17. **The correct answer is B.** The function $f(g(x))$ is a composition of two functions in which you plug in the expression for $g(x)$, which is $3x^2-x$, for x in the formula for $f(x)$, which is $1-2x$:

$$f\big(g(x)\big)=1-2\big(3x^2-x\big)$$
$$=1-6x^2+2x$$
$$=-\big(6x^2-2x-1\big)$$

In choice A, after correctly plugging in the expression for g(x) for in the formula for f(x), you did not distribute the -2 to both terms of the binomial. Choice C is the reverse composition, g(f(x)). In choice D, you factored out the -1 incorrectly. In choice E, you multiplied f(x) times g(x) instead of solving the composition.

18. **The correct answer is H.** Set up a proportion equating the ratio of snowfall per hour to the ratio of snowfall per x hours, and cross-multiply to solve for x:

$$\frac{1}{0.50} = \frac{x}{S}$$
$$S = 0.50x$$
$$x = \frac{S}{0.50} = 2S$$

Choice F is incorrect because you should divide by 0.50, not multiply by it; you likely inverted half of the proportion to get this answer. Choice G is the reciprocal of the correct expression. Choice J is incorrect because when solving the equation $0.50x = S$, you must divide by 0.50, not add it to both sides. Choice K is incorrect because when solving the equation $0.50x = S$, you must divide by 0.50, not subtract it from both sides.

19. **The correct answer is D.** The job costs $m + l$ to complete each hour, so if it takes h hours, the expression would be $h(m + l)$. Choices A and B are incorrect because you should be adding m and l, not multiplying them, and then you should multiply the resulting sum by h. Choice C is just the cost per hour; you must multiply by the number of hours, h. Choice E is incorrect because you should be adding mh and lh, not multiplying them.

20. **The correct answer is K.** First, multiply M by 3 and then subtract the matrices component-wise:

$$3M - N = 3\begin{bmatrix} 0 & 2 \\ -1 & 3 \end{bmatrix} - \begin{bmatrix} -5 & 2 \\ 0 & 1 \end{bmatrix}$$
$$= \begin{bmatrix} 0 & 6 \\ -3 & 9 \end{bmatrix} - \begin{bmatrix} -5 & 2 \\ 0 & 1 \end{bmatrix}$$
$$= \begin{bmatrix} 0-(-5) & 6-2 \\ -3-0 & 9-1 \end{bmatrix}$$
$$= \begin{bmatrix} 5 & 4 \\ -3 & 8 \end{bmatrix}$$

Choice F is just $M - N$. Choice G is $3(M - N)$. Choice H is just $3M$. Choice J is $3M + N$.

Chapter 7

Intermediate Algebra and Coordinate Geometry

CHAPTER 8: PLANE GEOMETRY AND TRIGONOMETRY

OVERVIEW

- Angles
- Triangles
- Quadrilaterals
- Circles
- Solids
- Right Triangle Trigonometry
- Trigonometric Identities
- Solving Trigonometric Equations
- Summing It Up
- Practice

Our final math review chapter will cover two of the most visual portions of the ACT Mathematics test: plane geometry and trigo-nometry. Our intent in this chapter is to expose you to the visuals, formulas, and terminology that will come up on the ACT. We can't say it enough—a huge part of doing well on the ACT Mathematics test is knowing *which* formulas to use *when*. That's why we accompany all of the concepts we explain with sample ACT questions so you can see them in action, rather than just looking at numbers and variables in a table.

The last part of this chapter covers the basic concepts of trigonometry, starting with right triangle trigonometry and then moving to the trigonometric functions and their graphs and trigonometric identities. These are pretty advanced concepts—they're the highest-level math featured on the ACT. The good news is that only 5 to 10 percent of mathematics questions might cover these concepts. The better news is that this chapter covers the breadth of what you can expect to see on test day. Review the concepts we give you and practice the questions, and you'll be all set.

Now, on to the final lesson!

You likely have a general understanding of the terms *point, line, line segment, ray,* and *angle,* so we will not linger there. Rather, let's focus on classifying angles and their relationships—understanding how these smaller elements of geometry relate to one another will be an important factor in your success on the exam. ACT questions rarely ask about single components; rather, they want you to figure out how smaller geometry elements fit together.

Mastering the concepts and vocabulary in the first part of this chapter that covers geometry is a big step on the way to excelling with ACT geometry questions—almost all questions will require that you are very familiar with the terms that follow. Let's begin!

ANGLES

Angles are classified according to their **measure.** Angle units are expressed in **degrees** (and often **radians** when studying trigonometry), and the notation m $\angle$ (name of angle) is used to denote the measure of a given angle.

These are the various angle characterizations you should know—these terms will likely come up somewhere on the ACT:

Term	Definition	
Acute Angle		An angle with a measure between 0 and 90 degrees
Right Angle		An angle with a measure of 90 degrees
Obtuse Angle		An angle with a measure between 90 and 180 degrees
Straight Angle		An angle with a measure of 180 degrees
Complementary Angles		Two angles with measures that sum to 90 degrees
Supplementary Angles		Two angles with measures that sum to 180 degrees
Congruent Angles		Two angles that have the same measure

It's not only important that you understand individual angle classifications, but also how pairs of angles relate to each other. Knowing these relationships will help you figure out angle values in figures and perform more complex calculations.

Take a look at the following image and the table that follows. You will likely be presented with a figure on the ACT test that has some angle values filled in, and then be asked to determine missing values in order to solve a problem. We suggest that you review and memorize these angle relationships until they're second nature to you—they are sure to come in handy when you take the test.

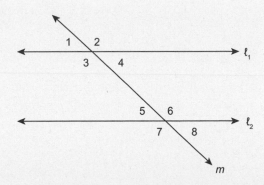

Term	Examples from Diagram
Corresponding Angles	$\angle 1$ and $\angle 5$, $\angle 3$ and $\angle 7$ In a diagram such as the one above, if the lines l_1 and l_2 are parallel, then corresponding angles are congruent.
Adjacent Angles	$\angle 1$ and $\angle 2$, $\angle 5$ and $\angle 7$
Vertical Angles	$\angle 1$ and $\angle 4$, $\angle 6$ and $\angle 7$ Vertical angles are *always* congruent!
Alternate Interior Angles	$\angle 4$ and $\angle 5$, $\angle 3$ and $\angle 6$ In a diagram such as the one above, if the lines l_1 and l_2 are parallel, then alternate interior angles are congruent.

Remember: typically parallelism is denoted by two vertical hash marks, like $l_1 \parallel l_2$. Congruence is generally denoted by a single hash mark.

If two lines cut by a transversal are NOT parallel, then pairs of corresponding angles and pairs of alternate interior angles are *not* necessarily congruent.

Let's look at a sample problem dealing with lines and angles.

Points *A*, *D*, and *E* lie on the same line in the figure below. What is the measure of angle *BEC*?

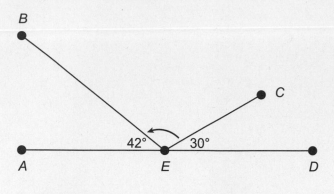

F. 60°
G. 48°
H. 90°
J. 108°
K. 150°

The correct answer is J. In the diagram, the three angles form a straight line and therefore, their measures must sum to 180°.

$$m\angle AEB + m\angle BEC + m\angle CED = 180°$$
$$42° + m\angle BEC + 30° = 180°$$
$$m\angle BEC = 180° - 42° - 30°$$
$$= 108°$$

TRIANGLES

Triangles come in all different sizes and are classified using their angles and sides as follows.

Classified by Angles		
Term	**Definition**	
Right	One of the angles is a right angle (the other two, therefore, must be acute)	
Acute	All three angles are acute	
Obtuse	One of the angles is obtuse (the other two, therefore, must be acute)	

Classified by Sides	
Term	**Definition**
Equilateral	All three sides have the same length; that is, all three sides are **congruent**
Isosceles	At least two sides have the same length; that is, at least two sides are **congruent**
Scalene	All three sides have different lengths

All triangles obey the **triangle sum rule** and the **triangle inequality**. The triangle sum rule says that the sum of the measures of the three angles in any triangle must be 180°. The triangle inequality says that the sum of the lengths of any two sides of a triangle must be strictly larger than the length of the third side.

Let's put some of these rules into practice with this sample problem.

What is the measure of angle *DEF*?

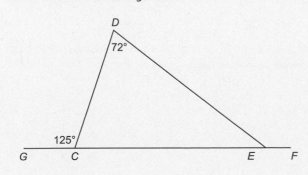

A. 127°
B. 125°
C. 108°
D. 90°
E. 53°

The correct answer is A. Angle *DCE* is supplementary to angle *DCG*, so its measure is 180° − 125° = 55°. The interior angles of a triangle sum to 180°, so the measure of angle *DEC* is 180° − 55° − 72° = 53°. Finally, angle *DEF* is supplementary to angle *DEC*, so its measure is 180° − 53° = 127°.

RIGHT TRIANGLES AND THE PYTHAGOREAN THEOREM

The lengths of the sides of right triangles are always related by the **Pythagorean theorem**. Consider the right triangle shown here:

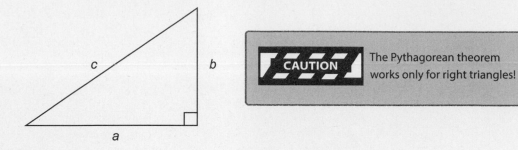

The Pythagorean theorem works only for right triangles!

The sides with lengths *a* and *b* are called **legs,** and the side opposite the right angle is the **hypotenuse.** The hypotenuse is the longest side of a right triangle.

> Two common right triangles have sides that measure 3-4-5 and 5-12-13, or multiples thereof. Be on the lookout for these **Pythagorean triples**—recognizing them within a problem can make calculating a missing side easier.

The Pythagorean theorem says that $a^2 + b^2 = c^2$.

Two special right triangles are 30-60-90 and 45-45-90 triangles; the numbers indicate the triangles' angle measures. The ratio of the side lengths for these special triangles are given below.

45-45-90 Triangle

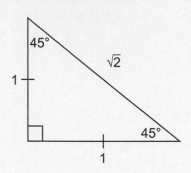

30-60-90 Triangle

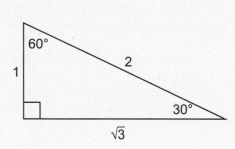

Again, familiarize yourself with these values and be on the lookout for triangles with these angle measures—there is sure to be at least one ACT question where knowing them will help you answer quickly and confidently.

TRIANGLES AND MEASUREMENT

We say two triangles *ABC* and *DEF* are **congruent** if all three corresponding pairs of angles are congruent *and* all three corresponding sides are congruent. Always identify **corresponding** sides of two triangles using the order in which their vertices (i.e., points where two sides meet) are written. As noted here in our description, vertex *A* corresponds to vertex *D*, *B* to *E*, and *C* to *F*.

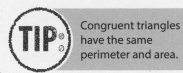

TIP: Congruent triangles have the same perimeter and area.

TIP: Corresponding angles in two similar triangles must be congruent.

Two triangles *ABC* and *DEF* that are *not* congruent can still be proportional to each other in the sense that the ratios of the three pairs of corresponding sides are the same—that is, $\frac{AB}{DE} = \frac{BC}{EF} = \frac{AC}{DF} = k$, where *k* is a positive number.

In such cases, we say triangles *ABC* and *DEF* are **similar.**

The **perimeter** of a closed plane figure is the distance around the figure and is computed by adding the lengths of all segments/sides forming its outer boundary. Some common units used when measuring length are *inches, feet, yards,* etc.; the metric system is also commonly used (*centimeters, meters,* etc.) The perimeter of a triangle is the sum of the lengths of its three sides. Often, a question will require you to compute the perimeter of a right triangle, but you will not explicitly be given the lengths of all the sides. In such case, do not forget that you have the Pythagorean theorem!

The **area** of a two-dimensional plane figure is the number of **unit squares** needed to cover it. The standard units of measure of area are *square inches, square feet, square yards,* etc.; the metric system is also commonly used (*square centimeters, square meters,* etc.) The area formula for a triangle with base *b* and height *h*, as illustrated below, is $A = \frac{1}{2}b \bullet h$.

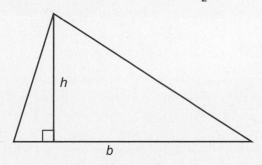

The height of a triangle must be perpendicular to its base. That means there are three possible pairings of heights with bases for any triangle—each base has its own height.

Take a look at a problem like you may see on the ACT that deals with the area of a right triangle.

What is the area in square inches of a right triangle with sides of 27 inches, 36 inches, and 45 inches?

   F.   972
   G.   486
   H.   192
   J.   96
   K.   Cannot be determined from the given information

The correct answer is G. This is a multiple of a 3-4-5 right triangle: 3(9) = 27, 4(9) = 36, 5(9) = 45. (We told you they would come up! Whenever you are given three side values of a right triangle, check to see if they are multiples of a Pythagorean triple.) Since it is a right triangle, the legs serve as the base and height. So its area is half the product of its legs: $\frac{1}{2}(27)(36) = 486$ square inches.

ALERT: Be careful with units. Every now and then, all quantities in a problem will NOT be expressed using the same units (some may be in feet and others in inches, for instance). The first thing to do in such case is to convert all quantities to the same units.

Let's look at a couple of problems dealing with measurement.

The open area in front of a museum is a square lawn bordered by footpaths 250 feet long on each side. The museum plans to create a diagonal footpath that would connect the northwest corner of the lawn to the southeast corner of the lawn. Approximately how many feet shorter would the new path be than the shortest possible route on the existing footpaths?

    A. 500
    B. 354
    C. 250
    D. 146
    E. 125

The correct answer is D. The current paths require a trip of 500 feet (250 feet for each of the two sides one must travel along to get from one corner to the other). A diagonal path would form a 45°–45°–90° isosceles right triangle with the existing paths being its legs. As such, the length of the diagonal path would be $250\sqrt{2}$ feet, or approximately 354 feet. The new path would shorten the route by approximately 500 – 354 = 146 feet.

A certain triangle has sides of lengths 50, 120, and 130 centimeters. If a similar triangle has a perimeter of 1,500 centimeters, what is the length (in centimeters) of the triangle's shortest side?

    F. 50
    G. 130
    H. 250
    J. 600
    K. 650

The correct answer is H. The two triangles are similar, so their sides are in proportion. The first triangle has a perimeter of 50 + 120 + 130 = 300 centimeters. The second triangle has a perimeter that is 5 times this: 1,500 centimeters. Thus, the sides of the second triangle are exactly 5 times as long as the sides of the first triangle: 250, 600, and 650 centimeters. So the length of the shortest side is 250 centimeters.

Proving Geometric Theorems

The notion of proving theorems in geometry is not tested very often on the ACT, but it does come up from time to time, usually in the context of triangles. In this section, we will review congruence and some typical methods of proof used to establish the congruence of two triangles.

Two figures F and G are **congruent** if they have the same size and shape. We denote this fact by writing $F \cong G$. The following two facts are obvious, but very important:

- Two line segments are congruent *if and only if* they have the same length.

- Two angles are congruent *if and only if* they have the same measure.

Two triangles *ABC* and *DEF* are *congruent* if the following conditions hold:

Picture	Segments	Angles
A *D* *B* *C* *E* *F* **Note:** Vertex *A* is identified with vertex *D*; *B* is identified with *E*; and *C* is identified with *F*.	$AC \cong DF$ $AB \cong DE$ $BC \cong EF$	$m\angle A = m\angle D$ $m\angle B = m\angle E$ $m\angle C = m\angle F$

Although all six conditions must hold in order for the two triangles to be congruent, we do not need to verify all six. Rather, there are different congruence properties that tell us that if we verify certain subsets of these conditions, the others must hold true as a consequence.

Congruence Property	Conditions That Must Be Satisfied
SAS Property	Two pairs of corresponding sides are congruent, and the corresponding angles between them must be congruent.
ASA Property	Two pairs of corresponding angles are congruent, and the included sides between them must be congruent.
SSS Property	All three pairs of corresponding sides are congruent.

Isosceles Triangle Theorem

If the triangle *ABC* is isosceles, then the angles that are opposite the congruent sides (base angles) will also be congruent.

 A typical question on the ACT test that involves proofs consists of a statement and the lines of the proof in scrambled order. The question will ask you to provide the correct order of the statements so that the result constitutes a proof of the statement.

Here is the step-by-step proof:

1) Given that triangle *ABC* is isosceles with $AB \cong AC$.
2) Draw angle bisector *AD*, such that $\angle BAD \cong \angle CAD$.
3) $AD \cong AC$ using the reflexive property.
4) Therefore, by the SAS property, $\triangle BAD \cong \triangle CAD$.

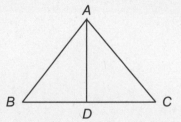

Using CPCTC (corresponding parts of congruent triangles are congruent), $\angle B \cong \angle C$.

The proof is complete.

Hypotenuse-Leg (HL) Theorem

If the hypotenuse and one leg of a right triangle are congruent to the corresponding parts of another right triangle, then the two triangles are congruent.

Here is the step-by-step proof:

1) Given triangles *ADB* and *ADC* are right triangles and $AB \cong AC$.

2) *AB* is the hypotenuse of $\triangle ADB$ and *AC* is the hypotenuse of $\triangle ADC$ (opposite the right angles).

3) $AD \cong AD$ using the reflexive property.

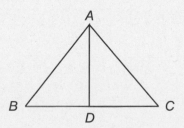

Since the hypotenuse and leg of $\triangle ADB$ are congruent to the corresponding hypotenuse and leg of $\triangle ADC$, the two triangles are congruent using the HL Theorem.

The proof is complete.

QUADRILATERALS

Quadrilaterals are four-sided plane figures in which each side is a line segment. The following are the most common quadrilaterals you are likely to come across on the ACT:

Quadrilateral	Defining Characteristics	Illustration
Square	Two pairs of parallel sides, all four sides congruent, and all four angles congruent (all are right angles)	
Rectangle	Two congruent pairs of parallel sides and all four angles congruent (all are right angles)	
Parallelogram	Two congruent pairs of parallel sides	
Rhombus	Two pairs of parallel sides and all four sides are congruent	
Trapezoid	Exactly one pair of parallel sides	
Isosceles Trapezoid	Exactly one pair of parallel sides and one pair of opposite sides are congruent	

You have likely learned many facts about the properties of these quadrilaterals in geometry, such as diagonals of a parallelogram bisect each other, and if the parallelogram is a rectangle, the diagonals are perpendicular to each other. Typically, questions involving deeper properties of the quadrilaterals rarely occur on the ACT, so we're going to focus more on the formulas and facts you'll need for test questions.

Like with triangles, two quadrilaterals of the same type are called **congruent** if all of their corresponding sides are congruent. They are called **similar** if the four ratios of their corresponding sides are equal. You compute the perimeter of any quadrilateral by adding together the lengths of its four sides.

Here are two useful **perimeter formulas** you should know for quadrilaterals:

1. Perimeter of a square with side length s is $P = 4s$.
2. Perimeter of a rectangle with length l and width w is $P = 2l + 2w$.

Likewise, the following are useful **area formulas** for the most common quadrilaterals that surface on the ACT:

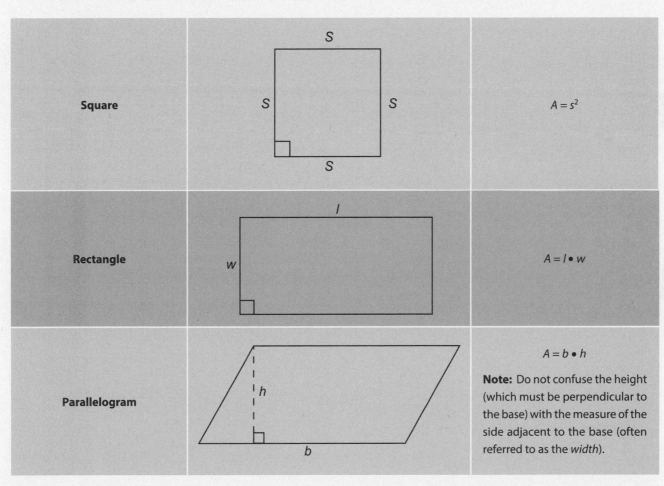

Square		$A = s^2$
Rectangle		$A = l \bullet w$
Parallelogram		$A = b \bullet h$ **Note:** Do not confuse the height (which must be perpendicular to the base) with the measure of the side adjacent to the base (often referred to as the *width*).

A common ACT mathematics question will give you the perimeter or area of a square or rectangle and ask you to identify the length of a side. When variables are involved, this requires you to use your algebra skills, as in the problem below.

. . . .

The area of a rectangle is $4x^2 + 4x - 3$ square units. If its length is $2x + 3$ units, what is its width, in units?

    A. $\dfrac{4x^2 + 4x - 3}{2}$

    B. $4x + 1$

    C. $2x + 1$

    D. $x - 1$

    E. $2x - 1$

The correct answer is E. The area of a rectangle is equal to *lw*, where *l* and *w* are its length and width, respectively. You are given that the area of the rectangle is $4x^2 + 4x - 3$ square units and that its length is $2x + 3$. You need to find the other factor that, when multiplied by $(2x + 3)$, produces $4x^2 + 4x - 3$. The only factor that works is the one given in choice E.

. . . .

Other questions may ask you to determine vertices or areas of figures plotted on the standard coordinate (x, y) plane, as in the following samples:

. . . .

If, in the given figure, the point is the vertex of a square with perimeter of 12 units, which of the following could be another vertex of this square?

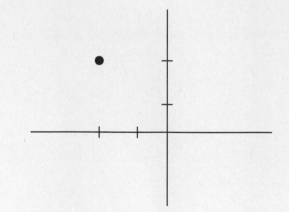

The correct answer is K. The perimeter of a square with side length *s* is given by $P = 4s$. Since the perimeter of this square is 12, *s* must be 3. The given point has coordinates $(-2, 2)$, so any other vertex of the same square must have an *x*-coordinate that is either equal to or 3 units away from -2. This means that the *x*-coordinate can be -5, -2, or 1. The square must have a *y*-coordinate of -1, 2, or 5. Only choice K, $(-5, 5)$, meets these conditions.

    F. $(3, 2)$

    G. $(7, 2)$

    H. $(-9, 2)$

    J. $(-3, -7)$

    K. $(-5, 5)$

What is the area in square units of the rectangle shown below in the standard (x, y) coordinate plane?

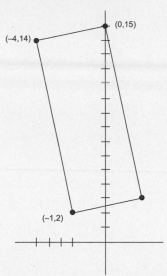

A. 17
B. 51
C. $3\sqrt{17}$
D. 153
E. $8\sqrt{17}$

The correct answer is B. You must first determine the width and length of the rectangle. Recall what we learned in Chapter 7—you can find the lengths when given two points by using the distance formula:

$$w = \sqrt{(-4-(-1))^2 + (14-2)^2} = \sqrt{9+144} = \sqrt{153} = 3\sqrt{17} \text{ units}$$

$$l = \sqrt{(-4-0)^2 + (14-15)^2} = \sqrt{16+1} = \sqrt{17} \text{ units}$$

So the area of the rectangle is $\left(3\sqrt{17}\right)\left(\sqrt{17}\right) = 51$ square units.

CIRCLES

The set of all points in the plane that are a given distance r from a fixed point P is a **circle.** Here is the basic terminology involving circles you should know before you take the ACT. Most of these are sure to surface on the exam, so you should absolutely memorize these definitions.

Term	Illustration	Definition
Center		The point P equidistant from all points on the circle
Radius		The common distance r that points on the circle are from the center

Diameter		A line segment that passes through the center of the circle and has endpoints on the circle (its length is twice the radius)
Central Angle		An angle formed between two radial segments
Arc		A portion of the circle that lies between two points
Sector		The portion of the inside of a circle that lies between two radial segments

You will use these terms when configuring values of circles, as in the following formulas. Circumference and area of circles are the formulas that come up most frequently on the ACT.

Circumference of a Circle		Since the diameter d is $2r$, there are two expressions for this formula: $P = 2\pi r = \pi d$
Length of an Arc of a Circle		$P = \dfrac{\theta}{180°} \cdot \pi r$
Area of a Circle		$A = \pi r^2$

Area of a Sector of a Circle	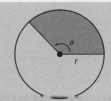	$A = \dfrac{\theta}{360°} \cdot \pi r^2$

Follow along with this sample problem.

- -

The length of the radius of circle A is 4 times as long as the radius of circle B. If the radius of circle B is x units, what is the area (in square units) of circle A?

The correct answer is J. The radius of circle A is 4x. So its area is $\pi(4x)^2 = 16\pi x^2$.

    F. $16x$

    G. $\dfrac{x}{16}$

    H. $\dfrac{x}{4}$

    J. $16\pi x^2$

    K. $\dfrac{\pi x^2}{16}$

- -

Problems like these come in different varieties, but they all involve using the same formulas. Sometimes, you will be given a diameter instead of a radius, or you will be given an area or perimeter of a sector and asked to identify the radius or diameter. The key is to be flexible with using the formulas in various ways, depending on what information is provided.

Chapter 8

Plane Geometry and Trigonometry

SOLIDS

The solids that show up most frequently on the ACT Mathematics test are cubes, prisms, and cylinders. Let's take a look at formulas (yes, more formulas!) you should know for the test. Understanding the variable parts that make up these formulas well in advance will make it easier for you to translate the words given in ACT geometry problems into values you can calculate.

You should remember the formulas for the cube and rectangular prism, but the test providers will supply the other formulas. Just be sure you are comfortable using them!

Solid	Illustration	Surface Area Formula	Volume Formula
Cube		$6A = 6s^2$	$V = s^3$
Rectangular Prism		$SA = 2(lw + lh + wh)$	$V = lwh$
Cylinder		$SA = 2\pi r^2 + 2\pi rh$	$V = \pi r^2 h$

Now try working out some problems on your own.

Examples:

Answer the following computational questions involving these solids.

1. If the volume of a cube is 512 cubic inches, what is the area of one of its faces? _____

2. If the volume of a cylinder is 200π cubic feet and its height is 5 feet, what is the diameter of its base? _____

3. If three distinct sides of a rectangular box have lengths of 4 cm, 10 cm, and 15 cm, what is its surface area? _____

Solutions:

1. Let s represent an edge of the cube. Then, $s^3 = 512$, and $s = 8$ inches. So an area of *one* face is $8^2 = 64$ square inches.

   Again, don't forget to read questions slowly and carefully to make sure you know exactly what value the question is seeking. Then, after you select your answer, check *again*. You don't want to have wasted math done correctly by selecting a value that answers another question.

2. Using the formula $V = \pi r^2 h$, we are given $V = 200\pi$ and $h = 5$. Plug those in and solve for r:

$$200\pi = \pi r^2 \bullet 5$$
$$\frac{200\pi}{5\pi} = r^2$$
$$40 = r^2$$
$$2\sqrt{10} = r$$

   The diameter of the base is 2r, which is $4\sqrt{10}$ feet.

3. Using the formula $SA = 2(lw + lh + wh)$, simply plug in 4 cm, 10 cm, and 15 cm for l, w, and h—it does not matter which value you associate with which letter:

$$SA = 2(lw + lh + wh)$$
$$= 2(4 \bullet 10 + 4 \bullet 15 + 10 \bullet 15) \text{ square centimeters}$$
$$= 500 \text{ square centimeters}$$

Such solids occur within application problems as well. For instance, consider the following example.

Example:

Michael wishes to apply primer to the four walls and the ceiling of a tool shed. The ceiling has dimensions 8 feet by 12 feet and the height of the shed is 9 feet. If each can of primer is used to seal 200 square feet of wall, how many cans must he purchase? _____

Solution:

First, we must determine the total surface area to be painted. The shed is in the shape of a rectangular prism; its surface area formula is given above. We must account for four walls and a ceiling, but NOT the floor. So the surface area is

$$\underbrace{(8 \bullet 12)}_{\text{Ceiling}} + \underbrace{2(8 \bullet 9) + 2(12 \bullet 9)}_{\text{Walls}} = 456 \text{ square feet.}$$

Since each can coats 200 square feet, he must purchase three cans of primer.

Transformations

A **transformation** is a sequence of steps that moves a planar figure around in the *xy*-plane without changing its actual size or shape. The result of applying a transformation to a figure creates an **image** of that figure. If *P* is a point on the original figure, then the image of *P* is typically denoted by *P'*.

There are various movements that can be performed to transform figures.

Transformation	Description	Illustration
Translation	All points on a figure are moved in the same direction and distance.	(Here, each point on *PQR* was moved two units to the right and one unit up.)
Rotation	All points on a figure are connected to a common point (called the **center of rotation**) and are rotated clockwise or counter-clockwise by the same angle.	(This illustrates a 180-degree rotation counterclockwise of figure *PQR* about the center marked *O*.)
Reflection	All points on a figure are reflected over a given line in the plane. To do so, a line segment is drawn from a point on the figure perpendicularly to the line over which it is being reflected. The image of that point is obtained by going the same distance on the opposite side of the reflection line.	(This illustrates quadrilateral *PQRS* being reflected over the line *x* = 3.)

Use the information in the table of transformations to solve the following problems.

Examples:

Consider the point $P(1, 2)$ in the plane. Determine the image of this point under the indicated transformation.

1. Translated 5 units up and 2 units left. _____

2. Reflected over the line $y = 8$. _____

Solutions:

1. The image P' is $(-1, 7)$.

2. The image P' is $(1, 14)$.

RIGHT TRIANGLE TRIGONOMETRY

Trigonometric functions were defined, in part, to identify the lengths of sides of a right triangle when one side and one angle (instead of two sides) are known. The names of these six functions, with their abbreviations, are as follows. If given on the ACT, you will likely only see the abbreviated form of the name.

Trigonometric Function	Abbreviation
Cosine	cos
Sine	sin
Tangent	tan
Secant	sec
Cosecant	csc
Cotangent	cot

Let's explore what these trigonometric functions mean. Consider the following right triangle. In this triangle, θ represents an angle:

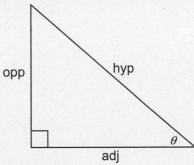

Using this image gives you a visual representation to follow when understanding how trigonometric functions are defined in what we'll call **right triangle trigonometry.** When asked to find the values of these functions on the ACT, you will use the following formulas:

$$\sin\theta = \frac{\text{opposite}}{\text{hypotenuse}}$$

$$\cos\theta = \frac{\text{adjacent}}{\text{hypotenuse}}$$

$$\tan\theta = \frac{\text{opposite}}{\text{adjacent}} = \frac{\sin\theta}{\cos\theta}$$

$$\cot\theta = \frac{\text{adjacent}}{\text{opposite}} = \frac{\cos\theta}{\sin\theta} = \frac{1}{\tan\theta}$$

$$\sec\theta = \frac{\text{hypotenuse}}{\text{adjacent}} = \frac{1}{\cos\theta}$$

$$\csc\theta = \frac{\text{hypotenuse}}{\text{opposite}} = \frac{1}{\sin\theta}$$

The problems related to trigonometry on the ACT Mathematics test come in two main varieties:

1) Compute a trigonometric function or determine a side of a triangle using given information.

2) Solve a word problem that can be modeled using a right triangle.

Let's take a look at a few sample ACT–type trigonometry problems.

· ·

In right triangle ABC, $\sin A = \frac{1}{2}$. What is the value of $\cos A$?

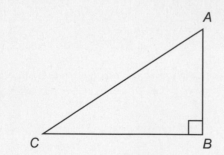

F. $\sqrt{3}$

G.   2

H. $\dfrac{\sqrt{3}}{3}$

J. $\dfrac{1}{2}$

K. $\dfrac{\sqrt{3}}{2}$

The correct answer is K. Remember that sine is $\dfrac{\text{opposite}}{\text{hypotenuse}}$ and that cosine is $\dfrac{\text{adjacent}}{\text{hypotenuse}}$. From what is given, $\dfrac{CB}{AC} = \dfrac{1}{2}$.

We label the lengths of CB and AC in the triangle:

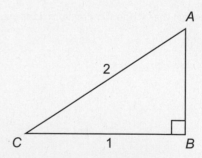

To find the cosine of angle A, you need to know the length of the side adjacent to it, namely segment AB. Since the length of a leg of this triangle is related to the length of its hypotenuse in the ratio of 1:2, remember from earlier in this chapter that this is a 30-60-90 right triangle, whose three sides are related in the ratio of $1:\sqrt{3}:2$. Therefore, $AB = \sqrt{3}$, so $\cos A = \dfrac{\sqrt{3}}{2}$.

In the isosceles right triangle below, what is the value of $\sin(z°) + \cos(z°)$?

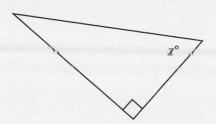

A. $\dfrac{\sqrt{2}}{2}$

B. 1

C. $\sqrt{2}$

D. $\dfrac{\sqrt{3}}{2}$

E. $\sqrt{3}$

The correct answer is C. Remember that in an isosceles right triangle, the angles are 45°-45°-90°, the legs have the same length of 1, and the hypotenuse has a length of $\sqrt{2}$. (Familiarizing yourself with all of the charts will really help you out!) So both $\sin(z°)$ and $\cos(z°)$ equal $\dfrac{1}{\sqrt{2}}$. Hence, $\sin(z°) + \cos(z°) = \dfrac{2}{\sqrt{2}} = \sqrt{2}$.

A 95-foot cable attached to the top of a telephone pole is anchored to the ground. If the wire rises at a 64° angle with the ground, how tall is the telephone pole (in feet)?

A. 95 tan 64°
B. 64 cos 95°
C. 95 cos 64°
D. 95 sin 64°
E. 64 sin 95°

The correct answer is D. As shown in the diagram below, the height of the telephone pole, x, is opposite a 64° angle, and the hypotenuse of the triangle is 95 feet.

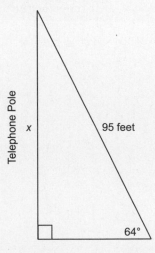

Since sine equals $\dfrac{\text{opposite}}{\text{hypotenuse}}$, we get the formula

$$\dfrac{x}{95} = \sin 64°; x = 95 \ \sin 64°.$$

GRAPHS OF TRIGONOMETRIC FUNCTIONS

In order to graph trigonometric functions, we use a value called **radian measure** instead of degrees to measure angles. To find radian measure, you form the ratio of the arc length of a circle's sector to its radius. Place the vertex of the angle at the center of a circle of radius r and denote the length of the arc of the circle formed by the two rays of this angle by s:

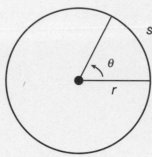

The **radian measure** of the angle θ is given by $\theta = \dfrac{s}{r}$.

Let's say that $\theta = 90°$. Since the circumference of the entire circle is $2\pi r$, and the central angle of an entire circle is 360°, it follows that an angle with measure $\theta = 90°$ cuts off an arc with a length that is $\dfrac{1}{4}$ of the entire circle; that is, $s = \dfrac{1}{4}(2\pi r)$. As such, the measure of angle θ in radians is $\theta = \dfrac{s}{r} = \dfrac{\frac{1}{4}(2\pi r)}{r} = \dfrac{\pi}{2}$ radians.

So $90° = \dfrac{\pi}{2}$ radians. And that means that an entire 360° circle has a measure of 2π radians. The same type of reasoning works to determine the radian measure corresponding to any degree measure.

The graphs of $f(x) = \sin(x)$ and $g(x) = \cos(x)$ for $0 \le x \le 2\pi$ are as follows:

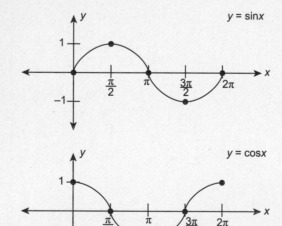

Note: The graphs on the intervals $2\pi \le x \le 4\pi$, $4\pi \le x \le 6\pi$, etc. are identical to the graph above. We say these functions are **periodic**. The **period** is the length of the smallest interval that can be used to produce a graph by replicating what it looks like on that interval on abutting intervals of the same length. Here, the period is 2π—starting after 2π, that exact curve will repeat.

Consider the function $f(x) = \sin(2x)$. As x moves from 0 to π, the angles swept out by $2x$ actually go from 0 to 2π. So an entire period of inputs is swept out by letting x go from only 0 to π in this case. So the period of $f(x) = \sin(2x)$ is $\dfrac{2\pi}{2} = \pi$.

Similarly, the period of $f(x) = \sin(5x)$ is $\dfrac{2\pi}{5}$. The same analysis applies for $g(x) = \cos(x)$. In general, the period of $f(x) = \sin(Bx)$ and $g(x) = \cos(Bx)$ is $\dfrac{2\pi}{B}$.

Now, consider the function $f(x) = 3\sin(x)$. The period is still 2π, but notice the outputs this time go from -3 to 3. If you don't see this, try plotting some points. So multiplying by 3 on the inside to get $\sin(3x)$ changes the period, while multiplying $\sin(x)$ by 3 on the outside to get $3\sin(x)$ changes the maximum and minimum values.

The same goes for the cosine function. We say the **amplitude** of a periodic function equals $\dfrac{\text{maximum value} - \text{minimum value}}{2}$.

🔔 **ALERT**: $\sin(mx)$ does not equal $m\sin(x)$—you cannot pull out the m!

See if you can solve this cosine function problem.

. . . .

How many cycles does the function $y = 3\cos(8x)$ complete when $0 \le x \le 2\pi$?

A. $\dfrac{1}{8}$

B. $\dfrac{1}{2}$

C. 1

D. 3

E. 8

The correct answer is E. The coefficient of x determines the period of a cosine function, while the coefficient in front (in this case, 3) determines the amplitude and has no effect on the period. Since we know the period of $g(x) = \cos(Bx)$ is $\dfrac{2\pi}{B}$ and the same is true for $g(x) = A\cos(Bx)$ for any nonzero number A, we conclude that the graph of $y = 3\cos(8x)$ completes 8 full cycles in the interval $0 \le x \le 2\pi$.

. . . .

TRIGONOMETRIC IDENTITIES

Trigonometric identities are useful equalities that are always true—you can use them on questions that ask you to simplify expressions involving trigonometric functions or to determine the sine or cosine of an angle when the cosine or sine of that angle is known. The following table features just a few of the most commonly used identities you might see on the ACT test—don't expect anything beyond this to show up on the test.

Name	Identity
Pythagorean Identity	$\cos^2\theta + \sin^2\theta = 1$
Periodicity Identities	$\sin(2n\pi + \theta) = \sin(\theta)$, where n is an integer $\cos(2n\pi + \theta) = \cos(\theta)$, where n is an integer
Symmetry Identities	$\sin(-\theta) = -\sin(\theta)$ $\cos(-\theta) = \cos(\theta)$
Complementary Angle Identities	$\cos\left(\dfrac{\pi}{2} - \theta\right) = \sin\theta$ $\sin\left(\dfrac{\pi}{2} - \theta\right) = \cos\theta$
Double-Angle Identities	$\sin(2\theta) = 2\sin\theta\cos\theta$ $\cos(2\theta) = \cos^2\theta - \sin^2\theta$

One term that you might see on the ACT is the **terminal side** of an angle. The terminal side of an angle θ swept out from the positive x-axis in the counterclockwise direction is the radial segment that forms the angle, along with the positive x-axis:

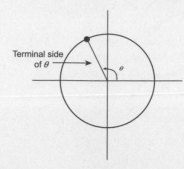

The signs of cos θ and sin θ are determined by the quadrant in which the terminal side lies.

Quadrant in Which the Terminal Side Lies	Illustration	Sign of cos θ	Sign of sin θ
I		+	+
II		–	+
III		–	–
IV		+	–

Now, let's explore how to use these identities to solve a ACT problem together.

Example:

Suppose $\cos\theta = -\dfrac{1}{5}$ and the terminal side of θ intersects the unit circle in Quadrant II. Compute $\sin\theta$.

Solution:

Use the Pythagorean identity $\sin^2\theta + \cos^2\theta = 1$ to find two possible values for $\sin\theta$. Then, use the fact that the sine of an angle whose terminal side is in Quadrant II must be positive to choose the correct value:

$$\sin^2\theta + \cos^2\theta = 1$$
$$\sin^2\theta + \left(-\frac{1}{5}\right)^2 = 1$$
$$\sin^2\theta + \frac{1}{25} = 1$$
$$\sin^2\theta = \frac{24}{25}$$
$$\sin\theta = \pm\frac{\sqrt{24}}{5} = \pm\frac{2\sqrt{6}}{5}$$

Since the terminal side is in Quadrant II, we conclude that the correct value is $\dfrac{2\sqrt{6}}{5}$.

Now try one on your own.

. . . .

Suppose that $\sin\theta = \dfrac{3}{5}$ and that the terminal side of θ is in Quadrant II. Which of the following equals $\cos 2\theta$?

A. $\dfrac{4}{5}$

B. $-\dfrac{4}{5}$

C. $\dfrac{7}{25}$

D. $-\dfrac{3}{5}$

E. $\dfrac{9}{5}$

The correct answer is C. First, use the Pythagorean identity $\sin^2\theta + \cos^2\theta = 1$ to find two possible values for $\cos\theta$. Then, use the fact that the cosine of an angle whose terminal side is in Quadrant II must be negative to choose the correct value. Finally, use the double-angle formula $\cos 2\theta = \cos^2\theta - \sin^2\theta$:

$$\sin^2\theta + \cos^2\theta = 1$$
$$\left(\frac{3}{5}\right)^2 + \cos^2\theta = 1$$
$$\cos^2\theta = 1 - \frac{9}{25}$$
$$\cos\theta = \pm\frac{4}{5}$$

Since the terminal side is in Quadrant II, we conclude that $\cos\theta = -\dfrac{4}{5}$.

Therefore,

$$\cos 2\theta = \cos^2\theta - \sin^2\theta = \left(-\frac{4}{5}\right)^2 - \left(\frac{3}{5}\right)^2 = \frac{16}{25} - \frac{9}{25} = \frac{7}{25}.$$

. . . .

309

SOLVING TRIGONOMETRIC EQUATIONS

Just as there are linear equations, quadratic equations, and equations involving radicals of an unknown, there are equations involving the trigonometric functions. The general aim is the same—you need to find values of the input that will make the equation true.

In the case of trigonometric equations, it will be very helpful for you to remember these common values of trigonometric functions. If you can recall these, you will be able to save several steps if faced with a trigonometric equation on the ACT. These problems will not turn up frequently on the test—but if they do, there's a good chance that they will include one or more of the values from the following table:

x	$\sin(x)$	$\cos(x)$
0	0	1
$\dfrac{\pi}{6}$	$\dfrac{1}{2}$	$\dfrac{\sqrt{3}}{2}$
$\dfrac{\pi}{4}$	$\dfrac{\sqrt{2}}{2}$	$\dfrac{\sqrt{2}}{2}$
$\dfrac{\pi}{3}$	$\dfrac{\sqrt{3}}{2}$	$\dfrac{1}{2}$
$\dfrac{\pi}{2}$	1	0
π	0	−1
$\dfrac{3\pi}{2}$	−1	0
2π	0	1

Let's take a look at how this table can help you on the exam.

. . . .

Which of the following is a solution of the equation $\cos(3x) = 1$?

A. π

B. $\dfrac{2\pi}{3}$

C. 2π

D. $\dfrac{\pi}{6}$

E. $\dfrac{\pi}{4}$

The correct answer is B. Looking at the table above, you can see any value of x for which $3x = 0$ or 2π is a solution of this equation (it will lead to a value of 1, which is what you are seeking). So $x = 0$ and $x = \dfrac{2\pi}{3}$ are both solutions. Of these, only the latter is a choice, so the answer is B.

. . . .

SUMMING IT UP

- Angles are classified according to their "size" or measure; the units in which this is expressed are **degrees** or **radians.**
  - ° An angle with a measure between 0 and 90 degrees is **acute**.
  - ° An angle with a measure of 90 degrees is a **right** angle.
  - ° An angle with a measure between 90 and 180 degrees is **obtuse**.
  - ° An angle with a measure of 180 degrees is a **straight** angle.

- Two angles with measures that sum to 90 degrees are **complementary;** two angles with measures that sum to 180 degrees are **supplementary.**

- Two angles that have the same measure are **congruent.** Vertical angles are *always* congruent.

- A **right** triangle is one that has a right angle; an **acute** triangle is one in which all three angles are acute; an **obtuse** triangle has one obtuse angle.

- An **equilateral** triangle is one in which all three sides have the same length; an **isosceles** triangle has at least two sides with the same length; a **scalene** triangle has three sides of different lengths.

- The **triangle sum rule** says that the sum of the measures of the three angles in any triangle must be $180°$. The **triangle inequality** says that the sum of the lengths of any two sides of a triangle must be strictly larger than the length of the third side.

- The **Pythagorean theorem** states that for a right triangle with legs a and b and hypotenuse c, $a^2 + b^2 = c^2$.

- Two triangles $\triangle ABC$ and $\triangle DEF$ are **congruent** if all three corresponding pairs of angles are congruent AND all three corresponding sides are congruent. Two triangles $\triangle ABC$ and $\triangle DEF$ are **similar** if the ratios of the three pairs of corresponding sides are the same; that is, $\dfrac{AB}{DE} = \dfrac{BC}{EF} = \dfrac{AC}{DF} = k$, where k is a positive number.

- The **area formula** for a triangle with base b and height h is $A = \dfrac{1}{2}b \bullet h$.

- Two quadrilaterals of the same type are **congruent** if their corresponding sides are all congruent, and they are called **similar** if the four ratios of their corresponding sides are equal.

- The **perimeter of a square** with side length s is $P = 4s$. The **area of a square** with side length s is $A = s^2$.

- The **perimeter of a rectangle** with length l and width w is $P = 2l + 2w$. The **area of a rectangle** with length l and width w is $A = l \bullet w$.

- The **circumference of a circle** with radius r (or diameter $d = 2r$) is $C = 2\pi r = \pi d$. The **area of a circle** with radius r is $A = \pi r^2$.

- The **volume of a cube** with side length s is $V = s^3$.

- The **volume of a rectangular box** with side lengths l, w, and h is $V = lwh$.

- The **volume of a cylinder** with base radius r and height h is $V = \pi r^2 h$.

- **Trigonometric functions** are used to identify the lengths of sides of a right triangle when one side and one angle (instead of two sides) are known. There are six trigonometric functions: **cosine** (cos), **sine** (sin), **tangent** (tan), **secant** (sec), **cosecant** (csc), and **cotangent** (cot).

- **Trigonometric formulas** are used to find the values of trigonometric functions:

$$\sin\theta = \frac{\text{opposite}}{\text{hypotenuse}} \quad \text{and} \quad \cos\theta = \frac{\text{adjacent}}{\text{hypotenuse}}$$

$$\tan\theta = \frac{\text{opposite}}{\text{adjacent}} \quad \text{and} \quad \cot\theta = \frac{\text{adjacent}}{\text{opposite}} = \frac{1}{\tan\theta}$$

$$\sec\theta = \frac{\text{hypotenuse}}{\text{adjacent}} = \frac{1}{\cos\theta} \quad \text{and} \quad \csc\theta = \frac{\text{hypotenuse}}{\text{opposite}} = \frac{1}{\sin\theta}$$

Chapter 8

Plane Geometry and Trigonometry

- **Trigonometric identities** are useful equalities that are always true that can help you to simplify expressions involving trigonometric functions or to determine the sine or cosine of an angle when the cosine or sine of that angle is known. The most commonly used identities are as follows:

  ○ **Pythagorean identity:** $\cos2\,\theta + \sin2\,\theta = 1$

  ○ **Periodicity identities:** $\sin(2n\pi + \theta) = \sin(\theta)$, $\cos(2n\pi + \theta) = \cos(\theta)$, where n is an integer

  ○ **Symmetry identities:** $\sin(-\theta) = -\sin(\theta)$, $\cos(-\theta) = \cos(\theta)$

  ○ **Complementary angle identities:** $\cos\left(\dfrac{\pi}{2} - \theta\right) = \sin\theta$, $\sin\dfrac{\pi}{2} - \theta = \cos\theta$

  ○ **Double-angle identities:** $\sin(2\theta) = 2\sin\theta\cos\theta$, $\cos(2\theta) = \cos^2\theta - \sin^2\theta$

WANT TO KNOW MORE?

Access more practice questions, lessons, helpful hints, and strategies for the following math topics in *Peterson's ACT Online Course.*

- Lines and Angles
- Triangles
- Quadrilaterals
- Circles
- Solids
- Multiple Figures
- Trigonometry Functions
- Trigonometry Functions and Identities

To purchase and access the course, go to ***www.petersons.com/act***.

PRACTICE

It's time for your final mathematics practice quiz. When you're finished answering all 20 questions, check the answers and explanations that follow to figure out how well you did and why you may have selected some incorrect answer choices.

1. In the figure shown, what is the value of *x*?

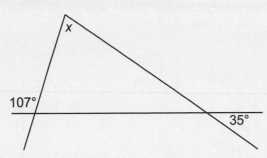

SHOW YOUR WORK HERE

   A.   35°
   B.   38°
   C.   72°
   D.   107°
   E.   145°

2. Angle *Q* measures (180 − *x*) degrees. If angle *Q* is a positive acute angle, which of the following is true of *x*?

   F. $0 < x < 60$
   G. $0 < x < 90$
   H. $90 < x < 180$
   J. $180 < x < 270$
   K. $200 < x < 250$

3. Which of the following sets of triangle side lengths represents a right triangle?

   A.   1, 2, 5
   B.   2, 3, 4
   C.   4, 5, 21
   D.   5, 12, 13
   E.   6, 9, 11

4. In triangle *RST*, if *RS* = *RT* = *TS*, then which of the following statements is FALSE?

   F.   All three angles must be acute.
   G.   The triangle can be a right triangle.
   H.   There is no obtuse angle.
   J.   The sum of any two angles in the triangle exceeds 90 degrees.
   K.   The sides cannot satisfy the Pythagorean theorem.

5. In the following figure, *ABDC* is a square. What is the area of triangle *AFE*?

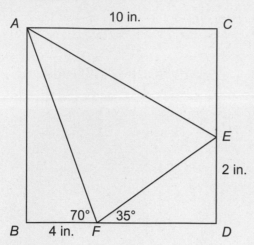

A. 20 square inches
B. 34 square inches
C. 40 square inches
D. 60 square inches
E. 66 square inches

6. In the figure below, triangles *ACB* and *FED* are similar. What is the length of segment *DE*?

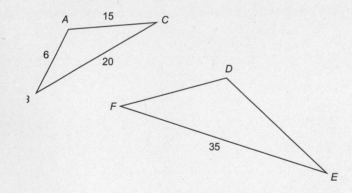

F. 10

G. 21

H. 30

J. $\frac{60}{7}$

K. $\frac{140}{3}$

314

Chapter 8

Plane Geometry and Trigonometry

7. What is the area of an equilateral triangle with a perimeter of 30 feet?

   A. $\dfrac{25}{2}\sqrt{3}$ square feet

   B. $100\sqrt{3}$ square feet

   C. 10 square feet

   D. $50\sqrt{3}$ square feet

   E. $25\sqrt{3}$ square feet

8. If the area of triangle *YVZ* is 6 square centimeters and the length of segment *XV* is 12 centimeters, what is the perimeter of parallelogram *WXYZ*?

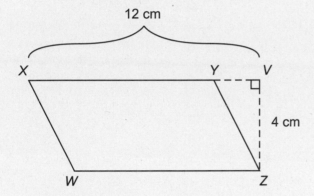

   F. 10 centimeters
   G. 18 centimeters
   H. 24 centimeters
   J. 26 centimeters
   K. 28 centimeters

315

Chapter 8

Plane
Geometry and
Trigonometry

9. The length of a narrow rectangular room is 11 yards more than three times its width. If the area of the room is 4 square yards, how many yards long is the room?

   A. $\dfrac{1}{3}$

   B. 1

   C. 12

   D. $24\dfrac{2}{3}$

   E. 36

10. In the given parallelogram, what is the measure of angle *CAB*?

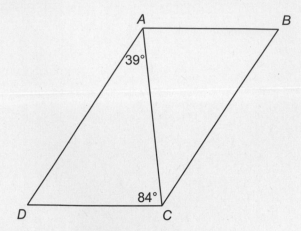

- **F.** 39°
- **G.** 57°
- **H.** 123°
- **J.** 100°
- **K.** 84°

11. In the given figure, a circle is inscribed within a square. If the perimeter of the square is 80 inches, what is the area of the shaded region in square inches?

- **A.** 400 − 10π
- **B.** 400 + 100π
- **C.** 80 + 20π
- **D.** 80 − 20π
- **E.** 400 − 100π

12. Points *X*, *W*, and *Y* lie on the circle with center *O*. If the unshaded sectors *XOW* and *XOY* comprise $\frac{1}{10}$ and $\frac{3}{5}$ of the area of the entire circle, respectively, what is the measure of angle *WOY*?

SHOW YOUR WORK HERE

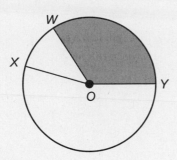

- **F.** 54°
- **G.** 36°
- **H.** 90°
- **J.** 108°
- **K.** 252°

13. What is the surface area of the following solid?

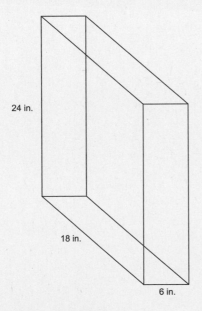

24 in.

18 in.

6 in.

- **A.** 342 square inches
- **B.** 684 square inches
- **C.** 1,368 square inches
- **D.** 2,052 square inches
- **E.** 2,592 square inches

317

Chapter 8

Plane Geometry and Trigonometry

14. A cube has side length *s*. A new cube is formed whose sides are twice as long as the original cube. Which of the following statements is true?

SHOW YOUR WORK HERE

    F. The volume of the new cube is twice the volume of the original cube.

    G. The volume of the new cube is four times the volume of the original cube.

    H. The volume of the new cube is one-half the volume of the original cube.

    J. The volume of the new cube is eight times the volume of the original cube.

    K. The volume of the new cube is six times the volume of the original cube.

15. Using the following triangle, what is the value of *x*?

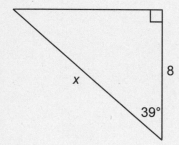

    A. $\dfrac{8}{\cos 39°}$

    B. $\dfrac{8}{\sin 39°}$

    C. $\dfrac{\cos 39°}{8}$

    D. $8 \sin 39°$

    E. $8 \cos 39°$

16. The ratio of the side lengths of a right triangle is $1 : \sqrt{3} : 2$. What is the cosine of the largest non-right angle in this triangle?

    F. 0

    G. $\dfrac{1}{2}$

    H. $\sqrt{3}$

    J. $\dfrac{\sqrt{3}}{2}$

    K. 2

17. For $0° < \theta < 90°$, if $\cos \theta = \dfrac{5}{7}$ then $\cot \theta = $ _____

   A. $\dfrac{5}{24}$

   B. $\dfrac{5\sqrt{6}}{12}$

   C. $\dfrac{2\sqrt{6}}{7}$

   D. $\dfrac{7}{5}$

   E. $2\sqrt{6}$

18. Consider rectangle $ABCD$ below. What is $\sin \theta$?

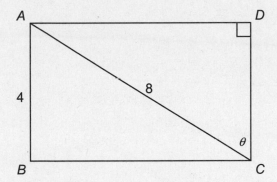

   F. $\dfrac{\sqrt{3}}{2}$

   G. 1

   H. $\dfrac{1}{2}$

   J. $4\sqrt{3}$

   K. $\dfrac{\sqrt{2}}{2}$

19. What is the period of the graph of $y = 5\cos\dfrac{x}{2}$?

   A. $\dfrac{\pi}{2}$

   B. π

   C. $\dfrac{3\pi}{2}$

   D. 2π

   E. 4π

319

Chapter 8

Plane
Geometry and
Trigonometry

20. What is the smallest positive value of x for which $\sin 3x = 0$?

F. 0

G. $\dfrac{\pi}{6}$

H. $\dfrac{\pi}{3}$

J. π

K. $\dfrac{2\pi}{3}$

1. **The correct answer is C.** Use the Triangle Sum Rule to determine x. To do this, you need the values of the other two angles in the triangle. First, the vertical angle to the one marked 35° also has a measure of 35° since vertical angles are congruent. Then, the angle adjacent to the one marked 107° has a measure of 73° because those two angles are supplementary. Therefore, the sum of x, 35°, and 73° is 180°. So solving for x yields:

$$x + 35° + 73° = 180°$$
$$x + 108° = 180°$$
$$x = 72°$$

Choice A is the measure of the base angle that is vertical to the one with the same measure, but it does not equal x. In choice B, you mistakenly used 107° as one of the angles in the triangle. Choice D is incorrect because angles on opposite sides of this leg of the triangle are not congruent—they are not alternate interior angles formed by cutting two parallel lines with a transversal. Choice E is the supplementary angle to the one marked 35°, but it is not equal to x.

2. **The correct answer is H.** An acute angle is, by definition, one that measures between 0° and 90°. In order for angle Q to satisfy this definition, its measure of $(180 - x)$ degrees must be between 0 and 90. Algebraically, $0 < 180 - x < 90$. Solving the inequality for x:

$-180 < -x < -90$, so that $90 < x < 180$

Therefore, choice H is correct.

Choices F and G are incorrect because Q would be obtuse. Choices J and K are incorrect because they would make Q acute, but negative.

3. **The correct answer is D.** The sides of any right triangle are related by the Pythagorean theorem, which states that the sum of the squares of the legs is equal to the square of the hypotenuse. This is often written as $a^2 + b^2 + c^2$, where a and b are the legs and c is the hypotenuse (the longest of the three sides). Test each set of sides to see which satisfies the Pythagorean theorem and is therefore a right triangle. In choice D, $\underset{=169}{5^2 + 12^2} = \underset{=169}{13^2}$. For all other choices, this relationship does not hold.

4. **The correct answer is G.** In any triangle, the angles opposite equal sides are equal to each other. Since all three sides are congruent, it follows that all three angles are congruent. Since the sum of the three angles of a triangle must be 180°, the measure of each angle is 60°. As such, it is not possible for the triangle to be a right triangle.

Choice F cannot be correct because all angles in such a triangle measure 60°, and so they are all acute. Choice H also cannot be correct because all the angles are acute (and measure 60°), so none of them is obtuse. Choice J cannot be correct since the sum of any two angles in such a triangle is 120°. Choice K cannot be correct because only *right* triangles satisfy the Pythagorean theorem, and such a triangle cannot be right because all the angles are acute (and have measure 60 degrees).

5. **The correct answer is B.** The strategy is to find the areas of the other three right triangles inside square $ABCD$ and then subtract their sum from the area of the square. To do so, you must identify the height and base of each triangle. Since all sides of the square have a length of 10 inches, these are the lengths of other segments:

$CE = 8$ inches, $FD = 6$ inches, $AB = 10$ inches

Using the area formula $A = \frac{1}{2}bh$, where b is the base and h is the height of a triangle, you can calculate the areas:

- Area of triangle $ABF = \frac{1}{2}$ (10 in.)(4 in.) = 20 sq. in.

- Area of triangle $EDF = \frac{1}{2}$ (6 in.)(2 in.) = 6 sq. in.

- Area of triangle $ACE = \frac{1}{2}$ (10 in.)(8 in.) = 40 sq. in.

The area of the square $ABCD$ is (10 in.)(10 in.) = 100 sq. in. So the area of triangle AFE is 100 − (20 + 6 + 40) = 100 − 66 = 34 square inches.

Choice A is the area of triangle ABF. Choice C is the area of triangle ACE. Choice D is the sum of the areas of triangles ABF and ACE. Choice E is the area of the region inside the square but *outside* triangle AFE.

321

Chapter 8

Plane
Geometry and
Trigonometry

6.   **The correct answer is K.** Since the two triangles are similar, the corresponding sides are in proportion: $\frac{AB}{FD}=\frac{AC}{FE}=\frac{BC}{DE}$. Using the second equality, solve for DE, as follows:

$$\frac{15}{35}=\frac{20}{DE}$$
$$15DE=20(35)$$
$$DE=\frac{20(35)}{15}=\frac{4(35)}{3}=\frac{140}{3}$$

Choice F is incorrect; since triangle FED is larger than triangle ACB, the length of its side cannot be less than the length of the corresponding side of ACB. In choices G and H, you don't simply subtract the same amount from the length of one side to get another when dealing with similar triangles. Rather, the side lengths are in proportion. In choice J, you set up the proportion incorrectly—one of your fractions needs to be flipped.

7.   **The correct answer is E.** All sides of an equilateral triangle have the same length, so an equilateral triangle with a perimeter of 30 feet must have sides with a length of 10 feet. This means that the base of the triangle is 10 feet, and the height is the line that divides the equilateral triangle into two 30-60-90 triangles. Since each of these 30-60-90 triangles has a shorter leg of 5 feet (half the base) and a hypotenuse of 10, the longer leg h (the height) must satisfy the Pythagorean theorem: $h^2 + 5^2 = 10^2$ so that $h^2 = 75$; so $h = \sqrt{75} = 5\sqrt{3}$ feet.

Now, substitute these numbers into the area formula:

$$\frac{1}{2}bh=\frac{1}{2}(10)(5\sqrt{3})=25\sqrt{3} \text{ square feet}$$

Choice A is incorrect because the height of the triangle is not 5 feet. In choice B, you multiplied by 2 instead of $\frac{1}{2}$ in the area formula for a triangle.

Choice C is incorrect because you cannot use two sides in the area formula since they are not perpendicular to each other and so cannot play the role of the height. In choice D, you forgot to divide by 2; remember that the area of a triangle is $\frac{1}{2}$ times the base times the height.

8.   **The correct answer is K.** Since the area of triangle YVZ is 6 square centimeters and its height, segment VZ, has a length of 4 centimeters, the base, segment YV, must have a length of 3 centimeters. As such, using the

Pythagorean theorem, segment YZ must have a length of 5 centimeters. Given that XV has length 12 centimeters, it follows that XY has a length of 9 centimeters. As such, since opposite sides of a parallelogram have the same length, it follows that the perimeter is $(9 + 9+ 5 + 5)$ centimeters = 28 centimeters.

In choice F, you only added the lengths of the two shorter sides. In choice G, you only added the lengths of the two longer sides. Choice H is twice the length of x, not the perimeter. In choice J, you mistakenly used VZ as a side of the parallelogram—you should have used YZ.

9.   **The correct answer is C.** Start by letting w represent the width, and then translate to find the length. "11 yards more than 3 times the width" is the same as $3w + 11$. You're given that the area is 4 square yards, and you have a specific length and width. Substitute them all into the area formula to solve for w:

$$w(3w+11)=4$$
$$3w^2+11w-4=0$$
$$(3w-1)(w+4)=0$$
$$w=\frac{1}{3},\ \cancel{-4}$$

Solving for w yields two possibilities: –4 and $\frac{1}{3}$. However, the width of a rectangle cannot be negative, so w must be equal to $\frac{1}{3}$. Thus, the length is $3\times\frac{1}{3}+11=12$ yards.

Choice A is the width of the room. Choice B is the width of the room in feet. Choice D is the perimeter of the room. Choice E is the length of the room in feet, not yards.

10.   **The correct answer is K.** Opposite sides of a parallelogram are parallel. This means that $\overline{AD}\|\overline{DC}$, and $\overline{AC}$ is a transversal. Alternate interior angles formed by such a transversal are congruent. Therefore, m$\angle CAB = 84°$.

Choice F is the measure of angle ACB. Choice G is the measure of angle ADC. Choice H is the measure of angle BCD. Choice J cannot be correct since alternate interior angles formed by such a transversal are congruent.

11.   **The correct answer is E.** The area of the shaded region is the difference between the area of the square and the area of the circle. The perimeter of the square is 80 inches, so each of its sides is $80 \div 4 = 20$ inches. If you

draw a diameter through the center of the circle, you will see that it is congruent to a side of the square, so the diameter of the circle is also 20 inches.

Now, find the areas of the large square and the circle. The area of a square is equal to s^2, so the area of this square is $20^2 = 400$ square inches. The area of a circle is equal to πr^2. Since the diameter of the circle is 20 inches, its radius is 10 inches, making its area $\pi(10)^2 = 100\pi$ square inches. Therefore, the area of the shaded region is $400 - 100\pi$ square inches.

In choice A, you forgot to square the radius when computing the area of the circle. Choice B is incorrect because you should be subtracting the area of the circle from the area of the square. Choice C is the sum of the perimeters of the square and circle, not the differences in their areas. In choice D, you subtracted the perimeters of the square and circle, not their areas.

12. **The correct answer is J.** The unshaded sectors XOW and XOY comprise a total of $\frac{1}{10} + \frac{3}{5} = \frac{7}{10}$ of the circle. This means that the shaded region, sector WOY, takes up the remaining $\frac{3}{10}$ of the circle. A circle has 360 total degrees, so set up a proportion to find the measure of angle WOY:

$$\frac{3}{10} = \frac{m\angle WOY}{360°}$$
$$10(m\angle WOY) = 1080°$$
$$m\angle WOY = 108°$$

Choice F is incorrect because a circle has 360 degrees, not 180. Choice G is the measure of the angle WOX. Choice H is incorrect because you can't eyeball the sector. Choice K is the measure of $360 - WOY$, not just AOC.

13. **The correct answer is C.** The surface area of a rectangular box is the sum of the areas of the six rectangular faces. The dimensions of the faces are as follows:

$$24 \text{ in.} \times 18 \text{ in.}$$
$$24 \text{ in.} \times 6 \text{ in.}$$
$$6 \text{ in.} \times 18 \text{ in.}$$

There are two faces with each set of dimensions. So find the area of each face, multiply it by 2, and add them:

$$2[24(18) + 24(6) + 6(18)] = 1,368 \text{ square inches}$$

In choice A, you took half the area of each face instead of multiplying the areas by 2. Choice B is half the surface area—you must double the area of each

face. In choice D, you multiplied the area of each face by 3, not 2. Choice E is the volume, not the surface area.

14. **The correct answer is J.** We need to determine expressions for both cubes and then compare them. The volume of the original cube is $V_{original} = s^3$. The length of a side of the new cube is $2s$. So the volume of the new cube is $V_{new} = (2s)^3 = 8s^3$. Comparing the two formulas, we see that the volume of the new cube is eight times the volume of the original cube. Choice J is the correct answer.

Choice F is incorrect because *each* side is doubled, and so the volume increases by a factor larger than 2. Choice G is incorrect because this would be the amount by which the surface area increases, not the volume. Choice H is incorrect because the new cube is larger than the original cube, and so it cannot have a smaller volume than the original cube. Choice K is incorrect because $2^3 = 8$, not 6.

15. **The correct answer is A.** You have the side adjacent to the 39° angle, as well as the hypotenuse. Choose the trig function that uses both of these sides of a right triangle. Note that $\cos 39° = \frac{8}{x}$. If we solve for x, we obtain:

$$\cos 39° = \frac{8}{x}$$
$$x \cos 39° = 8$$
$$x = \frac{8}{\cos 39°}$$

In choices B and D, using sin 39° would require you to have the side opposite the 39° angle, which you do not have. Choice C is the reciprocal of the correct answer. In choice E, you should be dividing 8 by cos 39°, not multiplying by it.

16. **The correct answer is G.** Since the sides are in the proportion $1 : \sqrt{3} : 2$, you can use those as the actual side lengths or any constant multiple of them. For simplicity, assume that the actual lengths are 1, $\sqrt{3}$, and 2. The largest non-right angle in a triangle is opposite the larger of the two legs, so in this triangle, it would be opposite the side of length $\sqrt{3}$. In relation to this angle, the adjacent would be 1 and the hypotenuse would be 2. Since cosine $= \frac{\text{adjacent}}{\text{hypotenuse}}$, the cosine of this angle would be $\frac{1}{2}$.

Choice F is the cosine of the largest angle—but the largest angle is the right angle, which is not what was asked for. Choice H is the length of the longer of the two legs, not the cosine of the angle across from it. Choice J is cos(30), which is of the smaller of the two non-right angles. Choice K is the reciprocal of the correct answer.

17. **The correct answer is B.** Since $\cos\theta = \dfrac{5}{7}$, create a right triangle with an adjacent side of 5 and a hypotenuse of 7. Solve for the opposite leg using the Pythagorean theorem:

$$5^2 + b^2 = 7^2$$
$$b^2 = 49 - 25$$
$$b = \sqrt{24}$$
$$= 2\sqrt{6}$$

Therefore, $\cot\theta$ is equal to $\dfrac{1}{\tan\theta} = \dfrac{\text{adjacent side to } \theta}{\text{opposite side to } \theta}$, which equals $\dfrac{5\sqrt{6}}{12}$.

In choice A, you forgot that when using the Pythagorean theorem, you must square both legs and the hypotenuse. Choice C is sine of θ. Choice D is secant of θ. Choice E is the length of the side opposite of θ.

18. **The correct answer is F.** Since opposite sides of a rectangle are congruent, CD has length of 4 units. However, you need AD and are not given BC (the side to which it is congruent). So, you must use the Pythagorean theorem to compute its length:

$$4^2 + \left(BC\right)^2 = 8^2$$
$$\left(BC\right)^2 = 48$$
$$BC = 4\sqrt{3}$$

Therefore, AD also has length $4\sqrt{3}$.

Since $\sin\theta = \dfrac{\text{opposite side to } \theta}{\text{hypotenuse}}$, we see that

$$\sin\theta = \dfrac{4\sqrt{3}}{8} = \dfrac{\sqrt{3}}{2}.$$

Choice G is incorrect because it would require the angle θ to be 90°. Choice H is $\cos\theta$. Choice J is the length of BC. Choice K is incorrect because it would require the angle θ to be $45°$ and triangle ABC would need to be isosceles, but it is not.

19. **The correct answer is E.** The graph of $y = \cos x$ has a period of 2π. However, if you graph $y = 5\cos\dfrac{x}{2}$, the period doubles in length to 4π. Note that the coefficient of the cosine, 5, affects only the amplitude—not the period. All of the other choices are incorrect because the period for $y = A\cos Bx$ is $\dfrac{2\pi}{B}$. Each of these choices is the result of not remembering this fact correctly.

20. **The correct answer is H.** First, find the angles with a sine of 0; you will get 0° and 180°, which are equal to 0 and π radians, respectively. Since you want only the positive value of x, this means that $3x = \pi$, so that $x = \dfrac{\pi}{3}$.

Choice F is incorrect because 0 is a solution, but it is not positive. Plugging choice G in for x gives $\sin\dfrac{\pi}{2}$, which is 1, not 0. So this is not a solution. While choices J and K are solutions, neither is the smallest value of x that makes the equation true.

PART V: READING STRATEGIES FOR THE ACT®

Chapter 9: Social Studies and Natural Sciences Passages

Chapter 10: Literary Narrative/Prose Fiction and Humanities Passages

READING STRATEGIES FOR THE ACT® TEST

While odds are you've been reading for a *while* at this point, reading comprehension for test-taking and assessment purposes is a slightly different ball game. When you read for fun, you generally seek to follow the story and recognize or identify with the characters. You might attempt to understand their motivation, to the extent it clarifies what happens in the narrative, but you probably only read for an appreciative understanding—and even then, only once.

The ACT Reading test wants you to read to . . . answer questions correctly. It's a bonus if you enjoy the passages you read, but your main goal in this test section is to read critically and carefully, so you know for certain the *who, what, when, where,* and (most important) *why* of a passage and the author who wrote it.

The ACT Reading test will contain four excerpts in total. Three of them will be single, longer passages, and one will contain a pair of two shorter passages. Each excerpt represents a different subject category. The subject categories represented in the passages include social studies, natural sciences, literary/narrative prose fiction, and humanities. On test day, you will have 35 minutes to answer 40 multiple-choice questions.

To help you develop your critical reading skills for this section of the ACT, the next two chapters will introduce you to crucial reading strategies, including active and close reading techniques, as well as tools for identifying the main idea, recognizing essential details, making inferences, drawing generalized conclusions, making comparisons, and more. Chapter 9 emphasizes reading techniques, and selected passages come from the Natural Sciences and Social Studies categories; Chapter 10 features passages from the Literary Narrative/Prose Fiction and Humanities categories and teaches you how to recognize and decode question types.

These chapters include sample test passages and practice questions with detailed answer explanations and tips and suggestions for how to effectively read and analyze the passages on test day. At the end of each chapter, you'll find a 20-question practice exam featuring two representative passages, each paired with 10 questions for analysis.

Turn the page to learn more about how to read for ACT success!

327

Part V:

Reading
Strategies
for the
ACT® Test

CHAPTER 9:
SOCIAL STUDIES AND NATURAL SCIENCES PASSAGES

OVERVIEW

- Active Reading Techniques
- Reading for the Main Idea
- Reading for Significant Details
- Analyzing the Author's Voice and Method
- Summing It Up
- Practice

The ACT Reading test will contain four excerpts (or three longer passages and two shorter passages), each representing a different subject category. This chapter will cover the first two categories, Social Studies and Natural Sciences, and the next chapter will cover the other two, Literary Narrative/Prose Fiction and Humanities. We'll begin with active reading techniques and critical thinking skills that will help you feel prepared to tackle these sections, then we'll take a look at each question type you're likely to see and how to recognize its signal phrases.

The Social Studies category may include passages covering any of the following topics:

- Anthropology, the study of societies around the world
- Archaeology, the study of human activity in the past
- Biography, nonfiction narratives about people's lives
- Business, issues of commerce and corporations
- Economics, the study of production, distribution, and consumption
- Education, the study of the process of imparting knowledge
- Geography, the science of interpreting Earth's topography
- History, the examination of past events
- Political Science, the study of principles and institutions of government
- Psychology, the science of the mind and mental states
- Sociology, the study of how human society functions

The Natural Sciences category includes passages in the following content areas:

- Anatomy, the science of the physical structure of animals and plants
- Astronomy, the science of space outside Earth's atmosphere
- Biology, the science of life in all its forms
- Botany, the science of plants
- Chemistry, the science of composition and properties of substances

329

Chapter 9

Social
Studies and
Natural
Sciences
Passages

- Ecology, the study of organisms and their interactions with their environment
- Geology, the study of the physical history and elements of Earth
- Medicine, the science of diagnosing and treating disease and illness
- Meteorology, the science of atmosphere, weather, and climate
- Microbiology, the science of the structure, function, and existence of microscopic organisms
- Natural History, the earth sciences and study of their origins
- Physiology, the study of organisms and their processes
- Physics, the science of matter, energy, motion, and force
- Technology, the study and use of industrial arts, engineering, and applied sciences
- Zoology, the study of animals

Past passages have included reports, articles, and excerpts from nonfiction books, essays, and textbooks. Of course you're not going to be familiar with all of the above topics—you probably won't be familiar with most of them! We're going to teach you the best way to approach these passages. In cases where the language is dense or hard to follow, you'll need to be able to stay calm and mine for relevant information.

 ALERT: You will *not* need any background or outside experience with these science or history topics in order to answer the reading questions on the ACT. You will be able to derive everything you need to answer the questions from the passage itself.

ACTIVE READING TECHNIQUES

An important key to success when taking the ACT Reading test is to be an active reader. No; that doesn't mean reading while you work out—being an active reader means that you read material with the goal of understanding and evaluating it with a specific purpose in mind. In this case, the purpose is to correctly answer the questions on the ACT. The acronym ACTIVE can help you to remember the goals of active reading:

ACTIVE readers **Ask** questions, make **Connections**, **Track** down important information, **Infer** and predict, **Visualize**, and **Evaluate**, making decisions and discoveries as they explore a text.

We're going to look at a few ways that active reading can help you break down passages so you can determine what's important. Knowing that will help you as you go through the questions associated with each passage.

The most crucial first step to doing well on the ACT Reading test is to read the passage *twice*. The first time, lightly underline any details that seem most essential and use a system of your own devising to indicate questions, key terms, the main idea, and any supporting details. This technique is called **close reading.** Some close reading suggestions: use question marks in the margins for questions, draw big boxes around key terms, draw double lines under main idea or thesis statements, and use wavy lines for supporting details—but you should come up with a system that works for you and practice it often so it becomes a habit by test day.

As you read the passage the second time, think about the probable context of the passage. Word choice, tone, and internal references can give you a sense of *when* the text was written. A text that refers to up-to-date technology is obviously recent; a passage with archaic vocabulary or outdated information could have been chosen for historical significance. Think also about *why* a text was written. Is the author trying to inform? Entertain? Persuade? Disagree with an established context? Synthesize multiple views? Offer a counterargument? Call you to action? Then, try to get inside the test maker's head! Why did they choose *this* text? Because it's a classic? Because it's confusing? Because it has obvious distractions? Because it shows off technical writing abilities?

330

Chapter 9

Social
Studies and
Natural
Sciences
Passages

Let's look at a Social Studies passage on the psychology of advertising. Read this excerpt all the way through once, and then skim the questions that follow.

. . . .

Advertising is an appeal to the attention, to the memory, to the feeling, to the impulses of the reader. Every printed line of advertisement is thus a lever that is constructed to put some mental mechanism in motion. The science of the mental machinery is psychology, which works on principles with the exact methods of the experiment. It seems unprogressive, indeed, if just this one industry neglects the help that experimental science may furnish. A few slight beginnings, to be sure, have been made, but not by the individuals whose practical interests are involved. They have been made by psychologists who, in these days of carrying psychology into practical life, have pushed the laboratory method into the field of advertising.

The beginnings indicated at once that much of what is sanctioned by the traditions of economic life will have to be fundamentally revised. Psychologists, for instance, examined the memory value of the different parts of the page. Little booklets were arranged in which words were placed in the four quarter pages. The advertiser is accustomed patiently to pay an equal amount for his quarter page, whether it is on the left half or the right, on the lower or on the upper part of the page. The experiment demonstrated that the words on the upper right-hand quarter had about twice the memory value of those on the lower left. The advertiser who is accustomed to spend for his insertion on the lower left the same sum as for that on the upper right throws half his expenditure away. He reaches only half of the customers, or takes only half a grasp of those whom he reaches. This case, which can be easily demonstrated by careful experiments, is typical of the tremendous waste that goes on in the budget of the advertising community. And yet the advertiser would not like to act like the poet who sings his song not caring whose heart he will stir.

According to the second paragraph of the passage, what is one major benefit psychology may have for advertisers?

A. Knowing how best to influence their customers
B. Knowing what mental mechanisms are stirred by print ads
C. Knowing when to hire writers with fresh perspectives
D. Knowing how to strategically place their ads

The passage establishes all of the following EXCEPT:

F. the advertising value of the upper right corner of the page is twice the value of the lower left corner of the page.
G. advertising is a logical field for psychologists to study and influence.
H. the content of an ad is not nearly as important as its placement.
J. many advertising budgets contain wasteful spending.

. . . .

Here's an example of the passage with close reading annotations. Make use of the margins, underlining, starring, boxing, or note-taking on scrap paper. Keep the questions in mind as you read. These questions ask you for a "major benefit" of advertising and for you to identify significant details that are—and are not—mentioned in the passage.

For this sample close-read, we'll use the following notations:

- Brackets/margin comments to identify big picture ideas
- Underlining to note background information
- Asterisks (*) to help keep track of references to "benefits of advertising"

[Advertising is an appeal to the attention, to the memory, to the feeling, to the impulses of the reader.] Every printed line of advertisement is thus a lever that is constructed to put some
> **Topic Sentence:** We can assume the rest of the passage will be about the science behind advertising.

mental mechanism in motion.* [The science of the mental machinery is psychology, <u>which works on principles with the exact methods of the experiment.</u>] It seems unprogressive, indeed, if just this one industry neglects the help that experimental science may furnish. A few slight beginnings, to be sure, have been made, but not by [the individuals whose practical interests are involved. They have been made by psychologists] who, in these days of carrying psychology into practical life, have pushed the laboratory method into the field of advertising.
> This tells us the name for that science is psychology.

> Advertisers are not the ones examining the benefits of incorporating psychology—psychologists are.

[The beginnings] indicated at once that much of what is sanctioned by the traditions of economic life will have to be
> Refers back to the previous paragraph, in reference to the research findings.

fundamentally revised. [Psychologists, for instance, examined the memory value of the different parts of the page.] Little booklets were arranged in which words were placed in the four quarter pages. <u>The advertiser is accustomed patiently to pay an equal amount for his quarter page</u>, whether it is on the left half or the right, on the lower or on the upper part of the page. [The experiment demonstrated that the words on the upper right-hand quarter had about twice the memory value of those on the lower left.]* The advertiser who is accustomed to spend for his insertion on the lower left the same sum as for that on the upper right throws half his expenditure away. [He reaches only half of the customers or takes only half a grasp of those whom he reaches.] This case, which can be easily demonstrated by careful experiments, is typical of the tremendous waste that goes on in the budget of the advertising community. And yet the advertiser would not like to act like the poet who sings his song not caring whose heart he will stir.
> Description of an experiment relevant to advertising.

> Results of the experiment.

> Conclusion derived from the findings of the experiment.

Now you're ready to close read the questions. You'll notice that the first adopts a more macro (or big-picture) approach, asking for a main idea expressed by the passage. It gives you a specific location within the passage to focus on (the second paragraph) and requires that you make an inference from the evidence presented. Key phrases in the question are in **bold** type so you can start to think like a question maker.

According to the **second paragraph of the passage**, what is **one major benefit** psychology may have for advertisers?

A. Knowing how best to influence their customers

This may be the main idea of the section from which this excerpt is drawn, but it is not the most specific answer supported by this paragraph.

B. Knowing what mental mechanisms are stirred by print ads

Similarly, this is definitely a benefit of psychology implied in the opening sentences of this passage, but the question asks you to focus on the second paragraph and the specific benefit it implies.

C. Knowing when to hire writers with fresh perspectives

While the advertiser may need to hire writers who can play off the insights provided by psychology in their ad copy, this idea is not specifically supported by the passage.

D. Knowing how to strategically place their ads

*Most of the discussion in this paragraph is regarding the memory impact of page placement, so it's reasonable to infer the awareness of this tactic would be a major benefit to advertisers. **This is the correct answer**.*

The second question requires you to identify a significant detail; pay careful attention to the *EXCEPT*, which indicates that three of the four answer choices are taken from the passage. The answer choice that is *not* included in the passage is the correct answer to this question. If you zoom past the *except*, you risk selecting the first answer you recognize—a careless mistake that's easy to avoid.

The passages establishes all of the following EXCEPT:

F. the advertising value of the upper right corner of the page is twice the value of the lower left corner of the page.

As covered by the previous question, this IS established by the passage.

G. advertising is a logical field for psychologists to study and influence.

The opening paragraph clearly makes this point.

H. the content of an ad is not nearly as important as its placement.

*The passage stops short of implying this, though it refers to advertisers who might think more about the content than the placement. **This is the correct answer.***

J. many advertising budgets contain wasteful spending.

While you might find this evidence not particularly well-supported, it's presented by the passage as fact.

Another key component of understanding a main idea in a passage is generalizing—thinking outside of what you have read to form an idea that is not explicitly stated. Take a look at this question, which requires you to derive clues from statements within the text.

TIP

Always reread the specific paragraphs, lines, or phrases mentioned in the question or answer choices, even if you're confident. Double-check that you're not misremembering the main idea as described in the question with the main idea you actually read.

The author of this passage would most likely agree with which of the following?

   A. In order to keep up with other industries, advertisers need to be more calculated about reaching the most susceptible audience for their message.
   B. If their products are good, advertisers can trust that their message will reach their best customers.
   C. A picture is worth a thousand words.
   D. Advertisers have a lot to learn from poets, who have the broadest reach of all.

The correct answer is A. Based on the last line, "And yet the advertiser would not like to act like the poet who sings his song not caring whose heart he will stir," we can conclude that the author is unlikely to agree that poets have the best targeted marketing plan (so choice D is incorrect). The author refers specifically to "printed words" in the opening paragraph and never mentions images, so choice C is also incorrect. The focus on potential improvements from incorporating psychological insights should suggest to you that the author does *not* think the product is as important as the message, so choice B is incorrect. Choice A is the most reasonable inference based on the sentence in the first paragraph, which says, "It seems unprogressive, indeed, if just this one industry neglects the help that experimental science may furnish." If advertising is "just this one industry" that would be neglecting the help, it implies that every other industry is making use of these innovative techniques.

READING FOR THE MAIN IDEA

A **topic** is the general prompt that leads someone to write an essay. The main idea, however, is the **thesis**—the major takeaway an author wants someone to infer after reading his or her work. It might involve the author's feelings about the topic, a crucial piece of information the author wants to highlight, or a realization the author wants the reader to have about the topic. The main idea is usually featured in the first third of an excerpt or is the idea most often referred to or repeated throughout the passage. The rest of the passage is made up of background information, evidence, and supporting details.

Sometimes questions will ask you outright, "What is the main idea of this passage?" Other times you'll be asked either to refer to explicit information to determine the main idea or to use your critical reasoning abilities to infer it.

Take a look at this archaeology passage from a 1920 guide for travelers in the Middle East.

The hints that it is the object of this volume to convey are not meant for experienced archaeologists. They are rather addressed to those who, while anxious to observe and record the antiquities which they may see on their travels, are likely, 5 owing to lack of training, to miss things that may be of importance, or, having observed them, to bring home an imperfect record. It is hoped also that they may catch the attention of some of those who are not interested in the subject, but, coming into possession of antiquities, may unwittingly do incalculable 10 harm by allowing them to be destroyed or dispersed before any record has been made.

Most, if not all, of the countries with which we are concerned, have their Laws of Antiquities. It cannot be too strongly insisted that those laws, even if they might be better than they are, 15 should be obeyed by the traveller. He should familiarize himself

with their main provisions, which are summarized in an Appendix. The traveller who makes it his object to loot a country of its antiquities, smuggling objects out of it and disguising the sources from which they are obtained, does a distinct dis-
20 service to archaeological science. Although he may enrich collections, public or private, half or more than half of the scientific value of his acquisitions is destroyed by the fact that their provenance is kept secret or falsely stated. Such action is equivalent to tearing out whole pages from a history and
25 destroying them forever, for each antiquity, whatever it may be, is in its way a part of history, whether of politics, arts, or civilization. For the same reason anything like unauthorized excavation, especially by unskilled hands, is gravely to be deprecated. To dig an ancient site unskillfully or without keeping
30 a proper record is to obliterate part of a manuscript that no one else will ever be able to read. The tendency of recent legislation is to allow more generous terms in the matter of licenses for export to excavators and collectors, and the harsher provisions of some of the existing laws are likely soon to be
35 amended.

Excerpt from "Chapter I, Introductory," by G.F. Hill, from *How To Observe In Archaeology: Suggestions For Travellers In The Near And Middle East* (1920)

One of the author's main points about traveling in historically significant areas is:

F. undiscovered antiquities are ripe for the taking in remote or unexplored areas.

G. legislation governing the acquisition and use of antiquities is due for an update.

H. visitors have obligations to be respectful and travel with guided tour groups.

J. smuggling objects out of their country of origin has repercussions for history.

The correct answer is J. The stakes of this passage rest on the long-term impact amateur excavations, theft, and looting can have on the legacy of arts and culture. Choice F is incorrect—the author never suggests these artifacts are available to be recovered. While the author does mention laws "might be better than they are," that aside is countered by the final statement, which says the laws are likely to be loosened in the near future. Choice H is incorrect because there is no reference to guided tours; the author might even believe tourism is as bad for the integrity of these sites as the unscrupulous travelers.

Let's examine another passage in search of the main idea, from the Social Studies subcategory of education. The question that follows asks you to refer to information that is explicitly stated in the passage.

The influence of art upon the life of a young child is difficult to measure. It may freely be said, however, that there is little or no danger in exaggerating its influence, and considerable danger in underrating it. It is difficult to measure because the
5 influence is largely an unconscious one. Indeed, it may be questioned whether that form of art which gives him the most conscious and outspoken pleasure is the form that in reality is the most beneficial; for, unquestionably, he will get great sat-isfaction from circus posters, and the poorly printed, abominably
10 illustrated cheap picture-books afford him undeniable joy. He is far less likely to be expressive of his pleasure in a sun-shiny nursery, whose walls, rugs, white beds, and sun-shiny windows are all well designed and well adapted to his needs. Nevertheless, in the end the influence of this room is likely to be the greater
15 influence and to permanently shape his ideas of the beautiful; while he is entirely certain, if allowed to develop artistically at all, to grow past the circus poster period.

This fact—the fact that the highest influence of art is a secret influence, exercised not only by those decorations and pictures
20 which flaunt themselves for the purpose, but also by those

quiet, necessary, everyday things, which nevertheless may most truly express the art spirit—this fact makes it difficult to tell what art and what kind of art is really influencing the child, and whether it is influencing him in the right directions.

Excerpt from "Art and Literature on Child Life," from *Study of Child Life*, by Marion Foster Washburne. (1907) [http://www.gutenberg.org/files/13467/13467-h/13467-h.htm#art]

Which of the following is directly supported by the passage?

A. Elegant decorations are more influential on a child's development than popular, flashy artwork and poorly printed children's books.

B. While it is undeniable that art has an impact on child development, it is difficult to evaluate what elements are most influential.

C. Popular art that a child enjoys is the most significant contributor to artistic development and social maturity.

D. The art we are exposed to as children affects us in specific, measurable ways.

The correct answer is B. The opening and closing sentences of the excerpt directly support this option. Choices A and C are both outright rejected by the passage, which mainly discusses how hard it is to differentiate between specific influences. Similarly, choice D is incorrect because there are no specific, measurable impacts under discussion in the passage.

. . . .

For this next excerpt, from the Natural Sciences subcategory of botany, you will be asked to *infer* a main idea. This calls for using your reasoning skills to determine implicit meaning—so the main idea may not be directly stated.

. . . .

In 55 B.C., then-governor Julius Caesar invaded the south of what would later become Great Britain with his nearly 10,000 soldiers, under orders of Emperor Claudius.

It may be safely assumed that, two thousand years ago, before Caesar set foot in southern Britain, the whole countryside visible from the windows of the room in which I write, was in what is called "the state of nature." Except, it may be, by raising a few
5 sepulchral mounds, such as those which still, here and there, break the flowing contours of the downs, man's hands had made no mark upon it; and the thin veil of vegetation which overspread the broad-backed heights and the shelving sides of the coombs was unaffected by his industry. The native grasses and weeds,
10 the scattered patches of gorse, contended with one another for the possession of the scanty surface soil; they fought against the droughts of summer, the frosts of winter, and the furious gales which swept, with unbroken force, now from the Atlantic, and now from the North Sea, at all times of the year; they filled up,
15 as they best might, the gaps made in their ranks by all sorts of underground and overground animal ravagers. One year with another, an average population, the floating balance of the unceasing struggle for existence among the indigenous plants, maintained itself. It is as little to be doubted, that an essentially
20 similar state of nature prevailed, in this region, for many thousand years before the coming of Caesar; and there is no assignable reason for denying that it might continue to exist through an equally prolonged futurity, except for the intervention of man.

Excerpt from "Evolution and Ethics. Prolegomena."[1894], from *Evolution and Ethics and Other Essays*, by Thomas H. Huxley.

From information in the passage, it can be reasonably inferred that:

F. the arrival of Caesar had no effect on the grasses and vegetation of southern Britain.
G. the weather in southern Britain is exceptionally clement and allows for all kinds of growth and plant life.
H. the "state of nature" in southern Britain included a wide variety of animal species.
J. the intervention of humans has destroyed or disrupted the natural ecology of southern Britain.

The correct answer is J. Even though it is never directly stated, the descriptions of Britain prior to the arrival of Caesar and his troops, plus the last line, "it might continue to exist through an equally prolonged futurity, except for the intervention of man," allow for the reasonable assumption that Caesar's invasion had impacts on the natural landscape. Choice F is incorrect because there's no other reason the author would have framed the passage with Caesar's presence in Britain. Choice G is an inaccurate summary of the passage, which describes the British climate as rough and prone to "furious gales." Choice H reflects one supporting point in the passage, but it is not significant enough to qualify as a main idea (nor does it require an inference on the part of the reader).

Finally, we'll revisit drawing generalizations from the main idea of the passage with this passage from the work of Nikola Tesla, an inventor and scientific innovator who lived from 1856 to 1943.

. . . .

In how far we can understand the world around us is the ultimate thought of every student of nature. The coarseness of our senses prevents us from recognizing the ulterior construction of matter, and astronomy, this grandest and most positive of
5 natural sciences, can only teach us something that happens, as it were, in our immediate neighborhood: of the remoter portions of the boundless universe, with its numberless stars and suns, we know nothing. But far beyond the limit of perception of our senses the spirit still can guide us, and so we may hope that even
10 these unknown worlds—infinitely small and great—may in a measure become known to us. Still, even if this knowledge should reach us, the searching mind will find a barrier, perhaps forever unsurpassable, to the *true* recognition of that which *seems* to be, the mere *appearance* of which is the only and slender basis of
15 all our philosophy.

According to the passage, students of nature should:

A. be guided by the five senses to guide their understanding of the world.

B. stay alert to the distinction between what *is* and what *seems* to be.

C. give up on trying to see beneath the *appearance* of our world.

D. focus on the most recent advancements in technology.

The correct answer is B. Choice A is in direct opposition to the passage, in which Tesla refers to the "coarseness" of our senses. Choice C doesn't seem at all related to Tesla's hope that we will keep searching beyond the surface of the world and its mysteries. Choice D might be a reflection of Tesla's values, but there is nothing in the passage on which to base this inference. Choice B is the best answer—the clue that allows for this inference is the final sentence, "the searching mind will find a barrier, perhaps forever unsurpassable, to the true recognition of that which seems to be, the mere appearance of which is the only and slender basis of all our philosophy." Tesla opened this chapter by addressing himself to all "students of nature"—it's reasonable to generalize that he'd want these students to keep pushing beyond the barrier of appearances.

337

Chapter 9

Social
Studies and
Natural
Sciences
Passages

. . . .

READING FOR SIGNIFICANT DETAILS

Up to this point, the questions have emphasized extracting main ideas from the passage; we've examined shortened excerpts in order to help you focus. Now we'll look at extended versions of some of the same passages and identify the strategies and techniques that will help you "work micro," i.e., find significant details in the passage to answer questions.

TAKING NOTES

As we mentioned at the start of the chapter, the most essential technique is taking notes on your own—before you even know what the questions are going to ask, you can make sure you're mining the passage for all its worth.

Let's revisit this archaeology passage. We'll put brackets around the relevant text, make notes in the margins, and then compile the notes at the bottom in a bulleted list.

[The hints which it is the object of this volume to convey are not meant for experienced archaeologists. They are rather addressed to those who, while anxious to observe and record the antiquities which they may see on their travels, are likely, owing to lack of training, to miss things that may be of importance, or, having observed them, to bring home an imperfect record.] It is hoped also that they may catch the attention of some of those who are not interested in the subject, but, coming into possession of antiquities, may unwittingly do incalculable harm by allowing them to be destroyed or dispersed before any record has been made.

The intended audience is not experienced archaeologists, but amateurs.

Most, if not all, of the countries with which we are concerned, have their Laws of Antiquities. It cannot be too strongly insisted that those laws, even if they might be better than they are, should be obeyed by the traveller. He should familiarize himself with their main provisions, which are summarized in an Appendix. The traveller who makes it his object to loot a country of its antiquities, smuggling objects out of it and disguising the sources from which they are obtained, does a distinct disservice to archaeological science. [Although he may enrich collections, public or private, half or more than half of the scientific value of his acquisitions is destroyed by the fact that their provenance is kept secret or falsely stated.] Such action is equivalent to tearing out whole pages from a history and destroying them for ever, for each antiquity, whatever it may be, is in its way a part of history, whether of politics, arts, or civilization. For the same reason anything like unauthorized excavation, especially by unskilled hands, is gravely to be deprecated. [To dig an ancient site unskillfully or without keeping a proper record is to obliterate part of a manuscript which no one else will ever be able to read.] The tendency of recent legislation is to allow more generous terms in the matter of licenses for export to excavators and collectors, and the harsher provisions of some of the existing laws are likely soon to be amended.

Even if a museum pays for a find, the loss of legitimate origin damages its value.

Damaging antiquities has long-term impacts on historical and cultural records.

Before leaving home, the traveller will be well advised to make inquiries at the [museums or at the headquarters of the archaeological societies] which concern themselves specially with the places which he intends to visit. It is hardly necessary to warn him that archaeological training cannot be acquired in a few days, and that he will have to buy his experience in various ways; but the more time he can devote to [working through the collections in this country,] the more useful will be his observations abroad. He will be able to learn what kind of antiquities it is especially desirable to look for, not merely with the object of filling gaps in the public collections, but for the advancement of archaeological knowledge in general.

Resources for travelers.

Travelers can spend time becoming informed about what collections already exist so they have some sense of value of their finds.

[The object of archaeological travel and excavation is not to collect antiquities so that they may be arranged according to the existing catalogues of museums, but to collect fresh information to amplify and correct what we now know, to make our knowledge of the past more complete and useful.]

— A mission statement for travelers: Find something new.

On arrival in the country of his choice, he is recommended to continue at the National Museum the study, which we suppose he has already begun in the museums at home, of the kind of antiquities which he is likely to come across. [But he should also take an early opportunity of getting into touch with the local British Archaeological School or other similar institution, where he will receive advice what to look for and where and how to look, and assistance in procuring suitable equipment.] The best

— The traveler should consult experts— what does it mean that the author assumes there will be a British school or institution in any place a traveler might wish to go?

maps of the district will also be accessible for examination [(but the traveller is recommended to make inquiries in this respect before leaving England)]; the libraries will provide the literature dealing with the routes he proposes to take; and such a collection as the type–series of pottery and the [Finlay collection of prehistoric sculptures, grave goods, and vases] at the British School at Athens may be useful to supplement his previous studies at museums, and enable him to observe with intelligence [the potsherds, &c.,] that he may find on an ancient site. In return, he will be expected to report his results either to the School or to some other scientific society or museum at home. It should be unnecessary to remind him that the conditions of the law of the land relating to the reporting of discoveries to the competent authorities should be strictly observed. [Such authorities should also be informed of any destruction or removal of monuments which may be noticed.]

— The author assumes the reader/ traveler is British.

— Specific kinds of specimens.

— Unfamiliar word "potsherds"; from context: broken shards of pottery? Unfamiliar term "&c."; from context: etc.?

— The author appears to sign off on the destruction or removal of less noticeable monuments!

Excerpt from "Chapter I, Introductory," by G.F. Hill, from *How To Observe In Archaeology: Suggestions For Travellers In The Near And Middle East* (1920)

339

Chapter 9

Social Studies and Natural Sciences Passages

NOTES

- The intended audience is not experienced archaeologists, but amateurs.
- Even if a museum pays for a find, the loss of legitimate origin decreases its value.
- Damaging antiquities has long-term impacts on historical and cultural records.
- Resources for travelers: museums, archaeological society headquarters
- Travelers can spend time becoming informed about what collections already exist so they have some sense of value of their finds.
- A mission statement for travelers: Find something new.
- The traveler should consult experts—what does it mean that the author assumes there will be a British school or institution in any place a traveler might wish to go?
- The author assumes the reader/traveler is British.
- Specific kinds of specimens: "prehistoric sculptures, grave goods, and vases"
- Unfamiliar word "potsherds"; from context: broken shards of pottery; unfamiliar term "&c."; from context: etc.?
- The author appears to sign off on the destruction or removal of less noticeable monuments!

In this compilation of notes, we've essentially captured what's sometimes called a "reverse outline" of the passage. By recording a main idea from each paragraph, we can document the scope of the excerpt and have a shorter, succinct version to refer back to. We also recorded a question we had about the assumed British presence all around the world. You don't need to be familiar with world politics of 1920 to infer the British had at that time a presence in international societies where prized antiquities exist.

Now, let's see how taking notes can directly lead you to correct answers quickly and efficiently.

340

Chapter 9

Social
Studies and
Natural
Sciences
Passages

What are some examples of the antiquities mentioned in the passage?

   I.   Rare manuscripts
   II. Sculptures
   III. Broken pottery
   IV. Taxidermy

F. I, III
G. II, IV
H. II, III
J. I, IV

The correct answer is H. Notice how helpful it is to have notes about where specific examples were located! It was easy to return to the bullet points and select the correct combination of answers. Choice I, rare manuscripts, is a figurative reference within the passage. Choice IV, taxidermy, is the skin of a dead animal stuffed to appear lifelike—such items are not usually well preserved in tombs or ancient structures, and moreover, they are not mentioned in the passage.

According to the author in Paragraph 4, the goal of archaeological expeditions is to:

A. renegotiate export licenses, not to contribute new map features.

B. make new discoveries, not to further augment existing collections.

C. give a crash course in excavation, not to prioritize treasure hunting goals.

D. share findings with sponsoring institutions, not to replenish museums' stores of pottery shards.

The correct answer is B. This type of question and its answer choices can be tricky because the answer choices are all paraphrased from the passage—if you rely on mere recognition to point you to the correct answer, you'll be in trouble. Instead, carefully return to your notes. What is the goal of this type of visit? Our shorthand version was, "A mission statement for travelers: Find something new." Which answer choice most nearly reflects that statement? Choice B.

Now it's your turn to practice active note taking. Remember, the goal is to allow you to more easily identify crucial details and answer the questions that check for this up-close kind of understanding.

The influence of art upon the life of a young child is difficult to measure. It may freely be said, however, that there is little or no danger in exaggerating its influence, and considerable danger in underrating it. It is difficult to measure because the influence
5 is largely an unconscious one. Indeed, it may be questioned whether that form of art which gives him the most conscious and outspoken pleasure is the form that in reality is the most beneficial; for, unquestionably, he will get great satisfaction from circus posters, and the poorly printed, abominably illustrated
10 cheap picture-books afford him undeniable joy. He is far less likely to be expressive of his pleasure in a sun-shiny nursery, whose walls, rugs, white beds, and sun-shiny windows are all well designed and well adapted to his needs. Nevertheless, in the end the influence of this room is likely to be the greater
15 influence and to permanently shape his ideas of the beautiful; while he is entirely certain, if allowed to develop artistically at all, to grow past the circus poster period.

This fact—the fact that the highest influence of art is a secret influence, exercised not only by those decorations and pictures
20 which flaunt themselves for the purpose, but also by those quiet, necessary, every-day things, which nevertheless may most truly express the art spirit—this fact makes it difficult to tell what art and what kind of art is really influencing the child, and whether it is influencing him in the right directions.

Color

25 Until he is three years old, for example, and often until he is past that age, he is unable to distinguish clearly between green, gray, and blue; and hence these cool colors in the decorations around him, or in his pictures, have practically no meaning for him. He has a right, one might suppose, to the gratification of
30 his love for clear reds and yellows, for the sharp, well-defined lines and flat surfaces, whose meaning is plain to his groping little mind. Some of the best illustrators of children's books have seemed to recognize this. For example, Boutet de Monvil in his admirable illustrations of Joan of Arc meets these requirements
35 perfectly, and yet in a manner which must satisfy any adult lover of good art. The Caldecott picture books, and Walter Crane's are also good in this respect, and the Perkins pictures issued by the Prang Educational Co. have gained a just recognition as excellent pictures for hanging on the nursery wall. Many of the illustrations
40 in color in the standard magazines are well worth cutting out, mounting and framing. This is especially true of Howard Pyle's work and that of Elizabeth Shippen Green.

Classic Art

Since photogravures and photographs of the masterpieces can be had in this country very inexpensively, there is no
45 reason why children should not be made acquainted at an early age with the art classics, but there is danger in giving too much space to black and white, especially in the nursery where the children live. Their natural love of color should be appealed to deepen their interest in really good pictures.

50 Nevertheless, it is a matter of considerable difficulty still to find colored pictures which are inexpensive and yet really good. The Detaille prints, while not yet cheap, are not expensive either, and are excellent for this purpose; but the insipid little pictures of fairies, flowers, and birds may be
55 really harmful, as helping to form in the young child's mind too low an ideal of beauty—of cultivating in him what someone has called "the lust of the eye."

Plastic Art

What holds true of the pictorial art holds equally true of the plastic art. As Prof. Veblin of the University of Chicago
60 has scathingly declared, our ideals of the beautiful are so mingled with worship of expense that few of us can see the genuine beauty in any object apart from its expensiveness. For this reason as well as, perhaps, because of a remnant of barbarism in us, we love gold and glitter, and a great deal of
65 elaboration in our vases, and are far from being over-critical of any piece of statuary which costs a respectable sum.

Excerpt from "Art and Literature on Child Life," from *Study of Child Life*, by Marion Foster Washburne. (1907) [http://www.gutenberg.org/files/13467/13467-h/13467-h.htm#art]

Chapter 9

Social Studies and Natural Sciences Passages

Now it's your turn. Use this space to record your own notes from this passage—whether you compile your margin comments, reverse outline, record questions, or document main ideas and supporting details, do your own excavating for information so that when you approach the question that follows, you've already begun distilling the passage down into the most useful information.

_____

_____

_____

_____

_____

_____

_____

_____

_____

_____

_____

Now, using only your notes, see if you can identify the correct answer to the question.

Chapter 9

Social
Studies and
Natural
Sciences
Passages

According to the passage, what are the first colors a child is able to perceive?

F. Black and white
G. Green, gray, and blue
H. Green, red, and yellow
J. Purple, brown, and orange

The correct answer is F. Although the passage acknowledges yellow and red (given in choice H) as the more clearly visible colors, it indicates children aren't able to "distinguish clearly between green, gray, and blue" until they are at least three years old, eliminating choices G and H. A child's ability to perceive black and white (choice F) is implied in the next paragraph, about classic art, making it the correct answer. There is no mention of purple, brown, or orange in the passage (choice J).

Did you find the answer in your notes? If you discerned that the order in which a child sees colors could be an important point and jotted it down, you saved yourself time by not having to refer back to the passage. You want to be especially aware of managing your time when taking the ACT Reading test. Being an effective active reader will help you with that skill.

Vocabulary in Context

Another purpose of extensive close reading is to help you identify and define key vocabulary or concepts via context. Even if you're unfamiliar with specialized vocabulary—which may be more likely in the sciences or social studies fields—you can derive meaning from the surrounding sentences.

When you come across a word you don't know, read the sentence, cover the unknown word, and think of a word that you do know that might fit in the sentence. Then, compare your word to the answer choices. Chances are you will find a good fit.

Let's go back to the passage on page 341. Here's a sample question that asks you to practice this technique; pay particular attention to the "most nearly" phrasing to help you distinguish between similar answer choices.

In line 64 the word *barbarism* most nearly means:

   A. a quality of being foreign.
   B. the practice of hair-cutting techniques.
   C. an absence of culture and civilization.
   D. extreme cruelty or brutality.

The correct answer is C. If you recognize that barbarism is related to *barbarian* and *barbaric*, you might remember its connotation with cruelty (choice D) and being foreign (choice A). However, in this particular context, *barbarism* is more related to a lack of *taste* than to a lack of compassion or a connection with outsider status, so choice C is the correct answer. You can determine this from nearby references to vases, décor, as well as the topic of the passage as a whole, art and aesthetics. The author is not suggesting our modern ideals lead us to callous or violent behavior, merely that our sense of exalted art objects is diluted by an appreciation for the tacky or gilded.

Cause and Effect

Another kind of detail-oriented question asks you to identify the logical links between ideas in the passage or determine a cause-and-effect relationship. These questions will identify a key concept and then ask you to determine why the author made that point, or how it is supported by information elsewhere in the passage.

Referring back to the passage on page 341, let's take a look at an example of a cause-and-effect example.

The passage suggests that pictures of fairies, flowers, and birds are not appropriate choices for a nursery because:

   F. they are too fantastical to encourage a child's understanding of the world.
   G. the colorful prints are too expensive for a short-term decorating investment.
   H. they are insipid artistic subjects that will warp a child's artistic tastes.
   J. they appeal to a child's natural love of color insufficiently.

The correct answer is H. The passage both refers to fairies, flowers, and birds as insipid *and* suggests they may cultivate a "lust of the eye" (which is a whole other interpretive question—you can infer from the context that it is deemed negative by the author, however). Choice F is incorrect because only fairies are actually imagination-based; flowers and birds might be "insipid," but they are factual. Choice G is incorrect; while the passage does consider the expense of finding good prints, it also recommends pages from color magazines, which would certainly be cost-effective. Choice J is incorrect; the passage indicates that fairy, birds, and flowers are an excellent way to appeal to a child's love of color.

For this next passage, pay attention to which of the questions that follow asks for a big picture "main idea" reading and which one requires a detail-oriented close read.

It may be safely assumed that, two thousand years ago, before Caesar set foot in southern Britain, the whole country-side visible from the windows of the room in which I write, was in what is called "the state of nature."
5 Except, it may be, by raising a few sepulchral mounds, such as those which still, here and there, break the flowing contours of the downs, man's hands had made no mark upon it; and the thin veil of vegetation which overspread the broad-backed heights and the shelving sides of the
10 coombs was unaffected by his industry. The native grasses and weeds, the scattered patches of gorse, contended with one another for the possession of the scanty surface soil; they fought against the droughts of summer, the frosts of winter, and the furious gales which swept, with
15 unbroken force, now from the Atlantic, and now from the North Sea, at all times of the year; they filled up, as they best might, the gaps made in their ranks by all sorts of underground and overground animal ravagers. One year with another, an average population, the floating balance
20 of the unceasing struggle for existence among the indigenous plants, maintained itself. It is as little to be doubted, that an essentially similar state of nature prevailed, in this region, for many thousand years before the coming of Caesar; and there is no assignable reason for denying that
25 it might continue to exist through an equally prolonged futurity, except for the intervention of man.

Reckoned by our customary standards of duration, the native vegetation, like the "everlasting hills" which it clothes, seems a type of permanence. The little Amarella
30 Gentians, which abound in some places to-day, are the descendants of those that were trodden underfoot by the prehistoric residents who have left their flint tools, about, here and there; and they followed ancestors which, in the climate of the glacial epoch, probably flourished
35 better than they do now. Compared with the long past of this humble plant, all the history of civilized men is but an episode.

Yet nothing is more certain than that, measured by the liberal scale of time-keeping of the universe, this present
40 state of nature, however it may seem to have gone and to go on forever, is but a fleeting phase of her infinite variety; merely the last of the series of changes which the earth's surface has undergone in the course of the millions of years of its existence. Turn back a square foot of the thin turf,
45 and the solid foundation of the land, exposed in cliffs of chalk five hundred feet high on the adjacent shore, yields full assurance of a time when the sea covered the site of the "everlasting hills"; and when the vegetation of what land lay nearest, was as different from the present Flora of the Sussex downs,
50 as that of Central Africa now is.

No less certain is it that, between the time during which the chalk was formed and that at which the original turf came into existence, thousands of centuries elapsed, in the course of which, the state of nature of the ages during which the chalk
55 was deposited, passed into that which now is, by changes so slow that, in the coming and going of the generations of men, had such witnessed them, the contemporary conditions would have seemed to be unchanging and unchangeable.

Excerpt from "Evolution and Ethics. Prolegomena."[1894], from *Evolution and Ethics and Other Essays*, by Thomas H. Huxley. [http://www.gutenberg.org/cache/epub/2940/pg2940-images.html]

According to the passage, Paragraph 3 most closely identifies the shift from discussing:

A. botany (the study of plants) to geology (the study of the earth's surface).

B. the geography of Great Britain to the geography of Central Africa.

C. anthropology (the study of humans) to zoology (the study of animals).

D. ancient geology to the modern landscape.

The correct answer is A. This question requires you to pinpoint a shift between two larger ideas, and this answer choice showcases a moment where the author literally moves from the surface to the subterranean features of the landscape when he says, "Turn back a square foot of the thin turf, and the solid foundation of the land, exposed in cliffs of chalk five hundred feet high on the adjacent shore, yields full assurance of a time when the sea covered the site of the 'everlasting hills.'" (lines 44–48). Choice B picks up on a comparison made by the passage, but the paragraph is not actually moving on to a discussion of Central Africa. Choice C is not reflected in the passage. Choice D is a distraction meant to mislead you by referring to the passage of time; while the paragraph does mention "the course of millions of years," it does not signal a shift to discussing the modern landscape.

344

Chapter 9

Social
Studies and
Natural
Sciences
Passages

Which of the following would the author be MOST likely to recommend?

F. Studying the history of the Holy Roman Empire
G. Excavating the burial mounds of early inhabitants of the British Isles
H. Mining the coast of Britain for its chalk and mineral resources
J. Establishing a nature preserve to cultivate southern Britain's original plant life

The correct answer is J. You can make this inference by gauging the author's appreciative tone toward the original flora and fauna of this part of England and his resistance to the arrival of Caesar. Choice F is incorrect because the author's attention is primarily on the natural history of Britain, not the history of the invading populations (who, in any case, would have been unable to properly perceive the shifts in landscape do to their limited lifespans). Choice G is incorrect; the author does not seem particularly interested in the burial mounds of the early inhabitants, nor in exploiting the mineral elements in the region (choice H).

. . . .

For this next passage, look for the distinction between a question that asks about the sequence of events and a question more focused on cause and effect.

. . . .

The theory of the origin of sleep that has gained the widest credence is the one that attributes it to anæmia of the brain. It has been shown by Mosso, and many others, that in men with defects of the cranial wall the volume of the brain decreases
5 during sleep. At the same time, the volume of any limb increases as the peripheral parts of the body become turgid with blood. In dogs, the brain has been exposed, and the cortex of that organ has been observed to become anæmic during sleep. It is a matter of ordinary observation that in infants, during sleep,
10 the volume of the brain becomes less, since the fontanelle is found to sink in. It has been supposed, but without sufficient evidence to justify the supposition, that this anæmia of the brain is the cause and not the sequence of sleep. The idea behind this supposition has been that, as the day draws to an
15 end, the circulatory mechanism becomes fatigued, the vasomotor center exhausted, the tone of the blood vessels deficient, and the energy of the heart diminished, and the circulation to the cerebral arteries lessened.

By means of a simple and accurate instrument (the Hill-
20 Barnard sphygmometer), with which the pressure in the arteries of man can be easily reckoned, it has been recently determined that the arterial pressure falls just as greatly during bodily rest as during sleep. The ordinary pressure of the blood in the arteries of young and healthy men averages 110–120 mm. of
25 mercury. In sleep, the pressure may sink to 95–100 mm.; but if the pressure be taken of the same subject lying in bed, and quietly engaged on mental work, it will be found to be no higher. By mental strain or muscular effort, the pressure is, however, immediately raised, and may then reach 130–140
30 mm. of mercury. It can be seen from considering these facts that the fall of pressure is concomitant with rest, rather than with sleep. As, moreover, it has been determined on strong evidence

that the cerebral vessels are not supplied with vasomotor nerves, and that the cerebral circulation passively follows every
35 change in the arterial pressure, it becomes evident that sleep cannot be occasioned by any active change in the cerebral vessels. This conclusion is borne out by the fact that to produce in the dog a condition of coma like to sleep, it is necessary to reduce, by a very great amount, the cerebral circulation.

40 Thus, both carotids and both vertebral arteries, can be frequently tied at one and the same time without either producing coma or any very marked symptoms. The circulation is, in such a case, maintained through other channels, such as branches from the superior intercostal arteries which enter
45 the anterior spinal artery. While total anæmia of the brain instantaneously abolishes consciousness, partial anæmia is found to raise the excitability of the cortex cerebri. By estimation of the exchange of gases in the blood which enters and leaves the brain, it has been shown that the consumption
50 of oxygen and the production of carbonic acid in that organ is not large. Further, it may be noted that the condition of anæsthesia is not in all cases associated with cerebral anæmia. Thus, while during chloroform anæsthesia the arterial pressure markedly falls, such is not the case during anæsthesia pro-
55 duced by ether or a mixture of nitrous oxide and oxygen.

The arterial pressure of man is not lowered by the ordinary fatigue of daily life. It is only in extreme states of exhaustion that the pressure may be found decreased when the subject is in the standing position. The fall of pressure which does
60 occur during rest or sleep is mainly occasioned by the diminished rate of the heart. The increase in the volume of the limbs is to be ascribed to the cessation of muscular movement and to the diminution in the amplitude of respiration. The duty of

the heart is to deliver the blood to the capillaries. From the veins the blood is, for the most part, returned to the heart by the compressive action of the muscles, the constant change of posture and by the respiration acting both as a force and suction pump. All of these factors are at their maximum during bodily activity and at their minimum during rest. On exciting a sleeper by calling his name, or in any way disturbing him, the limbs, It has been recorded, decrease in volume while the brain expands. This is so because the respiration changes in depth, the heart quickens, the muscles alter in tone, as the subject stirs in his sleep in reflex response to external stimuli. Considering all these facts, we must regard the fall of arterial pressure, the depression of the fontanelle, and the turgescence of the vessels of the limbs as phenomena concomitant with bodily rest and warmth, and we have no more right to assign the causation of sleep to cerebral anæmia than to any other alteration in the functions of the body, such as occur during sleep.

We may well here summarize these other changes in function:

- The respiratory movement becomes shallow and thoracic in type.
- The volume of the air inspired per minute is lessened by one-half to two-thirds.
- The output of carbonic acid is diminished by the same amount.
- The bodily temperature falls.
- The acidity of the cortex of the brain disappears.
- Reflex action persists; the knee jerk is diminished, pointing to relaxation in tone of the muscles; consciousness is suspended.

Analyzing more closely the conditions of the central nervous system, it becomes evident that, in sleep, consciousness alone is in abeyance. The nerves and the special senses continue to transmit impulses and to produce reflex movements. If a blanket, sufficiently heavy to impede respiration, be placed upon the face of a sleeping person, we know that it will be immediately pushed away. More than this, complicated movements can be carried out; the postilion can sleep on horseback; the punkah-wallah may work his punkah and at the same time enjoy a slumber; a weary mother may sleep, and yet automatically rock her infant's cradle. Turning to the histories of sleep walkers, we find it recorded that, during sleep, they perform such feats as climbing slanting roofs or walking across dangerous narrow ledges and bridges. The writer knew of the case of a lad who, when locked in his room at night to prevent his wandering in his sleep, climbed a partition eight to ten feet in height which separated his sleeping compartment from the next, and this without waking.

The brain can carry out not only such complicated acts as these, but it has been found to maintain during sleep its normal inhibitory control over the lower reflex centers in the spinal cord.

Excerpt from "Sleep and the Theories of Its Cause" (*Scientific American Supplement*, Pg. 18768, Vol. XLV., No. 1178, June 25, 1898). [https://www.gutenberg.org/files/18265/18265-h/18265-h.htm#art16]

According to the passage, the process of falling asleep involves all of the following EXCEPT:

A.   lower blood pressure.
B.   increase in the blood stored in the limbs.
C.   slowed respiration volume.
D.   expansion of the brain.

The correct answer is D. The passage states, "On exciting a sleeper by calling his name, or in any way disturbing him, the limbs, it has been recorded, decrease in volume while the brain expands," which implies the brain normally contracts during sleep. Choices A, B, and C are all mentioned specifically in the passage.

The passage indicates that in adults, blood pressure falls during sleep because:

F.   the fontanelle sinks in.
G.   the muscles stop moving.
H.   the heart rate slows down.
J.   cerebral vessels contract.

The correct answer is H. The heart is responsible for pumping blood throughout the body, and when it slows, the pressure generated through circulation is reduced as blood stands in the limbs. Choice F is incorrect because the question specifically asks about adults, and the fontanelle is only present in infant skulls. Choice G is incorrect because muscle relaxation is one of the causes of a slowing heart rate—it's a degree removed from the change in blood pressure, and besides, involuntary muscle movement occurs during sleep. Choice J is incorrect—the passage indicates that cerebral blood vessels contract along with the other processes of sleep, as opposed to being their cause.

The next set of questions involves a variety of approaches to reading for implicit and explicit details.

Geology deals with the rocks of the earth's crust. It learns from their composition and structure how the rocks were made and how they have been modified. It ascertains how they have been brought to their present places and wrought to their
5 various topographic forms, such as hills and valleys, plains and mountains. It studies the vestiges which the rocks preserve of ancient organisms which once inhabited our planet.

To obtain a general idea of the nature and method of our science before beginning its study in detail, we may visit some
10 valley on whose sides are rocky ledges. Here the rocks lie in horizontal layers. Although only their edges are exposed, we may infer that these layers run into the upland on either side and underlie the entire district; they are part of the foundation of solid rock which everywhere is found beneath the loose
15 materials of the surface.

The ledges of the valley are of sandstone. Looking closely at the rock we see that it is composed of myriads of grains of sand cemented together. These grains have been worn and rounded. They are sorted also, those of each layer being about of a size.
20 By some means they have been brought hither from some more ancient source. Surely these grains have had a history before they here found a resting place,—a history which we are to learn to read.

The successive layers of the rock suggest that they were built
25 one after another from the bottom upward. We may be as sure that each layer was formed before those above it as that the bottom courses of stone in a wall were laid before the courses which rest upon them.

We have no reason to believe that the lowest layers which
30 we see here were the earliest ever formed. Indeed, some deep boring in the vicinity may prove that the ledges rest upon other layers of rock which extend downward for many hundreds of feet below the valley floor. Nor may we conclude that the highest layers here were the latest ever laid; for elsewhere we
35 may find still later layers lying upon them.

A short search may find in the rock relics of animals, such as the imprints of shells, which lived when it was deposited; and as these are of kinds whose nearest living relatives now have their home in the sea, we infer that it was on the flat sea floor
40 that the sandstone was laid. Its present position hundreds of feet above sea level proves that it has since emerged to form part of the land; while the flatness of the beds shows that the movement was so uniform and gentle as not to break or strongly bend them from their original attitude.

45 The surface of some of these layers is ripple-marked. Hence the sand must once have been as loose as that of shallow sea bottoms and sea beaches today, which is thrown into similar ripples by movements of the water. In some way the grains have since become cemented into firm rock.

50 Note that the layers on one side of the valley agree with those on the other, each matching the one opposite at the same level. Once they were continuous across the valley. Where the valley now is was once a continuous upland built of horizontal layers; the layers now show their edges, or outcrop, on
55 the valley sides because they have been cut by the valley trench.

The rock of the ledges is crumbling away. At the foot of each step of rock lie fragments which have fallen. Thus the valley is slowly widening. It has been narrower in the past; it will be wider in the future.

60 Through the valley runs a stream. The waters of rains which have fallen on the upper parts of the stream's basin are now on their way to the river and the sea. Rock fragments and grains of sand creeping down the valley slopes come within reach of the stream and are washed along by the running water. Here
65 and there they lodge for a time in banks of sand and gravel, but sooner or later they are taken up again and carried on. The grains of sand which were brought from some ancient source to form these rocks are on their way to some new goal. As they are washed along the rocky bed of the stream they slowly rasp
70 and wear it deeper. The valley will be deeper in the future; it has been less deep in the past.

Excerpt from *The Elements of Geology*, by William Harmon Norton.

From information in the passage, it can be reasonably inferred that:

A. the topographical features of a given region are in their permanent state.
B. every geologic survey is recording details that are relatively temporary.
C. the presence of water is the single greatest factor in climate change
D. fossils occur only in areas with arid, dry climates.

The correct answer is B. The passage consistently discusses that each observation is of a current state: the valley used to be narrower; it will be wider in the future; the valley used to be shallower, it will be deeper in the future. Choice A is incorrect as it directly contradicts the message of the passage. Choice C is incorrect—while water is clearly a vital element of geological

347

Chapter 9

Social
Studies and
Natural
Sciences
Passages

transformation, there is no reference to climate change in the passage. Choice D is incorrect—the passage refers to fossils that used to live under water but now reside in the rocks in this valley, which also has water running through the bottom of it.

According to the passage, which of the following most closely identifies the effect of slowly ebbing tides on stone?

    F. The rough, jagged texture of crumbling rock

    G. The matching heights of the cliffs on either side of the valley

    H. The gradual angle of the river bed showing the sand was cemented into rock

    J. The presence of embedded fossils

The correct answer is H. The passage indicates that the rippled-texture of the lower walls of the valley suggests "the movement was so uniform and gentle" that it didn't break the rock roughly or abruptly, so choice F is incorrect. Choice G is incorrect because the height of the cliffs doesn't reflect the method of water-based erosion, merely that there was a level plain before the intrusion of a flowing body of water. Choice J is incorrect because fossils are deposited by moving water or the consequence of sediment layers as they contract into rock.

ANALYZING THE AUTHOR'S VOICE AND METHOD

Now we're going to spend time close reading for clues about the author. What can we find out about intentions, background, or motivations in writing the excerpt? Let's begin with this archaeology-themed excerpt we read earlier in the chapter. (You may recall our notes on it included several questions about the author's intention!)

On arrival in the country of his choice, he is recommended to continue at the National Museum the study, which we suppose he has already begun in the museums at home, of the kind of antiquities which he is likely to come across. But he should also
5 take an early opportunity of getting into touch with the local British Archaeological School or other similar institution, where he will receive advice what to look for and where and how to look, and assistance in procuring suitable equipment. Thus the traveller who starts from Athens or Jerusalem should apply at
10 the British School of Archaeology. He may there be given all possible assistance in obtaining such articles of equipment as are available on the spot. (Photographic supplies and all scientific instruments should be brought out from England.) The best maps of the district will also be accessible for examination (but the
15 traveller is recommended to make inquiries in this respect before leaving England); the libraries will provide the literature dealing with the routes he proposes to take; and such a collection as the type–series of pottery and the Finlay collection of prehistoric antiquities at the British School at Athens may be useful to sup-
20 plement his previous studies at museums, and enable him to observe with intelligence the potsherds, &c., that he may find on an ancient site. In return, he will be expected to report his results either to the School or to some other scientific society or museum at home. It should be unnecessary to remind him that
25 the conditions of the law of the land relating to the reporting of discoveries to the competent authorities should be strictly

observed. Such authorities should also be informed of any destruction or removal of monuments which may be noticed.

What is the author's point of view?

    A. An egalitarian attitude that everyone who can travel to historic sites should take advantage of the opportunity

    B. An international awareness of the stakes for those who travel abroad to excavate antiquities

    C. A British-centric sense of entitlement to the resources of institutions and any undiscovered assets belonging to foreign nations

    D. A healthy sense of humility about disturbing the relics of ancient civilizations.

The correct answer is C. The author repeatedly refers to British institutions, museums, and materials as the most promising resources for a traveler. The author doesn't encourage anyone to travel to historic sites (choice A), nor does he indicate there are risks to the *travellers* so much as to the antiquities themselves, particularly earlier in the passage (choice B). The author certainly isn't humble about suggesting British explorers help themselves to foreign relics, so long as they notify the authorities.

Read the following excerpt from another passage you've seen before, from *Study of Child Life*, and let's walk through another question together.

The influence of art upon the life of a young child is difficult to measure. It may freely be said, however, that there is little or no danger in exaggerating its influence, and considerable danger in underrating it. It is difficult of measurement because 5 the influence is largely an unconscious one. Indeed, it may be questioned whether that form of art which gives him the most conscious and outspoken pleasure is the form that in reality is the most beneficial; for, unquestionably, he will get great satisfaction from circus posters, and the poorly printed, abominably 10 illustrated cheap picture-books afford him undeniable joy. He is far less likely to be expressive of his pleasure in a sun-shiny nursery, whose walls, rugs, white beds, and sun-shiny windows are all well designed and well adapted to his needs. Nevertheless, in the end the influence of this room is likely to be the greater 15 influence and to permanently shape his ideas of the beautiful; while he is entirely certain, if allowed to develop artistically at all, to grow past the circus poster period.

The author feels that a neutral, bright, and well lit environment is:

F. the best possible influence on a baby's aesthetic development of taste.

G. only as valuable as the entertaining posters and artwork displayed there.

H. no reason to try to measure the influence of art upon the life of a young child.

J. not something a child will ever notice or enjoy.

The correct answer is F. As indicated by the passage's final sentence, a well-lit room will permanently influence a child's idea of the beautiful. Choice G is incorrect because the author believes a child will outgrow the circus posters or picture books. Choice H is incorrect—the author mentions that it is difficult to measure the influence, but also says it would be dangerous to underrate it, and difficult to overrate. Choice J is incorrect—the author acknowledges it's difficult to determine whether a child is most benefited by what they notice consciously or unconsciously, but can't definitely say that a child *doesn't* notice his or her environment.

Here's another example of how the ACT will ask you to get inside the mind of a passage's author to infer what he or she believes. Remember—all you have is the passage in front of you. Leave aside any outside biases, and use only the text you see and the message it has to make assumptions about an author.

There is one industry in the world which may be called, more than any other, a socializing factor in our modern life. The industry of advertising binds men together and tightly knits the members of society into one compact mass. Every one in 5 the big market-place of civilization has his demands and has some supply. But in order to link supply and demand, the offering must be known. The industry which overcomes the isolation of man with his wishes and with his wares lays the real foundation of the social structure. It is not surprising that 10 it has taken gigantic dimensions and that uncounted millions are turning the wheels of the advertising factory. The influence and civilizing power of the means of propaganda go far beyond the help in the direct exchange of goods. The advertiser makes the modern newspaper and magazine possible. These mightiest 15 agencies of public opinion and intellectual culture are

supported, and their technical perfection secured, by those who pay their business tax in the form of advertisements.

Surely there is an abundance of clever advertisement writers at work, and great establishments make some careful tests 20 before they throw their millions of circulars before the public. Yet even their so-called tests have in no way scientific character. They are simply based on watching the success in practical life, and the success is gained by instinct. Common sense tells even the most superficial advertiser that a large announcement 25 will pay more than a small one, an advertisement in a paper with a large circulation more than in a paper with a few subscribers, one with a humorous or emotional or exciting text more than one with a tiresome and stale text. He also knows that the cover page in a magazine is worth more than the 30 inner pages, that a picture draws attention, that a repeated

Social Studies and Natural Sciences Passages

Peterson's ACT® Prep Guide

insertion helps better than a lonely one. Yet even a score of such rules would not remove the scheme of advertising from the common places of the trade. They still would not show any trace of the fact that the methods of exact measurement and of lab-
35 oratory research can be applied to such problems of human society.

When the author says, "Surely there is an abundance of clever advertisement writers at work, and great establishments make some careful tests before they throw their millions of circulars before the public. Yet even their so-called tests have in no way scientific character," it is a reflection of his or her belief that:

A. large agencies have a variety of useful tools at their disposal to maximize their influence.

B. brilliant copywriters can accomplish everything that a scientific approach could.

C. psychology will provide more structure and accuracy to the practice of advertising.

D. the tests that advertisers perform add nothing to the strategic impact of their product placement.

The correct answer is C. As you may have remembered from the earlier excerpt from this passage, the author firmly believes in the potential benefits psychological insight can have for the advertising industry. Choice A gets off to the right start, by paraphrasing the author's acknowledgment that advertising companies do have experience-based tests to guide their budgeting choices, but the author doesn't believe these tests are maximizing the advertisers' influence. Choice B is incorrect—the author doesn't think that "clever advertisement writers" have as much to offer as tests with scientific character. Choice D is incorrect because the author acknowledges the "careful tests" the advertisers perform.

· ·

Now we're going to look at less familiar passages so you can practice making inferences about the author with much less to go on. Our first example is from a biography of activist Susan B. Anthony (1820–1906), who fought for women's right to vote (or suffrage) as well as legal property rights in the mid- to late-nineteenth century. The temperance movement was a woman-led initiative to ban the production and sale of alcohol in the United States.

· ·

350

Teachers' conventions, however, were only a minor part of her new crusade, plans for which were still simmering in her mind and developing from day to day. Going back to many of the towns where she had held temperance meetings, she found that
5 most of the societies she had organized had disbanded because women lacked the money to engage speakers or to subscribe to temperance papers. If they were married, they had no money of their own and no right to any interest outside their homes, unless their husbands consented.

10 Discouraged, she wrote in her diary, "As I passed from town to town I was made to feel the great evil of woman's entire dependency upon man for the necessary means to aid on any and every reform movement. Though I had long admitted the wrong, I never until this time so fully took in the grand idea of pecuniary
15 and personal independence. It matters not how overflowing with benevolence toward suffering humanity may be the heart of woman, it avails nothing so long as she possesses not the power to act in accordance with these promptings. Woman must have a purse of her own, and how can this be, so long as the *Wife*
20 is denied the right to her individual and joint earnings. Reflections like these, caused me to see and really feel that there was no true

freedom for Woman without the possession of all her property rights, and that these rights could be obtained through legislation only, and so, the sooner the demand was made of the Legislature,
25 the sooner would we be likely to obtain them."

Excerpt from *Susan B. Anthony, Rebel, Crusader, Humanitarian*, by Alma Lutz.

Susan B. Anthony's statement, "Reflections like these, caused me to see and really feel that there was no true freedom for Woman without the possession of all her property rights, and that these rights could be obtained through legislation only" most nearly illustrates:

A. her belief that the key to women's liberation was the temperance movement.

B. her faith in the judicial system to administer women's rights.

C. her passion for women's suffrage.

D. her realization that women's legal empowerment was the key to all the rights that would follow.

The correct answer is D. Her use of "reflections like these, causes me to see and really feel" signals this statement represents a realization, and she clearly identifies property rights as the foundation of women's freedom. Elsewhere in the passage she indicates the temperance movement was in the past, so choice A is incorrect. The quote in the question indicates she was shifting her focus to the legislative branch of government, not the judicial branch, choice B. Choice C is incorrect—even though Anthony was undoubtedly devoted to suffrage, this quote is not the best illustration of that passion.

Of course, scientific papers or journal articles cannot be shown on the ACT in their entirety. Sometimes, the test will ask you to infer what later parts of a passage might discuss—ones that you obviously can't see.

We have seen that the usual shape of celestial bodies themselves is spherical. Of what form then are their paths, or *orbits*, as these are called? One might be inclined at a venture to answer "circular," but this is not the case. The orbits of the planets cannot

5 be regarded as true circles. They are ovals, or, to speak in technical language, "ellipses." Their ovalness or "ellipticity" is, however, in each case not by any means of the same degree. Some orbits—for instance, that of the Earth—differ only slightly from circles; while others—those of Mars or Mercury, for example—are markedly

10 elliptic. The orbit of the tiny planet Eros is, however, far and away the most elliptic of all, as we shall see when we come to deal with that little planet in detail.

When the author says "The orbit of the tiny planet Eros is, however, far and away the most elliptic of all, as we shall see when we come to deal with that little planet in detail," it is most likely an indication that:

F. the rest of the text will primarily deal with the orbit of Eros.

G. the rest of the text will explore different aspects of the solar system in detail.

H. understanding Eros' orbit is the key to comprehending the rest of the planets.

J. Eros' orbit is not properly an orbit at all.

The correct answer is G. The amount of time spent on other planets and their orbits in the paragraph should tell you the author does not intend to focus only on Eros in the rest of their work. Choices H and J are unsupported by the passage.

SUMMING IT UP

- The **Social Studies and Natural Science** categories feature passages with varying degrees of technical or context-dependent information. You will always be able to answer the questions from the information provided.

- **Active reading can** help **you to successfully navigate through the ACT Reading test passages.** ACTIVE readers **Ask** questions, make **Connections**, **Track** down important information, **Infer** and predict, **Visualize**, and **Evaluate**, making decisions and discoveries as they explore a text. Master the following before taking the ACT Reading test:

  - **Close reading:** Before beginning to answer questions, take time to read through the passage. Using your own system (or borrowing ours), mark up the text as you read. Underline key concepts, jot down questions in the margins, asterisk supporting details, etc. This will help you focus on the main idea of a passage, and its evidence.

  - **Note taking:** On a separate sheet of paper, or using the margins, reverse outline or take notes paraphrasing/summarizing each paragraph. This will help you retain facts and information for detail-oriented review questions.

  - **Finding the main idea:** The main idea is the "thesis" or major argument you as the reader take away from the passage.

  - **Referring to what is explicitly stated:** These types of questions will ask you cite specific examples from the text.

  - **Reasoning to determine implicit meaning:** These types of questions will ask you to draw conclusions from implications or suggested ideas.

  - **Locating and interpreting significant details:** These types of questions will ask you to use a variety of techniques (read more about them in the next chapter)—you'll be asked to determine the definitions of context-dependent words, select accurate summaries/paraphrases of passage content, understand sequential and cause and effect relationships, and make comparisons within a text.

  - **Analyzing the author's voice and method:** You'll also be asked to read into the author's motivations and intentions using context clues.

ONLINE PREP

WANT TO KNOW MORE?

Access more practice questions, lessons, helpful hints, and strategies for the following reading topics in *Peterson's ACT Online Course*:

- Understanding Social Studies Content

- Understanding Natural Sciences Passages

- Hard Science Passages

To purchase and access the course, go to ***www.petersons.com/act***.

PRACTICE

Now you're ready for a two-passage practice review quiz. In the real ACT, you'll have 35 minutes to answer 40 questions. Here, you will be answering questions based on a Natural Science and a Social Studies passage.

PASSAGE I

NATURAL SCIENCE: This passage is an excerpt from *The Automobilist Abroad* by Francis Miltoun (1907).

In the library of the Patent Office in London the literature of motor road vehicles already fills many shelves. The catalogue is interesting as showing the early hopes that inventors had in connection with steam as a motive power for light road vehicles,
5 and will be of value to all who are interested in the history of the movement or the progress made in motor-car design.

In France, the Bibliothèque of the Touring Club de France contains a hundred entries under the caption "Automobiles," besides complete files of eleven leading journals devoted to
10 that industry. With these two sources of information at hand, and aided by the records of the Automobile Club de France and the Automobile Club of Great Britain and Ireland, the present-day historian of the automobile will find the subject well within his grasp.

15 There are those who doubt the utility of the automobile, as there have been scoffers at most new things under the sun; and there have been critics who have derided it for its "seven deadly sins," as there have been others who have praised its "Christian graces." The parodist who wrote the following news-
20 paper quatrain was no enemy of the automobile in spite of his cynicism.

"A look of anguish underneath the car,

Another start; a squeak, a grunt, a jar!

The Aspiration pipe is working loose!

25 The vapour can't get out! And there you are!"

"Strange is it not, that of the myriads who

Have Empty Tanks and know not what to do,

Not one will tell of it when he Returns.

As for Ourselves, why, we deny it, too."

30 The one perfectly happy man in an automobile is he who drives, steers, or "runs the thing," even though he be merely the hired chauffeur. For proof of this one has only to note how readily others volunteer to "spell him a bit," as the saying goes. Change of scene and the exhilaration of a swift rush through
35 space are all very well for friends in the *tonneau*, but for real "pleasure" one must be the driver. Not even the manifold responsibilities of the post will mar one's enjoyment, and there is always a supreme satisfaction in keeping one's engine running smoothly.

40 "Nothing to watch but the road," is the general motto for the automobile manufacturer, but the enthusiastic automobilist goes farther, and, for his motto, takes "stick to your post," and, in case of danger, as one has put it, "pull everything you see, and put your foot on everything else."

45 The vocabulary of the automobile has produced an entirely new "jargon," which is Greek to the multitude, but, oh, so expressive and full of meaning to the initiated.

An automobile is masculine, or feminine, as one likes to think of it, for it has many of the vagaries of both sexes. The French
50 Academy has finally come to the fore and declared the word to be masculine, and so, taking our clue once more from the French (as we have in most things in the automobile world), we must call it *him*, and speak of it as *he*, instead of *her*, or *she*. That other much overworked word in automobilism, *chauffeur*,
55 should be placed once for all. The driver of an automobile is not really a *chauffeur*, neither is he who minds and cares for the engine; he is a *mécanicien* and nothing else—in France and elsewhere. We needed a word for the individual who busies himself with, or drives an automobile, and so we have adapted
60 the word *chauffeur*. Purists may cavil, but nevertheless the word is better than *driver*, or *motor-man* (which is the quintessence of snobbery), or *conductor*.

The word, *chauffeur*, the Paris *Figaro* tells us, was known long before the advent of automobiles or locomotives. History tells
65 that about the year 1795, men strangely accoutered, their faces covered with soot and their eyes carefully disguised, entered, by night, farms and lonely habitations and committed all sorts of depredations. They garroted their victims, demanded information as to the whereabouts of their money and jewels, or
70 dragged them before a great fire where they burned the soles of their feet. Hence they were called *chauffeurs*, a name which frightened our grandfathers as much as the scorching *chauffeur* today frightens our grandchildren.

1. Which of the following statements is supported by the passage?

    A. Early automobile drivers were resentful and fearful of the newly available technology.

    B. Early automobile owners always employed professional drivers to minimize the risks to themselves.

    C. Early automobile drivers enjoyed their vehicles so much they composed poems and essays in their honor.

    D. Early automobile drivers formed clubs to record the development and experience of driving and maintaining cars.

2. One of the author's main points about the literature of motor road vehicles found in the London Patent Office is:

    F. it compiles essential facts and trivia that all drivers should read in order to travel safely and enjoy their time on the road.

    G. it reflects the depth and breadth of interest and knowledge compiled by automobile enthusiasts in Europe.

    H. there's no substitute for the pleasure of being behind the wheel, no matter how entertaining the written materials are.

    J. it ranges from entertaining anecdotes to investigative reports, from descriptions of road trips to the implications of common driving terminology.

3. Based on the context in the passage, it is reasonable to infer the original meaning of the word *chauffeur* (line 32) is:

    A. steering wheel.

    B. driver.

    C. heater.

    D. engine.

4. The slogan "Nothing to watch but the road" used by automobile manufacturers most likely refers to the:

    F. clarity of the new glass windscreens.

    G. absence of the horses that were previously needed to pull carriages.

    H. popularity of long road trips among new car owners.

    J. security of doors that could lock, keeping out vandals.

5. The sentence, "The vocabulary of the automobile has produced an entirely new 'jargon,' which is Greek to the multitude, but, oh, so expressive and full of meaning to the initiated," marks a shift in the passage from:

    A. a broad examining of driving literature to the exploration of the French influence on British driving culture.

    B. an introduction to the history of the automobile to a study of the automobile's gender identity.

    C. the various reactions to the invention of the automobile to the history of vandalism in France.

    D. a discussion of the highlights of automobile enthusiast publications to an examination of specialized terminology relevant to drivers.

6. As used in the passage, *accoutered* (line 65) is most likely defined as:

    F. equipped.

    G. named.

    H. walking.

    J. employed.

7. The passage suggests that you can tell drivers are the happiest person in the car because:

    A. the change of scene and exhilaration of a swift rush are impossible to beat.

    B. the other passengers will offer to take the wheel and drive for a while.

    C. they get to control the radio.

    D. they have a working knowledge of the car's mechanical functions.

8. According to the passage, all of the following are true EXCEPT:

    F. the automobile has been declared masculine by the French Academy.

    G. the "motor-man" is considered arrogant.

    H. the arrival of the automobile was universally celebrated by society.

    J. driving comes with various responsibilities of mechanical ability and operation.

9. Which of the following would the author be LEAST likely to recommend?

    A. The establishment of a monthly road trip society

    B. The adoption of the term *motor-man* for paid drivers

    C. A visit to the British Patent Office

    D. A thorough understanding of the jargon surrounding driving

10. The passage suggests drivers adopted the word *chauffeur* (line 63) because:

    F. *mechanic* was taken.

    G. they needed a word for the person who tends and drives a car.

    H. they wanted to frighten children into practicing automobile safety.

    J. the French were very influential in the development of British automobiles.

PASSAGE II

SOCIAL STUDIES: This passage is an excerpt from "The Story of Aaron Burr," from *Famous Affinities of History: The Romance of Devotion, Volumes 1–4, Complete* by Lyndon Orr.

There will come a time when the name of Aaron Burr will be cleared from the prejudice which now surrounds it, when he will stand in the public estimation side by side with Alexander Hamilton, whom he shot in a duel in 1804, but whom in many
5 respects he curiously resembled. When the white light of history shall have searched them both they will appear as two remarkable men, each having his own undoubted faults and at the same time his equally undoubted virtues.

Burr and Hamilton were born within a year of each other—
10 Burr being a grandson of Jonathan Edwards, a famous Calvinist preacher, and Alexander Hamilton being the illegitimate son of a Scottish merchant in the West Indies. Each of them was short in stature, keen of intellect, of great physical endurance, courage, and impressive personality. Each as a young man
15 served on the staff of Washington during the Revolutionary War, and each of them quarreled with him, though in a different way.

On one occasion Burr was quite unjustly suspected by Washington of looking over the latter's shoulder while he was
20 writing.

Washington leaped to his feet with the exclamation:

"How dare you, Colonel Burr?"

Burr's eyes flashed fire at the question, and he retorted, haughtily:

25 "Colonel Burr DARE do anything."

This, however, was the end of their altercation. The cause of Hamilton's difference with his chief is not known, but it was a much more serious quarrel; so that the young officer left his staff position in a fury and took no part in the war until the
30 end, when he was present at the battle of Yorktown.

Burr, on the other hand, helped Montgomery to storm the heights of Quebec, and nearly reached the upper citadel when his commander was shot dead and the Americans retreated. In all this confusion Burr showed himself a man of mettle. The
35 slain Montgomery was six feet high, but Burr carried his body away with wonderful strength amid a shower of musket-balls and grape-shot.

Hamilton could never obtain an elective office, though Washington's magnanimity and clear-sightedness made
40 Hamilton Secretary of the Treasury. Burr, on the other hand, continued his military service until the war was ended, routing the enemy at Hackensack, enduring the horrors of Valley Forge, commanding a brigade at the battle of Monmouth, and heading the defense of the city of New Haven. He was also
45 attorney-general of New York, was elected to the United States Senate, was tied with Jefferson for the Presidency, and then became Vice-President in 1801.

Both Hamilton and Burr were effective speakers; but, while Hamilton was wordy and diffuse, Burr spoke always to the
50 point, with clear and cogent reasoning. Both were lavish spenders of money, and both were engaged in duels before the fatal one in which Hamilton fell. Both believed in dueling as the only way of settling an affair of honor. Both lost children under tragic circumstances. Neither of them was averse to
55 love affairs, though it may be said that Hamilton sought women, while Burr was rather sought by women. When Secretary of the Treasury, Hamilton was obliged to confess an adulterous amour in order to save himself from the charge of corrupt practices in public office. So long as Burr's first wife
60 Theodosia lived, he was a devoted, faithful husband to her, though she was married when they first became romantically involved. Hamilton confessed his illicit acts while his wife, formerly Miss Elizabeth Schuyler, was living. She spent her later years working to restore Hamilton's legacy, raising funds
65 for the Washington Monument, and establishing the first private orphanage in New York City.

The most extraordinary thing about Aaron Burr was the magnetic quality that was felt by every one who approached him. The roots of this penetrated down into a deep vitality.
70 He was always young, always alert, polished in manner, courageous with that sort of courage which does not even recognize the presence of danger, charming in conversation, and able to adapt it to men or women of any age whatever. His hair was still dark in his eightieth year. His step was still elastic,
75 his motions were still as spontaneous and energetic, as those of a youth.

11. What is a reasonable inference to make about the author's intention in writing this biography?

   A. To reveal Burr as the power-mad, resentful politician that he was

   B. To rehabilitate Burr's reputation, which is often reduced to his role in the Hamilton duel

   C. To introduce readers to key figures in the Revolutionary War

   D. To tell the story of Eliza Hamilton's orphanage

12. According to the passage, a reader learning about this period in American history should:

   F. acknowledge George Washington's flashes of temper.

   G. recognize the similarities between Burr and Hamilton.

   H. understand the importance of the Battle of Quebec.

   J. appreciate Burr's attractiveness in later life.

13. Which of the following statements is NOT a quality that Hamilton and Burr shared?

   A. A short stature

   B. A great courage

   C. A fondness for courting women

   D. A restrained oratory style

14. Compared to Burr, Hamilton:

   F. worked tirelessly for social change.

   G. achieved greater influence without ever being elected to office.

   H. was more faithful to his wife.

   J. was less appreciated by George Washington.

15. Which quotation from the passage most vividly illustrates Burr's courage?

   A. "Colonel Burr DARE do anything." (line 25)

   B. "The most extraordinary thing about Aaron Burr was the magnetic quality that was felt by every one who approached him." (lines 67–69)

   C. "Burr spoke always to the point, with clear and cogent reasoning." (lines 49–50)

   D. "Each as a young man served on the staff of Washington during the Revolutionary War." (lines 15–16)

16. From the mix of personal and political details of Burr's and Hamilton's lives it can be reasonably inferred that:

   F. Burr and Hamilton had more uniting them than they had dividing them.

   G. they were destined to be enemies due to their conflicting political ambitions.

   H. Elizabeth Hamilton's efforts made a major difference in restoring Hamilton's legacy at the expense of Burr's.

   J. Burr's strength and clarity would have outlasted Hamilton's diffuse speaking habits and personal frailties, if not for their tragic showdown.

17. When the author mentions "Both were lavish spenders of money, and both were engaged in duels before the fatal one in which Hamilton fell," (lines 50–51) she is most nearly illustrating her main idea that:

   A. neither Hamilton nor Burr deserved their illustrious reputations.

   B. both had a habit of shooting their mouths off thoughtlessly.

   C. Burr was also a flawed individual, though his strengths were considerable.

   D. Hamilton had more money than sense.

18. Which of the following most clearly distinguishes between Hamilton's and Burr's quarrels with George Washington?

   F. Hamilton's was more drastic; Burr's was a misunderstanding.

   G. Burr's was more pivotal in American history; Hamilton's was overrated.

   H. Hamilton's was a result of his hot temper; Burr's was attributable to his pride.

   J. Burr's made him famous; Hamilton's disgraced him.

19. Which of the following qualities best explains Burr's appeal to his contemporaries?

   A. His youthful walk and vitality

   B. His polished manners and unselfconscious courage

   C. His belief in dueling as the only way of settling an affair of honor

   D. His renowned grandfather, Jonathan Edwards

20. Which of the following answer choices reflects the correct chronological arrangement of Hamilton's and Burr's lives?

    I.   Hamilton is killed in a duel with Burr.

    II.   Burr becomes Vice-President.

    III.   The Battle of Yorktown.

    IV.   Both men join the Revolutionary army

F.   III, IV, I, II

G.   IV, III, II, I

H.   IV, II, III, I

J.   II, IV, I, III

ANSWERS AND EXPLANATIONS

1. **The correct answer is D.** While there is a satirical poem in the passage, it is only one example of its type and insufficient evidence for the conclusion that most or even many early drivers wrote poems or essays about their cars, choice C. Choice A is incorrect because the entire passage is about the joy drivers found behind the wheel; while the passage mentions professional drivers, there's no implication that many or most drivers employed chauffeurs, so choice B is not the best answer.

2. **The correct answer is G.** The opening paragraphs make clear the author has discovered a wide variety of information in the publications of automobile clubs. Choice F is incorrect—there's no indication the author thinks the information he found is crucial to being a safe driver. Choice H is incorrect because the author goes on to discuss other social context issues like the effect on language, which are just as much of interest as being behind the wheel. Choice J is incorrect because there is no discussion of investigative reports.

3. **The correct answer is C.** The context clues that would help you decode this are in the final paragraph: the masked bandits dragged their victims "before a great fire where they burned the soles of their feet. Hence they were called…."The *hence* is especially helpful because it connects the burning of feet to the meaning of the name.

4. **The correct answer is G.** The rest of the paragraph indicates that drivers were adjusting to the technological demands of driving automobiles, and the reasonable inference is that they were adapting their driving skills from days driving wagons or carriages. The passage does not specifically discuss features like windscreens (choice F), door locks (choice J), or the duration or distance of the driving opportunities available (choice H).

5. **The correct answer is D.** This choice is the best balancing of the specific examples of the first half of the passage and the linguistic close reading of the second half of the passage. In choice A, the second half of the answer is too specific; the passage is not specifically looking at French influence so much as vocabulary, which happens to be French. Choice B is incorrect because the first half is not as broad as an introduction to the entire history of the automobile, nor is a car's gender identity the main focus

of the second half. Choice C is incorrect because the second half of the passage is not primarily devoted to vandalism in France.

6. **The correct answer is F.** The context clues that would help you determine this definition were the subsequent descriptions of "faces covered with soot and their eyes carefully disguised."While you might not recognize the root of *accouterments* (accessories), you could determine that *strangely* doesn't refer to the men's names (choice G), walking (choice H), or employment (choice J).

7. **The correct answer is B.** You can rule out choice A with the excerpt, "for real 'pleasure' one must be the driver." Choice C is incorrect—based on the implied time period of this passage, cars do not yet have radios. Choice D is incorrect—while keeping the engine running smoothly is a source of satisfaction, according to the passage, it does not provide the same enjoyment that driving does.

8. **The correct answer is H.** It is the lone answer choice not represented somewhere in the passage. The excerpt directly states choices F, G, and J.

9. **The correct answer is B.** The author indicates his feeling about the term *motor-man* in the second-to-last paragraph when he calls it "the quintessence of snobbery." Based on the passage, it's reasonable to infer that choices A, C, and D would all be supported by the author.

10. **The correct answer is G.** If you speak French you might recognize the reference to *mecanicien* (or mechanic), but even without that outside knowledge, choice G is the only option that reflects a specific quote from the passage. Choices H and J are risky inferences to make based on the information contained in the passage.

11. **The correct answer is B.** The evidence can be found in the opening paragraph, when the author declares Burr's name "will be cleared from the prejudice which now surrounds it" and encourages readers to esteem Burr as highly as they regard Hamilton and his role in establishing the country. The tone of the passage does not support choice A; its content is not sufficiently broad to support choice C, and Eliza Hamilton's orphanage is barely mentioned, so it cannot be choice D.

12. **The correct answer is G.** The clue to this inference is the prolonged comparison between the two men. Choices F and H are not given enough attention to be a main idea in the passage; the goal of the passage is not primarily to draw attention to Burr's physical condition (choice J).

13. **The correct answer is D.** The passage distinguishes between Burr's and Hamilton's speaking styles when it says "while Hamilton was wordy and diffuse, Burr spoke always to the point, with clear and cogent reasoning." In the other respects mentioned by answer choices A, B, and C, the two men were similar.

14. **The correct answer is G.** Hamilton's legacy as Treasury Secretary was far more fundamental to the formation of America's financial system than Burr's legacy in any of his elected offices at the state or national levels. Both men worked to effect change throughout their lives; Hamilton was infamously unfaithful to his wife; and Hamilton received political appointments from George Washington while Burr never received the same recognition from his commander in chief, so choices F, H, and J are incorrect.

15. **The correct answer is A.** In context, it depicts Burr standing up to the pre-eminent American general in history. The question also asks for vividness—choices B, C, and D are descriptive, not illustrative.

16. **The correct answer is J.** Based on the author's stated intent, the emphasis on Burr's achievements was to reshape the reader's perception of this maligned historical figure; this choice would be a reasonable conclusion to reach if you found the evidence persuasive. Choice F is a theme of the passage, but it is not an inference based on the mix of personal and political details, so this choice is incorrect. Choice G is incorrect because there is no discussion of destiny, nor does the dual discussion suggest any fated outcome. Choice H is insufficiently supported by the passage—it's not clear that Elizabeth's work had any effect on Burr's public perception.

17. **The correct answer is C.** The main idea of the passage was to rehabilitate Burr's image; one way to do that is replacing mythology with a more realistic depiction. Referring to Burr's flaws is a compelling example of his humanity. It also humanizes Hamilton by portraying him as someone who believed in participating in duels, but doesn't go so far as to discard the reputations of both men (choice A), dismiss both as hotheads (choice B), or disparage Hamilton's character (choice D).

18. **The correct answer is F.** According to the passage, Burr was "quite unjustly suspected by Washington," while Hamilton's quarrel, whatever the cause, led to his abrupt departure from Washington's service. Choice G is incorrect because Burr's disagreement was not particularly significant in history, at least not as represented in the passage. Choice H is incorrect because we don't have sufficient information to know what triggered Hamilton's argument with Washington. Choice J is incorrect because Burr was not made famous until after his service in the war.

19. **The correct answer is B.** Notice the question asks for what BEST explains Burr's appeal. His personality is a more compelling explanation than his gait and energy level (choice A), his views on dueling (choice C), or his family lineage (choice D).

20. **The correct answer is G.** Hamilton and Burr were both working with George Washington's staff by 1777 (statement IV). The Battle of Yorktown (statement III) occurred in 1781 (which you can also determine from its organization within the passage, and logically— America couldn't have a president or vice-president until after the revolution, and Thomas Jefferson was clearly president after George Washington). Burr became Vice-President in 1801 (statement II), as mentioned in the passage, and shot Hamilton in 1804 (statement I), which is specified in the introductory paragraph.

359

Chapter 9

Social Studies and Natural Sciences Passages

CHAPTER 10:
LITERARY NARRATIVE/ PROSE FICTION AND HUMANITIES PASSAGES

OVERVIEW

- Determine the Main Idea
- Locate and Interpret Significant Details
- Character Description
- Relationships
- Understand Sequences of Events
- Comprehend Cause-and-Effect Relationships
- Make Comparisons

- Determine the Meaning of Context-Dependent Words, Phrases, and Statements
- Draw Generalizations
- Analyze the Author or Narrator's Voice and Method
- Summing It Up
- Practice

As we learned in the last chapter, when we discussed Social Studies and Natural Science–themed passages, the ACT Reading test is all about inferences—what you can reasonably conclude from having read the passage presented.

Many of the same test-taking strategies apply to the passages we'll cover in this chapter:

- Read the passage carefully and mark up your test booklet with observations and questions, or take notes separately if you're taking the exam online.
- Read the questions carefully, looking out for tricky phrases like "all of the following EXCEPT" or "Which of the following is NOT an example of… "
- Consider all the answer choices before you choose the most accurate response (ACT question writers love "most nearly" or "most closely resembles" or "best approximates"—the right answer choice might not perfectly match the answer you came up with on your own, but it should be the closest one to it).
- Refer back to the passage when you answer questions—don't trust your short-term memory! You may be rattled by nerves or unfamiliarity with the text. Always double back and refer to the specific paragraphs, lines, or phrases mentioned in the question or answer choices.

As a reminder, each ACT Reading test will have either a Literary Narrative or a Prose Fiction passage and a Humanities passage. Passages may be anywhere from 350 to 1,000 words long and are likely excerpts from longer works. Some sections will have one long passage; others will have two short passages. In the event there are two shorter passages, some of the questions may ask you to compare and contrast the two texts. Occasionally, you may recognize a passage from elsewhere, but you'll be able to answer all questions based only on the available content, even if you're seeing it for the first time.

LITERARY NARRATIVES/PROSE FICTION

Literary narratives can refer to essays, memoirs, short stories, or novels; prose fiction refers only to short stories or novels. Essays and memoirs are considered nonfiction—i.e., based on fact. The narrator is generally the author, who is most often writing in the first person. Short stories and novels are fictional—although they may be based in reality, the author's imagination is responsible for the plot, characters, and dialogue. The narrator may be omniscient, or a character may be speaking in the first person (Don't confuse the character's point of view with what the author says or believes!). A novel is a long-form piece of writing, so you may be presented with an excerpt from one without a sense of where it falls in the larger plot. Everything you need to answer any question presented will always be in the passage provided to you—you do *not* need to have read the larger work outside of the exam to get every question right.

HUMANITIES

The Humanities category may include passages that talk about a *wide* range of topics: architecture, art, dance, ethics, film, language, literary criticism, music, philosophy, radio, television, theater, memoirs, and personal essays.

- An architecture passage might examine the history of a particular building, landmark, or famous architect's life.
- An art passage may span from a range of artistic periods and include visual art like paintings, or multimedia works like sculptures or installations.
- A film passage might be a portion of a film script or a critical discussion of a scene in a film (television and radio passages would be along the same lines).
- A passage on language might examine the etymology of a word or phrase or a sociological issue related to linguistics.
- A literary criticism passage is the discussion of prose in which its merits and flaws are assessed and evaluated.
- A music-related passage might examine a famous performance, a composer, or a piece of music that an author wishes to interpret.
- A theater passage might look at a play or a critique of a performance.
- A philosophy passage could be an excerpt of a well-known scholar's work, a more recent interpretation of that work, or even a modern exploration of a moral or ethical issue.

A representative sample of these genres will be incorporated for review throughout the chapter and in the end-of-chapter practice.

362

Chapter 10

Literary
Narrative/
Prose Fiction
and
Humanities
Passages

Now, let's examine the types of questions you're likely to see on the ACT Reading test. For each type, you'll learn to recognize key words and signal phrases that tell you what to look for in the passage. For the purposes of our review, the excerpted passages for each question may be shorter than the versions you'll see on the exam. You'll have a chance to practice with full-length passages at the end of the chapter.

DETERMINE THE MAIN IDEA

The Main Idea question category is the easiest to recognize on the ACT Reading test. You will see questions such as the following:

- *The main idea in this excerpt is*
- *One of the author's main points about [_____] is [_____].*
- *Which of the following most closely represents the main idea of the passage?*
- *Which of the following statements is supported by the passage? (main idea/inference)*

When you see questions phrased this way, they're basically asking, "What was the point of this excerpt?" Let's look at an example. Remember, read through the passage once just to get acquainted, then revisit it and read actively. You might underline ideas that are emphasized by repetition or intensity, mark pieces of dialogue that give you hints about character, or take note of other elements that strike you.

The following narrative prose passage is taken from Jane Austen's *Pride and Prejudice*. Read through it and then observe the type of main idea question that you may be asked on the ACT.

. . . .

It is a truth universally acknowledged, that a single man in possession of a good fortune, must be in want of a wife.

However little known the feelings or views of such a man may be on his first entering a neighbourhood, this truth is
5 so well fixed in the minds of the surrounding families, that he is considered the rightful property of some one or other of their daughters.

"My dear Mr. Bennet," said his lady to him one day, "have you heard that Netherfield Park is let at last?"

10 Mr. Bennet replied that he had not.

"But it is," returned she; "for Mrs. Long has just been here, and she told me all about it."

Mr. Bennet made no answer.

"Do you not want to know who has taken it?" cried his
15 wife impatiently.

"*You* want to tell me, and I have no objection to hearing it."

This was invitation enough.

"Why, my dear, you must know, Mrs. Long says that Netherfield is taken by a young man of large fortune from
20 the north of England; that he came down on Monday in a chaise and four to see the place, and was so much delighted with it, that he agreed with Mr. Morris immediately; that he is to take possession before Michaelmas, and some of his servants are to be in the house by the end of next week."

25 "What is his name?"

"Bingley."

"Is he married or single?"

"Oh! Single, my dear, to be sure! A single man of large fortune; four or five thousand a year. What a fine thing for
30 our girls!"

"How so? How can it affect them?"

"My dear Mr. Bennet," replied his wife, "how can you be so tiresome! You must know that I am thinking of his marrying one of them."

35 "Is that his design in settling here?"

"Design! Nonsense, how can you talk so! But it is very likely that he may fall in love with one of them, and therefore you must visit him as soon as he comes."

"I see no occasion for that. You and the girls may go, or
40 you may send them by themselves, which perhaps will be still better, for as you are as handsome as any of them, Mr. Bingley may like you the best of the party."

* * *

"But consider your daughters. Only think what an estab- lishment it would be for one of them. Sir William and Lady
45 Lucas are determined to go, merely on that account, for in general, you know, they visit no newcomers. Indeed you must go, for it will be impossible for us to visit him if you do not."

"You are over-scrupulous, surely. I dare say Mr. Bingley will
50 be very glad to see you; and I will send a few lines by you to assure him of my hearty consent to his marrying whichever he chooses of the girls; though I must throw in a good word for my little Lizzy."

363

Chapter 10

Literary
Narrative/
Prose Fiction
and
Humanities
Passages

"I desire you will do no such thing. Lizzy is not a bit better
55 than the others; and I am sure she is not half so handsome
as Jane, nor half so good-humoured as Lydia. But you are
always giving her the preference."

"They have none of them much to recommend them,"
replied he; "they are all silly and ignorant like other girls; but
60 Lizzy has something more of quickness than her sisters."

"Mr. Bennet, how can you abuse your own children in such
a way? You take delight in vexing me. You have no compassion
for my poor nerves."

"You mistake me, my dear. I have a high respect for your
65 nerves. They are my old friends. I have heard you mention
them with consideration these last twenty years at least."

"Ah, you do not know what I suffer."

"But I hope you will get over it, and live to see many
young men of four thousand a year come into the
70 neighbourhood."

"It will be no use to us, if twenty such should come, since
you will not visit them."

"Depend upon it, my dear, that when there are twenty,
I will visit them all."

 TIP The main idea is often found in the first/topic sentence or in the last few sentences of a passage.

The main point of this excerpt is to:

A. indicate that real estate in this neighborhood is at a premium.
B. establish that marrying off daughters is a high priority.
C. suggest the Bennets are likely to divorce.
D. get the reader invested in Mr. Bingley as a character.

The correct answer is B. You can identify the correct answer to this Main Idea question from the frequency and intensity with which marriage is discussed. In the very opening sentence, Jane Austen signals her readers that the main plot of this novel is going to be the pursuit of marriage. Rather than explaining this explicitly, she then illustrates it with engaging dialogue between two of the novel's more memorable characters.

Notice how insistently Mrs. Bennet invokes marriage to her husband—how in her mind (and apparently, that of her neighbors too), it is the primary reason a wealthy young man would have moved into the neighborhood. There are not enough references to real estate for choice A to be the main idea of the passage. There's no indication the Bennet marriage is in serious trouble (choice C), nor are we given information about Mr. Bingley that might make us care about him as a person (choice D). Instead, this spirited exchange about acting in their daughters' best interests establishes the Bennets' presence in the foreground of the novel.

Variations on this question type might ask you to close read for a particular term or concept in order to make an inference, as in these sample questions.

Based on the passage, the primary purpose of a young single man is to:

F. become a landowning citizen.
G. find a wife.
H. move to the country.
J. have a large family.

The correct answer is G. You can answer this question by taking a look at the passage's opening line. The other answer choices are perfectly fine aspirations—and ones that the characters of *Pride and Prejudice* might support—but they're not the dominant idea of *this* excerpt. Remember—the answers to the questions are right there in the passage in front of you; don't bring in any outside biases.

364

Chapter 10

Literary
Narrative/
Prose Fiction
and
Humanities
Passages

According to the passage, a young man's best qualification for marriage is a:

A. large fortune.
B. notable family.
C. gift of conversation.
D. willingness to travel.

The correct answer is A. Again, the answer is established in the opening line of the passage. To emphasize the point, recall that Mrs. Bennet knew nothing about Mr. Bingley other than his yearly earnings, but was insistent upon the possibility of a marriage between him and one of her daughters. You should have been able to recognize this point through your earlier close reading.

- -

Another variation of Main Idea questions asks you to determine which of the answer choices is most *representative* of the passage's main idea. Let's consider this excerpt from *The Atlantic Monthly* magazine article, "Doings of the Sunbeam":

- -

Few of those who seek a photographer's establishment to have their portraits taken know at all into what a vast branch of commerce this business of sun-picturing has grown. We took occasion lately to visit one of the principal
5 establishments in the country, that of Messrs. E & H.T. Anthony, in Broadway, New York. We had made the acquaintance of these gentlemen through the remarkable instantaneous stereoscopic views published by them, and of which we spoke in a former article in terms which some might think
10 extravagant. Our unsolicited commendation of these marvelous pictures insured us a more than polite reception. Every detail of the branches of the photographic business to which they are more especially devoted was freely shown us, and "No Admittance" over the doors of their inmost sanc-
15 tuaries came to mean for us, "Walk in, you are heartily welcome."

The guests of the neighboring hotels, as they dally with their morning's omelet, little imagine what varied uses come out of the shells which furnished them their anticipatory
20 repast of disappointed chickens. If they had visited Mr. Anthony's upper rooms, they would have seen a row of young women before certain broad, shallow pans filled with the glairy albumen which once enveloped those potential fowls.

The one next takes a large sheet of photographic paper,
25 (a paper made in Europe for this special purpose, very thin, smooth, and compact,) and floats it evenly upon the surface of the albumen. Presently she lifts it very carefully by the turned-up corners and hangs it *bias*, as a seamstress might say, that is, cornerwise, on a string, to dry. This "alb-
30 umenized" paper is sold most extensively to photographers,

who find it cheaper to buy than to prepare it. It keeps for a long time uninjured, and is "sensitized" when wanted, as we shall see by-and-by.

"Doings of the Sunbeam" (*The Atlantic Monthly*, pp. 1–3, Volume 12, No 69, July 1863)

Which of the following statements is supported by the passage?

F. People on vacation never know what's happening around them.
G. People might be surprised at the process required to produce photo paper.
H. There are various uses for chicken eggs and their contents.
J. Photography is a fascinating professional industry.

The correct answer is G. This phrasing requires you either to identify a moment when a key concept is being applied or to make an inference—a reasonable guess based on the evidence at hand—about the main idea of the passage. While the photo process does feature multiple uses for the albumen that fills an egg, "uses for eggs" (choice H) is not the main motivation for the passage, which is to describe how photo paper is produced. Since that's the main idea, and it could easily be new information to most readers, this passage supports choice G. Choice F is a distractor designed to draw your attention to the hotel-dwellers having omelets near the studio. While photography is fascinating, this passage doesn't even get to the process of taking pictures, so choice J can't be the main idea of the passage.

365

Chapter 10

Literary
Narrative/
Prose Fiction
and
Humanities
Passages

- -

TIP
The big realization here is that there are multiple approaches to acquiring the same information and that, once you learn to recognize the cues, finding the main idea is easier than ever.

LOCATE AND INTERPRET SIGNIFICANT DETAILS

Significant Detail questions are designed to assess your ability to distinguish what is significant from what is incidental or unimportant. They also test your ability to use context to understand an unfamiliar word or phrase.

Questions might be phrased like any of the following:

- *This passage establishes all of the following EXCEPT:*
- *According to the passage, which of the following most closely identifies...*
- *Based on the passage, the primary purpose of [_____] was to...*
- *According to the passage, use of the word _____ instead of ____ implies which of the following?*
- *When the author does [_____], she is most nearly illustrating her point that:*
- *As used in the passage, the phrase [_____] most nearly means:*
- *The [_____] in the passage best symbolizes what?*
- *The sentence [_____] most closely means:*
- *All of the following are true EXCEPT:*
- *At the time the passage was written, what was most likely true?*

Let's refer again to the *Atlantic Monthly* excerpt to see how this question type might come into play on the ACT with the same passage:

. . . .

Few of those who seek a photographer's establishment to have their portraits taken know at all into what a vast branch of commerce this business of sun-picturing has grown. We took occasion lately to visit one of the principal
5 establishments in the country, that of Messrs. E & H.T. Anthony, in Broadway, New York. We had made the acquaintance of these gentlemen through the remarkable instantaneous stereoscopic views published by them, and of which we spoke in a former article in terms which some might think
10 extravagant. Our unsolicited commendation of these marvelous pictures insured us a more than polite reception. Every detail of the branches of the photographic business to which they are more especially devoted was freely shown us, and "No Admittance" over the doors of their inmost sanc-
15 tuaries came to mean for us, "Walk in, you are heartily welcome."

The guests of the neighboring hotels, as they dally with their morning's omelet, little imagine what varied uses come out of the shells which furnished them their anticipatory
20 repast of disappointed chickens. If they had visited Mr. Anthony's upper rooms, they would have seen a row of young women before certain broad, shallow pans filled with the glairy albumen which once enveloped those potential fowls.

The one next takes a large sheet of photographic paper,
25 (a paper made in Europe for this special purpose, very thin, smooth, and compact,) and floats it evenly upon the surface of the albumen. Presently she lifts it very carefully by the turned-up corners and hangs it *bias*, as a seamstress might say, that is, cornerwise, on a string, to dry. This "alb-
30 umenized" paper is sold most extensively to photographers, who find it cheaper to buy than to prepare it. It keeps for a long time uninjured, and is "sensitized" when wanted, as we shall see by-and-by.

"Doings of the Sunbeam" (*The Atlantic Monthly*, pp. 1–3, Volume 12, No 69, July 1863)

Based on the context of the passage, what is *albumen* (line 23)?

- **A.** the white of an egg
- **B.** egg shells
- **C.** a photo-developing fluid
- **D.** egg yolk

The correct answer is A. The author's reference to neighboring hotel guests eating omelets, coming from the "shells which furnished them their anticipatory repast of disappointed chickens" (i.e., the yolks), creates an associative picture of the clear, viscous liquid that fills an egg.

. . . .

366

Chapter 10

Literary
Narrative/
Prose Fiction
and
Humanities
Passages

Let's look at another example. This is the first time Jim, the narrator of Robert Louis Stevenson's *Treasure Island*, meets the infamous Long John Silver. Read between the lines to see what Jim is seeing in the moment, and what the author is hinting Jim will understand later.

. . . .

As I was waiting, a man came out of a side room, and at a glance I was sure he must be Long John. His left leg was cut off close by the hip, and under the left shoulder he carried a crutch, which he managed with wonderful dexterity, hopping
5 about upon it like a bird. He was very tall and strong, with a face as big as a ham—plain and pale, but intelligent and smiling. Indeed, he seemed in the most cheerful spirits, whistling as he moved about among the tables, with a merry word or a slap on the shoulder for the more favoured of
10 his guests.

Now, to tell you the truth, from the very first mention of Long John in Squire Trelawney's letter I had taken a fear in my mind that he might prove to be the very one-legged sailor whom I had watched for so long at the old Benbow.
15 But one look at the man before me was enough. I had seen the captain, and Black Dog, and the blind man, Pew, and I thought I knew what a buccaneer was like—a very different creature, according to me, from this clean and pleasant-tempered landlord.

20 I plucked up courage at once, crossed the threshold, and walked right up to the man where he stood, propped on his crutch, talking to a customer.

"Mr. Silver, sir?" I asked, holding out the note.

"Yes, my lad," said he; "such is my name, to be sure. And
25 who may you be?" And then as he saw the squire's letter, he seemed to me to give something almost like a start.

"Oh!" said he, quite loud, and offering his hand. "I see. You are our new cabin-boy; pleased I am to see you."

And he took my hand in his large firm grasp.

30 Just then one of the customers at the far side rose suddenly and made for the door. It was close by him, and he was out in the street in a moment. But his hurry had attracted my notice, and I recognized him at glance. It was the tallow-faced man, wanting two fingers, who had come first to the Admiral
35 Benbow.

"Oh," I cried, "stop him! It's Black Dog!"

"I don't care two coppers who he is," cried Silver. "But he hasn't paid his score. Harry, run and catch him."

One of the others who was nearest the door leaped up
40 and started in pursuit.

"If he were Admiral Hawke he shall pay his score," cried Silver; and then, relinquishing my hand, "Who did you say he was?" he asked. "Black what?"

"Dog, sir," said I. "Has Mr. Trelawney not told you of the
45 buccaneers? He was one of them."

"So?" cried Silver. "In my house! Ben, run and help Harry. One of those swabs, was he? Was that you drinking with him, Morgan? Step up here."

The man whom he called Morgan—an old, grey-haired,
50 mahogany-faced sailor—came forward pretty sheepishly, rolling his quid.

"Now, Morgan," said Long John very sternly, "you never clapped your eyes on that Black—Black Dog before, did you, now?"

55 "Not I, sir," said Morgan with a salute.

"You didn't know his name, did you?"

"No, sir."

"By the powers, Tom Morgan, it's as good for you!" exclaimed the landlord. "If you had been mixed up with the like of that,
60 you would never have put another foot in my house, you may lay to that. And what was he saying to you?"

"I don't rightly know, sir," answered Morgan.

"Do you call that a head on your shoulders, or a blessed dead-eye?" cried Long John. "Don't rightly know, don't you!
65 Perhaps you don't happen to rightly know who you was speaking to, perhaps? Come, now, what was he jawing—v'yages, cap'ns, ships? Pipe up! What was it?"

"We was a-talkin' of keel-hauling," answered Morgan.

"Keel-hauling, was you? And a mighty suitable thing, too,
70 and you may lay to that. Get back to your place for a lubber, Tom."

And then, as Morgan rolled back to his seat, Silver added to me in a confidential whisper that was very flattering, as I thought, "He's quite an honest man, Tom Morgan, on'y stupid.
75 And now," he ran on again, aloud, "let's see—Black Dog? No, I don't know the name, not I. Yet I kind of think I've—yes, I've seen the swab. He used to come here with a blind beggar, he used."

367

Chapter 10

Literary
Narrative/
Prose Fiction
and
Humanities
Passages

"That he did, you may be sure," said I. "I knew that blind
80 man too. His name was Pew."

"It was!" cried Silver, now quite excited. "Pew! That were
his name for certain. Ah, he looked a shark, he did! If we run
down this Black Dog, now, there'll be news for Cap'n
Trelawney! Ben's a good runner; few seamen run better than
85 Ben. He should run him down, hand over hand, by the powers!
He talked o' keel-hauling, did he? I'LL keel-haul him!"

All the time he was jerking out these phrases he was
stumping up and down the tavern on his crutch, slapping
tables with his hand, and giving such a show of excitement
90 as would have convinced an Old Bailey judge or a Bow Street
runner. My suspicions had been thoroughly reawakened on
finding Black Dog at the Spy-glass, and I watched the cook
narrowly. But he was too deep, and too ready, and too clever
for me, and by the time the two men had come back out of
95 breath and confessed that they had lost the track in a crowd,
and been scolded like thieves, I would have gone bail for the
innocence of Long John Silver.

Robert Louis Stevenson uses all of the following to describe
Long John Silver EXCEPT:

- **F.** plain and pale
- **G.** clean and pleasant-tempered
- **H.** intelligent and smiling
- **J.** trustworthy and innocent

The correct answer is J. While each of the other choices appears
in the description of Long John Silver, it is the narrator, Jim, who
is (temporarily) convinced Silver is innocent. The last paragraph,
when Jim says "he was too deep, and too ready, and too clever
for me" is meant to foreshadow Silver's later misdeeds.

···

CHARACTER DESCRIPTION

Think about your favorite books or even movies—how do they introduce a character? Do they paint a picture with words from
head to toe? How do they communicate crucial information about the character's traits and habits without straight description?

Character description questions on the ACT Reading test might take on the following forms:

- *Based on the passage, [_____] could be characterized as:*
- *The passage suggests that [_____] could be most nearly described as:*
- *What physical attributes of [character] can be inferred from the passage?*
- *According to the passage, [character] is:*

Take a closer look at a portion of the excerpt from *Treasure Island*. What physical details did Stevenson use to create a picture of
Long John Silver?

As I was waiting, a man came out of a side room, and at a glance I was sure he must be Long John. His left leg was
cut off close by the hip, and under the left shoulder he carried a crutch, which he managed with wonderful dexterity,
hopping about upon it like a bird. He was very tall and strong, with a face as big as a ham—plain and pale, but intelligent
and smiling. Indeed, he seemed in the most cheerful spirits, whistling as he moved about among the tables, with a
merry word or a slap on the shoulder for the more favoured of his guests.

Did you find these details?

- *one leg, amputated from the hip*
- *hopping like a bird*
- *plain and pale*
- *tall and strong*
- *big intelligent, smiling face*
- *cheerful demeanor*

368

Chapter 10

Literary
Narrative/
Prose Fiction
and
Humanities
Passages

When approaching an ACT Reading passage, you can draw clues not only from close reading and identifying significant details, but also from making inferences from the key details an author chooses to include. From the sometimes contradictory description of Silver—plain and pale *and* intelligent and smiling—and Jim's doubt and ensuing decision to trust him, we can infer the author wants us uncertain of his true character.

Let's look at an example from that master of the inference, Sherlock Holmes. This excerpt is taken from Sir Arthur Conan Doyle's *A Study in Scarlet*. As you read, notice how the author creates a sense of Holmes' character. On the ACT Reading test, you will find questions posed like the two examples that follow the passage.

. . . .

This was a lofty chamber, lined and littered with countless bottles. Broad, low tables were scattered about, which bristled with retorts, test-tubes, and little Bunsen lamps, with their blue flickering flames. There was only one student in the
5   room, who was bending over a distant table absorbed in his work. At the sound of our steps he glanced round and sprang to his feet with a cry of pleasure. "I've found it! I've found it," he shouted to my companion, running towards us with a test-tube in his hand. "I have found a re-agent which is pre-
10 cipitated by haemoglobin, and by nothing else." Had he discovered a gold mine, greater delight could not have shone upon his features.

"Dr. Watson, Mr. Sherlock Holmes," said Stamford, introducing us.

15 "How are you?" he said cordially, gripping my hand with a strength for which I should hardly have given him credit. "You have been in Afghanistan, I perceive."

"How on earth did you know that?" I asked in astonishment.

20 "Never mind," said he, chuckling to himself. "The question now is about haemoglobin. No doubt you see the significance of this discovery of mine?"

"It is interesting, chemically, no doubt," I answered, "but practically—"

25 "Why, man, it is the most practical medico-legal discovery for years. Don't you see that it gives us an infallible test for blood stains? Come over here now!" He seized me by the coat-sleeve in his eagerness, and drew me over to the table at which he had been working. "Let us have some fresh blood,"
30 he said, digging a long bodkin into his finger, and drawing off the resulting drop of blood in a chemical pipette. "Now, I add this small quantity of blood to a litre of water. You perceive that the resulting mixture has the appearance of pure water. The proportion of blood cannot be more than
35 one in a million. I have no doubt, however, that we shall be able to obtain the characteristic reaction."

As he spoke, he threw into the vessel a few white crystals, and then added some drops of a transparent fluid. In an instant the contents assumed a dull mahogany colour, and a
40 brownish dust was precipitated to the bottom of the glass jar.

"Ha! ha!" he cried, clapping his hands, and looking as delighted as a child with a new toy. "What do you think of that?"

45 "It seems to be a very delicate test," I remarked.

"Beautiful! beautiful! The old guaiacum test was very clumsy and uncertain. So is the microscopic examination for blood corpuscles. The latter is valueless if the stains are a few hours old. Now, this appears to act as well whether
50 the blood is old or new. Had this test been invented, there are hundreds of men now walking the earth who would long ago have paid the penalty of their crimes."

"Indeed!" I murmured.

"Criminal cases are continually hinging upon that one
55 point. A man is suspected of a crime months perhaps after it has been committed. His linen or clothes are examined, and brownish stains discovered upon them. Are they blood stains, or mud stains, or rust stains, or fruit stains, or what are they? That is a question which has puzzled many an
60 expert, and why? Because there was no reliable test. Now we have the Sherlock Holmes' test, and there will no longer be any difficulty."

His eyes fairly glittered as he spoke, and he put his hand over his heart and bowed as if to some applauding crowd
65 conjured up by his imagination.

"You are to be congratulated," I remarked, considerably surprised at his enthusiasm.

* * *

"I have to be careful," remarked Sherlock Holmes, sticking a small piece of plaster over the prick on his finger and
70 turning to me with a smile, "for I dabble with poisons a good deal." He held out his hand as he spoke, and I noticed that it was all mottled over with similar pieces of plaster, and discoloured with strong acids. He seemed delighted at the idea of sharing his rooms with me. "I have my eye on a suite

75 in Baker Street," he said, "which would suit us down to the ground. You don't mind the smell of strong tobacco, I hope?"

"I always smoke 'ship's' myself," I answered.

"That's good enough. I generally have chemicals about, and occasionally do experiments. Would that annoy you?"

80 "By no means."

"Let me see—what are my other shortcomings? I get in the dumps at times, and don't open my mouth for days on end. You must not think I am sulky when I do that. Just let me alone, and I'll soon be right. What have you to confess 85 now? It's just as well for two fellows to know the worst of one another before they begin to live together."

I laughed at this cross-examination. "I keep a bull pup," I said, "and I object to rows because my nerves are shaken, and I get up at all sorts of ungodly hours, and I am extremely 90 lazy. I have another set of vices when I'm well, but those are the principal ones at present."

"Do you include violin-playing in your category of rows?" he asked, anxiously.

"It depends on the player," I answered. "A well-played violin 95 is a treat for the gods—a badly-played one——."

"Oh, that's all right," he cried, with a merry laugh. "I think we may consider the thing as settled—that is, if the rooms are agreeable to you."

"When shall we see them?"

100 "Call for me here at noon tomorrow, and we'll go together and settle everything," he answered.

"All right—noon exactly," said I, shaking his hand.

We left him working among his chemicals, and we walked together towards my hotel. "By the way," I asked suddenly, 105 stopping and turning upon Stamford, "how the deuce did he know that I had come from Afghanistan?" My companion smiled an enigmatical smile. "That's just his little peculiarity," he said. "A good many people have wanted to know how he finds things out." "Oh! a mystery is it?" I cried, rubbing my hands.

370

Chapter 10

Literary
Narrative/
Prose Fiction
and
Humanities
Passages

Compared to Holmes, Watson is more:

A. cautious.
B. arrogant.
C. introverted.
D. elegant.

The correct answer is A. If you pay close attention to Watson's responses to Holmes, you can see he offers diplomatic, deliberate responses after reading Holmes' reaction—while Holmes launches into the discussion of his new process without stopping to consider whether his listeners are interested. It would be difficult to be more arrogant than Holmes (choice B), who congratulates himself on an invention that hasn't proven itself useful yet. Although Watson says he "objects to rows" and mentions having his nerves shaken, he's not more introverted (choice C) than Holmes, who says "I get in the dumps at times, and don't open my mouth for days on end." While Holmes doesn't come across as elegant, with his hands bandaged and burned, Watson's description of himself as lazy, Holmes' assessment that he's fresh from Afghanistan, and the fact that they're each seeking a roommate, proves that neither is particularly elegant (choice D).

Sherlock Holmes observes that Dr. Watson has come from Afghanistan because:

F. he wants to put Watson at ease.
G. it's related to a case he's solving.
H. he wants to show off his mysterious skills.
J. he wants to travel with him.

The correct answer is H. The main clues are the way Holmes refuses to answer when Watson asks how he knows and the joy he takes in his discovery (and general intellectual superiority) elsewhere in the passage. While the men in the excerpt do discuss the applications of Holmes' experiment for unsolved crimes, that discussion is not related to Afghanistan, (choice G). Holmes seems to enjoy confounding Watson, so choice F is incorrect, and although they're planning to become roommates, there's no indication Holmes wants to travel, much less to visit Afghanistan (choice J).

RELATIONSHIPS

Imagine you're a novelist. What tools do you have at your disposal to illustrate a character? Basically, your main ones are straight physical or behavioral description, as we've seen, and expositional backstory. Relationship questions on the ACT usually take the following formats:

- *What can be inferred from the passage about [character's relationship with character]?*
- *The [thing] represents what to [character]?*

Or, you might see questions phrased like the next two that follow. Take another look at the excerpt from *Pride and Prejudice* to answer the following examples. Notice how the first question asks you to make an inference based on what a character says.

It is a truth universally acknowledged, that a single man in possession of a good fortune, must be in want of a wife.

However little known the feelings or views of such a man may be on his first entering a neighbourhood, this truth is
5 so well fixed in the minds of the surrounding families, that he is considered the rightful property of some one or other of their daughters.

"My dear Mr. Bennet," said his lady to him one day, "have you heard that Netherfield Park is let at last?"

10 Mr. Bennet replied that he had not.

"But it is," returned she; "for Mrs. Long has just been here, and she told me all about it."

Mr. Bennet made no answer.

"Do you not want to know who has taken it?" cried his
15 wife impatiently.

"*You* want to tell me, and I have no objection to hearing it."

This was invitation enough.

"Why, my dear, you must know, Mrs. Long says that Netherfield is taken by a young man of large fortune from
20 the north of England; that he came down on Monday in a chaise and four to see the place, and was so much delighted with it, that he agreed with Mr. Morris immediately; that he is to take possession before Michaelmas, and some of his servants are to be in the house by the end of next week."

25 "What is his name?"

"Bingley."

"Is he married or single?"

"Oh! Single, my dear, to be sure! A single man of large fortune; four or five thousand a year. What a fine thing for
30 our girls!"

"How so? How can it affect them?"

"My dear Mr. Bennet," replied his wife, "how can you be so tiresome! You must know that I am thinking of his marrying one of them."

35 "Is that his design in settling here?"

"Design! Nonsense, how can you talk so! But it is very likely that he may fall in love with one of them, and therefore you must visit him as soon as he comes."

"I see no occasion for that. You and the girls may go, or
40 you may send them by themselves, which perhaps will be still better, for as you are as handsome as any of them, Mr. Bingley may like you the best of the party."

* * *

"But consider your daughters. Only think what an estab-lishment it would be for one of them. Sir William and Lady
45 Lucas are determined to go, merely on that account, for in general, you know, they visit no newcomers. Indeed you must go, for it will be impossible for us to visit him if you do not."

"You are over-scrupulous, surely. I dare say Mr. Bingley will
50 be very glad to see you; and I will send a few lines by you to assure him of my hearty consent to his marrying whichever he chooses of the girls; though I must throw in a good word for my little Lizzy."

"I desire you will do no such thing. Lizzy is not a bit better
55 than the others; and I am sure she is not half so handsome as Jane, nor half so good-humoured as Lydia. But you are always giving her the preference."

"They have none of them much to recommend them," replied he; "they are all silly and ignorant like other girls; but
60 Lizzy has something more of quickness than her sisters."

Chapter 10

Literary
Narrative/
Prose Fiction
and
Humanities
Passages

"Mr. Bennet, how can you abuse your own children in such a way? You take delight in vexing me. You have no compassion for my poor nerves."

"You mistake me, my dear. I have a high respect for your
65 nerves. They are my old friends. I have heard you mention them with consideration these last twenty years at least."

"Ah, you do not know what I suffer."

"But I hope you will get over it, and live to see many young men of four thousand a year come into the
70 neighbourhood."

"It will be no use to us, if twenty such should come, since you will not visit them."

It can reasonably be inferred from the passage that Mr. Bennet:

   A. does not care about finding husbands for his daughters.
   B. thinks only Lizzy deserves to be married.
   C. is eager to assuage Mrs. Bennet's worry over visiting their neighbor.
   D. frequently teases Mrs. Bennet about her anxieties.

The correct answer is D. Mr. Bennet's teasing is reflected in lines 64–66 when he comments on his wife's nerves, or in lines 8–17 when he refuses to engage on her favorite topic of conversation. Choice A picks up on his detached attitude, but his teasing tone makes it difficult to conclude that he simply does not care. Choice B refers to his remark that Lizzy

has more sense than her sisters, but doesn't support an inference that he doesn't think the rest deserve to be married. Choice C is incorrect because Mr. Bennet clearly has no intention of reassuring his wife.

"You take delight in vexing me. You have no compassion for my poor nerves."

"You mistake me, my dear. I have a high respect for your nerves. They are my old friends. I have heard you mention them with consideration these last twenty years at least."

This excerpt most likely suggests what about the Bennets' relationship?

   F. They are great friends.
   G. They are constantly bickering.
   H. Mrs. Bennet doesn't understand her husband's sense of humor.
   J. Mr. Bennet is considerate and respectful of his wife's feelings.

The correct answer is H. "You take delight in vexing me" indicates that while Mr. Bennet might be having fun at his wife's expense, she is not in on the joke. The one-sidedness of his teasing should tell you that choice J isn't correct; they might actually be great friends, but this passage doesn't give us any insight into any mutually beneficial aspects of their relationship. Similarly, we can't tell from this snapshot whether they *always* bicker—or indeed, if this is "bickering" or just a moment of pique.

372

Chapter 10

Literary
Narrative/
Prose Fiction
and
Humanities
Passages

UNDERSTAND SEQUENCES OF EVENTS

Comprehending both humanities and literary texts often involves being able to understand the order in which things happen (a baby step toward understanding cause and consequence reactions, which we'll cover later). Look for questions like:

- *Line [___] marks a shift in the passage from _____ to _____…*
- *What is the first _____ [character] experiences?*
- *Which of the following statements best explains [_____]?*

Let's look at a passage with a sequence to detect and interpret, taken from Louisa May Alcott's *Jo's Boys*:

· ·

Things always went by contraries with Jo. Her first book, laboured over for years, and launched full of the high hopes and ambitious dreams of youth, foundered on its voyage, though the wreck continued to float long afterward, to the
5   profit of the publisher at least. The hastily written story, sent away with no thought beyond the few dollars it might bring, sailed with a fair wind and a wise pilot at the helm into public favour, and came home heavily laden with an unexpected cargo of gold and glory.

10   A more astonished woman probably never existed than Josephine Bhaer when her little ship came into port with flags flying, cannon that had been silent before now booming gaily, and, better than all, many kind faces rejoicing with her, many friendly hands grasping hers with cordial congratul-
15   ations. After that it was plain sailing, and she merely had to load her ships and send them off on prosperous trips, to bring home stores of comfort for all she loved and laboured for.

The fame she never did quite accept; for it takes very little fire to make a great deal of smoke nowadays, and notoriety
20   is not real glory. The fortune she could not doubt, and grate-fully received; though it was not half so large a one as a generous world reported it to be. The tide having turned continued to rise, and floated the family comfortably into a snug harbour where the older members could rest secure
25   from storms, and whence the younger ones could launch their boats for the voyage of life.

* * *

This was the sweet and sacred side of the change; but it had its droll and thorny one, as all things have in this curious world of ours. After the first surprise, incredulity, and joy,
30   which came to Jo, with the ingratitude of human nature, she soon tired of renown, and began to resent her loss of liberty. For suddenly the admiring public took possession of her and all her affairs, past, present, and to come. Strangers demanded to look at her, question, advise, warn, congratulate, and
35   drive her out of her wits by well-meant but very wearisome attentions. If she declined to open her heart to them, they reproached her; if she refused to endow pet charities, relieve private wants, or sympathize with every ill and trial known to humanity, she was called hard-hearted, selfish, and
40   haughty; if she found it impossible to answer the piles of letters sent her, she was neglectful of her duty to the admiring public; and if she preferred the privacy of home to the ped-estal upon which she was requested to pose, 'the airs of literary people' were freely criticized.

45   She did her best for the children, they being the public for whom she wrote, and laboured stoutly to supply the demand always in the mouths of voracious youth—'More stories; more right away!' Her family objected to this devotion at their expense, and her health suffered; but for a time she
50   gratefully offered herself up on the altar of juvenile literature, feeling that she owed a good deal to the little friends in whose sight she had found favour after twenty years of effort.

But a time came when her patience gave out; and wearying of being a lion, she became a bear in nature as in name, and
55   returning to her den, growled awfully when ordered out. Her family enjoyed the fun, and had small sympathy with her trials, but Jo came to consider it the worse scrape of her life; for liberty had always been her dearest possession, and it seemed to be fast going from her. Living in a lantern soon
60   loses its charm, and she was too old, too tired, and too busy to like it.

According to the passage, Jo first attained success as an author with:

A. her first book, over which she labored carefully and ambitiously.

B. her second book, which she wrote quickly and with much less thought.

C. a series of articles that she later turned into children's stories.

D. a memoir about a sea voyage that was well received.

The correct answer is B. In the first paragraph, the author describes Jo's first book, (choice A) as a wreck that foundered and continues the ship metaphor to describe the unexpected success of her next book. While she later describes her stories as juvenile literature, they did not begin as articles and later become something else (choice C), nor did she ever *actually* go to sea (choice D).

It can be inferred from the last paragraph that Jo:

F. still has a thriving literary career with many admirers.

G. initially appreciated the glowing reception her novels received.

H. tours regularly in support of her latest book.

J. no longer enjoys the celebrity that comes with literary success.

The correct answer is J. The author signals the reader by writing that Jo "considered it the worse scrape of her life" and didn't like "living in a lantern." Choices F and G may be reflected elsewhere in the passage, but they're not the note the author chose to end on. There is no mention of going on a book tour (choice H)—in fact, fans of Jo's work come to her house in search of her!

. . . .

Now, let's look at sequence of questions accompanying a Humanities passage, excerpted from Vitruvius's *The Ten Books on Architecture*.

. . . .

Methods of Building Walls

1. There are two styles of walls: *opus reticulatum*, now used by everybody, and the ancient style called *opus incertum*. Of these, the reticulatum looks better, but its construction makes it likely to crack, because its beds and builds spread out in every direction. On the other hand, in the opus incertum, the rubble, lying in courses and imbricated, makes a wall which, though not beautiful, is stronger than the reticulatum.

2. Both kinds should be constructed of the smallest stones, so that the walls, being thoroughly puddled with the mortar, which is made of lime and sand, may hold together longer. Since the stones used are soft and porous, they are apt to suck the moisture out of the mortar and to dry it up. But when there is an abundance of lime and sand, the wall, containing more moisture, will not soon lose its strength, for they will hold it together. But as soon as the moisture is sucked out of the mortar by the porous rubble, and the lime and sand separate and disunite, the rubble can no longer adhere to them, and the wall will in time become a ruin.

3. This we may learn from several monuments in the environs of the city, which are built of marble or dimension stone, but on the inside packed with masonry between the outer walls. In the course of time, the mortar has lost its strength, which has been sucked out of it by the porousness of the rubble; so the monuments are tumbling down and going to pieces, with their joints loosened by the settling of the material that bound them together.

4. He who wishes to avoid such a disaster should leave a cavity behind the facings, and on the inside build walls two feet thick, made of red dimension stone or burnt brick or lava in courses, and then bind them to the fronts by means of iron clamps and lead. For thus his work, being no mere heap of material but regularly laid in courses, will be strong enough to last forever without a flaw, because the beds and builds, all settling equally and bonded at the joints, will not let the work bulge out, nor allow the fall of the face walls which have been tightly fastened together.

5. Consequently, the method of construction employed by the Greeks is not to be despised. They do not use a structure of soft rubble polished on the outside, but whenever they forsake dimension stone, they lay courses of lava or of some hard stone, and, as though building with brick, they bind the upright joints by interchanging the direction of the stones as they lie in the courses. Thus they attain to a perfection that will endure to eternity. These structures are of two kinds. One of them is called *isodomum*, the other *pseudisodomum*.

6. A wall is called isodomum when all the courses are of equal height; pseudisodomum, when the rows of courses do not match but run unequally. Both kinds are strong: first, because the rubble itself is of close texture and solid, unable to suck the moisture out of the mortar, but keeping it in its moist condition for a very long period; secondly, because the beds of the stones, being laid smooth and level to begin with, keep the mortar from falling, and, as they are bonded throughout the entire thickness of the wall, they hold together for a very long period.

The *opus reticulatum* walls tend to crumble and spread out because the:

A. facings are too close to the courses.
B. inner courses weren't spaced far enough apart.
C. joints aren't properly bound by alternating the orientations of the stones.
D. stones absorb moisture from the mortar and it dries out.

The correct answer is D. The answer is located in the first and second steps, where the author examines currently crumbling monuments and detects the shared imperfection in their construction.

. . . .

COMPREHEND CAUSE-AND-EFFECT RELATIONSHIPS

In literature, authors often seize an opportunity to create outside associations or imply broader meaning by drawing connections between seemingly unrelated events. Often they do this by taking out the middle steps that got their main character from point A to point G. You might be asked to see if you can tell how the author leapt straight from one point to the other. Alternatively, a question might ask for more factual details, to ensure you understand who set a series of events in motion.

Look for questions like these:

- *The passage indicates [_____] happened because…*
- *The passage suggests that [character] did [_____] in order to…*
- *Based on the excerpt, one reason [_____] happened was due to…*
- *According to [_____], the main reason for [_____] was:*
- *Which organization is responsible for [_____]?*

Let's see a passage that could be accompanied by this type of ACT question. Read the following, from from *Heroes Every Child Should Know* by Hamilton Wright Mabie.

. . . .

We do not know anything about Robin Hood, who he was, or where he lived, or what evil deed he had done. Any man might kill him and never pay penalty for it. But, outlaw or not, the poor people loved him and looked on him as their
5 friend, and many a stout fellow came to join him, and led a merry life in the greenwood, with moss and fern for bed, and for meat the King's deer, which it was death to slay. Tillers of the land, yeomen, and some say knights, went on their ways freely, for of them Robin took no toll; but lordly churchmen
10 with money-bags well filled, or proud bishops with their richly dressed followers, trembled as they drew near to Sherwood Forest—who was to know whether behind every tree there did not lurk Robin Hood or one of his men?

One day Robin was walking alone in the wood, and reached
15 a river spanned by a very narrow bridge, over which one man only could pass. In the midst stood a stranger, and Robin bade him go back and let him go over. "I am no man of yours," was all the answer Robin got, and in anger he drew his bow and fitted an arrow to it, "Would you shoot a man who has
20 no arms but a staff?" asked the stranger in scorn; and with shame Robin laid down his bow, and unbuckled an oaken stick at his side. "We will fight till one of us falls into the water," he said; and fight they did, till the stranger planted a blow so well that Robin rolled over into the river.

25 "You are a brave soul," said he, when he had waded to land, and he blew a blast with his horn which brought fifty good fellows, clad in green, to the little bridge. "Have you fallen into the river that your clothes are wet?" asked one; and Robin made answer, "No, but this stranger, fighting on the
30 bridge, got the better of me, and tumbled me into the stream."

At this the foresters seized the stranger, and would have ducked him had not their leader bade them stop, and begged the stranger to stay with them and make one of themselves. "Here is my hand," replied the stranger, "and my heart with
35 it. My name, if you would know it, is John Little."

"That must be altered," cried Will Scarlett; "we will call a feast, and henceforth, because he is full seven feet tall and round the waist at least an ell, he shall be called Little John." And thus it was done; but at the feast Little John, who always
40 liked to know exactly what work he had to do, put some questions to Robin Hood. "Before I join hands with you, tell me first what sort of life is this you lead? How am I to know whose goods I shall take, and whose I shall leave? Whom I shall beat, and whom I shall refrain from beating?"

45 And Robin answered: "Look that you harm not any tiller of the ground, nor any yeoman of the greenwood—no knight, no squire, unless you have heard him ill spoken of. But if bishops or archbishops come your way, see that you spoil them, and mark that you always hold in your mind the High
50 Sheriff of Nottingham, the bitterest enemy the foresters have."

375

Chapter 10

Literary
Narrative/
Prose Fiction
and
Humanities
Passages

According to the passage, why would churchmen and bishops tremble when passing through Sherwood Forest?

F. They had no money to pay Robin Hood's toll.

G. They were scared Robin Hood would turn them in to the king for slaying deer.

H. They carried a lot of money and dressed flashily.

J. They did not want to get lost in the forest.

The correct answer is H. The first and last paragraphs in the passage make it clear that people who work hard and are not wealthy can pass freely through Sherwood Forest. The author specifically sets up a comparison between the hard-working people who come through the forest and the "lordly churchmen" and "proud bishops" who are loaded with money and act rich. This directly contradicts choice F—the churchmen and bishops clearly had money. There's no information in the passage about who, aside from Robin Hood's men, was eating the forbidden deer, so choice G is incorrect. In addition, there is no information given to support the idea that churchmen and bishops would get lost in the forest (choice J). Choice H is correct because it arrives at the conclusion that the churchmen and bishops are afraid because they are unlike the humble tillers and yeomen who can make their way through the forest without paying Robin Hood's toll.

Which of the following best explains why John Little joined Robin Hood's group?

A. Robin Hood was angry and wanted to kidnap the stranger.

B. The High Sheriff of Nottingham sent him to infiltrate the group.

C. By defeating Robin Hood in the fight, he was allowed to replace Robin Hood as head of the group.

D. He earned their respect by fighting fairly.

The correct answer is D. After Robin Hood falls into the water, his response is not anger (choice A). Rather, he compliments John Little by saying, "You are a brave soul." Later, he goes on to stop his men from getting revenge on John Little for pushing Robin Hood into the water. These responses on Robin Hood's part eliminate choice A. The passage shows no information about whether the High Sheriff of Nottingham might be involved, so you can rule out choice B as well. There is also no information to support that John Little replaces Robin Hood (choice C); the passage merely says that he is invited to join them and change his name. Choice D is correct because Robin Hood specifically admits that John Little "got the better of me" after insisting on a fair fight without weapons, and then invites him to become one of the group. Of all the choices, the passage gives the most information to support choice D.

376

Chapter 10

Literary
Narrative/
Prose Fiction
and
Humanities
Passages

Now, try an example of determining cause and effect in a Humanities passage. The following was excerpted from *Hamlet at the Lyceum*, by Oscar Wilde.

It sometimes happens that at a *première* in London the least enjoyable part of the performance is the play. I have seen many audiences more interesting than the actors, and have often heard better dialogue in the *foyer* than I have on
5 the stage. At the Lyceum, however, this is rarely the case, and when the play is a play of Shakespeare's, and among its exponents are Mr. Irving and Miss Ellen Terry, we turn from the gods in the gallery and from the goddesses in the stalls, to enjoy the charm of the production, and to take delight in
10 the art. The lions are behind the footlights and not in front of them when we have a noble tragedy nobly acted. And I have rarely witnessed such enthusiasm as that which greeted on last Saturday night the two artists I have mentioned. I would like, in fact, to use the word ovation, but a pedantic
15 professor has recently informed us, with the Batavian buoyancy of misapplied learning, that this expression is not to be employed except when a sheep has been sacrificed. At the Lyceum last week I need hardly say nothing so dreadful

occurred. The only inartistic incident of the evening was the
20 hurling of a bouquet from a box at Mr. Irving while he was engaged in pourtraying the agony of Hamlet's death, and the pathos of his parting with Horatio. The Dramatic College might take up the education of spectators as well as that of players, and teach people that there is a proper moment for
25 the throwing of flowers as well as a proper method.

As regards Mr. Irving's own performance, it has been already so elaborately criticised and described, from his business with the supposed pictures in the closet scene down to his use of 'peacock' for 'paddock,' that little remains to be said; nor,
30 indeed, does a Lyceum audience require the interposition of the dramatic critic in order to understand or to appreciate the Hamlet of this great actor. I call him a great actor because he brings to the interpretation of a work of art the two qualities which we in this century so much desire, the qualities of
35 personality and of perfection. A few years ago it seemed to

many, and perhaps rightly, that the personality overshadowed the art. No such criticism would be fair now. The somewhat harsh angularity of movement and faulty pronunciation have been replaced by exquisite grace of gesture and clear precision
40 of word, where such precision is necessary. For delightful as good elocution is, few things are so depressing as to hear a passionate passage recited instead of being acted. The quality of a fine performance is its life more than its learning, and every word in a play has a musical as well as an intellectual
45 value, and must be made expressive of a certain emotion. So it does not seem to me that in all parts of a play perfect pronunciation is necessarily dramatic.

When the words are 'wild and whirling,' the expression of them must be wild and whirling also. Mr. Irving, I think,
50 manages his voice with singular art; it was impossible to discern a false note or wrong intonation in his dialogue or his soliloquies, and his strong dramatic power, his realistic power as an actor, is as effective as ever. A great critic at the beginning of this century said that Hamlet is the most difficult
55 part to personate on the stage, that it is like the attempt to 'embody a shadow.' I cannot say that I agree with this idea. Hamlet seems to me essentially a good acting part, and in Mr. Irving's performance of it there is that combination of poetic grace with absolute reality which is so eternally
60 delightful. Indeed, if the words easy and difficult have any meaning at all in matters of art, I would be inclined to say that Ophelia is the more difficult part. She has, I mean, less

material by which to produce her effects. She is the occasion of the tragedy, but she is neither its heroine nor its chief
65 victim. She is swept away by circumstances, and gives the opportunity for situation, of which she is not herself the climax, and which she does not herself command. And of all the parts which Miss Terry has acted in her brilliant career, there is none in which her infinite powers of pathos and her imaginative
70 and creative faculty are more shown than in her Ophelia.

According to the excerpt, one of the main reasons Wilde thought the production of *Hamlet* was excellent was due to the:

F. fascinating foyer conversation of the audience.
G. actors' fusion of a poetic speaking style with emotional realism.
H. actors' impeccable diction.
J. actors' allowing their personalities to shine through.

The correct answer is choice G. Wilde found the lead actor and actress' success a result of their "wild and whirling" words and expressiveness. Wilde is very particular about the fact that a play cannot live on actor persona (choice J) or brilliant elocution (choice H) alone, and in the opening paragraph he indicates this was *not* one of those productions where the audience was more interesting than the play.

MAKE COMPARISONS

Along the same lines as cause and effect, making comparisons is a way for readers to come to a deeper understanding of a text. It begins with an observation—for example, one text is portraying mothers sympathetically, while another text takes a dark view of mothers—that you then develop into an argument with textual support, like so: "These texts each use conflict to make a statement about motherhood. Text A reflects the pressure of poverty, while text B shows the benefits of a financially secure family environment."

 Keep an eye out for obvious key words like "compare," and for two shorter excerpts instead of one longer one. As you read, consider what the passages have in common, and what distinguishes them.

Questions with paired passages will look something like these:

- *Which of the following statements provides the most accurate comparison of the tone of each passage?*
- *Compared to the narrator of Passage A, the narrator of Passage B …*
- *It can reasonably be inferred that compared to [_____], the narrator of [_____] felt [_____].*

Let's practice answering questions that accompany paired passages and ask you to relate one to the other. Passage A comes from Gene Stratton-Porter's *A Girl of the Limberlost*. Passage B is excerpted from Lucy Maud Montgomery's *Rilla of Ingleside*.

. . . .

Passage A
by Gene Stratton-Porter

Elnora looked into her mother's face and smiled. It was a queer sort of a little smile, and would have reached the depths with any normal mother.

"I see you've been bawling," said Mrs. Comstock. "I thought
5 you'd get your fill in a hurry. That's why I wouldn't go to any expense. If we keep out of the poor-house we have to cut the corners close. . ."

Elnora again smiled that pitiful smile.

"Do you think I didn't know that I was funny and would
10 be laughed at?" she asked.

"Funny?" cried Mrs. Comstock hotly.

"Yes, funny! A regular caricature," answered Elnora. "No one else wore calico, not even one other. No one else wore high heavy shoes, not even one. No one else had such a
15 funny little old hat; my hair was not right, my ribbon invisible compared with the others, I did not know where to go, or what to do, and I had no books. What a spectacle I made for them!" Elnora laughed nervously at her own picture. "But there are always two sides! The professor said in the algebra
20 class that he never had a better solution and explanation than mine of the proposition he gave me, which scored one for me in spite of my clothes."

"Well, I'm glad you got enough of it!"

"Oh, but I haven't," hurried in Elnora. "I just got a start. The
25 hardest is over. Tomorrow they won't be surprised. They will know what to expect. . .

I'm willing to bear the hard part to pay for what I'll learn. Already I have selected the ward building in which I shall teach in about four years. I am going to ask for a room with
30 a south exposure so that the flowers and moths I take in from the swamp to show the children will do well."

"You little idiot!" said Mrs. Comstock. "How are you going to pay your expenses?"

"Now that is just what I was going to ask you!" said Elnora.
35 "You see, I have had two startling pieces of news today. I did not know I would need any money. I thought the city furnished the books, and there is an out-of-town tuition, also. I need ten dollars in the morning. Will you please let me have it?"

"Ten dollars!" cried Mrs. Comstock. "Ten dollars! Why don't
40 you say a hundred and be done with it! I could get one as easy as the other. I told you! I told you I couldn't raise a cent. Every year expenses grow bigger and bigger. I told you not to ask for money!"

"I never meant to," replied Elnora. "I thought clothes were
45 all I needed and I could bear them. I never knew about buying books and tuition."

"Well, I did!" said Mrs. Comstock. "I knew what you would run into! But you are so bull-dog stubborn, and so set in your way, I thought I would just let you try the world a little and
50 see how you liked it!"

Elnora pushed back her chair and looked at her mother. "Do you mean to say," she demanded, "that you knew, when you let me go into a city classroom and reveal the fact before all of them that I expected to have my books handed out to
55 me; do you mean to say that you knew I had to pay for them?"

Mrs. Comstock evaded the direct question.

"Anybody but an idiot mooning over a book or wasting time prowling the woods would have known you had to pay. Everybody has to pay for everything. Life is made up of pay,
60 pay, pay! It's always and forever pay! If you don't pay one way you do another! Of course, I knew you had to pay. Of course, I knew you would come home blubbering! But you don't get a penny! I haven't one cent, and can't get one! Have your way if you are determined, but I think you will find the
65 road somewhat rocky."

Passage B
by Lucy Maud Montgomery

The big living-room at Ingleside was snowed over with drifts of white cotton. Word had come from Red Cross head-quarters that sheets and bandages would be required. Nan and Di and Rilla were hard at work. Mrs. Blythe and Susan
5 were upstairs in the boys' room, engaged in a more personal task. With dry, anguished eyes they were packing up Jem's belongings. He must leave for Valcartier the next morning. They had been expecting the word but it was none the less dreadful when it came.

10 Rilla was basting the hem of a sheet for the first time in her life. When the word had come that Jem must go she had

378

Chapter 10

Literary
Narrative/
Prose Fiction
and
Humanities
Passages

her cry out among the pines in Rainbow Valley and then she had gone to her mother.

"Mother, I want to do something. I'm only a girl—I can't
15 do anything to win the war—but I must do something to help at home."

"The cotton has come up for the sheets," said Mrs. Blythe. "You can help Nan and Di make them up. And Rilla, don't you think you could organize a Junior Red Cross among the
20 young girls? I think they would like it better and do better work by themselves than if mixed up with the older people."

"But, mother—I've never done anything like that."

"We will all have to do a great many things in the months ahead of us that we have never done before, Rilla."

25 "Well"—Rilla took the plunge—"I'll try, mother—if you'll tell me how to begin. I have been thinking it all over and I have decided that I must be as brave and heroic and unselfish as I can possibly be."

Mrs. Blythe did not smile at Rilla's italics. Perhaps she did
30 not feel like smiling or perhaps she detected a real grain of serious purpose behind Rilla's romantic pose. So here was Rilla hemming sheets and organizing a Junior Red Cross in her thoughts as she hemmed; moreover, she was enjoying it—the organizing that is, not the hemming. It was interesting
35 and Rilla discovered a certain aptitude in herself for it that surprised her. Who would be president? Not she. The older girls would not like that. Irene Howard? No, somehow Irene was not quite as popular as she deserved to be. Marjorie Drew? No, Marjorie hadn't enough backbone. She was too
40 prone to agree with the last speaker. Betty Mead—calm, capable, tactful Betty—the very one! And Una Meredith for treasurer; and, if they were very insistent, they might make her, Rilla, secretary. As for the various committees, they must be chosen after the Juniors were organized, but Rilla knew
45 just who should be put on which. They would meet around— and there must be no eats—Rilla knew she would have a pitched battle with Olive Kirk over that—and everything should be strictly business-like and constitutional. Her minute book should be covered in white with a Red Cross on the
50 cover—and wouldn't it be nice to have some kind of uniform which they could all wear at the concerts they would have to get up to raise money—something simple but smart?

"You have basted the top hem of that sheet on one side and the bottom hem on the other," said Di.

55 Rilla picked out her stitches and reflected that she hated sewing. Running the Junior Reds would be much more interesting.

Compared to the mother-daughter relationship in Passage B, the mother-daughter relationship dynamic in Passage A could be best described as:

A. more antagonistic.
B. more perfunctory.
C. more distant.
D. more loving.

The correct answer is A. Without knowing more about the book to speculate about Mrs. Comstock's motivations, the moments in the text where she calls her daughter "you little idiot" or where it's clear she deliberately sent Elnora into a humiliating school experience illustrate that Elnora and Mrs. Comstock's relationship is much more hostile and fraught than Rilla and Mrs. Blythe's. When Rilla asks for help, Mrs. Blythe has suggestions for how to help and supports her daughter's efforts to contribute to the war effort. A mother and daughter in a perfunctory relationship would hardly take notice of each other, and Elnora and her mother are at least having this heated conversation.

It can be inferred from both passages that:

F. interpersonal relationships between young women are complicated.
G. Elnora and Rilla are both resilient and resourceful.
H. running a Junior Red Cross is harder than earning money for school.
J. girls have fewer opportunities than boys in both of these societies.

The correct answer is G. While the struggles they face are different, and their degree of family support is highly contrasted, both Elnora and Rilla demonstrate determination and focus as they approach their respective obstacles. While it is undoubtedly true that young women's interpersonal relationships are complicated, that is not the main idea of either passage (choice F). While the implicit stakes for Rilla's Red Cross Society are related to the impending war, Elnora's poverty impedes her ability to get an education, which makes choice H an oversimplification of their individual problems. Though Rilla does say she's "only a girl," that's not sufficient to make choice J correct.

DETERMINE THE MEANING OF CONTEXT-DEPENDENT WORDS, PHRASES, AND STATEMENTS

One of the relatively preferable aspects of the ACT is that it doesn't ask you to memorize long lists of vocabulary words or define them in your own words. Instead, you'll be asked to flex the same muscles you strengthened identifying crucial details and use context to determine the meaning of a word.

Meaning-in-context questions on the ACT will look like this:

- *Which of the following most fully [explains/lists/addresses things considered by the author]?*
- *Which of the following most clearly distinguishes between [key term] and [other key term]?*
- *The passage states that all of the following are [key concept] EXCEPT:*

Looking at one of our earlier examples, let's try a sample question based on the Alcott passage.

. . . .

Things always went by contraries with Jo. Her first book, laboured over for years, and launched full of the high hopes and ambitious dreams of youth, foundered on its voyage, though the wreck continued to float long afterward, to the
5 profit of the publisher at least. The hastily written story, sent away with no thought beyond the few dollars it might bring, sailed with a fair wind and a wise pilot at the helm into public favour, and came home heavily laden with an unexpected cargo of gold and glory.

10 A more astonished woman probably never existed than Josephine Bhaer when her little ship came into port with flags flying, cannon that had been silent before now booming gaily, and, better than all, many kind faces rejoicing with her, many friendly hands grasping hers with cordial congratul-
15 ations. After that it was plain sailing, and she merely had to load her ships and send them off on prosperous trips, to bring home stores of comfort for all she loved and laboured for.

The fame she never did quite accept; for it takes very little fire to make a great deal of smoke nowadays, and notoriety
20 is not real glory. The fortune she could not doubt, and grate-fully received; though it was not half so large a one as a generous world reported it to be. The tide having turned continued to rise, and floated the family comfortably into a snug harbour where the older members could rest secure
25 from storms, and whence the younger ones could launch their boats for the voyage of life.

* * *

This was the sweet and sacred side of the change; but it had its droll and thorny one, as all things have in this curious world of ours. After the first surprise, incredulity, and joy,
30 which came to Jo, with the ingratitude of human nature, she soon tired of renown, and began to resent her loss of liberty. For suddenly the admiring public took possession of her and all her affairs, past, present, and to come. Strangers demanded to look at her, question, advise, warn, congratulate, and
35 drive her out of her wits by well-meant but very wearisome attentions. If she declined to open her heart to them, they reproached her; if she refused to endow pet charities, relieve private wants, or sympathize with every ill and trial known to humanity, she was called hard-hearted, selfish, and
40 haughty; if she found it impossible to answer the piles of letters sent her, she was neglectful of her duty to the admiring public; and if she preferred the privacy of home to the ped-estal upon which she was requested to pose, 'the airs of literary people' were freely criticized.

45 She did her best for the children, they being the public for whom she wrote, and laboured stoutly to supply the demand always in the mouths of voracious youth—'More stories; more right away!' Her family objected to this devotion at their expense, and her health suffered; but for a time she
50 gratefully offered herself up on the altar of juvenile literature, feeling that she owed a good deal to the little friends in whose sight she had found favour after twenty years of effort.

But a time came when her patience gave out; and wearying of being a lion, she became a bear in nature as in name, and
55 returning to her den, growled awfully when ordered out. Her family enjoyed the fun, and had small sympathy with her trials, but Jo came to consider it the worse scrape of her life; for liberty had always been her dearest possession, and it seemed to be fast going from her. Living in a lantern soon
60 loses its charm, and she was too old, too tired, and too busy to like it.

Which of the following most fully explains what Louisa May Alcott meant by "living in a lantern" where she says of Jo, "Living in a lantern soon loses its charm, and she was too old, too tired, and busy to like it." (lines 59–61)?

A. Life so close to the flame of genius is exhausting.

B. Jo considers her surroundings fragile or unstable.

C. Because of her writing, Jo feels isolated from her family.

D. As a famous author, Jo doesn't enjoy the amount of scrutiny she receives.

The correct answer is D. The lantern reference evokes an image of living in a glass house that everyone can see inside. Choice A is not correct because nowhere in the passage does Alcott indicate Jo is tired of being a writer. Choices B and C are incorrect because Jo's family is described as supportive and even as finding her plight humorous.

· ·

Now let's see the same question type, but this time with a Humanities passage. The below is from *How to Sing*, by Lilli Lehmann.

· ·

What is a vocal register?

A series of tones sung in a certain way, which are produced by a certain position of the vocal organs—larynx, tongue, and palate. Every voice includes three registers—chest, middle, and head. But all are not employed in every class
5 of voice.

Two of them are often found connected to a certain extent in beginners; the third is usually much weaker, or does not exist at all. Only very rarely is a voice found naturally equalized over its whole compass.

10 Do registers exist by nature? No. It may be said that they are created through long years of speaking in the vocal range that is easiest to the person, or in one adopted by imitation, which then becomes a fixed habit. If this is coupled with a natural and proper working of the muscles of the vocal
15 organs, it may become the accustomed range, strong in comparison with others, and form a register by itself. This fact would naturally be appreciated only by singers.

If, on the other hand, the muscles are wrongly employed in speaking, not only the range of voice generally used, but
20 the whole voice as well, may be made to sound badly. So, in every voice, one or another range may be stronger or weaker; and this is, in fact, almost always the case, since mankind speaks and sings in the pitch easiest or most accustomed, without giving thought to the proper position of the organs
25 in relation to each other; and people are rarely made to pay attention as children to speaking clearly and in an agreeable voice. In the most fortunate instances the range thus

practised reaches limits on both sides, not so much those of the person's power, as those set by his lack of skill, or
30 practice. Limitations are put on the voice through taking account only of the easiest and most accustomed thing, without inquiring into the potentialities of the organs or the demands of art.

The author discusses limitations on the voice in order to:

A. discourage amateurs from injuring their voices.

B. introduce the concept of improving through conscious study.

C. explain why not every singer is aware of their register.

D. motivate readers to think of their voice even in speaking.

The correct answer is choice D. The author introduces the idea of limitations in order to shift the focus onto the demands of art or the voice's potential and to encourage aspiring singers to think beyond the natural limits they've set on their own voices by the way they speak. There are no specific tips given to prevent vocal damage (choice A), and the author does not appear to be urging non-singers to undertake singing lessons (choice B). Choice C is incorrect because the author indicates that singers are the ones most likely to appreciate their individual registers—it's non-singers who lack an understanding of this concept.

Which of the following most clearly distinguishes between the three types of registers?

F. Head comes naturally to everyone; chest and middle are hard to tell apart.
G. Only middle can be improved by rigorous practice.
H. Chest and middle are often found in beginners; head voice needs to be developed.
J. Head voice uses the same muscles as in speech and therefore is the strongest.

The correct answer is H. The answer lies in the third paragraph—your practice at identifying sequences should have come in handy here in helping you match up "first and second" with the registers to which they referred. Choice F is incorrect because head is the hardest register and requires the most practice; chest and middle may be difficult to tell apart for some listeners, but it is not discussed overtly in the passage. Choice G is incorrect because the author is very clear that every speaker can improve his or her register with attentive practice—though only singers may appreciate it. Choice J is incorrect because each person's vocal range is different, so the muscles and their relative strength are specific to the individual speaker or singer.

DRAW GENERALIZATIONS

Where detecting crucial details requires you to zoom in on a text, drawing generalizations asks you to pan out, identify a key concept, and transport it to another context where it can add meaning. A simple example is a friend who owns purple sneakers, purple jeans, a purple phone case—it is reasonable to infer that a purple backpack would make a good gift for her. Some ACT examples will be subtler than others, so learn to recognize key phrases like these question templates:

- *From information in the passage, it can be reasonably inferred that [_____].*
- *According to the passage, a [person interacting with key concept] should…*
- *This passage states that in terms of [key concept], [action should be possible]…*
- *In [text] the narrator's description of [thing] suggests she sees [thing] as ultimately…*

The most obvious source of broad generalizations in classic literature is *Aesop's Fables*. Usually featuring animals, these fables end with a practical lesson or moral. For instance, in the fable, "The Fox and the Crane," we read about a fox that invites a crane over for dinner and learn a valuable lesson about hosting—despite the fact that we are neither foxes nor cranes.

Let's work through another example. Read the following fable, "The Man and the Lion," and answer the questions that follow.

A man and a lion traveled together through the forest. They soon began to boast of their respective superiority to each other in strength and prowess. As they were disputing, they passed a statue carved in stone, which represented "a lion strangled by a man." The traveler pointed to it and said: "See there! How strong we are, and how we prevail over even the king of beasts." The lion replied: "This statue was made by one of you men. If we lions knew how to erect statues, you would see the man placed under the paw of the lion."

The author of this fable would most likely agree with which of the following?

A. The one who lives to tell the story has a historical advantage.
B. The powerful have the right to dominate the weak.
C. He who laughs last, laughs longest.
D. There's no point in competing with your friends.

The correct answer is A. This kind of question more overtly asks you to make generalizations—you must draw a conclusion from the passage that allows you to speculate about how an author would interpret a different scenario. Since the lion and the man are ultimately depicted as equals (or at least equally as braggy!) in the fable, it's reasonable to

382

Chapter 10

Literary
Narrative/
Prose Fiction
and
Humanities
Passages

infer Aesop would agree that the individual who gets to tell the story benefits more than the one whose story isn't told. Choice B is not supported by the passage; while choice D might seem true, it doesn't reflect the outcome of the fable. Choice C is the moral to a different fable—neither the lion nor the man is laughing because the stakes of being right are too high.

The moral of this story is most likely:

- **F.** Misfortune tests the sincerity of friends.
- **G.** To the victor go the spoils.
- **H.** One story is good, till another is told.
- **J.** Evil companions bring more hurt than profit.

The correct answer is H. The traveler's evidence is momentarily persuasive, until the lion weighs in with his interpretation of the statue. There is no misfortune depicted in the passage, nor does either partner seem particularly evil, choices F and J. Choice G might be a tempting distractor, but it doesn't refer as directly to the passage in the question.

. . . .

Let's explore drawing generalizations in a Humanities passage now. The following is from David Hume's *An Enquiry Concerning the Principles of Morals*.

. . . .

We may observe that, in displaying the praises of any humane, beneficent man, there is one circumstance which never fails to be amply insisted on, namely, the happiness and satisfaction, derived to society from his intercourse and
5 good offices. To his parents, we are apt to say, he endears himself by his pious attachment and duteous care still more than by the connexions of nature. His children never feel his authority, but when employed for their advantage. With him, the ties of love are consolidated by beneficence and
10 friendship. The ties of friendship approach, in a fond observance of each obliging office, to those of love and inclination. His domestics and dependents have in him a sure resource; and no longer dread the power of fortune, but so far as she exercises it over him. From him the hungry receive food, the
15 naked clothing, the ignorant and slothful skill and industry. Like the sun, an inferior minister of providence he cheers, invigorates, and sustains the surrounding world.

As these topics of praise never fail to be employed, and with success, where we would inspire esteem for any one;
20 may it not thence be concluded, that the utility, resulting from the social virtues, forms, at least, a PART of their merit, and is one source of that approbation and regard so universally paid to them?

When we recommend even an animal or a plant as USEFUL
25 and BENEFICIAL, we give it an applause and recommendation suited to its nature. As, on the other hand, reflection on the baneful influence of any of these inferior beings always inspires us with the sentiment of aversion. The eye is pleased with the prospect of corn-fields and loaded vine-yards; horses
30 grazing, and flocks pasturing: but flies the view of briars and brambles, affording shelter to wolves and serpents.

* * *

In general, what praise is implied in the simple epithet USEFUL! What reproach in the contrary!

With which of the following would David Hume, author of this excerpt, be LEAST likely to agree?

- **F.** The primary purpose of life is to be of use to one's fellows.
- **G.** There is a high value in beauty for its own sake.
- **H.** Utility is a large part of how we estimate value.
- **J.** Humans hate that which is not useful.

The correct answer is G. Choices F, H, and J all summarize parts of Hume's observations about the overlap between virtue and usefulness.

. . . .

ANALYZE THE AUTHOR OR NARRATOR'S VOICE AND METHOD

This category is where distinguishing between genres comes in handy. Remember, if it's fiction, the narrator is not necessarily the author—but you can close read to see what the author is doing to convey the character's opinion or perspective. If it's nonfiction (like an essay or memoir), it may be in first-or second person, but the narrator is generally the author—even if the author is thinking of him- or herself as a character.

Look for these kinds of phrases to signal that you should be looking beyond the text into who's doing the talking.

- *What is the point of view (POV)?*
- *Why did the author choose that POV?*
- *What best illustrates that POV?*
- *From the passage, what is a reasonable inference about the narrator's motivation?*
- *Which of these observations can be inferred as something the narrator/author would agree/disagree with?*
- *Which of the following best states the author's response to [_____]?*
- *When the author says, "_____," she is most likely suggesting…*
- *Which of the following would the author be LEAST/MOST likely to recommend?*
- *The narrator most nearly suggests [_____] because…*
- *The narrator's statement is most nearly meant to…*
- *The excerpt indicates that compared to the narrator's expectation about [_____], the reality was…*
- *What do you notice about the author's tone in this passage?*

The following example is an excerpt from the Foreword of Anne Brontë's *The Tenant of Wildfell Hall*.

My object in writing the following pages was not simply to amuse the Reader; neither was it to gratify my own taste, nor yet to ingratiate myself with the Press and the Public: I wished to tell the truth, for truth always conveys its own
5 moral to those who are able to receive it.

But as the priceless treasure too frequently hides at the bottom of a well, it needs some courage to dive for it, especially as he that does so will be likely to incur more scorn and obloquy for the mud and water into which he has ven-
10 tured to plunge, than thanks for the jewel he procures; as, in like manner, she who undertakes the cleansing of a careless bachelor's apartment will be liable to more abuse for the dust she raises than commendation for the clearance she effects.

15 Let it not be imagined, however, that I consider myself competent to reform the errors and abuses of society, but only that I would fain contribute my humble quota towards so good an aim; and if I can gain the public ear at all, I would rather whisper a few wholesome truths therein than much
20 soft nonsense.

As the story of 'Agnes Grey' was accused of extravagant over-colouring in those very parts that were carefully copied from the life, with a most scrupulous avoidance of all exaggeration, so, in the present work, I find myself censured for
25 depicting con amore, with 'a morbid love of the coarse, if not of the brutal,' those scenes which, I will venture to say, have not been more painful for the most fastidious of my critics to read than they were for me to describe.

I may have gone too far; in which case I shall be careful
30 not to trouble myself or my readers in the same way again; but when we have to do with vice and vicious characters, I maintain it is better to depict them as they really are than as they would wish to appear. To represent a bad thing in its least offensive light is, doubtless, the most agreeable course
35 for a writer of fiction to pursue; but is it the most honest, or the safest? Is it better to reveal the snares and pitfalls of life to the young and thoughtless traveller, or to cover them with branches and flowers?

Oh, reader! if there were less of this delicate concealment
40 of facts—this whispering, 'Peace, peace,' when there is no peace, there would be less of sin and misery to the young of both sexes who are left to wring their bitter knowledge from experience.

Which of these most accurately reflects the tone of Anne Brontë in this excerpt?

- **A.** Apologetic
- **B.** Defiant
- **C.** Bewildered
- **D.** Hopeful

The correct answer is A. Phrases like "I may have gone too far; in which case I shall be careful not to trouble myself or my readers in the same way again" and her description of writing the scenes in *Agnes Grey* that critics found most difficult indicate that she regrets writing something that readers found troubling. While she is also resolute about continuing to tell the truth as she sees it, she is not defiant (choice B), or bewildered (choice C). You could argue she arrives in a more hopeful tone at the end of the passage (choice D), but that is not the dominant note of the excerpt.

You will also likely be asked to make assumptions about the author's purpose for writing a piece, as in the following.

Based on this excerpt, which of these is the most accurate inference about Brontë's intention in writing this book?

- **F.** To gently introduce readers to the consequences of bad behavior, without upsetting or shocking them
- **G.** To honestly convey the brutal vices and flaws that destroy lives in order to dissuade other young people from making these same mistakes
- **H.** To atone for her previous book by writing in a more lady-like fashion about socially acceptable topics
- **J.** To entertain readers with lurid and graphic stories of dissipation and gossip

The correct answer is G. While Anne Brontë was dismayed to receive such negative reviews for *Agnes Grey*, this introductory essay demonstrates that she thinks writing frankly and honestly is the only way to make negative stories meaningful. Choice F is not correct because Brontë doesn't believe it's helpful to "cover [snares and pitfalls] with branches and flowers." Similarly, choice H is incorrect because Brontë doesn't think writing in a "lady-like" fashion is adequate when lives are in the balance. However, her purpose is not simply to revel in what is "coarse" or "brutal," so choice J is incorrect.

SUMMING IT UP

- Questions in the **Literary Narrative** category are based on passages from short stories, novels, memoirs, and personal essays.

- Questions in the **Prose Fiction** category are based on passages from short stories and novels. Test-takers will see either Literary Narrative or Prose Fiction passages on the ACT.

- Questions in the **Humanities** category are based on passages in the content areas of architecture, art, dance, ethics, film, language, literary criticism, music, philosophy, radio, television, and theater. Questions may also be based on passages from memoirs and personal essays.

- **ACT Reading test questions** fall into the following types:

  - **Determine main idea:** What is the author getting at? What is the defining idea of the passage? Is there a key concept being introduced or interpreted? Are you meant to be persuaded of something?

  - **Locate and interpret significant details:** This is where you're asked to close-read the passage and identify a specific fact, term, plot point, or key concept.

  - **Character description:** Remember to look not only at what the author *says* about the characters, but also how they behave and how others react to them.

  - **Relationships:** Sometimes relationships are made explicit, other times you have to closely read interactions between characters and infer how they feel about one another.

  - **Understand sequences of events:** Some passages recount events chronologically, others in order of priority—be able to decode this choice and indicate what happened first, second, third, etc.

  - **Comprehend cause-and-effect relationships:** This is another category where the answer may have been made evident by the author or require you to make an inference. Transfer your insights into relationships to this category and understand when one action is responsible for, or the result of, another.

  - **Make comparisons:** Sometimes you'll be asked to compare two elements within the same passage, or more often, to compare two different passages. How are they alike? How are they different? And most important, why does it matter? What is the impact of these differences?

  - **Determine the meaning of context-dependent words, phrases, and statements:** Often, an author's chosen context can change or more precisely identify the meaning of a key term or concept; be able to make a reasonable guess about the author's intention and understand how that might shift a reader's understanding of the passage in question.

  - **Draw generalizations:** Be able to transfer an understanding of one context to other contexts—if an author agrees with X, and X is similar to Y, then it's probable that an author would agree with Y.

  - **Analyze the author or narrator's voice and method:** Approaching these types of questions may vary by genre—be sure you know whether you're reading fiction or nonfiction, and make your inferences about the author/narrator accordingly. Look for literary devices or connotative words that offer insight beyond what is literally being said.

    - **Tone:** Look to features of the text such as word choice, subtext, tense, and pacing to evaluate an author's tone.

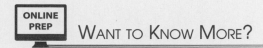
WANT TO KNOW MORE?

Access more practice questions, lessons, helpful hints, and strategies for the following reading topics in *Peterson's ACT Online Course*:

- Answering Humanities Questions
- Understanding Difficult Text
- Hard Prose Passages
- Hard Reading Questions
- Advanced Reading Test Strategies

To purchase and access the course, go to ***www.petersons.com/act***.

387

Chapter 10

**Literary
Narrative/
Prose Fiction
and
Humanities
Passages**

actice everything we've covered in this chapter. This time, you'll see the passages in full and accompanied by a
estions—the sets will look like the ones you will see on the actual ACT. The first 10 questions accompany a Prose
passage, and the second 10 accompany a Humanities passage. After you have completed all 20 questions, you will find detailed
answer explanations that walk you through every answer choice.

PASSAGE I

PROSE FICTION: Passage A is an excerpt from a novel, *The Tenant of Wildfell Hall,* by Anne Brontë. Passage B is an excerpt from Charlotte Brontë's debut novel, *Jane Eyre.*

Passage A
by Anne Brontë

I believe it was on that very evening that I ventured on another invasion of Wildfell Hall. From the time of our party, which was upwards of a week ago, I had been making daily efforts to meet its mistress in her walks; and always disappointed (she must
5 have managed it so on purpose), had nightly kept revolving in my mind some pretext for another call.

At length I concluded that the separation could be endured no longer (by this time, you will see, I was pretty far gone); and, taking from the book-case an old volume that I thought she
10 might be interested in, though, from its unsightly and somewhat dilapidated condition, I had not yet ventured to offer it for perusal, I hastened away,—but not without sundry misgivings as to how she would receive me, or how I could summon courage to present myself with so slight an excuse.

15 But, perhaps, I might see her in the field or the garden, and then there would be no great difficulty: it was the formal knocking at the door, with the prospect of being gravely ushered in by Rachel, to the presence of a surprised, uncordial mistress, that so greatly disturbed me. My wish, however, was not gratified.

20 Mrs. Graham herself was not to be seen; but there was Arthur playing with his frolicsome little dog in the garden. I looked over the gate and called him to me. He wanted me to come in; but I told him I could not without his mother's leave. "I'll go and ask her," said the child. "No, no, Arthur, you mustn't do that; but if
25 she's not engaged, just ask her to come here a minute. Tell her I want to speak to her." He ran to perform my bidding, and quickly returned with his mother.

How lovely she looked with her dark ringlets streaming in the light summer breeze, her fair cheek slightly flushed, and her
30 countenance radiant with smiles. Dear Arthur! what did I not owe to you for this and every other happy meeting? Through him I was at once delivered from all formality, and terror, and

constraint. In love affairs, there is no mediator like a merry, simple-hearted child—ever ready to cement divided hearts, to
35 span the unfriendly gulf of custom, to melt the ice of cold reserve, and overthrow the separating walls of dread formality and pride.

"Well, Mr. Markham, what is it?" said the young mother, accosting me with a pleasant smile.

"I want you to look at this book, and, if you please, to take it,
40 and peruse it at your leisure. I make no apology for calling you out on such a lovely evening, though it be for a matter of no greater importance."

"Tell him to come in, mamma," said Arthur.

"Would you like to come in?" asked the lady.

45 "Yes; I should like to see your improvements in the garden."

"And how your sister's roots have prospered in my charge," added she, as she opened the gate. And we sauntered through the garden, and talked of the flowers, the trees, and the book, and then of other things.

50 The evening was kind and genial, and so was my companion. By degrees I waxed more warm and tender than, perhaps, I had ever been before; but still I said nothing tangible, and she attempted no repulse, until, in passing a moss rose-tree that I had brought her some weeks since, in my sister's name, she
55 plucked a beautiful half-open bud and bade me give it to Rose.

"May I not keep it myself?" I asked.

"No; but here is another for you." Instead of taking it quietly, I likewise took the hand that offered it, and looked into her face. She let me hold it for a moment, and I saw a flash of ecstatic
60 brilliance in her eye, a glow of glad excitement on her face—I thought my hour of victory was come—but instantly a painful recollection seemed to flash upon her; a cloud of anguish darkened her brow, a marble paleness blanched her cheek and lip; there seemed a moment of inward conflict, and, with a
65 sudden effort, she withdrew her hand, and retreated a step or two back.

"Now, Mr. Markham," said she, with a kind of desperate calmness, "I must tell you plainly that I cannot do with this. I like your company, because I am alone here, and your conversation
70 pleases me more than that of any other person; but if you cannot

388

Chapter 10

Literary
Narrative/
Prose Fiction
and
Humanities
Passages

be content to regard me as a friend—a plain, cold, motherly, or sisterly friend—I must beg you to leave me now, and let me alone hereafter: in fact, we must be strangers for the future."

75   "I will, then—be your friend, or brother, or anything you wish, if you will only let me continue to see you; but tell me why I cannot be anything more?" There was a perplexed and thoughtful pause. "Is it in consequence of some rash vow?"

"It is something of the kind," she answered. "Some day I
80   may tell you, but at present you had better leave me; and never, Gilbert, put me to the painful necessity of repeating what I have just now said to you," she earnestly added, giving me her hand in serious kindness.

How sweet, how musical my own name sounded in her
85   mouth!

"I will not," I replied. "But you pardon this offence?"

"On condition that you never repeat it."

"And may I come to see you now and then?"

"Perhaps—occasionally; provided you never abuse the
90   privilege."

"I make no empty promises, but you shall see."

"The moment you do our intimacy is at an end, that's all."

"And will you always call me Gilbert? It sounds more sisterly, and it will serve to remind me of our contract."

95   She smiled, and once more bid me go; and at length I judged it prudent to obey, and she re-entered the house and I went down the hill.

Passage B
by Charlotte Brontë

The vehemence of emotion, stirred by grief and love within me, was claiming mastery, and struggling for full sway, and asserting a right to predominate, to overcome, to live, rise, and reign at last: yes,—and to speak.

5   "I grieve to leave Thornfield: I love Thornfield:—I love it, because I have lived in it a full and delightful life,—momentarily at least. I have not been trampled on. I have not been petrified. I have not been buried with inferior minds, and excluded from every glimpse of communion with what is
10   bright and energetic and high. I have talked, face to face, with what I reverence, with what I delight in,—with an original, a vigorous, an expanded mind. I have known you, Mr. Rochester; and it strikes me with terror and anguish to feel I absolutely must be torn from you for ever. I see the
15   necessity of departure; and it is like looking on the necessity of death."

"Where do you see the necessity?" he asked suddenly.

"Where? You, sir, have placed it before me."

"In what shape?"

20   "In the shape of Miss Ingram; a noble and beautiful woman,—your bride."

"My bride! What bride? I have no bride!"

"But you will have."

"Yes;—I will!—I will!" He set his teeth.

25   "Then I must go:—you have said it yourself."

"No: you must stay! I swear it—and the oath shall be kept."

"I tell you I must go!" I retorted, roused to something like passion. "Do you think I can stay to become nothing to you? Do you think I am an automaton?—a machine without
30   feelings? and can bear to have my morsel of bread snatched from my lips, and my drop of living water dashed from my cup? Do you think, because I am poor, obscure, plain, and little, I am soulless and heartless? You think wrong!—I have as much soul as you,—and full as much heart! And if God
35   had gifted me with some beauty and much wealth, I should have made it as hard for you to leave me, as it is now for me to leave you. I am not talking to you now through the medium of custom, conventionalities, nor even of mortal flesh;—it is my spirit that addresses your spirit; just as if both had passed
40   through the grave, and we stood at God's feet, equal,—as we are!"

"As we are!" repeated Mr. Rochester—"so," he added, enclosing me in his arms. Gathering me to his breast, pressing his lips on my lips: "so, Jane!"

Questions 1–4 ask about Passage A.

1.   The main idea of this passage is:

   A.   Gilbert enjoys being neighborly and visiting Mrs. Graham.

   B.   Mrs. Graham wants Gilbert to leave her alone.

   C.   Gilbert is using her son Arthur to make a good impression on Mrs. Graham.

   D.   Gilbert Markham is determined to pursue Mrs. Graham, despite her reticence.

2. Which of the following moments in the passage represents a tonal shift in the dynamic between Gilbert and Mrs. Graham?

F. When Arthur runs to ask Mrs. Graham to come out and speak to Gilbert

G. When Gilbert takes Mrs. Graham's hand after she offers him a rose

H. When Gilbert finally comes up with an excuse to come visit Mrs. Graham

J. When Mrs. Graham and Gilbert walk in the garden and talk comfortably

3. According to the passage, we can infer that Gilbert is all of the following EXCEPT:

A. infatuated with Mrs. Graham.

B. manipulative.

C. determined.

D. spontaneous.

4. What is the reader meant to infer from Mrs. Graham's abrupt change in demeanor?

F. She really doesn't like Gilbert.

G. She feels awkward about socializing romantically in front of her son.

H. She is hiding something.

J. Gilbert has unwittingly offended her.

Questions 5–8 ask about Passage B.

5. Jane confesses her feelings to Rochester because:

A. she believes he's in love with her.

B. her passionate nature overcomes her sense of propriety.

C. she wants to manipulate him into letting her stay.

D. she wants him to call off his wedding.

6. In line 9, *communion* most nearly means:

F. a religious ritual.

G. a collaborative mode of living.

H. an exchange of intimate feelings.

J. the recognition of a central authority.

7. Charlotte Brontë may have selected to tell this scene from Jane's point of view for all of the following reasons EXCEPT:

A. to illustrate the strength of Jane's character.

B. to maintain the mystery surrounding Rochester's past.

C. to reveal Jane's insecurities about her position relative to Rochester's.

D. to instill a sense of magical realism.

8. According to the passage, which of the following would Rochester MOST likely recommend as a successful way to show romantic interest in another person?

F. Inventing an imaginary romantic partner to make your love interest jealous.

G. Signing up for the same classes as the object of your affections.

H. Engineering a meeting outside in a romantic wooded area.

J. Having a frank and friendly conversation about your feelings.

Questions 9 and 10 ask about both passages.

9. Compared to the first passage, the characters in the second passage are:

A. more in love than Gilbert and Mrs. Graham are.

B. less bound by social convention.

C. not hiding anything from one another.

D. parodying the romance novel genre.

10. Considering Charlotte and Anne Brontë were living and writing at the same time, what can you conclude about the difference in their respective styles from these two excerpts?

F. Charlotte's work was more passionately romantic; Anne's work was more grimly realistic.

G. Anne's novel was more innovative; Charlotte's was more traditional.

H. Charlotte's work was influenced by real life; Anne's was based solely in her imagination.

J. Anne's novels were less sensational; Charlotte's were more scandalous.

PASSAGE II

HUMANITIES: This passage is excerpted from the introduction to *The Autobiography of Benjamin Franklin*.

The thing that makes Franklin's *Autobiography* different from every other life story of a great and successful man is the human aspect of the account. Franklin told the story of his life, as he himself says, for the benefit of his posterity. He
5 wanted to help them by the relation of his own rise from obscurity and poverty to eminence and wealth. *He is not unmindful of the importance of his public services and their recognition, yet his accounts of these achievements are given only as a part of the story, and the vanity displayed is incidental*
10 *and in keeping with the honesty of the recital.* There is nothing of the impossible in the method and practice of Franklin as

he sets them forth. The youth who reads the fascinating story is astonished to find that Franklin in his early years struggled with the same everyday passions and difficulties that he

15 himself experiences, and he loses the sense of discouragement that comes from a realization of his own shortcomings and inability to attain....

The life of Benjamin Franklin is of importance to every American primarily because of the part he played in securing

20 the independence of the United States and in establishing it as a nation. Franklin shares with Washington the honors of the Revolution, and of the events leading to the birth of the new nation. While Washington was the animating spirit of the struggle in the colonies, Franklin was its ablest

25 champion abroad. To Franklin's cogent reasoning and keen satire, we owe the clear and forcible presentation of the American case in England and France; while to his personality and diplomacy as well as to his facile pen, we are indebted for the French alliance and the funds without which

30 Washington's work must have failed. His patience, fortitude, and practical wisdom, coupled with self-sacrificing devotion to the cause of his country, are hardly less noticeable than similar qualities displayed by Washington. In fact, Franklin as a public man was much like Washington, especially in the

35 entire disinterestedness of his public service....

Franklin is a good type of our American manhood. Although not the wealthiest or the most powerful, he is undoubtedly, in the versatility of his genius and achievements, the greatest of our self-made men. The simple yet

40 graphic story in the *Autobiography* of his steady rise from humble boyhood in a tallow-chandler shop, by industry, economy, and perseverance in self-improvement, to eminence, is the most remarkable of all the remarkable histories of our self-made men. It is in itself a wonderful illustration

45 of the results possible to be attained in a land of unequaled opportunity by following Franklin's maxims.... Franklin has indeed been aptly called "many-sided." He was eminent in science and public service, in diplomacy and in literature. He was the Edison of his day, turning his scientific discoveries

50 to the benefit of his fellow-men. He perceived the identity of lightning and electricity and set up the lightning rod. He invented the Franklin stove, still widely used, and refused to patent it. He possessed a masterly shrewdness in business and practical affairs. Carlyle called him the father of all the

55 Yankees. He founded a fire company, assisted in founding a hospital, and improved the cleaning and lighting of streets. He developed journalism, established the American Philosophical Society, the public library in Philadelphia, and the University of Pennsylvania. He organized a postal system

60 for the colonies, which was the basis of the present United States Post Office. Bancroft, the eminent historian, called

him "the greatest diplomatist of his century." He perfected the Albany Plan of Union for the colonies. He is the only statesman who signed the Declaration of Independence,

65 the Treaty of Alliance with France, the Treaty of Peace with England, and the Constitution. As a writer, he has produced, in his *Autobiography* and in *Poor Richard's Almanac*, two works that are not surpassed by similar writing. He received honorary degrees from Harvard and Yale in the United States,

70 from Oxford and St. Andrews in England, and was made a fellow of the Royal Society, which awarded him the Copley gold medal for improving natural knowledge. He was one of the eight foreign associates of the French Academy of Science....

75 Franklin's place in literature is hard to determine because he was not primarily a literary man. His aim in his writings as in his life work was to be helpful to his fellow-men. For him writing was never an end in itself, but always a means to an end. Yet his success as a scientist, a statesman, and a

80 diplomat, as well as socially, was in no little part due to his ability as a writer. "His letters charmed all, and made his correspondence eagerly sought. His political arguments were the joy of his party and the dread of his opponents. His scientific discoveries were explained in language at once so

85 simple and so clear that plow-boy and exquisite could follow his thought or his experiment to its conclusion."...

... Franklin was essentially a journalist. In his swift, terse style, he is most like Daniel Defoe, who in addition to writing *Robinson Crusoe*, was the first great English journalist and

90 master of the newspaper narrative. The style of both writers is marked by homely, vigorous expression, satire, burlesque, repartee. Here the comparison must end. Defoe and his contemporaries were authors. Their vocation was writing and their success rests on the imaginative or creative power

95 they displayed. To authorship Franklin laid no claim. He wrote no work of the imagination. He developed only incidentally a style in many respects as remarkable as that of his English contemporaries. He wrote the best autobiography in existence, one of the most widely known collections of maxims,

100 and an unsurpassed series of political and social satires, because he was a man of unusual scope of power and usefulness, who knew how to tell his fellow-men the secrets of that power and that usefulness.

11. Based on the passage, Ben Franklin was responsible for invention or innovation in all of the following areas EXCEPT:

A. the cleaning and lighting of streets.

B. the implementation of a postal system.

C. the development of a new kitchen stove.

D. the establishment of a national bank.

12. The author characterizes Benjamin Franklin's rise "from obscurity and poverty to eminence and wealth" in order to:

F. diminish his status as a member of early America's elite.

G. encourage young readers who might be struggling with the same issues Franklin did as a young man.

H. dispel the myth that Franklin was born to be a leader.

J. explain why Franklin was so dedicated to spreading knowledge of his discoveries.

13. The phrase, "Although not the… the greatest of our self-made men." (lines 37–39) marks a shift in the passage from:

A. a consideration of his impoverished early years to his wealth and consequence in later life.

B. an examination of his long-term contributions to society to the presentation of his smaller reforms and initiatives.

C. a domestic perspective on Franklin to a survey of his international reputation abroad.

D. a discussion of Franklin's patriotic public service to a recounting of his varied literary and scientific discoveries.

14. Benjamin Franklin received honorary degrees from which of the following American universities?

F. Harvard

G. Stanford

H. Oxford

J. King's College

15. One of the author's main points about Benjamin Franklin in this passage is:

A. he was more essential to the American Revolution than George Washington.

B. he is the only statesman who signed the Declaration of Independence, the Treaty of Alliance with France, the Treaty of Peace with England, and the Constitution.

C. his contributions to early America were so varied and significant that everyone should read his autobiography.

D. his autobiography was hugely important at the time of its publication but has little to offer young activists and writers today.

16. According to the author of the passage, Franklin is responsible for the:

F. reconciliation of England and its former colonies.

G. foreign alliance with and funding from France.

H. popularity of autobiography as a genre.

J. invention of satire.

17. From the tone and content of this passage, you can reasonably infer that its purpose was to:

A. elevate Benjamin Franklin to equal status with George Washington.

B. serve as an introduction to Franklin's autobiography.

C. consign Franklin's life and work to its appropriate place in history.

D. reimagine Franklin as a journalist instead of a statesman.

18. Compared to novelist Daniel Defoe, Franklin:

F. was less gifted as a writer.

G. had more imagination and creativity.

H. used writing as a means to an end, rather than as a craft unto itself.

J. was wittier and more prolific.

19. Which of the following best reflects the definition of *exquisite* as used in line 85?

A. Extremely beautiful and, typically, delicate person

B. A person with intense feelings

C. A highly sensitive or discriminating person

D. A man who is affectedly concerned with his clothes and appearance; a dandy

20. "He is not unmindful… the honesty of the recital" (lines 6–10) indicates that compared to the author's expectation, Benjamin Franklin's attitude toward his own accomplishments was:

F. vain, self-aggrandizing, and boastful.

G. humble, focused on improving posterity.

H. bemused, as though they happened by accident.

J. resentful, because he was disappointed not to obtain more recognition.

ANSWERS AND EXPLANATIONS

1. **The correct answer is D.** Choice A is incorrect because it does not recognize Gilbert's deliberate intentions (he even says "invasion"!) in selecting a book to loan Mrs. Graham or complimenting her gardens. You might select choice B if you noticed that Mrs. Graham was avoiding Gilbert in the opening paragraph, but she appears to be happy to see him until he starts giving her romantic hints. Similarly, Gilbert certainly *is* using Arthur to get close to Mrs. Graham (choice C), but it is not the main idea of this passage.

2. **The correct answer is G.** To quote Anne Brontë, "She let me hold it for a moment, and I saw a flash of ecstatic brilliance in her eye, a glow of glad excitement on her face—I thought my hour of victory was come—but instantly a painful recollection seemed to flash upon her; a cloud of anguish darkened her brow, a marble paleness blanched her cheek and lip; there seemed a moment of inward conflict, and, with a sudden effort, she withdrew her hand, and retreated a step or two back." Before this moment, they're enjoying one another's company. Afterward, Mrs. Graham is putting Gilbert at arm's length and making him promise to stay there. Choices F, H, and J represent increases in their intimacy, rather than a tonal shift.

3. **The correct answer is D.** Gilbert is frank about having fallen in love with Mrs. Graham, deliberate about his machinations to get close to her, and insistent about maintaining their burgeoning friendship, choices A, B, and C respectively. The fact that he's been seeking opportunities to drop by or meet her by chance suggests he's more scheming than spontaneous.

4. **The correct answer is H.** The "radiant smiles" with which Mrs. Graham greets Gilbert signal that she actually does like him, so choice F is incorrect; Gilbert even notices that having Arthur around helps them both relax and be less formal, so choice G is incorrect, as well. She offers him her hand in "serious kindness" even after telling him not to behave romantically, so choice J is not correct either. This is instead a moment of foreshadowing before the reveal of Mrs. Graham's big secret a few chapters later.

5. **The correct answer is B.** In the opening paragraph, Jane describes the warring emotions she's feeling, and in paragraph 12, she defiantly describes their equal status, despite their difference in social status. Choice A is incorrect because there is no evidence she thinks Rochester might reciprocate her feelings. Choice C is

incorrect because it is not supported by the passage—Jane is defiantly insisting she will go to Ireland despite her feelings, not trying to convince Rochester to ask her to remain in his employ. Choice D is incorrect for similar reasons—there is no indication Jane expects Rochester to cancel his engagement.

6. **The correct answer is H.** The clues to this answer lie in the context; Jane remarks she has been surrounded by "what is bright and energetic and high" and had the chance to engage with Rochester's "original...vigorous... and expanded mind." Choice F is incorrect—this may be the most recognizable meaning of *communion*, but given the context, it is not the correct choice. Choice G is incorrect because the idea of communal living is not supported by the passage. Choice J is incorrect because there is no discussion of a higher religious or governing authority.

7. **The correct answer is D.** Presenting the scene from Jane's perspective allows readers to see her determined and passionate character (choice A), and her awareness of the gap of age, wealth, and experience between herself and Rochester. It even successfully keeps Rochester and his intentions mysterious (choice B). However, there is no sense of magical realism in the passage.

8. **The correct answer is F.** Based on his behavior in this passage, Rochester has been pretending he intends to marry someone else in order to provoke Jane into declaring her feelings. He shies away from doing anything direct like talking directly to Jane about his feelings (choice J) or arranging a rendezvous (choice H). Finding out your love interest's schedule (choice G), Rochester might suggest, can backfire if you come across as anything less than favorable.

9. **The correct answer is B.** You can determine this by Jane's description of herself as "poor, obscure, plain, and little" yet spiritually equal to her wealthy noble employer. In contrast, Gilbert and Mrs. Graham are tightly bound by social mores. There is not enough context to determine whether Rochester and Jane are hiding anything from one another (choice C), and there's no way to measure whether they are more in love. The intensity and sincerity of the prose makes it unlikely this is a parody scene (choice D)—nothing is ridiculous or played for laughs at the characters' expense.

393

Chapter 10

Literary
Narrative/
Prose Fiction
and
Humanities
Passages

10. **The correct answer is F.** Both Charlotte and Anne's work, as represented by these scenes, had innovative elements—the way Charlotte's poor governess is allowed to speak openly to her high-status employer, the way Anne thwarted the typical script for a love scene—as well as traditional components—Mrs. Graham guarding her honor, Mr. Rochester being brooding and vague, so choices G and J are incorrect. There is not enough information in these passages to know which novel was influenced more by the authors' lives.

11. **The correct answer is D.** The passage mentions Franklin's contributions to city street maintenance (choice A), the post office (choice B), and the invention of the Franklin stove (choice C), but while he worked in a chandler's (or candle merchant) shop, there's no mention of his involvement in the establishment of a national bank.

12. **The correct answer is G.** In the opening paragraph, the author writes, "The youth who reads the fascinating story is astonished to find that Franklin in his early years struggled with the same everyday passions and difficulties that he himself experiences, and he loses the sense of discouragement that comes from a realization of his own shortcomings and inability to attain." Choice F is incorrect because based on the amount of praise and appreciation in it, nothing in the passage is intended to diminish Benjamin Franklin. Choice H is incorrect because there is no common wisdom that Franklin was born to power or wealth. Choice J is incorrect because correlation is not causation—being a self-made man may well have factored into Franklin's interest in making his discoveries public, but the passage does not make this conjecture.

13. **The correct answer is D.** The author opens with Franklin's best-known accomplishments during the American Revolution and immediately afterward, then moves to his lesser-known but equally long-lasting achievements. Choice A is incorrect because Franklin's wealth is not the motive for the shift; choice B is incorrect because the author repeatedly makes the point that Franklin's contributions endure across the spectrum and that some of his less-nationalistic works are the most significant. Choice C is incorrect because the passage adopts the opposite approach, moving from Franklin's international influence to his domestic presence.

14. **The correct answer is F.** Read the question carefully—it asks for American universities only. Choices G and J are not mentioned in the passage, and Oxford University

(choice H) is in England, so Harvard is the only correct answer.

15. **The correct answer is C.** Choice C reflects the most accurate big-picture summary of the author's attitude toward Benjamin Franklin. Choice A is broad, but not accurate; choice B is accurate but has too narrow a focus. Choice D is not supported by the passage—the author seems to believe the opposite.

16. **The correct answer is G.** The author of the passage says, "while to his personality and diplomacy as well as to his facile pen, we are indebted for the French alliance and the funds without which Washington's work must have failed." Choice F is incorrect; if anything, Franklin's satire and public writing helped make the American colonies' case for independence. Choice H is incorrect—while the passage cites Franklin's autobiography as among the greatest, he does not get credit for its invention; the same goes for his work with satire (choice J).

17. **The correct answer is B.** The passage functions as an overview of the *Autobiography*, with an explicit argument for the work's significance in literature and history. Choice A is incorrect; though the author repeatedly mentions the two together in paragraph 3, it was not the purpose of the passage. Choice C is incorrect because there is no indication the author was trying to diminish or cut Franklin's legacy down to size—on the contrary, he makes every effort to highlight its extraordinary (yet attainable) aspects. Choice D is incorrect because the author repeatedly reflects on the multifaceted nature of Franklin's life and achievements.

18. **The correct answer is H.** The author compares Franklin and Defoe in terms of style and ability, but distinguishes between them on the basis of writing as a tool versus as a vocation. Choice F is incorrect because the author clearly regards them as equal practitioners with different intentions. Choice G is incorrect because the author says, "Defoe and his contemporaries were authors. Their vocation was writing and their success rests on the imaginative or creative power they displayed. To authorship Franklin laid no claim," meaning he used the world around him to inspire his writing, not his imagination. Choice J is incorrect because the author did not compare the sizes of the literary output of the two writers, and clearly both writers are witty.

394

Chapter 10

Literary
Narrative/
Prose Fiction
and
Humanities
Passages

19. **The correct answer is D.** The context clue is the intended contrast in the comparison with the plow boy—a plow boy could be beautiful (choice A), have intense feelings (choice B), or be sensitive (choice C), but is not generally defined as someone concerned with their appearance or personal style.

20. **The correct answer is G.** The author acknowledges Franklin was aware of the importance of his accomplishments, which rules out choices H and J, but the use of *yet* suggests the author might have expected Franklin to brag about his achievements, when in fact his intention was to provide future generations with tools to succeed.

395

Chapter 10

Literary
Narrative/
Prose Fiction
and
Humanities
Passages

Peterson's ACT® Prep Guide

PART VI: SCIENCE STRATEGIES FOR THE ACT®

Chapter 11: Data Representation

Chapter 12: Research Summaries

Chapter 13: Conflicting Viewpoints

SCIENCE STRATEGIES FOR THE ACT®

Each section of the ACT tests a wide array of knowledge and problem-solving skills, and the Science test is no different. The ACT Science test focuses on your ability to consider science-based questions. You will use your general knowledge of the natural sciences and call upon your reading comprehension, data analysis, and reasoning skills to understand experiments presented to you, interpret and analyze data, and draw logical conclusions. You will be given 35 minutes to complete 40 questions in this section.

The ACT Science test covers a very wide range of material, focusing on the four main natural science disciplines:

- **Biology,** the study of life and living organisms. The field of biology includes a wide range of topics that includes cells, genetics, evolution, taxonomy, anatomy and physiology, and ecology.

- **Chemistry,** the study of matter, including its structure, properties, and reactivity. At its most basic, chemistry examines elements and atoms, which form chemical bonds to create molecules. Both elements and molecules can undergo chemical reactions that change their identities and properties.

- **Physics** is also the study of matter, but physics is more concerned with the relationship between matter and energy. As such, physics includes the study of such topics as mechanics (motion), radiation, and gravity.

- **Earth and space sciences.** Earth science, or geoscience, refers to the study of our home planet, including its composition and atmosphere. Space science, or astronomy, expands this range of knowledge to include the sun and planets of our solar system, along with the universe that exists beyond the boundaries of the Milky Way galaxy.

Together, these four disciplines (biology, chemistry, physics, and earth and space sciences) will provide the content of the ACT Science test, but your ability to reason through topics in these areas will be the main indicator of your success on the test.

While it's true that this section will require some recall of the science you have learned, the fact is that recall is *not* the most important aspect of this test. You won't be expected to have memorized the chemical formula of magnesium tungstate or the name of Saturn's second largest satellite ($MgWO_4$ and Rhea, FYI). As far as information recall goes, you will be responsible only for knowing the basics in each of the four main science disciplines. What is far more important is your ability to *apply* what you know about these disciplines and reason through these applications. For example, you might be asked to interpret a data table that tells you about the phenotypes associated with a number of different genotypes. In order to answer this question, you will need to know the basics about what genes are, and what the words *genotype* and *phenotype* mean.

TIP

It definitely will be helpful to look over books and notes from the natural science classes you have taken throughout high school. Reviewing topics you've studied over the course of your high school career can make these topics seem less scary or imposing if you happen to encounter them on the ACT Science test.

But here's another inside tip: even if you didn't know what these vocabulary words meant, you will be presented with enough information in the passage that you could probably figure it out. The take-home message here is that you can certainly study the various scientific disciplines in order to become familiar again with topics you've studied in the past, but you will not be expected to know everything about every scientific discipline. The most important skills to practice as you prepare for the ACT Science test are your problem-solving and reasoning skills, because most of the questions you'll encounter on this test fall under this category. That's where Part VI of this book comes in handy.

NOTE: There will not be any advanced mathematics on the science test, and you will not be permitted to use a calculator.

So how will the ACT Science test assess your ability to think analytically? There are three types of questions that you will encounter as you make your way through the test: Data Representation, Research Summaries, and Conflicting Viewpoints.

Data Representation questions will provide you with tables or graphs that contain scientific data, just like you would find if you were to read a science journal. These questions will require you to examine the data, figure out what information is provided by the data, and draw conclusions based on this information.

Research Summary questions focus more on experimental design and the results of these experiments. This is where you will come across questions that ask you to think about science procedures and reason through how they can help you answer particular questions. You may also be asked to analyze the results of these experiments.

Conflicting Viewpoints questions will give you a few different viewpoints or hypotheses that are not consistent. Your job will be to compare these viewpoints and analyze whether or not the viewpoints are valid. Conflicting Viewpoints questions are just like a scientific debate; you get the opportunity to be the judge and determine if the arguments are supported by scientific knowledge or experimental data.

The next three chapters of this book will provide you with an in-depth look at each of these three ACT Science test question types, with each chapter focusing exclusively on one of the three. Each chapter will include a description of what the question type entails and what the passages are like, a walkthrough of the concepts tested for the question type and how to handle them, common mistakes made, and examples of how to reason through answers from sample passages. There will also be a practice set at the end of each chapter that will give you the opportunity to practice each question type, and then you can check your answers when you're finished.

When it comes to the ACT Science test, the best way to prepare is to practice. If you know what to expect when you walk in on test day, you'll be much less nervous and much more confident because you will know exactly how to think about the questions you're about to see. Let's get started!

CHAPTER 11:
DATA REPRESENTATION

OVERVIEW

- What Information Does the Figure Provide?
- What Conclusions Can I Draw from the Data?
- How Can I Analyze the Data Graphically?
- How Valid Is This Data?
- What Additional Experiments Can Be Done Based on the Data?
- Common Traps in the Science Test
- Summing It Up
- Practice

On the ACT Science test, you will be able to recognize Data Representation questions immediately because you will usually see some kind of a graph, scatterplot, figure, or table that you will be required to understand and interpret. Data Representation questions—which comprise 30 to 40 percent of ACT Science test questions—tend to be rather straightforward conceptually, so the key to answering these questions is figuring out what the data actually means and what conclusions can be drawn.

A Data Representation passage always begins with a written introduction that presents the scientific topic covered or question that is being asked, provides some key terminology, and introduces the data you will have to analyze. The introduction paragraph is usually no longer than a few sentences or so; this is because the most important part of a Data Representation passage is the diagram, figure, or chart. In addition to the introduction paragraph, most passages will include an additional written paragraph (or a few paragraphs) to provide details about the experiment and the data.

Each Data Representation passage is usually accompanied by five questions that test you on several key skills in data analysis: understanding the data, drawing conclusions from the data, analyzing graphical figures, assessing the validity of the data, and thinking about future work based on the data. To tackle Data Representation questions, you will have to ask yourself several (or all) of the following questions, each of which is accompanied by a very simple example to give you an idea of how the questions might appear when you're taking the ACT Science test.

If the written portions of a Data Representation question are confusing, the visuals can usually help you to figure out what is going on in the described scenario.

WHAT INFORMATION DOES THE FIGURE PROVIDE?

This question is the launching point of your data analysis. In order to answer any of the questions in a set, you have to be able to look at the provided figure and determine what it is telling you. Once you are able to read a figure and extract information from it, you can start to draw conclusions and think about the data critically.

When you are attempting to read a figure, the best way to start is to read the introductory and surrounding paragraphs and determine the question the data is supposed to answer; in other words, what is the purpose of the experiment being conducted? Every scientific experiment is performed in order to answer some kind of scientific question—that question will almost always be directly addressed in these paragraphs. The paragraphs may also include a **hypothesis**, which is an educated prediction about the outcome of the experiment. Alternatively, you might be asked to choose a logical hypothesis for the given experiment in the questions themselves.

TIP It may help to circle key words as you read the introductory and surrounding paragraphs to help you zoom in on the most important concepts.

The introductory and surrounding paragraphs may also provide details about the independent variable and dependent variable in the experiment. The **independent variable** is the condition that the experimenter is altering throughout the experiment, while the **dependent variable** is the condition that the experimenter is measuring throughout the experiment. Any conditions that do not change throughout the experiment, regardless of changes made in the independent variable, are called **constants**. Experiments may also include a **control variable**, which is an experimental trial that minimizes the effect of whatever the independent variable is testing.

For example, say an experiment is testing the effect of five different temperatures on the growth rate of pea plants.

- The independent variable is temperature.
- The dependent variable is the change in pea plant height.
- Constants might include amount of sunlight and amount of water provided because all pea plants receive the same amounts of each.
- A possible control variable could be a pea plant grown under the same conditions as the others, but at standard room temperature.

If you find the introductory and surrounding paragraphs confusing in a Data Representation question, or if you don't understand some of the terminology or vocabulary used, don't worry! Here's a neat insight: the figure itself can tell you all you need to know. If the figure is a diagram or picture, examine it closely, focusing on what is actually happening in the experiment and what is being measured. If the figure is a table, look at the headers along the top of the table to see which variables are being changed or measured. Usually, the headers in a table will include the independent and dependent variables. If the figure is a graph or scatterplot, look at the axes; the *y*-axis (the vertical axis) will usually be the dependent variable, while the *x*-axis (the horizontal axis) will usually be the independent variable. Understanding the passages will definitely help you to understand the specifics of the experiment more easily, but most of the time, you can figure out what is happening in the experiment based on the diagrams and figures alone.

Take a look at the following practice question. We will use the same passage and data throughout the first few examples in this chapter so you can get a sense of the different question types that will come up within a Data Representation set.

Five pea plants were planted in identical pots containing the same amount and type of soil. Each plant was placed in temperature-controlled boxes at different temperatures ranging from 0 to 80°C. Each plant was provided with the same sunlight exposure and volume of water at the same times each day. The height of each plant was measured and recorded at 12 p.m. every eighth day.

Pea Plant Air Temperature (°C)	Pea Plant Height (cm) After x Days				
	0	8	16	24	32
0°	0	5.2	20.2	26.0	34.3
20°	0	5.3	23.4	28.2	35.0
40°	0	3.2	17.5	22.4	25.7
60°	0	2.7	13.0	15.2	19.0
80°	0	1.2	8.8	12.3	14.2

Which of the following would be an appropriate hypothesis for this experiment?

- **A.** If pea plants tend to favor colder temperatures, then increasing the air temperature will result in faster growth rates.
- **B.** If pea plants tend to favor colder temperatures, then increasing the air temperature will result in slower growth rates.
- **C.** If pea plants tend to favor colder temperatures, then increased water volume will result in faster growth rates.
- **D.** If pea plants tend to favor colder temperatures, then increased water volume will result in slower growth rates.

The correct answer is B. The introduction tells us that the five plants are grown under identical conditions, with the exception of varying temperatures, and that plant height was measured every eight days. That means that the independent variable is temperature, because temperature is the condition that the experimenter is changing. We can also see that the dependent variable is plant height, because this is the variable that the experimenter is measuring. Both of these variables appear in the table; the independent variable is the header of the first column, while the dependent variable is the header of the rest of the columns. So even if we had no idea what the introductory paragraph was discussing, we can determine the scientific question simply by looking at the provided table. Since the experimenter is measuring the changes in height over time, or the growth rates, of pea plants grown at different temperatures, the scientific question might be: *How does temperature affect the growth rate of pea plants?*

The question asks us to choose an appropriate hypothesis. We have to choose a hypothesis that provides a predicted answer to the scientific question we've just asked. If we look at the four possible answer choices, we can immediately rule out both choice C and choice D. These choices both provide predictions that involve changes in water volume, which the passage explicitly states was *not* changed. Choices A and B both relate to temperature. The first part of each hypothesis is "If pea plants tend to favor colder temperatures…" The logical prediction would be that if pea plants favor colder temperatures, they will grow more quickly at lower temperatures.

403

Chapter 11

Data Representation

WHAT CONCLUSIONS CAN I DRAW FROM THE DATA?

Once you've successfully read a figure and determined its purpose, you will almost always be asked to use the figure to answer questions or draw conclusions. When examining a data set, you will probably notice patterns and trends. Recognizing these trends will be extremely helpful when you're trying to draw conclusions because the conclusions will usually be based on these observations. Questions that ask you to draw conclusions from the data might ask you to describe a pattern from the data, to predict a result that is not displayed in the figure, or to apply the data to a different but relevant scenario. Patterns and trends in the data will usually be fairly straightforward; for instance, if a few different conditions are tested for a particular independent variable, the results for each condition will be distinctive enough for you to tell them apart and draw conclusions.

If you're a visual thinker, you will probably have an easier time seeing trends and patterns in graphs or scatterplots. These kinds of figures show rather than tell—you will be able to see a line with a positive slope on a graph, or a progressive decrease in magnitude of a variable on a scatterplot. If you're better with numbers, you might prefer tables, on which you can compare values for different conditions. Regardless, you can always convert tables to graphs and vice versa. For example, if you're struggling to understand a scatterplot, you can write up your own small table with numerical estimates of the values from the scatterplot. Or if you're given a table and prefer a graph, you can always sketch a small graphical version of the numbers you've been given.

Once you've figured out the pattern or trend specified in the question, you can apply that trend to answer the question. If a question asks you directly about the trend, choose the answer that most accurately describes the pattern you found. If a question asks you to predict a result that is not given in the figure, you can apply the trend accordingly and predict how the new condition will compare to the conditions provided. If you're asked to apply that trend to a new situation altogether, simply imagine the use of that trend in the new situation and predict how it will apply.

Let's take a look at an example in action.

Five pea plants were planted in identical pots containing the same amount and type of soil. Each plant was placed in temperature-controlled boxes at different temperatures ranging from 0 to 80°C. Each plant was provided with the same sunlight exposure and volume of water at the same times each day. The height of each plant was measured and recorded every eighth day at 12 p.m.

Pea Plant Air Temperature (°C)	Pea Plant Height (cm) After x Days				
	0	8	16	24	32
0°	0	5.2	20.2	26.0	34.3
20°	0	5.3	23.4	28.2	35.0
40°	0	3.2	17.5	22.4	25.7
60°	0	2.7	13.0	15.2	19.0
80°	0	1.2	8.8	12.3	14.2

If you were to grow a pea plant under the same conditions at 50°C, during which time period would you expect to see the most rapid growth rate?

- **F.** 0–8 days
- **G.** 8–16 days
- **H.** 16–24 days
- **J.** 24–32 days

The correct answer is G. This question asks us to make a prediction about the growth rate of a plant grown at 50°C based on the data provided for these five other temperatures. For each of the five plants described in the table, the most rapid increase in height occurs between 8 days and 16 days. For example, the pea plant grown at 0°C grows 5.2 cm between Day 0 and Day 8, 15.0 cm between Day 8 and Day 16, 5.8 cm between Day 16 and Day 24, and 8.3 cm between Day 24 and Day 32. The largest difference in height over the course of eight days occurs between Day 8 and Day 16. For confirmation, you could repeat this procedure for the plants at the other temperatures. Since this trend is consistently seen for all five plants, which includes plants grown at temperatures above and below 50°C, it would be reasonable to predict that a plant grown at 50°C would also experience its most rapid growth rate between Day 8 and Day 16.

HOW CAN I ANALYZE THE DATA GRAPHICALLY?

Graphs are an extremely useful way to convey scientific data. You will almost certainly be asked to graph data or interpret graphs on the ACT Science test, particularly in Data Representation questions. Therefore, it is important to understand the various types of graphs and how they are used.

On a coordinate plane, graphs consist of points that are plotted based on their location along the x and y axes. (3-D graphs may include a z-axis, directed out of the page at you, but you will rarely, if ever, see these on the ACT Science test.)

Graphs that are straight lines indicate **linear functions**, while curved lines represent **exponential functions**. In linear functions, lines that increase from left to right have positive slopes, while lines that decrease from left to right have negative slopes. A perfectly horizontal line has a slope of zero, while a perfectly vertical line is usually described as "undefined" or "infinite." In exponential functions, the line can also increase or decrease; however, in exponential functions, the line is curved, which means that the slope is not constant. In a positive exponential function, the curve approaches zero (or a minimum) to the left and infinity to the right. In a negative exponential function, the curve approaches zero (or a minimum) to the right and infinity to the left.

The key difference between linear and exponential functions is that linear functions have a constant slope, which means that the change in y value per x value is the *same* for all intervals, while exponential functions have a slope that either increases (positive exponential function) or decreases (negative exponential function) from left to right.

There are other types of graphs, including parabolas (U-shaped graphs) and hyperbolas (curved graphs that approach, but never quite reach, invisible lines called *asymptotes*). However, linear and exponential functions are far and away the most common graphs you'll find on the ACT Science test and are the two types you should focus on when reviewing.

When interpreting a graph, it is important to determine which variable is represented by each axis. If you are given a graph as your figure, this will be quite obvious because the axes will usually be labeled. However, if you are given a table and asked to predict the shape of a graph, it may be a bit trickier. As a general rule, the x-axis is usually the independent variable, or the variable that the experimenter alters, while the y-axis is usually the dependent variable, or the variable that is being measured in the experiment. Once you recognize which variable is which on a table, converting the values into a graphical form is not so difficult. Questions that ask you to analyze graphs might ask you about graph types and shapes, patterns and trends, or axes and variables.

Five pea plants were planted in identical pots containing the same amount and type of soil. Each plant was placed in temperature-controlled boxes at different temperatures ranging from 0 to 80°C. Each plant was provided with the same sunlight exposure and volume of water at the same times each day. The height of each plant was measured and recorded every eighth day at 12 p.m.

Pea Plant Air Temperature (°C)	Pea Plant Height (cm) After x Days				
	0	**8**	**16**	**24**	**32**
0°	0	5.2	20.2	26.0	34.3
20°	0	5.3	23.4	28.2	35.0
40°	0	3.2	17.5	22.4	25.7
60°	0	2.7	13.0	15.2	19.0
80°	0	1.2	8.8	12.3	14.2

Over the course of the first 16 days of height measurement, the growth rate for the pea plants can best be described as:

- **A.** increasing linearly.
- **B.** decreasing linearly.
- **C.** increasing exponentially.
- **D.** decreasing exponentially.

The correct answer is C. This question asks for a graphical type/shape interpretation based on the numbers provided in a table. You can tell if a graph is linear if the measured dependent variable value increases or decreases by the same amount over the same given independent variable interval.

This particular question asks us to look at the shape over the first 16 days. First, let's take a look at Day 0 through Day 8 for the first plant. The height increases by 5.2 cm. Now let's look at Day 8 through Day 16. The height increases by 15.0 cm. Both of these time intervals are eight days, so if this was a linear trend, the height increases should be the same. They are not the same, however, so this must be an exponential trend. We can therefore rule out choice A and choice B because these answers both refer to linear changes. The difference between choice C and choice D is whether the change in height over time is an increase or decrease. Logically, plants don't decrease in height over time, but as always, we just have to look at the numbers for confirmation. The height of each plant increases over time—therefore, we can rule out choice D.

HOW VALID IS THIS DATA?

When it comes to analyzing scientific data, a scientist must always think critically about his or her work in order to determine whether or not the collected information is valid. One common method for assessing data validity is to use statistics. Specifically, scientists look at accuracy and precision in order to get a sense of whether or not their experiment can be trusted.

Accuracy describes the degree to which a numerical measurement or calculation agrees with a known value or standard. For example, let's say a scientist performs a set of experiments to determine the standard heat of formation for liquid water at 25°C. After she does the experiments, the scientist can compare her final measured value to an actual known value because the standard heat of formation for liquid water is a well-established number that has been determined numerous times in the past.

Let's see what this looks like in real time. Just so you know for this experiment, and in case you happen to come across it again, standard heat of formation for any substance is the change in enthalpy (or heat energy) when one mole of a substance is formed from its pure elements under standard conditions. For liquid water at 25°C, the standard heat of formation is −286 kJ/mol, which means that 286 kJ of energy is released when liquid H_2O forms from its pure elements, gaseous H_2 and O_2.

Accuracy can be described numerically using a percent error calculation:

$$\text{Percent Error} = \left| \frac{\text{Known Value} - \text{Measured Value}}{\text{Known Value}} \right| \times 100\%$$

So in this sample experiment, if the scientist experimentally found that the standard heat of formation for liquid water is −143 kJ/mol, the percent error, using the calculation above, would be calculated like this:

$$\text{Percent Error} = \left| \frac{(-286) - (-143)}{(-286)} \right| \times 100\% = 50\%$$

This value tells us that the scientist's experimental value is half, or 50%, of the actual known value. If multiple trials of the same experiment are performed, the measured value you should use here is the **mean**, or average, value of the trials. For example, if the scientist performs two experimental trials to determine the standard heat of formation of liquid water and gets −144 kJ/mol and −142 kJ/mol, the scientist's measured value would be the average of these two values:

$$\text{Average} = \frac{\text{Sum of Values from All Trials}}{\text{Number of Trials}} = \frac{(-144) + (-142)}{2} = -143 \text{ kJ/mol}$$

Scientific research is aimed at learning new information and discovering the undiscovered. Therefore, known values are not always available. Even though you can't always determine accuracy, you *can* always determine precision when multiple trials of the same experiment are performed.

 In most scientific experiments, you will not know an actual value, so you may not always be able to determine accuracy.

Precision describes how close the measured values are to each other for the same kind of experiment. You can often tell if data is precise simply by looking. If the numbers you measure for several trials of the same experiment are close to one another, your data is probably precise. On the other hand, if the numbers don't agree and are not close to one another at all, the data is probably not precise.

When data is more precise, it means that same experiment, when repeated multiple times, yields consistent numbers. It is important in science to be able to repeat the same experiment and get similar results each time because it helps to confirm that a result is not a fluke. This is why scientists conduct the same experiment repeatedly. Each repeated experiment is called a **trial**. Precision can be measured numerically by calculating **standard deviation**, which indicates how far a set of measured numbers are from their average—in this way, standard deviation describes how precise data is.

 You won't have to calculate standard deviations on the ACT; however, it is important to know that a low standard deviation means that the data is generally close to the average and is precise, while a high standard deviation means that the data is less precise.

Data is often considered to be more valid when it is precise, or when the standard deviation is as low as possible. If multiple trials for a particular experiment give precise results, but one trial gives a result that is very different, this data point is called an **outlier**. If you see an outlier for a particular trial, you can usually conclude that an error occurred in this trial because the obtained result was so different from the others.

Remember that you won't have to do any advanced calculations on the ACT Science test. You will usually be able to tell simply by looking at the given values if they are accurate and/or precise. If you come across terms like *mean* and *standard deviation*, you'll be all set if you remember that they refer to accuracy and precision, respectively.

In addition to looking at accuracy and precision, there are other ways to assess data validity. If an experiment is described on the ACT Science test, you might notice a flaw in its design that could cause you to question whether or not the obtained data is valid. For instance, you might notice that the experiment did not control a particular condition while testing another condition, or you might notice that the scientist did not choose the best possible technique to measure a certain value. Observations like these might cause you to question the quality of the results obtained in an experiment.

Another way that the ACT Science test might assess your ability to evaluate data validity is to ask questions about errors that may have occurred during an experiment. For example, you might be asked to suggest an error that would cause the measured value in an experiment to be either too high or too low. Alternatively, you might be asked to predict how a particular error would affect the measured value. For instance, if you are testing the effect of temperature on the growth of a pea plant and you add more water to one plant than to the others, this error could result in a larger height increase for that one plant because it received extra nutrients that the other plants did not receive.

Five pea plants were planted in identical pots containing the same amount and type of soil. Each plant was placed in temperature-controlled boxes at different temperatures ranging from 0 to 80°C. Each plant was provided with the same sunlight exposure and volume of water at the same times each day. The height of each plant was measured and recorded every eighth day at 12 p.m.

Pea Plant Air Temperature (°C)	Pea Plant Height (cm) After x Days				
	0	8	16	24	32
0°	0	5.2	20.2	26.0	34.3
20°	0	5.3	23.4	28.2	35.0
40°	0	3.2	17.5	22.4	25.7
60°	0	2.7	13.0	15.2	19.0
80°	0	1.2	8.8	12.3	14.2

Because the most drastic change in pea plant height was observed at 20°C, the scientist decides to repeat this experiment two additional times. The following plant heights were obtained:

Pea Plant Air Temperature (°C)	Pea Plant Height (cm) After x Days				
	0	8	16	24	32
20°	0	5.2	23.8	28.3	35.2
	0	5.3	23.6	28.2	35.0

Based on the additional trials for pea plant growth at 20°C, it can be concluded that the height data over the 32-day range is:

F. accurate.

G. not accurate.

H. precise.

J. not precise.

The correct answer is H. This question asks you to assess the data among the three 20°C trials for accuracy and precision. This particular experiment is measuring pea plant growth over time. No actual or "known" values are provided, so we can't judge accuracy in this experiment. As such, we can rule out choice F and choice G right away. In order to judge precision, we have to look at the height values among the three trials and see if they are close to one another. At all time points, the height values are very close to one another. Therefore, we can conclude that this data is precise. In general, results that are not precise will be very obvious; for example, one plant might not have grown at all. In this example, however, the numbers are close, so we can say that this data is precise.

WHAT ADDITIONAL EXPERIMENTS CAN BE DONE BASED ON THE DATA?

In scientific research, one experiment usually leads to another experiment; when you learn something new from one experiment, you can do additional experiments to learn more about the topic of interest. Additional experiments can be based on what was learned in the original experiment, or they can test a new variable that was not the focus of the original experiment.

Questions that ask you to suggest additional experiments will often state a goal, and you will have to select the response that would most successfully achieve that goal. In order to answer these questions, identifying the independent and dependent variables will be key. Given a particular goal, you can figure out what you are varying and what you are measuring. Once you have identified these variables, you can look at the answer choices and pick the one that uses these variables.

A good strategy for questions like these is process of elimination. You will often be able to rule out answers describing experiments that very obviously vary the wrong conditions or take the wrong measurement. Questions that ask you to suggest further experimentation are more commonly seen in the Research Summaries passages, but you might see them occasionally in Data Representation questions, so it is best to be prepared!

Five pea plants were planted in identical pots containing the same amount and type of soil. Each plant was placed in temperature-controlled boxes at different temperatures ranging from 0 to 80°C. Each plant was provided with the same sunlight exposure and volume of water at the same times each day. The height of each plant was measured and recorded every eighth day at 12 p.m.

Pea Plant Air Temperature (°C)	Pea Plant Height (cm) After x Days				
	0	8	16	24	32
0°	0	5.2	20.2	26.0	34.3
20°	0	5.3	23.4	28.2	35.0
40°	0	3.2	17.5	22.4	25.7
60°	0	2.7	13.0	15.2	19.0
80°	0	1.2	8.8	12.3	14.2

The scientist wants to focus on which temperature provides the most rapid germination period of pea plant growth. Germination is the process by which a plant sprouts from a seed. This can best be accomplished by:

A. repeating the experiment at 20°C only, varying the soil type between plants.

B. repeating the experiment at all temperatures, measuring plant heights after much smaller time increments.

C. repeating the experiment at all temperatures, using a variety of plant types.

D. repeating the experiment at all temperatures, extending the eight-day measurements to 40 days rather than 32 days.

The correct answer is B. Remember, with the questions that ask you to suggest additional experiments, it is important to identify the independent and dependent variables right away. This question asks you to suggest an experiment that will measure germination rate, or the rate at which the plant sprouts from the seed, at different temperatures. That means that the independent variable will again be temperature, and that the dependent variable will again be plant height. You can therefore rule out choice A, because if you use only one temperature, you cannot compare germination rates between plants at different temperatures. Choice A does not satisfy the desired independent variable. Based on the question alone, you can also rule out choice C. The goal is to look at germination growth rates in pea plants only, so using different plant types at different temperatures will not help to accomplish this goal. Choices B and D both have temperature as the independent variable and plant height as the dependent variable, so you must choose the better answer between the two. Since germination refers to the sprouting of a plant from its seed, the new experiment should focus on the earliest stages of pea plant growth. Based on the original data provided, the plants reach heights of 3–5 centimeters after eight days, so the initial germination process is not included in the original experiment. Extending the overall measurement time to 40 days, as described in choice D, will not accomplish the goal of focusing on germination. Choice B, on the other hand, involves measuring after shorter time periods. The experiment described in choice B involves taking more measurements between 0 and 8 days, which will give a much better sense of how quickly each plant at the different temperatures emerges from its seed.

COMMON TRAPS IN THE SCIENCE TEST

Now that we've gone over Data Representation questions and how to tackle the concepts you'll come across in these types of questions, let's talk about some common pitfalls that test takers encounter in these questions and how to avoid them. Discussing common missteps is important—if you're aware in advance of mistakes that others have made in the past, you can avoid them yourself because you will be aware of what you might come across while answering these kinds of questions.

CHALLENGING TERMINOLOGY

Given the huge range of topics that the ACT Science test can potentially cover, it is likely that you're going to come across a passage describing a subject with which you have little familiarity. Maybe you forgot what mitosis is, or what a double displacement chemical reaction entails. Or you know you've heard the word *capacitance* before but can't quite put your finger on what it means.

First and foremost, it is important that you stay calm and don't assume you won't be able to figure out what an unfamiliar word means. Sometimes the passage will provide you with the definition. In other cases, you will be provided with enough information in the passage to figure out what the word means. In still other cases, you might not even need to determine the definition of the term because it may not be needed to answer the questions. If experimental data provides numbers to show that one liquid has a higher boiling point than another, you don't really need to know what a boiling point is to be able to point out that the boiling point value for Substance A is a higher number than the boiling point value for Substance B.

So if you come across a challenging term in a Data Representation question and have no idea what it means, read the full passage and see if it provides you with any hints about the word's meaning. If it does, proceed with your reading and keep this newly determined definition in mind. If you still don't know what the word means, continue on to the questions and see if you even need to know the precise definition of the word to answer the questions. In the event that you can't figure out a word's definition and you *do* need it to answer a question, make an educated guess about the word's definition given the context. Even if you do come across such a rare word, it is unlikely that more than a question or two will rely on its definition. Enough information will usually be provided in the passage and in the diagrams to help you understand what is going on, so it is unlikely that you will come across a word and have no idea what it describes.

. . . .

Surface tension is an important property of liquids that is caused by cohesion, the attraction of molecules to one another. A scientist wants to compare the surface tension of water, ethanol, and cyclohexane by measuring the number of drops of each liquid she can fit on a small metal disk, which has a small lip around its edge, before the liquid overflows and spills off of the disk. Using an eyedropper that delivers the same volume of liquid per drop, the scientist obtains the following results:

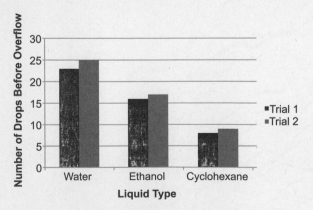

Which of the three tested liquids has the highest surface tension?

    F. Water

    G. Ethanol

    H. Cyclohexane

    J. All three liquids have the same surface tension.

The correct answer is F. This passage describes a surface tension experiment, and the question asks you to draw a conclusion based on the provided data. The question requires that you know what surface tension is, and while the passage explains that surface tension is caused by cohesion, it does not specifically provide its definition. Fortunately, you can figure it out based on the information and data provided. If surface tension is caused by cohesion, the attraction of a liquid's molecules to one another, then it would make sense that a liquid that exhibits higher cohesion also exhibits higher surface tension. In this experiment, the scientist is adding drops of liquid to a disk until the liquid overflows. That means that the liquid with the greatest cohesion, and therefore the highest surface tension, will be the liquid for which more drops can fit on the disk, because if more drops can fit on the disk, it means that the liquid molecules have a greater attraction for one another and are able to stick together longer before falling apart and overflowing off of the disk. Based on the data, a graph, more drops of water are able to fit onto the disk than any other liquid. The liquid, of the three tested liquids, with the highest surface tension is therefore water, so the correct answer is choice F. Even without knowing the exact definition of surface tension when starting the question, you can figure out the answer based on the information provided in the passage.

. . . .

UNNECESSARY INFORMATION

Another common mistake test takers make is getting caught up in extraneous information. Passages might include interesting details about the given topic, or specific tidbits about experimental design. You might find this information interesting, or you might be baffled by its inclusion; either way, if you identify right away that the information is not essential to understanding the passage or the associated questions, cast this information aside for the time being and focus on what is important.

For example, a passage might provide you with some historical information about the discoverer of a particular phenomenon, or a list of properties of a substance. If the provided information does not enhance your understanding of the data provided in the question, then don't spend too much time on this information. Focus on the important information and set the extra details aside. You have 35 minutes to complete 40 questions, and while this is plenty of time to complete the test, it is best to spend your time on the most useful information instead of working through facts you won't actually need to complete the questions.

Max Planck originally proposed the idea of *blackbody radiation* in 1900, suggesting that radiation is quantized. In 1905, Albert Einstein took this concept a step further by describing the *photoelectric effect*, in which radiation is still quantized after absorption by a metal. The photoelectric effect is the observation that when light is shone upon many types of metal, electrons are emitted from the metal. The photoelectric work function is the minimum energy required to eject an electron from the surface of the metal; a photon of light with energy less than the work function will never be able to eject electrons.

An apparatus was set up consisting of an evacuated quartz tube with photosensitive metal plates. The plates were connected separately to negative and positive terminals of a battery, and then they were connected to one another using wires to form a circuit. An ammeter was included in the circuit to measure current. When electrons were ejected by the photosensitive plates, they created a current that was measured by the ammeter. The work functions for three metals, used in the plates, were determined using this setup:

Metal	Work Function (eV)
Aluminum	4.1
Nickel	5.0
Sodium	2.3

If a photon of light of a particular energy strikes the aluminum plate at its work function and creates a current, which of the following must be true?

- **A.** The same light source will eject an electron from the nickel plate only.
- **B.** The same light source will eject an electron from the sodium plate only.
- **C.** The same light source will eject an electron from both the nickel and sodium plates.
- **D.** The same light source will not eject an electron from the nickel or sodium plates.

The correct answer is B. This is a physics question that asks you to look at measured data and apply the definition of a work function to the results. The first two sentences of the first paragraph provide history context for the photoelectric effect. The first sentence mentions blackbody radiation. While this is an important concept in physics, you will realize as you continue reading that this passage focuses on the photoelectric effect. Blackbody radiation studies were critical studies that contributed to discovery of the photoelectric effect, but you need not focus on this at all because it is unrelated to the data presented. The historical information is interesting, but it too is unnecessary for the analysis of the data. It doesn't matter if you don't know what blackbody radiation is; you can move on because the description of blackbody radiation is simply included to provide historical context for the subject of interest, the photoelectric effect.

In answering the provided question, we can use the definition of "work function" provided in the passage. The passage indicates that the photoelectric work function is the minimum energy required to eject an electron from the surface of the metal, so a photon of light with energy less than the work function will never be able to eject electrons. If a photon of light has the energy of aluminum's work function, this same photon of light will *not* be able to eject electrons from metals with a higher work function, but it *will* be able to eject electrons from metals with a lower work function. The work function of nickel is higher than that of aluminum, while the work function of sodium is lower than that of aluminum. Therefore, the photon will be able to eject an electron from a sodium plate, but not from a nickel plate.

UNEXPECTED RESULTS

It is important to not assume you know a result without looking at the data. Why is this? Science experiments do not always work perfectly. There may be design flaws in the procedure or errors that took place during the experiment, all of which could affect results. A simple experiment could give completely unexpected results, and even if it is clear the results are incorrect, it is important to analyze the data.

For example, experimental data in a passage may indicate that ice is more dense than liquid water, even though liquid water is actually more dense than ice; in this case, make sure that if you are asked to draw conclusions based on the data, you draw your conclusions based on the numbers you see rather than on the results you would expect. For the most part, data included on the ACT Science test will be exactly what you would expect. Still, it is important to pay attention to the numbers and not assume a result without looking closely at the data first.

A student mixes canola oil, ethanol, and pure water, three liquids that are immiscible and form three separate layers without mixing, at room temperature. The student's task is to determine which layer is which within the mixture.

The student decides to use density for this experiment. Density is a measure of mass per unit volume. For each liquid, the student removed a sample from the stock and used a balance to measure the mass of the liquid sample by subtracting the mass of the beaker from the combined mass of the beaker and liquid. The student then used a graduated cylinder to measure the volume of each sample. The results are shown in the table:

Liquid Sample Identity	Mass of Liquid (g)	Volume of Liquid (mL)
Canola Oil	9.00	9.92
Ethanol	7.90	10.00
Water	6.00	4.00

Based on the data, the identity of Layer 2 is:

F. canola oil.

G. ethanol.

H. water.

J. either canola oil or ethanol.

The correct answer is F. In order to answer this question, you must estimate the densities of the three liquids. Based on the data provided, canola oil has a density of just over 0.90 g/mL, ethanol has a density of 0.79 g/mL, and water has a density of 2.0 g/mL. (In reality, water has a density of 1.5 g/mL at room temperature, so this number is actually incorrect, but the question must be answered based on the data. In terms of relative densities, this inaccurate number doesn't actually change the order of liquid densities, but it is important still to base conclusions on the data regardless.) Of the three liquids, water has the highest density, canola oil has the second highest density, and ethanol has the lowest density. Therefore, Layer 1 is water, Layer 2 is canola oil, and Layer 3 is ethanol. The question asks you to determine the identity of the liquid in Layer 2, so the correct answer is canola oil (choice F).

Unusual Data Presentation

Sometimes you will see a graph that is not a simple XY scatter, or a table that is more complicated than a few sets of columns. There is no need to feel flustered if you see data presented in an unusual way.

If the test includes a type of data presentation that you've never seen before, focus on the written introduction, because understanding the kind of data collected will help you to hone in on the most important part of the data table or graph. As always, it will very much help to identify the independent and dependent variables in the experiment. Once you've identified these variables, find where each occurs on the data table or graph. A data figure might include extra information that you may need for some questions but not others; while trying to get a handle on the basics of the data figure, ignore any supplementary information and focus on the independent and dependent variables. Simplifying figures in your mind by blocking out extra information is a solid strategy for understanding the basics of an experiment on a data figure that is new to you.

> **TIP** As a general rule, the more complicated or strange a data representation may look, the more explanation you will receive in the introductory or surrounding paragraphs.

Protein X is an enzyme that degrades substrate S in humans. The rate at which Protein X degrades S was studied *in vitro* using UV-vis spectroscopy. A number of solutions were made that contained Protein X at the same concentration. Then, S was added to each solution at overall concentrations that ranged from 0 to 1,400 nM. UV-vis spectroscopy was used to observe the initial rate, over the first five seconds of activity, by which Protein X degraded S in each solution. The initial rates of degradation were graphed as a function of the concentrations of S for the various solutions:

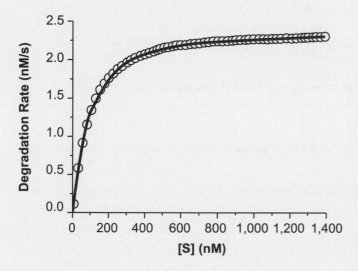

Why does the initial rate of S degradation flatline around 500 nM S?

A. The concentration of Protein X overwhelms the concentration of S at this point, halting the increase in degradation rate.

B. Protein X appears to be inactivated in the presence of 500 nM S, giving a degradation rate of 0 nM/s.

C. The reaction reverses at this point, and S begins to be produced.

D. The concentration of substrate S overwhelms the concentration of Protein X at this point, halting the increase in degradation rate.

The correct answer is D. This passage presents a Michaelis-Menton curve, which is a type of graph used to study the kinetics of protein activity. You've likely never seen a graph like this before, but using the passage and the figure, we can easily determine what is happening here. According to the passage, the independent variable is the substrate concentration, because this is what is different in each sample. This appears on the graph on the *x*-axis. The dependent variable is the initial rate of substrate S degradation, because this is what is being measured. This variable appears on the graph on the *y*-axis. From 0 to 500 nM S, the initial rate of S degradation increases as S concentration increases. From approximately 500 nM S and higher, substrate S is still being degraded, but the rate of degradation is no longer increasing.

Now that you understand the experiment and graph, you can answer the question. The question asks why the graph flatlines around 500 nM S. Remember, the concentration of S is increasing while the concentration of Protein X remains the same. As such, choice A cannot be correct because you are seeing an increase in

S, not Protein X, as you move from left to right on the graph. Choice B states that starting at 500 nM S, the degradation rate is 0 nM/s. While the slope of the line here is approximately 0, the *y*-axis is degradation rate, the dependent variable, and at 500 nM and over, the degradation remains fairly constant at around 2.4 nM/s. Choice B, therefore, is incorrect. Choice C indicates that the reaction reverses, and that substrate S starts to be produced rather than degraded.

This is definitely not true because the degradation rates are all positive, meaning that at every concentration, we are seeing substrate S being degraded. Choice D indicates that the flat curve is a result of the concentration of substrate S overwhelming that of Protein X. This makes sense because the concentration of S is increasing.

SUMMING IT UP

- **Data Representation** passages present you with a graph, table, or figure that describes some kind of scientific experiment or phenomenon.

- **Read the introductory and surrounding paragraphs to determine the questions the data is supposed to answer.** Even if you don't understand the terminology or vocabulary used, the figure itself can usually tell you all you need to know.

- **Recognizing patterns and trends in data sets will be helpful when you're trying to draw conclusions**—questions accompanying data sets will usually ask about these types of observations.

- If you need to change data from a table into a graph, remember that the *x*-axis is usually the **independent variable** (the variable that the experimenter alters), and the *y*-axis is usually the **dependent variable** (the variable being measured in the experiment).

- **Precision** means that the same experiment, when repeated multiple times, will yield consistent numbers—precision can be measured by calculating **standard deviation,** which indicates how far a set of measured numbers are from their average. If the numbers measured for several trials of the same experiment are close to another, the data is probably **precise**; if the numbers don't agree and are not close to one another at all, the data is probably not precise.

- An **outlier** is a result very different from the other multiple and precise results of a trial. An outlier usually means that an error occurred in an experiment.

- **Identifying the dependent and independent variables is key to answering questions that ask you to suggest additional experiments**—you can look at the answer choices and pick the one that uses these variables. A good strategy for these questions is process of elimination. You can rule out answers describing experiments that very obviously vary the wrong conditions or take the wrong measurement.

- **If you come across a challenging term and have no idea what it means, read the full passage and see if it provides you with any hints.** If you still don't know what the word means, continue on to the questions and see if you actually need to know the definition to answer the questions—many times, you won't!

- **Don't spend too much time on information within a passage that does not enhance your understanding of the data provided**—it's likely extraneous and worth casting aside.

- **Don't assume you know a result and skip over looking at the data.** A simple experiment could give completely unexpected results. Even if they are incorrect, the ACT questions ask about the exact experiment presented as is. Analyze exactly what you see.

- **A figure might include extra information you don't need to answer the questions.** Simplify figures by blocking out extra information as you answer each question. When in doubt, define and search for the independent and dependent variables.

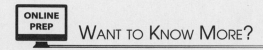

Want to Know More?

Access more practice questions, lessons, helpful hints, and strategies for the following science topics in *Peterson's ACT Online Course*:

- Data Representation and Research

- Data Representation and Interpretation

To purchase and access the course, go to ***www.petersons.com/act***.

415

Chapter 11

Data Representation

PRACTICE

Now that we've worked through a series of Data Representation questions together, it's time to try a practice set on your own. When you're finished answering all 20 questions, check the answers and explanations that follow to figure out how well you did and why you may have selected any incorrect answer choices.

PASSAGE I

Rocks are naturally occurring solids composed of one or more kinds of minerals. The outermost solid layer of the earth, the lithosphere is composed of rock. Pumice is a type of volcanic rock that is usually light in color and rough in texture. It is created when very hot, highly pressurized rock is ejected violently from volcanoes. After ejection, the fast rate of cooling and decrease in pressure causes the formation of bubbles on the rock's surface due to lowered internal gas solubility. As a result, pumice is extremely porous. The density of pumice averages around 0.25 g/mL. Granite, on the other hand, is a type of igneous rock that is composed of a wide array of solid chemical compounds. It is very hard, nonporous, and often used for construction. The density of granite averages around 2.75 g/mL.

Your lab group wants to test the absorbency of pumice and granite by examining these rocks' ability to absorb water, with the goal of determining whether rock porosity correlates with the mass of water rock can hold. The masses of three pieces of pumice and three pieces of granite were measured. The six rocks were then submerged completely in water, held down with identical straps. Each hour, the rocks were removed from the water, patted dry, and measured for mass on a balance. This process was repeated over the course of six hours. The rocks were handled carefully throughout the experiment to prevent chipping or loss of rock mass. For each hour mark, the average masses and standard deviations were calculated for each rock type, and the following data was collected, with error bars representing one standard deviation upward and downward:

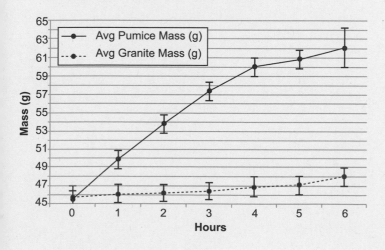

1. Based on the information provided in the passage and the figure, why must the rocks be fastened beneath the water in this and future related experiments?

   A. Pumice is air-sensitive and would corrode upon exposure to oxygen.
   B. Granite is air-sensitive and would corrode upon exposure to oxygen.
   C. Pumice would, based on its density, otherwise float to the surface of the water.
   D. Granite would, based on its density, otherwise float to the surface of the water.

2. What mass of water, on average, did the granite samples absorb after 6 hours?

   F. Slightly less than 1 g of water
   G. Slightly more than 1 g of water
   H. Slightly less than 2 g of water
   J. Slightly more than 2 g of water

3. The least precise set of trials was collected at:

   A. 0 hours for granite.
   B. 0 hours for pumice.
   C. 6 hours for granite.
   D. 6 hours for pumice.

4. Based on the data, which of the following conclusions would appropriately summarize the experimental results?

   F. Regardless of rock type, rocks with larger dry weight absorb more water after 6 hours than rocks with smaller dry weight.
   G. Regardless of rock type, rocks with smaller dry weight absorb more water after 6 hours than rocks with larger dry weight.
   H. As rock porosity increases, the water absorbance capacity of rocks also increases.
   J. As rock porosity increases, the water absorbance capacity of rocks decreases.

5. Which of the following statistical analyses would best account for the fact that all six rocks did not start at exactly the same mass?

   A. Graph the average percentage increase in mass rather than the average increase in mass.
   B. Calculate the collective average of granite and pumice masses at each time point and graph these values.
   C. Subtract the average dry weight of each rock type from each data point.
   D. Swap the variables graphed on the x- and y-axes.

PASSAGE II

To determine the spring constant k of a spring found in the laboratory, your lab group decides to apply Hooke's law, which states that the force required to extend or compress a spring by a given distance is proportional to that distance. This can be expressed by the equation $F = -kx$, where F is force, k is the spring constant, and x is the displacement magnitude, a distance.

The spring was hung vertically from a hook. Its resting position was marked as $x = 0$ cm. Various masses were hung at the bottom of the spring, and the spring was allowed to extend as needed. The figure below shows the resting spring and the extended spring with a 40-g weight:

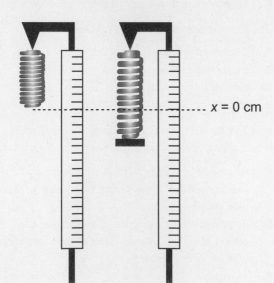

$x = 0$ cm

This process was repeated using four different masses, with displacement measured for each mass. Since weight is equivalent to the product of mass and the acceleration of gravity, each mass was converted to a weight in millinewtons. The data is shown below:

Mass Added to Spring (g)	Weight Added to Spring (mN)	Displacement (cm)
51	500	3.5
102	1,000	7.0
153	1,500	10.5
204	2,000	14.0

In order to determine the spring constant, the weight added to the spring was plotted as a function of displacement, and the slope of the line was determined.

6. What displacement magnitude would be expected for a 3,000-mN weight?

   F. 1.75 cm
   G. 17.5 cm
   H. 21.0 cm
   J. 28.0 cm

7. The plotted line used to determine the spring constant k would most resemble which of the following graphs?

A.
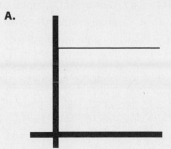

B.
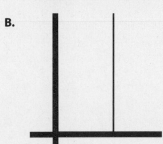

C.
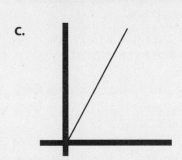

D.
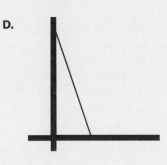

8. Each of the masses was converted to weight for the application of Hooke's law because:

F. mass and force have the same units, but weight does not.

G. weight and force have the same units, but mass does not.

H. mass and force are proportional to one another, but not to weight.

J. weight and force are proportional to one another, but not to mass.

9. How would the spring constant change if this identical experiment were performed on the surface of Mercury, a planet that is much smaller in radius than Earth, assuming similar temperatures?

A. The spring constant would remain the same because the difference in gravitational pull between Earth and Mercury would affect both weight and displacement similarly.

B. The spring constant would remain the same because the difference in gravitational pull between Earth and Mercury Is negligible.

C. The spring constant would increase due to the difference in gravitational pull between Earth and Mercury, which would alter the weight on the y-axis.

D. The spring constant would decrease due to the difference in gravitational pull between Earth and Mercury, which would alter the weight on the y-axis.

10. A mass is applied to the spring displayed in the first figure. The mass is pulled downward slightly and released. This action has turned the setup into:

F. a pulley.

G. a motor.

H. a harmonic oscillator.

J. a torsion spring.

Aqueous solutions of hydrochloric acid and sodium sulfide react to form hydrogen sulfide and sodium chloride, according to the following chemical reaction:

$$2HCl(aq) + Na_2S(aq) \rightarrow H_2S(g) + 2NaCl(aq)$$

The apparatus displayed in the figure below allows for the reactants to be added, the flask to be sealed, and then the reaction to be mixed; immediately after reactant addition in a flask, a cork containing a syringe is used to seal the reaction flask and collect in the syringe any gas produced by the reaction. The plunger, fully depressed to start, is pushed out as gas fills the syringe. After allowing the reaction to continue to completion, the volume reading on the syringe indicates the amount of hydrogen sulfide gas produced in the reaction.

Your lab group has three sodium sulfide solutions (A, B, and C) whose concentrations are 6 M, 10 M, and 14 M; however, you have no idea which is which. To assign the appropriate concentrations to the solutions, a 50-mL sample of each sodium sulfide solution was separately mixed with 50 mL of concentrated hydrochloric acid in identical flask apparatuses like the one above, with the reaction setup ensuring that hydrochloric acid is well in excess. The following volumes of gas were collected when each reaction was allowed to continue to completion:

Solution	Gas Volume Produced (mL)
A	40.0
B	50.7
C	50.7

The experiment was repeated by mixing 5-mL samples of the sodium sulfide solutions with 95 mL of concentrated hydrochloric acid in the apparatuses. The following data was obtained:

Solution	Gas Volume Produced (mL)
A	2.0
B	8.9
C	4.7

11. Based on the data collected, the sodium sulfide solution with the highest concentration (14 M) is:

    A. Solution A.
    B. Solution B.
    C. Solution C.
    D. unable to be determined.

12. Lower volumes of gas were produced in the second round of experiments because:

    F. the mole ratio of reactivity for hydrochloric acid and sodium sulfide was altered by the volume changes.
    G. the reaction shifted to produce more sodium chloride rather than hydrogen sulfide, resulting in a lower gas volume.
    H. the sodium sulfide solutions were more diluted in the reaction mixtures and provided less reactant for the reaction.
    J. the reaction was reversed by the increased volume of hydrochloric acid relative to sodium sulfide.

13. Why did Solutions B and C produce identical gas volumes in the first round of experiments but different gas volumes in the second round of experiments?

    A. Hydrochloric acid was the limiting reagent for Solutions B and C in the first round, while sodium sulfide was limiting for every other experiment.
    B. Sodium sulfide was the limiting reagent for Solutions B and C in the first round, while hydrochloric acid was limiting for every other experiment.
    C. Solutions B and C must have the same concentration.
    D. Human error disrupted the results during the first round.

14. If this experiment is repeated using 5 mL of Solution A and 195 mL of hydrochloric acid, what volume of gas would be produced?

F. 0.0 mL

G. 1.0 mL

H. 2.0 mL

J. 4.0 mL

15. What is another method you could use to identify each of the three sodium sulfide solution concentrations?

A. Paper chromatography

B. Filtration

C. Titration

D. Distillation

PASSAGE IV

The disease hereditary nonpolyposis colorectal cancer (HNPCC) is caused by mutations in human genes that repair errors in DNA. The gene *MLH3* codes for such a DNA repair protein. In an experiment, this gene was modified so that when the protein is expressed, it will be attached to a dye called GFP (green fluorescence protein), which allows for the MLH3 protein to be detected using fluorescence when it is expressed in the cells. The cells were observed using live cell imaging and confocal microscopy, and accumulation of MLH3 was detected at the centrosomes. Centrosomes are the organelles in animal cells where microtubules are organized and which regulate cell division.

Fluorescence recovery after photobleaching (FRAP) is a technique that was used to detect MLH3 at the centrosomes in human cells to determine its stability. An initial burst of light decreases the fluorescence in the centrosomes and when fluorescence is restored in this region, it shows how quickly the protein moves back into the region. Fluorescence measurements were taken over the course of 32 seconds after this initial burst of light. Eight separate trials were performed, and error bars were calculated based on the standard deviations from these trials. The figure shows the two foci, or regions, where the measurements were taken.

These foci appear as light-colored dots in the figure. The data is shown below:

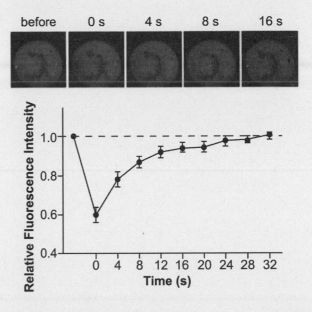

Source: Roesner, Lennart M.; Mielke, Christian; Faehnrich, Silke; Merkhoffer, Yvonne; Dittmar, Kurt E.J.; Drexler, Hans G.; Dirks, Wilhelm G. 2014. "Localization of MLH3 at the Centrosomes." *Int. J. Mol. Sci.* 15, no. 8: 13932–13937.

16. The most rapid rate of fluorescence recovery occurred:

F. before 0 seconds.

G. between 0 and 4 seconds.

H. between 8 and 12 seconds.

J. between 24 and 28 seconds.

17. The advantage of FRAP over live cell imaging alone is the ability to:

A. acquire quantitative data rather than visual data.

B. take advantage of the linked fluorescent protein.

C. collect data without the use of additives.

D. complete the study without harming the cells.

18. The time at which the displayed curve reaches the dotted line indicates:

F. the time required for the foci to photobleach completely.

G. the time required for 100% fluorescence recovery.

H. the time it takes the light burst to decrease fluorescence to its lowest point before recovery begins.

J. the overall time over which all data points were taken throughout the experiment.

Chapter 11

Data Representation

19. For time points where multiple independent measurements were taken, which of the following statements is true?

A. Measurement precision increases over time.

B. Measurement precision decreases over time.

C. Measurement accuracy increases over time.

D. Measurement accuracy decreases over time.

20. Based on its organelle association, MLH3 likely plays a key role in successful:

F. apoptosis.

G. phagocytosis.

H. pinocytosis.

J. mitosis.

ANSWERS AND EXPLANATIONS

PASSAGE I

The first passage is an earth sciences topic. The passage describes an experiment to test water absorbency of pumice and granite, two very different types of rock with very different porosities.

1. **The correct answer is C.** This question asks you to think about the specifics of the experimental design, based on the described experiment, for this experiment and any future experiments of the same variety. The passage and figure include no information whatsoever about air sensitivity or corrosiveness; plus, if the rocks are being taken out of the water every hour, it would be disastrous if the rocks were air-sensitive. Therefore, eliminate choices A and B right away. You might already know that the density of water is approximately 1 g/mL at room temperature, but even if you didn't, you can easily figure it out. The passage provides the numerical densities of both pumice and granite. The density of pumice is much less than that of granite, and a less dense rock will be the more likely rock to float in water. This should help you choose choice C as the correct answer. It is true that pumice will get heavier as it absorbs water, but this question is fairly general; granite will never really require the fasteners, but pumice certainly will, particularly at the earliest time points in the experiment.

2. **The correct answer is J.** This question asks you to interpret the graph. If we look at the granite line at 6 hours, the average mass of the rock and water is approximately 48 g. We can find the dry mass of the rock by looking at the granite line at 0 hours. The dry mass is just under 46 g. The difference between these masses, just over 2 g, represents the average mass of water absorbed by the granite.

3. **The correct answer is D.** This question asks you to assess the validity of the data by looking at precision. The passage indicates that the error bars represent standard deviation. The least precise set of trials will be the set of trials with the largest error bar, as a large standard deviation indicates that the individual data points were generally further from the mean. The largest error bar on the graph can be found on the pumice line at 6 hours.

4. **The correct answer is H.** This question asks you to look for trends in the data and draw a conclusion. Choices F and G draw conclusions based on rock dry weight rather than rock type; since the dry weights for all rocks were more or less the same, these answers can be eliminated. Furthermore, the question proposed in the passage was to test porosity, so it wouldn't make sense to draw conclusions that do not address the proposed question. The graph indicates that pumice clearly absorbs much more water than granite. Pumice is much more porous than granite. Therefore, the correct conclusion is that more porous rocks absorb more water, so the answer is choice H.

5. **The correct answer is A.** This question asks you to consider other ways to analyze the data statistically. Choice B is incorrect because it eliminates the distinction between rock types, which is really the basis of the whole proposal. Choice C is incorrect because the graph would look exactly the same, and it does not account for any differences in initial dry mass. Choice D is incorrect because it would just transform the graph without extracting any helpful new information. Using percentage increases rather than mass increases would show how a particular rock absorbs water relative to its own initial mass, thereby eliminating any issues with the fact that all six rocks did not begin at perfectly identical masses.

PASSAGE II

This is a physics passage about springs, Hooke's law, and the calculation of spring constants.

6. **The correct answer is H.** The first question for this passage asks you to use the data to predict a displacement for a weight that has not been tested. Based on the data table, when weight doubles, so does the displacement. It is a linear trend. 3,000 mN is twice the weight of 1,500 mN, which exhibited a displacement of 10.5 cm. Doubling this should give the displacement for 3,000 mN. $10.5 \times 2 = 21.0$ cm, so the correct answer is choice H.

7. **The correct answer is C.** This question asks you to predict what the described graph looks like. The passage indicates that weight was plotted as a function of displacement, and the data shows that as weight increases, displacement also increases. The only graph that shows this positive correlation between these variables is choice C.

8. **The correct answer is G.** This question asks you to think about why the scientists converted mass to weight in order to apply Hooke's law. If you remember that

Newtons are the correct unit for force, this answer will be obvious, but even if you don't, you can use logic to figure it out. We can immediately rule out choices H and J because the various equations in the passage show that force is proportional to both mass and weight, so neither of these answers can be correct. Now we must decide whether force has the same units as mass or weight. Force can be measured in Newtons, just like weight is here, so the correct answer is choice G. If you didn't know that force is measured in Newtons, simply think about the process: the scientists took the extra step of converting masses to weights. Why would they do this unless weight had the units necessary to apply Hooke's law? The conversion would be redundant otherwise. This is an example of how you can figure out an answer using logic even if you don't know a particular scientific fact.

9. **The correct answer is A.** This question asks you to predict what would happen if the same experiment were repeated under different conditions. In the situation described in the question, the new condition is lower gravitational pull. If the same experiment is performed on Mercury, the major relevant difference is that the gravitational pull would be significantly lower than on Earth. Gravitational pull comes into play when graphing weight as a function of displacement, but gravity will affect both weight and displacement in the same way. If temperatures are assumed to be similar, decreased gravity-influenced weight on Mercury would be accompanied by a decreased displacement. These variables would change in the same way, resulting in no change in line slope. We can rule out choice B because the reason k stays the same is *not* because the gravitational pull between Earth and Mercury is negligible. We can also rule out choices C and D, which indicate that the spring constant would change because only the weight would be affected; these answers do not consider that displacement would also change if the experiment is performed under different gravitational conditions. The answer is therefore choice A. In general, remember that numbers described as "constants" will stay the same under most conditions.

10. **The correct answer is H.** This question asks you to look at the picture of the experimental setup and choose the term that best describes what you would see. This question does require that you have at least some understanding of each of these terms, though really you are all set if you know the term in the correct answer. A pulley is a wheel on an axle that supports movement of a belt and can change direction of motion along its

circumference. The figure includes no such setup, so this cannot be a pulley. The answer is not choice F. We can also rule out choice G; a motor, in general, is a machine that converts electrical energy into mechanical energy. The only major energy conversion occurring in the described situation is an interconversion between potential and kinetic energy, so this answer is also incorrect. A torsion spring describes a spring that functions by twisting, which is the definition of *torsion*. No twisting is happening here, so we can rule out choice J. A harmonic oscillator is a system that experiences a restoring force proportional to its displacement when displaced from its equilibrium position. Even if you had no idea what a harmonic oscillator was, you might recognize the root word *oscillate*, which means to vary in magnitude regularly around a central point. When you pull the spring down a bit, the mass will move up and down, above and below the original resting equilibrium position.

PASSAGE III

This is a chemistry passage that describes the use of a gas-collecting apparatus to match three sodium sulfide solutions with their concentrations. This experiment relies on the idea that if the three sodium sulfide solutions are mixed with the same amount of hydrochloric acid, the differences in H_2S gas volume produced will indicate which original sodium sulfide solution contained the greatest concentration of sulfide. As the two rounds of experimentation show, however, this experiment is useful only if hydrochloric acid is in excess; it seems that HCl was in excess in the second round of experimentation, giving useful results there, but not in the first round of experimentation.

11. **The correct answer is B.** This question asks you to interpret the data and draw a conclusion. In order to figure out which sodium sulfide has the highest concentration, you have to determine which solution produced the greatest volume of gas. The first round of experiments will not be helpful because Solutions B and C both produced the same gas volumes. The second round of experimentation clearly distinguishes among the three solutions, with Solution B producing the most gas. Therefore, the correct answer is choice B.

12. **The correct answer is H.** This question asks you to explain the discrepancies in data between the first and second rounds of experimentation. Looking at the possible answers, we can rule out choice F right away because volume changes will not affect the mole ratio. A chemical equation will not change (unless, in specific cases, environmental conditions change), so F can be

ruled out. This same concept helps us to rule out choice G because the reaction will not shift to produce one product over the other. Per stoichiometric concepts, the ratios of reactants and products remain constant for a particular chemical equation. Finally, we can rule out choice J because the reaction is not a reversible reaction; the reaction would have been written with arrows pointing in both directions if it was reversible. The correct answer is choice H because the answer to this question is fairly straightforward; in the first round of experiments, the sodium sulfide solution comprises 50% of the reaction mixture volume, while in the second round of experiments, the sodium sulfide solution comprises 5% of the reaction mixture volume.

13. **The correct answer is A.** This question asks you look at the data and predict why the results were not identical in each round. The key here is that significantly more sodium sulfide was used in the first round of experiments than in the second round. This is important because the reaction will run to completion until the limiting reagent is completely used up. In the first round of experiments, the same amount of HCl was used in every experiment, while the three sodium sulfide solutions had different concentrations. The fact that Solutions B and C yielded the same gas volume indicates that the HCl was limiting in the first round of experiments, when the better experiment for determining relative sodium sulfide concentrations would have HCl in excess. This is exactly what was done in the second round of experiments. The gas volume for Solution B in particular should not be taken at face value, since HCl could potentially still be limiting for that solution, but the second round of experiments clearly confirms that Solutions A and C have lower concentrations than Solution B. Therefore, this discrepancy between rounds is based on limiting reagents, and choice A correctly describes this. Choice B has the solutions backwards and is incorrect. The fact that different gas volumes were measured in the second round of experiments clearly shows that Solutions B and C have different concentrations, so the answer is not choice C. Human error is always a possibility, but it is unlikely that human error would have resulted in Solutions B and C giving exactly the same volume of 50.7 mL.

14. **The correct answer is H.** This question asks you to think about future experimentation. In the described scenario, the sodium sulfide solution volume remains the same as the volume used in the second round of experiments, but the volume of HCl is greatly increased. Since HCl is already the excess reactant in the second

round, increasing the amount of HCl will *not* change the amount of gas produced. With sodium sulfide as the limiting reactant, no more H_2S can be produced, regardless of how much extra HCl is added. 5 mL of Solution A reacts with excess HCl to form 2.0 mL of gas, according to the data obtained in the second round of experimentation. This same volume will be obtained under the described conditions, so the correct answer is H.

15. **The correct answer is C.** This question asks you to think of another method for determining which sodium sulfide solution is which. Paper chromatography, choice A, is a method for separating components of a mixture based on affinity for a solid, so this is not relevant for concentration determination. Filtration, choice B, is a method for separating solids from liquids in a mixture, so this answer is not relevant here either. Distillation, choice D, is a method used to separate components of a mixture based on boiling point. With three of the four answers being physical separation techniques, we can use process of elimination to figure out that the correct answer is choice C. If you know what a titration is going in, however, you could pick this answer out as correct right away! A titration is a technique that uses an indicator to allow for determination of the concen-tration of an unknown solution, and indicators exist that can be used to determine the concentration of a sodium sulfide solution.

PASSAGE IV

This is a biology passage in which a technique called FRAP is described to show the high mobility of the MLH3 protein as it localizes at the centrosomes in a human cell.

16. **The correct answer is G.** This question asks you to read and interpret the provided graph. The most rapid rate of fluorescence recovery occurs where the slope of the line is highest. This occurs between 0 and 4 seconds, so the answer is choice G. Note that a steep slope is also observed before 0 seconds, but this is a negative slope and the direct result of the light burst photobleaching the sample, so this is not part of the fluorescence recovery process.

17. **The correct answer is A.** This question asks you to think about the described techniques and consider why each kind of collected data is useful. FRAP offers a way to quantify MLH3 mobility at the centrosomes, so its advantage is that numerical, or quantitative, data can be collected. Choice B is incorrect because both methods take advantage of fluorescence, and choice D

is incorrect because neither method harms the cells; if anything, FRAP is more harmful than live cell imaging because it destroys the fluorescence properties of fluorophores in the cell. Additives do not play a major role in either technique, so choice C can also be ruled out.

18. **The correct answer is G.** This question asks you to interpret the data and explain why the data was presented in the manner in which it was presented. The significance of the dotted line is that it represents 100% fluorescence recovery. Therefore, the time it takes for the fluorescence readings to reach the line indicates the time required for 100% fluorescence recovery, choice G. Choice F is incorrect because photobleaching is the process of *losing* fluorescence, not gaining fluorescence. Choice H is incorrect for the same reason; it refers to the loss, rather than gain, of fluorescence in the region of interest. Choice J is incorrect because data points were taken before time zero, which means that the time at which the data points reach the dotted line will actually be shorter than the total overall time of data point collection over the course of the entire experiment. It is important that you notice that the *x*-axis does not begin with time zero at the far left; otherwise, you might be tempted to choose this answer.

19. **The correct answer is A.** This question asks about the validity of the data by asking you to assess precision and accuracy of the data points. We can rule out choices C and D immediately. Accuracy is determined relative to a known value, and we have no known values here with which to compare the data. Therefore, we cannot assess accuracy. We can assess precision by looking at the error bars, which are based on standard deviation, a statistical measure of precision. Over time, the magnitude of the error bars generally decreases, indicating increased precision. The correct answer, therefore, is choice A.

20. **The correct answer is J.** This question asks you to apply the information in the passage and data with your knowledge of cell biology and processes. The key here is to recognize that centrosomes play a key role in one of these processes but not the others. You might also pick up on the fact that MLH3 is a DNA mismatch repair protein, and DNA is heavily involved in only one of the four listed processes. That process is mitosis. Centrosomes represent the constricted regions of mitotic chromosomes and are the organelle to which spindle fibers attach during mitosis. Apoptosis is programmed cell death, and while it involves a cascade of proteins, maintaining DNA integrity is not so important here, so we can rule out choice F. Phagocytosis mostly occurs in phagocytes and protists, so it is unlikely that MLH3 is important in this process since the passage describes human (animal) cells. Furthermore, DNA is not a key participant in phagocytosis, so there would be no need for a protein like MLH3. The same goes for pinocytosis, so we can rule out choices G and H. That leaves mitosis, which is the part of the cell cycle in which chromosomes in a cell nucleus are split into two identical sets of chromosomes, with each assigned to its own nucleus. This is very much relevant to centrosomes, MLH3, and DNA, so mitosis is the process that makes the most sense here.

CHAPTER 12:
RESEARCH SUMMARIES

OVERVIEW

- What to Expect
- What Is the Scientific Question or Purpose of This Experiment?
- What Hypothesis Can Be Proposed to Predict the Outcome of This Experiment?
- How Can the Scientific Question Be Addressed Experimentally?
- How Can the Provided Data Be Analyzed?
- What Conclusions Can Be Drawn Based on the Experiment and Results?
- Common Mistakes to Avoid
- Summing It Up
- Practice

427

Chapter 12

Research
Summaries

Now that we've reviewed Data Representation questions, we will move on to Research Summaries. Research Summaries are the most frequently featured question on the ACT Science test. These questions make up 45–55 percent of the Science test, which means that over half of the science questions you see could be Research Summaries. In the real world of science research, research summaries appear everywhere: in science journals, magazines, newspapers, and even in textbooks for historically important research investigations. Therefore, it makes a lot of sense that such a significant part of the science test focuses on this kind of stimulus passage.

In many ways, questions based on Research Summaries will require a lot of the same skills you used when answering Data Representation questions because both question types require you to analyze data. Furthermore, information from the same natural science disciplines (biology, chemistry, physics, and astronomy/earth sciences) provides the passage source material. The added challenge of Research Summaries passages is that you are often given more background information about the experiment and the thought that went into its design. As such, Research Summaries questions might ask you to identify the purpose of an experiment or to propose a possible hypothesis for the question the experiment is addressing. You might need to identify independent, dependent, or control variables, or suggest methods or alternative techniques that will help answer the question. The similarity to Data Representation questions lies in the fact that you will also be presented with experimental results, which you will be expected to analyze in order to draw conclusions. For questions that involve analyzing data and drawing conclusions, you will certainly be able to apply many of the same skills we've already discussed, but we will still talk about how to use these skills in the context of Research Summaries questions in this chapter.

Peterson's ACT® Prep Guide

WHAT TO EXPECT

Research Summaries typically begin with a written introduction that provides background information about a scientific topic before introducing the experiment. Included in this background information may be important vocabulary words, reminders about principles and topics you may have learned about in the past, and specific details about the featured topic.

After the background information is provided, the passage will then give a description of the experiment that was performed. From this information, you should be able to identify the **independent variable, dependent variable,** and **control variables,** which we discussed in Chapter 11. The written parts of Research Summaries will almost certainly be longer and more in-depth than the written parts of Data Representation. The goal of Data Representation passages is to present you with data to analyze, whereas Research Summaries place a far greater emphasis on experimental design and the scientific method in full. Experimental descriptions may include an image to help you visualize the setup described in the passage.

Following the experimental description is data of some kind. This can include a table, a graph, or sometimes a written description of the results obtained. In addition, you may even be provided with a conclusion reached by the scientists who performed the experiment.

Because these passages focus more equally on the experiment and the results (rather than just the results), the questions that accompany Research Summaries cover more ground than the questions that accompany Data Representation questions. As such, there are usually five or six questions that follow each passage of this type, slightly more on average than you might see for Data Representation questions.

> **TIP**
> Any provided conclusions should be taken with a grain of salt, because the questions that follow the passage may ask you to support or refute the given conclusion.

The questions that follow Research Summaries will test you on a number of important skills: identifying the purpose of a research project, formulating hypotheses to make predictions, proposing experiments or alternative experimental methods, analyzing data, and drawing conclusions based on experimental data. Keep these skills in mind as you read through Research Summaries, because it is very likely you will have to answer relevant questions that test your proficiency in some or all of these areas. In order to give you an idea of how each of these skills may be tested within the context of Research Summaries, consider the following questions, each of which is followed by a sample question so you know what to expect when you come across them on the exam.

WHAT IS THE SCIENTIFIC QUESTION OR PURPOSE OF THIS EXPERIMENT?

Whenever you read about any kind of scientific experiment, the first thing you must do is identify the **scientific question,** mentioned back in Chapter 11. The scientific question is also called the **purpose** of the experiment. Basically, you need to ask yourself:

- Why should anyone bother doing this experiment?
- Why was this particular topic chosen?
- What will this experiment test?
- Why will the results of this experiment be important?

Stating the purpose of an experiment is always the first step of the scientific method because a scientist must establish exactly *why* he or she is performing an experiment before actually performing it. If the purpose of the experiment is not clearly identified, then it will be very difficult to design an experiment because it may not be exactly clear what the scientist is trying to accomplish.

>
> **TIP**
> When you are trying to state the purpose of an experiment, it always helps to identify and include the dependent variable (what is being measured) and the independent variable (what the scientists change) in the statement, which we previously discussed in more depth in Chapter 11.

Almost always, background research is needed to flesh out a scientific question or purpose. Background research helps a scientist to narrow down a general topic to something more specific. For example, if a scientist wants to study the effect of seaweed population on photosynthetic efficiency in a body of water, background research can help the scientist to choose specifically to monitor dissolved oxygen levels in the water as a means of quantifying photosynthesis (since, as you may recall from your biology class, photosynthesis is the process by which plants convert carbon dioxide and water to glucose and oxygen).

As a test taker, you won't have the luxury of being able to do your own background research on a particular topic. Fortunately, Research Summaries save you time by providing you with all the background information you will need to clearly identify the purpose of the experiment of interest! Given the general topic description and background information and then looking ahead at the experimental design (which we will discuss further in a bit), you should be able to determine the purpose for any experiment posed in Research Summaries you come across.

It was important to identify the purpose of an experiment in Data Representation passages so you knew what to look for in the provided data tables or graphs. In Research Summaries, you may be required to delve into this a bit more. For example, you might be asked to choose a relevant scientific question or statement of purpose from four choices, or you could be asked to formulate a different but related question about the topic of interest.

Let's look at a test-style question in action. As in the last chapter, we will use the same passage and data throughout the first few examples in this chapter so you can get a sense of the different question types that will come up within a Research Summary set.

· ·

Photosynthesis is a biological process that generates stored energy through the formation of glucose from carbon dioxide and water, according to the following chemical reaction:

$$6\,CO_2 + 6\,H_2O \rightarrow C_6H_{12}O_6 + 6\,O_2$$

Cellular respiration works in opposition, using oxygen to break down the sugar and release that energy to form ATP:

$$C_6H_{12}O_6 + 6\,O_2 \rightarrow 6\,CO_2 + 6\,H_2O$$

Carbon dioxide reacts with water to form carbonic acid. Phenolphthalein is an indicator that remains colorless in acid and turns pink in base. Three drops of phenolphthalein can be added to a small water sample, and the amount of NaOH needed to turn a clear sample pink (its neutralization point) gives an indication of the concentration of carbonic acid in the sample.

Many plants and algae are capable of both photosynthesis and respiration. Among these is an algal species called stonewort, of

the genus *Chara*. Stonewort grows well in lime-rich waters, which results in the formation of calcium carbonate deposits on the algae.

A group of students wants to test the rates of photosynthesis and respiration in stonewort in different light conditions. The students acquire two 6.00-g stonewort samples and place each in a beaker containing 250 mL of spring water. One beaker was incubated in the dark at 25°C, while the other beaker was incubated in the light at 25°C. Over the course of one day, two 1-mL water samples were removed from each beaker every six hours. One of each pair of water samples was used to detect dissolved oxygen concentration using an oxygen electrode, which measures O_2 concentration in units of parts per million (ppm). The second water sample per pair was used to test carbon dioxide levels using phenolphthalein and 0.04 M NaOH. Both tests were performed immediately after sample extraction to avoid sample disruption. The following results were obtained:

Stonewort Sample	Measurement	Time (hours)				
		0	6	12	18	24
Light	Dissolved O_2 (ppm)	2.35	2.81	4.61	5.02	5.30
	Volume 0.04 M NaOH (µL)	21.0	18.3	14.0	13.3	12.8
Dark	Dissolved O_2 (ppm)	2.36	2.37	2.01	1.84	1.79
	Volume 0.04 M NaOH (µL)	22.2	23.0	26.1	28.7	30.0

Which of the following questions best summarizes the purpose of this research project?

A. How do the concentrations of O_2 and CO_2 in water affect stonewort survival in dark and light conditions?

B. How do O_2 concentrations impact CO_2 production in stonewort submerged in water?

C. How do light and dark conditions impact net O_2 and CO_2 concentrations in water due to stonewort energy cycles?

D. What is the effect of acidic and basic water conditions on stonewort O_2 and CO_2 production in dark and light conditions?

The correct answer is C. This question requires you to read the passage, recognize precisely what the scientists are trying to discover, and understand the kind of data that was collected. The passage itself gives you most of your answer in one sentence: *A group of students wants to test the rates of photosynthesis and respiration in stonewort in different light conditions.* However, this must be altered to include the kind of data collected. In this experiment, the net production or loss of CO_2 and O_2 was measured in the dark and light as a means of determining whether the rate of photosynthesis surpasses the rate of its reverse, respiration, or vice versa. The only answer choice, among the four provided options, that correctly identifies dark/light conditions as the independent variable and net CO_2/O_2 concentrations as the dependent variable is choice C.

Choice A is incorrect because it indicates that CO_2/O_2 concentrations are the independent variable—as well as dark/light conditions—rather than the dependent variable, and that stonewort survival is the dependent variable, which it is not. Choice B is incorrect because it indicates that O_2 concentration is the independent variable and CO_2 concentration is the dependent variable, without making any mention of light/dark conditions. Choice D is incorrect because it indicates that acidic and basic water conditions were the independent variable, though it does correctly identify O_2/CO_2 concentrations as the dependent variable. While CO_2 does react with water to form an acid, carbonic acid, and while NaOH was indeed used in the phenolphthalein test, the research project is not focused on testing the effects of acidic or basic conditions under light and dark conditions.

WHAT HYPOTHESIS CAN BE PROPOSED TO PREDICT THE OUTCOME OF THIS EXPERIMENT?

A **hypothesis** is an educated prediction about the outcome of a particular experiment. When developing a hypothesis, a scientist must consider cause and effect and rely on both logic and background research. For example, if you had to hypothesize whether a ball will reach a higher speed when dropped from 20 inches or 20 feet, it is perfectly fine to rely on logic. A reasonable prediction might be that the ball dropped from 20 feet will reach a higher speed because it has a longer distance along which to accelerate due to gravitational acceleration.

On the other hand, if you had to predict the effect of different buffers on the stability of a specific protein in solution, you would need more background information about the protein and its amino acid content in order to make a reasonable prediction. In most cases, hypotheses are based on a combination of logic *and* background research. Hypotheses are often framed in the "if–then" format, where the first clause provides the reasoning for your prediction (the cause) and the second clause provides the prediction itself (the predicted effect). An example could be: "If a greater drop distance provides a falling object with more distance over which to accelerate, then the ball dropped from 20 feet will reach a higher maximal speed than the ball dropped from 20 inches." Hypotheses are not absolutely required to take on the "if–then" format, but it is a helpful way to frame predictions and is quite widely used. On the ACT Science test, your ability to develop hypotheses may be tested primarily in two different ways.

1) **Choose a hypothesis.** The most straightforward question type might ask you to select which of the given choices is the most suitable hypothesis for an experiment. In this case, you would have to choose the answer that makes a logical prediction based on the background information you've been given. You should double-check that your answer also satisfies the correct independent and dependent variables described in the passage. For example, if your experiment is measuring the speed of a ball dropped from two different heights, your chosen hypothesis must also relate to speed as the dependent variable. In this example, your hypothesis should not be about, say, which ball will make the most noise or which ball will create the bigger crater when it hits the sand below.

2) **Make a prediction.** Another ACT science question type might ask you to make a prediction based on the background information provided. In a question like this, you might be given four choices that are all valid hypotheses for the given experiment—but based on the background information, there may be one choice that makes logical sense where the others do not.

One important thing to remember is that hypotheses are *predictions*, not results. A hypothesis will not always correctly predict the outcome of an experiment. A hypothesis might predict one result, but the experiment might demonstrate something entirely different. This is perfectly fine, and it happens all the time in science. Results of experiments often disprove hypotheses, and this is often how scientists make revolutionary discoveries.

 Your hypothesis must always correctly address the appropriate independent and dependent variables.

When a particular experiment consistently gives a result that isn't exactly what you expected, then it opens the door to further experiments to explain why this may be the case. So keep in mind that a hypothesis is still valid even if it is does not correctly predict an experimental result. You may find after performing the experiment that the results do not support your hypothesis, but the hypothesis is simply an attempt to make a prediction and won't always necessarily be correct.

Let's try another question.

. . . .

Photosynthesis is a biological process that generates stored energy through the formation of glucose from carbon dioxide and water, according to the following chemical reaction:

$$6\,CO_2 + 6\,H_2O \rightarrow C_6H_{12}O_6 + 6\,O_2$$

Cellular respiration works in opposition, using oxygen to break down the sugar and release that energy to form ATP:

$$C_6H_{12}O_6 + 6\,O_2 \rightarrow 6\,CO_2 + 6\,H_2O$$

Carbon dioxide reacts with water to form carbonic acid. Phenolphthalein is an indicator that remains colorless in acid and turns pink in base. Three drops of phenolphthalein can be added to a small water sample, and the amount of NaOH needed to turn a clear sample pink (its neutralization point) gives an indication of the concentration of carbonic acid in the sample.

Many plants and algae are capable of both photosynthesis and respiration. Among these is an algal species called stonewort, of the genus *Chara*. Stonewort grows well in lime-rich waters, which results in the formation of calcium carbonate deposits on the algae.

A group of students wants to test the rates of photosynthesis and respiration in stonewort in different light conditions. The students acquire two 6.00-g stonewort samples and place each in a beaker containing 250 mL of spring water. One beaker was incubated in the dark at 25°C, while the other beaker was incubated in the light at 25°C. Over the course of one day, two 1-mL water samples were removed from each beaker every six hours. One of each pair of water samples was used to detect dissolved oxygen concentration using an oxygen electrode, which measures O2 concentration in units of parts per million (ppm). The second water sample per pair was used to test carbon dioxide levels using phenolphthalein and 0.04 M NaOH. Both tests were performed immediately after sample extraction to avoid sample disruption. The following results were obtained:

Stonewort Sample	Measurement	Time (hours)				
		0	6	12	18	24
Light	Dissolved O_2 (ppm)	2.35	2.81	4.61	5.02	5.30
	Volume 0.04 M NaOH (µL)	21.0	18.3	14.0	13.3	12.8
Dark	Dissolved O_2 (ppm)	2.36	2.37	2.01	1.84	1.79
	Volume 0.04 M NaOH (µL)	22.2	23.0	26.1	28.7	30.0

Based on the provided information, which of the following might be a logical hypothesis to predict what will happen in the phenolphthalein/NaOH tests?

F. If light drives photosynthesis but not respiration, then the light samples should exhibit higher O_2 levels than the dark samples over the course of 24 hours.

G. If light drives photosynthesis but not respiration, then the light samples should exhibit lower O_2 levels than the dark samples over the course of 24 hours.

H. If light drives photosynthesis but not respiration, then the light samples should exhibit higher CO_2 levels than the dark samples over the course of 24 hours.

J. If light drives photosynthesis but not respiration, then the light samples should exhibit lower CO_2 levels than the dark samples over the course of 24 hours.

The correct answer is J. This question asks you to choose a valid hypothesis from four choices. All four choices have the same "cause" stem: "If light drives photosynthesis but not respiration…" That means that, based on the background information, we should choose a logical conclusion based on this stem.

We can immediately eliminate choices F and G because the "effect" portions of these hypotheses refer to O_2 levels, and the passage indicates that the phenolphthalein/NaOH test detects CO_2 levels. Now we can hone in on choices H and J. To come up with a reasonable hypothesis, we should focus on the chemical equations for photosynthesis and respiration. According to the passage, the chemical equation for photosynthesis is: $6\ CO_2 + 6\ H_2O \rightarrow C_6H_{12}O_6 + 6\ O_2$. The chemical equation for respiration is: $C_6H_{12}O_6 + 6\ O_2 \rightarrow 6\ CO_2 + 6\ H_2O$. If the "cause" stem of the hypothesis predicts that light will drive photosynthesis but not respiration, then the predictions for CO_2 levels in the light versus dark samples should reflect this. Per this stem, the light samples should promote photosynthesis and decrease CO_2 levels, while respiration should not be affected. Therefore, the light samples should exhibit lower CO_2 levels than the dark samples over 24 hours, based on the "cause" portion of the stem.

HOW CAN THE SCIENTIFIC QUESTION BE ADDRESSED EXPERIMENTALLY?

After identifying the purpose of a research project and formulating a hypothesis to predict the outcome, the next section on which you should focus in Research Summaries questions is the experiment. The experiment describes the methods and techniques used in the laboratory to explore the question of interest. Sometimes the experiment will be based on techniques you've seen before, but at other times you'll come across techniques you've never heard of. Fortunately, experimental descriptions in Research Summaries provide enough detail about the experimental design itself, as well as the independent and dependent variables, that you can figure out what's going on. Since Research Summaries will never be pages long, the techniques will not be overly complicated—in many cases, they will be extremely simple and straightforward. But if you do ever come across a technique with which you are unfamiliar, the passage will provide you with the background you need; you won't ever be left completely in the dark about what a particular method does.

TIP

You may have to apply your science background in order to understand the basics about a particular technique, but there will always be enough content in the passage for you to understand what's happening.

When it comes to ACT questions that ask about an experimental design, there are a few different ways you might be tested.

1) **Recognize and identify.** Some questions might simply ask you to recognize the basics: for example, identifying variables and controls, understanding how the technique works based on the information provided, and recognizing how the experiment answers the scientific question posed.

2) **Critique and improve.** You might be asked to critique the experiment and suggest possible improvements.

3) **Provide alternative methods.** You could also come across a few kinds of questions that ask you to think beyond the obvious. For instance, you could be asked to suggest an alternative experimental method. If, for example, a passage describes a study to investigate the rate of a chemical reaction and the scientist measures product formation, an alternative method might be to track reactant disappearance; both are valid ways to acquire data about reaction rate, but they are *different* ways to study the reaction rate.

4) **Consider future experiments.** Another less-than-obvious question type that may be asked about experimental design pertains to future experiments. Questions that ask about future experiments require you to think beyond what is in front of you. Most often, you will be asked to build off what has been provided in order to recommend a logical next step. For example, if an experiment discovers that plants grow better in the light than in the dark, a logical follow-up experiment might be to test optimal light intensity, or optimal duration of light exposure, or some other dependent variable that is related to what was tested in the original described experiment. Again, with this type of question, you won't be expected to know about any specialized techniques off the top of your head; these answers will usually be based on logic, or on some variation of the experiment described in the original passage.

• •

Photosynthesis is a biological process that generates stored energy through the formation of glucose from carbon dioxide and water, according to the following chemical reaction:

$$6\,CO_2 + 6\,H_2O \rightarrow C_6H_{12}O_6 + 6\,O_2$$

Cellular respiration works in opposition, using oxygen to break down the sugar and release that energy to form ATP:

$$C_6H_{12}O_6 + 6\,O_2 \rightarrow 6\,CO_2 + 6\,H_2O$$

Carbon dioxide reacts with water to form carbonic acid. Phenolphthalein is an indicator that remains colorless in acid and turns pink in base. Three drops of phenolphthalein can be added to a small water sample, and the amount of NaOH needed to turn a clear sample pink, its neutralization point, gives an indication of the concentration of carbonic acid in the sample.

Many plants and algae are capable of both photosynthesis and respiration. Among these is an algal species called stonewort, of

the genus *Chara*. Stonewort grows well in lime-rich waters, which results in the formation of calcium carbonate deposits on the algae.

A group of students wants to test the rates of photosynthesis and respiration in stonewort in different light conditions. The students acquire two 6.00-g stonewort samples and place each in a beaker containing 250 mL of spring water. One beaker was incubated in the dark at 25°C, while the other beaker was incubated in the light at 25°C. Over the course of one day, two 1-mL water samples were removed from each beaker every six hours. One of each pair of water samples was used to detect dissolved oxygen concentration using an oxygen electrode, which measures O_2 concentration in units of parts per million (ppm). The second water sample per pair was used to test carbon dioxide levels using phenolphthalein and 0.04 M NaOH. Both tests were performed immediately after sample extraction to avoid sample disruption. The following results were obtained:

Stonewort Sample	Measurement	Time (hours)				
		0	6	12	18	24
Light	Dissolved O_2 (ppm)	2.35	2.81	4.61	5.02	5.30
	Volume 0.04 M NaOH (µL)	21.0	18.3	14.0	13.3	12.8
Dark	Dissolved O_2 (ppm)	2.36	2.37	2.01	1.84	1.79
	Volume 0.04 M NaOH (µL)	22.2	23.0	26.1	28.7	30.0

All of the following steps could significantly improve the reliability of the experiment EXCEPT:

A. using a magnetic stir bar to ensure constant gas composition throughout the beakers.

B. decreasing the concentration of NaOH used in the phenolphthalein test to more efficiently detect acidity.

C. increasing the number of samples taken from each beaker at each time point.

D. decreasing the number of time points over 24 hours to minimize disruption of the beakers.

The correct answer is D. This question asks you to suggest improvements to the experiment to increase the reliability of the results. You must decide which of the given suggestions would be *least likely* to improve the experiment. Choice A provides a method of ensuring that the dissolved gas composition is consistent throughout the beaker, which is something that was not addressed in the original experiment. This is certainly an improvement, so it is not the correct answer here. Choice B suggests decreasing the concentration of NaOH added during the phenolphthalein test. While this would involve adding a greater volume of NaOH to the test sample, this step improves the reliability of the experiment because it allows for smaller concentration increment increases in NaOH base, allowing the students to more closely estimate the solution acidity rather than overshooting it. This is also an improvement. Choice C, increasing the number of experimental trials, is *always* an improvement because increasing the number of trials means you are basing your average numbers on a greater sample size, which improves reliability.

That leaves choice D. While minimizing beaker disruption would be ideal, decreasing the number of time points decreases the number of data points you obtain, and it decreases your chances of seeing more subtle changes. In terms of the data acquired in this particular experiment, there were certain time periods (e.g., 6–12 hours) that experienced more dramatic changes in dissolved gases relative to others, and this would all be missed if the number of time points were decreased.

HOW CAN THE PROVIDED DATA BE ANALYZED?

Beyond analysis of the question, hypothesis, and experiment itself, the rest of the material covered by questions that accompany Research Summaries should look very familiar. That's because we've already discussed data analysis and drawing conclusions in Chapter 11. All of the principles of data analysis that applied to Data Interpretation questions also apply here.

To review, those key skills are as follows:

- Understand the provided data.

- Draw conclusions based on the data.

- Analyze or construct graphs.

- Assess the validity of the data.

- Consider future work based on the data.

We'll focus on drawing conclusions in the next section, but the rest of these data analysis skills are relevant here. Understanding the data means identifying the variables and controls, and then determining how the data express these variables and controls. Analyzing and constructing graphs becomes essential in data analysis because you have to be able to read data provided in graphical form, but you also might be asked to interpret trends in tabulated data and present that data in graphical form. Finally, considering future work based on data is a bit different than what we just discussed in the previous section, though only slightly. While the previous section focused on the experimental side of considering future work, here the future work is more idea- and data-based. In other words, this aspect of future work is geared more toward building new hypotheses based on data rather than just focusing on experimental variations. Still, the two go hand-in-hand and overlap in many respects.

For our purposes, the following examples fall under the category of considering characteristics of data and possible trends for the future, but in the context of the sample passage we've been working with throughout this chapter.

Be sure to review Chapter 11 for more detailed information about each of these subcategories of data analysis.

Which of the following graphs best represents the trend in dissolved oxygen as a function of time for the stonewort grown in the light?

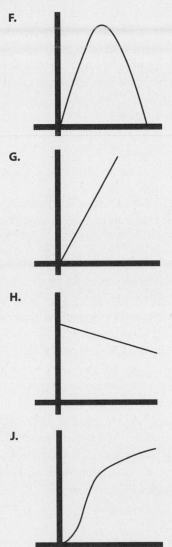

F.

G.

H.

J.

The correct answer is J. This question asks you to construct a chart based on the data provided in the table. Whenever you're asked to construct a graph based on a set of numerical data, the first thing you should do is identify the independent and dependent variables. Based on our data table, as well as the description of the experiment, the independent variable is *time*, and the dependent variable is *the concentration of dissolved oxygen*, as measured by an oxygen electrode.

The next step is to look for the general trend in the numbers—in other words, examine whether the data increase, decrease, or fluctuate throughout the experiment. In this case, we're looking at the dissolved oxygen data for stonewort grown in the light; this would be the first row of data in the data table. As time

increases, the concentration of dissolved oxygen also increases. There is never a decrease in oxygen concentration, so we can immediately rule out choices F and H because both exhibit some kind of a decrease in dissolved oxygen concentration over the measured time period. In order to distinguish between choices G and J, we must now determine whether or not the increase in dissolved oxygen is linear. To test this out, check out the increase in dissolved oxygen concentration over a few equivalent time periods; if the increase is the same, the increase is linear.

For this example, let's look at the 0–6 hour and 6–12 hour time periods. From 0 to 6 hours, the dissolved oxygen concentration increases by 0.46 ppm, but from 6 to 12 hours, the dissolved oxygen concentration increases by 1.80 ppm. These are clearly not the same, and if we check out each time point, we can confirm that we are not looking at a linear trend. The answer, then, cannot be choice G. The correct answer, which displays a graph that fits our trend, is choice J.

In this experiment, the more reliable gas measurement is:

A. dissolved oxygen, because it is a direct measurement of gas concentration.
B. carbon dioxide, because it is a direct measurement of gas concentration.
C. dissolved oxygen, because the same trend in concentration is observed in the light and dark.
D. carbon dioxide, because the same trend in concentration is observed in the light and dark.

The correct answer is A. This question asks you to analyze the two types of gas measurements acquired in this experiment and determine which technique is more reliable. We can look at the data to immediately rule out choices C and D; opposite trends are clearly seen in the light and dark conditions, so this reasoning does not work. In the dark, the concentration of CO_2 increases, while in the light, the concentration of CO_2 decreases. In the dark, the concentration of O_2 decreases, while in the light, the concentration of O_2 increases.

The dilemma is now deciding between choices A and B by deciding which technique is more direct. With the CO_2 measurements, CO_2 reacts with water in the presence of phenolphthalein to form acid, which is then measured by adding NaOH. There are a few places where this experiment could give unreliable results; for instance, the experiment relies on a chemical reaction, and not all of the CO_2 may have been converted to acid at the time of detection. Furthermore, a color change is used as a marker of acidity, not even CO_2 concentration specifically. This method is indirect. An oxygen probe, like any probe, directly measures the gas of interest. Therefore, the best answer is choice A.

WHAT CONCLUSIONS CAN BE DRAWN BASED ON THE EXPERIMENT AND RESULTS?

Once you've progressed through the question, hypothesis, experiment, and data, the final feature of Research Summaries on which you'll be tested is your ability to draw conclusions based on the data. Drawing conclusions was a major part of analyzing Data Representation questions, on which we focused heavily in Chapter 11. To review, the goal of drawing conclusions is to answer the posed scientific question by finding trends and patterns in the data. Applying an observed pattern or trend in order to answer a scientific question is really the main point of doing scientific research; performing experiments and gathering data are most beneficial to the scientific community if conclusions can be drawn. The ACT Science test therefore assesses you in this area because drawing conclusions is such an important feature of Research Summaries. If you can look at data, identify trends, and apply these trends in a relevant way to a scientific question, then you have successfully shown your ability to think like a scientist.

Let's see how you might be tested on this skill.

. . . .

Photosynthesis is a biological process that generates stored energy through the formation of glucose from carbon dioxide and water, according to the following chemical reaction:

$$6\,CO_2 + 6\,H_2O \rightarrow C_6H_{12}O_6 + 6\,O_2$$

Cellular respiration works in opposition, using oxygen to break down the sugar and release that energy to form ATP:

$$C_6H_{12}O_6 + 6\,O_2 \rightarrow 6\,CO_2 + 6\,H_2O$$

Carbon dioxide reacts with water to form carbonic acid. Phenolphthalein is an indicator that remains colorless in acid and turns pink in base. Three drops of phenolphthalein can be added to a small water sample, and the amount of NaOH needed to turn a clear sample pink, its neutralization point, gives an indication of the concentration of carbonic acid in the sample.

Many plants and algae are capable of both photosynthesis and respiration. Among these is an algal species called stonewort, of

the genus *Chara*. Stonewort grows well in lime-rich waters, which results in the formation of calcium carbonate deposits on the algae.

A group of students wants to test the rates of photosynthesis and respiration in stonewort in different light conditions. The students acquire two 6.00-g stonewort samples and place each in a beaker containing 250 mL of spring water. One beaker was incubated in the dark at 25°C, while the other beaker was incubated in the light at 25°C. Over the course of one day, two 1-mL water samples were removed from each beaker every six hours. One of each pair of water samples was used to detect dissolved oxygen concentration using an oxygen electrode, which measures O_2 concentration in units of parts per million (ppm). The second water sample per pair was used to test carbon dioxide levels using phenolphthalein and 0.04 M NaOH. Both tests were performed immediately after sample extraction to avoid sample disruption. The following results were obtained:

Stonewort Sample	Measurement	Time (hours)				
		0	6	12	18	24
Light	Dissolved O_2 (ppm)	2.35	2.81	4.61	5.02	5.30
	Volume 0.04 M NaOH (μL)	21.0	18.3	14.0	13.3	12.8
Dark	Dissolved O_2 (ppm)	2.36	2.37	2.01	1.84	1.79
	Volume 0.04 M NaOH (μL)	22.2	23.0	26.1	28.7	30.0

Based on the data, which of the following conclusions can be drawn about the effect of light and dark conditions on photosynthesis and respiration in stoneworts?

F. The rates of photosynthesis and respiration increase under light conditions relative to dark conditions.

G. The rates of photosynthesis and respiration decrease under light conditions relative to dark conditions.

H. The rate of photosynthesis exceeds the rate of respiration in the light, but the rate of respiration exceeds the rate of photosynthesis in the dark.

J. The rate of respiration exceeds the rate of photosynthesis in the light, but the rate of photosynthesis exceeds the rate of respiration in the dark.

The correct answer is H. This question simply asks you to examine the data and draw a conclusion to answer the scientific question based on the data. The answer choices for this question refer to both photosynthesis and respiration under light and dark conditions, so it is important that we examine the data to include all of these relevant variables.

Based on the data, we can immediately rule out choices F and G, because the trends observed for carbon dioxide and oxygen, respectively, are not the same under light and dark conditions. We must now distinguish between choices H and J. To begin, look at the dissolved oxygen data. Under light conditions, the concentration of oxygen increases over time, but under dark conditions, the concentration of oxygen decreases over time. Oxygen is a product of photosynthesis and a reactant in respiration, so these data indicate that photosynthesis occurs more rapidly than respiration under light conditions and more slowly than respiration under dark conditions. The carbon dioxide data lead us to the same conclusion. Under light conditions, the carbon dioxide concentration decreases, but under dark conditions, the carbon dioxide concentration increases. Carbon dioxide is a reactant in photosynthesis and a product of respiration, so the same conclusion can be drawn from the carbon dioxide data. Based on these trends, the correct answer is choice H. In order to see these net gas increases and decreases, photosynthesis must be stimulated under light conditions, while respiration prevails under dark conditions. If you have any background knowledge of photosynthesis, this conclusion may be obvious, as photosynthesis depends on light absorption.

COMMON MISTAKES TO AVOID

In Chapter 11, some of the common traps we covered for Data Representation questions were challenging terminology, unnecessary information, unexpected results, and unusual data representation. These same pitfalls apply to Research Summaries, so feel free to head back to Chapter 11 to review the relevant explanations and examples again. However, there are a few other common mistakes that test takers make that are more specific to Research Summaries; we'll discuss those here.

PASSAGE SKIMMING

When you're taking the ACT, you will probably experience at least a small amount of stress and urgency. After all, you're being asked to answer quite a few questions in a relatively short period of time. As we've seen already, some of the questions you'll come across will be simple recall and reading comprehension from the passage, while others may require a bit more thinking. Regardless of exactly what kinds of questions you face, you will have plenty of time and should use that time efficiently. Unfortunately, students under stress will often turn to a skimming strategy—they go directly to the questions to see what information they will need, and then they skim through the passage in order to find the specific answers to the questions. While skimming might work sometimes for questions that require simple recall, it is a flawed strategy and can cause problems if you use it throughout the ACT Science test.

By definition, skimming through a passage involves rapid reading; you look for keywords without completely comprehending the meaning of the entire passage. Sure, you might be able to skim the passage to understand what paper chromatography does or to find the equation to calculate a coefficient of friction, but you will miss a lot of important details, too. You could even miss the basic premise of the passage, and this could be devastating for Research Summaries because if you don't understand the scientific question, you will not be clear on the kind of data you need to collect and the kinds of conclusions you should be drawing.

TIP: Instead of skimming through a passage after looking at the questions, you should start with the passage itself.

Read through and jot down some notes in the margins of your test. The test booklets are there for you to work out your thoughts, so you might as well use them! As you read, identify the scientific question, and write down some notes about important details you'll want to remember or underline key words you may want to return to later. As you approach the experimental design, jot down the dependent and independent variables, as well as any controls you feel are worth noting. Then, you'll be all set to take on the questions because you've established the basic premise of the passage. This is particularly important because the incorrect answers that follow the questions are often tied very closely to the premise. That means if you simply skim the passage to find the correct answer without actually understanding the passage, you might mistakenly choose a wrong answer simply because it seems closely tied to the topic, when in fact there might be a better answer among the choices.

This question highlights the importance of carefully reading the passage.

Pectinase is an enzyme that breaks down pectin, a polysaccharide found in plant cell walls. Pectin compounds hold together dispersed particles in suspension in fruit juices. As such, pectins increase the viscosity of juice.

A group of students wanted to compare the activities of pectinases from three different plant species (A, B, and C). The students placed 30 mL of applesauce into each of four beakers, labeled 1–4. In beaker 1, 1 mL of distilled water was added. In each of beakers 2–4, 1 mL of pectinase from one of the species A, B, and C

was added. The contents of each beaker were thoroughly stirred using separate glass stirring rods, and then the four beakers were allowed to sit at room temperature for 15 minutes. After the 15 minutes, cheesecloth was placed into four separate funnels, each of which was placed onto a 50-mL graduated cylinder. Using the glass stirring rod to move the mixtures along, the contents of each beaker were poured into each of the graduated cylinders, and the filtrate was collected for each. The amount of juice was measured, and the results are shown in the table below:

Beaker (Pectinase Species)	Volume of Filtrate Collected (mL)
1 (Distilled Water)	10.1
2 (Species A)	27.5
3 (Species B)	22.3
4 (Species C)	26.0

The control in this experiment is:

    A. the volume of filtrate collected for each sample.
    B. the sample to which no pectinase was added.
    C. the use of a glass stirring rod for each sample.
    D. the applesauce sample containing pectinase.

The correct answer is B. The passage describes an experiment for pectinase activity measurement using applesauce, and at its surface, the question is quite straightforward: identify the control in this experiment. The control is the unaffected sample to which all affected samples are compared. In order to figure out what the control is, we must first determine the variables. The independent variable is the *species from which the different pectinases have been extracted*. The dependent variable is the *volume of juice, or filtrate, acquired after applesauce incubation with pectinase*. Choice A, therefore, describes the dependent variable, not the control, and can be ruled out as a correct answer. Choice C, the use of a glass stirring rod for each sample, is a constant, not a control, because it is an experimental feature common to all samples.

In deciding between choices B and D, we are looking for the unaffected sample, which would be the sample to which no pectinase is added. That means that the correct answer is choice B. If you had just skimmed the passage, you might not have been drawn to choice B right away because all four answer choices are directly relevant to the experiment in some way, and two of the distractors (choices A and C) are important variables or constants that are very much relevant to the experiment. If you'd been jotting notes about such variables during your initial reading, you would be able to eliminate these choices right away. So when it comes to Research Summaries, take the time to read carefully and take some notes, because skimming for answers is far from a foolproof strategy.

INFORMATION INFERENCE AND ASSUMPTION

When you read through Research Summaries, it is important to avoid inferring information that is not actually given in the passage. This goes hand in hand with the "Unexpected Results" trap we discussed in Chapter 11. With unexpected results, the take-home advice was to use the data you're given and base your conclusions on those data, rather than assume you know what *should* happen in an experiment and base conclusions on that. This advice is even more relevant to experimental procedures, which is why it is important to discuss here.

Research Summaries provide fairly in-depth descriptions of experimental procedures and the data obtained from those procedures. Research Summary questions may ask you to suggest an improvement to the experiment or to come up with a way to ensure condition uniformity among your experimental groups. When you're asked questions like these, don't assume the scientists who performed the experiments already made the adjustments. Earlier in the chapter (on page 434), we asked you to choose the one method among the provided choices that would *not* improve the reliability of an experiment. If you look at the three distractors, which in this example are solid ways to improve the reliability of the experiment, you might think that these are obvious steps one would take in this experiment. However, these steps are not explicitly stated in the passage, so you can't assume they were performed, as obvious as they may seem.

The same tip can be applied to the passage as a whole. For instance, if a scientific question is posed and an experiment is performed to test that question, you can't always assume that the results answer the question. Sometimes, the data obtained may not tell you anything new. Other times, you might see unexpected data that answer a different scientific question. The important things to remember are that no science experiment is perfect, and errors or experimental design flaws are always possible. But don't worry about picking up on these on your own—if an experiment contains a major design flaw that you're supposed to notice, there will always be a question that addresses it so you know what to look out for, as in the following example.

. . . .

Pectinase is an enzyme that breaks down pectin, a polysaccharide found in plant cell walls. Pectin compounds hold together dispersed particles in suspension in fruit juices. As such, pectins increase the viscosity of juice.

A group of students wanted to compare the activities of pectinases from three different plant species (*A*, *B*, and *C*). The students placed 30 mL of applesauce into each of four beakers, labeled 1-4. In beaker 1, 1 mL of distilled water was added. In each of beakers 2-4, 1 mL of pectinase from one of the species *A*, *B*, and *C*

was added. The contents of each beaker were thoroughly stirred using separate glass stirring rods, and then the four beakers were allowed to sit at room temperature for fifteen minutes. After the fifteen minutes, cheesecloth was placed into four separate funnels, each of which was placed onto a 50-mL graduated cylinder. Using the glass stirring rod to move the mixtures along, the contents of each beaker were poured into each of the graduated cylinders, and the filtrate was collected for each. The amount of juice was measured, and the results are shown in the table below:

Beaker (Pectinase Species)	Volume of Filtrate Collected (mL)
1 (Distilled Water)	10.1
2 (Species *A*)	27.5
3 (Species *B*)	22.3
4 (Species *C*)	26.0

Which of the following additional constants should be maintained among the samples to allow the different pectinase results to be compared?

F. The organism from which the pectinases are extracted

G. The volume of filtrate collected for each sample

H. The concentration of pectinase in the 1 mL added per sample

J. The use of the same glass stirring rod for all four samples

The correct answer is H. The passage describes a fairly straightforward way to test for pectinase activity by looking at how much juice is collected from applesauce upon the addition of pectinase. This question asks you to choose a variable that should be kept constant for all samples in order to allow for comparison of the activities of the different pectinases. Choice F is incorrect; the passage indicates that the three tested pectinases are from different species, so this answer doesn't make sense. Even if the passage did not specify that the pectinases are from different organisms, the answer makes no logical sense because you can certainly compare the same protein from different organisms—scientists all over the world devote their research to this very cause! Choice G is not correct because it essentially describes the dependent variable of this experiment. If you adjusted your experiment so that all samples collected the same volume of filtrate, then you really wouldn't be accomplishing much, since the filtrate volume is what you're measuring. Choice J is also incorrect. The glass stirring rod is used only for indirect functions, like stirring the solutions or transferring the solutions to the funnels. Using the same glass stirring rod would only increase the likelihood of cross-contamination between samples and would not really improve sample comparability. That leaves choice H, which indicates that the concentration of pectinase added should be the same for all samples. This makes sense; concentration represents the amount of a substance per unit volume, so if you're adding 1 mL of different pectinases at the same concentration to each sample, you ensure you're adding the same amount of enzyme per sample. You can't assume this was done, as it is not stated in the passage, so this is the correct answer.

New Techniques

Because different test takers will have different amounts of exposure to various scientific techniques, this challenge will be more applicable to students who are perhaps less experienced than others. But don't worry if you're not familiar with a particular technique described in the passage—if a more complicated technique is described, you will be provided with enough information in the passage to figure out how it works. In the event that a new technique is presented and you still don't quite understand how it works, you can use clues throughout the passage to figure it out. For example, if a passage describes the separation of components in a mixture using paper chromatography, and you have no idea what paper chromatography is, you can look at the experimental description for hints about how it works and at the data to identify the independent and dependent variables. The independent and dependent variables are almost always included somewhere in any table or graph that contains data, so even if you're not 100 percent sure about how a new technique works, you can still figure out the most important features of the experiment from the given protocol, and you can determine the variables from the experimental description and provided data. Remember, you'll never be expected to know how specific scientific techniques work off the top of your head; you will always be given enough background information to figure out what you need to know about the technique (or set of techniques) discussed in the passage. Let's go back to our sample passage to illustrate.

Pectinase is an enzyme that breaks down pectin, a polysaccharide found in plant cell walls. Pectin compounds hold together dispersed particles in suspension in fruit juices. As such, pectins increase the viscosity of juice.

A group of students wanted to compare the activities of pectinases from three different plant species (A, B, and C). The students placed 30 mL of applesauce into each of four beakers, labeled 1-4. In beaker 1, 1 mL of distilled water was added. In each of beakers 2-4, 1 mL of pectinase from one of the species A, B, and C was added. The contents of each beaker were thoroughly stirred using separate glass stirring rods, and then the four beakers were allowed to sit at room temperature for fifteen minutes. After the fifteen minutes, cheesecloth was placed into four separate funnels, each of which was placed onto a 50-mL graduated cylinder. Using the glass stirring rod to move the mixtures along, the contents of each beaker were poured into each of the graduated cylinders, and the filtrate was collected for each. The amount of juice was measured, and the results are shown in the table below:

Beaker (Pectinase Species)	Volume of Filtrate Collected (mL)
1 (Distilled Water)	10.1
2 (Species A)	27.5
3 (Species B)	22.3
4 (Species C)	26.0

Based on the collected data, which pectinase sample exhibited the highest activity when added to applesauce?

A. Pectinase from Species *A*.
B. Pectinase from Species *B*.
C. Pectinase from Species *C*.
D. All three pectinases exhibited the same level of activity.

The correct answer is A. For this question, you are asked to draw a conclusion based on the provided data. But in order to do this, you must understand what is actually happening in the experiment. The passage indicates that pectinase breaks down pectin compounds and that pectin compounds hold particles together in fruit juices, making them more viscous. This means that if you add pectinase to a fruit juice sample, or in this example, applesauce, pectinase will break down the particle clumps in the sample and produce more liquid from the applesauce. This particular experiment uses filtration to separate the liquid from the rest of the applesauce, measuring the volume of filtrate.

If you know what filtration, or "filtering," is, you're all set. The more active pectinase will be the sample that produces more juice, or filtrate. If filtration is new to you, you can figure out what it is based on the protocol and data. The protocol describes the use of a funnel and cheesecloth, a porous material that allows liquid through while keeping solid material in the funnel. Another hint about how the technique works is the set of phrases "filtrate was collected" and "amount of juice was measured." These phrases indicate that the juice, a liquid, is what is being collected, and that the juice is therefore the filtrate. The data tell you that the dependent variable is the volume of filtrate, confirming that this technique separates liquid juice from the rest of the applesauce and measures its volume. So even if you don't know what filtration is, or what a "filtrate" is, you can figure it out from the passage and data. To answer the question, we want to know which pectinase sample was most active, so we want to identify the sample for which the greatest volume of liquid juice, or filtrate, was collected. Based on the data table, the highest volume of juice was collected from the Species *A* pectinase, especially compared to the water control, so the correct answer is choice A.

SUMMING IT UP

- **Research Summaries pose a scientific question and describe an experiment or set of experiments to answer that question.** They will also include the experimental results obtained, in the form of a table, graph, or chart.

- **Identify the scientific question** or **purpose of the experiment first** whenever you encounter a scientific experiment in an ACT Science passage. Ask yourself why the experiment is being conducted and what it's testing. Research Summaries provide you with all the background information you will need to identify the purpose of the given experiment.

- **Some ACT questions might ask you to choose the most suitable hypothesis for an experiment.** Your hypothesis must always correctly address the appropriate independent and dependent variables. Hypotheses are *predictions*, and a hypothesis will not always correctly predict the outcome of an experiment. Results of experiments often disprove hypotheses, which is okay!

- **Some ACT questions will ask you to identify variables and controls and recognize why the experiment was designed a certain way and how it answers the scientific question posed.** Research Summaries always provide enough detail so that you can figure out what's going on. The techniques will not be overly complicated—the passage will provide you with the background you need.

- **Drawing conclusions about data presented to you means finding trends and patterns in the data.** When reading over an experiment and its accompanying data, take note of any obvious trends—you are sure to be asked about them and how they relate to the experiment's hypothesis.

- **Don't skim ACT Science passages to simply look for key words you see in the questions—you will miss a lot of important details.** If you don't understand the scientific question, you will not be clear on the data you need to collect and the conclusions you should draw.

- **Avoid making any inferences or assumptions about experiments or data—you should consider *only* what is in front of you in the given passage as true.** If an experiment contains an error or flaw, it's supposed to be there! You will likely see a question asking about it.

- **Don't be daunted by new and unfamiliar scientific techniques you might see in passages.** You are not expected to know about every branch of science off the top of your head! You will always be given enough background information to figure out what you need to know.

441

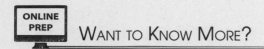

WANT TO KNOW MORE?

Access more practice questions, lessons, helpful hints, and strategies for the following science topics in *Peterson's ACT Online Course*:

- Data Interpretation of Experiments
- Research Summaries and Conflicting Viewpoints

To purchase and access the course, go to **www.petersons.com/act**.

PRACTICE

Now that you are more familiar with Research Summary questions, it's time to try a practice set on your own. When you're finished answering all 21 questions, check the answers and explanations that follow to figure out how well you did and why you may have selected any incorrect answer choices.

PASSAGE I

Gravitational acceleration is 9.8 m/s², and this is the force that pulls an object down an inclined plane. A student is interested in how roller coasters work and wants to test the effect of an angle of an inclined plane on the acceleration of a moving object. To investigate, the student sets up four tracks of the same 1-meter length, d, made of the same type of smooth wood. Each track varies in angle, θ, as measured using a protractor and ranging from 5° to 50°.

A marble was released at the top of each inclined plane, and the time, t, was recorded that it took for the marble to reach the end of the plane. Two trials were performed for each inclined plane, and the times were averaged. The data was analyzed by calculating the acceleration of the marble at each angle, using the equation $d = \frac{1}{2}at^2$.

Finally, the sine of each angle was calculated, and each acceleration was plotted as a function of sin θ to acquire a linear best-fit line.

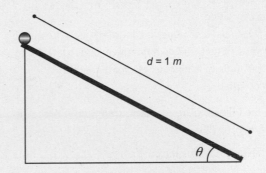

$d = 1\ m$

θ

Table 1			
Angle of Incline, θ (°)	**Average Travel Time (s)**	**Acceleration (m/s²)**	**Sin θ**
5	1.56	0.82	0.0872
20	0.748	3.57	0.342
35	0.599	5.57	0.574
50	0.514	7.57	0.766

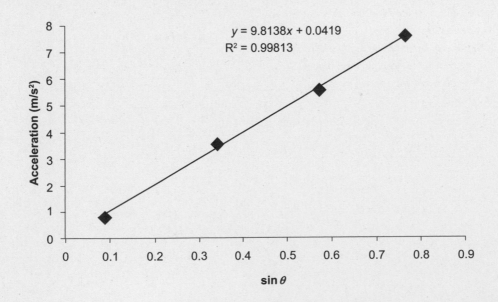

$y = 9.8138x + 0.0419$
$R^2 = 0.99813$

1. Which of the following hypotheses predicts the outcome of this experiment?

   A. If increased angles of incline allow for a greater effect of vertical gravitational pull, then increasing the angle of incline will increase marble acceleration.

   B. If increased angles of incline allow for a greater effect of vertical gravitational pull, then increasing the angle of incline will decrease marble acceleration.

   C. If decreased angles of incline allow for a greater effect of vertical gravitational pull, then increasing the angle of incline will increase marble acceleration.

   D. If decreased angles of incline allow for a greater effect of vertical gravitational pull, then increasing the angle of incline will decrease marble acceleration.

2. All of the following are constants throughout this experiment EXCEPT:

   F. the length of the inclined plane.
   G. the friction of the inclined plane.
   H. the height of the marble from the ground at its starting point.
   J. the height of the marble from the ground at its ending point.

3. The complete equation relating acceleration and time is $d = v_i t + \frac{1}{2} at^2$, where v_i is the initial velocity of the moving object. The student was able to simplify this equation to $d = \frac{1}{2} at^2$ because:

   A. the starting time was 0 seconds for each trial.
   B. the marble's initial velocity was 0 m/s for each trial since it started at rest.
   C. the marble was stopped to a velocity of 0 m/s after reaching the bottom of each inclined plane.
   D. the distance d did not vary between each of the trials.

4. The graph of acceleration as a function of $\sin \theta$ shows that:

   F. there is an exponential relationship between acceleration and $\sin \theta$, with the y-intercept approximately equal to gravitational acceleration.

   G. there is a linear relationship between acceleration and $\sin \theta$, with the y-intercept approximately equal to gravitational acceleration.

   H. there is a linear relationship between acceleration and $\sin \theta$, with the slope approximately equal to gravitational acceleration.

   J. there is no significant correlation between acceleration and $\sin \theta$.

5. If the experiment were repeated using an inclined plane that has a length of 2.0 m, which is twice the length of the plane used in the original experiment, how would the provided graph change?

   A. The slope of the new line would be double that of the original line.
   B. The slope of the new line would be half that of the original line.
   C. The slope of the new line would be the same as that of the original line.
   D. The y-intercept of the new line would be double that of the original line.

6. One way to improve this experiment would be to:

   F. use angles of incline up to 90°.
   G. increase the number of trials at each angle of incline.
   H. get the marble rolling in advance and start the time when it is halfway down the inclined plane.
   J. measure the times in minutes rather than seconds.

PASSAGE II

The radioactive decay of uranium produces the noble gas radon. Radon-222 is the most significant isotope of radon, occurring at a much higher concentration than any other radon isotopes, which are barely detectable in the environment. Radon-222 has a relatively long half-life of 3.8 days and appears at measurable levels in the environment. As radon decays, it dissolves into soil pores and fluid, migrating into groundwater, soil gas, and the atmosphere. Many scientists have hypothesized that radon levels might serve as precursors to earthquakes.

A telemetric radon station collected measurements of radon levels, temperature, and air pressure prior to a pair of shallow earthquakes that occurred in Prokopion, Greece, on November 17, 2014. The data are shown in the graphs below, with dates on the x-axis formatted as day/month.

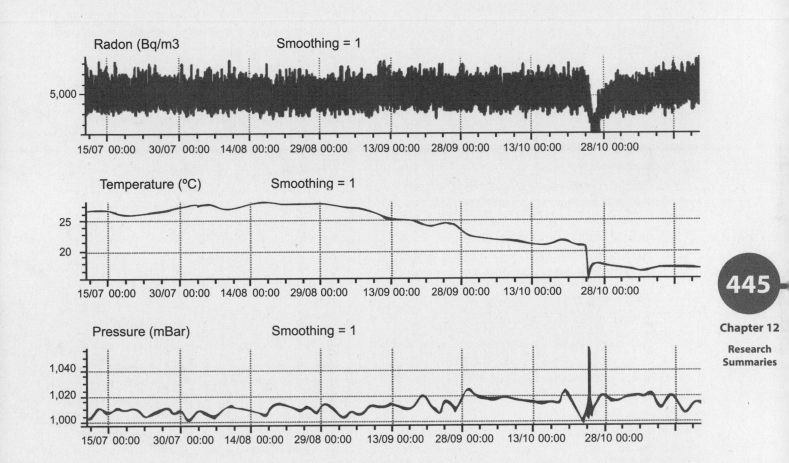

Source: [http://www.omicsonline.org/open-access/longmemory-trends-in-disturbances-of-radon-in-soil-prior-to-the-twin-ml-earthquakes-of-november-greece-2157-7617.1000244.pdf (open access)]

7. Which of the following identifies the scientific question or purpose of the collected data?

    A. How does pressure affect radon levels and temperatures over time?
    B. How do radon levels, temperature, and air pressure vary with altitude?
    C. How do radon levels, temperature, and air pressure change while earthquakes take place?
    D. How might radon levels, temperature, and air pressure be predictive of earthquake occurrence?

8. The date on which the highest air pressure is recorded is:

    F. July 15, 2014.
    G. September 28, 2014.
    H. October 28, 2014.
    J. November 17, 2014.

9. To increase the reliability of the acquired data, investigators could:

    A. measure the levels of the other radon isotopes in the environment.
    B. collect the same data from another local telemetric station for this region.
    C. calculate a best-fit line for all three types of data in order to predict future levels of each.
    D. plot the dependent variables on the same graph, using the same x- and y-axes units for comparison.

10. A constant among all variables measured in this experiment is the:

    F. regional location of all measurements.
    G. type of instrument or probe used to collect all measurements.
    H. amplitudes of all signals collected.
    J. inclusion of the date of the earthquakes on the x-axis.

11. Which of the following conclusions can be drawn based on the collected data?

    A. Simultaneous declines in radon-222, temperature, and air pressure levels might indicate an impending earthquake.
    B. Simultaneous declines in radon-222 and temperature levels, and a spike in air pressure might indicate an impending earthquake.
    C. Simultaneous spikes in radon-222, temperature, and air pressure levels might indicate an impending earthquake.
    D. Simultaneous spikes in temperature and air pressure levels, and a decline in the radon-222 level might indicate an impending earthquake.

PASSAGE III

Alloys are uniform mixtures that consist of a metal and at least one other kind of element. Steel is an alloy that is composed of iron and a variety of other elements; carbon steel is a mixture of iron and mostly carbon and a bit of chromium, while stainless steel is a mixture of iron and mostly chromium. Bronze is an alloy consisting mostly of copper and tin. Electrum is an alloy consisting of gold and silver.

After observing the formation of rust on their cars, several students were interested in testing the reactivity of these four alloys with air. The students hypothesize that the two types of steel will rust because they contain iron, while the other two alloys will not, based on their knowledge that iron reacts with oxygen gas in air to form iron oxide, or rust, which is a solid product of the reaction.

To test their hypothesis, the students weighed 5 g of each solid alloy and fastened it to the bottom of a test tube. They then inverted each test tube and placed it into a beaker containing 30 mL of water. The students took an initial measurement of the distance of the column of air, from the water level in the test tube to the bottom of the inverted test tube. The students also placed an empty inverted test tube into a beaker of 30 mL water as a control.

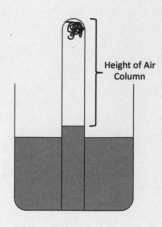

Height of Air Column

The students measured the height of the air column every three days for 12 days. The control test tube air column remained constant at 19.0 cm throughout the experiment. The alloy results are shown in the following graph.

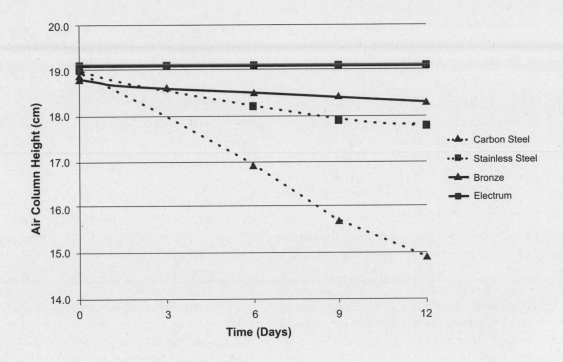

12. Based on their hypothesis, what would the students predict would happen in the bronze and electrum samples?

F. The heights of the air columns will increase significantly.

G. The heights of the air columns will decrease significantly.

H. The heights of the air columns will stay fairly constant.

J. The height of electrum's air column will decrease, while the height of bronze's air column will increase.

13. The dependent variable in this experiment is the:

A. time, in days, at which the measurements were taken.

B. air column heights.

C. types of alloys tested.

D. volumes of water in each beaker.

14. Measuring the mass of the metal in a test tube every three days for 12 days would not be an especially useful alternative method to this experiment because:

F. water is an essential part of the rusting reaction.

G. a key reactant of the rusting reaction is a gas.

H. oxygen is not the predominant gas in air.

J. the key product of the rusting reaction is a solid.

15. Which feature of the collected data most strongly and directly supports the students' hypothesis?

A. The alloys that contain iron exhibit a more significant air column decrease than those that do not contain iron.

B. The alloys that do not contain iron react more extensively with air than the alloys that do contain iron.

C. The minimal decreases in air column volume observed for bronze and electrum are likely due to alternative reactions of the alloys with gases in the air.

D. Bronze exhibited a more significant air column decrease than electrum.

447

Chapter 12

Research Summaries

16. A conclusion that can be drawn by comparing the data for carbon steel and stainless steel is:

    F. carbon in an alloy may protect iron from rusting.
    G. chromium in an alloy may protect iron from rusting.
    H. gold in an alloy may promote iron rusting.
    J. tin in an alloy may promote iron rusting.

PASSAGE IV

Garlic is a spice that has proven useful in treating a range of ailments, from colds and the flu to heart disease and high blood pressure. The two main substances found in garlic are alliin, a sulfur-rich amino acid, and an enzyme called alliinase. When garlic is crushed, alliinase mixes with alliin to form a compound called allicin. Alliin has no odor, but allicin formation gives garlic its characteristic pungent odor and taste.

A student wanted to test whether or not allicin has antibacterial properties. The student decided to test *Escherichia coli,* a gram-negative bacterial species found in an array of environments. The student wanted to use both solid and liquid growth media to test bacterial growth. First, the student used Luria broth (LB) growth media to make plates that contained kanamycin, an antibiotic to which her strain of *E. coli* is resistant. One set of plates contained solid LB with kanamycin, one set of plates contained LB solidified with kanamycin and 0.3 mM allicin, and one set of plates contained LB solidified with kanamycin and 1.0 mM allicin. There were three plates per set. The plates were grown

overnight at 37°C, and the number of colonies was counted for each plate. The average numbers of colonies per plate per set are displayed in the following table:

Plate Content	Average Number of Colonies per Plate
LB + kanamycin	20.7
LB + kanamycin + 0.3 mM allicin	5.3
LB + kanamycin + 1.0 mM allicin	1.3

The student then tested the growth of *E. coli* in liquid medium by growing five different samples in 50 mL of growth media. Samples 1–3 were initially grown in LB with kanamycin. Sample 1 was left alone. In Sample 2, allicin was added to the sample to a final concentration of 0.3 mM after 120 minutes of growth. In Sample 3, allicin was added to the sample to a final concentration of 1.0 mM after 2 hours of growth. Samples 4 and 5 were grown in LB and kanamycin that contained 0.3 and 1.0 mM allicin, respectively, from the start. The cells were grown at 37°C with constant shaking for 6 hours. Each hour, the student measured cell density by removing a sample of the growth and checking its optical density, or absorbance, at a wavelength of 600 nm. The growth curves obtained are shown below:

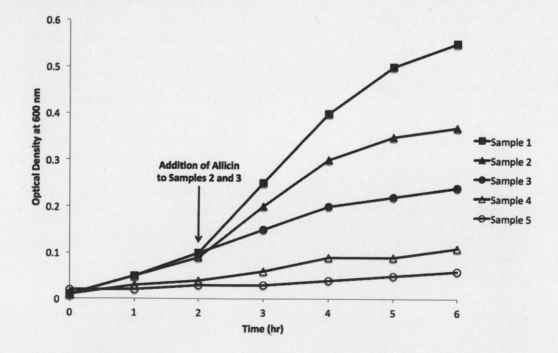

17. These experiments were designed to test the effect of:

A. temperature on *E. coli* bacterial growth.
B. solid and liquid media on allicin concentrations in *E. coli*.
C. cell density on *E. coli* bacterial growth.
D. varying concentrations of allicin on *E. coli* bacterial growth.

18. Based on the graph, what is the optical density for the allicin-free control after 5 hours?

F. 0.2
G. 0.35
H. 0.5
J. 0.55

19. The second set of plates, containing LB, kanamycin, and 0.3 mM allicin, most closely correspond with which liquid growth trial?

A. Sample 1
B. Sample 2
C. Sample 3
D. Sample 4

20. The purpose of adding kanamycin to the growth media for all samples is to:

F. slow *E. coli* growth to make for easier tracking.
G. prevent contamination by other microorganisms.
H. promote any effects of allicin on *E. coli* cells.
J. accelerate *E. coli* growth within the experimental timeframe.

21. Based on the data, which of the following conclusions can be drawn about the effect of allicin on *E. coli* bacterial growth?

A. Increased allicin concentrations promote *E. coli* growth, even when added during the growth process.
B. Increased allicin concentrations promote inhibition of *E. coli* growth, even when added during the growth process.
C. Increased allicin concentrations promote inhibition of *E. coli* growth, but only when included from the beginning of the growth process.
D. Increased allicin concentrations promote *E. coli* growth, but only when included from the beginning of the growth process.

449

Chapter 12

Research Summaries

Answers and Explanations

PASSAGE I

The first passage is a physics passage. It describes an experiment that tests the effect of an angle of incline on the acceleration of a marble.

1. **The correct answer is A.** The question asks you to choose the hypothesis that predicts the outcome of the experiment. Of the two hypothesis stems provided in the answer choices, the only one that makes sense and which also corresponds with the observed outcome in the data is, "If increased angles of incline allow for a greater effect of vertical gravitational pull." This allows you to immediately rule out choices C and D. The data show that as the angle of incline increases, the acceleration also increases. This means that you can rule out choice B, which states the opposite.

2. **The correct answer is H.** This question asks you to look at the experimental design and select the answer that is *not* held constant for every trial. The length of the inclined plane is 1 m for every trial, so you can rule out choice F. The friction of the inclined plane is also the same for every trial because the same material was used for all trials, so choice G can also be ruled out. The marble always reaches the ground at its ending point, so you can eliminate choice J. The starting height of the marble differs per trial because the 1-m board is set up at various angles of incline, so the correct answer is choice H.

3. **The correct answer is B.** The only difference between the complete equation and the simplified equation is the term $v_i t$. To eliminate this term, one of the two values must be zero. Since t also appears elsewhere in the equation, t cannot be zero, so the initial velocity must have been equal to zero. Thus, the correct answer is choice B. The other answers would not affect the equation in any way.

4. **The correct answer is H.** The graph of acceleration as a function of $\sin \theta$ is provided in the passage. You don't even have to know anything about how to calculate $\sin \theta$ to determine this answer. You can immediately rule out choice F because the relationship is clearly linear, not exponential. This is confirmed by the passage because it states that a best-fit line was determined for the data set. You can rule out choice J because there is a significant correlation between acceleration and $\sin \theta$, as they are related in a linear fashion according to the provided graph. The passage tells you that

gravitational acceleration is equal to 9.8 m/s². To distinguish between choices G and H, you have to look at the equation given on the graph. The slope, not the y-intercept, is about equal to 9.8, so the correct answer is choice H.

5. **The correct answer is C.** This question asks you to think about how the data would look if you doubled the length of the plane. This experiment measures a constant acceleration of a marble rolling down a plane. Doubling the length of the plane will give a different measured time, but the calculated acceleration should be identical. If the angles of incline and the determined accelerations are the same, the graph shouldn't change at all.

6. **The correct answer is G.** This question asks you to suggest an improvement to the experiment. Using angles of incline up to 90° would not improve the experiment because the marble would nearly be in freefall, so the experiment wouldn't really work; you can rule out choice F. Getting the marble rolling in advance before starting time collections would not be an improvement because we cannot assume that the initial velocity of the ball is zero, which means we cannot use the simplified acceleration equation; you can rule out choice H. Measuring the times in minutes rather than seconds wouldn't improve the experiment in any way; it would only give much smaller time values, so you can rule out choice J. Increasing the number of trials is always an improvement because it improves experimental reliability.

PASSAGE II

This passage falls under the earth sciences category. It describes radon, temperature, and air pressure data collected by a telemetric radon station in the months prior to a pair of twin earthquakes in Prokopion, Greece.

7. **The correct answer is D.** This question asks about the scientific question posed by the passage. Technically, the passage measures three dependent variables, radon levels, temperature, and air pressure, so an appropriate scientific question should address all three of these. This fact alone allows you to rule out choice A, which incorrectly uses pressure as the independent variable rather than the dependent variable. You can rule out choice B because the passage has nothing to do with

altitude. You can also rule out choice C because the experiment looks at three measurements *before* the earthquake, not *during* the earthquake (the key incorrect word here is *while*). We know that the earthquake is *not* included because the passage gives the earthquake date (Nov. 17), which does not appear on the *x*-axis in any of the graphs. The hypothesis posed in choice D correctly identifies the three independent variables, as well as the correct pre-earthquake time frame. (Notice the use of the word *predictive*, since the scientists were looking for changes in the levels in the days leading up to the earthquake in order to enhance forecasting.)

8. **The correct answer is H.** This question simply requires you to read the data. Based on the air pressure plot, the highest air pressure occurs on October 28, 2014, and there is a dramatic spike in air pressure on that day.

9. **The correct answer is B.** This question asks you to suggest a way to increase the reliability of the data in the experiment. You can eliminate choice A because the passage states that the other radon isotopes are not abundant enough in the environment to be detected. You can eliminate choice C because, even though it indicates the predictive purpose of the data, it incorrectly suggests using a best-fit line for data points that are clearly not linear. You can rule out choice D because it would not be possible to plot all three dependent variables together with the same axis units because each variable has different units, as displayed on the graphs. Collecting the same kind of data from a different station could confirm the obtained results and increase the reliability.

10. **The correct answer is F.** This question asks you to identify a constant in the experiment. Choice G is incorrect because all measurements require different instruments (i.e., a radon probe measures radon levels, a thermometer measures temperature, and a barometer measures air pressure). Choice H is incorrect because this is essentially the dependent variable and is not a constant among all of the variables. The earthquake date is not included on the *x*-axis, so you can rule out choice J. Choice F is correct; all measurements occur for the same region in Greece.

11. **The correct answer is B.** This question asks you to draw a conclusion based on the collected data. There is a clear anomaly, or deviation from what was expected, for all three tested variables on 10/28/2014. At this point, there is a clear drop in radon-222 and temperature levels, as well as a visible dramatic spike in air pressure.

The only answer that correctly describes these patterns as a predictive indicator of an impending earthquake is choice B.

PASSAGE III

This is a chemistry passage that describes an experiment that tests rusting reactions in four alloys, two of which contain iron, by measuring the volume of oxygen that disappears from an inverted test tube over water.

12. **The correct answer is H.** This question asks you to use the students' hypothesis to predict the outcome of the experiment. Since the students predicted that iron-containing alloys would use up oxygen during the rusting process, and since bronze and electrum do not contain iron, the result that would support the students' hypothesis is a decrease in their air column heights, as oxygen from the air is used up.

13. **The correct answer is B.** This question asks you to identify the dependent variable, which is the variable that is being measured in the experiment. The time is an independent variable, so choice A is incorrect. The types of alloys tested are also technically independent variables because they are varied among trials, so choice C is not correct. The volume of water in each beaker is a constant because it is 30 mL for all setups, so choice D is incorrect. The experiment measures the air column heights, so this is the dependent variable.

14. **The correct answer is J.** This question asks you to critique an alternative method, measuring the metal mass rather than oxygen usage. Choice F can be ruled out because the metal never contacts the water, so water is not an essential part of the reaction. You can also rule out choice G; while oxygen is a key reactant in the rusting reaction, it is not a reason why the alternative technique wouldn't work. Choice H is a true statement, but it is also not a reason why the alternative technique wouldn't work. Since rust is a solid, measuring changes in mass would be ineffective because you really cannot distinguish between the solid reactant and solid product in that way.

15. **The correct answer is A.** This question asks you to determine which data most strongly and directly supports the students' hypothesis that iron-containing alloys will use up more oxygen as they rust. Choice B expresses the opposite of this, so you can rule out this answer. Choice C may be a true statement, but the students did not hypothesize about these alternative side reactions. Choice D is true, but it does not distinguish between alloys that do and do not contain iron.

Choice A essentially restates the students' hypothesis as a conclusion supported by the data.

16. **The correct answer is G.** This question asks you to compare the data for the two types of steel used. If carbon protects iron from rusting, then carbon steel should rust more slowly than stainless steel; it does not, so choice F is false and can be ruled out. We can also rule out choices H and J because none of the alloys are a mixture of gold (choice H) or tin (choice J) with iron, so there is no data that measures these metals' potential effects on the rate of iron rusting. Stainless steel contains chromium and rusts more slowly than carbon steel; therefore, it seems that chromium could protect iron from rusting.

PASSAGE IV

This is a biology passage that describes an experiment that tests the effect of allicin, a compound from garlic, on the growth of E. coli in solid and liquid LB media.

17. **The correct answer is D.** This question basically asks you to state the purpose of the experiments. Choice A is incorrect because it incorrectly identifies temperature as the independent variable. Choice B is incorrect because it identifies allicin concentration as the dependent variable, when bacterial growth is the dependent variable. Choice C is incorrect because cell density is a means of measuring bacterial growth, so the independent variable is not correctly defined. Choice D correctly identifies that the experiments measure growth rate (OD per hour) at different allicin concentrations.

18. **The correct answer is H.** This question asks you to read the graph, which displays the data for bacterial growth in liquid media under different allicin concentrations. The allicin-free control is sample 1. If you find 5 hours on the x-axis, move vertically until you reach the graph of sample 1, and then move horizontally to the y-axis, you can find that the optical density after 5 hours was approximately 0.5.

19. **The correct answer is B.** This question asks you to compare the procedure for the solid and liquid media. The second set of plates contains LB, kanamycin, and 0.3 mM of allicin right from the start, since you can't change any concentrations in solidified media. Sample 1 contains no allicin, so you can eliminate choice A. Sample 3 contains 1 mM of allicin, so you can eliminate choice C. Sample 4 contains the correct allicin concentration, but it is added after 2 hours rather than right from the start, so choice D is incorrect. Sample 2 contains all of the correct chemicals right from the start of the experiment.

20. **The correct answer is G.** This question asks you to reason about the purpose of kanamycin based on the passage. The passage states that kanamycin is an antibiotic, which means that it kills off bacteria, but the passage also states that the *E. coli* used in the experiment is resistant to kanamycin. Therefore, kanamycin will kill off any microorganisms that are not *E. coli*, including unwanted contaminants that could interfere with the optical density measurements.

21. **The correct answer is B.** This question asks you to draw a conclusion about the effect of allicin on *E. coli* growth based on the data. Choice A states that increased allicin concentrations improve *E. coli* growth under all conditions, which is not true according to the data, so it is incorrect. Choice C states that increased allicin concentrations inhibit *E. coli* growth, except when the allicin is added midway through the growth process; this latter part of the statement is untrue based on Samples 2 and 3, so it is incorrect. Choice D indicates that allicin promotes *E. coli* growth when included from the beginning of the growth process, which is untrue based on the liquid media results from Samples 4 and 5. Choice B correctly indicates that increased allicin concentrations always inhibit *E. coli* growth, regardless of whether it is added at the beginning of or midway through the growth process.

CHAPTER 13:
CONFLICTING VIEWPOINTS

OVERVIEW

- Reading Comprehension, Science Style
- Can You Use Reading Comprehension Skills to Understand Details?
- What Do the Viewpoints Have in Common?
- What Are Key Differences Between the Viewpoints?
- How Can the Viewpoints Be Related or Understood by Inference?
- Common Mistakes to Avoid
- Summing It Up
- Practice

Together, the passages in the Data Representation and Research Summaries categories make up the majority of the ACT Science test. The last 15–20 percent of the test that we have not yet discussed consists of Conflicting Viewpoints passages. Even though this is easily the shortest section of the ACT Science test, Conflicting Viewpoints passages are important because they test your ability to read about different views and hypotheses about the same topic and then analyze the pros and cons of each. While the Data Representation and Research Summaries passages have a lot in common with typical research articles in scientific journals, Conflicting Viewpoints passages are more similar to perspective pieces, commentaries, or short communications. These passages briefly convey at least two viewpoints about a particular topic, and it is your job to answer questions based on these views.

READING COMPREHENSION, SCIENCE STYLE

Conflicting Viewpoints passages may seem a bit out of place in the ACT Science test. That's because these passages are extremely similar to reading comprehension passages you might see in the ACT Reading test. Sure, it will absolutely help if you have some background science knowledge in the covered areas, as you may have an easier time wading through the vocabulary or understanding the content. But when it really comes down to it, the ACT Science test is simply a test of reading comprehension in science-based passages.

Conflicting Viewpoints passages will usually pose two or three short descriptions of viewpoints, summaries, or hypotheses about the same science topic or about related science topics. The questions will then test your understanding of the viewpoints as individual pieces and in light of one another. In other words, it will be important to understand each of the viewpoint summaries on its own, but you will then be asked to compare and contrast the summaries or to draw connections between the summaries to show how one might affect the other. Each passage is usually accompanied by seven questions.

As a reminder, a **hypothesis** is an educated guess about the outcome of a particular experiment or scientific phenomenon. Hypotheses are constantly posed to try to explain observations in nature and may be based on collected data, comparisons to similar phenomena, or basic logic, but they are considered hypotheses because they are still predictions rather than well-supported conclusions. A **theory** is often used as a synonym for a hypothesis, but a theory is usually based on a more substantial number of experiments and observations. So a theory is usually less specific but more corroborated than a hypothesis.

Both hypotheses and theories are often based on general principles of a scientific topic that are commonly regarded as correct or true, but they are still considered proposed explanations rather than established fact. When it comes to common viewpoints passages, you will often be presented with two hypotheses or theories that either differ or focus on different features of a particular phenomenon. These explanations are therefore considered to be "viewpoints" in this passage category because they are hypotheses or theories.

A number of well-known theories include the Big Bang theory, the theory of relativity, and the theory of evolution. These are all considered theories, and not scientific fact, because there is a lot of scientific evidence to support them, but they are still conjectural and subject to experimentation.

However, not all of the passages will be based on well-known scientific theories or hypotheses. You will also see passages in which hypothetical students tackle simpler questions by doing some research and presenting their findings. The practice passages at the end of the chapter will include an example of each type of passage so you know what to expect in each case.

The most basic skill you will need when tackling Conflicting Viewpoints passages is reading comprehension. This skill is really vital to tackling all of the passages and questions in Conflicting Viewpoints clusters (and, in general, to all passages and questions on the Science test), but in addition, there are a few simple steps you can take to make sure you're extracting the appropriate information from Conflicting Viewpoints passages. Each Conflicting Viewpoints passage will begin with a brief paragraph that introduces the topic of interest.

After identifying the topic of interest, you can move on to the viewpoints themselves. Each viewpoint will be discussed in a paragraph or two and will usually provide supporting data in its explanation. When reading the viewpoints, it is important to figure out the opinions expressed. Underline key words and use the margin to write down the basic theory provided by each viewpoint in a clear and succinct way, so that when you have to start answering questions, you'll know where to look for the correct answers.

Make sure you clearly identify the topic of interest before proceeding with the rest of the passage. Jot down a note or two in the margins to make sure you don't forget later.

After you've identified the basic hypothesis or theory provided by each scientist, look for the data that support each viewpoint. Feel free to circle the data so you can look at it later. By identifying supporting data for each viewpoint, you can see whether or not the data for one viewpoint might support or refute the other viewpoint, and vice versa. Picking out the key data will also help you to compare and contrast the viewpoints because each piece of data will likely support one theory more strongly than the other; otherwise, the scientist would not bother to include it.

To summarize, the basic strategy to employ when reading Conflicting Viewpoints passages is as follows:

1) Identify the topic.
2) Identify the basic hypotheses or theories of the scientists.
3) Identify the relevant data used to support each of the two viewpoints discussed in the passage.

When you are posed with a set of Conflicting Viewpoints, you will likely be posed with questions that test your ability to understand details, compare the conflicting viewpoints, contrast the conflicting viewpoints, and make inferences either to relate the viewpoints to one another, or to use data (either real or hypothetical) to support or refute the conflicting viewpoints. These are the areas we will focus on in our preparation for these passage types.

CAN YOU USE READING COMPREHENSION SKILLS TO UNDERSTAND DETAILS?

The most straightforward question type you will encounter with Conflicting Viewpoints passages simply asks you to recall details from the passages. Questions may ask you about statements found explicitly in the passages or about implications based on statements found in the passage. For example, if a passage describes the short-term and long-term effects of mutations on human evolution, a question might ask you to choose the event that would most immediately follow a mutation; while all four answer choices may be correct based on the passage, you would have to choose the short-term effect rather than any of the long-term effects based on the use of the word *immediately* in the question. This is an example of why it is important to pay attention to details. When you're reading a question, make sure you understand what you are being asked so that you don't simply choose what appears to be the first correct statement you see, when in fact the question is asking you about something entirely different.

As a general rule, you won't have to bring an abundance of background information to the table when it comes to understanding details in Conflicting Viewpoints passages. Of course, having background knowledge about a particular topic won't hurt; for instance, if you know a lot about deep-sea vents, that background knowledge will certainly be helpful to you if you encounter a Conflicting Viewpoints passage that introduces vocabulary related to deep-sea vents. However, you won't be expected to be an expert on any of the topics presented. Reading comprehension is all about understanding what you read, and the vast majority of information you'll need to answer questions about Conflicting Viewpoints passages can be found in the passages themselves. Occasionally you'll need to figure out a vocabulary definition based on the information provided, but everything you need will be in the passage.

There are usually one to three detail-oriented recall questions per question set for Conflicting Viewpoints questions, and they usually refer to just one viewpoint at a time. You will often see one detail-based reading comprehension question per viewpoint; this setup makes sense because it makes sure you have read both of the passages.

TIP If you pay attention to details and take notes as you read, you should have no trouble at all identifying the topic and comprehending the details in Conflicting Viewpoints passages.

Let's look at how the ACT Science test will present these questions. As in the other science chapters, we will use one passage and data set for the majority of practice questions in this chapter.

There are numerous theories concerning the origin of life on Earth, focusing on how primitive Earth was able to chemically create biomolecules essential for biological life to arise. Two such ideas are the Theory of Volcanic Origin of Life and the RNA World Hypothesis.

Theory of Volcanic Origin of Life

A widely accepted theory for the origin of life is that lightning and gases from volcanic eruptions may have given rise to the very first life on Earth. The Miller-Urey experiment, performed in 1952, was a chemical experiment that simulated the conditions of primitive Earth. In this experiment, a mixture of gases thought to have been present in the primitive atmosphere (most prominently, H_2O, CH_4, NH_3, and H_2) was stored in a vial connected by a pipe to a heated water tank that simulated the evaporation of the ocean. In that vial, electrodes created a spark, simulating lightning, and reaction products were collected by re-liquefying the water vapor. The setup is shown in the illustration:

The Miller-Urey experiment showed that simple organic compounds, namely amino acids and various sugars, including ribose, can be produced from the gases in the atmosphere of primitive Earth with the addition of energy.

More recently, scientists performed a similar experiment with CO_2, CO, and N_2, an updated conception of Earth's early atmosphere, and these gases allowed for the production of an even wider array of biomolecules. The addition of volcanic gases like H_2 and CH_4 increased variety and supplied hydrogen, and follow-up experiments have shown that a simple volcanic gas called carbonyl sulfide (COS) helps free-floating amino acids to form peptides, the precursors to proteins, under various conditions,

and that metal ions help to intensify this reaction by up to 80 percent. However, since carbonyl sulfide decomposes rather quickly, it is unlikely to be present in large quantities in the atmosphere. Instead, scientists propose that this gas would be most predominant at hydrothermal vents on the seafloor, forming peptide chains that would stick to rocks and continue to lengthen.

RNA World Hypothesis

Francis Crick, among other scientists, first posed the RNA World Hypothesis in the 1960s. RNA has the unique ability to act as both genes and enzymes, which make RNA a sensible first biomolecule in the origin of life. A long-standing weakness of the RNA world hypothesis had been the inability of prebiotic Earth to form the molecule's nucleotides from its basic ingredients.

Recently, however, lab simulations, have demonstrated that pyrimidine nucleotides cytosine and uracil can form a number of plausible prebiotic molecules under early-Earth conditions, an atmosphere that included H_2O, CH_4, NH_3, and H_2, and that the simplest building blocks of sugars, glycolaldehyde and glyceraldehyde, can be derived from the prebiotic molecule HCN. There is no evidence of formation of the other two nucleotides present in RNA, adenine and guanine, but current research is moving in that direction. *In vitro* experiments under primordial conditions have demonstrated the ability to produce RNA molecules that perform a number of functions, including self-replication and the ability to copy other RNA molecules. These capabilities of RNA make it a very promising "first biomolecule" because RNA is the only biomolecule currently known to be capable of replication, catalysis, and containing genes itself, so RNA could have preceded DNA and proteins in evolution because RNA can self-catalyze to make protein, which can then replicate DNA.

The function of the condenser in the Miller-Urey experiment is to:

A. increase the temperature of the gases for analysis of reaction products.

B. convert the water vapor to liquid for reaction product collection.

C. condense the reacting gases into solid form for product detection.

D. produce RNA from gas precursors capable of self-replication.

The correct answer is B. This passage presents two different views on the origin of life. The first viewpoint describes the theory that atmospheric and volcanic gases, using energy from volcanic lightning, were capable of forming amino acids and simple sugars. The second viewpoint describes the hypothesis that RNA was the first biomolecule because there is some evidence that some of its nucleotides can be formed by the prebiotic atmosphere, and because RNA is genetic, self-replicates, and can act as a catalyst.

The question posed is a recall question that asks you to look back at the viewpoints and use the information to determine the purpose of the condenser in the Miller-Urey experiment. Since the Miller-Urey experiment is exclusively described in the first viewpoint, the answer to the question is found in the first viewpoint. Based on the diagram, there is a cold-water bath around the condenser; a decrease in temperature would promote the conversion of water vapor to liquid water. Even if you didn't catch

that, the passage itself indicates that the water vapor was re-liquefied for product collection, and in the diagram, the condenser is the link between the simulated atmosphere and the area where cooled water delivers the reaction products. Choice A is incorrect because the cool water won't increase the temperature; it decreases the temperature. Choice C is incorrect because even though the word *condenses* is in the answer, there is no deposition—conversion of a gas to a solid—taking place in this reaction. Choice D is incorrect; while this answer accurately describes one of the experiments mentioned in the second viewpoint, it is unrelated to this particular question.

WHAT DO THE VIEWPOINTS HAVE IN COMMON?

Each passage will present you with two conflicting viewpoints; by definition, *conflicting* seems to indicate that the viewpoints are in opposition to one another. However, in Conflicting Viewpoints passages, this doesn't necessarily mean that the two viewpoints are arguing in favor of opposite ideas; in many cases, the viewpoints are simply arguing in favor of *different* ideas. They are considered to be "conflicting" only because the arguments are not one and the same. In the previous example, both viewpoints could technically be correct, as both ideas seem to be valid based on experiments done thus far. However, they are Conflicting Viewpoints because they are arguing that their theory or hypothesis is the key first step that ignited the development of life on Earth.

When different viewpoints are presented (and even if they are in direct opposition to one another), it is almost always possible to find commonalities between the two. Often, the viewpoints will describe the same effect, but they will propose different causes for that effect. In other cases, viewpoints may be nearly identical, except for a detail or two that leads to a completely different conclusion. In still other situations, two viewpoints may propose entirely different theories about a particular phenomenon, but they could have a feature or two in common. Regardless of the viewpoints you encounter, there will always be some kind of parallel you can draw between them, and more often than not, one of the questions accompanying the passage will draw attention to one of those parallels. The easiest way to identify such parallels is to use the strategy we've already discussed—take notes in the margin to identify the shared topic, viewpoint presented by each author, and supporting data presented in favor of each viewpoint. These notes, however brief, can draw attention to details or data that are relevant to both of the viewpoints. If you come across a question that asks you to compare the conflicting viewpoints, you can use your notes to easily pinpoint where you should focus your efforts when narrowing down your answer choices.

Let's look at this type of question in action.

There are numerous theories concerning the origin of life on Earth, focusing on how primitive Earth was able to chemically create biomolecules essential for biological life to arise. Two such ideas are the Theory of Volcanic Origin of Life and the RNA World Hypothesis.

Theory of Volcanic Origin of Life

A widely accepted theory for the origin of life is that lightning and gases from volcanic eruptions may have given rise to the very first life on Earth. The Miller-Urey experiment, performed in

1952, was a chemical experiment that simulated the conditions of primitive Earth. In this experiment, a mixture of gases thought to have been present in the primitive atmosphere (most prominently, H_2O, CH_4, NH_3, and H_2) was stored in a vial connected by a pipe to a heated water tank that simulated the evaporation of the ocean. In that vial, electrodes created a spark, simulating lightning, and reaction products were collected by re-liquefying the water vapor. The setup is shown in the illustration.

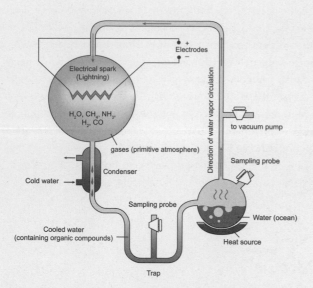

The Miller-Urey experiment showed that simple organic compounds, namely amino acids and various sugars, including ribose, can be produced from the gases in the atmosphere of primitive Earth with the addition of energy.

More recently, scientists performed a similar experiment with CO_2, CO, and N_2, an updated conception of Earth's early atmosphere, and these gases allowed for the production of an even wider array of biomolecules. The addition of volcanic gases like H_2 and CH_4 increased variety and supplied hydrogen, and follow-up experiments have shown that a simple volcanic gas called carbonyl sulfide (COS) helps free-floating amino acids to form peptides, the precursors to proteins, under various conditions, and that metal ions help to intensify this reaction by up to 80 percent. However, since carbonyl sulfide decomposes rather quickly, it is unlikely to be present in large quantities in the atmosphere. Instead, scientists propose that this gas would be most predominant at hydrothermal vents on the seafloor, forming peptide chains that would stick to rocks and continue to lengthen.

RNA World Hypothesis

Francis Crick, among other scientists, first posed the RNA World Hypothesis in the 1960s. RNA has the unique ability to act as both genes and enzymes, which make RNA a sensible first biomolecule in the origin of life. A long-standing weakness of the RNA world hypothesis had been the inability of prebiotic Earth to form the molecule's nucleotides from its basic ingredients.

Recently, however, lab simulations, have demonstrated that pyrimidine nucleotides cytosine and uracil can form a number of plausible prebiotic molecules under early-Earth conditions,

an atmosphere that included H_2O, CH_4, NH_3, and H_2, and that the simplest building blocks of sugars, glycolaldehyde and glyceraldehyde, can be derived from the prebiotic molecule HCN. There is no evidence of formation of the other two nucleotides present in RNA, adenine and guanine, but current research is moving in that direction. *In vitro* experiments under primordial conditions have demonstrated the ability to produce RNA molecules that perform a number of functions, including self-replication and the ability to copy other RNA molecules. These capabilities of RNA make it a very promising "first biomolecule" because RNA is the only biomolecule currently known to be capable of replication, catalysis, and containing genes itself, so RNA could have preceded DNA and proteins in evolution because RNA can self-catalyze to make protein, which can then replicate DNA.

A feature that the two viewpoints have in common is:

F. the type of proposed "first biomolecule" that led to the development of life.

G. the predicted gas content of the Earth's prebiotic atmosphere.

H. the argument that proteins are required for any kind of catalysis to occur.

J. the formation of the "first biomolecule" near deep-sea vents.

The correct answer is G. This question asks you to find a feature that the two viewpoints have in common with one another. Since the question stem itself does not specify a particular feature of the viewpoints on which to focus, the easiest way to go about answering this question is to go through each answer choice and decide whether or not it is true.

Choice F indicates that both viewpoints point to the same biomolecule as the "first biomolecule" in the origin of life. This is not the correct answer because the first viewpoint indicates that prebiotic conditions allowed for the production of amino acids and peptides as the "first biomolecule," as well as some sugars, while the second viewpoint argues that RNA was the "first biomolecule." Choice G indicates that both viewpoints agree on the prebiotic atmospheric content. Based on some of the listed gases in the passage, this is definitely a possibility. Choice H indicates that both viewpoints indicate that proteins are required for catalysis. This is not specifically mentioned in the first viewpoint, but a key argument in the second viewpoint is that RNA, which is a nucleic acid and not a protein, is capable of catalysis, so it cannot be correct. Choice J indicates that the viewpoints agree that the formation of the "first biomolecule" occurred in deep-sea vents; this is really only specified in the first viewpoint in reference to carbonyl sulfide, so this cannot be correct. The correct answer, therefore, is choice G.

WHAT ARE KEY DIFFERENCES BETWEEN THE VIEWPOINTS?

If you're going to be asked to compare the viewpoints, it makes sense that you would also be asked to contrast the viewpoints. You can approach the contrast question types in exactly the same way you would approach the comparison questions. If a question asks you to contrast the viewpoints with respect to a particular topic mentioned in the question stem, look through your notes or underlined words and phrases to find that topic within each viewpoint. If a question asks you to find differences between the viewpoints in general, you might need to take the same approach we took with the last example, by going through each answer choice and eliminating incorrect answers until you determine the correct answer.

> **NOTE:** In general, approximately half of the questions that follow a Conflicting Viewpoints passage will ask you to compare and contrast the viewpoints.

When Conflicting Viewpoints differ dramatically in approach to the subject at hand, it may be a little more difficult to pinpoint differences between the viewpoints, but use the questions to your advantage. The ACT Science test consists entirely of multiple-choice questions, and it is a perfectly valid strategy to look at the answers if you aren't sure about exactly what the question is asking you to determine from the viewpoints.

· ·

There are numerous theories concerning the origin of life on Earth, focusing on how primitive Earth was able to chemically create biomolecules essential for biological life to arise. Two such ideas are the Theory of Volcanic Origin of Life and the RNA World Hypothesis.

Theory of Volcanic Origin of Life

A widely accepted theory for the origin of life is that lightning and gases from volcanic eruptions may have given rise to the very first life on Earth. The Miller-Urey experiment, performed in 1952, was a chemical experiment that simulated the conditions of primitive Earth. In this experiment, a mixture of gases thought to have been present in the primitive atmosphere (most prominently, H_2O, CH_4, NH_3, and H_2) was stored in a vial connected by a pipe to a heated water tank that simulated the evaporation of the ocean. In that vial, electrodes created a spark, simulating lightning, and reaction products were collected by re-liquefying the water vapor. The setup is shown in the illustration.

The Miller-Urey experiment showed that simple organic compounds, namely amino acids and various sugars, including ribose, can be produced from the gases in the atmosphere of primitive Earth with the addition of energy.

More recently, scientists performed a similar experiment with CO_2, CO, and N_2, an updated conception of Earth's early atmosphere, and these gases allowed for the production of an even wider array of biomolecules. The addition of volcanic gases like H_2 and CH_4 increased variety and supplied hydrogen, and follow-up experiments have shown that a simple volcanic gas called carbonyl sulfide (COS) helps free-floating amino acids to form peptides, the precursors to proteins, under various conditions, and that metal ions help to intensify this reaction by up to 80 percent. However, since carbonyl sulfide decomposes rather quickly, it is unlikely to be present in large quantities in the atmosphere. Instead, scientists propose that this gas would be most predominant at hydrothermal vents on the seafloor, forming peptide chains that would stick to rocks and continue to lengthen.

RNA World Hypothesis

Francis Crick, among other scientists, first posed the RNA World Hypothesis in the 1960s. RNA has the unique ability to act as both genes and enzymes, which make RNA a sensible first biomolecule in the origin of life. A long-standing weakness of the RNA world hypothesis had been the inability of prebiotic Earth to form the molecule's nucleotides from its basic ingredients.

Recently, however, lab simulations, have demonstrated that pyrimidine nucleotides cytosine and uracil can form a number of plausible prebiotic molecules under early-Earth conditions,

459

Chapter 13

Conflicting Viewpoints

Electrodes
+
−

Electrical spark
(Lightning)

H_2O, CH_4, NH_3,
H_2, CO

gases (primitive atmosphere)

Condenser

Cold water

Direction of water vapor circulation

to vacuum pump

Sampling probe

Sampling probe

Water (ocean)

Cooled water
(containing organic compounds)

Heat source

Trap

an atmosphere that included H_2O, CH_4, NH_3, and H_2, and that the simplest building blocks of sugars, glycolaldehyde and glyceraldehyde, can be derived from the prebiotic molecule HCN. There is no evidence of formation of the other two nucleotides present in RNA, adenine and guanine, but current research is moving in that direction. *In vitro* experiments under primordial conditions have demonstrated the ability to produce RNA molecules that perform a number of functions, including self-replication and the ability to copy other RNA molecules. These capabilities of RNA make it a very promising "first biomolecule" because RNA is the only biomolecule currently known to be capable of replication, catalysis, and containing genes itself, so RNA could have preceded DNA and proteins in evolution because RNA can self-catalyze to make protein, which can then replicate DNA.

A key difference in biomolecule formation from the atmosphere, as described by these two viewpoints, is:

A. experimental evidence that the prebiotic atmosphere can form the full array of amino acid monomers, but not all of the RNA nucleotide monomers.

B. experimental evidence that the prebiotic atmosphere can form the full array of RNA nucleotide monomers, but not all of the amino acids.

C. experimental evidence that indicates the prebiotic atmosphere directly forms peptides and proteins, bypassing amino acid formation, while RNA nucleotide monomers must be formed first.

D. experimental evidence that indicates the prebiotic atmosphere directly forms RNA, bypassing nucleotide formation, while protein monomers, amino acids, must be formed first.

The correct answer is A. This question asks you to focus on differences in the modes of biomolecule formation. The answer choices are all related to experimental evidence, so if you took the time to underline the experimental data while reading, it would pay off heavily here because that is exactly the topic of focus for this question.

The answer choices are paired answers; choices A and B represent opposite ideas, and choices C and D represent opposite ideas. This means that one of these answer pairs is completely wrong altogether, while the other answer pair contains the correct answer. Choice A states that there is experimental evidence that shows that prebiotic atmosphere can form all of the amino acids, but not all of the nucleotides; this is true, according to the viewpoints, because the first viewpoint indicates that all amino acids have been formed experimentally, while the second passage indicates that only cytosine and uracil have currently been formed experimentally. This evidence indicates that choice A is correct, and that choice B is effectively incorrect.

To confirm our answer, let's check out choices C and D. Choice C indicates that peptide and protein formation bypasses the formation of amino acid monomers, while choice D indicates that RNA formation bypasses the formation of nucleotide monomers. The aforementioned experimental data appears to refute both of these statements, as the experimental evidence shows formation of amino acids and nucleotides rather than direct formation of full-fledged peptides and RNA. This makes sense, as it is much easier to form a smaller subunit of a biomolecule than a more complex one. Therefore, we can rule out choices B, C, and D.

HOW CAN THE VIEWPOINTS BE RELATED OR UNDERSTOOD BY INFERENCE?

So far, the question types we've discussed have been fairly straightforward reading comprehension questions for which you can find the answers simply by reading and understanding the passages. The last category of questions you might encounter will ask you to make inferences or to determine implied information, for one of two purposes:

1) To connect or relate the two viewpoints in some way
2) To introduce real or hypothetical data that might affect one or both of the viewpoints

Inference-based questions are still reading comprehension questions, but they require that you go beyond simply what is written in the text. The first inference question type might ask you to tweak one viewpoint so that it might work in collaboration with the second viewpoint or to indicate whether or not the two viewpoints are mutually exclusive. The second inference question type is much more common because it can be applied to any set of viewpoints, regardless of how similar or different they may be.

On one hand, you may be provided with a particular piece of real or hypothetical data, and you must determine how this new information will impact the two theories. For instance, a new hypothetical discovery might refute one viewpoint and support the other, or it might refute both viewpoints, or it might even be unrelated to either viewpoint. This kind of question requires that you fully understand both viewpoints, because you may have to apply new information to both in order to determine its effect on the two viewpoints.

The other version of this question type works in the reverse, in that you may be asked to choose a particular piece of information that supports or refutes one or both of the viewpoints. This question type may ask you to relate data to both viewpoints or to focus on only one viewpoint; in either case, you'll have to have a thorough understanding of what each viewpoint is conveying so that you know how new data could support or refute it.

The following examples will cover both types of data-based inference questions so you can get a sense of how they work.

. . . .

There are numerous theories concerning the origin of life on Earth, focusing on how primitive Earth was able to chemically create biomolecules essential for biological life to arise. Two such ideas are the Theory of Volcanic Origin of Life and the RNA World Hypothesis.

Theory of Volcanic Origin of Life

A widely accepted theory for the origin of life is that lightning and gases from volcanic eruptions may have given rise to the very first life on Earth. The Miller-Urey experiment, performed in 1952, was a chemical experiment that simulated the conditions of primitive Earth. In this experiment, a mixture of gases thought to have been present in the primitive atmosphere (most prominently, H_2O, CH_4, NH_3, and H_2) was stored in a vial connected by a pipe to a heated water tank that simulated the evaporation of the ocean. In that vial, electrodes created a spark, simulating lightning, and reaction products were collected by re-liquefying the water vapor. The setup is shown in the illustration.

The Miller-Urey experiment showed that simple organic compounds, namely amino acids and various sugars, including ribose, can be produced from the gases in the atmosphere of primitive Earth with the addition of energy.

More recently, scientists performed a similar experiment with CO_2, CO, and N_2, an updated conception of Earth's early atmosphere, and these gases allowed for the production of an even wider array of biomolecules. The addition of volcanic gases like H_2 and CH_4 increased variety and supplied hydrogen, and follow-up experiments have shown that a simple volcanic gas called carbonyl sulfide (COS) helps free-floating amino acids to form peptides, the precursors to proteins, under various conditions, and that metal ions help to intensify this reaction by up to 80 percent. However, since carbonyl sulfide decomposes rather quickly, it is unlikely to be present in large quantities in the atmosphere. Instead, scientists propose that this gas would be most predominant at hydrothermal vents on the seafloor, forming peptide chains that would stick to rocks and continue to lengthen.

RNA World Hypothesis

Francis Crick, among other scientists, first posed the RNA World Hypothesis in the 1960s. RNA has the unique ability to act as both genes and enzymes, which make RNA a sensible first biomolecule in the origin of life. A long-standing weakness of the RNA world hypothesis had been the inability of prebiotic Earth to form the molecule's nucleotides from its basic ingredients.

Recently, however, lab simulations, have demonstrated that pyrimidine nucleotides cytosine and uracil can form a number of plausible prebiotic molecules under early-Earth conditions, an atmosphere that included H_2O, CH_4, NH_3, and H_2, and that the simplest building blocks of sugars, glycolaldehyde and glyceraldehyde, can be derived from the prebiotic molecule HCN. There is no evidence of formation of the other two nucleotides present in RNA, adenine and guanine, but current research is moving in that direction. *In vitro* experiments under primordial conditions have demonstrated the ability to produce RNA molecules that perform a number of functions, including self-replication and

The illustration shows the Miller-Urey experimental setup with the following labels: Electrodes (+/−), Electrical spark (Lightning), H_2O, CH_4, NH_3, H_2, CO, gases (primitive atmosphere), Condenser, Cold water, Cooled water (containing organic compounds), Sampling probe, Direction of water vapor circulation, to vacuum pump, Sampling probe, Water (ocean), Heat source.

the ability to copy other RNA molecules. These capabilities of RNA make it a very promising "first biomolecule" because RNA is the only biomolecule currently known to be capable of replication, catalysis, and containing genes itself, so RNA could have preceded DNA and proteins in evolution because RNA can self-catalyze to make protein, which can then replicate DNA.

If continued research indicates that the prebiotic atmosphere is unlikely to have been able to synthesize adenine and guanine, which of the following statements is most correct?

F. All described components of the Theory of Volcanic Origin of Life should be regarded as inaccurate.
G. Proteins could be confirmed as the "first biomolecules" per the Theory of Volcanic Origin of Life.
H. All described components of the RNA World Hypothesis should be regarded as inaccurate.
J. RNA may still be a key early biomolecule, but its synthesis requires non-RNA catalysts.

The correct answer is J. This question asks you to use a piece of hypothetical data, the inability of the prebiotic atmosphere to synthesize adenine and guanine, to draw a conclusion about the viewpoints. This piece of hypothetical data seems to clearly impact the RNA World Hypothesis moreso than the Theory of Volcanic Origin of Life, but it is important to make sure by reasoning through each of the answer choices.

Choice F indicates that this new piece of data refutes the entire Theory of Volcanic Origin of Life. This is incorrect because this particular finding would not impact this theory since it does not propose that RNA is the "first biomolecule." Choice G indicates that this piece of data confirms proteins as the "first biomolecule." The need for a new catalyst to make RNA might strongly suggest that proteins are required for its synthesis, but this is a bit of a leap, as nothing about this piece of data specifically confirms that proteins are required for RNA synthesis. Therefore, choice G is incorrect. Choice H indicates that all components of the RNA World Hypothesis can be rejected with the introduction of this piece of data. This is not correct—the RNA World Hypothesis may indicate that RNA was likely the "first biomolecule," which this piece of data seems to reject, but the description of RNA's ability to contain genetic material, self-replicate, and act as a catalyst

for propagation are all still very valid points. Therefore, the correct answer is choice J, which indicates that this piece of data rejects RNA as the "first biomolecule," but RNA still performs important functions, particularly in self-propagation, that could make it an important early biomolecule. Therefore, only the "first biomolecule" aspect of the RNA World Hypothesis would be refuted; the rest is still valid.

Which of the following pieces of data would best support the Theory of Volcanic Origin of Life?

A. It is thermodynamically favorable for water to break down peptide chains via hydrolysis reactions.
B. Nucleic acids cannot be converted to proteins without cell machinery already in existence.
C. Pumice, the porous rock that forms when a volcano cools rapidly, can trap gas and nutrients to support microbe growth.
D. There were no metal ions present in the deep sea vent environment.

The correct answer is C. This question asks you to choose a piece of data that best supports one of the two viewpoints; in this case, the question asks you to choose the piece of data that best supports the Theory of Volcanic Origin of Life. To answer this question, we must go through each piece of data in order to determine how it affects the specified theory.

Choice A is incorrect. In fact, this piece of data would oppose the Theory of Volcanic Origin of Life. Since amino acid polymerization requires dehydration synthesis, the thermodynamically favorable breakdown of peptides by water would refute the theory, which indicates that the origin of life occurred at the deep-sea vents, located in water. Choice B is incorrect because the Theory of Volcanic Origin of Life does not indicate that nucleic acids are converted into protein. Choice D is incorrect because, if anything, this piece of data would decrease support for the Theory of Volcanic Origin of Life. Therefore, the correct answer is choice C. Pumice is a volcanic rock that could potentially support microbe life by trapping gas and nutrients in its pores, which would be extremely important in the deep sea environment.

COMMON MISTAKES TO AVOID

In the previous two chapters, we discussed a number of mistakes and pitfalls to avoid during the ACT Science test. Here, we will talk about a few more mistakes test takers sometimes make that are more specific to Conflicting Viewpoints passages. The mistakes we'll discuss are focusing on too many of the details during your first read-through, mixing up the viewpoints, relying on key words in answer choices, and failing to find support for your answers in the text. The previous examples have already highlighted several of these, but we'll go over each again specifically to make sure you don't fall into any traps when you encounter Conflicting Viewpoints passages.

FOCUSING ON TOO MANY DETAILS DURING THE FIRST READ-THROUGH

When you're reading a set of viewpoints in a Conflicting Viewpoints passage, it is definitely important to pay attention to what you're reading. However, you won't be able to remember absolutely everything. That's why it is so important to take the advice mentioned earlier and take notes. Identifying the overarching topic of the passage, the specific views or theories described by each viewpoint, and any key data will help you to cut out the extraneous information during the first read-through. If a question refers to any of this extra information, you can certainly go back and read through the viewpoints again to find that information. However, during the first read-through, it is essential that you gain a solid understanding of the topic, views, and supporting data, because once you are confident about these three key features of the passage, you will have a much easier time with the questions because you'll know exactly where to look.

. . . .

There are numerous theories concerning the origin of life on Earth, focusing on how primitive Earth was able to chemically create biomolecules essential for biological life to arise. Two such ideas are the Theory of Volcanic Origin of Life and the RNA World Hypothesis.

Theory of Volcanic Origin of Life

A widely accepted theory for the origin of life is that lightning and gases from volcanic eruptions may have given rise to the very first life on Earth. The Miller-Urey experiment, performed in 1952, was a chemical experiment that simulated the conditions of primitive Earth. In this experiment, a mixture of gases thought to have been present in the primitive atmosphere (most prominently, H_2O, CH_4, NH_3, and H_2) was stored in a vial connected by a pipe to a heated water tank that simulated the evaporation of the ocean. In that vial, electrodes created a spark, simulating lightning, and reaction products were collected by re-liquefying the water vapor. The setup is shown in the illustration.

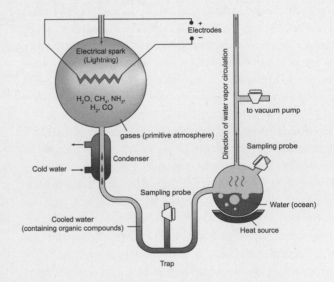

The Miller-Urey experiment showed that simple organic compounds, namely amino acids and various sugars, including ribose, can be produced from the gases in the atmosphere of primitive Earth with the addition of energy.

More recently, scientists performed a similar experiment with CO_2, CO, and N_2, an updated conception of Earth's early atmosphere, and these gases allowed for the production of an even wider array of biomolecules. The addition of volcanic gases like H_2 and CH_4 increased variety and supplied hydrogen, and follow-up experiments have shown that a simple volcanic gas called carbonyl sulfide (COS) helps free-floating amino acids to form peptides, the precursors to proteins, under various conditions, and that metal ions help to intensify this reaction by up to 80 percent. However, since carbonyl sulfide decomposes rather quickly, it is unlikely to be present in large quantities in the atmosphere. Instead, scientists propose that this gas would be most predominant at hydrothermal vents on the seafloor, forming peptide chains that would stick to rocks and continue to lengthen.

RNA World Hypothesis

Francis Crick, among other scientists, first posed the RNA World Hypothesis in the 1960s. RNA has the unique ability to act as both genes and enzymes, which make RNA a sensible first biomolecule in the origin of life. A long-standing weakness of the RNA world hypothesis had been the inability of prebiotic Earth to form the molecule's nucleotides from its basic ingredients.

Recently, however, lab simulations, have demonstrated that pyrimidine nucleotides cytosine and uracil can form a number of plausible prebiotic molecules under early-Earth conditions, an atmosphere that included H_2O, CH_4, NH_3, and H_2, and that the simplest building blocks of sugars, glycolaldehyde and glyceraldehyde, can be derived from the prebiotic molecule HCN. There is no evidence of formation of the other two nucleotides present in RNA, adenine and guanine, but current research is moving in that direction. *In vitro* experiments under primordial conditions have demonstrated the ability to produce RNA molecules that perform a number of functions, including self-replication and the ability to copy other RNA molecules. These capabilities of RNA make it a very promising "first biomolecule" because RNA is the only biomolecule currently known to be capable of replication, catalysis, and containing genes itself, so RNA could have preceded DNA and proteins in evolution because RNA can self-catalyze to make protein, which can then replicate DNA.

The main topic on which both of the viewpoints focus is the:

    F. chemical means by which biomolecules self-replicate.

    G. chemical means by which gases formed the first biomolecules.

    H. process by which gases can synthesize nucleotides.

    J. role of proteins and sugars in the origin of life.

The correct answer is G. This is a comparison question, but it is also a general question that you should answer for every Conflicting Viewpoints passage you encounter. This question basically asks you for the main topic of the entire passage, encompassing both of the viewpoints.

Choice F contains the buzzword "biomolecule," which appears constantly throughout the passage, but it is not correct because the main topic of the passage is not biomolecule self-replication. Choice G correctly states that the main topic of the passage is the chemical means by which gases formed the first biomolecules; even though each viewpoint offers a different take on how the first biomolecules were created, and importantly, which biomolecule came first, both viewpoints deal with the chemical processes by which the gases in the prebiotic atmosphere could have created biomolecule monomers. Choice H specifies that the topic of the passage is the means by which atmospheric gases form nucleotides, but this is really only the main topic of the second viewpoint, for the RNA World Hypothesis; it is unrelated to the first viewpoint. Choice J indicates that the main topic of the passage is the roles played by proteins and sugars in the origin of life. This is perhaps an indirect summary of the first viewpoint, but it is not especially relevant to the second viewpoint. Therefore, the correct answer is choice G.

If you focused too much on the details in the passage, you might have missed the big picture, and the big picture is exactly what this question focused on. You will likely encounter at least one or two big picture questions per Conflicting Viewpoints passage, so be sure you don't miss the big picture in favor of details that ultimately might not be as important.

MIXING UP THE VIEWPOINTS

This potential mistake might seem extremely obvious, but it happens more often than you would think. A question accompanying a passage might ask you about one viewpoint and then include a decoy answer that provides a correct response in relation to the other viewpoint. It may seem like an easy mistake to avoid, but under the pressure of a timed exam, it might also be an easy mistake to make. Read and then reread the questions you encounter to make sure you're looking in the right place for your answer, and then choose the appropriate response. Double-checking is really the only safeguard for this potential error, and careful reading throughout any Conflicting Viewpoints questions will help you to avoid it.

The next question illustrates how extremely important it is to read carefully and avoid mixing up the passages. If a question asks about a particular passage, check and double-check to make sure you are choosing the answer from the correct passage, because there will likely be a decoy answer among the choices that provides a correct answer from the wrong passage.

· ·

There are numerous theories concerning the origin of life on Earth, focusing on how primitive Earth was able to chemically create biomolecules essential for biological life to arise. Two such ideas are the Theory of Volcanic Origin of Life and the RNA World Hypothesis.

Theory of Volcanic Origin of Life

A widely accepted theory for the origin of life is that lightning and gases from volcanic eruptions may have given rise to the very first life on Earth. The Miller-Urey experiment, performed in 1952, was a chemical experiment that simulated the conditions of primitive Earth. In this experiment, a mixture of gases thought to have been present in the primitive atmosphere (most prominently, H_2O, CH_4, NH_3, and H_2) was stored in a vial connected by a pipe to a heated water tank that simulated the evaporation of the ocean. In that vial, electrodes created a spark, simulating lightning, and reaction products were collected by re-liquefying the water vapor. The setup is shown in the illustration.

The Miller-Urey experiment showed that simple organic compounds, namely amino acids and various sugars, including ribose, can be produced from the gases in the atmosphere of primitive Earth with the addition of energy.

More recently, scientists performed a similar experiment with CO_2, CO, and N_2, an updated conception of Earth's early atmosphere, and these gases allowed for the production of an even wider array of biomolecules. The addition of volcanic gases like H_2 and CH_4 increased variety and supplied hydrogen, and follow-up experiments have shown that a simple volcanic gas called carbonyl sulfide (COS) helps free-floating amino acids to form peptides, the precursors to proteins, under various conditions, and that metal ions help to intensify this reaction by up to 80 percent. However, since carbonyl sulfide decomposes rather quickly, it is unlikely to be present in large quantities in the atmosphere. Instead, scientists propose that this gas would be most predominant at hydrothermal vents on the seafloor, forming peptide chains that would stick to rocks and continue to lengthen.

RNA World Hypothesis

Francis Crick, among other scientists, first posed the RNA World Hypothesis in the 1960s. RNA has the unique ability to act as both genes and enzymes, which make RNA a sensible first biomolecule in the origin of life. A long-standing weakness of the RNA world hypothesis had been the inability of prebiotic Earth to form the molecule's nucleotides from its basic ingredients.

Recently, however, lab simulations, have demonstrated that pyrimidine nucleotides cytosine and uracil can form a number of plausible prebiotic molecules under early-Earth conditions, an atmosphere that included H_2O, CH_4, NH_3, and H_2, and that the simplest building blocks of sugars, glycolaldehyde and glyceraldehyde, can be derived from the prebiotic molecule HCN. There is no evidence of formation of the other two nucleotides present in RNA, adenine and guanine, but current research is moving in that direction. *In vitro* experiments under primordial conditions have demonstrated the ability to produce RNA molecules that perform a number of functions, including self-replication and the ability to copy other RNA molecules. These capabilities of RNA make it a very promising "first biomolecule" because RNA is the only biomolecule currently known to be capable of replication, catalysis, and containing genes itself, so RNA could have preceded DNA and proteins in evolution because RNA can self-catalyze to make protein, which can then replicate DNA.

According to the RNA World Hypothesis, the first biopolymer was a:

    A. lipid.
    B. protein.
    C. carbohydrate.
    D. nucleic acid.

The correct answer is D. This is a question about details and supporting data from the passage. Previous sample questions have focused on this concept, so the reasoning behind the correct answer shouldn't be a surprise. Choice A is an irrelevant decoy answer. Neither viewpoint refers to lipids, so this is clearly not the correct answer.

You can probably tell choice D is correct simply from the name "RNA World Hypothesis" alone. As the name—and the passage—indicate, the first biopolymer was an RNA molecule. The Theory of Volcanic Origin of Life refers to sugar formation briefly, but its focus is on proteins, which makes choice C incorrect.

However, choice B is the main decoy to watch out for here because if you look at the wrong viewpoint, you might be tempted to choose this answer. The Theory of Volcanic Origin of Life argues in favor of proteins as the first biopolymer, but that theory is not what the question is asking about.

. . . .

This question demonstrates the importance of keeping the viewpoints straight. Maybe one viewpoint in a set stood out to you because it included a helpful image or diagram, or perhaps one viewpoint in a set was memorable because it was the last one you read. Maybe you just understood one viewpoint better than the other. When it comes to answering a question that refers to a specific viewpoint, you have to make sure you are looking at the right one.

Relying on Key Words in Answer Choices

This potential pitfall may seem a bit tricky at first glance because looking for key words is a common strategy in reading comprehension. Using key words to distinguish between viewpoints, or writing down key words to mark your place while reading passages are perfectly valid strategies, and you should definitely employ them. Where key words can throw you off is in the answer choices for the questions themselves, and this really only becomes an issue if you rely too heavily on key words.

So what exactly does this mean? Let's say you read through a passage that presents three viewpoints about what caused the extinction of dinosaurs, with the three passages attributing the phenomenon to asteroid impact, climate changes, and atmospheric changes. One of the questions might ask you about a detail related to the theory of climate changes. One or more of the decoy answers may relate to asteroid impact or atmospheric changes, so these can be ruled out, but there may be a few answers containing key words related to climate changes. If you simply choose the first answer choice with a climate-related vocabulary word, there are no guarantees that you've chosen the correct answer.

Key vocabulary words can definitely help you to narrow down choices by eliminating incorrect choices related to incorrect passages or by eliminating incorrect choices that are irrelevant to the main topic altogether. However, you have to understand what you're reading, and when several incorrect decoy answers contain key words related to the question stem, you cannot rely solely on these key words. It is important to take notes as you read and understand the viewpoints, rather than choose an answer based solely on key words. Even if you come across an answer that seems correct, make sure you check all of the answers to ensure that there is not a better answer among the rest of the choices.

There are numerous theories concerning the origin of life on Earth, focusing on how primitive Earth was able to chemically create biomolecules essential for biological life to arise. Two such ideas are the Theory of Volcanic Origin of Life and the RNA World Hypothesis.

Theory of Volcanic Origin of Life

A widely accepted theory for the origin of life is that lightning and gases from volcanic eruptions may have given rise to the very first life on Earth. The Miller-Urey experiment, performed in 1952, was a chemical experiment that simulated the conditions of primitive Earth. In this experiment, a mixture of gases thought to have been present in the primitive atmosphere (most prominently, H_2O, CH_4, NH_3, and H_2) was stored in a vial connected by a pipe to a heated water tank that simulated the evaporation of the ocean. In that vial, electrodes created a spark, simulating lightning, and reaction products were collected by re-liquefying the water vapor. The setup is shown in the illustration.

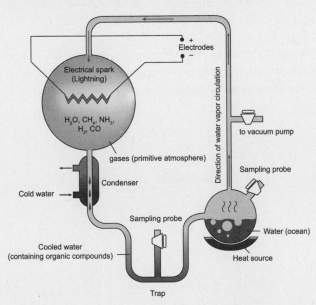

The Miller-Urey experiment showed that simple organic compounds, namely amino acids and various sugars, including ribose, can be produced from the gases in the atmosphere of primitive Earth with the addition of energy.

More recently, scientists performed a similar experiment with CO_2, CO, and N_2, an updated conception of Earth's early atmosphere, and these gases allowed for the production of an even wider array of biomolecules. The addition of volcanic gases like H_2 and CH_4 increased variety and supplied hydrogen, and follow-up experiments have shown that a simple volcanic gas called carbonyl sulfide (COS) helps free-floating amino acids to form peptides, the precursors to proteins, under various conditions, and that metal ions help to intensify this reaction by up to 80 percent. However, since carbonyl sulfide decomposes rather quickly, it is unlikely to be present in large quantities in the atmosphere. Instead, scientists propose that this gas would be most predominant at hydrothermal vents on the seafloor, forming peptide chains that would stick to rocks and continue to lengthen.

RNA World Hypothesis

Francis Crick, among other scientists, first posed the RNA World Hypothesis in the 1960s. RNA has the unique ability to act as both genes and enzymes, which make RNA a sensible first biomolecule in the origin of life. A long-standing weakness of the RNA world hypothesis had been the inability of prebiotic Earth to form the molecule's nucleotides from its basic ingredients.

Recently, however, lab simulations, have demonstrated that pyrimidine nucleotides cytosine and uracil can form a number of plausible prebiotic molecules under early-Earth conditions, an atmosphere that included H_2O, CH_4, NH_3, and H_2, and that the simplest building blocks of sugars, glycolaldehyde and glyceraldehyde, can be derived from the prebiotic molecule HCN. There is no evidence of formation of the other two nucleotides present in RNA, adenine and guanine, but current research is moving in that direction. *In vitro* experiments under primordial conditions have demonstrated the ability to produce RNA molecules that perform a number of functions, including self-replication and the ability to copy other RNA molecules. These capabilities of RNA make it a very promising "first biomolecule" because RNA is the only biomolecule currently known to be capable of replication, catalysis, and containing genes itself, so RNA could have preceded DNA and proteins in evolution because RNA can self-catalyze to make protein, which can then replicate DNA.

A key piece of evidence from the passage that places the origin of life in the deep sea is:

F. the requirement for metal ions to promote peptide formation.

G. the inability of carbonyl sulfide to tolerate a water-based environment.

H. the derivation of glycolaldehyde and glyceraldehyde from HCN.

J. the instability of carbonyl sulfide in the prebiotic atmosphere.

The correct answer is choice J. This is a question about details and supporting data from the passage. In particular, this question asks for the evidence that places the physical location for the origin of life at the bottom of the ocean. Since only the Theory of Volcanic Origin of Life refers to deep-sea vents, this question is clearly referring to this viewpoint. If we look through the answers, each answer contains key words that refer back to the passage, but the answers are obviously not all correct.

We can immediately eliminate choice H. This answer contains key words from the passage, but from the wrong passage. The second viewpoint refers to the derivation of glycolaldehyde and glyceraldehyde from HCN, but it is in no way related to the placement of the origin of life in the deep sea. Choice F refers to metal ions, which are discussed in the first viewpoint in the section that describes the deep sea proposal. At first glance, therefore, this might seem like the correct answer based on the key words, but the metal ions are not what caused the proposal for the deep sea location of the origin of life. Choice G contains all of the right key words, particularly "carbonyl sulfide" and the reference to water, but the answer says all of the wrong things. If carbonyl sulfide cannot tolerate a water-based environment, then the origin of life should *not* be pinpointed in the ocean. The correct answer is therefore choice J, which correctly specifies that carbonyl sulfide is not stable and breaks down in the atmosphere, which would be why the origin of life would be more likely to occur in the deep sea.

FAILING TO FIND SUPPORT FOR YOUR ANSWERS IN THE TEXT

At its heart, the analysis of a Conflicting Viewpoint passage is essentially science-based reading comprehension. This means that any answer you choose for a particular question should have some kind of textual support. If an answer choice for a question seems to come out of nowhere and has no textual context based on the passage, it is probably not the correct answer. If you go back and look over all of the examples that have been covered so far in this section, you'll see that this is true of each and every correct answer; you can trace every correct answer back to the passage and find textual evidence that supports that correct answer.

As such, a useful strategy to employ while dealing with Conflicting Viewpoints passages is to find textual support for any answer you've decided on as a correct answer, and if you want to confirm your answer, make sure there is no textual evidence that supports the other answers with respect to the question asked. Think of Conflicting Viewpoints questions like an open-book test, where all of the answers are given to you in some way in the passage.

There are numerous theories concerning the origin of life on Earth, focusing on how primitive Earth was able to chemically create biomolecules essential for biological life to arise. Two such ideas are the Theory of Volcanic Origin of Life and the RNA World Hypothesis.

Theory of Volcanic Origin of Life

A widely accepted theory for the origin of life is that lightning and gases from volcanic eruptions may have given rise to the very first life on Earth. The Miller-Urey experiment, performed in 1952, was a chemical experiment that simulated the conditions of primitive Earth. In this experiment, a mixture of gases thought to have been present in the primitive atmosphere (most prominently, H_2O, CH_4, NH_3, and H_2) was stored in a vial connected by a pipe to a heated water tank that simulated the evaporation of the ocean. In that vial, electrodes created a spark, simulating lightning, and reaction products were collected by re-liquefying the water vapor. The setup is shown in the illustration.

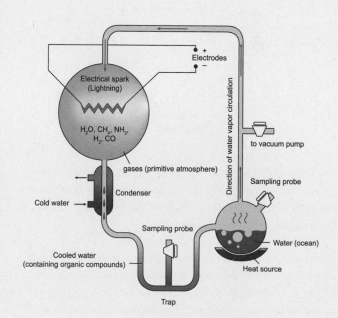

The Miller-Urey experiment showed that simple organic compounds, namely amino acids and various sugars, including ribose, can be produced from the gases in the atmosphere of primitive Earth with the addition of energy.

More recently, scientists performed a similar experiment with CO_2, CO, and N_2, an updated conception of Earth's early atmosphere, and these gases allowed for the production of an even wider array of biomolecules. The addition of volcanic gases like H_2 and CH_4 increased variety and supplied hydrogen, and follow-up experiments have shown that a simple volcanic gas called carbonyl sulfide (COS) helps free-floating amino acids to form peptides, the precursors to proteins, under various conditions, and that metal ions help to intensify this reaction by up to 80 percent. However, since carbonyl sulfide decomposes rather quickly, it is unlikely to be present in large quantities in the atmosphere. Instead, scientists propose that this gas would be most predominant at hydrothermal vents on the seafloor, forming peptide chains that would stick to rocks and continue to lengthen.

RNA World Hypothesis

Francis Crick, among other scientists, first posed the RNA World Hypothesis in the 1960s. RNA has the unique ability to act as both genes and enzymes, which make RNA a sensible first biomolecule in the origin of life. A long-standing weakness of the RNA world hypothesis had been the inability of prebiotic Earth to form the molecule's nucleotides from its basic ingredients.

Recently, however, lab simulations, have demonstrated that pyrimidine nucleotides cytosine and uracil can form a number of plausible prebiotic molecules under early-Earth conditions, an atmosphere that included H_2O, CH_4, NH_3, and H_2, and that the simplest building blocks of sugars, glycolaldehyde and glyceraldehyde, can be derived from the prebiotic molecule HCN. There is no evidence of formation of the other two nucleotides present in RNA, adenine and guanine but current research is moving in that direction. *In vitro* experiments under primordial conditions have demonstrated the ability to produce RNA molecules that perform a number of functions, including self-replication and the ability to copy other RNA molecules. These capabilities of RNA make it a very promising "first biomolecule" because RNA is the only biomolecule currently known to be capable of replication, catalysis, and containing genes itself, so RNA could have preceded DNA and proteins in evolution because RNA can self-catalyze to make protein, which can then replicate DNA.

Both viewpoints indicate that prebiotic conditions were capable of:

A. converting atmospheric gases into organic amino acids.

B. using carbonyl sulfide as a means of peptide formation.

C. synthesizing lipids from molecules found in the atmosphere and deep sea.

D. forming sugars and sugar precursors from available chemical compounds.

The correct answer is D. This is a comparison question that asks you to find a similarity between the two viewpoints. To answer this question, we can look for textual support from each answer choice in the passage. Choice A indicates that both viewpoints believe that the atmospheric gases were capable of amino acid formation. There is only textual evidence for this in the first viewpoint, but there is no evidence of the sort in the second viewpoint, so this answer is incorrect. Choice B indicates that the passages agree that carbonyl sulfide was likely used for peptide formation. Again, there is only textual evidence for this in the first viewpoint, but there is no evidence for this at all in the second passage. There is no textual evidence anywhere in either viewpoint to support the concept of lipid synthesis, so choice C is incorrect. Choice D indicates that both viewpoints suggest that sugars and sugar precursors could be formed from the available chemical compounds on prebiotic Earth. The first viewpoint states that various sugars can be produced from the gases in the atmosphere of primitive Earth, while the second viewpoint states that the prebiotic molecule HCN is capable of forming glycolaldehyde and glyceraldehyde, which are sugar precursors. There is textual evidence to support this answer for both passages, so it is correct.

SUMMING IT UP

- **Conflicting Viewpoints passages provide two (or sometimes three) arguments** that put forth a hypothesis or theory, along with supporting evidence, that are related to a particular common topic.

- **Follow these steps when you encounter a Conflicting Viewpoints passage on the ACT:**

    1) Identify the topic.
    2) Identify the basic hypotheses or theories of the scientists.
    3) Identify the relevant data used to support each of the two viewpoints discussed in the passage.

- **Reading comprehension is all about understanding what you read.** The vast majority of information you'll need to answer questions about Conflicting Viewpoints passages can be found in the passages themselves.

- **Look for commonalities.** There will always be some kind of parallel you can draw, and one of the questions accompanying the passage will draw attention to one of those parallels.

- **Take notes in the margin as you read Conflicting Viewpoints passages.** Doing so will help you to identify the shared topic, viewpoint presented by each author, and supporting data presented in favor of each viewpoint.

- **The ACT Science test is made up entirely of multiple-choice questions.** Use this to your advantage by looking at the answers if you aren't sure about what the question is asking so you can determine it from the viewpoints.

- **Conflicting Viewpoints questions require you to fully understand the ins and outs of each viewpoint.** Understanding the information completely will help you to figure out how new data could support or refute it.

- **When reading through a passage for the first time, identify three components:**

    1) The main topic of the passage
    2) The theories described by each viewpoint
    3) Any data that will help you to cut out the extraneous information

- **Read and reread questions to make sure you're looking in the right passage for your answer.**

- **Take notes as you read to understand the viewpoints presented.** Don't just choose an answer based solely on its inclusion of key words, which is a common trap.

WANT TO KNOW MORE?

Access more practice questions, lessons, helpful hints, and strategies for the following science topics in *Peterson's ACT Online Course*:

- Conflicting Viewpoints
- Hard Science Reasoning Questions
- Time Emergency: Science Test

To purchase and access the course, go to **www.petersons.com/act**.

PRACTICE

You now know the ins and outs of Conflicting Viewpoints questions, so it's time to try a full practice set on your own. When you're finished answering all 20 questions, check the answers that follow to read full explanations of all answer choices.

PASSAGE I

There are a number of theories that have been proposed to explain how the moon was formed. Two of those theories are the Fission Theory and the Giant Impact Theory.

Fission Theory

Many scientists support the Fission Theory of moon formation, which indicates that the moon was spun off from Earth when early Earth was rapidly rotating on its axis. This theory was first proposed by George Darwin in the 1800s. The piece of Earth that separated to form the moon may be from the Pacific Ocean basin. Key evidence that supports Fission Theory is the common composition between Earth's mantle and the moon. Siderophile ("metal-loving") elements, including molybdenum and rhenium, occur in both Earth's mantle and on the moon, though their concentrations in lunar rocks are significantly lower than concentrations found in Earth's mantle. Furthermore, the densities of moon rocks are very similar to those of Earth rocks found just below the crust. Additionally, the core of the moon is largely composed of metallic iron, alloyed with a small amount of sulfur and nickel. A 2010 study of seismic data on deep moonquakes confirmed that the outer core of the moon is iron-rich, and that the solid inner core is made of pure iron. The figure below shows the layers of the moon:

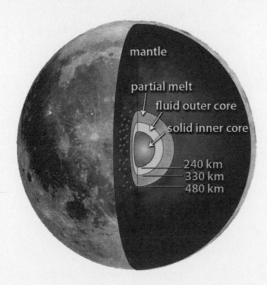

The analysis of the composition of the moon's core is relevant to Fission Theory because it is again very similar to that of Earth, though far smaller in radius. Earth would have to have been spinning extremely rapidly for the mode of moon formation proposed by Fission Theory to be true, but there is currently no evidence to suggest that this was the case.

Giant Impact Theory

The Giant Impact Theory is perhaps the most widely accepted theory for moon formation. According to this theory, an indirect collision between Earth and an astronomical body the size of Mars, called Theia, occurred 4.5 billion years ago; rock aging techniques indicated that Earth and the moon are approximately this same age. In consequence, the impact blasted pieces of Earth and Theia into Earth's orbit. Over time, the debris from the impact then eventually came together to form the mass that is the moon. Moon rocks have exhibited signs of having been molten at some point in the ancient past, which is atypical of Earth rocks, indicating that the moon was formed under very hot conditions. Additionally, Earth has a tilt and ecliptic plane orientation that differs from most other planets in the solar system, a possibly permanent effect of the collision of Earth with a Mars-sized mass. Furthermore, a similar collision was recently observed in 1994 between the gas giant Jupiter and the Shoemaker-Levy comet; despite the small size of the comet, the comet's collision with Jupiter resulted in its breakdown into a number of fragments. Finally, the stable isotope ratios of rocks from Earth and the moon were found to be identical, implying a common origin. These data support the theory that the moon formed as a result of Earth's impact with another sizeable astronomical body, Theia.

1. According to the first viewpoint, how does siderophile composition compare between Earth and the moon?

   A. Earth and the moon contain the same kinds and concentrations of siderophiles.
   B. Earth and the moon contain the same kinds of siderophiles, but the siderophiles are not present in the same concentrations in each.
   C. Earth and the moon contain different kinds of siderophiles, but the concentrations of the siderophiles are very similar.
   D. Earth and the moon contain different kinds of siderophiles that are present in very different concentrations.

2. Which piece of data from the passage indicates that the moon formed under extremely hot conditions?

   F. The average temperature of the moon's atmosphere is significantly higher than the average temperature of Earth's atmosphere.
   G. Earth has a tilt and ecliptic plane orientation inconsistent with most other planets in the solar system.
   H. Siderophiles are present on both Earth and the moon.
   J. Moon rocks were found to have been liquefied during the development of the young moon.

3. The moon does not have an overall magnetic field like Earth, but scientists decided to study the magnetic properties of its surface rocks. Which piece of evidence would most support both of the described theories for moon formation?

   A. The moon surface rocks show signs of having had a magnetic field early in the moon's history.
   B. The moon surface rocks likely had no magnetic field early on, but they have since developed that property.
   C. The moon surface rocks proved to be capable of conducting electricity under standard atmospheric conditions.
   D. There is no indication that there was ever any magnetic field in the histories of the moon surface rocks.

4. Scientists decided to look at oxygen isotopes because planets and moons have a distinct oxygen fingerprint that indicates the exact environmental conditions in which they were formed. They find that some of the moon rocks contain a slightly *higher* amount (12 ppm more) of the rare isotope oxygen-17 than Earth rocks do. If this difference is considered to be significant, this piece of data would most support:

   F. the Fission Theory of moon formation.
   G. the Giant Impact Theory of moon formation.
   H. both the Fission Theory and the Giant Impact Theory of moon formation.
   J. neither the Fission Theory nor the Giant Impact Theory of moon formation.

5. An additional theory of moon formation, the Capture Theory, proposes that the moon was formed somewhere else in the solar system and was later captured by the gravitational field of Earth. Which piece of data from the passage best supports the Fission Theory and Giant Impact Theory and refutes the Capture Theory?

   A. Rock aging data indicates that the rocks from Earth and the moon are approximately the same age of 4.5 billion years.
   B. The moon has a solid inner core, but its outer core is fluid.
   C. The moon's crust is thinner on the side nearest Earth.
   D. The Shoemaker-Levy comet fragmented upon collision with Jupiter.

6. With which statement would supporters of the Fission Theory be most likely to agree?

   F. The Pacific Ocean basin was created by the impact of an astronomical body.
   G. Moon rocks should have formed more recently than Earth rocks.
   H. Early Earth was very stable and compact.
   J. Moon rocks and Earth rocks should be very similar to one another in terms of their composition.

7. The Giant Impact Theory most deviates from the Fission Theory because it involves:

   A. superheating of moon rocks during early development.
   B. the existence of an iron core in the moon.
   C. the interaction of Earth with another massive object.
   D. pieces of Earth contributing to the formation of the moon.

PASSAGE II

Two students became involved in a debate of nature versus nurture, arguing whether human behavior is influenced more by one's genes or by one's upbringing. The students focus on academic success, the ability to do well in school. Each student did some research and wrote a brief argument in favor of either nature or nurture as the predominant force in academic success.

Student 1

One's genes are far more important for academic success than one's upbringing. A study compared identical twins and non-identical twins in their 20s, a reflection on the effect of genetics versus environment because identical twins share 100% of their genes, while non-identical twins share only 50% of their genes. The study found that identical twins performed similarly in tests of English, science, and math, but showed more variation in personality, behavior and health, indicating that genes are more closely linked with academic performance.

In addition, there are a number of single-gene genetic disorders, including dyslexia, and neural disorders, like autism and Down syndrome, that affect cognitive ability, which demonstrates another effect of genes on academic performance. Also, researchers have recently found that genetic variation affects expression of the *NPTN* gene, which encodes an NPTN protein that affects how brain cells communicate and results in a thinner brain cortex in the left cerebral hemisphere. Teenagers with this gene also performed worse on intelligence tests. Similar effects were seen for the same gene in mice. However, this gene only seems to affect 0.5% of total variation in intelligence.

Student 2

A person's environmental upbringing is more important for his or her academic success than genetics. A recent study, based on a pool of over 100,000 people, picked out 69 gene variants linked to educational achievement and cross-checked the list with gene variants found to be related to higher IQ based on cognitive tests taken by 24,000 people. Three gene variants were found to be linked to both educational achievement and high IQ. However, the researchers calculated that each variant contributed to an average of 0.3 points on an IQ test, in which two-thirds of the population normally scores between 85 and 115. This means that a person with all three variants would only score 1.8 points higher on an intelligence test than a person with none of them, which is hardly any effect at all. Furthermore, there are a dozen different single-nucleotide polymorphisms (SNPs) in DNA that correlate with IQ scores in certain humans, but with a statistically significant sample size, none are really linked to intelligence.

Genes aside, however, there are many environmental influences that can affect intelligence and academic performance. Nutrition, stress, and exposure to violence have all been associated with lower school grades and lower IQs. Even a child's position in birth order was found to influence intelligence, with firstborn children generally scoring higher, though these studies did not control for age or family size. Access to education and socioeconomic status can also influence one's performance in school.

8. Based on Student 1's viewpoint, increased expression of the *NPNT* gene would result in:

F. lower levels of NPNT protein.
G. a thicker brain cortex in the left cerebral hemisphere.
H. a decreased effect of stress on academic performance.
J. lower scores on intelligence tests.

9. Based on Student 2's viewpoint, which of the following factors would have the most significant negative impact on a teenager's academic performance?

A. Readily available educational resources
B. The expression of the *NPNT* gene
C. A demanding and stressful part-time job
D. The presence of SNPs in the teenager's DNA

10. Students 1 and 2 might agree that:

F. individual genes will not have a significant effect on intelligence across a population.
G. genetic and neural disorders have no effect on academic performance.
H. a child's home life will be the most important determinant of academic success.
J. the effect of hormones outweighs the effects of genes or environment in a student's academic success.

11. A common strategy used by both students to support their arguments is:

A. surveying small samples of people for information on environmental backgrounds.
B. focusing on twin studies in their approaches.
C. finding genetic studies that support their respective views.
D. connecting brain and neuronal development to the academic success of individuals.

12. What is a major weakness of Student 1's argument compared to Student 2's argument?

F. Student 1 fails to focus on environmental effects, while Student 2 uses both environmental and genetic evidence.
G. Student 1 fails to focus on genetic effects, while Student 2 uses both environmental and genetic evidence.
H. Student 1 uses a wide variety of genetic evidence to support his viewpoint.
J. Student 1 uses a wide variety of environmental evidence to support his viewpoint.

13. A new study finds that the presence of a particular gene product significantly decreases one's IQ and intelligence test scores. This result would support the viewpoint of:

A. Student 1.
B. Student 2.
C. both Student 1 and Student 2.
D. neither Student 1 nor Student 2.

14. The twin study described by Student 1 provides strong support for his argument, assuming that:

F. all of the twins express the NPNT protein.
G. none of the twins express the NPNT protein.
H. their genomes have been fully sequenced.
J. the twins were brought up in similar environments.

PASSAGE III

Two students were interested in investigating the pros and cons of acquiring and burning fossil fuels as an energy source. Fossil fuels are hydrocarbons, mostly oil, coal and natural gas, that form from the remains of decomposed organic matter. The students did some research to support their conflicting views on using fossil fuels as an energy source, and they presented their results here.

Student 1

Burning fossil fuels may be an effective and safe means for acquiring energy at this point, but it will not remain that way for long. Fossil fuels will become increasingly expensive to extract as they become scarcer on the planet. It will also become more dangerous to acquire fuel, as mines must go deeper into the earth, and oil rigs must travel further out to sea. In addition, burning fossil fuels also has negative environmental effects. Pollution from burning fossil fuels contributes to global warming and acid rain, and the means of fuel acquisition increases the risk of oil spillage. Fossil fuels contain high amounts of carbon, and burning these fuels leads to the release of high levels of CO_2 and greenhouse gases that cause damage to the ozone layer. The graph below shows global fossil carbon emissions over the last 200 years.

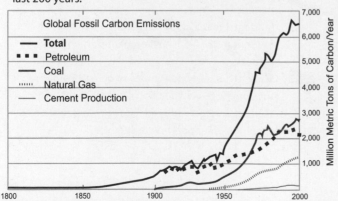

Controlling this pollution requires additional expense, and fuel prices will rise accordingly. Additionally, continued fossil fuel usage is unsustainable and nonrenewable. There are a limited amount of fossil fuels available that could take millions of years to naturally replenish.

Therefore, it is important to look into alternative energy sources, including solar, wind, wave, and water (hydro) power, all of which are renewable and sustainable. Alternative energy sources provide environmental benefits due to low or zero carbon emission, they are sustainable, and they also provide a stable and cost-effective energy supply that could decrease the country's reliance on international supply.

Student 2

It is relatively cheap to burn fossil fuels, and the process is an extremely effective way to acquire energy. Advanced technologies have been developed to ensure safe extraction, at least given the current extraction techniques, and plenty of technology has already been developed for the extraction process, including petrol-driven engines. Fossil fuels are also easily transported and can readily be converted to liquid, solid, or gas forms. Though it is costly, the means of controlling fuel-derived pollution exists, but the fuels also provide a source of income because fuel sales can improve the country's economy. The fossil fuel industry is a stable source of employment too.

There are currently no other energy sources that can replace fossil fuels completely and safely. Fossil fuel usage makes up the majority of U.S. energy acquisition, as the 2011 U.S. energy breakdown below shows.

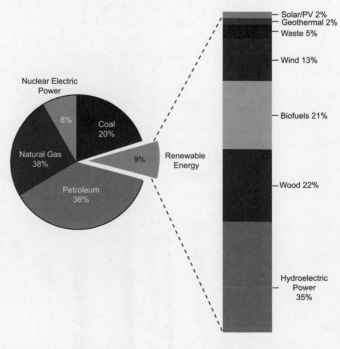

Alternative energy sources tend to be inefficient, and they do not currently have the capability of meeting the required energy demands. Therefore, it does not make sense to try to replace an energy source that is clearly such a significant source of energy in the country.

15. With which of the following statements would Student 1 disagree?

   A. The use of fossil fuels is an efficient means of energy acquisition.
   B. Alternative energy sources provide a way to decrease carbon emissions into the atmosphere.
   C. Fossil fuel usage has increased dramatically over the last few centuries.
   D. Fossil fuel renewal is timely enough to ensure resource sustainability.

16. Which of the following statements best summarizes Student 2's view on alternative energy sources?

   F. Alternative energy sources currently comprise the majority of the U.S.'s energy supply.
   G. Alternative energy sources are more costly but more efficient than fossil fuel usage.
   H. It will be difficult for alternative energy sources to provide sufficient energy for what is required by the U.S. currently.
   J. The burning of fossil fuels is a major contributor to acid rain, global warming, and oil spills.

17. The resource sustainability of fossil fuels is a concern posed by:

   A. Student 1.
   B. Student 2.
   C. both students.
   D. neither student.

18. Students 1 and 2 would agree that:

   F. the U.S. should continue to rely on fossil fuels because additional natural energy sources will always be found.
   G. fossil fuels are currently the most efficient source of energy in the U.S.
   H. carbon emissions are not a major concern in the 21st century.
   J. alternative energy sources are sufficient and sustainable enough to replace fossil fuels in the near future.

19. Concern for the economy is expressed specifically by:

   A. Student 1.
   B. Student 2.
   C. both students.
   D. neither student.

20. Which of the following hypothetical new technologies would best satisfy the main concern of Student 2 regarding the use of fossil fuels and alternative energy sources?

   F. The development of a process to efficiently absorb and use carbon byproducts from fossil fuel burning
   G. The creation of a new mode of transport for fossil fuels
   H. The discovery of a new, highly efficient natural alternative energy source
   J. Increased safety features with regard to fossil fuel technology

475

Chapter 13

Conflicting Viewpoints

ANSWERS AND EXPLANATIONS

The first passage is an earth sciences/astronomy passage that provides two theories for how Earth's moon was formed.

1. **The correct answer is B.** This question is a detail question that asks you to use the first viewpoint to compare the siderophile concentration between Earth and the moon. The first viewpoint indicates that same types of siderophiles are present on Earth and the moon, but that the moon has lower concentrations of these same siderophiles. The answer choice that best describes this relationship is choice B.

2. **The correct answer is J.** This question is also a detail question. The reference to the hot conditions that existed when the moon was formed occurs in the second viewpoint. Choice F has no textual support and is incorrect. Choice G is a true statement that occurs near the discussion of the hot moon formation in the second viewpoint, but it is irrelevant to the question. Choice H is also a true statement, but it is from the first passage and is also irrelevant to the question. Therefore, the correct answer is choice J. The second viewpoint describes the moon rocks as having been "molten" early on, which indicates that the rocks were probably in liquid form during the development of the moon.

3. **The correct answer is A.** This question requires both comparison and inference, as it involves new hypothetical information that pertains to both passages. Both theories posit that a significant portion of the moon's rocks came from Earth, so if Earth rocks are magnetic, it is likely that moon rocks were at least magnetic initially when they were derived from Earth. The correct answer, therefore, is choice A. Choice B states the opposite, choice C is irrelevant to the question, and choice D does not really support either theory.

4. **The correct answer is G.** This is an inference question. If the oxygen fingerprint gives a sense of rock origin, the newly presented piece of data suggests that some of the moon rocks are not derived from Earth since they have different oxygen fingerprints. These moon rocks may have been derived from Theia, the non-Earth astronomical body that may have collided with Earth and contributed to the rock composition of the moon, so this piece of data only supports the Giant Impact Theory because the Fission Theory indicates that the moon rocks were only derived from Earth.

5. **The correct answer is A.** This is an inference question that asks you to select the piece of data that supports the two posed theories, but refutes the newly introduced Capture Theory, which proposes that the moon was formed elsewhere in the solar system and was captured by Earth's gravitational field. Choice A indicates that the earth and moon rocks are approximately the same age, as this indicates that the rocks have the same origin and are likely not from some other

source elsewhere in the solar system. Choice B is irrelevant to the question; choice C is a true statement that is not mentioned in either viewpoint; and choice D, though true, does not particularly refute the Capture Theory.

6. **The correct answer is J.** This is an inference and detail question. Supporters of the Fission Theory would not agree that the Pacific Ocean basin was created by the impact of an astronomical body; while they would indicate that this it the source of moon rock, it would not be due to any impact, so the answer is not choice F. The answer is not choice G, as Fission Theory supporters would expect the earth and moon rocks to have the same age. The answer is also not choice H; if early Earth was extremely stable and compact, then pieces of rock would not be flying off to form the moon due to high-velocity spinning. The answer, therefore, is choice J, as similar composition between moon and Earth rocks indicates common origin.

7. **The correct answer is C.** This question asks you to contrast the two theories. The key difference between the theories is the involvement of impact, which occurs in the Giant Impact Theory but not in Fission Theory, so the correct answer is choice C. Choices A and B are not especially relevant to the question, and choice D is a similarity, not a difference, between the theories.

The second passage is a biology passage that uses the format in which two students debate a topic after researching their respective viewpoints. In this passage, the students are debating the classic nature vs. nurture question with respect to academic performance.

8. **The correct answer is J.** This question is a detail question. Based on the explanation in the first viewpoint of how the *NPNT* gene works, increased expression of *NPNT* would result in higher levels of NPNT protein, a thinner brain cortex in the left cerebral hemisphere, and lower scores on intelligence tests. This means that choices F and G are incorrect and choice J is correct. Choice H brings into the picture a nurture-based effect on intelligence and key vocabulary mentioned in the second viewpoint, but it is not relevant to this question because the question asks about the first viewpoint, not the second viewpoint.

9. **The correct answer is C.** This question is a detail question that asks you to predict which factor would have the most negative effect on a student's academic performance, according to the second viewpoint. The second viewpoint argues in favor of the domination of "nurture" over "nature." Therefore, we can immediately eliminate choices B and D because both are genetic factors discussed in the first viewpoint. Choices A and C both describe nurture-based factors, but logically, choice A should have a positive effect on academic

performance, not a negative effect. The answer, therefore, is choice C, which is also mentioned in the second viewpoint as a factor that can affect academic performance due to the key word *stress*.

10. **The correct answer is F.** This question asks you to compare the two viewpoints. While the first viewpoint favors nature over nurture, and the second viewpoint favors nurture over nature, both viewpoints include experimental evidence that individual genes do not significantly affect intelligence across a population. The first passage uses this information to imply that gene systems are more complex than that, while the second passage uses this information in an attempt to dismiss the effect of genes on intelligence. Choices G and H are both mentioned in only one of the viewpoints each, and choice J is mentioned in neither viewpoint.

11. **The correct answer is C.** This question also asks you to compare the viewpoints in terms of strategies each student used to make his or her argument. Choice A is incorrect because large sample sizes were used, and because the second viewpoint focused on environmental backgrounds, though it is implied that the first student inquired about environmental backgrounds in the twin studies. Choice B is incorrect because only Student 1 employed this strategy. Student 1 alluded to brain and neuronal development in the discussion of the NPNT protein, but there was no mention of this topic in Student 2's argument. Both students referred to genetic studies, so the correct answer is choice C.

12. **The correct answer is F.** This question asks you to compare and contrast the two viewpoints. We can immediately eliminate choices H and J because using a wide variety of genetic evidence would be a strength, not a weakness. Between choices F and G, the correct answer is choice F because Student 1 does not explicitly explore environmental effects, while Student 2 explores both genetic and environmental effects to show why environment effects might predominate over genetic effects.

13. **The correct answer is A.** This is an inference question. If new hypothetical data finds that a gene significantly affects intelligence and academic performance, it would clearly strengthen the argument posed by Student 1, who is arguing in favor of nature (genetics) over nurture (environment and upbringing).

14. **The correct answer is J.** This is an inference question that asks you to consider implied information. The conclusions drawn by Student 1 from the twin studies can be considered valid only if the twins are considered to have been brought up in similar environments; that way, genetics would be the only thing causing a difference between the two. Because the twins exhibited different personality traits but similar academic performances, the student's argument is strengthened because it indicates that twins with the same genes perform similarly academically, even though their personalities are not identical. In fact, the difference in personalities might be considered a

difference in "nurture," so if twins perform similarly academically, it would seem that the genes, and not the personality differences, correlate with the academic performance.

The final passage is a chemistry passage, with some biological implications. The conflicting viewpoints explore the pros and cons of using fossil fuels as an energy source.

15. **The correct answer is D.** This is a detail question. Even though the first student is arguing against the use of fossil fuels, the student still acknowledges that fossil fuels are an efficient mode of energy acquisition, so the answer is not choice A. Choice B essentially sums up the student's argument, and choice C supports the data the student provides, so neither of these answers is correct. The student indicates that fossil fuel turnover is not rapid enough to sustain the resource, so the student would disagree with choice D.

16. **The correct answer is H.** This is a detail question. Choice F is not true according to either viewpoint, nor is choice G, so these answers can be ruled out. Choice J is a true statement discussed by Student 1, but it is not relevant to this question. Choice H correctly sums up Student 2's view on alternative energy sources: that these sources will have a tough time providing enough energy for U.S. demand.

17. **The correct answer is A.** This is a detail question, though it might also be considered a compare/contrast question also. The question asks you to determine which student or students addressed resource sustainability of fossil fuels. Only Student 1 does this, so the correct answer is A.

18. **The correct answer is G.** This question asks you to compare the viewpoints. Choice F is incorrect because Student 1 specifically argues against the use of fossil fuels, while Student 2 would disagree with the implication that natural energy sources are infinite and plentiful. Choice H is incorrect because the data provided by Student 1 specifically show that carbon emissions are very much a concern today, and the student notes several negative effects caused by carbon emissions. Choice J is incorrect because Student 2 indicates that alternative energy sources are not sufficient or sustainable enough to replace fossil fuels. The correct answer is choice G, as both students acknowledge that fossil fuels are currently the most efficient energy source in the U.S., even though Student 1 is more concerned with the negative effects of the use of fossil fuels as an energy source.

19. **The correct answer is C.** This is a detail and compare/contrast question. The question asks you to choose which student or students expressed economic concerns in each viewpoint. Student 1 discusses the increased cost of finding increasingly scarce fossil fuels as the current stock is depleted, as well as the expense of pollution control. Student 2 discusses the economic benefits of fossil fuels on an international scale and as a

source of employment. Therefore, both students express economic concerns.

20. **The correct answer is H.** This is an inference question. This question asks you to choose the hypothetical technology that would most satisfy the key concern of Student 2 regarding fossil fuels and alternative energy sources. Student 2 was not so concerned with environmental impacts, so we can rule out choice F. Student 2 was also satisfied with the current mode of fossil fuel transport, so this was not a concern in the student's viewpoint. Student 2 also referred to fossil fuel extraction technology practices as "safe," so safety was not the student's main concern either. The answer is not choice J. Student 2 was not in favor of eliminating fossil fuels because there is not efficient replacement natural alternative energy source, so the development of such an energy source would address this concern. Such a technology would likely also get Students 1 and 2 on the same page because, as long as this new natural alternative energy source is safe, all of the arguments Student 2 makes in favor of fossil fuels could also be made in favor of the new energy source, minus the environmental concerns discussed by Student 1.

478

Chapter 13

Conflicting Viewpoints

PART VII:
WRITING STRATEGIES
FOR THE ACT®

Chapter 14: Mastering the ACT® Writing Test

WRITING STRATEGIES FOR THE ACT®

Doing well on every section of the ACT Test—including the writing test—is a great way for you to stand out from the crowd of college applicants and will increase your chances of getting into the college of your choice. If you've purchased this book and have decided to take preparing for the ACT *seriously*, you've already taken a great step forward toward achieving your goals.

This chapter provides you with everything you need to know to do your best on the ACT Writing test—including an overview of the test, what to expect on test day, how the writing test is scored, and what the official test readers are looking for in a high-scoring essay—as well as how to avoid getting a low score. You'll also find plenty of advice and strategies for building your writing skills, tackling essay prompts, and using your time effectively to plan and construct a great essay on test day. Then you'll be able to sharpen your skills with effective practice and review using sample prompts and model essays to compare your work against.

Use the information in this chapter to help you do your best on the writing section of the ACT test, impress the official ACT essay readers, and get a great score.

CHAPTER 14:
MASTERING THE ACT®
WRITING TEST

OVERVIEW

- Should You Take the ACT Writing Test?
- Test Overview
- The Essay Prompt
- The Essay Perspectives
- The Essay Task
- Planning Your Essay
- Writing Your Essay
- Sample ACT Essays
- Summing It Up
- Practice

The ACT Writing test is one of five test sections on the ACT, but it is the only test section of the ACT that is *optional*—which means that you get to decide whether or not taking the writing test is the right decision for you.

SHOULD YOU TAKE THE ACT WRITING TEST?

Whether or not the colleges that you're applying to require you to submit an ACT Writing test score should help guide your decision to take this optional test. Requirements vary by school, so make sure you check with your target schools well in advance. You have a few options:

- Look up the information on the school's website.
- Ask your high school counselor for assistance.
- Contact the schools directly.

ACT Writing Test: It's Your Call

Your decision to take—or not take—the ACT Writing test will not impact your scores on the other ACT subject area tests or your overall composite score. However, the *only* way to receive an English Language Arts (ELA) test score is by taking the ACT Writing test.

Even if your target colleges don't *require* an ACT Writing test score, you can still take the test and submit your score. If you're a confident writer and feel that you'll get a great score on test day and you'd like to include it as part of your college applications, you have the option of doing so—it could really help college admissions personnel make a decision regarding acceptance, as well as help guide later decisions regarding course placement.

TEST OVERVIEW

The ACT Writing test is a 40-minute essay-writing exam designed to do the following:

- Measure your English-language writing capabilities
- Test your ability to focus thoughtfully on a provided topic
- Assess your analytical ability
- Gauge your ability to develop ideas using logical reasoning

You'll use your experience and breadth of knowledge from English classes and writing projects throughout your academic career to create an argumentative essay that responds to a provided essay prompt.

The best test preparation for the ACT Writing test is—you guessed it—writing practice. We've got you covered: You'll get to practice writing using essay prompts that are similar to what you might see on the ACT later on in this chapter. You'll also get to see sample essays at each score level, to help you evaluate your own writing and determine what you need to work on to get a great score on test day!

The ACT Writing test can be taken on all six of the official national test dates (which includes the United States, U.S. territories, Canada, and Puerto Rico), as well as the five official international test dates and special or arranged test dates.

The test is taken using a pencil (remember to bring a few sharpened, non-mechanical No.2 pencils with you on test day), and you'll write your essay in an answer folder provided to you by the test administrator. If you require specific test accommodations, please visit the official ACT website for additional information.

ACT Writing Test Enhancements

If you've taken the ACT Writing test prior to September 2015 or have used older study materials to prepare, you'll notice that the test has changed—a lot. Don't worry, we'll provide everything you need to know right here!

Although at its core the ACT Writing test is still just what the name implies—a test of your writing abilities—the official ACT test developers have made a few recent enhancements that you should be aware of. Here's what is now included:

- **Increased time for essay planning and writing:** Previously, test-takers had 30 minutes to plan and write their essays. Test-takers now have 40 minutes to do so.
- **More guidance and structure for essay planning:** The test now features prewriting guidance for structuring and crafting a written response. We'll cover the essay information you'll receive on test day later on in this chapter.
- **Wider range of subjects:** Previous essay prompts focused mainly on school-based subject matter. Now, essay prompts will draw from a wider array of engaging subjects and topical issues.
- **Broader topic perspectives provided:** Test-takers will get three diverse perspectives on the issue provided in the essay prompt, allowing for a more multifaceted analytical engagement.
- **More reflective of real-world topic discussion:** Previously, students provided a response to the issue provided in the prompt. Now, their responses are built alongside, and in dialogue with, varying perspectives.
- **More comprehensive scoring:** The ACT Writing test now provides test-takers with scoring in four specific writing proficiency domains: **Ideas and Analysis, Development and Support, Organization,** and **Language Use and Conventions.** You'll also receive a writing score and a scaled English Language Arts (ELA) score (ranging from 1–36, similar to the other test sections on the ACT). Additional scoring information appears later in this chapter.

How the ACT Writing Test Is Scored

The enhanced ACT Writing test is designed to provide a comprehensive assessment of your abilities across a range of fundamental writing proficiency domains. You'll have the opportunity to respond to a writing prompt based on a carefully chosen topic, which will be presented alongside three distinct perspectives, each of which will be suggestive of a certain way of thinking about the issue.

During the essay writing process, you'll be tasked as follows:

- Analyze and evaluate the perspectives given
- State and develop your own perspective on the issue
- Explain the relationship between your perspective and those given

As you plan and structure your written response, your unique perspective on the issue can agree with any of the three perspectives provided, agree partially, or be completely distinct. Really, your opinion doesn't matter, as long as you have one! And as long as you *have* one and develop it, you're on the right track. Regardless of your perspective, you'll need to develop and support your essay using careful analysis, solid reasoning, sound ideas, and compelling examples.

As previously mentioned, your essay will be scored by two separate (and highly experienced) certified ACT essay readers in four specific writing proficiency domains.

1) Ideas and Analysis

This grading area measures how well you can organize critical analysis toward a provided prompt and perspectives on a given topic, and then develop effective ideas to build your own perspective. A high-scoring essay will demonstrate a solid understanding of the topic and provide a compelling, relevant argument in support of a clear perspective.

2) Development and Support

This grading area measures your ability to generate an effective written argument with sound ideas, solid reasoning, a clear rationale, and thoughtful support. A high-scoring essay will demonstrate a clear flow of thoughts alongside a solid stance on the issue provided in the prompt and strong support in defense of your perspective, creating a clear, convincing piece of argumentative writing.

3) Organization

This grading area measures your ability to carefully and thoughtfully organize your ideas to create a convincing, coherent essay. A high-scoring essay will be a clear, on target, and purposeful piece of writing that demonstrates a solid understanding of essay structure and an effective flow of ideas, from introduction to conclusion.

4) Language Use and Conventions

This grading area measures your ability to effectively utilize English-language writing principles such as spelling, vocabulary, grammar, syntax, and language mechanics. A high-scoring essay will be a clear, polished, and effective piece of writing that demonstrates a solid understanding of language use and conventions.

If you need a refresher on grammar, language mechanics, and sentence structure, you're in luck! Part III of this book offers comprehensive coverage of how to recognize proper usage, mechanics, and rhetoric for the ACT English test; applying the rules and tips to your writing will help you create a strong ACT essay! We strongly suggest you review chapters 4 and 5 if you need a confidence boost with language use and conventions.

The two readers who will be scoring your essay will provide a score from 1–6 in each of these four domains. Your total domain score for each of the four areas will be the sum of the two scores and will range from 2–12. (If the scores of the two readers in any domain area differ by more than one point, a third reader will be used to resolve the discrepancy.)

Your domain scores will reflect the essay readers' impressions of your abilities as follows:

Score 6: Your essay demonstrates a highly effective skill level in this domain area.
Score 5: Your essay demonstrates a well-developed skill level in this domain area.
Score 4: Your essay demonstrates an adequate skill level in this domain area.
Score 3: Your essay demonstrates some developing ability in this domain area.
Score 2: Your essay demonstrates a weak or inconsistent skill level in this domain area.
Score 1: Your essay demonstrates a deficient skill level in this domain area.

The test readers will calculate your individual domain scores based on the following ACT scoring rubric:

Score Level	Ideas and Analysis	Development and Support	Organization	Language Use and Conventions
Score 6	Essay demonstrates: • Effective critical engagement with perspectives • Nuance and purpose-driven precision • Excellent depth and contextual insight on the topic • Thoughtful analysis of the prompt issue(s) and implications of the writer's perspective	Essay demonstrates: • A deep and insightful level of effective idea development to promote understanding • Skilled reasoning and use of relevant and varied support to strengthen a perspective	Essay demonstrates: • A skilled ability to capably organize ideas into a cogent piece of writing • An effective and insightful central narrative theme that unifies the text • A thorough understanding of standard essay structure and flow, including effective transitions between sentences and thoughts	Essay demonstrates: • Skillful deployment of standard English language principles • Excellent use of varied and engaging vocabulary and sentence structures • A clear, authoritative, and effective voice and tone • Few or no errors in grammar, mechanics, and syntax
Score 5	Essay demonstrates: • Productive critical engagement with perspectives • Purpose-driven precision • Depth and contextual insight on the topic • Commendable analysis of the prompt issue(s) and acknowledgment of the implications of the writer's perspective	Essay demonstrates: • A commendable level of idea development to deepen understanding • Solid reasoning and use of relevant and varied support to strengthen a perspective	Essay demonstrates: • A solid ability to capably organize ideas into a cogent piece of writing • A solid central narrative theme that unifies the text • A commendable understanding of standard essay structure and flow, including effective transitions between sentences and thoughts	Essay demonstrates: • Commendable deployment of standard English language principles • Strong use of varied and engaging vocabulary and sentence structures • A capable and effective voice and tone • Few or no errors in grammar, mechanics, and syntax

Chapter 14

Mastering the ACT® Writing Test

Score Level	Ideas and Analysis	Development and Support	Organization	Language Use and Conventions
Score 4	**Essay demonstrates:** • Critical engagement with perspectives • Noticeable clarity and purpose • Insight on the topic • Analysis of the issue(s) in the essay prompt	**Essay demonstrates:** • A good level of idea development that provides clarity • Good reasoning and use of relevant and varied support to strengthen a perspective	**Essay demonstrates:** • An ability to organize ideas into a coherent piece of writing • A central narrative theme that demonstrates a real effort to unify the text • A good understanding of standard essay structure and flow, including evidence of clear transitions between sentences and thoughts	**Essay demonstrates:** • A good use of standard English language principles • Use of varied and engaging vocabulary and sentence structures • A good attempt to establish voice and tone • Some errors in grammar, mechanics, and syntax, which may occasionally impede meaning
Score 3	**Essay demonstrates:** • A limited engagement with perspectives • Noticeable clarity and purpose • Some discernible insight on the topic • Some analysis of the issue(s) in the essay prompt	**Essay demonstrates:** • Some general but simplistic idea development • Some evidence of reasoning in an attempt to clarify the argument	**Essay demonstrates:** • An attempt to organize ideas into a piece of writing with a basic structure • A grouping of ideas in some logical order • An attempt to provide a structure and flow between sentences and thoughts that the reader can follow	**Essay demonstrates:** • Attempt to deploy standard English language principles, with occasional errors • Attempt to display some varied range of vocabulary and sentence structures, though errors are present • A discernible voice and tone, though largely hard to discern • Noticeable errors in grammar, mechanics, and syntax that impede meaning

Score Level	Ideas and Analysis	Development and Support	Organization	Language Use and Conventions
Score 2	**Essay demonstrates:** • A weak engagement with perspectives • Limited clarity and purpose • Deficient insight on the topic • Poor analysis of the issue(s) in the essay prompt	**Essay demonstrates:** • Weak or deficient idea development • An effort to offer reasoning in an attempt to clarify the argument, though largely ineffective or off target	**Essay demonstrates:** • A weak organization of ideas and deficient structure • Ideas are weakly ordered, adversely affecting comprehensibility • A largely ineffective attempt at providing sound structure and flow between sentences and thoughts	**Essay demonstrates:** • A deficient attempt to deploy standard English language principles, with several noticeable errors • A weak or deficient vocabulary range and basic, often flawed, sentence structures • A weak, ineffective voice and tone, largely hard to discern • Several obvious errors in grammar, mechanics, and syntax that strongly impede meaning
Score 1	**Essay demonstrates:** • No engagement with perspectives • Lack of clarity and purpose • No insight on the topic • Lack of analysis of the issue(s) in the essay prompt	**Essay demonstrates:** • An absence of appropriate idea development • No appropriate or discernible effort to offer reasoning in an attempt to clarify the argument	**Essay demonstrates:** • No organization of ideas and a lack of basic structure • A lack of thoughtful order of ideas, severely affecting comprehensibility • An absent attempt at providing sound structure and flow between sentences and thoughts	**Essay demonstrates:** • No attempt to deploy standard English language principles, with serious errors • A very basic and often erroneous use of vocabulary, and many serious errors in sentence structure • A largely absent or indistinct voice and tone • Serious and widespread errors in grammar, mechanics, and syntax that profoundly impact meaning and comprehension

Your overall subject-level writing score is determined from your domain scores and will be reported on a scale of 1–36. You'll also receive a scaled English Language Arts (ELA) score ranging from 1–36. If you decide to take the ACT Writing test, your score reports will be released approximately 5 to 8 weeks after your test date. The colleges to which you decide to release your ACT score report will also be able to view your complete ACT Writing test essay.

Now that you know what to expect on test day, you're ready to take a closer look at what the ACT Writing test essay will look like, so you can take your preparation to the next level.

At some point, after making it through the ACT registration and preparation processes, and completing the required four ACT tests, you'll find yourself sitting at a desk with a pencil and paper, poised to write an essay that will hopefully dazzle the test readers and earn you a great score that will impress your target colleges. The best way to make this happen is by looking at what an actual ACT essay prompt might look like, as well as sample essays at each scoring level—so you'll have a better idea of what the essay readers might be looking for on test day. Let's get started!

THE ESSAY PROMPT

On test day, you'll be given a prompt from which you'll craft a thoughtfully constructed, well-written, and compelling essay that will reflect your perspective on the issue(s) provided. The essay prompt can be based on a myriad of topics, so the best way to prepare is to be prepared for anything.

It's a good idea to read the essay prompt *at least* twice.

- Your first read-through should focus solely on the information provided. Make sure you know exactly what the issue being presented is and what questions and ideas you are being asked to address in your essay response. Don't rush into furiously writing your essay without first knowing what it should cover!
- Your second read-through should confirm that you are clear on the essay task at hand and should also be an opportunity to start preliminary brainstorming ideas that you plan to include in your essay.

Don't race off into writing your own essay after your second read-through just yet. A major component of your essay will be to take into account the three perspectives provided alongside the essay prompt and task.

Here's a sample essay prompt, in the format you'll encounter on test day:

The Focus of Education: STEM vs. STEAM

In recent years, there has been a concerted effort by some educational policy makers to reposition the focus of academic curricula to a STEM model, an acronym that stands for science, technology, engineering, and math. Proponents believe that these four core academic areas reflect the primary knowledge bases that individuals will most need to be successful and vital in the twenty-first century, and that less resources should be allocated to the arts, history, and physical education, as their importance will decrease in our technology-focused world.

Critics of this approach contend that a STEAM model (science, technology, engineering, arts, and math) is a better, more comprehensive model, one that reflects the value and contributions that the arts make—both at an individual level and at every level of society including education, culture, and shaping the future.

Given the limited resources available and America's desire to reassert its commitment to education so that its citizens are prepared to tackle the challenges of the twenty-first century and succeed on a global scale, it is worth examining the debate regarding educational models, as well as exploring additional ideas for shaping policy in this area.

Make sure you carefully read, analyze, and consider the entire essay prompt. Notice that the prompt includes conflicting viewpoints, designed to help stimulate your thinking on the issue provided. You'll likely find a format similar to this in your test day prompt. This prompt serves as the foundation for the perspectives you will encounter next, and it should get you thinking about your own opinion on the topic.

After reading the prompt, you shouldn't go into full essay planning mode just yet, but feel free to start taking a few notes at this point if something important crosses your mind that would fit well into your essay.

ACT Writing Test: The Best Way to Prepare? Stay Aware!

It's important to stay aware of what's going on in the world and in the news—it's your best chance at preparing yourself to tackle any essay prompt on test day. Make it a habit to stay aware of the issues and current events that people are talking about—online, in magazines and newspapers, on TV, and in debates and conversations that are taking place around you. Get involved in these conversations as often as possible. Getting comfortable arguing your perspective on a range of issues is valuable practice. One of these issues just might be the foundation for your essay prompt when you take the ACT.

Now you're ready to move on to the three perspective snapshots provided.

THE ESSAY PERSPECTIVES

As we've discussed, you'll be given three varying perspectives on the issue provided in the essay prompt. You'll be asked to carefully consider each of these three perspectives as you begin to plan—and eventually construct—your essay.

As you read the three perspectives, think about how they fit or contrast with *your* thoughts on the issue. As with your second read-through of the essay prompt, use the ideas provided to help you begin to structure and refine your own perspective.

This is a great opportunity to do some additional brainstorming. Feel free to take notes—whether on paper or in your head—in whatever way has worked for you in your previous writing experiences. These notes will help you outline the core structure of your essay when you move fully into the planning phase.

The following are three perspectives on "The Focus of Education: STEM vs. STEAM":

Read and carefully consider these perspectives. Each suggests a particular way of thinking about the notion of instituting a STEM- or STEAM-based curriculum model.

PERSPECTIVE ONE

Schools nationwide, and at every grade level, should strictly follow a STEM curriculum model. The direction that the twenty-first century is taking has become quite clear in its early decades—the primacy of science and technology in every facet of society is apparent—and education programs should be able to shift and pivot to accurately reflect society. However, educational institutions are forced to deal with severe limitations in money, time, and resources. Making sure that the limited resources that are available are used in the wisest and most beneficial areas, those that will most benefit students as they become the workers and innovators of the future—locally, nationally, and globally—is the best way to position the United States for future success.

A collective failure to acknowledge the importance of the arts in education is both tragic and dangerous—for future generations and society at large. Providing students with a deep and comprehensive education in science, technology, engineering, and mathematics is important to prepare them for success beyond the classroom, but there is clearly both room and importance for tempering this model with an education in the liberal arts. It isn't wise to assume that there won't be a need or place for the arts in the future, and demonstrating or advocating a collective "devaluing" of the arts, or history, or music doesn't bode well for society. In order to create a future that allows individuals to fully flourish, express themselves, and grow and live in a world where there's room for wonderful innovations in technology and the arts, a STEAM model is the wisest approach.

Mandating a rigid educational model for every student, at every level, is confining at best—and potentially stifling. A "one size fits all" approach to life is rarely beneficial to the individuals who make up the "all," and this is true in education as well. While it's true that there are benefits to both STEM and STEAM models, a truly progressive society that's eager to refocus education for the future should allow students to individually tailor their academic experiences to match their unique interests and goals. In recent years, there has been a growing concern over the general lack of focus and attention students give to school; perhaps if they had a greater opportunity to create learning programs that engage them, they'd be more inclined to give school the attention it deserves—and all facets of society will benefit as a result.

Read these perspectives carefully, and think about how each point of view might complement—or not complement—your own perspective on the issue of utilizing a STEM vs. STEAM education model.

Read each perspective *critically*, analyzing how each tackles the issues provided in the essay prompt. As you move forward, continue thinking about the issues, brainstorming ideas, and formulating your essay's plan of attack.

Before you start actually drafting your essay, *make sure* you review the essay task provided. You want to be 100 percent positive you are planning to take a stance on the exact issue(s) raised by the prompt. Don't waste your time and energy creating an essay that does not address what the test wants you to address!

Remember—a great piece of writing that fails to fully address the essay prompt and task will not earn you great scores on test day.

THE ESSAY TASK

Now that you've fully digested the essay prompt and carefully considered each of the three perspectives provided and how they fit with your specific perspective, you'll be given a specific essay task. Be sure to read this *carefully*—the test readers will be checking to make sure your essay capably addresses the task provided, and it will factor into your final scores.

492

Chapter 14

Mastering
the ACT®
Writing Test

www.petersons.com

Read the following essay task for "The Focus of Education: STEM vs. STEAM":

Write a cohesive, logical essay in which you consider multiple perspectives on the STEM vs. STEAM education model. In your essay, be sure to:

- examine and assess the perspectives given
- declare and explain your own perspective on the issue
- discuss the relationship between your perspective and those given

Your perspective may be in full or partial agreement, or in total disagreement, with any of the others. Whatever the case, support your ideas with logical reasoning and detailed, persuasive examples.

NOTE: The wording on the actual ACT task is slightly different, but the task remains the same: form an opinion about the given topic, read and evaluate the perspectives, and present your opinion while relating the perspectives to your own.

Okay—you've read the essay prompt, considered your take on the issue alongside the three perspectives provided, and you're fully aware of the essay task at hand. The next step is to move forward and structure your essay!

PLANNING YOUR ESSAY

The first thing to acknowledge about essay planning is that there's no single, proven method that works for everyone. Just as everyone has a different way and style of writing, everyone has a unique way to prepare. At this point in your academic career, you've written lots of essays—perhaps some more successful than others. Do you like to write an outline or plan in your head? How do you like to brainstorm ideas?

Although your essay will be unique and reflect your distinct perspective on the issue provided in the prompt, an effective piece of argumentative writing should follow a basic structure.

INTRODUCTION

Use your essay opening to introduce your thoughts on the topic and explain why you think it's an important issue worth exploration. Also be sure to begin to discuss—or fully assert—the central idea or thesis of your essay. This should directly address the topic in the prompt and make your perspective on the issue quite clear for readers.

BODY

The body paragraphs of your essay should bolster the claims made in your central thesis, through thoughtful analysis, effective idea development, and strong support. Make sure your essay considers all three perspectives provided alongside the essay prompt. A high-scoring essay will be an in-depth, complex piece of writing that covers all possible viewpoints (including opposing ones!) while strengthening your central thesis.

CONCLUSION

Here's where you'll wrap up your essay, tying up all of the ideas you've provided in your essay while reasserting your position. Relevant, insightful ideas for further exploration and consideration can also be included here. It's always a good idea to end your work on a powerful concluding note—always remember, a great closing will leave a positive and lasting impression on your readers.

TAKING NOTES

One suggestion we like is to make a quick list of ideas you want to include in each structural element of your essay: introduction, body paragraphs, and conclusion. Your ideas can include any questions you'd like to ask yourself (and eventually answer!) while you write. When you read the prompt, perspectives, and task, what major questions arose in your mind? Jotting these down will eventually help you analyze all sides of the essay prompt in greater depth and will lead to a more comprehensive written response.

Don't waste time making these into grammatically perfect, well-constructed sentences—this should simply be a rough collection of thoughts that you'll soon develop into the polished, carefully organized, and compelling sentences that will make up your essay.

Let's take a look at a sample brainstorming list for this essay task:

Introduction Ideas

- STEAM is a better educational model
- Discuss power of education, to highlight issue importance (give quote?)
- Why so important at this moment in history?
- Discuss local, national, global implications, for present and future

Body Paragraph Ideas

- Why is STEAM a better model than STEM?
- Advantages of liberal arts education
  - More well-rounded students
  - Culture and arts to feed our souls and enhance society
  - Provide richness and meaning to life
- Acknowledge importance of STEM learning for future innovation, etc.
- Discuss "real" educational problem—lack of sufficient money and resources
  - How should this be addressed?
  - How should policy change or should it stay the same?

Conclusion Ideas

- Advantages/disadvantages/realistic limitations regarding education/focus
- Supplement school learning with home learning—"H" in STEAM?
- Reiterate importance of this issue, for current and future generations

As you can see, by using this method, your essay is already starting to take shape! Don't be surprised if the act of writing your ideas down in a list helps to stimulate new ideas as you move forward.

494

Chapter 14

Mastering
the ACT®
Writing Test

Feel free to refer back to your brainstorming list as you write your essay. It will help keep you on track and can act as a checklist to make sure you include all of your ideas and thoughts in your final work.

Take *no more than 10 minutes* to plan your essay before you start writing your first draft. Again, this is where practice before test day comes in handy! Use the practice essay at the end of this chapter to see if the 10 minutes of preplanning/30 minutes of writing and editing approach works for you, and don't be afraid to tweak it if necessary!

TIP

The best strategy for essay planning—and writing—is to use the strategies that have worked well for you in the past. If you're one of those lucky people who can jot down a plan in 3 minutes and head straight into writing, go for it. The main takeaway from this chapter: find the method that works for *you*, practice it, and stick with it.

After you've taken about 10 minutes to develop a solid plan or outline for your essay, take a deep breath and pick up your pencil, because you're ready to start writing your first draft!

WRITING YOUR ESSAY

When you're ready, find a quiet place to work, get a pencil and some paper, set a timer for 40 minutes, and get started.

Take the first 10 minutes to think about the issue and the information provided, and use the worksheet on the next page to brainstorm ideas that will help you construct your final work.

ACT Writing Test: Use Your Time Wisely

Use this guide to make the most of your time on test day:

Total test time: 40 minutes
Brainstorming: 10 minutes
Essay writing: 20–25 minutes
Editing and revising: 5–10 minutes

Brainstorming Ideas for:
"The Focus of Education: STEM vs. STEAM"

Introduction

_____
_____
_____
_____
_____

Body Paragraphs

_____
_____
_____
_____
_____
_____
_____
_____

Conclusion

_____
_____
_____
_____

Okay, you've used your first 10 minutes to brainstorm and construct a solid list of ideas, thoughts, and questions, which will help form the core of your essay—consider this time well spent!

Now it's time to begin crafting your essay on "The Focus of Education: STEM vs. STEAM." Remember that although your essay will be unique and reflect your distinct perspective on the issue provided in the prompt, an effective piece of argumentative writing should follow a basic structure of an introduction, then supporting body paragraphs, and finally a conclusion.

Once again, make sure your essay thoroughly addresses the prompt and task and includes the core structural elements mentioned above. Use the time you have left, which should be around 30 minutes, to write your essay.

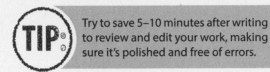 Try to save 5–10 minutes after writing to review and edit your work, making sure it's polished and free of errors.

After you've written and edited your essay and your total 40 minutes are up, take some time to review the following sample essays—there's one at each score level. Use them to help you figure out at what level you're writing and what you need to do between now and test day to prepare for success.

You'll also find sample scoring explanations for each of the four tested writing domains for the highest and lowest scoring essays. Use these to determine the level of your writing and the areas of strength and weakness and to help you structure your preparation plan between now and test day.

497

Chapter 14

**Mastering
the ACT®
Writing Test**

SAMPLE ACT ESSAYS

SAMPLE ESSAY—SCORE 1

Ideas and Analysis:	Score = 1
Development and Support:	Score = 1
Organization:	Score = 1
Language Use and Conventions:	Score = 1

> *Each person shuld be able to decide if go to school why should someone else tell people what to do with their time or even what they should be studied about. Some people like some classes what does bother most people is when they have to get up too late so this way they can sleep later and go to classes when they wake up? Some classes too long and students cant think about what teacher is talking about or saying, so can some of the classes be shorter even please.*
>
> *School is expensive and people should pay what they can to make it happen if they get into colleges they aplly to. Students should spend more time on computers and learning on technologee like phones cause thats how people learn and communicate these days so schools should know that and teachers should know that too. Why shuld someone else tell students what to study and which classes they should even care about. Let everybody tell everyone which classes they want to go to and then they should get the chance to go and learn more.*

SCORING EXPLANATION

Ideas and Analysis: Score = 1

This essay attempt fails to provide a discernible level of insight or analysis into the issue of utilizing a STEM vs. STEAM education model. The essay quickly falls off target and fails to establish a relevant perspective or appropriate unifying theme that addresses the prompt; as a result, we have no idea what the writer's thoughts on this issue are. The purpose and intent of the writer's essay is tangential at best ("Students should spend more time on computers and learning on technologee like phones"), and it reflects a poor level of analysis of the topic.

Development and Support: Score = 1

This essay response demonstrates a serious lack of idea development, and a complete lack of relevant support to bolster the writer's perspective on the merits of STEM vs. STEAM. Rather, it seems as if the writer failed to fully digest the essay topic and task, and instead simply provided a brief and scattered response that loosely discusses his or her college plans ("Each person should be able to decide if go to school why should someone else tell people what to do with their time or even what they should be studied about"); the end result is an unsuccessful essay that completely misses the mark.

Organization: Score = 1

This essay is a rough, disjointed piece of writing that greatly suffers from a serious lack of cohesive organization and structure. Rather than provide a relevant, engaging, and thoughtful perspective that effectively addresses the prompt and task, the essay offers an incoherent series of jumbled ideas on taking college classes ("Let everybody tell everyone which classes they want to go to") and how class decisions should be made ("Some classes too long and students cant think about what teacher is talking about or saying, so can some of the classes be shorter even please"). The essay is hard to follow, and the writer's intent is confusing and murky at best.

503

Chapter 14

Mastering the ACT® Writing Test

Language Use and Conventions: Score = 1

There are serious errors in language use and conventions throughout this essay, which seriously impact its overall effectiveness. Errors in word choice and vocabulary ("aplly," "technologee"), grammar (run-ons, punctuation), and usage ("or even what they should be studied about") demonstrate both a profound weakness in writing skills and a failure to appropriately review and edit the finished work.

SAMPLE ESSAY— SCORE 2

Ideas and Analysis:	Score = 2
Development and Support:	Score = 2
Organization:	Score = 2
Language Use and Conventions:	Score = 2

Technology is important and that what students learn in the classroom should show that they think its good. Students should give time learning about science and math and these things for the future, so they can be ready when they graduate and get good jobs. This is important for them and everyone.

Art and English and history, and classes like that are important, and that students that are interested in things like this should be able to learning more about them. Studnets that aren't interested can use more time learning about computers and science and hopefully they can be the ones who make all the great new inventions in the future when they finish with school.

Students would like to go to a school where the students did get to decide what classes they take. Its important that students know something about all kinds of different subjects but they should be able to spend most of their time in class lerning about the things that they want to focus on when they get jobs after school. Getting students ready to get good jobs is important.

SAMPLE ESSAY—SCORE 3

Ideas and Analysis:	Score = 3
Development and Support:	Score = 3
Organization:	Score = 3
Language Use and Conventions:	Score = 3

It's clear that technology is the wave of the future. Every day the news reports about some great new invention that's designed to help make lives a little easier, to improve and advance our society. All of these great thinkers, and inventors, and innovators have who help shape our world one thing in common. They all sat in classrooms during their early years, where their brains were stimulated and challenged with new conceps.

Who knows how many great ideas started behind desks while listen to teachers speak? Schools are definitely important, and what happens in classrooms can help build young minds and shape the future. Therefore, what type of model that schools follow couldn't be more importent.

Since technology is so important to our future, the classes that students should have to take should be science and technology based. The classes mentioned in the essay instructions, science, technology, engineering, and math should be the class model that schools use. If students learn a lot about these subjects they will be ready to get really great jobs and help our society advance and improve. They will be the ones who make computers and cell phones better and invent new things for example, and medecines and make all of lives better.

In conclusion, everyone can see how important these subjects are to the world, and to keep the world moving forward, so the time that students spend in classrooms, and learning, should be spent in these areas. There's no better way to ensure that society has the best futures possible than by giving students the education and knowledge they need to be succesful.

Sample Essay—Score 4

Ideas and Analysis:	Score = 4
Development and Support:	Score = 4
Organization:	Score = 4
Language Use and Conventions:	Score = 4

There's no better way to ensure our nation's prosperity than to make sure that those who will be responsible for carrying society into the future—the young learners who now sit in classrooms but who will soon inherit the future—are well-equipped to do so. They'll require the knowledge and skills to lead and innovate, to make sure that the country continues to remain at the forefront of advancement and achievement.

The crucial first steps, and perhaps the most important steps, will occur in our nation's classrooms. The guidance, direction, support, and mental fuel that students receive in school will directly contribute to America's ongoing success. Therefore, this question, about what curriculum model the nation should follow, couldn't be more important. A STEM model would best allow the United States to use and focus its resources to educate its students for ongoing success on a global scale.

Making the firm and clear decision to focus educational resources on the classes and programs that really matter for the future, which includes science, technology, engineering, and mathematics, is a bold but necessary step. These are the fields in which great societal advancements will likely be made—in science, and computer technology, and medicine, among others—and instilling an interest and yearning to learn and explore these fields in the nation's fertile young minds is critical.

There will likely be some people who feel that the STEAM model offers some advantages, that students will be better off learning about the arts as well as the other science and technology classes. It's ok to learn about these subjects, but people can learn about them outside of the classroom and on their own time. Students spend too much time these days doing unimportant things. They can learn STEM classes in the classroom and after school they can explore the arts and other things they're interested in.

There have been quite a lot of disturbing stories in the news about the poor state that our country's educational system is currently in. If the United States is going to be serious about using its resources wisely, and wants to fix the problems that plague education today, then policymakers will have to rethink and refocus the model schools use to teach students, which should reflect the subjects that are most important. The STEM model is America's best shot at ensuring that students lead society bravely and boldly through this century and beyond.

505

Chapter 14

Mastering
the ACT®
Writing Test

Sample Essay—Score 5

Ideas and Analysis:	Score = 5
Development and Support:	Score = 5
Organization:	Score = 5
Language Use and Conventions:	Score = 5

The United States is at a pivotal moment in its development. Throughout the rapid industrialization that characterized twentieth century global expansion and progression, the America was positioned at the vanguard of innovation and the bold exploration of new ideas. However, significant segments of the developed world—including the United States—have entered into the "technological era" that has characterized the dawning and early years of the twenty-first century thus far. And it's no longer clear that America stands at the forefront of this exciting time, or that its doing everything it can to best position itself to lead and inspire the world through the technological era, and what lies ahead. However, there is a way forward.

Any great structure is only as good as its foundation, and the cornerstone of America's foundation is a living thing that's capable of change—it's the boundless minds and imaginations of the people, and they're inspired to grow, create, and soar when properly nurtured behind the desks of its classrooms.

The resources available for education in America are certainly abundant compared to many other nations, but they aren't limitless. Therefore, policymakers need to allocate precious and finite funds in the most beneficial areas. Utilizing a STEM-focused educational model represents the collective best interests of the nation. Beyond a wise allocation of limited resources, it will hopefully send a clear and inspiring signal to hungry and eager student minds—and to the entire world—that the United States recognizes the role that science, technology, engineering, and math will play in building a better tomorrow and brighter future, and that it has made a serious commitment and investment towards making sure that today's students become tomorrow's skilled and trained leaders.

Beyond financial resources, the attention and focus of today's students are more atomized than ever before, and harder than ever to grab a hold of. With endless pervasive media outlets and technological gadgets vying for student's attention, educational policymakers need to acknowledge that opportunities to effectively engage with students are limited, and that the most important classes, which fall under the STEM umbrella, should take clear and established primacy.

The consequences of adopting a STEM-centric educational model would be that certain liberal arts classes would receive less, or little, attention. However, it's foolhardy to eradicate them completely, or to fear that individuals would lose their interest in the arts if they weren't taught as extensively—or at all—in the classroom. Students at all grade levels should have opportunities to supplement a core STEM education with elective coursework in classes they're interested in. These electives don't have to be liberal arts based, but the option should exist. Beyond the classroom, interest in the liberal arts can flourish in other ways—through extracurricular activities, on weekends and at home after class, and alongside friends and family.

It isn't too late—in fact it never will be—to change our present in the service of our future. All it will ever take is for enough people to recognize a need for change and the will to follow through until it happens. This includes the focus and direction of the nation's educational system. Making a change this large wouldn't be easy. Change is rarely easy, but some things in life are worth the effort.

Sample Essay—Score 6

Ideas and Analysis:	Score = 6
Development and Support:	Score = 6
Organization:	Score = 6
Language Use and Conventions:	Score = 6

Nelson Mandela once said, "Education is the most powerful weapon which you can use to change the world." Throughout history, the progressive march of nations worldwide has been fueled by improved access to education, and continued refinement to educational models and processes, which makes instinctual sense; as a nation evolves, so should its method and model for educating it's people. The 21st century, thus far a heady mix of rapid technological and social progression, has left the United States at a true inflection point. The entrenched educational models utilized to stimulate and expand the minds of future leaders and innovators feel outdated, and out of step with the pace of our current technological era. To make a complicated issue even more challenging, resources for system-wide educational overhaul remain woefully limited. Regardless, great nations become great in times of adversity, when challenges are met and overcome, with real forward progress as lasting proof of wise decisions having been made precisely when decisions were needed.

The best education has no walls beyond those in the classroom. The hungry minds of America should be nourished with the full range of "fruits" that this great nation has to offer. In this regard, a STEAM-based model offers the best of both worlds: a solid education in science, technology, engineering, and math—the fields that will continue to drive progress and innovation through this century and beyond; and the arts—the fields that allow citizens to learn from a society's collective and individual experiences and histories, celebrate life and distinct, varied cultures, and feed souls through creative expression in art, writing, music, film, and more. If a STEM education allows individuals to build their houses, the "A" in STEAM allows people to make them homes, to bring richness and meaning to living. Who could argue that a model that's missing any of these is a step forward?

The true issue at the heart of America's "educational problem" is the fact that a choice has to be made in the first place. A truly progressive nation should place a higher value on education, and find a way to provide the resources needed to ensure that it doesn't have to choose one or the other. Educational policy should be among a nation's highest priorities. Furthermore, funds given to education should not be looked at as an expense but rather as an investment in the future.

Until this happens, educational policymakers need to make the most of available, albeit limited, resources. This means that hard choices need to be made; a focus on STEM-centric model with time allocated for core liberal arts curricula—in history, English, and elective programs that engage students by letting them pursue the areas they're most interested in—is a wise approach given the circumstances.

However, an additional letter should be added to the acronym—an "H" for home. Educational administrators and policymakers need to do a better job of spreading the message that learning doesn't just happen in the classroom. Teachers need to work with families and parents to spread the message that learning at school can, and should, be supplemented by learning at home. This way, no subject gets shortchanged. In sum, if part of our educational focus is to spread the message that learning is an ongoing, lifelong process that occurs in all of the rooms that we find ourselves in throughout our lives, not just the classroom, we'll all be better off—and the pace of progress in all areas of life will be more of a confident march than a tentative stroll.

507

Chapter 14

Mastering the ACT® Writing Test

SCORING EXPLANATION

Ideas and Analysis: Score = 6

This essay offers an engaging, nuanced, and thoughtful analysis of the issue of STEM vs. STEAM and takes it a step further—the writer expands on the issue and provides ideas on what he or she perceives to be core problems regarding the direction and focus of education today ("A truly progressive nation should place a higher value on education, and find a way to provide the resources needed to ensure that it doesn't have to choose one or the other"); the idea to add a greater focus on learning outside of the classroom was a particularly insightful addition. The overall result is an in-depth, multifaceted, and carefully considered argument.

Development and Support: Score = 6

The writer of this essay provides an exceptional level of development and support to bolster his or her argument—from the opening quote from Nelson Mandela regarding the transformative power of education to the stirring salvo at the conclusion highlighting the role learning plays in dictating the pace of global progress. The writer establishes his preference for an all-inclusive educational model and develops a stirring case for why it's a wise choice. The overall level of sophistication and depth in the writing greatly supports the writer's perspective and leads to a persuasive argument.

Organization: Score = 6

It's clear the writer of this essay has a strong command of the basic principles of essay structure, and was able to effectively deploy them in service of his or her position on the essay prompt. A strong introduction, well-reasoned review of both sides of the prompt, additional insight on the core issues facing education, and holistic approach to idea generation results in a very successful essay.

Language Use and Conventions: Score = 6

An impressive display of vocabulary and varied word choice throughout the piece, use of engaging analogies (i.e., comparing STEM vs. STEAM to a house vs. a home), and sophisticated sentences and transitions clearly indicate a high level of writing proficiency. The writer was able to infuse a great deal of passion into his or her essay and to capture the reader's attention from beginning to end. The essay is largely free from errors, resulting in a highly polished and provocative piece.

At the end of the chapter, you'll also have the opportunity to practice writing another essay and review your work against some high- and low-scoring samples. Hopefully, as you continue to practice writing essays, you'll notice that your work is continually improving!

SUMMING IT UP

- **Understand the prompt material.** Read the instructions, the essay prompt, the perspectives, and the essay task *carefully*. Be sure you understand the issue and know *exactly* what you're being asked to write before you write it. Use the perspectives provided to help shape your work.

- **Use what you know.** The essay prompt that you'll encounter on test day can be based on a wide array of topics. Since you won't know your topic, the best way to prepare is to be ready to draw upon your wealth of experience to help you develop a well-rounded essay with sufficient real-world support—including your academic and life experiences. Stay aware of the issues and current events taking place around you.

- **Use your time wisely.** You'll have 40 minutes to plan and write your essay. Use this time efficiently. Practice planning and writing essays in the time provided—it'll help you find a comfortable writing pace and put you in great shape to impress the readers on test day.

- **Plan carefully.** When you feel the pressure and clock ticking on test day, your first instinct may be to pick up your pencil as quickly as possible and write furiously, to get as much down on the pages before the end of the test. Resist this urge. Instead, take a few minutes to analyze and think critically about the issue and the perspectives presented and plan your written response, creating an outline that will help you properly structure your essay. It will be time well spent.

- **Write purposefully.** Use the writing techniques and strategies that you've learned throughout your academic career as you craft your essay. Establish a clear perspective and focus for the reader and craft compelling, well-structured sentences that support your argument and address the essay prompt and perspectives provided, as well as the implications and potential consequences of your ideas.

- **Edit your work.** Do your best to leave a few minutes to review and edit your work after writing your essay. Think about the four writing domains that your essay will be judged on as you review your work:

    o Does your essay present a wealth of compelling ideas and nuanced analysis that responds to the prompt and fulfills the writing task?
    o Are the ideas in your essay fully developed, and do they contain sufficient support to bolster your perspective?
    o Is your essay well-structured and organized?
    o Do you effectively utilize English language principles and mechanics in your essay?
    o Polishing your first draft—checking for errors, proper word choice, grammar, sense, and sentence usage—is a great way to ensure that your final work is as good as it can possibly be.

- **Practice makes perfect.** Use the time you have between now and test day to practice writing essays on a variety of subjects. Choose a topic that's getting a lot of news attention or, better still, work with a writing partner who'll help you choose writing topics and who'll also review your work. Your partner may also be able to provide you with different perspectives to work with. If you can find a practice reader who's capable of reviewing your work along the four ACT test domains and providing you helpful critical feedback, that's even better!

509

Chapter 14

Mastering the ACT® Writing Test

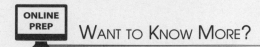

ONLINE PREP | WANT TO KNOW MORE?

Access more practice questions, lessons, helpful hints, and strategies for the following writing topics in *Peterson's ACT Online Course*:

- Introduction to Writing
- Essay Writing Method
- Organize and Develop Ideas
- Effective Style in Essays
- Avoid Common Errors
- Putting It All Together

To purchase and access the course, go to ***www.petersons.com/act***.

510

Chapter 14

**Mastering
the ACT®
Writing Test**

PRACTICE

As previously stated, there's no better way to build your writing skills than by practicing. Here's another sample essay prompt to help you get your writing into test-conquering shape. Use everything that you've learned in this chapter to help you craft a high-scoring essay that effectively responds to the following prompt. Be sure to review the model high-scoring and low-scoring essays that follow to gauge how well you did.

The Price of Higher Education: Cost *vs*. Value

The expense of obtaining a college education has steadily increased in recent decades—some would argue to an alarming degree—leading many politicians, legislators, and educational policy makers to wonder if the cost of higher education has reached a point where it's unclear if the potential benefits justify the daunting expense.

Some people strongly feel that the cost of a college degree is out of control, and real system-wide reform is urgently needed before an entire generation of students gets stuck with the financial burdens of overpriced educations and sizable loans to help finance their academic endeavors. Others feel that the value of a college degree justifies the price—including data that highlights the enhanced earning potential and greater professional fulfillment and options of college graduates vs. nongraduates.

Given the increased attention on the rising costs of obtaining a college degree, as well as questions regarding its relative value in a changing employment landscape, it is worth examining the debate regarding this issue, as well as how policy should be affected moving forward.

Read and carefully consider these perspectives. Each suggests a particular way of thinking about the cost of college and what should be done about it.

PERSPECTIVE ONE

The cost of college has certainly become too expensive, and it has finally reached the point where the potential benefits of obtaining a diploma need to be seriously weighed against the alarmingly bloated expense. There needs to be a serious overhaul of both the cost of college and the student loan industry, which is reaping tremendous profits from students and their families. Educational policymakers should seriously commit to exploring alternative measures. Schools should work toward finding ways to trim their expenses so they can operate effectively without having to charge enormous tuition sums. Improved financial aid packages should be implemented. If something isn't done regarding this issue, one thing is clear—generations of students will continue to buckle and fold under the crushing financial burden of a college education.

PERSPECTIVE TWO

It's true that school is expensive, but it's a realistic expense, considering both the costs of operating an institution of higher education and the return value of a college diploma. It's a wise investment in one's future—there's no denying that, on average, college graduates earn more money over their lifetimes and experience greater professional fulfillment, happiness, and success. There are financial aid tools in place that are designed to help students at all financial levels afford the cost of college, including scholarships, work-study programs, and student loans. Furthermore, there are a wide variety of schools, with widely varying tuitions, from community colleges to public and private universities. Every potential student's financial background is different, and there are schools and aid programs to help all qualified students cover the expenses.

It's tricky to make a general, blanket statement such as "college is too expensive"; the truth is, college is a big expense for *some*, but not so much for others who possess the financial means to handle the expense. It's also challenging to quantify the return on such an investment, so it's tough to determine whether or not it's a worthwhile investment over the long term. Instead of racing to the conclusion that the cost of higher education is objectively "out of control," a wiser use of time and resources would be to consider each student and his or her financial means individually, and make an effort to make school affordable for each of them. Perhaps implementing a realistic sliding scale cost program, so families can pay what they truly can afford, would be a worthwhile endeavor.

ESSAY TASK

Write a cohesive, logical essay in which you consider multiple perspectives on the cost of college. In your essay, be sure to:

- examine and assess the perspectives given
- declare and explain your own perspective on the issue
- discuss the relationship between your perspective and those given

Your perspective may be in full agreement with any of the others, in partial agreement, or wholly different. Whatever the case, support your ideas with logical reasoning and detailed, persuasive examples.

SAMPLE ESSAYS

SAMPLE ESSAY—SCORE 1

Ideas and Analysis:	Score = 1
Development and Support:	Score = 1
Organization:	Score = 1
Language Use and Conventions:	Score = 1

Yeah students should really hope to get a scolarship for college, even better if there good in most sports, they should get something for that and they can even agree to play for free and go to all of their classes. The best sport is football and good athletes in school hope that they can even play in college and maybe even professional NFL, that would be a dream to many students. Most people have their parents paying for college and plan on going somewhere warm and nice to school if they can, like California or somehwre like that. Parents whant there kids to go to college closer to home sometimes but students in high school want to be adults already! and live like there in charge of themself even if they have to get help to pay for college. There kids can even pay them back if they want to. Everyone should want to go to college and get great jobs and do what they always wanted to do as a job and make money for them and their family. If someone else needs help paying for college they can just ask family or someone they know for help or even ask the school to help them out with money or whatever they need. Theres always someone to help you out if you need it and ask nice.

Sample Essay—Score 6

Ideas and Analysis:	Score = 6
Development and Support:	Score = 6
Organization:	Score = 6
Language Use and Conventions:	Score = 6

Earning a college degree is an undeniably important and admirable achievement, but should it come at the expense of a student's future financial well being? In a word, no. Should an industrious, high achieving student, who worked hard in every grade—from kindergarten through high school—and gets accepted into the college of her dreams, but who doesn't have the means to pay for it, be forced to bear the catastrophic weight of a gigantic tuition bill in order to bring her academic dreams to fruition? Parents tell their children to work hard in school, to study hard, and to earn good grades in order to achieve their goals. But if they follow those lessons and get into the college of their dreams, but don't come from a family that can easily afford the cost, has their hard work and achievement just earned them a big, expensive problem?

Available statistical data regarding the average cost of a college education is both clear and startling—tuition, fees, and expenses have been skyrocketing for decades, and the number of families that can comfortably afford to send their children to college gets smaller every day. It's simply too much of a financial weight to bear, particularly when set alongside the dwindling promise of gainful, stable employment upon graduation. If the nation's goals include thriving generations of newly minted college graduates who can afford a level of social mobility, educational administrators and key policymakers need to implement sound policy that will help make the cost of getting an education manageable.

Perhaps this would entail reducing the budgets of other federal programs and reallocating funds to help subsidize educational costs. Perhaps it means a reinvention of the student loan industry, so students aren't saddled with large interest payments on top of their loan amounts. Perhaps colleges and universities nationwide need to explore ways to operate more efficiently on lower budgets, and pass on the savings to students. An expansion of federal work-study programs nationwide would help students shoulder the expense of school and gain valuable work experience in the process; this could include a government deployment of corporate incentives for businesses and industries that participate. These are just some of the areas that could be looked at in an effort to make college more affordable.

Clearly, serious change and drastic reform in this area will not be easy; there's no quick way to instantaneously overhaul the financial architecture of the higher education system in order to make it more affordable to students. But just because it might be difficult doesn't mean it isn't a worthwhile endeavor.

The arguments on the other side of this debate are clear. Yes, there are already tools in place for helping to pay for college, including scholarships, grants, and paid employment opportunities. But often this is not nearly enough and not available for every student. Some individuals argue that there are schools to match every budget, including 2-year and 4-year schools, and public and private universities. But this is a competitive society, one in which where people go to college can seriously affect their opportunities after they graduate. Shouldn't the best students who have achieved the best grades have opportunities to go to the best colleges and not get crushed—or worse deterred altogether—by the costs?

The ripple effects of system-wide reform can be deep and profound. Bright individuals with real potential who previously would've avoided applying to college for fear that they couldn't afford it will have new opportunities to achieve their goals. Students who previously would have graduated with the suffocating weight of student loans on their backs will now have opportunities to thrive and plan for securing their financial futures. They'll have more money to invest and support businesses and industries rather than feed the student loan beast. In sum, all will benefit from reform.

Its clear that this problem will not be solved overnight. However, at the very least, it's a troubling issue worth seriously exploring to keep the American dream of a college education from becoming a nightmare.

PART VIII: PRACTICE TESTS FOR THE ACT®

Chapter 15: ACT® Practice Tests

Chapter 16: Scoring Your ACT® Practice Tests

PRACTICE TESTS FOR THE ACT®

No matter where you are in your preparation process, taking a full-length practice exam is the best way to test your skills, assess your strengths and weaknesses, and determine where you should focus your study plan in the time leading up to test day. The first of the final two chapters of this guide, Chapter 15, contains four full-length practice exams that mirror the ones you will see when you take the actual ACT test. The last chapter, Chapter 16, contains the information you need to score your exams to give you a good idea of the results you would get on the official score report.

Chapter 15:
ACT® Practice Tests

OVERVIEW

- Practice Test 1
- Practice Test 2
- Practice Test 3
- Practice Test 4

It's practice test time—time to see how much you've learned and how close you are to being ready to take the ACT. Before you start taking your practice tests, consider the following reminders and suggestions.

When you take each exam, do your best to simulate the most test-like conditions possible. Be sure to get your answer sheets ready—you can either cut them out of the book or photocopy them. Set aside a 3-hour and 30-minute chunk of time, and find a quiet spot free from distractions. Yes, it's hard to find hours of free time to devote to taking a practice exam, but the end result is worth it—by the time you sit down to take the real ACT test, you will be used to the exact format, length, and process.

Test Day Preparation: Simulate the Silence

Even if you feel you work best with noise in the background, you won't have that option on test day. It's best to work under the same conditions you will have when taking your actual exam. Don't have a television on in the background or music blaring from your computer. Most importantly, switch all of your electronic devices to silent (or turn them off!)—as much as you think you can resist the temptation of checking a new text or email, you probably can't.

After you take each practice test, you should: 1) calculate your scores using the information and charts in Chapter 16; and 2) review your answers with the detailed explanations given at the end of each test. Calculating your score will assign a numerical value to each test you take, so you can get a sense of where you started and how you improve throughout your study plan. You can also get a sense of which sections are giving you the most trouble, so you can focus your review on a specific test section (or even a specific subsection) before you take your next practice exam. The answer explanations in this book are extremely helpful, as they not only explain why the correct answer is right, but they also go into detail about why each incorrect answer is wrong. You will see the mistakes you tend to repeat, which will help you avoid them in the future.

At this point, you're ahead of the game—you've dedicated yourself to preparation and practice, which is a huge step in the direction of ACT success. So don't get too discouraged if the results to your first few practice tests aren't exactly at your goal score. If you put in the time and focus, assess your test results, and tailor your study plan to hit the areas where you need help, you will reach the results you want by test day.

**Good
Luck!**

WRITING TEST

PLAN YOUR ESSAY

_____
_____
_____
_____
_____
_____
_____
_____
_____
_____
_____
_____
_____
_____
_____
_____
_____
_____
_____
_____
_____
_____
_____
_____
_____
_____
_____
_____
_____
_____

WRITING TEST

WRITE YOUR ESSAY

ENGLISH TEST

45 Minutes—75 Questions

DIRECTIONS: In this section, you will see passages with words and phrases that are underlined and numbered. In the right-hand column you will see a question corresponding to each number which provides alternatives to the underlined part. In most of the items, you are to choose the best alternative. If no change is needed, choose NO CHANGE.

In other items, there will be either a question about an underlined portion of the passage or a question about a section of the passage, or about the passage as a whole. This question type will correspond to a number or numbers in a box.

For each question, choose the best alternative or answer and fill in the corresponding circle on the answer sheet.

PASSAGE I

Fossey's Quest

[1]

Dian Fossey was a researcher, a visionary, and a pioneer in the field of animal conservation. <u>More specifically Fossey dedi-cated her life</u> to preserving the endangered mountain gorilla in Africa.

1.
A. NO CHANGE
B. More specifically, Fossey dedicated her life
C. More specifically Fossey, dedicated her life
D. More specifically, Fossey dedicated, her life

[2]

<u>She was born in San Francisco, Fossey made her first trip to Africa in 1963.</u> At the time, she was 31 years old. In the course of

2.
F. NO CHANGE
G. Fossey, was born in San Francisco, made her first trip to Africa in 1963.
H. Fossey was born in San Francisco and made her first trip to Africa in 1963.
J. Born in San Francisco, in 1963 Fossey made her first trip, to Africa.

her trip, she met <u>Dr. Louis Leakey. A prominent</u> archaeologist and anthropologist. Dr. Leakey believed in the importance of

3.
A. NO CHANGE
B. Dr. Louis Leakey. Who was a prominent
C. Dr. Louis Leakey a prominent
D. Dr. Louis Leakey, a prominent

research on large apes, and he <u>encourages</u> Fossey to undertake it. Fossey took up the challenge, deciding to study mountain gorillas.

4.
F. NO CHANGE
G. was encouraging
H. will encourage
J. encouraged

[3]

Fossey began her work in the African country of Zaire, but was forced to leave because of political unrest. She moved to

CONTINUE

---

another African country, Rwanda, where she established a

research camp in a national park. There, she spent thousands of
                                      5

hours observing the behavior of gorillas. Her steadfast patience

won the trust of the animals;
                        6

and they began to accept her presence among them. As a result,
          7
she was able to observe gorillas' behavior that had previously

never been seen by humans.

[4]

Spending so much time to observe the gorillas,
                      8

Fossey naturally distinguished among them and had particular
        9

favorites. One of these favorites, a young male gorilla named
                        10

Digit. Still, Digit was killed by a poacher, an illegal hunter of
       11
protected animals. Fossey was stunned and saddened. She began

a public campaign to raise awareness of the problem of gorilla

poaching, a practice that threatened the continued existence of

mountain gorillas. The rhinoceros, too, from poaching has faced
                  12
grave danger. Fossey's campaign earned worldwide attention
   12
and support, and she continued to live and work in Africa for

many years thereafter.

[5]

In 1980, Fossey took a teaching position at Cornell University

and wrote a book, *Gorillas in the Mist*, that brought further

5. **A.** NO CHANGE
    B. However, there,
    C. And so there,
    D. Meanwhile,

6. **F.** NO CHANGE
    G. animals
    H. animals,
    J. animals.

7. **A.** NO CHANGE
    B. began to accept and also tolerate
    C. began to show an acceptance, even, and also a
        tolerance
    D. began to show that they accepted

8. **F.** NO CHANGE
    G. Because she spent so much time observing the
        gorillas
    H. Spending much time in observation of the
        gorillas
    J. Being very sure to observe the gorillas

9. **A.** NO CHANGE
    B. Fossey naturally distinguishing
    C. the naturally distinguished Fossey
    D. Fossey was naturally distinguished

10. **F.** NO CHANGE
    G. favoring to a
    H. favorites were a
    J. favorites was a

11. **A.** NO CHANGE
    B. Unfortunately
    C. In fact
    D. Because

12. **F.** NO CHANGE
    G. The rhinoceros, too, has faced grave danger from
        poaching.
    H. From poaching as well, has the rhinoceros faced
        grave danger.
    J. OMIT the underlined portion.

attention to the crisis of diminishing numbers of mountain

gorillas. <u>After, though, to Rwanda Fossey returned,</u> and spent
　　　　　13

the rest of her life working to protect the mountain gorilla. Her

work continues even after her death. 14

[6]

Today, the population of mountain gorillas in Rwanda is

rising, thanks to the legacy of Dian Fossey.

13. **A.** NO CHANGE
    B. Afterward, Fossey returned to Rwanda
    C. Still, to Rwanda, Fossey returned,
    D. And yet, Fossey returned, to Rwanda

14. Which of the following sentences, when inserted after the second sentence in Paragraph 5, would provide a concrete example of a statement made by the author?

    F. She loved gorillas very much.
    G. She remains well-known among conservationists.
    H. Her efforts included organizing patrols to protect gorillas from poachers.
    J. Another primate conservationist who was influenced by Louis Leakey was Jane Goodall.

Question 15 asks about the passage as a whole.

15. Suppose the author of this passage had been assigned to write an essay that discussed whether Fossey's goals justified her very controversial methods. Would this essay successfully address that topic?

    A. Yes, because the author details the controversy Fossey inspired.
    B. Yes, because the author describes Fossey's important legacy in the field of conservation.
    C. No, because the author never offers an opinion as to whether Fossey's work was of any benefit to the mountain gorilla.
    D. No, because the author does not mention that any of Fossey's methods were controversial.

PASSAGE II

The Smoke That Thunders

[1]

The Zambezi River rushes <u>along which</u> the border of the
　　　　　　　　　　　　　　　　16
African countries of Zambia and Zimbabwe. This is no ordinary

river: it is home to one of the most stunning achievements of

nature, <u>this is truly a spectacular</u> waterfall that is twice as large
　　　　　　17

16. **F.** NO CHANGE
    G. which
    H. along
    J. OMIT the underlined portion.

17. **A.** NO CHANGE
    B. a truly spectacular
    C. this sight which will be truly spectacular
    D. the spectacularly large

CONTINUE

as North America's Niagara Falls. The Kololo tribe, who <u>have been</u>
18
<u>living</u> in the area in the 1800s, called the falls "Mosi-oa-Tunya," or
18
"The Smoke That Thunders." Around the same time, British

explorers who saw the falls for the first time dubbed it "The

Victoria Falls," after their queen.

18.
- **F.** NO CHANGE
- **G.** were lived
- **H.** has been lived
- **J.** lived

[2]

The waterfall, <u>which is composed of five actually separate</u>
19
<u>falls</u>, is considered to be one of the seven wonders of the natural
19

world—<u>and for good reason</u>. Visitors to the falls can spot columns
20
of spray from up to 25 miles away, as millions of cubic meters of

water per minute plunge 100 meters over a cliff. Anyone

<u>observing who witnesses</u> this wonder will understand the name
21

"Smoke That Thunders." The <u>roaring, crashing</u> falls send up
22

soaking billows of <u>spray. Imagine</u> —a rushing, two-kilometer-wide
23
river makes a sudden plunge downward for over 100 meters,

slamming into the gorge below.

19.
- **A.** NO CHANGE
- **B.** which of five separate falls actually is composed
- **C.** which is actually composed of five separate falls
- **D.** it is actually composed of five separate falls

20.
- **F.** NO CHANGE
- **G.** one of the others is the Grand Canyon
- **H.** some people don't think it's that spectacular
- **J.** Africa contains many wonders

21.
- **A.** NO CHANGE
- **B.** who witnesses
- **C.** who looks to see
- **D.** observing to see

22.
- **F.** NO CHANGE
- **G.** roaring crashing
- **H.** roaring, and crashing
- **J.** roaring, crashing,

23.
- **A.** NO CHANGE
- **B.** spray, imagine
- **C.** spray. To imagine
- **D.** spray imagining

[3]

Opposite the cliff, across the gorge, <u>stand's</u> a spectacular
24

stretch of rain forest. This forest provides another perspective

on the <u>grandiosity</u> of the falls.
25

24.
- **F.** NO CHANGE
- **G.** stands
- **H.** standing
- **J.** OMIT the underlined portion.

25.
- **A.** NO CHANGE
- **B.** generosity
- **C.** fruitfulness
- **D.** peacefulness

Visitors can enjoy, a walk along a path through the lush forest
26
and a breathtaking, spray-soaked vision of the falls. The Knife
Edge Bridge provides a particularly spectacular view of the falls
and of the Boiling Pot, a dramatic turn in the river. As some would
27
say, "a watched pot never boils." Many visitors choose to view the
27
sights from above, taking advantage of the services of pilots who
fly small planes filled with tourists over the falls.

[4]

While the waterfall is the attention-grabbing attraction of
the area, the surrounding Mosi-oa-Tunya National Park is full of
wonders as well. The natural beauty of the local wildlife is to be
28
admired by visitors. Among the animals who make their homes
28
at the Mosi-oa-Tunya National Park are zebras, giraffes, several
species of antelope, wildebeests, a dazzling array of birds, and
rare white rhinos.

[5]

Whichever attractions visitors choose to view during their
time at the Mosi-oa-Tunya National Park, they will surely never
forget the striking power and beauty of the falls. The image of
the massive wall of water is one that lasts a lifetime.

26.
F. NO CHANGE
G. enjoy, a,
H. enjoy a
J. be enjoying, a

27.
A. NO CHANGE
B. Some say a watched pot never boils.
C. Never watch a pot that you're waiting to boil.
D. OMIT the underlined portion.

28.
F. NO CHANGE
G. Visitors can admire the natural beauty of the local wildlife.
H. By visitors can the natural beauty of the local wildlife be admired.
J. OMIT the underlined portion.

Questions 29–30 ask about the passage as a whole.

29. Suppose the author had been asked to write an essay describing why it is more worthwhile to see Victoria Falls than the other six wonders of the natural world. Would this essay meet the assignment?

A. Yes, because it describes in detail how marvelous Victoria Falls is.
B. Yes, because it does not mention most of the other wonders of the natural world.
C. No, because it does not attempt to compare Victoria Falls to any other attractions.
D. No, because the author does not seem to think that Victoria Falls is a very interesting place to visit.

30. The writer wishes to insert a paragraph about a place where visitors can buy locally made crafts. This paragraph would most logically be inserted:

F. between Paragraph 1 and Paragraph 2.
G. between Paragraph 2 and Paragraph 3.
H. between Paragraph 3 and Paragraph 4.
J. between Paragraph 4 and Paragraph 5.

CONTINUE

PASSAGE III

Snow Experts

[1]

My family had just <u>moved to, Connecticut</u> from Florida in
31
the winter of 1990. I was eight years old, and my brothers and I
hated the North. We missed our friends back in Florida; we missed
catching the lizards that scaled the outside walls of houses. We
<u>even also</u> missed the steamy heat that lasted month after month.
32
We were convinced that we would never be happy up North.

[2]

One thing we <u>look forward to</u> was seeing snow. We had
33

seen snow on television <u>and, in movies,</u> of course. In movies,
34
snow always fell miraculously just when everyone wanted it.
On cartoons, snow would begin to fall on bare ground, and

<u>instantly right away</u> children were shooting through town on
35

sleds and <u>building</u> snowmen.
36

[3]

The first time snow fell right before our own eyes <u>were</u> on
37
a raw November morning. My brothers and I were eating cereal

in the kitchen before school. Our mother, <u>that</u> was almost as
38
excited as we were, pointed wordlessly to the window. Yelling,
my brothers and I raced to the window, our spoons clattering
into our cereal bowls. Sure enough, a few white flakes blew around

31. A. NO CHANGE
  B. moved to, Connecticut,
  C. moved, to Connecticut,
  D. moved to Connecticut

32. F. NO CHANGE
  G. even
  H. also had
  J. were also even finding that we

33. A. NO CHANGE
  B. look back at
  C. looked forward to
  D. sought out to

34. F. NO CHANGE
  G. and in movies,
  H. and, in movies
  J. and in movies

35. A. NO CHANGE
  B. instantly and right away
  C. instant
  D. instantly

36. F. NO CHANGE
  G. build
  H. had built
  J. were to build

37. A. NO CHANGE
  B. is
  C. are
  D. was

38. F. NO CHANGE
  G. which
  H. whom
  J. who

the bare tree branches. We looked at each other, and we were all thinking the same thing: that afternoon, after school, we would be initiated into the glamorous, Northern world of Snow. 39 We would build forts, engage in snowball fights, create snow angels, and construct towering snowmen. We would drag our new sled from the closet and whip down hills until, soggy, red-cheeked, and laughing, we would drag ourselves back home for

mugs of cocoa. Our plan for the games we'd play in the snow
                    40
were elaborate.

[4]

Hurriedly, we finished our breakfast, and yanked on our heavy jackets. We raced outside and were bewildered to discover
                                            41
that the flakes had gone over to a thin, cold rain. We looked at each other in horror. It certainly wasn't very cold outside.
                                    42
[5]

Later that winter, of course, we experienced true, heavy snowfalls. We experienced slush in our winter boots, numb toes, getting smacked by rogue snowballs thrown by other kids. We learned that you had to earn a downhill sled ride with a long, cold trudge up the hill, and that snow had to be shoveled from driveways and walkways.

[6]

And the more we learned about snow, the more we loved it. By the end of that winter, we considered ourselves to be experts on the stuff. Looking at the sky, we'd speculate: would this snowfall stick, or would it melt the instant it hit the ground? Would it be

39. Should the writer begin a new paragraph at this point?

   A. Yes, because the following sentence introduces a different topic.
   B. Yes, because separate details should have separate paragraphs.
   C. No, because the following sentence continues the same idea as the previous one.
   D. No, because the following sentence does not provide enough information about the children's plans.

40. F. NO CHANGE
    G. plans for
    H. plan toward
    J. plan to involve

41. A. NO CHANGE
    B. are bewildered
    C. was bewildered
    D. is bewildered

42. Which alternative sentence illustrates the feeling of surprise conveyed in the previous sentence?

    F. NO CHANGE
    G. We didn't like snow, after all.
    H. Was this someone's idea of a joke?
    J. We had never experienced such cold weather in Florida.

CONTINUE

good, wet packing snow, or powdery stuff that couldn't form a

decent snowball? <u>Some children</u> were, in short, Northern kids,
43

and our <u>once-held prejudices</u> had melted like an early snowfall.
44

43. **A.** NO CHANGE
   B. They
   C. Who
   D. We

44. **F.** NO CHANGE
   G. prejudices, once, held
   H. prejudices, once held,
   J. prejudices, once,

Question 45 asks about the passage as a whole.

45. The writer wants to insert the following material into the essay:

   We missed swimming outdoors virtually year-round.

   This new material would most logically be placed in Paragraph:

   A. 1.
   B. 2.
   C. 3.
   D. 6.

PASSAGE IV

Conserving a Natural Resource

[1]

   The Great Smoky Mountains National Park <u>is created of</u> over
46
half a million acres of the Appalachian Mountains, straddling the

border between Tennessee and North Carolina. It attracts more

visitors each year than any other national park. This may be in

large part to its central location—it is within a day's drive for

more than half of the American population—but surely most

wouldn't make the trip if the mountains were not so majestic.

The blue mist that gives the mountains their name <u>rise above</u> its
47
peaks. The mountains are rich with streams, waterfalls, vegetation,

and wildlife. Hikers choose among many trails, ranging from a

brisk, uphill <u>walk, a truly</u> challenging three-hour hike to the
48
dramatic view from a mountain peak. However, it's likely that

many of the visitors who enjoy the scenery are unaware of how

this stunning stretch of land came to be preserved as a

national park.

46. **F.** NO CHANGE
   G. is owned by
   H. consists of
   J. establishes

47. **A.** NO CHANGE
   B. rising above
   C. rises above
   D. rose above

48. **F.** NO CHANGE
   G. walk to a truly
   H. walk for a truly
   J. walk, then toward a

[2]

The idea of establishing a national park in the mountains of the Southeastern United States first emerged in the 1880s, when conservationists wished to protect the vast acres of forest area. The decision was a politically tricky one that required balancing logging interests with conservation concerns. Recognizing that trying to ban logging was <u>unrealistic</u>, conservationists sug-

49

gested that in a national park area, the government could regulate the logging <u>that, unchecked;</u> threatened to destroy the entire

50

forest. 51

49. **A.** NO CHANGE
    B. unrealistically
    C. unreal
    D. not real

50. **F.** NO CHANGE
    G. that unchecked
    H. that, unchecked
    J. that, unchecked,

51. The purpose of Paragraph 2, as it relates to the rest of the essay, is primarily to:
    A. give us a feeling for the motives behind the establishment of the park.
    B. encourage us to conserve endangered land by creating more national parks.
    C. argue that logging is a threat to America's national parks.
    D. provide background for further discussion of the conflict between environmentalists and loggers.

[3]

[1] In 1926, Congress approved the idea of a national park in the Southeast. [2] Next, it had to determine what the location of this park would be. [3] This was no easy task; initially, about sixty different sites were proposed for the park. [4] After the decision was made, the United States Geological <u>Survey an</u>

52

<u>organization</u> that explored and mapped land in the United States,

52

52. **F.** NO CHANGE
    G. Survey, an organization
    H. Surveyed an organization
    J. Survey, having an organization

CONTINUE

created a topographical chart of a proposed park stretching from western North Carolina to eastern Tennessee. 53

[4]

To make this plan become a reality, it would be no easy task.
54
Unlike the vast stretches of land in the American West that had

been preserved as national parks, much of the designated land

was owned in privacy. It would have to be purchased and then
55
deeded to the federal government. This, of course, meant that

an enormous amount of dollars would have to be raised to
56

purchase land from private owners and lumber companies, some

of whom recognized their leverage and hiked their prices. 57

[5]

Fundraisers in North Carolina and Tennessee collected over

two million dollars from private citizens. Each of the two states'

legislatures provided over a million dollars, and—just as the

53. Suppose the writer wanted to add the following sentence to Paragraph 3:

After much debate, the Smoky Mountains region emerged as the winner.

This sentence would most logically be added:

A. before Sentence 1.
B. between Sentence 1 and Sentence 2.
C. between Sentence 3 and Sentence 4.
D. after Sentence 4.

54. **F.** NO CHANGE
G. It would not be, making this plan a reality, an easy task.
H. No easy task would it be, making this plan become a reality.
J. Making this plan a reality would be no easy task.

55. **A.** NO CHANGE
B. privately owned
C. owned as a private
D. owned in a private manner

56. **F.** NO CHANGE
G. amount of money
H. number of monies
J. dollar

57. The writer's description of the landowners who hiked their prices makes the acquisition of the land seem even more:

A. challenging.
B. heroic.
C. foolish.
D. immoral.

park's supporters feared—they had fallen <u>short; they hadn't</u>
                                                    58
<u>raised enough money.</u> Just as it appeared that the conservationists
      58
had failed, the Rockefeller family rushed to the rescue by donating

an additional five million dollars. The federal government pro-

vided the final one and a half million dollars needed to complete

the purchase. On June 15, 1934, over 800 majestic square miles

of forested peaks were designated a national park.

PASSAGE V

A Mayan Worldview

[1]

The ancient Mayans inhabited the area that now consists

of Mexico, Guatemala, Belize, Honduras, and El Salvador. Their

<u>rich civilization flourished</u> from the third through the ninth
      61

centuries. <u>Plus</u> the many notable achievements of this society
            62
was the Mayan understanding of astronomy, which was manifest

not only in Mayan science but in every aspect of the culture.

58. **F.** NO CHANGE
   G. short—they hadn't raised enough money.
   H. short: they hadn't raised enough money.
   J. short.

Questions 59–60 ask about the passage as a whole.

59. Suppose the writer wanted to more closely examine the conflict between loggers and environmentalists. In order to expand upon material already present, this information would most logically be added to Paragraph:

   A. 1.
   B. 2.
   C. 3.
   D. 4.

60. Suppose that the writer had been asked to write an essay detailing the attractions that tourists can enjoy when they visit the Great Smoky Mountains National Park. Would this essay successfully fulfill that assignment?

   F. Yes, because it describes the park's beauty.
   G. Yes, because it mentions the park's popularity with visitors.
   H. No, because it concentrates on how the park was established.
   J. No, because it does not describe the park as being someplace that tourists would want to visit.

61. **A.** NO CHANGE
   B. civilization flourished and it was rich
   C. civilization richly flourished
   D. civilization was rich, flourished

62. **F.** NO CHANGE
   G. Despite
   H. Among
   J. Between

CONTINUE

[2]

Ancient Mayans kept meticulous records of the movements of the sun and moon, the planets, and the stars that were visible to the naked eye. Based on the solar year, they created a calendar which they used to keep track of time. So were <u>astute</u> the Mayans' observations that they could predict such events as solar and lunar eclipses, and the movement of the planets.

63. A. NO CHANGE
B. (Place before *were*)
C. (Place before *So*)
D. (Place before *Mayans'*)

[3]

For the ancient Mayans, astronomy was <u>not just</u> a science; it was a combination of science, religion, and philosophy that

64. F. NO CHANGE
G. merely
H. just
J. not

<u>was found</u> into many aspects of their lives, including architecture.

65. A. NO CHANGE
B. had to find
C. found its way
D. could be found

Mayan ceremonial buildings, for example, were <u>exact</u> aligned

66. F. NO CHANGE
G. exactly
H. to be exact
J. exacting

with compass points, so that at the fall and spring equinoxes, light would flood the interior of the building. These buildings were designed and built as acts of worship to the <u>Mayan gods:</u>

67. A. NO CHANGE
B. Mayan gods,
C. Mayan gods;
D. Mayan gods

science, architecture, and religion, then, were all intricately and beautifully blended. [68]

68. Which of the following words best expresses the writer's tone in this paragraph?

F. Gleeful
G. Indifferent
H. Resentful
J. Admiring

[4]

Government, too, was inextricably linked with astronomy. The beginning and ending of the reigns of Mayan leaders appear to have been timed to coincide with astronomical events. Ancient

Mayan artwork, carvings and murals—show royalty wearing
69
symbols relating to the sun, moon, and sky. The Mayans

believed that the sun and moon were guided across the sky

by benevolent gods, and that these gods needed human help

to thwart the evil gods and wanted to stop them. Human
70
intervention took the form of different rituals, including sac-

rifice. It was considered an honor to die for this cause, and

those who were sacrificed were believed to have gained
71
eternal life.

[5]

The planet Venus, which can often be seen by the unaided

eye, played a large role in Mayan life. Mayans appeared to
72
Venus in the sky as a means of timing when they attacked
72
enemies. The night sky, then, among its other duties, served

as a call to war.

[6]

In short, the ancient Mayans, in looking to the night sky
73

for guidance; discovered a natural order around which they were
74
able to base a rich and textured civilization.

69. **A.**   NO CHANGE
   B.   artwork, carvings, and murals, show
   C.   artwork, including carvings and murals—shows
   D.   artwork shows

70. **F.**   NO CHANGE
   G.   who wanted
   H.   which are wanting
   J.   they want

71. **A.**   NO CHANGE
   B.   and felt they
   C.   that they would soon have
   D.   one day they would have

72. **F.**   NO CHANGE
   G.   Venus, to all appearances,
   H.   The Mayans used the appearance of Venus
   J.   Venus appeared to be to the Mayans

73. **A.**   NO CHANGE
   B.   Shortly, the
   C.   To sum up the
   D.   Lastly, the

74. **F.**   NO CHANGE
   G.   guidance, discovered
   H.   guidance discovering
   J.   guidance: discovered

75. Suppose the writer were to add the following
   sentence at the end of the last paragraph:

   *The ancient Babylonians, too, were astronomers of
   remarkable accomplishment.*

   This change would have which of the following
   effects on the last paragraph?

   A.   It would make the paragraph into a more
   effective conclusion.
   B.   It would make the paragraph serve as a transition
   to another topic.
   C.   It would provide an illustrative detail.
   D.   It would contradict the information in the rest of
   the passage.

STOP

MATHEMATICS TEST

60 MINUTES—60 QUESTIONS

DIRECTIONS: For each of the following items, solve each problem, choose the correct answer, and then fill in the corresponding circle on the answer sheet. If you encounter problems that take too much time to solve, move on. Solve as many problems as you can, then return to the others in the time remaining for the test.

You may use a calculator on this test for any problems you choose, but some of the problems may best be solved without the use of a calculator.

SHOW YOUR WORK HERE

Note: Unless otherwise stated, assume the following:

1. Illustrative figures are NOT necessarily drawn to scale.
2. Geometric figures lie in a plane.
3. The word *line* indicates a straight line.
4. The word *average* indicates arithmetic mean.

---

1. A baseball team lost exactly 20% of the games it played last season. If the team lost 30 games, how many games did it play?

    A. 36
    B. 60
    C. 90
    D. 120
    E. 150

$$\frac{30}{X} = \frac{20}{100} \Rightarrow x = 150$$

2. If $a = 5$, what value of b solves the proportion below?

$$\frac{\overset{5}{a}}{6} = \frac{b}{15}$$

    F. 14
    G. $12\frac{1}{2}$
    H. 10
    J. $2\frac{1}{2}$
    K. 2

$$6b = 75$$
$$b = 12.5$$

3. In the figure below, points X, Y, and Z lie on the same line. What is the measure of ∠WYZ?

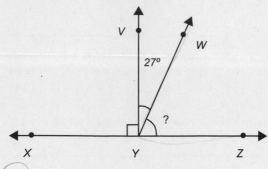

A. 63°
B. 73°
C. 90°
D. 117°
E. 153°

4. What is the fifth term of the sequence 3, –6, 12, …? −24, (48) _ _ ☐

F. –48
G. –24
H. 10
J. 24
K. 48

5. Martha cuts four pieces of ribbon, each 1.5 feet long, from a spool of ribbon. If 27.5 feet of ribbon are now left on the spool, how many feet of ribbon did it originally contain?

6

A. 21.5
B. 26
C. 29
D. 33.5
E. 39.5

6. If $y = -4$, then $2(5 - y) + y =$

$2(5 + 4) = 4 = x$
$2(9) - 4 = x$
$18 - 4 = x$

F. –72
G. –22
H. 6
J. 14
K. 22

7. If $\sqrt{x}$ lies between 5 and 6, then which of the following could be the value of x?

A. 11
B. 25
C. 31
D. 36
E. 56

SHOW YOUR WORK HERE

8. Points *A*, *B*, *C*, and *D* lie on the same line. If point *C* bisects segment *BD*, all of the following must be true EXCEPT:

    F. $2BC = BD$

    G. $BC = CD$

    H. $AD = 3CD$

    J. $CD = \dfrac{BD}{2}$

    K. $BD - CD = BC$

9. $|-3| - |3 - 9| =$

    A. −18
    B. −9
    C. −3
    D. 3
    E. 9

10. A bag contains only red, blue, and green marbles. There are a total of 20 marbles in the bag, and the probability of NOT selecting a blue marble is $\dfrac{1}{4}$. How many blue marbles are in the bag?

    F. 4
    G. 5
    H. 8
    J. 10
    K. 15

11. Line *a* is perpendicular to line *b*. If line *a* is defined by the equation $2x + 3y = 11$, what is the slope of line *b*?

    A. $-\dfrac{11}{3}$

    B. $-\dfrac{3}{2}$

    C. $-\dfrac{2}{3}$

    D. $\dfrac{2}{3}$

    E. $\dfrac{3}{2}$

12. Kecia uses a formula to prepare a chemical mixture of Solutions *A*, *B*, and *C*. The formula calls for 5 times as much Solution *B* as Solution *A*, and 12 more ounces of Solution *C* than Solution *A*. If the mixture contains *x* ounces of Solution *C*, how many ounces of Solution *B* does it contain, in terms of *x*?

    F. $5x + 60$
    G. $5x$
    H. $x - 12$
    J. $5x - 12$
    K. $5x - 60$

CONTINUE

13. A square with a side length of 5 is graphed in the standard (x, y) coordinate plane. If the coordinates of one of its corners are $(-2, 3)$, which of the following CANNOT be the coordinates of another of its corners?

    A. $(-7, 3)$
    B. $(-2, 8)$
    C. $(3, 3)$
    D. $(-2, -3)$
    E. $(-7, -2)$

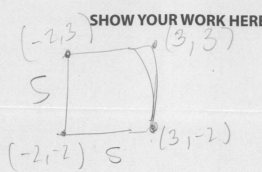

SHOW YOUR WORK HERE

14. Several years ago Joan bought a house for $75,000. If she wants to sell it for 5% more than she paid for it, for how much will she sell it?

    F. $75,500
    G. $78,750
    H. $80,000
    J. $82,500
    K. $112,500

15. For all x and y, $5x - (3y - x) =$

    A. $3(2x - y)$
    B. $4x - 3y$
    C. $6x + 3y$
    D. $2(x - y + 1)$
    E. $5x + 3xy$

16. Which of the following is a root of the equation $x^2 + x - 2 = 0$?

    F. -4
    G. -3
    H. -2
    J. 6
    K. 12

17. In the triangle below, what is the measure of angle ACB?

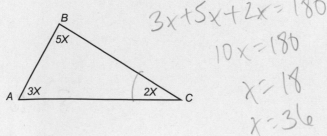

    A. $18°$
    B. $36°$
    C. $54°$
    D. $72°$
    E. $90°$

18. A jacket that normally sells for $75 is on sale for $50. By what percent is the original price discounted for this sale?

SHOW YOUR WORK HERE

F. 20%

G. 25%

H. $33\frac{1}{3}$%

J. 50%

K. 75%

19. If $4a + b = 2$ and $a - 3b = 7$, what is the value of b?

A. −13

B. −2

C. 1

D. 7

E. 10

20. If an inch of wire costs $0.20, how much will 5.25 feet of wire cost?

F. $1.05

G. $2.40

H. $12.60

J. $63

K. $315

21. For all a and b such that $a \neq 2$, $\dfrac{6a^4b + 2a^3b}{3a^2 - 5a - 2} =$

A. $\dfrac{8a^7b^2}{3a^2 - 5a - 2}$

B. $\dfrac{8a^7b^2}{-4a^3}$

C. $\dfrac{3a+1}{(a-2)}$

D. $\dfrac{2a^3b}{a-2}$

E. $2a^2b$

22. A rectangle has a length of 8 inches and a width of 3 inches. What is the width, in inches, of a rectangle whose length and width are in the same proportion, and whose perimeter is 44 inches?

F. 6

G. 11

H. 12

J. 16

K. 22

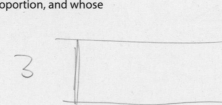

CONTINUE

Practice Test 1

23. A car rental company charges $19 per day of rental. Customers receive 100 free miles for each day of the rental period but must pay $0.18 for each mile above this allowance. If *d* is the number of days for which the car was rented, and *m* is the total number of miles driven, which of the following expressions could be used to calculate the cost of a car rental with this company?

    A. $19 + $0.18(m − d)$

    B. $19 + $0.18(100m − d)$

    C. $19d + $0.18(m − 100)$

    D. $19d + $0.18(m − 100d)$

    E. $19d + $0.18m$

$19d$

24. The garden in the figure below was created by adding equal semicircles to the four faces of a square. If the perimeter of this garden is 16π feet, what is its area in square feet?

    F. $64 + 8\pi$

    G. $64 + 32\pi$

    H. $64 + 64\pi$

    J. $256 + 32\pi$

    K. $256 + 64\pi$

$C = 2\pi r$

$16\pi = 2\pi r$ reduce

$$\frac{16\pi}{2\pi}$$

$8 = r \Rightarrow r = 4$

$A = \pi \cdot 8^2$

64π

25. Which of the following best describes the graph on the number line below?

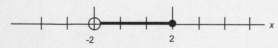

    A. $-2 \leq x < 2$

    B. $-2 < x \leq 2$

    C. $-2 \leq x \leq 2$

    D. $-2 < x < 2$

    E. $x > 2$

26. The remainder when n is divided by 9 is 6. What is the remainder when $7n$ is divided by 9?

- **F.** 1
- **G.** 2
- **H.** 3
- **J.** 6
- **K.** 13

SHOW YOUR WORK HERE

27. If the perimeter of a square is 36 meters, what is its area in square meters?

- **A.** 9
- **B.** 18
- **C.** 36
- **D.** 81
- **E.** 162

28. For all $a > 0$, $\dfrac{a}{5} - \dfrac{5}{a} =$

- **F.** $\dfrac{a-5}{5-a}$
- **G.** $a - 5$
- **H.** $\dfrac{5a-25}{5a}$
- **J.** $\dfrac{a^2-5a}{5a}$
- **K.** $\dfrac{a^2-25}{5a}$

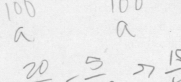

29. Two sides of a triangle have lengths 7 and 2. Which of the following could be the perimeter of this triangle?

- **A.** 9
- **B.** 11
- **C.** 14
- **D.** 16
- **E.** 18

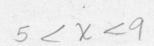
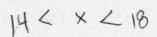

30. If $a^2 + b^2 = 34$ and $ab = -15$, which of the following could be the value of $a - b$?

- **F.** 0
- **G.** 2
- **H.** 8
- **J.** 16
- **K.** 64

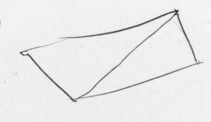

CONTINUE

31. John decides to give away his collection of baseball cards. When he divides the cards equally among 6 friends, he has one card left over. When he divides the cards equally among 7 friends, he again has one card left over. When he divides the cards equally among 8 friends, he again has one card left over. What is the smallest possible number of baseball cards in John's collection?

- **A.** 337
- **B.** 210
- **C.** 169
- **D.** 58
- **E.** 22

32. In right triangle ABC, $AB = 6$ and $BC = 8$. What is the length of segment AC?

- **F.** 10
- **G.** $2\sqrt{7}$
- **H.** 28
- **J.** 2
- **K.** Cannot be determined from the given information

33. The length of a square is increased by 5, and its width is decreased by 2 to create a rectangle. If the perimeter of the square is $4s$, what is the area of the rectangle, in terms of s?

- **A.** $4s + 6$
- **B.** $2s + 3$
- **C.** $s^2 - 10$
- **D.** $s^2 + 3s - 10$
- **E.** $s^2 + 7s + 10$

SHOW YOUR WORK HERE

34. In the isosceles right triangle *XYZ* below, $\cos\angle YXZ = \dfrac{\sqrt{2}}{2}$. What is the value of tan $\angle ZYX$?

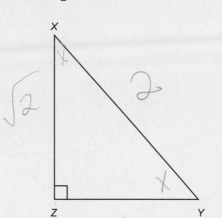

F. $\dfrac{1}{2}$

G. $\dfrac{\sqrt{2}}{2}$

H. 1

J. $\sqrt{2}$

K. 2

35. There are twice as many boys as girls in Mr. Botti's math class. The class's average grade on a recent test was 84. If the girls' average grade was 91, what was the boys' average grade?

A. 70

B. 77

C. 80.5

D. 87.5

E. 98

36. Which of the following is the graph of the solution set of $|3x - 2| < x$?

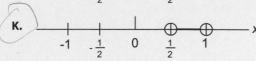

F.

G.

H.

J.

K.

37. The figure below was formed by combining two equal squares, such that a vertex of one square is at the center of the other square. The area of the shaded region is *x*. In terms of *x*, what is the area of the unshaded region?

$9 = x$

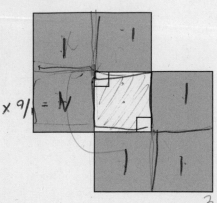

$x \, 9 / 1 = \mathbf{M}$

SHOW YOUR WORK HERE

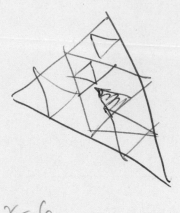

$x = \frac{3}{4} \times 2$

$x = 6$

.275

A. $\dfrac{6x}{7}$

B. $\dfrac{3x}{4}$

C. $\dfrac{x}{6}$

D. $\dfrac{x}{7}$

E. $\dfrac{x}{8}$

38. The average of three different positive integers is 99. What is the greatest possible value for one of these integers?

F. 33
G. 96
H. 294
J. 295
K. 296

$$\frac{x + y + z}{3} = 99$$

$x + y + z = 297$

39. In right triangle *ABC*, what is the measure of angle *BCA*?

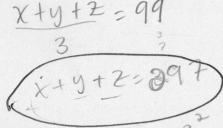

$(3\sqrt{3})^2 + \underline{\quad} = 9^2$

$27 + x = 81$

$x = 54$

$\tan x = \dfrac{9}{3\sqrt{3}}$

A. 90°
B. 60°
C. 45°
D. 30°
E. Cannot be determined from the given information

40. What are the coordinates of the point at which the lines represented by the equations $y + 2x = -4$ and $3y - x = 9$ intersect?

    F. $(0, -2)$
    G. $(0, 3)$
    H. $(-1, -2)$
    J. $(2, -3)$
    K. $(-3, 2)$

SHOW YOUR WORK HERE

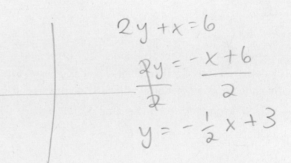

$y = -2x - 4$

$\dfrac{3y}{3} = \dfrac{x + 9}{3}$

$y = \dfrac{x}{3} + 3$

41. In the figure below, lines l_1 and l_2 are parallel. What is the value of n?

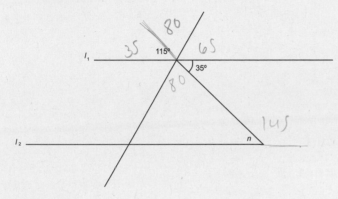

    A. $35°$
    B. $65°$
    C. $80°$
    D. $115°$
    E. $145°$

42. In the standard (x, y) coordinate plane, what is the slope of the line $2y + x = 6$?

    F. $-\dfrac{1}{2}$
    G. 0
    H. 1
    J. 2
    K. 3

$2y + x = 6$

$\dfrac{2y}{2} = \dfrac{-x + 6}{2}$

$y = -\dfrac{1}{2}x + 3$

43. Which of the following numbers is closest to 0.000000301 on a number line?

    A. 3.16×10^6
    B. 3.21×10^{-6}
    C. 4.01×10^{-7}
    D. 2.01×10^{-8}
    E. 2.99×10^{-9}

CONTINUE

44. In triangle *XYZ* below, what is the length of segment *XZ*?

SHOW YOUR WORK HERE

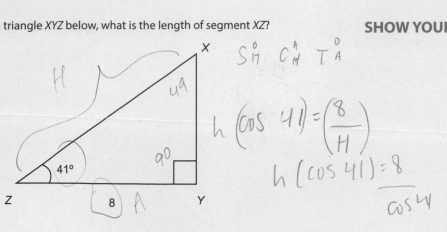

$sin \ \overset{O}{\underset{}{}} \ cos \ \overset{A}{\underset{H}{}} \ tan \ \overset{O}{\underset{A}{}}$

$h \ (cos \ 41) = \left(\dfrac{8}{H} \right)$

$h \ (cos \ 41) = 8$

$\dfrac{}{cos \ 4}$

F. 8 cos 41°

G. 8 sin 41°

H. $\dfrac{8}{\cos 41°}$

J. $\dfrac{8}{\sin 41°}$

K. 8 tan(41)

45. If $f(x) = x^2 + 2x + 1$ and $g(x) = x + 1$, then $f(g(x))$ is:

$(x+1)(x+1) + 2(x+1) + 1$

$x^2 + 2x + 1 + 2x + 2 + 1$

$x^2 + 4x + 4$

A. $x^2 + 2x + 2$

B. $x^2 + 4x + 4$

C. $x^2 + 2x + 4$

D. $x^2 + 3x + 4$

E. $x + 1$

46. A student has a 20-section spinner with 12 sections labeled red and 8 sections labeled blue. She wants to change some red sections to blue so that the probability of landing on a red section becomes $\dfrac{1}{4}$. How many red sections should be changed to blue?

20   12 R
        8 B

$\dfrac{1}{4} \to 20 = 5$

F. 7

G. 5

H. 4

J. 3

K. 2

47. Of the 24 guests who attended a barbecue, 8 guests ate hot dogs and 12 guests ate chicken. If 4 people ate both hot dogs and chicken, what fraction of the guests ate neither?

- **A.** $\dfrac{2}{3}$
- **B.** $\dfrac{1}{2}$
- **C.** $\dfrac{1}{3}$
- **D.** $\dfrac{1}{5}$
- **E.** $\dfrac{1}{6}$

48. $\dfrac{x-y}{x^2-y^2} =$

- **F.** $\dfrac{1}{x-y}$
- **G.** $\dfrac{1}{x+y}$
- **H.** $\dfrac{1}{-2xy}$
- **J.** $\dfrac{1}{y-x}$
- **K.** $x+y$

49. In right triangle *ABC*, the measure of angle *A* is 45°. If the hypotenuse of the triangle has length 5, what is the length of segment *BC*?

- **A.** $2\dfrac{1}{2}$
- **B.** $\dfrac{5\sqrt{2}}{2}$
- **C.** $\dfrac{5\sqrt{3}}{2}$
- **D.** $5\sqrt{2}$
- **E.** $5\sqrt{3}$

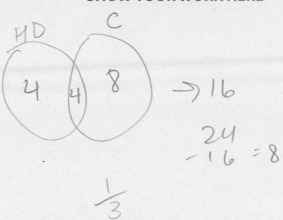

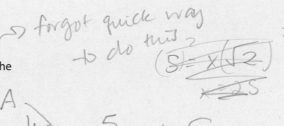

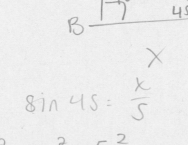

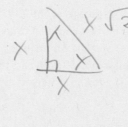

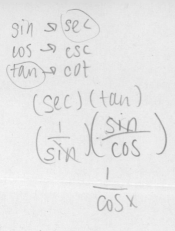

SHOW YOUR WORK HERE

50. $(\sec x)(\tan x) =$

    F. $\csc x$

    G. $\sin x$

    H. $\dfrac{1}{\cos x}$

    J. $\dfrac{\cos x}{\sin^2 x}$

    K. $\dfrac{\sin x}{\cos^2 x}$

51. How often does the parabola defined by the equation $y = x^2 + 2x - 3$ intersect the x-axis?

    A. Never

    B. Exactly once

    C. Exactly twice

    D. Exactly three times

    E. An infinite number of times

52. A drawer contains 7 black socks, 5 white socks, and 4 green socks. If 1 black sock is removed from the drawer, what is the probability that the next sock removed at random will NOT be black?

    F. $\dfrac{1}{15}$

    G. $\dfrac{3}{8}$

    H. $\dfrac{2}{5}$

    J. $\dfrac{9}{16}$

    K. $\dfrac{3}{5}$

53. If line 1 is defined by the equation $2y + x = 4$, and line 2 is defined by the equation $3y + 6x = 6$, then which of the following statements must be true?

    A. Line 1 is parallel to line 2.

    B. Line 1 is perpendicular to line 2.

    C. Line 1 and line 2 both have positive slopes.

    D. Line 1 and line 2 both pass through the origin.

    E. Line 1 and line 2 intersect at $(0, 2)$.

SHOW YOUR WORK HERE

54. The ratio of the circumference of circle *A* to the circumference of circle *B* is 4:9. What is the ratio of the area of circle *A* to the area of circle *B*?

    F. 2:3
    G. 4:9
    H. 8:27
    J. 16:81
    K. 81:16

55. If $ab > 0$ and $bc > 0$, then which of the following must be true?

    A. $b > 0$
    B. $ac > 0$
    C. $abc > 0$
    D. $ab^2 > 0$
    E. $\dfrac{b}{ac} > 0$

56. Janey goes to the movies with 5 friends. They decide to sit in a row that contains exactly 7 seats. In how many different ways can they arrange themselves if Janey insists on sitting in the middle seat?

    F. 24
    G. 35
    H. 120
    J. 720
    K. 5,040

57. A rectangular solid has dimensions *l*, *w*, and *h*. Doubling each dimension will increase the volume of the solid to how many times its original size?

    A. 2
    B. 6
    C. 8
    D. 12
    E. 16

58. Greg buys a stock on Monday. The price of the stock holds steady on Monday, remaining at the price Greg paid for it. On Tuesday the price of the stock increases by 20%. On Wednesday, the price of the stock falls by 25%. By what percentage must the stock price rise on Thursday to regain the original price Greg paid for it on Monday?

    F. 45%
    G. $22\frac{2}{9}\%$
    H. $11\frac{1}{9}\%$
    J. 10%
    K. 5%

CONTINUE

59. Square *WXYZ* is inscribed within circle *O* as shown in the figure below.

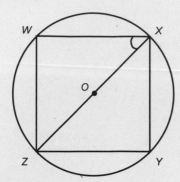

If the sine of $\angle WXZ = \dfrac{a}{b}$, which of the following represents the area of the circle?

A. $a^2\pi$

B. $b^2\pi$

C. $b\pi$

D. $\dfrac{b^2\pi}{4}$

E. $\dfrac{b\pi}{2}$

60. What is the units digit of 338^{340}?

F. 8

G. 6

H. 4

J. 2

K. 0

X
STOP

READING TEST

35 Minutes—40 Questions

DIRECTIONS: There are several passages in this test. Each passage is followed by several questions. Read each passage, choose the best answer, and fill in the corresponding circle on the answer sheet. You may refer back to the passages at any time.

PASSAGE I

PROSE FICTION: Passage A is an excerpt from the novel *House of Mirth* by Edith Wharton. Passage B is an excerpt from the novel *Emma* by Jane Austen.

Passage A
by Edith Wharton

Selden paused in surprise. In the afternoon rush of the Grand Central Station his eyes had been refreshed by the sight of Miss Lily Bart.

It was a Monday in early September, and he was returning to
5 his work from a hurried dip into the country; but what was Miss Bart doing in town at that season? If she had appeared to be catching a train, he might have inferred that he had come on her in the act of transition between one and another of the country-houses which disputed her presence after the close of the
10 Newport season; but her desultory air perplexed him. She stood apart from the crowd, letting it drift by her to the platform or the street, and wearing an air of irresolution which might, as he surmised, be the mask of a very definite purpose. It struck him at once that she was waiting for some one, but he hardly knew
15 why the idea arrested him. There was nothing new about Lily Bart, yet he could never see her without a faint movement of interest: it was characteristic of her that she always roused speculation, that her simplest acts seemed the result of far-reaching intentions.

20 An impulse of curiosity made him turn out of his direct line to the door, and stroll past her. He knew that if she did not wish to be seen she would contrive to elude him; and it amused him to think of putting her skill to the test.

"Mr. Selden—what good luck!"

25 She came forward smiling, eager almost, in her resolve to intercept him. One or two persons, in brushing past them, lingered to look; for Miss Bart was a figure to arrest even the suburban traveller rushing to his last train.

Selden had never seen her more radiant. Her vivid head,
30 relieved against the dull tints of the crowd, made her more conspicuous than in a ball-room, and under her dark hat and veil she regained the girlish smoothness, the purity of tint, that she was beginning to lose after eleven years of late hours and indefatigable dancing. Was it really eleven years, Selden found
35 himself wondering, and had she indeed reached the nine-and-twentieth birthday with which her rivals credited her?

"What luck!" she repeated. "How nice of you to come to my rescue!"

Passage B
by Jane Austen

Sixteen years had Miss Taylor been in Mr. Woodhouse's family, less as a governess than a friend, very fond of both daughters, but particularly of Emma. Between them it was more the intimacy of sisters. Even before Miss Taylor had ceased to hold
5 the nominal office of governess, the mildness of her temper had hardly allowed her to impose any restraint; and the shadow of authority being now long passed away, they had been living together as friend and friend very mutually attached, and Emma doing just what she liked; highly esteeming Miss Taylor's
10 judgment, but directed chiefly by her own.

The real evils, indeed, of Emma's situation were the power of having rather too much her own way, and a disposition to think a little too well of herself; these were the disadvantages which threatened her many enjoyments. The danger, however,
15 was at present so unperceived, that they did not by any means rank as misfortunes with her.

Sorrow came—a gentle sorrow—but not at all in the shape of any disagreeable consciousness—Miss Taylor married. It was Miss Taylor's loss which first brought grief. It was on the wed-
20 ding-day of this beloved friend that Emma first sat in mournful thought of any continuance. The wedding over, and the bride-people gone, her father and herself were left to dine together, with no prospect of a third to cheer a long evening. Her father

---

CONTINUE ➤

composed himself to sleep after dinner, as usual, and she had
25 then only to sit and think of what she had lost.

The event had every promise of happiness for her friend. Mr. Weston was a man of unexceptionable character, easy fortune, suitable age, and pleasant manners; and there was some satisfaction in considering with what self-denying, generous friendship
30 she had always wished and promoted the match; but it was a black morning's work for her. The want of Miss Taylor would be felt every hour of every day. She recalled her past kindness—the kindness, the affection of sixteen years—how she had taught and how she had played with her from five—years—old—how
35 she had devoted all her powers to attach and amuse her in health—and how nursed her through the various illnesses of childhood. A large debt of gratitude was owing here…the equal footing and perfect unreserve which had soon followed Isabella's marriage, on their being left to each other, was yet a dearer,
40 tenderer recollection.

She had been a friend and companion such as few possessed: intelligent, well-informed, useful, gentle, knowing all the ways of the family, interested in all its concerns, and peculiarly interested in herself, in every pleasure, every scheme of hers—one
45 to whom she could speak every thought as it arose, and who had such an affection for her as could never find fault.

How was she to bear the change?—It was true that her friend was going only half a mile from them; but Emma was aware that great must be the difference between a Mrs. Weston, only half a
50 mile from them, and a Miss Taylor in the house; and with all her advantages, natural and domestic, she was now in great danger of suffering from intellectual solitude. She dearly loved her father, but he was no companion for her. He could not meet her in conversation, rational or playful.

Questions 1-3 ask about Passage A.

1. Miss Lily Bart's behavior suggests that she:

   A. is late for a train she desperately needs to catch.

   B. is more interested in meeting someone than catching a train.

   C. is not very fond of Mr. Selden and wants to avoid him.

   D. is deciding whether or not to move back to town.

2. Miss Lily Bart's behavior toward Mr. Selden can best be described as:

   F. affectionate.

   G. mysterious.

   H. desperate.

   J. friendly.

3. Mr. Selden believes that Miss Lily Bart might:

   A. be older than people say she is.

   B. think he is being too forward.

   C. not want to talk to him.

   D. not remember who he is.

Questions 4-6 ask about Passage B.

4. As it is used in line 23, the word *cheer* most nearly means:

   F. encouragement.

   G. joy.

   H. applaud.

   J. brighten.

5. In the passage, Emma thinks about Miss Taylor's marriage:

   A. right before the wedding.

   B. while talking to Mr. Weston.

   C. after having dinner with her father.

   D. after getting into bed.

6. Mr. Weston's qualities include:

   I. pleasant manners.

   II. unexceptional character.

   III. high self-regard.

   F. I only

   G. I and II only

   H. II and III only

   J. I, II, and III

Questions 7-10 ask about both passages.

7. Both Miss Lily Bart in Passage A and Emma in Passage B:

   A. begin their respective passages without a companion.

   B. lose companions over the course of their respective passages.

   C. reminisce about companions they have lost.

   D. meet new companions.

8. One can infer from the passages that Miss Lily Bart and Emma:

   F. love to go dancing.

   G. both want to meet someone.

   H. have a tendency to get depressed.

   J. would not get along with each other.

9. Both passages are about:

   A. ways to get along without companionship.

   B. relationships that come to abrupt endings.

   C. the excitement of forming a new friendship.

   D. the need for human interaction.

10. According to the passages, Miss Lily Bart and Emma are both:

- **F.** at least in their twenties.
- **G.** city dwellers.
- **H.** waiting for trains.
- **J.** going to attend weddings.

PASSAGE II

SOCIAL SCIENCE: This passage is adapted from a historical essay.

Modern-day ambassadors have amenities in their host countries that anyone would envy. They are usually provided with such luxuries as limousines, mansions, and servants. There is a historic precedent to the manner in which ambassadors are
5 treated. In Europe, for instance, ambassadors have been a part of politics since the Middle Ages. Whenever the rulers of two kingdoms needed to make a peace treaty, trade agreement, or other cooperative alliance, they sent ambassadors to do the job. Because an ambassador was himself a representative of his ruler,
10 he was treated almost like royalty. The ambassador would be given a luxurious place to stay, be invited to fabulous feasts, and be showered with valuable gifts. If the ambassador was skillful enough to strike a deal that pleased both sides, then he might be rewarded with bags of gold to take back home.

15 The first ambassadors who actually stayed in their host countries long-term were not so fortunate. An ambassador's trip to his host country was slow and arduous, taking several weeks. The ambassador traveled on a small ship with several servants, horses, and supplies. Travel by sea was dreadful, and there were
20 often delays resulting from lack of wind or heavy storms. It was only at the end of the fourteen hundreds that rulers first offered permanent appointments to some of the ambassadors, and their decision to do so was practically an afterthought. Prior to this time, once the ambassadors' initial missions were completed,
25 their rulers would just leave them in their host countries to serve as their eyes and ears rather than incurring the costs involved with bringing them back home. However, these first permanent ambassadors found that their hosts were not as hospitable once the "honeymoon" period was over.

30 The size of an ambassador's entourage represented his home country's wealth and the importance of his task. This display of wealth was significant because the other foreign ambassadors would report this information back to their own countries' rulers. Horses were used for transportation, but they were also status
35 symbols, in the way that luxury cars are today. If an ambassador only brought ten horses with him, he would be considered poor. Twenty horses indicated average wealth, and thirty horses would be sure to impress one and all. If an ambassador did not have many horses, then he might make up for the deficiency by wearing
40 some gold chains around his neck. One of these chains could be

worth ten or twenty times more than the ship on which he sailed. Servants were another sign of status. Ambassadors traveling for a specific task often had many servants assisting them with such duties as making travel arrangements, shopping, and tending to
45 the horses. But ambassadors who stayed permanently would have only one or two servants, if that, as their rulers saw them as additional mouths to feed.

Living abroad was expensive, and the letters that the long-term ambassadors wrote home to their rulers often included requests
50 for more money. One of the first permanent ambassadors to England, Dr. Rodrigo Gonzalez de Puebla of Spain, discovered for himself the monetary woes of his occupation. He was originally sent to London by King Ferdinand and Queen Isabella in 1495 to arrange a marriage between their daughter, Katharine, and Arthur,
55 the son of King Henry VII. Although the marriage only lasted six months, de Puebla's stay in England lasted for several years. When his initial funds began to run out, de Puebla stayed at a modest inn that served simple meals, such as meat pies. He often visited the royal court for the sole purpose of enjoying a fine meal. Once,
60 when King Henry VII asked what de Puebla's business was on a particular visit, the king's assistant replied that de Puebla was just there for the food.

A permanent ambassador's principal task was to gather information—in other words, to spy. Such surveillance required a
65 combination of diplomacy and charm, as a good deal of information was exchanged through informal talk among the ambassadors in the court. Popularity was also an important factor; if the king did not like a particular ambassador, then he would not be able to gain access to the court, the center of information. For
70 example, after France invaded Italy during the mid-1490s, everyone in Henry's court avoided the French ambassador.

Gathering reliable information was quite difficult: public statements were not very useful, and private conversations were often full of deceptions. Since the ambassadors often did not
75 understand much of each other's native tongues, they had to depend largely on being able to interpret one another's body language. Upon learning that ambassadors were judging and interpreting his every word and gesture, King Henry VII became less expressive in the court and let his archbishops do most of
80 the talking.

Nevertheless, conversations in the court did not challenge the ambassadors nearly as much as communication with their rulers back home. Letters were the primary means of correspondence, but they took weeks to deliver, were often lost, and
85 occasionally fell into the wrong hands. Sending news and waiting for a reply could take two or three months. Ferdinand and Isabella

CONTINUE

often accused de Puebla of not writing often enough, and told him to send duplicate letters to ensure that they arrived. Sometimes an ambassador's letter was intercepted and read by
90 his hosts, to determine whether the ambassador was making any treacherous plans. Ambassadors tried to avoid giving away critical information by writing part or all of a letter in code. This method of encryption was a relatively new concept—and a flawed one at that, because the ambassadors and their own
95 rulers often could not figure out each other's system of codes. De Puebla, for instance, used Roman numerals for his code words, which confused Ferdinand and Isabella. The king and queen were enraged when de Puebla tried to solve the problem by sending a codebook along with one of his letters.

100 Eventually, after much pleading and complaining, de Puebla and the other first permanent ambassadors were allowed to return home. None of the ambassadors had been content with enduring years of prejudice, subtly spying on their hosts, begging for money from their rulers, and being so far away from their
105 own families, customs, and homes. Despite the drawbacks of ambassadorship, the positions, which were considered invaluable by rulers, continued to be filled. Little by little, as the art of diplomacy and the quality of transportation and communication improved, the role of being a permanent ambassador became
110 an increasingly desirable one.

11. Based on the information in the passage, one can infer that in the late fourteen hundreds, European rulers:

   A. did not allow ambassadors into their royal courts.
   B. made ambassadors do most of their work for them.
   C. paid their permanent ambassadors regularly with bags of gold.
   D. realized it was useful to have their ambassadors stay abroad.

12. The third paragraph (lines 30–47) implies that an ambassador with a small entourage would be perceived as:

   F. having low status.
   G. being admirably thrifty.
   H. being in need of higher pay.
   J. seeking to switch his allegiance to a wealthier country.

13. The author explains that, compared with modern ambassadors, the first permanent ambassadors in Europe:

   A. had fewer horses and servants.
   B. were more dishonest.
   C. had few luxuries.
   D. were treated much better.

14. According to the third paragraph (lines 30–47), an ambassador's entourage included his:

   I. king.
   II. horses.
   III. servants.

   F. I only
   G. II only
   H. III only
   J. II and III only

15. Information in the seventh paragraph (lines 81–99) supports which of these statements?

   A. Encryption of sensitive information was a well-established tradition by the 1400s.
   B. Communication between the early ambassadors and their rulers was slow and unreliable.
   C. King Henry VII read all of de Puebla's letters to see whether he was being lied to.
   D. Ferdinand and Isabella requested that de Puebla send a codebook with his letters.

16. In the fourth paragraph (lines 48–62), the author includes the story about de Puebla visiting King Henry VII to support the idea that:

   F. de Puebla's popularity had declined at Henry's court.
   G. meat pies were de Puebla's favorite dish.
   H. Ferdinand had given de Puebla a promotion.
   J. permanent ambassadors were poorly paid.

17. The last paragraph (lines 100–110) explains that the first permanent ambassadors in Europe were eventually replaced mainly because:

   A. they did not succeed in their tasks.
   B. they did not write letters often enough.
   C. their jobs were politically important.
   D. their hosts asked them to return to their homes.

18. In the second paragraph (lines 15–29), the main idea is that the first permanent ambassadors:

   F. did not enjoy the luxuries that modern-day ambassadors have.
   G. had a difficult time traveling between their homes and their host countries.
   H. had to achieve a specific task before they could return home.
   J. brought along many status symbols, such as horses, servants, and gold chains.

19. The author explains that, for the ambassadors, "gathering reliable information was quite difficult" because:

    I. most official statements were not reliable.
    II. people in the court often lied to each other.
    III. the codes were difficult to understand.

    A. I only
    B. I and II only
    C. II and III only
    D. I, II, and III

20. De Puebla originally went to England to:

    F. have King Henry sign a peace treaty.
    G. spy in the royal court.
    H. request that Katharine get divorced.
    J. arrange a royal marriage.

PASSAGE III

HUMANITIES: This passage is adapted from a scholarly musicological essay.

Morocco has many rich musical traditions stemming from its unique geographical conditions and a long history of intermingled cultures. For the past century, Morocco has attracted musicians and other artists from the west who wanted to learn
5 from the country's creative and hospitable people. For instance, Jimi Hendrix's style of guitar playing was influenced by his travels to Marrakesh and Essaouira, where he discovered the rhythmic music of the Ganawa tribe. The Rolling Stones were fascinated with Morocco's music and made several trips there to hear it.
10 During one of the Stones' stays, Brian Jones recorded an album of village folk music. Jazz musicians such as Pharoah Sanders and Ornette Coleman have also made pilgrimages, in search of Morocco's earthy, trance-inducing rhythms and complex melodies.

15   Morocco is located on the northeastern corner of Africa. It is only a few miles from the southern tip of Spain across the Strait of Gibraltar. Mountain ranges form the "backbone" of the country, running from the northeast to the southwest. Fertile plains stretch from the northern side of these mountains to the
20 Mediterranean Sea and Atlantic Ocean. This area, covered with farmland and several large cities and towns, is the most prosperous part of the country. Although the mountains themselves are quite rugged and rocky, there is plenty of water to support isolated villages of goatherds and fruit orchards. The southern
25 side of the mountains is more arid, with rocky plateaus and several fertile river valleys descending gradually into the Sahara Desert. The river valleys are dotted with towns and villages that get smaller as the rivers dry up along the desert's edge. Several nomadic tribes travel among the villages and desert oases.

30   Throughout the ages, the Berbers have been the largest ethnic group in Morocco. Their ancestors once lived all along the North African coast, until frequent invasions brought foreign rulers to many of the countries, including Morocco. Invading Greeks, Romans, Vandals, and Turks found it all but impossible to control
35 the Berbers who lived in the rugged and isolated mountain ranges. Despite ruling the country, foreigners could not conquer the stubborn Berber spirit. The Romans gave them their name, which eventually evolved into the term "barbarian," although this is a misnomer of such gracious and hospitable people.

40   Beginning in the seventh century, Arab legions invaded Morocco on several occasions. These invasions began to impact the region not only politically, but religiously as well. Eventually, the Berbers and most of the other indigenous tribes became Islamic and adopted some elements of Arabic culture, including
45 classical Arabic music. The strongest Arabic musical influence is found in their lyrics, which often praise Allah or refer to the Koran.

Despite these additional influences, the Berbers were still able to maintain most of their own beliefs and traditions. Traditional Berber music was performed solo or in larger ensembles, some-
50 times accompanied by dancers. Musicians could be found performing in the medina marketplaces in the older parts of towns. The musicians often started a performance with improvisational banter, referring to one another and to people in the gathering crowd. Then they began to warm up their instruments as they
55 continued jesting: drum skins that had been heated over lanterns were thumped, a few chords were played on a flute or a lute, some castanets clacked, or a few dance steps were stomped out. This buildup not only set the dramatic tone for the frenzied music about to be played; it also encouraged the audience to
60 toss out a few more coins.

Tribes of Saharan nomads, such as the Ganawa and the Tuareg, brought the music of West Africa up to Morocco. This rhythmic music traveled with the gold and salt caravans through Timbuktu and up to Marrakesh just across the Atlas Mountains. Their most
65 notable instruments were large, metal, double-castanets clapped between the fingers to make a galloping rhythm. Hand clapping, fast drumming, and harmonized chanting were also common elements of these southern Moroccan tribes.

Morocco's musical traditions were additionally influenced by
70 the country's northern neighbor, Spain. Arabs had lived in southern Spain for several centuries until they were driven out during the Spanish Inquisition. Arab musicians from the Spanish region of Andalucia brought a sophisticated and intricate style

CONTINUE

75 of music back to North Africa. Much of this Andalucian music was played on an oud, an Arabian lute with a pear-shaped body, three rounded soundholes, a short, fretless neck, and five pairs of strings. Andalucian music, with its distinctly western classic
80 sound, had in fact influenced the troubadours who played in the medieval courts of Europe. A good deal of southern European folk music, such as flamenco, was also influenced by Andalucian music.

Today many Moroccan musicians adeptly blend these various
85 musical styles, perhaps playing an Andalucian melody over a Ganawa rhythm while chanting in praise of Allah. Their lively mixes are as naturally eclectic as the rest of Moroccan culture. A few musicians, such as Nouamane Lahlou, have taken practically the reverse path of Jimi Hendrix and Ornette Coleman, blending
90 their Moroccan musical traditions with modern styles. Yet the result is similar: they have created popular songs that have a more international appeal.

21. The passage indicates that the Arab legions who invaded Morocco:

A. were unable to control the Berber people in the mountainous regions.

B. were the first group to have a significant cultural impact on the Berbers.

C. brought the first musical traditions to the people of Morocco.

D. arrived from the Andalucian region of southern Spain.

22. According to the passage, traditional Berber music might include which of the following instruments?

I. castanets
II. an oud
III. drums

F. I only
G. I and II only
H. I and III only
J. I, II, and III

23. Andalucian music is described as differing from the music of the Ganawa people in that it:

A. primarily uses double castanets.
B. has a galloping rhythm to it.
C. comes from West Africa.
D. sounds similar to classical music.

24. The passage explains that many popular musicians in the west:

F. once gathered in Marrakesh to play a music festival.
G. have invited Moroccan musicians to perform with them.
H. have traveled to Morocco to learn more about its music.
J. were first inspired to play music after visiting Morocco.

25. Which of these statements is supported by information from the second paragraph (lines 15–29)?

A. Morocco has a diverse range of geographical features and climates.
B. Most Moroccans live in small villages in the countryside.
C. Moroccan music has a wide variety of influences and styles.
D. Berbers have lived in Morocco for longer than any other ethnic group.

26. As it is used in line 5, the word *hospitable* most nearly means:

F. hostile.
G. talented.
H. dominant.
J. friendly.

27. The passage states that medieval court music and flamenco were influenced by:

A. Berber music.
B. Andalucian music.
C. Arabian music.
D. Tuareg music.

28. The main point of the third paragraph (lines 30–39) is that the Berber people in Morocco:

F. were able to preserve their culture despite many invasions.
G. once invaded many other North African countries.
H. mainly lived in the isolated mountain ranges.
J. like to get the crowd excited before they perform their music.

29. It can be inferred from the passage that a current trend in Moroccan music is to:

A. avoid mixing musical styles from different geographical regions.
B. mimic the sound of western artists.
C. blend traditional and modern musical styles.
D. concentrate on vocal, rather than instrumental, music.

30. The author suggests that Berber "musicians often started a performance with improvisational banter" (lines 52–53) to:

    F. show praise for Allah.
    G. compete with other musicians.
    H. warm up their instruments.
    J. attract a paying audience.

PASSAGE IV

NATURAL SCIENCE: This passage is adapted from an article in a popular scientific publication.

A heartbeat is the main sound made by a complicated function that pumps the heart tens of thousands of times per day. The heart contains four chambers that act as two pumps. The *right atrium* and the *right ventricle* are two chambers that form one

5 of the pumps. The right atrium receives oxygen-poor (blue) blood from the body and pumps it into the right ventricle. Then the right ventricle sends these blue blood cells to the lungs to absorb more oxygen. The other pump consists of the *left atrium* and the *left ventricle*. The left atrium receives oxygen-rich (red)

10 blood from the lungs and pumps it into the left ventricle. Then the left ventricle sends the red blood cells to nourish the rest of the body.

The two ventricles expand and contract in unison, each receiving and pumping the same amount of blood with each

15 heartbeat. The heart chambers have one-way valves that allow blood to flow through the heart in only one direction. The *cardiac muscle* of the heart works separately from the nervous system, due to its own natural pacemaker that sets the pace of the heartbeat. These contractions are regulated by the heart's elec-

20 trical conducting system, which consists primarily of three sets of specialized muscle tissues.

The "ignition key" to the heart's electrical conducting system is its natural pacemaker, the *sinoatrial node (SA node)*. The SA node is able to set the normal pace of the heart's contractions

25 without monitoring by the central nervous system; skeletal muscles receive their electrical signals from the central nervous system, but the SA node tells the heart to beat at a steady rate. Since the SA node dictates the heartbeat, the heart will still maintain a beat during a heart transplant, even though it is not

30 connected to a body. This steady rate is often modified according to the body's needs by the *cardioregulatory center*, which is located near the top of the spinal cord in the *medulla oblongata*. The cardioregulatory center can send signals to speed up the heart during strenuous activity, or to slow the rate down while

35 the body is resting.

The SA node is located on the wall of the right atrium, where it originates the electrochemical stimulation for the heart. It depolarizes itself about 70-80 times per minute. Each time it does so, an electrochemical signal is sent to the adjacent atrial

40 muscle cells, depolarizing them as well. This wave of electrical conduction spreads through all of the muscle cells of the right atrium, then to the muscle cells of the left atrium, signaling them to contract.

This atrial conduction also races along "highways" from the

45 SA node to the *atrioventricular node* (AV node). The AV node is located at the base of the right atrium, where it connects to the right ventricle. The AV node controls the contractions of the ventricles, and does so by delaying the signals from the SA node by a fraction of a second. This delay allows the atria to contract,

50 pushing more blood into the relaxed ventricles; the ventricles take the opportunity to fill with blood before the signal finally reaches them, causing them to contract and pump the blood back out of the heart. If the SA node becomes diseased or damaged, then the AV node can take over as the heart's pace-

55 maker, though the heart will beat at a slower rate of about 40-50 beats per minute.

Another set of "highways" connects the AV node to the *AV bundle*. The AV bundle branches into two strips, one going down the length of each ventricle. From the AV bundle, the electro-

60 chemical signal to contract is distributed uniformly across the cells of the ventricles, ensuring regular pumping of the blood. If neither the SA node nor the AV node is functioning properly, then the AV bundle may act as a backup pacemaker, but its rhythm is only 20-40 beats per minute. In this case, the heart

65 will probably need to have an artificial pacemaker connected to it as well.

An artificial pacemaker is an electronic device that takes over the role of the SA node, providing electric signals to regulate the pace of the heart's contractions. An artificial pacemaker is

70 worn on the chest, with its electrical leads implanted into the heart. A simple operation involves passing these leads through the patient's jugular vein, which forms a direct path down to the right atrium and right ventricle. The ends of the leads send the electrical signals to the heart at a steady pace.

75 There are three basic types of artificial pacemakers. One type acts only as a backup system to the heart's natural pacemaker, sending signals to the heart only when it detects that the heartbeat is slower than the preset rate on the device. Another type of device functions regularly, delivering signals to the heart

80 at a constant, preset rate. The third type of artificial pacemaker

CONTINUE

can receive impulse signals from the SA node. Whenever the SA node fails to release its own electrochemical signals, then the device sends signals at a steady rate.

31. The passage suggests that the SA node is like an "ignition key" (line 22) because the node:

    A. sends the initial signal telling the heart's muscles to contract.
    B. turns the heart on during activity and turns it off during rest.
    C. opens the heart's valves to let blood in, then locks them shut again.
    D. generates body heat in the heart that is transferred to other organs.

32. The passage states that the AV node delays the signal it sends to the:

    F. lungs.
    G. brain.
    H. ventricles.
    J. atria.

33. According to the passage, if an SA node is failing, its function may be taken over by:

    I. the AV node.
    II. the AV bundle.
    III. an artificial pacemaker.

    A. III only
    B. I and II only
    C. I and III only
    D. I, II, and III

34. According to the first paragraph (lines 1–12), the heart is made up of:

    F. two main chambers.
    G. four main chambers.
    H. two chambers and four pumps.
    J. four chambers, an atrium, and a ventricle.

35. According to the passage, cardiac muscles differ from skeletal muscles mainly because they are:

    A. smaller and more firmly packed together.
    B. directly attached to the veins and arteries.
    C. not all receiving signals simultaneously.
    D. not controlled by the central nervous system.

36. As defined by the passage, the AV node:

    I. is located at the base of the right atrium.
    II. controls the contractions of the ventricles.
    III. branches into two strips that go down the ventricles.

    F. II only
    G. I and II only
    H. I and III only
    J. II and III only

37. The first two paragraphs mainly cover the:

    A. purpose of heart transplant operations.
    B. different types of artificial pacemakers.
    C. electrical conducting system of the heart.
    D. basic functions of the heart.

38. According to the passage, an artificial pacemaker is usually needed when the heart rate:

    F. falls below 70-80 beats per minute.
    G. falls below 40-50 beats per minute.
    H. falls below 20-40 beats per minute.
    J. is not regulated by the medulla oblongata.

39. The passage mentions that the blue blood cells passing through the heart:

    A. carry too much oxygen.
    B. carry very little oxygen.
    C. are coming from the lungs.
    D. are going to the rest of the body.

40. All three of the basic types of artificial pacemakers:

    F. send electric signals that make the heart contract.
    G. monitor the activity of the SA node.
    H. function constantly to keep the heart beating.
    J. function only when the SA node fails.

STOP

SCIENCE TEST

35 Minutes—40 Questions

DIRECTIONS: There are seven passages in this test. Each passage is followed by several questions. Read each passage, choose the best answer, and fill in the corresponding circle on the answer sheet. You may refer back to the passages at any time.

Remember, you are NOT allowed to use a calculator on this test.

PASSAGE I

Diabetes, a disease in which the body does not produce or properly use insulin to convert sugar into usable energy, is marked by elevated blood sugar levels. A *glycated hemoglobin* test reveals a person's average blood sugar level for the past three months. A result of 5% or more is considered high. A glycated hemoglobin reading above 7% is a strong indicator of diabetes.

Table 1 indicates the breakdown of glycated hemoglobin levels among 100 non-diabetics tested.

Table 1	
Glycated Hemoglobin Reading	**Number of Test Subjects**
3%	12
4%	21
5%	19
6%	29
7%	17
8%	2
9%	0

time: 2:46

Scientists estimated the risk of developing cardiovascular disease associated with various glycated hemoglobin levels, first among a group of non-diabetics, and then among a group of diabetics. The results are represented in Figure 1.

Figure 1

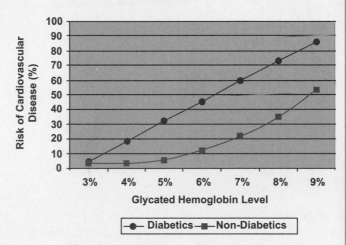

1. According to the data in Figure 1, as glycated hemoglobin levels increase, the risk of cardiovascular disease generally increases for:

   A. diabetics but not for non-diabetics.
   B. non-diabetics but not for diabetics.
   C. both diabetics and non-diabetics.
   D. neither diabetics nor non-diabetics.

2. A non-diabetic man's risk of cardiovascular disease is estimated to be approximately 70%. If the trend depicted in Figure 1 holds true, one could predict that his glycated hemoglobin level is:

   F. less than 5%.
   G. 7%.
   H. 9%.
   J. greater than 9%.

CONTINUE

3. The majority of the test subjects represented in Table 1:

   A. have high glycated hemoglobin levels.
   B. are probably diabetics.
   C. have a risk of cardiovascular disease greater than 10%.
   D. do not have high glycated hemoglobin levels.

4. Figure 1 indicates that the change in the risk of cardiovascular disease associated with each 1% increase in glycated hemoglobin level is:

   F. always greater for non-diabetics than for diabetics.
   G. more consistent for diabetics than for non-diabetics.
   H. positive for diabetics and negative for non-diabetics.
   J. most similar for diabetics and non-diabetics at the 6% glycated hemoglobin level and below.

5. The information in Table 1 suggests that:

   A. non-diabetics are at a lower risk for cardiovascular disease than are diabetics.
   B. a glycated hemoglobin test is not a perfectly reliable predictor of diabetes.
   C. none of the subjects tested has a risk of developing diabetes in the near future.
   D. cardiovascular disease has a positive correlation with glycated hemoglobin levels.

PASSAGE II

In the nineteenth century, Rocky Mountain locusts regularly ravaged the plains of the western United States, from California east to Minnesota and south to Texas. An 1875 swarm invaded the Great Plains at half a mile high, 110 miles wide, and 1,800 miles long, containing an estimated 3.5 trillion locusts. This largest locust swarm in recorded history laid siege to crops, animals, and property, leaving a vast trail of destruction in its wake. Twenty-eight years later, this fearsome pest had disappeared entirely, with the last known live Rocky Mountain locust observed in 1902. Several theories attempt to account for this species' sudden disappearance.

Ecological Changes Theory

Large-scale changes in the ecology of the Great Plains region caused the extinction of the Rocky Mountain locust. The once-plentiful bison created and maintained pools and small ponds known as *wallows*, which provided water and minerals for the bison herd. These wallows also served as shelter and nourishment centers for many other species. The bison were largely eradicated from the western United States, and with them disappeared the wallows that provided a critical habitat for the locusts. Moreover, large changes in regional climate also altered the locusts' prairie habitats. These changes in climate and the bison population altered the ecosystem to the point that the Rocky Mountain locust could no longer survive.

Human Intervention Theory

Small-scale but deeply pervasive interventions by humans into the Great Plains environment brought about the extinction of the Rocky Mountain locust. In between massive swarms every seven to twelve years, the locusts retreated to fertile river valleys scattered throughout the west. Settlers began cultivating these same valleys for their own needs, introducing insect-eating birds and habitat-altering crops. They raised cattle that stomped the ground, disrupting locust nests, and they eradicated the beaver population, causing the elimination of dams and the subsequent flooding of locust egg sanctuaries. In addition, field plowing uncovered and destroyed many hundreds of locust egg masses. Thus, while unsuccessfully attempting to combat the scourge with fire and primitive weapons, the settlers inadvertently brought about the extinction of the Rocky Mountain locust by disrupting the heart of its favored breeding grounds.

Concealment Theory

This theory posits that the Rocky Mountain locust is not extinct but rather concealed from humans in hidden habitats. Some adherents to this theory believe that Rocky Mountain locusts remain hidden because biological changes and environmental adaptations have eliminated the species' ability to swarm. Others contend that certain factors brought about by humans have temporarily made conditions non-conducive to swarming, but that Rocky Mountain locusts may one day swarm again.

6. Which of the following statements most accurately reflects the differences among the three theories presented?

   F. The Concealment Theory and the Human Intervention Theory differ most from the Ecological Changes Theory.
   G. The Human Intervention Theory and the Ecological Changes Theory differ most from the Concealment Theory.
   H. The Ecological Changes Theory and the Concealment Theory differ most from the Human Intervention Theory.
   J. The differences among the theories are equal in magnitude.

7. The facts of the Human Intervention Theory suggest that beavers were known to:

   A. help Rocky Mountain locusts by creating conditions favorable to locust offspring.

   B. help the settlers by killing Rocky Mountain locusts.

   C. hurt Rocky Mountain locusts by flooding their egg sanctuaries.

   D. hurt the settlers by creating ponds that nourished Rocky Mountain locusts.

8. Proponents of the Human Intervention Theory could reasonably argue that part of the Ecological Changes Theory supports their position as long as they can show that:

   F. humans had no control over the factors cited in the Ecological Changes Theory.

   G. the Rocky Mountain locust is, in fact, not extinct but merely hidden from human observation.

   H. the environment of the western United States was not impacted by settlers in the nineteenth century.

   J. hunters in the nineteenth century helped to bring about the decline in the bison population.

9. According to the passage, some proponents of the Concealment Theory would disagree with other proponents of that theory regarding which of the following assertions?

   A. The Rocky Mountain locust still exists.

   B. The Rocky Mountain locust is capable of swarming again.

   C. Human intervention was the cause of the Rocky Mountain locust's extinction.

   D. The Rocky Mountain locust is currently swarming in some region undetected by humans.

10. It can be inferred that some adherents to the Concealment Theory would disagree with supporters of the Human Intervention Theory with regard to whether:

   F. human activities have influenced the condition of the Rocky Mountain locust.

   G. the effects on the Rocky Mountain locust, as a result of activities cited in the Human Intervention Theory, are reversible.

   H. the activities outlined in the Human Intervention Theory actually took place.

   J. the depletion of bison wallows contributed to the disappearance of the Rocky Mountain locust.

11. Monarch butterflies have been extremely populous over the entire United States, but congregate in remote forests of Mexico during the winter months. These areas have seen large increases in logging activities, and now the Monarch butterfly is nearing extinction.

Concerning the fate of the Rocky Mountain locust, this evidence supports:

   A. none of the theories presented in the passage.

   B. the Concealment Theory, because it shows that although the Monarch butterfly is endangered, it is not yet fully extinct.

   C. the Ecological Changes Theory, because it demonstrates how changes to an ecosystem, brought about by alterations in the population or behavior of one species, may affect the survival of another species.

   D. the Human Intervention Theory, because it bolsters the notion that a species may become particularly vulnerable to human actions during a certain phase of its life cycle.

12. In terms of its relationship to the Rocky Mountain locust, the bison described in the Ecological Changes Theory is most analogous to the:

   F. cattle described in the Human Intervention Theory.

   G. settlers described in the Human Intervention Theory.

   H. beavers described in the Human Intervention Theory.

   J. birds described in the Human Intervention Theory.

PASSAGE III

Heart rate, a measure of the number of heart beats per minute, rises as the body strives to meet the demands of physical activity. Fitness generally increases as one's resting heart rate decreases and as the degree of change in heart rate during exercise increases. *Recovery rate* is the decrease in the number of beats per minute calculated for each minute following the cessation of physical activity, until heart rate returns to normal resting levels. Greater fitness correlates with higher recovery rates.

Scientists conducted three studies to investigate how heart rate fluctuates during and after two kinds of physical activity.

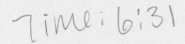

CONTINUE

Study 1

A high school swimmer and a high school basketball player participated for 10 continuous minutes in their respective sports, while an electronic device measured their heart rates in beats per minute (bpm) over the course of their exertions. Both began with their heart rate at normal resting levels. Both athletes ceased physical activity after 10 minutes, whereupon the devices continued to monitor their heart rates during 5 minutes of subsequent inactivity. The results are indicated in Figure 1.

FIGURE 1

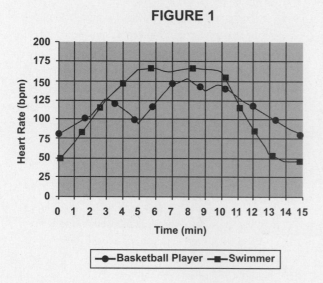

Study 2

Next, researchers analyzed a videotape of the basketball player's recorded activities during Study 1 and classified his movements into the following categories: walking; jogging; sprinting; shuffling (slight intense movements back and forth or side to side); and jumping. Figure 2 shows the percentage of time that the basketball player performed each kind of movement.

FIGURE 2

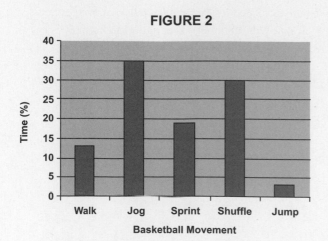

Study 3

Researchers then instructed the athletes to repeat the exercise according to the same parameters observed in Study 1, except this time with the swimmer playing basketball and the basketball player swimming. The athletes' heart rates after 10 minutes, and the decreases in their heart rates during the 5 minutes following that, are recorded in Table 1.

Table 1

	Basketball Player Swimming	Swimmer Playing Basketball
Heart rate after 10 minutes	145	150
Decrease in heart rate between 10 and 11 minutes	15	40
Decrease in heart rate between 11 and 12 minutes	15	35
Decrease in heart rate between 12 and 13 minutes	11	30
Decrease in heart rate between 13 and 14 minutes	10	0
Decrease in heart rate between 14 and 15 minutes	10	0

13. The results of Study 2 are most relevant to an explanation of:

    A. why the basketball player's heart rate decreases after swimming, as noted in Table 1.

    B. why there is a difference between the basketball player's decreased heart rate following swimming and the swimmer's decreased heart rate following basketball.

    C. the difference between the general shapes of the line graphs from minutes 0-10 in Figure 1.

    D. the basketball player's fitness level.

14. The results of Study 1 suggest that:

    F. the swimmer is more fit than the basketball player.

    G. the basketball player is more fit than the swimmer.

    H. swimming is a more strenuous activity than basketball.

    J. basketball is a more strenuous activity than swimming.

Time: 4:51

15. The researchers most likely designed Study 3 to investigate whether:

- **A.** swimmers are generally more fit than basketball players.
- **B.** swimmers are better at basketball than basketball players are at swimming.
- **C.** recovery rates are influenced by the type of physical activity in which one engages.
- **D.** the degree of change in heart rate during exercise is related to overall fitness.

16. The swimmer's recovery rate in the first minute after he stopped swimming is:

- **F.** less than 25 bpm.
- **G.** more than 50 bpm.
- **H.** equal to the basketball player's recovery rate in the first minute after he stopped playing basketball.
- **J.** greater than his recovery rate between minutes 13 and 14.

17. The zeros in Table 1 indicate that the:

- **A.** swimmer is in worse physical condition than the basketball player.
- **B.** swimmer's heart stopped three minutes after he had stopped playing basketball.
- **C.** swimmer disobeyed instructions and played basketball for 13 minutes instead of for 10 minutes.
- **D.** swimmer's heart rate had returned to normal resting levels by 3 minutes after he finished playing basketball.

18. In order to compare the relative demands placed on the heart by swimming and basketball, it would be most fruitful for scientists to study the heart rates of:

- **F.** professional swimmers and professional basketball players while they engaged in their respective sports.
- **G.** a large and diverse cross-section of the population while they both swam and played basketball.
- **H.** the same two athletes during numerous additional trials of the kind described in Study 1.
- **J.** the same two athletes competing against one another in swimming and basketball.

PASSAGE IV

Mitochondria are the source of energy within every living cell. Scientists conducted studies on a wasp species known as the European beewolf to investigate the mitochondria's role in species survival.

Study 1

Upon observing beewolf behavior, researchers noted that beewolves attack larger honeybees, which they sting, paralyze, and then feed to their young. The researchers tracked the breeding and hunting activities of six beewolves and compiled their findings in Table 1.

Table 1		
Beewolf	**Number of Offspring**	**Average number of honeybees fed to each offspring**
A	22	3
B	7	1
C	35	4
D	12	2
E	5	1
F	29	4

Study 2

The researchers then calculated, for 100 beewolves, the density of folded membranes inside the mitochondria of flight muscles. They were able to establish a general relationship between the density of these membranes and mitochondrial energy output (see Figure 1).

FIGURE 1

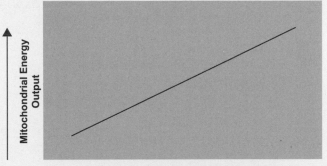

Mitochondrial Energy Output

Density of Flight Muscle Mitochondrial Membranes

CONTINUE

Study 3

Next the researchers measured the density of flight muscle mitochondrial membranes, expressed in folds per cubic centimeter (f/cc), of the original six beewolves observed in Study 1. The results are depicted in Table 2.

Table 2	
Beewolf	**Density of Flight Muscle Mitochondrial Membranes (f/cc)**
A	78
B	9
C	168
D	30
E	6
F	140

19. The main purpose of the studies described is to investigate a relationship between:

    A. honeybees and beewolves.
    B. mitochondrial density and energy output.
    C. mitochondrial energy output and species survival.
    D. flight muscles and honeybee offspring.

20. The results of the studies suggest that mitochondrial energy output is directly related to:

    F. the honeybee-hunting proficiency of beewolves.
    G. the number of flight muscles a beewolf possesses.
    H. a beewolf's risk of being killed by a honeybee.
    J. the mortality rate of beewolf offspring.

21. Study 1 provides information regarding all of the following EXCEPT the:

    A. number of honeybees killed by the observed beewolves.
    B. energy level of the observed beewolves.
    C. fighting methods of the observed beewolves.
    D. breeding statistics for the observed beewolves.

22. The result of Study 2 has what significance in the context of the overall investigation?

    F. It undermines the basis for speculating that mitochondrial energy output is related to species survival.
    G. It depicts a direct correlation between mitochondrial energy and species survival.
    H. It enables the data in Study 3 to indicate the relative mitochondrial energy output of the beewolves observed in Study 1.
    J. It determines the density of flight muscle mitochondrial membranes of the beewolves observed in Study 1.

23. If the researchers conclude from the studies' results that mitochondrial energy output is directly related to species survival, this conclusion would be most strengthened by a further study showing that:

    A. the density of flight muscle mitochondrial membranes is directly related to mitochondrial energy output.
    B. beewolf species survival is enhanced in proportion to the volume and nourishment of offspring.
    C. the density of honeybee mitochondrial membranes is equal to or greater than that of beewolves.
    D. beewolves with higher mitochondrial energy output tend to have fewer offspring than beewolves with lower mitochondrial energy output.

24. Scientists studying a different beewolf, beewolf G, found that it killed 25 honeybees to feed to its offspring. In accordance with the study results, one can predict that beewolf G has:

    F. less mitochondrial energy than beewolf B.
    G. more folds per cubic centimeter in its flight muscle mitochondrial membranes than beewolf A.
    H. flight muscle mitochondrial membranes with a density between 90 and 120 f/cc.
    J. flight muscle mitochondrial membranes with a density between 20 and 50 f/cc.

PASSAGE V

A *mineral* is a naturally occurring inorganic solid with a definite chemical composition and an ordered atomic arrangement. Minerals are composed of elements combined in various proportions. Figure 1 indicates the percentage amounts of five elements—magnesium (Mg), aluminum (Al), hydrogen (H), sulfur (S), and oxygen (O)—contained in six different minerals.

FIGURE 1

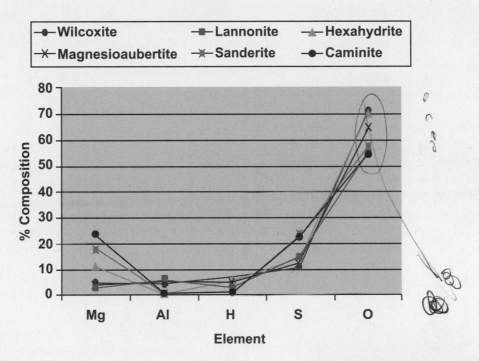

25. Approximately what percentage of caminite is made up of oxygen?

 A. 45%
 B. 50%
 C. 55%
 D. 60%

26. Which of the following elements accounts for the most consistent percentage composition among the six minerals listed?

 F. Magnesium
 G. Hydrogen
 H. Sulfur
 J. Oxygen

27. The lines in Figure 1 descending to meet the *x*-axis signify the:

 A. absence of aluminum in three minerals.
 B. presence of magnesium in three minerals.
 C. absence of hydrogen in two minerals.
 D. presence of oxygen in six minerals.

28. Which of the following minerals has the greatest percentage composition consisting of elements other than those represented in the graph?

 F. Hexahydrite
 G. Caminite
 H. Lannonite
 J. Sanderite

29. If a single additional element were added to the graph to the right of oxygen on the *x*-axis, one would expect which of the following to emerge on the line graphs between oxygen and the new element?

 A. A slightly upward line
 B. A horizontal line
 C. An upward line followed by a downward line
 D. A steep downward line

CONTINUE

PASSAGE VI

The rubbing between solid objects is called *friction*, while the rubbing between a solid object and a liquid or gas is called *drag*. Each produces a resistance force, measured in newtons (N), that works against the momentum of moving objects subjected to these forces. Both friction and drag produce heat. Researchers performed the following experiments to investigate the various properties of and relationships between these phenomena.

Experiment 1

A 20-kg box was placed on top of a long, inclined ramp and released such that it slid down the ramp, ranging in velocity from 0 km/hr at the top of the ramp to 30 km/hr at the bottom. A monitoring device was positioned to record the friction resistance force slowing the box's descent at five different velocities during five different trials. A boat on a river also accelerated from 0 km/hr to 30 km/hr, and the drag resistance force impeding its progress was measured during the course of five trials at the same five velocities at which the box friction was measured. The results are depicted in Figure 1.

FIGURE 1

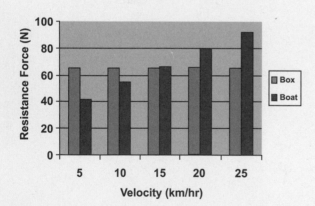

Experiment 2

Researchers repeated the ramp and box experiment, replacing the original box with a 10-kg box, a 30-kg box, and a 40-kg box. The friction resistance force working against each box was recorded at the point each attained a velocity of 20 km/hr. Moreover, the level of heat generated at that point was measured. The results are noted in Table 1.

Table 1		
Box	Friction Resistance Force	Heat Generated
10 kg	55 N	3.5°C
30 kg	75 N	10.5°C
40 kg	85 N	14°C

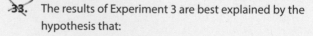

20 km/hr

Experiment 3

The ramp used in Experiment 1 was coated with a layer of sand and the original 20-kg box was released from the same spot, reaching a velocity of 18 km/hr at the bottom of the ramp. The sand was then fully cleared away and running water was sprayed down the ramp as the same box was again released from the same spot, this time achieving a velocity of 39 km/hr at the bottom.

30. When the box in Experiment 1 attained a velocity of 20 km/hr, one can deduce that the heat generated at that point would be closest to which of the following?

    F. 2.5°C
    G. 7°C
    H. 12°C
    J. 16.5°C

31. Experiment 2 demonstrates a positive correlation between:

    A. velocity and drag.
    B. weight and drag.
    C. heat and weight.
    D. friction and velocity.

32. It can be concluded from the investigation that friction differs from drag in that friction:

    F. produces a resistance force.
    G. produces heat.
    H. varies with weight.
    J. does not vary with velocity.

33. The results of Experiment 3 are best explained by the hypothesis that:

    A. both water and sand decrease the resistance force between the ramp and the box.
    B. both water and sand increase the resistance force between the ramp and the box.
    C. sand decreases the resistance force between the ramp and the box, while water increases it.
    D. water decreases the resistance force between the ramp and the box, while sand increases it.

English Test

1. Ⓐ Ⓑ Ⓒ Ⓓ	16. Ⓕ Ⓖ Ⓗ Ⓙ	31. Ⓐ Ⓑ Ⓒ Ⓓ	46. Ⓕ Ⓖ Ⓗ Ⓙ	61. Ⓐ Ⓑ Ⓒ Ⓓ
2. Ⓕ Ⓖ Ⓗ Ⓙ	17. Ⓐ Ⓑ Ⓒ Ⓓ	32. Ⓕ Ⓖ Ⓗ Ⓙ	47. Ⓐ Ⓑ Ⓒ Ⓓ	62. Ⓕ Ⓖ Ⓗ Ⓙ
3. Ⓐ Ⓑ Ⓒ Ⓓ	18. Ⓕ Ⓖ Ⓗ Ⓙ	33. Ⓐ Ⓑ Ⓒ Ⓓ	48. Ⓕ Ⓖ Ⓗ Ⓙ	63. Ⓐ Ⓑ Ⓒ Ⓓ
4. Ⓕ Ⓖ Ⓗ Ⓙ	19. Ⓐ Ⓑ Ⓒ Ⓓ	34. Ⓕ Ⓖ Ⓗ Ⓙ	49. Ⓐ Ⓑ Ⓒ Ⓓ	64. Ⓕ Ⓖ Ⓗ Ⓙ
5. Ⓐ Ⓑ Ⓒ Ⓓ	20. Ⓕ Ⓖ Ⓗ Ⓙ	35. Ⓐ Ⓑ Ⓒ Ⓓ	50. Ⓕ Ⓖ Ⓗ Ⓙ	65. Ⓐ Ⓑ Ⓒ Ⓓ
6. Ⓕ Ⓖ Ⓗ Ⓙ	21. Ⓐ Ⓑ Ⓒ Ⓓ	36. Ⓕ Ⓖ Ⓗ Ⓙ	51. Ⓐ Ⓑ Ⓒ Ⓓ	66. Ⓕ Ⓖ Ⓗ Ⓙ
7. Ⓐ Ⓑ Ⓒ Ⓓ	22. Ⓕ Ⓖ Ⓗ Ⓙ	37. Ⓐ Ⓑ Ⓒ Ⓓ	52. Ⓕ Ⓖ Ⓗ Ⓙ	67. Ⓐ Ⓑ Ⓒ Ⓓ
8. Ⓕ Ⓖ Ⓗ Ⓙ	23. Ⓐ Ⓑ Ⓒ Ⓓ	38. Ⓕ Ⓖ Ⓗ Ⓙ	53. Ⓐ Ⓑ Ⓒ Ⓓ	68. Ⓕ Ⓖ Ⓗ Ⓙ
9. Ⓐ Ⓑ Ⓒ Ⓓ	24. Ⓕ Ⓖ Ⓗ Ⓙ	39. Ⓐ Ⓑ Ⓒ Ⓓ	54. Ⓕ Ⓖ Ⓗ Ⓙ	69. Ⓐ Ⓑ Ⓒ Ⓓ
10. Ⓕ Ⓖ Ⓗ Ⓙ	25. Ⓐ Ⓑ Ⓒ Ⓓ	40. Ⓕ Ⓖ Ⓗ Ⓙ	55. Ⓐ Ⓑ Ⓒ Ⓓ	70. Ⓕ Ⓖ Ⓗ Ⓙ
11. Ⓐ Ⓑ Ⓒ Ⓓ	26. Ⓕ Ⓖ Ⓗ Ⓙ	41. Ⓐ Ⓑ Ⓒ Ⓓ	56. Ⓕ Ⓖ Ⓗ Ⓙ	71. Ⓐ Ⓑ Ⓒ Ⓓ
12. Ⓕ Ⓖ Ⓗ Ⓙ	27. Ⓐ Ⓑ Ⓒ Ⓓ	42. Ⓕ Ⓖ Ⓗ Ⓙ	57. Ⓐ Ⓑ Ⓒ Ⓓ	72. Ⓕ Ⓖ Ⓗ Ⓙ
13. Ⓐ Ⓑ Ⓒ Ⓓ	28. Ⓕ Ⓖ Ⓗ Ⓙ	43. Ⓐ Ⓑ Ⓒ Ⓓ	58. Ⓕ Ⓖ Ⓗ Ⓙ	73. Ⓐ Ⓑ Ⓒ Ⓓ
14. Ⓕ Ⓖ Ⓗ Ⓙ	29. Ⓐ Ⓑ Ⓒ Ⓓ	44. Ⓕ Ⓖ Ⓗ Ⓙ	59. Ⓐ Ⓑ Ⓒ Ⓓ	74. Ⓕ Ⓖ Ⓗ Ⓙ
15. Ⓐ Ⓑ Ⓒ Ⓓ	30. Ⓕ Ⓖ Ⓗ Ⓙ	45. Ⓐ Ⓑ Ⓒ Ⓓ	60. Ⓕ Ⓖ Ⓗ Ⓙ	75. Ⓐ Ⓑ Ⓒ Ⓓ

Math Test

1. Ⓐ Ⓑ Ⓒ Ⓓ Ⓔ	16. Ⓕ Ⓖ Ⓗ Ⓙ Ⓚ	31. Ⓐ Ⓑ Ⓒ Ⓓ Ⓔ	46. Ⓕ Ⓖ Ⓗ Ⓙ Ⓚ
2. Ⓕ Ⓖ Ⓗ Ⓙ Ⓚ	17. Ⓐ Ⓑ Ⓒ Ⓓ Ⓔ	32. Ⓕ Ⓖ Ⓗ Ⓙ Ⓚ	47. Ⓐ Ⓑ Ⓒ Ⓓ Ⓔ
3. Ⓐ Ⓑ Ⓒ Ⓓ Ⓔ	18. Ⓕ Ⓖ Ⓗ Ⓙ Ⓚ	33. Ⓐ Ⓑ Ⓒ Ⓓ Ⓔ	48. Ⓕ Ⓖ Ⓗ Ⓙ Ⓚ
4. Ⓕ Ⓖ Ⓗ Ⓙ Ⓚ	19. Ⓐ Ⓑ Ⓒ Ⓓ Ⓔ	34. Ⓕ Ⓖ Ⓗ Ⓙ Ⓚ	49. Ⓐ Ⓑ Ⓒ Ⓓ Ⓔ
5. Ⓐ Ⓑ Ⓒ Ⓓ Ⓔ	20. Ⓕ Ⓖ Ⓗ Ⓙ Ⓚ	35. Ⓐ Ⓑ Ⓒ Ⓓ Ⓔ	50. Ⓕ Ⓖ Ⓗ Ⓙ Ⓚ
6. Ⓕ Ⓖ Ⓗ Ⓙ Ⓚ	21. Ⓐ Ⓑ Ⓒ Ⓓ Ⓔ	36. Ⓕ Ⓖ Ⓗ Ⓙ Ⓚ	51. Ⓐ Ⓑ Ⓒ Ⓓ Ⓔ
7. Ⓐ Ⓑ Ⓒ Ⓓ Ⓔ	22. Ⓕ Ⓖ Ⓗ Ⓙ Ⓚ	37. Ⓐ Ⓑ Ⓒ Ⓓ Ⓔ	52. Ⓕ Ⓖ Ⓗ Ⓙ Ⓚ
8. Ⓕ Ⓖ Ⓗ Ⓙ Ⓚ	23. Ⓐ Ⓑ Ⓒ Ⓓ Ⓔ	38. Ⓕ Ⓖ Ⓗ Ⓙ Ⓚ	53. Ⓐ Ⓑ Ⓒ Ⓓ Ⓔ
9. Ⓐ Ⓑ Ⓒ Ⓓ Ⓔ	24. Ⓕ Ⓖ Ⓗ Ⓙ Ⓚ	39. Ⓐ Ⓑ Ⓒ Ⓓ Ⓔ	54. Ⓕ Ⓖ Ⓗ Ⓙ Ⓚ
10. Ⓕ Ⓖ Ⓗ Ⓙ Ⓚ	25. Ⓐ Ⓑ Ⓒ Ⓓ Ⓔ	40. Ⓕ Ⓖ Ⓗ Ⓙ Ⓚ	55. Ⓐ Ⓑ Ⓒ Ⓓ Ⓔ
11. Ⓐ Ⓑ Ⓒ Ⓓ Ⓔ	26. Ⓕ Ⓖ Ⓗ Ⓙ Ⓚ	41. Ⓐ Ⓑ Ⓒ Ⓓ Ⓔ	56. Ⓕ Ⓖ Ⓗ Ⓙ Ⓚ
12. Ⓕ Ⓖ Ⓗ Ⓙ Ⓚ	27. Ⓐ Ⓑ Ⓒ Ⓓ Ⓔ	42. Ⓕ Ⓖ Ⓗ Ⓙ Ⓚ	57. Ⓐ Ⓑ Ⓒ Ⓓ Ⓔ
13. Ⓐ Ⓑ Ⓒ Ⓓ Ⓔ	28. Ⓕ Ⓖ Ⓗ Ⓙ Ⓚ	43. Ⓐ Ⓑ Ⓒ Ⓓ Ⓔ	58. Ⓕ Ⓖ Ⓗ Ⓙ Ⓚ
14. Ⓕ Ⓖ Ⓗ Ⓙ Ⓚ	29. Ⓐ Ⓑ Ⓒ Ⓓ Ⓔ	44. Ⓕ Ⓖ Ⓗ Ⓙ Ⓚ	59. Ⓐ Ⓑ Ⓒ Ⓓ Ⓔ
15. Ⓐ Ⓑ Ⓒ Ⓓ Ⓔ	30. Ⓕ Ⓖ Ⓗ Ⓙ Ⓚ	45. Ⓐ Ⓑ Ⓒ Ⓓ Ⓔ	60. Ⓕ Ⓖ Ⓗ Ⓙ Ⓚ

Practice Test 1 — ANSWERS

Practice Test 1—Answer Sheet

Reading Test

1. Ⓐ Ⓑ Ⓒ Ⓓ	11. Ⓐ Ⓑ Ⓒ Ⓓ	21. Ⓐ Ⓑ Ⓒ Ⓓ	31. Ⓐ Ⓑ Ⓒ Ⓓ
2. Ⓕ Ⓖ Ⓗ Ⓙ	12. Ⓕ Ⓖ Ⓗ Ⓙ	22. Ⓕ Ⓖ Ⓗ Ⓙ	32. Ⓕ Ⓖ Ⓗ Ⓙ
3. Ⓐ Ⓑ Ⓒ Ⓓ	13. Ⓐ Ⓑ Ⓒ Ⓓ	23. Ⓐ Ⓑ Ⓒ Ⓓ	33. Ⓐ Ⓑ Ⓒ Ⓓ
4. Ⓕ Ⓖ Ⓗ Ⓙ	14. Ⓕ Ⓖ Ⓗ Ⓙ	24. Ⓕ Ⓖ Ⓗ Ⓙ	34. Ⓕ Ⓖ Ⓗ Ⓙ
5. Ⓐ Ⓑ Ⓒ Ⓓ	15. Ⓐ Ⓑ Ⓒ Ⓓ	25. Ⓐ Ⓑ Ⓒ Ⓓ	35. Ⓐ Ⓑ Ⓒ Ⓓ
6. Ⓕ Ⓖ Ⓗ Ⓙ	16. Ⓕ Ⓖ Ⓗ Ⓙ	26. Ⓕ Ⓖ Ⓗ Ⓙ	36. Ⓕ Ⓖ Ⓗ Ⓙ
7. Ⓐ Ⓑ Ⓒ Ⓓ	17. Ⓐ Ⓑ Ⓒ Ⓓ	27. Ⓐ Ⓑ Ⓒ Ⓓ	37. Ⓐ Ⓑ Ⓒ Ⓓ
8. Ⓕ Ⓖ Ⓗ Ⓙ	18. Ⓕ Ⓖ Ⓗ Ⓙ	28. Ⓕ Ⓖ Ⓗ Ⓙ	38. Ⓕ Ⓖ Ⓗ Ⓙ
9. Ⓐ Ⓑ Ⓒ Ⓓ	19. Ⓐ Ⓑ Ⓒ Ⓓ	29. Ⓐ Ⓑ Ⓒ Ⓓ	39. Ⓐ Ⓑ Ⓒ Ⓓ
10. Ⓕ Ⓖ Ⓗ Ⓙ	20. Ⓕ Ⓖ Ⓗ Ⓙ	30. Ⓕ Ⓖ Ⓗ Ⓙ	40. Ⓕ Ⓖ Ⓗ Ⓙ

Science Test

1. Ⓐ Ⓑ Ⓒ Ⓓ	11. Ⓐ Ⓑ Ⓒ Ⓓ	21. Ⓐ Ⓑ Ⓒ Ⓓ	31. Ⓐ Ⓑ Ⓒ Ⓓ
2. Ⓕ Ⓖ Ⓗ Ⓙ	12. Ⓕ Ⓖ Ⓗ Ⓙ	22. Ⓕ Ⓖ Ⓗ Ⓙ	32. Ⓕ Ⓖ Ⓗ Ⓙ
3. Ⓐ Ⓑ Ⓒ Ⓓ	13. Ⓐ Ⓑ Ⓒ Ⓓ	23. Ⓐ Ⓑ Ⓒ Ⓓ	33. Ⓐ Ⓑ Ⓒ Ⓓ
4. Ⓕ Ⓖ Ⓗ Ⓙ	14. Ⓕ Ⓖ Ⓗ Ⓙ	24. Ⓕ Ⓖ Ⓗ Ⓙ	34. Ⓕ Ⓖ Ⓗ Ⓙ
5. Ⓐ Ⓑ Ⓒ Ⓓ	15. Ⓐ Ⓑ Ⓒ Ⓓ	25. Ⓐ Ⓑ Ⓒ Ⓓ	35. Ⓐ Ⓑ Ⓒ Ⓓ
6. Ⓕ Ⓖ Ⓗ Ⓙ	16. Ⓕ Ⓖ Ⓗ Ⓙ	26. Ⓕ Ⓖ Ⓗ Ⓙ	36. Ⓕ Ⓖ Ⓗ Ⓙ
7. Ⓐ Ⓑ Ⓒ Ⓓ	17. Ⓐ Ⓑ Ⓒ Ⓓ	27. Ⓐ Ⓑ Ⓒ Ⓓ	37. Ⓐ Ⓑ Ⓒ Ⓓ
8. Ⓕ Ⓖ Ⓗ Ⓙ	18. Ⓕ Ⓖ Ⓗ Ⓙ	28. Ⓕ Ⓖ Ⓗ Ⓙ	38. Ⓕ Ⓖ Ⓗ Ⓙ
9. Ⓐ Ⓑ Ⓒ Ⓓ	19. Ⓐ Ⓑ Ⓒ Ⓓ	29. Ⓐ Ⓑ Ⓒ Ⓓ	39. Ⓐ Ⓑ Ⓒ Ⓓ
10. Ⓕ Ⓖ Ⓗ Ⓙ	20. Ⓕ Ⓖ Ⓗ Ⓙ	30. Ⓕ Ⓖ Ⓗ Ⓙ	40. Ⓕ Ⓖ Ⓗ Ⓙ

34. At the point at which it is descending the ramp at 10 km/hr, the 30-kg box tested in Experiment 2 would be expected to experience a friction resistance force of:

    F. less than 55 N.
    G. 75 N.
    H. 85 N.
    J. more than 85 N.

35. Which of the following most accurately reflects the design of Experiment 2?

    A. One factor is kept constant so that the relationship between other factors may be observed.
    B. Two variables are altered so that the effect on a third variable may be observed.
    C. An earlier experiment is repeated in order to verify its results.
    D. Conditions are arranged such that a previous hypothesis may be disproved.

PASSAGE VII

Wind speed is influenced by the obstacles it confronts on Earth's surface. Scientists have classified various types of Earth's terrain into *roughness classes:* the higher the roughness class, the rougher the terrain. Roughness class 0 represents water surfaces, roughness class 2 represents sparsely populated agricultural land, and roughness class 4 represents very large cities with tall buildings.

Table 1 shows mean wind speeds observed at three different heights above Earth's surface, in three different roughness classes. Observation heights are represented in meters (m), and wind speed is represented in meters per second (m/s).

Table 1		
Height Above Ground (m)	**Roughness Class**	**Wind Speed (m/s)**
50	0	13.73
50	2	10.7
50	4	8.1
100	0	14.4
100	2	11.7
100	4	9.39
150	0	14.8
150	2	12.29
150	4	10.14

Wind turbines convert wind power into electricity. The power generated from wind is expressed in watts per square meter, according to the formula $W/m^2 = (0.5)(1.225)(v^3)$, where v is wind speed in meters per second. Table 2 indicates the power of the wind at various wind speeds.

Table 2			
Wind Speed (m/s)	**Wind Power (W/m²)**	**Wind Speed (m/s)**	**Wind Power (W/m²)**
0	0	8	313.6
1	0.6	9	446.5
2	4.9	10	612.5
3	16.5	11	815.2
4	39.2	12	1058.4
5	76.2	13	1345.7
6	132.3	14	1680.7
7	210.1	15	2067.2

36. For a given height above the ground, the data indicates that as the roughness of the terrain increases, wind speed:

    F. decreases.
    G. decreases, then increases.
    H. increases.
    J. increases, then decreases.

37. Table 1 indicates that as the height above the ground decreases, wind speed:

    A. increases more rapidly in rougher terrain.
    B. declines more rapidly in rougher terrain.
    C. increases more rapidly in smoother terrain.
    D. declines more rapidly in smoother terrain.

38. Officials in a large city with skyscrapers are deciding between installing a 50-meter-high wind turbine and a 150-meter-high wind turbine. Based on the information in the passage, the difference in the power generated by the two turbines would be approximately:

    F. 200 W/m².
    G. 250 W/m².
    H. 300 W/m².
    J. 350 W/m².

CONTINUE

39. Based on the information in Table 1, which of the following locations exhibits the greatest mean wind speed?

 A. 50 meters above sparsely populated agricultural land
 B. 150 meters above a very large city with tall buildings
 C. 50 meters above a very large city with tall buildings
 D. 100 meters above sparsely populated agricultural land

40. According to Table 2, as wind speed increases from 0 m/s to 15 m/s, wind power:

 F. increases at a constant rate.
 G. decreases at a constant rate.
 H. increases at a decreasing rate.
 J. increases at an increasing rate.

STOP

WRITING TEST

40 Minutes

> **DIRECTIONS:** This is a test of your writing skills. You have forty (40) minutes to write an essay in English. Be sure to carefully read the issue and three perspectives presented before planning and writing your essay so you understand clearly the task you are being asked to do. Your essay will be graded on the evidence it provides of your ability to analyze the issue; evaluate and analyze the perspectives; state and develop a personal perspective; and describe the relationship between the given perspectives and your own, while effectively using organization, logic, and language according to the conventions of standard written English.

ARE 3D PRINTERS DANGEROUS?

As humankind marches bravely through the current era of rapid technological innovation, we continue to create wondrous new inventions that help us live easier, work faster, and enhance our collective and individual experiences. A curious new gadget that has arisen in recent years is the 3D printer, which allows users to "print" solid three-dimensional objects through a complex shaping and molding process. 3D printing technology, which will continue to evolve and improve over time and become more accessible to the average consumer, also brings with it a growing concern—that 3D printers will be used to create potentially dangerous weapons, like guns, for criminal use, or for counterfeiting objects. With that in mind, some feel that the sale of such technology should be subject to government oversight and regulation.

Read and carefully consider these perspectives. Each suggests a particular way of thinking about how to address the potential dangers of 3D printers.

PERSPECTIVE ONE

The potential dangers of 3D printers use are too great to allow private citizens to be able to own this new technology. They may at first seem to be a fascinating innovation and a great way to be creative, but as they continue to evolve and become more sophisticated, they come with the real potential for misuse. Imagine a world in which anyone with a 3D printer can create untraceable weapons and use them to commit crimes. It's hard enough for the government to deal with the volume of dangerous and illegal weapons now; how would it handle a society where we can create them at will from our own homes? To market and sell 3D printers to the general population would be irresponsible and not in the best interest of society.

PERSPECTIVE TWO

People should be allowed to freely use 3D printers. It isn't rational to automatically assume that they will be routinely misused for nefarious purposes, like creating plastic guns or other weapons. Just because something has the potential for danger doesn't mean that it needs to be automatically stripped from the hands of the public. Anyone can freely buy a set of kitchen knives, or a baseball bat, and both have the potential to cause harm—should they be taken off the market? Then, why should access to 3D printers be handled differently? These printers are exciting new outlets for creative thinking and future innovation, and banning them out of fear would be a sad and tragic move.

PERSPECTIVE THREE

While it is true that 3D printers carry the potential risk of abuse, they also have the potential to be amazing outlets for creative expression and technological innovation. We can't discard this intriguing new technology just because of a possible risk for misuse. Granted, it would be unwise to just let individuals "run free" and use 3D printers however they see fit. However, systems and rigid guidelines are already in place for handling the sale and purchase of other potentially dangerous items, such as handguns. These rules could easily be extended to include 3D printers; guidelines for sellers and purchasers and registration can be decided on at a state or national level. Careful and pragmatic product regulation is not a new concept; extending it to 3D printers would help ensure that they are used responsibly.

ESSAY TASK

Write a cohesive, logical essay in which you consider multiple perspectives addressing the concerns about 3D printing technology. In your essay, be sure to:

- examine and assess the perspectives given
- declare and explain your own perspective on the issue
- discuss the relationship between your perspective and those given

Your perspective may be in full or partial agreement, or in total disagreement, with any of the others. Whatever the case, support your ideas with logical reasoning and detailed, persuasive examples.

PLAN AND WRITE YOUR ESSAY

Use the first two pages of the Writing test answer sheet (found at the beginning of the test) to generate ideas and plan your essay. Then use the following four pages to write your essay. Consider the following as you compose your essay:

What are the strengths and weaknesses of the three perspectives provided?

- Identify the insights they present and what they fail to consider.
- Ascertain why a given perspective might persuade or fail to persuade.

How can you apply your own experience, knowledge, and values?

- Express your perspective on the issue, identifying the perspective's strengths and weaknesses.
- Formulate a plan to support your perspective in your essay.

ENGLISH

1.	B	20.	F	39.	C	58.	J
2.	H	21.	B	40.	G	59.	B
3.	D	22.	F	41.	A	60.	H
4.	J	23.	A	42.	H	61.	A
5.	A	24.	G	43.	D	62.	H
6.	H	25.	A	44.	F	63.	B
7.	A	26.	H	45.	A	64.	F
8.	G	27.	D	46.	H	65.	C
9.	A	28.	G	47.	C	66.	G
10.	J	29.	C	48.	G	67.	C
11.	B	30.	J	49.	A	68.	J
12.	J	31.	D	50.	J	69.	D
13.	B	32.	G	51.	A	70.	G
14.	H	33.	C	52.	G	71.	A
15.	D	34.	G	53.	C	72.	H
16.	H	35.	D	54.	J	73.	A
17.	B	36.	F	55.	B	74.	G
18.	J	37.	D	56.	G	75.	B
19.	C	38.	J	57.	A		

1. **The correct answer is B.** In this sentence, "more specifically," is an introductory phrase. An introductory phrase must be followed by a comma to indicate a pause, so the choices are narrowed to choices B and D since no comma follows the phrase in choice C. Choice D contains an unnecessary comma between "dedicated" and "her life."

2. **The correct answer is H.** As it appears in the passage, this sentence is confusing and contains a comma splice (a comma separating two complete sentences). Choice G is incorrect because the first comma stands between the subject (Fossey) and the verb (was), and because the second comma should precede a conjunction (such as *and*). Choice J is incorrect because the comma placed after *trip* gives the impression that it was her first trip ever, instead of her first trip to Africa. Choice H correctly separates the two parts of the sentence with a conjunction, and it is the most logical and straightforward of all of the choices.

3. **The correct answer is D.** As it appears in the passage, "A prominent archaeologist and anthropologist" is a sentence fragment because it contains no verb. Choice B also leaves the second sentence a fragment. Choice C is incorrect because it lacks a comma before the descriptive phrase about Dr. Leakey and merges the two

phrases into a run-on sentence. Choice D is correct because it connects the two phrases together into a complete sentence, with a comma between "Dr. Louis Leakey" and the descriptive phrase that follows.

4. **The correct answer is J.** This is a verb tense question. The sentence describes something that happened in the past (Dr. Fossey met Dr. Leakey, and because of his influence, she decided to study the apes), so you need the past tense form of *encourage*. The correct answer is choice J, *encouraged*. As originally written, the verb was written in the present tense, so choice F is incorrect. Choice G is in the past continuous tense and choice H is in the future tense.

5. **The correct answer is A.** In this case, the simplest form of the sentence is the one that makes the most sense. *There* refers to Rwanda (mentioned in the previous sentence), the place where Fossey "spent thousands of hours observing the behavior of gorillas." Choice B is incorrect because *however* implies a contrast, as if she spent thousands of hours of research in Rwanda despite her previous actions in Zaire, which is not the author's intention. Choice C is incorrect because "And so" implies

Practice Test 1 — ANSWERS

Answer Keys and Explanations

cause-and-effect. Choice D is incorrect because *Meanwhile* seems to say that Fossey spent the thousands of hours researching gorillas before she had finished establishing the research camp.

6. **The correct answer is H.** A comma correctly separates the two halves of this sentence. If the sentence did not contain a conjunction ("and"), then the semicolon would be correct, but this is not the case, so choice F is wrong. As it is, a comma must come before the conjunction. Choice J uses a period, which would create a fragment, and choice G fails to use any punctuation at all.

7. **The correct answer is A.** The sentence is correct as it is written. Choice B is redundant because *tolerate*, in this sentence, means approximately the same thing as *accept*. Choice C features the same problem but is even more verbose. Choice D, "began to show that they accepted," is not significantly different from the existing phrase, but it is wordy, and in this case, the simplest option is the best one.

8. **The correct answer is G.** "Spending so much time to observe the gorillas" is incorrect because the infinitival form "to observe" does not agree with the rest of the sentence; the proper verb form is *observing*. This becomes clearer if you cut the "spending so much time" modifier: saying "To observe the gorillas, Fossey naturally distinguished among them" would imply that Fossey distinguished among the gorillas *in order to* observe them, not that she distinguished among them *by* observing them. The only option that contains the correct verb form is choice G. Choice H would also be too wordy in any context. Choice J would be correct if the sentence took place in the present, but it is incorrect in this context.

9. **The correct answer is A.** The sentence is correct as it is written in the passage. The past tense fits well with the rest of the passage, which discusses Fossey's actions while she was studying the gorillas in Rwanda. Choices B and C create fragments, and choice D changes the meaning of the sentence.

10. **The correct answer is J.** The sentence as written is a fragment because it lacks a verb. Choice G does not correct this problem. Choice H is incorrect because the verb needs to modify *one*, not *favorites*. Choice J uses the correct singular verb *was* to accomplish this.

11. **The correct answer is B.** This question asks you to pick the best introductory phrase for the sentence. Since the sentence describes an unhappy turn of events,

Unfortunately is the best choice. Choice A, *Still*, would be a good choice if the sentence set up a contrast to the one before it—as in "Still, despite all of Fossey's efforts, Digit was killed"—but Fossey, prior to this point, had not engaged in any efforts to save gorillas from poachers. Choice C, "In fact," would be a good choice only if the sentence provided support or an example for the sentence before it. Choice D, *Because*, generally would not stand alone as an introductory phrase, though if it were part of such a phrase, it would signal cause-and-effect, which is inappropriate here.

12. **The correct answer is J.** This awkward sentence should be eliminated rather than rewritten, because there is no reason to include information about a rhinoceros in a passage that is about Dian Fossey's life, research, and conservation efforts among mountain gorillas in Africa. Choice G does not improve upon this problem in the original sentence, and choice H introduces the additional problem of confusing syntax.

13. **The correct answer is B.** The word *though* is inappropriate, because it provides a contrast; the author is not trying to contrast Fossey's return to Rwanda with other possible courses of action. *Still* and *yet* in choices C and D create the same problem. Only choice B eliminates the unnecessary contrast and makes the sentence flow properly.

14. **The correct answer is H.** The author says that Fossey spent the rest of her life "working to protect the mountain gorilla." A concrete example would be a specific description of some sort of action she took to protect the mountain gorilla, which is provided by choice H. Choices F and G provide opinions about Fossey but no description of her work, while choice J concerns another prominent anthropologist and thus can't serve as an example of a specific step that Fossey took.

15. **The correct answer is D.** The author of this essay does not discuss any controversy surrounding Fossey, so eliminate choice A. Eliminate choice B as well, because while the author does describe Fossey's important legacy in the field of conservation, this has nothing to do with whether the author fulfilled the assignment of writing an essay about Fossey's controversial methods. The author clearly states that Fossey's work was of benefit to the mountain gorilla, so eliminate choice C. The author simply does not discuss the controversial nature of Fossey's methods and, therefore, would not successfully meet the assignment described in the question, so the best choice is D.

16. **The correct answer is H.** A river rushes *along* a border, implying that the river follows the border of these two countries. *Which* is unnecessary, but *along* is important. Therefore, choices F, G, and J can be eliminated, and choice H can be confirmed as correct.

17. **The correct answer is B.** The underlined portion of the sentence begins a descriptive phrase that follows "one of the most stunning achievements of nature." Choices A and C are incorrect because the phrase does not need another subject (*this*). Choice D is redundant and should also be eliminated. Only choice B is worded correctly.

18. **The correct answer is J.** The phrase "in the 1800s" is key to solving this question. It indicates that the action in the sentence took place in the past. Choice F, "who have been living," makes it sound as though the Kololo tribe still lives in the area. It is incorrect to say that anyone "were lived" (choice G) or "has been lived" (choice H), both of which makes it sound like living was an action performed on the subject. The best answer is the past tense verb, choice J, *lived*.

19. **The correct answer is C.** The sentence as written seems to emphasize how separate the five falls are from each other, as though readers already understand that there are five of them. The sentence *should* emphasize that rather than being one waterfall, Victoria Falls is a collection of five separate falls. Choice C does the best job at clarifying this. Choice B is awkwardly written, and choice D makes matters worse by inserting a standalone sentence.

20. **The correct answer is F.** The underlined phrase should be a bridge into the description of why Victoria Falls is considered one of the seven wonders of the natural world. Of all the answer choices, choice F provides the best transition from the fact that the falls is one of the seven wonders of the natural world to the reasons why it is on this list. The others introduce separate subjects— the Grand Canyon (choice G), people's differing opinions (choice H), the other wonders of Africa (choice J)—that are not directly relevant to why the falls is considered one of the world's natural wonders.

21. **The correct answer is B.** *Observing* and *witnessing* are describing the same action, so you need to choose an option that eliminates one of these words as redundant. Choice B is the correct one. The others express some redundancy, with choice C using the redundant words *looks* and *see* and choice D using *observing* and *see*.

22. **The correct answer is F.** The phrase is correct as written, with a comma separating the two adjectives, no conjunction between them, and no comma between the last adjective and the subject. Choice G lacks the necessary comma, choice H adds the unnecessary conjunction *and*, and choice J adds an extra unnecessary comma.

23. **The correct answer is A.** The sentences are correctly separated. Choices B and D would create run-on sentences. In the second sentence, *Imagine* is a command to the reader, and does not need the *to* added in choice C.

24. **The correct answer is G.** The apostrophe in the existing word implies possession, which is not correct here, so eliminate choice F. *Standing* (choice H), is an adjective in this case (describing where the rain forest stands), not a verb. Omitting the word entirely, as choice J suggests, creates a series of dependent clauses with no verb. Only choice G uses the correct form of *stand* for this sentence.

25. **The correct answer is A.** This word choice question asks you to understand the point that the author is trying to make about the falls. Contextual clues indicate that what the author is trying to describe is the size and splendor of the falls. In that case, neither *generosity* (choice B) nor *fruitfulness* (choice C) fits the description. Likewise, *peacefulness* (choice D) is a bad fit with the rest of the passage: words such as *crashing* and *roaring* in the previous paragraph do not imply that the falls are particularly peaceful. *Grandiosity*, however, is certainly in keeping with earlier descriptions of the falls as *spectacular* and "twice as large as…Niagara Falls."

26. **The correct answer is H.** The phrase "enjoy a walk" should not be split by any commas to indicate a pause, which eliminates choices F, G, and J. Only choice H deletes the unnecessary comma without adding any new ones.

27. **The correct answer is D.** Other than echoing the words *pot* and *boil* from the previous sentence, this sentence has no relevance to the passage and should be eliminated. Rewording the sentence does not make it any more relevant, so choices B and C are not correct.

28. **The correct answer is G.** The subject matter of this sentence fits into the rest of the paragraph, which is about the additional natural attractions of the park. It should not be eliminated (choice J), just rewritten with the active voice—"is to be admired by" (choice F) is an example of the passive voice, which typically adds a phrase like "can be" or "will be" to a verb that should stand on its own. Choice H uses the passive voice and is lengthy and awkward.

29. **The correct answer is C.** Choice A can be eliminated; the essay does describe how marvelous Victoria Falls is, but that alone does not make it fulfill an assignment to describe why the falls are more worthwhile than other attractions. In order to do so, it would have to specifically describe the other six wonders of the natural world and give specific reasons why Victoria Falls is superior, so choice B is incorrect and choice C is correct. The writer does think Victoria Falls is interesting, so choice D misidentifies the reason the essay would fail to meet the assignment.

30. **The correct answer is J.** A paragraph about buying locally made crafts would have to come after the introduction of the idea that there are other, non-falls attractions in the park. Since that idea is introduced in Paragraph 4, a paragraph about crafts would most logically come between Paragraphs 4 and 5. Choices F, G, and H would all place it too early in the essay, which would disrupt its logical flow.

31. **The correct answer is D.** There is no need for a pause in the middle of the phrase "moved to Connecticut"; therefore, the commas in choices A, B, and C are unnecessary. Only choice D lacks all unnecessary commas.

32. **The correct answer is G.** The phrase as written is redundant. To test for this redundancy, try eliminating either *even* or *also*. If the sentence makes sense with only one of these words, you've found a redundancy. In this case, *even* is the best replacement for the redundant phrase (choice G), because it implies that the family in the passage missed the steamy heat of Florida—*even* though this sort of weather condition had been undesirable while they were in Florida. Choice H adds an unnecessary *had* to *also*, distorting the tense of the sentence. Choice J is even more redundant than the current version.

33. **The correct answer is C.** The phrase as written implies that the family hasn't yet moved from Florida to Connecticut but is looking forward to seeing snow. Since the rest of the passage is written as if the narrator is reflecting on the experience *after* he or she moved to Connecticut, you need the past tense here as well, as in choice C. Choice B makes it seem like the family was reminiscing about the snow in the past, which changes the intended meaning of the sentence. Choice D uses past tense but tries to join two verb clauses that make no sense together.

34. **The correct answer is G.** A comma should separate the phrases "and in movies" and "of course", but not *and* and "in movies." "Of course" clarifies "and in movies," but "in movies" does not clarify *and*. Therefore, you don't need a pause between the parts of this phrase, so you can eliminate choices F and H. Choice J lacks the comma needed after *movies*. Only choice G handles both parts correctly.

35. **The correct answer is D.** Because *instantly* and "right away" mean the same thing, both the existing sentence and choice B are redundant. A better choice is to eliminate one of the extra phrases. *Instantly* is an adverb that modifies the verb phrase "were shooting." *Instant* is an adjective that would incorrectly modify *children* (as in "instant children"), so choice C is incorrect. Only choice D is correct.

36. **The correct answer is F.** *Building* and *shooting* are both verbs in the same phrase and should remain in the same tense as they are in the original sentence. Choices G, H, and J change the tense of *build* senselessly.

37. **The correct answer is D.** The verb refers to "the first time," not *eyes*, so it must be a singular verb to match the singular subject; eliminate choices A and C. The action also refers to a past event, so eliminate choice B as well. Choice D is the correct past tense singular verb.

38. **The correct answer is J.** The underlined word must be a subject pronoun that refers to "our mother." *That* (choice F) and *which* (choice G) are generally used to describe things, but in this case, we're trying to describe a person. *Whom* (choice H) is always an object, not a subject. In this sentence, the most appropriate pronoun for the mother is *who* (choice J), which describes the identity of the person being referred to.

39. **The correct answer is C.** The sentence starting with "We would build forts" does not introduce a new topic. It provides support for the previous sentence by describing in detail how the children "would be initiated into the glamorous, Northern world of Snow." Therefore, choices A and B are wrong. Choice D misidentifies the reason the writer should not begin a new paragraph; the following sentence contains plenty of information about the children's plans.

40. **The correct answer is G.** The key word in this sentence is *were*, which signals that the noun to which it refers must be plural. If you ignore the extra information in the middle of the sentence, you can see that the sentence would correctly state, "Our plans were elaborate." Choices F and J both uses singular verbs, so they can be eliminated. Choice J would not make sense; in what would the children be involving their plan? Only choice

G uses the correct tense without introducing inappropriate vagueness.

41. **The correct answer is A.** This phrase should remain plural and in the past tense, because it modifies the same subject, *we*, as "raced outside." Choices B and D are in the present tense. Choice C is singular.

42. **The correct answer is H.** In the previous sentence, the characters look at each other "in horror" when they discover that their first snowfall has quickly changed to rain. Choices F and J are both factual statements that do not convey horror or surprise. Choice G is not supported by the rest of the passage because the characters do end up enjoying the snow, although they haven't decided that at this point in the story. Choice H is the best choice because it shows the characters' surprise and disbelief in the form of the question, "Is this someone's idea of a joke?"—meaning, "Is this really what snow is like?"

43. **The correct answer is D.** The story is narrated from a first-person point of view, using *I* and *we* to describe the observations and actions of the characters. The underlined phrase in this question refers to the characters in the story, not some other group of strangers, so it should also be in the first person. Choices A and B would be used only if the narrator was not discussing a group of children to which he or she belonged. Choice C makes no sense.

44. **The correct answer is F.** In this phrase, *once-held* serves as a single adjective; one word does not make sense in this context without the other. When two words join together to form one adjective, they should be hyphenated. Choices G and H do not retain the necessary hyphenation, while choice J loses *held*, which is necessary to complete the idiom. All of the incorrect choices also jumble the syntax by placing *prejudices* before *once*.

45. **The correct answer is A.** The sentence to be inserted is a description of something the children miss about their home state of Florida. It belongs in the paragraph that describes other things the children miss about Florida, which is the first paragraph of the passage. Placing it later in the passage would disrupt its logical flow, so choices B, C, and D are incorrect.

46. **The correct answer is H.** Based on the rest of the sentence, the underlined word or words should mean something like "is made up of," as in "over half a million acres make up the Great Smoky Mountains National Park." "Is created of" (choice F) is awkward because the

verb *create* generally does not take a modifier such as *of*. *Consists*, on the other hand, is frequently paired with *of*, and communicates the same meaning as "is made up of." So choice H is correct. Mountains cannot own anything, so choice G makes no sense. Similarly, a park cannot establish mountains, which eliminates choice J.

47. **The correct answer is C.** The sentence as written is incorrect, because the verb phrase "rise above" should have a plural subject. In this sentence, however, the subject is "the blue mist," not "the mountains." Choice C uses the appropriate singular form, "rises above." Choice B creates a sentence fragment, and choice D creates a sentence that uses both present and past tenses.

48. **The correct answer is G.** This is a complex sentence that lists several options for the hiker. Since the sentence begins by saying that hikers can choose walks "ranging from a brisk, uphill walk…," you can predict that the rest of the sentence will tell you the other end of the range of choices: "ranging *from* a brisk, uphill walk *to* a truly challenging three-hour hike." The *from… to* construction is common in a sentence that tries to provide a brief sketch of different extremes; that is exactly what this sentence attempts to do, and choice G is the only answer that fits the demand. Choice F contains a comma splice. While choices H and J simply fail to complete the *from…to* construction.

49. **The correct answer is A.** *Unrealistic* is the adjective that conveys that conservationists knew a ban on logging was not likely to happen. This is the author's meaning in the context. Slightly rephrased, the author is trying to say that because the conservationists knew that a full ban on logging was not likely to be effective, they suggested a compromise. *Unrealistic* implies that they recognized that a ban was unlikely, and is thus the correct adjective. Choice B converts *unrealistic* to its adverb form, so it does not modify anything. Choices C and D make it seem as though an attempt to ban logging was something that could not happen.

50. **The correct answer is J.** In this sentence, *unchecked* is extra information that needs to be set off by commas. In other words, you could eliminate *unchecked* and the sentence would have a similar meaning, but *unchecked* helps make the author's meaning clearer. A semicolon is used only to separate two independent clauses, so it isn't a good choice here. Therefore, choice F is incorrect. Choice G is missing all necessary commas, while choice H is missing one.

51. **The correct answer is A.** This question asks you what function the second paragraph serves in the passage.

The essay as a whole is about the establishment of the Great Smoky Mountains National Park, so this paragraph should further that point. Paragraph 2 describes the initial reason for the establishment of the park—it was a compromise struck by conservationists and loggers. This idea is best described by choice A. The essay does not go on to describe further conflict between loggers and conservationists; nor is this an important part of the essay's topic. Therefore, choice D is incorrect. As a historical account of the events leading up to the establishment of the park, it may have a viewpoint but does not argue for one particular political or social viewpoint over another, so eliminate choices B and C.

52. **The correct answer is G.** A phrase that contains extra information about the subject, in this case "an organization that explored and mapped land in the United States," must be set off by commas. The phrase modifies "United States Geological Survey," so the comma comes between *Survey* and "an organization…." As originally written, the phrase lacks the necessary comma. Choice H turns a word in an organization's title into a verb. Choice J would result in an awkward and illogically constructed sentence.

53. **The correct answer is C.** The sentence in the question needs to be placed logically in a series of events. Logically, a sentence saying that the Smoky Mountains region emerged as a winner would have to come after a sentence explaining what the competition was, but before a sentence detailing what happened next. Sentences 2 and 3 explain the competition: the location of the park had to be determined, and there were sixty proposed sites. The logical place to describe the decision would come next, right before Sentence 4 begins, "After the decision was made…." The sentence is clearly the continuation of a previous idea, which makes it a poor introductory statement, so choice A is wrong. Choice B places it too early in the passage, which would disrupt its logical flow. Choice D places it too late.

54. **The correct answer is J.** As it is written, the sentence contains an unnecessary pronoun, *it*. Since you already know that the object in this sentence is the *plan*, there is no need for the additional *it* to clarify matters. The option that uses the smallest number of words and eliminates redundancy is usually your best bet, and that is choice J. Both choices G and H add extra words and commas and lack clear syntax.

55. **The correct answer is B.** All of these choices have different shades of meaning. *Privacy* (choice A) means "seclusion or lack of exposure," implying that the ownership carries a certain secrecy; this is different from "private ownership," which indicates that something is not common or public property. "Privately owned" conveys the meaning: that this land would be difficult to acquire because it belonged to many private individuals. *Private*, not *privacy*, should modify the verb, and choice B is the most concise answer. Choice C is incorrect because use of the noun form of *private* (the lowest rank in the military) makes no sense in the context of the sentence. Choice D is an awkward rewording of the correct answer.

56. **The correct answer is G.** This question tests the fine distinction between *amount* and *number*. The underlined phrase, "amount of dollars," tries to describe countable items (dollars) with an indefinite quantifier (amount). *Amount* describes things that cannot be individuated (*e.g.*, the *amount of rain* that fell), whereas *number* describes things that can be specifically counted (e.g., the *number of inches* that fell). What is needed here, therefore, is either "number of dollars," which is not listed, or "amount of money" (choice G). While "number of monies" (choice H) is slightly more correct than the original, it is awkward and generally not an accepted phrasing. Choice J distorts the meaning of the sentence, implying that the park's founders sought paper currency that was physically much larger than standard monetary bills.

57. **The correct answer is A.** The detail about the landowners hiking their prices is intended to show the reader that purchasing the land was a challenging task. *Heroic* (choice B) might provide an alternative, since the author clearly approves of the purchasing of the land, but *challenging* is the better choice because the author is trying to give a straightforward account of the difficulties of establishing the park. *Heroic* does not necessarily imply difficulty, just as difficulty does not necessary imply heroism. The fact that the author approves of the purchasing of the land eliminates the negative descriptions *foolish* (choice C) and *immoral* (choice D).

58. **The correct answer is J.** "They had fallen short" is the same thing as "they hadn't raised enough money." To write both is redundant, so you should omit the phrase "they hadn't raised enough money" entirely. Choices F, G, and H fail to eliminate this redundancy.

59. **The correct answer is B.** This question requires you to go back to the passage and find a paragraph that already contains material about the conflict between

loggers and conservationists; Paragraph 2 discusses how compromises between conservation interests and logging interests led to the founding of the park, so this would be the best place to add this information. Paragraph 1 (choice A) is about how visitors are attracted to the Great Smoky Mountains National Park's location. Paragraph 3 (choice C) is about Congress' approval of the park. Paragraph 4 (choice D) is about the purchase of the park.

60. **The correct answer is H.** While the first paragraph does mention a few of the park's attractions, it serves only as an introduction to an essay about the establishment of the park. Because only a small fraction of the essay discusses this theme, and someone who would want to know more about visiting the park would probably prefer knowing about the park's features rather than its history, the passage would not successfully respond to the assignment. Therefore, choice H is correct, and choices F and G can be eliminated. Choice J misidentifies the reason the essay would not fulfill the assignment; the essay does describe the park as a place tourists like to visit.

61. **The correct answer is A.** In this sentence, the simplest version works best, so the phrase does not need to be changed. Choice B has the same meaning, but it is unnecessarily awkward. Choice C changes the meaning of the sentence by using *richly* as an adverb to describe *flourished*. Choice D is missing a conjunction.

62. **The correct answer is H.** *Among* is the correct choice because it indicates that the Mayan understanding of astronomy was one of many notable achievements. *Plus* (choice F) doesn't make sense because it means "in addition to"—in other words, in addition to "notable achievements," the Mayans had a profound understanding of astronomy. Astronomy is *one* of these notable achievements, so the word choice needs to acknowledge this. *Despite* (choice G) means "in spite of," which would contradict the meaning of the sentence, and *Between* (choice J) works only when there are exactly two achievements, not many.

63. **The correct answer is B.** The description *astute* must appear before the verb *were* because *astute* functions as an adjective, describing the observations that will follow the verb. Choices A, C, and D all result in poor syntax.

64. **The correct answer is F.** The underlined words are correct as written. The sentence intends to convey that astronomy is more than a science. Choice G, *merely*, and choice H, *just*, make the sentence mean that astronomy

is nothing more than a science; this is not the author's argument. Choice J claims that astronomy is not a science at all, which clearly contradicts what follows the semicolon.

65. **The correct answer is C.** *Found* (or *find*) and *into* as a combination of words doesn't work, because it's impossible to *find* something *into* many aspects, so choice A is wrong. By realizing that *found* must have an object paired with it, you can choose the one option that pairs *found* with an object. "Found its way" provides this pairing. Something cannot "find" (choice B) or "found" (choice D) into something else.

66. **The correct answer is G.** Because *exact* modifies the verb *aligned*, it must be an adverb. Choices F, H, and J do not use the adverb form of *exact*. Most adverbs end with -*ly*, making choice G the correct answer.

67. **The correct answer is C.** A semicolon connects two related clauses that could stand on their own as sentences. A colon, on the other hand, indicates that the author is about to make a list without a subject. Since *were* is the verb in the second part of the sentence, a semicolon is a better choice, despite the list that appears at the beginning of the clause. Therefore, choice A is incorrect and choice C is correct. Choice B uses a comma where a semicolon is needed, and choice D fails to use any punctuation at all.

68. **The correct answer is J.** The author's tone is one of praise, which is most apparent in the reference to the "notable achievements" of the Mayans in the first paragraph. There is an evident admiration of the civilization's accomplishments, so choice J is the best answer. While *gleeful* (choice F) is a positive word, it does not capture the author's tone as well as *admiring* does. *Indifferent* (choice G) and *resentful* (choice H) are both negative words.

69. **The correct answer is D.** On the ACT, the choice that makes the sentence the simplest is usually the correct choice. Carvings and murals are examples of artwork, so choice D simplifies the sentence by eliminating redundancy. Choices A, B, and C retain the redundant words *carvings* and *murals*. They all contain unnecessary punctuation between *murals* and *shows* too.

70. **The correct answer is G.** The pronoun *who* is generally used when referring to people (or even gods with human characteristics). *Which* (choice H) refers to non-human subjects. A relative pronoun is needed in this case to make clear that it is the evil gods who wanted to stop the benevolent gods, and *they* (choice J)

is a personal pronoun. As the sentence reads in the original, the verb appears to refer to the benevolent gods, which does not fit the context of the sentence. The evil gods, not the benevolent gods, are the ones attempting to stop the progress of the sun and moon.

71. **The correct answer is A.** Again, the simplest form is usually correct. "Believed to have gained" correctly indicates that those who died were believed by the Mayans to have gained eternal life. "And felt they" (choice B) makes the sentence redundant because *believed* and *felt* mean approximately the same thing in the context. While "they soon would have" (choice C) and "one day they would have" (choice D) express similar ideas, they do so awkwardly and with more words.

72. **The correct answer is H.** Word order is very important here. To determine it, you need to look at the context. The Mayans did not appear in the sky; Venus did. Therefore, you can eliminate the original sentence. The Mayans were using Venus to make a decision; choice H is the only choice that indicates this fact, so it is the correct answer. Choices G and J use awkward, grammatically incorrect wording.

73. **The correct answer is A.** The phrase "In short" accurately indicates that this paragraph will serve as a summary for the rest of the passage. *Shortly*, however, because it is an adverb, would have to modify the closest verb. "Shortly, in looking to the night sky for guidance" is not the author's meaning, so choice B is wrong. Choice C, "to sum up the," implies that everything about ancient Mayan culture is encapsulated by this passage, which is certainly an exaggeration. *Lastly* indicates the final item in a list, and since that is not what the final sentence in the essay is, choice D is incorrect.

74. **The correct answer is G.** The phrase "in looking to the night sky for guidance" is extra information that should be set off by commas. The two halves of the sentence cannot stand on their own as sentences, so the punctuation mark cannot be a semicolon. Therefore choice F is wrong. A colon is not the correct punctuation either, so choice J is wrong too. Choice H fails to use any punctuation at all.

75. **The correct answer is B.** Since the passage is not about the ancient Babylonians, mentioning them would signal a transition to another topic. A new topic or supporting detail would not be introduced as part of a conclusion, which is meant to summarize the information already presented, so choice A is wrong. The sentence does not illustrate (choice C) or contradict (choice D) any of the passage's information either.

MATHEMATICS

1.	E	16.	H	31.	C	46.	F
2.	G	17.	B	32.	K	47.	C
3.	A	18.	H	33.	D	48.	G
4.	K	19.	B	34.	H	49.	B
5.	D	20.	H	35.	C	50.	K
6.	J	21.	D	36.	K	51.	C
7.	C	22.	F	37.	C	52.	K
8.	H	23.	D	38.	H	53.	E
9.	C	24.	G	39.	B	54.	J
10.	K	25.	B	40.	K	55.	B
11.	E	26.	J	41.	A	56.	J
12.	K	27.	D	42.	F	57.	C
13.	D	28.	K	43.	C	58.	H
14.	G	29.	D	44.	H	59.	D
15.	A	30.	H	45.	B	60.	G

1. **The correct answer is E.** Twenty percent is the same as $\frac{1}{5}$, so 30 is $\frac{1}{5}$ of the games played. Therefore, the total number of games played must be 5(30) = 150. You could also have taken 20% of each answer choice to see which one yielded 30. Choice A takes $\frac{1}{5}$ of 30 and adds it to 30, applying the fraction to the wrong quantity. Choice B is a result of losing 50%, not 20%. Choice C implies a loss of $\frac{1}{3}$ of the games, not $\frac{1}{5}$ of them. Choice D implies a loss of $\frac{1}{4}$ of the games, not $\frac{1}{5}$ of them.

2. **The correct answer is G.** Plugging in $a = 5$ gives you $\frac{5}{6} = \frac{b}{15}$. Cross-multiply to solve for b:

$$(5)(15) = 6b$$
$$75 = 6b$$
$$b = \frac{75}{6}$$
$$= 12\frac{1}{2}$$

To get choice F, you subtracted 1 from the denominator to get a new fraction, which does not yield an equivalent fraction to the other side of the proportion. For choice H, you multiplied the numerator and denominator of a single fraction and divided that product by 15; you must cross-multiply in the

proportion instead. To get choice J, you divided 15 by 6, but this does not yield b; you must cross-multiply in the proportion instead. For choice K, the resulting fraction on the right side of the proportion would be much smaller than the one on the left.

3. **The correct answer is A.** Since $\overleftrightarrow{XYZ}$ is a straight line, angles VYX, VYW, and WYZ must total 180°. Therefore:

$$90° + 27° + \angle WYZ = 180°$$
$$\angle WYZ = 180° - 90° - 27°$$
$$= 63°$$

Choice B is likely an arithmetic error, since angles VYW and WYZ should sum to 90 degrees. Choice C is the value of either VYZ or VYX, but not WYZ. Choice D is supplementary to the correct value of WYZ. Choice E is incorrect because VYW and WYZ are complementary, not supplementary.

4. **The correct answer is K.** In a geometric sequence, each term is multiplied by some value to produce the following term. In this case the first term is 3 and the second is −6; since −2(3) = −6, you know that the multiplier for this sequence is −2. Since the third term is 12, the fourth is −2(12) = −24; the fifth term is −2(−24) = 48. Choice F is the negative of the correct answer. Choice G is the fourth term, not the fifth. Choice H is the result of viewing the sequence as being arithmetic, not geometric. Choice J is the opposite of the fourth term.

Answer Keys and Explanations

5. **The correct answer is D.** Martha cuts 4(1.5 feet) = 6 feet of ribbon from the spool. If 27.5 feet remain, then originally there were 6 + 27.5 = 33.5 feet of ribbon. For choice A, you subtracted 6 from 27.5, instead of adding. To get choice B, you subtracted the length of 1 piece of ribbon from 27.5, but you should have *added* 4 lengths to 27.5. For choice C, you added the length of 1 piece of ribbon, but you should have added the lengths of *4* pieces. To get choice E, you added 8 pieces of ribbon, not 4.

6. **The correct answer is J.** Plug $y = -4$ into the expression and solve:

$$2\left[5-(-4)\right]+(-4)=2(5+4)-4$$
$$=2(9)-4$$
$$=18-4$$
$$=14$$

For choice F, you multiplied 18 and −4 instead of adding them. In choice G, you multiplied by −2 instead of 2. For choice H, you plugged in $y = 4$, not $y = -4$. For choice K, the first part of the expression was evaluated correctly, but you mistakenly changed the sign on the second portion.

7. **The correct answer is C.** Squaring all terms, $\left(\sqrt{x}\right)^2$ lies between 5^2 and 6^2, or x lies between 25 and 36. The only choice that falls within this range is 31, choice C. Choices A and B are too low—if you know the square root of x is greater than 5, x must be greater than 25. Choice D and E are too high—if you know the square root of x is greater than 6, x must be less than 36.

8. **The correct answer is H.** You're told that C bisects $\overline{BD}$. This means that C divides $\overline{BD}$ into two equal parts, $\overline{BC}$ and $\overline{CD}$. With this knowledge you can look at each choice, to evaluate which is not necessarily true. If that seems a bit abstract, you can pick some numbers. If $BD = 10$, then $BC = CD = 5$. You can use these values to prove that choices F, G, J, and K must all be true. Choice H, $AD = 3CD$, may or may not be true. Since you are not given any information about where point A lies in relation to the other points, you cannot determine anything about the relationship between the lengths of $\overline{AD}$ and $\overline{CD}$.

9. **The correct answer is C.**

$$\left|-3\right|-\left|3-9\right|=3-\left|-6\right|$$
$$=3-6$$
$$=-3$$

Choice A is incorrect because you multiplied the two absolute values together instead of subtracting them. Choice B is incorrect because it misapplies the

absolute value to −3; note that $|-3| = 3$, not −3. In choice D, you took the absolute value of the final answer. Choice E is incorrect because $-|-6| = -6$, not 6.

10. **The correct answer is K.** If the probability of NOT selecting a blue marble is $\dfrac{1}{4}$, then the probability of selecting a blue marble is $\dfrac{3}{4}$: $\dfrac{3}{4}(20)=15$; therefore, there are 15 blue marbles in the bag. Choice F represents $\dfrac{1}{5}$ of the bag, not $\dfrac{3}{4}$. Choice G represents how many marbles in the bag are NOT blue. Choice H represents $\dfrac{2}{5}$ of the bag, and choice J represents $\dfrac{1}{2}$ of the bag.

11. **The correct answer is E.** The slopes of perpendicular lines are negative reciprocals. Rewrite the equation for line a in slope-intercept form ($y = mx + b$) to identify its slope:

$$2x+3y=11$$
$$3y=-2x+11$$
$$y=-\frac{2}{3}x+\frac{11}{3}$$

Now you can see that the slope of line a is $-\dfrac{2}{3}$, so the slope of line b must be the negative reciprocal of $-\dfrac{2}{3}$, or $\dfrac{3}{2}$. In choice A, you changed the sign of the y-intercept, but this does not affect the slope and hence has no impact on whether or not the two lines are perpendicular. For choice B, remember that the product of the slopes of two lines that are perpendicular is −1, not 1. Choice C is the slope of a line *parallel* to the given line. In choice D, you made the slope the opposite sign, but you did not do the reciprocal.

12. **The correct answer is K.** There are x ounces of C. There are 12 more ounces of C than A, so there are $x - 12$ ounces of Solution A. There are 5 times as many ounces of B as A, so there are $5(x - 12) = 5x - 60$ ounces of Solution B, choice K. In choice F, the number of ounces of A is $x + 12$, not $x - 12$. For choice G, you must multiply 5 by the number of ounces of A, not C. Choice H is the number of ounces of A. Choice J does not distribute the 5 through both terms in the product $5(x - 12)$.

13. **The correct answer is D.** The coordinates of one corner of the square are (−2, 3). The square has a side length of 5, which means that the distance between any two consecutive corners must be 5. To find the distance

between two points that have one coordinate in common, find the difference of their non-identical coordinates. Choice A runs 5 units from $x = -2$ to $x = -7$. Choice B runs 5 units from $y = 3$ to $y = 8$. Choice C runs 5 units from $x = -2$ to $x = 3$. Choice E, slightly trickier, runs 5 units from $x = -2$ to $x = -7$ *and* 5 units from $y = 3$ to $y = -2$, creating an opposite far corner. Choice D, however, runs 6 units from $y = 3$ to $y = -3$ and cannot be part of the same square.

14. **The correct answer is G.** Calculate 5% of the purchase price: $\$75{,}000 \times .05 = \$3{,}750$. Therefore, in order to make a 5% profit, Joan must sell the house for $\$75{,}000 + \$3{,}750 = \$78{,}750$. Choices F, H, J, and K are the result of computing the percentage incorrectly.

15. **The correct answer is A.** Combine like terms and factor:

$$5x - (3y - x) = 5x - 3y - (-x)$$
$$= 5x - 3y + x$$
$$= 6x - 3y$$
$$= 3(2x - y)$$

In choice B, you distributed only the negative to $3y$, but not the $-x$ in the second portion of the expression. In choice C, you applied the negative to $-x$, but not $3y$. Choice D has a constant term after simplifying, but the given expression in the problem does not. For choice E, you treated the expression $-(3y - x)$ incorrectly; you should not multiply all of the terms.

16. **The correct answer is H.** A root is a value of x that makes a quadratic equation true. To find possible values, use reverse FOIL:

$$x^2 + x - 2 = 0$$
$$(x + 2)(x - 1) = 0$$
$$x = -2 \text{ or } 1$$

Only one of these, -2, is among the answer choices. You could also have worked backward from the answer choices, plugging them all into the equation; again, only choice H works:

$$(-2)^2 + (-2) - 2 = 0$$
$$4 - 2 - 2 = 0$$

17. **The correct answer is B.** The interior angles of a triangle add up to 180°. Therefore:

$$2x + 3x + 5x = 180$$
$$10x = 180$$
$$x = 18$$

The measure of angle ACB is $2x$, so plugging in $x = 18$ gives you $2(18) = 36$. Choice A is the value of x, not $2x$. Choice C is the measure of angle BAC. Choice D is the value of $4x$, which is none of the angles shown. Choice E is the measure of angle ABC.

18. **The correct answer is H.** The jacket is discounted by $\$75 - \$50 = \$25$. $\text{Percent} = \dfrac{\text{part}}{\text{whole}} \times 100\%$ (keep in mind that the whole must be the original price of $75), so this is a discount of $\dfrac{\$25}{\$75} \times 100\% = \dfrac{1}{3} \times 100\% = 33\dfrac{1}{3}\%$.

The percentage in choice F is too low—the discount would need to be $15 for it to be true. For choice G, while the jacket is discounted by $25, $25 does not mean 25%. To get choice J, you used $50 as the whole instead of $75. For choice K, $75 does not mean 75%.

19. **The correct answer is B.** Use one equation to solve for one variable in terms of the other, and then plug this expression into the second equation to find a numerical value. Since you're looking for the value of b, use the second equation to solve for a in terms of b:

$$a - 3b = 7$$
$$a = 7 + 3b$$

Now plug this expression for a into the first equation to solve for b:

$$4a + b = 2$$
$$4(7 + 3b) + b = 2$$
$$28 + 12b + b = 2$$
$$28 + 13b = 2$$
$$13b = -26$$
$$b = -2$$

When solving the equation $13b = -26$, you must divide both sides by 13, not add it to both sides as in choice A. Choice C is the value of a, not b. Choices D and E are both results of algebraic errors when solving the system. If you plug each of these values in for b in both equations, you will see that you get two equations involving a that have different solutions. This tells you that b cannot be either of these values.

20. **The correct answer is H.** If 1 inch of wire costs $0.20, 1 foot costs $12(\$0.20) = \$2.40$. Therefore, 5.25 feet of wire cost $(\$2.40)(5.25) = \$12.60$. In choice F, you calculated the price of 5.25 inches, not feet, of wire. Choice G is the cost of 1 foot of wire, not 5.25 feet. In choice J, you multiplied the correct answer by 5. Choice K is the correct answer multiplied by 25. These latter two errors are the likely result of unit conversion problems.

21. **The correct answer is D.** Factor the numerator and denominator of the fraction individually, canceling out any factors they have in common:

$$\frac{6a^4b+2a^3b}{3a^2-5a}=\frac{2a^3b(3a+1)}{(3a+1)(a-2)}$$

$$=\frac{2a^3b}{a-2}$$

In choices A and B, you cannot combine the terms in the numerator and denominator in this manner because they are not like terms. For choice C, you likely factored correctly, but then canceled factors incorrectly. To get choice E, you ignored the second term in both the numerator and denominator. You must factor the numerator and denominator separately and then cancel factors common to them both.

22. **The correct answer is F.** The lengths of the sides of the two rectangles are proportional. The perimeter of a rectangle is $2(l + w)$, where l and w are the length and width, respectively. Therefore, the perimeter of the original rectangle is $2(8 + 3) = 2(11) = 22$. The perimeter of the similar figure is 44, so each of its dimensions must be twice that of the original rectangle. Since the width of the original rectangle is 3, the width of the similar rectangle must be $2(3) = 6$. Choice G is the sum of the width and length of the given rectangle, not the width of the proportionally larger rectangle. Choice H is twice the width of the proportionally larger rectangle. Choice J is the length of the proportionally larger rectangle, not its width. Choice K is the perimeter of the given rectangle.

23. **The correct answer is D.** The company charges $19 per day, so a rental of d days will include a charge of $19d$; since choices A and B don't reflect this charge, they can be eliminated. The company also includes a charge of $0.18 for each mile driven in excess of 100 each day. This means that a rental including a total of m miles driven will include a charge of $0.18(m - 100d)$, where $100d$ represents the number of free miles. Therefore, the total rental price is $19d + 0.18(m - 100d)$, choice D. For choice C, you need to multiply 100 by d since the expression given is just the number of free miles for one day, not d days. For choice E, you should have multiplied 0.18 by $(m - 100d)$ since you get $100d$ free miles.

24. **The correct answer is G.** The perimeter is composed of four equal semicircles, so each must have a circumference of $16\pi \div 4 = 4\pi$. That means that the circumference of an entire circle would be 8π, and its diameter would be 8. Since the diameter of each semicircle lies on a face of the center square, each side of the square is

also 8. The area of a square is equal to a side length squared, or 64 square feet. Since the diameter of each semicircle is 8, its radius is 4. The area of a circle is πr^2, where r is a radius of a circle, so the area of an entire circle is 16π. This makes the area of each semicircle 8π, so the combined area of all four semicircles is 32π. Therefore, the area in square feet of the entire garden is $64 + 32\pi$. Choice F accounts only for one of the four congruent semicircles. Choice H accounts for four congruent *circles*, not semicircles. In choice J, the area of the square is 64 square units, not 256; the diameter here is doubled. In choice K, the area of the square is not 256 units, and you accounted for four congruent circles, not semicircles.

25. **The correct answer is B.** The closed circle at 2 indicates that the solution set to the inequality includes 2; eliminate choices A, D, and E since they do not include 2. The open circle at –2 indicates that the solution set does not include –2; eliminate choice C since it includes –2. This leaves only choice B, which says that x is greater than –2 and less than or equal to 2.

26. **The correct answer is J.** Pick a value for n. Since the remainder when n is divided by 9 is 6, the easiest value to pick is $9 + 6 = 15$. This means $7n = 7(15) = 105$. $105 \div 9 = 11$, remainder 6, so choice J is correct. This shows that all other choices are impossible.

27. **The correct answer is D.** A square has four equal sides, so the length of one side is equal to its perimeter divided by 4: $36 \div 4 = 9$. The area of a square is equal to a side length squared: $9^2 = 81$ square meters. Choice A is the length of one side. Choice B is the result of incorrectly computing 9^2 by multiplying base times exponent. Choice C is incorrect because the area and perimeter of such a square are not equal. Choice E is twice the area.

28. **The correct answer is K.** Find a common denominator in order to combine the two fractions. Since the denominator of the first fraction is 5 and that of the second is a, their common denominator is $5a$:

$$\left(\frac{a}{a}\right)\frac{a}{5}-\frac{5}{a}\left(\frac{5}{5}\right)=\frac{a^2}{5a}-\frac{25}{5a}$$

$$=\frac{a^2-25}{5a}$$

Choice F is incorrect because you don't subtract fractions by subtracting their numerators and denominators, respectively; you must first get a common denominator and then subtract the numerators. For choice G, you likely combined the fractions correctly, but then canceled like *terms* instead of like *factors* in the numerator and denominator. In choice H, the first term in the numerator is wrong. In choice J, the second term in the numerator is wrong; you should have multiplied by 5, not *a*.

29. **The correct answer is D.** The third side of a triangle must be greater than the positive difference of its other two sides, and less than their sum. In this triangle:

$$(7-2) < \text{third side} < (7+2)$$
$$5 < \text{third side} < 9$$

If the third side must be between 5 and 9, then:

$$(7+2+5) < \text{perimeter} < (7+2+9)$$
$$14 < \text{perimeter} < 18$$

The only choice within this range is 16, so choice D must be correct. Choices A, B, and C are too small, and choice E is too big.

30. **The correct answer is H.** Use your knowledge of common quadratics and plug in the given values:

$$(a-b)^2 = a^2 - 2ab + b^2$$
$$= a^2 + b^2 - 2ab$$
$$= 34 - 2(-15)$$
$$= 34 + 30$$
$$= 64$$

Since $(a-b)^2 = 64$, $a - b$ could be 8 or –8. Only 8 is an answer choice, so it must be correct.

Choice F implies that $a = b$, but it is not possible for $a^2 = -15$. For choice G, when simplifying $(a-b)^2$ you got 34 – 30 = 4 instead of 34 + 30 = 64. Choice J is twice the correct answer. Choice K is the value of $(a-b)^2$.

31. **The correct answer is C.** Since John has one card left over when he tries to divide them equally among 6, 7, and 8 friends, you know that his total number of cards must be 1 greater than a number that is a multiple of 6, 7, and 8. Subtract 1 from an answer choice, and then check to see whether this difference is divisible by all three numbers. You want to find the smallest number that satisfies this condition, so check the choices from smallest to largest. Choices D and E are too small, but 169 – 1 = 168 is divisible by all three numbers. In choice B, when the number is divided by 8, you get remainder 2. The number in choice A satisfies the criterion, but there is a smaller choice listed that also does.

32. **The correct answer is K.** Beware of choice F! Triangle *ABC* could be a 6-8-10 right triangle, but it doesn't *have* to be. You're told that 6 and 8 are sides of the triangle, but not that they are its legs. Remember that it is also possible for 8 to be the *hypotenuse* of the triangle, in which case:

$$6^2 + AC^2 = 8^2$$
$$AC^2 = 64 - 36 = 28$$
$$AC = \sqrt{28} = 2\sqrt{7}$$

Since either value, 10 or $2\sqrt{7}$, is possible, choice K is correct. For choice H, you need to take the square root. For choice J, the square root of a difference of two numbers is not equal to the difference of the square roots of the two numbers, in general; you made this arithmetic error when applying the Pythagorean theorem.

33. **The correct answer is D.** A square has four equal sides, so each side of the square has a length of $4s \div 4 = s$. Adding 5 makes its length $s + 5$; subtracting 2 makes its width $s - 2$. The area of a rectangle is equal to length times width, or $(s + 5)(s - 2)$. Using FOIL, you find that the area of this rectangle is $s^2 - 2s + 5s - 10 = s^2 + 3s - 10$. Choice A is the perimeter of the new rectangle, not its area, and choice B is half the perimeter of the rectangle. In choice C, you forgot the middle term when squaring the binomial. For choice E, the width is $s - 2$, not $s + 2$.

34. **The correct answer is H.** The cosine of an angle is equal to $\dfrac{\text{adjacent side}}{\text{hypotenuse}}$. Since the cosine of angle *YXZ* is $\dfrac{\sqrt{2}}{2}$, we can set *XZ* equal to $\sqrt{2}$ and *XY* equal to 2 for the purposes of this question. The tangent of an angle is equal to $\dfrac{\text{opposite side}}{\text{adjacent side}}$, so you need the length of segment *YZ*, the side adjacent to angle *Y*, in order to solve. Since one leg of this right triangle is $\sqrt{2}$ and its hypotenuse is 2, it is an isosceles right triangle with sides in a ratio of $1:1:\sqrt{2}$. That means that $YZ = \sqrt{2}$, and the tangent of angle *ZYX* is $\dfrac{\sqrt{2}}{\sqrt{2}} = 1$. Choice F is too small (in fact, it is half the correct result). Choice G is the sine of *ZYX*. Choice J is the secant of *ZYX*, and choice K is the length of *XY*.

Alternatively, once you realize that the triangle is isosceles, you know that the opposite side and the adjacent side are of equal length, so the tangent of angle *ZYX* must be the ratio of two equal values, or 1.

35. **The correct answer is C.** There are twice as many boys as girls in the class, so let x equal the number of girls and $2x$ equal the number of boys. This means that there are $3x$ total students in the class. Given a class average of 84, calculate the total of all students' grades:

$$\text{average} = \frac{\text{sum of values}}{\text{number of values}}$$

$$\text{sum of grades} = \text{average grade} \times \text{number of students}$$

$$= 84(3x)$$

$$= 252x$$

You're also given that the girls' average is 91, so:

$$\text{sum of girls' grades} = \text{average grade} \times \text{number of girls}$$

$$= 91x$$

If the total score for the class is $252x$ and the girls' total score is $91x$, then the boys' total score must be their difference, $161x$. Therefore, the boys' average is $\frac{161x}{2x} = 80.5$. You could also have started off by saying that the ratio of boys to girls is 2:1, which means that the average is weighted 2 to 1 in favor of boys. Given that the girls' average, 91, is higher than the class average, 84, by 7 points, it follows that the boys' average must be *lower* than the class average (eliminate choices D and E right away) by exactly *half* of this difference: $84 - 3.5 = 80.5$. Similarly, choices A and B are too small and can also be eliminated.

36. **The correct answer is K.** When solving inequalities that contain absolute value signs, you must consider and solve for two cases: the value with a positive sign and the value with a negative sign. Remember to reverse the direction of the inequality sign when you make the value negative:

$$\begin{array}{ll} 3x-2 < x & 3x-2 > -x \\ 2x-2 < 0 & 4x-2 > 0 \\ 2x < 2 & 4x > 2 \\ x < 1 & x > \frac{1}{2} \end{array}$$

So $\frac{1}{2} < x < 1$, which is represented by the graph for choice K. In choice F, you ignored one half of the inequality; you also need to account for the fact that $x < 1$. In choice G, you also ignored one half of the inequality and did not account for the fact that $x > \frac{1}{2}$. Choice H is the reflection of the correct interval over $\frac{1}{2}$; you likely used a wrong definition of absolute value.

In choice J, the left endpoint is wrong; it should be $\frac{1}{2}$, not $-\frac{1}{2}$.

37. **The correct answer is C.** Based on the given description and figure, the unshaded square is exactly one fourth of either larger square, so within one of the larger squares the ratio of shaded area to unshaded area is 3:1. However, there is a second square that has an identical shaded region but no additional unshaded region, so over both squares the ratio of shaded area to unshaded area becomes 6:1. Therefore, if the shaded area is x, the unshaded area must be $\frac{x}{6}$. Choice A is the portion of the overall region (formed using the two overlapping squares) that is shaded, but x represents the area of just the shaded region, not including the unshaded square in the middle. For choice B, it is true that 3 of 4 congruent small squares are shaded within a single larger square, but $\frac{3}{4}$ is not the correct proportion of the entire shaded area that describes the unshaded region. For choice D, you included the unshaded region as part of the region whose area is x. For choice E, you included the unshaded region *twice* in the region whose area is x.

38. **The correct answer is H.**

Since $\text{average} = \frac{\text{sum of terms}}{\text{number of terms}}$, it follows that the sum of terms is equal to the product of the average and the number of terms. Therefore, the sum of these three positive integers is $3(99) = 297$. You can find the greatest possible value for one number by setting the other two numbers equal to their smallest possible values. Since each term is a different positive integer, the smallest integer is 1, and the next smallest is 2. That makes the greatest possible value for one of the numbers $297 - 1 - 2 = 294$.

Choice F is $\frac{99}{3}$, so it cannot be one of the biggest integers of three total that average to 99. Choice G is also way too small; you can make one of the integers very large as long as you make the others very small. Choice J is too big, since the smallest the other two integers can be is 1 and 2, and the average of 1, 2, and 295 exceeds 99. Choice K can be eliminated for the same reason as choice J.

39. **The correct answer is B.** The key to this question is recognizing that triangle ABC is a 30-60-90 right triangle. In such a triangle the sides are related in a ratio of $1:\sqrt{3}:2$. Since $BC = 3\sqrt{3}$, it follows that $AB = \left(\sqrt{3}\right)\left(3\sqrt{3}\right) = 9$. Therefore, angle BCA, the angle

opposite segment *AB*, must measure 60°. Choice A is impossible because the sum of all three angles in a triangle is 180 degrees. Choice C uses the wrong proportions; this is a 30-60-90 triangle, not a 45-45-90 triangle. Choice D is the measure of angle *BAC*. Choice E is not true because you can use the Pythagorean theorem with the proportions of a 30-60-90 triangle.

40. **The correct answer is K.** If two lines intersect at a point, the *x*- and *y*-coordinates of the point must satisfy the equations of both lines. Solve the system of equations and you will find this point. If you multiply the second equation by 2, you can add the equations so that the *x*-terms drop out:

$$y + 2x = -4$$
$$+2(3y - x = 9)$$
$$\overline{7y = 14}$$
$$y = 2$$

Plug *y* = 2 into either equation to find the value of *x*: 2 + 2*x* = –4, 2*x* = –6, *x* = –3. Therefore, the coordinates of the point of intersection of these two lines is (–3, 2). Plugging choices F, G, H, and J into both equations shows that at most, only one equation holds in each case.

41. **The correct answer is A.** First, use your knowledge of angles in a straight line to figure out the measure of the additional angles noted in the figure below.

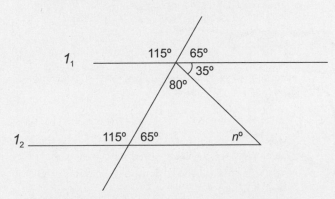

The figure shows two parallel lines with two different transversals. If you extend the lines of the transversal on the right (the downward-sloping side of the triangle), you'll see that it forms acute angles measuring 35° and *n*. Since all acute angles that are formed when a transversal crosses parallel lines must be equal, *n* = 35°. Choices B, C, and D are all angles that occur in the diagram (see above), but they are not the value of *n*. Choice E is the supplement of angle *n*.

42. **The correct answer is F.** Rewrite 2*y* + *x* = 6 in slope-intercept form:

$$2y = -x + 6$$
$$y = -\frac{1}{2}x + 3$$

Therefore, its slope is $-\frac{1}{2}$. Choice G would make the line horizontal, since having no *x*-term in the equation means the slope is 0. Choice H is incorrect because you must divide by the coefficient of *y* and take *x* to the right side before identifying the slope of the line. Choice J is incorrect because the coefficient of *y* is not the slope of the line. Choice K is the *y*-intercept.

43. **The correct answer is C.** Each choice represents a number in scientific notation by raising a numerical value between 1 and 10 to a power of 10. Rewriting the given value of 0.000000301 in this way yields 3.01×10^{-7}. Since changing the power of 10 would most significantly change the overall value, the answer choice with the *same* power of 10, choice C, will be closest.

All other choices are off by at least a factor of 10 and are obtained by making an error when converting to scientific notation.

44. **The correct answer is H.** You're given the side of the triangle adjacent to the angle marked 41° and asked about its hypotenuse. The cosine of an angle is equal to $\frac{\text{adjacent side}}{\text{hypotenuse}}$, so:

$$\cos 41° = \frac{8}{XZ}$$
$$(XZ)(\cos 41°) = 8$$
$$XZ = \frac{8}{\cos 41°}$$

In choices F and G, you solved the cosine equation incorrectly. Choice J is incorrect because you must use cos(41) instead of sin(41) since you are given the adjacent side to that angle and you want to find the hypotenuse. Choice K = *XY*, not *XZ*.

45. **The correct answer is B.** To find *f*(*g*(*x*)), plug the expression that defines *g*(*x*)—that is, *x* + 1—into *f*(*x*) for *x* and evaluate:

$$f(g(x)) = f(x + 1)$$
$$= (x + 2)^2 + 2(x + 1) + 1$$
$$= x^2 + 2x + 1 + 2x + 2 + 1$$
$$= x^2 + 4x + 4$$

Answer Keys and Explanations

Choice A is equal to $g(f(x))$. In choice C, when simplifying $(x + 1)^2$, you likely forgot to include the middle term. The coefficient of x is wrong in choice D; this is the likely result of an error using the distributive property. Choice E is just $g(x)$; you need to plug this in for x in the formula for $f(x)$ to get the composition.

46. **The correct answer is F.** There are 20 sections on the spinner, and we want the probability of landing on red to be $\frac{1}{4}$. Use a proportion to determine how many sections need to be red in order for this to happen:

$$\frac{1}{4} = \frac{r}{20}$$
$$4r = 20$$
$$r = 5$$

So for the probability of landing on red to be $\frac{1}{4}$, 5 of the 20 sections must be red. The spinner currently has 12 red sections, so 7 of them must be changed to blue. Choice G is the final number of sections you want to be red, not how many red sections should change to blue. Choice H is the reciprocal of the goal number of red sections. Choice J subtracts 5 from the total number of blue sections, instead of using it as the final goal number of red sections. Choice K would result in 10 final red sections, not 5.

47. **The correct answer is C.** Create a Venn diagram showing what the guests ate:

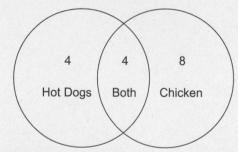

Now you can see that the number of people who ate hot dogs, chicken, or both is $4 + 4 + 8 = 16$. That means that $24 - 16 = 8$ guests ate neither, which is $\frac{8}{24} = \frac{1}{3}$ of the guests. Choice A is the fraction who ate either hot dogs, chicken, or both. Choice B is the fraction who ate chicken. Choice D is too small, and note that $\frac{1}{5}$ of 24 would not produce an integer. Choice E is the fraction who ate both, not neither.

48. **The correct answer is G.** Factor the denominator of the fraction and cancel out any factors it has in common with the numerator:

$$\frac{x - y}{x^2 - y^2} = \frac{x - y}{(x + y)(x - y)} = \frac{1}{x + y}$$

In choice F, you cannot cancel *terms* in the numerator and denominator; you can only cancel like *factors*. For choice H, you mistreated $x^2 - y^2$ as $(x - y)^2$. In choice J, you factored $x^2 - y^2$ incorrectly as $(x - y)(y - x)$. Choice K is the reciprocal of the correct answer.

49. **The correct answer is B.** In a right triangle, the two acute angles total 90°. Since one of the acute angles in this triangle is 45°, the other must be 45° as well. This means that it is an isosceles right triangle with sides in a ratio of $1 : 1 : \sqrt{2}$. If the hypotenuse of the triangle is 5, then the length of each leg must be

$$\frac{5}{\sqrt{2}} = \left(\frac{\sqrt{2}}{\sqrt{2}}\right)\frac{5}{\sqrt{2}} = \frac{5\sqrt{2}}{2}.$$

Choice A is incorrect because the length of the leg is not one-half the hypotenuse. For choices C and E, you likely mistook the triangle as having proportions $1 : 2 : \sqrt{3}$. For choice D, you should be dividing by $\sqrt{2}$, not multiplying by it.

50. **The correct answer is K.** The secant is the reciprocal of the cosine, and tangent is equal to $\frac{\text{sine}}{\text{cosine}}$. Therefore, $(\sec x)(\tan x) = \frac{1}{\cos x} \times \frac{\sin x}{\cos x} = \frac{\sin x}{\cos^2 x}$. For choice F, recall that $\sec(x) = \frac{1}{\cos(x)}$, not $\frac{1}{\sin(x)}$. For choice G, recall that $\tan(x) = \frac{\sin(x)}{\cos(x)}$, not the reciprocal of this quantity. Choice H is just $\sec(x)$; you must multiply it by $\tan(x)$. In choice J, the $\cos(x)$ and $\sin(x)$ terms should be interchanged.

51. **The correct answer is C.** The points at which a parabola intersects the x-axis are equal to the roots of the quadratic equation that defines the parabola, and this allows you to predict something about the parabola. The discriminant of the quadratic equation reveals whether it has 0, 1, or 2 real roots. Since the number of roots is the same as the number of x-intercepts, you can use the discriminant to predict the number of points at which a parabola will intersect the x-axis. The discriminant of a quadratic equation is $b^2 - 4ac$. When it is positive, the equation has two real roots and intersects the x-axis at two points; when it is 0, the equation has

one real root and intersects the x-axis at one point; and when it is negative, the equation has no real roots and intersects the x-axis at zero points. Find the discriminant of $y = x^2 + 2x - 3$: $2^2 - 4(1)(-3) = 4 + 12 = 16$. Since it is positive, the equation has two real roots, and the parabola intersects the x-axis in two places. This reasoning shows why choices A, B, D, and E are not feasible.

52. **The correct answer is K.** After 1 black sock is removed, there are 6 black, 5 white, and 4 green socks, for a total of 15 socks. The probability of NOT selecting a black sock is equal to the probability of selecting a white or green sock, or $\frac{5+4}{15} = \frac{9}{15} = \frac{3}{5}$. Choice F is the probability of a single sock (irrespective of color) of being selected from the drawer. In choice G, you kept the sample size as 16 instead of changing it to 15. Choice H is the probability of the complement of the event. For choice J, you included the removed black sock among those in the drawer for the second selection.

53. **The correct answer is E.** Putting both equations into slope-intercept form will make them easier to work with:

$2y + x = 4$
$2y = -x + 4$
$y = -\frac{1}{2}x + 2$

$3y + 6x = 6$
$3y = -6x + 6$
$y = -2x + 2$

When a line is in slope intercept form, $y = mx + b$, its slope is m and its y-intercept is b. Lines 1 and 2 both have y-intercepts of 2, which means that they both pass through point (0, 2), so choice E is correct. Because the slopes of the lines are $-\frac{1}{2}$ and -2, choice C cannot be correct. If the lines were parallel, their slopes would be equal, so choice A cannot be correct either. If the lines were perpendicular, their slopes would be negative reciprocals, so choice B can also be eliminated. If both lines passed through the origin, the coordinates (0, 0) would satisfy both equations; however, if you plug (0, 0) into the equations, it satisfies neither equation, eliminating choice D as well.

54. **The correct answer is J.** The ratio of the areas of two figures is equal to the square of the ratios of their corresponding linear measurements. Since the ratio of the circumferences, a linear measurement, is 4:9, the ratio of the areas must be $4^2 : 9^2 = 16:81$, choice J. In choice F, you took the square root when you should have squared the values. Choice G is the ratio of the circumferences, not the areas. For choice H, you should

have squared each portion, not multiplied by their respective square roots. In choice K, the ratio is written in the wrong order.

55. **The correct answer is B.** If $ab > 0$, then ab is positive. This means that both a and b are positive or both a and b are negative. Likewise, since bc is positive both b and c are positive, or both b and c are negative. So if b is positive, then all three variables are positive, and if b is negative, then all three variables are negative. Evaluate each choice with this in mind:

Choice A: $b > 0$: If b is positive, this is true; if b is negative, it is not true. Eliminate.

Choice B: $ac > 0$: If b is positive, both a and c are positive and their product is positive; if b is negative, both a and c are negative and their product is positive. Since the expression is true in either case, this choice is correct.

Choice C: $abc > 0$: If b is positive, all three variables are positive and their product is positive; if b is negative, all three variables are negative and their product is negative. Eliminate.

Choice D: $ab^2 > 0$: If b is positive, a is positive and this product is positive; if b is negative, a is negative and this product is negative. Eliminate.

Choice E: $\frac{b}{ac} > 0$: If b is positive, all three variables are positive and this expression is positive; if b is negative, all three variables are negative and this expression is negative. Eliminate.

56. **The correct answer is J.** Janey must sit in the middle, so one of the 7 seats is taken. This leaves 6 choices for the first friend, then 5 choices for the second friend, 4 choices for the third friend, 3 choices for the fourth friend, and 2 choices for the fifth friend. So the total number of possible arrangements of the 6 people is $1 \times 6 \times 5 \times 4 \times 3 \times 2 = 720$. Choice F is the number of ways of arranging four seats, not six. In choice G, you multiplied the two numbers in the problem, but this is not the way to compute the number of arrangements. Choice H is the number of ways of arranging five friends in five seats, not six seats. Choice K is the number of ways to arrange six people in seven seats, but Janey's seat is fixed. So you must arrange five friends in six seats.

57. **The correct answer is C.** Volume of a rectangular solid is lwh. Doubling each dimension would give you a volume of $(2l)(2w)(2h) = 8lwh$, which is 8 times the original volume. Choice A does not double each of the three dimensions. In choice B, $2^3 = 8$, not 6.

For choice D, you seemed to properly double two of the dimensions, but then tripled the third; all three dimensions should be doubled. Choice E is incorrect because there are three 2's being multiplied, not four.

58. **The correct answer is H.** Pick a number for the original price of the stock. Choose 100, since it's the easiest number to use with percentages. On Tuesday, the price increases by 20%, so the price increases to $100 + $20 = $120. On Wednesday, the price falls by 25%; 25% of 120 is 30, so the price drops to $120 – $30 = $90. The original price was $100, so the price of the stock must increase by $10. As a percent of the stock price, this is:

$$\frac{10}{90} \times 100\% = \frac{1}{9} \times 100\% = \frac{100\%}{9} = 11\frac{1}{9}\%$$

Choice F is the result of adding the percentages together instead of applying them to specific amounts. Choice G is double the correct percentage. In choice J, the dollar increase in the stock is $10, not 10%. Choice K is incorrect because you cannot subtract percentages like this; they must each be applied to specific values.

59. **The correct answer is D.** The sine of an angle is $\frac{\text{opposite side}}{\text{hypotenuse}}$. Since the sine of $\angle WXZ = \frac{a}{b}$, $WZ = a$ and $XZ = b$.

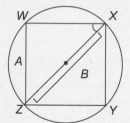

Since segment XZ passes through the center of the circle, it is a diameter of the circle. The area of a circle is equal to πr^2, where r is a radius of the circle. The diameter of the circle is b, so its radius is half of this, or $\frac{b}{2}$. Plugging this into the area formula gives you:

$$\pi\left(\frac{b}{2}\right)^2 = \pi \times \frac{b^2}{4}$$
$$= \frac{b^2\pi}{4}$$

Choice A is incorrect because a is not the radius of the circle. Choice B is incorrect because b is the diameter, not the radius. Choice C is the circumference of the circle, not its area. Choice E is incorrect because you must square the radius when computing the area.

60. **The correct answer is G.** Since the units digit of 338 is 8, the units digits of its powers will follow the pattern of powers of 8. You can use your calculator to figure the first few powers of 8 and find this pattern:

$$8^1 = \underline{8} \qquad\qquad 8^5 = 32,76\underline{8}$$
$$8^2 = 6\underline{4} \qquad\qquad 8^6 = 262,14\underline{4}$$
$$8^3 = 51\underline{2} \qquad\qquad \text{etc.}$$
$$8^4 = 4,09\underline{6}$$

The pattern here is 8, 4, 2, 6. That means that every fourth power of 8 (and, in turn, of 338) will have a units digit of 6. In this question, the number is raised to the 340th power; since 340 is evenly divisible by 4 with no remainder, the 340th power corresponds to the 4th term in the pattern, 6. Choices F, H, J, and K are all possible digits that arise, but none is the units digit for the specified power.

READING

1.	B	11.	D	21.	B	31.	A
2.	J	12.	F	22.	H	32.	H
3.	C	13.	C	23.	D	33.	D
4.	J	14.	J	24.	H	34.	G
5.	C	15.	B	25.	A	35.	D
6.	G	16.	J	26.	J	36.	G
7.	A	17.	C	27.	B	37.	D
8.	G	18.	F	28.	F	38.	H
9.	D	19.	B	29.	C	39.	B
10.	F	20.	J	30.	J	40.	F

1. **The correct answer is B.** If Miss Lily Bart was late for a train, she probably would be more concerned with getting on it than chatting with Mr. Selden, so choice A is not likely. If she were not fond of him, she probably would not go out of her way to chat with him in the first place, so you can eliminate choice C too. While Mr. Selden wonders what Miss Lily Bart is doing in town at this time of year, there is no reason to conclude that she is deciding whether or not to move back to town, so choice D is not the best answer. The best answer is choice B, since Miss Lily Bart seems like she has come to a place where there are a lot of people so she can meet someone, and she does go out of her way to meet Mr. Selden, who has already reached this conclusion.

2. **The correct answer is J.** Miss Lily Bart is not physical with Mr. Selden, so *affectionate* (choice F) does not describe her behavior accurately. Although Mr. Selden believes there is an air of mystery to Miss Lily Bart, her behavior toward him is hardly mysterious, so choice G is incorrect. Her comment that Mr. Selden has come to her rescue is meant jokingly and not literally, so choice H is not the best answer. The best answer is choice J, since Miss Lily Bart is merely being friendly with Mr. Selden.

3. **The correct answer is C.** Mr. Selden imagines that Miss Lily Bart may try to "elude" him, which suggests that she might not want to talk to him, so choice C is the best answer. At the end of the passage, Mr. Selden wonders if Miss Lily Bart has reached the birthday "with which her rivals credited her," which suggests the opposite of choice A. He never expresses concern that she might think he is being too forward (choice B) or that she might not remember who he is (choice D).

4. **The correct answer is J.** *Cheer* is used as a verb in line 23. Since *encouragement* and *joy* are both nouns, choices F and G can be eliminated. Choice H, app*laud*, is

a verb, but it does not make much sense to applaud a long evening. However, it does make sense to brighten an evening, so choice J is the best explanation of how *cheer* is used in the context of the sentence.

5. **The correct answer is C.** This is a detail question. The last sentence of Paragraph 3 reveals that Emma has just finished having dinner with her father, and the next paragraph finds her thinking about Miss Taylor's marriage. So choice C is the correct answer. The wedding has already taken place before this passage begins, so choice A is incorrect. Emma never speaks to Mr. Weston in this passage, so choice B cannot be correct. It is Emma's father who goes to bed after dinner, not Emma, so choice D is not correct.

6. **The correct answer is G.** Paragraph 4 confirms that Mr. Weston has "pleasant manners" and "unexceptional character." However, there is no indication that he has "high self-regard," though Paragraph 2 does mention that Emma thinks "a little too well of herself." Since that quality does not apply to Mr. Weston, any answer choice that includes Statement III can be eliminated, which means choices H and J. Choice F makes the mistake of failing to acknowledge the fact that Mr. Weston had unexceptional character. Only choice G includes the qualities mentioned in the passage without including the quality that is not mentioned.

7. **The correct answer is A.** As each passage begins, the two characters are without companions, though Miss Lily Bart may have made a new one by the end of Passage A. In Passage B, Emma has lost a companion, but this happened before the passage even began, so choice B is true of neither her nor Miss Lily Bart. Only Emma reminisces about a companion she has lost, so choice C is not the best answer, and only Miss Lily Bart

may have met a new companion, so choice D is wrong too.

8. **The correct answer is G.** Miss Lily Bart goes out of her way to meet Mr. Selden in Passage A, and Emma laments the fact that she does not have a companion in Passage B, so choice G is the best answer. However, only Miss Lily Bart is described as a dancer, so choice F is not the best answer. Emma seems a bit depressed in Passage B, but Miss Lily Bart does not in Passage A, so choice H is unlikely. There is no reason to conclude that these two characters would or would not get along, so you can eliminate choice J.

9. **The correct answer is D.** In Passage A, two people make an effort to interact with each other and in Passage B a woman misses the fact that she no longer has a governess to interact with, so choice D is the best answer and choice A can be eliminated. Only Emma's relationship with her governess has ended, so choice B is not the best description of the passages' main ideas. Only Miss Lily Bart seems to have formed a new friendship, so choice C does not describe both passages either.

10. **The correct answer is F.** According to Passage A, Miss Lily Bart "has reached the nine-and-twentieth birthday," which means she is 29 years old or older. Passage B states that Emma was five years old when she first came to know Miss Taylor and it is now sixteen years later, which means that Emma is at least twenty-one years old. Therefore, choice F is true. There are no details about whether or not they live in cities (choice G). Only Miss Lily Bart is at a train station, and she may not actually be waiting for a train, so choice H is incorrect. Only Emma has attended a wedding, which is over before Passage B even begins, so choice J is wrong.

11. **The correct answer is D.** This is an inference question about rulers at the end of the fifteenth century. There is nothing to support choices A or B. Choice C is the opposite of the truth; the passage says that permanent ambassadors typically had money problems. The next-to-last line of the second paragraph supports choice D as being the right answer.

12. **The correct answer is F.** This is both an inference question and a cause-and-effect question. According to the third paragraph, the size of an ambassador's entourage "represented his home country's wealth and the importance of his task." You can infer that if an ambassador had a small entourage, he would not be considered very important. Choices G, H, and J are not supported by the passage, so choice F is the correct answer.

13. **The correct answer is C.** This is a detail question that compares the first permanent ambassadors in Europe with modern ambassadors. Choice A is incorrect because modern ambassadors don't have horses. There is no support for choice B. Much of the passage describes the challenges of being a permanent ambassador, making choice C correct. The opposite of choice D is true, as indicated by much of the passage.

14. **The correct answer is J.** This is a detail question. According to the paragraph, ambassadors would send information back home to their rulers. You can infer, then, that an ambassador's king was not part of his entourage, so you can eliminate choice F, which is the only one that includes Statement I. Both horses, Statement II, and servants, Statement III, are mentioned in the paragraph. The only choice containing both of these statements is choice J. Choices F and G each fails to include one of the correct statements.

15. **The correct answer is B.** The word *supports* indicates that this is an inference question about the seventh paragraph. Choice A is wrong because the paragraph states that encryption was a "relatively new concept." The second and third sentence of the seventh paragraph support choice B as being the right answer. There is no support for choice C. The last sentence of the paragraph counters choice D.

16. **The correct answer is J.** This question asks you to understand why the author made a particular choice—in this case, the choice to include the anecdote about de Puebla showing up at the King's court for the food. The paragraph in which this anecdote appears says that living abroad was expensive, and that when funds ran low, de Puebla had to move into a "modest inn" with "simple meals." You can infer that the free meals he got while conducting business with King Henry VII were much better than the meat pies he got at his inn. The story, then, supports the idea that permanent ambassadors didn't receive enough money to live very well, choice J. Choices F, G, and H are not supported by the passage.

17. **The correct answer is C.** This is a detail question regarding the final paragraph. There is no support for choices A and B. The next-to-last sentence in the final paragraph directly mentions political value, so choice C is the right answer. There is no support for choice D.

18. **The correct answer is F.** This is a main idea question regarding the second paragraph. The paragraph describes the difficult journey to the ambassador's host country, and concludes by stating that ambassadors

found their hosts less than welcoming. That makes choice F the correct answer. Choice G supports the main idea but is not the general or main idea of the paragraph. There is no support for choice H. The importance of status symbols, choice J, is addressed in the third paragraph, not the second.

19. **The correct answer is B.** This is a detail question. The phrase appears in the first sentence of the sixth paragraph. Statements I and II are supported by the rest of the sentence. Statement III does not apply, so choice D can be eliminated. Choices A and C each fails to include one of the correct statements. Therefore, the correct answer is choice B.

20. **The correct answer is J.** This is a detail question about de Puebla. The third sentence of the fourth paragraph provides the exact answer, choice J. Choices F and H are not correct. Choice G might have been one of de Puebla's duties, but the passage states that he originally went to England to arrange a marriage, so it is a wrong choice.

21. **The correct answer is B.** This is a detail question about the Arab legions. Relevant information appears in the fourth paragraph. Choice A refers to the foreign invaders mentioned in the preceding paragraph. Choice B is supported as being correct, starting with the second sentence of the fourth paragraph. There is no support for choice C; if the Arab legions influenced Berber music, then they must have had existing music before this time. The passage does not support choice D.

22. **The correct answer is H.** This detail question asks you to go back into the passage and do a little research. The fifth paragraph discusses instruments used in traditional Berber music, including castanets and drumskins that are thumped (in other words, drums). The oud is mentioned two paragraphs later as part of Andalucian music, not Berber music, so choices G and J, which include Statement II, can be eliminated. Choice F fails to include both of the correct statements. The correct answer is choice H.

23. **The correct answer is D.** This is a detail question. Double castanets (choice A) and galloping rhythm (choice B) appear in the third sentence of the sixth paragraph and refer to music of the Ganawa, not Andalucian music. Choice C also refers to Ganawa music, as stated in the first sentence of the sixth paragraph. Choice D is correct, supported by the next-to-last sentence in the seventh paragraph.

24. **The correct answer is H.** This is a detail question about popular musicians in the West in regard to Moroccan music. There is no support for choices F and G. The second half of the opening paragraph supports choice H as being correct. Choice J is incorrect because the musicians that the author cites were presumably already playing music when they visited Morocco.

25. **The correct answer is A.** The entire second paragraph discusses the variety of geographic features and climates in Morocco, supporting choice A as being correct. Choice B is incorrect; the passage mentions that there are prosperous villages in the mountains, but it does not state whether the majority of Moroccans live in these villages. This paragraph does not discuss music (choice C) or Berbers (choice D).

26. **The correct answer is J.** This is a vocabulary-in-context question appearing in the final sentence of the third paragraph. Choice F is the opposite of *hospitable*. *Hostile* would not make sense in the sentence. Choices G and H also would not make sense; neither *talented* nor *dominant* would really contradict the Berber's stubborn or courageous spirit. Choice J is correct, as *hospitable* means friendly and welcoming.

27. **The correct answer is B.** This is a detail question. Medieval court music and flamenco are discussed in the second half of the seventh paragraph. The entire paragraph is about the influence of Andalucian music, making choice B the only possible answer. The passage never suggests that Berber music (choice A), Arabian music (choice C), or Tuareg music (choice D) influenced medieval court music and flamenco.

28. **The correct answer is F.** This is a main point question about the third paragraph. The entire paragraph discusses the different invaders of Morocco, making choice F the correct answer. The Berber people are being invaded; they are not the invaders (choice G). Choice H is a detail from the third-from-last sentence. Choice J does not apply to this paragraph.

29. **The correct answer is C.** This is an inference question. Current Moroccan musicians are discussed in the final paragraph, which says that many Moroccan musicians are blending the different traditional musical styles of Morocco and also incorporating modern styles. That's choice C. Choice A is the opposite of that, and there is no support in the passage for choices B and D.

30. **The correct answer is J.** This is an inference question about the provided phrase. The quote is from the fourth sentence of the fifth paragraph. There is no mention

here of Allah (choice F), who is discussed in the fourth paragraph. The second half of the sentence containing the phrase says the musicians refer to, not compete with, each other, as choice G might suggest. The next sentence states that the musicians warm up their instruments *after* they banter (choice H). The final sentence supports choice J as the correct answer.

31. **The correct answer is A.** This is an inference question about the phrase "ignition key," which is the SA node, as indicated in the first sentence of the third paragraph. Choice A is supported by the first sentence of the fourth paragraph, with the phrase, "originates the electro-chemical stimulation of the heart." Likewise, an ignition key originates the signal for a car or plane to start. Choice B refers to the *medulla oblongata*, as described in the final sentence of the third paragraph. There is no support for choices C or D.

32. **The correct answer is H.** This is a detail question about the AV node. The third sentence of the fifth paragraph provides the exact answer, choice H. That concrete answer makes choices F, G, and J impossible.

33. **The correct answer is D.** This is a two-part detail question. Statement I is supported by the last sentence of the fifth paragraph. Statement II is supported by the next-to-last sentence of the sixth paragraph. Statement III is supported by the final two sentences of the sixth paragraph. The only answer containing all three statements is choice D. Choices A, B, and C each fails to include at least one of the correct statements.

34. **The correct answer is G.** This is a detail question relating to the first paragraph. The second sentence specifically provides the correct answer, choice G. There is no support for choices F, H, or J.

35. **The correct answer is D.** This is a detail question comparing the cardiac muscles with the skeletal muscles. The third sentence of the second paragraph states that the cardiac muscles work separately from the nervous system. The third sentence of the third paragraph says that the skeletal muscles receive their electrical signals from the central nervous system. Therefore, choice D is correct. There is no support for choices A, B, or C.

36. **The correct answer is G.** This is a two-part detail question about the AV node. Statement I is supported by the second sentence of the fifth paragraph. Statement II is supported by the third sentence of the fifth paragraph. Statement III refers to the *AV bundle*, mentioned in the second sentence of the sixth

paragraph, so you can eliminate choices H and J since they both include Statement III. The only answer containing Statements I and II, but not Statement III, is choice G. Choice F fails to include both of the correct statements.

37. **The correct answer is D.** This is a main idea question about the first two paragraphs. Heart transplants (choice A) are not discussed. Choice B is covered in the seventh and eighth paragraphs. Choice C is discussed in the third and fourth paragraphs. The first two paragraphs discuss the basic functions of the heart, choice D.

38. **The correct answer is H.** This is a detail question that also requires you to make an inference. Choice F refers to depolarization of the SA node, as mentioned in the second sentence of the fourth paragraph. Choice G refers to the AV node, as mentioned in the final sentence of the fifth paragraph. It can be inferred that choice H is the right answer from the information in the final two sentences of the sixth paragraph. The medulla oblongata (choice J) is not mentioned in relation to pacemakers.

39. **The correct answer is B.** This is a detail question about blue blood cells, which are mentioned in the first paragraph. The phrase "oxygen-poor (blue)," mentioned in the fourth sentence, supports choice B as being correct. This same information eliminates choice A. The fifth sentence says the blue blood cells get sent to the lungs, so choice C is not correct. The final sentence of the paragraph, relating to choice D, discusses red, not blue, blood cells.

40. **The correct answer is F.** This is an inference question. The information appears in the final paragraph. The paragraph describes when each of the three kinds of artificial pacemakers would send electrical signals, making choice F correct. The passage indicates that a different artificial pacemaker applies to choices G, H, and J.

SCIENCE

1.	C	11.	D	21.	B	31.	C
2.	J	12.	H	22.	H	32.	J
3.	A	13.	C	23.	B	33.	D
4.	G	14.	F	24.	J	34.	G
5.	B	15.	C	25.	C	35.	A
6.	G	16.	J	26.	G	36.	F
7.	A	17.	D	27.	A	37.	B
8.	J	18.	G	28.	H	38.	H
9.	B	19.	C	29.	D	39.	D
10.	G	20.	F	30.	G	40.	J

1. **The correct answer is C.** While the risk of cardiovascular disease increases at a generally steeper and more consistent pace for diabetics than for non-diabetics, it nonetheless increases for both groups as glycated hemoglobin levels increase. The upward slope of both lines attests to this fact. Choices A, B, and D all claim one or both groups do not show an increase.

2. **The correct answer is J.** Figure 1 indicates that a non-diabetic with a glycated hemoglobin level of 9% has just over a 50% chance of developing cardiovascular disease. Stretching that line out in the same direction, according to the trend thus far established in the graph, one would expect it to hit the 70% risk level some place to the right of the 9% glycated hemoglobin level. This person would thus be expected to have a glycated hemoglobin level greater than 9%. Choices F, G, and H are all levels already marked on the graph, so you can see they're not correct.

3. **The correct answer is A.** A high glycated hemoglobin level is defined as a level of 5% or greater. There are $19 + 29 + 17 + 2$, or 67 total people in this category, which represents a majority. This makes choice A correct and choice D incorrect.

   Choice B is incorrect because the passage explicitly states that the people represented in Table 1 are all non-diabetics. Don't be fooled by the fact that some people in the study have glycated hemoglobin levels of 7% and above, which are levels deemed a "strong indicator of diabetes." The notion of a strong indicator concerns probabilities, which does not supersede the out-and-out assertion that the 100 people represented in Table 1 do not have the disease.

   Choice C is also incorrect. 48 of the 100 people studied—that is, a minority—have a glycated

hemoglobin level of 6% or more. Checking the data in Figure 1, only people with glycated hemoglobin levels of 6% or more have a greater than 10% chance of cardiovascular disease. Thus, a majority of test subjects represented in Table 1 do not have a risk of cardiovascular disease greater than 10%.

4. **The correct answer is G.** Choice G can be arrived at by noticing the difference in the shapes of the two upward lines on the graph. The diabetics' line is very nearly straight, indicating a steady and consistent rise in cardiovascular disease risk for each 1% increase in glycated hemoglobin. The non-diabetics' line, however, does not increase at all between 3% and 4% glycated hemoglobin and barely increases between 4% and 5%. The rise in risk for each 1% increase gets larger and larger until by the end, between 8% and 9%, it approximates the risk increase for diabetics. As correct choice G points out, the risk associated with each 1% increase in glycated hemoglobin level is much more consistent across the graph for diabetics than for non-diabetics. Choice F is incorrect, as evidenced by the fact that there appears to be no increase at all in risk for non-diabetics between the 3% and 4% hemoglobin levels, while diabetic risk increases significantly at this level. Choice H is incorrect because there is no decrease in risk for non-diabetics indicated anywhere in the graph. As glycated hemoglobin levels rise, the increase in cardiovascular risk appears to be 0 between 3% and 4% and then is positive from there on. Choice J is incorrect, for at 6% and below, the two lines in the graph are most *dissimilar*. The lines appear to better resemble one another between the 6% and 9% levels.

Practice Test 1—ANSWERS

Answer Keys and Explanations

5. **The correct answer is B.** Choice B can be deduced from a combination of the table figures and information provided in the passage's introduction. We're told that a glycated hemoglobin reading above 7% is a strong indicator of diabetes. Yet Table 1 indicates two non-diabetics with a glycated hemoglobin level of 8%. Knowing that these people do not have diabetes allows us to conclude that one cannot infallibly predict diabetes via a glycated hemoglobin test, since a person with a reading that might normally point toward the existence of the disease may not, in fact, have diabetes. Choices A and D are incorrect because Table 1 provides no information on diabetics or the risk of cardiovascular disease. Moreover, the correlation referred to in choice D is suggested in Figure 1, not Table 1. Choice C is incorrect, as the table provides no information regarding what may happen in the future. All we know for sure is that the 100 individuals did not have diabetes at the time they were tested.

6. **The correct answer is G.** The most striking difference among the theories is that both the Ecological Changes Theory and the Human Intervention Theory maintain that the Rocky Mountain locust is indeed extinct, while the Concealment Theory argues that it is not. So while the first two differ from one another in particulars, they both at least agree that this pest is gone for good and go on to explain, in their own ways, why this is so. The Concealment Theory denies this basic premise and thus differs most from the other two. This reasoning makes choices F, H, and J not the best choices.

7. **The correct answer is A.** According to the Human Intervention Theory, settlers "eradicated the beaver population, causing the elimination of dams and the subsequent flooding of locust egg sanctuaries." It can be inferred from this chain of events that prior to the beaver disappearance, beaver dams helped the locusts by preventing the type of flooding that, in their absence, damaged their egg sanctuaries. The beavers would thus have provided favorable conditions for the propagation of the locust population. Choices B and C represent the opposite of what's suggested by the beaver scenario. As noted above, the beavers helped the locusts, not the settlers, and they didn't flood locust egg sanctuaries but rather built dams that presumably prevented such flooding. Choice D is incorrect, as it refers to the types of ponds created by the bison that nourished the locusts, discussed as part of the Ecological Changes Theory. The evidence here suggests that beaver dams kept water from damaging locust eggs; there's nothing connecting these dams with the creation of nourishing ponds.

8. **The correct answer is J.** The Human Intervention Theory focuses on activities of people that brought about the demise of the Rocky Mountain locust. Part of the Ecological Changes Theory posits that the disappearance of the bison had something to do with this species' demise. This is not entirely inconsistent with the Human Intervention Theory, especially if one could show that human hunters played a part in the extinction of the bison. If that were true, the Human Intervention proponents could reasonably use the bison evidence from the Ecological Changes Theory to support their own case. Choice F would emphatically *not* support the Human Intervention Theory, which is based upon the negative effects of human activities on the locust population. Choice G does not reconcile the Ecological Changes Theory with the Human Intervention Theory, but rather lends support to the main premise of the Concealment Theory. Choice H does not demonstrate that the Ecological Changes Theory may be compatible with the Human Intervention Theory, but rather contradicts the basic premise of the Human Intervention Theory.

9. **The correct answer is B.** The passage indicates that one faction of Concealment theorists believes that changes have "eliminated the species' ability to swarm," while another faction thinks the conditions encouraging the locusts to remain hidden may be temporary and that the locusts "may one day swarm again." These two groups within the Concealment camp disagree, therefore, as to whether the Rocky Mountain locust is capable of swarming in the future.

Choices A and C are incorrect, since every proponent of the Concealment Theory believes that the Rocky Mountain locust is not extinct. All adherents to this theory would, therefore, view these assertions in the same manner: they would agree with choice A and disagree with choice C. Choice D is incorrect because there is consensus among the Concealment Theory supporters that there is no swarming currently taking place; they disagree over *why* this is so.

10. **The correct answer is G.** Some of those who believe in the Concealment Theory hold that "certain factors brought about by humans have temporarily made conditions non-conducive to swarming, but that Rocky Mountain locusts may one day swarm again." While these people believe that external events, including factors cited in the Human Intervention Theory, may have grounded the locusts for the time being, they feel that these effects are reversible; that is, that the locusts may regain their ability to swarm. The Human

Interventionists, who contend that locusts are extinct, clearly feel that the human influence in this matter is irreversible. Choices F and H are incorrect. Supporters of the Concealment Theory do not deny that human activities, as outlined in the Human Intervention Theory, took place, or that these activities have influenced the condition of the Rocky Mountain locust. The supporters simply don't believe that these activities have killed the locusts off entirely. Choice J is incorrect, as the bison wallow issue is part of the Ecological Changes Theory, not the Human Intervention Theory.

11. **The correct answer is D.** The example of the Monarch butterfly shows how human intervention in an eco-system can adversely affect a species that depends on that environment. The retreat of the Monarch butterfly to the forests of Mexico in winter is most similar to the Rocky Mountain locust's retreat to fertile river valleys in the western U.S. every seven to twelve years. The butterfly example thus best supports the Human Intervention Theory as presented in choice D. Choice A is incorrect. The Monarch example supports the Human Intervention Theory. Choice B is incorrect. The butterfly example does not support the Concealment Theory because the main premise of that theory is that a species may be extant yet unseen. An example that better supports the Concealment Theory would be the rediscovery of a species thought to be extinct. Choice C is incorrect, as the Monarch example does not involve changes for one species influencing the survival of another species. Logging, a human activity, is the factor said to be affecting the butterfly species.

12. **The correct answer is H.** Both the bison and the beavers, though presumably acting entirely in their own interests, created conditions favorable to the survival and proliferation of the locusts. The bison created wallows that nourished and sheltered the locusts, and the beavers created dams providing dry areas for locust eggs to mature. According to the theories, when each disappeared from its ecosystem, the Rocky Mountain locust suffered. The bison and beavers are thus analogous with respect to their beneficial (albeit probably unintentional) effect on the locusts. In contrast, the activities of the cattle, settlers, and birds mentioned in choices F, G, and J directly hurt the locusts.

13. **The correct answer is C.** While swimming is inferably a fairly constant activity, Figure 2 indicates that basketball is a sport consisting of numerous types of physical

motions, some very strenuous (e.g., sprinting), some not (e.g., walking). This helps explain why the heart rate curve of the basketball player depicted in Figure 1 shows sudden and dramatic dips, while the swimmer's curve does not. Choices A and B refer to the recovery rates noted in Study 3. However, Study 2, which breaks up basketball activity, does not address recovery rates. Choice D is incorrect. The fact that basketball is made up of numerous types of physical activities does nothing to explain this particular basketball player's fitness level. On its own, the nature of the game doesn't tell us whether this individual is fit.

14. **The correct answer is F.** The passage's introduction indicates that, as a general rule, increasing fitness correlates with lower resting heart rates, a greater degree of change in heart rate during exercise, and greater recovery rates. The swimmer wins on all three counts. The swimmer's resting heart rate is under 50, while the basketball player's is over 75. His heart rate increases faster during exercise than does the bas-ketball player's (note the swimmer's steeper curve as his heart rate shoots from under 50 to around 160 at the 5-minute mark). Finally, the swimmer's steep downward curve from 10 to around 13 minutes when his heart rate is back to normal indicates a higher recovery rate than that of the basketball player. All of these clues allow us to deduce that the swimmer is fitter, which both confirms choice F and eliminates choice G. Choices H and J are incorrect because Study 1 provides data only on the heart rates of these two individuals. That, by itself, is not enough to state that one sport is more demanding overall. Observing a single individual participating in both sports might shed light on this issue, but Study 1 alone is insufficient to do so.

15. **The correct answer is C.** Study 3 deals exclusively with minutes 10–15, which constitute the resting period following the end of physical activity. This study was, therefore, designed to explore some aspect of recovery rates. Having the athletes switch activities allows one to compare the recovery rates observed in Study 3 with those observed in Study 1 and, thus, to hypothesize whether the kind of activity one engages in changes one's recovery rate. Choice A is incorrect, because a study focusing on only two athletes cannot yield enough information to allow one to compare the overall fitness level of swimmers with that of basketball players. Choice B is incorrect, because the relative quality of the swimming and basketball playing is not an issue in the studies, which are concerned only with how heart rate is affected by these activities. Study 3 was not constructed

to determine which athlete is better at the other's sport. Choice D is incorrect, because it merely restates an accepted fact given in the passage's introduction. Scientists already know that the degree of change in heart rate during exercise correlates with overall fitness; they don't need to design another study to discover this.

16. **The correct answer is J.** According to the introduction, recovery rate is the decrease in the number of beats per minute for each minute after activity stops. Only Study 1 addresses the swimmer's heart rate while and after swimming, so we need to analyze Figure 1 to approximate the swimmer's recovery rates. The question asks us to focus on the first minute after he stops swimming, which corresponds to the time between 10 and 11 minutes on the graph. At the 10-minute mark, his heart rate was halfway between 150 and 175, or roughly 163. After 11 minutes, his heart rate was just below 125. That means his heart rate dropped off by more than 25 beats per minute but less than 50, so choices F and G are incorrect. His recovery rate between 13 and 14 minutes is significantly less, as indicated by the leveling off of the line. Estimating, we would have to say that the drop-off between 13 and 14 minutes is much less than 25 beats per minute, which is why choice J is correct. Choice H is incorrect because the basketball player's drop-off between the 10- and 11-minute marks is less than the swimmer's, as illustrated by the swimmer's steeper curve between these points.

17. **The correct answer is D.** The numbers in Table 1 represent the decrease in heart rate at each 1-minute interval following the end of activity. The fact that the swimmer who had just played basketball has zeros as his final two entries shows that his heart rate is no longer decreasing following the 13-minute mark. This indicates that his heart rate has returned to normal resting levels 3 minutes after he has stopped playing. Choice A is incorrect, as the zeros actually represent the opposite. The swimmer's heart rate has returned to normal faster than the basketball player's heart rate, which is still decreasing 3 to 5 minutes after he finished swimming. The faster recovery indicated in the table suggests that the swimmer is in better shape. Choice B is incorrect, as the numbers in the table represent *decreases* in heart rate, not heart rate itself. A heart rate of zero would presumably suggest cardiac arrest, but in this case the zeros simply mean that the swimmer's heart rate is back to normal and is no longer descending from an elevated level. Choice C is incorrect, as nothing supports the hypothesis that the swimmer kept playing

after he was told to stop. In fact, the large decreases in the swimmer's heart rate, as indicated in the first three rows of the table, suggest that he did indeed stop playing at the appointed time.

18. **The correct answer is G.** The studies allow comparisons only between the two participating individuals, and we can't tell from such comparisons which sport is harder on the heart since the particularities of these individuals make it impossible to form such a broad conclusion. To compare the relative exertions associated with the two sports in general, one would need to observe many people playing both sports. Moreover, one would wish to have all kinds of people in the study to account for possible differences in fitness levels. The results would be most informative, therefore, if the study included a large sample of the population participating in both sports. One might then be able to deduce which sport is more taxing on the heart. Choice F is incorrect. If each group is limited to participating in its own sport, there would be no way to compare the demands of basketball to the demands of swimming. Choices H and J are incorrect. Merely repeating Study 1 or pitting the two athletes against each other would only yield more information on these two individuals, not make it easier to conclude anything about the physical demands of these two sports.

19. **The correct answer is C.** The main clue in answering this question is the introductory paragraph, which explicitly states that the scientists' purpose was "to investigate the mitochondria's role in species survival." Further evidence is that the studies do indeed unfold in such a way as to suggest a link between the mitochondrial energy output of an individual beewolf and the amount of food that a beewolf is able to provide its young, an issue related to species survival. Choices A, B, and D focus on subsidiary connections contained in the studies, while overlooking the main purpose clearly stated up front.

20. **The correct answer is F.** Study 2 shows that the denser the flight muscle mitochondrial membranes, the more energy is produced by the mitochondria. Bringing Studies 1 and 3 into the equation, we see that the beewolves with the highest density of flight muscle mitochondrial membranes (and, therefore, the highest mitochondrial energy output) are the same ones with the highest honeybee kill rates noted in Study 1. So it is reasonable to infer that mitochondrial energy output is directly related to beewolves' skill at procuring honeybees for their young. This reasoning contradicts choice J, as we'd expect beewolf mortality rate to

decrease as mitochondrial energy output increases. Choice G is incorrect because Study 3 concerns the density of certain membranes within beewolf flight muscles, not the number of flight muscles a beewolf possesses overall. Choice H distorts the investigation, which focuses on beewolves killing honeybees, not the other way around. If anything, the results suggest the opposite of choice H—that the more mitochondrial energy a beewolf possesses, the more success it will have in killing honeybees.

21. **The correct answer is B.** The energy levels of the beewolves in Study 1 are suggested by the table in Study 3, but not in Study 1 itself. The information listed in the other choices is provided or suggested by Study 1, as follows: Multiplying the number of offspring by the average number of honeybees fed to each yields an approximate number of honeybees killed by each beewolf in the study (choice A). The beewolf fighting method (choice C) is spelled out in the introduction to Study 1, where we learn that beewolves sting and paralyze larger honeybees, which they then feed to their young. The number of offspring of each honeybee, listed in the second column of the table, represents the breeding statistics referred to in choice D.

22. **The correct answer is H.** As we saw in the first question in this set, the primary purpose of this investigation is to determine the effect of mitochondrial energy output. However, nothing about the energy output of the beewolves studied is included in Study 1, and Study 3 provides information only on the density of flight muscle mitochondrial membranes in observed beewolves. It falls to Study 2 to provide the information that allows us to determine the relative mitochondrial energy output of beewolves A through F. Study 2's result—the fact that density of flight muscle mitochondrial membranes is directly related to mitochondrial energy output—allows us to apply the numbers in Study 3 to the beewolves in Study 1. That is, we can go back to Study 1 and say that the beewolves with the larger numbers in Study 3 are the ones with the greater mitochondrial energy. Then we can see how that fact relates to the number of honeybees killed by each. It is reasonable to infer that this is a proper use of Study 2, since the passage's overall introduction indicates that the effect of mitochondrial energy output is the main focus. Choice F is incorrect, as the positive correlation indicated in Study 2, coupled with the results of Studies 1 and 3, supports the speculation that mitochondrial energy output is related to species survival. Choice G is incorrect because, as noted above, the result of Study 2

provides a *link* between Studies 1 and 3 that allows speculation regarding the connection between mitochondrial energy and species survival. Study 2 does not, by itself, depict a direct correlation between these things. Choice J is incorrect. Study 3, not Study 2, makes the cited density determination.

23. **The correct answer is B.** The three studies, taken together, seem to imply that the higher the mitochondrial energy output of an individual beewolf, the more offspring it has and the more food it provides to each. Comparing the numbers in Study 3 with the results of Study 1, one finds a positive linear correlation to that effect, taking into account Study 2's indication that greater flight muscle mitochondrial density means more mitochondrial energy output. However, even with this implicit correlation in place, we still haven't gotten to the original point of the study—that is, to connect mitochondrial energy output with *species survival*. The way to do this would be to find a connection between species survival and the thing we have found correlated with mitochondrial energy output—namely, the volume of beewolf offspring and their nourishment. If beewolf species survival is enhanced in proportion to these things—a reasonable inference, but *one never stated anywhere in the passage*—then the conclusion that mitochondrial energy output is related to species survival would be more tenable. Choice B fills in this missing link, connecting the implications of the studies to the investigation's original speculation. No further study is needed to indicate the correlation in choice A, since Study 2 provides this already. The density of honeybee membranes (choice C) is irrelevant to the investigation and provides no further link between the study results and species survival. The study result cited in choice D contradicts the implication of the three studies described in the passage, so this result does not support the original speculation regarding species survival.

24. **The correct answer is J.** Killing 25 honeybees puts beewolf G on a close par with beewolf D, which averaged 2 honeybees for each of its 12 offspring, or 24 honeybees total. Based on the linear correlations indicated by the combination of study results, we'd expect this new beewolf to have roughly the same density of flight muscle mitochondrial membranes and roughly the same mitochondrial energy output as beewolf D. We'd therefore expect beewolf G to have flight muscle mitochondrial membranes with a density of approximately 30 f/cc, which falls within the range provided in correct choice J. We would expect beewolf

G to have more mitochondrial energy than beewolf B, which killed only approximately seven honeybees. This makes choice F incorrect. Since beewolf A killed roughly 66 honeybees, we would expect beewolf A to have more folds per cubic centimeter in its flight muscle mitochondrial membranes than new beewolf G, given the linear positive relationship among folds, mitochondrial energy, and honeybees killed. This contradicts choice G. Choice H is incorrect as well; this answer might result from mistaking 25 as the number of offspring rather than honeybees, observing that this value lies between beewolf A and beewolf E (based on Table 1), and then assuming a density between 78 and 140 (based on Table 2).

25. The correct answer is C. The caminite line intersects the oxygen portion of the graph between the 50% and 60% lines, making the other choices incorrect.

26. The correct answer is G. The key to the question is deciphering what it is asking you to determine. The element with "the most consistent percentage composition" is the one whose values are most nearly the same for all six minerals. In terms of the graph, that means the element whose values are most bunched together, which in this case is hydrogen, ranging from just above 0% for caminite to around 6–7% for wilcoxite. This range is smaller than the range associated with the other elements. Aluminum is closest, but is not among the choices. Magnesium has a range of roughly 20 percentage points, while the range of sulfur and oxygen values among the six minerals is over 10 percentage points. Hydrogen, therefore, is the element with the most consistent percentage composition.

27. The correct answer is A. The lines for three minerals— hexahydrite, sanderite, and caminite—descend from the magnesium portion of the graph to intersect the x-axis at the element aluminum. The x-axis represents the 0% point, so the part of the graph described in the question signifies that three of the minerals do not contain any aluminum. The other choices are incorrect because the lines on the graph do not meet the x-axis at any element besides aluminum. Choices B and D are also wrong because the x-axis signifies the absence of an element, not the presence of one.

28. The correct answer is H. The key to this question is to transform the vague wording into a clear task. Neither the passage's introduction nor the graph itself suggests that the five elements listed need be the *only* elements contained in these minerals. If the percentage values of the five elements for any given mineral add up to 100%,

then it stands to reason that there are no other elements in that mineral. If, however, these five elements do not add up to 100% for a given mineral, then that mineral must contain at least one other element. This question is essentially looking for the mineral with the lowest total percentage composition as indicated in the graph; that would be the element that must therefore contain the greatest percentage of *other* elements. The task is thus one of estimation and addition. Let's see how each choice plays out.

Choice F: Analyzing hexahydrite's line on the graph, we can estimate that it is composed of 10% magnesium, 5% hydrogen, 15% sulfur, and 70% oxygen. That's roughly 100%, so it's not likely that a significant percentage of other elements exists in this mineral.

Choice G: Moving on to caminite, we see that its aluminum content and its hydrogen content are negligible, but its magnesium and sulfur content fall between 20% and 25% each, which we can estimate accounts for around 45% of the mineral between them. Oxygen, at roughly 55%, makes up the rest, bringing this one close or equal to 100% composition from the listed elements.

Choice H: Lannonite does not match the totals of the previous two choices. We can estimate that its magnesium, aluminum, and hydrogen content, taken together, makes up roughly 10% of the mineral. It is composed of roughly 15% sulfur, bringing the total to around 25%. Its oxygen content is somewhere around 55%, bringing the grand total to approximately 80% and leaving roughly 20% unaccounted for, which makes this an excellent candidate for the right choice. All that's left is to estimate the values of sanderite to make sure that element isn't missing more than 20%.

Choice J: The content of sanderite is nearly fully accounted for, according to the following approximated values. We can safely discount its aluminum and hydrogen content by observing that the values for these elements are at or just above the x-axis— that is, the zero point. Eyeballing the graph also allows us to determine that its magnesium content is just below the 20% line, while its sulfur content is just above that same 20% line. Combining these gives us roughly 40%. When we observe that sanderite is composed of nearly 60% oxygen, we can conclude that another element, if any, must account for much less than the nearly 20% figure estimated for the additional elements in lannonite, confirming choice H as the correct answer.

29. **The correct answer is D.** As we saw in the previous question, the full compositions of most of the minerals are nearly accounted for by the five elements listed, so if additional elements were added to the line graph, we'd expect their values to hover around zero in many cases, or in the most extreme scenario, in the case of lannonite, to be around 20% to account for the missing content of that mineral (see the explanation of the previous question for this calculation). In any case, we would expect a steep decline from the oxygen values to the values of this new hypothetical element, which would be represented on the graph by a steep downward line between the two. Any sort of horizontal or upward line would indicate that the new element accounted for at least the same percentage of the mineral as oxygen, which is impossible given that oxygen alone (not even considering the other elements listed) makes up more than 50% of each mineral. Choice C is, in fact, impossible—the inclusion of a single additional element cannot result in a line moving in two different directions.

30. **The correct answer is G.** Heat generation is studied in Experiment 2, where we see a fairly proportional increase in heat generated as the box weight increases from 10 to 30 to 40 kg. Increasing the weight by 20 kg, from 10 to 30 kg, the difference in heat generated is 7°C. Increasing it by another 10 kg, from 30 to 40 kg, results in a jump half as large, 3.5°C. We can infer from these numbers that each 10 kg increase in weight corresponds roughly to a temperature increase of 3.5°C. The number that would best approximate the heat generated by a 20-kg box would be about halfway between 3.5°C and 10.5°C, or 7°C. These specifications make the other choices incorrect.

31. **The correct answer is C.** The table indicates that as the weight of the boxes observed increases from 10 to 30 to 40 kg, the heat generated at the point the box reaches a speed of 20 km/hr increases as well. That constitutes a positive correlation between weight and heat. Choice A is incorrect, because the correlation between velocity and drag is evident in Experiment 1, not Experiment 2. Drag, in fact, is not part of Experiment 2 at all—the resistance created between the ramp and box is friction—so choice B must also be incorrect. Choice D suggests another relationship involving velocity, but Experiment 2 is arranged such that velocity is kept constant.

32. **The correct answer is J.** The bars in Figure 1 representing the friction between the box and the ramp are constant at every velocity, roughly 65 N. In contrast, the drag on the boat increases at every velocity listed. These results indicate that unlike drag, friction does not vary with velocity. Choices F and G contradict the passage's introduction, which states that both friction and drag produce a resistance force and heat. These choices, therefore, do not represent a point of differentiation. Choice H is incorrect, because nothing in any of the experiments suggests that drag is unaffected by weight. While we know from Experiment 2 that friction does indeed vary with weight, we cannot conclude from the information given that drag does not.

33. **The correct answer is D.** In Experiment 1, the original 20-kg box reached a velocity of 30 km/hr at the bottom of the untreated ramp. Experiment 3 shows that the same box on a sandy ramp hits the bottom of the ramp at 18 km/hr, while on a wet ramp, the box reaches the bottom moving at 39 km/hr. This means that the box moves slower than normal on a ramp covered with sand and faster than normal on a ramp covered with water. The most logical explanation is that sand provides greater resistance to the box's movement and water provides less resistance, making all the other choices incorrect.

34. **The correct answer is G.** According to Experiment 2, the 30-kg box has a friction resistance force of 75 N at 20 km/hr. The results of Experiment 1 demonstrate that friction does not vary with velocity, so we would expect the box to have the same friction resistance force at 10 km/hr. Since friction does not vary, choices F, H, and J are incorrect.

35. **The correct answer is A.** The measurements in each case are taken when the boxes reach a speed of 20 km/hr, so it's reasonable to infer that the experimenters wished to keep velocity constant so that the relationship among weight, resistance, and heat could be observed. Choice B is incorrect. The only variable in Experiment 2 is the weight of the box, which varies from 10 to 30 to 40 kg. All other figures noted in the table represent the results at these various weights. Choices C and D are incorrect, for while the researchers repeated certain aspects of Experiment 1, a new variable is introduced (multiple box weights), and a new result (heat) is measured in Experiment 2. So we cannot say that the original experiment has been merely repeated for verification, or that the researchers set out consciously to overturn a previously stated hypothesis.

36. The correct answer is F. At all three heights listed in Table 1, as roughness increases from 0 to 2 to 4, wind speed decreases. Using 50 meters above ground as an example, the wind speed at roughness class 0 is 13.73, at class 2 is 10.7, and at class 4 is 8.1. The figures corresponding to 100 and 150 meters above ground exhibit the same pattern of consistently decreasing wind speeds as roughness increases. Since there is this constant decrease, all the other choices are incorrect.

37. The correct answer is B. There are two important things to notice that help answer this question. First, we're asked to notice something about what happens when height above the ground decreases, and we're looking to compare the magnitude of wind speed changes in various kinds of terrain. In all three terrains, wind speed decreases as height above the ground decreases. For example, follow the numbers for class 4 at 150 meters, then 100 meters, then 50 meters; you'll see that the wind speeds decrease. That observation eliminates choices A and C from consideration. The issue is now the rate of the decrease—do the numbers drop more quickly in rougher terrain or in smoother terrain? Let's use the figures in the table to determine this.

In the roughest terrain, class 4, wind speed drops from 10.14 at 150 meters above ground to 9.39 at 100 meters and 8.1 at 50 meters. This is a drop of approximately 0.7 and 1.3, respectively. In a less rough terrain, class 2, the corresponding decrease is from 12.29 to 11.7 to 10.7, which represents a drop of roughly 0.6 and 1.0. This drop is less dramatic, and the decrease in roughness class 0 even less so—from 14.8 to 14.4 (a drop of 0.4) to 13.73 (a drop of 0.67). Therefore, the drop-off in wind speed as height above ground decreases is more rapid in rougher terrains.

38. The correct answer is H. The first clue is the large city with skyscrapers—which tells us we're interested in the figures in roughness class 4 that correspond to the heights listed in the question. At 50 meters above ground, the mean wind speed in roughness class 4 is 8.1, and at 150 meters above ground the class 4 figure is 10.14. We can then consult Table 2 to determine the power generated from these wind speeds. There we see that a wind speed of 8 m/s generates wind power of 313.6 W/m^2, while a wind speed of 10 m/s generates wind power of 612.5 W/m^2. The difference is approximately 300 W/m^2.

39. The correct answer is D. Table 1 indicates that 100 meters above ground at roughness class 2, the level that corresponds to sparsely populated agricultural land, the mean wind speed is 11.7 m/s. The corresponding values for the locations listed in choices A, B, and C are 10.7 m/s, 10.14 m/s, and 8.1 m/s, respectively.

40. The correct answer is J. Table 2 shows that wind power increases as wind speed increases from 0 to 15 m/s—the numbers increase at every level. This eliminates choice G. To decide among the rest, we have to determine exactly how the wind power numbers increase. Let's observe the increases at the first few levels. From a wind speed of 0 m/s to a wind speed of 1 m/s, the increase in wind power is 0.6. From wind speeds of 1 to 2 m/s, the wind power increase is 4.3, a greater number. From 2 to 3, the increase is 11.6, an even greater increase than the change between 1 and 2. The pattern should begin to be clear: the increases in wind power are getting bigger at each successive wind speed level, and you can test out a few more cases if you wish to verify this. As correct choice J states, wind power is increasing at an increasing rate as we read through the table from 0 to 15 m/s. Further support for this is contained in the wind power formula itself. The formula shows that wind power is proportional to the cube of wind speed (v^3), which provides an element of exponential growth in wind power associated with each 1 m/s increase in wind speed.

SAMPLE ESSAY: SCORE 1

Ideas and Analysis:	Score = 1
Development and Support:	Score = 1
Organization:	Score = 1
Language Use and Conventions:	Score = 1

> I never saw no 3D printer what am I supposed to do with it I can buy the things I need at any store or online so why bother whith this thing. I cant imagine anything you pretend to create will be as good as real as the real thing so its not gonna fool anybody or make people think that we don't need stores or place to buy things anymore. how does it even work I don't understand does it just work like a printer at the library where you make copies of books or papers and they just come out? What makes this better than the prinders we already have to use, if someone can convince me that I need a new printer I'll think of ways to use and do things with it but I don't think anyone should be worried or think that people are gonna do bad things with it so that's what I think about it.

Scoring Explanation

Ideas and Analysis: Score = 1

The writer of this essay does not address the questions provided; instead, he or she provides a weak, peripheral set of random ideas on the value of 3D printers ("I cant imagine anything you pretend to create will be as good as real as the real thing") and barely mentions the notion that they may be dangerous or used improperly ("I don't think anyone should be worried or think that people are gonna do bad things with it"). This off-task response is ultimately an unsuccessful and confusing piece of writing.

Development and Support: Score = 1

A few scattered, poorly developed thoughts that largely veer off topic ("I cant imagine anything you pretend to create will be as good as real as the real thing so its not gonna fool anybody or make people think that we don't need stores or place to buy things anymore.") make up this essay response. The writer's perspective on the potential dangers of 3D printers is barely mentioned and thoughts on government regulation are completely absent, resulting in a wholly ineffective essay.

Organization: Score = 1

This essay demonstrates a complete lack of careful forethought toward creating an effective, well-structured essay. Instead of crafting a persuasive argument to convince readers of the author's perspective regarding the concerns of 3D printers, we are given a confusing response that invites more off-target questions than answers ("how does it even work I don't understand does it just work like a printer at the library"). There is no clear introduction, thesis statement, body, or conclusion, and it is not evident that the writer has a firm grasp on the fundamentals of essay structure.

Language Use and Conventions: Score = 1

This essay is hampered by an abundance of errors in spelling ("whith," "prinders"), grammar (run-ons), and punctuation (missing question marks, etc.). Sentences are weak, simplistic, and poorly developed, and the level of word choice is relatively basic. This response seems hastily written and in need of serious revision.

Sample Essay: Score 6

Ideas and Analysis:	Score = 6
Development and Support:	Score = 6
Organization:	Score = 6
Language Use and Conventions:	Score = 6

In our current era of technological innovation, we have been fortunate enough to witness an explosion of new ideas, gadgets, and processes, which are reshaping how we work, live, and interact. Many of these technological marvels have ushered in dramatic, lasting, and positive impacts (imagine going back to a world without smartphones). Others have, thus far, shown themselves to be little more than opportunities to show off the creativity and skill of their creators (sorry, Segway). There's also another category of innovation that deserves our attention—those that come with an unexpected social cost, namely the potential for serious misuse and abuse. It can be argued that 3D printers have earned this dubious distinction. However, that doesn't mean that we should try and stuff this exciting new technology back into Pandora's Box. It is worth our collective time to explore the potential societal hazards and benefits of the 3D printer and make a carefully considered, responsible decision regarding its use.

Although still in its relative technological infancy, 3D printing offers a great deal of exciting promise in nearly every field of endeavor—art, medicine, and architecture are just a few examples. Imagine a world in which advanced 3D printers create artificial limbs or braces, produce amazing and creative sculptures, and even help reduce the costs and labor involved in new construction projects. Like all new technology, the best way to refine it, improve it, and make it evolve is by putting it in the hands of the people. As a society, and as individuals, we think of fantastic new ways to enhance gadgets and ideas by using them. Taking 3D printers out of the hands of average citizens would be a big mistake and would not be in the best interests of the technology or society as a whole.

However, as previously stated, 3D printers do possess the potential for misuse. They can be used to create dangerous, untraceable weapons, and even make counterfeit items. And, unfortunately, as the technology evolves, the ability to misuse it will expand and improve as well. This wouldn't be the first innovation with a negative social cost. Nuclear technology and automobiles can be added to this list—both of these have led to unfortunate accidents and deaths, but as the technology improves and we better understand and adopt new ways to use them responsibly, the social benefits clearly begin to outweigh the costs.

The evolution of 3D printing technology can follow a similar trajectory—exploring new safety features and allowing responsible levels of government regulation and oversight—all designed to protect users and society at large as we enjoy and make the most of this new innovation. An avenue of research regarding 3D printing should be to explore ways that possible template or molding limits can be implemented for certain dangerous objects like guns, as well as items where there's a counterfeiting concern. Perhaps we can adjust 3D printing technology so that all items created in each machine is marked with the appropriate registration number, which can be traced to the owner.

There should be a mandatory registration process for individuals who purchase 3D printers, which can be done quickly online or through an application process. Having people register or even obtain licensure in order to purchase potentially dangerous items is not a new concept, and its purpose is a noble one—to make us all safer. Furthermore, the way we approach, react, and respond to a new invention often evolves alongside the technology; as we gain increased exposure to 3D printers, and learn more about them and how they're used, our strategies for ensuring their responsible use will continue to become refined. Societies and cultures often follow a trajectory similar to new products—forward, sometimes in leaps and bounds and other times in small, cautious steps, occasionally with fits and starts through trial and error, but confidently and assuredly heading in a positive direction. When we're bolstered and supported by creative new ideas and wondrous, innovative marvels like 3D printing, we're truly putting our best foot forward.

Scoring Explanation

Ideas and Analysis: Score = 6

This essay response contains a wealth of ideas on how we could address the potential dangers of 3D printing ("exploring new safety features and allowing responsible levels of government regulation and oversight"), as well as how to react to the potential for misuse that many new innovations bring ("I think that the way we approach, react, and respond to a new invention often evolves alongside the technology"). Ideas are deeply explored and responsibly weighed, both for this instance as well as the larger social context ("as the technology improves and we better understand and adopt new ways to use them responsibility, the social benefits clearly begin to outweigh the costs"). The end result is a carefully considered and multi-faceted response to the essay task, with a confident, clear, and convincing perspective.

Development and Support: Score = 6

The writer of this essay clearly gave careful thought to the topic, and developed a compelling response that serves his or her perspective quite well. He or she provides a clear point of view ("taking 3D printers out of the hands of average citizens would be a big mistake, and would not be in the best interests of the technology or society as a whole," while acknowledging the need to find "new ways to use them responsibly"), took the time to consider the perils of restrictive use of technology, and wisely offers other innovations for comparison (automobiles and nuclear technology) to bolster the position. The essay concludes with a stirring call for an acceptance of the risky yet potentially wonderful outcomes that can result from bold and innovative technological exploration and discovery.

Organization: Score = 6

From its engaging introduction to its memorable conclusion, this essay is a strong example of persuasive, impassioned writing, all of which supports a central unifying notion ("I feel that it is worth our collective time to explore the potential societal hazards and benefits of the 3D printer, and make a carefully considered, responsible decision regarding its use"). Although verbose, the writing is crisp, on target, and well organized, and the writer delivers a successful argument.

Language Use and Conventions: Score = 6

The author of this essay has a strong command of English language conventions and deploys them effectively throughout this piece of writing. The piece is largely free from errors in grammar and spelling, and a rich and varied word choice is on display, as are well-developed and interesting sentences and transitions. The result is a compelling essay that successfully responds to the task provided.

WRITING TEST

Plan Your Essay

WRITE YOUR ESSAY

ENGLISH TEST

45 Minutes—75 Questions

DIRECTIONS: In this section, you will see passages with words and phrases that are underlined and numbered. In the right-hand column you will see a question corresponding to each number which provides alternatives to the underlined part. In most of the items, you are to choose the best alternative. If no change is needed, choose NO CHANGE.

In other items, there will be either a question about an underlined portion of the passage or a question about a section of the passage, or about the passage as a whole. This question type will correspond to a number or numbers in a box.

For each question, choose the best alternative or answer and fill in the corresponding circle on the answer sheet.

PASSAGE I

A Bad Omen

[1]

Helen Thayer threw herself a birthday party, <u>only it's being</u> held at the South Pole and she was the only one invited. Helen

1. **A.** NO CHANGE
   B. but it was
   C. yet its being
   D. the kind to be

walked part of the way, skied over longer <u>distances and pulling</u> her own sled loaded with the gear and food she needed to survive. Why would a mature woman want to journey to a bleak,

2. **F.** NO CHANGE
   G. distances, and pulled
   H. distances. Pulling
   J. distances, while—you won't believe this—pulling

nearly featureless landscape of unbroken white and ice, <u>lit only</u>
₃

<u>by a sun never setting</u>, to visit a place that doesn't exist? ☐4
₃

3. **A.** NO CHANGE
    B. never lit by sunset
    C. only lighted by a sun that is not the kind to set
    D. lit only by a never-setting sun

4. Which of the following sentences, if added here, would best conclude and support the main idea of the first paragraph?

    F. To know Helen Thayer, one would have to explore the mind of an explorer and ask the ultimate question of why one climbs a mountain just because it is there.

    G. The answer, it seems, lies in the fact that Helen and her husband, Bill, once decided to live in many different countries and keep themselves in superb athletic shape.

    H. While part of her motivation was obviously the quest for adventure, she was also drawn to the Pole—which is not a physical location, but a point defined by scientists to describe Earth's magnetic field.

    J. And why would she have flown to Punta Arenas, a city in Chile, and boarded a Hercules aircraft intending to begin a challenge with another challenge in itself—a safe landing in hostile conditions?

[2]

Helen's journey began along the Antarctic coastline, at a place called Hercules Inlet. In what may later have seemed to be a bad omen, her boot buckle snapped off before she took her first step. Helen commented later <u>in her e-mail messages</u> that
₅
she was discouraged but decided to make repairs and start fresh the next day. Soon after getting underway, she faced miles of *sastrugi*, a type of ice formation marked by hard mounds and jagged ridges <u>of frozen water that formed</u> a nearly insurmountable
₆

barrier to the pole. <u>Overwhelmed by frustration,</u> Helen trusted
₇
her compass and global positioning system to guide her through.

5. **A.** NO CHANGE
    B. (place after *Helen*)
    C. (place after *discouraged*)
    D. (place after *fresh*)

6. **F.** NO CHANGE
    G. of frozen water which was formed
    H. formed by frozen water into
    J. that formed

7. The writer intends here to provide readers a description of the type of personality Helen Thayer possessed that allowed her to survive this challenge. Assuming all are true, which alternative best accomplishes this?

    A. NO CHANGE
    B. Fighting off frustration and relying on patience,
    C. Knowing that she'd face these conditions for some time,
    D. OMIT the underlined portion.

[3]

The problem of high and sustained winds turned out to be a <u>most daunting</u> challenge than the danger of falling into ice
8
crevasses. Helen had to lash a line around her waist and place an ice screw into a massive wall of ice to keep from being blown away. ⑨

<u>After the winds passed, total whiteout followed, Helen had</u>
10
<u>to go slowly, any step could be into a crevasse.</u> ⑪
10

8. **F.** NO CHANGE
   G. daunting
   H. most dauntless
   J. more daunting

9. Assuming all are true, which of the following sentences, if added here, would best contribute to the narration of events in this paragraph?

   A. The seasonal storm called El Niño was roaring through the Antarctic, causing these high winds.
   B. Huddled against the roar of 100-mile-per-hour winds, she felt like she was inside a jet engine, hanging on for her very life.
   C. She was passing through one of the most lifeless areas on the planet.
   D. Some of the crevasses could be as wide as twenty feet and required extensive detours around them.

10. **F.** NO CHANGE
    G. After the winds passed, total whiteout followed. Helen had to go slowly; any step could be into a crevasse.
    H. After the winds passed; total whiteout followed; Helen had to go slowly; any step could be into a crevasse.
    J. After the winds passed. Total whiteout followed. Helen had to go slowly; any step could be into a crevasse.

11. Which of the following best introduces a secondary element to the article's focus and provides an appropriate transition between paragraphs?

    A. NO CHANGE
    B. She next climbed a high ridge to scout for upcoming dangers in the form of the black lines of crevasses.
    C. As she carefully made her way, Helen thought of her first adventure to the North Pole years earlier and remembered how even in fine weather, things can go wrong—and soon they did.
    D. The next day, Helen celebrated her birthday with a frozen cupcake that she had carried in her pack.

CONTINUE

[4]

(1) A few days later, in an area that seemed safe, Helen plunged into a crevasse, finding herself in a <u>most troublesome</u>
₁₂ predicament few sixty-year-old women ever face. (2) As she fell, her <u>ski's tips</u> scraped against the wall and flipped her. (3) Its length
₁₃ was wider than the crevasse and had bridged the gap above, saving her. (4) Helen found herself hanging from the pull ropes of her sled. (5) Through some fancy maneuvering, she eventually was able to get herself back on solid ground. ☐14

[5]

Helen Thayer never made it to the South Pole. Not long after the crevasse incident, she was badly injured in another fall. She considered braving her difficulties and continuing her journey in pain. But in the end, she gave herself and her many friends a birthday present by radioing for help.

12. F. NO CHANGE
    G. more troublesome
    H. most dangerous
    J. OMIT the underlined portion.

13. A. NO CHANGE
    B. skis' tips
    C. skies' tips
    D. tips of her skis

14. For the sake of logic and coherence, Sentence 3 should be placed:

    F. where it is now.
    G. before Sentence 1.
    H. before Sentence 2.
    J. after Sentence 4.

Question 15 asks about the passage as a whole.

15. Suppose the writer had been assigned to write an essay about the personal challenges faced by Helen Thayer. Would this passage successfully fulfill the assignment?

    A. No, because the writer has failed to provide details of Helen's thinking when she was injured or alone or doubting herself.
    B. No, because the reader learns little about her motivations and how she supported this expensive adventure.
    C. Yes, because the reader can sense what the ordeal was like after reading this account of her trip.
    D. Yes, because the basic physical challenges she faced have been outlined and covered.

PASSAGE II

Rescuing the Palouse

[1]

The Palouse is an area in the southeastern corner of Washington that has rolling hills, actual "amber waves of grain" (more on that later), and historic nineteenth-century towns
16

as picturesque as the surrounding farmlands are. The complex
17

geology of this region is being formed through massive volcanic
18

action, monstrous floods, and scouring winds, resulting in topsoil
19
as deep in places as 3–4 feet in depth. [20]
19

16. F. NO CHANGE
    G. grain"; more on that later;
    H. grain," more on that later,
    J. grain,"

17. A. NO CHANGE
    B. more picturesque than
    C. just as picturesque than
    D. most picturesque as

18. F. NO CHANGE
    G. has formed
    H. formed
    J. has been formed through

19. A. NO CHANGE
    B. topsoil, in places that are 3–4 feet deep.
    C. topsoil as deep in places as 3–4 feet.
    D. 3–4-feet deep, thick topsoil.

20. The writer is considering adding the following sentence here:

    The giant Missoula flood contained more water than all the rivers in the world today, including the Amazon and the Nile.

    Would this be a logical and relevant addition at this point in the essay?

    F. Yes, because it would further expand on the geological activity that formed the unique features of this area.
    G. Yes, because it introduces the types of plants and animals that live in the Palouse, leading into the next paragraph.
    H. No, because it adds details that are unnecessary, and its inclusion would require further explanation of the significance of those details.
    J. No, because the facts it contains seem too fantastic to believe and might cause the reader to doubt the author's accuracy.

CONTINUE

[2]

Wind-blown volcanic dust built up loess, a rich type of soil found in this special biome. Rare bunchgrass, peculiar wildflowers, and giant earthworms three feet long flourished. Deer and elk abounded; <u>small ground feeders</u>, hawks, and badgers were the
21
dominant smaller animals. One plant, the intensely blue and

21. At this point, the writer wants to provide readers with a detail that will clearly distinguish this prairie region from other well-known areas of the western prairies. Assuming all are true, which of the following best accomplishes this?

   A. NO CHANGE

   B. abounded; small ground feeders (squirrels, gophers, and voles)

   C. abounded but bison were rare; small ground feeders,

   D. abounded; small ground feeders, insects

ubiquitous *camas*, <u>were</u> particularly influential in the region
22

22. **F.** NO CHANGE

   G. was

   H. will be

   J. has been

because <u>they're root and bulb</u> were harvested for centuries by
23
Native Americans.

23. **A.** NO CHANGE

   B. their root and bulb

   C. its roots and bulbs

   D. their roots and bulbs

[3]

The Nez Perce burned large tracts of the Palouse to encourage the growth of the camas flower. Early European explorers reported seeing patches of camas so wide and blue that they looked like bodies of water in the distance, <u>a phenomenon that demonstrates the success of this burning.</u>
24

24. Which choice would most logically comment on the effectiveness of the burning by the Nez Perce?

   F. NO CHANGE

   G. a phenomenon that indicates how greatly the prairie has changed today.

   H. a phenomenon that makes one wonder how effective burning as a tool really is.

   J. a phenomenon that suggests that the plant didn't really need the help of the clearing flames.

[4]

The first European-Americans in the Palouse were land-hungry and money-grubbing prospectors who arrived in
25
the 1860s. Settlers who came later thought the land would be

good only for cattle grazing. The coarse grasses in abundance
26
indicated the region's unsuitability for large-scale farming crops.
26
Yet when the first gardens and hay for livestock were planted,

the resulting bounty encouraged farmers to try planting wheat.

Things worked out pretty well after that.
27

[5]

Today, the Palouse has become a major producer of wheat

and legumes. The lentil-growing capital of the world. This culti-
28
vation of the land is a great achievement, yet many observers

wonder whether the insects that once pollinated the carpets of

25. **A.** NO CHANGE
   B. various kinds of
   C. foreign-born and gold-digging
   D. OMIT the underlined portion

26. Which of the choices best fulfills these two requirements: 1) explains clearly what the settlers thought
   about the land, and 2) shows the writer's love of the
   Palouse's native plant life?

   F. NO CHANGE
   G. abundance, which were actually the hardy Idaho
   fescue and bluebunch wheatgrass, made the
   settlers think the land wouldn't support
   H. abundance, which the settlers hated, were
   nothing like
   J. abundance, which grew throughout the area,
   were unlike

27. Which choice provides the most effective conclusion
   for Paragraph 4?

   A. NO CHANGE
   B. The famous "amber waves of grain" soon
   followed.
   C. After that, they tried other crops.
   D. Soon, farmers couldn't hire men and horses fast
   enough to plant their wheat.

28. **F.** NO CHANGE
   G. legumes, as well as the
   H. legumes. Surprisingly, the
   J. legumes, making it the

CONTINUE

Indian Paintbrush and Prairie Smoke will soon <u>disappear as most</u> <u>of the wildflowers have?</u> Ninety-four percent of wild Palouse prairie is now cropland. The remaining native plants, insects, and soils must be preserved by those who love the Palouse.
₂₉

29. **A.** NO CHANGE
  B. disappear as, most of the wildflowers have.
  C. disappear. As most of the wildflowers have?
  D. disappear as most of the wildflowers have.

Question 30 asks about the passage as a whole.

30. Suppose the writer wished to add the following sentence to the essay:

The Palouse is bounded by the Snake River, the Idaho panhandle mountains, and central Washington.

This new sentence would most logically be placed in Paragraph:

  F. 1.
  G. 2.
  H. 3.
  J. 4.

PASSAGE III

A Park Under the Sea

[1]

Someday it will be Smokers International Park or the Atlantis Massif Preserve. You and other nature lovers will journey to the middle of the ocean to see wonders rivaling Old Faithful or the Grand Canyon. <u>In addition to that, you</u> also will have to board a
₃₁

31. **A.** NO CHANGE
  B. Additionally, you
  C. However, you
  D. You

deep-sea submersible to travel thousands of feet below the waves to visit underwater hot springs. [32]

32. Would it contribute to the understanding of the passage to define the term *submersible* at this point?

  F. No, because it would distract from the intro-duction of the passage.
  G. Yes, because it may be confused with a word most readers know, "submarine."
  H. Yes, because there will be many technical words in a science passage and the reader can become overwhelmed.
  J. No, because the word is implicitly defined in the first sentence of the next paragraph.

[2]

Powerful spotlights <u>nearly will illuminate all of the</u> black
                        33
depths, revealing odd formations. Two monstrous mineral towers

resembling ragged chimneys spew what looks like black smoke,

yet <u>neither of these towers have</u> a fire inside.
        34

<u>The clouds are tiny metallic sulfide particles, the enormous heat</u>
                                    35
<u>and pressure cause the particles to precipitate, the minerals settle</u>
                                    35
<u>out, they build up quickly (over a meter a day) into towers, shelves,</u>
                                    35
<u>and icicles.</u> Hot water collects under the shelves into upside down
        35
reflecting pools. [36]

33. **A.** NO CHANGE
    B. will nearly illuminate all of the
    C. will illuminate nearly all of the
    D. will illuminate all of the nearly

34. **F.** NO CHANGE
    G. neither of these towers had
    H. neither tower have
    J. neither of these towers has

35. **A.** NO CHANGE
    B. The clouds are tiny metallic sulfide particles. The enormous heat and pressure cause the particles to precipitate. The minerals settle out; they build up quickly into towers, shelves, and icicles.
    C. The clouds are tiny metallic sulfide particles; the enormous heat and pressure cause the particles to precipitate; the minerals settle out; they build up quickly into towers, shelves, and icicles.
    D. The clouds are tiny metallic sulfide particles: the enormous heat and pressure cause the particles to precipitate. The minerals settle out; they build up quickly into towers, shelves, and icicles.

36. In Paragraph 2, should the final sentence be omitted?

    F. No, because it adds a vivid image to the description.
    G. No, because it adds an element of mystery to the surroundings and will keep the reader interested in the narrative.
    H. Yes, because it is confusing and it introduces an element that would need further description to be clear.
    J. Yes, because it incorrectly describes what you might see.

CONTINUE

[3]

Turning, you see "snowblowers," churning plumes of white
                    37
powder that shoot out from the ocean bottom. Of course, it isn't

snow in this seawater that is three times hotter than boiling, but
                                  38
is rather the byproducts of bacteria living inside vents under the

ocean bottom. Life abounds in this otherwise lifeless

world. [39] You have entered the realm of chemosynthesis.

The animals down here depend not on sunlight but on chemical

reactions. [40]

The reason microbes thrive is because they create energy
                          41
by metabolizing hydrogen sulfide in the water. They grow in

enormous white mats that cover everything and over 300 different
                                  42

37. A. NO CHANGE
    B. "snowblowers"
    C. "snowblowers";
    D. snowblowers, being

38. F. NO CHANGE
    G. three times more hot than
    H. the hottest water next to
    J. triple hot

39. At this point, the writer wants to emphasize the main theme of the passage. Assuming all are true, which choice best accomplishes this?

    A. NO CHANGE
    B. Volcanic activity under the seafloor brings heat and chemicals to these unique environments.
    C. At this great depth, there is little food or shelter for organisms.
    D. Technology will someday allow the average vacationer the opportunity to journey to this type of extreme habitat.

40. Which of these choices most effectively shortens the length of Paragraph 3 while preserving the author's original meaning?

    F. NO CHANGE
    G. Place a paragraph break before the previous sentence.
    H. Place a paragraph break after the next sentence.
    J. Place a paragraph break at this spot.

41. A. NO CHANGE
    B. is when
    C. because
    D. is that

42. F. NO CHANGE
    G. everything over
    H. everything, and over
    J. everything. Over

species feed on them <u>directly, including</u> blind shrimp, giant
                              43
mussels, amphipods, limpets the size of small bullets, octopuses,

and bright red tube worms, which can grow to twelve feet

in length.

[4]

44 This place is more like the frozen oceans of Jupiter's moon

Europa or the Martian ice caps than anywhere above water on

Earth. Indeed, scientists wonder whether life on Earth began

under oceans and spread upward to land. Some speculate that

life in outer space hides in an equally bizarre environment, beyond

our detection—for now.

43. **A.** NO CHANGE
    B. directly. These will include:
    C. directly, including,
    D. directly, including;

44. Given that all are true, which of the following
    sentences, if added here, would best enhance the
    author's method of bringing the reader to this hostile
    environment and introduce the last paragraph?

    F. Have you ever visited outer space and experi-
    enced its hostility?

    G. As your time on the bottom draws to a close, you
    may feel that you've been on another planet.

    H. What can live in a hostile world of 400° F water
    chilled to 36° F an inch or so from the vents
    under extremes of pressure reaching 6,000
    pounds per square inch?

    J. The concentration of chemicals in the water here
    is so corrosive that it leaches minerals out of
    stone and would kill ordinary sea life.

| **Question 45 asks about the passage as a whole.** |

45. If this passage were revised to include a paragraph on
    how various life forms have come to these underwater
    hot springs, the new paragraph would most logically
    follow Paragraph:

    A. 1
    B. 2.
    C. 3.
    D. 4.

CONTINUE

PASSAGE IV

Dialogues with the Dead

[1]

In sub-Saharan Africa, the living provide their <u>previously</u>
₄₆
<u>alive</u> ancestors with a functional role in everyday life. While many
₄₆

Western anthropologists have described <u>it</u> as an ancestor cult or
₄₇
worship, more properly, the role of elders, both living and

deceased, functions as a controlling factor among kinsmen. The

living elders of the Suku <u>as protectors</u> from southeastern Kinshasa
₄₈
go to the graves of the dead to appeal to them during times of

illness or misfortune. A monologue with the dead ensues, often

following a traditional form and in normal conversational tones.

"Your junior is sick. Are you angry? Have you been <u>offended!</u>
₄₉

<u>Other</u> lineages are doing fine. Why do you not look after us?" [50]
₄₉

46.
F. NO CHANGE
G. previously lively
H. previous living
J. OMIT the underlined portion.

47.
A. NO CHANGE
B. them
C. these roles
D. this phenomenon

48.
F. NO CHANGE
G. (move to after *elders*)
H. (move to after *dead*)
J. (move to after *them*)

49.
A. NO CHANGE
B. offended, other
C. offended? Other
D. offended. Other

50. The writer wishes to close Paragraph 1 with a sentence that will define the topic and sharpen the focus on the particular subject of this essay. Assuming all are true, which of the following would most effectively accomplish this?

F. The dead are expected to be as much a part of generational authority as the living.

G. The ancestors are also expected to lend assistance for other affairs of the lineage, such as marriage proposals and the success of a newborn.

H. The Suku go to any grave of any ancestor who was older than them to make these appeals.

J. This is a generalized pattern for most African ancestor cults with some local variations to be expected.

[2]

(1)The Suku do not even have a word for ancestor, <u>while</u>
                                                     51
<u>they do have a term for *grave* and long ago.</u> (2) The role of the
     51

dead is <u>much the same as it was when they were living which is</u>
                                    52
<u>that they</u> are merely on another level in the rigid structure of
    52

elder relationships within the lineage. (3) A <u>Suku, of any age, calls</u>
                                               53
<u>himself, Kusu, the name of his lineage</u> until someone senior to
         53
him arrives and is then called Kusu. (4) Appeals for authority,

help, and advice are made only to the generation of elders slightly

older, never skipping a generation. (5) <u>As such,</u> the last living
                                          54
elders turn to their elders even if they are deceased. (6) Authority

is <u>fluid any</u> man is an elder until an older Suku appears. [56]
     55

51. Which choice most effectively and appropriately
expands the idea introduced in the sentence?

   A. NO CHANGE

   B. but they have a term for *grave* and *long ago*,
which signifies their acknowledgment of the
dead

   C. while they have many terms that relate to elders
and lines of authority

   D. yet the single term *mbuta* refers to all elders
without distinguishing between the living and
the dead

52. **F.** NO CHANGE

   G. much the same as it was when they were living;
they

   H. the same as when they were living and they

   J. that they

53. **A.** NO CHANGE

   B. Suku of any age calls himself Kusu, the name of
his lineage

   C. Suku, of any age, calls himself Kusu the name of
his lineage

   D. Suku of any age calls himself, "Kusu," the name of
his lineage

54. **F.** NO CHANGE

   G. Granted that,

   H. On the contrary,

   J. For example,

55. **A.** NO CHANGE

   B. fluid; any

   C. fluid, any

   D. fluid—any

56. Which of the following provides the most logical
ordering of the sentences in Paragraph 2?

   F. NO CHANGE

   G. 1, 3, 2, 4, 5, 6

   H. 1, 2, 4, 5, 3, 6

   J. 1, 2, 4, 5, 6, 3

CONTINUE

[3]

Elders intervene in the lives of their juniors <u>due to the fact</u>
₅₇
<u>that</u> the dead are expected to affect the lives of the living. The
₅₇
powers of the elders derive from the powers of their ancestors.

The Suku worship both dead and living elders, believing that

each male in the lineage <u>is an elder, even if you happen</u> to
₅₈
be dead. [59]

57.
A. NO CHANGE
B. like as has often been demonstrated before that
C. because it goes without saying that
D. in much the same manner that

58.
F. NO CHANGE
G. are elders, even if they happen
H. is an elder, even if he happens
J. is an elder, even if it happens

59. The writer wishes to add another relevant example to Paragraph 3 in order to show how the Suku honor the dead like the living. Which of the following sentences would best further the writer's purpose?

A. A sheep sacrifice to an elder is not a prayer offering but a tribute or gift the elder would have received if alive.

B. The oldest of the living Suku elders will go to a grave or crossroads at night and bury food the ancestor enjoyed in life.

C. The place of the dead in Suku lineage is paralleled by the European custom of leaving an empty chair at the table to signify a missing elder.

D. Other tribes, like the Songye, transfer attention from the dead to the living by believing the ancestors are reincarnated in the grandchildren and thus honor newborns.

Question 60 asks about the essay as a whole.

60. Which of the following statements most effectively summarizes the essay as a whole?

F. The ancestors of the Suku are worshiped because they exercise authority over all the elders and owe protection to the entire lineage.

G. The Suku have arranged their society into complex levels of eldership, each determined by age or death.

H. The Suku give tribute to their elders for their authority, advice, and assistance whether those elders are alive or dead.

J. The ancestors of the Suku are not dead in a Western sense, because their powers are not supernatural but are the same powers the living elders possess.

PASSAGE V

Departures

[1]

One of my more favorite destinations in my youth was the
airport, even though I never went anywhere. Departure wasn't

even part of my realm of possibilities in those days because

cherished relatives only came from afar to visit my family and

my parents always taked me along on their drives back to the
airport when my relatives would abandon me until the next visit.

The glorious flying machines—so shiny and aerodynamic—taxied
imperiously before picture windows the size of movie screens.

It was like Tinsel-town—like one of the Saturday matinees I so
loved to attend. Who wouldn't delight in soaring through the
clouds in these sleek missiles?

[2]

On my first flight, I was filled with unadulterated joy and

wonder. Having never been thousands of feet up in the air before.

61. **A.** NO CHANGE
  B. my favorite destinations when I was young
  C. my favoritest destinations in my youth
  D. my most youthful favorite destinations

62. **F.** NO CHANGE
  G. (move to after *Departure*)
  H. (move to after *even*)
  J. (move to after *afar*)

63. **A.** NO CHANGE
  B. family; my
  C. family. My
  D. family because my

64. **F.** NO CHANGE
  G. had always taked
  H. always taken
  J. always took

65. The writer intends here to emphasize how unfamiliar, mysterious, and alluring the planes and the idea of travel were to him. Given that all of the statements are true, which choice would best accomplish the writer's goal?

  A. NO CHANGE
  B. identical except in size to my toy models back home
  C. promising adventures I had yet to experience
  D. terrifying with their whirling blades and screaming engines

66. **F.** NO CHANGE
  G. It was like Tinsel-town—I could almost taste the popcorn.
  H. It was like Tinsel-town—movies were the only way I had ever seen air travel before.
  J. OMIT the underlined portion.

67. **A.** NO CHANGE
  B. wonder, having
  C. wonder having
  D. was wonderful having

CONTINUE

I was enjoying a vacation, caring little about life's problems, and

that flying was less mystifying than I expected. However, my next
68

experience in an airport transformed my attitude towards the

place (and forever ruined the innocence of comings and goings.)
69

My father was offered a job overseas and would not return for a

year. Standing in the waiting area by the gate, I sensed the lone-

liness, the loss, the unhappy good-byes all around me. ⬚70

68. **F.** NO CHANGE
    G. that I had expected flying to be more mystifying than it was.
    H. to be flying, which I had expected to be mystifying.
    J. flying through the air with the greatest of ease.

69. **A.** NO CHANGE
    B. place. And forever ruined the innocence of comings and goings.
    C. place and forever ruined the innocence of comings and goings.
    D. place; and forever ruined the innocence of comings and goings.

70. The writer wishes to add another sentence to the end of this paragraph that would emphasize his theme of how the connotations of a place can change. Which of the following sentences does that best?

    F. The brand new plastic smell of airplanes brought back memories of the magic found here.
    G. He had been offered an excellent salary and a great promotion, and he couldn't say no.
    H. Other businessmen boarded the plane without a wave, but airports to them were all business, nothing more.
    J. The gate area had changed little since I was a child, only now I noticed that it could use a paint job.

[3]

Before too many years had passed, I would be on the

other end of that boarding ramp, the part that connects to
71

the hatch door on the airplane itself. After receiving a schol-
71

arship to a distant university, I found myself blowing kisses to

tear-stained faces, trembling chins, and stiff upper lips. I had

to be their brave, unwavering, football, player who wouldn't let
72

family and friends feel left behind.

71. **A.** NO CHANGE
    B. ramp, which is the bridge-like structure that connects the airplane hatch to the gate
    C. ramp, walking down the part that connects to the hatch door on the airplane itself
    D. ramp

72. **F.** NO CHANGE
    G. brave unwavering football player
    H. brave, unwavering, and football player
    J. brave, unwavering football player

[4]

Today, when my family and I pick up loved ones at the airport, my children are as excited <u>as me.</u>
73

<u>But unfortunately, as I dance with ghosts, awash in lost moments,</u>
74
<u>the rushing, the lost bags, the missed connections, the never</u>
74
<u>coming home again.</u> They can close all of the airports down as
74

far as I'm concerned. I'll go by rail. <u>I'm not effected</u> one way or
75
the other by train stations.

73. **A.** NO CHANGE
    B. as I used to be
    C. as we all are
    D. as I am

74. **F.** NO CHANGE
    G. But unfortunately, as I dance with ghosts, awash in lost moments, the rushing, the lost bags, the missed connections are the never coming home again.
    H. But unfortunately, as I dance with ghosts, awash in lost moments, airports will forever be to me the rushing, the lost bags, the missed connections, the never coming home again.
    J. But unfortunately, as I dance with ghosts, awash in lost moments, there is the rushing, the lost bags, the missed connections, and the never coming home again.

75. **A.** NO CHANGE
    B. I show no affects
    C. I am not effected
    D. I'm not affected

STOP

MATHEMATICS TEST

60 MINUTES—60 QUESTIONS

> **DIRECTIONS:** For each question, solve each problem, select the correct answer, and fill in the corresponding circle on the answer sheet.
>
> Do not spend too much time on problems that you cannot solve quickly. Answer as many questions as you can; then return to the others in the time remaining for this test.
>
> You are allowed to use a calculator on this test. Although you may use your calculator for any problem on this test, keep in mind that some of the problems may be solved more efficiently without using a calculator.

SHOW YOUR WORK HERE

Note: Unless otherwise stated, assume the following:

1. Illustrative figures are NOT necessarily drawn to scale.
2. Geometric figures lie in a plane.
3. The word *line* indicates a straight line.
4. The word *average* indicates arithmetic mean.

---

1. A cat food company conducted a poll of people who bought their product. When they asked 400 people to select one of three colors for their new packaging, 150 people chose blue, 200 people chose red, and the rest chose green. Of the people questioned, what percentage chose green?

   A. 12.5%
   B. 25%
   C. 37.5%
   D. 50%
   E. 87.5%

2. A *hand* is a unit of length equivalent to 4 inches. If the height of a horse's back is 57 inches, what is the height of the horse's back in hands?

   F. 10
   G. 14.25
   H. 53
   J. 142.5
   K. 228

3. In a certain parking lot, $\frac{1}{8}$ of the cars are convertibles and $\frac{3}{4}$ of the convertibles are red. If there are 22 convertibles in the lot that are NOT red, what is the total number of cars parked in the lot?

   A. 88
   B. 176
   C. 526
   D. 616
   E. 704

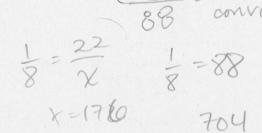

$$\frac{1}{4} = 22$$

$$\boxed{\frac{66}{88}} = \text{red}$$ convertibles

$$\frac{1}{8} = \frac{22}{x} \qquad \frac{1}{8} = 88$$

$$x = 176 \qquad 704$$

CONTINUE

SHOW YOUR WORK HERE

4. What value of *z* makes the following proportion true?

    $$\frac{15}{3z} = \frac{10}{4}$$

    F. 2
    G. $2\frac{1}{2}$
    H. 5
    J. 6
    K. 30

    30z = 60
    z = 2

5. Airplane A travels at a constant speed of 540 miles per hour for 3 hours. Airplane B travels at a constant speed of 400 miles per hour for 3 hours and 30 minutes. What is the total number of miles traveled by the two airplanes?

    A. 1,400
    B. 1,620
    C. 3,020
    D. 3,090
    E. 6,110

    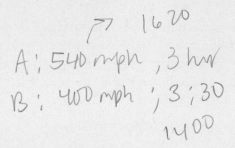

    1620
    A: 540 mph, 3 hrs
    B: 400 mph, 3:30
    1400

6. The price of a $250 television is reduced by 9%. What is the new price of the television?

    F. $205
    G. $227.50
    H. $241
    J. $259
    K. $272.50

7. What is the value of $2a + 4(a - 7)$ if $a = -4$?

    A. 52
    B. 36
    C. −8
    D. −44
    E. −52

    2(−4) + 4(−4 −7)
    −8 +

8. If $f(x) = 2x^2 - 3x + 6$, what is the value of $f(3)$?

    F. 5
    G. 6
    H. 9
    J. 15
    K. 33

    f(3) =
    2(3)² − 3(3) + 6

9. A line segment connects the points (5, −3) and (1, 7) on the standard (*x*, *y*) coordinate plane. What are the coordinates of the midpoint of the segment?

    A. (2, −5)
    B. (3, 2)
    C. (1, 2)
    D. (−15, 7)
    E. (3, −3)

    average

    (1, 7)
    10
    (3,
    (5, −3)

10. For the complex number i such that $i = \sqrt{-1}$, what is the product of $4 + i$ and $2 - 2i$?

    F. $6 - i$

    G. $10 - 6i$

    H. $-6 + 10i$

    J. $6 - 6i$

    K. $5 - 3i$

11. A student listened to a radio station six separate times during the same day, each time listening for four minutes. The table below indicates how many seconds of commercials each four-minute period contained.

Period	1	2	3	4	5	6
Seconds of commercials	120	180	240	0	120	180

What is the average number of seconds of commercials per minute?

    A.   24

    B.   35

    C.   140

    D.   168

    E.   210

12. If $(m + 4)(m - 2) = 0$, which of the following is a possible value of m?

    F.   0

    G.   2

    H.   4

    J.   6

    K.   8

13. What is the value of $|7| + |-9|$?

    A. -63

    B. -2

    C.   2

    D.   16

    E.   63

SHOW YOUR WORK HERE

CONTINUE

14. Points P, Q, and R lie on the same line in the figure below. What is the measure of angle SQT?

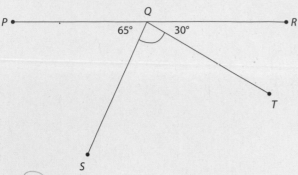

F. 85°
G. 90°
H. 95°
J. 105°
K. 115°

15. If x is a real number and $x^3 = 100$, then x lies between which two consecutive integers?

A. 2 and 3
B. 3 and 4
C. 4 and 5
D. 9 and 10
E. 10 and 11

16. Which of the following sets contains two elements whose greatest common factor is 4 and whose least common multiple is 48?

F. {4, 24}
G. {12, 16}
H. {12, 48}
J. {16, 32}
K. {24, 48}

17. How many times does the graph of $y = x^2 + 4x - 21$ intersect the x-axis?

A. 0
B. 1
C. 2
D. 3
E. 4

18. If ray PR bisects angle QPS, then which of the following must be true?

F. $\angle QPS \cong \angle RPS$
G. $\angle QPS \cong \angle RPQ$
H. $\angle QPR \cong \angle SPR$
J. $\angle RPQ \cong \angle SPQ$
K. $\angle SPQ \cong \angle RPS$

19. In which of the following equations is p directly proportional to the square root of q and inversely proportional to the square of r?

A. $\dfrac{r^2}{\sqrt{q}} = p$

B. $\dfrac{\sqrt{p}}{r^2} = q$

C. $\dfrac{\sqrt{r}}{q^2} = p$

D. $\dfrac{\sqrt{q}}{p^2} = r$

E. $\dfrac{\sqrt{q}}{r^2} = p$

20. A line in the (x, y) coordinate plane contains the points $(5, -3)$ and $(-2, -1)$. Which of the following expressions gives the slope of this line?

F. $\dfrac{5 - (-2)}{-3 - (-1)}$

G. $\dfrac{-3 - (-1)}{-2 - 5}$

H. $\dfrac{-2 - (-1)}{5 - (-3)}$

J. $\dfrac{-3 - (-1)}{5 - (-2)}$

K. $\dfrac{-3 - 1}{5 - 2}$

21. $-(-5) - |-5| =$

A. -25

B. -10

C. 0

D. 10

E. 25

22. A book that normally sells for $15.95 is on sale for 30% off. What is the sale price, to the nearest dollar?

F. $4

G. $5

H. $11

J. $12

K. $13

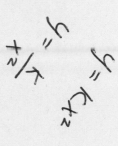

$$\frac{(-1) - (-3)}{(-2) - (5)} \rightarrow$$

CONTINUE

23. If $2x^2 + 9x - 5 = 0$ and $x > 0$, what is the value of x?

    A. $\frac{1}{2}$

    B. 2

    C. $2\frac{1}{2}$

    D. 5

    E. 9

SHOW YOUR WORK HERE

(handwritten work):
$2x^2 + 9x - 5 = 0$
$(2x - 1)(x + 5)$
$2x^2 + 10x - x - 5$
$2x - 1 = 0 \Rightarrow x = \frac{1}{2}$
$x + 5 = 0 \rightarrow x = -5$

24. In a group of 40 students, each student is asked to identify math, history, or art as his or her favorite class. The probability that a student chosen randomly from this group did NOT say math is his or her favorite is $\frac{1}{5}$.

    How many students said math is their favorite?

    F. 8

    G. 10

    H. 20

    J. 32

    K. 36

(handwritten work):
$\frac{1}{5} = \frac{8}{40}$

25. In the parallelogram below, what is the measure of angle *RSQ*?

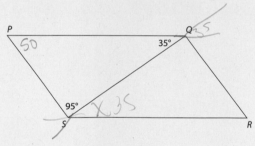

(handwritten annotations): 50, 35, x=35, 95°, 35°

    A. 25°

    B. 35°

    C. 50°

    D. 55°

    E. 60°

26. There are 8 fluid ounces in a cup. If 9 cups of imported olive oil cost $23.04, what is the cost per fluid ounce?

    F. $0.24

    G. $0.32

    H. $1.36

    J. $2.56

    K. $2.88

(handwritten work): 72 ounces

27. A wall in a bedroom has the dimensions shown below. How many square feet of wallpaper are needed to cover the wall without covering the window or door?

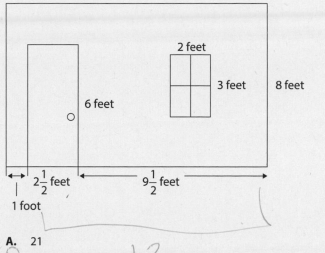

A = 104 ▭

▦ = 6

▢ = 15

A. 21
B. 83
C. 84
D. 89
E. 98

13

28. What is the y-intercept of the line represented by the equation $6x + 3y = 15$?

$3y = -6x + 15$

$y = 2x + 5$

F. −5
G. 2
H. 3
J. 5
K. 6

29. In the figure below, if $p \parallel q \parallel r$ and $t \parallel s$, what is the value of x?

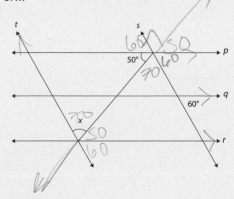

A. 20°
B. 50°
C. 60°
D. 70°
E. 170°

CONTINUE

30. In triangle *PQR* below, what is the tangent of angle *P*?

SHOW YOUR WORK HERE

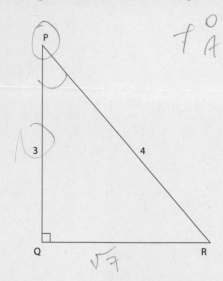

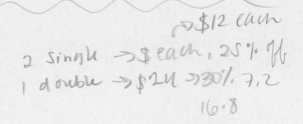

$$3^2 + x^2 = 4^2$$
$$9 + x^2 = 16$$
$$x^2 = 7$$
$$x = \sqrt{7}$$

F. $\dfrac{4}{\sqrt{7}}$

G. $\dfrac{\sqrt{7}}{4}$

H. $\dfrac{4}{3}$

J. $\dfrac{3}{\sqrt{7}}$

K. $\dfrac{\sqrt{7}}{3}$

31. Maria bought music CDs for her club. She bought 2 single CDs and 1 double CD, all on sale. The single CDs, regularly $16 each, were 25% off, and the double CD, regularly $24, was 30% off. Assuming no sales tax, how much in total did Maria pay for her CDs?

A. $16.80
B. $24
C. $28.80
D. $40.80
E. $56

32. The average of a set of 7 integers is 13. When an eighth number is included in the set, the average of the set decreases to 12. What is the eighth number?

F. 4
G. 5
H. 8
J. 13
K. 25

33. For all nonzero values of m, n, and y, $\dfrac{-20m^2n^4y}{5mn^6y^2} =$

$$\frac{-4m}{n^2y}$$

A. $-4mn^2y$

B. $-4m^2n^{10}y^3$

C. $\dfrac{-4n^2y}{m}$

D. $\dfrac{-4m^3}{n^{10}y^3}$

E. $\dfrac{-4m}{n^2y}$

34. If the area of the rectangle below is 24, what is the length of segment QR?

$A=24$

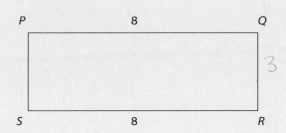

3

F. 2

G. 3

H. 4

J. 8

K. 16

35. A fair coin is tossed 3 times. What is the probability of obtaining exactly one head?

A. $\dfrac{1}{3}$

B. $\dfrac{3}{8}$

C. $\dfrac{1}{2}$

D. $\dfrac{2}{3}$

E. $\dfrac{7}{8}$

CONTINUE

SHOW YOUR WORK HERE

36. If $M = \begin{bmatrix} 4 & 1 \\ -3 & 5 \end{bmatrix}$ and $N = \begin{bmatrix} -4 & 0 \\ -2 & 8 \end{bmatrix}$, then $2(M + N) =$

   F. $\begin{bmatrix} 0 & 1 \\ -5 & 13 \end{bmatrix}$

   G. $\begin{bmatrix} 0 & 2 \\ -10 & 26 \end{bmatrix}$

   H. $\begin{bmatrix} 8 & 1 \\ -1 & -3 \end{bmatrix}$

   J. $\begin{bmatrix} -2 & 8 \\ 2 & 40 \end{bmatrix}$

   K. $\begin{bmatrix} 16 & 2 \\ -2 & -6 \end{bmatrix}$

   $2\begin{bmatrix} 0 & 9 \\ -5 & 13 \end{bmatrix} = \begin{bmatrix} 0 & 2 \\ -10 & 26 \end{bmatrix}$

37. In the standard (x, y) coordinate plane, how many times does the graph of $y = (x - 2)(x + 3)(x + 4)$ intersect the x-axis?

   A. 2
   B. 3
   C. 4
   D. 5
   E. 9

38. If $\log_2 x = 5$, what is the value of x?

   F. $\sqrt{5}$

   G. $\dfrac{5}{2}$

   H. $\dfrac{5}{\log 2}$

   J. 25

   K. 32

   $\log_2 x = 5$

   $x = 2^5$

39. The ratio of the side lengths of a right triangle is $1 : \sqrt{3} : 2$. What is the cosine of the smallest angle in this triangle?

   A. $\dfrac{\sqrt{3}}{3}$

   B. $\dfrac{1}{2}$

   C. $\sqrt{3}$

   D. $\dfrac{\sqrt{3}}{2}$

   E. 2

   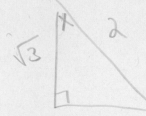

   $\dfrac{A}{H}$ $\dfrac{\sqrt{3}}{2}$

40. The circle with equation $(x - 5)^2 + (y - 7)^2 = 16$ lies completely inside a square. What is the least possible length of one of the square's sides?

- **F.** 4
- **G.** 8
- **H.** 10
- **J.** 14
- **K.** 16

41. For real numbers a, b, and c, $a > b$ and $c < 0$. Which of the following inequalities must be true?

$a > b \quad c < 0$

- **A.** $ab > 0$
- **B.** $ac < 0$
- **C.** $\dfrac{a}{b} > \dfrac{c}{b}$
- **D.** $\dfrac{a}{c} > \dfrac{b}{c}$
- **E.** $\dfrac{a}{c} < \dfrac{b}{c}$

42. The rectangular picture shown below has a shaded frame that is 2 inches wide. What is the area, in square inches, of the frame?

30 inches

26

2 ⌐ ¬ 2

18

22 inches

- **F.** 468
- **G.** 192
- **H.** 132
- **J.** 96
- **K.** 48

43. If $|x + y| = |x| + |y|$, then which of the following must be true?

- **A.** x and y have opposite signs
- **B.** x and y have the same sign
- **C.** x and y are integers
- **D.** $|x| = |y|$
- **E.** $x = -y$

$|2 + 3| = |2| + |3|$

$|5| = |2| + |3|$

CONTINUE

44. The system of linear equations below has no unique solution.

$$-20x - 12y = -28$$
$$5x + ky = -2$$

What must be the value of k?

F. -4

G. -3

H. $\dfrac{3}{5}$

J. $-\dfrac{3}{5}$

K. 3

45. In the standard (x, y) coordinate plane, if the graphs of $y = -3x - 4$ and $y = mx + 7$ are perpendicular, then what is the value of m?

A. $-\dfrac{7}{4}$

B. $-\dfrac{4}{7}$

C. $-\dfrac{1}{3}$

D. $\dfrac{1}{3}$

E. -3

46. A right triangle has a hypotenuse of 17 and a leg of 15. What is the length of the other leg?

F. 4

G. $\sqrt{32}$

H. 8

J. $\sqrt{514}$

K. 64

47. The distance between points $(4, b)$ and $(b, 6)$ in the standard (x, y) coordinate plane is 10 coordinate units. Which of the following could be the value of b?

A. -4

B. 2

C. 5

D. 10

E. 12

48. The temperature at 9 a.m. is –15.5°C. The temperature at 10 a.m. is –13.0°C. If the temperature changes by the same amount each hour, what will the temperature be at 1 p.m.?

   F. −20.5°C

   G. −8.0°C

   H. −5.5°C

   J. 2.5°C

   K. 7.5°C

SHOW YOUR WORK HERE

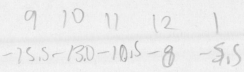

49. A line in the standard (x, y) coordinate plane passes through the point $\left(\dfrac{3}{4}, \dfrac{1}{3}\right)$ and the origin. What is the slope of this line?

   A. $\dfrac{5}{12}$

   B. $\dfrac{1}{3}$

   C. $\dfrac{4}{9}$

   D. $\dfrac{3}{4}$

   E. $\dfrac{9}{4}$

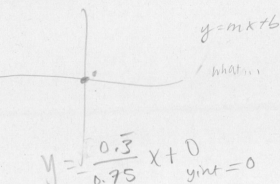

50. From the top of an airport control tower, the angle between a horizontal line and an approaching airplane is 27°, as shown below. If the distance between the control tower and the airplane is 35,000 meters, what is the difference, in meters, between the altitude of the plane and the top of the control tower?

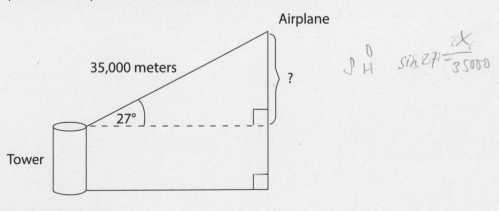

   F. $35{,}000 \times \sin 63°$

   G. $35{,}000 \times \sin 27°$

   H. $35{,}000 \times \cos 27°$

   J. $\dfrac{35{,}000}{\sin 27°}$

   K. $\dfrac{35{,}000}{\cos 27°}$

CONTINUE

51. The length of a rectangular room is 4 meters less than 3 times its width. If the area of the room is 84 square meters, how many meters long is the room?

    SHOW YOUR WORK HERE

    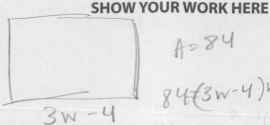

    A. 6
    B. 12
    C. 14
    D. 18
    E. 21

52. A balanced six-sided die with faces 1, 2, 3, 4, 5, 6 is rolled twice. What is the probability of getting one 5 and one 6?

    F. $\frac{1}{3}$

    G. $\frac{17}{18}$

    H. $\frac{1}{18}$

    J. $\frac{5}{9}$

    K. $\frac{1}{6}$

53. What is the area of a circle with diameter 16?

    A. 8π
    B. 16π
    C. 32π
    D. 64π
    E. 256π

54. There is only one solution for x in the equation $x^2 - kx = -1$. What is one possible value of k?

    F. -2
    G. -1
    H. $-\frac{1}{2}$
    J. $\frac{1}{2}$
    K. 1

55. What is the value of x in the pentagon below?

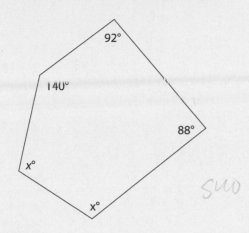

A. 220
B. 200
C. 110
D. 40
E. 20

56. If $f(x) = x - 2$ and $g(x) = 2x^2 + 1$, what is the value of $g(f(x))$?

F. $2x^2 - 7$
G. $2x^2 - 1$
H. $2x^2 - 8x + 9$
J. $4x^2 - 8x + 9$
K. $2x^2 - 4x + 5$

57. The figure below shows a glass tank partially filled with water. If the water occupies 60% of the glass tank and has a volume of 792 cubic centimeters, what is the surface area, in square centimeters, of the tank?

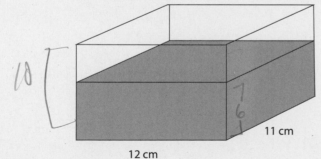

12 cm

11 cm

A. 362
B. 460
C. 504
D. 724
E. 1,320

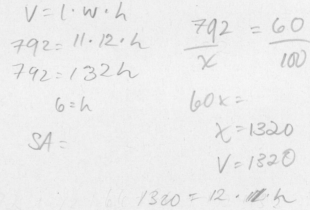

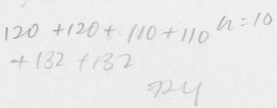

$(n-2) * 180$

540

$2(x-2)(x-2)) + 1$
$2(x^2 - 4x + 4) + 1$
$2x^2 - 8x + 8 + 1$

$V = l \cdot w \cdot h$
$792 = 11 \cdot 12 \cdot h$
$792 = 132h$
$6 = h$
$SA =$

$\dfrac{792}{x} = \dfrac{60}{100}$

$60x =$
$x = 1320$
$V = 1320$

$1320 = 12 \cdot h$
$h = 10$

$120 + 120 + 110 + 110$
$+ 132 + 132$
724

SHOW YOUR WORK HERE

58. The formula for the surface area of a cylinder is $2\pi rh + 2\pi r^2$, where r is the radius of the base and h is the height. If both the radius and the height of a cylinder are tripled, by what factor is its surface area increased?

F. 3
G. 6
H. 9
J. 27
K. 81

59. How many cycles does the function $y = 3 + 5 \cos 4x$ complete when $0 \le x \le 2\pi$?

A. $\dfrac{1}{4}$
B. 1
C. 3
D. 4
E. 16

60. For every point on a certain line in the standard (x, y) coordinate plane, two times the x-coordinate plus three times the y-coordinate is equal to 12. What is the slope of this line?

F. $-\dfrac{3}{2}$
G. $-\dfrac{2}{3}$
H. $\dfrac{1}{6}$
J. $\dfrac{2}{3}$
K. 4

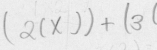

$$(2(x)) + (3(y)) = 12$$
$$2x + 3y = 12$$
$$3y = -2x + 12$$
$$y = -\frac{2}{3}x + 4$$

Ⓧ
STOP

READING TEST

35 Minutes—40 Questions

> **DIRECTIONS:** There are four passages in this test. Each passage is followed by several questions. Read each passage, select the best answer to each related question, and fill in the corresponding circle on the answer sheet. You may look back at the passages as often as you need.

PASSAGE I

PROSE FICTION: Passage A is an excerpt from *The Time Machine* by H.G. Wells. Passage B is an excerpt from *Twenty Thousand Leagues Under the Sea* by Jules Verne.

Passage A
by H.G. Wells

The thing the Time Traveller held in his hand was a glittering metallic framework, scarcely larger than a small clock, and very delicately made. There was ivory in it, and some transparent crystalline substance. And now I must be explicit, for this that
5 follows—unless his explanation is to be accepted—is an absolutely unaccountable thing. He took one of the small octagonal tables that were scattered about the room, and set it in front of the fire, with two legs on the hearthrug. On this table he placed the mechanism. Then he drew up a chair, and sat down. The only
10 other object on the table was a small shaded lamp, the bright light of which fell upon the model. There were also perhaps a dozen candles about, two in brass candlesticks upon the mantel and several in sconces, so that the room was brilliantly illuminated. I sat in a low arm-chair nearest the fire, and I drew this
15 forward so as to be almost between the Time Traveller and the fireplace. Filby sat behind him, looking over his shoulder. The Medical Man and the Provincial Mayor watched him in profile from the right, the Psychologist from the left. The Very Young Man stood behind the Psychologist. We were all on the alert. It
20 appears incredible to me that any kind of trick, however subtly conceived and however adroitly done, could have been played upon us under these conditions.

The Time Traveller looked at us, and then at the mechanism. 'Well?' said the Psychologist.

25 'This little affair,' said the Time Traveller, resting his elbows upon the table and pressing his hands together above the apparatus, 'is only a model. It is my plan for a machine to travel through time. You will notice that it looks singularly askew, and that there is an odd twinkling appearance about this bar, as though it was
30 in some way unreal.' He pointed to the part with his finger. 'Also, here is one little white lever, and here is another.'

The Medical Man got up out of his chair and peered into the thing. 'It's beautifully made,' he said.

'It took two years to make,' retorted the Time Traveller. Then,
35 when we had all imitated the action of the Medical Man, he said: 'Now I want you clearly to understand that this lever, being pressed over, sends the machine gliding into the future, and this other reverses the motion. This saddle represents the seat of a time traveller. Presently I am going to press the lever,
40 and off the machine will go. It will vanish, pass into future Time, and disappear. Have a good look at the thing. Look at the table too, and satisfy yourselves there is no trickery. I don't want to waste this model, and then be told I'm a quack.'

Passage B
by Jules Verne

Clearly we could do nothing but submit, and afterwards Captain Nemo showed me his wondrous craft … It was indeed a thing of marvels; for, besides the dining-room, it contained a large library of twelve thousand volumes, a drawing-room measuring
5 thirty feet by eighteen, and fifteen high. The walls of this apartment were adorned with masterpieces of the great painters, and beautiful marbles and bronzes. A large piano-organ stood in one corner, and there were glass cases containing the rarest marine curiosities which a naturalist
10 could wish to see. A collection of enormous pearls in a cabinet must have been worth millions, and Captain Nemo told me he had rifled every sea to find them.

The room assigned to me was fitted up with every luxury, yet the captain's own apartment was as simply furnished as a
15 monastic cell, but in it were contained all the ingenious instruments that controlled the movements of the *Nautilus*, as his submarine was named. The electricity was manufactured by a process of extracting chloride of sodium from the sea-water, but the fresh air necessary for the life of the crew could only
20 be obtained by rising to the surface. The engine-room was sixty-five feet long, and in it was the machinery for producing electricity as well as that for applying the power to the propeller.

The *Nautilus*, Captain Nemo explained, was capable of a speed
25 of fifty miles an hour, and could be made to sink or rise with

CONTINUE

precision by flooding or emptying a reservoir. In a box, raised somewhat above the hull and fitted with glass ten inches thick, the steersman had his place, and a powerful electric reflector behind him illumined the sea for half a mile in front.

30 The submarine also carried a small torpedo-like boat, fitted in a groove along the top, so that it could be entered from the *Nautilus* by opening a panel, and, after that was closed, the boat could be detached from the submarine, and would then bob upwards to the surface like a cork. The importance of this and its bearing
35 on my story will appear in due time.

It was on a desert island that Captain Nemo had carried out the building of the *Nautilus*, and from many different places he had secured the various parts of the hull and machinery, in order to maintain secrecy.

40 Deeply interested as I was in every detail of this extraordinary vessel, and excited beyond measure at the wonders which awaited me in exploring the world beneath the waves, I had still the feeling of a prisoner who dared scarcely hope that liberty might some day be obtained. But when the metal plates which
45 covered the windows of the saloon were rolled back as we sailed under the water, and on each hand I could see a thronging army of many-coloured aquatic creatures swimming around us, attracted by our light, I was in an ecstasy of wonder and delight.

Questions 1–3 ask about Passage A.

1. According to the first paragraph (lines 1–22), the model of the time travelling apparatus contains:

   A. glitter.
   B. crystal.
   C. ivory.
   D. wax.

2. It can be reasonably inferred from the passage that the Time Traveller is:

   F. worried his time travelling apparatus will not work.
   G. not concerned about what people think of him.
   H. trying to make fools of his colleagues.
   J. proud of his time travelling apparatus.

3. As depicted in the passage, the Medical Man's feelings toward the model of the time travelling apparatus can best be described as:

   A. amused.
   B. ambivalent.
   C. fearful.
   D. admiring.

Questions 4–6 ask about Passage B.

4. It can be inferred that Captain Nemo:

   F. values extravagance.
   G. has specific goals.
   H. avoids people.
   J. values function over comfort.

5. The passage suggests that the narrator feels:

   A. completely honored to have access to the *Nautilus*.
   B. both amazed and uneasy in the *Nautilus*.
   C. like a co-owner of the *Nautilus*.
   D. terrified being underwater in the *Nautilus*.

6. As it is used in line 1, the word *submit* most nearly means:

   F. surrender.
   G. quit.
   H. humor.
   J. send.

Questions 7–10 ask about both passages.

7. Both the Time Traveller and Captain Nemo:

   A. invite people into their machines.
   B. build dangerous weapons.
   C. build unusual machines.
   D. explore the oceans.

8. Which of the following is known about the *Nautilus* but NOT known about the time machine?

   F. How long it took to build
   G. Where it was built
   H. Who built it
   J. How it looks

9. It can be inferred from the passages that the Time Traveller and Captain Nemo are both:

   A. tiresome eccentrics.
   B. plotting something evil.
   C. original thinkers.
   D. wary of danger.

10. Which of the following is something Captain Nemo needs that the Time Traveller DOES NOT?

    F. Secrecy
    G. Credibility
    H. Music
    J. Adventure

PASSAGE II

SOCIAL SCIENCE: This passage is adapted from an online essay about the history of gold.

Gold is valuable for a wide variety of reasons—some logical, and some not so logical. It is a very soft metal, so craftspeople have found it easy to work with. It also happens to have a bright, shiny glow that people find irresistible. Gold can be easily melted
5 down and formed into coins to be used for money and trade, or into beautiful jewelry that is worn to represent status. Gold has helped to build empires, and it has played a hand in the collapse of many of them as well. Likewise, gold has played a role in many personal fortunes being gained, glorified, and
10 ultimately lost.

Some of the earliest known gold jewelry was found near the Euphrates and Tigris Rivers in Iraq in royal tombs. The tombs, created during the Sumer civilization, date back to about 3000 B.C. Gold objects uncovered in the region that Is now Eastern
15 Europe include a statuette of a bull that dates back to about 2300 B.C. Beginning around 1500 B.C., the tombs of Egyptian pharaohs were literally filled with amazing gold objects.

Gold has played a significant role throughout the history of civilization. In the western world, gold production gradually
20 increased during the Egyptian, Greek, and Roman Empires. The ancient Egyptians probably mined only about one ton of gold per year. During the Roman Empire, production of gold increased to between five and ten tons annually. After the fall of the Roman Empire, western civilization moved into the Middle Ages and a
25 period of decline. Gold production dropped drastically during this time, to probably less than one ton per year.

Gold production in the western world did not increase again until the Spanish invasions of great South American civilizations, including the Aztecs and the Incas. These civilizations' methods
30 of gold mining and craftsmanship were much more sophisticated than that of the Europeans at that time. An early method the Peruvians used involved hammering the gold into thin sheets that had been cut with knives made of rock; they would then engrave decorative drawings into the sheets. Southern Peruvians
35 developed a method of melting gold and pouring it into shaped molds. Once the gold cooled and hardened, its ceramic cast was broken and removed, and the piece was polished and decorated.

The Incas took their gold very seriously. They considered the
40 sun to be a god and the gold to be this god's "sweat." In Cuzco, the Inca capital, royal gardens were often filled with golden plants and animals, and the walls of the Incan Temple of the Sun were covered in gold.

After Columbus reached America in 1492, European kings and
45 queens sent adventurers to the New World in pursuit of riches. They heard legends of such cities as Cuzco, supposedly made of silver and gold, and went in search of them. By the early sixteenth century, Cortes found the Aztecs in what is now Mexico. In an effort to befriend Cortes and his men, the Aztec Emperor,
50 Montezuma, gave them splendid gifts—many made of gold. Unfortunately, the conquistadors had come for much more than a few gifts; they had their sights set on acquiring it all. Cortes conquered the Aztec people and filled ship after ship with plundered silver and gold.

55 Not long thereafter, Francisco Pizarro invaded the Incas and captured their emperor, Atahualpa. For the next few months, the Incas gathered tons of gold to be used as ransom for their leader. In the end, Pizarro had the emperor executed, yet continued to demand more gold. Pizarro had most of the unique
60 gold artifacts melted down to facilitate shipment back to Spain. Several thousand of these treasures have been preserved, but they represent only a fraction of what the skilled artisans originally created.

The European empires continued to search for gold in the New
65 World, until most of the ancient treasures were seized and brought back to Europe. The transfer of such vast amounts of gold encouraged the growth of European civilizations; however, this growth was at the expense of the destruction of much of South American civilization.

70 A huge transition in gold mining occurred after gold was discovered in a river at Sutter's Mill in California, in 1848. This discovery started a gold rush, and over the next several years, prospectors excavated between seventy and ninety tons annually in California. During the last half of the nineteenth century,
75 several other gold rushes occurred in various other parts of the world; three of the biggest were in South Africa, Australia, and the Yukon Territory of Canada. The first of these ended up producing the largest portion of the world's supply of gold, at an estimated 40 percent. By the beginning of the twentieth century,
80 about four hundred tons of gold were being mined per year worldwide. However, production actually declined throughout the century until the price of gold rose dramatically in 1980. This huge demand for gold resulted in old mines being reopened and new ones being explored. Production peaked in 1990 at
85 over seventeen hundred tons. Before the gold rush in California, perhaps only about ten thousand tons of gold had been excavated in all. In the hundred and fifty years that have since passed, over a hundred thousand additional tons of gold have been mined.

90 Due to its perpetually high value, gold has been considered too expensive to waste, so it has always been recycled. Even new gold objects that are made today often have some recycled gold that may originally have been dug out of a mine in Africa before the Bronze Age, or in Peru long before Europeans knew of the
95 so-called New World. So if you buy a gold watch or ring, or even a gold tooth, it's possible that some of the gold inside was once part of an old European coin, an Inca vase, or an African chief's bedpost.

11. From the statement" It also happens to have a bright, shiny glow that people find irresistible" (lines 3–4), it can be inferred that:

    A. part of the value of gold comes from its visual appeal.
    B. gold would be worthless if people didn't like to look at it.
    C. gold is worth more than silver because it is more beautiful.
    D. people select building materials for their beauty more than for their strength.

12. What is the main idea of the last paragraph (lines 90–98)?

    F. Gold has always been reused because it is so valuable.
    G. A new watch might have some recycled gold in it.
    H. There have been many gold rushes around the world since 1848.
    J. Most of the world's gold has been mined in the past 150 years.

13. The passage mentions that about 40 percent of the world's supply of gold has come from:

    A. California.
    B. Australia.
    C. Yukon Territory.
    D. South Africa.

14. The author mentions that the Incas:

    I. used ceramic casts to make gold objects.
    II. considered gold to be the sweat of the sun god.
    III. melted gold artifacts to ship them home.

    F. I only
    G. II only
    H. I and II only
    J. I, II, and III

15. According to the fourth paragraph (lines 27–38), the Incas' skill in working with gold was much better than that of:

    A. California prospectors.
    B. the Aztecs.
    C. the Australians.
    D. the Europeans.

16. The author's statement that "the Incas gathered tons of gold to be used as ransom for their leader" (lines 57–58) means that they wanted to:

    F. buy his freedom.
    G. pay for his funeral.
    H. elect him again.
    J. have him assassinated.

17. As it is used in line 65 , the word *seized* most nearly means:

    A. understood.
    B. stopped.
    C. afflicted.
    D. taken.

18. According to this passage, European explorers obtained gold from South America mainly by:

    F. mining it.
    G. stealing it.
    H. trading ships for it.
    J. buying it with silver.

19. The author mentions that the oldest gold artifacts were found in:

    A. tombs in Iraq.
    B. tombs in Egypt.
    C. Eastern Europe.
    D. South Africa.

20. One can tell by reading the passage that gold production in the twentieth century:

    F. steadily increased.
    G. steadily decreased.
    H. was greater than before the California gold rush.
    J. was in decline since 1980.

PASSAGE III

HUMANITIES: This passage is adapted from an essay on the history of the printed word.

Desktop publishing existed long before copy machines and personal computers. Moreover, multimedia art has been around for quite some time. William Blake, who is primarily remembered as a poet, developed a complex and unique system of "illumi-
[5] nated" printing that yielded beautiful results. William's brother, Robert, apparently envisioned the method and, shortly before his death, described it to William. Blake created and printed a series of books containing poetry and illustrations that were often intermingled on the page, something that was not possible
[10] to do at that time with conventional printing methods. He called these "illuminated books," probably referring to the handwritten, illuminated manuscripts of the Middle Ages that combined text and pictures.

William Blake was born in London in 1757 and served as an
[15] apprentice for a printer. The technical craft of printing enabled him to earn a modest income for the rest of his life, and provided him with the skills to make his brother's concept of illuminated printing a reality.

In Blake's day, books were typically printed using moveable type
[20] that was set in a letterpress by a skilled artisan. Another artisan pressed the inked type onto paper as many times as necessary. Illustrations were made from etchings made on copper plates; these required a different press, because it took a different amount of pressure to print the ink from the etched (carved)
[25] lines.

The method of printing that Blake developed involved engraving text and images onto the same copper plate, similar to a woodcut block. The raised surface made the actual imprint, as opposed to the etched lines of the standard method. To create a plate,
[30] Blake etched away the parts that would *not* print onto the paper. His first step was to draw model sketches of the text and images. Then, he drew the images in reverse on the copper plate with a solution that was resistant to the acid. This process was a tedious one, and, at times, the acid burned the wrong parts of
[35] the plate, compelling Blake to start over again. Once a plate was completed, however, he could make as many prints as he desired. Blake added colored inks to the copper plate, then made one or more pressings. After the ink dried on the page, he sometimes used watercolor paints to add background washes or subtle
[40] details, such as rosy cheeks.

Blake believed that his invention could empower writers, musicians, and other artists to create their own works, without the need to find a publisher who would approve of the work and print it. Blake claimed that this capability could liberate those
[45] artists who would otherwise be unable to publish their creative

visions due to financial or moral restrictions. Such issues were of particular concern to artists during Blake's time, whose works were often censored by the Church, the Crown, or both. Although illuminated printing could be done in one's home rather inex-
[50] pensively, it still required technical skills that most artists did not have. Even Blake himself could produce only a very limited number of books because their production was so labor-intensive. Therefore, Blake's invention was actually more of a self-publishing hope for artists than a practical reality.

[55] Blake's first illuminated book, completed in 1789, was a series of pastoral poems entitled *Songs of Innocence*. This volume, describing the innocence and grace of nature and youth, became his most popular work; Blake printed and sold many copies of it throughout his life. In 1794, he combined the work with the
[60] complementary *Songs of Experience,* in order to show "the Two Contrary States of the Human Soul."

The world's revolutions became another source of inspiration for Blake's works. Blake and many other artists were excited about the democratic changes that took place during the
[65] American Revolution and, subsequently, the French Revolution. Blake's works during this era were a series of prophetic myths created as commentary on the social, political, and religious shifts that were occurring. *The Marriage of Heaven and Hell* (1790) and *Visions of the Daughters of Albion* (1793) showed how the
[70] events in France were affecting life in Britain. *America, a Prophecy* (1793) and *Europe, a Prophecy* (1794) were the first of his apocalyptic works, suggesting that the transformational changes taking place could not be reversed by the Church and State. In his works, Blake attempted to comment on these changes. To
[75] avoid censorship and persecution, he disguised these comments in his own allegories, which were difficult to decipher.

These prophetic works were darker and more forbidding than his early pastoral poems. They also showcased the development of his technical and artistic methods. William Blake's new text
[80] and illustrations became more beautiful and vivid. They were more integrated as well, with tiny creatures roaming among the words, flames appearing to burn the page, and other dramatic interplay between his text and images. His final works represented the peak of his artistic vision. *Milton, a Poem* is a reflection
[85] on an introspective time in Blake's life, and a tribute to Milton, a poet whose work inspired Blake. *Jerusalem*, containing one hundred etched copper plates, was a grand synthesis of all of Blake's past myths.

Although Blake never became prosperous as an artist during
[90] his lifetime, he refused to see the major aspects of his life, poetry,

CONTINUE

painting, and printmaking as being separate. He believed that one's art, work, and life are the same, and that all are ultimately combined to express one's reverence for life. The conflict between the ideals of his creative vision and his materialistic limitations 95 was a driving force in his works, and a parallel to the conflicts that the world was experiencing in that era. In this way, Blake's works were able to both reflect and inspire a revolution of consciousness.

21. As it is used in line 16, the word *modest* most nearly means:

A. extravagant.
B. virtuous.
C. prudish.
D. moderate.

22. It can be inferred from the passage that Blake:

F. directly challenged his king and religious leaders.
G. was subtly critical of the British government and the Church.
H. earned most of his money from selling copies of his illuminated books.
J. must have traveled to France before he wrote *Europe, a Prophecy*.

23. In suggesting that "Blake's works were able to both reflect and inspire a revolution of consciousness" (lines 96–98), the author meant that:

A. Blake's books demonstrated his vision of how human consciousness was growing.
B. other artists also etched the reflected images of their works onto copper plates to print.
C. Blake worked long, hard hours on his revolutionary printing technique.
D. the French Revolution was inspired by Blake's prophetic works.

24. The passage explains that the traditional method of printing required separate copper plates for:

F. color and black ink.
G. text and images.
H. front and back.
J. artisans and writers.

25. The main point of the fifth paragraph (lines 41–54) is that William Blake's:

A. brother is credited with the initial idea for the printing technique that he later developed.
B. printing process was an innovative way to combine text and images together on the same page.
C. hope was that his printing technique would help other artists, though it was too complicated for them to use.
D. invention enabled many artists to self-publish, which freed them from financial and social restrictions.

26. Which of the following statements is supported by the fourth paragraph (lines 26–40)?

F. Blake's earliest and most popular illuminated books were pastoral poems.
G. William Blake's brother might have given him the idea for illuminated printing.
H. Blake found his new printing process easier and faster than the traditional method.
J. The raised surface of Blake's copper plates made the impression on paper.

27. The passage explains that during William Blake's life, censorship:

A. prevented many artists from being published.
B. slowed down the changes brought about by the revolutions.
C. was used to maintain a balance between Church and State.
D. was mainly used on allegorical works.

28. According to the passage, Blake wrote *Songs of Innocence*:

F. after he wrote a tribute to Milton.
G. after he wrote *Jerusalem*.
H. before he wrote *Songs of Experience*.
J. before he wrote his first illuminated book.

29. The author suggests that Blake's illuminated books are:

A. more popular than his poems.
B. an early form of desktop publishing.
C. reproductions of the illuminated manuscripts.
D. easily reproduced with moveable type.

30. As it is used in line 34, the word *tedious* most likely means:

F. somewhat destructive.
G. relatively simple.
H. unique and interesting.
J. long and tiresome.

PASSAGE IV

NATURAL SCIENCE: This passage is adapted from several popular science periodicals.

[handwritten: tech breakthrough]

In January 2003, the discovery of a new planet created many breakthroughs for the field of astronomy. The planet, named OGLE-TR-56b, is larger, hotter, farther away from Earth, and closer to its parent star than any previously known planet. The technique
5   used to discover the planet is also new. This exciting new technique, called *transiting*, makes finding planets easier and less costly; it also increases the number of star systems in which astronomers may now search for planets.

OGLE-TR-56b is probably the hottest known planet, with a surface
10 temperature of about 1600 degrees Celsius. Showers of molten iron rain down on the already boiling surface. The same side of this planet constantly faces its parent star, just as the same side of the moon always faces the Earth. Such a phenomenon is a result of the strong gravitational pull that the larger body exerts
15 on the smaller one. This means that on one side of OGLE-TR-56b, it's constantly day, and on the other side it's always nighttime.

[handwritten left margin: day/night from Earth]

Like Jupiter and Saturn, OGLE-TR-56b is a gaseous planet, a fact that contradicts previous thinking about planets with smaller orbits. Until recently, astronomers believed that gaseous planets
20 could not survive in the high temperatures that result from their proximity to their parent stars. These astronomers contended that only rocky planets—such as Mercury, Venus, Earth, and Mars—could exist in such close orbits. However, the many recently discovered gaseous planets with small orbits, including
25 OGLE-TR-56b, provide evidence suggesting that these huge gas balls originally formed farther away from their stars, and that over time, they gradually spiraled inward along "sticky" paths of gas and dust, so they now have much smaller orbits.

[handwritten left margin: gas planets orig got trapped]

Out of about 100 recently discovered gaseous planets, OGLE-
30 TR-56b has the fastest and smallest orbit. It takes only about 29 hours for it to make one orbit around its sun, which makes for an extremely short year. The diameter of its orbit is approximately 40 times smaller than Earth's, making OGLE-TR-56b's orbit much smaller than even Mercury's. Before OGLE-TR-56b was discovered,
35 astronomers believed that the diameter of a planet's orbit could not be less than about 25 times smaller than Earth's, due to the intense radiation that exists in such close proximity to a star. OGLE-TR-56b and its sun are so close that, when viewed from this hot planet, its sun appears to be about as large as a bowling
40 ball in the sky. By contrast, our own sun looks no larger than a marble when viewed from Earth.

[handwritten left margin: close to sun]

At about 5,000 light years away from Earth, OGLE-TR-56b is the most distant planet that astronomers have discovered.

[handwritten top: is "realization" factor]

Astronomers stumbled upon this remote planet almost by
45 accident while they were studying the brightness of stars. Until recently, most planets had been discovered by using the Doppler method, which measures slight movements in stars resulting from the gravitational pull of their planets. But in order to cause a noticeable movement in their parent stars, planets had to be
50 very large, much larger than Earth. Astronomers discovered OGLE-TR-56b by detecting a slight decrease in the light emitted by its parent star when the planet eclipsed it. It has since become possible for planets much smaller than OGLE-TR-56b to be detected while similarly moving in front of their parent stars.

55 Astronomers at Warsaw University first used this transiting technique to observe the brightness of 50,000 stars. The study, called OGLE (Optical Gravitational Lensing Experiment), was not originally intended to discover new planets. By studying the brightness of these stars, however, astronomers noticed that 59
60 of the stars had light reductions that were potentially caused by planets crossing in front of them.

[handwritten: ↓ when planets pass]

After the astronomers at Warsaw University announced their findings in February 2002, other astronomers began research to determine whether any of these light reductions were actually
65 caused by planets. They used the Doppler method to find the mass of the objects causing the light reductions. Most of the noted incidences of light reduction turned out to be false alarms caused by such factors as twin stars. However, astronomers from the Harvard-Smithsonian and the California Institute of
70 Technology proved one of the incidences to be evidence of a planet—the quick, hot planet named after the original study, OGLE-TR-56b.

[handwritten: mostly false alarms but # planet]

An advantage of the transiting technique is that it actually works with *less* technology than the Doppler method does. The Doppler
75 method requires the biggest and most expensive telescopes, which can detect planets orbiting only the brightest stars visible in our night sky. On the other hand, an astronomer can use any large, store-bought telescope, point it at stars—even dim ones— and detect possible cases of transiting. Thus literally tens of
80 thousands of other stars can be observed to find out whether any planets cross in front of them. Astronomers, however, still rely on the Doppler method in order to confirm the findings of the transiting technique. Therefore, they can still do most of the busywork of detecting potential planets simply and cheaply in
85 their own backyards, before graduating to the more expensive telescopes to follow up on their initial findings.

[handwritten right margin: less tech; doppler still relied on]

Another advantage of the transiting technique is that it can be used to detect much smaller planets. However, as the hazy

atmosphere of Earth can obstruct the viewing of such small
90 planets, the telescopes are better located in space where a clearer
view can be obtained. Plans have already been made by NASA
and the European Space Agency to launch such telescopes before
the end of the decade. So on Earth and in space, the technique
of transiting affords astronomers the opportunity to find hundreds
95 of new planets in distant galaxies. These new discoveries will
continue to challenge our existing theories about planets and
provide exciting opportunities to learn more about distant solar
systems.

31. The author claims that the technique of transiting is
exciting because:

- **A.** everyone enjoys learning about planets and stars.
- **B.** now astronomers can see whether OGLE-TR-56b is a planet.
- **C.** it makes it easier to discover new planets.
- **D.** it measures the brightness of the stars.

32. The passage defines an *eclipse* as:

- **F.** when a planet moves in front of its parent star.
- **G.** when it is always nighttime on one side of a planet.
- **H.** rain showers of molten iron.
- **J.** the inspiration for the transiting technique.

33. The passage explains that the Doppler method detects:

- I. the slight movement of a star.
- II. the gravitational pull of a planet.
- III. when a planet passes in front of a star.

- **A.** I and II only
- **B.** I and III only
- **C.** II and III only
- **D.** I, II, and III

34. One can tell by reading the passage that the transiting
technique of finding planets:

- **F.** makes the Doppler method no longer necessary.
- **G.** was used long before the Doppler method was developed.
- **H.** can be used on many more stars than the Doppler method.
- **J.** is much more expensive to use than the Doppler method.

35. It can be inferred from the passage that OGLE-TR-56b:

- **A.** has a 29-hour day.
- **B.** orbits our own sun.
- **C.** is a very rocky planet.
- **D.** is larger than Earth.

36. The passage states that OGLE-TR-56b:

- I. is about 5,000 light years away.
- II. is hotter than any known planet.
- III. has a very small orbit.

- **F.** I only
- **G.** I and III only
- **H.** II and III only
- **J.** I, II, and III

37. According to the last paragraph (lines 87–98), Earth's
hazy atmosphere makes it difficult to:

- **A.** launch large, powerful telescopes into outer space.
- **B.** find small planets by using telescopes located on the earth.
- **C.** calculate the gravitational pull of planets on their parent stars.
- **D.** tell whether a newly discovered planet is rocky or gaseous.

38. The passage claims that from the surface of OGLE-TR-56b, its sun appears:

- **F.** to have a twin sun facing it.
- **G.** to have hot iron poured on its surface.
- **H.** to be about the size of a bowling ball.
- **J.** to be about the size of a marble.

39. At Warsaw University, astronomers originally used the
transiting technique to:

- **A.** follow up a study from the California Institute of Technology.
- **B.** discover a gaseous planet named OGLE-TR-56b.
- **C.** search for planets around 59 stars.
- **D.** study the brightness of 50,000 stars.

40. What is the main idea of the fourth paragraph (lines 29–41)?

- **F.** The orbit of OGLE-TR-56b is about 40 times smaller than Earth's.
- **G.** OGLE-TR-56b's small orbit changed an assumption previously held by scientists.
- **H.** OGLE-TR-56b is one of the hottest planets ever discovered.
- **J.** Because OGLE-TR-56b is gaseous, astronomers have changed all of their ideas about planets.

STOP

SCIENCE TEST

35 Minutes—40 Questions

> **DIRECTIONS:** There are seven passages in this test. Each passage is followed by several questions. Read each passage, select the best answer to each related question, and fill in the corresponding circle on the answer sheet. You may look back at the passages as often as you need.
>
> You are NOT allowed to use a calculator on this test.

PASSAGE I

According to quantum theory, light consists of individual particles called *photons*. When photons with enough energy strike a bare metal surface, they can eject negatively charged electrons from that surface. The energy of a single photon is transferred to a single electron, called a *photoelectron*, in a phenomenon known as the *photoelectric effect*.

The photoelectric effect, one of the first important tests of quantum theory, can be observed with the use of an apparatus similar to the one shown in Figure 1. A metal plate and a small electrode are placed within a glass tube called a *photocell*. The photocell is connected to a circuit through which electric current can flow. The circuit contains an ammeter, a device that measures electric current. When the photocell is in the dark, the ammeter shows a reading of zero; when light shines on the photocell, the ammeter indicates a current flowing in the circuit. This current is produced by the photoelectrons emitted from the metal plate.

FIGURE 1

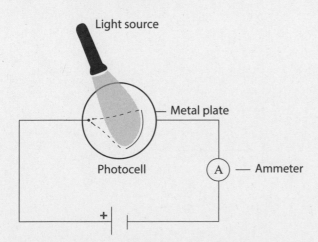

In 1986, at a physics workshop in Boulder, Colorado, a group of high school teachers studied the photoelectric effect in a two-part experiment.

Study 1

In the first part of the experiment, the teachers placed a light source at different distances from the photocell and measured the *photocurrent*, which is proportional to the number of photoelectrons being ejected from the surface. The experiment was conducted with two different color filters, blue and green, as different colors of light have different wavelengths. A filter transmits only one wavelength of light—a green filter, for example, allows only green light to pass through it. The results of this part of the experiment are shown in Table 1. (Current is being measured in microamperes, µA.)

Table 1			
Distance to light source with green filter (m)	**Photocurrent in µA (a)**	**Distance to light source with blue light filter (m)**	**Photocurrent in µA (a)**
0.10	430	0.10	350
0.20	100	0.20	90
0.30	50	0.30	45
0.40	25	0.40	20

CONTINUE

Study 2

A voltage can be applied to a circuit to either speed up or stop the flow of photoelectrons. The voltage required to stop the flow of photoelectrons is known as the *stopping potential*.

In the second part of the experiment, the teachers measured the stopping potential. Four different color filters were used, and the stopping voltage was measured three times for each color filter as well as for no filter at all. The distance to the light source was held constant. Table 2 is a summary of the data from this part of the experiment.

Table 2: Stopping Potential (volts)			
Color of filter	Trial 1	Trial 2	Trial 3
Red	0.0	0.0	0.0
Yellow	0.4	0.4	0.4
Green	0.65	0.65	0.65
Blue	1.0	1.1	1.1
No filter (white)	1.2	1.1	1.0

1. Which of the following graphs best represents the relationship between light source distance (m) and photocurrent (a) in Study 1?

A.

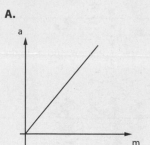

B.

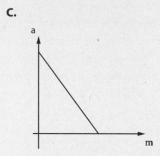

C.

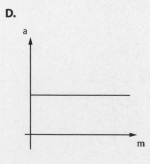

D.

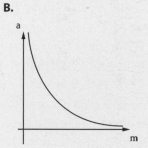

2. The data in Table 2 suggests that stopping potential:

   F. depends on the intensity of light.
   G. depends on the wavelength of light.
   H. depends on the characteristics of the metal plate.
   J. is constant for all wavelength of light.

3. Light intensity obeys an inverse square law, meaning that if the distance is halved, the light intensity is increased by a factor of 4. What conclusion can be drawn from the first part of the experiment?

   A. The greater the light intensity, the greater the number of photoelectrons ejected from the metal plate.
   B. The greater the light intensity, the smaller the number of photoelectrons ejected from the metal plate.
   C. Photoelectrons are not emitted from the metal plate until the light intensity reaches a threshold level.
   D. The number of photoelectrons ejected from the metal plate is independent of light intensity.

4. Which of the following best explains the behavior of red light in the second part of the experiment?

   F. The red light was too dim.
   G. Red light does not contain photons.
   H. Red light photoelectrons do not have sufficient energy to be detected.
   J. Red light photons do not have sufficient energy to eject photoelectrons.

5. What is the dependent variable in Study 1?

   A. The distance from the light source
   B. The magnitude of the photocurrent
   C. The color of the filter
   D. The thickness of the metal surface

6. Suppose the teachers were to use an orange filter in Study 2. One would expect the stopping potential with this filter to be:

   F. between 0 and 0.4 volts.
   G. between 0.4 and 0.65 volts.
   H. between 0.65 and 1.1 volts.
   J. greater than 1.1 volts.

PASSAGE II

Although different regions of Earth's surface are assigned specific names, it is dominated by a single ocean that covers about 70 percent of the surface. The continents and oceans are not evenly distributed around Earth. If you look at Earth from a viewpoint in the South Pacific, as shown in Figure 1, you can see that almost one-half of the planet has no land masses larger than small islands. In fact, in the Southern Hemisphere, between the latitudes of 50° S and 65° S, there are essentially no land masses at all.

FIGURE 1

Figure 2 considers various elevations and depths and indicates the percentage of Earth's surface that lies at each level.

FIGURE 2

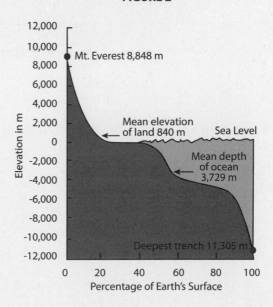

CONTINUE

Ocean water is saltwater, which means that the water contains dissolved salts and other minerals. The most abundant salt found in ocean water is sodium chloride. Sodium chloride is the most soluble of all the common minerals, so it dissolves readily out of rocks and soil and washes into the ocean.

The amount of dissolved salts and minerals in ocean water contributes to its density. The *density* of a substance is the mass of the substance per unit of volume. The greater the amount of dissolved salts, the greater the density. The percentage of dissolved salts is known as *salinity*.

Density is also affected by temperature. Pure water, which freezes at 0°C, reaches its maximum density at around 4°C. Adding salt and other minerals to water lowers both the freezing point and the temperature at which maximum density occurs. Figure 3 shows the relationship among the salinity of water, its freezing point, and temperature of maximum density.

FIGURE 3

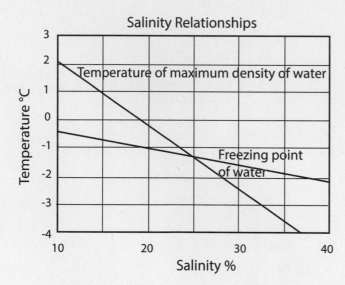

7. Approximately what portion of Earth's surface consists of land?

   A. 70%
   B. 50%
   C. 30%
   D. 10%

8. Oceans moderate weather. One would expect to find less extreme weather in the:

   F. Northern Hemisphere, because of the presence of large land masses.
   G. Southern Hemisphere, because of the presence of large oceans.
   H. Northern Hemisphere, because of the presence of large oceans.
   J. Southern Hemisphere, because of the presence of large land masses.

9. According to Figure 2, about what percentage of Earth's surface lies underwater but above an ocean depth of 4,000 meters?

   A. About 10%
   B. About 30%
   C. About 60%
   D. About 90%

10. In Figure 3, at what salinity does the temperature of maximum density drop below the freezing point?

   F. 15%
   G. 20%
   H. 25%
   J. 30%

11. An ocean with an average salinity of 50% would be expected to have an approximate freezing point of:

   A. 4.25°C.
   B. 0°C.
   C. –2.5°C.
   D. –7°C.

PASSAGE III

About 460 years ago, a Spanish soldier observed indigenous people of Brazil using darts to hunt wild animals. The tips of the darts had been dipped in a natural gum. As centuries passed, scientists discovered the following facts about the gum:

- It was a poison that came from a high-climbing vine of the *pareira* family.
- Its active ingredient was an alkaloid called *tubocurarine* or, simply, curare.
- It killed prey by paralyzing the muscles that controlled breathing. The muscles became paralyzed in the relaxed state rather than in the contracted state.

In an attempt to discover exactly how curare caused paralysis, French physiologist Claude Bernard performed the following experiments.

Experiment 1

Bernard tied one leg of a living frog with a string in such a way that blood could not circulate through the leg. He was careful to pass the string under the sciatic nerve, the nerve through which impulses (electric messages) travel from the brain to the leg. Because he did not constrict the nerve, impulses were still able to pass through the nerve into the leg. Figure 1 illustrates this setup.

He then injected curare into the upper body of the frog. He observed that all of the frog's muscles became paralyzed, *except* those in the leg that had been tied. These muscles were able to contract, thereby moving the bones to which they were attached.

FIGURE 1

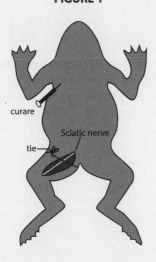

Experiment 2

Barnard placed an electrode, a device that produces an electric current, directly into the paralyzed muscle of the frog's leg that had not been tied with the string, as shown in Figure 2. He then passed an electric current into the muscle. Bernard observed that the muscle contracted.

FIGURE 2

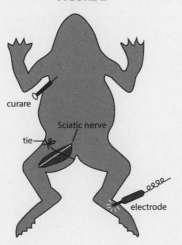

Experiment 3

From another frog's leg, Bernard removed the large muscle along with its nerve. He placed the nerve in a dish of curare but left the muscle outside the dish, as Figure 3 illustrates. He then stimulated the nerve and observed that the muscle contracted.

FIGURE 3

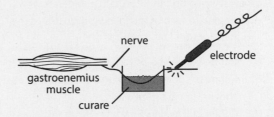

12. Which of the following hypotheses should be rejected as a result of Experiment 1?

    F. Curare attacks the brain.
    G. Curare does not attack muscles.
    H. Curare attacks nerves.
    J. Curare does not travel through the circulatory system.

13. Based on the results of Experiment 2, it can be concluded that:

    A. curare prevents electrical impulses from traveling through the body.
    B. curare attacks nerves directly.
    C. muscles are not directly attacked by curare.
    D. curare attacks bones.

14. The purpose of Experiment 3 was to reject or support the hypothesis that curare attacks:

    F. the circulatory system.
    G. muscles.
    H. the brain.
    J. nerves.

15. A human who eats an animal that was killed by curare is not harmed by the poison. Based on the information in the passage, which of the following best explains this observation?

    A. Curare is broken down as it acts on the animal and is no longer present in the body.
    B. The effects of curare wear off over time.
    C. Curare is not effective on humans.
    D. Curare is effective only when in the bloodstream.

CONTINUE

16. For a muscle cell to contract, a nerve impulse must be carried across a gap from a nerve cell to a muscle cell. The impulse is carried by a substance called *acetylcholine*. When acetylcholine binds to receptor molecules on the muscle cell, the muscle cell contracts. An enzyme, *acetylcholine esterase*, then removes the acetylcholine from the receptor site so the muscle can relax. Scientists suspected that curare interfered with some part of this process. Based on this information and Bernard's experiments, which of the following illustrates the action of curare?

   F. Curare blocks the action of acetylcholine esterase.
   G. Curare occupies the receptor site before acetylcholine can get there.
   H. Curare blocks nerve impulses from reaching the end of the nerve.
   J. Curare blocks nerve impulses from leaving the brain.

17. In controlled doses, curare can be used as a medicine. For which of the following purposes would one expect curare to be most effective?

   A. As a general anesthesia
   B. As a painkiller
   C. To immobilize broken bones
   D. To produce muscle contractions

PASSAGE IV

All matter is composed of atoms. An *atom* consists of a positively charged nucleus surrounded by negatively charged particles called *electrons*. Some atoms join, or bond, together by transferring or sharing electrons.

The nature of the electron bonds between two atoms is largely determined by the *electronegativity* of each atom. Electronegativity is the ability of an atom to attract the electrons of other atoms. A greater electronegativity value signifies a superior ability to attract electrons. Figure 1 shows the electronegativities of selected groups of elements in the periodic table.

FIGURE 1

Electronegativities of Groups 1A–7A

1A	2A		3A	4A	5A	6A	7A
H 2.2							
Li 1.0	Be 1.6		B 1.8	C 2.5	N 3.0	O 3.4	F 4.0
Na 0.93	Mg 1.3		Al 1.6	Si 1.9	P 2.2	S 2.6	Cl 3.2
K 0.82	Ca 1.0		Ga 1.8	Ge 2.0	As 2.2	Se 2.6	Br
Rb 0.82	Sr 0.9		In 1.8	Sn 1.8	Sb 2.0	Te 2.1	I 2.7
Cs 0.79	Ba 0.9		Tl 2.0	Pb 2.3	Bi 2.0	Po 2.0	At 2.2

Atoms with very similar electronegativities form molecules that are *nonpolar*. The electrons of these atoms are shared equally, and their molecules are said to be electrically symmetrical. The electron bond is equidistant between the nuclei of each atom.

Atoms with moderately different electronegativities form *polar covalent bonds*. In this case, one atom attracts electrons more than the other atom does; these molecules are said to be electrically asymmetrical. The electron bond between such atoms is closer to the more electronegative atom. Molecules that contain such atoms have a relative concentration of negativity at the end that is closer to the more electronegative atom.

The greater the difference in electronegativity, the more polar the molecule is.

18. In Figure 1, elements are arranged in vertical columns called groups or *families* and in horizontal rows called *periods*. Based on the patterns of electronegativity values among the families and periods, one would predict that the approximate electronegativity of bromine (Br) is:

   F. 2.6.
   G. 3.0.
   H. 3.6.
   J. 4.0.

19. Which element has the strongest electron attraction?

   A. Hydrogen (H)
   B. Cesium (Cs)
   C. Astatine (At)
   D. Fluorine (F)

20. Which of the following molecules is most likely to be nonpolar?

    F. NaCl
    G. MgO
    H. Cl_2
    J. HCl

21. Which of the following bonds is likely to be the most polar?

    A. K–Cl
    B. Ba–Se
    C. Na–S
    D. Be–O

22. The relative concentration of negativity in a molecule of lithium bromide (LiBr) is likely to reside:

    F. closer to the bromide atom.
    G. closer to the lithium atom.
    H. equidistant between the nuclei of each atom.
    J. outside the molecule.

PASSAGE V

In 2001, members of a national health foundation who were interested in examining possible links between cigarette smoking and cancer in the United States gathered relevant data from ten selected states.

First, they surveyed residents in each state to determine what percentage of the state's residents were cigarette smokers. For the purpose of consistency, smokers were defined as those who smoked every day or most days and who had smoked at least 100 cigarettes in their lifetime. Smokers were further asked whether they had ever attempted to quit smoking. For the purpose of consistency, a quit attempt was defined as having gone one day or longer without a cigarette in a deliberate effort to stop smoking. In both cases, percentages were weighted to reflect population characteristics.

The foundation's members then collected information from medical facilities, disease control centers, and other health organizations to reflect numbers of cancer-related deaths. They compared these numbers with the population figures in each state.

The members separated each state's data by gender and reported their findings. Table 1 summarizes the data.

Table 1					
State	**Cigarette Smoking Rate**		**Number of Cancer Deaths per 100,000 Population**		**Percent of Smokers Who Attempt to Quit**	
	Females	Males	Females	Males	Females	Males
California	13.3%	19.6%	156.7	212.8	63.6%	62.9%
Colorado	19.4%	21.4%	150.7	200.4	57.7%	52.7%
Florida	20.6%	23.4%	155.3	229.8	55.3%	48.4%
Indiana	25.7%	29.7%	172.9	271.9	61.0%	51.6%
Kentucky	30.3%	34.7%	182.0	297.6	53.6%	42.9%
Maine	21.0%	26.4%	170.5	262.7	62.2%	60.2%
Ohio	25.0%	28.3%	173.5	261.4	53.8%	49.5%
Rhode Island	20.9%	24.0%	167.7	253.9	64.4%	66.6%
Utah	11.4%	14.1%	117.2	181.0	72.1%	64.6%
West Virginia	27.2%	29.7%	186.0	267.9	48.9%	47.3%

CONTINUE

Figure 1 plots these same ten states' cancer mortality rates against the percentage of their residents who smoke. Data in this graph is not separated by gender.

FIGURE 1

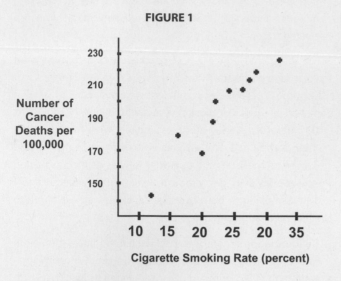

Cigarette Smoking Rate (percent)

23. Figure 1 indicates that cancer mortality rates among the ten selected states:

   A. cause higher cigarette smoking rates.
   B. vary directly with cigarette smoking rates.
   C. vary inversely with cigarette smoking rates.
   D. have no correlation with cigarette smoking rates.

24. Which of the following statements is NOT supported by Table 1?

   F. Kentucky has a higher percentage of smokers than any other listed state.
   G. Within each listed state, the percentage of males who smoke is higher than the percentage of females who smoke.
   H. Rhode Island has the highest listed percentage of males who attempt to quit smoking.
   J. Within each listed state, the percentage of females who attempt to quit smoking is higher than the percentage of males who attempt to quit smoking.

25. Some of the health foundation's members sought to prove that cigarette smoking causes cancer in the United States. Are the findings reported here sufficient to support such a conclusion?

   A. Yes, because states with a higher percentage of smokers have more cancer-related deaths.
   B. Yes, because states with a higher percentage of smokers who attempt to quit have fewer cancer-related deaths.
   C. No, because the survey results were altered to strengthen the health foundation's case.
   D. No, because the study failed to consider other possible causes for cancer.

26. In New Jersey, nearly 177 out of every 100,000 females died from cancer in 2001. Based on the information in Table 1, out of every 100,000 males in New Jersey in 2001, a likely estimate of the number who died from cancer would be:

   F. 246.
   G. 177.
   H. 150.
   J. 118.

27. Suppose the foundation wanted to test a hypothesis that quitting smoking would reduce the risk of cancer-related death. Which of the following would best accomplish this?

   A. Offer smoking cessation programs in states with the highest percentage of smokers.
   B. Compare cancer mortality rates of smokers who attempt to quit with those of smokers who do not.
   C. Compare cancer mortality rates of people who have successfully quit smoking with those of people who still smoke.
   D. Compare mortality rates from lung cancer with those from other forms of cancer.

PASSAGE VI

During the history of life on Earth, millions of new species evolved. Those species that were best adapted to conditions in their environment survived and produced generations of offspring. Some of these offspring differed from their parents in certain ways. If such differences aided survival, the offspring tended to live and produce many generations like themselves but unlike their parents. This process, called *speciation*, accounts for the diversity of species on Earth. Two opposing models have been proposed to characterize the development of species on Earth.

Phyletic Gradualism

In this model, species that descend from a common ancestor vary only slightly from their parent species, meaning that the structure of each new species is very much like its parent species. The variations occur gradually, continuously, and uniformly in small steps. Only after a very long time does a species finally emerge whose structure is dramatically different from that of the original parent species. Figure 1 shows a phyletic gradualistic view of an evolutionary tree.

FIGURE 1

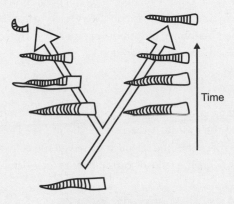

Punctuated Equilibrium

In this model, species that descend from a common ancestor vary significantly from their parent species, meaning that the structure of the new species is significantly different from that of its parent species. The variations occur abruptly, and the time span between changes in structure is relatively long. In other words, there is a long static period, or period of *equilibrium*, before a new species evolves. This period of equilibrium is *punctuated* by the sudden evolution of a new species from a previous one. Figure 2 shows a punctuated equilibrium view of an evolutionary tree.

FIGURE 2

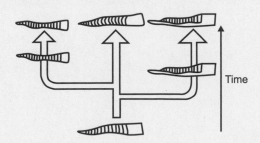

The geological illustrations in Figure 3 depict four different patterns of fossils found in different layers of rock.

FIGURE 3

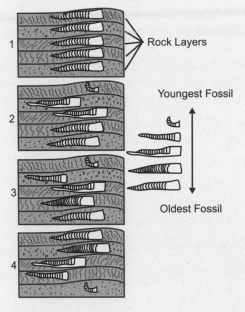

28. According to the passage, the time that elapses before the development of a new species is:

    F. equal in both the phyletic gradualism and punctuated equilibrium models.
    G. greater in the phyletic gradualism model than in the punctuated equilibrium model.
    H. greater in the punctuated equilibrium model than in the phyletic gradualism model.
    J. irrelevant to the study of evolution.

29. Which of the following characteristics is shared by the two models of evolution?

    A. Both models describe relatively rapid development of species.
    B. Both models describe gradual changes in structure.
    C. Both models describe continuous development of species.
    D. Both models describe species that eventually differ from their parent species.

CONTINUE

30. Figures 1 and 2 represent models of evolutionary change. As compared with Figure 1, what makes Figure 2 an appropriate model of punctuated equilibrium?

    F. It depicts gradual changes within species that occur in small steps.

    G. It depicts abrupt changes in species that occur after periods of equilibrium.

    H. It depicts a longer survival time of offspring.

    J. It depicts uniform changes in species that vary only slightly from the parent species.

31. The hypothesis behind the phyletic gradualism model could best be tested by examining the fossil record of a particular prehistoric era to determine:

    A. the extent of the variations between fossilized species.

    B. why each fossilized species became extinct.

    C. how each fossilized species survived its particular environment.

    D. whether different fossilized species are related to one another.

32. In Figure 3, which fossil pattern would you expect to find if the model of punctuated equilibrium is a better reflection of evolutionary processes than the model of phyletic gradualism?

    F. Pattern 1

    G. Pattern 2

    H. Pattern 3

    J. Pattern 4

33. In Figure 3, which fossil pattern would you expect to find if the model of phyletic gradualism is a better reflection of evolutionary processes than the model of punctuated equilibrium?

    A. Pattern 1

    B. Pattern 2

    C. Pattern 3

    D. Pattern 4

34. Which of the following is characteristic of the punctuated equilibrium model but NOT the phyletic gradualism model?

    F. A new species has significantly different structural characteristics from its parent species.

    G. A new species varies in structural characteristics only slightly from its parent species.

    H. A new species is identical to its parent species.

    J. A new species has nothing structurally in common with its parent species.

PASSAGE VII

Researchers have discovered that rattlesnakes have a number of sensory organs. These include eyes, heat sensors in two pits located beneath the eyes, and odor sensors on the roof of the mouth. In addition, rattlers are equipped with venom glands located on each side of the head. When a rattler strikes its prey, venom is delivered into the prey through a pair of hollow fangs. Typically, the rattler then releases the prey, which subsequently runs off. After a few minutes, the prey dies as a result of the venom. By this time, the prey is some distance from the rattler. The rattler can no longer see the prey or sense the prey's body heat—yet the snake invariably finds the prey. How does the rattlesnake accomplish this extraordinary tracking feat? Intrigued researchers performed the three experiments described here in an attempt to answer this question.

Experiment 1

Scientists exposed a rattlesnake to a live mouse. The rattlesnake observed the mouse. It then struck the mouse. During this sequence of events, the scientists observed the activity of the snake's tongue. The table below summarizes this data.

Rattlesnake Behavior	
Time (minutes)	**Tongue Flicks**
1	2
2	1
3	2
4*	2
5	76
6	80
7	74
8	79
	* Rattlesnake strikes mouse

Experiment 2

The scientists placed a live mouse out of reach of the rattlesnake. They again observed the activity of the snake's tongue. The table below summarizes this data.

Rattlesnake Behavior	
Time (minutes)	Tongue Flicks
1	2
2	1
3	3
4	2
5	1
6	3
7	2
8	1

Experiment 3

The scientists exposed a rattlesnake to two different dead mice. One had been killed by rattlesnake venom; the other had been killed in a humane, nonpoisonous manner by the scientists. The snake flicked its tongue more frequently at the poisoned mouse.

35. If the snake in Experiment 2 had been allowed to strike the mouse at 8 minutes, a likely number of tongue flicks during the ninth minute would be:

   A. 1.
   B. 3.
   C. 40.
   D. 76.

36. Which of the following statements is best supported by the data in Experiment 2?

   F. Rattlesnakes respond to visual stimuli.
   G. Rattlesnakes respond to heat stimuli.
   H. Rattlesnakes respond to olfactory stimuli.
   J. Rattlesnakes do not respond to prey that is out of reach.

37. Comparing the results of Experiments 1 and 2 would lead to the conclusion that:

   A. mouse odors stimulate tongue flicking.
   B. live mice stimulate tongue flicking.
   C. live mice inhibit tongue flicking.
   D. snake striking stimulates tongue flicking.

38. What can be inferred from the results of Experiment 3?

   F. Rattlers can kill prey without using venom.
   G. The means of killing the mouse is significant.
   H. Tongue flicking is a learned behavior.
   J. Dead mice stimulate tongue flicking.

39. Which of the following graphs most accurately describes the relationship between time (t) and number of tongue flicks (f) in Experiment 2?

   A.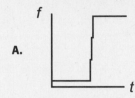

   B.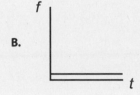

   C.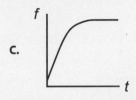

   D.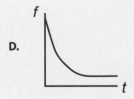

40. How would you test a hypothesis suggesting that a rattlesnake follows the scent of its own venom?

   F. Remove the rattlesnake's tongue and observe the behavior of the snake.
   G. Make a trail with a dead mouse that has NOT been bitten by a rattlesnake and observe the behavior of the snake.
   H. Make a trail with rattlesnake venom and observe the behavior of the snake.
   J. Make a trail with a live mouse that has NOT been bitten by a rattlesnake and observe the behavior of the snake.

Ⓧ
STOP

WRITING TEST

40 Minutes

> **DIRECTIONS:** This is a test of your writing skills. You have forty (40) minutes to write an essay in English. Be sure to carefully read the issue and three perspectives presented before planning and writing your essay so you understand clearly the task you are being asked to do. Your essay will be graded on the evidence it provides of your ability to analyze the issue; evaluate and analyze the perspectives; state and develop a personal perspective; and describe the relationship between the given perspectives and your own, while effectively using organization, logic, and language according to the conventions of standard written English.

LOOK WHO'S WATCHING

Have you ever heard the phrase, "Big Brother is watching"? It refers to the way governments and other institutions with power and influence can enact invasive surveillance measures upon groups of people. Although it's a line from a fictional story, some people feel that the massive increase in camera surveillance in public and private spaces comes close—or reaches—the eerie promise that we are constantly being watched and have lost our rights to privacy, immersed in a "culture of surveillance." Others feel that this is an acceptable infringement, as surveillance provides us a record of events to help settle disputes and also helps to deter and solve crimes. Whether we applaud the advantages or decry the disadvantages of increased surveillance in public and private spheres, we all must acknowledge the role of surveillance as technology rapidly evolves and continues to become a part of every aspect of our lives.

Read and carefully consider these perspectives. Each suggests a particular way of thinking about the increase in surveillance.

PERSPECTIVE ONE

Institutions with power and influence, such as governments and corporations, have littered the skies with surveillance equipment that has become so advanced and powerful that we must now live with the notion that very little of our lives are lived in private. The surveillance culture has even trickled down to the level of small businesses and homeowners. Not only is Big Brother watching, Little Brother and Sister are watching too. We must reverse this trend before it gets any worse.

PERSPECTIVE TWO

Although it's true that increased surveillance has affected our lives and impacted our privacy, its overall effect has been a positive one on society, and is well worth any perceived social costs. Surveillance helps deter and solve crimes, settle all manner of disputes by providing a tangible record, and protects business and property owners. In an increasingly complex society, we need increasingly sophisticated methods for protecting citizens. Surveillance technology provides the necessary means for doing this, and its value more than outweighs any perceived detriment.

PERSPECTIVE THREE

Surveillance is a potentially helpful tool in a wide variety of situations, but its use should not be impulsive or flippant; instead, it should be carefully considered in each instance. There are places where surveillance technology can be beneficial, such as in areas with traditionally high crime rates or valuable items. But if surveillance technology is used to watch us walk down the street, have private conversations, and record people who come into our homes, then we've gone too far. We've reached the point where we need to make more judicious use of a tool that can easily—and quickly—be misused. The next step should be open conversations about ways that we can ensure the responsible use of surveillance technology.

Essay Task

Write a cohesive, logical essay in which you consider multiple perspectives on the rise of surveillance. In your essay, be sure to:

- examine and assess the perspectives given
- declare and explain your own perspective on the issue
- discuss the relationship between your perspective and those given

Your perspective may be in full or partial agreement, or in total disagreement, with any of the others. Whatever the case, support your ideas with logical reasoning and detailed, persuasive examples.

Plan and Write Your Essay

Use the first two pages of the Writing test answer sheet (found at the beginning of the test) to generate ideas and plan your essay. Then use the following four pages to write your essay. Consider the following as you compose your essay:

What are the strengths and weaknesses of the three perspectives provided?

- Identify the insights they present and what they fail to consider.
- Ascertain why a given perspective might persuade or fail to persuade.

How can you apply your own experience, knowledge, and values?

- Express your perspective on the issue, identifying the perspective's strengths and weaknesses.
- Formulate a plan to support your perspective in your essay.

ENGLISH

1.	B	20.	H	39.	B	58.	H
2.	G	21.	C	40.	G	59.	A
3.	D	22.	G	41.	D	60.	H
4.	H	23.	C	42.	J	61.	B
5.	A	24.	F	43.	A	62.	F
6.	J	25.	D	44.	G	63.	C
7.	B	26.	G	45.	C	64.	J
8.	J	27.	B	46.	J	65.	C
9.	B	28.	G	47.	D	66.	J
10.	G	29.	D	48.	J	67.	B
11.	C	30.	F	49.	C	68.	J
12.	J	31.	D	50.	F	69.	C
13.	B	32.	F	51.	D	70.	H
14.	J	33.	C	52.	G	71.	D
15.	A	34.	J	53.	B	72.	J
16.	J	35.	B	54.	F	73.	B
17.	A	36.	H	55.	B	74.	H
18.	J	37.	A	56.	J	75.	D
19.	C	38.	F	57.	D		

1. **The correct answer is B.** This birthday party was something out of the ordinary, so the author is taking note of its difference. *Only* suggests this exception; however, "it's being" is in the present tense, while the story takes place in the past, so choice A is incorrect. *But* (choice B) uses the correct tense and retains the meaning of the original. You might choose *yet* because it is another contrast word, but *its* is a possessive pronoun, and there is no need to indicate that the party owned anything, so choice C is incorrect. Choice D indicates that there is a well-known kind of birthday party that is held at the South Pole, which is not true.

2. **The correct answer is G.** Commas separate items in a series such as the activities that Helen did; parallel structure must be observed when listing the activities. *Pulling* should be *pulled* (choice G) to match *walked* and *skied* unless, as in choice J, the author is noting that Helen walked while doing something else. Choice J is incorrect, however, because of the added and unnecessary "you won't believe this." Pulling her own sled is no harder to believe than the other things Helen did, and "you won't believe this" is more informal in tone than the rest of the selection. Choice H creates a sentence fragment that is missing a subject.

3. **The correct answer is D.** In this case, the original is slightly awkward because it inverts the noun, *sun*, and its description, "never setting." The choice closest to the original works best, with the addition of a hyphen between *never* and *setting* to indicate that both of these words form a compound to describe the noun, *sun*. Choice B, "never lit by sunset," changes the sentence's meaning, and choice C, "only lighted by a sun that is not the kind to set," uses far too many words.

4. **The correct answer is H.** Choice H achieves the dual purpose proposed by the question. It concludes the paragraph by answering the previous question, while echoing the first sentence by addressing why Helen decided to spend her birthday alone in a far-off place. It also explains the reference to "a place that doesn't exist." Choice J asks another question and causes us to continue wondering what motivated Helen. There are references to Helen's motivations in choices F and G, yet choice G would make us wonder more about these additional elements in Helen's character rather than keep us focused on the trip that is the topic of this selection. Choice F is vague—it doesn't answer any questions. Because this question might

require you to reread the first paragraph, you may want to delay answering it until you have finished the rest of the passage.

5.   **The correct answer is A.** This phrase produces different meanings depending upon where it is placed in the sentence. Choice A is correct because it puts the modifier "in her e-mail messages" close to the word being modified, *commented*. Choices C and D both create misplaced modifiers. Helen was discouraged in life, not in her e-mail messages (choice C). She is starting fresh on the journey, not in her e-mail messages (choice D). Choice B, though not incorrect, is awkward compared with choice A.

6.   **The correct answer is J.** Although most readers are not familiar with all of the conditions found in Antarctica, we don't need to be reminded that ice is frozen water. The sastrugi has already been defined as an ice formation. Choices F, G, and H add the same unnecessary information in different ways.

7.   **The correct answer is B.** We want the correct choice to give us a sense of Helen's character by showing how she handled this particular obstacle. The original sentence doesn't tell us enough about how she deals with her frustration; if anything, the sentence gives the impression that she was likely to give in. Choice B offers an example of her coping strategy and how it helps her to survive, making it the best answer. Choice C doesn't reveal much more to us than facts. Eliminating the phrase, as choice D suggests, would not tell the reader anything about Helen and thus not accomplish the writer's purpose.

8.   **The correct answer is J.** *Problem* and *danger* are being compared by the adjective *daunting*, so the superlative form *most*, which appears in choices F and H, is incorrect because only two items are being compared. Choice H also changes the word to *dauntless*, which makes no sense in context. It also doesn't make sense to use *than* without any kind of comparative adjective, as in choice G. Choice J appropriately uses the *more ... than* construction to compare the two items.

9.   **The correct answer is B.** The correct answer is choice B because it adds to Helen's story of using an ice screw as an anchor against the wind. It further describes the experience of the wind and helps the reader envision what Helen had to endure. Choice A introduces causes for the wind but it distracts from the description of the effects of this wind. Neither of the facts added in choice C, that the area was lifeless, nor choice D, that the

crevasses were huge, builds on the main idea of the paragraph, which is how Helen dealt with the winds.

10. **The correct answer is G.** The original sentence (choice F) doesn't seem to know where to end or how to link ideas—it's a run-on sentence. Choice H replaces all the commas in the original with semicolons and still doesn't order and link the different ideas properly. Choice J places a period after the first subordinate clause, creating a fragment. Choice G correctly divides separate ideas with a period, keeps the comma after the opening subordinate clause in the first sentence, and then links related but independent ideas with a semicolon in the second sentence.

11. **The correct answer is C.** The correct answer should introduce us to ideas we haven't encountered up to this point. Choice C does this by referring to past experiences and then leading right into events that will soon follow in the next paragraph. A birthday cupcake (choice D) is also a new idea, but it fails to connect this paragraph with the next. Choice B is linked to the adventure in the crevasse but introduces no additional element to the story; it also doesn't make sense, as she couldn't scout in a whiteout. Choice A doesn't introduce a secondary element.

12. **The correct answer is J.** Any predicament is by definition a fair bit of trouble, so "most troublesome" is redundant and wordy. There is no point in changing *most* to *more* (choice G), as *more* is used when two things are being compared, and there is no comparison here. Changing *troublesome* to *dangerous* (choice H) retains the same problem of redundancy and wordiness as seen in choice F. The best choice is to omit the underlined portion entirely.

13. **The correct answer is B.** *Skis* is a plural noun and forms its possessive by adding an apostrophe after the *s*. Choice B shows this correct form. Choice A uses the singular possessive, which is incorrect in this case because two ski tips were jammed. The plural form is incorrectly spelled in choice C, making it a plural possessive form of *sky*. The change to a prepositional phrase (choice D) might sound better except for the fact that *her* is repeated, and this repetition is awkward.

14. **The correct answer is J.** As the paragraph is written, it's not clear what *Its* refers to at the start of Sentence 3, and there's a problem with the order of events. Putting Sentence 3 before Sentence 1 or 2 (choices G and H) doesn't solve either problem; in fact, doing so makes the paragraph more confusing. Choice J is the only

choice that gives *Its* a proper antecedent and orders the events and facts so they make sense.

15. **The correct answer is A.** The assignment proposed to this writer was to create an intimate portrayal of personal challenges. The article would have had to provide us with her thinking and feelings and evidence of how she personally dealt with the ups and downs of the trip. Choice B introduces the idea of motivation, which would be part of an intimate portrayal, but also brings in financial support, which wouldn't necessarily be included in an intimate account of personal challenges. You may sense what the trip was like (choice C), but it's not a clear account of her feelings and emotions while she experienced these trials. And you do find out the basics of her trip (choice D), but not intimate details. Choice A is correct because, during the events narrated, we aren't informed in any great detail about how Helen felt.

16. **The correct answer is J.** The phrase "more on that later" is an example of a writer's device that attempts to create a clumsy connection between two parts of the paragraph. Good writing doesn't need such devices. "Amber waves of grain" is a phrase known well enough that it doesn't need further justification that the author will explain its meaning later, so choice F is not the best answer. The punctuation used to set it off from the rest of the paragraph in choices G and H does not obscure the fact that the phrase isn't necessary.

17. **The correct answer is A.** You can read the choices out loud and hear that "just as picturesque than," (choice C) and "most picturesque as," (choice D) sound odd. Choice C violates the customary "just as…as" construction by misplacing *than*, and choice D uses *most* to compare only two items. This leaves choices A and B. We have to assume that the meaning in the original sentence, choice A—that the towns and the farmlands are equally picturesque—is the intended meaning. Since choice B, though correct, would change this meaning, and since "as picturesque as" is already an acceptable form, choice A is correct.

18. **The correct answer is J.** Reject this sentence as written because huge volcanoes and floods are not currently rearranging Washington. Although geologic change is always ongoing, the bulk of these violent upheavals occurred long ago. Both *has formed* (choice G) and *formed* (choice H) are active voice, making "volcanic action, monstrous floods, and scouring winds" the direct objects, and causing the sentence to incorrectly state that the geology was responsible for floods and

volcanoes when the opposite is true. Choice J is correct because "has been formed" is present perfect tense, showing that the action has taken place in the past but continues into the present. The verb form is also passive voice, indicating that the subject, *geology*, was acted upon and creating an accurate relationship between the subject and direct objects.

19. **The correct answer is C.** The original version (choice A) mentions the thickness of the topsoil twice ("as deep…in depth"). Choice C eliminates the unnecessary repetition of "in depth." You can hear the simplicity. Adding *thick* and turning the depth readings into a compound adjective (choice D) makes the sentence overly wordy and awkward. Choice B incorrectly implies that the places, and not the topsoil, are 3–4 feet deep.

20. **The correct answer is H.** Choice H explains why this added sentence wouldn't work in this position. The sentence does fit well with the informational tone of the passage and is highly believable, so choice J has to be wrong. In order for the sentence to work, however, the author would also have to provide some kind of connection to the earlier mention of floods and how this fact changed the Palouse. It might add to the factual detail and accuracy; however, in a short selection, there isn't space, and the lack of space is the reason that expansion of the geologic discussion (choice F) is also unnecessary. The essay already contains enough detail for us to understand the geology of the area. The added sentence would also fail to introduce the next paragraph (choice G), because it is unrelated to plants or animals.

21. **The correct answer is C.** The passage was clearly written for people with a non-specialist's knowledge of geology and natural history, so the answer you choose must not go into so much detail that it clouds the reader's distinction between this prairie region and other Western prairie regions. Giving more details about the small ground feeders (choice B) doesn't distinguish the region because most people wouldn't know what ground feeders were common throughout most of the prairies. Adding insects (choice D) doesn't help distinguish the area because we can assume insects were found in a variety of prairie areas. The mention of bison (choice C) works well because bison are generally identified with the prairies, and because the fact that they were rare in this area tells us something distinguishing and unusual. Not changing the sentence (choice A) gives us no recognizable detail.

22. **The correct answer is G.** Choice F is incorrect because the singular subject, *plant*, does not agree with the plural verb *were*. The rest of the paragraph has been in past tense, so it doesn't make sense to switch to future tense, choice H. Likewise, switching to present perfect tense (choice J) doesn't make sense. *Was* (choice G) is past tense like the rest of the paragraph and is also singular, so it agrees with the subject, *plant*.

23. **The correct answer is C.** The pronoun that begins this phrase must be possessive, because it describes something belonging to the camas plant. *They're* (choice A) means "they are" and is not a possessive pronoun. The plural form *their* (choices B and D) may seem correct referring to *camas*, but *camas* is not the antecedent of the pronoun; the pronoun refers to "one plant." *Its* is the correct singular possessive pronoun. Also, *roots* and *bulbs* must be plural to agree with the plural verb form *were*, so choice C is correct.

24. **The correct answer is F.** Choice F is correct because, if we substitute each of the other choices into the sentence, we see that they do not logically comment on the effectiveness of the Nez Perce's burning. The changes in the prairie today (choice G) are not being discussed. Choice H doesn't make sense—the profusion of camas would not make us question the effectiveness of burning, but, rather, point to the success of the burning. Choice J is contrary to logic; the fires were set to encourage growth, which doesn't suggest that the fires were unnecessary. The existing sentence makes sense and follows logically from the rest of the paragraph.

25. **The correct answer is D.** We've read enough of the style used in this piece to be jarred by choice A, "land-hungry and money-grubbing." The tone of this phrase does not match the factual, straightforward style of the selection up to this point. "Foreign-born and gold-digging" (choice C) repeats what we've already learned from the terms *European-Americans* and *prospectors*. "Various kinds of" (choice B) is not as specific a reference as the style we've seen earlier. Choice D is correct because adjectives or other modifiers are not really needed, and the ones given are not consistent with the style of the rest of the essay.

26. **The correct answer is G.** Choice F obliquely indicates that the settlers found the land unsuitable for farming, but it doesn't show the writer's involvement with the plant life. Choice H says that the settlers hated the coarse grasses but doesn't explain why; it also gives us nothing to show the writer's detailed involvement with

the Palouse's plant life. Choice J tells us only that the native plants were unlike large-scale farming crops and gives no indication of the writer's involvement with the plant life. Choice G explains clearly what the settlers thought about the land. The specific detail in choice G—the names of the two main prairie plants—shows the writer's detailed involvement with native plant life of the Palouse. This makes choice G the best answer.

27. **The correct answer is B.** Choice B picks up the reference made in the first paragraph to "amber waves of grain." It also successfully concludes the paragraph by indicating that wheat farming would soon transform the Palouse. The original sentence (choice A) is very vague—how did things turn out well? Noting that other crops were planted, as in choice C, adds a new element and doesn't conclude the paragraph. Although choice D follows from the previous statement by giving more information on the growing of wheat, it also adds a new element (the need for many men and horses) that needs further explanation and thus doesn't conclude the paragraph.

28. **The correct answer is G.** In Choice F, the first sentence is followed by a sentence fragment, which cannot stand on its own. Choice G correctly places a comma to separate the parts of the sentence, which incorporates the fragment about legumes but still avoids becoming a run-on sentence. Choice J is grammatically correct but doesn't make sense. The first part of the sentence talks about wheat and legumes, and wheat has nothing to do with making the Palouse the lentil-growing capital of the world, so the phrase "making it the lentil-growing capital of the world" doesn't logically follow. Merely adding *Surprisingly* (choice H) doesn't change the fact that the construction following the first sentence is still a fragment without a verb.

29. **The correct answer is D.** The sentence as written is a statement, not a question, so the question mark makes choice A incorrect. Choice B changes the question mark to a period but adds an unnecessary comma. Choice C creates a sentence and a sentence fragment. Choice D replaces the question mark with a period and does not introduce any new errors, making it correct.

30. **The correct answer is F.** The first paragraph (choice F) introduces the Palouse and provides some geographical information about the Palouse, so the new sentence giving more geographic detail would most logically fit there. The second paragraph (choice G) defines the plants and animals of the Palouse. The third paragraph (choice H) discusses the indigenous Nez Perce and

camas flowers. The fourth paragraph (choice J) discusses how early settlers converted the area to farming.

31.   **The correct answer is D.** The word *also* in the sentence makes choices A and B unnecessary and redundant. The use of *However* in choice C suggests the introduction of an opposing thought, but no opposing thought is being presented—just an additional step that you will need to take to reach the park under the sea. Choice D, which leaves out the modifier, is correct.

32.   **The correct answer is F.** The term is not defined in the next paragraph (choice J), so you might consider having it defined here. However, pausing to define a term just as the passage is being introduced is rather jarring. Choice G states that the word's similarity to *submarine* may confuse readers, but, in fact, that similarity is more likely to help readers guess the correct definition. *Submersible* (choice H) is not a technical term. Since its meaning is easy to determine from the context clues in the sentence ("travel thousands of feet below the waves"), choice F is correct.

33.   **The correct answer is C.** To determine the correct version of this sentence, ask yourself to what the word *nearly* is referring. The spotlights are showing you "nearly all" of the depths, so choice C is correct. The only variation among other answer choices is the placement of the word *nearly*, and choices A, B, and D do not use it in the appropriate place.

34.   **The correct answer is J.** The subject of the sentence is *neither*, not *towers*, so the verb must be the singular *has*, (choice J) to match *neither*. Choice F uses the plural *have*. Changing the verb to a past form *had* (choice G) is incorrect because the narrative of this paragraph is told in the present tense. "Neither tower have" (choice H) also fails to eliminate the mismatched state of the subject and predicate, and it sounds awkward.

35.   **The correct answer is B.** Choice B takes a cluster of statements and imposes order upon them through proper punctuation. Each new sentence has a subject and a verb. The third sentence pairs the two thoughts (the settling out of the minerals and their building up into towers, shelves, and icicles) that belong together because of their similar subject. Placing a colon between the first two statements (choice D) makes the second a definition of the first, which it isn't. Placing semicolons (choice C) or commas (choice A) after every sentence does not define places where there need to be periods to signify the ends of complete thoughts.

36.   **The correct answer is H.** You may have noticed that the reasons offered in each of these choices help to define the value of this sentence. It does offer an image (choice F) but it is a somewhat confusing visual that is jarring at this point before we know much about how these smokers function. We may be intrigued about the image (choice G), but it will take a longer explanation to help us understand why hot water rises in super-cold depths, and the purpose of the article is not to mystify the reader. We have no way of judging the accuracy of the image based on the passage (choice J) so that really isn't a good reason to eliminate it.

37.   **The correct answer is A.** *Snowblowers* is in quotes because it is being used as a term with a slightly different meaning than it most often has. The author is not referring to real snowblowers, so the quotation marks are needed to set it off. A comma is needed after the term (choice A) to set it off from the appositive phrase that follows and defines the term, so choice B is not correct. Adding a semicolon (choice C) turns what follows it into a sentence fragment. Adding *being* (choice D) is an awkward means of explaining the term.

38.   **The correct answer is F.** It is enough to say this water is "three times hotter than boiling" (choice F). *Hotter* is the correct comparative form, and "more hot" (choice G) is awkward. *Hottest* (choice H) is superlative and shouldn't be used to compare two items. "Triple hot" (choice J) is neither idiomatic nor clear. What is *triple hot*? If the writer never explains it, you shouldn't choose this option.

39.   **The correct answer is B.** Because the author's overall idea may not yet have become evident, this may be a good question to set aside and come back to later. The futuristic angle of visiting these extreme environments (choice D) is only part of the author's method and is not the main theme of the passage. The author has just begun to introduce the idea of life in this place, so replacing one mention of living things with another, (choice C) won't necessarily lead to the main theme. Also, many readers won't make the connection that bacteria are organisms in need of food and shelter, a fact that subsequent sentences explain. Left as is, as in choice A, the passage lacks the scientific explanation for why this place exists. Choice B is correct because it explains how life can be found in unexpected places.

40.   **The correct answer is G.** Choice F allows a rather unwieldy paragraph to remain. In order to consider how it should be broken up, the idea strands have to be sorted. The paragraph begins with snowblowers, brings

in other life and chemosynthesis, and then provides examples of living things. It's best to break somewhere in the middle of this chain when chemosynthesis has been introduced but before it's expanded upon further, as suggested by choice G. Placing a break after the sentence that follows (choice H) breaks up the discussion of microbes by separating two closely related sentences that should not be separated. That change also creates a too-short paragraph consisting of one sentence. Choice J leaves the paragraph hanging without much of a conclusion or promise of anything noteworthy to come.

41. **The correct answer is D.** The existing construction—"the reason...is because..."—is redundant, as *reason* already implies a cause. The appropriate construction is "the reason…is that…" as seen in choice D. "When" (choice B) is awkward and inappropriate. Choice C lacks a verb.

42. **The correct answer is J.** Choice G doesn't work because the preposition *over* could cause us to think *over* goes with *cover* instead of with *300*. As written, the compound sentence is too long and confusing and is missing the necessary comma before *and*. However, even adding a comma, as in choice H, still leaves us with the problem of a compound sentence that's too long and confusing. Choice J breaks the compound sentence into two separate sentences that are much clearer to read and understand.

43. **The correct answer is A.** You may want to break up what appears to be a rather long sentence, as choice B suggests, but you have already broken up this sentence in the previous question choice. Therefore, it makes the sentence read smoothly to leave it as it is, choice A. Neither a semicolon (choice D) nor a comma (choice C) would be necessary or appropriate here, when the sentence does not require further division.

44. **The correct answer is G.** Read each of the choices in the position indicated by the question. You'll notice that choices H and J both provide important information that could be added here, but they don't refer to the reader or lead into the subject of the last paragraph. The author's earlier method of taking you on a tour (choice G) is effectively echoed in this last paragraph. Choice F asks an absurd question and compromises what credibility the passage has gained so far.

45. **The correct answer is C.** The migration of life is discussed in the last paragraph (choice D); however, it is a brief mention and is part of the conclusion of the passage. Choice C is more appropriate because

Paragraph 3's discussion of life forms that exist now at these vents is enhanced by knowing how life came to these remote areas. Bringing in these ideas at the very start (choice A) would interfere with the opening, and the reader wouldn't be ready to consider the implications. The second paragraph (choice B) is concerned more with the smoker towers, not with life forms.

46. **The correct answer is J.** Choice J is correct because the word *ancestor* means a person from whom one is descended, and the term is generally used to refer to relatives who have died. Therefore, "previously alive" (choice F), "previously lively" (choice G), and "previous living" (choice H) are all redundant, regardless of whether they are properly formed adverb-adjective pairs.

47. **The correct answer is D.** Choice D is correct because it properly defines the reference being made to an element of the previous sentence. *It* (choice A) lacks a proper antecedent and is vague. *Them* (choice B) seems to refer to cults or anthropologists, which is confusing. "These roles" (choice C) is specific but obscures the meaning of the sentence. The reference is to the act of endowing by the living. "This phenomenon" is exactly what the passage is describing.

48. **The correct answer is J.** The underlined phrase is referring to the dead, not the "elders" or the "graves." It must be placed beside the word it is modifying, which is *them* (choice J). Placed after *elders* (choice G), it seems to say they are the protectors, when they're appealing to the dead for protection from illness or misfortune. Placed after *dead* (choice H), it actually modifies *graves* because *dead* is only telling us whose graves are being visited. If the sentence isn't changed (choice F), the elders again seem to be the protectors.

49. **The correct answer is C.** An exclamation point serves to show emotion, and while emotion is being expressed by an elder in his appeal, a question mark should be used to end a sentence that asks a question. Choice C does this correctly. A comma, as in choice B, would splice the two sentences together and create a run-on sentence. A period, as in choice D, would be used only for declarative sentences that do not express any particularly strong emotion. Leaving the punctuation to stand, as in choice A, would obscure a question with unnecessary emotion. The words themselves convey the feelings of the speaker.

50. **The correct answer is F.** This added sentence should both summarize the main theme of the passage and direct the reader's attention to larger issues that will be covered throughout the passage. Choice F is best

because it reiterates the role of the dead in light of the responsibilities of the living. It confirms what we have just read and points to the rest of the passage. Mentioning other details the ancestors tend to (choice G) fails to provide the broader picture for the remainder of the passage. Describing which grave is selected (choice H) is another less important detail and lacks an overall focus. Discussing a generalized pattern (choice J) would provide a significant fact but would not restate the theme of the passage.

51. **The correct answer is D.** The sentence as it is written (choice A) provides irrelevant details about words that are not crucial to this discussion. Choice D is correct because it offers another word that further delineates how the Suku see the dead and the living. It is a contribution to the ideas introduced earlier in the sentence. Further explanation of the irrelevant terms (choice B) does not make them relevant. The additional information about lines of authority (choice C) is notable, but not in this context.

52. **The correct answer is G.** This awkward sentence structure can really be adjusted only by removing unnecessary words and creating two sentences, as suggested by choice G. The other fixes either lose ideas or mash them together into unwieldy linkage. Leaving the sentence as it is (choice F) has too many connections that blur meaning. Removing *much* from "the same," as in choice H, changes the meaning. The addition of *and* also forces an awkward transition between two thoughts. Chopping down the verbiage, as choice J does, may read more smoothly, but the concept of the unchanging role of the dead is lost.

53. **The correct answer is B.** Commas are used to set off an appositive that defines an unfamiliar term or a person's name and role. *Suku* may be a proper name, but "of any age" does not define who or what a Suku is. Therefore, choices that keep this construction, such as choices A and C, are misusing the commas. *Kusu* is an unfamiliar term that needs to be defined. The description should be set off with commas, as in choices B and D. However, *Kusu* is not a direct quote but a term of reference, so it does not need to be set off by quotation marks and commas, as in choice D.

54. **The correct answer is F.** Certain words and phrases act as transitional devices between thoughts. Many are similar in meaning, yet the examples offered here link two thoughts in very different ways. "As such" (choice F) offers an additional, extended thought along the same lines. The writer is signaling that this sentence is a

related and continued expansion on the previous sentence. "Granted that" (choice G) suggests a concession, an admission that the previous thought has forced this next thought. "On the contrary" (choice H) states contrast, or opposition; this sentence, however, is not a rebuttal of the previous one. "For example" (choice J) implies a more specific demonstration of what was just said, but this additional thought is not a particular example.

55. **The correct answer is B.** Related ideas can be included as independent clauses within a single sentence or can stand alone as separate sentences. The choice is a matter of effect and clarity of meaning. The original construction creates a run-on sentence, offers no connection between these ideas, and blurs the meaning. Adding a comma, as choice C does, doesn't help; we still have a run-on sentence. Inserting a dash, as choice D does, would be an effective way to offer a thought that is relevant but incomplete, which this second sentence isn't. It is related but needs to stand alone, as in choice B, to give full weight to its contribution.

56. **The correct answer is J.** Sentence 3 is out of place. Leaving it where it is (choice F) makes it unrelated to its surrounding sentences. Switching it with the previous sentence (choice G) merely breaks the connection between Sentences 1 and 2. Moving it before Sentence 6 (choice H) deprives it of the thought that sets up its meaning. It flows properly after Sentence 6 as a demonstration of the fluid nature of authority in the Suku, so choice J is the best answer.

57. **The correct answer is D.** A connection has to be made here between what the elders do and what the dead do. The original suggests that the former action takes place because of something the dead have done; this is not true. The use of *like*, as in choice B, would make a direct comparison except that "as has often been demonstrated before" is quite awkward. The phrase "because it goes without saying," which appears in choice C, should usually take its own advice and be avoided—if it goes without saying, it shouldn't be said. This phrase also suggests that the elders intervened because of something the dead did; this also isn't true. Simply suggesting that the actions of the elders and the dead are similar, as choice D does, is a straightforward means of linking both.

58. **The correct answer is H.** *Each male* can refer to an individual or all the males together. In either sense, it functions as a singular antecedent, so the pronoun

should match. Choice G incorrectly uses the plural *are elders* and *they*. The use of *you* in choice F is also incorrect, because the pronoun in this position must refer back to the males. This is the same problem with *it* in choice J. Each male is not "it." The reference would have to be *he*, as in choice H, to match each individual male.

59. **The correct answer is A.** Each of these additions can be judged by how well it meets the criteria established in the question. Here, we need to find ideas that show how the dead are honored. Choice A works best because it explains how a sacrifice functions both as a tribute to the dead and an identical offering to the living elders, which is the theme of the paragraph and the passage. The mention of burying food, choice B, does show one way the dead are honored but fails to serve as a relevant detail because it doesn't echo the themes stressed throughout the passage. The reference to European customs (choice C) introduces another element of tribute but tells us little about the Suku and even less about how this relates to the entire passage. The introduction of other tribes' beliefs (choice D) makes an interesting side note about other ways the dead are honored like the living, but the topic isn't relevant to the themes of this paragraph or of the passage as a whole.

60. **The correct answer is H.** The role of the dead for the Suku has been stressed throughout the passage, so any summary must reiterate how ancestor worship is actually a continuation of the elder relationships that were present in life. Choice H is correct because it cites specific examples of these relationships and notes this continuation. The role of the ancestors as authority figures (choice F) fails to effectively explain their role both before and after death. Focusing on the levels of eldership (choice G) reveals only one side of what is, in fact, a rather simple arrangement of authority between generations that extends beyond death. The introduction of additional ideas about Western conceptions of death (choice J) fails to explain how the dead and the living share authority for the Suku people.

61. **The correct answer is B.** The phrase "more favorite," which appears in the original sentence, is awkward and also incorrectly implies comparison between two destinations. If *favorite* were to take a modifier it would be the superlative *most*, but since the word *favorite* already means "preferred above all others," the word alone is sufficient and choice B is correct. *Favoritest* in choice C might be tempting, but no such word exists.

The word *most* in choice D accompanies *youthful* instead of *favorite* and thus distorts the meaning.

62. **The correct answer is F.** Moving this prepositional phrase after *departure* (choice G) limits the meaning of the sentence. It seems to refer only to "departure" as being different back then from now; that's not the author's intention. Choice F is correct because the phrase modifies the idea that needs to be placed in a time context. The author's "realm of possibilities" is what has changed over time. When he or she was young, this scheme was different, and, presumably, now it has changed. Placing the phrase after *even* (choice H) could work, but the sentence is awkward. Placing the phrase after *afar* (choice J) suggests that the relatives come from shorter distances these days, which may or may not be true.

63. **The correct answer is C.** Choice C is correct because it breaks up a long, convoluted sentence whose meaning is unclear without some separation of ideas. A period best accomplishes this separation. A semicolon (choice B) should be used to create a compound sentence only when the ideas in the separate independent clauses are closely related. The substitution of *because* (choice D) links the ideas as a cause and effect, which they are not.

64. **The correct answer is J.** This sentence requires the past form of the verb *take*. The correct past tense is *took*, and choice J is the only answer containing *took*. Choices F and G both use a nonexistent form *taked*. Choice H contains the past participle, *taken*, which creates the wrong verb tense; it fails further because it's missing the required auxiliary verb, *has* or *had*.

65. **The correct answer is C.** Choice C is correct because it gives the reader a sense of how the author lacks any real connection to these mysterious machines, which are essential to travel. Having never experienced them, he finds them unreal. Describing them as "identical" to his own toy airplanes (choice B) makes them seem more familiar and less mysterious. Referring to them as "shiny" (choice A) creates only a visual image. Considering them as "terrifying" (choice D) is contradictory to the idea that they're alluring.

66. **The correct answer is J.** The author's use of the movie metaphor is overdone in the original (choice F). Mentioning popcorn (choice G) is equally redundant and adds little to the sentence. The third mention of the movie connection (choice H) is both wordy and repetitive. Eliminating this unnecessary element (choice J) is the wisest option.

67. The correct answer is B. The second part of the original (choice A) is a sentence fragment. It must be joined to the previous sentence, which choice B does correctly with a comma. Not using any punctuation or connection (choice C) is also confusing. Creating a different, seemingly parallel phrase (choice D) changes the meaning of the sentence and produces a construction that doesn't make sense.

68. The correct answer is J. You might be able to make sense of the original (choice F), but it lacks parallel construction, which would give the sentence consistent form and clearer meaning. Choice J is correct because it provides a form *flying*, which matches the other verb forms in this list, *enjoying* and *caring*. The original is a noun clause, and it is repeated in a different form (choice G) which fails to make it smoother. Changing it into a prepositional phrase (choice H) also defies parallel construction.

69. The correct answer is C. The important decision to make here is whether the parenthetical phrase indeed needs to be set off from the rest of the sentence. The use of parentheses, as in choice A, is reserved for ideas that have no essential relation to the rest of the sentence, such as an explanation, figures, data, or examples. The phrase here is very strongly related, however, so it should not be tucked away in parentheses. Choice C is correct because it properly joins the second part of the predicate to the rest of the sentence. Choices B and D, by adding either a period or semicolon, cause the second part of the sentence to stand alone as a fragment.

70. The correct answer is H. The author's additional sentence must amplify the ideas of the previous sentence without repeating them. The author's view of other businessmen in similar surroundings points to the change occurring within the author's mind. Airports will soon be different places for him. The loss and separation of that moment will become an accepted part of the airport experience from now on. The smell of airplanes (choice F) may have come from his youth, but it fails to pinpoint the changing connotations. Details about the father's job (choice G) do little to advance the author's theme. Observations about the physical condition of the gate area (choice J) may be a telling detail but the author's noticing wear and tear is not indicative of his feelings.

71. The correct answer is D. It's highly doubtful that the author needs to describe which part of the airport is being mentioned. The coming sentences make it clear

that he is the one leaving, not the one being left behind. Eliminating these irrelevant details (choice D) will improve the sentence and the paragraph. The other choices merely add more irrelevant detail. Further explaining the structure's shape (choice B) or adding a verb (choice C) do not tell the reader anything important.

72. The correct answer is J. Choice J is correct because the relationship between the adjectives in a series governs the use of commas to separate them. The term *football player* has to stay together as it is a word group whose meaning is defined by being united. The original (choice F) places a comma between *football* and *player*, which upsets the meaning. Having no commas, as in choice G, blurs all the adjectives together. The word *and* can't be placed between *unwavering* and *football player*, as in choice H, because *unwavering* describes the compound noun *football player*. There is no comma between the last adjective in a series and the noun being described. Therefore, choice J is correct in placing a comma only between *brave* and *unwavering*.

73. The correct answer is B. The original sentence uses the objective pronoun form *me*. To properly complete the parallel construction, a subject is needed, as in "they are as excited as I am/was." Choice C is confusing, because it is unclear to whom *we* refers. Choice D might seem to make better sense until we remember that the writer has revealed that airports are no longer exciting places for him. We are left with choice B, which is grammatically correct and makes sense in the context of the essay.

74. The correct answer is H. The original sentence (choice F) is a fragment—it lacks a predicate. Choice G is a complete sentence saying that the "rushing, lost bags, and missed connections" *are* the "never coming home again." The sentence doesn't make sense. Choice J is a complete sentence and makes sense, so we should consider it. However, choice H is a better option. It more clearly and completely explains the contrast between the children's excitement and the writer's adult feelings about airports.

75. The correct answer is D. Choice D is correct because the word the author intends to use is the verb *affected*, meaning "emotionally stirred or moved" or "influenced by." *Effect* is usually a noun, although in its occasional verb form it means "to bring about," which is inappropriate in the context of the original sentence (choice A). Used as a noun in choice B, the word *affects* means "feelings or emotions," but to say, " I feel no affects…by train stations" makes no sense grammatically. Changing the contraction *I'm* to *I am*, as in choice C, doesn't alter the misuse of *effected* as a verb.

MATHEMATICS

1.	A	16.	G	31.	D	46.	H
2.	G	17.	C	32.	G	47.	E
3.	E	18.	H	33.	F	48.	H
4.	F	19.	E	34.	G	49.	C
5.	C	20.	J	35.	B	50.	G
6.	G	21.	C	36.	G	51.	C
7.	E	22.	H	37.	B	52.	H
8.	J	23.	A	38.	K	53.	D
9.	B	24.	J	39.	D	54.	F
10.	G	25.	B	40.	G	55.	C
11.	B	26.	G	41.	E	56.	H
12.	G	27.	B	42.	G	57.	D
13.	D	28.	J	43.	B	58.	H
14.	F	29.	D	44.	K	59.	D
15.	C	30.	K	45.	D	60.	G

1. **The correct answer is A.** To figure out what percentage chose green, first determine *how many* chose green. Out of 400 total people, 150 chose blue and 200 chose red, leaving 400 − (150 + 200) = 50 people. So 50 out of 400 chose green. Now calculate the percentage:

$$\text{Percent} = \frac{\text{part}}{\text{whole}}$$
$$\frac{x}{100} = \frac{50}{400}$$
$$400x = 5,000$$
$$x = \frac{50}{4} = 12.5$$

Choices B and C are incorrect due to arithmetic errors. For choice D, while 50 out of 400 chose green, this does not amount to 50%. Choice E is the percentage who did not choose green.

2. **The correct answer is G.** You're given that 1 hand equals 4 inches, and you want to find out how many hands are in 57 inches. This can be best solved by setting up a proportion:

$$\frac{1}{4} = \frac{x}{57}$$
$$4x = 57$$
$$x = \frac{57}{4} = 14.25$$

Choice F is too low; you must divide 57 by 4 and make certain not to approximate the answer. For choice H, when solving the equation 4x = 57, you subtracted 4 from both sides, but you should have

divided both sides by 4. In choice J, the decimal point is off by one place. For choice K, when solving the equation 4x = 57, you multiplied both sides by 4 instead of dividing by it.

3. **The correct answer is E.** If $\frac{3}{4}$ of the convertibles are red, then $\frac{1}{4}$ of the convertibles are NOT red.

We're told that 22 convertibles are NOT red, so there must be a total of 4(22) = 88 convertibles.

Since we're also told that $\frac{1}{8}$ of the cars are convertibles, it follows that there are a total of 8(88) = 704 cars.

Choice A represents the number of convertibles. Choice B is twice the number of convertibles, but is not the number of cars in the lot. Choice C is $\frac{3}{4}$ of the number of cars; you likely misinterpreted the quantity to which $\frac{3}{4}$ is to be applied. Choice D is the number of cars minus the number of convertibles.

4. **The correct answer is F.** You're already given the properly laid out proportion, so cross-multiply to solve for z:

$$\frac{15}{3z} = \frac{10}{4}$$
$$30z = 60$$
$$z = 2$$

Answer Keys and Explanations

Beware of choice J, 6, which is a partial answer. This value satisfies 3z, the unknown denominator, but doesn't correctly answer the question.

If you plug in the values of z in choices G, H, and J into the proportion, you do not get equality.

5. **The correct answer is C.** To find the total number of miles traveled by the two airplanes, first find the distance traveled by each, remembering that distance = rate × time.

For Airplane A:
distance = (540 mph)(3 hours) = 1,620 miles.

For Airplane B:
distance = (400 mph)(3.5 hours) = 1,400 miles.

The total distance, therefore, is 1,620 miles + 1,400 miles = 3,020 miles.

Choice A is the number of miles Airplane B has traveled. Choice B is the number of miles Airplane A has traveled. For choice D, you multiplied the rate of Airplane B times the time for Airplane A, and vice versa. For choice E, you added the rates and times for both planes and multiplied those quantities.

6. **The correct answer is G.** The new price is 9% less than the original. To find the new price, first find the reduction amount by taking 9% of the original price:

$$\text{Percent} = \frac{\text{part}}{\text{whole}}$$
$$\frac{9}{100} = \frac{x}{\$250}$$
$$1000x = \$2,250$$
$$x = \$22.50$$

So the price is being reduced by $22.50, which makes the new price $250 – $22.50 = $227.50.

For choice F, you subtracted 18%, not 9%. Choices H and J are incorrect because $9 does not mean 9%; also, in choice J, the dollar amount should be subtracted from $250. For choice K, you added 9% instead of subtracting it.

7. **The correct answer is E.** To evaluate the expression, plug in –4 for every instance of a and remember to follow PEMDAS.

$$2a + 4(a - 7) = 2(-4) + 4(-4 - 7)$$
$$= -8 + 4(-11)$$
$$= -8 - 44$$
$$= -52$$

Choice A is the opposite of the correct answer—be careful not to ignore the negative signs. Choice B has the wrong sign for 4(a – 7); it should be –44, not 44. If you chose choice C, you forgot to include 4(a – 7) in the calculation, and if you chose choice D, you have forgotten to include 2a in the calculation.

8. **The correct answer is J.** To find f(3), plug in 3 for every instance of x in the function and remember to follow PEMDAS.

$$f(3) = 2(3)^2 - 3(3) + 6$$
$$= 18 - 9 + 6$$
$$= 15$$

Choice F is f(1), and choice G is f(0). In choice H, note that $3^2 = 9$, not 6. For choice K, you have ignored the negative sign in the expression –3x.

9. **The correct answer is B.** The x-coordinate of the midpoint is halfway between the x-coordinates of the given points, (5, –3) and (1, 7):

$$x = \frac{5+1}{2} = \frac{6}{2} = 3$$

The y-coordinate of the midpoint is halfway between the y-coordinates of the given points, (5, –3) and (1, 7):

$$y = \frac{-3+7}{2} = \frac{4}{2} = 2$$

Therefore, the midpoint of the segment is (3, 2).

For choice A, you have subtracted corresponding components and divided by 2 instead of adding the corresponding components and then dividing by 2. For choice C, you did not average the x-coordinates. For choice D, you multiplied the x-coordinates of each point, but this does not give the midpoint between the two points. For choice E, you did not average the y-coordinates.

10. **The correct answer is G.** Use the FOIL method and combine like terms:

$$(4 + i)(2 - 2i) = 8 - 8i + 2i - 2i^2$$
$$= 8 - 6i - 2(-1)$$
$$= 8 - 6i + 2$$
$$= 10 - 6i$$

Choice F is the result of adding the complex numbers instead of subtracting them. Choice H has the i on the wrong term. Choice J is incorrect because $i^2 = -1$, not 1. Choice K is off by a factor of 2.

11. **The correct answer is B.** Remember that

$$\text{average} = \frac{\text{sum of values}}{\text{number of values}}.$$

To find the average number of seconds of commercials per minute, therefore, divide the total number of seconds of commercials by the total number of minutes.

First, add all of the table values in the second row to determine the total number of seconds of commercials: $120 + 180 + 240 + 0 + 120 + 180 = 840$. Next, note that the student listened to the radio station for six 4-minute intervals, which is a total of 24 minutes.

So the average per minute is $\frac{840}{24} = 35$. (Beware of choice D, which is the average per *period*, not per *minute*.)

Choice A is the number of minutes it takes to air six commercials. For choice C, you divided by the number of commercials, not the duration of the total number of commercials. For choice D, you divided the sum by 5, not 6; you must include "0" data values in the total of all data points. For choice E, you divided 840 by 4 (the length of one commercial).

12. **The correct answer is G.** If the product of two expressions is zero, then one of those expressions must equal zero. So either $m + 4 = 0$ or $m - 2 = 0$.

$$
\begin{array}{ccc}
m + 4 = 0 & & m - 2 = 0 \\
m = -4 & \text{or} & m = 2
\end{array}
$$

Only 2 is among the answer choices, so it must be correct. If you substitute any of the values in choices F, H, and K in for m, you do not get zero.

13. **The correct answer is D.** This expression is read as "the absolute value of 7 plus the absolute value of –9." Remember that absolute value is always the positive distance from zero on a number line, so the sum of two absolute values can never be negative. Eliminate choices A and B.

The absolute value of a number is basically the number without a positive or negative sign, so

$$|7| + |-9| = 7 = 9 = 16.$$

In choice A, the absolute value signs are ignored and the numbers are multiplied; in choice B, the absolute value signs are ignored and the numbers are added. In choice C, $|7 + (-9)|$ is computed, not the given sum. In choice E, the numbers are multiplied instead of added.

14. **The correct answer is F.** In the diagram, the three angles form a straight line and must, therefore, add up to 180°.

$$
\begin{aligned}
m\angle PQS + m\angle SQT + m\angle RQT &= 180° \\
65° + m\angle SQT + 30° &= 180° \\
m\angle SQT &= 180° - 65° - 30° \\
&= 85°
\end{aligned}
$$

For choices G, H, and J, you might have tried to eyeball the angle measure. The sum $65 + 30 + SQT$ must be 180 since these three angles form a straight angle. For choice K, you did not account for the 30-degree angle measure; angles PQS and SQT do not form a straight angle.

15. **The correct answer is C.** You're not asked to find numbers that give you an exact answer of 100. Rather, you need to find one number that, when cubed, gives you a value smaller than 100, and another number that, when cubed, gives you a value larger than 100. Working backward is the best option, and since the answer choices are in ascending order, start in the middle with choice C.

If x is between 4 and 5, then 4^3 should be less than 100 and 5^3 should be greater than 100. Since $4^3 = 64$ and $5^3 = 125$, choice C meets the requirement, and you do not have to try choices A, B, D, and E.

16. **The correct answer is G.** Work backward to find the pair of numbers with a greatest common factor of 4 and a least common multiple of 48. If a choice doesn't meet one condition, don't bother testing for the other condition.

Choice F:　　{4, 24}
　　GCF = 4; LCM = 24; eliminate

Choice G:　　{12, 16}
　　GCF = 4; LCM = 48; correct

Choice H:　　{12, 48}
　　GCF = 12; eliminate

Choice J:　　{16, 32}
　　GCF = 16; eliminate

Choice K:　　{24, 48}
　　GCF = 24; eliminate

The only set that fulfills both requirements is {12, 16}.

17. **The correct answer is C.** You should recognize that $y = x^2 + 4x - 21$ is the equation of a parabola that opens upward. One of the characteristics of such a parabola is that it will always intersect the x-axis 0, 1, or 2 times, but never more. This means that you can eliminate choices D and E right away.

    Remember that the graph will intersect the x-axis only when y equals zero. To find the number of x-intercepts of a quadratic equation, $ax^2 + bx + c = 0$, evaluate the discriminant, $b^2 - 4ac$. If the discriminant is positive, there are two x-intercepts; if it's zero, there is one x-intercept; if it's negative, there are none. In this case:

    $$b^2 - 4ac = (4)^2 - 4(1)(-21)$$
    $$= 16 - (-84)$$
    $$= 100$$

    Since this is a positive discriminant, the graph will cross the x-axis exactly twice. Hence, choices A and B cannot be correct.

18. **The correct answer is H.** When an angle is bisected, its degree measure is divided in half and two congruent angles are formed. In this case, $\overline{PR}$ divides $\angle QPS$ into congruent angles QPR and SPR. Choices F and K are incorrect because angle RPS has half the measure of the other given angle. Choices G and J are incorrect because angle RPQ has half the measure of the given angle.

19. **The correct answer is E.** The equation must contain p, $\sqrt{q}$, and r^2. The only two answer choices to include these are A and E, so eliminate choices B, C, and D. Both A and E have the variable p by itself, so you need to determine which placement of the other two variables is correct. If p is directly proportional to $\sqrt{q}$ but inversely proportional to r^2, then $\sqrt{q}$ must appear in the numerator and r^2 must appear in the denominator. Choice E gets it right.

20. **The correct answer is J.** The slope of a line is determined by $\dfrac{\text{rise}}{\text{run}}$, which, for any two points on the line, is the difference between the y-coordinates divided by the difference between the x-coordinates.

    For the points (5, –3) and (–2, –1), the y-coordinates are –3 and –1, so they must appear in the numerator of the line's slope expression. Only choices G and J have the correct y-coordinates in the numerator, so eliminate choices F, H, and K.

    Choice G, $\dfrac{-3-(-1)}{-2-5}$, is incorrect because the x-coordinates are subtracted in the reverse order from how

    the y-coordinates are subtracted. Choice J, $\dfrac{-3-(-1)}{5-(-2)}$, is set up properly, giving the correct slope of the line.

21. **The correct answer is C.** This expression is read as "the opposite of –5 minus the absolute value of –5." The opposite of –5 is 5, and the absolute value of –5 is 5. Therefore, $-(-5) - |-5| = 5 - 5 = 0$.

    For choice A, you likely multiplied the quantities and affixed the wrong sign to the product. For choice B, $-(-5) = 5$, not –5. For choice D, $-|-5| = -5$, not 5. For choice E, you multiplied the quantities.

22. **The correct answer is H.** The new price is 30% less than the original. To find the new price, first find the reduction amount by taking 30% of the original price:

    $$\text{Percent} = \frac{\text{part}}{\text{whole}}$$
    $$\frac{30}{100} = \frac{x}{\$15.95}$$
    $$100x = \$478.50$$
    $$x \approx \$4.79$$

    So the price is being reduced by about $4.79, which makes the new price about $15.95 – $4.79 ≈ $11.16. Since the question asks you for the sale price to the nearest dollar, you can round $11.16 to $11. Choice F is the approximate amount by which the price is reduced, but rounded down. Choice G is the approximate amount by which the price is reduced, but rounded up. In choice J, you rounded up, but should have rounded down. Choice K is incorrect because $3 does not mean 30%.

23. **The correct answer is A.** Since reverse FOIL is difficult on this equation, you can use the Quadratic Formula to solve it:

    $$x = \frac{-b \pm \sqrt{b^2 - 4ac}}{2a}$$
    $$= \frac{-9 \pm \sqrt{(9)^2 - 4(2)(-5)}}{2(2)}$$
    $$= \frac{-9 \pm \sqrt{81 + 40}}{4}$$
    $$= \frac{-9 \pm \sqrt{121}}{4}$$
    $$= \frac{-9 \pm 11}{4}$$
    $$= \frac{2}{4} \text{ or } \frac{-20}{4}$$
    $$= \frac{1}{2} \text{ or } -5$$

This gives two possible values for x. However, the question tells you that $x > 0$, so the only possible answer is $\frac{1}{2}$.

If you substitute the values for choices B, C, D, and E into the expression, you do not get zero.

24. **The correct answer is J.** If the probability of NOT saying math is their favorite is $\frac{1}{5}$, then the probability of saying math IS their favorite is $1 - \frac{1}{5} = \frac{4}{5}$. Therefore, we have the following proportion:

$$\frac{4}{5} = \frac{\text{number of students who say math is their favorite}}{40}$$

Cross-multiplying yields $4(40) = 5 \times$ number of students who say math is their favorite, and then dividing both sides by 5 yields that the number of students who say math is their favorite is 32. Choice F is the number of students who do NOT say math is their favorite. Choice G would mean $\frac{1}{4}$, not $\frac{1}{5}$, of students who say math is NOT their favorite. Choice H would mean $\frac{1}{2}$ of the sample did NOT say math is their favorite, which is not the case. Choice K would mean $\frac{1}{10}$ of the sample did NOT say math is their favorite, which is not the case.

25. **The correct answer is B.** Parallelograms have opposite sides that are parallel. This means that $\overline{PQ}$ and $\overline{RS}$ are parallel, and $\overline{QS}$ is a transversal. Since $\angle RSQ$, the angle you're looking for, is an acute angle, it must be congruent to $\angle PQS$, the other acute angle formed by the same transversal. Therefore, $m\angle RSQ = 35°$. Choices A, C, and D cannot be correct since alternate interior angles for this geometric figure are congruent. Choice E is the measure of angle QPS.

26. **The correct answer is G.** You're given the number of fluid ounces in a cup and the cost of 9 cups, and you're asked to find the cost per fluid ounce. First, convert 9 cups into fluid ounces by setting up a proportion:

$$\frac{9 \text{ cups}}{x \text{ fl. oz.}} = \frac{1 \text{ cup}}{8 \text{ fl. oz.}}$$
$$x = 72$$

So you know that 72 fluid ounces cost $23.04. Use another proportion to find the cost of one fluid ounce:

$$\frac{72}{\$23.04} = \frac{1}{x}$$
$$72x = \$23.04$$
$$x = \frac{\$23.04}{72} = \$0.32$$

Choice F is calculated assuming 12 cups, not 9 cups. For choice H, you've added 8 fluid ounces and 9 cups without converting the units; you should have multiplied these quantities. For both choices J and K, you did not multiply the number of cups by 8 fluid ounces before dividing.

27. **The correct answer is B.** First, find the total area of the wall (including the window and door), which is a rectangle; then subtract the area of the window and the area of the door.

The length of the wall is $1 + 2\frac{1}{2} + 9\frac{1}{2} = 13$ feet, and the height of the wall is 8 feet, so the entire area including window and door is $8 \times 13 = 104$ square feet.

The window and door are also rectangles, so use their lengths and heights to calculate their areas. The area of the window is $2 \times 3 = 6$ square feet, and the area of the door is $2\frac{1}{2} \times 6 = 15$ square feet.

Subtracting the window and door areas from the entire area yields $104 - 6 - 15 = 83$ square feet.

Choice A is the area you do *not* want to cover. Choice C is likely the result of an arithmetic error. For choice D, you've forgotten to subtract the area of the window. For choice E, you've forgotten to subtract the area of the door.

28. **The correct answer is J.** Put the equation into slope-intercept form, $y = mx + b$, where b is the y-intercept:

$$6x + 3y = 15$$
$$3y = -6x + 15$$
$$y = -2x + 5$$

This shows that the y-intercept of the line is 5. Choice F is the negative of the correct answer. Choice G is the coefficient of x after dividing by the coefficient of y; this will not give the y-intercept. Choice H is the coefficient of y, not the y-intercept. Choice K is incorrect because the coefficient of x is not the y-intercept.

29. **The correct answer is D.** Line q is a transversal that cuts through parallel lines s and t, which means that all of the acute angles it forms must be equal. Therefore, inside the small triangle that includes x, the angle at the intersection of lines q and t must equal 60°.

To find the third angle inside this triangle, use the upward-sloping transversal that cuts through lines p and q. The given acute angle is 50°, which means that its corresponding angle inside the triangle must also equal 50°.

The three angles inside this triangle must equal 180°, so use the given values to solve for x:

$$x + 60° + 50° = 180°$$
$$x = 180° - 60° - 50°$$
$$= 70°$$

Choice A is way too small since the other angles are 50 and 60 degrees, and the sum of the three angles of a triangle must be 180. Choices B and C are the other two angles in the triangle. Choice E is way too large since the other angles are 50 and 60 degrees, and the sum of the three angles of a triangle must be 180.

30. **The correct answer is K.** In a right triangle, $tangent = \dfrac{opposite}{adjacent}$, so first you need to find QR, the length of the opposite side. Use the Pythagorean theorem:

$$(PQ)^2 + (QR)^2 = (PR)^2$$
$$QR = \sqrt{(PR)^2 - (PQ)^2}$$
$$= \sqrt{4^2 - 3^2}$$
$$= \sqrt{16 - 9}$$
$$= \sqrt{7}$$

Therefore, $\tan \angle P = \dfrac{\sqrt{7}}{3}$.

Choice F is csc(P). Choice G is sin(P). Choice H is sec(P). Choice J is cot(P).

31. **The correct answer is D.** First, calculate the discounted cost of each single CD and double CD. Single CDs are discounted by 25%, so the new individual price of a single CD is $16 − (0.25)($16) = $12. Double CDs are discounted by 30%, so the new individual price of a double CD is $24 − (0.3)($24) = $16.80.

Maria bought two singles and one double, so for the singles she paid 2($12) = $24, and for the double she paid $16.80. Therefore, the total amount she paid was $24 + $16.80 = $40.80.

Choice A is the price of a double CD. Choice B does not include the price of a double CD. For choice C, you only included one single CD, but you should have included two. For choice E, you did not apply the discount.

32. **The correct answer is G.** Since average is equal to $\dfrac{\text{sum of values}}{\text{number of values}}$, the sum is the product of the average and the number of values.

The average of the first 7 integers is 13, so their sum is $7 \times 13 = 91$. The average of all 8 integers is 12, so their sum is $8 \times 12 = 96$. The value of the eighth number must be equal to the difference between the two sums: $96 - 91 = 5$. Choice F is too small; the resulting average would be less than 12. Choice H would not reduce the average by 1. Choice J would result in the same average, 13, not a decreased average. Choice K would increase the average if added as an eighth number.

33. **The correct answer is E.** Divide like terms separately. Begin with the numbers: $\dfrac{-20}{5} = -4$.

Next, divide the powers of m: $\dfrac{m^2}{m} = m$.

Then divide powers of n: $\dfrac{n^4}{n^6} = n^{-2} = \dfrac{1}{n^2}$.

Finally, divide powers of y: $\dfrac{y}{y^2} = y^{-1} = \dfrac{1}{y}$.

Now put everything together:

$$-4 \times m \times \frac{1}{n^2} \times \frac{1}{y} = \frac{-4m}{n^2 y}.$$

Choice A is incorrect because the $n^2 y$ term should be in the denominator; the negative exponent was applied incorrectly. Choice B is incorrect because you must subtract exponents to combine quotients of powers of the same variable. In choice C, the term n^2y should be in the denominator and m should be in the numerator. For choice D, you added the powers, but still had a correct notion of where the resulting terms should be placed in the fraction.

34. **The correct answer is G.** The area of a rectangle is the product of its length and width, so in the given rectangle:

$$\text{Area} = PQ \times QR$$
$$24 = 8 \times QR$$
$$QR = \frac{24}{8}$$
$$= 3$$

Choice F is too small; the resulting area would be 16. Choice H would result in the perimeter being 24, not the area. Choice J would result in making the area 64. Choice K is the length of the labeled segments; this would make the area 128.

35. **The correct answer is B.** A fair coin has one head and one tail, so each coin toss has two possible outcomes. Independently tossing the coin 3 times, therefore, will have a total of $2 \times 2 \times 2 = 8$ possible outcomes.

You're asked to determine how many of these 8 outcomes will contain exactly one head. Consider that the head can be the result of the first, second, or third toss, and write out the possibilities:

H T T

T H T

T T H

So 3 of the 8 possible outcomes yield exactly one head, which is a probability of $\frac{3}{8}$.

For choices A and D, you did not account for the probability of getting a head when a fair coin is tossed. Choice C is the probability of getting a head in a single toss of the coin. Choice E is the probability of getting at least one head.

36. **The correct answer is G.** First, add the two matrices together, combining corresponding terms:

$$\begin{bmatrix} 4 & 1 \\ -3 & 5 \end{bmatrix} + \begin{bmatrix} -4 & 0 \\ -2 & 8 \end{bmatrix} = \begin{bmatrix} 4 + (-4) & 1 + 0 \\ -3 + (-2) & 5 + 8 \end{bmatrix}$$
$$= \begin{bmatrix} 0 & 1 \\ -5 & 13 \end{bmatrix}$$

This matches choice F. However, remember that the question asks you for *twice* the sum. Therefore:

$$2\begin{bmatrix} 0 & 1 \\ -5 & 13 \end{bmatrix} = \begin{bmatrix} 0 & 2 \\ -10 & 26 \end{bmatrix}$$

In choice F, you did not multiply by 2. Choice H is $M - N$, not $2(M + N)$. Choice J is MN, not $2(M + N)$. Choice K is $2(M - N)$.

37. **The correct answer is B.** The graph will intersect the *x*-axis whenever *y* equals zero. Set the expression equal to zero and solve for *x*:

$$0 = (x - 2)(x + 3)(x + 4)$$

$$x - 2 = 0 \quad \text{or} \quad x + 3 = 0 \quad \text{or} \quad x + 4 = 0$$
$$x = 2 \qquad\qquad x = -3 \qquad\qquad x = -4$$

So when *x* is 2, –3, or –4, the expression will equal zero. This means that the graph intersects the *x*-axis 3 times. Therefore, choices A, C, D, and E are impossible.

38. **The correct answer is K.** You can make most logarithmic equations easier by rewriting them in exponential form:

$$\log_2 x = 5$$
$$2^5 = x$$
$$32 = x$$

For choices F and G, you seem to have misunderstood how to write a logarithmic expression in exponential form. For choice H, you are taking $\log_2$ of *x*, not multiplying *x* by the symbol $\log_2$. For choice J, the base is not a power of the right side; rather, you raise the base to the right side to get an equivalent exponential form.

39. **The correct answer is D.** Suppose, for simplicity's sake, that the actual lengths are 1, $\sqrt{3}$, and 2. It's important to note that 1 is the smallest length and 2 is the largest.

The smallest angle in a triangle is opposite the shortest side, so in this triangle it would be opposite the side of length 1. In relation to this angle, therefore, the opposite side would be 1, the adjacent would be $\sqrt{3}$, and the hypotenuse would be 2.

Since $\cos ine = \dfrac{\text{adjacent}}{\text{hypotenuse}}$, the cosine of this angle would be $\dfrac{\sqrt{3}}{2}$.

Choice A is the tangent of the smallest angle. Choice B, is cos(60), but the smallest angle does not have a

Answer Keys and Explanations

measure of 60 degrees. Choice C is the cotangent of the smallest angle. Choice E is the cosecant of the smallest angle.

40. **The correct answer is G.** In order for the circle to lie completely inside the square, the side length of the square must be at least as large as the diameter of the circle.

To find this diameter, use the given equation of the circle, $(x - 5)^2 + (y - 7)^2 = 16$. Since the equation is already in standard form, the right side of the equation, 16, represents the square of the radius. So if $r^2 = 16$, the radius is 4. And if the radius is 4, the diameter is equal to 8. Therefore, each side of the square must be at least 8 units long. Choice F is just the radius; you need to use the diameter to get a side of the smallest such square. For choice H, you doubled the x-coordinate of the center, but this doesn't affect how large the circle is. In choice J, you doubled the y-coordinate of the center, but this doesn't affect how large the circle is. For choice K, you used the radius squared, but should have used the diameter instead.

41. **The correct answer is E.** Plug in numbers to solve this problem. Let $a = 0$, because this will quickly get rid of answer choices that might otherwise remain with "easier" numbers. Since $b < a$, we can use -3 to replace b. And since $c < 0$, let's pick -1. So $a = 0$, $b = -3$, and $c = -1$.

If you plug these numbers into each answer choice, you'll see that only choice E yields a valid result:

$$\frac{a}{c} < \frac{b}{c}$$
$$\frac{0}{-1} < \frac{-3}{-1}$$
$$0 < 3$$

Choice A is incorrect—use sample values like $a = 1$ and $b = -2$ to see that this need not be true. For choice B, use $a = -1$ and $c = -2$ to see that this need not be true. For choices C and D, use $a = -1$, $b = -2$, and $c = -2$ to see that this need not be true.

42. **The correct answer is G.** To find the area of the shaded frame, calculate the area of the entire picture (including frame) and then subtract the unshaded region (the picture alone).

The entire rectangle is 30 inches by 22 inches, so it has an area of $(30)(22) = 660$ square inches.

For the unshaded region, remember that the picture is surrounded by a 2-inch border on all four sides. So its length is $30 - 2 - 2 = 26$ inches, and its width is $22 - 2 - 2 = 18$ inches. This makes its area $(26)(18) = 468$ square inches.

Therefore, the area of the shaded frame is $660 - 468 = 192$ square inches.

Choice F is the area of the picture portion of the entire frame, not the shaded portion. In choice H, you likely made an arithmetic error. Choice J only accounts for half of the frame. Choice K is just one-fourth of the shaded portion.

43. **The correct answer is B.** If the correct answer *must be* true, then all you need to do to make an answer choice incorrect is find one case where it's false. This is best done by plugging in numbers.

Try $x = 1$ and $y = 1$. This works:

$|1 + 1| = |2| = 2$ *and* $|1| + |1| = 1 + 1 = 2$. Since x and y don't have to have opposite signs, choices A and E are incorrect.

What about $x = -3$ and $y = -2$? This works, too: $|-3 + -2| = |-5| = 5$ and $|-3| + |-2| = 3 + 2 = 5$. Since the absolute values of x and y don't have to be the same, choice D is incorrect.

We can use decimals, too. What about $x = 0.5$ and $y = 1.5$? This works:

$|0.5 + 1.5| = |2| = 2$ and $|0.5| + |1.5| = 0.5 + 1.5 = 2$.

Since x and y don't have to be integers, choice C is incorrect.

This leaves choice B; for the equation to hold, x and y must have the same sign.

44. **The correct answer is K.** For a system of equations to have no unique solution, all of the variables must cancel. To see how this is possible for the given system, multiply the bottom equation by 4:

$$-20x - 12y = -28$$
$$4(5x + ky) = 4(-2)$$

$$-20x - 12y = -28$$
$$20x + 4ky = -8$$

For both x and y to cancel, y must have a coefficient of 12. Since its given coefficient here is $4k$, $4k$ must equal 12, which means that k must equal 3. In choices F, H, and J, the resulting system has one solution. In choice G, the resulting system has no solution.

45. **The correct answer is D.** The two given equations, $y = -3x - 4$ and $y = mx + 7$, are already in slope-intercept form, so it's easy to see that their slopes are -3 and m, respectively. When two lines are perpendicular, their slopes are negative reciprocals. This means that m must be the negative reciprocal of -3, which is $\frac{1}{3}$.

In choices A and B, you seem to be relating the constant terms of the lines, which are the y-intercepts. The perpendicularity of two lines is determined by the slopes, not the y-intercepts. Choice C is incorrect because the product of the slopes of perpendicular lines must be -1, not 1. Choice E would make the lines parallel, not perpendicular.

46. **The correct answer is H.** Use the Pythagorean theorem to solve for the missing length:

$$a^2 + b^2 = c^2$$
$$15^2 + b^2 = 17^2$$
$$b = \sqrt{17^2 - 15^2}$$
$$= \sqrt{289 - 225}$$
$$= \sqrt{64}$$
$$= 8$$

Choice F is incorrect because the correct expression is $\sqrt{17^2 - 15^2}$, not $(17 - 15)^2$. For choice G, you treated the hypotenuse like a leg in the Pythagorean theorem and forgot to square each of the legs. For choice J, you treated the hypotenuse like a leg in the Pythagorean theorem. For choice K, you forgot to take the square root.

47. **The correct answer is E.** Using the distance formula to solve algebraically for b would be quite tedious, so it's better to work backward here, starting with choice C.

Choice C says that $b = 5$. Plugging all actual numbers into the distance formula yields the following:

$$10 = \sqrt{(5-4)^2 + (6-5)^2}$$
$$10 = \sqrt{1 + 1}$$
$$10 \neq \sqrt{2}$$

The distance was supposed to be 10, but substituting 5 for b gave us only $\sqrt{2}$. This makes choice C wrong because it's too small, and it means that choices A and B, which would make the distance even smaller, should be eliminated as well.

Since we need a larger number, let's try choice E, which says that $b = 12$:

$$10 = \sqrt{(12-4)^2 + (6-12)^2}$$
$$10 = \sqrt{64 + 36}$$
$$10 = \sqrt{100}$$
$$10 = 10$$

48. **The correct answer is H.** The temperature at 9 a.m. is $-15.5°$, and at 10 a.m. it is $-13.0°$. This is a difference of $-13.0° - (-15.5°) = 2.5°$. If the temperature increases by $2.5°$ each hour, then 3 hours later at 1 p.m. it will be $-13.0° + 3(2.5°) = -13.0° + 7.5° = -5.5°$.

For choice F, you assumed the temperature was decreasing by 2.5 degrees Celsius per hour, but it is increasing at this rate. Choice G is the temperature after two hours of such an increase, not three hours. Choice J is the amount by which the temperature increases, and choice K is the total amount by which the temperature increases.

49. **The correct answer is C.** Plug the given points $\left(\frac{3}{4}, \frac{1}{3}\right)$ and $(0, 0)$ into the slope formula:

$$\frac{y_2 - y_1}{x_2 - x_1} = \frac{\frac{1}{3} - 0}{\frac{3}{4} - 0}$$
$$= \frac{\frac{1}{3}}{\frac{3}{4}}$$
$$= \frac{1}{3} \times \frac{4}{3}$$
$$= \frac{4}{9}$$

Choice A is the quotient of the differences of the x and y coordinates of the given point, not the slope. Choice B is the change in y, but you need to divide by the change in x to get the slope. Choice D is the change in x, but you need to divide the change in y by it to get the slope. Choice E is the reciprocal of the correct slope.

Answer Keys and Explanations

50. The correct answer is G. The distances in the diagram form a right triangle. To find the height difference, h, between the altitude of the plane and the top of the control tower, use the sine function:

$$\text{sine} = \frac{\text{opposite}}{\text{hypotenuse}}$$

$$\sin 27° = \frac{h}{35,000}$$

$$h = 35,000 \times \sin 27°$$

Choices F and H are incorrect; both these answers equal the length of the base of the triangle. For Choice J, you did not multiply the numerator and denominator. For choice K, you should be using either sin(27) or cos(63) in place of cos(27), and you should be multiplying the numerator by it, not dividing these quantities.

51. The correct answer is C. You're given that the area is 84 and that the length is 4 less than 3 times the width. Start by letting w represent the width, and then translate to find the length. "4 less than 3 times the width" is the same as "4 less than $3w$," or $3w - 4$. Now that you have a specific length, width, and area, substitute them all into the area formula to solve for w.

$$\text{Area} = \text{length} \times \text{width}$$

$$84 = (3w - 4)w$$

$$84 = 3w^2 - 4w$$

$$0 = 3w^2 - 4w - 84$$

$$0 = (3w + 14)(w - 6)$$

$$\begin{array}{ccc} 3w + 14 = 0 & & w - 6 = 0 \\ 3w = -14 & \text{or} & w = 6 \\ w = -\dfrac{14}{3} & & \end{array}$$

Solving for w yields two possibilities: $-\frac{14}{3}$ and 6. However, it doesn't make sense for the width of a rectangle to be negative, so w must be equal to 6. Since the question asked you to find length, not width, remember that your answer is $3w - 4 = 3(6) - 4 = 14$.

Choice A is the width, and choice B is twice the width, which does not equal the length. For choice D, you forgot to subtract 4; the length is $3w - 4$, not $3w$. Choice E would be the length of a side if the shape were a square, not a rectangle.

52. The correct answer is H. Rolling a fair six-sided die twice gives $6^2 = 36$ outcomes. You must determine how many of these outcomes yield one 5 and one 6. The only rolls that can result in this scenario are (5, 6) or (6, 5). Since all rolls are equally likely, the probability of this occurring is $\frac{2}{36} = \frac{1}{18}$. Choice F is the probability of getting either a 5 or a 6 in one roll. Choice G is the probability of the complement of the event "getting one 5 and one 6." Choice J is the probability of getting at least one 5 or one 6 in two rolls. Choice K is the probability of getting a 5 in one roll.

53. The correct answer is D. You're given a circle's diameter and asked to find its area. To find area, you first need to know the radius. If the diameter is 16, then the radius is exactly half of that, or 8. Now plug this into the formula for the area of a circle:

$$A = \pi r^2$$

$$= \pi (8)^2$$

$$= 64\pi$$

Choice A is the area of $\frac{1}{8}$ of the circle. Choice B is the area of $\frac{1}{4}$ of the circle. Choice C is the area of a semi-circle. For choice E, you used 16 for the radius, but this is the diameter.

54. The correct answer is F. If a quadratic equation of the form $ax^2 + bx + c = 0$ has only one solution, or root, it means that its discriminant, $b^2 - 4ac$, must be equal to zero. First, put the given equation in standard form:

$$x^2 - kx = -1$$

$$x^2 - kx + 1 = 0$$

Given that $a = 1$, $b = -k$, and $c = 1$, set the discriminant equal to zero:

$$b^2 - 4ac = 0$$

$$(-k)^2 - 4(1)(1) = 0$$

$$k^2 - 4 = 0$$

$$k^2 = 4$$

$$k = \pm 2$$

This gives two possible values of k, 2 or –2, but only one answer choice matches, so k must equal –2 in this case.

Choices G, H, J, and K would not render the quadratic expression $x^2 - kx + 1$ as the factored form $(x - a)^2$ for some real number a. As such, all these other choices would result in quadratic equations that have two solutions, not just one.

55. **The correct answer is C.** First you'll need to figure out how many total degrees are in a pentagon. To find the sum of all angles in a polygon with n sides, use the formula $180°(n - 2)$. A pentagon has 5 sides, so its angles must add up to $180° \times 3 = 540°$.

Now use the given angles in the diagram to solve for x:

$$140 + 92 + 88 + x + x = 540$$
$$2x + 320 = 540$$
$$2x = 220$$
$$x = 110$$

In choice A, you forgot to divide by 2. In choice B, you used $180(6 - 2)$ as the sum of all interior angles instead of $180(5 - 2)$. In choice D, you used $180(4 - 2)$ as the sum of all interior angles instead of $180(5 - 2)$, and forgot to divide by 2. In choice E, you used $180(4 - 2)$ as the sum of all interior angles instead of $180(5 - 2)$.

56. **The correct answer is H.** The function $g(f(x))$ is a composite, or compound function, which means that you need to work from the inside out. The inner function, $f(x)$, is carried out first and then substituted into the outer function, $g(x)$. This means that everywhere you see an x in the function $g(x)$, replace it with the function $f(x)$, or $x - 2$:

$$g(x) = 2x^2 + 1$$
$$g(f(x)) = 2(f(x))^2 + 1$$
$$= 2(x - 2)^2 + 1$$
$$= 2(x^2 - 4x + 4) + 1$$
$$= 2x^2 - 8x + 8 + 1$$
$$= 2x^2 - 8x + 9$$

In choice F, you misinterpreted $(x - 2)^2$ as $x^2 - 4$—you forgot the middle term. Choice G is $f(g(x))$. In choice J, the coefficient of x^2 is wrong. For choice K, you only distributed the 2 in the expression $2(x^2 - 4x + 4)$ to the first term.

57. **The correct answer is D.** Given that the water volume is 792 cm³ and occupies 60% of the tank, start by setting up a proportion to calculate the volume of the entire tank:

$$\text{Percent} = \frac{\text{part}}{\text{whole}}$$
$$\frac{60}{100} = \frac{792}{x}$$
$$60x = 79,200$$
$$x = 1,320$$

So the volume of the tank is 1,320 cubic centimeters. However, the question asks you to find the *surface area* of the tank. First, use the given length and width—which are the same for both the water and the entire tank—and the volume you just calculated to determine the height of the tank:

$$V = lwh$$
$$1,320 = (12)(11)(h)$$
$$h = \frac{1,320}{12 \times 11}$$
$$= 10$$

This makes the dimensions of the tank 12 by 11 by 10. Use these dimensions to calculate the overall surface area:

$$SA = 2lw + 2lh + 2wh$$
$$= 2(12)(11) + 2(12)(10) + 2(11)(10)$$
$$= 2(132) + 2(120) + 2(110)$$
$$= 264 + 240 + 220$$
$$= 724$$

In choice A, you forgot to double the areas of each side of the box. In choices B and C, you forgot to include the area of two of the sides of the box. Choice E is the volume.

58. **The correct answer is H.** Since the algebra on this problem can be a bit messy, plug in numbers to find the answer. Let $r = 2$ and $h = 3$ so that the arithmetic is easy. Use the values to find the surface area before the increase:

$$2\pi rh + 2\pi r^2 = 2\pi(2)(3) + 2\pi(2)^2$$
$$= 12\pi + 8\pi$$
$$= 20\pi$$

Now triple both the radius and the height. This means that r will become 6, and h will become 9. Use these increased values to find the new surface area:

$$2\pi rh + 2\pi r^2 = 2\pi(6)(9) + 2\pi(6)^2$$
$$= 108\pi + 72\pi$$
$$= 180\pi$$

We want to know by what factor the surface area increased, so compare the two numbers. Tripling the radius and height resulted in a number that was

$$\frac{180\pi}{20\pi} = 9$$ times the original surface area. Choice F is

the factor by which each parameter (radius and height) is increasing—but when multiplied, this number will increase. In choice G, $3^2 = 9$, not 6. For choice J, the volume would increase by a factor of 27, not the surface area. Choice K is too large.

59. **The correct answer is D.** The coefficient of x determines the period and frequency of a graphed trig function. Remember that neither a coefficient of the function itself, which determines the amplitude, nor a constant added to the function, which shifts the graph vertically, has any effect on frequency. To determine the number of cycles for this function, therefore, just compare the graph of $\cos 4x$ with the graph of $\cos x$.

The graph of $\cos x$ completes exactly one cycle from $x = 0$ to $x = 2\pi$, and the cosine is first equal to zero when $x = \dfrac{\pi}{2}$. Changing the function to $\cos 4x$,

however, compresses the graph horizontally. This means that the cosine is first equal to zero when $x = \dfrac{\pi}{8}$, and that $\cos 4x$ will complete its first cycle at

$x = \dfrac{\pi}{2}$, so it will complete 4 cycles for every one

cycle that $\cos x$ completes.

Therefore, when $0 \leq x \leq 2\pi$, the function $y = 3 + 5$ $\cos 4x$ will complete exactly 4 cycles.

For choices A, B, and C, the period of $\cos 4x$ is $\dfrac{1}{2}$,

so all of these choices are too small. Choice E would

imply that the function had period $\dfrac{\pi}{8}$, which it

does not.

60. **The correct answer is G.** To find the slope of the line, we must first find the equation of the line. Translate the given information into algebra: "two times the x-coordinate plus three times the y-coordinate is equal to 12" means that $2x + 3y = 12$. Now put this equation into slope-intercept form, $y = mx + b$:

$$2x + 3y = 12$$
$$3y = -2x + 12$$
$$y = -\frac{2}{3}x + 4$$

Since m represents slope, the slope of this line is $-\dfrac{2}{3}$.

Choice F is the reciprocal of the correct slope. For choice H, you divided both sides by 12 and used the coefficient of x; instead, you should have divided both sides by the coefficient of y. For choice J, you have left out the negative sign. Choice K is the y-intercept, not the slope.

READING

1.	C	11.	A	21.	D	31.	C
2.	J	12.	F	22.	G	32.	F
3.	D	13.	D	23.	A	33.	A
4.	F	14.	H	24.	G	34.	H
5.	B	15.	D	25.	C	35.	D
6.	F	16.	F	26.	J	36.	J
7.	C	17.	D	27.	A	37.	B
8.	G	18.	G	28.	H	38.	H
9.	C	19.	A	29.	B	39.	D
10.	F	20.	H	30.	J	40.	G

1. **The correct answer is C.** This is a detail question, and the only substance in the apparatus the narrator identifies specifically is ivory (choice C). While the framework of the apparatus glittered, it did not necessarily contain glitter (choice A). The narrator also identifies a crystalline substance in the apparatus, but this merely means it contained a substance resembling crystal, not necessarily actual crystal, so choice B is not correct. Candles surrounded the apparatus after the Time Traveller laid it on a table, but the apparatus itself did not contain wax (choice D).

2. **The correct answer is J.** This is an inference question about the Time Traveller, and considering how he has gathered his colleagues together to examine the model of his time travelling apparatus, how he keeps pointing out its details, and how he boasts about how long it took him to make, it is clear he is proud of it. Therefore, choice J is the best answer. The fact that he has gathered his colleagues together also indicates that he does care about what they think, so choice G is wrong. The Time Traveller's pride and confidence make choice F an unlikely correct answer. Since the Time Traveller specifically says that he is not trying to trick his colleagues, and there is no evidence that he is lying, choice H is not the best answer.

3. **The correct answer is D.** The Medical Man only says that the model of the time travelling apparatus is "beautifully made," so you can only infer that he sincerely admires it. That means choice D is correct and choice B can be eliminated. There is no evidence that he finds the model amusing (choice A) or frightening (choice C).

4. **The correct answer is F.** Captain Nemo filled his submarine with extravagances such as fine art, a huge organ, enormous pearls, and large, opulent rooms. He

clearly values extravagance even though his own apartment is simplistic, which confirms choice F and eliminates choice J. However, we never learn what his goals for the *Nautilus* are in the passage, so choice G is not the best answer. The fact that he brings people into the *Nautilus* also proves he does not avoid them, which eliminates choice H.

5. **The correct answer is B.** While the narrator marvels at all the wonderments inside the *Nautilus*, he also says he feels like "a prisoner who dared scarcely hope that liberty might some day be obtained." Choice B sums up those conflicting feelings well. Choice A only hints at the narrator's positive feelings about the *Nautilus* while not indicating his negative ones. Choice D only exaggerates those negative feelings. There is no indication that he feels like a co-owner of the *Nautilus* (choice C).

6. **The correct answer is F.** Considering that there are hints Captain Nemo has taken the narrator on the *Nautilus* against his will, *surrender* is the likeliest definition of *submit* in this context. While *submit* can also mean *quit* (choice G), *humor* (choice H), or *send* (choice J), none of those words makes sense in the context of line 1.

7. **The correct answer is C.** Passage A specifies that the Time Traveller built his time machine and Passage B specifies that Captain Nemo built his luxurious submarine, both of which are very unusual machines. However, only Captain Nemo invites someone into his machine; the Time Traveller is merely showing off a model of his creation. Therefore, choice A is incorrect. The *Nautilus* submarine has a boat that looks like a torpedo, but there is no evidence that it contains an actual weapon in Passage B. Nothing about the Time

Traveller's machine is weaponlike at all. Therefore, choice B is incorrect. Only Captain Nemo explores the oceans, so choice D is wrong.

8. **The correct answer is G.** The answer to this detail question is at the beginning of the fifth paragraph of Passage B: "It was on a desert island that Captain Nemo had carried out the building of the *Nautilus* . . . ." Passage A contains no information about where the Time Traveller built his time machine. However, the Time Traveller does mention that it took him two years to build his machine, while we do not know how long it took Captain Nemo to build the *Nautilus*, so choice F is incorrect. Considering that the reader knows the Time Traveller built his time machine and Nemo built his *Nautilus* submarine, choice H can be eliminated. The appearances of both machines are described in their respective passages, so choice J is incorrect.

9. **The correct answer is C.** To solve this inference question, think about what the Time Traveller and Captain Nemo do in their respective passages: the Time Traveller builds a time machine and Nemo builds a submarine full of opulent rooms, strange machinery, and a gigantic organ. Clearly, they are both original thinkers, so choice C is the best answer. While such originality of thought may also signal eccentricity, the genuinely interested reactions of their colleagues indicate they are not tiresome, which eliminates choice A. While there is some indication that Captain Nemo has taken the narrator of Passage B prisoner, there is no evidence that the Time Traveller is plotting something evil (choice B), and their desire to travel through time and explore the ocean proves they are not wary of danger (choice D).

10. **The correct answer is F.** While the Time Traveller is very open about how his time machine works, Captain Nemo built his *Nautilus* on a desert island and secured its parts "from many different places . . . in order to maintain secrecy," according to the fifth paragraph of Passage B. This supports choice F. The Time Traveller says he does not want his colleagues to think he is a "quack," which indicates that he is concerned about his credibility, so choice G is wrong. Although Captain Nemo's inclusion of an organ in the *Nautilus* makes it clear that he needs music, there is nothing in Passage A that indicates that the Time Traveller does not need music, so choice H is not the best answer. Both characters clearly need adventure, so choice J is wrong.

11. **The correct answer is A.** This question asks you to make an inference from a statement in the passage. The

statement is part of a paragraph that describes the different reasons that gold is valuable. You can infer, then, that gold's beauty is one of the traits that makes it valuable (choice A). Choice B doesn't work because the first paragraph gives several other reasons why gold is valuable. There is no support for choices C and D.

12. **The correct answer is F.** This main idea question directs you to the last paragraph. The first sentence provides the correct answer, choice F. Choice G is a specific detail from the paragraph. Choice H is the main idea of the previous paragraph. Choice J is a specific detail from the previous paragraph.

13. **The correct answer is D.** This is a detail question that requires you to be careful. The third sentence of the next-to-last paragraph lists South Africa (choice D), Australia (choice B), and Yukon Territory (choice C). But the next sentence tells you that it was the "first of these" (referring to South Africa) that ended up providing an "estimated 40 percent" of the world's gold. This makes choice D correct. California (choice A) is mentioned earlier in the same paragraph but never in relation to the 40 percent.

14. **The correct answer is H.** The word *mentions* in the question suggests that this is a detail question. The discussion of Incas begins in the fourth paragraph. You will find Statement I mentioned specifically in the last sentence, so eliminate choice G for not containing Statement I. Statement II appears in the first sentence of the fifth paragraph, so eliminate choice F for not containing Statement II. Statement III is an incorrect detail—the final sentence of the sixth paragraph states that Cortes shipped "plundered" (stolen) gold and silver from the Aztecs' home—so eliminate choice J for containing Statement III. This leaves choice H, which affirms that Statements I and II are correct.

15. **The correct answer is D.** This straightforward detail question directs you right to the fourth paragraph. The second sentence provides the correct answer, choice D, by stating that the methods of Aztecs and Incas were "much more sophisticated than that of the Europeans." The paragraph doesn't compare Inca techniques with Aztec techniques (choice B). The paragraph doesn't even discuss Australians (choice C).

16. **The correct answer is F.** This is an inference question. You'll find the quote in the second sentence of the seventh paragraph, where you are told that the Incas gathered gold. The following sentence explains that Cortes had demanded money for Montezuma's life. Therefore, paying for his funeral (choice G), electing him

again (choice H), and having him assassinated (choice J) make no sense in context. *Ransom* means "money paid for someone's release," making choice F correct.

17. **The correct answer is D.** This is a vocabulary-in-context question. If you substitute each answer, you will discover that only choice D makes sense. The European empires searched for gold treasures until most of the treasures were *taken* from their rightful owners and brought to Europe. Although *seized* can be used to mean *understood* (choice A), *stopped* (choice B), or *afflicted* (choice C), none of those words makes sense in the context of line 65.

18. **The correct answer is G.** This is an inference question. The sixth paragraph says that Cortes plundered silver and gold. There is nothing following this to suggest that European explorers mined it (choice F) or traded ships for it (choice H). They certainly did not buy it with silver (choice J), because they were stealing silver as well. The only possible answer is choice G.

19. **The correct answer is A.** This is a detail question about the origins of some of the oldest gold artifacts. The first sentence of the second paragraph provides the correct answer by placing "some of the earliest known gold jewelry" near the Tigris and Euphrates rivers in Iraq. The gold artifacts from Ancient Egypt (choice B), Eastern Europe (choice C), and South America (choice D) are mentioned as coming after those in Iraq, so they would be younger, not older.

20. **The correct answer is H.** This is an inference question about the twentieth century. You will need to compare details to arrive at the correct answer. Find the first mention of the twentieth century in the fifth sentence of the next-to-last paragraph. The very next sentence, which says that "production actually declined throughout the century until the price of gold rose dramatically in 1980," proves choices F, G, and J wrong. If production declined and then sharply rose, then it did not "steadily" increase or decrease, and if it was said to decline *until* 1980, then it was not in decline *since* 1980. Only choice H remains, and it is correct. The next-to-last sentence states that only about ten thousand tons of gold were produced before the California gold rush. The last sentence states that over a hundred thousand tons have been produced since then. Based on the other numbers in the paragraph, the majority of that hundred thousand tons, and certainly an amount more than ten thousand tons, would have been produced in the twentieth century.

21. **The correct answer is D.** For this vocabulary-in-context question, look for the word *modest* in the second sentence of the second paragraph. Choice A, *extravagant*, means excessive. The first sentence of the ninth paragraph—"Blake never became prosperous as an artist during his lifetime"—refutes this as being the correct choice. In fact, it directly supports choice D, *moderate*, as being the right answer. A person's character, not his or her income, would be described as *virtuous* (choice B) or *prudish* (choice C).

22. **The correct answer is G.** Look at each choice for this inference question. Choice F contradicts the final sentence of the seventh paragraph. In fact, Blake disguised his comments in allegories, which makes choice G the right answer. Choice H might be tempting, because the second sentence of the sixth paragraph states that Blake sold many copies of *Songs of Innocence*. However, the second-to-last sentence in the fifth paragraph mentions that Blake could produce only a limited number of books; therefore, it's unlikely that he "earned most of his money from selling copies." The seventh paragraph says the French Revolution inspired some of Blake's work, but there is nothing to support that he visited France (choice J).

23. **The correct answer is A.** The word *suggested* indicates that this is an inference question. Put the quote, which appears in the last sentence of the passage, into your own words. Revolution has to do with change, and consciousness has to do with awareness. Looking at the options, choices B, C, and D simply do not make sense; only choice A does.

24. **The correct answer is G.** This detail question directs you to find information about the use of copper plates in traditional printing methods. Scan for "copper plates" throughout the passage. You'll find the answer in the final sentence of the third paragraph, which states that "illustrations . . . required a different press"; this makes choice G correct. The mention of color ink (choice F) relates to Blake's innovative method, not traditional etching. Choice H isn't mentioned in the passage. Choice J relates to who printed the plates.

25. **The correct answer is C.** This main idea question relates to the fifth paragraph. Blake's brother (choice A) is mentioned in the second paragraph. Choice B is the main idea of the first paragraph. Choice D might be tempting, but the fourth sentence in the fifth paragraph makes it clear that this wasn't the case. Choice C is correct. Blake did hope his technique would help other

artists (second sentence), but it was ultimately too complicated to use (fourth sentence).

26. **The correct answer is J.** The word *supports* indicates that this is an inference question for the fourth paragraph. Choices F and G aren't discussed in this paragraph. There is also nothing in the paragraph to support choice H. The third sentence supports choice J. If Blake etched away parts that would not print, then the remaining parts *would* print.

27. **The correct answer is A.** Consider each choice for this detail question about censorship during Blake's lifetime. The second and third sentences of the fifth paragraph provide the answer, choice A. This section says that many artists were "unable to publish their creative visions due to financial or moral restrictions," defining the latter as censorship "by the Church, the Crown, or both." The fifth sentence in the seventh paragraph disproves choice B. There is no support for choice C. Likewise, choice D is a broad statement without strong support.

28. **The correct answer is H.** This detail question requires you to figure out the order in which events occurred. The sixth paragraph says that Blake's first illuminated book was *Songs of Innocence*. *Songs of Experience* came out a year later. Both *Jerusalem* and Blake's tribute to Milton (*Milton, a Poem*) came out later in Blake's career, as mentioned in the next-to-last paragraph. Choices F, G, and J do not explain accurately when Blake wrote *Songs of Innocence*.

29. **The correct answer is B.** The word *suggests* indicates that this is an inference question. Nothing in the passage supports choice A. The first sentence of the passage mentions desktop publishing, and the rest of the passage discusses Blake's innovative publishing method, so choice B is a supportable inference. As for choice C, the author does not imply that Blake's works are copies of manuscripts from the Middle Ages, only that the term "illuminated books" was probably a reference to them. Nothing in the passage supports that Blake's method is easily reproduced (choice D).

30. **The correct answer is J.** The word for this vocabulary-in-context question is located in the sixth sentence of the fourth paragraph. Try each choice to see which fits. Choice F might be tempting, but the sentence says that the acid only sometimes burned the wrong part of the plate. Therefore, it wasn't "somewhat destructive" (although possibly *sometimes* destructive). The opposite of choice G is true. Choice H, "unique and interesting," doesn't make sense with the rest of the sentence.

Choice J is the only logical answer. *Tedious* means "dull or tiresome."

31. **The correct answer is C.** This is a detail question looking for specific support for the claim that transiting is exciting. The answer, choice C, appears in the first mention of transiting in the last sentence of the first paragraph: "This exciting new technique, called *transiting*, makes finding planets easier . . . ." There is no support for choice A. Although choices B and D are true statements, they do not answer the question, which asks what makes the technique exciting.

32. **The correct answer is F.** This is a vocabulary-in-context question for the term *eclipse*, which appears in the next-to-last sentence of the fifth paragraph. The phrase "moving in front of" in the next sentence provides the answer, choice F. Choice G appears in the last sentence of the second paragraph, but has nothing to do with an eclipse. The same holds true for choice H, which is an unrelated detail in the second sentence of the second paragraph. There is no evidence to support choice J.

33. **The correct answer is A.** For this two-part detail question about the Doppler method, you need to check all of the numbered statements. Scan for the term *Doppler*, which first appears in the fifth paragraph. The third sentence states that it is a method of "measuring slight movements in stars caused by the gravitational pull of their planets." This sentence supports both Statements I and II, so eliminate choices B and C for not containing both of these statements. Statement III does not apply to the Doppler method but rather to transiting, so eliminate choice D. You are left with the correct answer, choice A, as only Statements I and II are correct.

34. **The correct answer is H.** The phrase "one can tell" indicates that this is an inference question. The second sentence of the seventh paragraph states that the Doppler method was used to determine the mass of the object. Therefore, this method still provides useful information that the transiting technique does not, making choice F incorrect. Likewise, the third sentence in the fifth paragraph disproves choice G. The first three and last two sentences in the eighth paragraph refute choice J. Transiting can use store-bought telescopes, which are less expensive than those needed for the Doppler method. The next-to-last sentence of the final paragraph explains that "transiting affords astronomers the opportunity to find hundreds of new planets," making choice H correct.

35. **The correct answer is D.** Check each choice for this inference question about OGLE-TR-56b to find the correct answer. Choice A refers to a specific detail in the second sentence of the fourth paragraph, which actually cites 29 hours as the length of its *year*, not day. There is nothing to support choice B. Choice C Is a specific detail about other planets (Mercury, Venus, Earth, and Mars) that appears in the third sentence of the third paragraph. Choice D is the only valid inference. The second sentence of the first paragraph describes OGLE-TR-56b as being "larger...than any previously known planet," so it follows that it must be larger than Earth.

36. **The correct answer is J.** This is a two-part detail question. Statement I appears in the first sentence of the fifth paragraph. Statement II appears in the second sentence of the first paragraph. Statement III appears in the third sentence of the fourth paragraph. The only answer that includes all three statements is choice J. Choices F, G, and H do not cover all of the details about OGLE-TR-56b in the question.

37. **The correct answer is B.** This detail question about Earth's hazy atmosphere directs you to the final paragraph. The third sentence states that telescopes will indeed be launched, so choice A is incorrect. Furthermore, the reason that they will be sent into space is to overcome the problem of the Earth's hazy atmosphere, making choice B correct. There is no discussion in this paragraph about calculating gravitational pull (choice C), or about whether new planets are gaseous or rocky (choice D).

38. **The correct answer is H.** The word *claims* indicates that this is a detail question about what the sun looks like from the surface of OGLE-TR-56b. The only reference to "twin stars" (choice F) appears in the third sentence of the seventh paragraph, which does not discuss the way the sun appears from OGLE-TR-56b. The reference to "molten iron" (choice G) appears in the second sentence of the second paragraph, which refers to the surface of the planet, not the way the sun looks from its surface. Choice J is a detail from the last sentence of the fourth paragraph, which describes Earth, not OGLE-TR-56b. The previous sentence supports choice H as the correct answer.

39. **The correct answer is D.** Scan for Warsaw University to answer this detail question. There is no mention of the California study (choice A) in relation to the first use of transiting at Warsaw University, as discussed in the sixth paragraph. The first sentence of the third paragraph does say that OGLE-TR-56b is gaseous, but this detail doesn't relate to Warsaw University, so choice B is incorrect. The detail about 59 stars in choice C does relate to Warsaw University. However, this detail does not explain why transiting was first used there; it was an "indirect" discovery. The first sentence in the paragraph points to choice D as the right answer.

40. **The correct answer is G.** This is a main idea question about the fourth paragraph. Choice G is supported by all of the details in the paragraph, which explain that while scientists used to believe large planets couldn't have very small orbits, their discoveries about OGLE-TR-56b have changed that. Choice F is a specific detail found in the third sentence, not the main idea. Choice H is a detail from the first sentence of the second paragraph. Choice J Is wrong, because while the third paragraph discusses scientists' disproved beliefs about gaseous planets not having small orbits, there is no evidence that astronomers have now changed all of their ideas about planets.

SCIENCE

1.	B	11.	C	21.	A	31.	A
2.	G	12.	F	22.	F	32.	G
3.	A	13.	C	23.	D	33.	C
4.	J	14.	J	24.	J	34.	F
5.	B	15.	D	25.	D	35.	D
6.	F	16.	G	26.	F	36.	J
7.	C	17.	C	27.	C	37.	D
8.	G	18.	G	28.	H	38.	G
9.	B	19.	D	29.	D	39.	B
10.	H	20.	H	30.	G	40.	H

1. **The correct answer is B.** Both sets of data in Table 1 show inverse relationships between distance to light source (m) and the photocurrent in μA (a), meaning that they change in opposite directions. The change, however, is not linear; they do not necessarily change by the same amount. Choice B is the best choice because it depicts nonlinear, inverse variation. Choice A is incorrect because the graph is linear and varies directly, not inversely. Choice C is incorrect because the graph is linear, even if its inverse variation is appropriate. The data here do not have a linear relation. Choice D cannot be correct because it represents constant photocurrent, when the data clearly indicate changing values.

2. **The correct answer is G.** According to Table 2, the stopping potential varies with the color of light. The color of light is determined by its wavelength. Therefore, the stopping potential must depend on the wavelength. Choice F is incorrect because Study 2 did not vary the light intensity. Choice H is not correct because Study 2 did not vary the metal used. Choice J is not correct because the stopping potential changes for different colors of light. If it were constant, Table 2 would show the same value for all colors of light.

3. **The correct answer is A.** The fact that light intensity increases as distance decreases means that changing the distance to the light source is one way to change the light intensity. According to Table 1, the photo-current increases as the distance to the light source decreases. The photocurrent depends on the number of photoelectrons emitted from the metal plate. Therefore, the photocurrent increases as the light intensity increases. Choice B is incorrect because it states that the photocurrent decreases with increasing light intensity, an assertion that is the opposite of what the data show. Choice C is incorrect because there is nothing in Study 1

that tests for a threshold level. This conclusion cannot be reached based on the data provided. Choice D is incorrect because there is indeed a relationship between light intensity and photocurrent.

4. **The correct answer is J.** Energy is required to eject photoelectrons from a metal. According to Table 2, different wavelengths of light must have different amounts of energy to eject photoelectrons. Blue light must have the most energy of the colors tested because it requires the greatest stopping potential. Because the stopping potential for red is zero, red light must not have enough energy to eject photoelectrons. Choice F is incorrect because the intensity was constant throughout the experiment. Choice G contradicts the passage, which explains that light is made up of photons. Choice H is not indicated by the data or the passage. If photoelectrons were produced by red light, they could be detected.

5. **The correct answer is B.** The dependent variable is the factor that responds to a change in the independent variable. The independent variable in Study 1 is the distance to the light source, which is manipulated during the experiment. In response to these changes in distance, the magnitude of the photocurrent changes. Therefore, the magnitude of the photocurrent is the dependent variable. Choice A describes the independent variable. Choices C and D cite factors that are held constant in each part of the study and are, therefore, not dependent on any other factors.

6. **The correct answer is F.** Orange is a color between red and yellow, so use the stopping potential values from Table 2 to interpolate the approximate

Practice Test 2—ANSWERS

stopping potential of an orange filter. Since the three red trials yielded 0.0 volts and the three yellow trials yielded 0.4 volts, you can assume that a typical trial with an orange filter would yield a stopping potential between 0.0 and 0.4 volts. Choice G gives a stopping potential between those of yellow and green. Choice H gives one between those of green and blue. Choice J gives one greater than that of blue, which suggests a color closer to violet or white.

7. **The correct answer is C.** The passage states that about 70 percent of Earth's surface is water, so the remainder (100 percent – 70 percent = 30 percent) must be land. Choice A represents the percentage of Earth's surface covered by ocean. Choice B may be reminiscent of the paragraph that said almost half of the globe has no large land masses. However, ocean also covers portions of the remainder of the globe, adding up to 70 percent overall. Choice D is too small.

8. **The correct answer is G.** If oceans moderate weather, one would expect to find the mildest or least extreme weather in areas dominated by oceans. According to the passage, the Southern Hemisphere is dominated by oceans, so one would expect less extreme weather in the Southern Hemisphere. Choice F has the information reversed. The Northern Hemisphere is dominated by the continents, but that makes weather in the Northern Hemisphere generally more extreme than in the Southern Hemisphere. Choice H confuses the hemispheres. The Northern Hemisphere is dominated by land masses, not by oceans. Choice J also confuses the hemispheres. The Southern Hemisphere is dominated by oceans, not by land masses.

9. **The correct answer is B.** To find the answer, locate –4,000 m on the vertical axis. Then read over to the curve. Look down to the horizontal axis to identify the percentage associated with this point. You find that 60 percent of Earth's surface is above about –4,000 m. The question asks for the percentage above this depth, but still below sea level. You know from the passage and the graph that 30 percent of Earth's surface is above sea level, so the curve must cross the zero-meter mark at 30 percent. The difference between these two points, 60 percent – 30 percent, is the answer, 30 percent. Choice A is too small to be correct. Choice C is the percentage of Earth's surface above approximately –4,000 m, but the question does not ask for all of the surface above this point. Choice D is too large and suggests that only 10 percent of Earth's surface could be above sea level.

10. **The correct answer is H.** Look for the point at which the lines representing the temperature of maximum density and the freezing point of water intersect. This happens at the point corresponding to 25 percent on the horizontal axis, so above 25 percent salinity, the temperature of maximum density of water is below the freezing point of water, as opposed to below 25 percent salinity, where it is above the freezing point. For choices F and G, the freezing point of water is below the temperature of maximum density. For choice J, the freezing point of water has already been above the temperature of maximum density.

11. **The correct answer is C.** Use the graph of salinity vs. freezing point in Figure 3 to extrapolate the missing value. For every 10 percent gain in salinity, the freezing point drops approximately 0.5°C, going from about –1°C at 20 percent to about –1.5°C at 30 percent to just under –2°C at 40 percent. Continuing this trend, at 50 percent salinity the freezing point would be about –2.5°C. Choice A changes the wrong variable in the wrong direction, giving the temperature of maximum density at 0 percent salinity. Choice B also goes in the wrong direction, giving the freezing point at 0 percent salinity. Choice D goes in the right direction but again changes the wrong variable, giving the temperature of maximum density at 50 percent salinity.

12. **The correct answer is F.** If curare did attack the brain, all of the frog's muscles would have been paralyzed because the brain would not send nerve impulses to *any* part of the body. So the hypothesis that the brain is attacked by curare must be rejected. Choice G is incorrect because the leg muscle was still able to contract, signifying that curare does not attack muscles. Choice H is incorrect because curare failed to prevent the nerve impulse from passing through the sciatic nerve. Choice J is incorrect because all muscles fed by the circulatory system did become paralyzed. The only muscle that did not become paralyzed was the one from which incoming blood was blocked.

13. **The correct answer is C.** Experiment 2 revealed that the muscle itself was unaffected by curare. Because the muscle could be stimulated to contract by an electric current, curare had not directly attacked the muscle. Choice A is not correct because if curare prevented electric impulses from traveling through the body, the muscle would not have contracted when stimulated by the electric current. Choice B is incorrect because the experimental setup was the same as for Experiment 1. The muscle *did* contract under those conditions so one cannot conclude that curare directly attacked nerves.

Choice D is incorrect because the experiment never addresses the effects of curare on bones.

14. **The correct answer is J.** Experiment 3 separated the muscle from the nerve. Only the nerve was exposed to curare. Any effect on muscle contraction, therefore, must be attributed only to the effect of curare on the nerve. Choice F is incorrect because the circulatory system was eliminated as a factor. No blood was circulating through the isolated nerve and muscle. Choice G is incorrect because the muscle was a control in this experiment. It was not exposed to curare. Choice H is also incorrect because the brain was not part of the experiment.

15. **The correct answer is D.** Although curare does not attack the circulatory system, it is transported in blood. In Experiment 1, when blood was prevented from reaching a leg, nerve impulses were still able to reach the leg. Therefore, when curare is not added to the blood, it does not cause paralysis. Choice A is incorrect because there is no information describing a breakdown in curare. Choice B is incorrect because the animal dies from the effects of curare. There is no indication that the curare wears off before death occurs. Choice C is incorrect because no humans were tested for the effects of curare in these experiments. Humans and other animals may or may not be affected by curare.

16. **The correct answer is G.** Muscles remain in the relaxed state unless stimulated. Stimulation occurs when acetylcholine binds to a muscle receptor site. If that site is blocked because curare is already occupying the site, the muscle cell will not contract. The muscle will be paralyzed in the relaxed state. Choice F is not correct because acetylcholine esterase causes a muscle cell to relax after it has contracted. If curare interfered with the action of acetylcholine esterase, the muscle cells would become paralyzed in the contracted state. Choice H is not correct because Experiment 3 showed that nerve impulses could move through a nerve bathed in curare. Choice J is not correct because Experiment 1 showed that nerve impulses from the brain to muscles were not affected when blood circulation was cut off to the muscle.

17. **The correct answer is C.** In describing Experiment 1, the passage states that muscle contractions cause the attached bones to move. It follows that, by paralyzing muscles and preventing them from contracting, curare would also prevent broken bones from moving. Choice A is incorrect because, as Bernard discovered in Experiment 1, curare has no effect on the central nervous system, including the brain, where general anesthetics do their work. Curare does not put animals "to sleep"; it only paralyzes muscles. Choice B misses the mark because pain is transmitted from nerve to nerve, and Experiment 1 shows that curare does not interrupt the passage of impulses through nerves. Choice D says the opposite of what is true, because curare *prevents* contractions by paralyzing the muscles.

18. **The correct answer is G.** Notice that electronegativity increases from left to right in a given period, and it decreases from top to bottom in a given family. Therefore, the electronegativity of Br should be greater than that of Se (2.6) and between that of Cl (3.2) and I (2.7). In other words, it should be in the range of 2.8 – 3.1. Choices F, H, and J do not fall in this range.

19. **The correct answer is D.** Remember, a greater value for electronegativity means a greater attraction for electrons. No element on the list has a higher electronegativity (4.0) than fluorine. Choice A is incorrect as hydrogen's electronegativity is about half that of fluorine. Choice B reverses the criterion for electronegativity. Cesium has the smallest value for electronegativity (0.79), so it is the *least* electronegative element shown. Although choice C, astatine, belongs to the most electronegative group in the periodic table, it is the least electronegative element in that group.

20. **The correct answer is H.** The polarity of a molecule is determined by the difference in electronegativity between its atoms. A smaller difference in electronegativity means less polarity. In a nonpolar molecule, therefore, if you subtract the value of the smaller electronegativity from that of the larger electronegativity, you should get a result near zero. Since two atoms of the same element, such as Cl_2, have identical values for electronegativity, the result of subtracting one electronegativity from the other is exactly 0, making the molecule nonpolar. In choice F, the electronegativity values for Cl (3.2) and Na (0.93) yield a difference of: $3.2 – 0.93 = 2.27$. This is greater than the value for Cl_2, so choice F should be eliminated. In choice G, the difference in electronegativity values for O (3.4) and Mg (1.3) is: $3.4 – 1.3 = 2.1$. Thus, MgO is more polar than Cl_2. You can also eliminate choice J, since subtracting the value for Be (1.6) from that of O (3.4) yields 1.8, which is much greater than the value for Cl_2.

21. **The correct answer is A.** In this case, use the reverse reasoning from that used to find the answer to Question 20. Look for the *greatest* difference between the electronegativities of the bonded atoms. The difference for K–Cl (choice A) is 2.38, and none of the other

differences are as great. The difference for choice B, Ba–Se, is 1.7; for choice C, Na–S, the difference is 1.67; and for choice D, Be–O, it is 1.8. The question asks you to identify the electron bond that is *most* polar, so you can eliminate choices B, C, and D.

22. **The correct answer is F.** LiBr would be a polar molecule, because lithium and bromide have different electronegativities. The passage states that polar molecules have a relative concentration of negativity at the end that is closer to the more electronegative atom. In this case, bromide has a greater electronegativity (between 2.7 and 3.2) than that of lithium (1.0), so the relative concentration of negativity would reside at the end closer to the bromide atom. Choice G says the opposite of this. Choice H describes the behavior of a nonpolar molecule, in which both atoms have the same electronegativity. Choice J does not make sense.

23. **The correct answer is B.** Figure 1 plots cigarette smoking rates vs. number of cancer deaths. The resulting graph is a scatterplot in which both variables change in the same direction. As the percentage of cigarette smokers (horizontal) increases, the number of cancer-related deaths (vertical) tends to increase as well. This signifies a direct relationship. Choice A is incorrect because it takes this direct relationship a step too far. The fact that smoking rates and cancer deaths change in the same direction does not automatically imply cause and effect; even if it did, one would probably find it hard to believe that higher mortality rates cause more people to smoke. Choice C says the opposite of what is indicated by the graph. Choice D is wrong because the graph does indicate a pattern.

24. **The correct answer is J.** This is an except question, meaning that three of the four answer choices will be supported by Table 1. The correct answer will be the one that is *false*. Choices F, G, and H are all supported by the numbers in the table. Choice J, however, is *not* supported by the data, because the percentage of Rhode Island females who attempt to quit smoking is actually lower than the percentage of Rhode Island males.

25. **The correct answer is D.** Even if a correlation exists between cigarette smoking and cancer-related deaths, it's difficult to say that one definitely causes the other. To isolate cigarette smoking as a cause of cancer, those conducting the study would need to eliminate other possible causes, such as diet, environmental pollution, and exposure to toxic chemicals. Choice A is incorrect because, although there is a correlation between smoking rates and cancer-related deaths, the question

is based on proving that smoking causes the *incidence* of cancer itself. Dying from cancer and developing cancer are two separate variables and would, therefore, need to be tested separately. Choice B is incorrect for two reasons: there does not appear to be as strong an inverse correlation between quit attempts and cancer-related deaths, and, more importantly, those who are listed as having attempted to quit were still smokers. Choice C is incorrect because there's no reason to believe that the health foundation would have tampered with the results of its own study.

26. **The correct answer is F.** This question relates to the second data group in Table 1, number of cancer deaths. In all ten listed states, the number of males who died from cancer was significantly higher than the number of females who died from cancer. Having only these data to consult, it's reasonable to conclude that New Jersey would be likely to have a similar result. The only answer greater than 177, the number of females, is choice F, 246. Choices G, H, and J are too small to make sense.

27. **The correct answer is C.** To test the given hypothesis, the foundation would need to measure the effects of the independent variable, quitting smoking, on the dependent variable, cancer mortality. The best way to do this is to monitor two groups—one consisting of smokers and one consisting of people who have successfully quit smoking—and compare the number of cancer-related deaths within each group. Choice A is incorrect because helping people to quit smoking would do little to test the hypothesis unless some plan were also devised to measure the consequences. Choice B is incorrect because *attempts* to quit smoking may or may not result in actually quitting; all of the quit attempts described in the current study, for instance, were by those who still smoked. Choice D is incorrect because it introduces a specific comparison between lung cancer and other cancers, which has no bearing on the comparison between the two variables presented by the hypothesis.

28. **The correct answer is H.** The passage specifically tells us that the punctuated equilibrium model hypothesizes long periods of stasis before new species evolve, whereas the phyletic gradualism model sees changes as occurring continuously. This means that in the phyletic gradualism model, new species evolve over relatively short periods of time, as compared with punctuated equilibrium. Choice F can be eliminated because the passage specifically discusses differences in the evolutionary time frames that both models present. The time that elapses between the development of species,

therefore, cannot be equal in both models. Choice G is incorrect, again because the phyletic model views change as occurring constantly. Choice J is not supported; elapsed time is one of the crucial differences between these two models of evolution, so there must be some relevance.

29. **The correct answer is D.** Evolution involves the production of new species from old ones. Since both models picture evolutionary processes, both posit that new species eventually evolve from previous species. Choice A cannot be correct because only the phyletic gradualism model shows a relatively rapid development of species; in the punctuated equilibrium model, by contrast, new species evolve only after long periods of stasis. Choice B is also incorrect because, again, only the phyletic gradualism model shows gradual changes in structure. Choice C can be eliminated because in the punctuated equilibrium model, species form in abrupt spurts rather than through continuous change.

30. **The correct answer is G.** Figure 2 holds two clues that reflect the punctuated equilibrium model: longer periods of time between the evolution of species, and greater structural differences between new species and their parent species. Choice F is incorrect because Figure 1 depicts gradual changes occurring in short steps, which is characteristic of phyletic gradualism. Choice H can be eliminated because neither figure connotes a longer survival time than the other. The passage states that differences between offspring and parents can aid survival and promote speciation, but there is no evidence to indicate whether longer survival results from gradual, continuous evolution or from sudden changes after long periods of equilibrium. Choice J can also be eliminated, because Figure 2 depicts significant changes in species that vary more dramatically from the parent species than those changes reflected in Figure 1.

31. **The correct answer is A.** The phyletic gradualism model argues that changes between species occur very gradually. According to this model, long periods of time must elapse before significant changes in species can be observed. To test this hypothesis, it would be helpful to examine the fossil record to determine just how significant the differences were between new species and their parent species, as reflected in different layers of rock. Minor variations in species would support the phyletic gradualism model, whereas significant differences between the species would cast doubt on this model and lend support to the punctuated equilibrium view. Choices B and C are incorrect because

they suggest examining evidence that is irrelevant to the question of whether species changes were gradual, as the model proposes. A scientific test must help researchers to either support or refute a hypothesis. The hypothesis that "species changes occur gradually" cannot be addressed by determining *why* a species became extinct or *how* it survived its environment. Choice D can also be eliminated, because the question of *whether* species are related is less important to testing the hypothesis than knowing *how different* new species are from their parent species.

32. **The correct answer is G.** Compared with the phyletic gradualism model, the punctuated equilibrium model posits that a greater amount of time passes between the points at which new species appear. These larger time spans between new species account for the fact that some layers of rock hold fossils with the same structures. In the punctuated equilibrium model, intermediate species forms do not exist because the changes between species are abrupt. Choice F is incorrect because fossil pattern 1 shows no evidence of new species having evolved. Choice H can be eliminated because fossil pattern 3 shows relatively uniform and gradual evolutionary changes, which are characteristic of the phyletic gradualism model. Choice J is incorrect for two reasons: fossil pattern 4 shows gradual changes in relatively short spans of time and also has the evolutionary process reversed, with the youngest fossils found in the oldest layers of rock.

33. **The correct answer is C.** The fossils in pattern 3 show gradual changes in structure over time. Each layer of rock holds a slightly different shell. Choice A is incorrect because no evolutionary changes have occurred in fossil pattern 1. Choice B should be eliminated because fossil pattern 2 shows few and abrupt structural changes, which is more typical of the punctuated equilibrium model. Choice D is incorrect because, again, fossil pattern 4 has the evolutionary process reversed, with the youngest fossils found in the oldest layers of rock.

34. **The correct answer is F.** Reread the section describing punctuated equilibrium and you'll find the following statement: "...the structure of the new species is significantly different from that of its parent species." Choice G is incorrect because it describes a characteristic of the phyletic gradualism model. Choice H can be ruled out because both models of evolution describe how *changes* occur between parent species and new species. Choice J is incorrect because it is too extreme. The description of punctuated equilibrium states that a

new species differs significantly from its parent species, but it does not claim that the new species shares no structural commonalities with its parent species.

35. **The correct answer is D.** Table 1 shows that the rate of tongue flicking increases to 76 flicks per minute at a time 1 minute after the snake strikes. Therefore, in Experiment 2, one would expect a similar response 1 minute after a hypothetical strike at minute 8. Choice A is incorrect because the results of Experiment 1 indicate that a dramatic increase in tongue flicking follows a strike. Choice B is incorrect, too. If you chose this as the answer, you may have focused on the repeating pattern in Table 2. If this pattern were followed, a rate of 3 flicks per minute would be expected at minute 9. However, the pattern in Table 2 was generated in an experiment in which the snake did NOT strike. This question relates to a snake striking, which is reflected in the data for Experiment 1. Choice C is incorrect but is closer to the correct answer.

36. **The correct answer is J.** The rate of tongue flicking remained slow and the snake did not respond in any other way to the prey placed out of reach. The only explanation justified by the data is that rattlesnakes do not respond to prey that is out of reach. Although choices F, G, and H may be true statements, they are incorrect. Reread the question. It doesn't ask for what is *true*, but for what *conclusion can be drawn from the data*. Since the snake is not responding to the mouse in this experiment, there is no reason to conclude that it responds to *any* stimuli.

37. **The correct answer is D.** Data from Experiment 1 clearly shows that the rate of tongue flicking sharply rises directly after the snake strikes. In Experiment 2, the snake does *not* strike, and the rate of tongue flicking remains relatively constant at a low level. Therefore, it can be concluded that the act of striking stimulates tongue flicking. Choice A is wrong because when mouse odors were placed near the snake, no increase in tongue flicking occurred. Choice B is incorrect because in Experiment 1, tongue flicking remained low for the first 4 minutes even though the snake was exposed to a live mouse. Tongue flicking increased only after the snake struck. Choice C is also incorrect. You might reach this conclusion because in the first 4 minutes of Experiment 1, the snake was exposed to a live mouse and the rate of tongue flicking remained low. However, it increased after the snake struck and while the mouse was still alive. So a live mouse did not inhibit tongue flicking.

38. **The correct answer is G.** The rattlesnake's rate of tongue flicking varied from one mouse to the other. The only apparent difference between the mice was the way in which they were killed. So this difference was significant. Choice F is incorrect because it was the scientists that killed the mouse without venom. Choice H is wrong because the experiment is not designed to differentiate learned vs. unlearned behavior; the experiment provides no evidence for or against this hypothesis. Choice J is also not correct. If the state of the mouse being dead stimulated the rattlesnake's tongue flicking, then tongue flicking would have been high regardless of the means by which the mouse had been killed; however, this was not the result. The rate of tongue flicking remained low when the snake was exposed to the mouse that was killed by other means.

39. **The correct answer is B.** The data from Experiment 2 are summarized in Table 2, which shows the number of tongue flicks remaining relatively constant as time passes. The graph that describes this relationship should, therefore, resemble a horizontal line. Choice A is incorrect because it actually represents the data from Experiment 1, with the number of tongue flicks jumping from a low constant to a high constant halfway across the graph. Choice C is incorrect because it depicts a steady increase in tongue flicking during the first several minutes, which results in a constant high level. This is inaccurate even for Experiment 1. Choice D completely misses the mark by showing a steady decrease during the first several minutes, followed by a constant low level. This is vastly different from anything indicated by either table.

40. **The correct answer is H.** This experiment would eliminate all variables *except* rattlesnake venom. If the snake does not follow the trail of the venom, then the hypothesis will not be supported. If the snake does follow the trail of the venom, then the hypothesis will be supported. Choice F is not correct. Carefully reread the question and the opening paragraph. Snakes do use their tongues to sense odors, but depriving a snake of this sense cannot support or refute the hypothesis that a rattlesnake follows the scent of its own venom; under those conditions, it cannot follow the scent of anything. Choices G and J can be eliminated for the same reason. Neither answer can be correct because the question asks whether a snake follows the scent of its own venom; there is no way of answering the question if there is no venom in the experiment.

Sample Essay: Score 1

Ideas and Analysis:	Score = 1
Development and Support:	Score = 1
Organization:	Score = 1
Language Use and Conventions:	Score = 1

> I don't care if noone or anyone is watching me cause I'm not doing anything wrong or will be so why should I care? I see cameras wherever I go the movies and the mall and restaurants and they don't hurt me and I don't do anything that's worth being bothered about. Why should you care, are you doing illegal things? Cameras are used to make movies and TV shows and I watch a ton of videos so do you want people to stop making things on Youtube or put things on Instagram? I got a camera on my phone and I take pictures of things all the time, so should I stop doing that? I like that every time I buy a new phone that cameras get better and the pictures I can take wherever I go get much better, so I don't want to change that. You shouldn't want that either, so people should be able to make cameras better and use them too.

Scoring Explanation

Ideas and Analysis: Score = 1

The writer of this argument provides minimal ideas or insight that relates to the topic at hand; instead of offering an analysis of the advantages and disadvantages of surveillance, the essay quickly veers off on a tangent with scattered thoughts regarding phone cameras and making YouTube videos. The end result is an argument that widely misses the mark and fails to address the essay task.

Development and Support: Score = 1

There is little or no evidence of thoughtful idea development in this essay. The resulting essay is a loose collection of thoughts that fail to offer a cogent perspective on the benefits or dangers of the rise of so-called surveillance culture. There is also no support offered to bolster the writer's thoughts, and little provided to compel the reader into agreeing with his or her murky viewpoint.

Organization: Score = 1

The ideas presented in this argument are largely disconnected from a central unifying theme that addresses the specific essay task. There is no assertion of a clear position regarding surveillance and a lack of well-organized ideas to lend credence and support; instead, what's offered is a loose amalgam of disorganized thoughts on marginally related subjects.

Language Use and Conventions: Score = 1

The response provided shows a lack of basic grammar skills mastery and a deficiency in effective language mechanics. The weaknesses and errors demonstrated throughout the essay ultimately lead to an ineffective argument that fails to address the given task.

Practice Test 2—ANSWERS

SAMPLE ESSAY: SCORE 6

Ideas and Analysis:	Score = 6
Development and Support:	Score = 6
Organization:	Score = 6
Language Use and Conventions:	Score = 6

Perhaps Big Brother *is* watching—surveillance is a part of world and time in which we live, a time when increasingly sophisticated forms of technology exist not only to watch us, but also to heal us, to connect us, and to make our lives easier.

Is the rise of the so-called "surveillance culture" an unfortunate symptom of the expanding technological era? No. Surveillance equipment, like *most* technological advancements, is a benefit, providing tools whose purpose is to make our society better.

The assertion that expansive surveillance provides a benefit to society is not an abstract one. Two years ago, my aunt was walking to her car in a multi-level parking garage after a day of shopping. It was mid-afternoon, and out of nowhere she was attacked. She was knocked to the ground, her bags and purse were stolen—but that wasn't the worst of it. She also lost a sense of comfort and ease that day, and she became afraid to go into unattended public places. Around every corner and in every shady area she felt a real potential for danger. Worse still, the burglar had her identification and address. These feelings persisted long after the incident, and the *only* thing that made her feel better was when the person that robbed her was caught. How did they catch him? They reviewed surveillance footage of the incident and matched the image of the criminal to existing mug shots. Without surveillance, they may never have caught him, and the peace of mind that he stole from my aunt along with her things may have been lost forever. What better way to see the benefits of a technology than through a clear example of its success?

The purpose of surveillance technology is to keep a watchful eye on things and make people safer. Why should we limit that? Those who race to label us a "culture of surveillance" are merely referring to the increased use of a technology that has proven itself to be beneficial. Do we live in a "culture of penicillin" because of its increased use?

Some bemoan the notion that surveillance has gone too far, and has reached the point to where we've lost the right to expect some measure of personal privacy, but in reality that notion is an exaggeration. There are certainly places where we are not being watched, and any misuse of surveillance technology should not count as a strike against its very existence.

Besides, history is full of examples of technological advances that have improved society but have also included a social cost. Should doctors and hospitals get rid of X-rays because of the radiation they emit? Some argue that the Internet has created a generation of self-involved people with limited attention spans and an inability to make meaningful connections. Should we abandon all of the great things the Internet has provided? It often takes time to figure out how to responsibly use new technologies in their relative infancies. But as a society we learn and progress, often through trial and error. It's true, there is some measure of privacy that is traded away when surveillance technology is employed. But would you rather be safe or unwatched?

Scoring Explanation

Ideas and Analysis: Score = 6

This essay demonstrates a thoughtful, carefully considered analysis of the role surveillance should have in our society and the culture at large. The ideas are well integrated and support a clear, nuanced perspective on the issue—including insightful social commentary (i.e., "culture of penicillin," inherent trade-offs in historical technological advances) and a powerful personal angle (the writer's aunt's mugger getting caught thanks to surveillance footage). The end result is a compelling and convincing argument that capably frames the issue—from a personal perspective to its larger social relevancy.

Development and Support: Score = 6

From the writer's provocative opening notion ("Perhaps Big Brother *is* watching") to the thought-provoking conclusion ("would you rather be safe or unwatched?"), the writer galvanizes a well-stocked toolkit of capably developed ideas in support of the notion that surveillance is largely a benefit to society. This assertion is examined from various levels (impact on an individual; impact on society; impact on culture), with an impressive degree of development and deft deployment of support. The examination of quick cultural labels and their impact is particularly deft, and the writer's willingness to concede that surveillance may indeed contain a social cost demonstrates a confidence and willingness to examine the essay task from more than just a narrow lens.

Organization: Score = 6

This argument demonstrates an impressive mastery of structure and organization. The writer delivers a compelling piece of writing with clear focus, from its attention-grabbing opening and thoughtful, multi-faceted analysis to its memorable closing. Rather than simply offering a straightforward defense of one closed perspective on the value of surveillance technology, the writer capably weaves in micro and macro level thoughts, and an examination of hasty cultural labels and society's responsibility to learn how to best use new technology (often through trial and error).

Language Use and Conventions: Score = 6

The writer of this argument exhibits a commendable use of varied language and a skilled hand at writing conventions for crafting effective essays. The word choices made by the writer are rich, thoughtful, and varied without being dry or academic, and sentences are well-constructed, resulting in an impressive essay that's both enjoyable to read and convincing.

English Test

1. Ⓐ Ⓑ Ⓒ Ⓓ 16. Ⓕ Ⓖ Ⓗ Ⓙ 31. Ⓐ Ⓑ Ⓒ Ⓓ 46. Ⓕ Ⓖ Ⓗ Ⓙ 61. Ⓐ Ⓑ Ⓒ Ⓓ
2. Ⓕ Ⓖ Ⓗ Ⓙ 17. Ⓐ Ⓑ Ⓒ Ⓓ 32. Ⓕ Ⓖ Ⓗ Ⓙ 47. Ⓐ Ⓑ Ⓒ Ⓓ 62. Ⓕ Ⓖ Ⓗ Ⓙ
3. Ⓐ Ⓑ Ⓒ Ⓓ 18. Ⓕ Ⓖ Ⓗ Ⓙ 33. Ⓐ Ⓑ Ⓒ Ⓓ 48. Ⓕ Ⓖ Ⓗ Ⓙ 63. Ⓐ Ⓑ Ⓒ Ⓓ
4. Ⓕ Ⓖ Ⓗ Ⓙ 19. Ⓐ Ⓑ Ⓒ Ⓓ 34. Ⓕ Ⓖ Ⓗ Ⓙ 49. Ⓐ Ⓑ Ⓒ Ⓓ 64. Ⓕ Ⓖ Ⓗ Ⓙ
5. Ⓐ Ⓑ Ⓒ Ⓓ 20. Ⓕ Ⓖ Ⓗ Ⓙ 35. Ⓐ Ⓑ Ⓒ Ⓓ 50. Ⓕ Ⓖ Ⓗ Ⓙ 65. Ⓐ Ⓑ Ⓒ Ⓓ
6. Ⓕ Ⓖ Ⓗ Ⓙ 21. Ⓐ Ⓑ Ⓒ Ⓓ 36. Ⓕ Ⓖ Ⓗ Ⓙ 51. Ⓐ Ⓑ Ⓒ Ⓓ 66. Ⓕ Ⓖ Ⓗ Ⓙ
7. Ⓐ Ⓑ Ⓒ Ⓓ 22. Ⓕ Ⓖ Ⓗ Ⓙ 37. Ⓐ Ⓑ Ⓒ Ⓓ 52. Ⓕ Ⓖ Ⓗ Ⓙ 67. Ⓐ Ⓑ Ⓒ Ⓓ
8. Ⓕ Ⓖ Ⓗ Ⓙ 23. Ⓐ Ⓑ Ⓒ Ⓓ 38. Ⓕ Ⓖ Ⓗ Ⓙ 53. Ⓐ Ⓑ Ⓒ Ⓓ 68. Ⓕ Ⓖ Ⓗ Ⓙ
9. Ⓐ Ⓑ Ⓒ Ⓓ 24. Ⓕ Ⓖ Ⓗ Ⓙ 39. Ⓐ Ⓑ Ⓒ Ⓓ 54. Ⓕ Ⓖ Ⓗ Ⓙ 69. Ⓐ Ⓑ Ⓒ Ⓓ
10. Ⓕ Ⓖ Ⓗ Ⓙ 25. Ⓐ Ⓑ Ⓒ Ⓓ 40. Ⓕ Ⓖ Ⓗ Ⓙ 55. Ⓐ Ⓑ Ⓒ Ⓓ 70. Ⓕ Ⓖ Ⓗ Ⓙ
11. Ⓐ Ⓑ Ⓒ Ⓓ 26. Ⓕ Ⓖ Ⓗ Ⓙ 41. Ⓐ Ⓑ Ⓒ Ⓓ 56. Ⓕ Ⓖ Ⓗ Ⓙ 71. Ⓐ Ⓑ Ⓒ Ⓓ
12. Ⓕ Ⓖ Ⓗ Ⓙ 27. Ⓐ Ⓑ Ⓒ Ⓓ 42. Ⓕ Ⓖ Ⓗ Ⓙ 57. Ⓐ Ⓑ Ⓒ Ⓓ 72. Ⓕ Ⓖ Ⓗ Ⓙ
13. Ⓐ Ⓑ Ⓒ Ⓓ 28. Ⓕ Ⓖ Ⓗ Ⓙ 43. Ⓐ Ⓑ Ⓒ Ⓓ 58. Ⓕ Ⓖ Ⓗ Ⓙ 73. Ⓐ Ⓑ Ⓒ Ⓓ
14. Ⓕ Ⓖ Ⓗ Ⓙ 29. Ⓐ Ⓑ Ⓒ Ⓓ 44. Ⓕ Ⓖ Ⓗ Ⓙ 59. Ⓐ Ⓑ Ⓒ Ⓓ 74. Ⓕ Ⓖ Ⓗ Ⓙ
15. Ⓐ Ⓑ Ⓒ Ⓓ 30. Ⓕ Ⓖ Ⓗ Ⓙ 45. Ⓐ Ⓑ Ⓒ Ⓓ 60. Ⓕ Ⓖ Ⓗ Ⓙ 75. Ⓐ Ⓑ Ⓒ Ⓓ

Math Test

1. Ⓐ Ⓑ Ⓒ Ⓓ Ⓔ 16. Ⓕ Ⓖ Ⓗ Ⓙ Ⓚ 31. Ⓐ Ⓑ Ⓒ Ⓓ Ⓔ 46. Ⓕ Ⓖ Ⓗ Ⓙ Ⓚ
2. Ⓕ Ⓖ Ⓗ Ⓙ Ⓚ 17. Ⓐ Ⓑ Ⓒ Ⓓ Ⓔ 32. Ⓕ Ⓖ Ⓗ Ⓙ Ⓚ 47. Ⓐ Ⓑ Ⓒ Ⓓ Ⓔ
3. Ⓐ Ⓑ Ⓒ Ⓓ Ⓔ 18. Ⓕ Ⓖ Ⓗ Ⓙ Ⓚ 33. Ⓐ Ⓑ Ⓒ Ⓓ Ⓔ 48. Ⓕ Ⓖ Ⓗ Ⓙ Ⓚ
4. Ⓕ Ⓖ Ⓗ Ⓙ Ⓚ 19. Ⓐ Ⓑ Ⓒ Ⓓ Ⓔ 34. Ⓕ Ⓖ Ⓗ Ⓙ Ⓚ 49. Ⓐ Ⓑ Ⓒ Ⓓ Ⓔ
5. Ⓐ Ⓑ Ⓒ Ⓓ Ⓔ 20. Ⓕ Ⓖ Ⓗ Ⓙ Ⓚ 35. Ⓐ Ⓑ Ⓒ Ⓓ Ⓔ 50. Ⓕ Ⓖ Ⓗ Ⓙ Ⓚ
6. Ⓕ Ⓖ Ⓗ Ⓙ Ⓚ 21. Ⓐ Ⓑ Ⓒ Ⓓ Ⓔ 36. Ⓕ Ⓖ Ⓗ Ⓙ Ⓚ 51. Ⓐ Ⓑ Ⓒ Ⓓ Ⓔ
7. Ⓐ Ⓑ Ⓒ Ⓓ Ⓔ 22. Ⓕ Ⓖ Ⓗ Ⓙ Ⓚ 37. Ⓐ Ⓑ Ⓒ Ⓓ Ⓔ 52. Ⓕ Ⓖ Ⓗ Ⓙ Ⓚ
8. Ⓕ Ⓖ Ⓗ Ⓙ Ⓚ 23. Ⓐ Ⓑ Ⓒ Ⓓ Ⓔ 38. Ⓕ Ⓖ Ⓗ Ⓙ Ⓚ 53. Ⓐ Ⓑ Ⓒ Ⓓ Ⓔ
9. Ⓐ Ⓑ Ⓒ Ⓓ Ⓔ 24. Ⓕ Ⓖ Ⓗ Ⓙ Ⓚ 39. Ⓐ Ⓑ Ⓒ Ⓓ Ⓔ 54. Ⓕ Ⓖ Ⓗ Ⓙ Ⓚ
10. Ⓕ Ⓖ Ⓗ Ⓙ Ⓚ 25. Ⓐ Ⓑ Ⓒ Ⓓ Ⓔ 40. Ⓕ Ⓖ Ⓗ Ⓙ Ⓚ 55. Ⓐ Ⓑ Ⓒ Ⓓ Ⓔ
11. Ⓐ Ⓑ Ⓒ Ⓓ Ⓔ 26. Ⓕ Ⓖ Ⓗ Ⓙ Ⓚ 41. Ⓐ Ⓑ Ⓒ Ⓓ Ⓔ 56. Ⓕ Ⓖ Ⓗ Ⓙ Ⓚ
12. Ⓕ Ⓖ Ⓗ Ⓙ Ⓚ 27. Ⓐ Ⓑ Ⓒ Ⓓ Ⓔ 42. Ⓕ Ⓖ Ⓗ Ⓙ Ⓚ 57. Ⓐ Ⓑ Ⓒ Ⓓ Ⓔ
13. Ⓐ Ⓑ Ⓒ Ⓓ Ⓔ 28. Ⓕ Ⓖ Ⓗ Ⓙ Ⓚ 43. Ⓐ Ⓑ Ⓒ Ⓓ Ⓔ 58. Ⓕ Ⓖ Ⓗ Ⓙ Ⓚ
14. Ⓕ Ⓖ Ⓗ Ⓙ Ⓚ 29. Ⓐ Ⓑ Ⓒ Ⓓ Ⓔ 44. Ⓕ Ⓖ Ⓗ Ⓙ Ⓚ 59. Ⓐ Ⓑ Ⓒ Ⓓ Ⓔ
15. Ⓐ Ⓑ Ⓒ Ⓓ Ⓔ 30. Ⓕ Ⓖ Ⓗ Ⓙ Ⓚ 45. Ⓐ Ⓑ Ⓒ Ⓓ Ⓔ 60. Ⓕ Ⓖ Ⓗ Ⓙ Ⓚ

Practice Test 3—ANSWERS

Reading Test

1. Ⓐ Ⓑ Ⓒ Ⓓ   11. Ⓐ Ⓑ Ⓒ Ⓓ   21. Ⓐ Ⓑ Ⓒ Ⓓ   31. Ⓐ Ⓑ Ⓒ Ⓓ

2. Ⓕ Ⓖ Ⓗ Ⓙ   12. Ⓕ Ⓖ Ⓗ Ⓙ   22. Ⓕ Ⓖ Ⓗ Ⓙ   32. Ⓕ Ⓖ Ⓗ Ⓙ

3. Ⓐ Ⓑ Ⓒ Ⓓ   13. Ⓐ Ⓑ Ⓒ Ⓓ   23. Ⓐ Ⓑ Ⓒ Ⓓ   33. Ⓐ Ⓑ Ⓒ Ⓓ

4. Ⓕ Ⓖ Ⓗ Ⓙ   14. Ⓕ Ⓖ Ⓗ Ⓙ   24. Ⓕ Ⓖ Ⓗ Ⓙ   34. Ⓕ Ⓖ Ⓗ Ⓙ

5. Ⓐ Ⓑ Ⓒ Ⓓ   15. Ⓐ Ⓑ Ⓒ Ⓓ   25. Ⓐ Ⓑ Ⓒ Ⓓ   35. Ⓐ Ⓑ Ⓒ Ⓓ

6. Ⓕ Ⓖ Ⓗ Ⓙ   16. Ⓕ Ⓖ Ⓗ Ⓙ   26. Ⓕ Ⓖ Ⓗ Ⓙ   36. Ⓕ Ⓖ Ⓗ Ⓙ

7. Ⓐ Ⓑ Ⓒ Ⓓ   17. Ⓐ Ⓑ Ⓒ Ⓓ   27. Ⓐ Ⓑ Ⓒ Ⓓ   37. Ⓐ Ⓑ Ⓒ Ⓓ

8. Ⓕ Ⓖ Ⓗ Ⓙ   18. Ⓕ Ⓖ Ⓗ Ⓙ   28. Ⓕ Ⓖ Ⓗ Ⓙ   38. Ⓕ Ⓖ Ⓗ Ⓙ

9. Ⓐ Ⓑ Ⓒ Ⓓ   19. Ⓐ Ⓑ Ⓒ Ⓓ   29. Ⓐ Ⓑ Ⓒ Ⓓ   39. Ⓐ Ⓑ Ⓒ Ⓓ

10. Ⓕ Ⓖ Ⓗ Ⓙ   20. Ⓕ Ⓖ Ⓗ Ⓙ   30. Ⓕ Ⓖ Ⓗ Ⓙ   40. Ⓕ Ⓖ Ⓗ Ⓙ

Science Test

1. Ⓐ Ⓑ Ⓒ Ⓓ   11. Ⓐ Ⓑ Ⓒ Ⓓ   21. Ⓐ Ⓑ Ⓒ Ⓓ   31. Ⓐ Ⓑ Ⓒ Ⓓ

2. Ⓕ Ⓖ Ⓗ Ⓙ   12. Ⓕ Ⓖ Ⓗ Ⓙ   22. Ⓕ Ⓖ Ⓗ Ⓙ   32. Ⓕ Ⓖ Ⓗ Ⓙ

3. Ⓐ Ⓑ Ⓒ Ⓓ   13. Ⓐ Ⓑ Ⓒ Ⓓ   23. Ⓐ Ⓑ Ⓒ Ⓓ   33. Ⓐ Ⓑ Ⓒ Ⓓ

4. Ⓕ Ⓖ Ⓗ Ⓙ   14. Ⓕ Ⓖ Ⓗ Ⓙ   24. Ⓕ Ⓖ Ⓗ Ⓙ   34. Ⓕ Ⓖ Ⓗ Ⓙ

5. Ⓐ Ⓑ Ⓒ Ⓓ   15. Ⓐ Ⓑ Ⓒ Ⓓ   25. Ⓐ Ⓑ Ⓒ Ⓓ   35. Ⓐ Ⓑ Ⓒ Ⓓ

6. Ⓕ Ⓖ Ⓗ Ⓙ   16. Ⓕ Ⓖ Ⓗ Ⓙ   26. Ⓕ Ⓖ Ⓗ Ⓙ   36. Ⓕ Ⓖ Ⓗ Ⓙ

7. Ⓐ Ⓑ Ⓒ Ⓓ   17. Ⓐ Ⓑ Ⓒ Ⓓ   27. Ⓐ Ⓑ Ⓒ Ⓓ   37. Ⓐ Ⓑ Ⓒ Ⓓ

8. Ⓕ Ⓖ Ⓗ Ⓙ   18. Ⓕ Ⓖ Ⓗ Ⓙ   28. Ⓕ Ⓖ Ⓗ Ⓙ   38. Ⓕ Ⓖ Ⓗ Ⓙ

9. Ⓐ Ⓑ Ⓒ Ⓓ   19. Ⓐ Ⓑ Ⓒ Ⓓ   29. Ⓐ Ⓑ Ⓒ Ⓓ   39. Ⓐ Ⓑ Ⓒ Ⓓ

10. Ⓕ Ⓖ Ⓗ Ⓙ   20. Ⓕ Ⓖ Ⓗ Ⓙ   30. Ⓕ Ⓖ Ⓗ Ⓙ   40. Ⓕ Ⓖ Ⓗ Ⓙ

WRITING TEST

PLAN YOUR ESSAY

WRITE YOUR ESSAY

ENGLISH TEST

45 MINUTES—75 QUESTIONS

> **DIRECTIONS:** In this section, you will see passages with words and phrases that are underlined and numbered. In the right-hand column you will see a question corresponding to each number which provides alternatives to the underlined part. In most of the items, you are to choose the best alternative. If no change is needed, choose NO CHANGE.
>
> In other items, there will be either a question about an underlined portion of the passage or a question about a section of the passage, or about the passage as a whole. This question type will correspond to a number or numbers in a box.
>
> For each question, choose the best alternative or answer and fill in the corresponding circle on the answer sheet.

PASSAGE I

The Names of Flowers

[1]

I <u>look and stare</u> at the first green shoots sprouting up through
1

the dead leaves. The sight sets me trembling <u>with anticipation,</u>
2

and I kneel toward the earth to make sure <u>I'd seen</u> correctly. Yes,
3

the daffodils have already begun pushing toward the sun. <u>Like</u>
4
in a fever, I forget my work and wander about the garden

inspecting the mulched beds. Winter is almost <u>over, I</u> can taste
5
the coming delirium of flowers.

[2]

Gardening is something new to me, a delight this city boy

never imagined. As a child growing up in an apartment in New

York, it <u>seems</u> enough to know that there were flowers and trees.
6

1. A. NO CHANGE
   B. look, staring
   C. looking and staring
   (D.) stare

2. (F.) NO CHANGE
   G. to anticipate
   H. and anticipating
   J. OMIT the underlined portion.

3. (A.) NO CHANGE
   (B.) I've seen
   C. I can see
   D. I will see

   I have seen
   I had seen

4. F. NO CHANGE
   G. Just like
   (H.) As if
   J. Similar to

5. A. NO CHANGE
   B. over and I
   (C.) over, and I
   D. over, yet I

6. F. NO CHANGE
   G. does seem
   H. did seem
   (J.) seemed

<u>Culture marked even more than the seasons were by nature.</u>

7

Autumn was when we played football in the street, or when I

was older, tried to pick the peak foliage weekend to go camping.

We were familiar with the highlights that marked each season,

<u>whereas</u> the subtle particulars, the gradual way one transformed

8

into another. Such intimacy was reserved for buildings, crowds,

and subway trains. ⑨

[3]

Now the twilight of summer is marked for me by budding

<u>chrysanthemum's spilling</u> over the retaining wall at the side of

10

the house. In two seasons, they've grown huge and sprawling.

At the height of autumn they are as <u>bright yellow and red and</u>

11

<u>purple</u> as any foliage, and the season ends when they turn brown

11

and the last rose buds on the climbers leaning up the porch fail

to open.

[4]

Daffodils along the front walk <u>mark</u> the beginning of a long

12

Missouri spring that unfolds with crocuses and tulips, irises and

peonies under my study window, and forsythia and spirea around

the edges of the lawn. Summer means daisies swaying on the

hill, and later, black-eyed susans jostling along the fence.

7. **A.** NO CHANGE
   B. Even culture was marked more than the seasons than nature.
   C. Even the seasons were marked more by culture than by nature.
   D. Seasons were marked more even by culture than by nature.

8. **F.** NO CHANGE
   G. though not
   H. even though not
   J. and still not

9. The purpose of Paragraph 2 as it relates to the remainder of the essay is primarily to:
   A. provide background that helps to explain the significance of the garden to the writer.
   B. provide background that explains why the writer feels lucky to have escaped the city.
   C. portray the writer's childhood as vividly as the writer's garden.
   D. establish the writer's sensitive personality and ability to appreciate flowers.

10. **F.** NO CHANGE
    G. chrysanthemums' spillage
    H. chrysanthemum's that
    J. chrysanthemums that spill

11. **A.** NO CHANGE
    B. bright yellow red and purple
    C. bright, yellow, and red, and purple
    D. bright yellow, and red, and purple

12. **F.** NO CHANGE
    G. have marked
    H. marks
    J. marked

[5]

At thirty-five, I'm beginning to learn the names of flowers, and more than just the names. Names are our entry into the world, and I feel a fresh side of myself come alive as I become familiar with the words <u>standing</u> for all those vivid scents and
13
colors springing from the ground. It's nice to know that one can keep on growing, finding enough space inside for gardens and for subway trains.

ari become familiar with the words that stand who stand for standing

13. A. NO CHANGE
    B. that stand
    C. who stand
    D. whose stand

Questions 14 and 15 refer to the passage as a whole.

14. Is the writer's use of contractions appropriate in the essay?

    F. No, because it creates confusion when the writer switches from the present to the past.
    G. No, because it creates an informal tone that is inappropriate for the subject.
    H. Yes, because it creates an informal tone that is appropriate for the intimate nature of the subject.
    J. Yes, because it helps to focus the essay on the specific flowers in the garden.

15. The writer wishes to insert the following detail into the essay:

    I could tell you there were pines, but not distinguish them from cedar.

    The sentence would most logically be inserted into Paragraph:

    A. 1.
    B. 2.
    C. 3.
    D. 4.

PASSAGE II

Pasta and Tomatoes

[1]

As trade goes, <u>so also</u> goes the world. In these days of global
16
markets where people and goods crisscross the world, the idea

16. F. NO CHANGE
    G. so therefore,
    H. also
    J. so

that a development in Asia can have a major <u>affect on</u> America
17

17. A. NO CHANGE
    B. effect on
    C. effect over
    D. affect over

is taken for granted. Less widely understood <u>was</u> the fact that
18
exchange has always been a major force in world affairs.

18. F. NO CHANGE
    G. is
    H. had been
    J. could be

[2]

19 Agricultural techniques developed in the Near East spread
deeper into Asia, as well as Europe and Africa, evolving form as

19. Which of the following sentences, if inserted at this point, would provide the most effective transition to the second paragraph?

    A. Throughout history, agriculture has always played a major role in the development of civilizations.
    B. Throughout history, the movement of people and goods has been a major factor in changing human societies.
    C. Many examples of this can be found by studying the history of trade over the past 100 years.
    D. However, this phenomenon was never as important as it is in the modern world.

they went. <u>Goods, religion, knowledge, all of these things have</u>
20
<u>moved</u> about through the ages, adopted here by one people,
20
forced on another people there, and every wealth of interchange

also witnessed a wealth of transformation.

20. F. NO CHANGE
    G. Goods, religion, knowledge: all of these things have moved
    H. Movement has occurred in goods, religion, and knowledge
    J. Goods, religion, and knowledge have all moved

[3]

That is why Herodotus could marvel at the different practices
he found upon his <u>tour, of</u> the ancient Mediterranean, and why
21

21. A. NO CHANGE
    B. tour—of
    C. tour; of
    D. tour of

too his impressions <u>had been</u> passed on to generations born
22

22. F. NO CHANGE
    G. have been
    H. are
    J. will be

two millennia later. In fact, the ancient Greeks, <u>whom</u> were well
                                                    23
aware of the influences of Egypt on their civilization, did not pass

their wealth of knowledge directly on to the rest of Europe, which

claims Greece as its root. Greek thought was kept alive by Arab

scholars at the height of Islam's <u>power and Greek</u> texts had to
                                              24
be translated from Arabic into Latin before the likes of Thomas

Aquinas could open the intellectual door to the European

Renaissance.

[4]

But perhaps the clearest examples of this exchange and

transformation lay in a realm less heady and much closer to the

stomach. <u>How would modern Italy be</u> without pasta and
                        25

tomatoes? <u>Imagine</u> Switzerland without chocolate or Ireland and
              26

Eastern Europe without potatoes. ☐27

[5]

Marco Polo brought pasta back to Europe from China.

Tomatoes, potatoes, and <u>cacao, they</u> were all brought back from
                                28

23. **A.** NO CHANGE
    B. that
    C. who
    D. which

24. **F.** NO CHANGE
    G. power, and Greek
    H. power, but Greek
    J. power, therefore Greek

25. **A.** NO CHANGE
    B. What would modern Italy be like
    C. Where would modern Italy be
    D. Would modern Italy be

26. **F.** NO CHANGE
    G. Can you imagine
    H. It's like imagining
    J. Isn't it strange to imagine

27. Which of the alternatives provides the most logical
    conclusion for Paragraph 4?

    A. Yet none of these familiar staples was known in
           the Europe of the Middle Ages.
    B. These staples have become part of the very
           identity of these nations.
    C. They would not be the same countries that they
           are today.
    D. Cuisine is an important element of every culture.

28. **F.** NO CHANGE
    G. cacao,
    H. cacao
    J. cacao, which

> **CONTINUE**

the Americas and transformed into something else. <u>Therefore,</u>
                29

29. **A.** NO CHANGE
    B. Because
    C. Since
    D. For

while neither tomatoes nor pasta is originally Italian, <u>one cannot</u>
                                       30

<u>think of pasta and tomato sauce in all their glorious forms without</u>
                                      30

<u>thinking of Italy</u>.
    30

30. Which of the alternatives would conclude this sentence so that it supports the writer's point about culture?

    F. NO CHANGE
    G. they have been adapted by Italians.
    H. they are now important in Italian cooking.
    J. one cannot forget that they were once unknown in Italy.

PASSAGE III

The Uncharted Waters of Alternative Medicine

[1]

Enter any large natural foods store, head to the supplements section, and you are liable to find yourself bewildered by a sea of herbal <u>remedies, each</u> claiming a variety of medicinal
                    31

31. **A.** NO CHANGE
    B. remedies; each
    C. remedies, and each
    D. remedies each

properties. It is very difficult to know which works and <u>what</u>
                                             32
doesn't. Often, the choice comes down to trial and error mixed with a good dose of faith.

32. **F.** NO CHANGE
    G. who
    H. which
    J. why it

[2]

The same can be said of alternative healing techniques such as <u>the one called acupuncture</u>. No one has ever been able to
                    33
prove the existence of energy paths in the body, the theory upon which acupuncture is based. Yet a video clip of a Chinese woman <u>giving birth</u> while calmly eating a bowl of rice offers convincing
    34
evidence of acupuncture's effectiveness against pain.

33. **A.** NO CHANGE
    B. that which is called acupuncture
    C. acupuncture
    D. anything like acupuncture

34. **F.** NO CHANGE
    G. that gives birth
    H. who gave birth
    J. to give birth

[3]

(1) Yet perhaps one of the reasons why alternative medicine is booming today <u>has been</u> precisely that, in an era in which
35
invasive medical procedures and antibiotics are prescribed at the drop of a hat, people have become less trusting of medical science. (2) The medical profession has traditionally scoffed at the claims of alternative medicine. (3) When anecdotal evidence of <u>it's</u> successes has spread, doctors have routinely written it off
36
as the placebo effect. (4) Clearly drugs and technology, as valuable as each might be, <u>does not hold all of the answers.</u> 38
37

35.
- **A.** NO CHANGE
- **B.** is
- **C.** are
- **D.** will be

36.
- **F.** NO CHANGE
- **G.** its'
- **H.** its
- **J.** OMIT the underlined portion.

37.
- **A.** NO CHANGE
- **B.** holds not all the answers
- **C.** hold no answers
- **D.** do not hold all of the answers

38. Which of the following sentence sequences will make Paragraph 3 most logical sentence?
- **F.** NO CHANGE
- **G.** 2, 3, 1, 4
- **H.** 2, 4, 1, 3
- **J.** 4, 1, 2, 3

[4]

The antagonism between medical science and alternative medicine is <u>older, than</u> most people know. In fact, the American
39
Medical Association was founded in 1846 mostly in response to the nation's first medical association, the American Institute of Homeopathy. The AMA set the standard for medical <u>licenses; and</u>
40
was quick to exclude any doctor who had even associated with someone practicing homeopathy.

39.
- **A.** NO CHANGE
- **B.** older; than
- **C.** older than
- **D.** older: than

40.
- **F.** NO CHANGE
- **G.** licenses. And
- **H.** licenses and
- **J.** licenses: and

CONTINUE

[5]

[41] Younger doctors are beginning to acknowledge the

limits of biomedical understanding and admit that there <u>might</u>
42

<u>or might not indeed</u> be healing properties in plants or treatments
42

that may be effective, even if we don't know how they work.

Recently, a major drug company signed a contract with China

to develop pharmaceuticals from traditional Chinese medicine.

Finally, we are beginning to see serious attempts to evaluate

alternative medicine, rather than simply dismiss it. Perhaps within

the next decade, when <u>we approach</u> that sea of herbal remedies,
43

you will have a better sense of which ones really work and why.

41. Which of the following sentences, if inserted at this point, would provide the most effective transition to Paragraph 5?

- **A.** Homeopathy is still not fully accepted by the medical establishment.
- **B.** The rules of the AMA are not as strict as they once were.
- **C.** However, alternative medicine is making a comeback.
- **D.** Only now are there signs that this deep schism in the field of health is beginning to heal.

42. F. NO CHANGE
- **G.** is some possibility to
- **H.** might or might not
- **J.** might

43. A. NO CHANGE
- **B.** one approaches
- **C.** you approach
- **D.** we are approached by

Questions 44 and 45 ask about the passage as a whole.

44. If this essay were revised to include a paragraph on the philosophy behind homeopathic remedies used in alternative medicine, the new paragraph would most logically follow Paragraph:

- **F.** 2.
- **G.** 3.
- **H.** 4.
- **J.** 5.

45. Suppose the writer had been assigned to write an essay exploring the reasons for the present popularity of alternative medicine. Would this essay successfully fulfill the assignment?

- **A.** Yes, because it focuses on people's dissatisfaction with the medical establishment.
- **B.** Yes, because it touches on the reasons for alternative medicine's popularity in Paragraph 3.
- **C.** No, because it focuses on the question of the value of alternative medicine.
- **D.** No, because it restricts its focus to the antagonism of doctors toward alternative medicine.

PASSAGE IV

A Professional Lesson

[1]

When I first began working as a journalist in the 1970s, there

are few women in the field who are taken seriously. I had

no illusions, I would have to prove myself again and again.

[2]

Editors were surprised when my work turned out to be first

rate. It took me a long time to understand that the reason had

to do with the way I carried myself, not to mention the fact that

I was making no attempt with which to conceal my anxieties.

I had not yet learned to put on a professional face.

[3]

Editors who would try to hand me the softer stories, or the

stories with a "woman angle." "Maybe you could do a piece on

the charity work of the First Lady." I was undaunted by these

incidents, and by the inevitable sexist jokes and innuendoes.

After all, I had chosen a career that meant not breaking ground

in a traditional male bastion. Determination and a thick skin were

mandatory.

46. F. NO CHANGE
G. there are few women in the field who is taken seriously.
H. here were few women in the field who are taken seriously.
J. there were few women in the field who were taken seriously.

47. A. NO CHANGE
B. no illusions: I
C. no illusion in which I
D. no illusion that I

48. F. NO CHANGE
G. not to mention the fact that I made no attempt to conceal my anxieties
H. with the fact that I made no attempt to conceal my anxieties
J. I made no attempt to conceal my anxieties

49. A. NO CHANGE
B. Editors would try to hand me the softer stories,
C. The softer stories were the ones editors would try to hand me,
D. Editors who tried to hand me the softer stories,

50. F. NO CHANGE
G. could do the charity work of
H. could be doing it on the charity work of
J. could do a piece on charity work for

51. A. NO CHANGE
B. breaking ground in
C. it broke ground in
D. broken ground in

CONTINUE

[4]

There was, however; an aspect of professional life for which
                    52
many of us were not prepared. I remember that when I was

working on a difficult assignment and I checked in with the editor,

I would tell him about my worries, describe the obstacles I had

yet to surmount, or sometimes even complaining about the
                                    53
minor frustrations that had made for a bad day. I thought of it

as communication, being honest in my work. I never doubted

that I would get past these problems. They merely represented

the moment-to-moment process of doing my job. After all, life

was like that too—full of difficulties that I discussed with friends

as a way of getting through them. 54

[5]

I noticed, therefore, that when my male colleagues spoke
              55
to editors, no matter what doubts they had, they always said that

everything was under control. It seemed like lying. What were

these men afraid of? I didn't realize that by behaving the way in
                                                            56
which I'd been acting, my honesty was creating a negative
              56
impression with my editors. Editors assumed that if I was speaking

about my difficulties, then I must really be in trouble. Like all

managers, they wanted to know that everything was under

control. By sharing the struggles that are part of the process of

all work, I made my editors worry and at the same time reinforced

all those stereotypes about women that can't stand the pressure.
                                          57

52. **F.** NO CHANGE
    G. was however,
    H. was, however,
    J. was; however,

53. **A.** NO CHANGE
    B. was complaining
    C. complained
    D. complain

54. Would it add to the effectiveness of the essay if the writer inserted a paragraph at this point describing the way in which she discussed problems with a close friend?

    F. No, because the writer's description of how she interacted with her editor is already clear.
    G. No, because such a description belongs just before this paragraph.
    H. Yes, because the writer needs to more fully illustrate how she interacts with other people.
    J. Yes, because the writer needs to show why she wanted the "softer stories" she was assigned.

55. **A.** NO CHANGE
    B. somewhat
    C. in support of my ideas
    D. though

56. **F.** NO CHANGE
    G. my behavior and
    H. my behaving in that way and
    J. OMIT the underlined portion.

57. **A.** NO CHANGE
    B. who
    C. whom
    D. OMIT the underlined portion.

58. For the sake of unity and coherence, Paragraph 2 should be placed:

    F. where it is now.
    G. before Paragraph 1.
    H. after Paragraph 4.
    J. after Paragraph 5.

59. The writer is considering eliminating Paragraph 4. If the writer removed this paragraph, the essay would primarily lose:

    A. relevant details about the mistakes the writer made that led to her ultimate realization.
    B. historical information regarding women in the workplace.
    C. relevant details regarding the writer's male colleagues' behavior.
    D. a revealing anecdote about the writer's experience with her friends.

60. Which of the following assignments would this essay most clearly fulfill?

    F. Write a persuasive essay about the benefits of holding a job.
    G. Write an essay comparing current and past business environments for women.
    H. Write an essay about a lesson you learned from a professional experience.
    J. Write an essay about an experience in which your personal integrity was challenged.

PASSAGE V

Edwidge Danticat, A Born Writer

[1]

Those who live in countries where a large proportion of the population <u>is illegible</u> share their stories orally. In Haiti,
61

<u>it being a small country,</u> when someone has a tale to tell he or
62

61. **A.** NO CHANGE
    B. are ineligible
    C. is illiterate
    D. are illiterate

62. **F.** NO CHANGE
    G. as one of the world's smaller countries,
    H. being a small country
    J. OMIT the underlined portion.

CONTINUE

she will call out *Krik?* <u>Neighbors:</u> friends, and relatives will then
$\qquad$ 63

gather around with an answering call of *Krak!*, signaling <u>there</u>
$\qquad$ 64

willingness to listen.

63. A. NO CHANGE
    B. Neighbors;
    C. Neighbors
    D. Neighbors,

64. F. NO CHANGE
    G. they're
    H. their
    J. they are

[2]

The Haitian-born writer Edwidge Danticat <u>would have been</u> only
$\qquad$ 65

twenty-six when she took these two words and made them the

title for her collection of stories. The nine stories in *Krik?Krak!*

focus on the hardships of living <u>alongside a</u> dictatorship and the
$\qquad$ 66

struggles encountered by families who flee Haiti and seek new

<u>lives, in</u> the United States.
$\qquad$ 67

The book received <u>much critical</u> acclaim and even became a
$\qquad$ 68

finalist for the National Book Award.

65. A. NO CHANGE
    B. having been
    C. was being
    D. was

66. F. NO CHANGE
    G. under a
    H. without a
    J. in spite of a

67. A. NO CHANGE
    B. lives' in
    C. lives in
    D. life in

68. F. NO CHANGE
    G. many critically
    H. too critical
    J. much criticism

[3]

Born in Port-au-Prince in 1969, <u>her family moved to New</u>
$\qquad$ 69
<u>York City when Danticat was twelve.</u> She spoke little as a new
$\qquad$ 69

69. A. NO CHANGE
    B. Danticat moved to New York City when she was twelve
    C. New York City is where Danticat moved when she was twelve
    D. when she was twelve Danticat moved to New York City

immigrant, because when she did speak, other children made
fun of her heavily accented English. 70 Her thesis in graduate

70. Which of the following sentences, if added here,
would best provide a transition from the description
of Danticat as a young girl to that of Danticat as
an author?

F. Danticat refrained from criticizing them in return,
however, and was successful in the end.
G. Most Haitians speak Creole, and the language is
quite different from American English.
H. Many writers have had difficult childhoods.
J. Although she was silent much of the time,
Danticat watched and remembered, as if already
thinking like a writer.

school later became the novel *Breath, Eyes, Memory*. That novel,
which was subsequently chosen by Oprah Winfrey for her book
club, featured a heroine who, like the author, moved from Haiti
                                                            71
to New York City at the age of twelve. Danticat's third book, *The
Farming of Bones*, Is also set in Haiti.

71. A. NO CHANGE
    B. not unlike the author
    C. just as the author did
    D. in much the same manner as the author

[4]

This young authors chosen subject matter, as well as the
                    72
Creole-accented language she uses to tell her stories, demonstrate
that while Danticat has left Haiti for her adopted country of
America, she has forgotten both the land of her birth and its
                                                            73
brave people.

72. F. NO CHANGE
    G. authors'
    H. author's
    J. author

73. A. NO CHANGE
    B. either the land of her birth or its
    C. neither the land of her birth or its
    D. neither the land of her birth nor its

CONTINUE

Questions 74 and 75 refer to the passage as a whole.

74. The writer wishes to open the essay with a sentence that will set the theme and tone of the essay. Which of the following would most effectively accomplish this?

    F. Whether or not they can read, people all over the world love stories.

    G. One of my favorite books is a collection of stories set in Haiti.

    H. The problem of illiteracy results in a variety of consequences for people all over the world.

    J. Have you ever wondered what it feels like not to be able to read?

75. The writer wishes to give this essay a different title. Which of the following alternatives would be most appropriate?

    A. "How Edwidge Danticat Overcame Struggles as an Immigrant"

    B. "Life in Haiti"

    C. "A New Voice in Literature"

    D. "The Haiti I Will Never Forget"

STOP

MATHEMATICS TEST

60 MINUTES—60 QUESTIONS

DIRECTIONS: For each of the following items, solve each problem, choose the correct answer, and then fill in the corresponding circle on the answer sheet. If you encounter problems that take too much time to solve, move on. Solve as many problems as you can; then return to the others in the time remaining for the test.

You may use a calculator on this test for any problems you choose, but some of the problems may best be solved without the use of a calculator.

SHOW YOUR WORK HERE

Note: Unless otherwise stated, assume the following:

1. Illustrative figures are NOT necessarily drawn to scale.
2. Geometric figures lie in a plane.
3. The word *line* Indicates a straight line.
4. The word *average* indicates arithmetic mean.

---

1. Of the 80 children at a daycare center, 32 missed at least 1 day because of illness in January. What percent of the children at the center missed at least 1 day due to illness in January?

   A. 4%
   B. 16%
   C. 24%
   D. 32%
   E. 40%

2. Three lines intersect to form the triangle below. What is the value of *x*?

   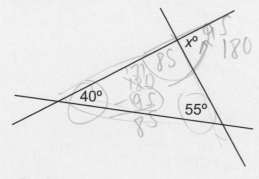

   F. 55
   G. 75
   H. 85
   J. 95
   K. 105

SHOW YOUR WORK HERE

3. A businessperson calculates that it costs her *p* dollars per hour in parts costs and *l* dollars per hour in labor costs to operate a certain piece of machinery. Which of the following expressions would provide her with the total cost of operating this machine for *x* hours?

   A. *plx*
   B. (*px*)(*lx*)
   C. *x*(*p* + *l*)
   D. *pl*
   E. *p* + *l*

   $p(x) + l(x)$

4. In the standard (*x*, *y*) coordinate plane, a straight line segment is drawn to connect (0, 0) and (4, 4). Which of the following sets of points, when connected by a straight line segment, will intersect the original segment?

   F. (0, −1) and (4, 3)
   G. (−1, 0) and (3, 4)
   H. (0, 1) and (4, 5)
   J. (1, 0) and (8, 4)
   K. (2, 1) and (2, 5)

5. A phone company charges $1 per calling card call plus 25 cents per minute for the length of the call. If Jacob makes 10 calling card calls, half of which last exactly 1 minute and half of which last exactly 3 minutes, what is his cost for the 10 calls?

   A. $5
   B. $10
   C. $11.25
   D. $13.75
   E. $15

   $.25(x) + 1$
   $.25(1) + 1 = 1.25(5) = 6.25$
   $.25(3) + 1 = 1.75(5) = 8.75$

6. $(3 + \sqrt{2})(4 - \sqrt{2}) =$

   F. $12 - 2\sqrt{2}$
   G. 10
   H. $10 + \sqrt{2}$
   J. 14
   K. $14 + 7\sqrt{2}$

   $12 - 3\sqrt{2} + 4\sqrt{2} - 2$
   $12 + \sqrt{2} - 2$
   $10 + \sqrt{2}$

7. Which of the following is equal to the sum of $\frac{2}{5}$, $\frac{1}{8}$, and 0.177?

   A. 0.525
   B. 0.577
   C. 0.602
   D. 0.692
   E. 0.702

8. In the figure below, $BC = 2$ and $BD = 10$. If the area of triangle ABC is 5 square inches, what is the area, in square inches, of triangle ACD?

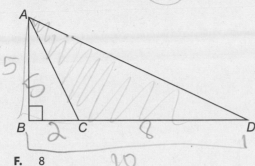

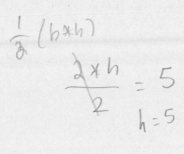

F. 8
G. 15
H. 20
J. 25
K. 30

9. What is the value of $m^2 - 4mn + n$ when $m = -1$ and $n = -3$?

A. −15
B. −14
C. −11
D. 8
E. 10

10. For all a, $(2a - 3)^2 =$

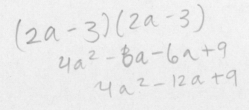

F. $4a - 6$
G. $4a^2 - 9$
H. $4a^2 - 6a + 9$
J. $4a^2 - 12a + 9$
K. $4a^2 - 12a - 9$

11. What is the measure of one of the interior angles of a regular hexagon?

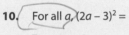

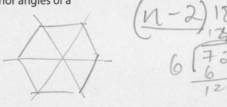

A. 60°
B. 90°
C. 100°
D. 110°
E. 120°

12. What pair of numbers shares a greatest common factor of 3 and a least common multiple of 90?

F. 6 and 15
G. 9 and 15
H. 15 and 18
J. 6 and 30
K. 18 and 45

CONTINUE

13. Colin earns an annual salary of C dollars, and Daryl earns an annual salary of D dollars. If the difference between Colin's and Daryl's average monthly salary is $500, which of the following represents the relationship between C and D?

SHOW YOUR WORK HERE

A. $|C - D| = 500$

B. $|C + D| = 500$

C. $\left|\dfrac{C + D}{2}\right| = 6,000$

D. $|C - D| = 6,000$

E. $|C + D| = 6,000$

14. $(0.01)^4 =$

F. 10^{-8}
G. 10^{-4}
H. 10^{-2}
J. 10^4
K. 10^8

15. In the figure below, segments AD and BC intersect at point E and $\overline{AB} \parallel \overline{CD}$. What is the measure of $\angle CED$?

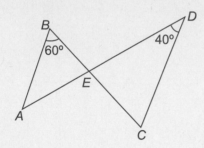

A. $40°$
B. $60°$
C. $80°$
D. $100°$
E. Cannot be determined from the given information

16. If $x < 0$ and $3x^2 - 7x = 6$, then $x =$

F. -6
G. -3
H. -2

J. $-\dfrac{3}{2}$

K. $-\dfrac{2}{3}$

17. What is the slope of the line $3x + y - 2 = 0$?

   A. -3

   B. $-\dfrac{3}{2}$

   C. $-\dfrac{1}{3}$

   D. 2

   E. 3

18. A painter calculates that one side of a house requires either exactly 4 large cans of paint or exactly 6 small cans of paint. If all 4 sides of the house require identical amounts of paint, which collection of paint cans will cover all 4 sides with no waste?

   F. 2 large and 24 small

   G. 4 large and 18 small

   H. 6 large and 16 small

   J. 8 large and 8 small

   K. 12 large and 12 small

19. At what value of x does the expression $\left| x - 5 \right| + 2$ reach its minimum?

   A. -5

   B. -2

   C. 0

   D. 2

   E. 5

20. In the figure below, triangles BCA and DEF are similar. What is the length of segment EF?

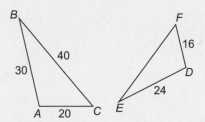

   F. 28

   G. 30

   H. 32

   J. 36

   K. 40

CONTINUE

SHOW YOUR WORK HERE

21. For all nonnegative values of a and b, $\sqrt{3^4 a^3 b^2} =$

    A. $9a^{\frac{2}{3}}b$

    B. $9a^{\frac{3}{2}}b$

    C. $9a^{-\frac{3}{2}}b$

    D. $81a^3b^2$

    E. $27a^6b^4$

22. The average of six test scores is 80. When two more tests are included, the average for all eight tests is 85. What is the average score of the two added tests?

    F. 70
    G. 85
    H. 90
    J. 95
    K. 100

23. What is the area of right triangle *ABC* below, in square centimeters?

    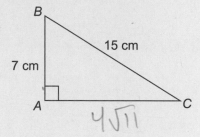

    A. 14
    B. $4\sqrt{11}$
    C. 26
    D. $14\sqrt{11}$
    E. $\dfrac{105}{2}$

24. It took Renee exactly 9 minutes and 20 seconds to download a 1,400-kilobyte file from the Internet to her computer. At that same rate, how long would it take Renee to download a 2,000-kilobyte file?

    F. 6 minutes and 30 seconds
    G. 12 minutes and 10 seconds
    H. 12 minutes and 40 seconds
    J. 13 minutes and 20 seconds
    K. 18 minutes and 40 seconds

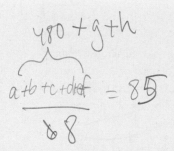

$$\frac{a+b+c+d+e+f}{8} = 85 \qquad 480+g+h=680$$
$$\frac{g+h}{2} = \frac{200}{2}$$
$$g+h = 100$$

$$49 + x^2 = 225$$
$$x^2 = 176$$
$$\boxed{13.26}$$

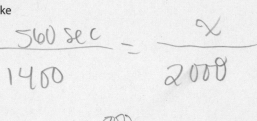

$$\frac{560 \text{ sec}}{1400} = \frac{x}{2000}$$
$$x = 800$$
$$13.20$$

25. A college campus's central green is a square lawn bordered by footpaths 100 feet long on each side. The college plans to create a diagonal footpath that would connect the southwest corner of the green to the northeast corner of the green. Approximately how many feet shorter would the new path be than the shortest possible route on the existing footpaths?

- **A.** 40
- **B.** 50
- **C.** 60
- **D.** 140
- **E.** 150

SHOW YOUR WORK HERE

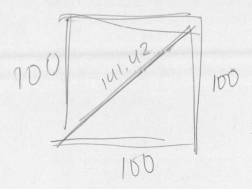

26. What is the smallest positive integer value of x for which $x - \sqrt{5} > 5$ is true?

- **F.** 9
- **G.** 8
- **H.** 7
- **J.** 6
- **K.** 5

27. Ben has won the bid to repaint the local high school football stadium. If one gallon of paint covers an area of 150 square feet, what is the minimum number of gallons he will need to paint two walls that are each 100 yards long and 15 yards high?

- **A.** 20
- **B.** 60
- **C.** 90
- **D.** 150
- **E.** 180

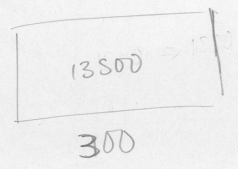

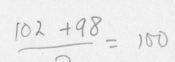

$$\frac{102 + 98}{2} = 100$$

$$\frac{200 + x}{3} = 102$$

$$200 + x = \frac{306}{200}$$

$$x = 106$$

28. In the figure below, *WXYZ* is a square. Points are chosen on each pair of adjacent sides of *WXYZ* to form four congruent right triangles, as shown below. Each of the triangles has one leg that is three times longer than the other leg. What is the ratio of the area of the four triangles to the area of the shaded region?

SHOW YOUR WORK HERE

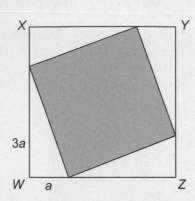

F. $\dfrac{3}{8}$

G. $\dfrac{2}{5}$

H. $\dfrac{1}{2}$

J. $\dfrac{3}{5}$

K. $\dfrac{3}{4}$

29. $\dfrac{0.018}{0.12}$ is equal to how many thousandths?

A. 0.150
B. 1.5
C. 15
D. 150
E. 667

30. Which of the following inequalities gives the complete solution set for $|x-1| \le 2$?

F. $-3 \le x \le 1$

G. $-1 \le x \le 3$

H. $0 \le x \le 4$

J. $x \ge -1$

K. $x \le 3$

31. In the figure below, $\overline{BE} \parallel \overline{CD}$. If $BC = 4$, $DE = 3$, and $AB = 10$, how many units long is $\overline{AE}$?

SHOW YOUR WORK HERE

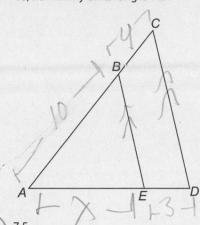

A. 7.5
B. 10.5
C. 12.0
D. 15.0
E. 26.0

$$\frac{4}{14} = \frac{3}{x+3}$$

$$4x = 42$$

$$x = 7.5$$

$$\boxed{\frac{10}{14}} = \frac{x}{x+3}$$

$$10x + 30 = 14x$$

$$30 = 4x$$

$$x = 7.5$$

32. For $0° < \theta < 90°$, if $\cos \theta = \dfrac{5}{7}$, then $\tan \theta =$

F. $\dfrac{2}{5}$

G. $\dfrac{7}{5}$

H. $\dfrac{2\sqrt{6}}{7}$

J. $\dfrac{2\sqrt{6}}{5}$

K. $\dfrac{24}{5}$

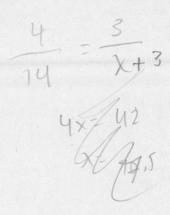

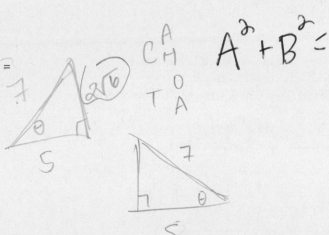

$$A^2 + B^2 = C^2$$

C$_H$
T$_O$A

33. The average of x numbers is 15. If two of the numbers are each increased by y, the new average will be increased by how much?

A. $2y$
B. y
C. $\dfrac{x}{2y}$
D. $\dfrac{y}{x}$
E. $\dfrac{2y}{x}$

$$\frac{(x) + y + y}{x + 2y} = 15$$

$$\frac{10 + 15 + 20}{3} = 15$$

$$\frac{10 + 21 + 26}{3} = 15$$

$$\frac{57}{3} = 19$$

CONTINUE

34. Points *A*, *B*, and *C* below lie on the circumference of a circle with center *O*. If the unshaded sectors *AOB* and *BOC* comprise $\frac{2}{5}$ and $\frac{1}{3}$ of the area of the circle, respectively, what is the measure of $\angle AOC$?

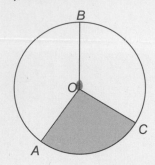

Handwritten work: $\frac{2}{5} + \frac{1}{3} = \frac{6}{15} + \frac{5}{15} = \frac{11}{15}$

$\frac{4}{15} \Rightarrow \frac{x}{360}$

- **F.** 48°
- **G.** 90°
- **H.** 92°
- **J.** 96°
- **K.** 264°

35. A 12-foot ladder is propped against a 10-foot house as outlined below. Approximately how many feet is the base of the ladder from the wall of the house?

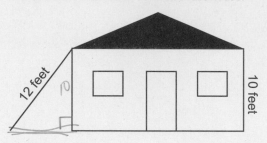

- **A.** 2.0
- **B.** 4.0
- **C.** 6.6
- **D.** 15.6
- **E.** 44

36. A circle with a radius of 3 feet has a circumference of how many feet?

- **F.** $\dfrac{3\pi}{2}$

Handwritten: circle with 3 labeled, $2\pi r$

- **G.** 3π
- **H.** 6π
- **J.** 9π
- **K.** 12π

37. If $\frac{3}{5}n + \frac{2}{7} = \frac{3}{7}n - \frac{2}{5}$, then $n =$

- **A.** −4
- **B.** −3
- **C.** 0
- **D.** 2
- **E.** 3

38. A line in the standard (x, y) coordinate plane is parallel to the y-axis and passes through the point $(2, 3)$. Which of the following is an equation of this line?

    F. $x = 2$
    G. $y = 3$
    H. $y = 2x$
    J. $y = 2x - 3$
    K. $y = x + 1$

39. What is the area of an equilateral triangle with a perimeter of 18?

    A. $9\sqrt{3}$

    B. 18

    C. $18\sqrt{3}$

    D. 36

    E. $36\sqrt{3}$

40. If the quadrants in the standard (x, y) plane are numbered as below, the graph of the circle defined by $(x - 4)^2 + (y + 6)^2 = 25$ lies entirely in which quadrants?

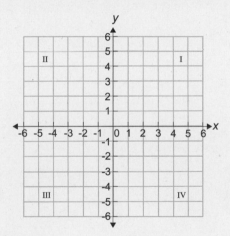

    F. I and II
    G. I and IV
    H. II and III
    J. II and IV
    K. III and IV

41. If the circle below has center at *C* and a radius of 9 feet, what is the length, in feet, of arc *XYZ*?

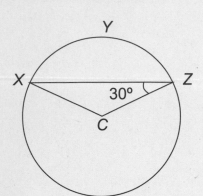

A. $\dfrac{3\pi}{2}$

B. 3π

C. 6π

D. 18π

E. 27π

42. What is the least possible value for the product *xy*, if $x + y = 24$ and *x* and *y* are both prime numbers?

F. 23

G. 44

H. 95

J. 119

K. 143

43. The area of a circle is 64 square inches. What is the diameter, in inches, of the circle?

A. 8

B. 16

C. $\dfrac{128}{\pi}$

D. $\dfrac{8}{\sqrt{\pi}}$

E. $\dfrac{16}{\sqrt{\pi}}$

44. If $2x = 4x + 1$, then $6x - 2 =$

F. −5

G. −3

H. −1

J. $-\dfrac{1}{2}$

K. 1

45. In the isosceles right triangle below, what is the value of tan $x°$?

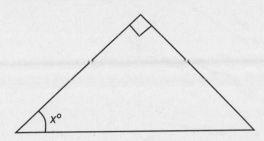

A. $\dfrac{\sqrt{2}}{2}$

B. 1

C. $\sqrt{2}$

D. $\dfrac{\sqrt{3}}{2}$

E. $\sqrt{3}$

46. What is the area of the rectangle shown below in the standard (x, y) coordinate plane?

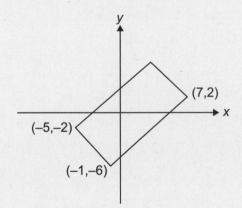

F. $32\sqrt{2}$

G. 64

H. $24\sqrt{2}$

J. 128

K. 144

CONTINUE

SHOW YOUR WORK HERE

47. If $\dfrac{x^3 y^2}{z}$ is positive, then which of the following could be true?

    I. x and z are both negative

    II. x is negative and z is positive

    III. x is zero

    A.   I only

    B.   II only

    C.   I and II

    D.   II and III

    E.   I, II, and III

48. What is the value of $\log_4 64$?

    F.   2

    G.   3

    H.   4

    J.   8

    K.   16

49. If x is inversely related to y and y is directly related to z, which of the following expressions gives one possibility for y in terms of x and z?

    A. $y = \dfrac{x}{z}$

    B. $y = \dfrac{z}{x}$

    C. $y = z^x$

    D. $y = x^z$

    E. $y = z^x$

50. A circle exists such that its center is at $C(1, -1)$ and it passes through $P(5, 2)$ in the standard (x, y) coordinate plane below. Which equation determines the circle described?

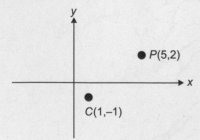

    F. $(x - 5)^2 + (y - 2)^2 = 25$

    G. $(x + 5)^2 + (y + 2)^2 = 25$

    H. $(x - 1)^2 + (y + 1)^2 = 25$

    J. $(x + 1)^2 + (y - 1)^2 = 25$

    K. $(x + 1)^2 + (y + 1)^2 = 25$

51. If $-[(x-4)-(3-2x)] = 3 - (5x+6)$, what is the value of x?

    A. -6
    B. -5
    C. -4
    D. -3
    E. -2

SHOW YOUR WORK HERE

52. What is the period of the graph of $y = 3\sin\dfrac{x}{2}$?

    F. $\dfrac{\pi}{2}$

    G. π

    H. $\dfrac{3\pi}{2}$

    J. 2π

    K. 4π

53. A rectangle is formed by increasing the length of a square by 4 inches and decreasing the width by 3 inches. If each side of the original square was s inches long, which of the following represents the area of the rectangle, in square inches?

    A. $s^2 + 1$
    B. $s^2 - 12$
    C. $s^2 - s + 12$
    D. $s^2 + s - 7$
    E. $s^2 + s - 12$

54. A positive number x is increased by 20 percent, and the result is then decreased by 30 percent. The final result is equal to which of the following?

    F. x decreased by 50 percent
    G. x decreased by 16 percent
    H. x decreased by 10 percent
    J. x increased by 10 percent
    K. x increased by 24 percent

55. A 50-foot wire is attached to the top of an electric pole and is anchored on the ground. If the wire rises in a straight line at a 70° angle from the ground, how many feet tall is the pole?

    A. $50 \sin 70°$
    B. $50 \cos 70°$
    C. $50 \tan 70°$

    D. $\dfrac{\cos 70°}{50}$

    E. $\dfrac{50}{\cos 70°}$

CONTINUE

56. What is the complete solution set for the equation

$|1-x| = x-1$?

  F. All real numbers

  G. $x \leq -1$

  H. $x < 1$

  J. $x \geq 1$

  K. $x = 1$

57. At which point in the standard (x, y) coordinate plane do the two lines below intersect?

$$\frac{x}{2} + y = 2$$
$$2x + y = 2$$

  A. $(2, 0)$

  B. $(1, -2)$

  C. $(0, 2)$

  D. $(-1, -1)$

  E. $(-2, 0)$

58. Lines m and n are perpendicular in the standard (x, y) coordinate plane below. Which of the following is the equation for line n?

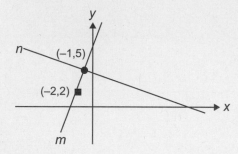

  F. $y = -x + 5$

  G. $y = -2x + 3$

  H. $2y = -x - 4$

  J. $3y = -x + 14$

  K. $3y = x + 16$

59. Five cards lettered A through E are placed in a hat. If two cards are drawn at random from the hat, what is the probability that the B and C cards will both be drawn?

  A. 0.05

  B. 0.1

  C. 0.20

  D. 0.25

  E. 0.4

60. While shopping at a clothing store, Ben finds that a shirt and two ties cost $105, while two shirts and one tie cost $135. If the store charges the same price for all of its shirts and the same price for all of its ties, what is Ben's cost if he wants to buy just one tie?

SHOW YOUR WORK HERE

- **F.** $15
- **G.** $25
- **H.** $30
- **J.** $50
- **K.** $55

STOP

READING TEST

35 Minutes—40 Questions

> **DIRECTIONS:** There are four passages in this test. Each passage is followed by several questions. Read each passage, select the best answer to each related question, and fill in the corresponding circle on the answer sheet. You may look back at the passages as often as you need.

PASSAGE I

PROSE FICTION: Passage A is an excerpt from *Pride and Prejudice* by Jane Austen. Passage B is an excerpt from *Middlemarch* by George Eliot.

Passage A
by Jane Austen

Mr. Bennet was among the earliest of those who waited on Mr. Bingley. He had always intended to visit him, though to the last always assuring his wife that he should not go; and till the evening after the visit was paid she had no knowledge of it. It

5 was then disclosed in the following manner. Observing his second daughter employed in trimming a hat, he suddenly addressed her with:

"I hope Mr. Bingley will like it, Lizzy."

"We are not in a way to know what Mr. Bingley likes," said her

10 mother resentfully, "since we are not to visit."

"But you forget, mamma," said Elizabeth, "that we shall meet him at the assemblies, and that Mrs. Long promised to introduce him."

"I do not believe Mrs. Long will do any such thing. She has

15 two nieces of her own. She is a selfish, hypocritical woman, and I have no opinion of her."

"No more have I," said Mr. Bennet; "and I am glad to find that you do not depend on her serving you."

Mrs. Bennet deigned not to make any reply, but, unable to

20 contain herself, began scolding one of her daughters.

"Don't keep coughing so, Kitty, for Heaven's sake! Have a little compassion on my nerves. You tear them to pieces."

"Kitty has no discretion in her coughs," said her father; "she times them ill."

25 "I do not cough for my own amusement," replied Kitty fretfully. "When is your next ball to be, Lizzy?"

"Tomorrow fortnight."

"Aye, so it is," cried her mother, "and Mrs. Long does not come back till the day before; so it will be impossible for her

30 to introduce him, for she will not know him herself."

"Then, my dear, you may have the advantage of your friend, and introduce Mr. Bingley to her."

"Impossible, Mr. Bennet, impossible, when I am not acquainted with him myself; how can you be so teasing?"

35 "I honour your circumspection. A fortnight's acquaintance is certainly very little. One cannot know what a man really is by the end of a fortnight. But if we do not venture somebody else will; and after all, Mrs. Long and her daughters must stand their chance; and, therefore, as she will think it an act of

40 kindness, if you decline the office, I will take it on myself."

The girls stared at their father. Mrs. Bennet said only, "Nonsense, nonsense!"

"What can be the meaning of that emphatic exclamation?" cried he. "Do you consider the forms of introduction, and the

45 stress that is laid on them, as nonsense? I cannot quite agree with you there. What say you, Mary? For you are a young lady of deep reflection, I know, and read great books and make extracts."

Mary wished to say something sensible, but knew not how.

Passage B
by George Eliot

Celia thought privately, "Dorothea quite despises Sir James Chettam; I believe she would not accept him." Celia felt that this was a pity. She had never been deceived as to the object of the baronet's interest. Sometimes, indeed, she had reflected

5 that Dodo would perhaps not make a husband happy who had not her way of looking at things; and stifled in the depths of her heart was the feeling that her sister was too religious for family comfort. Notions and scruples were like spilt needles, making one afraid of treading, or sitting down, or even eating.

10 When Miss Brooke was at the tea-table, Sir James came to sit down by her, not having felt her mode of answering him

at all offensive. Why should he? He thought it probable that Miss Brooke liked him, and manners must be very marked indeed before they cease to be interpreted by preconceptions either
15 confident or distrustful. She was thoroughly charming to him, but of course he theorized a little about his attachment. He was made of excellent human dough, and had the rare merit of knowing that his talents, even if let loose, would not set the smallest stream in the county on fire: hence he liked the prospect
20 of a wife to whom he could say, "What shall we do?" about this or that; who could help her husband out with reasons, and would also have the property qualification for doing so.

As to the excessive religiousness alleged against Miss Brooke, he had a very indefinite notion of what it consisted in, and
25 thought that it would die out with marriage. In short, he felt himself to be in love in the right place, and was ready to endure a great deal of predominance, which, after all, a man could always put down when he liked. Sir James had no idea that he should ever like to put down the predominance of this handsome
30 girl, in whose cleverness he delighted. Why not? A man's mind—what there is of it—has always the advantage of being masculine,—as the smallest birch-tree is of a higher kind than the most soaring palm,—and even his ignorance is of a sounder quality. Sir James might not have originated this estimate; but
35 a kind Providence furnishes the limpest personality with a little gunk or starch in the form of tradition.

"Let me hope that you will rescind that resolution about the horse, Miss Brooke," said the persevering admirer. "I assure you, riding is the most healthy of exercises."

40 "I am aware of it," said Dorothea, coldly. "I think it would do Celia good—if she would take to it."

"But you are such a perfect horsewoman."

"Excuse me; I have had very little practice, and I should be easily thrown."

45 "Then that is a reason for more practice. Every lady ought to be a perfect horsewoman, that she may accompany her husband."

"You see how widely we differ, Sir James. I have made up my mind that I ought not to be a perfect horsewoman, and so I
50 should never correspond to your pattern of a lady." Dorothea looked straight before her, and spoke with cold brusquerie, very much with the air of a handsome boy, in amusing contrast with the solicitous amiability of her admirer.

Questions 1–3 ask about Passage A.

1. Lizzy is described in the passage as the Bennets':
   - A. youngest daughter.
   - B. oldest daughter.
   - C. sensible daughter.
   - D. second daughter.

2. When Kitty coughs, she is met with what could best be described as:
   - F. apathetic dismissal.
   - G. angry mocking.
   - H. overblown annoyance.
   - J. exasperated silence.

3. When Mr. Bennet tells his wife that she should introduce Mr. Bingley to Lizzy, she feels that Mr. Bennet:
   - A. has lost his mind.
   - B. is breaching etiquette.
   - C. does not understand his wife.
   - D. does not love his wife.

Questions 4–6 ask about Passage B.

4. According to the passage, people seem to think that Miss Brooke is:
   - F. too rude.
   - G. too religious.
   - H. too happy.
   - J. too unscrupulous.

5. In the second and third paragraphs, all of the following qualities are used to describe Miss Brooke EXCEPT:
   - A. handsome.
   - B. ignorant.
   - C. clever.
   - D. charming.

6. As it is used in line 3, the word *pity* most nearly means:
   - F. sorry.
   - G. compassion.
   - H. sympathy.
   - J. shame.

Questions 7–10 ask about both passages.

7. Given the way they are presented in each passage, Mrs. Bennet and Miss Brooke are best described as:
   - A. demure.
   - B. disgusted.
   - C. short-tempered.
   - D. amusing.

8. In what way is Kitty in Passage A DIFFERENT from Miss Brooke in Passage B?

- **F.** Kitty is concerned about how others interpret her behavior.
- **G.** Kitty does not care about what is expected of women.
- **H.** Kitty uses hostility to mask her romantic feelings.
- **J.** Kitty is extremely selfish and hypocritical.

9. The narrators of Passage A and Passage B reveal the inner thoughts of which characters from each passage?

- **A.** Kitty and Celia
- **B.** Elizabeth and Miss Brooke
- **C.** Mr. Bingley and Sir James
- **D.** Mary and Celia

10. It can be inferred that Mr. Bingley in Passage A and Sir James in Passage B are both:

- **F.** extremely charming.
- **G.** uninterested in etiquette.
- **H.** unmarried men.
- **J.** in love with the women they meet.

PASSAGE II

SOCIAL SCIENCE: This passage is adapted from a sociological study of traditional Fiji culture conducted by Dr. Alfred Goldsborough Mayer.

Land tenure in traditional Fijian culture is a subject so complex that heavy volumes could be written about it. In general it may be said that the chief could sell no land without the consent of his tribe. In traditional Fiji society, cultivated land belonged to
5 the man who originally farmed it, and was passed undivided to all his heirs. Waste land was held in common. Native settlers who were taken into the tribes from time to time were permitted to farm some of the waste land, and for this privilege they and their heirs paid a yearly tribute to the chief either in produce
10 or in service. In essence, this amounted to paying rent to the chief.

Fijians appear never to have been wholly without a medium of exchange, for sperm-whale's teeth always had a recognized purchasing power. They also were especially regarded as a
15 means of expressing good will and honesty of purpose. A whale's tooth was as effective to secure compliance with the terms of a bargain in ancient Fiji as a signed contract is with modern Americans. Given Americans' penchant for wiggling their way out of contracts, a whale's tooth from a Fijian probably generated
20 much more trust that the agreement would be fulfilled.

As in all communities, including our own world of finance, a man's wealth consisted not only of what he possessed but even more so of the number of people from whom he could beg or borrow. Wilkes records an interesting example of this, for he
25 found that the rifle and other costly presents he had presented to King Tanoa were being seized by Tanoa's nephew who, as his vasu, had a right to take whatever he might select from the king's possessions. Indeed, in order to keep his property in sight, Tanoa was forced to give it to his own sons, thus escaping the
30 rapacity of his nephew.

In a traditional Fiji tribe, an individual as such can hardly be said to own property, for nearly all things belong to his family or clan, and are shared among cousins. This condition is partially responsible for the absence of personal ambition which once
35 struck Westerners as so illogical, but which was nevertheless the dominant feature of the social fabric of traditional Polynesians, and which prevented the introduction of "ideals of modern progress" until well into the twentieth century. The Fijians, for much of the last few centuries, were relatively happy;
40 why should they work when every reasonable want was already supplied? None were rich in material things, but none were beggars except in the sense that all were such. No one could be a miser, a capitalist, a banker, or a promoter in such a community, and thieves were almost unknown. Indeed, the honesty
45 of the traditional Fijians was one of those virtues that promoted the comment of travelers in previous centuries.

During Professor Alexander Agassiz's cruises in the late 1800s, in which he visited nearly every island of the Fijis, the natives came on board by the hundreds and not a single object was
50 stolen, although things almost priceless in native estimation lay loosely upon the deck. Once, indeed, when the deck was deserted by both officers and crew and fully a hundred natives were on board, the Professor found a man who had been gazing wistfully for half an hour at a bottle which lay upon the laboratory
55 table. Somehow he had managed to acquire a shilling, a large coin in Fiji at the time, and this he offered in exchange for the coveted bottle. As Agassiz tells us: "One can never forget his shout of joy and the radiance of his honest face as he leaped into his canoe after having received it as a gift."

60 As these Fijians said to Professor Agassiz, "The white man possesses more than we, but his life is full of toil and sorrow, while our days are happy as they pass."

But this was the Fiji of the past, when life was an evanescent thing, and only as real as the murmur of the surf when the sea
65 breeze comes in the morning. This was Fiji before capitalism took hold, before the forests were slashed and burned to make more land available for farming, and before the young people began to leave their ancient islands to look for "a better life."

CONTINUE

This life usually entails hoarding wealth and becoming enmeshed
70 in the rat race of modern civilization. Sadly, this race rarely has a happy ending.

Hoarded wealth inspired no respect in the Fiji of previous centuries, and indeed, were it discovered, its possession would have justified immediate confiscation. Yet man must raise idols
75 to satisfy his instinct to worship things above his acquisition, and thus rank was more revered because respect for property was low. Among traditional Fijian tribes, chiefs were greatly revered, and names themselves had more power than worldly goods.

80 One aspect to note is that names in traditional Fijian culture could change throughout one's life, depending on any important events that occurred. For instance, Chief Thakombau began life as "Seru," then after the civil war in which he overcame his father's enemies and reestablished Tanoa's rule in Mbau he was called
85 "Thakombau" (evil to Mbau). At the time he also received another name, "Thikinovu" (centipede) in allusion to his stealth in approaching to bite his enemy, but this designation, together with his given Christian name "Ebenezer" (he was converted by British missionaries), did not survive the test of usage.

11. The passage specifies that in traditional Fijian society, individual property was, for the most part:

    A. taken by Western explorers.
    B. collectively owned by the family or clan.
    C. owned solely by the chief of the tribe.
    D. thought to be possessed of evil phantoms.

12. Based on information in the passage, a contract from a traditional Fijian would most likely take the form of which of the following?

    F. a burnt offering to the gods
    G. a semiprecious stone
    H. the granting of a Fijian name
    J. a whale's tooth

13. The anecdote about King Tanoa's nephew described in the third paragraph is presented in order to illustrate the principle that:

    A. Western civilization has destroyed traditional Fijian values.
    B. the right to take or borrow from another was a notable indication of wealth in Fijian culture.
    C. all communities that value personal property levy heavy sanctions against theft.
    D. trust was not easily gained among Fijian tribes.

14. The author of the passage appears to feel that the question "What does modern civilization mean for the people of Fiji?" is best answered by the assertion that:

    F. Fiji, like most island civilizations, must give up its insular culture in order to compete in world markets.
    G. capitalism has helped the people of Fiji profit from their traditional values of honesty and egalitarianism.
    H. modern civilization has not made the people of Fiji any happier than they previously were.
    J. there is little chance that modern civilization will ever have an impact on the way of life enjoyed by most Fijians.

15. The author states in Paragraph 4 that "the introduction of 'ideals of modern progress'" was prevented "until well into the twentieth century" in Fiji because of a lack of:

    A. a sense of personal ownership.
    B. established religious customs.
    C. codified land laws.
    D. Western cultural indoctrination.

16. As it is used in line 16, the word *compliance* most nearly means:

    F. agreement.
    G. introduction.
    H. flexibility.
    J. resignation.

17. According to the passage, Chief Thakombau was granted this name after he:

    A. was born to distinguished parents.
    B. hoarded a large amount of wealth.
    C. was converted by British missionaries.
    D. restored Tanoa's rule in Mbau.

18. The author's analysis of traditional Fiji culture includes details concerning:

    I. ownership of land.
    II. how capitalism has changed Fijian culture.
    III. the shortage of natural resources in Fiji.

    F. I only
    G. I and II only
    H. II and III only
    J. I, II, and III

19. According to the first paragraph, a Fijian chief did NOT have the right to:

- **A.** declare war.
- **B.** start a new community on the same island.
- **C.** cultivate land.
- **D.** sell tribal land without the tribe's permission.

20. One of the main points made in the fourth paragraph is that although traditional Fijians did not have strong ambitions to acquire personal wealth, one benefit of this was the:

- **F.** lack of good jobs.
- **G.** promotion of industrialization.
- **H.** scarcity of theft in Fijian society.
- **J.** growth of friendship between Fijian chiefs.

PASSAGE III

HUMANITIES: This passage is adapted from *The Physical Michelangelo* by James Frederick Rogers.

Had Michelangelo been less poetic and more explicit in his language, he might have said there is nothing so conducive to mental and physical wholeness as saturation of body and mind with work. The great artist was so prone to over-anxiety and
5 met (whether needlessly or not) with so many rebuffs and disappointments that only constant absorption in manual labor prevented spirit from fretting itself free from flesh. He toiled "furiously" in all his mighty undertakings that body and mind remained one and in abundant health for nearly four score and
10 ten years.

Michelangelo's life was devoted with passion to art. Art became his religion and required of him the sacrifice of all that might keep him below his highest level of power for work. His father early warned him to have a care for his health. Said he,
15 "In your profession, if once you were to fall ill you would be a ruined man." To one so intent on perfection and so keenly alive to imperfection such advice must have been superfluous, for the artist could not but observe the effect upon his work of any depression of his bodily well-being. He was, besides, too thrifty
20 in all respects to think of lapsing into bodily neglect or abuse. He was severely temperate, save in those times when devotion to work caused him to sleep with his clothes on, so that he might not lose time in seizing the chisel when he awoke. He ate to live and to labor. When intent on some work he usually

25 confined his diet to a piece of bread which he ate in the middle of his labors. Few hours were devoted to sleep. He ate comparatively little and slept less than many men because he worked better. He dressed for comfort and not to mortify the flesh, sometimes leaving his high dog-skin boots on for so long that
30 when he removed them the scarf skin came away like the skin of a molting serpent.

His intensity of purpose and fiery energy expressed themselves in his features and form. His face was round, his brow square, ample, and deeply furrowed; the temples projected much
35 beyond the ears; his eyes were small rather than large, of a dark color and peered, piercingly, from under heavy brows. The flattened nose was the result of a blow from a rival apprentice. He evidently looked the part, though for such mental powers one of his colossal statues would seem a more fitting mold.

40 It was not until the age of seventy that an illness which seemed to mark any weakening of his bodily powers came upon Michelangelo. At seventy-five, symptoms of calculus (a disease common in that day at fifty) appeared, but, though naturally pessimistic, he writes, "In all other respects I am pretty much as
45 I was at thirty years." He wielded the brush and the chisel with consummate skill in his seventy-fifth year. With the later loss of his energy, he found vent more in the planning and supervising of architectural works, culminating in the building of St. Peter's. But even in these later years he took up the chisel as an outlet
50 for superfluous energy and to induce sleep. Though the product of his hand was not good, his health was the better for this mutual exercise of mind and body.

In his eighty-sixth year he is said to have sat drawing for three consecutive hours until pains and cramps in his limbs warned
55 him that he had not the endurance of youth. For exercise, when manual labor proved a disappointment, he often took horseback rides. There was no invalidism about this great spirit, and it was not until the day before his death that he would consent to go to bed.

60 His temperance, manual industry, and his extraordinary blamelessness in life and in every action had been his source of preservation. He was miserly, suspicious, quarrelsome, and pessimistic, but the effects of these faults were balanced by his better habits of thought and action. That he, like most great
65 men, felt keenly the value of health, is evidenced not only by his own practice, but by his oft repeated warnings to his nephew when choosing a wife to see that whatever other qualities she might have she be healthy. One of those who look beneath unusual human phenomena for signs of the pathologic finds

70 Michelangelo "affected by a degree of neuropathy bordering closely upon hysterical disease." What a pity that more of us do not suffer from such degrees of neuropathy and how much better for most of us if we had such enthusiasm for perfection, and such mania for work, at least of that health-bringing sort in
75 which there is absorbing unity of brain and hand. True it is that "there is no better way of keeping sane and free from anxiety than by being mad."

21. According to the passage, Michelangelo had to maintain his physical health because:

  A. poor health ran in his family.
  B. his father demanded that he did.
  C. if he got sick, he wouldn't be able to work.
  D. he could get seriously injured.

22. The author of the passage would most likely agree with which of the following statements?

  F. Michelangelo used the physicality of his work to help relieve his many anxieties and frustrations.
  G. Michelangelo was an easygoing, carefree man who possessed a unique genius for art.
  H. In order to be successful, all artists have to have the same passion Michelangelo had.
  J. Michelangelo's artistic skills remained completely intact until he died.

23. The passage states that Michelangelo began planning and supervising more architectural works when he was:

  A. under thirty.
  B. eighty-six.
  C. under seventy.
  D. over seventy-five.

24. According to the third paragraph, Michelangelo's physical appearance reflected:

  I. a coarse sense of humor.
  II. fierce devotion to his work.
  III. enormous mental capacity.

  F. I only
  G. III only
  H. II and III
  J. I, II and III

25. It can be inferred from the second paragraph that by limiting his food and sleep, Michelangelo was:

  A. able to fully realize his potential as an artist.
  B. driven to madness.
  C. unable to be as prolific as he might otherwise have been.
  D. able to control his health.

26. The passage suggests that during his youth as an apprentice painter Michelangelo:

  F. had not yet learned how to take proper care of his health.
  G. was overly generous with his friends.
  H. had a fight with a rival apprentice painter.
  J. often ignored the advice of his father.

27. The main idea of the passage is that:

  A. to live a long, healthy life, one must make the same sacrifices Michelangelo did.
  B. Michelangelo's supreme devotion to his work enabled him to live to a ripe old age with a unique merging of mind and spirit.
  C. through sheer force of will, Michelangelo was able to stay healthy.
  D. Michelangelo was insane.

28. According to Paragraph 6, Michelangelo's "source of preservation" was due in part to his:

  I. ascetic lifestyle.
  II. miserly nature.
  III. pessimistic outlook.

  F. I only
  G. I and II
  H. I and III
  J. II and III

29. Based on the information in the passage, which of the following is a fact rather than an opinion?

  A. Michelangelo's last sculptures were not of the same artistic caliber as his earlier works.
  B. Michelangelo's bad qualities were balanced by his good ones.
  C. We would all be better off if we had the same keen desire for perfection that Michelangelo did.
  D. Michelangelo did not rest until the day before his death.

30. The phrase "one of his colossal statues would seem a more fitting mold" in Paragraph 3 implies:

  F. many of Michelangelo's sculptures were self-portraits.
  G. Michelangelo's actual appearance was not as impressive as his work.
  H. his intellectual skills were not as great as his sculptural ability.
  J. Michelangelo didn't create small-scale sculptures.

PASSAGE IV

NATURAL SCIENCE: This passage is adapted from an excerpt of a biology text.

Imagine for a moment that you are a plant living in a bog. You strain to extract the nitrogen you need from the soil, but it's simply too acidic for the bacteria that break down dead plant matter to grow in.

5 So where do you get the nitrogen you need? If you're a pitcher plant, you get it from insects that you catch.

Like the Venus flytrap, the sundew, and the bladderwort, the pitcher plant is able to trap and consume insects. But unlike these other carnivorous plants, the pitcher plant does not
10 produce enzymes to digest the captured insects itself. Instead, the pitcher plant absorbs nutrients that are the result of a complex interaction between insect larvae that grow in the pitcher plant's deadly interior.

A pitcher plant has a sweet-smelling flower and purple-veined
15 leaves that form "pitchers" by curving in on themselves. These leaves have tiny downward-pointing hairs on them to prevent any insects that happen to wander into the pitcher's clutches from wandering out again. Below the downward-pointing hairs is a highly slippery part of the leaf. When insects reach this
20 slippery section, they fall into the heart of the pitcher plant: a highly acidic mixture of water and the plant's own secretions.

First, an insect is attracted to the pitcher plant by the sugary smell of its flower. Once the victim has drowned in the deadly water, the pitcher plant has its own unique system of extracting
25 needed nutrients from the deceased insect. Inside the pitcher plant, living in the deadly acid reservoir, are the larvae of three distinct insect species. The larvae of a fly, a mosquito, and a midge species all live in the noisome fluid of the pitcher plant. These larvae, which are amazingly found nowhere else in nature,
30 work together to break down the victim insects into base components that can be absorbed by the plant, and along the way the larvae also receive needed sustenance. Within the pitcher plant is a tiny ecosystem of plants and animals working together.

Each larva has a life span of about a year, which is also the
35 life span of each pitcher plant leaf. In July, adult insects deposit their young in the pitcher plant where for four months the larvae consume insects unlucky enough to fall into the watery pit. Then the larvae spend the cold winter months frozen inside of the pitcher plant. With the spring thaw, the larvae resume their
40 feast until early July. At that point they are fully mature insects, ready to fly off from their botanic home, find a mate and lay their eggs in a new pitcher plant receptacle.

The three different insect species do not actually compete for the insects that fall into the clutches of the pitcher plant.

45 The fly larvae are much larger than the midge and mosquito larvae. Floating at the top of the pitcher pool, the fly maggot chews on insects when they first enter the pool and drown. Underneath the fly maggot the mosquito and midge larvae lurk, waiting for carcasses or parts of carcasses that escape the
50 greedy jaws of the maggot.

Then the midge gets to work, gnawing on insects that sink below the fly. The mosquito has to wait for the midge to finish eating, since the mosquito can only consume very small particles of insect that the midge chews up first. The mosquito larvae
55 also consume the bacteria that grow on the surface of these insect particles.

Field biologists were able to examine the interaction of these species by taking clear plastic tubes, filling them with water from actual pitcher plants, and then sticking these tubes into
60 bogs. These tubes were then used in a variety of experiments to determine just how the insect larvae in pitcher plants process their food.

In one experiment, a fixed number of midges and mosquitoes were placed in various plastic pitchers. After a week, the plastic
65 tubes were taken to a lab and analyzed. Measurements were made of the amount of food particles in each tube, how much bacteria was in each pool, and the number of midges and mosquitoes that survived. Each midge and mosquito larva was also weighed to determine how healthy it was.

70 Biologists found that the more midges there were in a pitcher plant, the better off the mosquitoes were. This is because instead of competing for resources with the mosquitoes, the midges were actually preparing food for mosquitoes to consume. This is a unique interaction in the animal kingdom. Usually when
75 animals are in a symbiotic relationship they both benefit in some way, but in this case the mosquito population did not positively affect the midges in the experiments conducted. But since the mosquitoes brought no harm to the midges, this could not be considered a parasitic relationship. This relationship,
80 where one species produces food for another species, has been termed a "processing chain" by some biologists.

31. The passage mentions that biologists have conducted experiments demonstrating that mosquito larvae in the pitcher plant benefit from:

  A. an absence of midge larvae in the plant's basin.

  B. a dearth of fly larvae in the plant's basin.

  C. an increase in the number of midge larvae in the plant's basin.

  D. any change in the amount of bacteria in the plant's basin.

CONTINUE

32. According to the passage, the pitcher plant has:

    I.   long, penetrating roots.
    II. a sweet-smelling flower.
    III. leaves with tiny hairs on them.

    F. I only
    G. II only
    H. I and II
    J. II and III

33. The passage suggests that a pitcher plant leaf lives for approximately:

    A. one month.
    B. four months.
    C. one year.
    D. ten years.

34. It can reasonably be inferred from the passage that the water found in the basin of a pitcher plant is all of the following EXCEPT:

    F. full of enzymes produced by the pitcher plant.
    G. the home for several species of insect larvae.
    H. highly acidic in nature.
    J. the fluid from which the pitcher plant absorbs needed nutrients.

35. According to the passage, fly larvae differ from mosquito and midge larvae because fly larvae:

    A. do not present a danger to field biologists.
    B. always live on the bottom of the pitcher plant's basin.
    C. directly affect the number of midge larvae in the pitcher plant.
    D. are larger than mosquito and midge larvae.

36. The reason that the pitcher plant cannot extract nitrogen from the soil of a bog is due to the:

    F. pitcher plant's immature root system.
    G. surplus of water found in boggy locations.
    H. lack of a certain type of bacteria in the soil.
    J. insect larvae living in the plant's interior.

37. According to the passage, mosquito larvae cannot eat insect parts until the insects have first been:

    A. broken down by the midge larvae in the pitcher plant.
    B. dissolved by acids produced by the pitcher plant.
    C. frozen for several months in the interior of the pitcher plant.
    D. completely consumed by the fly larvae in the pitcher plant.

38. The passage states that biologists used plastic tubes in order to:

    F. trap mosquito larvae for testing.
    G. test the acidity of the soil found in the bog.
    H. simulate the form of the pitcher plant.
    J. give fly larvae a chance to compete with the midges and mosquitoes.

39. Based on information from the passage, the leaves of the pitcher plant have all of the following characteristics EXCEPT:

    A. downward-pointing hairs.
    B. a way to produce digestive enzymes.
    C. purple veins on them.
    D. a section that is highly slippery.

40. Which of the following would be the best example of a "processing chain" that mirrors the midge and mosquito relationship found in the interior of the pitcher plant?

    F. A human farmer grows grains to be consumed by both humans and farm animals.
    G. A vulture can eat a moose only after it has been killed and partially consumed by a wolf.
    H. A certain fish survives by eating the bacteria found on a shark's skin and the shark benefits from this relationship with healthier skin.
    J. A bird feeds her young by taking food from other smaller birds.

STOP

SCIENCE TEST

35 MINUTES—40 QUESTIONS

> **DIRECTIONS:** There are seven passages in this test. Each passage is followed by several questions. Read each passage, select the best answer to each related question, and fill in the corresponding circle on the answer sheet. You may look back at the passages as often as you need.
>
> You are NOT allowed to use a calculator on this test.

PASSAGE I

As power is supplied to a circuit, current flows through the circuit. An ammeter is the device used to measure the current, and many ammeters measure current in milliamperes (mA). The voltage responsible for the current can be measured by a voltmeter and is measured in volts. When a resistor is placed in a circuit, it dampens the current flowing through a circuit at a given voltage.

If there is a linear relationship between current and voltage when a resistor is placed in the circuit, the resistor is considered an ohmic device. If the temperature of the resistor changes, then it is not considered an ohmic device. Some resistors are sensitive to small external temperature changes and will show a change in resistance as a result of these temperature changes. These resistors are called *thermistors*. The change in resistance exhibited by a thermistor can be detected by a change in the observed current at a given voltage.

The following procedure was performed to investigate whether different resistors acted as ohmic devices in a circuit. The circuit was constructed as shown in Figure 1.

FIGURE 1

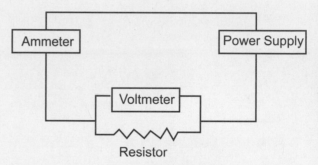

Resistor

After each resistor was connected to the circuit, the resistor was submerged in water to detect any changes in temperature as well as its sensitivity to different beginning temperatures. The power source was turned on and the voltages of the power source and the resulting current were recorded. The voltage was changed several times, and the corresponding current was noted.

Practice Test 3 — SCIENCE

CONTINUE

Table 1 summarizes the results when three different resistors were tested at two different temperatures. In all cases, no change in water temperature was observed.

Voltage (V)	Current (mA)	Current (mA)
Resistor A		
	23°C	**25°C**
0.25	25	25
0.50	50	50
1.00	100	100
2.00	200	200
3.00	300	300
4.00	400	400
4.50	450	450
5.00	500	500
Resistor B		
	23°C	**25°C**
0.25	150	150
0.50	195	195
1.00	230	230
2.00	295	295
3.00	345	345
4.00	405	405
4.50	420	420
5.00	445	445
Resistor C		
	23°C	**25°C**
0.25	5	4.5
0.50	10	9.0
1.00	20	18.0
2.00	40	36.0
3.00	60	54.0
4.00	80	72.0
4.50	90	81.0
5.00	100	90.0

Table 1

1. When the voltage is 3 volts and the temperature 23°C, what is the current of the circuit when Resistor B is used?
   - A. 54 mA
   - B. 60 mA
   - C. 300 mA
   - D. 345 mA

2. If 6.0 volts were used in the circuit with Resistor C at 25°C, approximately what would the current have read?
   - F. 108 mA
   - G. 140 mA
   - H. 485 mA
   - J. 600 mA

3. According to the data, which of the following resistors is NOT sensitive to temperature?
   - I. Resistor A
   - II. Resistor B
   - III. Resistor C

   - A. I only
   - B. III only
   - C. I and II
   - D. II and III

4. Which of the following observations supports the conclusion that one of the resistors is a thermistor?
   - F. Resistor A did not show a change in resistance when introduced to two different temperatures.
   - G. Resistor B had a greater measured current than Resistor A.
   - H. Resistor C had a change in resistance when introduced to two different temperatures.
   - J. Resistor C had a lower observed current than Resistor A.

5. Based on the data in Table 1, Resistor B does NOT appear to be an ohmic device because:
   - A. at a constant voltage, the current varies with temperature.
   - B. the current is unaffected by temperature.
   - C. the voltage and current have a linear relationship.
   - D. the voltage and current do not have a linear relationship.

6. Which of the following hypotheses would be disproved if there had been a noted temperature change in the water for all six trials?

- F. Resistor A is an ohmic device because of its linear relationship between voltage and current.
- G. Resistor B is affected by different starting temperatures.
- H. Resistor C is not an ohmic device because it does not have a linear relationship between voltage and current.
- J. Resistor C is not affected by different starting temperatures.

PASSAGE II

A state forestry commission engaged a group of ecologists to study the nutrient flow in a forest on federal land that was being considered for lease to a logging company. They were also asked to study the effects of clear-cutting in selected areas and predict what the long-term effects on the nutrient budget might be. The scientists selected several small sections of the forest for observation and experiment.

The first task was to estimate the average nutrient flow within the entire forest area. Table 1 shows their estimate based on six experimental areas chosen within the forest. Nutrients enter the forest ecosystem via precipitation, so rain gauges were set up in various locations in the study areas. Nutrients exit the ecosystem through runoff from streams and rivers, so the ecologists measured stream flows in the designated areas.

Table 1: Average Concentrations of Dissolved Substances in Bulk Precipitation and Stream Water in Six Undisturbed Experimental Watersheds

Substance	Precipitation	Stream Water	Percent Change
Calcium	0.21	1.51	−619%
Magnesium	0.05	0.37	−640%
Potassium	0.10	0.23	−130%
Sodium	0.12	0.94	−683%
Aluminum	0.01	0.24	−2,300%
Ammonium	0.22	0.05	340%
Sulfate	3.10	6.20	−100%
Nitrate	1.30	1.14	12%
Chloride	0.42	0.64	−52%
Silica	0.03	4.59	−15,300%

After estimating the overall nutrient flow in this forest, the ecologists had one 15-hectare* area cleared of trees in order to determine the amount of increase that would occur in runoff. The trees were removed from the area, but nothing else was disturbed. For the first two years after the logging, an herbicide was applied so that no vegetation would grow back. The ecologists then compared this cleared watershed with one of the intact watersheds under study. They measured the stream flow for the first three years after the logging took place. Table 2 summarizes the amounts of organic and inorganic matter found at the watershed basin. A net and filter system was utilized to catch finer matter as the runoff exited the watershed area.

*A hectare is a metric unit of measure equal to 2.471 acres.

Table 2: Annual Losses of Particulate Matter

Source of Output	Year	Watershed 1 Undisturbed Area		Watershed 2 Deforested Area	
		Organic	Inorganic	Organic	Inorganic
Ponding Basin	1	4.62	8.30	35.41	158.32
Net	1	0.43	0.02	0.26	0.01
Filter	1	2.64	2.80	4.23	4.80
Ponding Basin	2	11.39	31.00	45.13	321.88
Net	2	0.43	0.02	0.25	0.03
Filter	2	3.32	3.70	6.24	7.10
Ponding Basin	3	3.83	5.78	53.72	540.32
Net	3	0.42	0.01	0.27	0.04
Filter	3	2.61	2.97	8.73	12.98

Note: Data is given in kilograms per dry weight of materials per hectare of the watershed. Basin-caught materials are coarse, net-caught materials are fine, and filter-caught materials are superfine.

7. Based on the figures reported in Table 1, which is apparently true of the nutrient budget as estimated using the six experimental areas?

   A. There is a net loss for all measured nutrients entering the ecosystem.
   B. There is a net gain for all measured nutrients entering the ecosystem.
   C. There is a net loss for all measured nutrients, except for ammonium and nitrate
   D. There is a net gain for all measured nutrients, except for ammonium and nitrate.

8. According to the data obtained, which substances are most dramatically depleted in this ecosystem?

   F. Sodium and calcium
   G. Silica and aluminum
   H. Magnesium and potassium
   J. Chloride and nitrate

9. Which of the following best explains why the scientists chose to use three different collection methods?

   A. It enabled them to collect particulate matter at different watersheds.
   B. It enabled them to collect particulate matter of different sizes.
   C. All of the collected particulate matter was quite coarse.
   D. The collected particulate matter was dissolved in water.

10. Which of the following hypotheses concerning the effects of logging on the forest ecosystem is supported by the data?

    F. Logging decreases the loss of organic and inorganic matter from the forest ecosystem.
    G. Logging increases the loss of organic matter but has no effect on inorganic matter in the forest ecosystem.
    H. Logging increases the loss of inorganic matter but has no effect on organic matter in the forest ecosystem.
    J. Logging increases the loss of organic and inorganic matter from the forest ecosystem.

11. Based on the trend in the numbers over the first three years of observing the undisturbed and logged watershed areas reported in Table 2, it would be reasonable to predict that the runoff:

    A. would vary from year to year within narrow limits in the undisturbed area but steadily increase in the logged area.
    B. in both experimental areas would steadily increase over the years.
    C. in both experimental areas would vary from year to year.
    D. in the undisturbed area would remain constant, but the runoff in the logged area would vary from year to year.

12. The ecologists inform the state officials that the bark in trees contains a significant proportion of nutrients. If the state officials are committed to leasing a set amount of this federal land to a logging company, they might reduce the nutrient loss in that region by:

    F. removing all remains from the trees after they are cut down so that the area is clear for new growth.
    G. applying herbicide immediately after any logging operation.
    H. allowing the logging companies to use the cleared areas for roads.
    J. stripping the bark from all logged trees and leaving it behind in the cleared area.

PASSAGE III

Elements are categorized to help understand the similarities and differences between them. One way is to consider their similarities based on the number of negatively charged particles in a particular orbit. Alkali metals are reactive elements that contain one electron in what is considered an *s* orbital. Scientists have been able to observe different characteristics in alkali metals. Atomic number is the number of positively charged particles (protons) in an element. These positively charged particles are balanced with the same number of electrons in a neutrally charged atom.

Table 1 contains data for the alkali metals, including the atomic number, atomic weight, melting point, and density.

Table 1

Element	Atomic Number	Atomic Weight (amu)	Melting Point (°C)	Density (g/cm³)
Lithium	3	6.9	181	0.53
Sodium	11	23.0	98	0.97
Potassium	19	39.1	63	0.86
Rubidium	37	85.5	39	1.53
Cesium	55	132.9	29	1.87

13. The element with atomic weight of 85.5 amu has a melting point of:

A. 29°C.

B. 37°C.

C. 39°C.

D. 63°C.

14. According to the table, which of the following elements has a density of approximately twice that of sodium?

F. Lithium

G. Potassium

H. Rubidium

J. Cesium

15. The data seems to indicate that as the atomic number increases, the melting point:

A. increases.

B. decreases.

C. remains constant.

D. decreases, then increases.

16. It was hypothesized that the density will increase as atomic weight increases. Based on the data in the table, which of the following pairs of substances supports this hypothesis?

   I. Sodium and potassium

  II. Rubidium and cesium

  III. Lithium and potassium

F. I only

G. III only

H. I and II

J. II and III

17. If an alkali metal existed with an atomic number greater than that of cesium, which of the following would be the best predicted measurements for its melting point and density?

A. The melting point would be greater than 29°C, and density would be greater than 1.87 g/cm³.

B. The melting point would be less than 29°C, and density would be less than 1.87 g/cm³.

C. The melting point would be greater than 29°C, and density would be less than 1.87 g/cm³.

D. The melting point would be less than 29°C, and density would be uncertain.

PASSAGE IV

By studying rock samples, geologists can reconstruct much of an area's geologic history. Table 1 lists rock samplings taken along a line proceeding east and inland from a shoreline, in 20-mile intervals. The sampled rock found at each altitude and distance is shown, and the crystallization temperature and ages typical of each type of rock are listed. Figure 1 shows the cross-sectional area of measurement.

Table 1

Distance East (miles)	Altitude (feet)	Type of Rock in Sample	Crystallization Temperature*	Estimated Age (millions of years)
0 (shoreline)	0	Rhyolite	750°	10.0
20	6,000	Diorite	850°	250.0
40	5,000	Peridotite	1,200°	200.0
60	90	Shale	750°	0.1
80	−10	Limestone	800°	6.0
100	25	Breccia	750°	0.5
120	75	Andesite	950°	3.6
140	2,000	Andesite	900°	4.0
160	3,300	Gabbro	1,100°	300.0
180	13,900	Granite	700°	400.0

*Crystallization temperature is based on the mineral composition of the rock.

CONTINUE

FIGURE 1

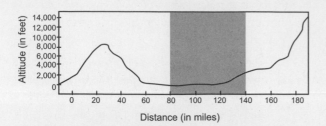

18. What is the relationship between the ages of rocks and altitude?

    F. The oldest rocks are generally found at lower altitudes.
    G. The oldest rocks are generally found at higher altitudes.
    H. There is no relationship between altitude and rock ages.
    J. Rocks less than 100 million years old are only found in areas less than 1,000 feet in altitude.

19. If higher crystallization temperatures generally produce darker-colored rocks, which of the following rocks is most likely to be dark-colored?

    A. Limestone
    B. Shale
    C. Gabbro
    D. Granite

20. Which of the following measurements is shown on the vertical axis in Figure 1?

    F. Altitude
    G. Distance inland from shoreline
    H. Temperature
    J. Age of rocks

21. Iron ore is usually found in rocks that crystallize at higher temperatures. From the data shown, how far east of the shoreline would a miner try to find large concentrations of iron?

    A. 40 miles
    B. 100 miles
    C. 120 miles
    D. 180 miles

22. Based on the data provided, what is the relationship between distance from shoreline and the ages of the rock samples?

    F. Rocks closer to the shoreline are always younger.
    G. Rocks closer to the shoreline are always older.
    H. The age of rocks gradually increases farther inland.
    J. There is no consistent relationship between the distance from shore and the ages of the rock samples.

23. Limestone is sedimentary rock that develops from the accumulated deposits of sea organisms with shells. Andesite is igneous rock deposited by lava flows from volcanoes. Which of the following is the best hypothesis about the geologic record of the shaded area?

    A. Part of this area was once a sea while volcanoes erupted to the east.
    B. Part of this area was once a sea; later, volcanoes erupted to the east.
    C. A volcano arose west of an inland sea in this area.
    D. A sea existed in part of this area after nearby volcanoes became extinct.

PASSAGE V

The apparent bird-dinosaur evolutionary connection has been a source of considerable debate among paleontologists during the second half of the twentieth century. This association was proposed on the basis of numerous anatomical similarities and has been supported by the discovery of fossils of a small number of seeming transitional forms uncovered in Europe and Asia. Yet scientists differ in their interpretation of the significance of these similarities and the nature of the fossil evidence as well.

Paleontologist A

The discovery of fossil reptiles equipped with feathers, wings, and beak-like snouts may be significant but more likely provides only limited support for the dinosaurs-into-birds hypothesis. Convergent evolution often provides animals of very distant lineages with similar appendages—witness, for example, the similarities in the body shape and presence of fins in fish and cetaceans such as whales and dolphins. We would never put forth the idea that orcas evolved from sharks based on the morphological similarities of these creatures; it would be immediately deemed absurd.

It is more likely the case that birds and dinosaurs share a very distant common ancestor, perhaps from among the thecodonts. These prototypical reptiles of the late Permian survived the largest mass extinction recorded in the planet's history to bring forth many more recent lines; crocodiles, dinosaurs, pterosaurs, and birds are the most notable among these.

Paleontologist B

In our studies of numerous dinosaur fossils, it has become obvious that the lifestyles of dinosaurs were amazingly varied. No longer is it acceptable to view dinosaurs only as lumbering, cold-blooded monsters; indeed, the most frightening dinosaurs did not lumber at all. They were agile, swift, and deadly predators who could run, leap, kick, and shred to pieces an animal they were intent upon consuming. Lightweight muscular body structure would be crucial to the success of this type of predator.

Based upon this observation, along with a number of obvious physical similarities and evidence from the fossil record, we are convinced that birds evolved from small, carnivorous dinosaurs called theropods. A mere examination of the forelimb, hindlimb, and feet of a theropod fossil, and a comparison to one of the five available specimens of *Archaeopteryx**, will bear this out. In addition, more recent discoveries of fossil dinosaurs with bird-like traits and habits, particularly the finds uncovered in the Liaoning province of China, lend further credible support for our position that birds are for all intents and purposes actual members of the lineage Dinosauria living and thriving in our midst.

Archaeopteryx was a feathered reptile of the late Jurassic Era thought to represent an intermediate form between dinosaurs and birds.

24. According to Paleontologist A, similarities in the body forms of dinosaurs and birds:

    F. represent a failed experiment of evolution.
    G. are the products of convergent evolution.
    H. are completely without significance.
    J. helped both types of organism survive a large mass extinction.

25. Which of the following types of evidence, if found, would lend strong support to the position of Paleontologist A?

    A. Discovery of thecodont fossils with characteristics of modern birds and existing dinosaur fossils
    B. Discovery of another possible intermediate form between dinosaurs and birds from the Jurassic Era
    C. Discovery of an avian prototype dating back to before the beginning of the era of dinosaur dominance
    D. A careful examination of several sets of theropod fossil remains

26. Which of the following is a criticism that Paleontologist A would make of the avian evolutionary hypothesis of Paleontologist B?

    F. It ignores the possibility of the existence of transitional forms.
    G. It ignores the impact of a very large mass extinction.
    H. It assumes that morphological similarities are a result of a direct lineage.
    J. It proposes that dinosaurs and birds arose from distant lineages.

27. Which of the following perspectives would be consistent with the views of Paleontologist B?

    A. Convergent evolution produces similar forms in diverse lineages.
    B. Dinosaurs and birds may be related via a common ancestor.
    C. Birds and dinosaurs arose from completely separate lineages.
    D. Birds arose from a lineage of dinosaurs.

28. If genetic evidence was established to date the avian lineage 85 million years prior to the rise of *Archaeopteryx*, this finding would tend to:

    F. support the theory of Paleontologist A.
    G. support the theory of Paleontologist B.
    H. support the theories of both paleontologists.
    J. refute the theories of both paleontologists.

29. If Paleontologist B could confirm that birds appeared much later in evolutionary history than any dinosaurs, which of the following statements would reconcile this fact with the theory of Paleontologist A?

    A. The ancestors of birds and the ancestors of dinosaurs were exposed to specific environmental conditions at the same time, and this caused the development of similar characteristics.
    B. The ancestors of birds and the ancestors of dinosaurs were exposed to specific environmental conditions that caused the development of similar characteristics, but the dinosaur ancestors were exposed to these environmental conditions later than the bird ancestors were.
    C. The rate of evolutionary change from the thecodont ancestor was much slower for the lineage that resulted in birds than for the lineage that resulted in dinosaurs.
    D. The rate of evolutionary change from the thecodont ancestor was much faster for the lineage that resulted in birds than for the lineage that resulted in dinosaurs.

CONTINUE

PASSAGE VI

Ecology graduate students wished to experiment with levels of diversity in a simple community to observe the relationship between increasing complexity and stability of populations. In particular, they were interested in the impact of changing certain conditions in a community on populations of two species of *Paramecium*, a common ciliated protozoan.

A *trophic* level is the number of steps a species is away from the producer species in a community. Producers are organisms that synthesize energy out of chemical products into nutrients. Table 1 shows the trophic level occupied by each type of organism involved in the experiments and the number of species that would be used on each level.

Table 1

Trophic Level	Organism	Number of Species Studied
First	Bacteria	3
Second	Paramecia	2
Third	Amoebae (predator of protozoa)	2

Experiment 1

The graduate students wished to study the relationship between one species of *Paramecium* and the number of species of bacteria available for consumption in the community. They created 300 "microcosms"—100 cultures each populated with communities of one, two, or three species of bacteria and one of the *Paramecium* species. After 20 days, they examined the cultures individually. The results are displayed in Table 2.

Table 2

Number of Bacterium Species	Number of Cultures in Which Paramecia Survived
1	32/100
2	61/100
2	70/100

Experiment 2

The students then decided to study how two species of *Paramecium* would be affected when different combinations of *Paramecium* and bacteria were mixed in the cultures. They created 100 dishes each of six separate types of communities—600 cultures with different combinations of the *Paramecium* and the three bacteria species. After 20 days, they examined the cultures and recorded their results. These results are reproduced in Table 3.

Table 3

Number of Bacterium/ Paramecium Species	Number of Cultures in Which Paramecia Survived
1/1	35/100
2/1	58/100
3/1	65/100
1/2	20/100
2/2	26/100
3/2	31/100

Experiment 3

The last condition that the graduate students studied was the addition of a third trophic level to their microcosms. They introduced two different species of *Amoebae* that feed on *Paramecium*. They decided to use five different versions in 100 culture dishes each, creating 500 communities for this last experiment. They allowed them to grow undisturbed for 20 days, and then examined the cultures and recorded their results in Table 4 displayed below.

Table 4

Number of Bacterium/ Paramecium/ Amoeba Species	Number of Cultures in Which Paramecia Survived
1/1/1	22/100
2/1/1	15/100
2/2/1	8/100
2/2/2	6/100
3/2/2	2/100

30. Which of the following factors was varied in Experiment 1?

F. The species of *Paramecium* in the community

G. The number of species of bacteria present in the community

H. The medium used to culture the microbes

J. The number of trophic levels in the community

31. According to the results of Experiments 1 and 2, increasing the number of bacteria species present in the community:

A. decreased the survival rates of the *Paramecium* in the community.

B. increased the survival rates of the *Paramecium* in the community.

C. had no effect on any species in the community.

D. decreased the survival rates of one type of bacteria in the community.

32. According to the results of Experiment 2, increasing the number of *Paramecium* species in the community was related to:

F. decreased survival rates for the *Paramecium*, depending on the number of bacteria species present in the community.

G. decreased survival rates for all species present in the community.

H. decreased survival rates for the *Paramecium* independent of the number of bacteria species present in the community.

J. increased survival rates for the *Paramecium*, depending on the number of bacteria species present in the community.

33. What new factor was introduced in Experiment 3?

A. An additional species of bacteria

B. A longer time for incubation of the experimental cultures

C. A new method for culturing the experimental microbes

D. An additional trophic level

34. After examining the results of Experiment 3, it would be reasonable to conclude that increased diversity in the experimental communities:

F. was beneficial to all species present in the communities.

G. had no effect on any species in the communities.

H. had a detrimental effect on the survival rate of one species of Amoeba only.

J. had a detrimental effect on the survival rates of both species of Paramecium under study.

PASSAGE VII

Classification of planets in our solar system has been a controversial issue, especially in the last decade. Advanced telescopes have allowed scientists to see more celestial objects in space, so scientists have observed characteristics among the objects that have caused them to reconsider whether certain planets should retain their "planet" status. Some of the characteristics that make these objects distinct include size, mass, and shape, as well as orbital characteristics. Two orbital characteristics of planets often compared by astronomers are orbital inclination and orbital eccentricity. Orbital inclination is the amount an object's orbit is tilted with respect to the plane of the solar system. Orbital eccentricity refers to the amount that an object's orbit deviates from a circular orbit.

In 2006, the International Astronomical Union (IAU) officially defined what a planet is and established a system of classification for celestial bodies other than satellites (moons). According to the definition, a planet is a celestial body that orbits the sun, has sufficient mass to be rounded in shape by its own gravity, and has cleared out other large rocks and bodies from its orbital path. The other classifications established were *dwarf planets* and *small solar system bodies*. Based on these new definitions, Pluto was reclassified from a planet to a dwarf planet.

CONTINUE

The table below summarizes many of the qualities of the eight planets in our solar system.

Table 1								
	Inner Planets				**Outer Planets**			
Celestial Body	**Mercury**	**Venus**	**Earth**	**Mars**	**Jupiter**	**Saturn**	**Uranus**	**Neptune**
Mass (kg)	3.3×10^{23}	4.9×10^{24}	6.0×10^{24}	6.4×10^{23}	1.9×10^{27}	5.7×10^{26}	8.7×10^{25}	1.0×10^{26}
Mean Density (kg/m³)	5,427	5,204	5,520	3,933	1,326	687	1,318	1,638
Black-body Temp. (°K)	442.5	238.9	247.3	216.6	90.6	63.9	35.9	33.2
Orbital Inclination (°)	7.000	3.390	0.000	1.850	1.305	2.484	0.770	1.769
Orbital Eccentricity (°)	0.2056	0.0068	0.0167	0.0934	0.0484	0.0542	0.0472	0.0086
Rotation Period (hrs.)	1,407.60	5,832.50	23.93	24.62	9.93	10.50	17.24	16.11

35. Neptune has a density greater than which of the following planets?

   A. Mars, Venus, and Mercury
   B. Saturn, Uranus, and Jupiter
   C. Earth, Jupiter, and Saturn
   D. Venus, Saturn, and Earth

36. Black-body temperature is the temperature that would result from the planet absorbing all received electro-magnetic radiation without reflection. If black-body temperatures are higher for objects closer to the sun, which of the following would be considered farthest from the sun based on the data presented?

   F. Mercury
   G. Uranus
   H. Jupiter
   J. Neptune

37. If an astronomer proposed that a celestial body does not qualify as a planet based solely on having an orbital inclination greater than 5 degrees and orbital eccentricity greater than 0.2, how many of the current planets would lose their planet classification?

   A. 4
   B. 3
   C. 2
   D. 1

38. The orbital eccentricity of a celestial body refers to the amount that its orbit deviates from a perfectly circular orbit. A value of 0 is a circular orbit. The higher the eccentricity value, the more distorted the orbit, which can result in objects displaying elliptical, parabolic, and hyperbolic orbits.

   Which pair lists the planet with an orbit that deviates the least from a perfect circle and the one that deviates the most?

   F. Earth; Mercury
   G. Mercury; Neptune
   H. Venus; Mercury
   J. Neptune; Venus

39. It was hypothesized that Jupiter, Saturn, Neptune, and Uranus were gaseous planets, whereas the others were composed of solid material. Which of the following statements best supports this hypothesis?

   A. Jupiter, Saturn, Neptune, and Uranus have lower temperatures than most of the other planets.

   B. Jupiter, Saturn, Neptune, and Uranus have densities much smaller than the densities of the other planets.

   C. Jupiter, Saturn, Neptune, and Uranus have greater masses than the other planets.

   D. Jupiter, Saturn, Neptune, and Uranus have rotation periods that are much shorter than the other planets.

40. Which of the following statements is NOT supported by the data?

   F. Mercury and Venus exhibit the longest rotation periods of all the planets.

   G. Rotation period decreases as black-body temperature decreases.

   H. The two planets with the greatest mass have the shortest rotation periods.

   J. Mars and Earth have rotation periods within one hour of length of each other.

ⓧ STOP

WRITING TEST

40 Minutes

DIRECTIONS: This is a test of your writing skills. You have forty (40) minutes to write an essay in English. Be sure to carefully read the issue and three perspectives presented before planning and writing your essay so you understand clearly the task you are being asked to do. Your essay will be graded on the evidence it provides of your ability to analyze the issue; evaluate and analyze the perspectives; state and develop a personal perspective; and describe the relationship between the given perspectives and your own, while effectively using organization, logic, and language according to the conventions of standard written English.

ALTERNATIVE ENERGY

The United States—and the entire world—is at a crossroads when it comes to our sources of energy. Traditional fossil fuels, including coal, petroleum, and natural gas, are our primary fuel sources, and are responsible for everything from powering our vehicles to warming our homes and providing electricity for our favorite gadgets. However, fossil fuels are also responsible for emitting carbon dioxide into the atmosphere, which most climate scientists feel adversely impacts the environment and contributes to global warming. As a result, some have called for increased exploration and investment in renewable, non-fossil sources of energy, including hydroelectric, solar, nuclear, and wind power, which are better for the environment and would also help reduce our dependence on foreign oil supplies. Efforts to find new, more efficient, and more cost-effective methods for harnessing the power of these alternative energy sources is already underway. As we continue to march through the twenty-first century, what are your thoughts on the advantages and disadvantages of alternative energy exploration and use? What roles should we play regarding strategies, investment, and incentives for alternative energy use?

Read and carefully consider these perspectives. Each suggests a particular way of thinking about if and how alternative energies should be used to meet the needs of the country

PERSPECTIVE ONE

The United States has sufficient fuel from coal, oil, and gas, and we should continue to use these fossil fuels for all of our energy needs. The media exaggerate their negative effects and the science isn't definitive. Our nation has thrived through the twentieth century thanks to these abundant and effective sources of power, and the government shouldn't waste time, energy, and resources on alternative energies, which are expensive, inefficient, and unable to fully meet the needs of the country.

PERSPECTIVE TWO

A serious and committed investment in alternative energy is not only needed right now, it's long overdue. Our reliance on fossil fuels has kept us dependent on energy sources that are destroying our planet. We cannot afford any further apathy, or to put off figuring out how to free ourselves from fossil fuels—even if it's expensive and difficult. We need to end our reliance on fossil fuels immediately. Our planet is worth the effort.

PERSPECTIVE THREE

A decision as large and important as the direction of energy sourcing in the United States should not be made impulsively. Available scientific evidence indicates that a continued long-term reliance on fossil fuels as our primary energy sources might not be the most responsible approach. However, quitting fossil fuels "cold turkey" or without a clear plan isn't realistic either. Our nation needs to develop a long-term plan that includes a tapering off from fossil fuels and an increased use of alternative, renewable energy sources. Furthermore, we need to work with other responsible countries around the world on decreasing fossil fuel reliance; only a worldwide effort will help us tackle this issue.

ESSAY TASK

Write a unified, coherent essay in which you evaluate multiple perspectives on alternative energy. In your essay, be sure to:

- examine and assess the perspectives given
- declare and explain your own perspective on the issue
- discuss the relationship between your perspective and those given

Your perspective may be in full or partial agreement, or in total disagreement, with any of the others. Whatever the case, support your ideas with logical reasoning and detailed, persuasive examples.

PLAN AND WRITE YOUR ESSAY

Use the first two lined pages of the Writing test answer sheet (found at the beginning of the test) to generate ideas and plan your essay. Then use the following four pages to write your essay. Consider the following as you compose your essay:

What are the strengths and weaknesses of the three perspectives provided?

- Identify the insights they present and what they fail to consider.
- Ascertain why a given perspective might persuade or fail to persuade.

How can you apply your own experience, knowledge, and values?

- Express your perspective on the issue, identifying the perspective's strengths and weaknesses.
- Formulate a plan to support your perspective in your essay.

ENGLISH

1.	D	20.	J	39.	C	58.	J
2.	F	21.	D	40.	H	59.	A
3.	B	22.	G	41.	D	60.	H
4.	H	23.	C	42.	J	61.	C
5.	C	24.	G	43.	C	62.	J
6.	J	25.	B	44.	F	63.	D
7.	C	26.	F	45.	C	64.	H
8.	G	27.	A	46.	J	65.	D
9.	A	28.	H	47.	B	66.	G
10.	J	29.	D	48.	H	67.	C
11.	A	30.	F	49.	B	68.	F
12.	F	31.	A	50.	F	69.	B
13.	B	32.	H	51.	B	70.	J
14.	H	33.	C	52.	H	71.	A
15.	B	34.	F	53.	D	72.	H
16.	J	35.	B	54.	F	73.	D
17.	B	36.	H	55.	D	74.	F
18.	G	37.	D	56.	J	75.	C
19.	B	38.	G	57.	B		

1. **The correct answer is D.** This option gets rid of the redundant phrasing caused by two similar verbs. Choices A and B use different forms of the two similar verbs. Choice C does not correct the mistake, but repeats it using grammatically incorrect forms of the verbs.

2. **The correct answer is F.** *With* is the appropriate preposition in this common phrase. Choice G introduces a grammatical error, and choice H changes the meaning of the sentence. The phrase should not be omitted because it explains the writer's trembling, so choice J is incorrect.

3. **The correct answer is B.** The verb here refers to an action (staring at the green shoots) that began in the immediate past and continues into the present; therefore, the present perfect tense is appropriate. The original sentence mistakenly uses the past perfect tense, so choice A is incorrect. Choice C would be used only if the sentence were written in the simple present tense, and choice D would be used if it was written in the simple future tense.

4. **The correct answer is H.** The comparison here involves a prepositional phase (*in a dream*), so *as if* is the proper wording to use. *Like* (choice F), *just like* (choice G), and *similar to* (choice J) should be used only before noun phrases.

5. **The correct answer is C.** The conjunction *and* is needed to correct the comma splice in the original sentence, which is the incorrect use of just a comma to connect two independent clauses. A comma before the *and* is also needed, because this conjunction is being used to coordinate two independent clauses with two separate subjects, so choice B is incorrect. The conjunction *yet (*choice D) is inappropriate, because there is no change in direction between the two clauses.

6. **The correct answer is J.** The past tense is appropriate because the writer is describing his childhood. Choices F, G, and H are all written in the present tense.

7. **The correct answer is C.** This option clearly states the writer's point that in New York, culture was the dominating element, even when it came to marking the passage of the seasons. Choices A, B, and D are all worded confusingly.

8. **The correct answer is G.** *Though not* is the appropriate conjunction to indicate the contrast between knowing the highlights and not knowing the particulars of the seasons. *Whereas* (choice F) indicates a contrast, but using it on its own creates a fragment. Choices H and J create awkward wording.

9. **The correct answer is A.** Paragraph 2 tells us that the writer grew up knowing little about nature. This fact is essential to understanding the garden's effect on the writer. The writer's current environment is quite different from a city, but he never suggests the city was something he felt lucky to have escaped, so choice B is wrong. Paragraph 2 may be a vivid recollection (choice C) or an indication of the writer's sensitivity (choice D), but neither of these describes the paragraph's main purpose.

10. **The correct answer is J.** The plural form *chrysanthemums* is appropriate here, and there is no need for a possessive apostrophe, so choices F, G, and H are incorrect. The most straightforward option is best: *chrysanthemums that spill*.

11. **The correct answer is A.** No comma should be used before yellow because *bright* modifies yellow and all the other colors. No commas are needed to separate the colors because the writer has chosen to link them with the conjunction *and*. Therefore, choices C and D are incorrect. Choice B, however, fails to link *yellow* and *red* with either a comma or *and*, so it is incorrect.

12. **The correct answer is F.** The present tense is appropriate for a general situation that is repeated year after year. The plural, *Daffodils*, demands the third-person plural form of the verb. Choices G and J are in the past tense. Choice H is a singular verb when a plural one is required.

13. **The correct answer is B.** A relative pronoun is needed to link the words with what they stand for. *That* is appropriate for objects. As originally written, the sentence lacks a relative pronoun. The pronouns *who* (choice C) and *whose* (choice D) refer to people, not objects.

14. **The correct answer is H.** The tone of the essay is personal and informal, so choice H is correct and choice G can be eliminated. Pronouns have no effect on time, so choice F does not make sense. Neither does choice J, since the use of pronouns does not really tighten the focus on specific flowers.

15. **The correct answer is B.** This detail is an example of how little the writer knew about nature; therefore, it belongs in the paragraph that discusses growing up in New York. Paragraphs 1 (choice A), 3 (choice C), and 4 (choice D) all take place in the present.

16. **The correct answer is J.** The idiomatic expression is: *as x goes, so goes y*, so choice J is correct. Choices F and G add unnecessary words. Choice H is simply awkward.

17. **The correct answer is B.** As these words are most commonly used, *affect* is the proper verb form, while *effect* is the noun form. Here the word is a noun, so the proper word to use is *effect*, which means you can eliminate choices A and D. The preposition that properly follows *effect* is *on*, so choice B is correct and choice C is incorrect.

18. **The correct answer is G.** The writer is speaking about our present understanding of trade in the past, so choice G is correct, and you can eliminate choices F and H, which are in the past tense. It is an assertion without any sense of the conditional, so choice J is incorrect.

19. **The correct answer is B.** This is the only sentence that stresses the historical importance of exchange and thereby links the previous paragraph to the examples of this phenomenon presented in Paragraph 2. Choice A is inappropriate, since agriculture is merely one detail in Paragraph 2 and not its main idea. Choice C would be a more fitting concluding sentence for Paragraph 1 than an introductory sentence for Paragraph 2, since a phrase such as "Many examples of this…" should continue a previous idea directly. Choice D introduces that same organizational error and focuses on the modern world, while Paragraph 2 focuses on the historical importance of exchange.

20. **The correct answer is J.** The clearest construction lists the subjects and proceeds directly to the verb without punctuation or unnecessary words. As originally written, the list lacks the conjunction *and* between the last two items in the list and misuses a comma to separate the list from the rest of the sentence. In choice G a colon is correctly used instead of a comma, but the conjunction *and* is still missing. Choice H changes the meaning of the sentence.

21. **The correct answer is D.** No punctuation should separate the noun from the prepositional phrase that identifies it. Choices A, B, and C all contain unnecessary punctuation.

22. **The correct answer is G.** The present perfect tense indicates the connection between the past and the present, between antiquity and today. Choices F, H, and J are all in the wrong tense.

23. **The correct answer is C.** *Greeks* is the subject of the relative clause, so the relative pronoun *who* is appropriate. *Whom* is a personal pronoun, so the original sentence is incorrect. Choices B and D are inappropriate because they refer to non-human subjects.

24. **The correct answer is G.** A comma is required before a coordinating conjunction when linking two independent clauses. *And* is the best choice because it indicates the non-contrasting relationship between the clauses, so choices F and H are incorrect. *Therefore* also expresses this relationship but cannot be used to link two independent clauses with only a comma; a semicolon would be required instead, so you can eliminate choice J.

25. **The correct answer is B.** This phrasing properly indicates that the question is about the character of modern Italy. Choices A, C, and D ask different questions.

26. **The correct answer is F.** The imperative form avoids unnecessary words and maintains the authoritative tone of the essay. Choices G and J ask questions and would be appropriate only if the sentence ended with a question mark. Choice H changes the meaning of the sentence.

27. **The correct answer is A.** This sentence makes the point that these foods are not indigenous to the nations that rely on them, and this point is crucial to the main idea of the essay. Choice C makes this point awkwardly, while choices B and D do not make this point at all.

28. **The correct answer is H.** The sentence begins with a series of subjects and should proceed to the verb without punctuation (choices F, G, and J) or unnecessary words (choices F and J).

29. **The correct answer is D.** *For* creates a smooth transition from the previous sentence without changing the meaning. *Therefore* (choice A) wrongly indicates that the way we think of Italy is a direct consequence of the transformation of exchanged goods. Choices B and C do not make grammatical sense in the context of this sentence.

30. **The correct answer is F.** This option emphasizes the creative transformation of tomatoes and pasta by Italian cooking. Choices G, H, and J do not express this crucial idea effectively.

31. **The correct answer is A.** A comma is necessary to separate the modifying phrase from *remedies*, the noun being modified. Choices B, C, and D would work only if the final phrase were an independent clause.

32. **The correct answer is H.** *Which* is an appropriate pronoun to use when asking a question involving a

choice of many. In this case, it is also required by parallel structure. Choices F, G, and J disrupt that structure. Choice G introduces an additional error because *who* refers to a person, not a thing such as an herbal remedy.

33. **The correct answer is C.** This option avoids unnecessary words and is the clearest. Choices A, B, and D are wordy and confusing.

34. **The correct answer is F.** There is no need for a conjugated verb (which would have to be in the continuous tense). The gerund phrase describes what the woman is doing and keeps the sentence flowing. Choices G, H, and J are all written in the wrong tense. Choice G introduces an additional error, since *that* refers to a non-human noun, yet the noun to which it refers in this sentence is *woman*.

35. **The correct answer is B.** The present tense is needed because the sentence speaks about today. Choice A is in the past tense, and choice D is in the future tense. *One of the reasons* is singular, so the third-person singular is required. Therefore, choice C is incorrect.

36. **The correct answer is H.** This option supplies the possessive pronoun for alternative medicine. As written, *it's* is a contraction of *it is*, so choice F is incorrect. Choice G includes an unnecessary apostrophe. Omitting the word would make the sentence vague, so choice J is not the best answer.

37. **The correct answer is D.** The compound subject of this sentence is *drugs and technology*, which is plural and requires the plural verb *do*. Therefore, choices A and B are incorrect. Since choice C changes the meaning of the sentence, choice D is the best answer.

38. **The correct answer is G.** *Yet* indicates the contrasting nature of Sentence 1. By placing it after Sentence 3, it counters the position of the medical establishment and serves as a bridge to the conclusion that medical science does not hold all the answers. Choices F, H, and J would disrupt the paragraph's logical flow.

39. **The correct answer is C.** *Than* is part of a comparison, so it should directly follow the comparative form of the adjective. Choices A, B, and D all contain unnecessary and incorrect punctuation.

40. **The correct answer is H.** The sentence has only one subject; the verb should not be separated from it by punctuation. Therefore, choice H is correct and choices F and J can be eliminated. Simply starting a new sentence with *And* creates a sentence fragment, so Choice G is incorrect.

41. The correct answer is D. This sentence declares that the antagonism of the previous paragraph is lessening and paves the way for the examples that follow. Choice A contradicts the main idea of Paragraph 5. That paragraph is not about AMA rules, so choice B is not a good introductory sentence. Choice C is too informal for this passage, so it is not as good a transitional sentence as choice D is.

42. The correct answer is J. This option expresses the intended possibility while avoiding the unnecessary words in choice G. Choices F and H undermine that intended possibility with the words "might not."

43. The correct answer is C. The pronoun *you* is used in the last part of the sentence, so the pronoun in the dependent clause must agree. This also refers back to the opening sentence, where the reader was addressed directly as *you*. Choices A, B, and D disrupt the parallel structure with different pronouns.

44. The correct answer is F. Paragraph 2 mentions the theory behind acupuncture and provides an example of its use. Therefore, an exploration of the philosophy behind another form of alternative medicine would logically follow this paragraph. Paragraph 3 (choice G) is about the professional medical community's distrust of homeopathy. Paragraph 4 (choice H) is about the AMA. Paragraph 5 (choice J) is about changing attitudes toward herbal remedies.

45. The correct answer is C. The essay discusses alternative medicine in terms of its possible but unproven value in the field of health. Dissatisfaction with the medical establishment is only a minor detail in Paragraph 3 and not the essay's main focus, so choice A can be eliminated. Similarly, the reasoning behind choices B and D inflate minor details into main ideas.

46. The correct answer is J. The phrase refers to the past, so the verbs must be in the past tense. Choices F and G are in the present tense, and choice G contains a singular verb (*is*) that does not agree with its plural antecedent (*women*). Choice H combines the present and past tenses.

47. The correct answer is B. The first sentence of the paragraph tells us that the writer must prove herself in reality. This answer is the only one that maintains such a meaning and is correctly punctuated with a colon to separate the two related independent clauses. As originally written, the sentence contains a comma splice. Choice C changes the sentence's meaning, and choice D is phrased awkwardly.

48. The correct answer is H. This option maintains the parallel structure set up by the preposition *with*, thus indicating that the two factors mentioned are sides of the same problem. As originally written, the phrase "not to mention the fact" suggests an incidental piece of information and not the explanatory information that actually follows the phrase. Choices G and J are phrased awkwardly.

49. The correct answer is B. This option turns the fragment (choice A) into a complete sentence and avoids the needless use of the passive voice in choice C. Choice D is also a fragment.

50. The correct answer is F. This option makes it clear that the writer is being asked to write a piece about the First Lady's charity work. Choices G and J change the sentence's meaning. Choice H is unnecessarily wordy.

51. The correct answer is B. The gerund phrase acts as a noun—in this case the object of the verb *meant*, creating a correct sentence. The verbs in choices C and D are in the wrong form. The form should be positive because the essay makes it clear that the author did break ground. As originally written, the sentence contradicts its own meaning by including the word *not*.

52. The correct answer is H. Commas are required before and after *however* to set it apart from the rest of the sentence. The original sentence and choice J use semicolons mistakenly. Choice G is missing one of the required commas.

53. The correct answer is D. The verb *would tell* in the previous part of the sentence sets up a parallel structure that requires *describe* and *complain*. Choices A, B, and C all disrupt the parallel structure with the wrong form of *complain*.

54. The correct answer is F. The suggested paragraph would add unnecessary details and distract from the writer's point. Since that suggested paragraph does not belong at any point in this essay, choices G, H, and J can all be eliminated.

55. The correct answer is D. This is the only answer choice indicating that the writer is contrasting her behavior in the previous paragraph with the behavior of her male colleagues. *Therefore* implies the result of a cause, so the sentence is wrong as originally written. Choice B would be used to soften a conclusion, not introduce a contrast. Choice C signals the introduction of supporting details.

56. **The correct answer is J.** This option avoids unnecessary wording and correctly conveys the writer's feeling that her complete honesty was inappropriate for her workplace. Choices F, G, and H would all leave the sentence wordy and unclear.

57. **The correct answer is B.** The relative subject pronoun *who* is needed because *women* is the subject of the relative clause. The original sentence is incorrect because *that* refers to a non-human subject. *Whom* is a personal pronoun, so choice C is incorrect. Omitting a word would create a fragment, so choice D is incorrect.

58. **The correct answer is J.** The opening sentence of the paragraph indicates that the writer has set up some kind of expectation that her work will not be first rate. Therefore, in order for this paragraph to be most effective, it should come at the end of the passage, after the writer has shown us what she has done to set up such an expectation. In addition, the last line of the paragraph serves to point out the lesson that has been learned, concluding the essay. The paragraph would disrupt the flow of the essay if placed anywhere else, so choices F, G, and H are wrong.

59. **The correct answer is A.** In Paragraph 4, the writer sets up important, relevant information regarding her behavior that ultimately helped her to understand why she needed to put on a professional face. Choice B is incorrect because there are no historical details about women in the workplace in the paragraph. The paragraph mentions nothing about the writer's male colleagues (choice C) or friends (choice D) either.

60. **The correct answer is H.** The writer is conveying an experience she had in her professional life that led to a personal revelation. The paragraph is a personal essay, not a persuasive (choice F) or comparative (choice G). The writer's personal integrity is not challenged in the essay, so choice J does not make sense.

61. **The correct answer is C.** *Illiterate* means unable to read, and *population* is a singular noun, so choice C is the correct answer and choice D, which uses the plural verb *are*, can be eliminated. The original sentence is incorrect because *illegible* means *unreadable*. Choice B uses the wrong verb form and the wrong word; *ineligible* means "not entitled."

62. **The correct answer is J.** The size of the country is irrelevant here, so the phrase should be omitted entirely. Choices G, and H do not make that information any more relevant than it is in the original sentence.

63. **The correct answer is D.** The word *Neighbors* is part of a list and should be separated from the next item by a comma. Choices A and B use incorrect punctuation, and choice C uses no punctuation at all.

64. **The correct answer is H.** The *willingness* refers to that of the neighbors, friends, and relatives, so the possessive pronoun *their* is appropriate. Choices F and G both use homonyms mistakenly: *there* means a particular spot, and *they're* is a contraction of *they* and *are*. Since *they are* does not make sense in this context under any circumstances, choice J is incorrect.

65. **The correct answer is D.** The sentence describes the age of the author at the specified time, requiring the simple past tense of the verb *to be*. Choice A would be used only if the subject did not get a chance to be something, which is not the case in this essay. Choice B is a perfect gerund that indicates a state of being no longer in effect, and it is not the clearest form to use in this sentence. Choice C indicates an ongoing action that occurred in the past.

66. **The correct answer is G.** *To live under* a dictatorship is the correct idiomatic phrase. Choices F and J are not proper idioms. Choice H contradicts the intended meaning of the sentence.

67. **The correct answer is C.** No punctuation is needed before the prepositional phrase that begins with *in*, so choice C is correct and choice A can be eliminated. The sentence discusses plural *families*, so they must be seeking new *lives*, which eliminates choice D. An apostrophe is used to show possession, yet the *lives* possess nothing in this sentence. Therefore, choice B is wrong.

68. **The correct answer is F.** Since *acclaim* is a noun, it should be modified by the adjective *critical*, not the adverb *critically* (choice G) or the noun *criticism* (choice J). Adding *too* in front of this adjective changes the connotation, so choice H is not as strong an answer as choice F.

69. **The correct answer is B.** The first word that follows the comma should be the subject of the modifying phrase *born in Port-au-Prince in 1969*. That would be *Danticat*, which is not the first word in choices A, C, or D. Choice C is also too wordy.

70. **The correct answer is J.** This option links Danticat's childhood behavior with her development as a writer. Choices F and G do not create such a link. Choice H is too vague.

71. **The correct answer is A.** This option notes the similarity between Danticat and the heroine in the clearest language. *Like* is the appropriate preposition to use when comparing nouns. The wordiness of choices B and D leaves the sentence unclear. Choice C suggests a comparison between actions, not people.

72. **The correct answer is H.** Only one author is being discussed, and the possessive form is used to indicate that the subject matter belongs to the author. Choices F and G indicate more than one author. Choice J lacks the elements needed to show possession.

73. **The correct answer is D.** This option is the most logical, given the author's subject matter. The proper negative construction is *neither . . . nor*. The constructions in choices A and B create sentences that contradict their own intended meanings. Choice C disrupts the proper negative construction by following *nor* with *or*.

74. **The correct answer is F.** This option introduces the informative, impersonal tone of the essay and provides an introduction to the theme of storytelling. Choice G is too personal. Choice H is too vague. Choice J is too informal and suggests the main theme of the essay is illiteracy, not storytelling.

75. **The correct answer is C.** The essay is primarily about an emerging writer, an idea suggested by choice C. The essay is not mainly about Danticat's status as an immigrant (choice A) or Haitian life in general (choice B). Choice D is wrong because the writer of the essay never refers to himself or herself in any capacity, let alone whether or not he or she has ever been to Haiti.

MATHEMATICS

1.	E	16.	K	31.	A	46.	G
2.	J	17.	A	32.	J	47.	A
3.	C	18.	G	33.	E	48.	G
4.	K	19.	E	34.	J	49.	B
5.	E	20.	H	35.	C	50.	H
6.	H	21.	B	36.	H	51.	B
7.	E	22.	K	37.	A	52.	K
8.	H	23.	D	38.	F	53.	E
9.	B	24.	J	39.	A	54.	G
10.	J	25.	C	40.	K	55.	A
11.	E	26.	G	41.	C	56.	J
12.	H	27.	E	42.	H	57.	C
13.	D	28.	J	43.	E	58.	J
14.	F	29.	D	44.	F	59.	B
15.	C	30.	G	45.	B	60.	G

1. **The correct answer is E.** Plug the given numbers into the percent formula, where 32 is the part, 80 is the whole, and x is the unknown percent:

$$\frac{32}{80} = \frac{x}{100}$$
$$80x = 3{,}200$$
$$x = 40$$

Choice A is the result of an arithmetic error; you are off by a multiple of 10. Choices B and C are incorrect because when taken out of 100, both 16 and 24 give a number less than $\frac{32}{80}$, so these percentages cannot be correct. Choice D would imply that the whole part being used is 100, but it is actually 80.

2. **The correct answer is J.** The sum measure of a triangle's interior angles is 180°, so the missing interior angle measures 180° – 40° – 55° = 85°. Since this angle is supplementary to the angle measuring $x°$, $x = 180 – 85 = 95$.

Choice F is incorrect because the angles labeled x and 55 in the diagram are not congruent alternate interior angles. Choices G and K are the likely result of an arithmetic error; you should be computing 180 – 85. Choice H is the measure of the third angle in the triangle, not the one labeled x.

3. **The correct answer is C.** The machine costs $p + l$ to operate each hour, so if it operates for x hours, the expression would be $x(p + l)$.

Choice A is incorrect because you should be adding p and l, not multiplying them. In choice B, you should be adding px and lx, not multiplying them. Choice D is incorrect because you should be adding p and l, not multiplying them, and you should multiply the resulting sum by x. Choice E is just the cost per hour—you must multiply by the number of hours, x.

4. **The correct answer is K.** If you sketch each of the segments on a coordinate plane, you'll find that only the segment connecting (2, 1) and (2, 5) intersects with the original segment. The line segments given in choices F, G, H, and J do not intersect the original segment.

5. **The correct answer is E.** Jacob pays a base $1 rate for each call, so his total base cost for all 10 calls is $10. Each 1-minute call costs 25 cents, so the total additional cost of these 5 calls is 5 × $0.25 = $1.25. Each 3-minute call costs 3 × 25 cents = 75 cents, so the total additional cost of these 5 calls is 5 × $0.75 = $3.75. Add these costs together: $10 + $1.25 + $3.75 = $15.

Choice A is the portion of the total charge from the length of the calls; you did not include the base charge. Choice B is just the base charge. In choice C, you did not include the cost of the three-minute calls. In choice D, you did not include the cost of the minute calls.

6. **The correct answer is H.** Even though there are no variables, you can still use FOIL to simplify the expression:

$$(3+\sqrt{2})(4-\sqrt{2}) = 12 - 3\sqrt{2} + 4\sqrt{2} - 2$$
$$= 10 + \sqrt{2}$$

Choice F is incorrect; $\sqrt{2} \cdot \sqrt{2} \neq 2\sqrt{2}$, and you forgot the middle term obtained when FOILing. In choice G, you omitted the middle terms obtained when FOILing. For choice J, you forgot the middle terms when FOILing, and when multiplying the last terms of the binomials, you should get -2, not 2. Choice K is the product of $(3+\sqrt{2})(4+\sqrt{2})$.

7. **The correct answer is E.** Convert the fractions to decimals: $\frac{2}{5} = 0.4$ and $\frac{1}{8} = 0.125$ Now add the three decimals: $0.4 + 0.125 + 0.177 = 0.702$.

In choice A, you dropped 0.177 from the sum. In choice B, you dropped $\frac{1}{8}$ from the sum. To get choice C, you forgot to carry one to the tenths place when adding. For choice D, you neglected to carry one to the hundredths place when adding.

8. **The correct answer is H.** The area of triangle ABC is 5 square inches. Plug this area and the length of the base, $\overline{BC}$, into the area formula to solve for the height, $\overline{AB}$:

$$A = \frac{1}{2}bh$$
$$5 = \frac{1}{2}(2)(AB)$$
$$AB = 5$$

Triangle ACD has the same height as triangle ABC. To find the length of its base, $\overline{CD}$, subtract BC from BD:

$10 - 2 = 8$. Therefore, the area of triangle ACD is

$\frac{1}{2}(8)(5) = 20$. Choice F is the length of CD, not the area. In choice G, you used 8 in place of 10 as the length of the base ABD. Choice J is the area of triangle ABD. In choice K, you should have subtracted the area of triangle ABC from the area of triangle ABD, not added it.

9. **The correct answer is B.** Plug the given values of m and n into the expression and evaluate:

$$m^2 - 4mn + n = (-1)^2 - 4(-1)(-3) + (-3)$$
$$= 1 - 12 - 3$$
$$= -14$$

In choice A, you dropped m^2 from the expression. In choice C, you dropped n from the expression. In choice D, you miscalculated the signs of all three parts of the expression. Choice E is incorrect because the product of an odd number of negative integers must be odd, therefore, $(-4)(-1)(-3) = -12$, not 12.

10. **The correct answer is J.** Write the expression as the product of two binomials, and use FOIL to do the multiplication:

$$(2a-3)^2 = (2a-3)(2a-3)$$
$$= 4a^2 - 6a - 6a + 9$$
$$= 4a^2 - 12a + 9$$

In choice F, you multiplied the base times the exponent, which is not the proper way to compute a power. In choice G, you forgot the middle term; $(a-b)^2$ does not equal $a^2 - b^2$. In choice H, you forgot one of the outer terms. In choice K, you forgot to multiply the two negative signs attached to the 3's to make a positive.

11. **The correct answer is E.** The sum of the interior angles of a polygon can be generalized by the formula $180(n-2)°$, where n is the number of sides of the polygon. The sum of the interior angles of a six-sided figure, therefore, is $180(6-2)° = (180 \times 4)° = 720°$. Since the six interior angles of a regular hexagon are all congruent, each angle measures $720° \div 6 = 120°$.

For choices A and B, you used $180(4-2)$ and $180(5-2)$, respectively, for the sum of the interior angles of a hexagon. For choice C, you used $n = 5$, which is for a pentagon, not a hexagon. Choice D is the likely result of an arithmetic error.

12. **The correct answer is H.** Go through the answers and use the process of elimination. In choice F, 6 and 15 share a greatest common factor (GCF) of 3, but their least common multiple (LCM) is 30. Eliminate this choice. In choice G, 9 and 15 share a GCF of 3, but their LCM is 45. Eliminate this choice. In choice H, 15 and 18 share a GCF of 3, and their LCM is 90. This is the correct answer. In choice J, 6 and 30 share a GCF of 6, and their LCM is 30. Eliminate this choice. In choice K, 18 and 45 share an LCM of 90, but their GCF is 9. Eliminate this choice.

13. **The correct answer is D.** The difference between Colin's and Daryl's average monthly salary is $500, so the difference between their annual salaries is $500 × 12 = $6,000. We don't know who earns more, but the difference between their annual salaries is $|C - D|$ dollars. Thus, $|C - D| = 6,000$.

Choice A is the difference of *monthly* salaries, not the *annual* salaries. Choice B is incorrect because you should be subtracting salaries, not adding them—even so, the right side would represent the difference of *monthly* salaries, not annual salaries. In choice C, the average of the annual salaries is 6,000, which is not given in the problem. In choice E, you should be subtracting, not adding salaries.

14. **The correct answer is F.** The value in parentheses, 0.01, can be rewritten as 10^{-2}. Therefore, $(0.01)^4 = (10^{-2})^4 = 10^{-8}$.

For choice G, note that 0.01 equals 10–2, not 10–1. For choice H, you forgot to raise this result to the fourth power. In choice J, 0.01 = 10, but it actually equals 10–2. For choice K, note that 0.01 equals 10–2, not 10^2.

15. **The correct answer is C.** When parallel lines are cut by a transversal, the alternate interior angles are equal. Therefore, $\angle DCE$ measures 60°. Since the measures of the angles in a triangle add up to 180°, $\angle CED$ measures 180° – 40° – 60° = 80°.

Choice A is incorrect because $\angle CED$ is neither corresponding nor alternate interior to $\angle CDE$, and so it is not congruent to it in this scenario. In choice B, $\angle CED$ is neither corresponding nor alternate interior to $\angle ABE$, and so it is not congruent to it in this scenario. For choice D, you must subtract this sum from 180 degrees to get the desired angle. Choice E is not true since you can use the various relationships among angles formed by two parallel lines cut by a transversal.

16. **The correct answer is K.** Rewrite the equation in standard quadratic form: $3x^2 - 7x - 6 = 0$. Then apply reverse FOIL to factor this equation:

$$3x^2 - 7x - 6 = 0$$
$$(3x + 2)(x - 3) = 0$$

This means that either $3x + 2 = 0$ or $x - 3 = 0$. If $3x + 2 = 0$, then $x = -\frac{2}{3}$. If $x - 3 = 0$, then $x = 3$. Since it's given that $x < 0$, x must equal $-\frac{2}{3}$.

If you substitute choices F, G, H, and J into the equation, you do not get a true statement.

17. **The correct answer is A.** Rewrite the equation in slope-intercept form, $y = mx + b$:

$$3x + y - 2 = 0$$
$$y = -3x + 2$$

When the equation is written in this form, the slope is equal to m, the coefficient of x. In this case, the slope is –3.

For choice B, you divided by the y-intercept, but you should have divided by the coefficient of y (which is just 1 in this case). In choice C, you solved for x, not y; to find the slope, you must put the equation in the form $y = mx + b$. Choice D is the y-intercept, not the slope. Choice E is incorrect because you must first solve for y before identifying the coefficient of x as the slope of the line.

18. **The correct answer is G.** Painting one side of the house requires 6 small cans, so painting all 4 sides requires 24 small cans. If 6 small cans are the same as 4 large cans, then the combination of 4 large and 18 small cans is equivalent to 6 + 18 = 24 small cans, which is exactly the amount needed to cover all 4 sides of the house.

Choice F results in 2 large cans left over. For choice H, note that 2 large cans is more paint than 2 small cans, and you only need 6 small cans to paint a side. Choice J would not be enough paint. Choice K is too much paint (by 6 small cans).

19. **The correct answer is E.** Since an absolute value can never be negative, its minimum is at 0. The absolute value of $x - 5$ equals 0 only when x is 5. Choices A and B give the values of 12 and 9, respectively, when plugged into the expression, and there are smaller values for other x values listed. Choice C is the minimum value of the absolute value expression, not the given sum. Choice D is the minimum value, not the x-value at which it's attained.

20. **The correct answer is H.** Set up a proportion between similar sides:

$$\frac{24}{30} = \frac{x}{40}$$
$$30x = 960$$
$$x = 32$$

None of the values in choices F, G, J, and K retain the proportionality.

Answer Keys and Explanations

21. The correct answer is B. Simplify the expression by taking the square root of each factor separately:

$$\sqrt{3^4 a^3 b^2} = \sqrt{3^4} \times \sqrt{a^3} \times \sqrt{b^2}$$
$$= 3^2 \times a^{\frac{3}{2}} \times b$$
$$= 9a^{\frac{3}{2}}b$$

In choice A, $\sqrt{a^3} = a^{\frac{3}{2}}$, not $a^{\frac{2}{3}}$. In choice C, the exponent of a should not be negative. In choice D, you ignored the square root sign. In choice E, you squared the expression instead of taking its square root, and computed $(3^4)^2$ by multiplying all three numbers.

22. The correct answer is K. The total of the 6 original scores is $(6)(80) = 480$ points. The total of all 8 tests is $(8)(85) = 680$ points. Since the total of the 2 added tests must be $680 - 480 = 200$, the average of these 2 tests is $200 \div 2 = 100$. The values listed in choices F, G, H, and J will all result in an average lower than 85.

23. The correct answer is D. First, find AC by plugging the two given lengths into the Pythagorean theorem:

$$7^2 + (AC)^2 = 15^2$$
$$49 + (AC)^2 = 225$$
$$(AC)^2 = 176$$
$$AC = \sqrt{176}$$
$$= 4\sqrt{11}$$

Now plug the legs of this triangle into the area formula as the base and height:

$$\frac{1}{2}bh = \frac{1}{2}\left(4\sqrt{11}\right)(7)$$
$$= 14\sqrt{11}$$

In choice A, you computed AC incorrectly as 4; you must use the Pythagorean theorem to find this length. Choice B is the length of AC, not the area. In choice C, when applying the Pythagorean theorem, you forgot to take the square root, and as a result said AC had length 8. For choice E, you used the hypotenuse instead of the base in the area calculation.

24. The correct answer is J. Convert the time to seconds: 9 minutes and 20 seconds = 560 seconds. Then set up a proportion:

$$\frac{560}{1,400} = \frac{x}{2,000}$$
$$1,400x = 1,120,000$$
$$x = 800 \text{ seconds}$$
$$= 13 \text{ minutes and 20 seconds}$$

Choice F is incorrect because it should take longer to download a larger file. Choices G, H, and K are likely the results of arithmetic errors involving unit conversions and setting up proportions correctly.

25. The correct answer is C. The current paths require a trip of 200 feet. A diagonal path would form an isosceles right triangle with the existing paths. By the rules of 45°-45°-90° triangles, the length of the path would be $100\sqrt{2}$ feet, or approximately 140 feet. The new path would shorten the route by about $200 - 140 = 60$ feet.

Choice A is likely the result of an arithmetic error. For choice B, you used the wrong triangle relationship; this is a 45-45-90 triangle, not a 30-60-90 triangle. Choice D is the approximate length of the path. For choice E, you used the wrong triangle relationship; this is a 45-45-90 triangle, not a 30-60-90 triangle, and this would be the length of the path.

26. The correct answer is G. Rewrite the inequality to solve for the range of x:

$$x - \sqrt{5} > 5$$
$$x > 5 + \sqrt{5}$$

Since $\sqrt{5}$ is between 2 and 3, $5 + \sqrt{5}$ must be between 7 and 8. Therefore, the smallest positive integer value of x is 8. Choice F is a larger integer for which the inequality is true. None of the values in choices H, J, and K is larger than $5 + \sqrt{5}$.

27. The correct answer is E. Each wall is 100 yards long and 15 yards high. Convert these yards to feet, since the paint coverage is measured in square feet. There are 3 feet in a yard, so each wall measures 300 feet by 45 feet, and the total square footage is $2 \times 300 \times 45 = 27,000$ square feet. One gallon of paint covers an area of 150 square feet, so calculate the number of gallons needed for this job:

$$27,000 \text{ square feet} \times \frac{1 \text{ gallon}}{150 \text{ square feet}} = 180$$

In choice A, you did not convert to feet when computing square footage. In choice B, you did not convert 100 yards to feet. In choice C, you did not account for the fact that there are two walls. Choice D is the information given to you; you must determine total square footage and then divide by 150.

28. **The correct answer is J.** First calculate the area of the four triangles. Since the area of a triangle is $\frac{1}{2}bh$, each triangle has an area of $\frac{1}{2}(a)(3a)=\frac{3}{2}a^2$. Thus, the total area of all four triangles is $4\times\frac{3}{2}a^2=6a^2$. The easiest way to calculate the area of the shaded region is to subtract the area of the four triangles from the area of square $WXYZ$, each side of which has a length of $a + 3a = 4a$. The area of square $WXYZ$ is $(4a)^2 = 16a^2$, so the area of the shaded region is $16a^2 - 6a^2 = 10a^2$. Therefore, the ratio of the area of the 4 triangles to the area of the shaded region is:

$$\frac{6a^2}{10a^2}=\frac{3}{5}$$

In choice F, you compared the area of four triangles to the area of the square $WXYZ$, not the shaded region. Choice G is incorrect because the area of the four triangles is $6a^2$, not $4a^2$. Choice H is incorrect because the area of the four triangles is $6a^2$, not $5a^2$. In choice K, the area of the shaded region is $10a^2$, not $8a^2$.

29. **The correct answer is D.** $\frac{0.018}{0.12}=0.150$, or 150 thousandths.

Choice A is incorrect because the problem asks how many thousandths, not simply the value of the decimal to which the quotient is equal. Choice B is off by a factor of 100; you probably did not move the decimal point correctly when dividing. Choice C is off by a factor of 10. For choice E, you divided in the wrong order.

30. **The correct answer is G.** If $\left|x-1\right|\le 2$, then $x - 1$ must be 2 or fewer units away from zero, in either a positive or negative direction. Set up a new inequality to solve for the range of x:

$$-2\le(x-1)\le 2$$
$$-1\le x\le 3$$

In choice F, when isolating x in the double inequality, you subtracted 1 from all parts of the inequality instead of adding it. For choice H, you added 2 to all parts of the double inequality, which would lead to $x + 1$ in the middle, not just x. For choice J, you forgot half of the inequality—remember, $|x - a| < b$ means

$-b < x - a < b$. In choice K, you forgot the left side of the inequality—remember, $|x - a| < b$ means $-b < x - a < b$.

31. **The correct answer is A.** You are dealing with similar triangles, so you can set up a proportion between the segments:

$$\frac{AB}{AC}=\frac{AE}{AD}$$
$$\frac{10}{14}=\frac{x}{x+3}$$
$$10(x+3)=14x$$
$$10x+30=14x$$
$$30=4x$$
$$x=7.5$$

For choice B, you inverted half of the proportion. Choice C is incorrect because AE does not equal the product of DE and BC. In choice D, you simplified the equation incorrectly; you should get $10x + 30 - 14x$, not $10x + 30 = 12x$. For choice E, when solving $30 = 4x$ for x, you subtracted 4 but should have divided by it.

32. **The correct answer is J.** Since $\cos\theta=\frac{5}{7}$, create a right triangle with an adjacent side of 5 and a hypotenuse of 7. Solve for the opposite leg using the Pythagorean theorem:

$$5^2+b^2=7^2$$
$$b^2=49-25$$
$$b=\sqrt{24}$$
$$=2\sqrt{6}$$

Therefore, $\tan\theta$ is equal to the opposite side divided by the adjacent side, or $\frac{2\sqrt{6}}{5}$.

Choice F is incorrect because when using the Pythagorean theorem, both legs and the hypotenuse should be squared. Choice G is the secant of θ. Choice H is sine of θ. In choice K, you forgot to take the square root when using the Pythagorean theorem to find the missing leg.

33. **The correct answer is E.** If the average of x numbers is 15, then the total of these numbers is $15x$. When two numbers are increased by y, $2y$ will be added to this total. The value of x does not change, so the new average will be $\frac{15x+2y}{x}=15+\frac{2y}{x}$. This is an increase of $\frac{2y}{x}$ over the original average.

Answer Keys and Explanations

Choice A is the amount added to the overall total before averaging. Choice B is just the amount by which each of the two numbers increased, not how much by which the average increases. Choice C is the reciprocal of the correct answer. The value given in choice D should be doubled, since *two* numbers were increased by *y*.

34. **The correct answer is J.** The unshaded sectors *AOB* and *BOC* comprise a total of $\frac{2}{5}+\frac{1}{3}=\frac{11}{15}$ of the circle. This means that the shaded region, sector *AOC*, takes up the remaining $\frac{4}{15}$ of the circle. A circle has 360 total degrees, so set up a proportion to find the measure of $\angle AOC$:

$$\frac{4}{15}=\frac{m\angle AOC}{360°}$$
$$15(m\angle AOC)=1,440°$$
$$m\angle AOC=96°$$

Choice F is incorrect because the number of degrees in a circle is 360, not 180. In choice G, you seem to have mistakenly said that the shaded region is $\frac{1}{4}$ of the circle—don't eyeball it! Choice H is close, but is likely the result of eyeballing the region rather than using the information provided in the problem. Choice K is the measure of $360 - \angle AOC$, not just $\angle AOC$.

35. **The correct answer is C.** The ladder forms a right triangle with the house and the ground, so use the Pythagorean theorem to solve for the distance:

$$10^2+b^2=12^2$$
$$b^2=144-100$$
$$b=\sqrt{44}$$
$$\approx 6.6$$

In choice A, when using the Pythagorean theorem, you forgot to square the legs and hypotenuse. For choice B, you computed the squares of the legs and hypotenuse incorrectly; note that a^2 does not equal $2a$. For choice D, you treated the hypotenuse as a leg in the Pythagorean theorem. For choice E, you forgot to take the square root.

36. **The correct answer is H.** The radius is 3 feet, so the circumference is $2\pi \times 3 = 6\pi$ feet.

In choice F, instead of dividing by 2, you should have multiplied by 2—remember, the circumference is $2\pi r$, not $\pi \cdot \frac{r}{2}$. In choice G, you forgot to multiply by

2. Choice J is the area. For choice K, you used the diameter in place of the radius—remember, the circumference is $2\pi r$, not $2\pi d$.

37. **The correct answer is A.** Multiply both sides of the equation by the LCM, 35, to eliminate the fractions. Then solve the resulting equation for *n*:

$$35\left(\frac{3}{5}n+\frac{2}{7}\right)=35\left(\frac{3}{7}n-\frac{2}{5}\right)$$
$$21n+10=15n-14$$
$$6n=-24$$
$$n=-4$$

If you substitute in the value of *n* for choices B, C, D, and E, you do not get a true statement.

38. **The correct answer is F.** In order for a line to be parallel to the *y*-axis, it must have the same *x*-coordinate at all points. Since the line passes through (2, 3), its equation must be $x = 2$.

Choice G is parallel to the *x*-axis, not the *y*-axis. Choices H, J, and K are not parallel to the *y*-axis; rather, they are diagonal with varying degrees of steepness.

39. **The correct answer is A.** An equilateral triangle has equal side lengths, so an equilateral triangle with a perimeter of 18 must have sides of length 6. This means that the base of the triangle is 6, and the height is the line that divides the equilateral into two 30-60-90 triangles. Since each of these 30-60-90 triangles has a shorter leg of 3 (half the base) and a hypotenuse of 6, the longer leg (the height) must be $3\sqrt{3}$. Now plug these numbers into the area formula:

$$\frac{1}{2}bh=\frac{1}{2}(6)(3\sqrt{3})$$
$$=9\sqrt{3}$$

Choice B is incorrect because the height of the triangle is not 6. In choice C, you forgot to divide by 2; remember that the area of a triangle is $\frac{1}{2}$ times the base times the height. For choice D, the height of the triangle is not 6, and you forgot to multiply by $\frac{1}{2}$ in the area formula. For choice E, you multiplied by 2 instead of $\frac{1}{2}$ in the area formula for a triangle.

40. **The correct answer is K.** The given circle has a center at (4, –6) and a radius of 5. The circle is centered in quadrant IV, and part of the circle—for example, the point (–1, –6)—also goes into quadrant III, but it never reaches quadrants I or II.

For choice F, the largest the *y*-value gets is –1, so it cannot even reach into these quadrants. For choice G, the largest the *y*-value gets is –1, so it cannot even reach into quadrant I. For choices H and J, the largest the *y*-values get are –1, so it cannot reach into quadrant II.

41. **The correct answer is C.** If $\angle Z$ measures 30°, then $\angle X$ also measures 30°, and $\angle C$ must measure $180° - 30° - 30° = 120°$. Arc *XYZ* is thus $\frac{120°}{360°} = \frac{1}{3}$ of the entire circumference of the circle. The circumference is $2\pi(9) = 18\pi$ feet, so arc *XYZ* has a length of $\frac{18\pi}{3} = 6\pi$ feet.

In choice A, you used the wrong proportion—it should be $\frac{1}{3}$ of the entire circle, not $\frac{1}{12}$. For choice B, you used the wrong proportion—it should be $\frac{1}{3}$ of the entire circle, not $\frac{1}{6}$. Choice D is the circumference of the entire circle. Choice E exceeds the circumference of the entire circle.

42. **The correct answer is H.** Three pairs of prime numbers add to 24: 5 + 19, 7 + 17, and 11 + 13. The smallest resulting product is $5 \times 19 = 95$, so 95 is the least possible value of *xy*.

Choice F gives you a prime, so it cannot be a product of prime numbers. You get choice G from the choice 2 + 22, but 22 is not prime. You get choice J from 7 and 17 and choice K from 11 and 13, but neither one yields the least product.

43. **The correct answer is E.** Use the area formula to find the radius of the circle:

$$\pi r^2 = 64$$
$$r^2 = \frac{64}{\pi}$$
$$r = \frac{8}{\sqrt{\pi}}$$

The diameter is twice the radius, or $\frac{16}{\sqrt{\pi}}$ inches.

In choice A, you dropped π from the area formula when finding the radius and forgot to double it to find the diameter. In choice B, you dropped π from the area formula when finding the radius. In choice C, you forgot to take the square root when finding the radius. Choice D is the radius, not the diameter.

44. **The correct answer is F.** First solve for *x*:

$$2x = 4x + 1$$
$$-2x = 1$$
$$x = -\frac{1}{2}$$

Then substitute this value into the second equation:

$$6\left(-\frac{1}{2}\right) - 2 = -3 - 2$$
$$= -5$$

In choice G, you forgot to subtract 2—this is 6*x* not $6x - 2$. Choice H is $6x + 2$, not $6x - 2$. Choice J is the value of *x*, not $6x - 2$. For choice K, note that $x = -\frac{1}{2}$, not $\frac{1}{2}$.

45. **The correct answer is B.** Tangent equals opposite divided by adjacent. In an isosceles right triangle, the legs are equal. In this case, that means the opposite and adjacent sides are equal, so $\tan x° = 1$. Choice A is either sine or cosine of 45 degrees. Choice C is either the secant or cosecant of 45 degrees. For choices D and E, you used the wrong triangle relationships—this is a 45-45-90 triangle, not a 30-60-90 triangle.

46. **The correct answer is G.** Solve for the width and length of the rectangle using the distance formula:

$$w = \sqrt{(-5 - (-1))^2 + (-2 - (-6))^2}$$
$$= \sqrt{16 + 16}$$
$$= \sqrt{32}$$
$$= 4\sqrt{2}$$

$$l = \sqrt{(-1 - 7)^2 + (-6 - 2)^2}$$
$$= \sqrt{64 + 64}$$
$$= \sqrt{128}$$
$$= 8\sqrt{2}$$

The area of the rectangle is $\left(4\sqrt{2}\right)\left(8\sqrt{2}\right) = 64$.

For choice F, note that $\sqrt{2} \bullet \sqrt{2} = 2$, not $\sqrt{2}$.

Choice H is the perimeter, not the area. Choice J is the square of the length of a side of the rectangle. For choice K, you seem to have assumed the rectangle was a square with side 12. You must use the distance formula to find a side length.

47. **The correct answer is A.** In order for the expression to be positive, x and z must either both be negative or both be positive. Choice B would produce a quotient involving an odd number of negative signs, which must be odd. Choice C is incorrect because option II is false—this would produce a quotient involving an odd number of negative signs, which must be odd. Choices D and E are incorrect because options II and III are false. Option II is false because this would produce a quotient involving an odd number of negative signs; option III is false because if $x = 0$, then the quotient is 0.

48. **The correct answer is G.** If $\log_4 64 = n$, then $4^n = 64$. Since $64 = 4^3$, $\log_4(64) = 3$.

Choice F is incorrect because $4^2 = 16$, not 64. You get choices H and J when you misunderstand the meaning of a logarithm. Note that $\log_4(64) = 3$ because $4^3 = 64$. For choice K, while $4(16) = 64$, this is not the meaning of a logarithm. Note that $\log_4(64) = 3$ because $4^3 = 64$.

49. **The correct answer is B.** For x to have an inverse relationship with y, it must be in the denominator of the right side. For z to have a direct relationship with y, it must be in the numerator of the right side. Only the equation $y = \dfrac{z}{x}$ does this.

Choice A is incorrect because the right side should be the reciprocal of what is listed here. Choice C is incorrect because it means y is inversely proportional to both z and x. For choice D, applying the logarithm rules, this would make $\log(y)$ inversely proportional to z and proportional to $\log(x)$. For choice E, applying the logarithm rules would make $\log(y)$ inversely proportional to x and proportional to $\log(z)$.

50. **The correct answer is H.** The general formula for a circle is $(x - h)^2 + (y - k)^2 = r^2$, where (h, k) is the center of the circle and r is the radius. Of the equations given, only $(x - 1)^2 + (y + 1)^2 = 25$ has a center at $(1, -1)$.

In choices F and G, the radius is correct, but the center is $(1, -1)$, not $(5, 2)$. For choices J and K, the signs of the center you used are incorrect.

51. **The correct answer is B.** Carefully solve the equation one step at a time:

$$-[(x - 4) - (3 - 2x)] = 3 - (5x + 6)$$
$$-(x - 4 - 3 + 2x) = 3 - 5x - 6$$
$$-(3x - 7) = -5x - 3$$
$$-3x + 7 = -5x - 3$$
$$2x = -10$$
$$x = -5$$

For choices A, C, D, and E, if you substitute the values in for x, you do not get a true statement.

52. **The correct answer is K.** The graph of $\sin x$ has a period of 2π. However, if you graph $\sin\dfrac{x}{2}$, the period doubles in length to 4π. Note that the coefficient of the sine, 3, affects only the amplitude, not the period.

To get choices F, G, H, and J, you did not account for the fact that the period for $y = A\sin Bx$ is $\dfrac{2\pi}{B}$.

53. **The correct answer is E.** The sides of the new rectangle are $s + 4$ and $s - 3$, so the area of the rectangle is the product of these two values. Use FOIL to multiply the binomials:

$$(s + 4)(s - 3) = s^2 - 3s + 4s - 12$$
$$= s^2 + s - 12$$

In choice A, you forgot the middle term when FOILing, and when multiplying the last terms of the binomials you actually added them. In choice B, you forgot the middle term when FOILing. In choice C, you got the signs wrong when FOILing. In choice D, you forgot the middle term when FOILing, and when multiplying the last terms of the binomials you actually added them.

54. **The correct answer is G.** Begin by plugging in 100 for x. If 100 is increased by 20 percent, the result is 120. This number is then decreased by 30 percent. Thirty percent of 120 is 36, so the final result is $120 - 36 = 84$. This is the same as decreasing 100 by 16 percent. Choice F is incorrect because the percentages are actually acting in different directions, so you cannot simply add them in this manner. Choices H and J are incorrect because you cannot just add percentages; they must be applied to a whole. For choice K, you assumed that x was initially decreased by 20% and then applied 30% to $0.80x$.

55. **The correct answer is A.** As shown in the diagram below, the height of the pole, x, is opposite a 70° angle, and the hypotenuse of the triangle is 50.

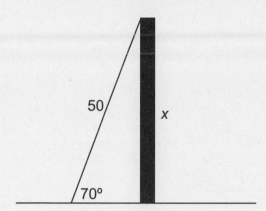

Sine equals opposite divided by hypotenuse:

$$\frac{x}{50} = \sin 70°$$
$$x = 50 \sin 70°$$

Choice B is the length of the unlabeled leg of the triangle. In choice C, you used an incorrect definition of tangent.

In choices D and E, you used an incorrect definition of cosine.

56. **The correct answer is J.** When solving for an absolute value, you must consider that the expression within the absolute value can be either positive or negative. If it is positive, then the absolute value does not change the expression:

$$1 - x = x - 1$$
$$-2x = -2$$
$$x = 1$$

If the expression is negative, then the absolute value changes the sign of the expression:

$$-(1 - x) = x - 1$$
$$x - 1 = x - 1$$

The last equation is true only if the expression within the absolute value is negative, and $1 - x$ is negative only when $x > 1$. Therefore, the complete solution of the equation is $x = 1$ or $x > 1$, which can be simplified as $x \geq 1$.

Choice F is incorrect because x-values less than 1 do not satisfy this inequality. Choice G is incorrect because none of these values satisfies the inequality. Choice H is the complement of the solution set,

meaning that these are precisely the x-values for which the inequality is false. Choice K presents one solution, but all values larger than it also work.

57. **The correct answer is C.** Subtract the first equation from the second equation to solve for x:

$$2x + y = 2$$
$$-\left(\frac{x}{2} + y = 2\right)$$
$$\overline{\frac{3}{2}x = 0}$$
$$x = 0$$

Then substitute 0 for x in the easier equation to solve for y:

$$2(0) + y = 2$$
$$y = 2$$

The point of intersection is (0, 2). Note that you could also have tested the answer choices in the given linear equations. The correct point is the one whose coordinates make both equations true.

Choice A is incorrect because the coordinates should be interchanged. For choices B, D, and E, none of these, when plugged in, satisfy both equations.

58. **The correct answer is J.** The equation for line m is $y = 3x + 8$. Since line n is perpendicular to line m, it must have a slope of $-\frac{1}{3}$. By putting the given equations in slope-intercept form, you can see that only the line represented by $3y = -x + 14$ has a slope of

$-\frac{1}{3}$: $y = -\frac{1}{3}x + \frac{14}{3}$. The slopes of the lines in choices F,

G, and H are not $-\frac{1}{3}$. Remember, the product of the

slopes of perpendicular lines must be –1. Choice K is incorrect because the slope of line m is 3. Since the product of the slopes of perpendicular lines must be –1, this cannot be the equation of line n.

59. **The correct answer is B.** Probability is the number of favorable outcomes divided by the total number of possible outcomes. The probability of picking either the B or C card on the first draw is $\frac{2}{5}$. After the first card has been drawn, both the number of favorable outcomes and the total number of possible outcomes decrease by one, so the probability of picking either the B or C card on the second draw is $\frac{1}{4}$. Therefore, the probability of both of these events happening is $\frac{2}{5} \times \frac{1}{4} = \frac{1}{10}$. This is the same as 0.1.

Choice A is incorrect because the probability for the first draw should be $\frac{2}{5}$, not $\frac{1}{5}$. In choice C, you have the probability of any single outcome on the first draw—you did not account for there being two outcomes of interest or for there being two draws. Choice D gives you the probability of picking whichever of B and C remains on the second draw— you did not account for the first draw. In choice E, you have the probability of picking B or C on the first draw, but you did not account for the second draw.

60. **The correct answer is G.** A shirt and two ties cost $105, which translates to $s + 2t = 105$. Two shirts and one tie cost $135, which translates to $2s + t = 135$. Multiply both sides of the first equation by 2: $2s + 4t = 210$. Then subtract the second equation from the first equation to solve for t, the price of one tie:

$$2s + 4t = 210$$
$$-(2s + t = 135)$$
$$3t = 75$$
$$t = 25$$

In choice F, when solving the system you added the t-terms but should have subtracted them. In choice H, you likely made an arithmetic error. In choice J, you have the cost of two ties, not one. In choice K, you calculated the cost of one shirt.

READING

1.	D	11.	B	21.	C	31.	C
2.	H	12.	J	22.	F	32.	J
3.	B	13.	B	23.	D	33.	C
4.	G	14.	H	24.	H	34.	F
5.	B	15.	A	25.	A	35.	D
6.	J	16.	F	26.	H	36.	H
7.	C	17.	D	27.	B	37.	A
8.	F	18.	G	28.	F	38.	H
9.	D	19.	D	29.	D	39.	B
10.	H	20.	H	30.	G	40.	G

1. **The correct answer is D.** Paragraph 1 states that Mr. Bennet addressed his second daughter, and the following line finds him addressing Lizzy, so choice D is correct and choice B can be eliminated. A second daughter could be the youngest one if there are only two daughters, but we know based on this passage that there are at least three daughters in the Bennet family (Lizzy, Kitty, and Mary), so choice A is not the correct answer. The only mention of anyone being sensible in this passage refers to Mary, not Lizzy, and she fails in her attempt to do so, so choice C is not the correct answer.

2. **The correct answer is H.** Kitty's parents both react with annoyance when she coughs, and because she does not really do anything wrong, their reactions are overblown, so choice H is best. The other answer choices are all negative, but none of them really describes Kitty's parents' reactions to her coughing. Since they react with annoyance rather than apathy, choice F is incorrect. They do not mock her, so you can eliminate choice G. Since they do react with words, choice J does not make sense.

3. **The correct answer is B.** After Mr. Bennet makes the suggestion, Mrs. Bennet dismisses it as a breach of etiquette, which is apparently very important in this story. According to etiquette, Mrs. Bennet cannot make the introduction when she does not know Mr. Bingley personally. Although Mrs. Bennet believes Mr. Bennet has made a poor suggestion, it is extreme to conclude that she thinks he has lost his mind (choice A), he does not understand her (choice C), or he does not love her (choice D).

4. **The correct answer is G.** Although Miss Brooke's behavior toward Sir James may be interpreted as rude, no one in the passage ever says she is too rude, so choice F is not the best answer. Although the words

happy and *scruples* are used in the first paragraph, neither word is used to describe Miss Brooke, so you can eliminate choices H and J. However, both Celia and Sir James are familiar with the notion that Miss Brooke is too religious, so choice G is the best answer.

5. **The correct answer is B.** Although the word *ignorance* is used in the third paragraph, it applies to Sir James, not Miss Brooke. However, he notes in Paragraph 2 that she is *charming* (choice D) to him, and in Paragraph 3 that she is *handsome* (choice A) and possesses *cleverness* (choice C).

6. **The correct answer is J.** The sentence reads: "Celia felt that this was a *pity*." It is clear from this sentence that the word *pity* is a noun, so you can eliminate choice F since *sorry* can be used only as an adjective. *Compassion* (choice G) and *sympathy* (choice H) have the same meaning, so they most likely cancel each other out. They also would not make sense if used in place of *pity* in the original sentence. The only answer choice that would is *shame*.

7. **The correct answer is C.** In Passage A, Mrs. Bennet has little patience for her daughters' comments, and Miss Brooke is abrupt and cold with Sir James, so the answer that best describes both women is choice C, *short-tempered*. *Demure* means *shy,* and neither woman has any reservations about expressing her opinions, so choice A does not make sense. *Disgusted* may describe Miss Brooke since she may "despise" Sir James, but it is too harsh a word to describe Mrs. Bennett, so choice B is not the best answer. The narrator of Passage B describes Miss Brooke's behavior as an amusing contrast to Sir James's solicitous amiability, but that

Practice Test 3— ANSWERS

Answer Keys and Explanations

word does not really describe her in general, and it does not really describe Mrs. Bennet either, so choice D is not the best answer.

8. **The correct answer is F.** This is an inference question. Kitty becomes fretful when her parents interpret her coughing as impudence. This implies that she is concerned about how others interpret her behavior. However, Miss Brooke says exactly what is on her mind no matter how others might interpret her words. So choice F describes a difference between the two characters. Choice G describes how Miss Brooke is different from Kitty, not the other way around. Choice H is Sir James's interpretation of Miss Brooke's behavior; it is not anyone's interpretation of Kitty's. Mrs. Bennet describes Ms. Long as selfish and hypocritical; no one describes Kitty this way, so choice J is wrong.

9. **The correct answer is D.** At the end of Passage A, the narrator reveals Mary's unspoken wish "to say something sensible." The first paragraph of Passage B reveals Celia's private thoughts. Choice D is the best answer. Kitty's inner thoughts are never revealed in Passage A, so choice A is incorrect. Neither Elizabeth nor Miss Brooke's inner thoughts are known in these passages, so choice B is wrong. Mr. Bingley never even appears in Passage A, so choice C cannot be correct.

10. **The correct answer is H.** In Passage A, the Bennets intend to introduce their daughter Lizzy to Mr. Bingley in the hope that there will be a romantic connection between them. In Passage B, Sir James expresses romantic interest in Miss Brooke. Therefore, you can infer that both men are unmarried. The other answer choices are difficult to confirm. Mr. Bingley does not actually appear in Passage A, so it is not possible to know whether or not he is extremely charming (choice F), uninterested in etiquette (choice G), or if he even meets Lizzy (choice J).

11. **The correct answer is B.** Paragraph 4 begins by stating that "In a traditional Fiji tribe an individual as such can hardly be said to own property, for nearly all things belong to his family or clan." Choice A is incorrect because the passage does not say that Westerners had taken Fijian property. Choice C is incorrect because, according to the first paragraph, the chief cannot sell land without "the consent of his tribe." Furthermore, Paragraph 4 states that property belongs to the "family or tribe." Choice D is incorrect because the passage does not mention evil phantoms or spirits.

12. **The correct answer is J.** Paragraph 2 states that a whale's tooth expressed "good will" and was comparable

to "a signed contract." The other choices are incorrect because the passage never mentions burnt offerings to the gods (choice F), semiprecious stones (choice G), or the granting of a Fijian name (choice H) as ways to represent a contract.

13. **The correct answer is B.** Paragraph 3 begins by stating that "a man's wealth consisted not only in what he possessed but even more so in the number of people from whom he could beg or borrow." The paragraph then presents the Tanoa story as an example of this principle. Choice A is incorrect because Western destruction of Fijian values is not mentioned anywhere in the passage. (Although Paragraph 7 decries the "capitalism" and "hoarding [of] wealth" that characterize "the rat race of modern civilization," this is in no way related back to the story of King Tanoa's nephew.) Choice C is incorrect because theft is not mentioned until Paragraph 4. Choice D is incorrect because the anecdote is not presented to show the difficulty of obtaining Fijian trust.

14. **The correct answer is H.** Paragraph 7 shows that the author believes that modern civilization (capitalism) "entails the hoarding of wealth and becoming enmeshed in the rat race of modern civilization. Sadly, this race rarely has a happy ending." Choice F is incorrect because competition in world markets is not mentioned in the passage. Choice G is incorrect because Paragraph 7 tells us that capitalism took Fijians *away* from their traditional values. This is contrasted with the end of Paragraph 6, in which the Fijians of the past proclaim, "our days are happy as they pass." Choice J is incorrect because Paragraph 7 clearly shows that modern civilization has had an impact on the lives of Fijians.

15. **The correct answer is A.** Paragraph 4 links the lack of personal property to the difficulty in introducing "ideals of modern progress" in Fiji. Choice B is incorrect because religious customs are never discussed. Choices C and D are incorrect because neither land laws nor Western cultural indoctrination is ever mentioned in relation to the introduction of "ideals of modern progress."

16. **The correct answer is F.** The paragraph discusses contracts and uses the word *compliance* to signify "agreement." Choices G and J are incorrect because *compliance* would never mean "introduction" or "resignation." Choice H is incorrect because while *compliance* can mean "flexibility," this meaning does not make sense in the context of this sentence with its discussion of contracts.

17. **The correct answer is D.** The final paragraph says that "Seru" was called "Thakombau" after the civil war in which he overcame his father's enemies and reestablished Tanoa's rule in Mbau. Choice A is incorrect because the final paragraph in the passage does not mention Chief Thakombau's parents. Choice B is incorrect because Paragraph 8 tells us that hoarded wealth was not respected in Fiji. Choice C is incorrect because the final paragraph in the passage says that Chief Thakombau's Christian name was "Ebenezer."

18. **The correct answer is G.** Statement I is mentioned in Paragraph 1 ("land tenure"), and Statement II is mentioned in Paragraph 7 ("Fiji before capitalism took hold"), so choice G is correct. Choice F can be eliminated since it only mentions one of the included details. Statement III is not mentioned in the passage, so choices H and J cannot be correct.

19. **The correct answer is D.** The second sentence of the passage states that "the chief could sell no land without the consent of his tribe." The passage never suggests the chief could not declare war (choice A), start a new community on the same island (choice B), or cultivate land (choice C).

20. **The correct answer is H.** Paragraph 4 ends with the statement that "No one could be a miser, a capitalist, a banker, or a promoter in such a community, and thieves were almost unknown." Choice F is incorrect because the lack of jobs in Fiji is never presented as a benefit of the lack of ambition to acquire personal property. Choice G is incorrect because the lack of ambition would not promote industrialization; in fact, it would have the opposite effect. Choice J is incorrect because the passage does not mention friendship between Fijian chiefs.

21. **The correct answer is C.** In Paragraph 2, Michelangelo's father states, "In your profession, if once you were to fall ill you would be a ruined man." Choice A is incorrect because there is no indication in the passage that anyone in Michelangelo's family was in poor health. Choice B is incorrect because although Michelangelo's father advised his son to take care of his health, there is nothing in the passage that implies Michelangelo's father meant this advice as a demand. Choice D is incorrect because although Michelangelo's work was extremely physical and the possibility of injury existed, this possibility is never explicitly mentioned, nor does it have any bearing on whether he maintained his long-term health.

22. **The correct answer is F.** Choice F paraphrases the Statement in Paragraph 1: "The great artist was so prone to over-anxiety and met (whether needlessly or not) with so many rebuffs and disappointments that only constant absorption in manual labor prevented spirit from fretting itself free from flesh." Choice G is incorrect because it contradicts the above statement and because, in Paragraph 6, the author describes him as "miserly, suspicious, quarrelsome, and pessimistic." Choice H is incorrect because the passage makes no reference to other artists or how they might aspire to Michelangelo's greatness. Choice J is incorrect because Paragraph 4 implies that Michelangelo was not able to produce work as skillfully and artistically impressive as he once had.

23. **The correct answer is D.** Paragraph 4 states that, while Michelangelo still painted and sculpted with the skill of a genius at age 75, he later lost the required energy for such work and turned to such works as St. Peter's and other architectural projects, so choices A, B, and C can be eliminated.

24. **The correct answer is H.** Both Statements II and III are supported by Paragraph 3 with the phrases "his intensity of purpose and fierce energy" and "for [Michelangelo's] mental powers one of his colossal statues would seem a more fitting mold." Statement I, however, is incorrect, which eliminates choices F and J. Although reference is made in Paragraph 2 to the coarse nature of Michelangelo's dress habits (he left his boots on for so long that when he took them off, they came away "like the skin of a molting serpent"), no mention is made of his sense of humor. In fact, from the description the author gives of Michelangelo in the last paragraph, one might think the artist had no sense of humor at all. Choice G fails to mention one of the statements that Paragraph 3 supports.

25. **The correct answer is A.** The beginning of Paragraph 2—"art became his religion and required of him the sacrifice of all that might keep him below his highest level of power for work"—indicates that the rest of the paragraph will describe the elements that Michelangelo sacrificed for his work. Sleep and food are two of these elements. Choice B is incorrect because, although the assertion in Paragraph 6 that Michelangelo was "affected by a degree of neuropathy bordering closely upon hysterical disease" implies that he was not of sound mind, the following lines ("What a pity that more of us do not suffer from such degrees of neuropathy and how much better for most of us if we had such enthusiasm for perfection") imply that, to the author,

such madness is desirable. Choice C is incorrect because there is no indication in the passage that Michelangelo was anything *but* prolific. In fact, in the first paragraph, the statement that "He toiled 'furiously' in all his mighty undertakings that body and mind remained one and in abundant health for nearly four score and ten years" indicates that, since Michelangelo worked throughout his almost ninety years, he was indeed prolific. Choice D is incorrect because, although Michelangelo was intent on controlling his health, the implication of the second paragraph is that he limited his food and health in order to devote every minute possible to his art.

26. **The correct answer is H.** Paragraph 3, which discusses the appearance of Michelangelo's face, states: "The flattened nose was the result of a blow from a rival apprentice." So presumably Michelangelo had a fight with the rival apprentice. Choice F is incorrect because Paragraph 2 notes that Michelangelo's attention to his health began very early in his life. Choice G is incorrect because Paragraph 2 discusses Michelangelo's thriftiness, and Paragraph 5 goes so far as to suggest that he was miserly. Thus he could not have been overly generous with his friends. Choice J is incorrect because, to the contrary, Michelangelo appeared to listen to his father's advice, particularly as it related to matters of health.

27. **The correct answer is B.** Choice B is the best answer because it is a paraphrase of the first paragraph—in particular, the lines "there is nothing so conducive to mental and physical wholeness as saturation of body and mind with work." Choice A is incorrect because, although the passage may imply that living the way Michelangelo did may help other people live as long as he did, it is not the main idea of the passage. Choice C is incorrect because in Paragraph 2, the author states that Michelangelo remained healthy not simply because he wished to but because he took scrupulous care of himself. He knew that if he did not remain healthy, he could not work. Also, in Paragraph 5, the author implies that Michelangelo stayed healthy because he remained active, even when he couldn't pursue manual labor as he once had. Choice D is incorrect because, although in Paragraph 6 the author refers to Michelangelo's devotion to his art as a type of madness, the author clearly does not consider the artist truly mad. He suggests that such devotion is an admirable, beneficial state of mind. In addition, the question of the artist's sanity is not the main idea of the passage.

28. **The correct answer is F.** Statement I is supported by Paragraph 2, which says that "he ate comparatively little and slept less than many men because he worked better." Statements II and III are incorrect, so choices G, H, and J can be eliminated. Paragraph 6 indicates that Michelangelo's miserliness and pessimism were undesirable qualities that his good qualities, the ones that helped preserve him, balanced out.

29. **The correct answer is D.** Paragraph 5 states that "it was not until the day before his death that he would consent to go to bed." This is a fact with biographical support. The statements in choices A, B, and C are all opinions.

30. **The correct answer is G.** The author's description of Michelangelo in Paragraph 3 is of a man whose appearance is flawed and not as befitting a man of his genius as one of his statues would be. Choice F is incorrect because the passage makes no reference to the subject matter of Michelangelo's work. Choice H is incorrect because several references are made to Michelangelo's great intellectual capacity. Paragraph 1 states that his "body and mind remained one and in abundant health for nearly four score and ten years." Paragraph 3 refers to his mental powers being equivalent in size to "one of his colossal statues." Choice J is incorrect because, although Paragraph 3 refers to Michelangelo's statues as "colossal," this does not mean he never created smaller-scale statues.

31. **The correct answer is C.** Paragraph 11 states that "the more midges there were in a pitcher plant, the better off the mosquitoes were." Choice A is incorrect because Paragraph 11 says that mosquitoes benefit from more midge larvae. Choice B is incorrect because the passage does not mention the effect that fly larvae have on mosquitoes. Choice D is incorrect because the passage does not suggest that mosquitoes benefit from "any change" in the amount of bacteria. Since mosquitoes eat the bacteria, it may be assumed that a decrease in the amount of bacteria would harm them.

32. **The correct answer is J.** Statements II and III are supported by Paragraph 4, which describes "a sweet-smelling flower" and "tiny downward-pointing hairs." Statement I is incorrect because the roots of the pitcher plant are never mentioned, so choices F and H can be eliminated. Choice G fails to acknowledge that Paragraph 4 supports Statement III as well as Statement II.

33. **The correct answer is C.** Paragraph 6 states that "each larva has a life span of about a year, which is also the life span of each pitcher plant leaf." That concrete information makes choices A, B, and D incorrect.

34. **The correct answer is F.** Paragraph 3 says that the pitcher plant "does not produce enzymes." Choice G is incorrect because Paragraphs 5–8 discuss the insect species living in the pitcher plant. Choice H is incorrect because Paragraph 4 states that the plant has "a highly acidic mixture." Choice J is incorrect because Paragraph 3 states that the pitcher plant "absorbs nutrients" from its internal ecosystem.

35. **The correct answer is D.** Paragraph 7 states, "The fly larvae are much larger than the midge and mosquito larvae." Choice A is incorrect because the passage does not mention fly larvae being a danger to anyone. Choice B is incorrect because, according to Paragraph 7, fly larvae float on the top of the pitcher pool. Choice C is incorrect because the passage does not state that fly larvae directly affect the number of midge larvae.

36. **The correct answer is H.** The first paragraph says that "it's simply too acidic for the bacteria that break down dead plant matter to grow in." Choice F is incorrect because the plant's root system is never mentioned. Choices G and J are also incorrect; neither the surplus of water nor the presence of insect larvae is mentioned as a reason that the pitcher plant cannot extract nitrogen from the soil.

37. **The correct answer is A.** Paragraph 8 states: "The mosquito has to wait for the midge to finish eating, since the mosquito can only consume very small particles of insect that the midge chews up first." Choice B is incorrect because the passage never indicates that acids produced by the pitcher plant dissolve the insects or aid the mosquito larvae in feeding off the insects. Choice C is incorrect because the passage does not say that the insect parts must be frozen to be eaten by the mosquito larvae. Choice D is incorrect because if the insect parts were completely consumed by the fly larvae, there would be no parts left for the midge or mosquito larvae to eat.

38. **The correct answer is H.** According to Paragraph 9: "These tubes were then used in a variety of experiments to determine just how the insect larvae in pitcher plants process their food." It can be assumed that, since the tubes were filled with pitcher plant water and used to examine the interactions within the plant, the tubes were designed to simulate the form of the plant. Choices F and G are incorrect because the passage does not say that the tubes were used to trap mosquitoes or to test the acidity of the bog soil. Choice J is incorrect because the passage does not say that fly larvae compete with other larvae in the pitcher plant.

39. **The correct answer is B.** Paragraph 3 states that the "pitcher plant does not produce enzymes." Choices A, C, and D are incorrect because downward-pointing hairs, purple veins, and a highly slippery section of the leaf are all mentioned in Paragraph 4.

40. **The correct answer is G.** The vulture example is the only example in which the consumer of the processed food (the vulture) eats what is left over by the original consumer (the wolf). This mirrors the relationship between midge and mosquito larvae as described in the passage. Choice F is incorrect because, unlike a person producing food for others, the midge and fly larvae consume what comes to them, leaving the scraps for the mosquito larvae. Choice H is incorrect because the shark benefits from the fish's cleaning, while the midge does not benefit from its food processing for the mosquito. Choice J is incorrect because it describes a competitive system (the "taking of food from other smaller birds"). Paragraphs 7 and 11 clearly state that midges and mosquitoes do not compete for resources in the pitcher plant.

SCIENCE

1.	D	11.	A	21.	A	31.	B
2.	F	12.	J	22.	J	32.	F
3.	C	13.	C	23.	B	33.	D
4.	H	14.	J	24.	G	34.	J
5.	D	15.	B	25.	A	35.	B
6.	F	16.	J	26.	H	36.	J
7.	C	17.	D	27.	D	37.	D
8.	G	18.	G	28.	F	38.	H
9.	B	19.	C	29.	C	39.	B
10.	J	20.	F	30.	G	40.	G

1. **The correct answer is D.** Looking at the table, Resistor B has a current of 345 mA when the temperature is 23°C and the voltage is 3 volts. Choice B would be the correct answer if the question asked about Resistor C, and choice C would be the correct answer if the question asked about Resistor A. The value for choice A cannot be found in the table.

2. **The correct answer is F.** Current for Resistor C at 5 volts and 25 degrees was 90 mA, and for every 1 volt increase, the current increases by 18 mA. The current at 6 volts would be 108 mA. Choices G, H, and J are all too big to make sense with the pattern of increase shown in the table.

3. **The correct answer is C.** When exposed to different temperatures, Resistor A and Resistor B are not affected. Both I and II are correct, making choice A incorrect. According to the table, Resistor C is affected by temperature, making choices B and D incorrect.

4. **The correct answer is H.** A thermistor is a device that shows different resistances based on sensitivity to temperature; therefore, Resistor C could be the one thermistor. Choice F is incorrect because Resistor A did *not* show a change in resistance due to temperature. Choices G and J do not address a change in temperature affecting current within one resistor.

5. **The correct answer is D.** Resistor B does not demonstrate a linear relationship between voltage and current. Choice A is incorrect—the current stays the same with the change in temperature. Choice B is incorrect because though the current is unaffected by temperature, this has nothing to do with an ohmic device. Choice C is incorrect because the relationship is *not* linear.

6. **The correct answer is F.** Resistor A seems to be an ohmic device because there is a linear relationship between voltage and current. If Resistor A released heat into the water, it would not be considered an ohmic device. Choice G is incorrect because according to the table, Resistor B is not affected by temperature change. Choice H is incorrect because temperature change would not affect this outcome. Choice J is incorrect because according to the table, temperature does affect the current of Resistor C.

7. **The correct answer is C.** Choice C is correct because, although most nutrients are decreasing (making choice B incorrect), the table shows a net gain for these two. Choice A is incorrect because two nutrients, ammonium and nitrate, have a net gain. Choice D is the opposite of the correct answer.

8. **The correct answer is G.** According to Table 1, the largest percentage decreases are shown for silica and aluminum. Choices F, H, and J are incorrect because the depletion of all these nutrients is not as great as the depletion of silica and aluminum.

9. **The correct answer is B.** The purpose of using the different techniques was to ensure that the scientists could capture the different sizes of material exiting the ecosystem. This makes choice C incorrect—if all the matter were coarse, different techniques would not be needed to capture it. Choice A is incorrect because different collection methods are not needed to test separate areas. Choice D is incorrect because nothing is mentioned about matter being dissolved in water.

10. **The correct answer is J.** This experiment was designed to track the effects of logging on watersheds that were already losing nutrients. The design of the experiment and the design/display of the results in Table 2 show the ecologists' concern about loss of nutrients to be of crucial importance.

Practice Test 3—ANSWERS

Answer Keys and Explanations

Choice J is the only option that reflects this concern. Choices F, G, and H are incorrect—Table 2 shows that the deforested area had a loss of both organic and inorganic matter.

11. **The correct answer is A.** Close examination of Table 2 shows that there is no pattern to the loss of substances in the undisturbed watershed and that the loss is relatively small. The logged area is losing nutrients, and this is increasing each year. The only answer that reflects this comparison is choice A. Choices B and D are incorrect because there is no pattern or constancy to the undisturbed area. Choice C is incorrect because the logged area does not vary—it is constantly losing nutrients.

12. **The correct answer is J.** Nutrients are more dramatically depleted in the logged area, so a way to retain some of the nutrients would be useful. If tree bark contains many nutrients, keeping it in the system would help toward this end. Choices F, G, and H do not leave any of the nutrients from the bark in the ecosystem, so they are incorrect.

13. **The correct answer is C.** The element with the atomic weight of 85.5 is rubidium, and its melting point is 39°C. Choice A is the melting point of cesium. Choice B is incorrect because 37 is the atomic number of rubidium. Choice D is the melting point of potassium.

14. **The correct answer is J.** Sodium's density is 0.97 g/cm³, and cesium's density is 1.87 g/cm³, which is nearly twice that of sodium. Choices F, G, and H are incorrect because their densities are too small to be two times sodium's density.

15. **The correct answer is B.** According to the table, as the atomic number increases, the melting point decreases. Choice A is incorrect—you might have mistakenly looked at another column in the chart. Choices C and D are incorrect—the numbers in the melting point column do nothing but increase.

16. **The correct answer is J.** Cesium has a higher atomic weight and density than rubidium. Potassium has a higher atomic weight and density than lithium. Choices F and H are incorrect because option I does not support the hypothesis—as the atomic weight increases from sodium to potassium, the density decreases. Choice G is incorrect because option II is also correct.

17. **The correct answer is D.** Melting point seems to constantly decrease as the atomic number increases, making choices A and C incorrect. If another metal existed with a greater atomic number, the melting point would be lower than that of cesium. Density does not

clearly increase or decrease as the atomic number increases, so it would be difficult to predict the density of the element, making choice B incorrect. Therefore, choice D is the best answer.

18. **The correct answer is G.** The oldest rocks are at the higher altitudes, according to the table; therefore, choices F and H incorrect. Choice J is incorrect—look at andesite, which is 4 million years old and found at 2,000 feet altitude.

19. **The correct answer is C.** Gabbro has the highest crystallization temperature of the rocks listed. Choices A, B, and D are all lower temperatures, so none of these can be the best choice.

20. **The correct answer is F.** The vertical axis is the altitude. Choice G is incorrect; distance inland from shoreline is the horizontal axis. Choices H and J are values in Table 1, not Figure 1.

21. **The correct answer is A.** The highest crystallization temperatures are found with peridotite. Peridotite is found 40 miles inland. Choices B, C, and D are incorrect because breccia, andesite, and granite do not have the highest crystallization temperatures, so choice A would yield the highest concentration of iron.

22. **The correct answer is J.** The age of rocks is not related to the distance from the shore that the rocks are found—this makes choices F, G, and H incorrect. The oldest rocks are found closest to the coast and farthest from the coast.

23. **The correct answer is B.** Limestone is found 80 miles inland, and andesite is found 120 to 140 miles inland. The andesite is farther east than the limestone. The limestone is 6.0 million years old. The andesite is 3.6 to 4.0 million years old. Andesite from volcanoes would have had to erupt after the deposit of the limestone. Choices A and D are incorrect because according to the chart, andesite is younger than limestone, so it could not have formed simultaneously to limestone or before it. Choice C is incorrect because the volcano arose east, not west.

24. **The correct answer is G.** Paleontologist A believes that morphological (body) similarities can just as reasonably be assumed to represent the effects of convergent evolution on distant lineages inhabiting similar environments. Choice F is incorrect—this paleontologist does not mention a failed experiment of evolution. Choice H is incorrect because even though the paleontologist does not think birds evolved directly from dinosaurs, a connection is acknowledged. Choice J is

incorrect—there is no discussion of what caused the thecodonts to survive extinction.

25. **The correct answer is A.** Paleontologist A believes that dinosaurs and birds share a common ancestor. A fossil find from before the age of the dinosaurs with common features would support this view. An intermediate form between dinosaurs and birds, choice B, or an avian prototype before dinosaur dominance, choice C, would not directly support the position of a common ancestor. Examining theropod remains, choice D, does not relate to Paleontologist A's theory—he/she talks about thecodonts.

26. **The correct answer is H.** Paleontologist B assumes that the body similarities between dinosaurs and early birds must be evidence that birds came forth from the dinosaur lineage. This view does subscribe to the idea of transitional forms. Mass extinction is not relevant to this view. Choice F is incorrect because Paleontologist B directly discusses transitional forms—shared features from immediate ancestors. Choice G is incorrect because extinction is not a main feature of Paleontologist A's argument. Choice J is incorrect—neither paleontologist thinks the lineages are distant.

27. **The correct answer is D.** Paleontologist B believes that birds arose from a lineage of dinosaurs, which makes choice C incorrect. Choice A is incorrect—Paleontologist B does not believe in convergent evolution. Choice B is the view of Paleontologist A.

28. **The correct answer is F.** This contradicts the theory of Paleontologist B, who suggests that birds arose from dinosaurs (making choices G and H incorrect). Paleontologist A suggests that the two arose from an extremely distant ancestor, and the theory of convergent evolution is not inconsistent with birds appearing before dinosaurs. Paleontologist A's view is present, so choice J is incorrect.

29. **The correct answer is C.** Paleontologist A postulates the existence of a very distant common ancestor for birds and dinosaurs. The development of birds much later than that of dinosaurs might seem to refute this argument. However, the rate of evolutionary change is not constant across different lineages. Dinosaurs may have developed relatively rapidly from thecodonts, for example, whereas birds did not evolve until much later. Choice D is the opposite of this correct answer. Choices A and B are unrelated to the timing of the appearance of birds and dinosaurs.

30. **The correct answer is G.** Close examination of Table 2 shows that the only factor being changed is the number of species of bacteria present. Choice F is incorrect—the explanation for the experiment states only one *Paramecium* species is present in each microcosm. The medium, choice H, is also unchanged. Trophic levels (choice J) are not mentioned in the experiment.

31. **The correct answer is B.** Examining the results in Tables 2 and 3 shows that increasing the number of species of their food sources, the bacteria, did produce a relative increase in the survival rate of *Paramecia*. Choice A states the opposite, so it is incorrect. Choice C is incorrect because there is a definite increase. Choice D is incorrect—the only variable being observed is *Paramecia*, which increased.

32. **The correct answer is F.** Looking at Tables 2 and 3, it appears that increasing the number of species of *Paramecium* from one to two was most detrimental to their overall survival. The number decreased, making choice J incorrect. Choice G is incorrect because it cannot be confirmed—the only variable being observed is *Paramecia*. Choice H is incorrect—according to Table 3, the number of species did have an effect on *Paramecia* survival.

33. **The correct answer is D.** Experiment 3 added a predator of *Paramecia*. Choices A, B, and C are incorrect: the number of bacteria species remained at 3, and we have no information that the time or the culture method was changed.

34. **The correct answer is J.** The results of this experiment suggest that increasing diversity in terms of trophic levels was ultimately harmful to the survival of the *Paramecium* species under study. Choices F and G are incorrect: it was not beneficial to all species because of the decreasing survival rates for the *Paramecia*, and it definitely had an effect on *Paramecia*. Choice H is incorrect, as we do not know the effect the experiment had on *Amoebae*.

35. **The correct answer is B.** Neptune's density is 1,638 kg/m^3. Saturn has a density of 687 kg/m^3, Uranus has a density of 1,318 kg/m^3, and Jupiter has a density of 1,326 kg/m^3. Choices A, C, and D all contain planets with a higher density than Neptune.

36. **The correct answer is J.** Neptune has the lowest temperature; based on that measure, it would seem to be the farthest from the sun. Mercury (choice F), Uranus (choice G), and Jupiter (choice H) all have higher black-body temperatures and so are closer to the sun.

37. The correct answer is D. Mercury has an orbital inclination of 7.000 degrees and an orbital eccentricity of 0.2056. Therefore, Mercury would be reclassified. Choices A, B, and C are incorrect because none of these planets have an orbital inclination greater than 5 or an orbital eccentricity greater than 0.2.

38. The correct answer is H. The orbital eccentricity of Venus is 0.0068; its orbit is the most circular in the solar system. Mercury has an orbital eccentricity of 0.2056; its egg-shaped orbit exhibits the greatest eccentricity in the solar system and thus deviates the most from a circular orbit. Choice F is incorrect—there is a planet with an orbital eccentricity closer to 0 than Earth. Choice G is incorrect—there is a planet with an orbital eccentricity closer to 0 than Neptune. Choice J is incorrect—there is a planet with an orbital eccentricity further from 0 than Neptune.

39. The correct answer is B. The gaseous planets would be expected to be less dense than the ones made of solid material. Choices A and D are incorrect—temperature and rotation period should not be affected whether a planet is a solid or a gas. Choice C is incorrect because these planets do not have greater masses than the others.

40. The correct answer is G. Choice F is incorrect because Venus and Mercury do have the longest rotation periods. Choice J is incorrect because Mars and Earth do have similar rotation periods. Choice H is incorrect because the planets with the greatest mass do have the shortest rotation periods. However, as black-body temperature decreases, the rotation periods do not necessarily decrease, making choice G the only false statement—and the correct answer.

SAMPLE ESSAY: SCORE 1

Ideas and Analysis:	Score = 1
Development and Support:	Score = 1
Organization:	Score = 1
Language Use and Conventions:	Score = 1

I'm not sure I don't use fossils for anything not something I care about even. I only plug in the stuff I used my phone and my laptop and I think my TV they're all plugged into the wall and I don't bother anybody with them. Keep the sound down low especially when its late and its late at night my parents say, so I do that and I know how to take care of my stuff! If anybody wants to use anything they want to make theyre stuff work and as long as theyre not hurting anybody its ok with me. If thyre hurting everybody they should stop and be nice people and use just the wall to plug theyre stuff in, it is safe and I use it all the time and noone gets hurt so everybody should do that.

Scoring Explanation

Ideas and Analysis: Score = 1

This essay reflects a poor grasp of the essay task and a weak understanding of the role of fossil fuels and available energy sources. As a result, ideas are scattered and confusing, the writer's argument fails to address the questions provided, and the argument veers off in a largely unrelated direction regarding his or her use of electricity and favorite electronic devices.

Development and Support: Score = 1

This argument suffers from a significant lack of development and support for a discernible perspective regarding the use of alternative energy vs. fossil fuels. This lack of idea development hinders comprehension and results in a disjointed essay that does not address the essay task at hand.

Organization: Score = 1

The writer provides a disjointed set of loosely connected thoughts with little or no thought given to effective essay construction or organization. There is no assertion of a clear perspective regarding the essay task, and the ideas provided don't follow a natural and coherent flow or support a unifying essay theme. The end result is a confusing piece of writing that falls off topic.

Language Use and Conventions: Score = 1

This essay demonstrates poor use of fundamental grammar and a deficient understanding of core English language rules. As a result, this piece of writing, which is full of errors in usage and mechanics, fails to competently address the given essay task.

SAMPLE ESSAY: SCORE 6

Ideas and Analysis:	Score = 6
Development and Support:	Score = 6
Organization:	Score = 6
Language Use and Conventions:	Score = 6

Let's be honest. It's nice to be able to drive to the beach on a warm summer day. It's a wonderful luxury to have air conditioning in our homes, heat during the winter, and enough electricity to power all of the electronic gadgets that make our lives more comfortable. But is it worth any cost? Is it worth the destruction of our environment, the safety and well-being of future generations who have not yet had the opportunity to enjoy the natural wonders of our world, the very future of our planet? Each of us can pretend that our use of energy doesn't matter much, that it doesn't have a huge impact on the Earth, but this is the sort of apathetic mindset that keeps us from meaningful change.

The hard truth is that fossil fuels power our planet and are weaved into our social fabric; extricating ourselves from such a complex intertwining won't be easy. But that doesn't mean it's an issue we should avoid, or push off onto future generations. However, calls for an immediate, rash, or unrealistic abatement of fossil fuel usage are unrealistic and prevent us from intelligently addressing the challenge at hand.

What might a realistic, considered approach look like? There needs to be vastly increased incentives for individuals and businesses of all sizes that are both utilizing renewable energy sources and working on innovative green energy solutions for society, including tax breaks, monetary compensation, and government support. Towns, cities, and states need to galvanize and energize their citizens, adopt greater alternative energy programs, and execute expanded information campaigns. Local and state governments need to offer realistic strategies for reduced fossil fuel consumption and increased use of alternative energy that are not cost prohibitive. Local, state, and federal budgets need to shift towards greater investment in this effort or we will surely stall before we make any further progress.

Our country needs to keep energy consumption change at the forefront of our list of challenges to overcome. How can each of us help make this happen? The power of the vote is a great place. We need to demand that our elected officials at all levels tackle these issues—if they want to stay in office. Our collective concern can continue to be made known to our elected officials through social media campaigns, petitions, and voting patterns. Nations around the world work together all the time and tackle tough issues. Worldwide collaboration to effect positive climate change and reduce carbon emissions have already begin, but it needs to move beyond its careful early steps and into larger and more audacious strategies. It's too important an issue to not face it bravely and boldly.

Here's the bottom line: we need to figure out a realistic approach for decreasing fossil fuel reliance at every level—individuals, towns, cities, states, countries, and nations working in unison can reduce non-renewable fuel consumption, advocate for and invest in alternative fuel use, and—perhaps most importantly—acknowledge that we're *all* responsible for the welfare of our planet. Until we decide to make the hard decisions to effect positive change we're placing our world in peril. Will it be easy? Certainly not. But, the cost of continued complacency is much larger and more onerous—for each of us, for our children, and for future generations.

Scoring Explanation

Ideas and Analysis: Score = 6

The writer of this essay provides a well-reasoned, insightful argument in support of a realistic, unilateral approach to reducing fossil fuel dependency and increasing investment, exploration, and use of alternative sources of fuel. The ideas are carefully considered and represent a confident perspective on the issue. Progressive ideas for taking bolder steps are provided at every level—from individuals to countries and political entities in-between, resulting in a cohesive, thoughtful piece of writing that clearly tackles this issue with the seriousness it deserves.

Development and Support: Score = 6

This argument is a capably structured response to a challenging essay task, one that touches on hot-button social and political issues and requires the writer to think on both micro and macro scales, which this response does quite well. From the provocative opening question about fossil fuels (is it worth any cost?), through the detailed exploration of possible strategies for reducing our non-renewable energy reliance and concluding plea for future generations, this essay demonstrates an impressive ability to develop and support a clear perspective.

Organization: Score = 6

This argument is a well-organized, cogent piece of writing that serves the writer's thoughts on the issue of alternative energy quite well. It contains a clear perspective and sharp focus, from the mature and realistic introduction to the thought-provoking conclusion. It does an especially admirable job of outlining what "a realistic, considered approach" aligned with the writer's thoughts on tapering off from fossil fuels might look like.

Language Use and Conventions: Score = 6

This essay demonstrates an impressive command of standard language use and conventions, especially pertaining to argumentative writing. The grammar and mechanics are strong throughout, and a wide array of engaging sentences and transitions are displayed. The varied, thoughtful word choices and careful construction all lead to a thorough and effective essay that more than meets the task at hand.

English Test

1. Ⓐ Ⓑ Ⓒ Ⓓ 16. Ⓕ Ⓖ Ⓗ Ⓙ 31. Ⓐ Ⓑ Ⓒ Ⓓ 46. Ⓕ Ⓖ Ⓗ Ⓙ 61. Ⓐ Ⓑ Ⓒ Ⓓ
2. Ⓕ Ⓖ Ⓗ Ⓙ 17. Ⓐ Ⓑ Ⓒ Ⓓ 32. Ⓕ Ⓖ Ⓗ Ⓙ 47. Ⓐ Ⓑ Ⓒ Ⓓ 62. Ⓕ Ⓖ Ⓗ Ⓙ
3. Ⓐ Ⓑ Ⓒ Ⓓ 18. Ⓕ Ⓖ Ⓗ Ⓙ 33. Ⓐ Ⓑ Ⓒ Ⓓ 48. Ⓕ Ⓖ Ⓗ Ⓙ 63. Ⓐ Ⓑ Ⓒ Ⓓ
4. Ⓕ Ⓖ Ⓗ Ⓙ 19. Ⓐ Ⓑ Ⓒ Ⓓ 34. Ⓕ Ⓖ Ⓗ Ⓙ 49. Ⓐ Ⓑ Ⓒ Ⓓ 64. Ⓕ Ⓖ Ⓗ Ⓙ
5. Ⓐ Ⓑ Ⓒ Ⓓ 20. Ⓕ Ⓖ Ⓗ Ⓙ 35. Ⓐ Ⓑ Ⓒ Ⓓ 50. Ⓕ Ⓖ Ⓗ Ⓙ 65. Ⓐ Ⓑ Ⓒ Ⓓ
6. Ⓕ Ⓖ Ⓗ Ⓙ 21. Ⓐ Ⓑ Ⓒ Ⓓ 36. Ⓕ Ⓖ Ⓗ Ⓙ 51. Ⓐ Ⓑ Ⓒ Ⓓ 66. Ⓕ Ⓖ Ⓗ Ⓙ
7. Ⓐ Ⓑ Ⓒ Ⓓ 22. Ⓕ Ⓖ Ⓗ Ⓙ 37. Ⓐ Ⓑ Ⓒ Ⓓ 52. Ⓕ Ⓖ Ⓗ Ⓙ 67. Ⓐ Ⓑ Ⓒ Ⓓ
8. Ⓕ Ⓖ Ⓗ Ⓙ 23. Ⓐ Ⓑ Ⓒ Ⓓ 38. Ⓕ Ⓖ Ⓗ Ⓙ 53. Ⓐ Ⓑ Ⓒ Ⓓ 68. Ⓕ Ⓖ Ⓗ Ⓙ
9. Ⓐ Ⓑ Ⓒ Ⓓ 24. Ⓕ Ⓖ Ⓗ Ⓙ 39. Ⓐ Ⓑ Ⓒ Ⓓ 54. Ⓕ Ⓖ Ⓗ Ⓙ 69. Ⓐ Ⓑ Ⓒ Ⓓ
10. Ⓕ Ⓖ Ⓗ Ⓙ 25. Ⓐ Ⓑ Ⓒ Ⓓ 40. Ⓕ Ⓖ Ⓗ Ⓙ 55. Ⓐ Ⓑ Ⓒ Ⓓ 70. Ⓕ Ⓖ Ⓗ Ⓙ
11. Ⓐ Ⓑ Ⓒ Ⓓ 26. Ⓕ Ⓖ Ⓗ Ⓙ 41. Ⓐ Ⓑ Ⓒ Ⓓ 56. Ⓕ Ⓖ Ⓗ Ⓙ 71. Ⓐ Ⓑ Ⓒ Ⓓ
12. Ⓕ Ⓖ Ⓗ Ⓙ 27. Ⓐ Ⓑ Ⓒ Ⓓ 42. Ⓕ Ⓖ Ⓗ Ⓙ 57. Ⓐ Ⓑ Ⓒ Ⓓ 72. Ⓕ Ⓖ Ⓗ Ⓙ
13. Ⓐ Ⓑ Ⓒ Ⓓ 28. Ⓕ Ⓖ Ⓗ Ⓙ 43. Ⓐ Ⓑ Ⓒ Ⓓ 58. Ⓕ Ⓖ Ⓗ Ⓙ 73. Ⓐ Ⓑ Ⓒ Ⓓ
14. Ⓕ Ⓖ Ⓗ Ⓙ 29. Ⓐ Ⓑ Ⓒ Ⓓ 44. Ⓕ Ⓖ Ⓗ Ⓙ 59. Ⓐ Ⓑ Ⓒ Ⓓ 74. Ⓕ Ⓖ Ⓗ Ⓙ
15. Ⓐ Ⓑ Ⓒ Ⓓ 30. Ⓕ Ⓖ Ⓗ Ⓙ 45. Ⓐ Ⓑ Ⓒ Ⓓ 60. Ⓕ Ⓖ Ⓗ Ⓙ 75. Ⓐ Ⓑ Ⓒ Ⓓ

Math Test

1. Ⓐ Ⓑ Ⓒ Ⓓ Ⓔ 16. Ⓕ Ⓖ Ⓗ Ⓙ Ⓚ 31. Ⓐ Ⓑ Ⓒ Ⓓ Ⓔ 46. Ⓕ Ⓖ Ⓗ Ⓙ Ⓚ
2. Ⓕ Ⓖ Ⓗ Ⓙ Ⓚ 17. Ⓐ Ⓑ Ⓒ Ⓓ Ⓔ 32. Ⓕ Ⓖ Ⓗ Ⓙ Ⓚ 47. Ⓐ Ⓑ Ⓒ Ⓓ Ⓔ
3. Ⓐ Ⓑ Ⓒ Ⓓ Ⓔ 18. Ⓕ Ⓖ Ⓗ Ⓙ Ⓚ 33. Ⓐ Ⓑ Ⓒ Ⓓ Ⓔ 48. Ⓕ Ⓖ Ⓗ Ⓙ Ⓚ
4. Ⓕ Ⓖ Ⓗ Ⓙ Ⓚ 19. Ⓐ Ⓑ Ⓒ Ⓓ Ⓔ 34. Ⓕ Ⓖ Ⓗ Ⓙ Ⓚ 49. Ⓐ Ⓑ Ⓒ Ⓓ Ⓔ
5. Ⓐ Ⓑ Ⓒ Ⓓ Ⓔ 20. Ⓕ Ⓖ Ⓗ Ⓙ Ⓚ 35. Ⓐ Ⓑ Ⓒ Ⓓ Ⓔ 50. Ⓕ Ⓖ Ⓗ Ⓙ Ⓚ
6. Ⓕ Ⓖ Ⓗ Ⓙ Ⓚ 21. Ⓐ Ⓑ Ⓒ Ⓓ Ⓔ 36. Ⓕ Ⓖ Ⓗ Ⓙ Ⓚ 51. Ⓐ Ⓑ Ⓒ Ⓓ Ⓔ
7. Ⓐ Ⓑ Ⓒ Ⓓ Ⓔ 22. Ⓕ Ⓖ Ⓗ Ⓙ Ⓚ 37. Ⓐ Ⓑ Ⓒ Ⓓ Ⓔ 52. Ⓕ Ⓖ Ⓗ Ⓙ Ⓚ
8. Ⓕ Ⓖ Ⓗ Ⓙ Ⓚ 23. Ⓐ Ⓑ Ⓒ Ⓓ Ⓔ 38. Ⓕ Ⓖ Ⓗ Ⓙ Ⓚ 53. Ⓐ Ⓑ Ⓒ Ⓓ Ⓔ
9. Ⓐ Ⓑ Ⓒ Ⓓ Ⓔ 24. Ⓕ Ⓖ Ⓗ Ⓙ Ⓚ 39. Ⓐ Ⓑ Ⓒ Ⓓ Ⓔ 54. Ⓕ Ⓖ Ⓗ Ⓙ Ⓚ
10. Ⓕ Ⓖ Ⓗ Ⓙ Ⓚ 25. Ⓐ Ⓑ Ⓒ Ⓓ Ⓔ 40. Ⓕ Ⓖ Ⓗ Ⓙ Ⓚ 55. Ⓐ Ⓑ Ⓒ Ⓓ Ⓔ
11. Ⓐ Ⓑ Ⓒ Ⓓ Ⓔ 26. Ⓕ Ⓖ Ⓗ Ⓙ Ⓚ 41. Ⓐ Ⓑ Ⓒ Ⓓ Ⓔ 56. Ⓕ Ⓖ Ⓗ Ⓙ Ⓚ
12. Ⓕ Ⓖ Ⓗ Ⓙ Ⓚ 27. Ⓐ Ⓑ Ⓒ Ⓓ Ⓔ 42. Ⓕ Ⓖ Ⓗ Ⓙ Ⓚ 57. Ⓐ Ⓑ Ⓒ Ⓓ Ⓔ
13. Ⓐ Ⓑ Ⓒ Ⓓ Ⓔ 28. Ⓕ Ⓖ Ⓗ Ⓙ Ⓚ 43. Ⓐ Ⓑ Ⓒ Ⓓ Ⓔ 58. Ⓕ Ⓖ Ⓗ Ⓙ Ⓚ
14. Ⓕ Ⓖ Ⓗ Ⓙ Ⓚ 29. Ⓐ Ⓑ Ⓒ Ⓓ Ⓔ 44. Ⓕ Ⓖ Ⓗ Ⓙ Ⓚ 59. Ⓐ Ⓑ Ⓒ Ⓓ Ⓔ
15. Ⓐ Ⓑ Ⓒ Ⓓ Ⓔ 30. Ⓕ Ⓖ Ⓗ Ⓙ Ⓚ 45. Ⓐ Ⓑ Ⓒ Ⓓ Ⓔ 60. Ⓕ Ⓖ Ⓗ Ⓙ Ⓚ

Practice Test 4—ANSWERS

Reading Test

1. Ⓐ Ⓑ Ⓒ Ⓓ   11. Ⓐ Ⓑ Ⓒ Ⓓ   21. Ⓐ Ⓑ Ⓒ Ⓓ   31. Ⓐ Ⓑ Ⓒ Ⓓ

2. Ⓕ Ⓖ Ⓗ Ⓙ   12. Ⓕ Ⓖ Ⓗ Ⓙ   22. Ⓕ Ⓖ Ⓗ Ⓙ   32. Ⓕ Ⓖ Ⓗ Ⓙ

3. Ⓐ Ⓑ Ⓒ Ⓓ   13. Ⓐ Ⓑ Ⓒ Ⓓ   23. Ⓐ Ⓑ Ⓒ Ⓓ   33. Ⓐ Ⓑ Ⓒ Ⓓ

4. Ⓕ Ⓖ Ⓗ Ⓙ   14. Ⓕ Ⓖ Ⓗ Ⓙ   24. Ⓕ Ⓖ Ⓗ Ⓙ   34. Ⓕ Ⓖ Ⓗ Ⓙ

5. Ⓐ Ⓑ Ⓒ Ⓓ   15. Ⓐ Ⓑ Ⓒ Ⓓ   25. Ⓐ Ⓑ Ⓒ Ⓓ   35. Ⓐ Ⓑ Ⓒ Ⓓ

6. Ⓕ Ⓖ Ⓗ Ⓙ   16. Ⓕ Ⓖ Ⓗ Ⓙ   26. Ⓕ Ⓖ Ⓗ Ⓙ   36. Ⓕ Ⓖ Ⓗ Ⓙ

7. Ⓐ Ⓑ Ⓒ Ⓓ   17. Ⓐ Ⓑ Ⓒ Ⓓ   27. Ⓐ Ⓑ Ⓒ Ⓓ   37. Ⓐ Ⓑ Ⓒ Ⓓ

8. Ⓕ Ⓖ Ⓗ Ⓙ   18. Ⓕ Ⓖ Ⓗ Ⓙ   28. Ⓕ Ⓖ Ⓗ Ⓙ   38. Ⓕ Ⓖ Ⓗ Ⓙ

9. Ⓐ Ⓑ Ⓒ Ⓓ   19. Ⓐ Ⓑ Ⓒ Ⓓ   29. Ⓐ Ⓑ Ⓒ Ⓓ   39. Ⓐ Ⓑ Ⓒ Ⓓ

10. Ⓕ Ⓖ Ⓗ Ⓙ   20. Ⓕ Ⓖ Ⓗ Ⓙ   30. Ⓕ Ⓖ Ⓗ Ⓙ   40. Ⓕ Ⓖ Ⓗ Ⓙ

Science Test

1. Ⓐ Ⓑ Ⓒ Ⓓ   11. Ⓐ Ⓑ Ⓒ Ⓓ   21. Ⓐ Ⓑ Ⓒ Ⓓ   31. Ⓐ Ⓑ Ⓒ Ⓓ

2. Ⓕ Ⓖ Ⓗ Ⓙ   12. Ⓕ Ⓖ Ⓗ Ⓙ   22. Ⓕ Ⓖ Ⓗ Ⓙ   32. Ⓕ Ⓖ Ⓗ Ⓙ

3. Ⓐ Ⓑ Ⓒ Ⓓ   13. Ⓐ Ⓑ Ⓒ Ⓓ   23. Ⓐ Ⓑ Ⓒ Ⓓ   33. Ⓐ Ⓑ Ⓒ Ⓓ

4. Ⓕ Ⓖ Ⓗ Ⓙ   14. Ⓕ Ⓖ Ⓗ Ⓙ   24. Ⓕ Ⓖ Ⓗ Ⓙ   34. Ⓕ Ⓖ Ⓗ Ⓙ

5. Ⓐ Ⓑ Ⓒ Ⓓ   15. Ⓐ Ⓑ Ⓒ Ⓓ   25. Ⓐ Ⓑ Ⓒ Ⓓ   35. Ⓐ Ⓑ Ⓒ Ⓓ

6. Ⓕ Ⓖ Ⓗ Ⓙ   16. Ⓕ Ⓖ Ⓗ Ⓙ   26. Ⓕ Ⓖ Ⓗ Ⓙ   36. Ⓕ Ⓖ Ⓗ Ⓙ

7. Ⓐ Ⓑ Ⓒ Ⓓ   17. Ⓐ Ⓑ Ⓒ Ⓓ   27. Ⓐ Ⓑ Ⓒ Ⓓ   37. Ⓐ Ⓑ Ⓒ Ⓓ

8. Ⓕ Ⓖ Ⓗ Ⓙ   18. Ⓕ Ⓖ Ⓗ Ⓙ   28. Ⓕ Ⓖ Ⓗ Ⓙ   38. Ⓕ Ⓖ Ⓗ Ⓙ

9. Ⓐ Ⓑ Ⓒ Ⓓ   19. Ⓐ Ⓑ Ⓒ Ⓓ   29. Ⓐ Ⓑ Ⓒ Ⓓ   39. Ⓐ Ⓑ Ⓒ Ⓓ

10. Ⓕ Ⓖ Ⓗ Ⓙ   20. Ⓕ Ⓖ Ⓗ Ⓙ   30. Ⓕ Ⓖ Ⓗ Ⓙ   40. Ⓕ Ⓖ Ⓗ Ⓙ

WRITING TEST

PLAN YOUR ESSAY

WRITE YOUR ESSAY

ENGLISH TEST

45 Minutes—75 Questions

> **DIRECTIONS:** In this section, you will see passages with words and phrases that are underlined and numbered. In the right-hand column you will see a question corresponding to each number which provides alternatives to the underlined part. In most of the items, you are to choose the best alternative. If no change is needed, choose NO CHANGE.
>
> In other items, there will be either a question about an underlined portion of the passage or a question about a section of the passage, or about the passage as a whole. This question type will correspond to a number or numbers in a box.
>
> For each question, choose the best alternative or answer and fill in the corresponding circle on the answer sheet.

PASSAGE I

Vaudeville

[1]

Ask people if they have ever <u>heard, of vaudeville, and</u> most
of them will have no idea what the word even means. However,
around 100 years ago, vaudeville was the most popular form of
entertainment in the United States. Between the years 1875 and
1932, <u>it was vaudeville bringing laughter and joy throughout
the country to millions of people.</u>

[2]

The fact that vaudeville had something for everyone led to
its <u>wonderful</u> appeal.

The variety of the <u>acts was</u> impressive. Each show featured
jugglers, horseback riders, musicians, and puppeteers to entertain

1. A. NO CHANGE
   B. heard of vaudeville, and
   C. heard, of vaudeville and
   D. heard of vaudeville and

2. F. NO CHANGE
   G. vaudeville brought laughter and joy to millions of people throughout the country.
   H. it was vaudeville that brought laughter and joy throughout the country to millions of people.
   J. vaudeville was bringing laughter and joy to people throughout the country in the millions.

3. A. NO CHANGE
   B. great deal of
   C. large
   D. mass

4. F. NO CHANGE
   G. acts, were
   H. acts were
   J. acts was,

the crowd. <u>The audience would laugh at the clowns and come-</u>
<u>dians, joining the singers in song, and in amazement of the magic</u>
<u>tricks and acrobats.</u> Since acts like magic, mime, and dancing

5. **A.** NO CHANGE
   B. The audience would laugh at the clowns and comedians, join the singers in song, and watch the magic tricks and acrobats in amazement.
   C. The audience would laugh at the clowns and comedians, join the singers in song, and being amazed by the magic tricks and acrobats.
   D. The audience would have laughed at the clowns and comedians, joining the singers in song, and be amazed by the magic tricks and acrobats.

required little to no <u>verbal communication or speaking,</u> many of
the new immigrants to this country did not need to speak English
to join in the fun. In addition, tickets to vaudeville shows were

6. **F.** NO CHANGE
   G. verbal communication, or speaking
   H. verbal communication or speech,
   J. verbal communication,

relatively <u>inexpensive. Making</u> it possible for people with limited
means to purchase them. Another reason for vaudeville's

7. **A.** NO CHANGE
   B. inexpensive, this made
   C. inexpensive, making
   D. inexpensive, yet making

popularity was the family-oriented nature <u>of the acts.</u> Vulgarity

8. **F.** NO CHANGE
   G. of the acts'.
   H. of the act's.
   J. of the act.

was not allowed, so when parents took their children, <u>we could</u>
enjoy the show without worrying about exposing them to
improper language or behavior.

9. **A.** NO CHANGE
   B. he or she could
   C. they could
   D. one could

[3]

[10] The word *vaudeville* comes from the French phrase *voix
de ville*, or "voices of the town." In France, people would gather
in the valleys to amuse each other with song and dance. Gradually,
vaudeville spread to America, into the saloons of the wild west.
There, performers delighted the audience with acts like singing

10. Which of the following sentences offers the best introduction to Paragraph 3?
    F. The French language has given us many words commonly used in English.
    G. People have always enjoyed singing and dancing.
    H. The origins of vaudeville can be traced to Europe.
    J. Historians have different theories about the origins of vaudeville.

and rope spinning. As the acts became <u>mostly creative</u> and

11. **A.** NO CHANGE
    B. the most creative
    C. more than creative
    D. more creative

diverse, they attracted a wider audience. <u>Rapidly growing in</u>
                                            12
<u>popularity, businesspeople began opening theaters all over the</u>
                                12
<u>country.</u> When vaudeville reached its peak in the 1920s, there
  12
were over 600 theaters showcasing 60,000 acts.

[4]

(1) W. C. Fields, Ethel Merman, and Will Rogers are just a few examples of performers who achieved celebrity status. (2) Some performers gained fame and stardom on the vaudeville stage. (3) Other famous vaudevillians include the Marx Brothers and Sarah Bernhardt. [13]

[5]

Despite its immense success, vaudeville would not last forever. The Great Depression as well as technological advances like the radio and movies contributed to the demise of a great form of entertainment.

12. **F.** NO CHANGE
     G. Noting its popularity, businesspeople began opening theaters all over the country.
     H. Rapidly growing in popularity, theaters all over the country were opened by businesspeople.
     J. Rapidly growing in popularity, businesspeople all over the country began opening theaters.

13. Which of the following sequences of sentences makes Paragraph 4 most logical?

     A. NO CHANGE
     B. 3, 1, 2
     C. 2, 3, 1
     D. 2, 1, 3

> **Questions 14 and 15 ask about the essay as a whole.**

14. For the sake of the unity and coherence of this essay, Paragraph 3 should be placed:

     F. where it is now.
     G. after Paragraph 4.
     H. before Paragraph 1.
     J. after Paragraph 1.

15. Suppose the author wanted to write an essay to convince readers that modern movie theaters should be replaced by vaudeville theaters. Which paragraph in the essay would offer the best support for his argument? Follow the original order of the paragraphs.

     A. Paragraph 1
     B. Paragraph 2
     C. Paragraph 3
     D. Paragraph 4

CONTINUE

PASSAGE II

The Huang He Flood

[1]

Rivers are an essential natural resource to human life. They
        16
provide fish, water for drinking and farming, and a means of

transportation. Unfortunately, rivers can also be a source of

16. **F.** NO CHANGE
 G. Rivers are to human life an essential natural resource.
 H. Rivers are an essential resource natural to human life.
 J. Rivers are a natural resource essential to human life.

destruction. The Huang He, which flows through China has
               17
brought both life and death to the people of the region.

17. **A.** NO CHANGE
 B. Huang He which flows through China,
 C. Huang He that flows through China
 D. Huang He, which flows through China,

[2]

The Huang He cuts a meandering path across the North

China Plain. Also known as the Yellow River, it gets its name from
                                              18

18. **F.** NO CHANGE
 G. get's it's
 H. get's its
 J. gets it's

the yellow mud that coats the riverbed. For centuries it is being
                                                      19

19. **A.** NO CHANGE
 B. it be
 C. it has been
 D. it is

a vital part of Chinese life. [20] The Huang He has an unfortunate

propensity for flooding, bursting its banks an average of two

20. At this point, the writer would like to add a sentence to Paragraph 2. Which of the following choices would provide the best transition between these two sentences?
 F. It has helped to sustain the people, but it has demanded a heavy price.
 G. The river deposits fertile mud each time it floods the nearby lowlands.
 H. It has been a valuable natural resource for the Chinese people.
 J. It is about 3,000 miles long, and its receding floodwaters have caused it to change course numerous times in the last few thousand years.

years in every three and washing away entire villages with their
                                                          21
raging floodwaters. The flood in the summer of 1935 was

21. **A.** NO CHANGE
 B. they're
 C. them
 D. its

devastating, which caused enormous suffering for the villagers
<u>22</u>
flooded out of their homes.

22. F. NO CHANGE
G. devastating and caused
H. devastating that caused
J. devastating, and which caused

[3]

In that tragic summer, the villagers and farmers <u>who</u> resided
23
along the river had endured a long drought. Their crops, which
included sweet potatoes, corn, wheat, and cucumbers, were in
serious need of rain. With their crops and lives in jeopardy, they
were <u>content</u> when the long-awaited rain finally arrived. However,
24
the rain turned into a torrential downpour. Some areas received
20 inches of rain in two days, more than some parts of the world
receive for <u>the period of</u> an entire year. The river swelled to
25
dangerously high levels, threatening to overflow the dikes along
the riverbank.

23. A. NO CHANGE
B. whom
C. which
D. whose

24. F. NO CHANGE
G. satisfied
H. pleased
J. elated

25. A. NO CHANGE
B. the duration of
C. the length of
D. OMIT the underlined portion.

[4]

<u>The villagers working desperately to raise the dikes, the</u>
26
<u>farms and houses in the fields below were on the verge of disaster.</u>
26

26. F. NO CHANGE
G. The villagers were working desperately to raise the dikes, the farms and houses in the fields below were on the verge of disaster.
H. The villagers worked desperately to raise the dikes and save the farms and houses in the fields below.
J. The villagers worked desperately to raise the dikes and the farms and houses in the fields below.

They reinforced the dikes with rocks and <u>kaoling stalks.</u> Sadly,
27
this did not prevent the Huang He from bursting its banks and

27. Kaoling is a plant similar to sugarcane. Would it be good strategy for the writer to define this word in the passage?

A. Yes, because the writer defines other unfamiliar words in the passage.
B. Yes, because defining a word unfamiliar to most readers would enhance the readers' understanding of the sentence.
C. No, because this passage is not about kaoling or sugarcane.
D. No, because most readers will know what *kaoling* means.

CONTINUE

rushing down in explosive and deadly power. The valley below was washed away in <u>floodwaters that like Niagara Falls swelled to six times the volume.</u> The river flooded 6,000 square miles of land. The results were disastrous.

28

28

[5]

Thousands of people drowned. Some were lucky and were able to flee in small boats. Others managed to climb to the roofs of the more stable buildings and wait for possible rescue. They suffered great hunger and thirst. Surrounded by floodwater, they were unable to drink from it because it contained sewage and the corpses of people who had been unable to escape. The situation turned even more tragic, as hundreds of thousands died from the famine that followed. The villagers were also beset by outbreaks of cholera and the bubonic plague. An earlier catastrophic flood occurred when the Huang He burst its banks in 1887, resulting in the deaths of possibly a million people. 29

[6]

It is little wonder that the Huang He has earned the nickname "China's Sorrow." It is a river of life, but it is also a river of tears.

28. **F.** NO CHANGE
    G. floodwaters, which like Niagara Falls swelled to six times the volume.
    H. floodwaters that swelled to six times the volume of Niagara Falls.
    J. floodwaters that swelled to six times the volume, like Niagara Falls.

29. In Paragraph 5, should the final sentence be kept or eliminated?

    A. Kept, because the passage is about floods.
    B. Kept, because it is an interesting detail.
    C. Eliminated, because the flood of 1887 is not a focus of this paragraph or the passage.
    D. Eliminated, because it happened too long ago to be historically important or relevant.

Question 30 asks about the passage as a whole.

30. Which of the following statements most effectively summarizes the passage as a whole?

    F. The Huang He floods the river valley along its banks every two out of three years.
    G. The Huang He Flood of 1935 caused massive devastation throughout the river valley.
    H. The villagers' failure to build stronger dikes left them vulnerable to the disastrous flood of 1935.
    J. The Huang He has brought both life and death to villagers of the river valley.

PASSAGE III

Never Again

[1]

It began harmlessly enough. My wife wanted to replace our old TV stand, so <u>she and I</u> ordered a new one from a catalog.
31

It was a nice <u>model it having shelves</u> for the cable box, VCR, and
32
videotapes. When it arrived, we opened the box excitedly. It was only a matter of minutes before our excitement turned into dismay. We stared into a box that was filled with panels, shelves, knobs, and enough screws to open up <u>your own</u> hardware store.
33
And welcoming us into the nightmarish world of do-it-yourself assembly, <u>we saw the dreaded instruction manual fastened to</u>
34
<u>the top panel.</u>
34

I sighed and retrieved <u>the box of tools that was</u> under the kitchen
35
sink. This was going to take a while.

[2]

(1) After spreading all of the parts on the floor, <u>we had begun</u>
36
to scrutinize the intricate, brain-numbing details of the instruction manual. (2) First, we had to separate the screws into piles of the same type. (3) <u>Not one of them was</u> easily distinguishable from
37
the others, so finding the right screw for the right pile was a tedious process. (4) Then the instructions told us to attach Panel

31. **A.** NO CHANGE
    B. she and me
    C. me and her
    D. her and I

32. **F.** NO CHANGE
    G. model, and it had shelves
    H. model holding shelves
    J. model with shelves

33. **A.** NO CHANGE
    B. our own
    C. its own
    D. one's own

34. **F.** NO CHANGE
    G. we saw the top panel, on which the dreaded instruction manual was fastened.
    H. the top panel held the dreaded instruction manual in place.
    J. the dreaded instruction manual was fastened to the top panel.

35. **A.** NO CHANGE
    B. the box of tools that were
    C. the box of tools being
    D. the toolbox that which was

36. **F.** NO CHANGE
    G. we begun
    H. we began
    J. we were beginning

37. **A.** NO CHANGE
    B. Not one of them were
    C. Not one of them is
    D. Not one of them became

CONTINUE

A to Panel B; Panel B to Panel C; Panel C to Panel D, which would also be attached to Panel A, but not to panel B, which would hold half the brackets for Shelves E and F, the other half to be found on Panel A. [38]

38. For best stylistic effectiveness, which of the following should the writer do with Sentence 4?

   F. Keep it as written.
   G. Make it shorter and more concise.
   H. Delete it from the paragraph.
   J. Move it as written to follow Sentence 1.

[3]

[39] (1) After two hours of sorting screws and attaching panels, the instructions directed us to position Supporting Bar

A over Slot 1 until it was in perpendicular position over the aforementioned slot. (2) Then we had to insert the bar five-eighths of an inch into the slot. (3) The other side of the bar would be inserted into Slot 2, at which point we would be ready to attach the handles to the <u>TV stands doors.</u>
                                                            40

39. Which of the following sentences offers the best introduction to Paragraph 3?

   A. After that, putting the TV stand together was a piece of cake.
   B. That's when we decided to take a break.
   C. We decided never to assemble anything ever again.
   D. Things quickly went from bad to worse.

40. F. NO CHANGE
   G. TV stand's doors
   H. TV stands' doors
   J. TV stands doors'

(4) <u>Unfortunately, two nearly identical types of screws were</u>
                                    41
<u>confusing, so we mixed them up.</u> (5) We had to unscrew the
         41
handles and start over.

41. A. NO CHANGE
   B. Unfortunately, two types of screws were nearly identical, so we mixed them up.
   C. Unfortunately, we confused two nearly identical types of screws, so we mixed them up.
   D. Unfortunately, we mixed up two nearly identical types of screws that were confused.

[4]

(1) The top panel required eight screws, but when we were ready to attach it, we discovered we had only seven screws left.

(2) Luckily, I was able to use one of the screws in my toolbox. (3) The toolbox had been a birthday present <u>from my wife who</u>
42
wanted me to do more around the house. (4) It took five and a half hours, but finally we arrived at the final step. (5) We attached the top panel and stood back to admire the fruit of our labors. 43

[5]

Something was terribly wrong. The stand looked like we had put it together in the dark—with our feet. It was just a big, crooked mess. My wife and I looked at each other and silently agreed. Our do-it-ourselves assembly days were over.

42. F. NO CHANGE
    G. from my wife who,
    H. from my wife, who
    J. from, my wife, who

43. For the sake of unity and coherence, which of the following sentences does NOT belong in Paragraph 4?
    A. Sentence 2
    B. Sentence 3
    C. Sentence 4
    D. Sentence 5

Questions 44 and 45 ask about the passage as a whole.

44. What function does Paragraph 5 serve in relation to the rest of the passage?
    F. It underscores the narrator's view that do-it-yourself assembly can turn into a big, pointless headache.
    G. It allows the reader to see that the writer has a sense of humor.
    H. It proves that the narrator is incompetent.
    J. It illustrates why the narrator does not do more around the house.

45. After finishing the passage, the writer decides to add the following sentence:

    The manual consisted of eight pages of diagrams and text in tiny print.

    If added to the passage, the sentence would most logically be placed after:
    A. Sentence 1 in Paragraph 2.
    B. Sentence 3 in Paragraph 2.
    C. Sentence 4 in Paragraph 2.
    D. Sentence 1 in Paragraph 3.

CONTINUE

PASSAGE IV

The Sport of Rowing

[1]

Have you ever wondered what it would be like to glide silently across the water, <u>using only your muscles but not an engine or sail to power your travel?</u> Thousands, in fact millions, of rowers worldwide experience this feeling every day as they train on their local rivers. <u>Rowing is such a popular sport that there are now clubs in cities and towns across the globe.</u>

46. **F.** NO CHANGE
    G. using only your muscles, not an engine or sail to power your travel
    H. using only your muscles, and not an engine or sail to power your travel
    J. using only your muscles, but not an engine, or sail to power your travel

47. **A.** NO CHANGE
    B. Rowing is such a popular sport, because there are now clubs in countless cities and towns across the globe.
    C. Rowing is such a popular sport, that there are now, rowing clubs in cities and towns across the globe.
    D. Rowing is such a popular sport. There are now rowing clubs in cities and towns across the globe.

[2]

<u>Its</u> not as effortless as it looks. <u>The best athletes made it look easy,</u> but in reality it takes an intense coordinated effort of body and mind to propel a rowing shell over the surface of the water.

48. **F.** NO CHANGE
    G. It's
    H. So that
    J. Since its

49. **A.** NO CHANGE
    B. The best athletes had made it look easy
    C. The best athletes make it look easy
    D. The best athletes makes it look easy

<u>When rowing in a team boat, the athletes must mimic</u> the exact movements of their teammates, right down to their breathing at times. <u>If they become unsynchronized, you see, even for a moment,</u> the boat will lose crucial speed necessary to thrust the boat through the water.

50. **F.** NO CHANGE
    G. When rowing together in a team boat; rowers must mimic
    H. When rowing together in a team boat. Rowers must mimic
    J. When rowing together in a team boat and rowers must mimic

51. **A.** NO CHANGE
    B. If they become unsynchronized, consequently, even for a moment
    C. If they become unsynchronized, just a bit, even for a moment
    D. If they become unsynchronized, even for a moment

[3]

Lost speed is not something rowers want to happen to their
52
boat, especially when racing. Sometimes races are won or lost
52
by thousandths of a second, which can be devastating for a team

that have trained as hard as elite rowers usually do. They often
53
train on the water two times a day (morning and night) and

spend hours in the weight room additionally the time they spend
54
on the water.

[4]

Races, which are usually 2000 meters in length, only last for
55
about 6 to 8 minutes, depending on the size of the boat and wind

conditions. Often rowers will train thousands of hours a year for

one important race, such as the World Championships. These are
56

a lot of training for such a short race! 57 Dedicated rowers,

however, will tell you that the sacrifice is well worth having the

chance to win a national or even Olympic medal one day.

---

52. F. NO CHANGE
G. Losing speed is not something rowers want happening to their boat
H. Losing speed (Is not something rowers want) happening to their boat
J. To lose speed is not something that should have happened to their boat

53. A. NO CHANGE
B. train
C. trains
D. were training

54. F. NO CHANGE
G. in addition to
H. because of
J. since

55. A. NO CHANGE
B. Races, that are usually 2,000 meters in length,
C. Races, which are usually 2,000 meters in length
D. Races which are usually 2,000 meters in length,

56. F. NO CHANGE
G. That
H. That been
J. That is

57. At this point in the essay, the author is considering the addition of the following sentence:

There are a few long-distance races that measure approximately 3.5 miles and are raced in a "chase" fashion with each boat starting in 10-second intervals.

Would this be a logical and relevant addition to the essay?

A. Yes, because it serves to further explain the types of races in which rowers participate.
B. Yes, because it serves to establish the main point of this paragraph.
C. No, because this paragraph is discussing only the World Championships for which rowers train many hours.
D. No, because it does not serve to emphasize the difference in the amount of training relative to the length of the races.

CONTINUE

[5]

The next time you travel near a river, be sure to notice any

long, skinny boats skimming lightly atop the water, silently

propelled by these well-trained athletes. You may be watching

a past, present, or <u>future Olympian. Or perhaps</u> you will see
                                          58

someone who just loves to spend his or her morning on the river,

<u>enjoyed by</u> the sport of rowing.
     59

58. How can the author best combine these
    two sentences?

    (F.) future Olympian, or perhaps

    G.   future Olympian: or perhaps

    H.   future Olympian and perhaps

    J.   future Olympian so perhaps

59. A. NO CHANGE

    B.   to enjoy

   (C.) enjoying

    D. had enjoyed

Question 60 asks about the essay as a whole.

60. Suppose the author had been assigned to write a
    brief essay detailing the technical aspects of the
    training and performance of elite rowers. Would this
    essay successfully fulfill the requirement?

   (F.) No, because the essay does not discuss any
    training or performance techniques in detail.

    G.   No, because the essay suggests that rowing is
    not a sport that requires much training or
    technique.

    H.   Yes, because the essay describes the length and
    time of rowing races.

    J.   Yes, because the essay tells us in great detail
    about the weight-room training schedule of
    elite rowers.

PASSAGE V

**A New Link Between Saturated Fats and
Alzheimer's Disease**

[1]

Recent studies seem to indicate <u>that</u> a diet high in fat is
                                       61
somehow linked to the onset of Alzheimer's disease and dementia.

A recent article in the *Archives of Neurology* <u>cite</u> experiments that
                                                   62
show how sticking to a diet rich in "good fats"—fats found in

61. (A.) NO CHANGE

    B.   for

    C.   in

    D. how

62. F. NO CHANGE

    G.   citation

    H.   citing

   (J.) cites

nuts, fatty fish, and vegetable oils—seems to lower the risk of mental disease. "Bad fats," otherwise known as saturated fats, seem to increase the risk. It was interesting that, the new studies
63
point out that antioxidant vitamins, once touted as possessing curative effects for Alzheimer's and dementia, now seem to be ineffective.

63. **A.** NO CHANGE
B. In a bit of interest, the
C. Interestingly enough, the
D. Enough to be interesting, the

[2]

The new studies seem to make a profound discovery satu-
64
rated fats and cholesterol are detrimental to overall brain func-
64
tions. In one study, scientists assembled a group of 815 senior citizens who reported no signs of deteriorated mental condition.

64. **F.** NO CHANGE
G. a profound discovery: saturated fats and cholesterol
H. a profound discovery with saturated fats and cholesterol
J. a profound discovery saturating fats and cholesterol

Each member of the group was asked to list the foods it ate
65
regularly. Two years later, each was asked again to list the foods

65. **A.** NO CHANGE
B. he or she
C. that they
D. that was

eaten on a regular basis. Then, for a period of four years followed
66
the second test, the research team tracked the health of each
66
member of the group. By the end of the observation period, 131 seniors had developed Alzheimer's.

66. **F.** NO CHANGE
G. that following the second
H. following the second
J. follow did the second

[3]

The data collected from this experiment showed that the seniors who had reported eating more saturated and hydroge-nated fats from foods such as red meat, fried foods, and packaged
67

67. **A.** NO CHANGE
B. like
C. with
D. because

goods such as cookies, chips, and cakes were more than double
68
as likely to develop Alzheimer's. Those who had recorded salmon, tuna, fruits, avocados, nuts, and grains as their favorite foods

68. **F.** NO CHANGE
G. over double
H. more than twice
J. plus more than twice

CONTINUE

carried less of a risk for dementia. These foods are rich in poly-unsaturated and monounsaturated fats.

[4]

A second experiment <u>attacks</u> a very popular and long-upheld
69
medical theory. Many researchers have gone on record

69. A. NO CHANGE
    B. does an attack on
    C. will attack
    D. did attack

<u>in supporting the notion that</u> unstable compounds in the blood-
70
stream, called "free radicals," are responsible for damaging nerve cells and causing the onset of dementia. Traditionally, vitamins such as C, E, and beta carotene <u>has</u> been singled out as agents
71
that can reduce the risk of free-radical damage within the human system.

70. F. NO CHANGE
    G. to supporting the notion that
    H. to support the notion that
    J. with support for the notion which

71. A. NO CHANGE
    B. have
    C. are
    D. will be

[5]

(1) During that time, 242 people developed Alzheimer's.
(2) Researchers tracked <u>the eating habits</u> of 980 elderly people
72
—none of whom displayed dementia symptoms—for four years.
(3) Lead researcher Jose A. Luchsinger, an associate at Columbia University in New York City, wrote: "Neither dietary, supplemental, nor intake of carotenes and vitamins C and E was associated with a decreased risk." (4) No link could be found between the afflicted people's dietary supplement intake and the prevention of disease. 73

72. F. NO CHANGE
    G. the eating habit's
    H. those eating habits
    J. those eating habit's

73. Which of the following ordering of the sentences will make Paragraph 5 most logical?
    A. NO CHANGE
    B. 3, 4, 1, 2
    C. 1, 2, 4, 3
    D. 2, 1, 4, 3

Questions 74–75 ask about the passage as a whole.

74. The writer wrote this piece in response to a school assignment. The assignment was to provide the reader with an overview of a recent scientific discovery. Was this objective accomplished?

  F. No, because the author does not offer valuable details concerning food sources for antioxidant vitamins.

  G. Yes, because the author outlines the findings of two new experiments, providing illustrations and details only as needed.

  H. No, because the author makes no attempt to provide counterpoints to the information supposedly gleaned by the experiments.

  J. Yes, because the author wisely references the work of Jose A. Luchsinger, a researcher from Columbia University.

75. After reading this article, readers should infer that in order to reduce their own risk of contracting Alzheimer's disease or dementia, they should:

  A. increase their dosage of antioxidant vitamins.

  B. maintain a diet rich in saturated fats rather than polyunsaturated and monounsaturated fats.

  C. maintain a diet rich in polyunsaturated and monounsaturated fats rather than saturated fats.

  D. remove antioxidant vitamins from their diet.

Ⓧ
STOP

MATHEMATICS TEST

60 Minutes—60 Questions

DIRECTIONS. For each of the following items, solve each problem, choose the correct answer, and then fill in the corresponding circle on the answer sheet. If you encounter problems that take too much time to solve, move on. Solve as many problems as you can; then return to the others in the time remaining for the test.

You may use a calculator on this test for any problems you choose, but some of the problems may best be solved without the use of a calculator.

SHOW YOUR WORK HERE

Note: Unless otherwise stated, assume the following:

1. Illustrative figures are NOT necessarily drawn to scale.
2. Geometric figures lie in a plane.
3. The word *line* indicates a straight line.
4. The word *average* indicates arithmetic mean.

---

1. On the final project in Juan's art class, 14 students earned a grade of B. Those 14 students were exactly 20% of the total number of students in the class. How many students were in the class?

   A. 28
   B. 34
   C. 56
   D. 70
   E. 84

2. What is the sixth term of the arithmetic sequence 3, 6, 9, 12, …?

   F. 13
   G. 15
   H. 18
   J. 21
   K. 24

3. What is the value of *x* in the following equation?

   $$\frac{16}{8} = \frac{6}{x}$$

   A. 2
   B. 3
   C. 9
   D. 12
   E. 18

CONTINUE

SHOW YOUR WORK HERE

4. In the figure below, points *G*, *H*, and *I* are on the same line. What is the measure of ∠*GHK* ?

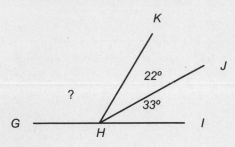

F. 35°
G. 55°
H. 75°
J. 125°
K. 147°

5. If line segment *XY* is bisected by point *Z*, then which of the following must be true?

A. $\overline{XZ} \cong \overline{ZY}$
B. $\overline{ZX} \cong \overline{XY}$
C. $\overline{ZY} \cong \overline{XY}$
D. $\overline{YZ} \cong \overline{YX}$
E. $\overline{XZ} \cong \overline{YX}$

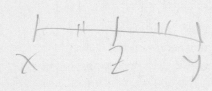

6. At a certain construction site, there is a pile containing 55 tons of sand. Four trucks, each of which holds 11.4 tons of sand, are filled from this pile. How many tons of sand remain in the pile?

F. 9.4
G. 20.8
H. 22.8
J. 43.6
K. 45.6

7. What is the value of 2(*x* – 3) + 15, if *x* = –2?

A. –3
B. 0
C. 5
D. 13
E. 25

8. |7| – |–7| – 7 =

F. –7
G. 0
H. 7
J. 14
K. 21

9. Rosie's boss is going to give her a raise of 8%. If her salary before the raise is $25,500, what will her salary be after the raise?

   A. $23,460
   B. $26,520
   C. $27,040
   D. $27,540
   E. $27,900

10. If x is a real number such that $x^3 = 80$, between which two consecutive integers does x lie on the number line?

    F. 2 and 3
    G. 3 and 4
    H. 4 and 5
    J. 5 and 6
    K. 6 and 7

11. If $67 + a = -191$, then $a =$

    A. -258
    B. -124
    C. 113
    D. 124
    E. 258

12. Joel is 8 years older than Karen, and Karen is twice as old as Lina. If Lina is x years old, how old is Joel in terms of x?

    F. $x + 8$
    G. $2x$
    H. $x - 8$
    J. $-2x$
    K. $2x + 8$

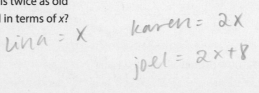

13. A rectangle is graphed in the standard (x, y) coordinate plane. Three of the rectangle's corners have coordinates $(-4, 5)$, $(2, 5)$, and $(-4, -2)$. What are the coordinates of the fourth corner?

    A. $(-5, 2)$
    B. $(4, -2)$
    C. $(-2, 2)$
    D. $(-4, 5)$
    E. $(2, -2)$

14. Which of the following is a simplified form of $3a + 9b - 2a$?

    F. $-6a + 9b$
    G. $a + 9b$
    H. $12ab - 2a$
    J. $3a + 7ba$
    K. $10a^2b$

Practice Test 4

15. In the parallelogram below, what is the measure of $\angle WZY$?

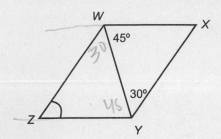

   A. 55°
   B. 75°
   C. 90°
   D. 105°
   E. 115°

16. What is the slope of the line $2x - 6y = 10$?

   F. $-\dfrac{5}{3}$
   G. $-\dfrac{1}{3}$
   H. 0
   J. $\dfrac{1}{3}$
   K. 2

$$2x - 6y = 10$$
$$-6y = -2x + 10$$
$$\frac{-6y}{-6} = \frac{-2x + 10}{-6}$$
$$y = \frac{1}{3}x - \frac{5}{3}$$

17. If x is positive, and $2x^2 - 7x - 9 = 0$, then what is the value of x?

   A. 1
   B. 2
   C. 4.5
   D. 7
   E. 9

$$2x^2 - 7x - 9$$

$$\overset{-18}{(2x^2 - 9x)(+2x - 9)}$$
$$x(2x - 9) + 1(2x - 9)$$
$$(x + 1)(2x - 9)$$
$$2x - 9 = 0$$
$$2x = 9$$
$$x = 9/2$$

18. A certain triangle has sides of lengths 40, 50, and 60 inches. If a similar triangle has a perimeter of 300 inches, how many inches long is that triangle's longest side?

   F. 40
   G. 60
   H. 80
   J. 100
   K. 120

P=150   P=300

19. A portable radio that normally sells for $29.55 is marked down by 20%. What is the sale price of the radio, rounded to the nearest dollar?

   A. $20
   B. $21
   C. $22
   D. $23
   E. $24

$23.64

20. Which of the following is the factored form of
$3d^4e^3 - 15de^2$?

    F. $3(d^4e^3 - 15de^2)$
    G. $3de^2(d^3e - 5)$
    H. $3(d^4e - 5de)$
    J. $3d^4e^3 - 15de^2$
    K. $-12d^3e$

21. If $2u + 2 = 20$, and $v - 2u = -2$, what is the value of v?

    A. -20
    B. 9
    C. 12
    D. 14
    E. 16

22. At a certain store, a 7.5-pound bag of rice costs $4.80. What is the cost per ounce of rice? (There are 16 ounces in a pound.)

    F. $0.02
    G. $0.03
    H. $0.04
    J. $0.05
    K. $0.15

23. On Farm X, farm workers work 6 days per week and earn $23 per day, plus $0.74 per bushel filled. If a certain farm worker earned $165.38 in a week, how many bushels did she fill in that week?

    A. 7
    B. 21
    C. 37
    D. 187
    E. 224

24. A garden needs to be covered with grass sod. The garden has the dimensions shown below. How many square feet of sod are required to cover the garden?

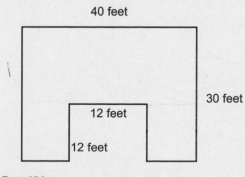

    F. 656
    G. 912
    H. 984
    J. 1,056
    K. 1,200

SHOW YOUR WORK HERE

$3d^4e^3 - 15de^2$

$3de^2(d^3e - 5)$

$2u + 2 = 20$
$v - 2u = -2$

$2 - v = 18$
$-v = 16$
$v = 16$

120 oz

138 ⊳ start

$0.74\overline{)27.38}$ ⇒ 37

$(40 \cdot 30) - (12 \cdot 12)$
$1200 - 144$
1056

SHOW YOUR WORK HERE

25. Which of the following is the graph of the solution set for $z + 2 < 8$?

    A.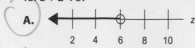

    2 4 6 8 10

    B.

    2 4 6 8 10

    C.

    2 4 6 8 10

    D.

    2 4 6 8 10

    E.

    2 4 6 8 10

    Handwritten: $z < 6$

26. The quantity $\dfrac{2}{3}$ is greater than which of the following?

    F. $\dfrac{5}{6}$

    G. $\dfrac{5}{9}$

    H. $\dfrac{7}{10}$

    J. $\dfrac{11}{15}$

    K. $\dfrac{14}{20}$

27. A right triangle has sides of length 15, 20, and 25 meters. What is the area of the triangle in square meters?

    A. 60
    B. 150
    C. 250
    D. 625
    E. 7,500

    Handwritten: $\dfrac{b \cdot h}{2} = \dfrac{20 \cdot 15}{2}$

    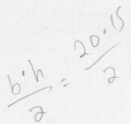

28. A store displays all the AA batteries it has in a display case on a wall. The batteries can be displayed in three columns of equal height. The batteries can also be displayed in four, five, or six columns of equal height. What is the smallest number of batteries that the store can have?

    F. 15
    G. 30
    H. 60
    J. 180
    K. 360

    Handwritten: LCM

29. Two sides of a triangle are 17 and 18 feet. Which of the following CANNOT be the length of the third side?

A. 2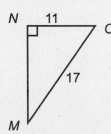

B. 8

C. 15

D. 18

E. 36

30. If x and y are positive numbers, $\dfrac{x}{4} - \dfrac{3}{y} =$

F. $\dfrac{xy - 12}{4 + y}$

G. $-\dfrac{3x}{4y}$

H. $\dfrac{x - 3}{4 - y}$

J. $\dfrac{xy - 3}{4y}$

K. $\dfrac{xy - 12}{4y}$

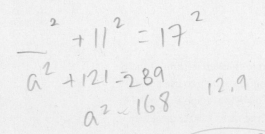

31. In the right triangle below, how long is side MN?

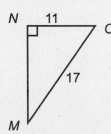

A. 6

B. $\sqrt{6}$

C. $\sqrt{17 - 11}$

D. $\sqrt{17^2 - 11^2}$

E. $\sqrt{17^2 + 11^2}$

32. A square has sides of length v feet. If the length of this square is increased by 2 feet and its width is decreased by 1 foot, what is the area of the resulting rectangle, in square feet?

F. $v + 2$

G. $v - 1$

H. $v^2 - 2$

J. $v^2 - v - 2$

K. $v^2 + v - 2$

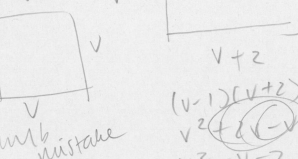

CONTINUE

SHOW YOUR WORK HERE

33. If the sine of a certain angle is $\frac{2}{7}$ and its cosine is $\frac{6}{7}$, what is the angle's tangent?

    A. $\frac{1}{3}$

    B. $\frac{4}{7}$

    C. $\frac{6}{2}$

    D. $\frac{8}{7}$

    E. $\frac{12}{49}$

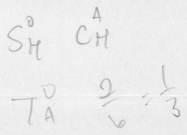

34. Which of the answer choices best describes the graph on the number line below?

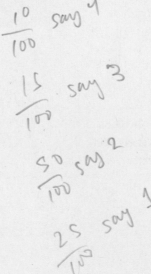

    F. $1 > x > -2.5$

    G. $1 < x < -2.5$

    H. $-1 < x < 2.5$

    J. $1 > |x| > -2.5$

    K. $1 < |x| < -2.5$

35. A large group of food tasters was asked to sample and rate a new cheesecake recipe. They were to use a scale of 1 to 5. 10% of the tasters gave the recipe a rating of 4. 15% gave a rating of 3. Half the tasters, 50%, gave the recipe a rating of 2. And 25% gave the recipe a rating of 1. What was the average rating for the cheesecake recipe, rounded to the nearest tenth?

    A. 2.0

    B. 2.1

    C. 2.2

    D. 2.3

    E. 2.4

SHOW YOUR WORK HERE

36. In the right triangle below, how many meters long is side *AC*?

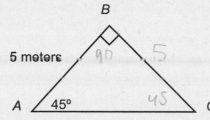

F. 5
G. 7.5
H. 10
J. $5\sqrt{2}$
K. $5\sqrt{3}$

37. What is the smallest possible sum of 2 positive integers whose product is 36?

A. 9
B. 10
C. 12
D. 13
E. 15

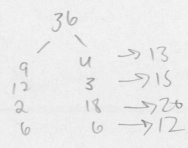

38. In the figure below, lines *a* and *b* are parallel to each other, and lines *c* and *d* are parallel to each other. If the two angles have measures 40° and 115°, as shown, what is the measure of angle *x*?

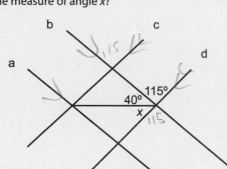

F. 25°
G. 35°
H. 50°
J. 65°
K. 75°

CONTINUE

39. The line $3x - 8y = 16$ is plotted on the (x, y) coordinate plane. What is the y-intercept of the line?

A. −4
B. −3
C. −2
D. 2
E. 4

SHOW YOUR WORK HERE

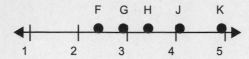

$3x - 8y = 16$

$-8y = -3y + 16$

$y = \frac{+3}{+8} y - 2$

40. Among the points on the number line below, which is closest to $\sqrt{6}$?

F. F
G. G
H. H
J. J
K. K

41. Angle H measures $(180 - x)$ degrees. If angle H is an obtuse angle, which of the following is true of x?

A. $0 < x < 60$
B. $0 < x < 90$
C. $90 < x < 180$
D. $180 < x < 270$
E. $135 < x < 180$

42. If $m - n = 2$ and $m + n = -\frac{1}{2}$, then what is the value of $\frac{n}{m+n}$?

F. $-\frac{5}{4}$
G. $\frac{3}{2}$
H. $\frac{5}{8}$
J. $\frac{5}{2}$
K. 5

43. A triangle has sides of lengths 10 feet, 24 feet, and 26 feet. What is the measure of the angle between the two shortest sides?

A. 30°
B. 60°
C. 90°
D. 120°
E. 150°

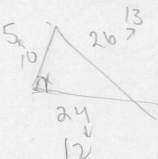

44. A line is graphed on the (x, y) coordinate plane. The value of the x-coordinate for each point on the line is 5 more than three times the value of the y-coordinate of that point. What is the slope of the line?

   F. $\dfrac{1}{3}$

   G. $\dfrac{1}{2}$

   H. 1

   J. 2

   K. 3

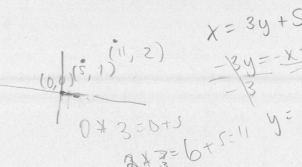

45. Two numbers have a greatest common factor of 6 and a least common multiple of 36. Which of the following could be the pair of numbers?

   A. 6 and 12

   B. 6 and 18

   C. 12 and 18

   D. 12 and 24

   E. 18 and 24

46. What is the length of the radius of a circle with an area of 4π?

   F. 1.25

   G. 2

   H. 2.25

   J. 2.5

   K. 4

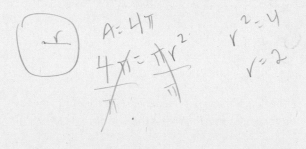

47. In the standard (x, y) coordinate plane, a line passes through the origin and the point $\left(-\dfrac{7}{8}, \dfrac{1}{6}\right)$. What is the slope of the line?

   A. $-\dfrac{4}{21}$

   B. $-\dfrac{17}{24}$

   C. $-\dfrac{7}{48}$

   D. $\dfrac{17}{24}$

   E. $-\dfrac{21}{4}$

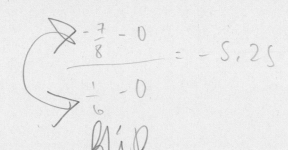

SHOW YOUR WORK HERE

CONTINUE

48. What is the area of the shaded region below, if the radius of the inner circle is 2.5 inches and the radius of the outer circle is 5 inches?

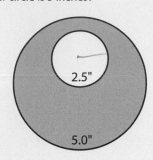

2.5"

5.0"

F. 1.5625π
G. 6.25π
H. 7.5π
J. 12.5π
K. 18.75π

SHOW YOUR WORK HERE

$r = 2.5$ $\pi(2.5)^2 \rightarrow 6.25\pi$
$r = 5$ $\pi(5)^2 \rightarrow 25\pi$

18.75π

49. The equation for a certain line is $3y - x = 12$. Which of the following points lies on the line?

A. $(0, -10)$
B. $(1, 4)$
C. $(5, 5)$
D. $(-6, 2)$
E. $(-20, -3)$

$3y - x = 12$
$3y = x + 12$
$y = \frac{1}{3}x + 4$

50. The figure below has the dimensions given and the two right angles shown. What is the sine of angle *BAD*?

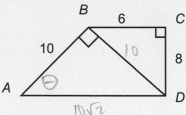

F. 1
G. $\sqrt{2}$
H. $\dfrac{\sqrt{2}}{2}$
J. $10\sqrt{2}$
K. $100\sqrt{2}$

$\overset{O}{S}_H$

$\sin\theta = \frac{10}{10\sqrt{2}}$ no

$\dfrac{10}{10\sqrt{2}}\left(\dfrac{\sqrt{2}}{\sqrt{2}}\right) = \dfrac{10\sqrt{2}}{10(2)} = \dfrac{\sqrt{2}}{2}$

51. What is the value of gh, if $3g - 12 = h$ and $\dfrac{h}{g} = -1\dfrac{1}{2}$?

- A. $-\dfrac{32}{3}$
- B. $-\dfrac{8}{3}$
- C. -4
- D. $\dfrac{8}{3}$
- E. $\dfrac{32}{3}$

52. X, Y, and Z are real numbers and $XYZ = \pi$. Which of the following must be true?

- F. $XYZ^2 = \pi^2$
- G. $\dfrac{XY}{Z} = \dfrac{\pi}{Z}$
- H. $XYZ\pi = 0$
- J. $\dfrac{XYZ}{\pi} = \pi^2$
- K. $ZY = \dfrac{\pi}{X}$

53. A square measuring w inches on each side is removed from a rectangle of length $(w + 6)$ inches and width $(w - 1)$ inches. What is the remaining area, in square inches, of the rectangle?

- A. w^2
- B. $5w - 6$
- C. $2w + 5$
- D. $w^2 + 5w - 6$
- E. $6 - 5w$

54. If three jazz CDs are added to a box of only classical CDs, the probability of randomly drawing a classical CD from the box becomes $\dfrac{4}{5}$. How many classical CDs are in the box?

- F. 6
- G. 9
- H. 12
- J. 15
- K. 18

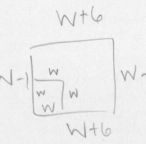
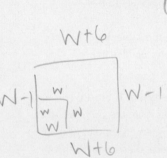

55. How many different integer values of x satisfy the inequality $\frac{1}{12} < \frac{2}{x} < \frac{1}{8}$?

SHOW YOUR WORK HERE

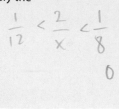

A. 3
B. 4
C. 5
D. 6
E. 7

56. What is the distance, on a standard (x, y) coordinate plane, between the point $(-2, 3)$ and the point $(-5, -4)$?

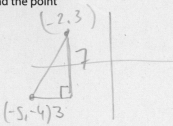

F. $\sqrt{26}$
G. $\sqrt{58}$
H. $\sqrt{10}$
J. 10
K. 58

57. Which of the following determines a unique plane in 3-dimensional Euclidean space?

A. Two intersecting perpendicular lines
B. Two distinct points
C. Three distinct points on the same line
D. Two non-intersecting, non-parallel lines
E. Three non-parallel lines

58. A tin of candy contains three flavors. There are twice as many grape candies in a tin as there are cherry candies. There are three times as many lemon candies as grape candies. If a number of apple candies, equal to the number of cherry candies already in the tin, is added to the tin, what is the probability of randomly selecting a lemon candy from the tin?

F. $\frac{1}{20}$
G. $\frac{1}{10}$
H. $\frac{1}{5}$
J. $\frac{3}{5}$
K. $\frac{2}{3}$

SHOW YOUR WORK HERE

59. In order to set up loudspeakers for a conference room, the following amounts of wire are needed for each speaker:

   2 wires at 15 feet each
   4 wires at 3.5 feet each
   2 wires at 8 inches each

   If the room requires 9 speakers, and wire costs $0.031 per inch, approximately how much will it cost to set up the speakers for the room?

   A. $112
   B. $152
   C. $168
   D. $360
   E. $544

60. In tossing a fair coin three consecutive times, what is the probability of getting heads on two consecutive tosses but NOT on three consecutive tosses? (A fair coin has an equal likelihood of a heads or tails outcome.)

   F. $\frac{1}{4}$

   G. $\frac{3}{8}$

   H. $\frac{1}{8}$

   J. $\frac{1}{2}$

   K. $\frac{3}{4}$

X STOP

READING TEST

35 MINUTES—40 QUESTIONS

DIRECTIONS: There are four passages in this test. Each passage is followed by several questions. Read each passage, select the best answer to each related question, and fill in the corresponding circle on the answer sheet. You may look back at the passages as often as you need.

PASSAGE I

PROSE FICTION: Passage A is an excerpt from *"Bartleby the Scrivener: A Story of Wall Street"* by Herman Melville. Passage B is an excerpt from *The Adventures of Tom Sawyer* by Mark Twain.

Passage A
by Herman Melville

At first Bartleby did an extraordinary quantity of writing. As if long famishing for something to copy, he seemed to gorge himself on my documents. There was no pause for digestion. He ran a day and night line, copying by sun-light and by
5   candle-light. I should have been quite delighted with his application, had be been cheerfully industrious. But he wrote on silently, palely, mechanically…

Now and then, in the haste of business, it had been my habit to assist in comparing some brief document myself, calling
10 Turkey or Nippers for this purpose. One object I had in placing Bartleby so handy to me behind the screen, was to avail myself of his services on such trivial occasions. It was on the third day, I think, of his being with me, and before any necessity had arisen for having his own writing examined, that, being much hurried
15 to complete a small affair I had in hand, I abruptly called to Bartleby. In my haste and natural expectancy of instant compliance, I sat with my head bent over the original on my desk, and my right hand sideways, and somewhat nervously extended with the copy, so that immediately upon emerging from his
20 retreat, Bartleby might snatch it and proceed to business without the least delay.

In this very attitude did I sit when I called to him, rapidly stating what it was I wanted him to do—namely, to examine a small paper with me. Imagine my surprise, nay, my consternation,
25 when without moving from his privacy, Bartleby in a singularly mild, firm voice, replied, "I would prefer not to."

I sat awhile in perfect silence, rallying my stunned faculties. Immediately it occurred to me that my ears had deceived me, or Bartleby had entirely misunderstood my meaning. I repeated
30 my request in the clearest tone I could assume. But in quite as clear a one came the previous reply, "I would prefer not to."

"Prefer not to," echoed I, rising in high excitement, and crossing the room with a stride. "What do you mean? Are you moon-struck? I want you to help me compare this sheet
35 here—take it," and I thrust it towards him.

"I would prefer not to," said he.

I looked at him steadfastly. His face was leanly composed; his gray eye dimly calm. Not a wrinkle of agitation rippled him. Had there been the least uneasiness, anger, impatience
40 or impertinence in his manner; in other words, had there been any thing ordinarily human about him, doubtless I should have violently dismissed him from the premises. But as it was, I should have as soon thought of turning my pale plaster-of-paris bust of Cicero out of doors. I stood gazing at him awhile,
45 as he went on with his own writing, and then reseated myself at my desk. This is very strange, thought I. What had one best do? But my business hurried me. I concluded to forget the matter for the present, reserving it for my future leisure.

Passage B
by Mark Twain

Monday morning found Tom Sawyer miserable. Monday morning always found him so—because it began another week's slow suffering in school. He generally began that day with wishing he had had no intervening holiday, it made the
5   going into captivity and fetters again so much more odious.

Tom lay thinking. Presently it occurred to him that he wished he was sick; then he could stay home from school. Here was a vague possibility. He canvassed his system. No ailment was found, and he investigated again. This time he thought he
10 could detect colicky symptoms, and he began to encourage them with considerable hope. But they soon grew feeble, and presently died wholly away. He reflected further. Suddenly he discovered something. One of his upper front teeth was loose. This was lucky; he was about to begin to groan, as a
15 "starter," as he called it, when it occurred to him that if he came into court with that argument, his aunt would pull it out, and

CONTINUE

that would hurt. So he thought he would hold the tooth in reserve for the present, and seek further.

Nothing offered for some little time, and then he remembered
20 hearing the doctor tell about a certain thing that laid up a patient for two or three weeks and threatened to make him lose a finger. So the boy eagerly drew his sore toe from under the sheet and held it up for inspection. But now he did not know the necessary symptoms. However, it seemed well worth while
25 to chance it, so he fell to groaning with considerable spirit…

Sid said: "Tom! Say, Tom!" [No response.] "Here, Tom! Tom! What is the matter, Tom?" And he shook him and looked in his face anxiously.

Tom moaned out: "Oh, don't, Sid. Don't joggle me."

30 "Why, what's the matter, Tom? I must call auntie…"

Sid flew down-stairs and said:

"Oh, Aunt Polly, come! Tom's dying!"

"Dying!"

"Yes'm. Don't wait—come quick!"

35 "Rubbage! I don't believe it!"

But she fled up-stairs, nevertheless, with Sid and Mary at her heels. And her face grew white, too, and her lip trembled. When she reached the bed-side she gasped out:

"You, Tom! Tom, what's the matter with you?"

40 "Oh, auntie, I'm—"

"What's the matter with you—what is the matter with you, child?"

"Oh, auntie, my sore toe's mortified!"

The old lady sank down into a chair and laughed a little, then
45 cried a little, then did both together. This restored her and she said:

"Tom, what a turn you did give me. Now you shut up that nonsense and climb out of this."

The groans ceased and the pain vanished from the toe. The
50 boy felt a little foolish, and he said:

"Aunt Polly, it *seemed* mortified, and it hurt so I never minded my tooth at all."

"Your tooth, indeed! What's the matter with your tooth?"

"One of them's loose, and it aches perfectly awful."

55 "There, there, now, don't begin that groaning again. Open your mouth. Well—your tooth is loose, but you're not going to

die about that. Mary, get me a silk thread, and a chunk of fire out of the kitchen."

Tom said:

60 "Oh, please, auntie, don't pull it out. It don't hurt any more. I wish I may never stir if it does. Please don't, auntie. I don't want to stay home from school."

"Oh, you don't, don't you? So all this row was because you thought you'd get to stay home from school and go a-fishing?
65 Tom, Tom, I love you so, and you seem to try every way you can to break my old heart with your outrageousness."

Questions 1–3 ask about Passage A.

1. As it is used in line 10, the word *object* means:

    A. thing.
    B. item.
    C. protest.
    D. purpose.

2. Why exactly doesn't Bartleby want to compare the sheet?

    F. He does not say.
    G. He thinks it is unworthy of his skills.
    H. He is in the middle of doing his own work.
    J. He wants to make his boss angry.

3. The boss stops insisting Bartleby compare the sheet:

    A. on Bartleby's first day working in the office.
    B. before Bartleby has a chance to say whether or not he will do the task.
    C. while Bartleby is in the middle of doing another task.
    D. after Bartleby says he would prefer not to do it for the third time.

Questions 4–6 ask about Passage B.

4. Aunt Polly reacts to Tom Sawyer's antics with:

    F. complete intolerance.
    G. terrifying scorn.
    H. loving exasperation.
    J. incredible boredom.

5. It is reasonable to infer from the passage that the author mentions that Tom Sawyer did not want to go into "captivity and fetters" (line 5) because:

    A. he thinks school is like a jail.
    B. he has committed a crime.
    C. he is claustrophobic.
    D. he lives in constant fear.

6. Which of the following most accurately describes how Sid feels about Tom Sawyer?

    F. Sid does not trust Tom.

    G. Sid is afraid to disobey Tom.

    H. Sid delights in assisting Tom's deceitfulness.

    J. Sid feels genuine concern for Tom.

Questions 7–10 ask about both passages.

---

7. Both passages are mainly about characters who:

    A. work in an office.

    B. do not want to do something.

    C. are trying to fool a relative.

    D. confuse all the people around them.

8. In what way are Bartleby in Passage A and Tom Sawyer in Passage B DIFFERENT?

    F. Bartleby is lazy and sloppy, and Tom Sawyer is hard-working but feeling sick.

    G. Bartleby gets what he wants by stating his position, and Tom Sawyer tries to get what he wants by being underhanded.

    H. Bartleby refuses to speak his mind, and Tom Sawyer cannot control his constant babbling.

    J. Bartleby regrets being defiant, but Tom Sawyer is proud of his ability to devise elaborate schemes.

9. Considering how Bartleby is portrayed in Passage A and Tom Sawyer is portrayed in Passage B, they would both most accurately be described as:

    A. lawbreakers.

    B. followers.

    C. nonconformists.

    D. geniuses.

10. In what way are Bartleby's boss in Passage A and Aunt Polly in Passage B DIFFERENT?

    F. Bartleby's boss is bothered by Bartleby's behavior, yet Aunt Polly is not bothered by Tom's behavior.

    G. Bartleby's boss conducts himself in a very professional manner, yet Aunt Polly is completely unprofessional.

    H. Bartleby's boss is surprised by Bartleby's behavior, yet Aunt Polly expects Tom to act as he does.

    J. Bartleby's boss is firm and controlling, yet Aunt Polly is meek and easygoing.

PASSAGE II

SOCIAL SCIENCE: The following passage is adapted from a history text that discusses the origins and uses of Yoga.

Contrary to the common perception in the West, Yoga is much more than just an exercise regimen. A centuries-old spiritual and physical way of life, Yoga derives its name from the Sanskrit word for "union." Yoga teaches that a person can become one
5 with the spiritual world through certain practices in exercise, breathing, posture, diet, and meditation. Beyond simply a workout fad, one of many that became popular in twentieth-century America and Europe, Yoga is in fact one of the six orthodox belief systems of Hindu philosophy, and it has a complex and
10 rich history, particularly in India.

The origins of Yoga are not entirely known. Early Indian religious texts speak of ecstatics, who, because of their association with religious trances and mystical transcendence, may well have been predecessors of the later yogis (followers and
15 teachers of Yoga). Although it most likely developed from other Hindu philosophical and spiritual disciplines, Yoga has been made into a separate school of thought. However, its influence and many of its practices have been felt in other areas of Hindu belief. Yoga's central tenets derive from the doctrine of Samkhya
20 (meaning "enumeration" or "number"). From this particular Hindu belief system, Yoga takes the idea that the achievement of spiritual liberation occurs when an individual is freed from the earth-bound limitations of matter, limitations that result from ignorance and worldly illusions. Yoga attempts to return
25 the practitioner to an "original" spiritual and physical state, one that has no need for the pleasures and concerns of this world—an individual can re-enter a condition of purity of body and consciousness. Once the aspirant (who aims towards a more elevated state of being through Yoga) has learned to control and suppress
30 the mundane activities of his or her mind, and has succeeded in letting go of strong attachments to material objects, he or she will be able to enter a state of deep concentration that results in a blissful, ecstatic union with the ultimate reality.

Though it is primarily a philosophical system, Yoga's practical
35 aspects seem to play the most significant role, even more so than its intellectual content. Generally, the Yoga process is described as being composed of eight stages, the first two of which are ethical preparations (restraint and observance). The next two stages are physical preparations during which the
40 practitioner performs exercises in physical posture and breathing, bringing about flexibility, stability, balance, and health. The fifth stage involves control of the senses and rests in the practitioner's ability to withdraw the attention of the senses from outward objects to the inner mind. The final three

CONTINUE

45 stages of Yoga are purely mental or internal; they are more difficult mental exercises in concentration, meditation, and contemplation.

Classical yoga, called raja-yoga (which translates as "royal yoga"), originated with a text dating from the second century 50 BC. This text, the *Yoga-sutra*, was composed over a long period of time by a man, or more likely several men, who wrote under the name Patanjali. Raja-yoga, which has to do with the essential difference between matter and self, seeks to free the self from the material world. The most popular form of Yoga is called 55 hatha-yoga. Those who practice hatha-yoga seek to improve their health and sense of well-being by learning body control through a series of breathing exercises, by assuming special postures, and through concentration. The special breathing exercises and the postures, such as the familiar lotus position, 60 are a part of hatha-yoga. There are, however, many different schools of Yoga that have become popular, particularly in the West, for their cardiovascular value and their emphasis on balance, flexibility, and physical control.

In the West, most people who study and practice Yoga are 65 likely to emphasize its health benefits as a form of exercise and relaxation rather than its religious and philosophical aspects. Though some medical professionals may be skeptical, there seems to be little question that many physiological processes— including blood pressure, respiration, and even body tem- 70 perature and heart rate—may be controlled and improved through the practice of Yoga. The first important organization for practitioners in the United States was the Self-Realization Fellowship, founded by Paramahansa Yogananda in 1920. Some 50 years later, instruction emphasizing both the physical and 75 spiritual benefits of Yoga techniques was available through a wide variety of sectarian Yoga organizations, nonsectarian classes, and television programs in the United States and Europe. Still, many people in the West regard Yoga as little more than a low-intensity workout and thereby fail to benefit from some of 80 its less obvious benefits.

11. According to the passage, which of the following does NOT accurately describe Yoga?

- **A.** A popular form of exercise
- **B.** An ancient way of life
- **C.** An orthodox belief system
- **D.** A money-making scheme

12. Yoga teaches that union with the divine can be reached by:

- I. letting go of the limitations of the material world.
- II. following certain rules of diet and exercise.
- III. giving up all worldly possessions and entering a life of poverty.

- **F.** I only
- **G.** II only
- **H.** III only
- **J.** I and II only

13. According to the passage, the "aspirant" in Yoga:

- **A.** seeks financial gains through propagating popular exercise regimens.
- **B.** teaches practitioners the correct postures and techniques to achieve union with the divine.
- **C.** seeks a higher quality of existence through the practice of Yoga.
- **D.** is an expert in raja-yoga.

14. The eight stages of Yoga include:

- I. one stage of sensory preparation.
- II. three purely internal, mental stages.
- III. four stages of ethical preparation.

- **F.** I only
- **G.** II only
- **H.** I and II only
- **J.** I and III only

15. The passage implies that Western practitioners of Yoga are most likely to be interested in its:

- **A.** spiritual benefits.
- **B.** benefits in terms of health and relaxation.
- **C.** philosophical components.
- **D.** value as an alternative to traditional medicine.

16. As it is used in line 12, the word *ecstatics* refers to:

- **F.** Yoga postures.
- **G.** predecessors of yogis.
- **H.** religious fundamentalists.
- **J.** energy felt when doing Yoga.

17. The author would most likely agree with which of the following statements regarding the Western attitude toward Yoga?

   A. Western practitioners of Yoga have a full understanding of its complexities as a philosophical as well as a practical system.

   B. By ignoring its potential benefits as a philosophical practice, some Westerners give up the chance to experience Yoga's more subtle advantages.

   C. In the West, people do not have a need for Yoga's philosophical and spiritual aspects, so it is not important to know about them.

   D. Western practitioners of Yoga have never given any consideration to Yoga's importance as something more than an exercise regimen, unfortunately.

18. The passage implies that Yoga returns the practitioner to a state of original consciousness by all of the following EXCEPT teaching the practitioner to:

   F. control and suppress the mundane activities of his or her mind.

   G. let go of attachments to the material world.

   H. use physical pain to reach a higher state of spirituality.

   J. enter a state of deep concentration.

19. In Yoga, which of the following seems to play the most significant role?

   A. Philosophical content
   B. Practical aspects
   C. Intellectual content
   D. Religious aspects

20. The central text of Yoga is the:

   F. "Way of Yoga," written by a health guru from Northern California.

   G. *Kama-sutra*, composed by the prophet Patanjali.

   H. *Yoga-sutra*, composed by an anonymous writer or writers.

   J. *Yoga-sutra*, composed by a man, or men, who wrote under the name Patanjali.

PASSAGE III

HUMANITIES: This passage is excerpted from a compendium of rural American music and musicians.

Bluegrass music is a truly American art form, a blend of influences and traditions that speaks to a broad audience while retaining a distinctive cultural character. Although bluegrass in its current form has existed only for a handful of decades, it has

5 been in the making for centuries, and it continues to grow in popularity today.

Bluegrass music's "high, lonesome sound," as musician Bill Monroe described it, is native to the rural mountain communities of the southeastern United States. There, its roots can be found
10 in the musical traditions of the Scotch, English, and Irish people who immigrated to America in the 1600s. These immigrants settled in the hills of the present-day southeastern United States, including the Carolinas, Tennessee, Kentucky, and Virginia. They brought with them traditional Irish, English, and Scottish dances,
15 which were eventually blended with other southern American musical forms, including folk, gospel, and blues.

The blend of styles resulted in a distinctive musical form. Until the 1940s, this music was simply called "old time country" or "mountain" music. It was characterized by the use of acoustic
20 (nonelectrical) instruments, particularly the fiddle and other stringed instruments. The music was fast-paced and energetic, with high-pitched vocals, performed whenever local communities congregated to dance and socialize. The subject matter of the music reflected the hardscrabble lives of the musicians,
25 for whom geographic isolation and economic hardship were commonplace. The tunes alternated between yearning expressions of love and loss, and declarations of religious faith, a result of the closely woven influence of gospel music.

In the early 1900s, the phonograph and radio began to spread
30 the sound beyond the hill country of its birth. In the first half of the twentieth century, talented musicians began appearing on the radio, particularly in several family groups who were popular in the 1920s and 1930s, including the Monroe Brothers. Charlie Monroe played the guitar, while his brother Bill played
35 the mandolin, and the two sang in harmony. The brothers dissolved their act in 1938, an event that would ultimately lead to bluegrass music as we know it today. After the split, each brother continued to play music. Bill Monroe formed a new band, and, being from Kentucky—the Bluegrass state—he
40 called the band Bill Monroe and the Blue Grass Boys.

Bill Monroe and the Blue Grass Boys launched the distinct musical genre now called bluegrass. Their sound wedded the traditional elements of mountain music with a new twist: hard-driving rhythms and a distinctive harmonic blend of voices.
45 Monroe's choice of instruments for the band (banjo, fiddle, mandolin, guitar, and bass) would become the standard orchestration for bluegrass music. The Blue Grass Boys sent the sound into mainstream America over the airwaves of the legendary Grand Ole Opry radio show, which broadcast country music
50 from the Ryman Auditorium in Nashville, Tennessee.

CONTINUE

To many bluegrass purists, the true realization of the art form did not occur until the mid-1940s, when banjo player Earl Scruggs joined the Blue Grass Boys. Scruggs introduced a three-fingered picking style that became a signature of blue-
55 grass. He later separated from the band with another of its members, and they formed a new group called The Foggy Mountain Boys. Their band introduced the use of the Dobro—a resonator guitar—along with the traditional instruments of country music. Some bluegrass bands today use the Dobro;
60 others eschew it, remaining true to the original combination of instruments in Bill Monroe's band.

From the late 1940s to the 1960s, The Foggy Mountain Boys toured the country, using concerts and television appearances to further ingrain bluegrass into American culture. By the 1950s,
65 the name "bluegrass music" had caught on to describe the musical form, and Bill Monroe had earned the title "Father of Bluegrass Music."

Bluegrass continued to grow in popularity and reached far beyond the mountains of its origin. Having edged its way into
70 American culture by way of radio and television, the music made its appearance in another form of American popular media: movies. In 1967, the soundtrack to the film *Bonnie and Clyde* featured bluegrass music, and in 2001, the popular soundtrack to the movie *O Brother, Where Art Thou* brought
75 renewed attention to bluegrass and a level of general cultural acceptance that the genre had yet to achieve.

Today, the music that emerged from the rural American hills is performed all over the world. Bluegrass festivals bring together musicians and fans; bluegrass clubs, web sites, publications,
80 and venues abound. As new generations discover this musical weave of American folk traditions, the rich cultural heritage of the mountains continues to inspire musicians and listeners from around the globe.

21. According to the passage, which of the following influenced bluegrass music?

   I. Gospel music
   II. English, Scotch, and Irish dances
   III. European classical music

  A. I only
  B. I and II only
  C. II and III only
  D. I, II, and III

22. It can be inferred from the passage that:

  F. the author believes that modern bluegrass should be played with electrical instruments.
  G. bluegrass musicians are more talented than other types of musicians.
  H. without radio, television, and movies, bluegrass might have remained a local art form.
  J. the influence of gospel on bluegrass was not as great as the influence of traditional folk music.

23. According to the information in the first paragraph, the author of this passage would most likely describe which of the following as being an attribute of an American art form?

  A. Uses acoustic instruments
  B. Draws on a variety of traditions
  C. Expresses the feelings of the musicians
  D. Remains unchanged over long periods of time

24. According to the passage, the breakup of the Monroe brothers was significant because:

  F. neither of the brothers was a particularly talented musician on his own.
  G. it marked the beginning of the demise of bluegrass music.
  H. each brother would later claim to have invented bluegrass music.
  J. it led to the formation of the band that launched bluegrass music.

25. As it is used in line 24, the word *hardscrabble* most nearly means:

  A. meaningful.
  B. uneventful.
  C. distressed.
  D. fascinating.

26. According to the passage, which of the following contributions did Bill Monroe make to bluegrass music?

   I. Instituting the specific combination of instruments that would become a signature of the musical style
   II. Organizing festivals to bring together bluegrass fans and musicians
   III. Playing the music on a popular radio show that reached a broad audience

  F. I only
  G. II and III only
  H. I and III only
  J. I, II, and III

27. Which of the following quotations best expresses the main point of the passage?

    A. "The subject matter of the music reflected the hardscrabble lives of the musicians."

    B. "The Blue Grass Boys sent the sound into mainstream America."

    C. "To many bluegrass purists, the true realization of the art form did not occur until the mid-1940s."

    D. "Bluegrass music is a truly American art form."

28. Which of the following descriptions most accurately and completely represents this passage?

    F. A comprehensive history of American musical styles

    G. An explanation of why the author enjoys bluegrass music

    H. A detailed biography of Bill Monroe

    J. A brief description of the evolution of bluegrass music

29. According to the passage, in which order did the following events occur?

    I. The Dobro was incorporated into bluegrass music.

    II. Bill Monroe and his band played on the Grand Ole Opry radio show.

    III. The name "bluegrass music" came into common use.

    A. I, II, III

    B. II, I, III

    C. III, II, I

    D. I, III, II

30. Based on the information in the passage, bluegrass music of the mid-1940s was different from early bluegrass music because:

    F. three-fingered picking was introduced.

    G. the music began to appear in movie soundtracks.

    H. the name "bluegrass" began to catch on.

    J. the songs first started to have religious themes.

PASSAGE IV

NATURAL SCIENCE: This is an excerpt from a scientific journal article.

Although stars account for only five percent of the estimated total mass of the universe, they are among some of the most visible objects in the night sky. For most of history, they were considered homogeneous bodies, devoid of distinguishing
5 characteristics; today, however, we know that no two stars are alike, and that all stars can be classified into one of several categories, based on attributes such as size and brightness.

To understand these categories, and where a particular star (such as our sun) might fall, it is necessary to examine how a
10 star is born. The differences between stars are readily apparent even at this stage, when the size of the star is determined by the size of the gas cloud out of which it is formed. A star is born when this cloud (a mixture of small particles, hydrogen, and helium) begins to spin very fast around a center point. As the
15 cloud gathers momentum, it collapses due to gravity, and the inner part of the star, called the protostar, is created. The part of the cloud that remains becomes what is often called the planetary disk: the particles and gas that are not incorporated into the star undergo a process of conglomeration, out of which
20 planets are born. Once the protostar has gathered sufficient mass, it becomes a full-fledged star.

All stars, at this point in their life cycle, produce the same chemical reaction. For every four hydrogen atoms in the core of the star, one atom of helium is produced. This reaction is
25 called "exothermic" because it produces energy. This is why stars appear to "shine"—an excess of energy is released as light. The reaction is also nuclear, which means that it can only occur at a very high temperature, about 27 million degrees Fahrenheit. Only at its core can a star maintain this temperature, so this is
30 where the conversion of hydrogen into helium and light occurs. The reaction also produces gas pressure, which counteracts the force of gravity. Gravity would otherwise cause a star to collapse inward because of the weight of its outer layers.

A star that is still converting hydrogen to helium is said to be
35 on the "main sequence." But when no more hydrogen remains in the core of the star, the star ages. Because the nuclear reaction is no longer occurring in the core of the star, the star begins to collapse due to gravity. When this happens, the temperature of the star rises high enough to ignite the additional layer of
40 hydrogen in the shell around the core. The star expands and its overall temperature falls, but, because of its size, the star appears brighter and, to observers on Earth, reddish in color. Stars at this stage are called "red giants." Eventually, they begin to pulsate and shed their outer layers. A dense core, a "white dwarf," is left
45 behind. This type of star does not produce chemical reactions, and eventually becomes completely dark.

This is the life cycle of a star about the size of our sun. Stars with masses 10 to 40 times greater than the mass of the sun, however, are subject to a more violent death. Their weight allows
50 them to collapse further, and, as a result of increased temperatures, burn helium (produced in the reaction $4H = He + energy$) to create carbon. A series of reactions at different levels of the

CONTINUE

star produce the other "heavy" elements—oxygen, magnesium,
and silicon. In time, the star resembles an onion, composed of
55 many different layers, each with a different chemical composition. Then, when iron is produced in the core, the star ceases
to undergo nuclear reactions. Why? Nuclear reactions that
convert iron into heavier elements use energy instead of producing it. With no gas pressure to balance gravity, the star
60 collapses on itself. The core remains, but the outer layers of the
star are released into space as a giant explosion of atoms. This
is a supernova, and the amount of energy it releases is equivalent
to 2.4×10^{28} megatons of TNT. Supernovae appear to us as giant,
brightly-colored clouds. Each element produced while the star
65 died is observed as a different color.

There is still one more possibility for a dying star. If it is more
than 40 times more massive than our sun, it lives only a short
time on the main sequence before it becomes a black hole. A
star that will become a black hole dies in an explosion like a
70 supernova star, but its core, instead of becoming a faint neutron
star, continues to collapse for an infinite period of time. No
reactions occur, so no gas pressure can balance gravity. A black
hole is so dense that not even light can escape from it.

Although our sun is not a massive star, the deaths of stars
75 more than 10 times greater than the size of the sun might play
a surprising and important role in the geologic history of Earth.
Elements that comprise our planet include silicon, iron, and
oxygen, but hydrogen and helium are considered the only
elements that existed at the beginning of the universe. Where
80 did the other elements originate? Speculatively, they were
created as massive stars grew old, and expelled into space when
they died, where they were incorporated into the clouds that
became the other stars and planets.

31. This passage asserts that stars with a masses more than
    10 times greater than that of the sun always:

    A. collapse into black holes.
    B. become red giants.
    C. explode in supernovae.
    D. are white dwarfs.

32. This passage states that main sequence stars do not
    collapse in on themselves because:

    F. gas pressure from their nuclear reactions
       balances gravity.
    G. they increase their temperature in response
       to gravity.
    H. they explode in supernovae.
    J. they become black holes.

33. The main point of the last paragraph is that:

    A. the sun is responsible for the iron and silicon
       on Earth.
    B. the heavy elements we find on Earth did not exist
       at the beginning of the universe; they originated
       in supernovae explosions.
    C. supernovae explosions resulted in the elements
       hydrogen and helium.
    D. hydrogen and helium were the only elements that
       existed at the beginning of the universe.

34. The word *speculatively* in the final paragraph refers to
    the fact that:

    F. we do not know for sure that four hydrogen atoms
       can burn to create helium.
    G. the theory about heavy elements on Earth has not
       been proven.
    H. the sun may be more massive than we think.
    J. supernovae may not occur.

35. As it is defined in the passage, a star on the
    main sequence:

    I. burns hydrogen into helium and energy.
    II. eventually becomes a supernova.
    III. will shrink to a white dwarf.

    A. I only
    B. II only
    C. I and II
    D. I, II, and III

36. It can be reasonably deduced from the passage that
    our sun will:

    F. remain on the main sequence indefinitely.
    G. become a white dwarf, then a supernova.
    H. collapse into a black hole after it has become a
       white dwarf.
    J. become a red giant, then a white dwarf.

37. The word *violent* in line 49 refers to the fact that
    massive stars:

    A. create carbon.
    B. fade to white dwarfs.
    C. explode in supernovae.
    D. do not allow light to escape them once they
       become black holes.

38. This passage states that black holes:

    I.   originate with stars that are 10–40 times the size of the sun.

    II. are in a perpetual state of collapse.

    III. are synonymous with neutron stars.

    F. I only

    G. II only

    H. I and II

    J. I, II, and III

39. You could reasonably conclude from lines 66–71 that a neutron star forms when a:

    A. black hole is created.

    B. faint white dwarf dies.

    C. massive star, 10–40 times the mass of the sun, is born.

    D. massive star, 10–40 times the mass of the sun, dies.

40. The passage states that planets are formed:

    F. out of the protostar cloud that creates the star.

    G. out of the remnants of neutron stars.

    H. when red giants expel their outer layers.

    J. when white dwarfs become faint.

Ⓧ
STOP

SCIENCE TEST

35 Minutes—40 Questions

DIRECTIONS: There are seven passages in this test. Each passage is followed by several questions. Read each passage, choose the best answer, and fill in the corresponding circle on the answer sheet. You may refer back to the passages at any time.

Remember, you are NOT allowed to use a calculator on this test.

PASSAGE I

Various methods are used to estimate the number of microorganisms in a culture. One method utilizes a *spectrophotometer* to measure the density of organisms in a broth medium. Density indicates the quantity of organisms in a given volume.

In this method, a beam of light is passed through the broth medium. The density of microorganisms in the broth is inversely proportional to the intensity of the light that passes through the broth. A meter is used to indicate the percentage of light transmitted through the medium.

FIGURE 1

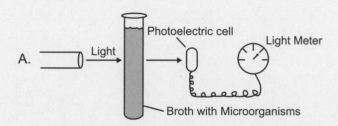

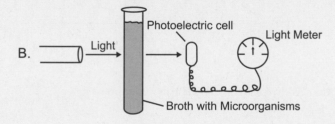

The spectrophotometric data are used to produce a graph, such as the one below, that relates optical density to cell number.

FIGURE 2

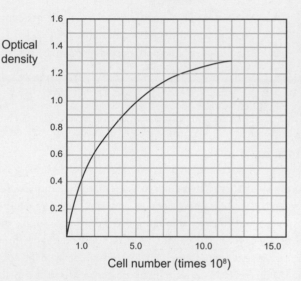

1. In Figure 1, how does the growth of microorganisms in setup A compare with the growth in setup B?

   A. The growth is equal in setups A and B.
   B. The greatest growth occurred in setup A.
   C. The greatest growth occurred in setup B.
   D. No growth occurred in either setup.

2. In Figure 2, an optical density of 0.9 coincides with a cell number of approximately:

   F. 3×10^8
   G. 4×10^8
   H. 40×10^8
   J. 5×10^8

CONTINUE

3. Based on the graph, the optical density for a cell number of 15.0×10^8 would fall between which two values?

   A. 0.9–1.1
   B. 1.1–1.3
   C. 1.3–1.5
   D. 1.5–1.7

4. In Figure 1, if broth were added to the test tube in setup B, what would you expect the *immediate* result to be?

   F. Optical density would decrease.
   G. Optical density would increase.
   H. The growth of microorganisms would double.
   J. The growth of microorganisms would decrease.

5. What inference can be made from the graph?

   A. The growth of microorganisms in a given medium doubles with the doubling of time.
   B. The growth of microorganisms is limited by space and available nutrients.
   C. Optical density is inversely proportional to cell number.
   D. Light stimulates the growth of microorganisms.

PASSAGE II

During incubation, a bird embryo, like a mammal embryo, uses oxygen to satisfy its energy needs. However, unlike a mammal embryo, a bird embryo cannot rely on its mother to supply the necessary oxygen. The oxygen must be supplied directly from the outside environment by *diffusion* through pores in the egg's shell. Diffusion is the movement of substances through a membrane from a region of higher concentration to a region of lower concentration.

Based on this fact, a group of scientists suspected that there might be a relationship between the mass of an egg and its total pore area. A *pore* is a channel through which substances can diffuse from one side of the membrane to the other.

To investigate this concept, the scientists collected the data shown in Table 1 and displayed in the graph of Figure 1.

Table 1		
Bird	**Average Egg Mass (g)**	**Average Pore Area (mm²)**
Pigeon	27.0	0.70
Warbler	1.4	0.02
Goose	250.0	15.00
Emu	800.0	55.00
Kestrel	8.5	0.20
Skua	90.0	6.00
Chicken	80.0	4.00
Ostrich	1100.0	250.00
Redwing Blackbird	6.0	0.80
Shearwater	60.0	2.00
Rhea	820.0	5.00

FIGURE 1

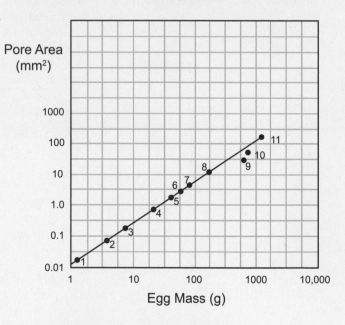

6. Which point on the graph represents data for the chicken?

   F. 4
   G. 5
   H. 6
   J. 7

7. Assuming a species of bird has an average egg mass of 500 g, what would be the predicted pore area of its eggs?

A. 1.5 mm²

B. 40 mm²

C. 750 mm²

D. greater than 750 mm²

8. Which type of bird egg has the greatest ratio of average egg mass to average pore area?

F. Skua

G. Rhea

H. Warbler

J. Redwing blackbird

9. Which of the following conclusions can be drawn from the data?

A. Egg mass and pore area exhibit an inverse relationship.

B. Egg mass and pore area exhibit a direct relationship.

C. There is no discernable relationship between egg mass and pore area.

D. The larger the bird, the larger the egg it produces.

10. Which of the following represents the process that is responsible for the diffusion of oxygen (O_2) through an eggshell? The terms *lower*, *equal*, and *higher* refer to oxygen concentration.

F.

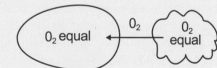

G.

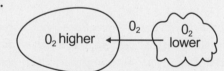

H.

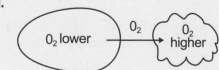

J.

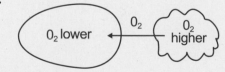

PASSAGE III

The orientation of plant parts, such as roots and stems, is influenced by such factors as light and gravity. Parts that grow toward or away from light are exhibiting phototropism—*photo* meaning "light," and *tropism* meaning "to turn toward (positive) or away from (negative) a stimulus." Plant parts that respond to gravity are said to be exhibiting *gravitropism*.

Scientists have long observed phototropic and gravitropic responses of plants. However, they were unaware of the processes that triggered these responses. The drawings below depict a number of experiments that shed light on these processes in roots.

FIGURE 1

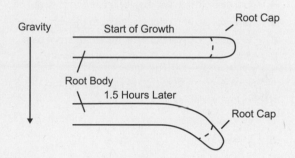

FIGURE 2

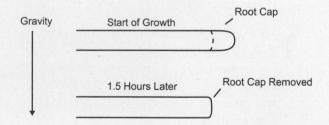

FIGURE 3

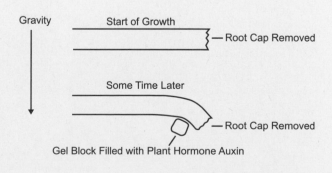

CONTINUE

11. What is the common factor in all three experiments?

   A. Root cap intact
   B. Root cap removed
   C. Auxin applied
   D. Gravity

12. What response is being shown in the lowest of the two roots that appear in Figure 1?

   F. Positive gravitropism
   G. Negative gravitropism
   H. Positive phototropism
   J. Neither gravitropism nor phototropism

13. What conclusion can be reached from the experiment shown in Figure 2?

   A. Gravitropic behavior is not related to the root cap.
   B. Gravitropic behavior is related to the root body.
   C. Gravitropic behavior is related to the root cap.
   D. The growth of a root is affected by gravity.

14. In the experiment depicted in Figure 3, what is the dependent variable?

   F. The root cap
   G. The root body
   H. Auxin
   J. The bending of the root

15. What inference can be made from the three experiments?

   A. Auxin in root caps produces negative gravitropism in roots.
   B. Auxin in root caps produces positive gravitropism in roots.
   C. Auxin in root bodies produces negative gravitropism in roots.
   D. Auxin in root bodies produces positive gravitropism in roots.

16. Scientists have observed that the bending of a root is accompanied by differential cell growth on the top and bottom surfaces of the root cap. Which of the following configurations of root cells would lead to a positive gravitropic response of a root?

   F.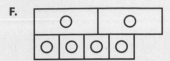

   G.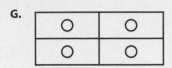

   H.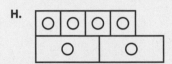

   J.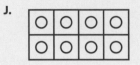

PASSAGE IV

Before the late seventeenth century, most people and many scientists were convinced that some forms of life were generated from nonliving objects. This concept came to be called *abiogenesis*, or *spontaneous generation*. According to supporters of this idea, organisms such as maggots (fly larvae) arose spontaneously from decaying meat, earthworms were born from soil inundated with rain, and a soiled shirt left in the dark and sprinkled with grain could give birth to mice. Later, after microorganisms were discovered, proponents of abiogenesis proposed that these microscopic organisms arose spontaneously from spoiling broth.

Some scientists, however, took exception to this concept. They believed in the concept of *biogenesis*, that is, that life arises only from living things. Several noteworthy scientists performed experiments to support their position.

Some of the earliest experiments were performed by Italian physician Francesco Redi in 1688. Two of his experimental setups are shown in Figures 1 and 2.

FIGURE 1

Control Group

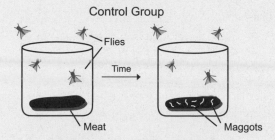

Experimental Group

Redi's First Experiment

Figure 4 shows an experiment performed in 1768 by Italian biologist Lazzaro Spallanzani. The broth he used was identical to that used by Needham.

FIGURE 4

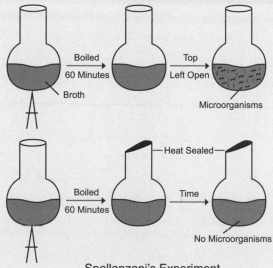

Spallanzani's Experiment

FIGURE 2

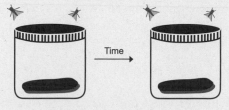

Redi's Second Experiment

In 1748, English naturalist John Needham performed the experiment shown in Figure 3. Needham believed that heating the meat for a short time to make broth would kill all living things in the broth.

In 1860, French chemist Louis Pasteur addressed this question by performing the experiment shown in Figure 5.

FIGURE 5

FIGURE 3

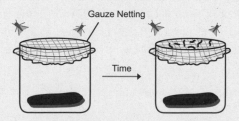

Needham's Experiment

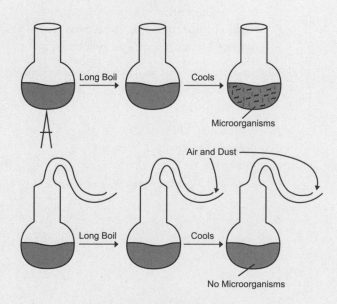

Pasteur's Experiment

CONTINUE

17. What conclusion can be drawn from Francesco Redi's first experiment?

    A. Maggots arise spontaneously from decaying meat.
    B. Air is required for maggots to arise spontaneously from decaying meat.
    C. Maggots arise from decaying meat only if flies are able to reach the meat.
    D. Maggots are not related to flies.

18. In what way did Redi's second experiment differ from his first experiment?

    F. New air was allowed to reach the meat in the jars.
    G. Meat was placed in the jars.
    H. Flies were allowed to reach the meat in the jars.
    J. Maggots appeared on the meat in the jars.

19. What criticism leveled by proponents of abiogenesis did Redi's second experiment address?

    A. Flies give rise to maggots.
    B. Maggots give rise to flies.
    C. A continuous supply of air is not required for spontaneous generation.
    D. A continuous supply of air is required for spontaneous generation.

20. What conclusion *seemed* to be supported by the results of Needham's experiment?

    F. Air is needed for the growth of microorganisms.
    G. Microorganisms arise spontaneously from broth.
    H. Microorganisms arise from other microorganisms.
    J. Microorganisms cannot arise from boiled broth.

21. What independent variable apparently was responsible for the different results of Spallanzani's and Needham's experiments?

    A. Components of the broth
    B. Characteristics of the microorganisms
    C. Boiling time
    D. Growth of the microorganisms

22. Spallanzani's experimental results support which conclusion?

    F. Microorganisms arise through abiogenesis.
    G. Microorganisms arise through biogenesis.
    H. Microorganisms are not alive.
    J. Broth is alive.

23. What conclusion could be reached by the results of Pasteur's experiment?

    A. Dust particles, not air, carry microorganisms.
    B. Air free of dust particles carries microorganisms.
    C. Microorganisms arise spontaneously from broth.
    D. Heating destroys a substance in broth that is required to support life.

PASSAGE V

One current theory for the formation of the planets in the solar system is known as the *solar nebula hypothesis*. This theory states that the planets condensed from a disk of gas and dust surrounding the sun. According to theoretical models, the temperature of the nebula was over 2,000 K at the interior edge of the cloud, but only 100 K at a distance of 10 AU. (K is the symbol for measurements of temperature using the Kelvin scale. AU stands for an astronomical unit, which is a unit of distance used to measure large distances in space.)

Figure 1 compares the temperature of the nebula to distance from the sun.

FIGURE 1

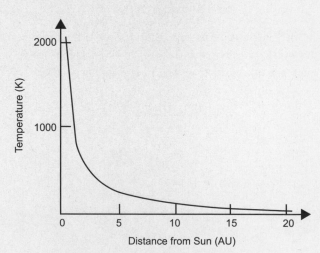

Table 1 lists the approximate temperatures at which various materials would have condensed from the solar nebula.

Table 1	
Material	Approximate Condensation Temperature
Metals	1,600 K
Rocky materials	950 K
Water ice	270 K
Ammonia ice	100 K

Table 2 lists the distances at which several of the planets formed.

Table 2	
Planet	Distance (AU)
Earth	1
Jupiter	5
Saturn	10
Uranus	20

24. Earth is composed primarily of rocky material, while Saturn and Uranus are composed mostly of gas, ammonia ice, and water ice. Which of the following is the best explanation for this difference?

- **F.** Saturn and Uranus formed more slowly, after the terrestrial planets had already formed.
- **G.** Saturn and Uranus melted after they were formed, releasing stored gases in the rocks.
- **H.** Saturn and Uranus formed at lower temperatures than Earth.
- **J.** Saturn and Uranus formed at higher temperatures than Earth.

25. Mercury formed much closer to the sun than Earth did. Which of the following is the most likely composition of Mercury?

- **A.** Mostly metal
- **B.** Mostly rock
- **C.** A mixture of rock and ice
- **D.** Mostly ice

26. Earth contains an iron core but consists mostly of rock. Mars formed a little farther out in the nebula, at approximately 1.5 AU. Which of the following is the most likely composition of Mars?

- **F.** Mostly iron
- **G.** Mostly rock with a little iron
- **H.** All rock with no iron
- **J.** Mostly ice

27. According to the theory, between which temperatures did Jupiter form?

- **A.** 100 K–500 K
- **B.** 500 K–1,000 K
- **C.** 1,000 K–1,500 K
- **D.** 1,500 K–2,000 K

28. If the solar nebula hypothesis is correct, how would the density of a planet in the solar system depend on its distance from the sun?

- **F.** The highest-density planets would be closest to the sun.
- **G.** The highest-density planets would be farthest from the sun.
- **H.** The density of the planets would reach a maximum around 1 AU.
- **J.** The density of the planets would reach a minimum around 1 AU.

CONTINUE

PASSAGE VI

Light, both visible and nonvisible, is described in terms of frequency (f) and wavelength (λ). Figure 1 shows the *electromagnetic spectrum*, which organizes types of light by frequency and wavelength.

FIGURE 1

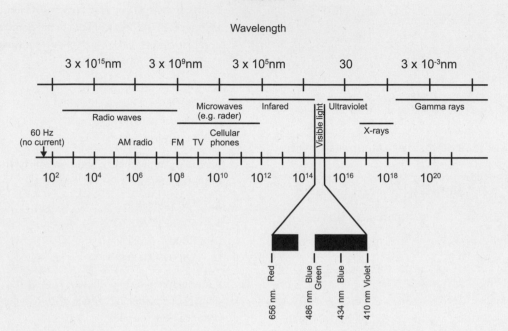

Under certain conditions, atoms can be made to emit light. When the light is analyzed through a spectroscope, a series of lines known as a *line spectrum* or *emission spectrum* is produced.

A great deal of research has been conducted on the emission spectra of different elements. The simplest line spectrum is produced by an atom of hydrogen.

In 1885, a scientist named J.J. Balmer researched the spectrum of hydrogen. He discovered that the visible lines in the hydrogen spectrum followed a predictable pattern.

Additional research by other scientists revealed a further series of lines in the hydrogen spectrum that also followed similar patterns.

FIGURE 2

Balmer Series of Lines

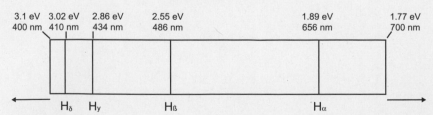

FIGURE 3

Live Spectrum for Hydrogen

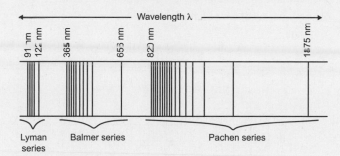

Why does an atom produce a line spectrum? The answer to this question came as a result of the research of Neils Bohr. Bohr suggested that electrons are found at discrete energy levels in an atom. When an atom is said to be excited, electrons jump to higher energy levels. This excited condition is not permanent. Eventually, the electrons return to their standard energy levels through one or more transitions. As electrons jump to lower energy levels, they release energy. The energy is not emitted in a continuous fashion, but instead in discrete amounts called *photons*. The amount of energy determines the nature of the light in the spectrum.

Table 1 lists the first six energy levels in a hydrogen atom.

Table 1	
Level $n =$	Energy
1	0 eV
2	10.2 eV
3	12.1 eV
4	12.8 eV
5	13.1 eV
6	13.2 eV

29. The Balmer series is produced when excited electrons transition down to the first excited state ($n = 2$). The transition from the $n = 4$ level (H_β) involves an energy change of 2.6 eV. Which of the energies relate to the transition from the $n = 5$ level to the $n = 2$ level?

    A. 1.9 eV
    B. 2.9 eV
    C. 3.0 eV
    D. 13.1 eV

30. In which portion of the electromagnetic spectrum does the Lyman series fall?

    F. Infrared
    G. Visible red
    H. Visible blue
    J. Ultraviolet

31. A researcher found that a population of excited hydrogen atoms has electrons in the $n = 4$ level. How many different photon energy transitions are possible as these atoms return to the lowest energy level?

    A. 1
    B. 2
    C. 6
    D. 8

32. Which of the following graphs best describes the relationship the researchers discovered between the energy and the wavelength of a photon?

    F.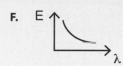

    G.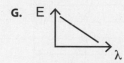

    H.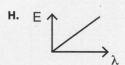

    J.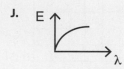

33. Which transition would most likely produce the H_γ line in the Balmer series?

    A. $n = 3$ to $n = 1$
    B. $n = 4$ to $n = 2$
    C. $n = 5$ to $n = 2$
    D. $n = 5$ to $n = 3$

34. Researchers confined excited hydrogen gas in a discharge tube. They found that it glows with a distinctive red color. This is probably due to which Balmer line?

    F. H_α
    G. H_β
    H. H_γ
    J. H_δ

CONTINUE

PASSAGE VII

The *climate* of a region is affected by several different factors, such as intensity of solar radiation, the amount of sunlight reflected back to space, the topography, and the distribution of land and water. Climate is not just the average *weather* for a region. Climate also includes the extremes of weather. The presence of an ocean or other large body of water can moderate extremes of temperature and humidity.

The temperature of a locale changes during a 24-hour period (*diurnal variation*). The temperature of a locale also varies during the year (*annual variation*). A group of students conducted a study into diurnal and annual variation. They recorded the average temperature over the course of one year at two different locations. Figure 1 is a graph of their data.

The students also recorded the average temperature over a 24-hour period at two different locations. Figure 2 is a graph of this data.

FIGURE 1

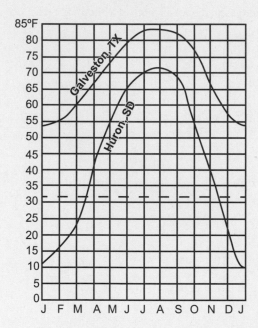

data from http://www.cdc.noaa.gov/USclimate/

FIGURE 2

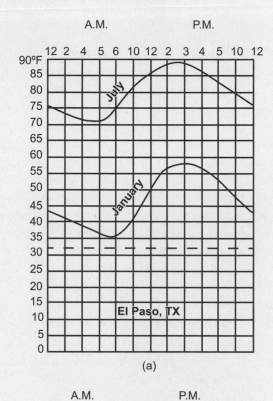

(a)

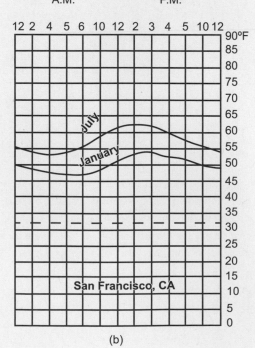

(b)

Finally, they determined the global mean annual temperature and the global mean annual temperature range as a function of latitude. Table 1 and Figure 3 represent this information.

Table 1		
Latitude	Global Mean Temperature (°F)	Temperature Range (°F)
90 to 80°	8	63
80 to 70°	13	60
70 to 60°	30	62
60 to 50°	41	49
50 to 40°	57	39
40 to 30°	68	29
30 to 20°	78	16
20 to 10°	80	7
10 to 0°	79	2
0 to -10°	79	3
-10 to -20°	78	6
-20 to -30°	73	12
-30 to -40°	65	12
-40 to -50°	53	11
-50 to -60°	42	14
-60 to -70°	27	30
-70 to -80°	10	57
-80 to -90°	-5	54

FIGURE 3

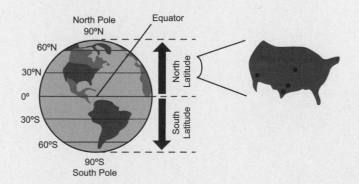

35. Which of the following statements might the students have used to describe climate as opposed to weather?

A. The low temperature this morning was 10°F.

B. The next two weeks are predicted to be warm.

C. Tomorrow will be partly cloudy with showers in the afternoon.

D. The hottest August was in 1954.

36. Based on this research, which of the following describes a location with extreme annual variation in temperature?

F. North Pole

G. Equator

H. North Latitude

J. South Latitude

37. According to the research, which of the following is the most likely explanation of why extreme annual variations of temperature are found at middle and high latitudes in the northern hemisphere?

A. High mountains in the North Pole block cold air from reaching middle latitudes.

B. The northern hemisphere is dominated by large land masses.

C. The southern hemisphere has no source of cold polar air.

D. Earth is closer to the sun in the southern hemisphere winter.

38. How might the students explain why Huron, South Dakota, has a much wider temperature variation than Galveston, Texas?

F. Huron is located much farther from any ocean.

G. Huron is closer to the Gulf of Mexico.

H. Huron is much farther north than Galveston.

J. Huron is at a higher elevation than Galveston.

39. Milwaukee, Wisconsin, is on the western shore of Lake Michigan. Grand Haven, Michigan, is at the same latitude on the eastern shore. The wind generally blows from west to east across Lake Michigan. Which statement is most likely accurate?

A. Grand Haven is warmer in winter and cooler in summer than Milwaukee.

B. Grand Haven is cooler in winter and warmer in summer than Milwaukee.

C. Grand Haven is warmer in winter and warmer in summer than Milwaukee.

D. Grand Haven is cooler in winter and cooler in summer than Milwaukee.

40. The research shows that El Paso, Texas, is colder in the winter and warmer in the summer than San Francisco, California. Which of the following is the most likely explanation?

- **F.** El Paso is much farther north.
- **G.** El Paso is much farther south.
- **H.** El Paso is much farther inland.
- **J.** El Paso is very near the ocean.

STOP

WRITING TEST

40 Minutes

> **DIRECTIONS:** This is a test of your writing skills. You have forty (40) minutes to write an essay in English. Be sure to carefully read the issue and three perspectives presented before planning and writing your essay so you understand clearly the task you are being asked to do. Your essay will be graded on the evidence it provides of your ability to analyze the issue; evaluate and analyze the perspectives; state and develop a personal perspective; and describe the relationship between the given perspectives and your own, while effectively using organization, logic, and language according to the conventions of standard written English.

A DANGEROUS SPORT

Is football too dangerous a sport to keep playing? Media coverage regarding the increasing number of football-related injuries at every level—from youth football leagues to the NFL—has placed this issue in the national spotlight. Football injuries, often career-ending, life-altering, and even life-threatening, have placed the game under more scrutiny than ever before. Former professional players, worried parents, and politicians have become more vocal in their concern regarding player safety, raising questions about the future of the sport. The number of people calling for a ban altogether is on the rise. What are your thoughts regarding the future of football? How should we address the growing concerns regarding the safety of this sport? Should the game of football be banned altogether? Should serious reform, which might alter the way the game is currently played but would make the game safer to play, be considered?

Read and carefully consider these perspectives. Each suggests a particular way of thinking about how the dangers of football should be addressed.

PERSPECTIVE ONE

Football should be banned immediately. It's simply too dangerous a sport to play, and people's lives should not be put at risk for a game. There have already been too many players who have been hurt, maimed, paralyzed, and even killed—and playing this game is not worth these risks. Professional football players whose careers aren't ended early due to injury are often saddled with a lifetime of pain and medical issues after retirement. Who wants to put their kids at risk of suffering a similar fate? Those who are interested in playing sports should choose to get involved in a safer one.

PERSPECTIVE TWO

The sport of football should be left alone! Generations of people have grown up on the game and have made following their favorite professional teams a big part of their lives—this shouldn't just be taken away from them. Football teaches discipline and teamwork, brings people together, and is a viable way for many individuals to succeed in their lives. Most players and organizations approach the game responsibly and carefully, and their lives are enhanced—not ruined—by their involvement with the game. Just because a few injuries have received media attention doesn't mean the game should be banned. Should everything that contains some level of risk be banned? If so, then add NASCAR, window washing, and mountain climbing to the list of things to ban. We live in a free society, and that includes the right to pursue athletic endeavors safely and responsibly.

PERSPECTIVE THREE

It's tough to deny that football is a dangerous sport. It's true, individuals who choose to get involved in this rough athletic activity are putting themselves at risk, even if they play carefully and responsibly and utilize the most current safety equipment. However, this doesn't mean that the sport should be banned altogether. There are lots of things in life that contain an element of risk, and banning them is against what a free society stands for. The fact is, people should have the right to choose whether or not they get involved in a rough sport like football, as adults or parents of children who play. The added media attention that football injuries have been receiving isn't a bad thing, but the conversation should turn to ways to make the game safer, such as improving safety equipment technology, greater information campaigns regarding the potential dangers of the game, and perhaps revising how the game is played to make it safer—not banning it altogether.

ESSAY TASK

Write a unified, coherent essay in which you evaluate multiple perspectives on the future of football. In your essay, be sure to:

- examine and assess the perspectives given
- declare and explain your own perspective on the issue
- discuss the relationship between your perspective and those given

Your perspective may be in full or partial agreement, or in total disagreement, with any of the others. Whatever the case, support your ideas with logical reasoning and detailed, persuasive examples.

PLAN AND WRITE YOUR ESSAY

Use the first two pages of the Writing test answer sheet (found at the beginning of the test) to generate ideas and plan your essay. Then use the following four pages to write your essay. Consider the following as you compose your essay:

What are the strengths and weaknesses of the three perspectives provided?

- Identify the insights they present and what they fail to consider.
- Ascertain why a given perspective might persuade or fail to persuade.

How can you apply your own experience, knowledge, and values?

- Express your perspective on the issue, identifying the perspective's strengths and weaknesses.
- Formulate a plan to support your perspective in your essay.

ENGLISH

1.	B	20.	F	39.	D	58.	F
2.	G	21.	D	40.	G	59.	C
3.	D	22.	G	41.	B	60.	F
4.	F	23.	A	42.	H	61.	A
5.	B	24.	J	43.	B	62.	J
6.	J	25.	D	44.	F	63.	C
7.	C	26.	H	45.	A	64.	G
8.	F	27.	B	46.	G	65.	B
9.	C	28.	H	47.	A	66.	H
10.	H	29.	C	48.	G	67.	A
11.	D	30.	G	49.	C	68.	H
12.	G	31.	A	50.	F	69.	A
13.	D	32.	J	51.	D	70.	H
14.	J	33.	B	52.	G	71.	B
15.	B	34.	J	53.	C	72.	F
16.	J	35.	A	54.	G	73.	D
17.	D	36.	H	55.	A	74.	G
18.	F	37.	A	56.	J	75.	C
19.	C	38.	F	57.	D		

1. **The correct answer is B.** The comma after *heard* should be removed because the word *vaudeville* is essential to the meaning of the sentence. The comma cuts off the first part of the sentence at the wrong place. The second comma is correct because a comma should come before a connecting word (*and*) joining two independent clauses, or complete sentences. This sentence is really two sentences joined by *and*. Choice C misplaces the comma, and choice D is missing it altogether.

2. **The correct answer is G.** The sentence is written awkwardly, so look for a better construction, one in which *vaudeville* is the subject. Choice G is the best way, because *It was vaudeville* is simplified to the subject *vaudeville*; the simple past tense of the verb, *brought*, is more concise and effective in this sentence; and reordering the words in the second half is also a stylistic improvement. Choice H is awkward, and choice J is unclear, using a modifier (*in the millions*) that is far from the subject it modifies (*people*).

3. **The correct answer is D.** The word *wonderful* would work better if it modified the noun *vaudeville*, to describe the entertainment itself. However, in this sentence *wonderful* is modifying *appeal*, making it seem as if the appeal, not vaudeville, is wonderful. Given the context of the sentence, a different adjective would best modify the word *appeal*. The word *great* by itself may

have fit the context and style of the sentence, but the phrase *great deal of* is an awkward replacement in this sentence, so choice B is incorrect. The word *large*, choice C, is most often used to describe physical objects, not abstract concepts like *appeal*. As used in this sentence, the word *mass* means something that involves or affects a large number of people. The sentence tells you that vaudeville "had something for everyone," so it had a *mass* appeal.

4. **The correct answer is F.** The subject in the sentence is *the variety of the acts*. Although the last word is *acts*, which is plural, this word does not represent the complete subject. In this sentence, what is impressive is the *variety* of the acts, not the acts themselves. Therefore, the sentence needs the singular verb *was*. The sentence is correct as written. Choice G introduces an unnecessary comma and uses the plural form of *was*, *were*. Choice H loses the comma but retains the incorrect verb *were*. Choice J has the correct verb form, but it adds another incorrect comma.

5. **The correct answer is B.** The original sentence suffers from poor construction in that it lacks parallelism. The audience takes three basic actions in the sentence: laughing, joining, and watching.

Notice how in this case, all of the verbs end in *ing*. That is an example of parallelism. The structure of each verb is parallel to the structure of the other verbs. This answer choice states that the audience would laugh, join, and watch. The verbs are all in the same tense, controlled by the helping verb *would*. This corrects the parallelism problem. Choices C and D do not solve the problem.

6. **The correct answer is J.** Speaking is a form of verbal communication, so the phrase is redundant as written. The only way to correct the redundancy is to take out either "verbal communication" or "speaking." Choices G and H do not do that, but choice J does.

7. **The correct answer is C.** As written, the sentence ending in *inexpensive* is grammatically correct. However, the sentence beginning with *making* is a fragment, not a complete sentence, and therefore needs to be changed. Choice C corrects the fragment by joining it to the other sentence with a comma. Choice B is incorrect because it creates a comma splice (two complete sentences separated by a comma). Choice D is wrong because the conjunction *yet* indicates contrast, which would be illogical in this sentence.

8. **The correct answer is F.** No apostrophe is needed since the word *acts* is not a possessive word in this sentence. Therefore, choices G and H are incorrect. The phrase "of the" serves to indicate possession, and it would be redundant to do so twice. The *s* is needed because the word is plural, so choice J is incorrect. Only the sentence as originally written is correct.

9. **The correct answer is C.** There is an error in this sentence as written. The word *we* refers to the parents who took their children to vaudeville shows. Because *parents* is in the third person and *we* is in the first person, the sentence needs a different pronoun. *Parents* is plural, so it cannot be referred to with the singular *he or she* (choice B) or *one* (choice D). The only word that works is *they*.

10. **The correct answer is H.** While choice F is a true statement, it is not the main idea of the paragraph, which is the origin of vaudeville. Choice G, too, might be true, but it is too general and does not introduce the main idea of the paragraph. Choice H is correct because it is about the origins of vaudeville and leads logically into the sentence that currently begins Paragraph 3. Choice J would work if the paragraph presented various theories on the origin of vaudeville, but it does not.

11. **The correct answer is D.** The word *mostly* isn't right in this sentence. The sentence explains that there was an increase in the creativity and diversity of the acts. You're looking for a word that shows comparison, to show that the acts changed (became more creative and diverse) over time. The word *more* accomplishes that, though *most* (choice B) does not. Choice C doesn't work because it changes the meaning of the sentence. Only choice D works.

12. **The correct answer is G.** This sentence has a dangling modifier, a type of error that can be difficult to spot. As written, it sounds like the businesspeople are growing in popularity. The modifier *rapidly growing in popularity* should refer to what grew popular, which is vaudeville in this case. In choices F and J, the sentences read as if the businesspeople grew in popularity. Choice H makes it seem as though the theaters grew in popularity. Changing the beginning of the sentence to *Noting its popularity* makes it correct to have *businesspeople* as the subject. They are doing the noting.

13. **The correct answer is D.** It doesn't make sense for the paragraph to begin with examples, so eliminate choice A. Logically, examples should go after a statement of some kind. Since Sentence 3 begins by referring to *other famous vaudevillians*, this means that some vaudevillians were already mentioned. You can guess that Sentence 3 goes after Sentence 1. Sentence 2 is the topic sentence, referring in general to the performers who gained fame. It should be followed by Sentence 1, which lists several specific examples. Sentence 3 should end the paragraph by providing some additional examples. This is the most logical sequence. Choices B and C do not improve the logical flow of Paragraph 4.

14. **The correct answer is J.** This paragraph should be placed early in the essay because it gives introductory information, such as the origin and meaning of the word *vaudeville*. Nonetheless, the first paragraph should remain where it is because it is most effective as the introduction, so you can eliminate choice H. Therefore, Paragraph 3 should come directly after Paragraph 1. Choice G would place the introductory information at the end of the essay.

15. **The correct answer is B.** Paragraph 1 (choice A) mentions the laughter and joy that vaudeville brought to millions, but Paragraph 2 makes the author's argument more convincing. It provides many details—the diversity of the acts, vaudeville's appeal to non-English speakers, and its focus on family fun—to make the author's argument more convincing. This is the

correct answer. Paragraph 3 (choice C) is mostly background on the roots of vaudeville. This does not advance the author's argument. Paragraph 4 (choice D) focuses on performers who became famous on the vaudeville stage. This would not help the author's argument.

16. **The correct answer is J.** Although the meaning of this sentence is clear, it is awkwardly constructed, so eliminate choice F. The word order in choice G is also awkward, placing the phrase *to human life* right between the verb and its object. The construction in choice H changes the meaning of the original sentence. Word order is crucial to the meaning of a sentence. The sentence reads most effectively when *essential* is not separated from the phrase *to human life*, as it is in the other answer choices. Only choice J expresses the meaning more clearly and smoothly.

17. **The correct answer is D.** This sentence contains a nonrestrictive element. Think of a nonrestrictive element as a little bit of extra information in a sentence. When it appears in the middle, it must be set off by two commas, not one. So you can eliminate choice A, which uses only one comma, and choice B, which does not use any. Using *that* and no commas (choice C) makes the phrase suggest that there is more than one Huang He, one of which flows through China.

18. **The correct answer is F.** The sentence is correct as written. As a verb, *gets* should have no apostrophe, so choices G and H are incorrect. Additionally, *its* is correctly used here as a possessive; *it's* is a contraction for *it is*. *It's* is used mistakenly in choices G and J.

19. **The correct answer is C.** The verb in the sentence is in present progressive tense, which indicates that the action is taking place at the time it is written about. In this sentence, it creates an awkward, confusing sense of time and ignores that the river has been vital in the past as well. *It be* is incorrect, so eliminate choice B. Eliminate choice D because just saying *it is* ignores the role the river has played throughout history—*for centuries*, according to the passage. The only choice that works is choice C, which describes something that began in the past but still has an effect at the time of the writing.

20. **The correct answer is F.** The correct answer should provide a logical transition between the sentence about the river's importance to Chinese life and the sentence about the devastation caused by its flooding, as it includes and relates both topics. Eliminate choice G, because the river's propensity for flooding is not mentioned until the sentence that follows, so choice G

creates an illogical sequence. Choice H just rephrases the idea in the previous sentence, that the river is crucial to life in China. It is a needless repetition, and doesn't introduce the idea of the river's devastation. Eliminate choice J because a description of the river's physical characteristics does nothing to provide the needed transition between sentences. Only choice F makes sense.

21. **The correct answer is D.** The antecedent to the pronoun *their* is the Huang He. Since *Huang He* is a singular antecedent, *their* must be replaced with a singular possessive pronoun. The contraction *they're* means "they are." It makes no sense to say "with they are raging waters," so eliminate choice B. *Them* is not a possessive, so eliminate choice C. *Its* is the correct possessive to use here.

22. **The correct answer is G.** This sentence reads as if *caused* is modifying (or referring to) *devastating*, when it should refer to *flood*. In choice G, both *devastating* and *caused* correctly and clearly modify the noun *flood*. Choices F, H, and J are awkward and create confusion over which noun *caused* modifies.

23. **The correct answer is A.** The pronouns *who* and *whom* are frequently confused. *Who* is in the subjective case, which means that it functions as a subject. *Whom* (choice B) is in the objective case, which means that it functions as an object. Since *who* refers to *villagers and farmers*, which is the subject of the sentence, the pronoun must be in the subjective case. The sentence is correct as written. The pronoun *which* is not used to refer to people, so eliminate choice C. The pronoun *whose* shows possession, or ownership, which is not needed here, so eliminate choice D.

24. **The correct answer is J.** The word *content,* choice F, indicates a sense of satisfaction, but it does not convey the stronger emotion that the villagers would have felt. Neither does *satisfied* (choice G) nor *pleased* (choice H). The word *elated*, which means overjoyed, expresses the extreme happiness that the villagers would have felt. The sentence tells you that their crops and lives were in jeopardy, so they would have felt more than contentment or satisfaction at the end of the long drought.

25. **The correct answer is D.** The original sentence is wordy. This is a problem with style, not grammar, which is why wordiness can be easy to miss. In good writing, every word counts. A year *is* a period, so there is no need to state the obvious. Choices B and C simply reword the original unnecessary phrase; they do not correct the problem.

26. **The correct answer is H.** The original sentence is confusing and awkward. It sounds as though *the villagers working desperately to raise the dikes* modifies the second part of the sentence, and it doesn't make sense. Choice G contains a comma splice; it's grammatically incorrect, so eliminate it. Choice J changes the meaning of the sentence, so eliminate it. Choice H correctly shows the cause-and-effect relationship between the two parts of the sentence.

27. **The correct answer is B.** Eliminate choice A because the writer does not define other unfamiliar words in the passage. While it is true that the word is not the focus of the passage, writers do often define words and terms in their works, even if not crucial to the passage as a whole. Eliminate choice C. It is unlikely that most readers will know the word, so eliminate choice D.

28. **The correct answer is H.** Choices F, G, and J read as if Niagara Falls also swelled to six times the volume. Also, it is unclear what *the volume* refers to. In fact, the only choice that is clear and makes sense is choice H.

29. **The correct answer is C.** Interesting details can enhance an essay. However, good writers are selective of the details they include in their writing. Just because a detail is interesting does not mean it belongs in the essay. The passage focuses on the flood of 1935. Paragraph 5 gives details of the tragic consequences of that particular flood. Throwing in one sentence about an earlier flood detracts from the unity of the paragraph and the passage, so choices A and B are wrong. Choice D misidentifies the reason the sentence should be eliminated.

30. **The correct answer is G.** Choice G mentions the specific flood that the passage describes. It is the best summary of the passage as a whole. Choices F and H are too narrow and choice J is too broad.

31. **The correct answer is A.** The sentence is correct as written. Both pronouns should be in the subjective case, meaning that they function as a subject. These pronouns were part of a compound subject, so testing each subject separately makes it easier to find the answer: *she ordered*; *I ordered*. *Me ordered* does not sound right, so choices B and C can be eliminated. *Her ordered* does not sound right either, which reinforces the fact that choice C is wrong and eliminates choice D.

32. **The correct answer is J.** In this case, the simplest phrase works best. As it is written, the sentence is grammatically incorrect, sticking two ideas together without punctuation, and using the wrong form of the verb *to have*. Choice J expresses the idea in the clearest, most effective way, eliminating extra words. Choice G separates the two parts of the sentence in an unnecessary way, and choice H is awkward.

33. **The correct answer is B.** There is an error in this sentence. The subject is in the first person, but the possessive pronoun *your* is in the second person. The sentence needs to maintain consistency. Because the subject is *we*, the correct possessive is *our*. Choice C makes an additional error since the pronoun *it* replaces a non-human noun. Choice D would be used only if the people doing the owning are not specifically identified, which they are in this sentence.

34. **The correct answer is J.** The sentence in the passage has a dangling modifier. The sentence begins by stating that something is welcoming the couple into the nightmarish world. This idea must be carried over into the second half of the sentence. The noun being modified by the first half of the sentence must immediately follow the comma. The original sentence and choice G make it seem as though the narrator and the narrator's wife welcomed themselves into the nightmarish world of do-it-yourself assembly. Choice H makes it seem like the top panel introduced them into that nightmarish world.

35. **The correct answer is A.** The sentence is correct as written. Eliminate choice B because the verb must agree with *box*, not *tools*. Choice C uses the wrong verb tense, and choice D doesn't make sense.

36. **The correct answer is H.** As the sentence is written, the verb is in the past perfect tense, but this tense should be used when an action that started in the past ended at a specified time. This sentence needs a simple past tense verb, so choice H is correct. Either *have* or *has* always proceeds *begun*, so choice G would be incorrect in any context. Choice J is in the past indicative tense.

37. **The correct answer is A.** The sentence is correct as written. The construction *one of them* is singular. A singular noun takes a singular verb, so *was* is correct, so choice B is incorrect. Choice C creates a change in tense not appropriate to the sentence. Assembling the stand took place in the past. Choice D is not a logical answer choice. The screws are not undergoing a transformation.

38. **The correct answer is F.** This sentence is long and could easily be shortened, for example, "Then the instructions told us to attach all of the panels according to their letter designations." However, the original sentence is more rhetorically effective. Detailing how the panels are

attached emphasizes the maddening complexities of the instruction manual. The paragraph proceeds logically as it is written, first describing the process of organizing the screws, and then describing the next step in the instructions. Choices G and H undermine the sentence's intended purpose. Sentence 2 follows Sentence 1 logically, and placing Sentence 4 between them would disrupt that logical flow. Therefore, choice J is incorrect.

39. **The correct answer is D.** The narrator's account of what followed hardly suggests that the assembly was a piece of cake, or very easy, so eliminate choice A. The passage never mentions that the narrator and his wife took a break, so eliminate choice B. Choice C might be true, but this statement would be better placed in the conclusion, where the narrator might reflect on the overall experience. The narrator's account of what happened next certainly reads as if things went from bad to worse, so choice D is correct.

40. **The correct answer is G.** There is an apostrophe error in this sentence. The narrator and his wife have to attach the handles to the doors *of* the TV stand—in other words, the TV stand's doors. Putting an apostrophe before the last *s* in *stands* corrects the problem by making the word possessive. Placing the apostrophe after the last *s* makes the *s* part of the subject, turning the singular *stand* into the plural *stands*. There is only one stand, so eliminate choice H. Eliminate choice J because it makes the wrong word possessive.

41. **The correct answer is B.** As it is written, the sentence is awkward and confusing. Eliminate choice C because the idea of confusion is needlessly repeated—*confused*, *mixed up*. Both parts of the sentence say nearly the same thing. Choice D is awkward and repetitive, and it makes it seem as if the screws—not the people—are confused! The only clear rewrite of the sentence is choice B, which shows the cause-and-effect relationship of the nearly identical screws and the confusion they caused.

42. **The correct answer is H.** This sentence has a comma error. The phrase that follows *who* is restrictive, or essential to the meaning of the sentence. It should not be preceded by a comma, so eliminate choice G. The phrase that follows *wife* is nonrestrictive, or nonessential. It is additional information not crucial to the reader's understanding of the sentence. Therefore, it should be set off with a comma from the rest of the sentence, as choice H does. Choice J includes an unnecessary extra comma between *from* and *my*.

43. **The correct answer is B.** Sentence 2 (choice A) explains how the narrator was able to resolve the problem of the missing screw, so it is important. The fact that the narrator's wife gave him the toolbox for his birthday is not essential to the paragraph or the passage, so Sentence 3 (choice B) can be left out. Sentence 4 (choice C) reminds the reader that putting together the TV stand was a long, tedious process, which is relevant to the paragraph and the passage, and Sentence 5 (choice D) expresses the natural conclusion to their efforts in putting together the TV stand.

44. **The correct answer is F.** The fact that the TV stand came out crooked after all the work that the narrator and his wife put into it demonstrates that do-it-yourself assembly can be a terrible, headache-inducing experience. The sentence might indicate that the writer has a sense of humor, but the focus of this passage is definitely on the narrator and his experience assembling the TV stand, so eliminate choice G. The narrator may well be incompetent, but it is not logical to make that characterization based on this one experience, so eliminate choice H. The passage is specific to do-it-yourself assembly, not housework in general, so eliminate choice J.

45. **The correct answer is A.** Sentence 1 in Paragraph 2 states that the narrator and his wife had just begun to study the instruction manual. The new sentence makes the most logical sense here. Sentence 3 tells about the similarity of the screws. The new sentence would seem illogical if placed here, so choice B is wrong. Sentence 4 provides details from the instructions. However, describing what the instruction manual looked like would make more sense earlier in the passage. Therefore, you can eliminate choice C. If placed after Sentence 1 in Paragraph 3, the new sentence would interrupt details about the assembly of the stand, so choice D is wrong.

46. **The correct answer is G.** This sentence requires a comma to set apart the two separate ideas of muscle power versus engine or sail power, and the original sentence is missing that comma. Choice G places the comma between the two ideas correctly. A conjunction such as *but* or *and* is not necessary and makes the construction of the sentence awkward, so choices H and J should be eliminated.

47. **The correct answer is A.** The conjunction *because* in choice B is incorrect since it changes the meaning of the original sentence (the popularity of rowing is illustrated by the number of clubs around the world). By adding

Answer Keys and Explanations

because, the sentence indicates that rowing is popular due to the number of clubs. Choice C contains two unnecessary commas that splice and interrupt the flow of the sentence. Finally, because the aim of the original sentence is to illustrate just how popular rowing has become worldwide, choice D should be eliminated (although it is not grammatically incorrect) because separating the original sentence into two does not convey the meaning that the author intends.

48. **The correct answer is G.** *It's* is the appropriate contraction for "it is." Choice F cannot be correct because *its* is a singular possessive pronoun, not the contraction that we need. Choice H does not contain a subject and, therefore, cannot be correct. Choice J once again contains the singular possessive, rather than the appropriate contraction, and the addition of *since* makes the sentence awkward.

49. **The correct answer is C.** Because the rest of this sentence is in the present tense, the verb *to make* must also be in the present tense and not in the past tense as it is in the original sentence. Choice B is still in the wrong tense and should be eliminated. Choice D is incorrect because it is the third-person singular and does not agree with the third-person plural subject *athletes*. Only choice C is written in the correct tense and makes no subject-verb errors.

50. **The correct answer is F.** The sentence is correct as written. Choice G is incorrect because the semicolon divides the independent and dependent clauses. The period in choice H creates the sentence fragment "When rowing together in a team boat." Choice J is also a sentence fragment and can be eliminated.

51. **The correct answer is D.** Choice A is incorrect because it contains an unnecessary phrase *you see*. Choice B can be eliminated because adding *consequently* does not make sense; the author has not given a possible reason for the rowers getting out of synch. Therefore, there is no consequence to discuss. Choice C is incorrect because it is redundant. *Just a bit* repeats the idea behind *even for a moment*. Only choice D is written correctly.

52. **The correct answer is G.** The present participles of the verbs *to lose* and *to happen* are in agreement in choice G. Choice F is incorrect because *lost speed* does not really "happen" to an object, such as a boat. The addition of parentheses is inappropriate in choice H because the words contained in the parentheses are grammatically related to the rest of the sentence and should not be separated by this form of punctuation. Choice J should

be eliminated because the infinitive *to lose* and the past participle *have happened* do not agree in tense.

53. **The correct answer is C.** It contains the third-person singular form of the verb, which agrees with the subject *team*. Choice A is incorrect because *have* is a plural verb form, but the subject, the collective noun, *team*, is singular. Choice B cannot be the answer because you would say *the team trains*, not *the team train*. Choice D can also be eliminated because *were* is a plural verb form, but we know that the subject is singular.

54. **The correct answer is G.** This is the appropriate compound preposition for this sentence. Choice F is incorrect because *additionally* is an adverb that is not modifying a verb in its current location. Choice H should be eliminated; the rowers do not spend time in the weight room as a result of training on the water. Choice J is incorrect because *since* is also an adverb and is grammatically incorrect.

55. **The correct answer is A.** The sentence is correct as written. Choice B is incorrect because the clause beginning with *that* should not be separated (by the comma) from the noun it modifies. By removing the second comma in the sentence, choice C isolates *races* and creates a comma splice. Choice D can be eliminated because the modifying clause beginning with *which* must begin and end with a comma.

56. **The correct answer is J.** *Is* provides the proper tense of the verb *to be* for this sentence. Choice F should be eliminated because *are* is the second-person plural form of *to be*, while the subject of the sentence is third-person singular. Choice G is incorrect because it does not provide a verb for the sentence. Choice H can also be eliminated because it is partially in the past perfect tense and is an incomplete form of this tense.

57. **The correct answer is D.** The mention of longer races does not support the point the author is making about training time versus time spent racing. Choice A is incorrect because the placement of this sentence would be at the end of the paragraph where it would not help to further explain races themselves, a concept introduced in the very beginning of the paragraph. Choice B can be eliminated because the main point of this paragraph is that time spent racing is far less than the time spent training. Choice C is incorrect due to the fact that the World Championships are not the sole focus of this paragraph.

58. **The correct answer is F.** The comma precedes *or* and serves to join the two independent clauses. The colon in

choice G is incorrect because it does not join the clauses. Choices H and J can be eliminated; they do not express the author's original intention of comparing one type of rower to another.

59. **The correct answer is C.** This clause requires the present participle of the verb *enjoy*. Choice A is incorrect because the tense is incorrect and does not agree with the rest of the sentence. Choice B should be eliminated because this is not an appropriate situation to use the infinitive of *enjoy*. Choice D is also incorrect because it causes a tense shift within the sentence.

60. **The correct answer is F.** While the essay does mention that rowers train many hours, it is not composed entirely of specific details of racing and training. Choice G is incorrect because the essay does in fact illustrate that rowing requires both intense training and good technique. While the fourth paragraph discusses the distance and typical time of a rowing race, there is no other mention of this throughout the rest of the essay, so we may eliminate choice H. Choice J is similarly incorrect, as there was only a brief mention, not great detail, concerning weight training schedules.

61. **The correct answer is A.** It offers the correct idiom. It is most common in our language to say: "…studies indicate that." We would never hear "…studies indicate for (choice B), or "…studies indicate in" (choice C). And while it might pass in ordinary conversation to say "…studies indicate how," this is not a proper construction, so choice D is incorrect.

62. **The correct answer is J.** It pairs the singular verb *cites* with the singular subject *article*. Eliminate choice F since it offers a plural verb to match with the singular subject: "A recent article …cite experiments …." Eliminate choice G since it offers a noun instead of a verb, and a verb is most definitely required for this spot. Choice H proposes the gerund (-*ing*) form of the verb, which is inappropriate for this situation because the underlined word bears the responsibility of being the operative verb for the sentence. *Citing* could only be used if another verb bears the brunt of that work, as in: "A recent article citing several noted neurobiologists stated that …." In this example, *stated* becomes the operative verb.

63. **The correct answer is C.** Essentially, this question asks us to find the most common expression of the idea carried in this phrase. If a study is particularly interesting, how might you write that in an introduction to a sentence? Choices B and D offer roundabout constructions you would never hear spoken or see written.

Choice A is a bit too colloquial for the written language; at any rate, the comma actually renders this choice grammatically incorrect. Choice C remains the best choice.

64. **The correct answer is G.** It proposes the best combination of proper punctuation and grammar to convey the meaning of the sentence. Choice F is a run-on sentence. There needs to be some sort of break in the prose after the word *discovery* since a new thought begins. Punctuation can be used, or perhaps an appropriate connecting word such as *and* or *because*. Choice H proposes the word *with*, but this is inappropriate since it connects rather than separates the different thoughts in the sentence. Choice J turns *saturated* (an adjective) into *saturating* (a verb). This confounds the grammar in the sentence. Choice G appropriately uses a colon to signal the reader that information on the new discovery is forthcoming.

65. **The correct answer is B.** This question primarily tests your command of pronouns. *Each member* is the operative subject of the sentence. *Each member* is a singular construction. Pronouns are used to refer to previously established nouns. Singular pronouns must be used in reference to singular nouns. Plural pronouns must be used to refer to plural nouns. *They* is a plural pronoun; therefore, eliminate choice C. Choice D suggests no pronoun at all; it, too, can be eliminated because a pronoun is necessary to provide clarity in the sentence. Although *it* is a singular pronoun, it is not used to refer to people, so choice A is also incorrect. To some ears, Choice B may sound cumbersome. It is, however, the most grammatically correct option available.

66. **The correct answer is H.** It provides a grammatically correct descriptive phrase for the sentence. The underlined portion is essentially a phrase modifying the *period of four years*. Each option attempts to convey the idea that the referenced period occurred after the second research test was administered. A gerund (the -*ing* form of a word) is the most commonly used construction for this type of work, so choices F and J are incorrect. We frequently hear "a period following" in our language. There is no need to insert *that* as offered by choice G—it only interrupts the flow of the sentence.

67. **The correct answer is A.** The studies show that eating foods rich in saturated and hydrogenated fats can increase a person's chance of developing Alzheimer's disease. For clarification, the author chooses to list examples of these foods. The correct phrase for listing

examples of a point is "such as. *Like* is often used incorrectly for this purpose. *Like* should be used when you are ascribing similar qualities to two things. Eliminate choice B since it offers *like*. Eliminate choices C and D since *with* and *because* are inappropriate words for listing examples of a concept.

68. **The correct answer is H.** This question asks you to find the most idiomatically acceptable expression of quantity. According to the author's information, a diet rich in saturated and hydrogenated fats will increase a person's chances of developing Alzheimer's disease. How much will it increase the chances? "More than twice." Why? Because *double* is either a verb or an adjective. It cannot stand in for "two times" like the word *twice* does. So eliminate choices F and G. Eliminate choice J because the word *plus* doesn't make sense there.

69. **The correct answer is A.** It offers the correct verb tense. Choice B offers a convoluted verb expression. While you may have heard a phrasing like *does an attack on* in English conversation, the rules of standard written language are more strict. Choice C proposes that the study *will attack* a theory in the future, but this doesn't hold up to the information contained in the rest of the essay: the study is currently being considered. Choice D's construction references the past tense—again, incorrect since the study is being considered in the present. Besides, *did attack* can be written more concisely as "attacked."

70. **The correct answer is H.** It offers a grammatically correct predicate phrase. The passage says, "Many researchers have gone on record," and then we need to choose an underlined portion that describes their stance. Choice F, *in supporting the notion that*, is awkward. Similarly, Choice G disrupts its own grammar by incorrectly pairing *to* with the gerund *supporting*. Choice J switches *that* to *which*. *Which* is used to establish a modifying clause, which does not exist in this case.

71. **The correct answer is B.** It offers a correct subject-verb agreement. The subject of the sentence is *vitamins,* a plural noun. It must be coupled with a plural verb. Choice A offers *has*, which is a singular verb and can be eliminated. Choice C proposes *are*, which does not fit with the rest of the sentence—"are been singled out" is never a proper construction in English. Choice D proposes a repetition of forms of the verb to be: "will be been." The best option is choice B, which notes that *vitamins have been* singled out as agents that can reduce the risk of free radical damage.

72. **The correct answer is F.** Apostrophes show ownership or denote contractions. In this sentence, the phrase "of 980 elderly people" implies ownership already—writing an apostrophe would be redundant. For this reason, eliminate choices G and J. Choice H inserts the word *those*, which is completely unnecessary in this case. Eliminate it, and you are left with the correct answer, choice F.

73. **The correct answer is D.** Choices A and C can be eliminated immediately. They propose to begin the paragraph with "during that time" without previously establishing a point of reference. In fact, Sentence 2 contains the increment of time to which Sentence 1 refers. Therefore, any correct ordering of the paragraph must put Sentence 2 before Sentence 1, which choice B does not do. The only option that does this is choice D.

74. **The correct answer is G.** Eliminate choice F since it focuses only on antioxidant vitamins. Antioxidants are merely a point of reference in the author's narrative, which provides his readers with an outline of these new scientific studies. Delving into more detail concerning antioxidants would only harm the author's mission to provide an overview of the studies. Eliminate choice H since there is no need to provide counterpoints in order to offer an overview of the studies. Eliminate choice J on the basis that the author's inclusion of a quote from Jose A. Luchsinger in no way validates his success of creating an overview of the studies cited. Only choice G explains how the essay fulfills the assignment accurately.

75. **The correct answer is C.** Eliminate choices A and D since the second study mentioned by the author maintains that despite widely held beliefs concerning antioxidants, they are apparently ineffectual for decreasing the risk of contracting Alzheimer's disease or dementia. Eliminate choice B since it maintains the exact opposite of what the cited studies show. Saturated fats have been linked to an increased chance of contracting Alzheimer's disease or dementia. Increasing your dosage of saturated fats will only increase your chances of contracting these two ailments. Therefore, choice C is the best answer.

MATHEMATICS

1.	D	16.	J	31.	D	46.	G
2.	H	17.	C	32.	K	47.	A
3.	B	18.	K	33.	A	48.	K
4.	J	19.	E	34.	F	49.	D
5.	A	20.	G	35.	B	50.	H
6.	F	21.	E	36.	J	51.	A
7.	C	22.	H	37.	C	52.	K
8.	F	23.	C	38.	F	53.	B
9.	D	24.	J	39.	C	54.	H
10.	H	25.	A	40.	F	55.	E
11.	A	26.	G	41.	B	56.	G
12.	K	27.	B	42.	J	57.	A
13.	E	28.	H	43.	C	58.	J
14.	G	29.	E	44.	F	59.	B
15.	D	30.	K	45.	C	60.	F

1. **The correct answer is D.** If 20% equals 14 students, then 100% equals 70 students. 100% is five times 20%, so 100% of the class is 5×14, or 70 students.

   Choice A is 40%, not 100%, of the total class. In choice B, you added 20 and 14, but 20 is a percent while 14 is a number of students—they cannot be added directly. Choice C is 80% of the total number of students in the class. In choice E, you added 14 to 100% of the class, which is actually 120% of the total class.

2. **The correct answer is H.** Since the numbers are a sequence, they must follow a pattern. In an arithmetic sequence, some number is added to each term to create the next. Here the pattern is to add 3 to the previous number. 6, 9, and 12 are each 3 more than the preceding number. So the next term in the sequence is $12 + 3 = 15$. But that's not the answer, as that is only the fifth term. We need the sixth term, which is $15 + 3 = 18$.

   Choice F is incorrect because you must add three to a term to get the next one in the sequence—this cannot even be the fifth term. Choice G is the fifth term of the sequence. Choice J is the seventh term of the sequence. Choice K is the eighth term of the sequence.

3. **The correct answer is B.** There are a couple of ways to approach this. One way is to realize that the fraction $\frac{16}{18}$ is equal to 2, so the second fraction must also equal 2.

Since $6 \div 3 = 2$, x must equal 3. Another way to solve is to cross-multiply. You get $48 = 16x$, and dividing both sides by 16 yields $x = 3$. If you substitute the values from choices A, C, D, and E into the equation, you do not get a true statement.

4. **The correct answer is J.** Since the three angles combine to form the straight line GI, the sum of the angles must equal 180°. You already know that $\angle JHI = 33°$ and $\angle KHJ = 22°$, so $\angle GHK = 180° - 33° - 22° = 125°$. Choice F is incorrect because the three angles form a straight angle, not a right angle. Choice G is incorrect because angle GHK is obtuse and cannot have measure equal to $KHJ + JHI$ (which is 55 degrees). Choice H is too small—the sum of all three angles must be 180 degrees. Choice K is $GHK + KHJ$, not just GHK.

5. **The correct answer is A.** By definition, if point Z bisects the line segment, then it cuts it in half. Therefore the two halves of the line segment are equal. Thus, the length from point X to midpoint Z is the same length as that from the midpoint Z to the other end point, point Y. All four of the incorrect choices compare one half of the line segment to the whole line segment.

   Choice B is incorrect because XY is double the length of ZX. Choice C is incorrect because XY is double the length of ZY. Choice D is incorrect

Answer Keys and Explanations

because *YX* is double the length of *YZ*. Choice E is incorrect because *YX* is double the length of *XZ*.

6. **The correct answer is F.** Each truck holds 11.4 tons, so all four trucks will hold $4 \times 11.4 = 45.6$ tons. With 45.6 tons in the trucks, there will be $55 - 45.6 = 9.4$ tons of sand left in the pile.

    In choice G, you subtracted what three trucks can hold, not four trucks. Choice H is the amount that two trucks can hold. In choice J, you subtracted the amount one truck can hold, not four. Choice K is the number of tons the four trucks can hold combined.

7. **The correct answer is C.** Substituting -2 for *x* in the expression, you have: $2(-2 - 3) + 15$. The quantity in the parentheses sums to -5. Thus, you have $2(-5) + 15$. Doing the multiplication leaves you with $-10 + 15$, which is equal to 5.

    Choice A is incorrect because $2(-2 - 3)$ equals -10, not -12—you multiplied -2 and -3 in the parentheses rather than subtracting them. In choice B, you mistook $2(-2 - 3)$ as $3(-2 - 3)$. In choice D, $-2 - 3 = -5$, not -1. In choice E, $-2 - 3 = -5$, not 5.

8. **The correct answer is F.** First determine the absolute values of the first two terms. Since 7 is positive, the absolute value of 7 is simply 7. Looking at the second term, the absolute value of -7 is also 7. Substituting, the expression now reads $7 - 7 - 7 = ?$ Since $7 - 7 = 0$, and $0 - 7 = -7$, the answer is -7.

    Choice G is incorrect because you ignored part of the expression. For choice H, $7 - |-7| = 7 - 7 = 0$, not 14. In choice J, you seem to have dropped the middle term when evaluating the expression. In choice K, you ignored all negative signs.

9. **The correct answer is D.** After the raise, Rosie's salary will be her current salary ($25,500) plus 8% of this ($25,500 × 0.08). Calculating the amount of the raise, $25,500 × 0.08 = $2,040. Now add the amount of the raise to the old salary to determine the new salary: $25,500 + $2,040 = $27,540.

    In choice A, you subtracted 8% instead of adding it. In choice B, you added 4%, not 8%. In choice C, you added $25,000 to 8% of $25,500. In choice E, note that 8% of $25,500 is $2,040, not $2,400.

10. **The correct answer is H.** The problem is asking you to find two consecutive integers, the first of which has a cube less than 80, and the second of which has a cube greater than 80. Use the answer choices to help you. The cubes of 2, 3, 4, and 5 are, respectively: 8, 27, 64, and 125. Since 80 falls between 64 and 125, you know that *x*

is between 4 and 5, and you don't need to go any further—choices F, G, J, and K are not possible.

11. **The correct answer is A.** This is a straightforward algebra problem. To isolate the variable *a*, subtract 67 from both sides. That leaves you with $a = -191 - 67$, which combines to $a = -258$.

    In choice B, you added 67 to both sides, but should have subtracted it. If you selected choices C and D, you likely made an arithmetic error. Choice E is the opposite of the correct answer.

12. **The correct answer is K.** You can either solve algebraically or by choosing actual values for the ages. Algebraically, you know that Lina is *x* years old. Karen is twice as old, so Karen is $2x$ years old. Joel is 8 years older than Karen, so he is $2x + 8$ years old, choice K. Alternatively, you could choose a value for *x*. Let's say $x = 10$. Then Lina is 10, Karen is 20, and Joel is 28. Only choice K yields 28 when you substitute 10 for *x*, so this must be the correct answer. Choice F likely represents your calculation for Joel's age in relation to Karen, and choice G likely represents your equation for Karen's age in relation to Lena—both do not answer what the question asks. Choices H and J are untenable.

13. **The correct answer is E.** Looking at the coordinates given, you know that two of the points will have an *x*-coordinate of -4 and two will have an *x*-coordinate of 2. Likewise, two will have a *y*-coordinate of 5 and two will have a *y*-coordinate of -2. What is missing from the 3 points given? You see that you are missing an *x*-coordinate of 2 and a *y*-coordinate of -2. You could also draw a picture to help you visualize this. In order to have a chance at being the vertex, the points must lie on one of these lines: $x = -4$, $x = 2$, $y = 5$, or $y = -2$. The points in choices A and C do not. In choice B, the *x*-coordinate is wrong. In choice D, the *y*-coordinate is wrong.

14. **The correct answer is G.** Simplifying is a matter of combining like terms. In this expression, $3a$ and $-2a$ can be combined, resulting in *a*. This cannot be combined with $9b$, so the simplified form of the expression is $a + 9b$.

    In choice F, you multiplied the coefficients of *a*, but you should have added them. In choice H, note that $3a + 9b$ does not equal $(3 + 9)ab$—you cannot combine these terms because they are not like terms. In choice J, note that $ab - 2a$ does not equal $(a - 2)ba$—you cannot combine these terms because they are not like terms. For choice K, you cannot simply add all coefficients and multiply all bases—only coefficients of like terms can be added.

15. **The correct answer is D.** Since this is a parallelogram, the opposite angles are equal. Thus, $\angle WZY = \angle WXY$. You know that the angles in a triangle sum to 180°, so $\angle WXY = 180° - 45° - 30° = 105°$. Therefore, $\angle WZY$ also equals 105°. In choices A, B, and C, WZY is obtuse, so its measure must be greater than 90 degrees. Choice E is likely the result of an arithmetic error.

16. **The correct answer is J.** To find the slope, first put the equation in $y = mx + b$ form. Then the value of m will be the slope. Subtracting $2x$ from both sides of the equation gives you $-6y = -2x + 10$. Dividing both sides by -6 yields $y = \dfrac{-2x}{-6} + \dfrac{10}{-6}$. So the slope is $\dfrac{-2}{-6}$ or $\dfrac{1}{3}$.

    Choice F is the y-intercept. Choice G is incorrect because you must solve for y before identifying the slope of the line. For choice H, since there is an x in the equation, the line is not horizontal—it cannot have a slope of 0. For choice K, you must solve for y before identifying the coefficient of x as the slope.

17. **The correct answer is C.** Start by factoring the binomial. $2x^2 - 7x - 9 = 0$ factors to $(2x - 9)(x + 1) = 0$. Next, solve for the values of x by setting each of the factors equal to 0. $2x - 9 = 0$ becomes $2x = 9$, so one possible value of x is $9 \div 2$, or 4.5. The other factor is $x + 1$. Setting that equal to 0 and solving for x yields $x = -1$. Since you're told x is positive, x must be 4.5.

    In choice A, you switched the signs when factoring; -1 is a solution, not 1. For choices B, D, and E, when these x values are plugged in, you do not get a true statement.

18. **The correct answer is K.** The two triangles are similar, so their sides are proportionate. The first triangle has a perimeter of $40 + 50 + 60 = 150$ inches. The second triangle has a perimeter exactly twice as large: 300 inches. Thus, the sides of the second triangle are exactly twice as long as the sides of the first triangle, and the second triangle has sides of 80, 100, and 120 inches. 120 inches, then, is the length of the longest side.

    Choice F is the length of the shortest side of the shorter triangle. Choice G is the length of the longest side of the shorter triangle. Choice H is the length of the shortest side of the larger triangle. Choice J is the length of the middle side of the larger triangle.

19. **The correct answer is E.** If the radio is marked down 20%, then the sale price is $100\% - 20\% = 80\%$ of the original price. Algebraically, the sale price $= 0.8 \times \$29.55$, which is equal to \$23.64. This rounds up to \$24.

    Choice A is incorrect because 20% does not mean \$20. Choices B and C are likely the result of an arithmetic error. Choice D is incorrect because you should have rounded up, not down.

20. **The correct answer is G.** To factor the expression, look for terms that are common to both quantities. 3 can be divided out of both terms, as can d and e^2. Thus, you can factor out $3de^2$, leaving $(d^3e - 5)$. So the factored form is: $3de^2(d^3e - 5)$. If you weren't sure how to factor, you could have multiplied out each of the answer choices to see which would result in the original expression.

    In choice F, you forgot to factor the 3 out of the second term. In choice H, you dropped the e^2 factor. In choice J, you haven't factored the expression; a greatest common factor can be pulled out of both terms. Choice K is incorrect because you cannot subtract unlike terms by subtracting their coefficients and exponents.

21. **The correct answer is E.** This system of equations can be solved by substitution or combination. In this case, combination is quicker. To do this, add $(2u + 2 = 20)$ and $(v - 2u = -2)$. Adding the two equations makes the u values cancel, and you are left with $v + 2 = 18$. Subtracting 2 from both sides gives you $v = 16$.

    Choice A is incorrect because $u = 9$, not -9. Choice B is the value of u, not v. Choice C is incorrect because $u = 9$, not 7, and choice D is incorrect because u does not equal 8.

22. **The correct answer is H.** First convert the units so that you are working with ounces. Since each pound has 16 ounces, a 7.5 pound bag of rice has $7.5 \times 16 = 120$ ounces of rice in it. To determine the cost per ounce, divide the total cost (\$4.80) by the number of ounces (120). That yields $\$4.80 \div 120 = \$0.04$. Choices F, G, J, and K are likely the result of an arithmetic error.

23. **The correct answer is C.** The work week is six days and each day a minimum of \$23 is earned. So without filling any bushels, the worker will earn $6 \times \$23 = \$138$. You can think of that as a base salary. The extra money earned by filling bushels is the remainder of her pay for the week, or $\$165.38 - \$138 = \$27.38$. That's the total "bonus" based on bushels. Since each bushel earns \$0.74, you can find the number of bushels filled by dividing the total (\$27.38) earned by the pay per bushel (\$0.74). $\$27.38 \div \$0.74 = 37$, so she filled 37 bushels.

    Choice A is way too small given the context of the question. In choice B, you multiplied (instead of dividing) the amount made for all bushels gathered times the cost paid per bushel. In choice D, you divided the amount earned for 6 days of work by the amount paid per bushel. In choice E, you did not subtract the amount earned for 6 days from the total earned in the week.

24. **The correct answer is J.** The problem is asking you to determine the area of the figure. There are a few ways to do this. You could break the figure into 3 rectangles and add their areas. However, a quicker method is to consider the figure a solid rectangle by drawing a line from one of the bottom "legs" to the other. The area of that rectangle would be 30 feet × 40 feet = 1,200 square feet. But that's too big; you have to subtract from this the area of the 12 foot × 12 foot square that isn't really part of the garden. That square is 12 × 12 = 144 square feet. 1,200 square feet − 144 square feet = 1,056 square feet, choice J.

Choice F is incorrect because the area of the large rectangle is 1,200, not 800. In choice G, you subtracted the areas of two such squares, not just one, from the area of the rectangle. In choice H, you subtracted the area of 1.5 such squares, not just one, from the area of the rectangle. Choice K is the area of the large rectangle; you did not subtract the area of the square portion that is not part of the garden.

25. **The correct answer is A.** Solve this by first isolating the inequality's variable. Subtracting 2 from each side of the inequality gives you the exact set of values for z: $z < 6$. Now look for the answer choice that depicts all the numbers less than 6. That choice will have an open circle over 6, since 6 is not included in the set, and an arrow highlighting all the numbers to the left of (less than) 6.

In choice B, you added 2 to both sides instead of subtracting it. In choice C, you forgot to subtract 2 from both sides of the inequality. Choice D is incorrect because the inequality is not a double inequality and so the solution set should be a ray, not an interval. In choice E, the ray is extending in the wrong direction.

26. **The correct answer is G.** $\frac{2}{3}$ is 0.666, repeating, so you can either compare that value to the decimal equivalents of the answer choices or find common denominators for each choice and $\frac{2}{3}$. Either way, the only one that is less than $\frac{2}{3}$ is $\frac{5}{9}$, since $\frac{2}{3}$ is actually equal to $\frac{6}{9}$. Choice F is incorrect because $\frac{2}{3}$ is approximately 0.667 and $\frac{5}{6}$ is approximately 0.833, so $\frac{2}{3}$ is not less than $\frac{5}{6}$.

Choice H is incorrect because $\frac{2}{3}$ is approximately 0.667 and $\frac{7}{10}$ is 0.7, so $\frac{2}{3}$ is not less than $\frac{7}{10}$. Choice J is incorrect because $\frac{2}{3}$ is approximately 0.667 and $\frac{11}{15}$ is approximately 0.733, so $\frac{2}{3}$ is not less than $\frac{11}{15}$.

Choice K is incorrect because $\frac{2}{3}$ is approximately 0.667 and $\frac{14}{20}$ is 0.7, so $\frac{2}{3}$ is not less than $\frac{14}{20}$.

27. **The correct answer is B.** The area of a triangle is $\frac{1}{2}$ × base × height. Since this is a right triangle, the height is the length of one of the legs of the triangle, and the base is the other leg of the triangle. Since the hypotenuse is always the longest side, the two legs of the triangle are the 15- and 20-meter sides. Using the formula shows the area to be $\frac{1}{2} \times 15 \times 20 = 150$ square meters.

Choice A is the perimeter, not the area. In choice C, you used the hypotenuse as one of the legs when computing the area. In choice D, you squared the hypotenuse to get the area, which is not the area formula. In choice E, you multiplied the lengths of all sides of the triangle, which is not how you calculate the area of a triangle.

28. **The correct answer is H.** Since the batteries can be evenly divided by 3, 4, 5, and 6, the answer will be the least common multiple of these numbers. The quickest approach is to consider the choices from smallest to largest. 15 is not a multiple of 4 or 6, so choice F is no good. 30 isn't a multiple of 4, so choice G is incorrect. 60, however, is evenly divisible by all four numbers. Choices J and K are divisible by 4, 5, and 6, but there is a smaller choice listed that also works.

29. **The correct answer is E.** In any triangle, the third side must be greater than the positive difference of the other two sides, and less than their sum. This means that the third side of this triangle must be greater than 18 − 17 = 1 and less than 17 + 18 = 35. Therefore, 36 is the only choice that is NOT a possible length for the third side.

All of the lengths listed in choices A, B, C, and D satisfy the triangle law and so can be the length of the third side of the triangle.

30. **The correct answer is K.** To solve, you need a common denominator. The common denominator is $4y$. To convert the first fraction, $\frac{x}{4}$, to a denominator of $4y$, multiply the top and bottom by y, like this: $\frac{y}{y} \times \frac{x}{4} = \frac{xy}{4y}$. To give the second fraction a denominator of $4y$, multiply its top and bottom by 4, like this: $\frac{4}{4} \times \frac{3}{y} = \frac{12}{4y}$. Since the denominators are now the same, you can now subtract: $\frac{xy}{4y} - \frac{12}{4y} = \frac{xy-12}{4y}$.

Choice F is incorrect because you should multiply the denominators, not add them. In choice G, you multiplied the numerators instead of subtracting them. Choice H is not the proper way to subtract fractions; you must first get an LCD. For choice J, you forgot to multiply 3 by 4.

31. **The correct answer is D.** Since this is a right triangle, you can use the Pythagorean theorem to solve. The square of the hypotenuse is equal to the sum of the squares of the legs, so $17^2 = 11^2 + MN^2$. Let x equal MN and solve. $17^2 = 11^2 + x^2$, so subtracting 11^2 from both sides gives you $17^2 - 11^2 = x^2$. Now take the square root of both sides to determine x, which is the length of $\overline{MN}$: $\sqrt{17^2 - 11^2} = x$.

For choice A, note that $\sqrt{(17-11)^2} \neq \sqrt{17^2 - 11^2}$.

In choice B, you forgot to square the legs inside the radical sign before subtracting. In choice C, you forgot to square the legs. Choice E is incorrect because you should be subtracting the terms within the radical sign since 17 is the hypotenuse.

32. **The correct answer is K.** The area of a rectangle is equal to length × width, so first determine these dimensions. All sides are originally v, but the length is extended by 2, resulting in $(v + 2)$, and the width is shortened by 1, resulting in $(v - 1)$. To find the area, simply multiply the terms. $(v + 2)(v - 1) = v^2 + v - 2$, choice K. Alternatively, you could have chosen a value for v. If $v = 10$, then the new rectangle has length 12 and width 9. Its area would be $12 \times 9 = 108$. Substituting the chosen value for v, 10, into the answer choices, only choice K gives the same area of 108.

Choice F is the length of the resulting rectangle. Choice G is the width of the resulting rectangle. In choice H, when FOILing $(v + 2)(v - 1)$, you forgot the middle term. In choice J, when FOILing $(v + 2)(v - 1)$, the sign of the middle term is wrong.

33. **The correct answer is A.** The key is knowing the definitions of sine, cosine, and tangent. The tangent is the side opposite the angle divided by the side adjacent to the angle. To solve, you just need those two measurements. The sine of the angle is the opposite side over the hypotenuse. Here the sine is $\frac{2}{7}$, so the opposite side is 2. The cosine is the adjacent side over the hypotenuse. Here the cosine is $\frac{6}{7}$, so the adjacent side is 6. Substituting these values into the definition of an angle's tangent, opposite ÷ adjacent, you get $\frac{2}{6}$, which reduces to $\frac{1}{3}$.

Choice B is incorrect because you should divide sine by cosine, not subtract them. Choice C is the cotangent of the angle. Choice D is incorrect because you should have divided sine by cosine, not added them. In choice E, you should have divided sine by cosine, not multiplied them.

34. **The correct answer is F.** The number line highlights the region between approximately −2.5 and 1. Thus, the best description of the range of numbers highlighted is choice F: the numbers greater than −2.5 but less than 1.

The inequality in choices G and K do not make sense because 1 is not less than −2.5. Choice H is the exact opposite of the correct answer. Choice J is incorrect because the middle term of the double inequality should be x, not $|x|$.

35. **The correct answer is B.** The average is the sum of the terms divided by the number of terms—in this case, the sum of all the ratings divided by the number of tasters. You don't know how many tasters there were, but that's not a problem. Since you know all the percentages, simply pick a number for the number of tasters and use it. Since the percentages are in multiples of 5, you'll want a number that is easily divisible by 20, since 5% is one out of 20. Let's use 20 to keep things simple. (You could have used 100 or any other number divisible by 20.) 10% of 20 is 2, so 2 tasters gave a rating of 4. That's $2 \times 4 = 8$ points total. 15% gave a rating of 3. 15% of 20 is 3, so that is $3 \times 3 = 9$ points. Half the testers, 10 of them, gave a rating of 2, so that makes another $10 \times 2 = 20$ points. Finally, 25%, or 5 tasters, gave a rating of 1. That's $5 \times 1 = 5$ more points. Total points awarded $= 8 + 9 + 20 + 5 = 42$ points. Divide that by the number of tasters used, 20, and the average rating is $\frac{42}{20} = 2.1$. Choices A, C, D, and E are close but likely the result of some small arithmetic error.

36. **The correct answer is J.** It pays to know the special triangles. This is a 45°–45°–90° right triangle. That means that the sides are in the ratio $1:1:\sqrt{2}$. You can use that proportion here to determine the length of the hypotenuse. One leg has length 5 meters, so the other leg has length 5 meters and the hypotenuse has length $5\sqrt{2}$ meters. Even if you forgot the special triangle, you could have used the Pythagorean theorem to solve:

$$AC^2 = 5^2 + 5^2$$
$$= 25 + 25$$
$$= 50$$
$$AC = \sqrt{50}$$
$$= 5\sqrt{2}$$

Choice F is the length of a leg, not the hypotenuse. Choice G is incorrect because the hypotenuse in a 45-45-90 triangle is $\text{leg} \cdot \sqrt{2}$, not $\text{leg} \cdot \frac{\sqrt{3}}{2}$. For choices H and K, you used the wrong triangle relationship—this is not a $1:\sqrt{3}:2$ triangle.

37. **The correct answer is C.** The quickest way to do this is just find the pairs of factors that produce 36 and add them. The factors are: 36 and 1, 18 and 2, 12 and 3, 9 and 4, and 6 and 6. If you add the integers in those pairs, $6 + 6$ gives the smallest sum, 12.

It is not possible to get these sums for choices A and B with factors of 36. Choice D comes from a viable pair (9,4), but there is a pair with a smaller sum. Choice E comes from a viable pair (12, 3), but there is a pair with a smaller sum.

38. **The correct answer is F.** Line *d* forms a 180° angle, as does every line. If you look at the intersection of lines *b* and *d*, you can see that 3 different angles make up this 180°. Two of the angles are labeled: one is 115° and another is 40°. The third angle is the one you need to find. You can do that by subtracting the sum of the two known angles from 180°: $180° - (115° + 40°) = 25°$. (Notice that the entire figure wasn't required to answer this question.) Choice G is the likely result of an arithmetic error. Choice H is the complement of the 40 degree angle, but when added to the sum of 40 and 115, the sum is not 180. Choice J is the supplement of the 115 degree angle, but when added to the sum of 40 and 115, the sum is not 180.

39. **The correct answer is C.** The *y*-intercept occurs when $x = 0$. To find it, substitute 0 for *x* in the equation: $3(0) - 8y = 16$. So $-8y = 16$, and $y = -2$. Another way to solve would be to convert the equation to the form $y = mx + b$, where *b* is the *y*-intercept. When you plug

each of the other values for *y*, along with $x = 0$, into the equation, you do not get a true statement.

40. **The correct answer is F.** $\sqrt{6}$ is equal to approximately 2.449, so all the question is really asking is which point is closest to 2.449 on the number line. That number is just about halfway between 2 and 3, so the closest point is F. Since choices G, H, J, and K are larger, they are not the correct answers.

41. **The correct answer is B.** An obtuse angle is, by definition, one that measures between 90° and 180°. In order for angle *H* to fit this definition, its measure of $(180 - x)$ must be more than 90 but less than 180. Algebraically, $90 < 180 - x < 180$. Solving the inequality for *x*, $-90 < -x < 0$, and $90 > x > 0$. This can also be written as $0 < x < 90$, so choice B is correct.

Choice A is incorrect because, *x* could be strictly between 60 and 90 degrees and H would still be obtuse. Choice C, would make H acute. Choice D would make H acute and negative. Choice E would make H acute.

42. **The correct answer is J.** You already have the value for the denominator, since you know that $m + n = -\frac{1}{2}$. To solve, you need to find the value of *n*. If $m - n = 2$, then $m = n + 2$. Substituting $(n + 2)$ for *m* in the second equation, you have $(n + 2) + n = -\frac{1}{2}$. This simplifies to $2n + 2 = -\frac{1}{2}$. Dividing both sides by 2 results in $n + 1 = -\frac{1}{4}$, and subtracting 1 from both sides yields $n = -\frac{5}{4}$. Now substitute the values for *n* and $m + n$ into the expression:

$$\frac{n}{m+n} = \frac{-\frac{5}{4}}{-\frac{1}{2}}$$
$$= -\frac{5}{4} \times -2$$
$$= \frac{5}{2}$$

In choice F, you did not account for the denominator—this is just *n*. Choice G is 2*m*. In choice H, you multiplied *n* and $m + n$. Remember, $\frac{a}{b} \div \frac{c}{d} = \frac{a}{b} \cdot \frac{d}{c}$.

Choice K represents the numerator, not the entire fraction.

43. **The correct answer is C.** Hopefully you realized that this is a special triangle. The sides of length 10, 24, and 26 fall into the ratio of a 5-12-13 right triangle. Since the

right angle always falls between the two shortest sides, the measure of this angle is 90°.

Choices A and B are angles when one side is the hypotenuse. Choices D and E are incorrect because this is a right triangle, so neither of these angles is possible since the sum of all three angles must be 180 degrees.

44. **The correct answer is F.** The hardest part of this problem is determining the equation of the line. If x is 5 more than 3 times y, the equation is $3y + 5 = x$. If you correctly translated the equation, you need only put the equation in $y = mx + b$ form. That gives you $3y = x - 5$, or

$$y = \frac{x}{3} - \frac{5}{3}.$$

Since the slope is the coefficient of x, the slope is $\frac{1}{3}$. Alternatively, you could have picked values for the points and then found the slope. When $y = 0$, x is 3 times that plus 5, or $3(0) + 5 = 5$. When $y = 1$, x is 3 times that plus 5, or $3(1) + 5 = 8$. The rise, or change in y, is 1, and the run, or change in x, is 3. So the slope is rise over run, or $\frac{1}{3}$.

Choices G, H, and J don't reflect the "three times the value" part of the relationship. Choice K is the reciprocal of the slope; you likely interchanged x and y when writing the description symbolically.

45. **The correct answer is C.** You know that the two numbers are both divisible by 6 and by no greater number. This eliminates choice D, as 12 is a common factor for 12 and 24. You also know that the least common multiple the two numbers share is 36. That knowledge eliminates choice A, as 12 is the least common multiple there. Choice B fails for the same reason, as 18 is a common multiple less than 36. Finally, choice E does not have 36 as a multiple of both numbers. Choice C has the only pair of numbers that fits the description.

46. **The correct answer is G.** The formula for the area of a circle is $A = \pi r^2$. The area of this circle is 4π, so $4\pi = \pi r^2$. To solve for r, divide both sides by π. The equation becomes $4 = r^2$ and $r = 2$. Choices F, H, and J are likely the result of using the wrong formula for the area, or an arithmetic error. For choice K, you forgot to take the square root.

47. **The correct answer is A.** The slope of a line is the change in the y-value divided by the change in the x-value. Since the point passes through the origin, the

changes in the values are simply the coordinates of the second point. So the slope, $y \div x$, is $\frac{1}{6} \div -\frac{7}{8}$, or

$$\frac{1}{6} \times -\frac{8}{7} = -\frac{4}{21}.$$

Choice B is incorrect because you don't add the coordinates of a point on the line to get the slope. Choice C is incorrect because you don't multiply the numerators and denominators of the x and y coordinates to get the slope. In choice D, you subtracted the x-coordinate from the y-coordinate, but this is not how you compute the slope. Choice E is the reciprocal of the correct answer; remember, slope is change in y divided by change in x.

48. **The correct answer is K.** The way to solve this is to compute the areas of both circles and subtract the area of the smaller from the area of the larger. The smaller circle has a radius of 2.5 inches. Using the formula Area $= \pi r^2$, you get area $= \pi(2.5)^2$, or 6.25π. The larger circle has an area of $\pi(5)^2$, which is 25π. Thus, the area of the shaded region is $25\pi - 6.25\pi = 18.75\pi$.

Choice G is the area of the small, unshaded circle. Choice F is the area of the small, unshaded circle if you used 2.5 as the diameter. For choice H, you just added the radii and multiplied the result by π. Choice J is the area of half the big circle.

49. **The correct answer is D.** The simplest way to solve is to plug in the coordinates of the listed points. The pair that makes the equation work is the point on the line. Choice D does so. If you plug in -6 and 2 for x and y, you get $3(2) - (-6) = 12$. That simplifies to: $6 + 6 = 12$, which is correct.

If the values in choices A, B, C, and E are substituted into the equation they will not result in a true statement.

50. **The correct answer is H.** You need to find the lengths of the opposite side and hypotenuse of the triangle BAD in order to compute the sine of $\angle BAD$. Thanks to the adjacent triangle, you can do this. The adjacent triangle is a right triangle with legs of 6 and 8. This is a multiple of the 3-4-5 right triangle. Thus, the hypotenuse of this triangle is 10. Now you have the lengths of both legs in triangle BAD as 10. This is, therefore, another special triangle: a 45°-45°-90° right triangle. The sides of such a triangle are in the ratio of $1:1:\sqrt{2}$. So the sides here must be 10, 10, and $10\sqrt{2}$. To find the sine, divide the

Answer Keys and Explanations

side opposite the angle, 10, by the hypotenuse, $10\sqrt{2}$, to get the sine: $\dfrac{10}{10\sqrt{2}} = \left(\dfrac{1}{\sqrt{2}} \times \dfrac{\sqrt{2}}{\sqrt{2}}\right) = \dfrac{\sqrt{2}}{2}$.

Choice F is the tangent of *BAD*. Choice G is the cosecant of *BAD*. Choice J is the length of *AD*. Choice K uses the correct sides, but you should be dividing their lengths—remember, sine is opposite divided by adjacent.

51. **The correct answer is A.** From the second equation, you know that $h = -1\frac{1}{2}g$. Substitute that value for h in the first equation: $3g - 12 = -1\frac{1}{2}g$.

Manipulating the equation to combine like terms, you have $4\frac{1}{2}g = 12$. Then solve for g:

$$g = \frac{12}{4\frac{1}{2}} \quad g = \frac{12}{\frac{9}{2}} \quad g = 12 \times \frac{2}{9} \quad g = \frac{24}{9} \quad g = \frac{8}{3}.$$

Since $h = -1\frac{1}{2}g$, it follows that $h = -1\frac{1}{2} \times \frac{8}{3} = -\frac{3}{2} \times \frac{8}{3} = -4$.

Now just multiply g and h: $-4 \times \dfrac{8}{3} = -\dfrac{32}{3}$.

Choice B is –g. Choice C is just h. Choice D is just g. In choice E, the sign should be negative since you are multiplying a positive real number times a negative real number.

52. **The correct answer is K.** You are told that the product of the three variables is equal to π. Knowing that, you must go through the choices to find the one that must be true. Choice F is wrong because it only squares one of the three variables. Choice G is wrong because it divides π by *Z*, but doesn't divide the product of *X*, *Y*, and *Z* by *Z* on the other side. Choice H is wrong because if you multiply *XYZ* by π, you have to multiply π by itself, which does not equal 0. Choice J has one side divided by π but the other multiplied by π. Choice K, however, correctly divides both sides by *X*.

53. **The correct answer is B.** Start with the rectangle. Its area is the product of its length and width. Thus the area is: $(w + 6)(w - 1) = w^2 + 5w - 6$. The area of the square is $w \times w = w^2$. To find the remaining area after removing the square, just subtract the area of the square from the area of the rectangle: $(w^2 + 5w - 6) - (w^2) = 5w - 6$.

Choice A is the area of the portion removed. Choice C is half the perimeter of the rectangle. Choice D is the area of the entire rectangle without the square being removed. In choice E, you subtracted in the wrong order.

54. **The correct answer is H.** If the probability of drawing a classical CD is $\dfrac{4}{5}$, then the probability of drawing a jazz CD is $1 - \dfrac{4}{5} = \dfrac{1}{5}$. This means that there are 4 classical CDs for each jazz CD. Since there are 3 jazz CDs, there are $3 \times 4 = 12$ classical CDs in the box.

Choices F, G, J, and K result from an error in determining the number of classical CDs per jazz CD in the collection.

55. **The correct answer is E.** This is a little trickier than it seems, because the numerator above the *x* is 2, not 1. You need to convert the other fractions so that they also have numerators of 2: $\dfrac{1}{12}$ becomes $\dfrac{2}{24}$ and $\dfrac{1}{8}$ becomes $\dfrac{2}{16}$. Now you can just list and count the fractions with 2 as a numerator that fall between $\dfrac{2}{24}$ and $\dfrac{2}{16}$ on the number line. There are 7 of them:

$\dfrac{2}{23}, \dfrac{2}{22}, \dfrac{2}{21}, \dfrac{2}{20}, \dfrac{2}{19}, \dfrac{2}{18}, \dfrac{2}{17}$. If you didn't take note of the 2 in the numerator, you probably chose choice A, 3, in error. Choices A, B, C, and D are the result of simple counting errors.

56. **The correct answer is G.** The key is to plot the points and draw a right triangle, such that the two points are the endpoints of the hypotenuse. If you do that, the other point making the right triangle is at $(-2, -4)$. [You could also use the point at $(-5, 3)$ if you like.] Now count the units making up the legs of the triangle. The distance from $(-2, 3)$ to $(-2, -4)$ is 7 units. The distance from $(-5, -4)$ to $(-2, -4)$ is 3 units. Now just solve by the Pythagorean theorem: the square of the hypotenuse is equal to $7^2 + 3^2 = 49 + 9 = 58$. Thus the hypotenuse, which is the distance between the two points, is $\sqrt{58}$.

You can also find the distance between any two points by using the distance formula:

$$\begin{aligned} d &= \sqrt{(x_1 - x_2)^2 + (y_1 - y_2)^2} \\ &= \sqrt{(-2 - (-5))^2 + (3 - (-4))^2} \\ &= \sqrt{(3)^2 + (7)^2} \\ &= \sqrt{9 + 49} \\ &= \sqrt{58} \end{aligned}$$

In choice F, you subtracted the coordinates of the individual points instead of subtracting the *x* coordinates and the *y* coordinates. In choice H, you forgot to square the differences in the *x* and *y* coordinates. In choice J, you forgot to square the differences in the *x* and *y* coordinates, and you forgot to take the square root. In choice K, you forgot to take the square root.

57. **The correct answer is A.** The only approach is to go through the choices to see which one determines a single plane. You don't have to go far, as choice A does so. Two lines meeting at right angles will give us exactly one plane. Think of the standard (x, y) coordinate plane. The *x* and *y* axes are intersecting, perpendicular lines, giving us a plane. As for the others, two points, choice B, give you a line, not a plane. Three points on the same line, choice C, just give you a line, not a plane. Two lines that don't intersect won't give you a plane unless they are parallel, so choice D is incorrect. And three non-parallel lines won't necessarily define a distinct plane. They could be in three different planes; therefore, choice E is also incorrect.

58. **The correct answer is J.** It's easiest to give numbers to the question, since none are provided. Let's make the tin have 1 cherry candy. We're told it has twice as many grape candies, so there are 2 grapes. There are three times as many lemon candies as grape, so that means the tin has $2 \times 3 = 6$ lemon candies. So the bag has 1 cherry, 2 grape, and 6 lemon candies. Next, a number of apple candies equal to the number of cherry candies is added. That means 1 apple candy is added, and the tin has $1 + 2 + 6 + 1 = 10$ candies total. 6 of the 10 are lemon, so the probability of selecting a lemon is $\frac{6}{10} = \frac{3}{5}$.

Choice F is way too low. There are 10 candies from which to choose, so the probability of any single outcome is $\frac{1}{10}$. Choice G is the probability of selecting an apple candy (or the probability of selecting a cherry candy). Choice H is the probability of selecting a grape candy. Choice K is the probability of selecting a lemon candy *before* adding the apple candy to the mix.

59. **The correct answer is B.** Let's get the total inches for each type of wire. Two 15 foot wires are $2 \times 15 = 30$ feet, which converts to $30 \times 12 = 360$ inches. Four 3.5 foot wires are $4 \times 3.5 = 14$ feet, which converts to $14 \times 12 = 168$ inches. And the last two wires are $2 \times 8 = 16$ inches. Now add up the inches: $360 + 168 + 16 = 544$ inches of wire per speaker. 544 inches per speaker $\times$ 9 speakers = 4,896 inches. That's the total amount of wire needed. At a cost of $0.031 per inch, the job will require $4,896 \times \$0.031 = \$151.776$, or about \$152. Choice A is likely the result of an arithmetic error. Choice C is the number of inches in four 3.5-foot wires. Choice D is the number of inches in two 15-foot wires. Choice E is the number of inches per speaker.

60. **The correct answer is F.** How can you have two consecutive heads but not three? The first two tosses could be heads and the third could be tails. Also, the last two tosses could be heads while the first is tails. Those are the only ways to achieve the desired outcome. So what are the probabilities? For the first desired outcome, you need heads, heads, tails. The probability of that outcome is $\frac{1}{2} \times \frac{1}{2} \times \frac{1}{2} = \frac{1}{8}$. There's a one out of two chance of getting the outcome we want on each toss, so the chance of getting all three outcomes in a row is $\frac{1}{2} \times \frac{1}{2} \times \frac{1}{2}$. That's not the answer though. You could also get the tails, heads, heads outcome. This too has a $\frac{1}{2} \times \frac{1}{2} \times \frac{1}{2} = \frac{1}{8}$ probability. Since either outcome is acceptable, you add the probabilities: $\frac{1}{8} + \frac{1}{8} = \frac{2}{8} = \frac{1}{4}$.

For choice G, you included the outcome in which the two heads were not consecutive, namely HTH, but this does not satisfy the criterion. Choice H is the probability of getting HHT, but you forgot about THH. Choice J is too high; there are only two of 8 possible outcomes that satisfy the criterion. Choice K is the probability of the complement of the desired event.

READING

1.	D	11.	D	21.	B	31.	C
2.	F	12.	J	22.	H	32.	F
3.	D	13.	C	23.	B	33.	B
4.	H	14.	H	24.	J	34.	G
5.	A	15.	B	25.	C	35.	A
6.	J	16.	G	26.	H	36.	J
7.	B	17.	B	27.	D	37.	C
8.	G	18.	H	28.	J	38.	G
9.	C	19.	B	29.	B	39.	D
10.	H	20.	J	30.	F	40.	F

1. **The correct answer is D.** If you were to replace the word *object* in line 10 with "purpose," it would still make sense, so choice D is the likeliest answer. Choices A and B have the same meaning, so they probably cancel each other out, and since neither makes sense in the context of the sentence, they are clearly wrong. Choice C does not make sense in context either.

2. **The correct answer is F.** When his boss asks him to compare the sheet, Bartleby merely says, "I prefer not to." He gives no real reason for refusing the task, so there is no reason to reach the conclusions in choices G, H, or J.

3. **The correct answer is D.** The opening paragraph of the passage makes it clear that Bartleby has been working in the office for a while, so you can eliminate choice A. If Bartleby is in the middle of doing his own work, he clearly stops doing it when his boss asks him to compare the sheet, so choice C is incorrect. In fact, the boss stops insisting Bartleby compare the sheet after the third time Bartleby says he would prefer not to do it. Therefore, choice B can be eliminated and choice D can be confirmed as the correct answer.

4. **The correct answer is H.** After Aunt Polly confirms that Tom is only faking having a sore tooth, she says, "Tom, I love you so, and you seem to try every way you can to break my old heart with your outrageousness," which expresses loving exasperation. The love she expresses makes choice H a better answer than choice F. She doesn't even yell at Tom, so she hardly reacts with terrifying scorn (choice G). Since she expresses some emotion, it would be inaccurate to say she reacts with incredible boredom (choice J).

5. **The correct answer is A.** In the passage, Tom does not want to go to school, and the author states that Tom feels that going to school is like being in "captivity and fetters," which suggests something jail-like. The phrase is

not meant literally, so choice B does not explain why the author uses it. There is no evidence that Tom does not want to go to school because he is claustrophobic, or has a fear of confining spaces (choice C). He does not seem to be very fearful at all, so choice D is not the best answer.

6. **The correct answer is J.** Sid seems to truly believe Tom is in pain and expresses true concern when he asks Aunt Polly to help Tom, so choice J is the best answer. That also means that choice F is incorrect. Tom does not force Sid to tell Aunt Polly that Tom is in pain, so there is no reason to conclude that choice G is correct. Also Sid does not seem to recognize that Tom is only faking having a sore tooth, so choice H is unlikely.

7. **The correct answer is B.** In Passage A, Bartleby does not want to do his job, and in Passage B, Tom Sawyer does not want to go to school, so choice B is the best answer. Only Bartleby works in an office, so you can eliminate choice A. You can eliminate choice C since only Tom Sawyer is trying to fool a relative. Bartleby's behavior confuses his boss, but Tom's aunt knows exactly what her nephew is trying to do, so choice D does not describe the main idea of both passages.

8. **The correct answer is G.** When Bartleby's boss asks him to do a task he does not want to do, Bartleby states "I'd prefer not to" clearly. When Tom Sawyer has to go to school but does not want to, he tries to trick his aunt by pretending he has a sore tooth. Bartleby's refusal to do his job may make him seem lazy, but the first paragraph of the passage contradicts this notion, so you can eliminate choice F. The fact that Bartleby states his position clearly eliminates choice H. He also shows no signs of regret, so choice J is wrong too.

Answer Keys and Explanations

9. **The correct answer is C.** A nonconformist is someone who refuses to do what society expects of him or her. Society expects workers like Bartleby to do their jobs and young boys like Tom Sawyer to go to school, yet they both refuse to accept those expectations. However, to say they are lawbreakers (choice A) is an extreme and inaccurate conclusion. As a pair of nonconformists, Bartleby and Tom Sawyer are the opposite of followers (choice B). While Tom is somewhat clever, neither he nor Bartleby can really be described as a genius, so choice D is not the most sensible answer.

10. **The correct answer is H.** Bartleby's refusal to do his job takes his boss by surprise, yet Aunt Polly realizes that Tom is faking a sore tooth to get out of school, so she must expect this kind of behavior from him. Bartleby's boss and Aunt Polly are bothered by Bartleby and Tom Sawyer's respective behavior, so choice F does not explain how they are different. Bartleby's boss is probably as professional as he can be under the circumstances, but Aunt Polly is not in a work-place situation in Passage B, so describing her as "unprofessional" is not appropriate. Therefore, choice G is not the best answer. Bartleby's boss allows Bartleby to shirk his office duties, so he is hardly a firm and controlling boss. Aunt Polly is not particularly meek or easygoing, so choice J is incorrect.

11. **The correct answer is D.** Given the passage's emphasis (beginning in the first paragraph but sustained throughout) on Yoga's importance as both an ancient way of a life and an orthodox philosophy, choices B and C cannot be correct here. Looking back at the first paragraph, the author describes Yoga as having substance *in addition to* its value as a popular exercise regimen, which logically implies that choice A cannot be correct either. Only choice D is not mentioned in the article as a legitimate descriptor of Yoga.

12. **The correct answer is J.** This question requires you to synthesize some of the basic information from paragraphs one and two, where diet and exercise as well as letting go of the material world, are mentioned in reference to achieving spiritual union with the divine. Statement III is not derived directly from the passage, which never mentions adopting a life of poverty in order to reach that union; therefore, you can eliminate choice H. Statements I and II are both mentioned in the first two paragraphs, so you can eliminate choices F and G in favor of choice J, the most complete answer.

13. **The correct answer is C.** Look back at the passage to see how "aspirant" is used in context. The last sentence of the second paragraph tells us in the parenthetical clause that the "aspirant" in Yoga is one who "aims towards a more elevated state of being." Neither choice A nor choice B fits in with the passage's contextual definition of the "aspirant." However, choice C does match this definition, since "higher quality of existence" is simply another way of saying "elevated state of being." There is no evidence for choice D; raja-yoga is mentioned in the fourth paragraph.

14. **The correct answer is H.** The third paragraph explains the eight stages of Yoga, so looking back to that paragraph is the quickest and safest way to answer this question. Statement I is true (the fifth stage is one of sensory preparation); Statement II is also true (the last three stages are internal); Statement III is not true (there are two stages, not four, of ethical preparation). Therefore, you can eliminate choice J. Choices F and G each fail to acknowledge one of the true statements.

15. **The correct answer is B.** Refer back to the final paragraph of the passage, which tells us about Yoga's reception in the West. According to that paragraph, choices A and C are incorrect. Choice D is not mentioned as an option in the passage. Choice B is mentioned as the most likely to appeal to Western practitioners of Yoga.

16. **The correct answer is G.** For vocabulary-in-context questions, be sure to go back and reread the part of the passage where the word is used. In this case, choice H is a distortion of the description of the "ecstatics," which tells us that they are mystical figures, not religious fundamentalists. Choices F and J are not directly mentioned in the passage. Within the context of the passage, only choice G is completely correct.

17. **The correct answer is B.** To answer this inference question, go back to the very last paragraph where the history of Yoga in the West is discussed. There, the passage states that although "…instruction emphasizing both the physical and spiritual benefits of Yoga techniques was available … many people in the West regard Yoga as little more than a low-intensity workout and thereby fail to benefit from some of its less obvious benefits." The author does not seem to think that Westerners have a full appreciation for Yoga's philosophical aspects, indicated by choice A, but neither does the author seem to think that the West has no appreciation at all for these aspects, as in choice D. As this is an article about Yoga's rich and complex history, it is not logical that the author would believe choice C,

that Westerners have no need for understanding more about Yoga. So the only logical inference is choice B.

18. **The correct answer is H.** The last sentence of the second paragraph states than an individual who can "control and suppress the mundane activities of his or her mind … will be able to enter a state of deep concentration that results in a blissful, ecstatic union with the ultimate reality." Of the options, choice H is the only one not directly referred to in the passage; choices F, G, and J are all mentioned in the passage.

19. **The correct answer is B.** The first sentence of the third paragraph states that "Yoga's practical aspects seem to play the most significant role, even more so than its intellectual content." Choices A, C, and D all refer to other important aspects of Yoga mentioned in the article, but nowhere else is one aspect referred to as more important or significant than any of the others.

20. **The correct answer is J.** The second sentence of the third paragraph describes a text dating from the second century BC. This text, the *Yoga-sutra*, was composed over a long period of time by a man, or more likely several men, who wrote under the name Patanjali. Choice H gives the text's correct name but does not mention the name assigned to the writer or writers; choice G gives the correct author name but not the correct name of the text. Choice F is not referred to in the passage.

21. **The correct answer is B.** The origins of bluegrass music are discussed in the second paragraph. Gospel music and European dances are mentioned in the paragraph. However, European classical music is not. Therefore, you can eliminate choices C and D. Choice A fails to acknowledge both of the influences of bluegrass music mentioned in the passage.

22. **The correct answer is H.** The answer to a question such as this tests your understanding of the author's purpose. Be wary of answer choices that provide the author with a strong opinion in this mostly scholarly passage. For example, choice F is incorrect because the author never gives an opinion about what should happen in bluegrass music, only what has happened in the past. Similarly, choice G is incorrect because while the author does mention other musical styles in describing the origins of bluegrass, he never compares the quality of the musicians. Regarding the influence of other musical styles, choice J is incorrect because the author does not emphasize the importance of one originating style over another. Choice H is correct because the author mentions several times how radio, television, and

movies brought bluegrass music to national attention; therefore, one could infer that without these media outlets, bluegrass would be a localized phenomenon.

23. **The correct answer is B.** The first sentence provides a definition of a "truly American art form": a blend of influences and traditions. That leads to choice D as the correct answer. Acoustic instruments are not mentioned in the first paragraph, so choice A is incorrect. Do not be fooled by choice C—the author says that bluegrass speaks to a broad audience, but he does not mention the feelings of the musicians. Choice D is incorrect because it is not stated in the first paragraph, and it is contradicted by the rest of the information in the passage.

24. **The correct answer is J.** The Monroe brothers are discussed in the fourth paragraph, but the answer is in the fifth paragraph, which describes the significance of Bill Monroe and the Blue Grass Boys. The breakup led to the formation of this new musical group that eventually created bluegrass as we know it today. This makes choice J correct. Choices F, G, and H are not indicated by the passage.

25. **The correct answer is C.** The sentence containing the word *hardscrabble* ends with "geographic isolation and economic hardship." These are negative things, so eliminate answer choices with a positive tone: choices A and D. Between choices B and C, choice C is more representative of the troubles of the musicians. Their lives were more distressed (or unsettled) than uneventful.

26. **The correct answer is H.** The fifth paragraph covers the contributions of Bill Monroe. The paragraph says that Monroe's choice of instruments became the standard for bluegrass music, making Statement I correct. The paragraph also states that Monroe sent the sounds of bluegrass to the American public by way of radio, which makes Statement III correct. There is no evidence of Statement II, so choices G and J cannot be correct answers. Choice F fails to acknowledge both correct statements; only choice H does without including an incorrect statement.

27. **The correct answer is D.** The answer to this question must be broad enough to encapsulate the entire passage. Eliminate answer choices that are too narrow. This includes choice A, which only covers the tough lives of early bluegrass musicians, and choice B, which only covers the accomplishments of Monroe's band. Choice C incorporates a larger swatch of the passage, but it still ignores the early paragraphs about the origins

of the music. Choice D is correct because it is general enough to include the entire passage—it is also the subject of the first sentence, which sets up the rest of the text.

28. **The correct answer is J.** By the end of this passage, you should be well-aware of its purpose: to provide an overview of the history of bluegrass music, or choice J. Choice F is far too broad, and choice H is far too narrow. The author probably does enjoy bluegrass music, but choice G does not "accurately and completely" represent the passage—this is a brief description, not a personal essay.

29. **The correct answer is B.** You can locate each of the statements and find the order, but go about it in a strategic way. Because the word *Dobro* is easy to scan for, and because two of the answer choices start with Statement I, research Statement I first. The Dobro does not appear until the last third of the passage, so eliminate choices A and D. Now all you have to do is find out if Bill Monroe came before the name "bluegrass music." Bill Monroe essentially created the style, but the name "bluegrass" did not come into common use until the 1950s with the help of The Foggy Mountain Boys. Therefore, choice C is incorrect and choice B is correct.

30. **The correct answer is F.** Scan the passage for the mid-1940s, and you will find yourself in the paragraph about the banjo player Earl Scruggs. His main contribution to bluegrass was a three-finger picking style, which makes choice F correct. Choices G and H occur later in the history of bluegrass, and choice J is true of the very earliest forms of the music.

31. **The correct answer is C.** Although a star with a mass that is more than 10 times greater than that of the sun can become a black hole, not all stars this massive become black holes, only stars more than 40 times the mass of the sun, so choice A is incorrect. All stars more than 10 times the mass of the sun go supernovae, however, so choice C is correct. Red giants (choice B) are stars that were once the size of our own sun. The same is true of white dwarfs (choice D) are stars at their final stage of life.

32. **The correct answer is F.** The passage discusses how gas pressure from the nuclear reaction 4H = He + energy balances gravity and describes how a star begins to collapse when nuclear reactions no longer produce pressure to counteract gravity, so choice F is the best answer. Choice G might seem like a possible answer because dying medium-sized stars, red giants, do increase their temperature to respond to gravity, but

the question reads "main sequence stars," not merely "medium-sized stars on the main sequence." The passage states that all stars, until they begin to die, produce the same chemical reaction and balance gravity against gas pressure in the same way, which makes choices H and J inaccurate.

33. **The correct answer is B.** The final paragraph discusses the origin of the heavy elements iron, silicon, and oxygen, all of which appear on Earth but are not believed to have existed at the beginning of the universe. The paragraph explains why supernovae are the possible cause of the heavy elements. Of all the choices, choice B is the only one that communicates all of this information. Choices A and C are not true: the passage states that only more massive stars can produce heavy elements and expel them in supernovae. Choice D is accurate, but represents only a small part of what the paragraph states about the significance of massive stars and supernovae.

34. **The correct answer is G.** The word *speculatively* appears at the head of the sentence about how the elements from supernovae explosions might have been incorporated into the composition of the earth. You can therefore assume that it has something to do with this subject. Process of elimination is the best way to answer the question. The author states for a fact earlier in the passage that four hydrogen atoms burn to create helium, that the sun is a medium-sized star, and that supernovae happen. She does not say anything about the earth's composition, however, until that sentence. It seems likely, therefore, that the earth's composition is a matter for speculation, but that the other possibilities in choices F, H, and J are actual facts.

35. **The correct answer is A.** This question requires you to think carefully about what the author states in the third and fourth paragraphs about main sequence stars. All stars are on the main sequence until they begin to die; this is where they differ. Only medium-sized stars become white dwarfs; only stars 10 times more massive than the sun become supernovae. Therefore, not all stars on the main sequence can be both white dwarfs and supernovae and any answer choice that includes statements II and/or III can be eliminated—that means choices B, C, and D. The only statement that is true is Statement I; choice A is the correct answer.

36. **The correct answer is J.** The fourth paragraph discusses the fate of a medium-sized star: it first becomes a red giant, and then a white dwarf. The author stated elsewhere that the sun is a medium-sized star; therefore, the sun will become a red giant, then shrink to a white

dwarf. She also indicates that no star can stay on the main sequence forever; therefore, you can eliminate choice F. She states that only massive stars can become supernovae or black holes, so choices G and H cannot be correct.

37. **The correct answer is C.** The fifth paragraph discusses supernovae: explosions that occur when a star is 10–40 times more massive than the sun. Carbon by itself doesn't indicate anything at all spectacular or violent about a star, so choice A is incorrect. You can conclude that your answer should have nothing to do with black holes, because black holes occur when a star is more than 40 times the mass of the sun, which makes choice D incorrect. You already know, from the fourth paragraph, that only medium-sized stars fade to white dwarfs, so you can eliminate choice B. Choice C is the only remaining possibility.

38. **The correct answer is G.** The sixth paragraph discusses the fact that black holes occur after a star more massive than 40 times the mass of the sun dies, so Statement I cannot be correct and choices F, H, and J can be eliminated. The paragraph does state that black holes are always collapsing on themselves, so Statement II is true. The paragraph also states that black holes form "instead of a neutron star," so a neutron star cannot be the same as a black hole and Statement III is not correct. Only choice G acknowledges the one correct statement and lacks all incorrect ones.

39. **The correct answer is D.** The passage never states exactly what a neutron star is, only that the most massive of massive stars, instead of becoming neutron stars, collapse into black holes. You can reason from this that the next largest category of stars, the ones 10–40 times the mass of the sun, form neutron stars after they have exploded in supernovae. Since this is part of a star's death, choice D is the correct answer. Since the passage mainly discusses the death of stars, choice D would have been the better guess, even if you weren't quite sure about the correct answer.

40. **The correct answer is F.** The second paragraph discusses the birth of stars out of a giant cloud of dust, and states that the remainder of this dust forms the planets. Choice G might distract you: "the remnants of neutron stars" could be interpreted as the supernova explosion that sent the heavy elements into the sky, but this possibility should be ruled out because it is not explicit enough. The ACT will not expect you to engage in this much reasoning. Choice H can also be eliminated; nothing is said about the outer layers of red giants. Likewise, it is difficult to see how white dwarfs becoming faint could create planets, so choice J is wrong.

SCIENCE

1.	C	11.	D	21.	C	31.	C
2.	G	12.	F	22.	G	32.	F
3.	C	13.	C	23.	A	33.	C
4.	F	14.	J	24.	H	34.	F
5.	B	15.	B	25.	A	35.	D
6.	H	16.	F	26.	G	36.	F
7.	B	17.	C	27.	A	37.	B
8.	G	18.	F	28.	F	38.	F
9.	B	19.	D	29.	B	39.	A
10.	J	20.	G	30.	J	40.	H

1. **The correct answer is C.** The meter reading is lower in setup B than in setup A. This means that less light is striking the photoelectric cell in setup B. This would be true only if the medium in which the microorganisms are growing in setup B is more optically dense due to the greater number of microorganisms in this setup. Hence, there has been more growth in setup B than in setup A. Choice A is incorrect because the meter readings are not equal in both setups, and these readings measure the growth of microorganisms. Choice B is incorrect because the data indicate that the opposite is correct. Choice D is incorrect because a comparison of meter readings in setups A and B indicates that something is occurring in one of the setups, presumably the growth of microorganisms, because the light transmission through the medium is being altered.

2. **The correct answer is G.** Reading across from the y-axis at an optical density value of 0.9, the curve intersects at a cell number of 4.0×10^8. Choice F is not correct because this is the cell number for an optical density of 0.8, not 0.9. Choice H is off by a factor of 10. Choice J shows the cell number for an optical density of 1.0, not 0.9.

3. **The correct answer is C.** The curve is rising very gradually and flattening out between cell counts of 10.0×10^8 and 12.0×10^8. The trend of the curve indicates that a cell count of 15.0×10^8 should coincide with an optical density of greater than 1.3 but less than 1.5. Choice A is incorrect because it would indicate a fall in the curve, which is counter to the trend of the curve. Choice B is incorrect because the curve is still rising at a value of 12.0×10^8 cells, which is already equivalent to an optical density of 1.3. Choice D would indicate a reversal of the trend to a steeper curve. There is no evidence for such an event.

4. **The correct answer is F.** The key word in the question is *immediate*. You would expect an increase in the growth of microorganisms due to an increase in nutrients. You would also expect a decrease in optical density due to a dilution of the broth. However, the *immediate* effect would be a decrease in optical density followed later by an increase in the growth of microorganisms. Choice G is incorrect because an increase in optical density results from an increase in the growth of microorganisms, which would not be *immediate*. Choice H is incorrect because there is no data to support any conclusion indicating by what factor growth might increase due to an increase in media. Choice J is not correct because, in general, an increase in food supply promotes increases in the population of any living thing, not the reverse.

5. **The correct answer is B.** It is reasonable to assume that the graph flattens due to limits of space and available nutrients. These are apparently the only independent variables in the experiment. Thus, either or both factors must be limiting the growth of microorganisms. Choice A is not correct because neither the graph nor the experimental setups describe a time-growth relationship. In other words, there is no data upon which to base the conclusion represented by choice A. Choice C is incorrect. Density can be thought of as "thickness." Increased growth produces a thicker medium that inhibits the passage of light. Hence, optical density increases with cell growth. They are *directly* proportional, not *inversely* proportional. Choice D cannot be concluded from the available data, so you can eliminate this choice as well.

Practice Test 4—ANSWERS

6. **The correct answer is H.** The data table shows that the average mass of a chicken egg is 80 g, and the average pore area of a chicken egg is 4.0 mm². These values are the coordinates for point 6. Choice F is incorrect because the coordinates for point 4 are 27 g and 0.7 mm², which are those of the pigeon. You can use similar analyses to eliminate choices G and J, points 5 and 7, which respectively represent the coordinates of the shearwater and the skua.

7. **The correct answer is B.** If you draw a vertical line upward from 500 g on the *x*-axis, it will intersect the graph at a point whose value for pore area is 40 mm². If you chose choice A or C, you may have incorrectly identified how values vary on the *x*-axis. Choice A gives a pore area of 1.5 mm² for an egg mass of 50 g, not 500 g, while choice C gives a pore area of 750 mm² for an egg mass of 5,000 g, not 500 g. Choice D can be eliminated because a pore area greater than 750 mm² would be found in a bird whose egg mass is greater than 5,000 g, not at 500 g.

8. **The correct answer is G.** To find the answer, you must compare the average egg mass to the average pore area. For the rhea, the ratio is 820:5.0, or 164. Choices F, H, and J are 15, 70, and 7.5, respectively. These ratios are all less than that of the rhea.

9. **The correct answer is B.** The slope of the graph increases from bottom left to top right. This is characteristic of a direct relationship between two factors. As one rises, the other rises. From the graph, you can spot that choice A is wrong. For the relationship to be inverse, the graph would have to slope from top left to bottom right, which is not the case. Choice C is incorrect because a straight line graph always implies a linear relationship. If you chose D, reread the question. Choice D may be true, but it cannot be drawn from the data provided.

10. **The correct answer is J.** In diffusion, gases move from areas of higher concentration to areas of lower concentration. As a bird embryo develops, it uses up oxygen in its immediate environment—the inside of the shell. This lowers the oxygen concentration inside the cell compared with the oxygen concentration outside the shell. The imbalance causes oxygen to move from outside the shell to inside the shell. If the concentrations inside and outside the shell are equal, as in choice F, there will be no net movement of a gas in *either* direction. So choice F is incorrect. Choice G is incorrect because in diffusion, gases do not move from areas of lower concentration to areas of higher concentration. The same holds true for choice H.

11. **The correct answer is D.** In the experiment depicted in Figure 1, gravity and root structures are constants. In the experiment depicted in Figure 2, gravity is a constant, but root structure is not a constant because the root cap has been removed from one root. In the experiment depicted in Figure 3, gravity and root structure are constants. The independent variable is the gel block filled with auxin. Thus, the only factor that is constant in all three experiments is gravity. Choice A is incorrect because the root caps are not intact in the experiments depicted in Figures 2 and 3. Choice B is also not correct because the root caps were not removed in the experiment depicted in Figure 1. Choice C is incorrect because auxin was a factor only in the experiment depicted in Figure 3.

12. **The correct answer is F.** Gravitropism is a movement in response to the stimulus of gravity. A movement in the direction of gravity, that is, downward, is positive gravitropism. You can eliminate choice G if you are clear about the meaning of *positive* and *negative* as they modify tropisms. "Positive" indicates a movement toward a stimulus. "Negative" indicates a movement away from a stimulus. Choice H can be eliminated because no light source is shown in Figure 1. Thus, phototropism is not being tested. Choice J is incorrect because gravitropism is a response that is being shown.

13. **The correct answer is C.** The independent variable in the experiment depicted in Figure 2 is the root cap. The removal of the root cap eliminated the gravitropic behavior of the root. Thus, gravitropic behavior is related to the root cap. Choice A is incorrect for the reason that choice C is correct. The conclusion expressed in choice B cannot be drawn because the root body is not a variable in the experiment depicted. Choice D presents a true statement, but it cannot be concluded from the data presented in Figure 2 because neither root is responding to the force of gravity.

14. **The correct answer is J.** To arrive at this choice, you first have to be clear about the difference between an independent variable and a dependent one. An independent variable is a factor an experimenter changes, or a cause. A dependent variable is the factor that consequently changes, or an effect. Exposing the bottom root to auxin, the independent variable, causes the root to bend downward, the dependent variable. You can eliminate choice F since both root caps have been removed. Root caps are not any sort of variable in the experiment. The same reasoning applied to root bodies can be used to eliminate choice G. Auxin is

causing the change in the roots' behavior. So auxin is the *independent*, not dependent, variable. Eliminate choice H.

15. **The correct answer is B.** It is consistent with the data of the experiments. The first experiment (Figure 1) shows that roots are positively gravitropic. The second experiment (Figure 2) shows that the root cap plays a role in the gravitropism of roots. The third experiment (Figure 3) implies that auxin in a root cap contributes to a root's positive gravitropic behavior. Eliminate choice A because it runs counter to the evidence presented in Figures 1 and 3. Roots grow downward (positive gravitropism), not upward (negative gravitropism). Choice C runs counter to the evidence in Figure 3. The bottom root, which is stimulated by auxin, is exhibiting positive gravitropism, not the reverse. Careful examination of Figures 1 and 2 leads to the conclusion that the root cap, not the root body, is involved in gravitropism. Therefore you can eliminate choice D.

16. **The correct answer is F.** To arrive at this choice, imagine a seesaw. If the weight on both sides is even, the seesaw stays level. But if weight is added to one side, that side goes down. Similarly, the elongation of the top layer of cells in choice F compared with the shorter dimensions of the bottom layer of cells will force the root to bend downward, or in a positive gravitropic direction. You can eliminate choices G and J because in both cases, the cells in each layer are identical in size, which should not produce a change in the direction of growth of the root. Choice H is incorrect because it would result in the root bending upward, or exhibiting negative gravitropism.

17. **The correct answer is C.** Maggots appeared on the meat only in the jars to which flies had access. Choice A can be eliminated because maggots did not arise from the meat in the sealed jars. The conclusion suggested by choice B cannot be reached because there is air in both the experimental and control jars, although no *new* air is allowed to enter the sealed jars. Eliminate choice D because the experiment implies that maggots are related to flies.

18. **The correct answer is F.** The jars of the experimental group in the first experiment were sealed tightly so that no new air could enter. The jars in the second experiment were covered with gauze through which air could enter. Choice G is incorrect because all the jars in both experiments contained meat. Choice H can be eliminated because flies were not allowed to reach the meat in the jars of the experimental groups of both experiments. Choice J should not be considered because

maggots did not appear in the jars of the experimental groups in either experiment.

19. **The correct answer is D.** By allowing new air to enter the jars of the second experiment and showing that even under these conditions maggots did not arise from the decaying meat, the notion that a continuous supply of air was necessary for abiogenesis was refuted. Choice A is not correct because proponents of abiogenesis never suggested that flies gave rise to maggots. On the contrary, they suggested that decaying meat, not flies, gave rise to maggots. Choice B is incorrect for similar reasons. Proponents of abiogenesis did not connect flies and maggots in any way. You should eliminate choice C because it states the opposite of what the proponents of abiogenesis suggested.

20. **The correct answer is G.** Needham believed that heating the broth would kill all living things in the broth. When such living things later appeared in the broth, he concluded that they arose spontaneously from the broth. Since air was not a variable in the experiment, the conclusion postulated in choice F cannot be drawn. Choice H is contrary to Needham's assumption that heating the broth killed microorganisms. Choice J is contrary to the experimental evidence, which showed that microorganisms could seemingly arise from boiled broth.

21. **The correct answer is C.** Both experimental setups were essentially identical. They differed primarily in the amount of time the broth was heated. Eliminate choice A because the broth used by Spallanzani was identical to that used by Needham. Since the microorganisms in both experiments were a mix of those ordinarily found in air, the characteristics of the organisms in both experiments were essentially the same. So eliminate choice B. Choice D can be eliminated because neither experiment measured or identified the growth characteristics of microorganisms.

22. **The correct answer is G.** Spallanzani's experiment showed that heating a broth for a relatively long period of time and then sealing the flask prevented microorganisms from reproducing. The contents of the flask did not contain living things. However, when the flask was left unsealed, living things entered and reproduced in the broth. The results support the concept of biogenesis. Microorganisms arise from other microorganisms. Choice F is contradicted by the experimental results. Microorganisms did not arise spontaneously in the heated and sealed flask. Choice H is incorrect because only living things can reproduce, and that is

what occurred in the unsealed flask. The experiments provide no evidence to support the contention that broth is an organism. Eliminate choice J.

23. **The correct answer is A.** Air was free to move back into the broth in the swan-necked flask. Air also moved freely into the flask that had a straight neck. However, microorganisms grew only in the broth in the straight-necked flask. This can be explained if microorganisms riding on dust particles become trapped in the downward bend of the swan-necked flask. The air enters the broth, but the microorganism-carrying dust does not. Choice B can be eliminated because air free of dust particles entered the swan-necked flask but did not result in the growth of microorganisms in the broth. Choice C is incorrect because no microorganisms arose spontaneously in the broth of the swan-necked flask. Choice D is also incorrect since the broth in the straight-necked flask was heated, but microorganisms grew in it anyway.

24. **The correct answer is H.** Table 2 shows that Saturn and Uranus formed at 10 and 20 AU, respectively. According to the graph, these distances correspond to temperatures lower than 250 K. Earth, however, formed at a distance of 1 AU, which corresponds to a temperature near 2,000 K. At the distances of Saturn and Uranus, the nebula was cold enough for gases and ices to collect. Choice F is incorrect because nothing in the passage indicates that these planets formed more slowly. Choice G is also incorrect because nothing in the passage indicates they melted. Choice J contradicts the graph, which indicates that these planets formed at lower temperatures.

25. **The correct answer is A.** Because Mercury formed in a portion of the solar nebula where it was so hot that only metals could condense, Mercury probably contains mostly metals. Choice B cannot be correct because the solar nebula was too hot for much rocky material to condense. Choices C and D are not likely to be correct because the nebula was far too hot at the distance of Mercury for ice to condense.

26. **The correct answer is G.** Mars formed farther from the sun, so it probably contains more rock and less iron than Earth. Choice F would be the best choice for a planet that formed much closer to the sun. Choice H suggests there would be no iron, but if rock materials condense, so would iron. Choice J would be correct for a planet much farther from the sun. At 1.5 AU, the solar nebula is too hot for ices to condense.

27. **The correct answer is A.** This question requires you to use data from Table 2 and the graph. The table tells you that Jupiter formed at 5 AU. According to the graph, 5 AU correlates with a temperature of around 300 K. Choice A provides a range between 100 K and 500 K, so this choice is correct. Choices B, C, and D do not provide proper ranges.

28. **The correct answer is F.** According to the solar nebula hypothesis, metals would have condensed closest to the sun, rocks further out, then water ice, and then ammonia ice. So the density of the planets should decrease with distance from the sun, choice F. Choice G is reversed. Nothing in the passage indicates the kind of variation indicated by choices H or J.

29. **The correct answer is B.** The simple math equation is $13.1\ eV - 10.2\ eV = 2.9\ eV$. Choice A is the value for a transition from $n = 3$ to $n = 2$. Choice C is the value for a transition from $n = 6$ to $n = 2$. Choice D is the value for a transition from $n = 5$ to $n = 1$.

30. **The correct answer is J.** The Lyman series falls between 91 nm and 122 nm, which corresponds to the ultraviolet region of the electromagnetic spectrum. Choices F, G, and H are incorrect because they describe other regions of the spectrum.

31. **The correct answer is C.** There are a total of six different transitions. According to the information provided, an excited electron may transition to any lower energy level. If that energy level is not the lowest, it can undergo still other transitions and emit photons with other energies. The following transitions are possible: 4 to 1, 4 to 2, 4 to 3, 3 to 1, 3 to 2, and 2 to 1. So choice C is the correct choice. Choice A neglects transitions to intermediate states. Choice B allows for only one intermediate state, but more are possible. Choice D may have resulted from counting some transitions twice. It does not matter how an electron gets to $n = 2$; it still emits the same energy in transitioning to $n = 1$.

32. **The correct answer is F.** Energy and wavelength are inversely related, which means that as one increases, the other decreases. The relationship, however, is not linear. Choice G shows energy decreasing as wavelength increases, but it shows a linear relationship. Choice H represents direct variation, not inverse. In this case, both values either rise or fall together. Choice J represents exponential variation, not inverse variation.

33. **The correct answer is C.** This transition involves 2.9 eV (13.1 eV – 10.2 eV). This corresponds most closely to the H_γ line, which is listed as 2.86 eV. Choice A would involve 12.1 eV. Choice B would involve 2.6 eV, which relates more closely to the H_β line. Choice D would involve 1.1 eV, which would be in the infrared region.

34. **The correct answer is F.** This value relates to H_α, which is near the red end of the visible spectrum. Choice G is incorrect because the H_β line is blue-green. Choice H is incorrect because the H_γ is blue, and choice J is incorrect because H_δ is violet.

35. **The correct answer is D.** Climate involves temperature extremes as well as temperature averages, so a statement about temperature records refers to climate. Choice A is a description of the short-term variation of temperature, which is a statement about weather. Choice B is also incorrect. Although the prediction is for two weeks, climate involves much longer variation. Choice C is a short-term prediction; hence, it refers to weather.

36. **The correct answer is F.** According to the table, the locations with the most extreme variations in temperature are at the northernmost and southernmost latitudes. The only choice that corresponds is choice F, the North Pole. Choice G is incorrect because the equator has the least variation in temperature. Choices H and J both describe large regions that include areas of high variation as well as areas of low variation.

37. **The correct answer is B.** According to the passage, oceans moderate temperature extremes, so extreme variations in temperature suggest an absence of oceans. This is consistent with the distribution of land masses on Earth (Figure 3). The northern hemisphere is dominated by land, while the southern hemisphere is dominated by ocean. There is not enough evidence for choice A—the data does not indicate mountainous regions versus flatlands. Choice C is also incorrect. The passage makes no mention of a lack of cold air in the southern hemisphere, and the South Pole is one of the coldest places on Earth. Choice D is incorrect because the passage makes no reference to the distance of Earth from the sun.

38. **The correct answer is F.** Huron is located far from any ocean or other large body of water. Choice G is incorrect because Huron is far from the Gulf of Mexico. Galveston is on the Gulf of Mexico. The information in the passage suggests that more extreme temperature variations are found far from any ocean. Choice H makes a correct statement: Huron is much farther north. However, this cannot be the explanation for the temperature variation. Choice J is incorrect for a similar reason. Huron may be at a higher elevation, but the information in the passage suggests that distance from the ocean is the factor to be considered in relation to temperature variation.

39. **The correct answer is A.** Winds across Lake Michigan would moderate the temperature variation in Grand Haven, making it warmer in winter and cooler in summer. Choice B has these two reversed. Because of winds, Milwaukee, not Grand Haven, has cooler winters and warmer summers. Choice C is only partially correct. To moderate the temperature, the effect of the lake must be to produce a cooler summer. Choice D is also only partially correct. To moderate the temperature, the effect of the lake must be to produce a warmer winter.

40. **The correct answer is H.** According to the passage, distance from an ocean or other large body of water is what determines extremes of temperature variation. Choice F is not a good choice for two reasons. One, El Paso is farther south. Also, it is nearness to water, not latitude, that moderates temperature extremes. Choice G is also a poor choice. El Paso is south of San Francisco, but the primary reason for the larger temperature variation is distance from water. Choice J cannot be correct because El Paso is not near the ocean.

Sample Essay: Score 1

Ideas and Analysis:	Score = 1
Development and Support:	Score = 1
Organization:	Score = 1
Language Use and Conventions:	Score = 1

Football is the best sport ever and I like baseball and basketball too but football is the best one by far. I'm going to keep playing even if I don't make it to the pros so why should I stop if I still get my homework done and keep doing everything else I need to be doing? Ive never been to a game but I like to go so if I can get tickets I would but I don't know they may cost too expensive and I got other thngs to pay for if I can just watch it on TV, right? Whoever gets hurt should wear a helmet and not be too crazy just to score some touchdowns and make the other team look bad but everyone who stops playing football can just let the rest of us to play and too watch but it shouldn't cost any more money than most people can afford to spend and that the truth.

Scoring Explanation

Ideas and Analysis: Score = 1

This essay is comprised of disparate ideas that don't address the essay task provided. Rather than an exploration of thoughts pertaining to the future of football and strategies for addressing related safety issues, the writer provides a loose amalgam of ideas on why he or she likes football and will continue to play and watch it (as long as it doesn't get "too expensive"). The result is an unsuccessful essay that falls off-task.

Development and Support: Score = 1

This largely confusing response demonstrates little ability to construct a cohesive argument that stays on topic. There is scant development and support of a clear perspective on the questions posed. There is also no sufficient exploration or on-topic analysis of the ideas that are provided by the writer, resulting in a piece of writing that is more a grouping of weak sentences than a cohesive argument.

Organization: Score = 1

This piece of writing is, at best, a loose and unstructured set of ideas that briefly touch on football (and other sports), with little regard to the topic of safety beyond "whoever gets hurt should wear a helmet and not be too crazy." There is no clear and obvious unifying theme or overarching perspective tying the essay to the given task; overall, it's an ineffective and unsuccessful essay attempt.

Language Use and Conventions: Score = 1

Beyond the deficits in idea development and organization, this essay suffers from numerous grammatical problems, limited word choice, and a weak grasp of standard conventions of English writing. It's clear that minimal effort was given to develop a convincing, nuanced argument; the end result suffers dramatically and is a deficient piece of writing.

Answer Keys and Explanations

SAMPLE ESSAY: SCORE 6

Ideas and Analysis:	Score = 1
Development and Support:	Score = 1
Organization:	Score = 1
Language Use and Conventions:	Score = 1

On and off the athletic fields of America, the debate regarding the dangers of full-contact sports such as football rages on. Professional players, both active and retired, are more vocal about the physical perils and toll the game takes on players during their comparatively brief careers. Concerned parents across the country are thinking twice before allowing their children to play football, for fear of serious injury. Media outlets large and small are giving increased attention to the issue, helping to shape our national debate on this issue: Is football too dangerous? Should it be banned, or should the game change to satisfy the critics? Once posed, we shouldn't ignore these tough questions. And sometimes, tough questions require tough answers.

Should the sport of football be banned? No. Football is inexorably woven into the fabric of American culture, and attempting to ban the game would be an unfair and rash decision to say the least. It can be argued that football is now our primary national pastime, as evidenced by massive TV ratings and revenue generated by the game. Attempting to strip it from our collective hands would only demonstrate our inability to take a measured, careful approach to this issue. A blind, blanket ban on anything deemed somewhat dangerous, including football, stands in diametrical opposition to the tenets of a free and democratic society.

Yes, football is a dangerous sport. Injuries both major and minor, from sprains and concussions to broken bones and life-altering catastrophic trauma, occur at all levels of the game—from the NFL down to pee-wee football and everything in between. We should adopt a careful, phased approach to address this issue. Initially, there should be a collective acknowledgement of the sport's inherent dangers and a strict adherence to all accepted and available safety precautions. The game should simply not be played without the use of appropriate safety equipment. A thorough information campaign should be deployed, so anyone playing the game or interested in playing should be aware of the possible risks. Furthermore, I think a significant portion of the enormous profits generated by football at the professional and college levels should be invested in the exploration and development of enhanced safety equipment for players. We have come far from the days of leather helmets, but there is always room for improvement.

Does the game itself need to change? This question needs to stay at the forefront of our national discussion, and a serious review and exploration of ways to make the game safer needs to occur—even if this entails an alteration of the game's core structure in some way. Perhaps if there's a way to reduce the bone-crunching tackles and brutal pile-ups that occur in defense of a team's end zone, they should be considered and tested.

Anyone who defends football can no longer do so in ignorance. The tragic suicide of former NFL player Junior Seau brought media attention to chronic traumatic encephalopathy (CTE), a disease that occurs from repeated head trauma, which has affected numerous NFL players. We're all aware of the risks. Mature and realistic adults should accept the notion that football, like many facets of modern life, contains risks, and it is our responsibility to address them and do our best to minimize these risks whenever possible.

Take airplane flying for example. It is a mode of transportation with inherent risk, including loss of life, but that doesn't mean we should abandon it altogether. We approach it responsibly and carefully, we follow strict, evolving safety protocols, and we always look for ways to make flying even safer, even if it comes at a cost—whether it be money, time, or convenience. We should approach the sport of football in much the same way.

Informed compromise is often the best approach to any debate, and we cannot let blind devotion to tradition keep us from making progress. Perhaps a restructuring of football will not only make the game safer, but may also make it more enjoyable and accessible to everyone.

Scoring Explanation

Ideas and Analysis: Score = 6

This argument offers an impressive level of insight and analysis regarding the dangers of football and how the debate regarding the safety and future of the game should be handled. The writer calls for a "measured, careful approach" to address the issue, but clearly has considered both sides of the argument—those that defend the sport (arguably "our primary national pastime") and those who demand it to change or be banned ("a serious review and exploration of ways to make the game safer needs to occur")—resulting in a nuanced, effective essay that thoughtfully addresses the essay task.

Development and Support: Score = 6

The essay acknowledges cogent points on both sides of the football debate (football is dangerous but is "inexorably woven into the fabric of American culture"), develops a clear perspective on the topic (a stricter adherence to all safety protocols and a review of the game, with an eye towards making it safer), and makes a compelling argument for a considered yet aggressive march forward to make football safer. Support is provided to lend credence to the writer's argument, and prior research in the field of football-related injuries (chronic traumatic encephalopathy) is mentioned. The in-depth examination of both sides and skillful development and support of the writer's viewpoint leads to an essay that successfully tackles the task at hand.

Organization: Score = 6

This written response displays a strong command of effective essay structure and organization. It begins with a compelling call for action that asserts the seriousness of the topic, but wisely offers fair coverage of both sides of the debate in a clear, streamlined fashion. The writer's point-of-view on the topic is evident, and a sufficient level of support is provided. The writer even chooses to weave in examples of other dangerous activities (flying) that aren't banned but rather are carefully regulated, to help assert his or her concluding plea for a "careful, phased approach" and "informed compromise" to make the sport of football safer for everyone involved.

Language Use and Conventions: Score = 6

The writer displays a firm command of standard English-language use and conventions. The argument is well constructed and grammatically sound and contains a varied array of sentences, transitions, and word choices. The resulting essay is both compelling and effective and capably addresses the task provided.

CHAPTER 16:
SCORING YOUR ACT® PRACTICE TESTS

OVERVIEW

- Scoring Your ACT® Multiple-Choice Questions
- Scoring Your ACT® Writing Essay
- How to Use Your Test Results
- Summing It Up
- Practice Test 1 Scoring Keys
- Practice Test 2 Scoring Keys
- Practice Test 3 Scoring Keys
- Practice Test 4 Scoring Keys
- Writing Test and ELA Scores
- Scale Score Conversion Charts

After you take each ACT practice test in this book, you'll want to assess your score as accurately as possible. This chapter will explain how the ACT calculates your test score and will provide all the information you need to calculate your own score on each practice test. Using this information, you can measure your progress as you go and see where you need the most focus throughout your study plan.

But first, let's take a minute to discuss what the scores mean and how they relate to your official score report. The scores you will want to determine for each practice test (and that will be most prominently displayed on your score report) are the **composite score** and **scale scores**.

Your composite score represents how you performed on the ACT as a whole. Your scale scores represent how you performed in each subject area. Scale subscores, which highlight your specific strengths and weaknesses within each subject area, are also listed on the report.

When a college or university lists its preferred range of ACT scores for admission, it displays the composite score and the subject area scale scores. These are the scores ACT, Inc., reports to you on your official report, to your high school, and to your requested colleges and scholarship agencies.

The goal of scoring your practice tests is to give you an idea of the composite and scale scores you would earn when you take the actual test. It's an important step in gauging your readiness to take the ACT, and it's not that complicated. Let's get started!

SCORING YOUR ACT® MULTIPLE-CHOICE QUESTIONS

We mentioned it before, and it bears repeating here—the ACT test counts *only* the questions you answer correctly. There is *no penalty* for guessing, which means you do not get any points deducted for wrong answers. Hopefully, as you gain a better understanding of how your score will be calculated, you'll be more inclined to make sure you don't leave many (if any) questions blank on test day.

We're going to begin with an overview of how to score your tests. Step-by-step instructions are also included in each scoring section, in case you need a reminder as you go through the process.

RAW SCORES

When scoring your exam, you will begin by counting the number of questions you answered correctly. The questions are assessed on two levels:

1) four ACT subject area tests (English, mathematics, reading, and science), and

2) seven ACT subscore areas (listed in the chart below).

The number of test items you answered correctly within each section is your **raw score** for that section.

ACT Test Layout of Sections and Subsections

Subject Area Tests	No. of Questions	Subscore Areas
English Test	75	• Usage/Mechanics • Rhetorical Skills
Mathematics Test	60	• Pre-Algebra/Elementary Algebra • Intermediate Algebra/Coordinate Geometry • Plane Geometry/Trigonometry
Reading Test	40	• Social Studies/Natural Sciences • Arts/Literature reading skills
Science Test	40	**No scored subsections**

908

Chapter 16
Scoring Your
ACT®
Practice
Tests

Your first step to calculating your score on each ACT test is to figure out your raw score:

1) Take the tests, using the answer sheets provided.

2) Review your answers using the answer key and explanations at the end of every test.

3) Using the **Scoring Keys** starting on page 911, score your practice tests. If you answered a question correctly, place a hash mark in the box next to the question number—every chart is already separated into the correct subscores for every subject test. Remember—do NOT place a mark of any kind if you left a question blank or answered it incorrectly.

4) Count the total number of questions you answered correctly for:

   a. each ACT test section (English, mathematics, reading, and science); and
   b. each subsection.

5) Write down your raw scores in the blanks provided on every chart.

Read on to find out how to turn these into recognizable ACT scores.

SCALE SCORES

After finding your raw scores for each subject area test, you then must convert each raw score to a **scale score**. The ACT converts raw scores for each subject area test into scale scores ranging from 1 to 36 using conversion tables that are unique for every test given.

The ACT also assigns a scale score of 1–18 for each of the 7 test subscores.

For the practice tests in this book, you can convert your raw scores into scale scores using the scale score conversion charts at the end of this chapter, starting on page 931. Each subject area has its own chart, followed by charts for individual subject area subsections. Take the following steps to convert your practice test raw score results:

> The ACT scales raw scores uniquely for every test to adjust for small differences occurring among different versions.

1) Find your raw score result in the **Scale Score Conversion Chart** by locating the number of questions you answered correctly in the **Raw Score** row of the table. The number located below that number in the **Scale Score** row is your final scale score result (ranging from 1–36) for that test section.

   NOTE: Sometimes one raw score will correspond to one scale score, and sometimes a range of raw scores will correspond to one scale score. For example, in the chart below, if your English raw score is 6, your scale score is 4. If your English raw score is 21, your scale score is 10.

English Scale Score Conversion Chart

Raw Score	0–1	2–3	4–5	6	7–9	10–11	12–14	15–16	17–19	20–22	23	24
Scale Score	1	2	3	4	5	6	7	8	9	10	11	12

2) Enter your scale score number in the appropriate column in **the Multiple-Choice Scale Scores Chart** on page 934.

3) Repeat steps 1–2 for every test section.

4) Repeat these steps to find and record your scaled subscore (ranging from 1–18) for each test in the corresponding **Scale Subscore Conversion Chart**.

You now have your scale scores and subscores for each test section, which will give you a basic idea of which test sections are your strengths, which are your weaknesses, and where you should focus your study in the time leading up to the ACT. Compare your results after you take each new practice test to track your improvement!

COMPOSITE SCORE

The only time ACT combines scores is to calculate the **composite score** by adding together your English, Mathematics, Reading, and Science scale scores, dividing the resulting number by four, and rounding to the nearest whole number (to find the rounded average of the four subject area scores). Just like a scale score, a composite score can range from 1 to 36.

For example, say a student earned the following scale scores on each of the four subject area tests:

English: 21

Mathematics: 26

Reading: 20

Science: 24

First, add the scores: $21 + 26 + 20 + 24 = 91$.

Then, divide the result by 4: $91 \div 4 = 22.75$.

Finally, round the result to the nearest whole number: 22.75 rounds to 23.

The student's composite score in this case is 23.

Because your composite score is an average, even if you performed very well on one test section, a lower score can bring the total score down.

You can keep a record of your composite score for each practice test you take in the **Multiple-Choice Scale Scores Chart** on page 934. Track how your composite score changes from test to test, especially if you put extra work into improving in test sections that give you trouble at the beginning of your study plan.

SCORING YOUR ACT® WRITING TEST ESSAY

Unfortunately, scoring an essay isn't as easy as simply checking a box to determine whether it is right or wrong. As you discovered in Chapter 14, there are many components that ACT Writing test graders look for when scoring and assessing individual student essays. The scoring rubric in Chapter 14 (page 487), which is based on the same grading scale official test reviewers use, will be your guide to determining your essay score.

You have a couple of options for calculating your score on your essay. The first, which is a difficult (but very useful!) exercise, is scoring your own essay using the official rubric to assign your work a score from 1–6 for each of the test's four domains:

1) Ideas and Analysis

2) Development and Support

3) Organization

4) Language Use and Conventions

The rubric clearly lays out the components an essay will have at each score level. While it's pretty hard to objectively read and evaluate your own work, doing so will ensure that you carefully and critically look at your work next to the criteria on which you will be graded. It's easy to write an essay and never look at it again—if you are forced to review it with a careful eye, you'll be able to see the crucial scoring areas that might be missing from your work. Becoming your own editor helps you grow as a writer and as a reader.

Another option is to also have someone else evaluate your essay for you in order to get an outside perspective—maybe a classmate, a tutor, a parent or other family member, or a teacher. If you prefer not to score your own essay, you could have two reviewers do it for you. Give your volunteer grader (or graders) your essay, the scoring rubric, and the sample graded essays on pages 503–508 to get a sense of what essays at different levels look like. Your reviewer should assign your practice essay a score of 1–6 for each of the four domains.

When you and/or your revewer have assigned a score for each domain, add together all four and take the average: if you gave yourself a 4 for Ideas and Analysis, a 3 for Development and Support, a 6 for Organization, and a 2 for Language Use and Conventions, your essay score would be as follows:

$$4 + 3 + 6 + 2 = 15$$

$$15 \div 4 = 3.75$$

Your self-scored essay would receive a 4.

Because your writing test score should be based on two ratings, you can either multiply your own rating times two, or add your rating and another reader's rating to calculate your subscore (2–12) for your practice writing test. You then find the average of this score with your English and Reading test scores to determine your English Language Arts (ELA) scale score, which ranges from 1-36, like the other test sections.

 Aim to improve your writing test score by hitting more and more points on the rubric with every practice essay you write.

910

Chapter 16
Scoring Your
ACT®
Practice
Tests

www.petersons.com

HOW TO USE YOUR TEST RESULTS

The purpose of taking the practice tests in this book is to familiarize yourself as much as possible with the format, timing, and content of the ACT. The more practice tests you take, the more comfortable you will be with the test, and the fewer surprises you will face on your actual test day.

As you score your tests, always take note of not only your final composite score, but also the individual test scores that comprise it. Your test results should help guide your study. Is there a specific test section giving you trouble? Is there an even more specific sub-section within that section where you seem to get stuck, especially under timed conditions? Use the information you find when scoring your tests with the charts at the end of this chapter to target where you will focus the most work before you take your next practice test.

As much as possible, aim to take the practice tests in this book under the most test-like conditions you can: time yourself and take the test straight through in a quiet room. If you stick to the same methods for every test, you can really get a sense of whether or not you are improving.

If your score isn't as high as you expected, don't get discouraged—use the information you learn from scoring your tests to your advantage. You've taken a huge step by prepping with this book and committing to extensive practice!

SUMMING IT UP

- **ACT does not penalize you for wrong answers.** Your score is based only on the number of correct answers for every test section. There is no penalty for guessing.

- **Your raw score is the number of questions you answer correctly.** To calculate your score for each test section, figure out your raw score and then convert each raw score to a **scale score** using the charts at the end of the chapter. Your scale scores are featured on your official score report and range from 1–36 for each test section. No matter when you take the ACT, your scale score will accurately compare you to all other students who take the test.

- Your **composite score** is the average of your four test scale scores, rounded to the nearest whole number.

- Your **subscores** can help you to identify which specific areas within each subject test you need to work on.

- **You will have to calculate your essay writing score yourself or with the help of a volunteer grader**. Using the scoring rubric, assign yourself a score from 1-6 for each domain, then average your scores for a final essay score. Add it to the score your grader gives you or multiply your self-score by two to find your final essay score.

- **Use your test results to guide your study plan**. Take note of the test sections and subsections that give you the most trouble, and then focus on learning, review, and improvement before you take your next practice test. Always try to take your practice tests in the most test-like conditions possible.

PRACTICE TEST 1 SCORING KEYS

SCORING KEYS FOR MULTIPLE-CHOICE QUESTIONS

To determine your raw scores using the Scoring Keys:

1) Put a hash mark in the box next to each question you answered correctly.

2) Add the hash marks and put the number of correctly answered questions in the blank corresponding to each subtopic.

3) Add the total number of questions you answered correctly. The total is your raw score.

Complete this process for all four tests (English, Mathematics, Reading and Science). Keep in mind that there are no subscores for the Science test. Simply put the number of correct answers in the blank provided to determine your raw score.

Practice Test 1 — English Scoring Key

912

Chapter 16
Scoring Your
ACT®
Practice
Tests

#	KEY	Usg/Mech	RhtSkls	#	KEY	Usg/Mech	RhtSkls	#	KEY	Usg/Mech	RhtSkls
1.	B		▓	26.	H		▓	51.	A	▓	
2.	H		▓	27.	D	▓		52.	G		▓
3.	D		▓	28.	G	▓		53.	C	▓	
4.	J		▓	29.	C	▓		54.	J		▓
5.	A	▓		30.	J	▓		55.	B	▓	
6.	H		▓	31.	D		▓	56.	G		▓
7.	A	▓		32.	G		▓	57.	A	▓	
8.	G		▓	33.	C		▓	58.	J	▓	
9.	A	▓		34.	G	▓		59.	B	▓	
10.	J		▓	35.	D	▓		60.	H	▓	
11.	B	▓		36.	F		▓	61.	A		▓
12.	J	▓		37.	D		▓	62.	H		▓
13.	B	▓		38.	J		▓	63.	B		▓
14.	H	▓		39.	C	▓		64.	F	▓	
15.	D		▓	40.	G	▓		65.	C		▓
16.	H		▓	41.	A		▓	66.	G	▓	
17.	B		▓	42.	H		▓	67.	C		▓
18.	J		▓	43.	D		▓	68.	J	▓	
19.	C		▓	44.	F	▓		69.	D		▓
20.	F	▓		45.	A	▓		70.	G	▓	
21.	B		▓	46.	H		▓	71.	A	▓	
22.	F		▓	47.	C		▓	72.	H		▓
23.	A		▓	48.	G	▓		73.	A		▓
24.	G		▓	49.	A	▓		74.	G		▓
25.	A	▓		50.	J		▓	75.	B	▓	

*Usg/Mech: Usage/Mechanics

RhtSkls: Rhetorical Skills

Raw Scores (Number of Correct Answers)

Usage/Mechanics (Usg/Mech)	_____	out of 40
Rhetorical Skills (RhtSkls)	_____	out of 35
English Raw Score (Usg/Mech + RhtSkls)	_____	out of 75

#	KEY	PA/EA	IA/CG	PG/T	#	KEY	PA/EA	IA/CG	PG/T	#	KEY	PA/EA	IA/CG	PG/T
		SubScore Topic*					SubScore Topic*					SubScore Topic*		
1.	E				21.	D				41.	A			
2.	G				22.	F				42.	F			
3.	A				23.	D				43.	C			
4.	K				24.	G				44.	H			
5.	D				25.	B				45.	B			
6.	J				26.	J				46.	F			
7.	C				27.	D				47.	C			
8.	H				28.	K				48.	G			
9.	C				29.	D				49.	B			
10.	K				30.	H				50.	K			
11.	E				31.	C				51.	C			
12.	K				32.	K				52.	K			
13.	D				33.	D				53.	E			
14.	G				34.	H				54.	J			
15.	A				35.	C				55.	B			
16.	H				36.	K				56.	J			
17.	B				37.	C				57.	C			
18.	H				38.	H				58.	H			
19.	B				39.	B				59.	D			
20.	H				40.	K				60.	G			

*PA/EA = Pre-Algebra/ Elementary Algebra

IA/CG = Intermediate Algebra/ Coordinate Geometry

PG/ T = Plane Geometry/ Trigonometry

Raw Scores (Number of Correct Answers)

Pre-Algebra/Elementary Algebra (PA/EA)	_____	**out of 24**
Intermediate Algebra/ Coordinate Geometry (IA/CG)	_____	**out of 18**
Plane Geometry/ Trigonometry (PG/T)	_____	**out of 18**
Mathematics Raw Score (PA/EA + IA/CG +PG/T)	_____	**out of 60**

Practice Test 1   Reading Scoring Key

#	KEY	LI/PF/Hu	SS/NatSci	#	KEY	LI/PF/Hu	SS/NatSci
		SubScore*				SubScore Topic*	
1.	B			21.	B		
2.	J			22.	H		
3.	C			23.	D		
4.	J			24.	H		
5.	C			25.	A		
6.	G			26.	J		
7.	A			27.	B		
8.	G			28.	F		
9.	D			29.	C		
10.	F			30.	J		
11.	D			31.	A		
12.	F			32.	H		
13.	C			33.	D		
14.	J			34.	G		
15.	B			35.	D		
16.	J			36.	G		
17.	C			37.	D		
18.	F			38.	H		
19.	B			39.	B		
20.	J			40.	F		

*LI/PF/Hu = Literary Narrative/Prose Fiction/Humanities

SS/NatSci = Social Studies/Natural Sciences

914

Chapter 16
Scoring Your
ACT®
Practice
Tests

Raw Scores (Number of Correct Answers)

Literary Narrative/Prose Fiction/Humanities (LI/PF/Hu)	_____	out of 20
Social Studies/Natural Sciences (SS/NatSci)	_____	out of 25
Reading Raw Score (LI/PF/Hu + SS/NatSci)	_____	out of 40

#	KEY		#	KEY	
1.	C		21.	B	
2.	J		22.	H	
3.	A		23.	B	
4.	G		24.	J	
5.	B		25.	C	
6.	G		26.	G	
7.	A		27.	A	
8.	J		28.	H	
9.	B		29.	D	
10.	G		30.	G	
11.	D		31.	C	
12.	H		32.	J	
13.	C		33.	D	
14.	F		34.	G	
15.	C		35.	A	
16.	J		36.	F	
17.	D		37.	B	
18.	G		38.	H	
19.	C		39.	D	
20.	F		40.	J	

Raw Scores (Number of Correct Answers)

Science Raw Score	_____	out of 40

915

Chapter 16

Scoring Your
ACT®
Practice
Tests

PRACTICE TEST 2 SCORING KEYS

SCORING KEYS FOR MULTIPLE-CHOICE QUESTIONS

To determine your raw scores using the Scoring Keys:

1) Put a hash mark in the box next to each question you answered correctly.

2) Add the hash marks and put the number of correctly answered questions in the blank corresponding to each subtopic.

3) Add the total number of questions you answered correctly. The total is your raw score.

Complete this process for all four tests (English, Mathematics, Reading and Science). Keep in mind that there are no subscores for the Science test. Simply put the number of correct answers in the blank provided to determine your raw score.

Chapter 16
Scoring Your
ACT®
Practice
Tests

Practice Test 2 — English Scoring Key

#	KEY	Usg/Mech	RhtSkls	#	KEY	Usg/Mech	RhtSkls	#	KEY	Usg/Mech	RhtSkls
1.	B		■	26.	G		■	51.	D		■
2.	G		■	27.	B	■		52.	G		■
3.	D		■	28.	G	■		53.	B		■
4.	H		■	29.	D	■		54.	F		■
5.	A	■		30.	F	■		55.	B		■
6.	J		■	31.	D		■	56.	J		■
7.	B	■		32.	F		■	57.	D		■
8.	J	■		33.	C		■	58.	H		■
9.	B	■		34.	J		■	59.	A	■	
10.	G	■		35.	B		■	60.	H	■	
11.	C	■		36.	H		■	61.	B	■	
12.	J	■		37.	A		■	62.	F	■	
13.	B	■		38.	F	■		63.	C		■
14.	J	■		39.	B	■		64.	J	■	
15.	A	■		40.	G		■	65.	C		■
16.	J		■	41.	D		■	66.	J		■
17.	A		■	42.	J		■	67.	B		■
18.	J		■	43.	A		■	68.	J	■	
19.	C		■	44.	G	■		69.	C		■
20.	H	■		45.	C	■		70.	H		■
21.	C		■	46.	J		■	71.	D	■	
22.	G		■	47.	D		■	72.	J	■	
23.	C		■	48.	J		■	73.	B		■
24.	F	■		49.	C	■		74.	H		■
25.	D	■		50.	F	■		75.	D		■

*Usg/Mech: Usage/Mechanics

RhtSkls: Rhetorical Skills

Raw Scores (Number of Correct Answers)

Usage/Mechanics (Usg/Mech)	_____	out of 40
Rhetorical Skills (RhtSkls)	_____	out of 35
English Raw Score (Usg/Mech + RhtSkls)	_____	out of 75

Practice Test 2 — Mathematics Scoring Key

918

Chapter 16
Scoring Your
ACT®
Practice
Tests

#	KEY	PA/EA	IA/CG	PG/T	#	KEY	PA/EA	IA/CG	PG/T	#	KEY	PA/EA	IA/CG	PG/T
1.	A	✓			21.	C			✓	41.	E		✓	
2.	G	✓			22.	H	✓			42.	G			✓
3.	E	✓			23.	A		✓		43.	B	✓		
4.	F	✓			24.	J	✓			44.	K		✓	
5.	C		✓		25.	B			✓	45.	D		✓	
6.	G		✓		26.	G	✓			46.	H			✓
7.	E		✓		27.	B			✓	47.	E		✓	
8.	J		✓		28.	J		✓		48.	H			✓
9.	B	✓			29.	D			✓	49.	C		✓	
10.	G	✓			30.	K			✓	50.	G			✓
11.	B	✓			31.	D			✓	51.	C			✓
12.	G	✓			32.	G	✓			52.	H	✓		
13.	D			✓	33.	E			✓	53.	D			✓
14.	F			✓	34.	G	✓			54.	F			✓
15.	C	✓			35.	B			✓	55.	C		✓	
16.	G	✓			36.	G	✓			56.	H		✓	
17.	C		✓		37.	B			✓	57.	D		✓	
18.	H		✓		38.	K		✓		58.	H			✓
19.	E	✓			39.	D			✓	59.	D		✓	
20.	J	✓			40.	G			✓	60.	G		✓	

*PA/EA = Pre-Algebra/ Elementary Algebra

IA/CG = Intermediate Algebra/ Coordinate Geometry

PG/ T = Plane Geometry/ Trigonometry

Raw Scores (Number of Correct Answers)

Pre-Algebra/Elementary Algebra (PA/EA)	_____	out of 24
Intermediate Algebra/ Coordinate Geometry (IA/CG)	_____	out of 18
Plane Geometry/ Trigonometry (PG/T)	_____	out of 18
Mathematics Raw Score (PA/EA + IA/CG +PG/T)	_____	out of 60

#	KEY	SubScore Topic* LI/PF/Hu	SS/NatSci	#	KEY	SubScore Topic* LI/PF/Hu	SS/NatSci
1.	C			21.	D		
2.	J			22.	G		
3.	D			23.	A		
4.	F			24.	J		
5.	B			25.	G		
6.	F			26.	J		
7.	C			27.	A		
8.	G			28.	H		
9.	C			29.	B		
10.	F			30.	J		
11.	A			31.	C		
12.	F			32.	F		
13.	D			33.	A		
14.	H			34.	H		
15.	D			35.	D		
16.	F			36.	J		
17.	C			37.	D		
18.	F			38.	H		
19.	B			39.	B		
20.	J			40.	F		

*LI/PF/Hu = Literary Narrative/Prose Fiction/Humanities

SS/NatSci = Social Studies/Natural Sciences

Raw Scores (Number of Correct Answers)

Literary Narrative/Prose Fiction/Humanities (LI/PF/Hu)	_____	out of 20
Social Studies/Natural Sciences (SS/NatSci)	_____	out of 25
Reading Raw Score (LI/PF/Hu + SS/NatSci)	_____	out of 40

919

Chapter 16

Scoring Your
ACT®
Practice
Tests

#	KEY		#	KEY	
1.	D		21.	A	
2.	G		22.	F	
3.	A		23.	B	
4.	J		24.	J	
5.	G		25.	D	
6.	J		26.	F	
7.	A		27.	C	
8.	H		28.	H	
9.	B		29.	D	
10.	J		30.	G	
11.	C		31.	A	
12.	F		32.	G	
13.	A		33.	C	
14.	H		34.	F	
15.	D		35.	D	
16.	J		36.	J	
17.	B		37.	D	
18.	H		38.	G	
19.	D		39.	B	
20.	G		40.	H	

Raw Scores (Number of Correct Answers)

Science Raw Score   _____   **out of 40**

920

Chapter 16
Scoring Your
ACT®
Practice
Tests

PRACTICE TEST 3 SCORING KEYS

Scoring Keys for Multiple-Choice Questions

To determine your raw scores using the Scoring Keys:

1) Put a hash mark in the box next to each question you answered correctly.

2) Add the hash marks and put the number of correctly answered questions in the blank corresponding to each subtopic.

3) Add the total number of questions you answered correctly. The total is your raw score.

Complete this process for all four tests (English, Mathematics, Reading and Science). Keep in mind that there are no subscores for the Science test. Simply put the number of correct answers in the blank provided to determine your raw score.

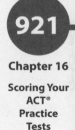

921

Chapter 16

**Scoring Your
ACT®
Practice
Tests**

#	KEY	SubScore Topic* Usg/Mech	SubScore Topic* RhtSkls	#	KEY	SubScore Topic* Usg/Mech	SubScore Topic* RhtSkls	#	KEY	SubScore Topic* Usg/Mech	SubScore Topic* RhtSkls
1.	D		▓	26.	F	▓		51.	B		▓
2.	F		▓	27.	A	▓		52.	H		▓
3.	B		▓	28.	H		▓	53.	D		▓
4.	H	▓		29.	D	▓		54.	F	▓	
5.	C		▓	30.	F	▓		55.	D		
6.	J		▓	31.	A		▓	56.	J		▓
7.	C		▓	32.	H		▓	57.	B		
8.	G		▓	33.	C			58.	J	▓	
9.	A	▓		34.	F		▓	59.	A	▓	
10.	J		▓	35.	B		▓	60.	H	▓	
11.	A		▓	36.	H		▓	61.	C		▓
12.	F		▓	37.	D	▓		62.	J		▓
13.	B		▓	38.	G	▓		63.	D		▓
14.	H	▓		39.	C		▓	64.	H		▓
15.	B		▓	40.	H		▓	65.	D		▓
16.	J		▓	41.	D		▓	66.	G	▓	
17.	B		▓	42.	J		▓	67.	C		▓
18.	G		▓	43.	C		▓	68.	F		▓
19.	B	▓		44.	F	▓		69.	B		▓
20.	J		▓	45.	C		▓	70.	J	▓	
21.	D		▓	46.	J		▓	71.	A		▓
22.	G		▓	47.	B		▓	72.	H		▓
23.	C		▓	48.	H	▓		73.	D		▓
24.	G	▓		49.	B	▓		74.	F	▓	
25.	B	▓		50.	F	▓		75.	C		▓

*Usg/Mech: Usage/Mechanics

RhtSkls: Rhetorical Skills

Raw Scores (Number of Correct Answers)

Usage/Mechanics (Usg/Mech)	_____	out of 40
Rhetorical Skills (RhtSkls)	_____	out of 35
English Raw Score (Usg/Mech + RhtSkls)	_____	out of 75

Practice Test 3 — Mathematics Scoring Key

Practice Test 3 — Mathematics Scoring Key

#	KEY	PA/EA	IA/CG	PG/T	#	KEY	PA/EA	IA/CG	PG/T	#	KEY	PA/EA	IA/CG	PG/T
1.	E				21.	B				41.	C			
2.	J				22.	K				42.	H			
3.	C				23.	D				43.	E			
4.	K				24.	J				44.	F			
5.	E				25.	C				45.	B			
6.	H				26.	G				46.	G			
7.	E				27.	E				47.	A			
8.	H				28.	J				48.	G			
9.	B				29.	D				49.	B			
10.	J				30.	G				50.	H			
11.	E				31.	A				51.	B			
12.	H				32.	J				52.	K			
13.	D				33.	E				53.	E			
14.	F				34.	J				54.	G			
15.	C				35.	C				55.	A			
16.	K				36.	H				56.	J			
17.	A				37.	A				57.	C			
18.	G				38.	F				58.	J			
19.	E				39.	A				59.	B			
20.	H				40.	K				60.	G			

*PA/EA = Pre-Algebra/ Elementary Algebra

IA/CG = Intermediate Algebra/ Coordinate Geometry

PG/ T = Plane Geometry/ Trigonometry

Raw Scores (Number of Correct Answers)

Pre-Algebra/Elementary Algebra (PA/EA) _____ out of 24

Intermediate Algebra/ Coordinate Geometry (IA/CG) _____ out of 18

Plane Geometry/ Trigonometry (PG/T) _____ out of 18

Mathematics Raw Score (PA/EA + IA/CG +PG/T) _____ out of 60

923

Chapter 16

Scoring Your ACT® Practice Tests

Peterson's ACT® Prep Guide

Practice Test 3 — Reading Scoring Key

#	KEY	LI/PF/Hu	SS/NatSci	#	KEY	LI/PF/Hu	SS/NatSci
		SubScore Topic*				SubScore Topic*	
1.	D			21.	C		
2.	H			22.	F		
3.	B			23.	D		
4.	G			24.	H		
5.	B			25.	A		
6.	J			26.	H		
7.	C			27.	B		
8.	F			28.	F		
9.	D			29.	D		
10.	H			30.	G		
11.	B			31.	C		
12.	J			32.	J		
13.	B			33.	C		
14.	H			34.	F		
15.	A			35.	D		
16.	F			36.	H		
17.	D			37.	A		
18.	G			38.	H		
19.	D			39.	B		
20.	H			40.	G		

*LI/PF/Hu = Literary Narrative/Prose Fiction/Humanities

SS/NatSci = Social Studies/Natural Sciences

924

Chapter 16
Scoring Your
ACT®
Practice
Tests

Raw Scores (Number of Correct Answers)

Literary Narrative/Prose Fiction/Humanities (LI/PF/Hu)	_____	out of 20
Social Studies/Natural Sciences (SS/NatSci)	_____	out of 25
Reading Raw Score (LI/PF/Hu + SS/NatSci)	_____	out of 40

#	KEY		#	KEY	
1.	D		21.	A	
2.	F		22.	J	
3.	C		23.	B	
4.	H		24.	G	
5.	D		25.	A	
6.	F		26.	H	
7.	C		27.	D	
8.	G		28.	F	
9.	B		29.	C	
10.	J		30.	G	
11.	A		31.	B	
12.	J		32.	F	
13.	C		33.	D	
14.	J		34.	J	
15.	B		35.	B	
16.	J		36.	J	
17.	D		37.	D	
18.	G		38.	H	
19.	C		39.	B	
20.	F		40.	G	

Raw Scores (Number of Correct Answers)

Science Raw Score	_____	out of 40

925

Chapter 16

Scoring Your
ACT®
Practice
Tests

PRACTICE TEST 4 SCORING KEYS

SCORING KEYS FOR MULTIPLE-CHOICE QUESTIONS

To determine your raw scores using the Scoring Keys:

1) Put a hash mark in the box next to each question you answered correctly.

2) Add the hash marks and put the number of correctly answered questions in the blank corresponding to each subtopic.

3) Add the total number of questions you answered correctly. The total is your raw score.

Complete this process for all four tests (English, Mathematics, Reading and Science). Keep in mind that there are no subscores for the Science test. Simply put the number of correct answers in the blank provided to determine your raw score.

926

Chapter 16
Scoring Your
ACT®
Practice
Tests

www.petersons.com

Practice Test 4 — English Scoring Key

#	KEY	Usg/Mech	RhtSkls	#	KEY	Usg/Mech	RhtSkls	#	KEY	Usg/Mech	RhtSkls
1.	B			26.	H			51.	D		
2.	G			27.	B			52.	G		
3.	D			28.	H			53.	C		
4.	F			29.	C			54.	G		
5.	B			30.	G			55.	A		
6.	J			31.	A			56.	J		
7.	C			32.	J			57.	D		
8.	F			33.	B			58.	F		
9.	C			34.	J			59.	C		
10.	H			35.	A			60.	F		
11.	D			36.	H			61.	A		
12.	G			37.	A			62.	J		
13.	D			38.	F			63.	C		
14.	J			39.	D			64.	G		
15.	B			40.	G			65.	B		
16.	J			41.	B			66.	H		
17.	D			42.	H			67.	A		
18.	F			43.	B			68.	H		
19.	C			44.	F			69.	A		
20.	F			45.	A			70.	H		
21.	D			46.	G			71.	B		
22.	G			47.	A			72.	F		
23.	A			48.	G			73.	D		
24.	J			49.	C			74.	G		
25.	D			50.	F			75.	C		

*Usg/Mech: Usage/Mechanics

RhtSkls: Rhetorical Skills

Raw Scores (Number of Correct Answers)

Usage/Mechanics (Usg/Mech)	_____	out of 40
Rhetorical Skills (RhtSkls)	_____	out of 35
English Raw Score (Usg/Mech + RhtSkls)	_____	out of 75

#	KEY	SubScore Topic* PA/EA	IA/CG	PG/T	#	KEY	SubScore Topic* PA/EA	IA/CG	PG/T	#	KEY	SubScore Topic* PA/EA	IA/CG	PG/T
1.	D				21.	E				41.	B			
2.	H				22.	H				42.	J			
3.	B				23.	C				43.	C			
4.	J				24.	J				44.	F			
5.	A				25.	A				45.	C			
6.	F				26.	G				46.	G			
7.	C				27.	B				47.	A			
8.	F				28.	H				48.	K			
9.	D				29.	E				49.	D			
10.	H				30.	K				50.	H			
11.	A				31.	D				51.	A			
12.	K				32.	K				52.	K			
13.	E				33.	A				53.	B			
14.	G				34.	F				54.	H			
15.	D				35.	B				55.	E			
16.	J				36.	J				56.	G			
17.	C				37.	C				57.	A			
18.	K				38.	F				58.	J			
19.	E				39.	C				59.	B			
20.	G				40.	F				60.	F			

*PA/EA = Pre-Algebra/ Elementary Algebra

IA/CG = Intermediate Algebra/ Coordinate Geometry

PG/ T = Plane Geometry/ Trigonometry

Raw Scores (Number of Correct Answers)

Pre-Algebra/Elementary Algebra (PA/EA)	_____	out of 24
Intermediate Algebra/ Coordinate Geometry (IA/CG)	_____	out of 18
Plane Geometry/ Trigonometry (PG/T)	_____	out of 18
Mathematics Raw Score (PA/EA + IA/CG +PG/T)	_____	out of 60

928

Chapter 16
Scoring Your
ACT®
Practice
Tests

www.petersons.com

#	KEY	SubScore Topic* LI/PF/Hu	SS/NatSci	#	KEY	SubScore Topic* LI/PF/Hu	SS/NatSci
1.	D			21.	B		
2.	F			22.	H		
3.	D			23.	B		
4.	H			24.	J		
5.	A			25.	C		
6.	J			26.	H		
7.	B			27.	D		
8.	G			28.	J		
9.	C			29.	B		
10.	H			30.	F		
11.	D			31.	C		
12.	J			32.	F		
13.	C			33.	B		
14.	H			34.	G		
15.	B			35.	A		
16.	G			36.	J		
17.	B			37.	C		
18.	H			38.	G		
19.	B			39.	D		
20.	J			40.	F		

*LI/PF/Hu = Literary Narrative/Prose Fiction/Humanities

SS/NatSci = Social Studies/Natural Sciences

929

Raw Scores (Number of Correct Answers)

Literary Narrative/Prose Fiction/Humanities (LI/PF/Hu)	_____	out of 20
Social Studies/Natural Sciences (SS/NatSci)	_____	out of 25
Reading Raw Score (LI/PF/Hu + SS/NatSci)	_____	out of 40

#	KEY		#	KEY	
1.	C		21.	C	
2.	G		22.	G	
3.	C		23.	A	
4.	F		24.	H	
5.	B		25.	A	
6.	H		26.	G	
7.	B		27.	A	
8.	G		28.	F	
9.	B		29.	B	
10.	J		30.	J	
11.	D		31.	C	
12.	F		32.	F	
13.	C		33.	C	
14.	J		34.	F	
15.	B		35.	D	
16.	F		36.	F	
17.	C		37.	B	
18.	F		38.	F	
19.	D		39.	A	
20.	G		40.	H	

Raw Scores (Number of Correct Answers)

Science Raw Score   **out of 40**

930

Chapter 16
Scoring Your
ACT®
Practice
Tests

SCALE SCORE CONVERSION CHARTS

Now that you know your raw scores for each test, you can convert them to scale scores using the following conversion tables. For each test section, find the number of questions you answered correctly in the **Raw Score** row of the table. The number located below in the **Scale Score** row is your scale score for that test. Enter your scale score in the **Multiple-Choice Scale Scores Chart** on page 934.

The scale subscores tables immediately follow the test section in which they belong. Find the number of questions you answered correctly in each subsection in the Raw Score row of the table. The number located below in the **Scale Score** row is your scale score for that test. Enter your scale subscore in the **Multiple-Choice Scale Scores Chart** on page 934.

SCALE SCORE CONVERSION CHARTS FOR MULTIPLE-CHOICE QUESTIONS

English Test

English Scale Score Conversion Chart

Raw Score	0–1	2–3	4–5	6	7–9	10–11	12–14	15–16	17–19	20–22	23–24	25–26
Scale Score	1	2	3	4	5	6	7	8	9	10	11	12
Raw Score	27–28	29–30	31–33	34–36	37–38	39–40	41–43	44–46	47–50	51–52	53–55	56–57
Scale Score	13	14	15	16	17	18	19	20	21	22	23	24
Raw Score	58–59	60–61	62–63	64	65	66–67	68	69	70	71	72–74	75
Scale Score	25	26	27	28	29	30	31	32	33	34	35	36

Usage/Mechanics Scale Subscore Conversion Chart

Raw Score	0–4	5–7	8–9	10–12	13–14	15–16	17–19	20–21	22–23
Scale Score	1	2	3	4	5	6	7	8	9
Raw Score	24–26	27–28	29–30	31	32–33	34–35	36–37	38–39	40
Scale Score	10	11	12	13	14	15	16	17	18

Rhetorical Skills Scale Subscore Conversion Chart

Raw Score	0–2	3–4	5–7	8–9	10–11	12	13–14	15–16	17–19
Scale Score	1	2	3	4	5	6	7	8	9
Raw Score	20–21	22–24	25–26	27–28	29	30–31	32–33	34	35
Scale Score	10	11	12	13	14	15	16	17	18

Mathematics Test

Mathematics Scale Score Conversion Chart

Raw Score	0	–	–	1	–	2	–	3	–	4	5–6	7
Scale Score	**1**	**2**	**3**	**4**	**5**	**6**	**7**	**8**	**9**	**10**	**11**	**12**
Raw Score	8–9	10–13	14–17	18–21	22–25	26–27	28–29	30–31	32	33–34	35–37	38–39
Scale Score	**13**	**14**	**15**	**16**	**17**	**18**	**19**	**20**	**21**	**22**	**23**	**24**
Raw Score	40–41	42–44	45–46	47–48	49	50	51–52	53	54–5	56	57–58	59–0
Scale Score	**25**	**26**	**27**	**28**	**29**	**30**	**31**	**32**	**33**	**34**	**35**	**36**

Pre–Algebra/Elem. Algebra Scale Subscore Conversion Chart

Raw Score	0	1	2	3–4	5	6–7	8–9	10–11	12–13
Scale Score	**1**	**2**	**3**	**4**	**5**	**6**	**7**	**8**	**9**
Raw Score	14	15	16–17	18	19	20	21	22	23–24
Scale Score	**10**	**11**	**12**	**13**	**14**	**15**	**16**	**17**	**18**

Int. Alg/Coord. Geometry Scale Subscore Conversion Chart

Raw Score	0	–	1	2	–	3	4	5	6–7
Scale Score	**1**	**2**	**3**	**4**	**5**	**6**	**7**	**8**	**9**
Raw Score	8	9	10–11	12	13–14	15	16	17	18
Scale Score	**10**	**11**	**12**	**13**	**14**	**15**	**16**	**17**	**18**

Plane Geometry/Trig Scale Subscore Conversion Chart

Raw Score	0	1	2	–	3	–	4	5	6–7
Scale Score	**1**	**2**	**3**	**4**	**5**	**6**	**7**	**8**	**9**
Raw Score	8	9	10–11	12–13	14	15–16	17	–	18
Scale Score	**10**	**11**	**12**	**13**	**14**	**15**	**16**	**17**	**18**

932

Chapter 16
Scoring Your
ACT®
Practice
Tests

Reading Test

Reading Scale Score Conversion Chart

Raw Score	0	1	–	2	–	3	4	5	–	6–7	8	9–10
Scale Score	1	2	3	4	5	6	7	8	9	10	11	12
Raw Score	11–12	13–14	15–16	17–18	19–20	21	22–23	24–25	26	27–28	29	30
Scale Score	13	14	15	16	17	18	19	20	21	22	23	24
Raw Score	31	32	33	34	35	36	–	37	38	39	–	40
Scale Score	25	26	27	28	29	30	31	32	33	34	35	36

Literary Narrative/Prose Fiction and Humanities Scale Subscore Conversion Chart

Raw Score	0	1	2	3	4	5	6	7	8
Scale Score	1	2	3	4	5	6	7	8	9
Raw Score	9	10	11–12	13	14	15	16	17–18	19–20
Scale Score	10	11	12	13	14	15	16	17	18

Social Studies/ Natural Sciences Scale Subscore Conversion Chart

Raw Score	0–1	–	2	3	4	–	5	6–7	8
Scale Score	1	2	3	4	5	6	7	8	9
Raw Score	9	10	11	12	13–14	15	16–17	18–19	20
Scale Score	10	11	12	13	14	15	16	17	18

Science Test

Science Scale Score Conversion Chart

Raw Score	0	–	1	–	2	3	–	4	5–6	7	8	9
Scale Score	1	2	3	4	5	6	7	8	9	10	11	12
Raw Score	10	11	12	13	14	15–16	17	18–19	20–21	22–23	24–25	26
Scale Score	13	14	15	16	17	18	19	20	21	22	23	24
Raw Score	27–28	29–30	31	32	33	34	35	36	–	37	38	39–40
Scale Score	25	26	27	28	29	30	31	32	33	34	35	36

MULTIPLE-CHOICE SCALE SCORES CHART

Multiple-Choice Scale Scores Chart

	Scale Score/Subscore			
	Test 1	Test 2	Test 3	Test 4
English				
Usage/Mechanics				
Rhetorical Skills				
Mathematics				
Pre-Algebra/Elementary Algebra				
Intermediate Algebra/Coordinate Geometry				
Plane Geometry/Trigonometry				
Reading				
Literary Narrative/Prose Fiction/Humanities				
Social Studies/Natural Science				
Science				
Total Scale Scores (Do NOT include subscores.)				
Composite Score (sum ÷ 4)				

934

Chapter 16
Scoring Your
ACT®
Practice
Tests

WRITING TEST AND ELA SCORES

Writing Test and ELA Scores Chart

To determine your Writing and English Language Arts (ELA) scores:

1) Refer to the scoring rubric in Chapter 14 (page 487) and evaluate your essay based on the four domains.

    a. Each domain can be given a score ranging from 1–6. Once you have assigned a score for each domain, add all four scores together and take the average (divide the total score by 4).

    b. Since the writing test score should be based on two ratings, be sure to either multiply your rating by two, or add your rating to another reader's rating to get your Writing test subscore.

2) Enter your domain scores and subscore in the **Writing Test /ELA Scores** chart.

3) Go back to the **Multiple-Choice Scale Scores Chart** and locate your English and Reading scale scores. Enter your English and Reading scale scores in the **Writing Test /ELA Scores** chart.

4) Add your English, Reading, and Writing test scale scores together and take the average (divide the total score by 3). This is your ELA score. Enter your ELA score in the **Writing Test /ELA Scores** chart.

Writing Test/ ELA Scores				
Domain	**Test 1**	**Test 2**	**Test 3**	**Test 4**
Ideas and Analysis				
Score 1				
Score 2				
Development/Support				
Score 1				
Score 2				
Organization				
Score 1				
Score 2				
Language Use/Conventions				
Score 1				
Score 2				
Total Essay Score				
Score 1				
Score 2				
Average (sum ÷ 4)				
Score 1				
Score 2				

935

Chapter 16

Scoring Your ACT® Practice Tests

Writing Test Subscore (Score 1 Average + Score 2 Average)				
English Test Scale Score				
Reading Test Scale Score				
Writing/ELA Scale Score (English + Reading + Writing ÷ 3)				

936

Chapter 16
Scoring Your
ACT®
Practice
Tests

NOTES

NOTES

NOTES

NOTES

NOTES

NOTES

NOTES

NOTES

NOTES

NOTES

NOTES

NOTES